Koren Talmud Bavli

THE NOÉ EDITION

ZEVAḤIM

Steinsaltz Center

KOREN

תלמוד בבלי

KOREN TALMUD BAVLI

THE NOÉ EDITION

זבחים

ZEVAḤIM

Daf 36b through Daf 66a

COMMENTARY BY

Rabbi Adin Even-Israel Steinsaltz

EDITOR-IN-CHIEF

Rabbi Dr Tzvi Hersh Weinreb

SENIOR CONTENT EDITOR

Rabbi Dr Shalom Z Berger

EXECUTIVE EDITOR

Rabbi Joshua Schreier

•

STEINSALTZ CENTER
KOREN PUBLISHERS JERUSALEM

Supported by the Matanel Foundation

Koren Talmud Bavli, The Noe Edition
Vol. 29c: Tractate Zevaḥim, Daf 36b through Daf 66a
Paperback, ISBN, 978-965-7767-19-1

First Hebrew/English paperback edition, 2025

Koren Publishers Jerusalem Ltd.
PO Box 4044, Jerusalem 91040, ISRAEL
PO Box 8531, New Milford, CT 06776, USA
www.korenpub.com

Steinsaltz Center

Steinsaltz Center is the parent organization of institutions established by Rabbi Adin Even-Israel Steinsaltz

PO Box 45187, Jerusalem 91450 ISRAEL
Telephone: +972 2 646 0900, Fax +972 2 624 9454
www.steinsaltz-center.org

הִנֵּה יָמִים בָּאִים, נְאֻם אֲדֹנָי יֱהֹוִה, וְהִשְׁלַחְתִּי רָעָב בָּאָרֶץ,
לֹא־רָעָב לַלֶּחֶם וְלֹא־צָמָא לַמַּיִם, כִּי אִם־לִשְׁמֹעַ אֵת דִּבְרֵי יהוה.

Behold, days are coming – says the Lord God – I will send a hunger to the land, not a hunger for bread nor a thirst for water, but to hear the words of the Lord. (AMOS 8:11)

The Noé edition of the Koren Talmud Bavli
with the commentary of Rabbi Adin Even-Israel Steinsaltz
is dedicated to all those who open its covers
to quench their thirst for Jewish Knowledge,
in our generation of Torah renaissance.

This beautiful edition is for the young, the aged,
the novice and the savant alike,
as it unites the depth of Torah knowledge
with the best of academic scholarship.

Within its exquisite and vibrant pages,
words become worlds.

It will claim its place in the library of classics,
in the bookcases of the Beit Midrash,
the classrooms of our schools,
and in the offices of professionals and business people
who carve out precious time to grapple with its timeless wisdom.

For the Student and the Scholar

DEDICATED BY LEO AND SUE NOÉ

Steinsaltz Center

Executive Director, Steinsaltz Center

Rabbi Meni Even-Israel

Managing Editor

Rabbi Jason Rappoport

Senior Content Editor

Rabbi Dr. Shalom Z. Berger

Editors

Rabbi Dr. Joshua Amaru, *Coordinating Editor*
Rabbi Yehoshua Duker, *Senior Editor*
Rabbi Yedidya Naveh, *Content Curator*
Rabbi Avishai Magence, *Content Curator*
Rabbi Yehonatan Eliav, *Hebrew Edition*
Rabbi Gershon Kitsis, *Hebrew Edition*
Menucha Chwat
Rabbi Yonatan Shai Freedman
Rabbi Ayal Geffon
Rabbi Uri Goldstein
Noam Harris
Yisrael Kalker
Rabbi Tzvi Chaim Kaye
Rabbi Yonatan Kohn
Sholom Licht
Catriel Lev
Elisha Loewenstern
Rafi Miller
Rabbi Jonathan Mishkin
Rabbi Eli Ozarowski
Rabbi David Sedley
Rabbi Jonathan Shulman
Rabbi Michael Siev
Avi Steinhart
Rabbi David Strauss

Copy Editors

Aliza Israel, *Coordinator*
Ita Olesker
Debbie Ismailoff
Shira Finson
Ilana Sobel
Deena Nataf
Eliana Kurlantzick Yorav
Erica Hirsch Edvi
Sara Henna Dahan
Oritt Sinclair

Language Consultants

Dr. Stéphanie E. Binder, *Greek & Latin*
Rabbi Yaakov Hoffman, *Arabic*
Dr. Shai Secunda, *Persian*
Shira Shmidman, *Aramaic*

Technical Staff

Tani Bednarsh
Adena Frazer
Yaakov Shmidman
Shaltiel Shmidman
Nava Wieder

KOREN

Design & Typesetting

Dena Landowne Bailey, *Typesetting*
Tani Bayer, *Jacket Design*
Raphaël Freeman, *Design & Typography*

Images

Eliahu Misgav, *Illustration & Image Acquisition*
Daniel Gdalevich, *Illustration & Image Acquisition*

Introduction by the Publisher

The Talmud has sustained and inspired Jews for thousands of years. Throughout Jewish history, an elite cadre of scholars has absorbed its learning and passed it on to succeeding generations. The Talmud has been the fundamental text of our people.

Beginning in the 1960s, Rabbi Adin Even-Israel Steinsaltz שליט״א created a revolution in the history of Talmud study. His translation of the Talmud, first into modern Hebrew and then into other languages, as well the practical learning aids he added to the text, have enabled millions of people around the world to access and master the complexity and context of the world of Talmud.

It is thus a privilege to present the *Koren Talmud Bavli*, an English translation of the talmudic text with the brilliant elucidation of Rabbi Steinsaltz. The depth and breadth of his knowledge are unique in our time. His rootedness in the tradition and his reach into the world beyond it are inspirational.

Working with Rabbi Steinsaltz on this remarkable project has been not only an honor, but a great pleasure. Never shy to express an opinion, with wisdom and humor, Rabbi Steinsaltz sparkles in conversation, demonstrating his knowledge (both sacred and worldly), sharing his wide-ranging interests, and, above all, radiating his passion. I am grateful for the unique opportunity to work closely with him, and I wish him many more years of writing and teaching.

Our intentions in publishing this new edition of the Talmud are threefold. First, we seek to fully clarify the talmudic page to the reader – textually, intellectually, and graphically. Second, we seek to utilize today's most sophisticated technologies, both in print and electronic formats, to provide the reader with a comprehensive set of study tools. And third, we seek to help readers advance in their process of Talmud study.

To achieve these goals, the *Koren Talmud Bavli* is unique in a number of ways:

- The classic *tzurat hadaf* of Vilna, used by scholars since the 1800s, has been reset for great clarity, and opens from the Hebrew "front" of the book. Full *nikkud* has been added to both the talmudic text and Rashi's commentary, allowing for a more fluent reading with the correct pronunciation; the commentaries of *Tosafot* have been punctuated. Upon the advice of many English-speaking teachers of Talmud, we have separated these core pages from the translation, thereby enabling the advanced student to approach the text without the distraction of the translation. This also reduces the number of volumes in the set. At the bottom of each *daf*, there is a reference to the corresponding English pages. In addition, the Vilna edition was read against other manuscripts and older print editions, so that texts which had been removed by non-Jewish censors have been restored to their rightful place.

- The English translation, which starts on the English "front" of the book, reproduces the *menukad* Talmud text alongside the English translation (in bold) and commentary and explanation (in a lighter font). The Hebrew and Aramaic text is presented in logical paragraphs. This allows for a fluent reading of the text for the non-Hebrew or non-Aramaic reader. It also allows for the Hebrew reader to refer easily to the text alongside. Where the original text features dialogue or poetry, the English text is laid out in a manner appropriate to the genre. Each page refers to the relevant *daf*.

- Critical contextual tools surround the text and translation: personality notes, providing short biographies of the Sages; language notes, explaining foreign terms borrowed from Greek, Latin, Persian, or Arabic; and background notes, giving information essential to the understanding of the text, including history, geography, botany, archaeology, zoology, astronomy, and aspects of daily life in the talmudic era.
- Halakhic summaries provide references to the authoritative legal decisions made over the centuries by the rabbis. They explain the reasons behind each halakhic decision as well as the ruling's close connection to the Talmud and its various interpreters.
- Photographs, drawings, and other illustrations have been added throughout the text – in full color in the Standard and Electronic editions, and in black and white in the Daf Yomi edition – to visually elucidate the text.

This is not an exhaustive list of features of this edition, it merely presents an overview for the English-speaking reader who may not be familiar with the "total approach" to Talmud pioneered by Rabbi Steinsaltz.

Several professionals have helped bring this vast collaborative project to fruition. My many colleagues are noted on the Acknowledgments page, and the leadership of this project has been exceptional.

RABBI MENACHEM EVEN-ISRAEL, DIRECTOR OF THE STEINSALTZ CENTER, was the driving force behind this enterprise. With enthusiasm and energy, he formed the happy alliance with Koren and established close relationships among all involved in the work.

RABBI DR. TZVI HERSH WEINREB שליט״א, EDITOR-IN-CHIEF, brought to this project his profound knowledge of Torah, intellectual literacy of Talmud, and erudition of Western literature. It is to him that the text owes its very high standard, both in form and content, and the logical manner in which the beauty of the Talmud is presented.

RABBI JOSHUA SCHREIER, EXECUTIVE EDITOR, assembled an outstanding group of scholars, translators, editors, and proofreaders, whose standards and discipline enabled this project to proceed in a timely and highly professional manner.

RABBI MEIR HANEGBI, EDITOR OF THE HEBREW EDITION OF THE STEINSALTZ TALMUD, lent his invaluable assistance throughout the work process, supervising the reproduction of the Vilna pages.

RAPHAËL FREEMAN, EXECUTIVE EDITOR OF KOREN, created this Talmud's unique typographic design which, true to the Koren approach, is both elegant and user friendly.

It has been an enriching experience for all of us at Koren Publishers Jerusalem to work with the Steinsaltz Center to develop and produce the *Koren Talmud Bavli*. We pray that this publication will be a source of great learning and, ultimately, greater *avodat Hashem* for all Jews.

Matthew Miller, Publisher
Koren Publishers Jerusalem
Jerusalem 5772

Contents

For the vocalized Vilna Shas layout, please open as a Hebrew book.

Introduction to Perek IV

And he shall slaughter the bull before the Lord, and Aaron's sons, the priests, shall present the blood, and sprinkle the blood roundabout against the altar that is at the door of the Tent of Meeting.

(Leviticus 1:5)

And the priest shall take of the blood of the sin offering with his finger, and put it upon the corners of the altar of burnt offering, and the remaining blood thereof he shall pour out at the base of the altar of burnt offering.

(Leviticus 4:25)

And you shall sacrifice your burnt offerings, the flesh and the blood, upon the altar of the Lord your God; and the blood of your offerings shall be poured against the altar of the Lord your God, and you shall eat the flesh.

(Deuteronomy 12:27)

This chapter concludes the discussion concerning *piggul* as well as disqualifying intentions in general. It starts by analyzing an improper intention that can lead to *piggul* in the presenting of the blood. Apropos to this case, the Gemara discusses at length the details of the presenting of the blood of various offerings. The chapter does not focus on the manner in which an offering is disqualified by intention, but on the prohibition of *piggul* itself: On which parts of an offering does *piggul* take effect, and on which parts does it not apply?

With regard to each offering one must distinguish between the factor that renders the offering permitted, i.e., through which it is accepted, and those parts of the offering that are rendered fit to be sacrificed or eaten by means of the permitting factor. An improper intention in the performance of a permitting factor, e.g., the presenting of the blood, renders the rest of the offering *piggul*. The basic *halakha* of *piggul* is derived from peace offerings, and therefore, as in the case of peace offerings, only those parts of the offering that are rendered permitted by a permitting factor are prohibited by *piggul* status.

This chapter clarifies which items do not have a permitting factor, either because they themselves render the rest of the offering permitted, or because the entire offering is sacrificed and consequently cannot be divided into permitting and permitted factors.

Furthermore, the Sages disagree about the status of additional parts of offerings, e.g., libations; whether they are considered part of the offering and therefore they have a permitting factor, or whether they have the status of a separate offering.

Incidental to the analysis of items on which the prohibition of *piggul* applies, the chapter also addresses other prohibitions that involve the consumption of offerings for which one can become liable to receive *karet*, specifically the prohibition against eating sacrificial meat in a state of ritual impurity and the prohibition against eating *notar*, i.e., sacrificial food that has been left over beyond its designated time. The Gemara discusses which parts of an offering are included in these prohibitions. The chapter concludes with a list of matters for the sake of which an offering must be slaughtered.

The clarification of these *halakhot* and their sources in the verses are the main issues of this chapter.

מתני׳ בית שמאי אומרים: כל הניתנין על מזבח החיצון, שנתן במתנה אחת – כיפר, ובחטאת – שתי מתנות. ובית הלל אומרים: אף חטאת שנתנה מתנה אחת – כיפר.

MISHNA **Beit Shammai say:** With regard to **all the** offerings **whose** blood is to be **placed**[N] **on the external altar,**[H] even those that require that the blood be sprinkled on two opposite corners of the altar so that it will run down each of its four sides, in a case **where** the priest **placed** the blood on the altar **with** only **one placement, he facilitated atonement. And in** the case of **a sin offering,** which requires four placements, one on each of the four corners of the altar, at least **two placements** are necessary to facilitate atonement. **And Beit Hillel say: Even** with regard to **a sin offering,** in a case **where** the priest **placed** the blood with **one placement, he facilitated atonement** after the fact.

לפיכך, אם נתן את הראשונה כתיקנה ואת השניה חוץ לזמנה – כיפר,

Therefore, since the priest facilitates atonement with one placement in all cases other than a sin offering according to Beit Shammai, and even in the case of a sin offering according to Beit Hillel, **if he placed the first** placement **in its proper manner,**[H] **and the second** with the intent to eat the offering **beyond its** designated **time, he facilitated atonement.** Since the second placement is not indispensable with regard to achieving atonement, improper intent while performing that rite does not invalidate the offering.

ואם נתן את הראשונה חוץ לזמנה ואת השניה חוץ למקומה – פיגול וחייבין עליו כרת.

And based on the same reasoning, **if he placed the first** placement with the intent to eat the offering **beyond its** designated **time**[N] **and** he placed **the second** placement with the intent to eat the offering **outside its** designated **area,** the second of which does not render an offering *piggul*, the offering is ***piggul***, an offering disqualified by improper intention, **and one is liable** to receive **excision from the World-to-Come** [***karet***] **for its** consumption. This is because the intent that accompanied the second placement does not supersede the *piggul* status of the offering.

כל הניתנין על המזבח הפנימי שאם חיסר אחת מן המתנות – כאילו לא כיפר. לפיכך, נתן כולן כתיקנן ואחת שלא כתיקנה – פסולה ואין בו כרת.

All this applies to those offerings whose blood is to be placed on the external altar. But with regard to **all** the offerings **whose** blood is to be **placed on the inner altar,**[NH] **if** the priest **omitted** even **one of the placements, it is as though he did not facilitate atonement. Therefore,** if **he placed all** the placements **in their proper manner, and one** placement **in an improper manner,** i.e., with the intent to eat the offering beyond its designated time, the offering is **disqualified,** as it is lacking one placement; **but there is no** liability for ***karet*** **for** one who partakes of the offering, as the improper intention related to only part of the blood that renders the offering permitted for consumption, and an offering becomes *piggul* only when the improper intention relates to the entire portion of the offering that renders it permitted for consumption.

NOTES

All whose blood is to be placed – כל הניתנין: As explained in Chapter Five, with regard to certain offerings a single pouring of the blood is required, from a vessel, onto one of the sides of the altar that has a base, i.e., not on the southeastern corner. These offerings are: The male firstborn of a kosher animal, an animal tithe offering, and the Paschal offering. Some other offerings require two sprinklings of blood, which are four. In other words, the blood must be sprinkled from a vessel onto two diagonally opposite corners of the altar so that the blood reaches all four of its sides. These offerings include the burnt offering, guilt offering, thanks offering, and peace offering. With regard to sin offerings that are to be placed on the external altar, their blood must be placed on all four corners of the altar, and not from a vessel but by the hand of the priest, *ab initio*.

Blood of the Paschal offering being passed to the altar and poured on the base

If he placed the first placement with the intent to eat the offering beyond its time – אם נתן את הראשונה חוץ לזמנה: As stated on 29a, if a priest sacrificed an offering with the intent to partake of it or burn it beyond its designated time, the offering is *piggul* and one who partakes of it is liable to receive *karet*, provided that the offering's permitting factor, the blood, was sacrificed in accordance with its mitzva, without any other disqualifying intentions. In this case, since only the first placement is indispensable, it is considered the permitting factor, and therefore the later intent to eat the offering outside its designated area does not negate its status as *piggul*, as the sacrifice is considered complete before the priest had that intent.

Whose blood is to be placed on the inner altar – הניתנין על מזבח הפנימי: These are the bull and goat of Yom Kippur (see Leviticus, chapter 16), the bull for an unwitting sin of the anointed priest, the bull for an unwitting communal sin (see Leviticus, chapter 4), and the goat for an unwitting communal sin of idol worship (see Numbers, chapter 15).

High Priest sprinkling blood on the inner altar on Yom Kippur

HALAKHA

All whose blood is placed on the external altar, etc. – כל הניתנין על מזבח החיצון וכו׳: With regard to all offerings whose blood is placed on the external altar, if the priest performed only one act of placement he facilitated atonement. Even in the case of a sin offering, which requires four placements *ab initio*, only one is indispensable to the rite, while the others are considered an additional mitzva. This is in accordance with the opinion of Beit Hillel (Rambam *Sefer Avoda*, *Hilkhot Pesulei HaMukdashin* 2:1).

If he placed the first placement in its proper manner – אם נתן את הראשונה כתיקנה: With regard to all blood that is placed on the external altar, the determinative placement is the first one. If one placed the first placement with proper intent, even if the other placements were performed with intent to eat the offering beyond its designated time or outside its designated area, the offering is valid and its owner has achieved atonement. If the first placement was performed with intent to eat the offering beyond its designated time, and the other placements were performed with the intent to eat the offering outside its designated area, the offering is *piggul* (Rambam *Sefer Avoda*, *Hilkhot Pesulei HaMukdashin* 17:1).

Whose blood is placed on the inner altar – הניתנין על מזבח הפנימי: With regard to all blood that is placed on the inner altar, if one placement was omitted the priest has not facilitated atonement, as all the placements are indispensable. The reason is that the verse specifies the precise number of placements: "Seven times" (Leviticus 4:6). Since all these are indispensable, if any of them are performed with improper intent, the offering is invalid. Nevertheless, the offering is *piggul* only if the priest placed all of them with the intent to eat the offering beyond its designated time, as all the placements are considered part of the same act (Rambam *Sefer Avoda*, *Hilkhot Pesulei HaMukdashin* 2:3, 17:1–2).

NOTES

And the blood of your offerings shall be poured – וְדַם זְבָחֶיךָ יִשָּׁפֵךְ: The verse does not state that the blood shall be poured around the altar as is written elsewhere, e.g., Leviticus 1:5. This indicates that one pouring is sufficient (Rashi).

גמ׳ תנו רבנן: מנין לניתנין על מזבח החיצון שנתנן במתנה אחת, שכיפר? תלמוד לומר: ״ודם זבחיך ישפך״. והאי להכי הוא דאתא? האי מיבעי ליה לכדתניא:

GEMARA **The Sages taught** in a *baraita*: **From where** is it derived **with regard to** those offerings whose blood is **placed on the external altar, that** if the priest **placed** the blood **with one placement, he facilitated atonement? The verse states: "And the blood of your offerings shall be poured**[N]" upon the altar of the Lord your God" (Deuteronomy 12:27), indicating that a single pouring of blood suffices. The Gemara asks: **But does this** verse **come to** teach **this** *halakha*? **That** verse **is necessary for that which is taught** in another *baraita* discussing a different matter:

Perek **IV**
Daf **37** Amud **a**

NOTES

Placement of blood on the base of the altar – מַתַּן דָּם לַיְסוֹד: This derivation is necessary because the *halakha* that the remainder of the blood must be poured onto the base of the altar is explicitly stated only with regard to a sin offering (see Leviticus 4:25), but not with regard to the other offerings.

This teaches that all the leftover blood – לִימֵּד עַל כָּל הַדָּמִים: Most commentaries, including Rashi, explain that it is derived from this verse that all offerings require the pouring of the remainder of the blood onto the base of the altar. The Ra'avad, citing Rabbeinu Efrayim, proposes an entirely different explanation of this passage, according to which no offerings, apart from the various types of sin offerings, require the pouring of the blood onto the base of the altar. He explains that the *halakha* mentioned here teaches that the blood must be sprinkled in an area of the altar that has a base, i.e., not on the southeastern corner (see 50a–b).

By sprinkling…by pouring – בִּזְרִיקָה...בִּשְׁפִיכָה: Sprinkling is performed by the priest at a distance from the altar; the blood is cast from a vessel onto the wall of the altar. In the case of pouring, the priest stands alongside the altar and pours the blood from the vessel onto the base of the altar (Rashi).

Sprinkling is not included in pouring – לֹא זְרִיקָה בִּכְלַל שְׁפִיכָה: Rashi explains this passage in the following manner: Rabbi Yishmael maintains that the blessing over the Paschal offering exempts one from reciting the blessing over the Festival offering, because if one poured the blood of a Festival offering in the manner that one does for a Paschal offering, he has fulfilled his obligation. By contrast, if the priest sprinkled the blood of a Paschal offering, in the manner that one does for a Festival peace offering, the offering is disqualified, and therefore the blessing over the Festival offering does not exempt one from reciting the blessing over the Paschal offering. In *Pesaḥim* (121a), Rashi explains that the issue here is not the sprinkling of the blood itself, but the treatment of the remainder of the blood: In the case of other offerings the remainder may be poured anywhere on the altar, whereas the blood of the Paschal offering must be poured onto the base of the altar.

Other commentaries claim that the very link between the blessing over an offering and the treatment of its blood is problematic (see *Tosafot* on *Pesaḥim* 121a). In fact, in the Jerusalem Talmud the dispute between Rabbi Yishmael and Rabbi Akiva is understood in an entirely different manner; the disagreement there is about the relationship between the consumption of these two offerings. Rabbi Yishmael holds that the primary mitzva is the eating of the Paschal offering, while the Festival peace offering is secondary, and there is a *halakha* that one recites a blessing over the primary food, and this exempts him from reciting a blessing over the secondary food (see *Berakhot* 44a). Conversely, Rabbi Akiva maintains that these are two separate mitzvot, and therefore the recitation of a blessing over one of them does not exempt one from reciting a blessing over the other. Re'em Horowitz explains that the disagreement concerns the blessing recited over the mitzva of placing the blood, and not blessing over the mitzva of partaking of the offerings.

מנין לכל הדמים שטעונים מתן דם ליסוד? תלמוד לומר: ״ודם זבחיך ישפך״! נפקא ליה מדרבי. דתניא, רבי אומר: ״והנשאר בדם ימצה״, שאין תלמוד לומר ״בדם״, ומה תלמוד לומר ״בדם״?

From where is it derived **that all** the **blood** that is left over from an offering after the requisite placement **requires placement of blood on the base** of the altar?[N] **The verse states: "And the blood of your offerings shall be poured** upon the altar of the Lord your God" (Deuteronomy 12:27). The Gemara answers: The *tanna* of the first *baraita* **derives** this **from** the verse cited **by Rabbi** Yehuda HaNasi, **as it is taught** in a *baraita*: **Rabbi** Yehuda HaNasi **says** with regard to a verse discussing a bird sin offering: **"And the rest of the blood shall be squeezed out** at the base of the altar; it is a sin offering" (Leviticus 5:9). **As** there is **no** need for **the verse to state "of the blood,"** because the entire verse is talking about the blood, **what** is the meaning when **the verse states "of the blood"?**

לפי שלא למדנו אלא לניתנין מתן ארבע שטעונין מתן דמים ליסוד, שאר דמים מנין? תלמוד לומר: ״והנשאר בדם ימצה״, שאין תלמוד לומר ״בדם״, ומה תלמוד לומר ״בדם״? לימד על כל הדמים שטעונין מתן דמים ליסוד.

The *baraita* continues: **Since we** have **learned only about** those offerings whose blood is **placed** on the altar with **four placements**, i.e., outer sin offerings, **that they require placement of the** leftover **blood on the base** of the altar, **from where** is it derived that the same applies to the leftover **blood** of all the **other** offerings? **The verse states: "And the rest of the blood shall be squeezed out** at the base of the altar; it is a sin offering" (Leviticus 5:9). **Since** there is **no** need for **the verse to state "of the blood,"** because the entire verse is talking about the blood, **what** is the meaning when **the verse states "of the blood"?** This **teaches that all the** leftover **blood**[N] from all the offerings **requires placement of blood on the base** of the altar.

ואכתי, להכי הוא דאתא? מיבעי ליה לכדתניא: מנין לניתנין בזריקה שנתנן בשפיכה יצא – תלמוד לומר: ״ודם זבחיך ישפך״!

The Gemara asks: **But still,** does **this** verse, Deuteronomy 12:27, **come to** teach **this** *halakha*, that if a priest placed the blood with one placement, he facilitated atonement? **That** verse **is necessary for that which is taught** in a *baraita*: **From where** is it derived **with regard to** those offerings whose blood is supposed to be **placed by** means of **sprinkling**[H] from a certain distance from the altar, **that** if the priest **placed** the blood **by pouring**[N] it from up close **he has fulfilled** his obligation? **The verse states: "And the blood of your offerings shall be poured** upon the altar of the Lord your God" (Deuteronomy 12:27).

סבר לה כרבי עקיבא, דאמר: לא זריקה בכלל שפיכה, ולא שפיכה בכלל זריקה.

The Gemara answers that the ruling in this *baraita* is in accordance with the opinion of Rabbi Yishmael, while the *tanna* of the earlier *baraita* **holds in accordance with** the opinion of **Rabbi Akiva, who says: Sprinkling is not included in pouring,**[N] **and** similarly **pouring is not included in sprinkling.** Rather, these are separate actions performed under different circumstances, and one does not fulfill his obligation to sprinkle the blood by pouring it. Therefore, the verse is available to him to teach that if a priest placed the blood with one placement, he facilitated atonement.

HALAKHA

With regard to those offerings whose blood is placed by sprinkling, etc. – לַנִּיתָּנִין בִּזְרִיקָה וכו׳: With regard to all offerings whose blood must be sprinkled, if the priest poured the blood he has fulfilled his obligation, as stated in the *baraita* (Rambam *Sefer Avoda, Hilkhot Pesulei HaMukdashin* 2:2 and *Kesef Mishne* there).

דְּתְנַן: בֵּרַךְ בִּרְכַּת הַפֶּסַח – פָּטַר אֶת שֶׁל זֶבַח,

The Gemara demonstrates that this is the opinion of Rabbi Akiva: This is **as we learned** in a mishna (*Pesaḥim* 121a): **If one recited the blessing over the Paschal offering,**[N] which is: Who sanctified us with His mitzvot and commanded us to eat the Paschal offering, **he has** also **exempted** himself from reciting a blessing over the Festival peace **offering,** i.e., the peace offering that is eaten together with the Paschal offering. The blessing for the Festival peace offering of the fourteenth of Nisan is: Who sanctified us with His mitzvot and commanded us to eat the offering.

שֶׁל זֶבַח – לֹא פָּטַר אֶת הַפֶּסַח, דִּבְרֵי רַבִּי יִשְׁמָעֵאל.

If he recited the blessing over the Festival **offering, he has not exempted** himself from reciting a blessing over **the Paschal offering.** This is **the statement of Rabbi Yishmael.** Rabbi Yishmael's reasoning is based on the *halakha* that the blood of the Paschal offering is poured, while the blood of the Festival offering is sprinkled. He maintains that sprinkling is included in the more general category of pouring, and therefore the blessing over the Paschal offering includes the Festival offering. Pouring is not included in the more limited category of sprinkling, and therefore reciting the blessing over the Festival offering does not exempt one from reciting a blessing over the Paschal offering.

רַבִּי עֲקִיבָא אוֹמֵר: לֹא זוֹ פּוֹטֶרֶת זוֹ, וְלֹא זוֹ פּוֹטֶרֶת זוֹ.

The mishna continues: **Rabbi Akiva says: This** blessing **does not exempt** one from reciting a blessing over **that one,**[H] **and that** blessing **does not exempt** one from reciting a blessing over **this one.** Sprinkling is not included in pouring, and pouring is not included in sprinkling. Therefore, there is a separate blessing for each offering.

אַכַּתִּי לְהָכִי הוּא דְּאָתָא? מִיבָּעֵי לֵיהּ לְכִדְתַנְיָא: רַבִּי יִשְׁמָעֵאל אוֹמֵר: מִתּוֹךְ שֶׁנֶּאֱמַר: ״אַךְ בְּכוֹר שׁוֹר אוֹ בְכוֹר כֶּשֶׂב אוֹ בְכוֹר עֵז״ וגו׳, לָמַדְנוּ לִבְכוֹר שֶׁטָּעוּן מַתַּן דָּמִים וְאֵימוּרִים לְגַבֵּי מִזְבֵּחַ, מַעֲשֵׂר וּפֶסַח מִנַּיִן? תַּלְמוּד לוֹמַר: ״וְדַם זְבָחֶיךָ יִשָּׁפֵךְ״!

The Gemara asks: **Still,** does **this** verse, Deuteronomy 12:27, **come** to teach **this** *halakha*, that if a priest placed the blood with one placement he facilitated atonement? That verse **is necessary for that which is taught** in a *baraita*: **Rabbi Yishmael says: Since it is stated: "But the firstborn of a bull, or the firstborn of a sheep, or the firstborn of a goat,** you shall not redeem; they are sacred. You shall sprinkle their blood upon the altar and shall burn their fat for an offering made by fire, for an aroma pleasing to the Lord" (Numbers 18:17), **we learned with regard to a firstborn** animal, which must be given to a priest to be offered on the altar in the Temple, **that it requires placement of** its **blood and sacrificial portions on the altar. From where** is it derived that the same applies to an animal **tithe** offering **and a Paschal offering?**[NH] **The verse states: "And the blood of your offerings shall be poured** upon the altar of the Lord your God" (Deuteronomy 12:27). This verse teaches that all offerings require placement of their blood on the altar.

סָבַר לָהּ כְּרַבִּי יוֹסֵי הַגְּלִילִי;

The Gemara answers that the *tanna* of the earlier *baraita*, who derives from Deuteronomy 12:27 the *halakha* that if a priest placed the blood with one placement he facilitated atonement, **holds in accordance with** the opinion of **Rabbi Yosei HaGelili.** Rabbi Yosei HaGelili maintains that the *halakha* that the blood and sacrificial parts of an animal tithe offering and a Paschal offering must be placed on the altar is derived from the aforementioned verse concerning a firstborn animal: "You shall sprinkle their blood upon the altar and shall burn their fat for an offering made by fire, for an aroma pleasing to the Lord" (Numbers 18:17).

דְּתַנְיָא, רַבִּי יוֹסֵי הַגְּלִילִי אוֹמֵר: ״דָּמוֹ״ לֹא נֶאֱמַר אֶלָּא ״דָּמָם״, ״חֶלְבּוֹ״ לֹא נֶאֱמַר אֶלָּא ״חֶלְבָּם״ – לִימֵּד עַל בְּכוֹר מַעֲשֵׂר וּפֶסַח שֶׁטְּעוּנִין מַתַּן דָּמִים וְאֵימוּרִין לְגַבֵּי מִזְבֵּחַ.

This is **as it is taught** in a *baraita*, that **Rabbi Yosei HaGelili says: It is not stated** in this verse: **Its blood, but** rather: **"Their blood."** Similarly, **it is not stated: Its fat, but** rather: **"Their fat."** The plural form **teaches with regard to** the **firstborn** animal, which is mentioned explicitly in the verse, as well as with regard to the animal **tithe** offering **and** the **Paschal offering,** which have a level of sanctity similar to that of a firstborn animal, **that** each **requires placement of** the **blood and sacrificial portions on the altar.**[H]

NOTES

If one recited the blessing over the Paschal offering – בֵּרַךְ בִּרְכַּת הַפֶּסַח: One brings the Festival peace offering together with the Paschal offering. The Festival peace offering is consumed first so that after eating the Paschal offering the person will be satiated.

From where is it derived that the same applies to an animal tithe and a Paschal offering – מַעֲשֵׂר וּפֶסַח מִנַּיִן: The Torah does not specify what must be done with the blood of these animals. Rabbi Yishmael therefore derives from Deuteronomy 12:27 that the blood of any offering whose rite is not explained elsewhere must be poured onto the altar.

HALAKHA

This blessing does not exempt that one, etc. – לֹא זוֹ פּוֹטֶרֶת זוֹ וכו׳: The blessing over the Paschal offering does not exempt one from reciting the blessing over the Festival peace offering, and likewise the blessing over the Festival peace offering does not exempt one from reciting the blessing over the Paschal offering, in accordance with the opinion of Rabbi Akiva (Rambam *Sefer Zemanim, Hilkhot Ḥametz UMatza* 8:7).

From where is it derived that the same applies to an animal tithe and a Paschal offering – מַעֲשֵׂר וּפֶסַח מִנַּיִן: The blood of the firstborn offering, of the animal tithe offering, and of the Paschal offering must be poured once against the base of the altar, on any side of the altar (Rambam *Sefer Avoda, Hilkhot Ma'aseh HaKorbanot* 5:17).

Sacrificial portions on the altar – אֵימוּרִין לְגַבֵּי הַמִּזְבֵּחַ: All offerings include portions that are consumed on the altar, which are placed there after the placement of the blood (Rambam *Sefer Avoda, Hilkhot Ma'aseh HaKorbanot* 5:18).

NOTES

Two *tanna'im* – **תְּרֵי תַּנָּאֵי**: According to the opinion that Rabbi Yishmael derives from this verse the *halakha* that the blood of the Paschal offering is poured, it cannot be that he derives from the same verse that sprinkling is included in pouring. Accordingly, this *baraita* would disagree with the presentation of the dispute in the mishna in *Pesaḥim*.

According to the opinion that Rabbi Yishmael derives from this verse that sprinkling is included in pouring, the blood of the Paschal offering is sprinkled, not poured, just like the blood of the Festival peace offering. Since, according to this opinion, the blood of the two offerings is treated in the same manner, the determination of which blessing exempts the other, if at all, cannot be established according to this criterion. Instead, Rabbi Yishmael's ruling is based on the *halakha* that one recites a blessing over a primary food, in this case the Paschal offering, and that blessing exempts one from having to recite a blessing over the secondary food, the meat of the Festival peace offering (Rashi).

וְרַבִּי יִשְׁמָעֵאל, הַאי קְרָא מַפֵּיק לֵיהּ לְהָכִי וּמַפֵּיק לֵיהּ לְהָכִי? תְּרֵי תַּנָּאֵי אַלִּיבָּא דְּרַבִּי יִשְׁמָעֵאל.

The Gemara asks: **But does Rabbi Yishmael derive** one *halakha* **from this verse and** then **derive** another *halakha* **from this** same verse? It was stated earlier that Rabbi Yishmael derives from the verse "And the blood of your offerings shall be poured" that sprinkling is included in pouring, and yet here he derives from that same verse that the blood of an animal tithe offering and that of a Paschal offering must be presented on the altar. The Gemara answers: These are the opinions of **two *tanna'im*,**[N] each of whom expressed his opinion **in accordance with** the opinion **of Rabbi Yishmael.**

בִּשְׁלָמָא לְרַבִּי יִשְׁמָעֵאל דְּמוֹקֵים לָהּ כּוּלֵּיהּ בִּבְכוֹר – הַיְינוּ דִּכְתִיב: "וּבְשָׂרָם יִהְיֶה לָּךְ",

The Gemara raises a question with regard to the disagreement about the interpretation of Numbers 18:17. **Granted, according to** the opinion of **Rabbi Yishmael, who interprets the entire** verse as referring **to a firstborn** animal, and according to whom the plural form in the verse is referring to three such firstborns, that of a bull, that of a sheep, and that of a goat, **this** explains that **which is written** immediately afterward: **"And their meat shall be yours"** (Numbers 18:18), in the plural, i.e., the meat of these firstborn animals shall be eaten by the priests.

אֶלָּא לְרַבִּי יוֹסֵי דְּמוֹקֵי לֵיהּ נַמִּי בְּמַעֲשֵׂר וּפֶסַח – מַעֲשֵׂר וּפֶסַח בְּעָלִים אָכְלִי לֵיהּ, מַאי "וּבְשָׂרָם יִהְיֶה לָּךְ"? אֶחָד תָּם וְאֶחָד בַּעַל מוּם,

But according to the opinion of **Rabbi Yosei, who interprets** this verse as referring **also to** an animal **tithe** offering **and a Paschal offering**, there is a difficulty, as an animal **tithe** offering **and a Paschal offering are eaten by their owners,** not by the priests. If so, **what** is the meaning of the phrase **"and their meat shall be yours"?** The Gemara answers that the plural term "their meat," is referring not to an animal tithe offering or a Paschal offering, but to different types of firstborns, i.e., **both an unblemished** animal, whose blood is poured on the altar, **and a blemished** one, which is not brought as an offering on the altar.

Perek **IV**
Daf **37** Amud **b**

HALAKHA

A blemished firstborn is given to a priest – **בְּכוֹר בַּעַל מוּם שֶׁנִּיתָּן לַכֹּהֵן**: If a male firstborn of a kosher animal has a blemish, whether it was born with the blemish or whether it developed the blemish later, it is given to a priest and it becomes that priest's property in all regards (Rambam *Sefer Korbanot*, *Hilkhot Bekhorot* 1:3).

לִימֵּד עַל בְּכוֹר בַּעַל מוּם שֶׁנִּיתָּן לַכֹּהֵן, שֶׁלֹּא מָצִינוּ לוֹ בְּכָל הַתּוֹרָה כּוּלָּהּ.

This verse **teaches that a blemished firstborn is given to a priest**[H] as a gift, and that he may eat its meat. This is a novel concept, **as we have not found in the entire Torah**[N] another *halakha* similar **to it,** where a blemished offering is given to the priests for consumption.

וְרַבִּי יִשְׁמָעֵאל? נָפְקָא לֵיהּ מִ"לְךָ יִהְיֶה" דְּסֵיפָא.

The Gemara asks: **And** according to **Rabbi Yishmael,** who interprets this verse differently, from where does he derive this *halakha* that a blemished firstborn is given to a priest? The Gemara answers: **He derives it from** the phrase: "As the breast of waving and as the right thigh, **it shall be yours"** (Numbers 18:18), **which is the latter clause** of that same verse. The repetition of the phrase "shall be yours" serves to teach that even the meat of a blemished firstborn shall be eaten by the priests.

NOTES

As we have not found in the entire Torah – **שֶׁלֹּא מָצִינוּ לוֹ בְּכָל הַתּוֹרָה כּוּלָּהּ**: Some explain that we have found no other source in the Torah for this *halakha* (Rashi). This interpretation is somewhat problematic, as there are many *halakhot* that are derived from a single source, and therefore it is unclear why the Gemara would deem it necessary to point out this fact in this particular case. Other commentaries explain that a unique *halakha* applies in the case of a firstborn. In general, when a consecrated animal develops a blemish, it is sold and the proceeds are used for the purchase of another animal that will be sacrificed on the altar. The firstborn is an exception in this regard, as when it develops a blemish it is given as a gift to a priest (*Tosafot*). Others add that the novelty is that a blemished firstborn belongs to a priest even if it developed the blemish while still in the possession of the owner (*Keren Ora*).

בִּשְׁלָמָא לְרַבִּי יוֹסֵי הַגְּלִילִי דְּמוֹקֵי לֵיהּ נַמִּי בְּמַעֲשֵׂר וּפֶסַח – הַיְינוּ דִּכְתִיב: ״לֹא תִפְדֶּה כִּי קֹדֶשׁ הֵם״ – הֵם קְרֵיבִין, וְאֵין תְּמוּרָתָן קְרֵיבָה,

§ The Gemara raises another question: **Granted, according to** the opinion of **Rabbi Yosei HaGelili, who interprets** the verse as referring **also to** an animal **tithe** offering **and a Paschal offering, this is as it is written** in the same verse: **"You shall not redeem; they are sacred"** (Numbers 18:17). The word "they" indicates that only **they are sacrificed** on the altar, **but their substitutes are not sacrificed.**[N] In general, if one substitutes a non-sacred animal for one designated as an offering, both the original and the substitute are considered to be consecrated, and they are therefore sacrificed. But if one substitutes a non-sacred animal for a firstborn, an animal tithe offering, or a Paschal offering, the substitute is not sacrificed.

דִּתְנַן: תְּמוּרַת בְּכוֹר וּמַעֲשֵׂר – הֵן וּוְלָדָן וּוְלַד וְלָדָן עַד סוֹף כָּל הָעוֹלָם – הֲרֵי הֵן כִּבְכוֹר וּמַעֲשֵׂר, וְיֵאָכְלוּ בְּמוּמָן לַבְּעָלִים;

This is **as we learned** in a mishna (*Temura* 21a): With regard to **the substitute of a firstborn and** of an animal **tithe** offering,[H] both **they,** the substitutes themselves, **and their offspring, and the offspring of their offspring,**[H] **forever,** i.e., for all future generations, **are as the firstborn and** the animal **tithe** offering, respectively, **and** therefore **they are eaten in their blemished** state **by the owners;** but unlike the firstborn and the animal tithe offering themselves, they are not sacrificed on the altar.

וּתְנַן, אָמַר רַבִּי יְהוֹשֻׁעַ: שָׁמַעְתִּי שֶׁתְּמוּרַת פֶּסַח קְרֵיבָה, וּתְמוּרַת פֶּסַח אֵינָהּ קְרֵיבָה, וְאֵין לִי לְפָרֵשׁ.

And likewise with regard to the substitute of a Paschal offering, **we learned** in a mishna (*Pesaḥim* 96b) that **Rabbi Yehoshua**[P] **says:** I have **heard** two rulings from my teachers: One ruling was **that the substitute of a Paschal offering**[H] **is sacrificed** as a peace offering after Passover, **and** another ruling was that **the substitute of a Paschal offering is not offered** as a peace offering after Passover; **and I cannot explain** these apparently contradictory rulings, as I do not remember the circumstances to which each ruling applies. And as will be explained, if the substitution took place after the sacrifice of the Paschal offering, the animal is sacrificed, as it is considered the substitute of a peace offering, whereas if the substitution occurred before the sacrifice of the Paschal offering, it is not sacrificed, as it is the substitute of a Paschal offering. This indicates that the substitute of a Paschal offering is not sacrificed, just like the substitute of a firstborn is not sacrificed.

אֶלָּא לְרַבִּי יִשְׁמָעֵאל דְּמוֹקֵי לֵיהּ כּוּלֵּיהּ בִּבְכוֹר, מַעֲשֵׂר וּפֶסַח דְּלָא קְרֵיבָה תְּמוּרָתָן מְנָא לֵיהּ? מַעֲשֵׂר גָּמַר עֲבָרָה עֲבָרָה מִבְּכוֹר.

But according to the opinion of **Rabbi Yishmael, who interprets the entire** verse as dealing **with a firstborn, from where does he** derive the *halakha* **that the substitute of** an animal **tithe** offering **and of a Paschal offering are not sacrificed?** The Gemara answers: With regard to an animal **tithe** offering, **he derives** this by means of a verbal analogy between the terms **passing,** and **passing** written **with regard to a firstborn.** Concerning a firstborn it is stated: "And you shall pass [*veha'avarta*] to the Lord all that opens the womb" (Exodus 13:12), and concerning an animal tithe it is stated: "Of whatever passes [*ya'avor*] under the rod" (Leviticus 27:32). From this verbal analogy it may be derived that just as the substitute of a firstborn is not sacrificed, so too, the substitute of an animal tithe offering is not sacrificed.

פֶּסַח – בְּהֶדְיָא כְּתַב בֵּיהּ: ״כֶּשֶׂב״, מַה תַּלְמוּד לוֹמַר: ״אִם כֶּשֶׂב״ – לְרַבּוֹת תְּמוּרַת הַפֶּסַח אַחַר הַפֶּסַח, שֶׁתִּקְרַב שְׁלָמִים. יָכוֹל אַף לִפְנֵי הַפֶּסַח כֵּן? תַּלְמוּד לוֹמַר: ״הוּא״.

With regard to the **Paschal offering,** this *halakha* is not derived through a verbal analogy, but rather this *halakha* **is explicitly written concerning it.** The verse referring to peace offerings states: "If he offers a lamb for his offering" (Leviticus 3:7). The Torah could simply have stated: **A lamb,** and proceed from there to teach the *halakhot* of a lamb peace offering. If so, **what** is the meaning when **the verse states: "If he offers a lamb"?** This serves **to include the substitute of a Paschal offering** that was substituted **after** the sacrifice of **the Paschal offering,** teaching **that it is sacrificed as a peace offering,** since the Paschal offering has the status of a peace offering after that time. One **might** have thought that **even before** the sacrifice of **the Paschal offering the same** should apply, i.e., that the substitute of a Paschal offering is sacrificed as a peace offering. Therefore, **the verse states** with regard to the Paschal offering: "It is the sacrifice of the Lord's Passover" (Exodus 12:27), which indicates that **it,** the Paschal offering itself, is sacrificed, but its substitute is not sacrificed.

NOTES

But their substitutes are not sacrificed – **וְאֵין תְּמוּרָתָן קְרֵיבָה**: Generally, the substitute of an offering is treated like the offering itself; the substitute of a burnt offering is sacrificed as a burnt offering, and the substitute of a peace offering is sacrificed as a peace offering. In the cases mentioned in the Gemara, however, the substitute is not sacrificed, as it states: "They are sacred" (Numbers 18:17), indicating that the offerings themselves are sacred, but that their substitutes are not. With regard to the substitute of an animal tithe offering, one waits until it develops a blemish, at which point it is eaten by the owner. The substitute of a firstborn is given to a priest. Rabbi Yehoshua adds that the substitute of a Paschal offering is also not sacrificed.

HALAKHA

The substitute of a firstborn and animal tithe – **תְּמוּרַת בְּכוֹר וּמַעֲשֵׂר**: The substitute of a firstborn offering is given to a priest, while the substitute of an animal tithe offering remains with its owner. Just as a firstborn offering or animal tithe offering that develops a blemish is not redeemed, likewise, its substitute is not redeemed (Rambam *Sefer Korbanot, Hilkhot Temura* 3:2).

Their offspring and the offspring of their offspring – **וְלָדָן וּוְלַד וְלָדָן**: The offspring of an animal tithe offering, the offspring of the substitute of an animal tithe offering, the offspring of the substitute of a male firstborn offering, and the offspring of all of these offspring in all subsequent generations, are not sacrificed upon the altar. Rather, they are left to graze until they develop blemishes, at which point they are eaten in the manner of a firstborn or animal tithe offering that developed a blemish (Rambam *Sefer Korbanot, Hilkhot Temura* 4:6).

The substitute of a Paschal offering – **תְּמוּרַת פֶּסַח**: With regard to one who lost his Paschal offering and separated another animal in its stead, and later found the first one so that both animals are available, he sacrifices whichever he chooses as a Paschal offering, and the other is sacrificed as a peace offering. If he found the first animal after the second had already been sacrificed, the first should be sacrificed as a peace offering. If he performed substitution on this first animal after the second was sacrificed, the substitute is sacrificed as a peace offering. If he found the first animal before the second was slaughtered, and performed substitution on this first animal, this substitute is not sacrificed but is left to graze until it develops a blemish, at which point it is sold and the money used for the purchase of a peace offering (Rambam *Sefer Korbanot, Hilkhot Korban Pesaḥ* 4:6).

PERSONALITIES

Rabbi Yehoshua – **רַבִּי יְהוֹשֻׁעַ**: Rabbi Yehoshua ben Ḥananya was one of the leading Sages in the generation following the destruction of the Second Temple. A Levite, he served as a singer in the Temple. After its destruction, he was among the students who followed their primary teacher, Rabban Yoḥanan ben Zakkai, to Yavne. Rabbi Yehoshua lived a life of poverty, worked as a blacksmith, and was recognized by all as a leading Torah authority. While he disagreed with Rabban Gamliel's rulings on several occasions, he ultimately accepted the authority of the *Nasi*. After Rabban Gamliel's death, he acted as a leader of the Sages.

וְכָל הָנָךְ תַּנָּאֵי דְּמַפְּקִי לֵיהּ לְהַאי ״דַּם זְבָחֶיךָ יִשָּׁפֵךְ״ לִדְרָשָׁא אַחֲרִינָא, הַאי כָּל הַנִּיתָּנִין עַל מִזְבֵּחַ הַחִיצוֹן שֶׁנְּתָנָן מַתָּנָה אַחַת שֶׁכִּיפֵּר, מְנָא לְהוּ? סָבְרִי לְהוּ כְּבֵית הִלֵּל, דְּאָמְרִי: אַף חַטָּאת שֶׁנְּתָנָהּ מַתָּנָה אַחַת כִּיפֵּר, וְיָלְפִינַן כּוּלְּהוּ מֵחַטָּאת.

The Gemara asks: **And** as for **all those *tanna'im* who derive a different exposition from this** verse: **"And the blood of your offerings shall be poured"** (Deuteronomy 12:27), **this** *halakha* that is recorded in the mishna, that with regard to **all** the offerings **whose** blood is to be **placed on the external altar,** in a case **where** the priest **placed** the blood on the altar with **one placement, he facilitated atonement, from where do they** derive this? The Gemara answers: Those *tanna'im* **hold in accordance with** the opinion of **Beit Hillel, who say: Even** with regard to **a sin offering,** in a case **where** the priest **placed** the blood with **one placement, he facilitated atonement** after the fact. **And they derive** the *halakha* applying to **all** the other offerings **from** that which applies to **a sin offering.**

״וְהַחַטָּאת – שְׁתֵּי מַתָּנוֹת״. אֲמַר רַב הוּנָא: מַאי טַעְמָא דְּבֵית שַׁמַּאי?

§ The mishna teaches that Beit Shammai maintain that in the case of **a sin offering,** which requires four placements, at least **two placements** are necessary to facilitate atonement, whereas Beit Hillel hold that even in the case of a sin offering one placement suffices. **Rav Huna said: What is the reasoning** for the opinion **of Beit Shammai?**

״קַרְנוֹת״ ״קַרְנוֹת״ ״קַרְנוֹת״ – הֲרֵי כָּאן שֵׁשׁ, אַרְבָּעָה לְמִצְוָה וּשְׁתַּיִם לְעַכֵּב.

He explains: The verse states: "And the priest shall take of the blood of the sin offering with his finger, and put it upon the **corners** of the altar" (Leviticus 4:25). Subsequently, the verse states: "The priest shall take of its blood with his finger, and put it on the **corners** of the altar" (Leviticus 4:30), and an additional verse states: "The priest shall take of the blood of the sin offering with his finger, and put it on the **corners** of the altar" (Leviticus 4:34). As the minimum amount justifying the use of the plural form, i.e., in the word "corners," is two, one may conclude that **there are six** references to the corners of the altar **here. Four** of them are mentioned **for a mitzva,** meaning that the priest should place the blood on all four corners of the altar *ab initio,* **and** the other **two** are mentioned **to invalidate** the offering if he did not present the blood on at least two corners.

וּבֵית הִלֵּל: ״קַרְנֹת״ ״קַרְנֹת״ ״קַרְנוֹת״ – הֲרֵי כָּאן אַרְבַּע, שָׁלֹשׁ לְמִצְוָה אַחַת לְעַכֵּב.

The Gemara asks: **And** what is the reasononing for the opinion of **Beit Hillel?** The Gemara answers: The matter should be understood according to the written consonantal text, i.e., the way in which the words are actually spelled. The word **"corners"** is written plene, i.e., with a *vav*, in one of the verses, which means that it must be read in the plural form. In the other two verses, **"corners"** and **"corners"** are written deficient, i.e., without a *vav*, in a way that can be vocalized in the singular form, i.e., as *karnat*. Therefore, **there are four** references to corners **here. Three** of these references are written **to** indicate the placements of blood are performed only as **a mitzva,** i.e., they are performed *ab initio*, and the remaining **one** is written **to** indicate that its absence **invalidates** the offering, i.e., the offering is not valid if the blood was not placed against at least one corner of the altar.

וְאֵימָא: כּוּלְּהוּ לְמִצְוָה! כַּפָּרָה בִּכְדִי לָא אַשְׁכַּחַן.

The Gemara asks: **But** according to this explanation of Beit Hillel, why not **say** that **all of them are** written **for** the **mitzva** and none are to invalidate, i.e., that the blood must be presented on all four corners *ab initio*, but the offering atones after the fact even if the blood was not presented at all? The Gemara rejects this possibility: **We have not found** anywhere in the Torah an example of an offering in which **atonement** can be achieved **with no** placement[N] of the blood.

וְאִיבָּעֵית אֵימָא, הַיְינוּ טַעְמָא דְּבֵית הִלֵּל: אִהֲנֵי מִקְרָא וְאַהֲנֵי מָסוֹרֶת, אַהֲנֵי מִקְרָא – לְטַפּוּיֵי חֲדָא, וְאַהֲנֵי מָסוֹרֶת – לְבַצּוּרֵי חֲדָא.

And if you wish, say instead that **this is the reason of Beit Hillel: The vocalized text** of the Torah, i.e., the way in which the words of the Torah are pronounced based on the tradition of what vowels the words contain, **is effective** in determining how the verses are to be expounded. **And** likewise, **the consonantal text**[B] of the Torah, i.e., the way in which the words are actually written, **is** also **effective** in determining how the verses are to be expounded. The Gemara elaborates: **The vocalized text is effective in adding one** more corner **and the consonantal text is effective in subtracting one** corner. Consequently, the verse is interpreted as referring to five corners, four of which are necessary for the mitzva *ab initio*, and one of which is indispensable after the fact.

NOTES

We have not found atonement with no placement – **כַּפָּרָה בִּכְדִי לָא אַשְׁכַּחַן:** The *Sefat Emet* notes that even according to this answer, the four mentions of corners in the Torah all are referring to the mitzva *ab initio*, as the claim that we have not found anywhere that atonement is achieved without placement is an axiomatic statement, not a *halakha* derived from a verse. Accordingly, the statement: Three of these placements are written to indicate that they are performed only as a mitzva, and the remaining one is written to indicate that its absence invalidates the offering, is not an exposition of the verses but is rooted in the axiom that atonement cannot be achieved without any placement of the blood.

BACKGROUND

Consonantal text – מָסוֹרֶת: Both the consonantal and vocalized texts of the Torah are rooted in the most ancient traditions, and the question as to which is authoritative must be addressed when one wishes to draw halakhic conclusions from one in instances where it contradicts the other. This issue is treated in several places in the Talmud. In fact, with regard to which version is authoritative, neither opinion entirely precludes the other, as everyone agrees that both the vocalization and the consonantal text must be taken into consideration.

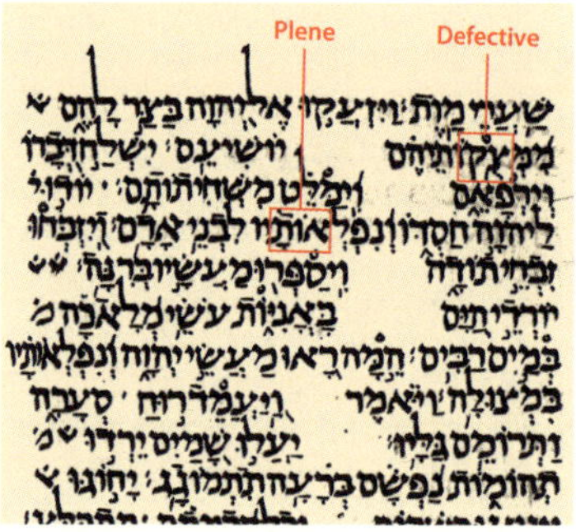

Excerpt from the book of Psalms in the Leningrad Codex, showing plene and defective spellings in the consonantal text

אֶלָּא מֵעַתָּה, ״לְטֹטָפֹת״ ״לְטֹטָפֹת״ ״לְטוֹטָפוֹת״ – הֲרֵי כָּאן אַרְבַּע, אַהֲנֵי קְרָא וְאַהֲנֵי מָסוֹרֶת – חֲמִשָּׁה בָּתֵּי בָּעֵי לְמֶיעֱבַד!

The Gemara asks: **But if that is so,** that this is the proper manner of expounding the verses, consider the case of the phylacteries of the head, about which it is stated: "And **for frontlets** [*totafot*] between your eyes" (Exodus 13:16), and: "They shall be **for frontlets** [*totafot*] between your eyes" (Deuteronomy 6:8), and subsequently: "They shall be **for frontlets** [*totafot*] between your eyes" (Deuteronomy 11:18). The word *totafot* is written once in plene form, i.e., with a *vav*, indicating the plural form, and twice in a deficient form, i.e., without a *vav*, indicating the singular. Accordingly, **there are four** frontlets **here,**[N] and from here the Sages derive that the phylacteries of the head consist of four compartments, which together form a cube. Why not say that **the vocalized text,** read in the plural, **is effective,** i.e., that it requires six compartments, **and** likewise, **the consonantal text,** read in the singular, **is effective,** i.e., it requires four compartments, and therefore one should be **required to prepare five compartments** for the phylacteries of the head?

סָבַר לַהּ כְּרַבִּי עֲקִיבָא, דְּאָמַר: ״טֹט״ בְּכַתְפֵּי שְׁתַּיִם, ״פַּת״ בְּאַפְרִיקִי שְׁתַּיִם.

The Gemara answers that Beit Hillel **hold in accordance with** the opinion of **Rabbi Akiva, who says** that the requirement to have four compartments in the phylacteries of the head is not derived from the number of times that the word *totafot* is mentioned, but rather from an exposition of the word *totafot* itself: ***Tot*** **in the Katpi** language means **two,** and ***pat*** **in the Afriki** language means **two,** for a total of four.

אֶלָּא מֵעַתָּה, ״בַּסֻּכֹּת״ ״בַּסֻּכֹּת״ ״בַּסּוּכּוֹת״ – אַהֲנֵי מִקְרָא וְאַהֲנֵי מָסוֹרֶת, חַמְשָׁא דָּפְנָתָא בָּעֵי לְמֶיעֱבַד!

The Gemara raises another objection to this method of exposition: **If that is so,** consider the case of a *sukka,* about which it is stated: "**In *sukkot*** [***basukkot***] shall you reside seven days; all that are home-born in Israel shall reside **in *sukkot*** [***basukkot***]. So that your future generations will know that I caused the children of Israel to reside **in *sukkot*** [***basukkot***] when I took them out of the land of Egypt: I am the Lord your God" (Leviticus 23:42–43). Two instances of the word *basukkot* are written in a deficient manner, i.e., without a *vav,* indicating the singular, and one instance is written in plene form, i.e., with a *vav,* indicating the plural form. The Sages derived from here that a *sukka* must have four walls. Why not say that **the vocalized text,** read in the plural, **is effective,** requiring six walls, **and** likewise, **the consonantal text,** read in the singular, **is effective,** requiring four walls, and therefore one should be **required to build** a *sukka* with **five walls?**

NOTES

For frontlets, there are four here – לְטוֹטָפוֹת הֲרֵי כָּאן אַרְבַּע: The commentaries note that according to the Masoretic text of the Torah the word *totafot* is always written without a second *vav* (*Tosafot*, citing Rabbeinu Tam). Rabbeinu Tam therefore explains that the exposition is based on the *vav* at the beginning of the word *uletotafot* (Exodus 13:16). This *vav* means "and," indicating an extra compartment. Alternatively, the reference is to the *vav* between the two instances of the letter *tet*, and the word is interpreted as though the *vav* appeared after the *peh*, which would indicate the plural. This is similar to the exegetical method of: The Sages subtract and add and interpret homiletically, in which letters are moved from one place to another for the purposes of an exposition.

The word *ultotafot* as written in a Torah scroll

Perek **IV**
Daf **38** Amud **a**

הָתָם חַד קְרָא כּוּלֵּיהּ לְגוּפֵיהּ, וְחַד לִסְכָכָה, אֲתַאי הִלְכְתָא וּגְרַעְתָּהּ לִשְׁלִישִׁית וְאוֹקִימְתָּהּ אַטֶּפַח.

The Gemara answers: **There, one** of the five indicated by the **verse** is needed **entirely for** the mitzva **itself,** i.e., to teach the basic *halakha* that one must dwell in a *sukka*. **And** another **one** of the five is needed **to** teach that a *sukka,* as is indicated by its name, must have **a covering** [*sekhakha*].[N] Accordingly, there are three left, alluding to the requirement that a *sukka* must have three walls. The Gemara adds that **the *halakha*** transmitted to Moses from Sinai **comes and reduces the** size of the **third** wall, teaching that it need not be complete, **and sets** its minimum length **at** only **one handbreadth.**[B]

BACKGROUND

Handbreadth – טֶפַח: This measure represents the width of a clenched fist. One handbreadth is equal to four fingerbreadths, which is equivalent to five times the width of the middle finger, or six times the width of the little finger. According to the measurements of Rabbi Ḥayyim Na'e, a handbreadth is 8 cm. According to the measurements of the *Ḥazon Ish*, it is 9.6 cm.

NOTES

And one to teach it must have a covering – וְחַד לִסְכָכָה: This exposition is apparently superfluous, as a *sukka* by definition includes a covering. Nevertheless, as the word *basukkot* is interpreted as addressing the structure of the *sukka* in that it refers to the number of walls, it is fitting that the other part of the structure of a *sukka*, its covering, should be mentioned as well (Rashi).

אֶלָּא מֵעַתָּה, "וְטָמְאָה שְׁבֻעַיִם" – שִׁבְעִים, אַהֲנֵי קְרָא וְאַהֲנֵי מָסוֹרֶת – אַרְבָּעִים וּתְרֵין בָּעֲיָא לְמֵיתַב!

The Gemara raises yet another objection: **If that is so,** that both the vocalized and the consonantal texts are taken into account, consider the case of a woman who gives birth to a female child. Concerning this woman the verse states: "But if she bear a female child, **then she shall be impure two weeks** [*shevu'ayim*],[B] as in her menstruation" (Leviticus 12:5). The way that the word is written allows it to be read as ***shivim***, seventy. Why not say that **the vocalized text** of the Torah **is effective,** teaching us that the woman is ritually impure for fourteen days, **and the consonantal text is** also **effective,** teaching us that she is impure for seventy days, and, therefore, **she** should be **required to sit** in a state of ritual impurity for **forty-two** days, which is the halfway point between fourteen and seventy days?

שָׁאנֵי הָתָם, דִּכְתִיב: "כְּנִדָּתָהּ".

The Gemara answers: **There it is different,** and the consonantal text is disregarded entirely, **as it is written: "As in her menstruation,"**[N] and a menstruating woman is impure for one week. Evidently, the verse is speaking in terms of weeks, and is not alluding to the number seventy at all.

וְתַנָּא מַיְיתֵי לַהּ מֵהָכָא: "וְכִפֶּר" "וְכִפֶּר" "וְכִפֶּר" מִפְּנֵי הַדִּין.

§ The Gemara further analyzes the opinion of Beit Hillel that even in the case of a sin offering, if the priest placed the blood on the altar with one placement, he facilitated atonement. **And a *tanna*** cites proof **for this from here,** as it was taught in a *baraita*: The verse states with regard to the sin offering brought by a king: **"And** the priest **shall make atonement** for him" (Leviticus 4:26), and with regard to the goat brought as a sin offering by an ordinary person: **"And** the priest **shall make atonement** for him" (Leviticus 4:31), and with regard to the sheep brought as a sin offering by an ordinary person: **"And** the priest **shall make atonement** for him" (Leviticus 4:35). The repetition of this term is **due to a logical inference.**

שֶׁיָּכוֹל, וַהֲלֹא דִּין הוּא: נֶאֶמְרוּ דָּמִים לְמַטָּה וְנֶאֶמְרוּ דָּמִים לְמַעְלָה, מָה מַתַּן דָּמִים הָאֲמוּרִים לְמַטָּה שֶׁנְּתָנָן בְּמַתָּנָה אַחַת כִּיפֵּר – אַף דָּמִים הָאֲמוּרִים לְמַעְלָה שֶׁנְּתָנָן בְּמַתָּנָה אַחַת כִּיפֵּר.

As one **might** have thought to say: **Could this not** be derived through **logical inference** as follows: It **is stated** that **blood** is placed **below** the red line, **and** it **is stated** that **blood** is placed **above** the red line. **Just as** with regard to the **blood concerning** which it **is stated** that it is placed **below** the red line, **when** the priest **placed** it on the altar **with one placement he facilitated atonement, so too,** with regard to the **blood concerning** which it **is stated** that it is placed **above** the red line, **when** the priest **placed** it on the altar **with one placement he facilitated atonement.**

אוֹ כְּלָךְ לְדֶרֶךְ זוֹ: נֶאֶמְרוּ דָּמִים בִּפְנִים וְנֶאֶמְרוּ דָּמִים בַּחוּץ, מָה דָּמִים הָאֲמוּרִים בִּפְנִים – חִיסֵּר אַחַת מִן הַמַּתָּנוֹת לֹא עָשָׂה וְלֹא כְלוּם, אַף דָּמִים הָאֲמוּרִין בַּחוּץ – חִיסֵּר אַחַת מִן הַמַּתָּנוֹת לֹא עָשָׂה וְלֹא כְלוּם!

Or perhaps, **go this way,** turning away from the previous explanation and toward this explanation: It **is stated** that **blood** is presented **on** the **inner** altar, i.e., with regard to a sin offering of the community or of the High Priest; the blood of these offerings is sprinkled on the incense altar that is inside the Sanctuary. **And** it **is stated** that **blood** is presented **on** the **external** altar, i.e., with regard to the sin offering of an ordinary person, which is offered on the outer altar that is in the courtyard. **Just as** with regard to the **blood concerning** which it **is stated** that it is presented **on** the **inner** altar, if the priest **omitted one of the placements he has done nothing,** i.e., the offering is not valid, **so too,** with regard to the **blood concerning** which it **is stated** that it is presented **on** the **external** altar, if the priest **omitted one of the placements he has done nothing.**

נִרְאֶה לְמִי דּוֹמֶה, דָּנִין חוּץ מֵחוּץ, וְאֵין דָּנִין חוּץ מִבִּפְנִים. אוֹ כְּלָךְ לְדֶרֶךְ זוֹ: דָּנִין חַטָּאת וְאַרְבַּע קְרָנוֹת מֵחַטָּאת וְאַרְבַּע קְרָנוֹת, וְאַל יוֹכִיחַ חוּץ, שֶׁאֵין חַטָּאת וְאַרְבַּע קְרָנוֹת!

The Gemara analyzes the two possibilities: **Let us see to which** of the two cases the blood of an animal sin offering is more **similar.** It can be claimed: We **derive** a *halakha* stated with regard to the **external** altar **from** a *halakha* stated with regard to the **external** altar, **but** we **do not derive** a *halakha* stated with regard to the **external** altar **from** a *halakha* stated with regard to the **inner** altar. **Or, go this way: We derive** a *halakha* stated with regard to **a sin offering** whose blood is to be placed on the **four corners** of the altar **from** a *halakha* stated with regard to **a sin offering** whose blood is to be placed on the **four corners** of the altar. **But** a sin offering consisting of a bird, **which is not a sin offering** whose blood is to be placed on the **four corners** of the altar, **cannot serve as proof** to the *halakha* concerning an animal sin offering, whose blood is to be placed on the four corners of the altar.

BACKGROUND

Impure two weeks – טָמְאָה שְׁבֻעַיִם: The Torah describes various *halakhot* that apply to a woman after she has given birth. A new mother is considered ritually impure for seven days if she gave birth to a boy, and for fourteen days if she gave birth to a girl. Later, after immersion in a ritual bath, she is ritually pure for the next thirty-three or sixty-six days, respectively, even if she experiences uterine bleeding. Nevertheless, during this total period of forty days for a boy and of eighty days for a girl, it is prohibited for the mother to enter the Temple or to partake of the meat of offerings. After the fortieth or eightieth day she brings a purification offering in the Temple. This offering consists of a male lamb that is in its first year, which is brought as a burnt offering; and a young pigeon or dove, which is brought as a sin offering. If she cannot afford the cost of a lamb for the burnt offering, she can bring two doves or two young pigeons, one as a burnt offering and the other as a sin offering. She may then enter the Temple and partake of sacrificial foods (see Leviticus 12:1–8).

Women after childbirth presenting purification offerings in the Temple

NOTES

As in her menstruation – כְּנִדָּתָהּ: Since the period of menstruation is one week, this indicates that one should follow the reading that employs units of weeks, i.e., two weeks. Admittedly, seventy can also be divided into weeks, but ten weeks is far longer than the period of menstruation (Rashi). Alternatively, the verse should be understood as follows: In addition to the number of days that a woman is ritually impure after giving birth to a male child, a woman who gives birth to a female is impure for another period equal to her period of menstruation, which is one week (see Leviticus 12:2); the total time is therefore two weeks (*Tosafot*).

תלמוד לומר: "וכפר" "וכפר" "וכפר" (מפני הדין), "וכפר" – אף על פי שלא נתן אלא שלש, "וכפר" – אף על פי שלא נתן אלא שתים, "וכפר" – אף על פי שלא נתן אלא אחת.

Since both of the above inferences are reasonable, neither can serve as the source of the *halakha*. Therefore, **the verse states:** "And the priest **shall make atonement,**" "And the priest **shall make atonement,**" "And the priest **shall make atonement,**" for a total of three times. The verses are interpreted as follows: "**And** the priest **shall make atonement," even if he placed only three** placements. Subsequently: "**And** the priest **shall make atonement," even if he placed only two** placements, and then: "**And** the priest **shall make atonement," even if he placed only one** placement. This interpretation is the source of Beit Hillel's opinion.

והאי מיבעי ליה לגופיה! אמר רבא: בר אדא מרי אסברה לי, אמר קרא: "וכפר... ונסלח" – זו היא כפרה זו היא סליחה.

The Gemara challenges: But each of these verses **is necessary for itself,** to teach that atonement is achieved for each of the sins through its respective sin offering. **Rava said: Bar Adda Mari explained** this matter **to me: The verse states** with regard to each of these sin offerings: "**And** the priest **shall make atonement...and he shall be forgiven**" (Leviticus 4:26, 31, 35). **This is atonement** and **this is forgiveness;** they are one and the same. Since it would have sufficed to say: "And he shall be forgiven," the superfluous mentions of the phrase: "And the priest shall make atonement," serve to teach that the priest facilitates atonement even if he has not performed all the placements.

אימא: "וכפר" – אף על פי שלא נתן אלא שלש למעלה ואחת למטה, "וכפר" – אף על פי שלא נתן אלא שתים למטה ושתים למעלה, "וכפר" – אף על פי שלא נתן למעלה אלא למטה!

The Gemara asks: But even if these phrases are superfluous, do they necessarily indicate that a priest who omitted placements has nevertheless facilitated atonement? Why not **say** that these phrases serve to teach that if the priest placed all the placements he facilitated atonement even if the placements were placed in the wrong place? And expound the verses as follows: "**And** the priest **shall make atonement," even if he placed** the blood on the altar with **only three** placements **above,** on the corners of the altar, **and one below,** on the lower portion of the altar; "**And** the priest **shall make atonement," even if he placed** the blood with **only two** placements **above and two below;** "**And** the priest **shall make atonement," even if he did not place** the blood **above** at all, **but** only **below.**[N]

אמר רב אדא בר יצחק: אם כן, ביטלת תורת ארבע קרנות. ואי רחמנא אמר – ליבטלון!

Rav Adda bar Yitzḥak says: If so, that the priest facilitates atonement even if he placed all the placements below, **you have abolished the requirement of four corners** that is stated with regard to the sin offering (see, e.g., Leviticus 4:34), as the four corners are on the upper portion of the altar. The Gemara is puzzled by Rav Adda bar Yitzḥak's claim: **But if the Merciful One states** that this is so, **let** this requirement **be abolished.**

אמר רבא: איזהו דבר שצריך שלש – הוי אומר: אלו קרנות.

As Rav Adda bar Yitzḥak's claim was rejected, **Rava said** there is a different reason why the previous claim cannot be accepted: **What is the item that requires three**[N] repetitions of "and the priest shall make atonement," i.e., to what are these verses referring? **You must say** that **these are the corners** of the altar. The Torah must teach that the priest facilitates atonement even if he did not place the blood on three of the four corners. But in order for the verses to teach that all four placements can be placed below, the phrase "and the priest shall make atonement" would have to be written four times.

NOTES

Even if he did not place it above but only below – אף על פי שלא נתן למעלה אלא למטה: The commentaries ask: Why does the Gemara move from a case of two placements above and two below to that of none above and all four below? Why not mention immediately a case of one above and three below, as the Gemara does later on? *Tosafot* answer that the Gemara first considers cases that either involve most of the placements being performed above, or where the placements performed below are carried out in the same manner that they are in the cases of those offerings whose blood is placed below. Since blood is placed below in the form of one placement that is two, i.e., on the corner so that the blood spreads in two directions, it is suggested here that two placements should be performed below. As three placements are not performed below for any other offering, that possibility is not entertained. Later, the Gemara will suggest that even if one does not find three placements below in any other case, perhaps this is still more reasonable than all four placements of a sin offering being performed below.

What is the item that requires three – איזהו דבר שצריך שלש: Some commentaries maintain that this question is not referring to the three instances of the phrase "And the priest shall make atonement," but to the three mentions of corners in the verses about the blood of a sin offering. The *Panim Meirot* explains as follows: If these three uses of corners are indeed stated only for a mitzva, and not a single corner is indispensable, there would be no reason for the word to appear three times; the verse could simply have stated: Corners, in the plural, twice, which would be referring to all four corners. The fact that the term is mentioned three times indicates that one of the placements on a corner is indispensable.

HALAKHA

He sprinkled from it one time upward, etc. – הִזָּה מִמֶּנּוּ אַחַת לְמַעְלָה וכו׳: On Yom Kippur, when the High Priest sprinkles the eight sprinklings onto the Ark Cover in the Holy of Holies and in the Sanctuary, from the blood of the bull and the blood of the goat, he sprinkles once upward and seven times downward. The blood is not sprinkled literally upward and downward, but in a kind of whipping motion, with each sprinkling below the previous one (Rambam *Sefer Avoda*, *Hilkhot Avodat Yom HaKippurim* 3:5).

אֵימָא: ״וְכִפֶּר״ – אַף עַל פִּי שֶׁלֹּא נָתַן אֶלָּא אַחַת לְמַעְלָה וְשָׁלֹשׁ לְמַטָּה!

The Gemara asks further: Even so, it is possible to interpret the three repetitions of the phrase "and the priest shall make atonement" as referring to the location of the placements, without abolishing the requirement of corners, as one can **say:** "And the priest shall make atonement," even though he placed the blood on the altar with only three placements above and one below; "And the priest shall make atonement," even though he placed the blood with only two placements above and two below; **"And** the priest **shall make atonement," even though he placed** the blood with **only one** placement **above and three below.**

לֹא מָצִינוּ דָּמִים שֶׁחֶצְיָין לְמַעְלָה וְחֶצְיָין לְמַטָּה. וְלָא? וְהָתְנַן: הִזָּה מִמֶּנּוּ אַחַת לְמַעְלָה וְשֶׁבַע לְמַטָּה!

The Gemara answers: This entire line of inquiry can be rejected, as **we do not find** a case involving **blood, half of which** is placed **above** the red line **and half of which** is placed **below** it. One either places all the blood on the lower half of the altar, as in the case of most offerings, or all of it on the upper half of the altar, as in the case of sin offerings. The Gemara asks: **And** is there really **no** case of that sort? **But didn't we learn** in a mishna (*Yoma* 53b): The High Priest took the blood of the bull into the Holy of Holies and **sprinkled from** the blood **one** time **upward**[H] **and** then **seven** times **downward?** Apparently, part of the blood of an offering can be sprinkled upward, toward the upper part of the Ark Cover, and part can be placed downward, toward the lower part of the Ark Cover.

כְּמַצְלִיף. מַאי ״כְּמַצְלִיף״? מַחֲוֵי רַב יְהוּדָה: כְּמַנְגְּדָנָא.

The Gemara rejects this: That is not a case where half the blood is sprinkled upward and half is sprinkled downward. Instead, that sprinkling was **like a *matzlif*.**[N] The Gemara explains: **What** is the meaning of **like a *matzlif*? Rav Yehuda demonstrated** with his hand; it means **like one who whips.** One who whips another does not strike repeatedly in one place but directs one lash beneath the other.

״הִזָּה עַל טָהֳרוֹ שֶׁל מִזְבֵּחַ שֶׁבַע פְּעָמִים״;

The Gemara further asks: And is there really no case of that sort? But didn't we learn in a mishna (*Yoma* 58b) about the Yom Kippur service: After the High Priest sprinkled blood on the four corners of the incense altar, **he sprinkled** blood **seven times on *tohoro* of the altar.**

NOTES

Like a *matzlif* – כְּמַצְלִיף: Rashi maintains that the sprinkling was not performed on two separate places, on the Ark Cover and on the Ark Cover's side. Rather, it was done like one who whips, directing his lashes from above to below. The Gemara in *Yoma* 55a explains that the phrase: One time upward and seven times downward, refers to the High Priest's palm, i.e., whether his palm is pointed upward or downward at the moment of the sprinkling (see *Tosafot Yeshanim* on *Yoma* 15a).

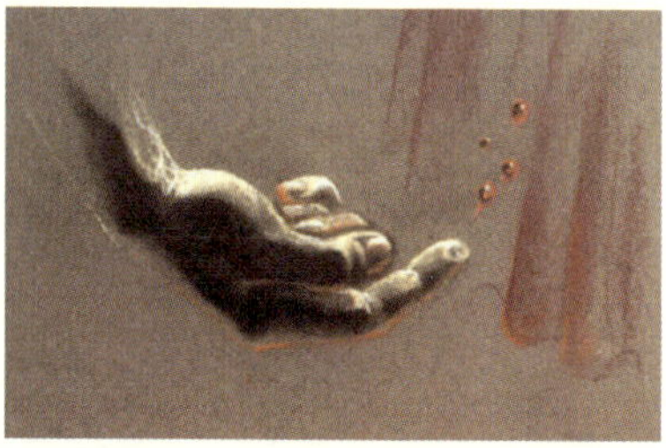

Position of priest's hand in sprinkling blood upward

High Priest sprinkling blood on the Ark Cover on Yom Kippur

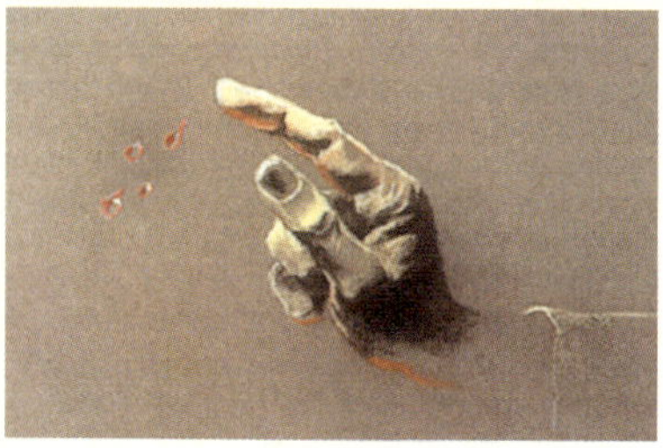

Position of priest's hand in sprinkling blood downward

מַאי לָאו אַפַּלְגֵיהּ דְּמִזְבֵּחַ, כִּדְאָמְרִי אֱינָשֵׁי "טְהַר טִיהֲרָא דְּיוֹמָא"? אֲמַר רָבָא בַּר שֵׁילָא: לָא, אַגִּילוּיֵיהּ, דִּכְתִיב: "וּכְעֶצֶם הַשָּׁמַיִם לָטֹהַר".

What, is it not referring **to the middle**[N] of the side **of the altar, as people say: Clear noon** [*tihara*], that is the middle **of the day?** Accordingly, the root *tet, heh, reish* denotes the middle; in the one case, the middle of the day, and in the other case, halfway up the altar. Now, since the blood was sprinkled on the altar seven times, inevitably some of the blood landed above the midpoint and some of it landed below the midpoint. **Rava bar Sheila said: No,** that is not the meaning of *tohoro*. Rather, *tohoro* means **on the revealed** part, i.e., the top, of the altar, **as it is written: "Like the very clear** [*latohar*] **sky"** (Exodus 24:10). *Tohoro* is referring to the top of the altar when it has been revealed, after the ashes of the incense are cleared and the pure gold is visible.

וְהָאִיכָּא שִׁירַיִם! שִׁירַיִם לָא מְעַכְּבִי.

The Gemara asks again: Is there not a case where some of the blood is presented above the red line and some of it is presented below? **But there is** the **remainder** of the blood, which is poured on the base of the altar even in the case of a sin offering, the main blood of which is placed on the upper portion of the altar. The Gemara answers: The pouring of the **remainder** of the blood on the base of the altar **is not indispensable** for atonement. Blood that is indispensable for atonement is in no instance presented half above the red line and half below it.

וְהָאִיכָּא שִׁירַיִם הַפְּנִימִים, דְּאִיכָּא דְּמַאן דְּאָמַר מְעַכְּבִי! בְּחַד מָקוֹם קָאָמְרִינַן.

The Gemara continues this line of questioning: **But there is the remainder** of the blood **of the inner** sin offerings, the main blood of which is sprinkled on the inner altar. The remainder of the blood of these offerings is poured on the base of the external altar, and **there is one who says** that this pouring of the blood is **indispensable** for atonement. The Gemara explains: When we said that there is no blood, half of which is presented above and half below, **we said** this **with regard to one place,** i.e., the same altar. The blood of inner sin offerings is sprinkled on the inner altar, while the remainder of that blood is poured on the base of the external altar. There is no case of blood, half of which is presented above and half of which is presented below on the same altar.

תַּנְיָא, רַבִּי אֱלִיעֶזֶר בֶּן יַעֲקֹב אוֹמֵר, בֵּית שַׁמַּאי אוֹמְרִים: שְׁתֵּי מַתָּנוֹת שֶׁבְּחַטָּאת, וְאַחַת שֶׁבְּכָל הַזְּבָחִים – מַתִּירוֹת.

§ The mishna teaches that according to the opinion of Beit Shammai, in the case of a sin offering two placements facilitate atonement, while with regard to other offerings a single placement is sufficient. Beit Hillel disagree and say that even in the case of a sin offering one placement suffices after the fact. With regard to this issue, it **is taught** in a *baraita* that **Rabbi Eliezer ben Ya'akov says: Beit Shammai say** that **two placements in** the case of **a sin offering, and one** placement **in** the case of other **offerings, they render** the offering **permitted** for eating since these actions facilitate atonement after the fact, despite the fact that blood was not placed on all four corners of the altar.

וּמְפַגְּלוֹת. בֵּית הִלֵּל אוֹמְרִים: אַחַת שֶׁבְּחַטָּאת, וְאַחַת שֶׁבְּכָל הַזְּבָחִים מַתֶּרֶת וּמְפַגֶּלֶת.

And similarly **they render** the offering ***piggul***.[B] That is to say, if the priest placed two placements of the blood of a sin offering or one placement of the blood of any another offering, intending to eat or burn the offering beyond its designated time, the offering is *piggul*. **Beit Hillel say: One** placement **in** the case **a sin offering, and** likewise **one** placement **in** the case of **all** the other **offerings,** if done with proper intent, renders the offering **permitted** for eating **and,** if done with improper intent, **renders** the offering ***piggul***.[H]

מַתְקִיף לָהּ רַב אוֹשַׁעְיָא: אִם כֵּן, לִיתְנְיֵיהּ גַּבֵּי קוּלֵּי בֵּית שַׁמַּאי וְחוּמְרֵי בֵּית הִלֵּל!

Rav Oshaya objects to this: If so, let this *halakha* **be taught** in the fourth chapter of tractate *Eduyyot* **alongside** the other rare cases of **Beit Shammai's leniencies and Beit Hillel's stringencies.** According to Beit Hillel, a sin offering is *piggul* even if the priest intended to partake of it beyond its designated time even while performing a single placement, whereas Beit Shammai maintain that the offering is *piggul* only if he had this improper intent during two placements.

NOTES

What, is it not to the middle – מַאי לָאו אַפַּלְגֵיהּ: Rashi explains that as it is impossible for the sprinkled blood to land exactly in the middle, some of the blood will inevitably fall on the upper part of the altar and some on the lower part. Other commentaries explain that the Gemara assumes that this is referring to the side of the inner altar, which is called: Below, in relation to the four corners of the altar above, where the High Priest had already sprinkled blood. The Gemara answers that even these seven sprinklings were performed above (*Shita Mekubbetzet*, citing *Tosafot*).

BACKGROUND

***Piggul* – פִּיגּוּל:** A thought of *piggul* is a disqualifying intent in the sacrifice of an offering, whether an animal, bird, or meal offering. If, while engaged in sacrificing an offering, a priest expresses intent to sprinkle the blood of the offering, burn its fats on the altar, or eat its meat, after the designated time, that intent disqualifies the offering. An offering that has assumed that status may not be sacrificed, and it does not fulfill the obligation of the one bringing it. One who eats from that offering intentionally is liable to receive *karet*. The Sages also decreed that an offering with *piggul* status imparts ritual impurity. The intent of the priest sacrificing the offering, and not the intent of the person bringing it, determines whether or not it is unfit due to improper intent.

HALAKHA

Renders it permitted and renders it *piggul* – מַתֶּרֶת וּמְפַגֶּלֶת: With regard to all blood placed on the external altar, if the priest performed only one placement he facilitated atonement. This *halakha* applies even in the case of a sin offering. Consequently, if the priest performed the first placement with the correct intent, and from the second placement onward he intended his action not for the sake of the offering being sacrificed, or he intended that it should be consumed or burned beyond its designated time or outside its designated area, this intent does not disqualify the offering. If he performed the first placement with the intent that the offering should be consumed or burned beyond its designated time, the offering is *piggul*, even if he intended to consume it or burn it outside its designated area while performing the other placements as well (Rambam *Sefer Avoda*, *Hilkhot Pesulei HaMukdashin* 2:1, 17:1).

אֲמַר לֵיהּ רָבָא: כִּי אִיתְּשִׁיל – לְהֶתֵּירָא אִיתְּשִׁיל, דְּהָווּ לְהוּ בֵּית שַׁמַּאי לְחוּמְרָא.

Rava said to Rav Oshaya: **When** this question **was** initially **asked,** and the Sages stated their opinions concerning the matter, **it was asked with regard to the permission**[N] to partake of the sin offering. In other words, the dispute arose as a result of an inquiry into the other relevant *halakha*, i.e., whether the priests may partake of a sin offering, the blood of which was placed only one time. In this case it is **Beit Shammai who are** more **stringent,** as they permit the meat of a sin offering only after two placements have been placed. For this reason, this case was not listed among the other leniencies of Beit Shammai and stringencies of Beit Hillel.

אָמַר רַבִּי יוֹחָנָן: שָׁלֹשׁ מַתָּנוֹת שֶׁבַּחַטָּאוֹת אֵינָן בָּאוֹת בַּלַּיְלָה, וּבָאוֹת לְאַחַר מִיתָה, וְהַמַּעֲלֶה מֵהֶן בַּחוּץ חַיָּיב.

§ **Rabbi Yoḥanan says:** Despite the fact that, according to the opinion of Beit Hillel, the last **three placements in** the case of **a sin offering**[H] are not indispensable to the atonement, they **may not be performed at night,** because the blood is invalidated at sunset. **And** these three placements **may be performed after** the **death** of the owner. If the owner of the offering died before any of the blood was placed on the altar, the blood may not be placed, and the offering is burned as a disqualified offering. But if he died after one placement, the priest may perform the other three placements, as he has already facilitated atonement by means of the first placement. **And** as it is a mitzva to perform these three placements on the altar, **one who offers** this blood **up** on an altar **outside** the Temple is **liable** to receive *karet*, the punishment received by one who offers a sacrifice outside the Temple.

אָמַר רַב פַּפָּא: יֵשׁ מֵהֶן כִּתְחִלָּתוֹ, וְיֵשׁ מֵהֶן כְּסוֹפוֹ;

Rav Pappa says: There are some respects in which the blood of the last three placements of a sin offering is treated **like** the blood presented **at the outset,**[N] i.e., like the blood of the first placement, **and there are some** respects in which the blood of the last three placements is treated **like** the blood presented **at the end,** i.e., like the remainder of the blood of a sin offering.

חוּץ, וְלַיְלָה, זָרוּת, וּכְלִי שָׁרֵת, קֶרֶן, וְאֶצְבַּע, כִּיבּוּס, וְשִׁירַיִם – כִּתְחִלָּתָן.

Rav Pappa elaborates: With regard to liability for presenting blood **outside** the Temple, **and** concerning the prohibition against presenting blood at **night,** and with regard to the disqualification of **a non-priest** from presenting blood and his liability for death at the hand of Heaven if he presents blood in the Temple, **and** with regard to the requirement that the blood that is to be presented must first be placed in **a service vessel,** and that the blood must be placed on the **corner** of the altar, **and** that the placement must be performed with the priest's **finger,** and concerning the obligation to **launder**[B] a garment onto which the blood of a sin offering sprayed, **and** finally with regard to the requirement of pouring the **remainder**[N] of the blood on the base of the altar, the last three placements are treated **like** blood presented at **the outset,** i.e., like the first placement.

NOTES

It was asked with regard to the permission – לְהֶתֵּירָא אִיתְּשִׁיל: In other words, the question concerned whether or not the priests may partake of the meat of this offering if only one placement had been performed and the rest of the blood spilled. In this case, the ruling of Beit Shammai is the more stringent, as they prohibit consumption of this meat. Rabbi Eliezer ben Ya'akov inferred from here that just as the meat may not be consumed after one placement, so too, according to the opinion of Beit Shammai, the sin offering is not rendered *piggul* by improper intent during one placement (Rashi).

There are some like at the outset – יֵשׁ מֵהֶן כִּתְחִלָּתוֹ: In other words, with regard to some matters these placements are considered like the first placement, while for the purposes of other *halakhot* they are considered like the remainder of the blood. Some commentaries explain the difference between these cases as follows: In matters relating to the status of the blood itself, the blood remaining after the first placement is certainly considered the blood of a sin offering, as the Torah commanded that this blood be placed on the altar. In matters relating to whether the blood renders the offering permitted for eating and facilitates atonement, the blood of the other placements is like the remainder of the blood (*Ḥazon Yeḥezkel*).

And the remainder – וְשִׁירַיִם: If the blood of the sin offering was received in four different vessels, and the priest placed one placement from each vessel, all the blood in each vessel must be poured onto the base of the altar, as is performed with the remainder of blood in a standard case.

HALAKHA

Three placements in a sin offering, etc. – שָׁלֹשׁ מַתָּנוֹת שֶׁבַּחַטָּאת וכו׳: If the priest performed one placement of the blood of a sin offering and then its owner died, the priest should complete the other three placements. If the priest performed one placement of the blood by day, he should not perform the others by night. If he performed one placement of the blood inside the Temple, and subsequently performed the others outside, he is liable for sacrificing outside the Temple. The *halakha* is in accordance with the opinion of Rabbi Yoḥanan (Rambam *Sefer Avoda*, *Hilkhot Pesulei HaMukdashin* 2:4–6).

BACKGROUND

Laundering – כִּיבּוּס: Should the blood of a sin offering spray onto clothing after it has been collected in a sacred vessel and before it has been placed on the altar, the clothes must be cleaned with water and a cleansing agent. This *halakha* is unique to sin offerings and is not required with regard to the blood of other types of offerings. In the event that blood is found on the clothing, only the affected area requires cleaning, not the entire garment.

Roman fresco depicting adults and children treading on laundry in tubs

וּבָאוֹת לְאַחַר מִיתָה, לָא שָׁרְיָא, וְלָא מְפַגְּלָא, וְלָא עַיְּילָא לְגַוַּאי – כְּסוֹפָן.

But these last three placements **may be performed after** the **death** of the owner; and they do **not** render the offering **permitted** for eating, as that was already achieved by means of the first placement; **nor** do they **render** the offering ***piggul*** if during these placements the priest intended to eat or burn the offering beyond its designated time; **and** similarly, they are **not** governed by the *halakha* that if the blood **enters inside** the Sanctuary the sin offering is disqualified. With regard to all these matters the blood of the last three placements is treated **like** the blood presented **at the end,** i.e., like the remainder of the blood of a sin offering.

אֲמַר רַב פַּפָּא: מְנָא אָמִינָא לָהּ? דִּתְנַן: נִיתַּז מִן הַצַּוָּאר עַל הַבֶּגֶד – אֵינוֹ טָעוּן כִּיבּוּס, מִן הַקֶּרֶן וּמִן הַיְּסוֹד – אֵינוֹ טָעוּן כִּיבּוּס; הָא מִן הָרָאוּי לַקֶּרֶן – טָעוּן כִּיבּוּס!

With regard to the obligation to launder a garment onto which the blood of a sin offering sprayed, **Rav Pappa said: From where do I say** that this *halakha* applies even to the blood of the last three placements? It is **as we learned** in a mishna (93a): If the blood of a sin offering **sprayed** directly **from the neck**[N] of the animal **onto a garment,**[H] that garment **does not require laundering,** as the blood had never been received in a vessel. Likewise, if the blood sprayed onto the garment **from the corner** of the altar after having been placed there, **or from the base** of the altar after the remainder was poured there, the garment **does not require laundering.** It may be inferred from here that blood that sprayed from the corner of the altar does not require laundering. **But** blood that is **fit** to be placed **on the corner,** as it has not yet been placed, **requires laundering,** and the blood of the last three placements is indeed fit to be placed on the corner of the altar.

וְלִיטַעֲמִיךְ, מִן הַיְּסוֹד אֵינוֹ טָעוּן כִּיבּוּס, הָא מִן הָרָאוּי לַיְּסוֹד טָעוּן כִּיבּוּס? "אֲשֶׁר יִזֶּה" כְּתִיב, פְּרָט לָזֶה שֶׁכְּבָר הוּזָּה!

The Gemara rejects this proof: **But according to your reasoning,** one can claim in the same manner that it is only blood that sprayed **from the base** of the altar that **does not require laundering; but** blood **that is fit for the base** of the altar, i.e., what remains of the blood after it has been placed on the corners, **requires laundering.** This is difficult, as **it is written:** "And **when there will be sprinkled** [*yizze*] of its blood upon any garment" (Leviticus 6:20). The future form of the word *yizze* serves to **exclude** this blood sprayed onto the garment from the corner of the altar, **as it has already been sprinkled.**[H]

הָא מַנִּי? רַבִּי נְחֶמְיָה; דִּתְנַן, רַבִּי נְחֶמְיָה אוֹמֵר: שְׁיָרֵי הַדָּם שֶׁהִקְרִיבָן בַּחוּץ – חַיָּיב.

The Gemara explains: In accordance with **whose** opinion **is this** ruling? It is in accordance with the opinion of **Rabbi Neḥemya,**[N] **as we learned** in a mishna (110b) that **Rabbi Neḥemya says:** With regard to the **remainder of the blood** of an offering, **which** was to be poured at the base of the altar, if **one presented it outside** the Temple, he is **liable.** Since Rabbi Neḥemya treats the remainder of the blood as blood with regard to liability for a service performed outside the Temple, he also treats the remainder of the blood of a sin offering as blood with regard to laundering. Accordingly, Rav Pappa's inference from the previously cited mishna is valid only according to Rabbi Neḥemya, but not according to the majority opinion of the Rabbis, who disagree with him.

אֵימַר דִּשְׁמַעְתְּ לֵיהּ לְרַבִּי נְחֶמְיָה לְעִנְיַן הַעֲלָאָה, מִידֵּי דַּהֲוֵי אֵאֵיבָרִים וּפְדָרִים, לְעִנְיַן כִּיבּוּס מִי שְׁמַעְתְּ לֵיהּ? אִין,

The Gemara challenges the proof even according to the opinion of Rabbi Neḥemya: **Say that you heard** that **Rabbi Neḥemya** ruled in this manner **with regard to the offering up** of the remainder of the blood outside the Temple, **just as** is the case **with regard to limbs and fats.** Even though the offering of the limbs and fats is not indispensable for atonement, one who offers them outside the Temple is liable. But **did you** also **hear him** say this **with regard to laundering,** that one must launder a garment sprayed with the remainder of the blood of a sin offering? The Gemara answers: **Yes,** we also heard Rabbi Neḥemya rule in this manner with regard to laundering.

NOTES

Sprayed from the neck – **נִיתַּז מִן הַצַּוָּאר**: It is derived from the verse: "And when there is sprinkled of its blood upon any garment" (Leviticus 6:20), that only blood that is fit for sprinkling is included in this *halakha*, not blood that has already been sprinkled or that has not yet been rendered fit for sprinkling.

In accordance with whose opinion is this, Rabbi Neḥemya – **הָא מַנִּי רַבִּי נְחֶמְיָה**: The commentary here follows Rashi, who understands that this is a continuation of the Gemara's rejection of the opinion of Rav Pappa. Rashi's interpretation can be summarized as follows: If one infers from the mishna as proposed, one should infer likewise with regard to the subsequent clause. This inference is possible only according the opinion of Rabbi Neḥemya, whereas according to the disputing opinion of the Rabbis there is no requirement to launder a garment in which the remainder of the blood of a sin offering has been absorbed. The Gemara proceeds to question whether this is in fact the opinion of Rabbi Neḥemya, and eventually concludes, on the following *amud*, that this is not the case.

Other commentaries maintain the opposite, that this paragraph is an answer to the previous difficulty raised against the opinion of Rav Pappa. Rav Pappa's proof from the mishna should not be rejected on account of the fact that one can infer in a similar manner from its latter clause, as according to Rabbi Neḥemya that inference is indeed valid. Admittedly, this means that the mishna is in accordance with the opinion of Rabbi Neḥemya, while the *halakha* is not in accordance with his opinion, but this does prove the basic point that the *halakha* of laundering a garment applies to blood for which one is liable for sacrificing outside the Temple (*Tosafot*). *Tosafot* provide an alternative explanation, that the suggested inference from the latter clause is according to the opinion of Rabbi Neḥemya, whereas the first part of the mishna is according to the opinion of the Rabbis, and therefore Rav Pappa's proof remains valid (see *Keren Ora*).

HALAKHA

Sprayed from the neck onto a garment – **נִיתַּז מִן הַצַּוָּאר עַל הַבֶּגֶד**: If the blood of a sin offering sprayed directly from the animal's neck, or from the altar, onto a garment, or if the blood spilled on the floor and was collected in a vessel and then sprayed onto a garment, the garment does not require laundering. The only blood that causes a garment to require laundering is the blood of a sin offering that was properly received into a service vessel and that is fit to be placed upon the altar (Rambam *Sefer Avoda, Hilkhot Ma'aseh HaKorbanot* 8:6).

Exclude this as it has already been sprinkled – **פְּרָט לָזֶה שֶׁכְּבָר הוּזָּה**: If the priest performed the four placements of a sin offering and afterward some of the remaining blood in the service vessel sprayed onto a garment, that garment does not require laundering (Rambam *Sefer Avoda, Hilkhot Ma'aseh HaKorbanot* 8:7).

וְהָתַנְיָא: דָּמִים הַטְּעוּנִין יְסוֹד – טְעוּנִין כִּיבּוּס, וּמַחְשָׁבָה מוֹעֶלֶת בָּהֶן, וְהַמַּעֲלֶה מֵהֶן בַּחוּץ חַיָּיב.

And this is as **it is taught** in a *baraita*: With regard to **blood that requires** the **base** of the altar, presumably a reference to the remainder of the blood of a sin offering, which must be poured on the base of the altar, it **requires laundering; and** improper **intent is effective with regard to it,** i.e., if the priest poured such blood with the intent to partake of the sacrificial meat beyond its designated time, the offering is *piggul;* **and one who offers it up outside** the Temple is **liable.**

וְדָמִים הַנִּשְׁפָּכִין לָאַמָּה – אֵין טְעוּנִין כִּיבּוּס, וְאֵין מַחְשָׁבָה מוֹעֶלֶת בָּהֶן, וְהַמַּעֲלֶה מֵהֶן בַּחוּץ פָּטוּר;

And conversely, with regard to **blood that is poured into the** Temple courtyard **drain**[N] that passed through the Temple and emptied into the Kidron River, which is blood that has been become disqualified, it **does not require laundering, and** improper **intent is not effective with regard to it, and one who offers it up outside** the Temple is **exempt.**

מַאן שָׁמְעַתְּ לֵיהּ דְּאָמַר: מַעֲלֶה מֵהֶן בַּחוּץ חַיָּיב – רַבִּי נְחֶמְיָה הִיא, וְקָאָמַר: טָעוּן כִּיבּוּס.

The Gemara inquires: About **whom did you learn that he said** that **one who offers up** the remainder of the blood **outside** the Temple **is liable? It is Rabbi Neḥemya** who says this, **and he states** in this *baraita* that a garment that was sprayed with such blood **requires laundering.**

וּמַחְשָׁבָה מוֹעֶלֶת בָּהֶן? וְהָתַנְיָא: יָצְאוּ שִׁירַיִם וְהַקְטָרַת אֵימוּרִין שֶׁאֵין מְעַכְּבִין אֶת הַכַּפָּרָה, שֶׁאֵין מַחְשָׁבָה מוֹעֶלֶת בָּהֶן!

The Gemara asks: **And is** improper **intent effective with regard to** blood that must be poured on the base of the altar? **But isn't it taught** in a *baraita* discussing the intent that renders an offering *piggul*: The possibility of *piggul* applies only with regard to a service that is indispensable for atonement. This serves to **exclude** pouring the **remainder** of the blood on the altar **and burning** the **sacrificial portions** on the altar, actions **that are not indispensable for atonement,** concerning which the *halakha* is **that** improper **intent is not effective with regard to them.**

כִּי תַּנְיָא הַהִיא – בְּשָׁלֹשׁ מַתָּנוֹת שֶׁבְּחַטָּאת.

Rather, **when that** *baraita* **is taught,** stating that blood that requires the base requires laundering, it is not referring to the remainder of the blood after the placements have been completed. Instead, it is referring **to** the blood that is to be used for the last **three placements** of the blood **of a sin offering.**[N]

אִי הָכִי, טְעוּנִין יְסוֹד? לַקֶּרֶן אָזְלִי! אֵימָא: נִיטְעֲנִין יְסוֹד. וּמַחְשָׁבָה מוֹעֶלֶת בָּהֶן? הָאָמְרַתְּ: לָא שָׁרְיָא וְלָא מְפַגְּלָא וְלָא עָיְילָא לְגַוַּאי, כְּסוֹפָן!

The Gemara asks: **If so,** is it correct to describe this blood as **requiring** the **base** of the altar? After all, this blood **goes to the corner** of the altar, not the base. The Gemara answers: **Say** that this means: Blood that becomes **required** for the **base,** i.e., blood that in the end, after the placements are completed, will be poured on the base of the altar. The Gemara further asks: **But is** improper **intent effective with regard to** the blood of the last three placements of the blood of a sin offering? **Didn't you say** that this blood does **not render** the offering **permitted** for eating, **nor** does it **render** the offering ***piggul*****,** **and** it is **not** governed by the *halakha* that if the blood **enters inside** the Sanctuary the sin offering is disqualified? With regard to all these matters the blood of the last three placements is treated **like** the blood presented at **the end,** i.e., like the remainder of the blood of a sin offering.

אֶלָּא, כִּי תַּנְיָא הַהִיא – בְּדָמִים הַפְּנִימִים.

The Gemara explains: **Rather, when that** *baraita* **is taught,**[N] stating that blood requiring the base requires laundering, and improper intent is effective with regard to it, and one who presents of it outside the Temple is liable, it is indeed referring to the remainder of the blood after the placements have been completed. It is stated not with regard to the remainder of the blood of a standard sin offering, but **with regard to** the remainder of **the blood of inner** sin offerings, which are brought on the inner altar located inside the Sanctuary.

NOTES

And blood that is poured into the Temple drain – וְדָמִים הַנִּשְׁפָּכִין לָאַמָּה: This is referring to blood that is entirely disqualified from being used for any service, e.g., blood from an animal's neck that was not received in a service vessel. This blood was poured into a drainage channel that passed through the Temple, from where it emptied into the Kidron River.

When that *baraita* is taught it is referring to the last three placements of a sin offering – כִּי תַּנְיָא הַהִיא בְּשָׁלֹשׁ מַתָּנוֹת שֶׁבְּחַטָּאת: According to Rashi, this statement is part of the Gemara's difficulty. In other words, one cannot prove from this *baraita* that according to Rabbi Neḥemya a garment that absorbs some of the remainder of the blood requires laundering, as the *baraita* is referring to the last three placements. Some commentaries maintain that the word: Rather, should be included in the text of the Gemara here. This term indicates a change from the previous line of thought. According to this explanation, the Gemara is emphasizing that Rav Pappa's proof is valid, as this *baraita* is evidently not in accordance only with the opinion of Rabbi Neḥemya but applies even in accordance with the opinion of the Rabbis (see *Tosafot* on 39a).

Rather, when that *baraita* is taught, etc. – אֶלָּא כִּי תַּנְיָא הַהִיא וכו׳: That is, the Gemara returns to the previous interpretation, that the term: Blood that requires the base, is a reference to the remainder of the blood. But it is not referring to a standard sin offering, sacrificed on the external altar; rather, it is referring to the blood of a sin offering sacrificed on the inner altar. According to certain opinions the pouring of the remainder of the blood of such sin offerings is indispensable, and therefore the *halakha* of *piggul* applies to them. If so, this *baraita* cannot be cited as proof with regard to Rabbi Neḥemya's opinion as to whether a garment that absorbs the blood of a sin offering sacrificed on the external altar requires laundering.

אֲבָל בְּדָמִים הַחִיצוֹנִים מַאי, פָּטוּר? אַדְּתָנֵי: דָּמִים הַנִּשְׁפָּכִין לָאַמָּה, לִיפְלוֹג וְלִיתְנֵי בְּדִידָהּ: בַּמֶּה דְּבָרִים אֲמוּרִים – בְּדָמִים הַפְּנִימִים, אֲבָל בְּדָמִים הַחִיצוֹנִים – פָּטוּר!

The Gemara asks: **But** if that is the case, **with regard to** the remainder of **the blood of external** sin offerings that are brought on the external altar, **what is the** *halakha*? Is one who presents them outside the Temple **exempt?** If so, **rather than teaching** the *halakha* of disqualified **blood that is poured into the** Temple courtyard **drain, let** the *baraita* **distinguish and teach** the *halakha* **within the** case of the remainder of the blood **itself,** in the following manner: **In what** case **is this statement said? In** a case of **the blood of** sin offerings brought on the **inner** altar. **But in** the case of **the blood of** sin offerings brought on the **external** altar, one who offers up such an offering outside the Temple is **exempt.**

הָא מַנִּי רַבִּי נְחֶמְיָה הִיא, דְּאָמַר: שְׁיָרֵי הַדָּם שֶׁהִקְרִיבָן בַּחוּץ חַיָּיב, וְלָא מַתְנֵי לֵיהּ תְּלָתָא פְּטוּרֵי לְבַהֲדֵי תְּלָתָא חִיּוּבֵי.

The Gemara answers: The *baraita* could not have made such a distinction, for in accordance with **whose** opinion **is this** ruling? **It is** in accordance with the opinion of **Rabbi Neḥemya,**[N] **who says:** With regard to the **remainder of the blood** of a sin offering brought on the external altar, in a case **where one presented it outside** the Temple, he is **liable. And** therefore, were the *tanna* to contrast the *halakha* of the blood of sin offerings brought on the external altar with that of the blood of sin offerings brought on the inner altar, **he would not** have been able to **teach three** rulings of **exemptions**[N] **corresponding to three** rulings of **liabilities,** as Rabbi Neḥemya maintains that even with regard to the remainder of the blood of a sin offering brought on the external altar, if one presents it outside the Temple he is liable. Therefore, the *tanna* preferred to compare the *halakhot* of the remainder of the blood of inner sin offerings to the disqualified blood that is poured into the Temple courtyard drain, so that he could list three lenient rulings alongside three stringent ones.

רָבִינָא אָמַר: מִן הַקֶּרֶן – מַמָּשׁ, מִן הַיְסוֹד – מִן הָרָאוּי לַיְסוֹד.

§ The Gemara returns to discuss the statement of Rav Pappa, that a garment sprayed by blood from the last three placements of the blood of a sin offering requires laundering, and to his proof from the mishna that states that if the blood of a sin offering sprayed onto a garment from the corner of the altar or from the base of the altar, the garment does not require laundering. **Ravina says,** in answer to the objection raised against Rav Pappa above, that according to Rav Pappa the mishna (93a) should be understood as follows: The term: **From the corner,** means from the corner, **literally,** after the blood was placed there, and therefore Rav Pappa could infer from this that blood that is fit to be placed on the corner, including the blood to be used for the last three sprinklings, requires laundering. But the term: **From the base** of the altar, does not mean from the base, literally. Rather, it means: **From** blood **that is fit for the base** of the altar, i.e., from the remainder of the blood, which is to be poured on the base.

אֲמַר לֵיהּ רַב תַּחְלִיפָא בַּר גַּזָּא לְרָבִינָא: אֵימָא אִידִי וְאִידִי רָאוּי הוּא? הַאי מַאי? הַשְׁתָּא רָאוּי לַקֶּרֶן אָמְרַתְּ לָא, רָאוּי לַיְסוֹד מִיבַּעְיָא? אֶלָּא מִן הַקֶּרֶן – מִן הַקֶּרֶן מַמָּשׁ, מִן הַיְסוֹד – מִן הָרָאוּי לַיְסוֹד.

Rav Taḥlifa bar Gazza said to Ravina: One can **say** a different explanation, that both **this and that,** i.e., the term: From the corner, and the term: From the base, are referring to blood that **is fit** for the corner or the base, in which case the mishna teaches that a garment sprayed by the blood that was to be used for the last three placements of a sin offering does not require laundering, contrary to the opinion of Rav Pappa. Ravina replied: **What is this** claim? **Now that you say** that blood which is **fit for the corner** does **not** require laundering, **is it necessary** to state that the same applies to blood that is merely **fit for the base** of the altar? That ruling would be unnecessary. **Rather,** it must be that the term: **From the corner,** means **from the corner, literally,**[N] i.e., that the blood has already been placed there, whereas the term: **From the base,** means **from** blood **that is fit for the base,** i.e., from the remainder of the blood, which is to be poured on the base.

NOTES

In accordance with whose opinion is this, it is Rabbi Neḥemya – הָא מַנִּי רַבִּי נְחֶמְיָה הִיא: Rashi explains that the liability for sacrificing part of an offering outside the Temple depends on whether the sacrifice of that part is indispensable for atonement. If the blood is indispensable for atonement, one who sacrifices it outside the Temple is liable.

He would not teach three exemptions – לָא מַתְנֵי לֵיהּ תְּלָתָא פְּטוּרֵי: Since the *tanna'im* would teach their rulings orally, they would frequently contrast cases that involve opposing rulings, as a memory aid. It is therefore likely that the *tanna* preferred to compare two cases whose rulings contrast, even if a greater novelty could have been taught by employing a different example. In any case, this *baraita* does not prove the ruling of Rabbi Neḥemya with regard to the remainder of the blood from a sin offering sacrificed on the external altar and whether a garment that absorbs this blood requires laundering. If so, Rav Pappa's proof from the mishna, that a garment that absorbed from the blood of the last three placements of a sin offering requires laundering, is rejected. Therefore, in the next paragraph Ravina attempts to explain this proof in a different manner.

NOTES

From the corner literally – מִן הַקֶּרֶן מַמָּשׁ: As proof for his opinion that a garment that absorbed from the blood of the last three placements of a sin offering requires laundering, Rav Pappa cited the statement of the mishna: If the blood sprayed from the corner or from the base the garment does not require laundering. Rav Pappa inferred from this statement that if the blood was fit for the corner, i.e., the blood of the last three placements of a sin offering, the garment does require laundering. The Gemara subsequently raised a difficulty against this proof: By the same reasoning one could infer that a garment that absorbs blood that is fit for the base requires laundering, and this is not the *halakha*. Ravina counters this claim by explaining that while the term: From the corner, means literally from the corner, the term: From the base, does not mean literally from the base, i.e., blood that sprayed from the base after the remaining blood has been poured there. His reasoning is that once it has been taught that a garment that absorbs blood sprayed from the corner does not require laundering it is unnecessary to say that the same applies to blood from the base. Instead, this clause is referring to blood that is fit for the base, i.e., the remainder of the blood before it has been poured. The mishna is teaching that although the mitzva of pouring has not yet been performed with this blood, a garment that absorbs this blood does not require laundering.

NOTES

Bull of Yom Kippur – **פַּר יוֹם הַכִּפּוּרִים**: The bull of Yom Kippur is not mentioned in this chapter of the Torah at all. Yet, since its service is similar to that of these bulls in that the High Priest sprinkles its blood seven times on the Curtain, one can derive the details of its service from the bull for an unwitting sin of the anointed priest.

״כׇּל הַנִּיתָּנִין עַל מִזְבֵּחַ הַפְּנִימִי״ כו׳. תָּנוּ רַבָּנַן: ״וְעָשָׂה...כַּאֲשֶׁר עָשָׂה״ – מָה בָּא לְלַמּוֹד?

§ The mishna teaches: With regard to **all** the offerings **whose** blood is to be **placed on the inner altar**, which are the bull and goat of Yom Kippur, the bull for an unwitting sin of the anointed priest, the bull for an unwitting communal sin, and the goat for an unwitting communal sin of idol worship, if the priest omitted even one of the placements, it is as though he did not facilitate atonement. **The Sages taught** in a *baraita*: The Torah first discusses the bull for an unwitting sin of the anointed priest and afterward the bull for an unwitting communal sin, concerning which it states: "And he shall do with the bull, as he did with the bull for a sin offering" (Leviticus 4:20). It may be asked: This phrase: **"And he shall do…as he did," what** does this **come to teach?** All the details stated with regard to the first bull, i.e., that of the anointed priest, seem to be stated explicitly with regard to the second bull as well.

לִכְפּוֹל בְּהַזָּאָתוֹ. וְלִמֵּד שֶׁאִם חִיסֵּר אַחַת מִכׇּל הַמַּתָּנוֹת – לֹא עָשָׂה וְלֹא כְלוּם. אֵין לִי אֶלָּא מַתַּן שֶׁבַע שֶׁמְּעַכְּבוֹת בְּכׇל מָקוֹם, מַתַּן אַרְבַּע מִנַּיִין? תַּלְמוּד לוֹמַר: ״כֵּן יַעֲשֶׂה״,

Rather, the verse comes **to repeat the** *halakha* of the **sprinkling of** the blood, as though it were written twice with regard to the same bull. This repetition of the *halakha* indicates that the sprinkling is indispensable, thereby **teaching that if** the priest **omitted one of the placements he has done nothing. I have** a derivation **only** with regard to the **seven placements** on the Curtain separating between the Sanctuary and Holy of Holies, that they are indispensable, as these seven **are indispensable in all cases,** as the Gemara will explain (40a). **From where** is it derived that the same applies to the **four placements** on the inner altar? **The verse states: "So shall he do"** (Leviticus 4:20).

״לַפָּר״ – זֶה פַּר יוֹם הַכִּפּוּרִים,

The *baraita* continues: The verse states: "And he shall do **with the bull**" (Leviticus 4:20); **this** alludes to a different bull whose service is similar, namely **the bull of Yom Kippur.**[N]

Perek **IV**
Daf **39** Amud **b**

BACKGROUND

Anointed priest – **כֹּהֵן מָשִׁיחַ**: When the anointing oil was available, until the time of King Josiah, who sequestered it together with the Ark of the Covenant and the tablets, the High Priest would be consecrated by anointment with this special oil. After that point, the High Priest was inaugurated without being anointed; the appointment was simply pronounced publicly, and the new High Priest would proceed to don the eight garments of the High Priest and perform his service.

HALAKHA

Goats for an unwitting communal sin of idol worship – **שְׂעִירֵי עֲבוֹדָה זָרָה**: The Torah does not specify what must be done with the blood of the goat for an unwitting communal sin of idol worship. The Sages derived that as this offering is brought to atone for an unwitting communal sin, it should be treated like the bull brought to atone for an unwitting communal sin, with regard to the sprinkling, the burning of the flesh, and the fact that they render ritually impure those individuals who burn the flesh (Rambam *Sefer Avoda, Hilkhot Ma'aseh HaKorbanot* 5:16).

״כַּאֲשֶׁר עָשָׂה לַפָּר״ – זֶה פַּר כֹּהֵן מָשִׁיחַ, ״הַחַטָּאת״ – אֵלּוּ שְׂעִירֵי עֲבוֹדָה זָרָה. יָכוֹל שֶׁאֲנִי מְרַבֶּה אַף שְׂעִירֵי הָרְגָלִים וּשְׂעִירֵי רָאשֵׁי חֳדָשִׁים? תַּלְמוּד לוֹמַר: ״לוֹ״.

"**As he did with the bull**" (Leviticus 4:20); **this** is a reference to the **bull** for an unwitting sin **of the anointed priest,**[B] teaching that all of the sprinklings of the blood of this bull are also indispensable. "**A sin offering"; these are** the **goats for** an unwitting communal sin of **idol worship,**[HN] teaching that they are offered in the same manner as the bull for an unwitting communal sin, their blood being sprinkled in the Sanctuary and their flesh burned. One **might** have thought **that I** should **include also the goats of the Festivals and the goats** sacrificed on the **New Moons,**[N] which are communal offerings as well, i.e., that their service should be performed inside the Sanctuary like that of the bull for an unwitting communal sin. Therefore, **the verse states:** "So shall he do **with this**" (Leviticus 4:20), which indicates that this service is performed only with this animal and not with the goats of the Festivals or the goats of the New Moons.

NOTES

Goats for an unwitting communal sin of idol worship – **שְׂעִירֵי עֲבוֹדָה זָרָה**: The offerings brought for an unwitting sin of idol worship are outlined in Numbers 15:22–31. The verses there state only the basic *halakha* that in addition to a bull as a burnt offering, a goat as a sin offering must be brought on behalf of the community. Since the Torah does not provide the details of the service of this goat, they are derived from the *halakhot* of the bull for an unwitting communal sin. The connection between these two offerings is clear, as the sacrifice of these animals serves to atone for an unwitting communal sin, i.e., in a case where the Sanhedrin issued a mistaken ruling with regard to idol worship and the community followed their ruling.

The goats of the Festivals and the goats sacrificed on the New Moons – **שְׂעִירֵי הָרְגָלִים וּשְׂעִירֵי רָאשֵׁי חֳדָשִׁים**: These goats are also communal sin offerings, and the verse uses an expression of atonement with regard to them (see Numbers 28:22). Consequently, one might have thought that their blood should also be sprinkled inside the Sanctuary and their flesh burned.

וּמָה רָאִיתָ לְרַבּוֹת אֶת אֵלּוּ וּלְהוֹצִיא אֶת אֵלּוּ? אַחַר שֶׁרִיבָּה הַכָּתוּב וּמִיעֵט, מְרַבֶּה אֲנִי אֶת אֵלּוּ שֶׁמְּכַפְּרִין עַל עֲבֵירַת מִצְוָה יְדוּעָה, וּמוֹצִיא אֲנִי אֵלּוּ שֶׁאֵין מְכַפְּרִין עַל עֲבֵירַת מִצְוָה יְדוּעָה.

The Gemara asks: **And what did you see to include these** goats for an unwitting communal sin of idol worship **and to exclude those** goats sacrificed on the Festivals and the New Moons? The Gemara answers: **After** noting **that the verse included** some offerings **and excluded** others, one can say: **I include these** goats for an unwitting communal sin of idol worship, **as they atone for the known transgression of a mitzva,** i.e., idol worship, and therefore they are similar to the bull for an unwitting communal sin, which is brought for an erroneous ruling of the Sanhedrin with regard to a specific mitzva. **And I exclude those** goats sacrificed on the Festivals and the New Moons, **as they do not atone for the known transgression of a mitzva,** but rather they atone for the unwitting defilement of the Temple or its sacrificial foods.

״וְכִפֶּר״ – אַף עַל פִּי שֶׁלֹּא סָמַךְ, ״וְנִסְלַח״ – אַף עַל פִּי שֶׁלֹּא נָתַן שִׁירַיִם.

The *baraita* resumes its interpretation of the verse. **"And the priest shall make atonement"**; this teaches that atonement is achieved **even if** the Elders **did not place** their **hands**[NH] on the head of the bull as they are commanded to do (see Leviticus 4:15). **"And they shall be forgiven"**; this teaches that atonement is achieved **even if** the priest **did not place** the **remainder**[H] of the blood on the base of the altar, as is required (see Leviticus 4:7).

וּמָה רָאִיתָ לִפְסוֹל בְּהַזָּאוֹת וּלְהַכְשִׁיר בִּסְמִיכָה וְשִׁירַיִם?

The Gemara again asks: **And** as the verse does not specify which aspects of the service are included and which are excluded, **what did you see to disqualify** the offering **in** the case of the seven **sprinklings**; how did you derive that the phrase "And he shall do… as he did" teaches that the seven sprinklings are indispensable? **And** what did you see **to render** the offering **fit in** the absence of **placing hands** on the head of the offering **and** pouring out the **remainder** of the blood on the base of the altar, based on the words "And the priest shall make atonement… and they shall be forgiven"?

אָמַרְתָּ, פּוֹסֵל בְּהַזָּאוֹת שֶׁמְּעַכְּבוֹת בְּכָל מָקוֹם, וּמַכְשִׁיר אֲנִי בִּסְמִיכָה וְשִׁירַיִם שֶׁאֵין מְעַכְּבוֹת בְּכָל מָקוֹם.

The Gemara answers: **You should say** the following logical argument: I **disqualify** the offering **in** the absence of the seven **sprinklings, as** these seven sprinklings **are indispensable in all cases,** as will be explained (40a), **and I render** the offering **fit in** the absence of **placing hands** on the head of the offering **and** in the absence of the pouring of the **remainder** of the blood onto the base of the altar, **as** these **are not indispensable in all cases,** and therefore it is reasonable to conclude that they are not indispensable here either.

NOTES

And he shall make atonement, even if they did not place hands – וְכִפֶּר אַף עַל פִּי שֶׁלֹּא סָמַךְ: The phrase "And the priest shall make atonement" indicates that atonement is achieved even when not all the actions stated in the Torah have been performed. Although placing hands is never indispensable, one might have thought that since the Torah is particular that the service of these offerings should be performed in an entirely correct manner, perhaps this includes even placing hands. The commentaries explain that the Gemara does not find it necessary to derive from a verse the fact that the sacrificial portions that are consumed on the altar are not indispensable, as they are consumed after all the actions involving the blood have been completed, whereas placing hands occurs before the animal is slaughtered (*Tosafot*).

HALAKHA

Even if they did not place their hands – אַף עַל פִּי שֶׁלֹּא סָמַךְ: Placing hands on the head of an offering is not indispensable for atonement. Nevertheless, one who neglects to do so is considered as though he has not achieved full atonement (Rambam *Sefer Avoda, Hilkhot Ma'aseh HaKorbanot* 3:12).

Even if he did not place the remainder – אַף עַל פִּי שֶׁלֹּא נָתַן שִׁירַיִם: One who pours the remainder of the blood outside the Temple is exempt, even in the case of the remainder of the blood of sin offerings brought in the Sanctuary. The reason is that the pouring of the remainder of the blood is not indispensable for achieving atonement (Rambam *Sefer Avoda, Hilkhot Ma'aseh HaKorbanot* 19:4).

אָמַר מָר: אֵין לִי אֶלָּא מַתַּן שֶׁבַע שֶׁמְּעַכְּבוֹת בְּכׇל מָקוֹם. הֵיכָא? אָמַר רַב פָּפָּא: בְּפָרָה וּבִנְגָעִים.

The Gemara analyzes the *baraita* in detail. **The Master said** in the *baraita*: **I have** a derivation **only** with regard to the **seven placements** on the Curtain separating between the Sanctuary and Holy of Holies, that they are indispensable, **as** these seven **are indispensable in all cases.** The Gemara asks: **Where** are the seven indispensable? **Rav Pappa says: In** the case of the red **heifer** (see Numbers 19:2–4), **and in** the purification process of one afflicted with leprous **marks** (see Leviticus 14:16).[BHN]

מַתַּן אַרְבַּע מִנַּיִן? תַּלְמוּד לוֹמַר: "כֵּן יַעֲשֶׂה". מַאי שְׁנָא מַתַּן שֶׁבַע – דִּכְתִיבָן וּכְפִילָן, מַתַּן אַרְבַּע נַמִי כְּתִיבָן וּכְפִילָן!

The *baraita* continues: **From where** is it derived that the same applies to the **four placements** on the inner altar? **The verse states: "So shall he do"** (Leviticus 4:20). The Gemara asks: **What is different** about **seven placements,** that they should be indispensable? If you say that the reason is **that** the seven placements **are written and repeated,** by means of the terms "And he shall do… as he did," which teaches that they are indispensable, I can say that the **four placements as well are written and repeated.** Why then should their *halakha* be any different?

אָמַר רַבִּי יִרְמְיָה: לָא נִצְרְכָא אֶלָּא לְרַבִּי שִׁמְעוֹן; דְּתַנְיָא, לְמַעְלָה אוֹמֵר: "קֶרֶן קַרְנוֹת" – שְׁתַּיִם, לְמַטָּה הוּא אוֹמֵר: "קֶרֶן קַרְנוֹת" – אַרְבַּע, דִּבְרֵי רַבִּי שִׁמְעוֹן;

Rabbi Yirmeya says: This **is necessary only according to** the opinion of **Rabbi Shimon,** who maintains that only two placements are written in this chapter, while the other two are derived through a juxtaposition. Consequently, a specific derivation is required for these. **As it is taught** in a *baraita* with regard to the placements on the inner altar: **Above,** in the case of the bull for an unwitting sin of the anointed priest, the verse **states corner** in the plural form of **corners** (see Leviticus 4:7), i.e., it says "corners [*karnot*]," in the plural, where it could have written corner, in the singular. These are **two** corners. And **below,** with regard to the bull for an unwitting communal sin, **it** again **states corner** in the plural form of **corners** (see Leviticus 4:18). Together these amount to **four**[N] corners. This is **the statement of Rabbi Shimon.**

רַבִּי יְהוּדָה אוֹמֵר: אֵינוֹ צָרִיךְ, הֲרֵי הוּא אוֹמֵר "בְּאֹהֶל מוֹעֵד" – עַל כׇּל הָאָמוּר בְּאֹהֶל מוֹעֵד. וְרַבִּי יְהוּדָה, "כֵּן יַעֲשֶׂה" מַאי עָבֵיד לֵיהּ?

Rabbi Yehuda says: This derivation **is not necessary,**[N] **as it states** in these same verses: "And he shall put of the blood upon the corners of the altar which is before the Lord, which is **in the Tent of Meeting"** (Leviticus 4:18).[BN] The superfluous expression "in the Tent of Meeting" teaches that the blood must be placed **on all** the corners of the altar **that are stated with regard to the Tent of Meeting,** i.e., on all four corners. The Gemara asks: **And Rabbi Yehuda, what does he do with** the phrase **"so shall he do,"** which Rabbi Shimon interprets as referring to the four placements?

BACKGROUND

Leprous marks – נְגָעִים: The *halakhot* of *tzara'at*, traditionally rendered as leprosy but not necessarily identified medically with that illness, are recorded in the Torah in Leviticus, chapters 13–14. They are detailed in tractate *Nega'im*, which deals exclusively with the different types of leprosy. The *halakha* distinguishes between the ritual impurity of a quarantined leper, i.e., a suspected leper who is isolated for a period of up to two weeks until his status is clarified, and that of a confirmed leper. A confirmed leper must grow his hair long, rend his garments, and cover his head in a particular way. Part of the purification process of a leper involves removing of all of his body hair.

Tent of Meeting – אֹהֶל מוֹעֵד: The term: Tent of Meeting, is another name for the Tabernacle (see Exodus 27:21). The name derives from the fact that this location was where man encountered the Divine. In the wilderness, it was the principal spot of God's communications to Moses.

HALAKHA

In the case of the red heifer and in the purification of leprous marks – בְּפָרָה וּבִנְגָעִים: If the priest performing the service of the red heifer omits one of the seven sprinklings that are sprinkled toward the Sanctuary, he has disqualified the heifer, as stated in the mishna in *Menaḥot* (27b). Likewise, with regard to the purification of a leper, if the *log* of oil was spilled after the priest had placed some of the oil on his palm and had started to sprinkle toward the Holy of Holies, but before he had completed all seven sprinklings, he must bring a new *log* and start the seven sprinklings afresh (Rambam *Sefer Tahara, Hilkhot Para Aduma* 4:7 and *Sefer Korbanot, Hilkhot Meḥusrei Kappara* 5:5).

NOTES

In the case of the red heifer and in the purification of leprous marks – בְּפָרָה וּבִנְגָעִים: In the case of the red heifer the priest sprinkles its blood seven times toward the Tent of Meeting, and the verse concerning it states: "Statute" (Numbers 19:2), which indicates that all services mentioned in that passage are indispensable. Similarly, the purification ritual of a leper involves seven sprinklings of oil, and the verse states concerning it: "This shall be the law of the leper" (Leviticus 14:2). The term "law" teaches that these services are indispensable (see *Menaḥot* 19a).

Corner, corners, four – קֶרֶן קַרְנוֹת אַרְבַּע: Although one of the terms "corners" is written in the context of the bull for an unwitting sin of the anointed priest while the other is written in the context of the bull for an unwitting communal sin, the *halakhot* of these two types of offerings are derived from each other, as it is stated in the *baraita*: "As he did with the bull" (Leviticus 4:20); this is the bull for an unwitting sin of the anointed priest.

Is not necessary – אֵינוֹ צָרִיךְ: Some commentaries explain that the dispute between Rabbi Shimon and Rabbi Yehuda concerns the issue of whether the manner in which the verses in the Torah are written is authoritative, and whether one can therefore derive *halakhot* based on the spelling of the words. Rabbi Yehuda holds that one does derive *halakhot* in this manner, and therefore one reads the verse as if it states: Corner [*karnat*], as the word *karnot* is written without the *vav* that indicates the plural form. Conversely, Rabbi Shimon holds that the vocalization of the Torah is authoritative, meaning that one derives *halakhot* based on the pronunciation of the words even when it diverges from the spelling, and accordingly, the word is read as a plural form (Ra'avad; see Rashi and *Tosafot*).

As it states, in the Tent of Meeting – הֲרֵי הוּא אוֹמֵר בְּאֹהֶל מוֹעֵד: This superfluous phrase is stated with regard to the bull for an unwitting communal sin: "And he shall put from the blood upon the corners of the altar that is before the Lord, which is in the Tent of Meeting" (Leviticus 4:18), and similarly in connection with the bull for an unwitting sin of the anointed priest (Leviticus 4:7). Since it is known that the incense altar is inside the Tent of Meeting, this phrase is interpreted as serving to teach that the priest must place the blood on all the corners of the inner altar.

מִיבְּעֵי לֵיהּ לְכִדְתַנְיָא: לְפִי שֶׁלֹּא לָמַדְנוּ לְפַר יוֹם הַכִּפּוּרִים לִסְמִיכָה וּשְׁיָרֵי הַדָּם, מִנַּיִן? תַּלְמוּד לוֹמַר: "כֵּן יַעֲשֶׂה".

The Gemara answers that Rabbi Yehuda **requires** this verse **for that which is taught** in a *baraita*: **As we did not learn** with regard **to the bull of Yom Kippur that placing hands** is required, i.e., that the High Priest must place his hands on this animal before it is slaughtered, **and** likewise it is not stated that the **remainder** of its **blood** must be poured on the base of the altar. **From where** is it derived that these actions must be performed? **The verse states: "So shall he do."**

וּלְפַר יוֹם הַכִּפּוּרִים לֹא לָמַדְנוּ? הָא אָמַרְתְּ: "לְפַר" – זֶה יוֹם הַכִּפּוּרִים!

The Gemara asks: **And did we not learn** with regard **to the bull of Yom Kippur** that these requirements apply? **But you said** earlier in the *baraita*: **"With the bull"** (Leviticus 4:20); **this** alludes to the bull of **Yom Kippur,** which indicates that all the rites performed in connection with the bull for an unwitting communal sin apply also to the bull of Yom Kippur.

אִיצְטְרִיךְ, סָלְקָא דַּעְתָּךְ אָמִינָא: הָנֵי מִילֵּי עֲבוֹדָה דִּמְעַכְּבָא כַּפָּרָה, אֲבָל עֲבוֹדָה דְּלָא מְעַכְּבָא כַּפָּרָה אֵימָא לָא, קָמַשְׁמַע לַן.

The Gemara answers: The derivation from the phrase "so shall he do" **was necessary,** as it could **enter your mind to say** that **this matter,** the comparison between the bull for an unwitting communal sin and the bull of Yom Kippur, applies only to **a service that is indispensable for atonement,** e.g., the sprinkling of the blood. **But** with regard to **a service that is not indispensable for atonement,** such as placing hands on the head of the animal or pouring out the remainder of the blood, one might **say** that these actions need **not** be performed. Therefore, the verse **teaches us:** "So shall he do," i.e., these services, too, must be performed with the bull of Yom Kippur.

וְרַבִּי שִׁמְעוֹן, הַאי "בְּאֹהֶל מוֹעֵד" מַאי עָבֵיד לֵיהּ? "בְּאֹהֶל מוֹעֵד" מִבְּעֵי לֵיהּ, שֶׁאִם נִפְחֲתָה תִּקְרָה שֶׁל הֵיכָל – לֹא הָיָה מַזֶּה. וְאִידָּךְ? מֵ"אֲשֶׁר". וְאִידָּךְ? "אֲשֶׁר" לָא דָּרֵישׁ.

The Gemara asks: **And Rabbi Shimon, what does he do with this** phrase: **"In the Tent of Meeting,"** from which Rabbi Yehuda derives that the blood must be placed on all four corners of the altar? The Gemara answers: Rabbi Shimon **requires** the phrase **"in the Tent of Meeting"** to teach **that if the roof of the Sanctuary**[B] **was breached**[NH] by a hole, the priest **would not sprinkle** the blood, as it would no longer be called the Tent of Meeting. The Gemara asks: **And the other** *tanna,* Rabbi Yehuda, from where does he derive this *halakha*? The Gemara explains that Rabbi Yehuda derives it **from** the superfluous term **"which is** in the Tent of Meeting" (Leviticus 4:7, 18). The Gemara asks: **And the other** *tanna,* Rabbi Shimon? **He does not interpret** the term **"which is"** as he maintains that this expression is not significant enough to serve as the source of a *halakha*.

אַבָּיֵי אָמַר: לְרַבִּי יְהוּדָה נַמִי אִיצְטְרִיךְ, סָלְקָא דַּעְתָּךְ אָמִינָא: מִידֵּי דַּהֲוָה אַסְּמִיכָה וּשְׁיָרֵי הַדָּם, דְּאַף עַל גַּב דִּכְתִיבָן וּכְפִילָן לָא מְעַכְּבָא – מַתַּן אַרְבַּע נַמִי לֹא תְּתַעַכֵּב, קָא מַשְׁמַע לַן.

Abaye said: According to the opinion of **Rabbi Yehuda as well,** it **was necessary** to learn from the phrase "so shall he do" that the four placements are indispensable. As it might **enter your mind to say** that **just as it is with regard to placing hands and** the **remainder of the blood, that even though they are written and repeated they are not indispensable,** so **too,** the **four placements** of blood **should not be indispensable.** Therefore, the phrase "so shall he do" **teaches us** that this is not the case, and the four sprinklings are indeed indispensable.

NOTES

That if the roof of the Sanctuary was breached – שֶׁאִם נִפְחֲתָה תִּקְרָה שֶׁל הֵיכָל: If the roof was breached, the Sanctuary, which corresponds to the Tent of Meeting in the Tabernacle, is no longer considered a tent, and therefore one may not place the blood on the inner altar.

HALAKHA

Roof of the Sanctuary was breached – נִפְחֲתָה תִּקְרָה שֶׁל הֵיכָל: If the roof of the Sanctuary opened, the High Priest would not perform the sprinklings of Yom Kippur (Rambam *Sefer Avoda, Hilkhot Avodat Yom HaKippurim* 5:23 and *Kesef Mishne* there).

BACKGROUND

Sanctuary – הֵיכָל: The Sanctuary was the inner section of the Temple, between the Entrance Hall and the Holy of Holies. It was a roofed area, one hundred cubits high, in the west of the Temple courtyard. It contained the seven-branched Candelabrum, the golden Table for the shewbread, and the incense altar, or golden altar. On its western side was the Holy of Holies. The term Sanctuary is sometimes used also in reference to the entire building.

Sanctuary in Solomon's Temple, which contained multiple Candelabra and Tables

"לְפַר" – זֶה פַּר יוֹם הַכִּפּוּרִים. לְמַאי הִילְכְתָא? אִי לְעַכֵּב – פְּשִׁיטָא, "חֻקָּה" כְּתִיבָה בֵּיהּ!

§ The *baraita* teaches: **"With the bull"** (Leviticus 4:20), **this** alludes to **the bull of Yom Kippur. To what *halakha*** does this statement relate? **If** it serves **to** teach that all matters stated with regard to the bull of Yom Kippur are **indispensable,** this is **obvious,** since the word **"statute" is written concerning it:** "And this shall be an everlasting statute to you" (Leviticus 16:29), and there is a principle that *halakhot* described as statutes are indispensable.

אָמַר רַב נַחְמָן בַּר יִצְחָק: לָא נִצְרְכָא אֶלָּא לְרַבִּי יְהוּדָה, דְּאָמַר: כִּי כְּתִיבָה "חֻקָּה" – אַדְּבָרִים הַנַּעֲשִׂים בְּבִגְדֵי לָבָן בִּפְנִים, שֶׁאִם הִקְדִּים מַעֲשֶׂה לַחֲבֵירוֹ – לֹא עָשָׂה וְלֹא כְלוּם.

Rav Naḥman bar Yitzḥak said: This statement **is necessary only according to** the opinion of **Rabbi Yehuda, who says: When** the term **"statute" is written** concerning the Yom Kippur service, indicating that no details may be altered, it is written only **with regard to actions performed in white garments**[HB] **inside** the Holy of Holies, e.g., burning the incense and sprinkling the blood, which are the essential services of the day, and it teaches **that if** the High Priest **performed** one of the **actions before another,** i.e., not in the proper order, **he has done nothing.**

אֲבָל דְּבָרִים הַנַּעֲשִׂים בְּבִגְדֵי לָבָן בַּחוּץ, הִקְדִּים מַעֲשֶׂה לַחֲבֵירוֹ – מַה שֶּׁעָשָׂה עָשׂוּי, אֵימָא מִדִּכְסִידְרָן לָא מְעַכְּבִי – הַזָּאוֹת נַמִי לָא מְעַכְּבִי, קָא מַשְׁמַע לַן.

But with regard to **those actions performed in white garments outside,** in the Sanctuary, if he **performed** one **action before another, what he did is done** and he is not required to repeat the rite. Consequently, one might **say** that **from** the fact **that their order is not indispensable,** it may be derived that the **sprinklings,** i.e., placements, **themselves are also not indispensable.** Therefore, the term "with the bull" **teaches us** that the placements are indeed indispensable.

מַתְקִיף לָהּ רַב פַּפָּא: וּמִי מָצֵית אָמְרַתְּ הָכִי? וְהָתַנְיָא: "וְכִלָּה מִכַּפֵּר אֶת הַקֹּדֶשׁ", אִם כִּיפֵּר – כִּילָּה, וְאִם לֹא כִּיפֵּר – לֹא כִּילָּה, דִּבְרֵי רַבִּי עֲקִיבָא;

Rav Pappa objects to this: And how can you say this, that Rabbi Yehuda derives from here that the placements are indispensable? **But isn't it taught** in a *baraita*: The verse discussing the Yom Kippur service states: **"And when he has finished atoning for the Sanctuary"** (Leviticus 16:20). This indicates that **if he performed the atonement,** i.e., the sprinklings, inside the Sanctuary, **he has finished**[N] the order of the service, even though he has not poured the remainder of the blood on the base of the altar; **and if he did not perform the atonement, he has not finished;** this is **the statement of Rabbi Akiva.**

אָמַר לוֹ רַבִּי יְהוּדָה: מִפְּנֵי מָה לֹא נֹאמַר: אִם כִּילָּה – כִּיפֵּר, וְאִם לֹא כִּילָּה – לֹא כִּיפֵּר!

Rabbi Yehuda said to him: For what reason **do we not say: If he finished** the entire service, which includes sprinkling the blood in the Sanctuary and pouring the remainder of the blood onto the base of the altar, **he has facilitated atonement;**[N] **and if he did not finish, he has not facilitated atonement?** This indicates that Rabbi Yehuda derives from this verse the *halakha* that the sprinklings in the Sanctuary are indispensable.

אָמַר רַב פַּפָּא: לָא נִצְרְכָא, אֶלָּא לְ"אֶת" דָּם וּבִטְבִילָה; "אֶת" – אָמַר רַב אַחָא בַּר יַעֲקֹב: לָא נִצְרְכָא, לְהַכְשִׁיר

Rav Pappa says: This reference to the bull of Yom Kippur in the term "with the bull," **is necessary only**[N] **to** apply to the bull of Yom Kippur three *halakhot* that are derived from that which is stated with regard to the bull for an unwitting sin of the anointed priest: "And the priest shall immerse his finger [*et etzba'o*] in the blood" (Leviticus 4:6). These *halakhot* can be summarized in the shortened form: ***Et*, blood, and with immersion.**[N] The Gemara elaborates: With regard to the word ***et*, Rav Aḥa bar Ya'akov says:** This word **is necessary only to render fit**

HALAKHA

Actions performed in white garments, etc. – דְּבָרִים הַנַּעֲשִׂים בְּבִגְדֵי לָבָן וכו׳: All the actions performed by the High Priest in white garments inside the Sanctuary on Yom Kippur must be performed in the correct order. If he performed these rites in the incorrect order, he has done nothing, in accordance with the opinion of Rabbi Yehuda (Rambam *Sefer Avoda*, *Hilkhot Avodat Yom HaKippurim* 5:1, and see *Leḥem Mishne* there).

BACKGROUND

White garments – בִּגְדֵי לָבָן: This term refers to the four garments that the High Priest wore when he entered the Holy of Holies on Yom Kippur. They were the tunic, the trousers, the mitre, and the sash. These garments were made entirely of white linen and lacked the gold threads present in the High Priest's usual garments. They resembled those garments worn by an ordinary priest throughout the year, except that the sash worn by an ordinary priest was made of a combination of wool and linen.

High Priest entering the Holy of Holies in white garments

NOTES

If he performed the atonement he has finished – אִם כִּיפֵּר כִּילָּה: In other words, if he has performed the act that facilitates atonement in all cases, which is the sprinkling of the blood, it is as though he has finished the entire service, as nothing else is indispensable. Although he must still pour the remainder of the blood, the main part of the service has been completed (Rashi).

If he finished he has facilitated atonement – אִם כִּילָּה כִּיפֵּר: That is, he facilitated atonement only if he finished the entire service, including pouring the remainder of the blood (Rashi). According to this interpretation, Rabbi Yehuda maintains that the pouring of the remainder of the blood is indispensable. Others contend the opposite, that Rabbi Yehuda is saying that if the High Priest finished the sprinkling he facilitated atonement, while pouring the remainder of the blood is not indispensable, whereas Rabbi Akiva maintains that the pouring of the remainder of the blood is indispensable to achieve atonement (Ra'avya, citing the Jerusalem Talmud).

Is necessary only, etc. – לָא נִצְרְכָא אֶלָּא וכו׳: In other words, the derivation of the *baraita* with regard to the bull of Yom Kippur is from the bull for the unwitting sin of the anointed priest, which is also alluded to in the verse discussing the bull for an unwitting communal sin. Since the bull of Yom Kippur and the bull for the unwitting sin of the anointed priest are both alluded to in this verse, they are considered to be juxtaposed with each other (Rashi). Rabbeinu Tam maintains that the fact that both are alluded to in that verse is insufficient for a juxtaposition. He contends that the *halakha* of the bull of Yom Kippur is not derived from the bull for the unwitting sin of the anointed priest but from the mention of blood with regard to the bull for an unwitting communal sin (see Leviticus 4:17).

***Et*, blood, and with immersion** – אֶת דָּם וּבִטְבִילָה: Since the same verse subsequently states: "And sprinkle of the blood" (Leviticus 4:6), it must certainly be referring to a priest who had already immersed his finger in the blood. If so, the entire phrase "and the priest shall immerse his finger in the blood" is superfluous and available for exposition (*Korban Aharon*).

אִמִּין שֶׁבְּאֶצְבַּע. ״בַּדָּם״ – שֶׁיְּהֵא בַּדָּם שִׁיעוּר טְבִילָה מֵעִיקָּרָא, ״וְטָבַל״ – וְלֹא מְסַפֵּג.

service performed by a priest who has **a wart** or blister **on** his **finger.**[N] These are not considered an interposition between his finger and the blood. With regard to the term **"in the blood"** (Leviticus 4:6), this teaches **that the blood** in the service vessel **must be of a** sufficient **measure for immersion**[H] **from the outset.** The priest must initially collect in the vessel enough blood for all the sprinklings, rather than adding blood to the vessel for each sprinkling. Finally, the term **"and** the priest **shall immerse**[N] his finger in the blood" indicates that there must be enough blood in the vessel such that the priest can immerse his finger in it **and not** have to **wipe** the sides of the utensil to collect blood for sprinkling.

וְאִיצְטְרִיךְ לְמִכְתַּב ״בַּדָּם״, דְּאִי כָּתַב רַחֲמָנָא ״וְטָבַל״, הֲוָה אָמִינָא: אַף עַל גַּב דְּלֵיכָּא שִׁיעוּר טְבִילָה מֵעִיקָּרָא – כָּתַב רַחֲמָנָא: ״בַּדָּם״;

The Gemara explains: **And** it **was necessary** for the verse to state both these last two terms. It had **to write "in the blood,"**[N] as had **the Merciful One written** only **"and** the priest **shall immerse," I would say** that the sprinklings are valid **even if there was not** a sufficient **measure** of blood **for immersion from the outset,** but only enough for a single sprinkling, provided that the priest then added more blood to the vessel for each sprinkling. Therefore, **the Merciful One writes "in the blood"** to teach that from the outset there must be enough blood in the vessel for all the sprinklings.

וְאִי כָּתַב רַחֲמָנָא ״בַּדָּם״, הֲוָה אָמִינָא: אֲפִילּוּ מְסַפֵּג – כָּתַב רַחֲמָנָא: ״וְטָבַל״.

And conversely, **had the Merciful One written** only **"in the blood," I would say** that **even** if there was enough blood in the vessel at the outset it is not necessary that there be enough blood for immersion for the last sprinklings, as the priest can **wipe** the sides of the utensil to collect blood for sprinkling. Therefore, **the Merciful One writes "and** the priest **shall immerse."**

״מִזְבַּח קְטֹרֶת סַמִּים״ לָמָּה לִי? שֶׁאִם לֹא נִתְחַנֵּךְ הַמִּזְבֵּחַ בִּקְטוֹרֶת הַסַּמִּים – לֹא הָיָה מַזֶּה.

The Gemara addresses another apparently superfluous phrase in the same chapter: "And the priest shall put some of the blood upon the corners of **the altar of sweet incense** before the Lord" (Leviticus 4:7). **Why do I need**[N] the verse to mention the sweet incense? It would have been enough to identify the altar as being "before the Lord" and one would have understood that the reference is to the inner altar. Rather, this serves to teach **that if the altar had not been inaugurated with sweet incense,**[H] the priest **would not sprinkle** blood on it.

תַּנְיָא כְּווֹתֵיהּ דְּרַב פַּפָּא: ״וְעָשָׂה...כַּאֲשֶׁר עָשָׂה״, מַה תַּלְמוּד לוֹמַר ״לַפָּר״? לְרַבּוֹת פַּר יוֹם הַכִּפּוּרִים לְכָל מַה שֶּׁאָמוּר בָּעִנְיָן, דִּבְרֵי רַבִּי.

The Gemara comments: **It is taught** in a *baraita* **in accordance with** the opinion **of Rav Pappa** that the superfluous phrase in the passage discussing the bull for an unwitting communal sin alludes to the bull of Yom Kippur in order to teach the three *halakhot* of *et*, in the blood, and immersion, from the case of the bull for an unwitting sin of the anointed priest, which is also alluded to in that verse. The *baraita* states: **"And he shall do** with the bull, **as he did** with the bull for a sin offering" (Leviticus 4:20). **What is the meaning when the verse states "with the bull"?** This serves **to include the bull of Yom Kippur for all that is stated in** this **matter,**[N] i.e., in the passage concerning the bull for an unwitting sin of the anointed priest, specifically the *halakhot* of *et*, in the blood, and immersion. This is **the statement of Rabbi** Yehuda HaNasi.

NOTES

A wart on his finger – אִמִּין שֶׁבְּאֶצְבַּע: This is derived from the word *et*, which can have the meaning: With. This indicates that some growths or substances on the finger are considered like the finger itself (see *Or HaYashar*).

And he shall immerse – וְטָבַל: The verse could have omitted this term, as in the case of the bull of Yom Kippur: "And he shall take from the blood of the bull, and sprinkle it with his finger" (Leviticus 16:14), and with regard to the goat brought by a *Nasi* for his unwitting sin: "And the priest shall take from the blood of the sin offering with his finger, and put it upon the corners of the altar" (Leviticus 4:25). Here the verse emphasizes the action of immersing the finger in blood.

In the blood – בַּדָּם: The definite article indicates that when the priest immerses his finger for the purpose of sprinkling he must do so in the same blood that was initially in the vessel. This teaches that from the outset the service vessel must contain enough blood for all the immersions. The priest may not add a small amount of blood to the vessel each time (Ra'avad, in his commentary to *Torat Kohanim*). Rashi writes that the priest may not receive the blood of the bull in two different vessels, each of which contains less than the requisite measure, and then join them together (see *Menaḥot* 7b).

The altar of sweet incense, why do I need – מִזְבַּח קְטֹרֶת סַמִּים לָמָּה לִי: It is unclear why this phrase is discussed here. Rashi states that as the Gemara on the previous *amud* had explained another apparently superfluous phrase in that same verse: "Which is in the Tent of Meeting," it analyzes this expression as well. Others say that this exposition is another example of a *halakha* that applies to the bull of Yom Kippur that is derived from the bull for an unwitting sin of the anointed priest (*Tosafot*).

For all that is stated in this matter – לְכָל מַה שֶּׁאָמוּר בָּעִנְיָן: This is referring to the *halakhot* of *et*, in the blood, and immersion, as explained by Rav Pappa. Furthermore, this broad statement also includes the inference from the term "Tent of Meeting" stated on the previous *amud*, and the *halakha* derived from "the altar of sweet incense," explained earlier. It cannot be referring to the *halakha* that the sprinklings are indispensable, as this is not stated in this matter, i.e., in these specific verses, but is derived from the term "statute" stated with regard to the Yom Kippur service (*Tosafot*).

HALAKHA

Must be of a sufficient measure for immersion – שֶׁיְּהֵא בַּדָּם שִׁיעוּר טְבִילָה: The blood of a sin offering must be sprinkled by the priest with his finger. The service vessel must contain a sufficient measure of blood for immersing, as the priest should not wipe his finger on the side of the vessel (Rambam *Sefer Avoda*, *Hilkhot Ma'aseh HaKorbanot* 5:9, and see *Kesef Mishne*, *Mishne LaMelekh*, and *Ḥiddushei HaGriz* there).

The altar had not been inaugurated with sweet incense – לֹא נִתְחַנֵּךְ הַמִּזְבֵּחַ בִּקְטוֹרֶת הַסַּמִּים: If the inner altar has not been inaugurated through the service of the incense, the priest may not sprinkle the blood on it (Rambam *Sefer Avoda*, *Hilkhot Avodat Yom HaKippurim* 5:24; see *Hilkhot Temidin UMusafin* 3:1).

אָמַר רַבִּי יִשְׁמָעֵאל: קַל וָחוֹמֶר, וּמָה בְּמָקוֹם שֶׁלֹּא הוּשְׁוָה קׇרְבָּן לְקׇרְבָּן – הִשְׁוָה מַעֲשִׂים לְמַעֲשִׂים, מָקוֹם שֶׁהֻשְׁוָה קׇרְבָּן לְקׇרְבָּן – אֵינוֹ דִּין שֶׁיַּשְׁוֶה מַעֲשֶׂה לְמַעֲשֶׂה?

Rabbi Yishmael said: This inclusion is unnecessary, as these *halakhot* can be derived via **an *a fortiori*** inference:[N] **Just as in a case in which** one **offering is not equated with** another **offering** of a different type of animal, the Torah **equated** the **actions** of sprinkling the blood in one offering **with the actions** of the blood in the other offering, as will be explained, in **a case in which** the Torah **equated** one **offering with** another **offering,**[N] i.e., the bull for an unwitting sin of the anointed priest and the bull of Yom Kippur, **isn't it logical that** the Torah **should equate** the **actions** of sprinkling the blood in the one offering **with** the **actions** of the blood in the other offering? Therefore, the derivation by way of a special inclusion is not necessary.

אֶלָּא מַה תַּלְמוּד לוֹמַר ״לַפָּר״ – זֶה פַּר הֶעְלֵם דָּבָר שֶׁל צִבּוּר, ״לַפָּר״ – זֶה פַּר כֹּהֵן מָשִׁיחַ.

Rather, what is the meaning when **the verse states:** "And he shall do with the bull, as he did with the bull for a sin offering"? With regard to the first instance of **"with the bull," this is the bull for an unwitting communal sin.**[NB] And with regard to the second instance of **"with the bull," this is the bull for** an unwitting sin of the **anointed priest.** And the verse serves to teach that just as in the first case, if the priest omitted one of the sprinklings, he has done nothing, the same is true in the second case.

אָמַר מָר: וּמָה בְּמָקוֹם שֶׁלֹּא הוּשְׁוָה קׇרְבָּן לְקׇרְבָּן. מַאי ״לֹא הוּשְׁוָה קׇרְבָּן לְקׇרְבָּן״?

The Gemara clarifies the *baraita*. **The Master said** above: **Just as in a case in which** one **offering is not equated with** another **offering. What** is the meaning of the expression: One **offering is not equated with** another **offering?** Which offerings are not brought from the same type of animal, but nevertheless the *halakhot* governing the sprinkling of their blood are the same?

אִילֵימָא פַּר יוֹם הַכִּפּוּרִים וּשְׂעִיר יוֹם הַכִּפּוּרִים – אִיכָּא לְמִיפְרַךְ: מָה לְהָנָךְ שֶׁכֵּן נִכְנָס דָּמָם לִפְנַי וְלִפְנִים!

If we say that Rabbi Yishmael is referring to **the bull of Yom Kippur and the goat of Yom Kippur,** and from them he derives by way of an *a fortiori* inference that the actions concerning the bull of Yom Kippur are the same as those concerning the bull for an unwitting sin of the anointed priest, which are the same animal, this **can be refuted** as follows: **What** is notable **about these** offerings, the bull and the goat of Yom Kippur? They are notable **in that their blood enters the innermost sanctum,**[N] the Holy of Holies. This is not so of the bull for an unwitting sin of the anointed priest, the blood of which is sprinkled only in the outer area of the Sanctuary.

אֶלָּא פַּר הֶעְלֵם דָּבָר שֶׁל צִבּוּר וּשְׂעִירֵי עֲבוֹדָה זָרָה – אִיכָּא לְמִיפְרַךְ: מָה לְהָנָךְ שֶׁכֵּן מְכַפְּרִין עַל עֲבֵירוֹת מִצְוָה יְדוּעָה!

Rather, say that the reference here is to **the bull for an unwitting communal sin and the goats for** an unwitting communal sin of **idol worship.**[N] But once again this claim **can be refuted: What** is notable **about these** offerings? They are notable **in that** they both **atone for the transgressions of a known mitzva,**[N] whereas the bull of Yom Kippur atones for unknown transgressions (see *Shevuot* 2a).

אֶלָּא פַּר הֶעְלֵם דָּבָר שֶׁל צִבּוּר וְשָׂעִיר שֶׁל יוֹם הַכִּפּוּרִים. וְהָכִי קָאָמַר: וּמָה בְּמָקוֹם שֶׁלֹּא הוּשְׁווּ קׇרְבָּן לְקׇרְבָּן, דְּהַאי פַּר וְהַאי שָׂעִיר – הוּשְׁווּ מַעֲשִׂים לְמַעֲשִׂים לְמַאי דִּכְתַב בְּהוּ, מָקוֹם שֶׁהוּשְׁוָה קׇרְבָּן לְקׇרְבָּן, דְּהַאי פַּר וְהַאי פַּר – אֵינוֹ דִּין

Rather, the reference here is to **the bull for an unwitting communal sin and the goat of Yom Kippur, and this** is what Rabbi Yishmael **is saying: Just as in a case in which** one **offering is not equated with** another **offering, as this is a bull and that** is **a goat,** nevertheless the **actions** of sprinkling the blood in one offering **are equated with** the **actions** of the blood in the other offering **with regard to that which is written concerning it, in a case in which** one **offering is equated with** another **offering,** i.e., the bull for an unwitting sin of the anointed priest and the bull of Yom Kippur, **as this is a bull and that** is **a bull, isn't it logical**

NOTES

A fortiori inference – קַל וָחוֹמֶר: This is not a standard *a fortiori* inference. Generally, an *a fortiori* inference involves a case where one derives that a restriction that applies to a lenient case certainly applies to a more severe case. Here, the *halakhot* that are applied from one case to another are not necessarily restrictions, as the allowance granted to a priest to perform the service with a wart on his finger is a leniency. Furthermore, the three *halakhot* in question, i.e., *et*, in the blood, and immersion, are not actually stated in the case from which the *a fortiori* inference is derived, which according to the conclusion of the Gemara is the goat of Yom Kippur. Rather, this inference merely serves to highlight the relationship between the two cases, similar to the exegetical method of: Disclosure of the matter, in which a similarity is emphasized.

A case in which the Torah equated one offering with another offering – מָקוֹם שֶׁהִשְׁוָה קׇרְבָּן לְקׇרְבָּן: In other words, as the service of the bull of Yom Kippur is performed inside the Sanctuary like the service of the bull for an unwitting communal sin, it is logical that the *halakhot* stated in this passage in Leviticus should apply also to the bull of Yom Kippur, including the three *halakhot* of *et*, in the blood, and immersion. The verse juxtaposes the bull for an unwitting communal sin with the bull for an unwitting sin of the anointed priest, which is where the *halakhot* of *et*, in the blood, and immersion are stated (Rashi). Some commentaries maintain that these three *halakhot* are derived from the *halakhot* of the bull for an unwitting communal sin itself (Rabbeinu Tam; see *Tosafot*).

With the bull, this is the bull for an unwitting communal sin – לַפָּר זֶה פַּר הֶעְלֵם דָּבָר שֶׁל צִבּוּר: On *daf* 41a the Gemara will pose the obvious question: Since this verse itself is discussing the bull for an unwitting communal sin, why is it necessary to include it by means of an exposition?

That their blood enters the innermost sanctum – שֶׁכֵּן נִכְנָס דָּמָם לִפְנַי וְלִפְנִים: By contrast, the blood of the bull for an unwitting communal sin and that of the bull for an unwitting sin of the anointed priest is sprinkled only inside the Sanctuary, not the Holy of Holies. This factor serves to refute the *a fortiori* inference, which is based on the idea that there is no specific reason to equate the two offerings of Yom Kippur, as they involve different animals. Once it has been shown that these two offerings do have a common element, i.e., that their blood enters the innermost sanctum, it can be claimed that this common element is the cause of their similar *halakhot*, and therefore the same *halakhot* need not necessarily apply to two different offerings even when they involve the same animal.

The bull for an unwitting communal sin and the goats for an unwitting communal sin of idol worship – פַּר הֶעְלֵם דָּבָר שֶׁל צִבּוּר וּשְׂעִירֵי עֲבוֹדָה זָרָה: The bull for an unwitting communal sin is sacrificed when the community sins unwittingly due to an erroneous ruling of the court with regard to a transgression whose intentional violation entails *karet*. The goats for an unwitting communal sin of idol worship are brought in a similar set of circumstances, in the particular case of the sin of idolatry. Accordingly, the goats for an unwitting communal sin of idol worship can be considered a particular type of offering for an unwitting communal sin.

The transgressions of a known mitzva – עֲבֵירוֹת מִצְוָה יְדוּעָה: The bull for an unwitting communal sin and the goats for an unwitting communal sin of idol worship are brought when the sin in question is known, but it was performed unwittingly. By contrast, the bull and goat of Yom Kippur atone for the defiling of the Temple, by entering it while ritually impure, or the defiling of its sacrificial foods, by partaking of them while ritually impure, when these transgressions are entirely unknown and there is merely a concern that they might have occurred (see *Shevuot* 2a).

BACKGROUND

The bull for an unwitting communal sin – פַּר הֶעְלֵם דָּבָר שֶׁל צִבּוּר: This bull serves as a communal sin offering. It is brought following an active unwitting transgression committed by the Jewish people as the result of an erroneous halakhic decision handed down by the Great Sanhedrin. Members of the Sanhedrin perform the ritual of placing their hands on the head of the offering. As in the case of the bull of the anointed priest, the blood of this sacrifice is sprinkled against the Curtain dividing the Sanctuary from the Holy of Holies, and on the inner altar. The sacrificial portions are burned on the altar, while the rest of the flesh and the skin are burned outside Jerusalem in the place of the ashes.

שֶׁהוּשְׁווּ מַעֲשִׂים לְמַעֲשִׂים?

that the **actions** of sprinkling the blood in one offering **are equated with** the **actions** of the blood in the other offering?[N] The blood of the goat of Yom Kippur is sprinkled even inside the Holy of Holies, which is not so concerning the blood of the bull. Nevertheless, with regard to the sprinkling in the Sanctuary, which is common to both, their actions are performed in the same manner, with the blood being sprinkled with a finger on the Curtain and on the corners of the altar.

וְאָתְיָא לֵיהּ פַּר יוֹם הַכִּפּוּרִים (נַמִי) לְ״אֶת בַּדָּם וּטְבִילָה״ מִפַּר כֹּהֵן מָשִׁיחַ, וְאָתֵי לֵיהּ שְׂעִיר יוֹם הַכִּפּוּרִים מִשְּׂעִירֵי עֲבוֹדָה זָרָה מִקַּל וָחוֹמֶר.

And by means of this *a fortiori* inference the case of **the bull of Yom Kippur is derived from** the case of **the bull of** an unwitting sin of the **anointed priest, with regard to** the *halakhot* summarized by the words ***et*****, in the blood, and immersion,** as they are both bulls. **And** likewise, the case of **the goat of Yom Kippur is derived from** the case of **the goats for** an unwitting communal sin of **idol worship,** with regard to the *halakhot* of *et*, in the blood, and immersion, **via** this ***a fortiori*** **inference,** as they are both goats.

וְכִי דָּבָר הַלָּמֵד בְּהֶיקֵּשׁ חוֹזֵר וּמְלַמֵּד בְּקַל וָחוֹמֶר? אֲמַר רַב פַּפָּא: קָסָבַר תָּנָא דְּבֵי רַבִּי יִשְׁמָעֵאל: דָּבָר הַלָּמֵד בְּהֶיקֵּשׁ חוֹזֵר וּמְלַמֵּד בְּקַל וָחוֹמֶר.

The Gemara asks: How can the *halakhot* of the goat of Yom Kippur be derived from the goats for an unwitting communal sin of idol worship? **But does a matter derived by juxtaposition,**[NB] i.e., a *halakha* that is not written explicitly in the Torah but that is learned by means of a comparison, **again teach by** ***a fortiori*** inference? There is a principle that a *halakha* derived by juxtaposition with regard to consecrated matters cannot subsequently teach another *halakha* via an *a fortiori* inference. The *halakhot* alluded to by the words *et*, in the blood, and immersion, are not explicitly stated with regard to the goats of an unwitting communal sin of idol worship. Rather, they are derived from the comparison found in the verse: "And he shall do… as he did" (Leviticus 4:20), which alludes to the goats for an unwitting communal sin of idol worship and the bull for an unwitting sin of the anointed priest. **Rav Pappa said: The school of Rabbi Yishmael maintains** that **a matter derived by juxtaposition does again teach by** ***a fortiori*** inference, even with regard to consecrated matters.

״לַפָּר״ – זֶה פַּר הֶעְלֵם דָּבָר שֶׁל צִבּוּר. הָא בְּצִיבּוּר גּוּפֵיהּ כְּתִיב! אֲמַר רַב פַּפָּא: מִשּׁוּם דְּבָעֵי אַגְמוּרֵי פַּר הֶעְלֵם דָּבָר שֶׁל צִבּוּר בְּיוֹתֶרֶת וּשְׁתֵּי כְלָיוֹת לִשְׂעִירֵי עֲבוֹדָה זָרָה,

The Gemara continues to analyze the statement of Rabbi Yishmael in the *baraita*: **"With the bull"; this is the bull for an unwitting communal sin.** The Gemara asks: Why is it necessary to derive this case by way of an exposition? **This** verse **itself is written in reference to** the bull for an unwitting **communal** sin. **Rav Pappa said:** The derivation is necessary **because** Rabbi Yishmael **wants** the case of the **bull for an unwitting communal sin to teach with regard to** the burning on the altar of the sacrificial portions, including the **diaphragm and** the **two kidneys,** that this obligation applies also **to the goats for** an unwitting communal sin of **idol worship,** despite the fact that this requirement is not stated with regard to them.

וּפַר הֶעְלֵם דָּבָר שֶׁל צִבּוּר בְּגוּפֵיהּ לָא כְּתִיב, בְּהֶיקֵּשָׁא אָתֵי – אִיצְטְרִיךְ ״לַפָּר״

Rav Pappa continues: **And** as the obligation to burn the diaphragm and the two kidneys on the altar is **not written with regard to the bull for an unwitting communal sin itself,** but rather it is **derived by juxtaposition** from the bull for an unwitting sin of the anointed priest, in which this requirement is explictly stated (see Leviticus 4:8–9), it **was necessary** to include the bull for an unwitting communal sin once again with the term **"with the bull."**

לְמֶיהֱוֵי כְּמַאן דִּכְתִיב בֵּיהּ בְּגוּפֵיהּ, וְלָא לֶיהֱוֵי דָּבָר הַלָּמֵד בְּהֶיקֵּשׁ חוֹזֵר וּמְלַמֵּד בְּהֶיקֵּשׁ.

The Gemara elaborates: This derivation is required in order **that it should be as though** this *halakha* of burning the diaphragm and the two kidneys **was written with regard to** the bull for an unwitting communal sin **itself. And** in this manner the derivation from this case, teaching the *halakha* in the case of the goats for an unwitting communal sin of idol worship, **should not be a matter derived by juxtaposition** that **again teaches by juxtaposition,** as such a derivation is not done with regard to consecrated matters.

NOTES

That the actions in one offering are equated with the actions in the other offering – שֶׁהוּשְׁווּ מַעֲשִׂים לְמַעֲשִׂים: Admittedly, the cases of the bull for an unwitting communal sin and the goat of Yom Kippur, from which this *a fortiori* inference is derived, are not entirely similar, as only the bull for an unwitting communal sin is juxtaposed to the bull for an unwitting sin of the anointed priest with regard to the three *halakhot* of *et*, in the blood, and immersion, while the goat is not. Nevertheless, the assumption here is that as their rites are similar, one case can be derived from the other with regard to the sprinkling of their blood (Rashi). Others explain that it is derived from the goats of an unwitting sin of idol worship that the *halakhot* of *et*, in the blood, and immersion, apply to the goat of Yom Kippur, and therefore the basis of the *a fortiori* inference is sound (*Tosafot*, citing Rabbeinu Shmuel).

But does a matter derived by juxtaposition – וְכִי דָּבָר הַלָּמֵד בְּהֶיקֵּשׁ: The Gemara in the next chapter (49b–51b) discusses at length a unique aspect of halakhic exegesis with regard to consecrated matters. In all other areas of *halakha*, once a detail has been applied to a case via any of the accepted exegetical methods, it is considered as though that detail was explicitly written in the Torah with regard to that case itself, and therefore it can serve as the source to teach that detail to another case. With regard to consecrated matters, there are limitations to the application of *halakhot* derived by exegesis, as certain exegetical methods may be used only once, after which they cannot serve as the basis for further derivations.

BACKGROUND

Juxtaposition – הֶיקֵּשׁ: When two matters appear in the same verse or in adjacent verses, the Talmud assumes that as they were juxtaposed, they are analogous. Consequently, inferences may be drawn by comparing the two cases. For example, the Torah states with regard to a woman being divorced: "And she departs his house, and goes and becomes another man's wife" (Deuteronomy 24:2). Since divorce and marriage appear in the same verse, the Talmud derives that many of the *halakhot* governing divorce apply to marriage, and vice versa. Juxtaposition is governed by the principle: There is no partial analogy based on juxtaposition. Therefore, inferences drawn through juxtaposition must be bilateral.

NOTES

It is taught in a *baraita* in accordance with the opinion of Rav Pappa – תַּנְיָא כְּוָותֵיהּ דְּרַב פָּפָּא: The *baraita* states, like Rav Pappa, that the term "with the bull" is referring to the bull for an unwitting communal sin, and it is stated solely to enable this case to serve as the source for the *halakha* of the goats for an unwitting sin of idol worship.

Their sin offering [*ḥattatam*]…for their error – חַטָּאתָם...עַל שִׁגְגָתָם: Just as the term *ḥattatam* can be referring both to their sin and to the offering brought for their sin, so too, the word "error," which is a synonym for sin, can be interpreted as referring both to a sin performed in error and to the offering brought for that error. Since it is stated: "For it was an error" (Numbers 15:25), the expression "for their error" is superfluous, and is expounded as referring to the offering sacrificed for the error. Accordingly, the phrase "their sin offering…for their error" means: Their sin offering in addition to the offering for their error, i.e., the two offerings are juxtaposed.

תַּנְיָא כְּוָותֵיהּ דְּרַב פָּפָּא: ״וְעָשָׂה...כַּאֲשֶׁר עָשָׂה״ – מַה תַּלְמוּד לוֹמַר ״לַפָּר״?

§ The Gemara comments: **It is taught** in a *baraita* **in accordance with** the opinion **of Rav Pappa:**[N] **"And he shall do** with the bull, **as he did"** (Leviticus 4:20); **what** is the meaning when **the verse states: "With the bull"?** It is clear that this verse is referring to the bull.

לְפִי שֶׁנֶּאֱמַר: ״וְהֵם הֵבִיאוּ אֶת קָרְבָּנָם אִשֶּׁה לַה׳״ וגו׳, ״חַטָּאתָם״ – אֵלּוּ שְׂעִירֵי עֲבוֹדָה זָרָה, ״שִׁגְגָתָם״ – זֶה פַּר הֶעְלֵם דָּבָר שֶׁל צִבּוּר, ״חַטָּאתָם...עַל שִׁגְגָתָם״ – אָמְרָה תּוֹרָה: חַטָּאתָם הֲרֵי הִיא לְךָ כְּשִׁגְגָתָם.

The *baraita* answers: **Because it is stated** with regard to the goats for an unwitting communal sin of idol worship: **"And they have brought their offering, an offering made by fire to the Lord,** and their sin offering before the Lord for their error" (Numbers 15:25), and this verse is interpreted as follows: **"Their sin offering"; these are the goats for** an unwitting communal sin of **idol worship,** alluded to in that passage. **"Their error"; this is the bull for an unwitting communal sin,** which is brought for an inadvertent transgression of the community. The juxtaposition of these offerings in the verse: **"Their sin offering…for their error,"**[N] indicates that the **Torah** means to **say: Their sin offering is for you like their error,** i.e., all the portions consumed on the altar in the case of the bull for an unwitting communal sin are also burned on the altar in the case of the goats for an unwitting sin of idol worship.

שִׁגְגָתָם מֵהֵיכָן לָמַדְתָּ – לָאו בְּהֶיקֵּשָׁא? וְכִי דָּבָר הַלָּמֵד בְּהֶיקֵּשׁ חוֹזֵר וּמְלַמֵּד בְּהֶיקֵּשׁ?

The Gemara asks: With regard to the offering brought for **their error,** i.e., the bull for an unwitting communal sin, **from where did you learn** this *halakha*? Was it **not via juxtaposition** from the bull for an unwitting sin of the anointed priest, as the diaphragm and the two kidneys are not explicitly mentioned with regard to the bull for an unwitting communal sin? **But** this is difficult, as **does a matter derived via juxtaposition again teach via juxtaposition?**

תַּלְמוּד לוֹמַר: ״לַפָּר״ – זֶה פַּר הֶעְלֵם דָּבָר שֶׁל צִבּוּר, ״לַפָּר״ – זֶה פַּר כֹּהֵן מָשִׁיחַ.

Therefore, **the verse states:** "And he shall do with the bull, as he did with the bull for a sin offering" (Leviticus 4:20). With regard to the first instance of **"with the bull," this is the bull for an unwitting communal sin.** And with regard to the second instance of **"with the bull," this is the bull for** an unwitting sin of the **anointed priest.** Due to this juxtaposition, it is as though the burning of the diaphragm and the two kidneys was explicitly written with regard to the bull for an unwitting communal sin, and therefore the *halakha* can be taught by juxtaposition with regard to the goats for an unwitting sin of idol worship, as stated by Rav Pappa.

אָמַר מָר: ״חַטָּאתָם״ – אֵלּוּ שְׂעִירֵי עֲבוֹדָה זָרָה. תֵּיפּוֹק לֵיהּ מִקְּרָא קַמָּא, דְּאָמַר מָר: ״הַחַטָּאת״ – לְרַבּוֹת שְׂעִירֵי עֲבוֹדָה זָרָה! אָמַר רַב פָּפָּא: אִיצְטְרִיךְ, סָלְקָא דַּעְתָּךְ אָמֵינָא: הָנֵי מִילֵּי הַזָּאוֹת דִּכְתִיבָן בְּגוּפֵיהּ,

The Gemara analyzes the previous *baraita*. **The Master said** above: **"Their sin offering," these are** the **goats for** an unwitting communal sin of **idol worship,** which are juxtaposed in this verse to the bull for an unwitting communal sin. The Gemara asks: But **let** the *tanna* **derive this from the earlier verse** stated with regard to the bull for an unwitting communal sin, **as the Master said** in the *baraita* cited earlier (39b): **"A sin offering"** (Leviticus 4:20), this serves **to include the goats for** an unwitting communal sin of **idol worship. Rav Pappa said:** This derivation **was necessary,** as if there were only the juxtaposition from Leviticus 4:20, it would **enter your mind to say: This matter** applies only to the acts of **sprinkling, which are written with regard to** the bull for an unwitting communal sin **itself.**

Perek **IV**
Daf **41** Amud **b**

אֲבָל יוֹתֶרֶת וּשְׁתֵּי כְלָיוֹת, דְּלָא כְּתִיבָן בְּגוּפֵיהּ – אֵימָא לָא, קָא מַשְׁמַע לָן.

But with regard to the burning of the **diaphragm and** the **two kidneys, which are not written with regard to** the bull for an unwitting communal sin **itself,** you might **say** that this *halakha* should **not** be derived from it. Therefore, this additional derivation of "their sin offering" **teaches us** that the two offerings are similar with regard to this detail as well.

אָמַר לֵיהּ רַב הוּנָא בְּרֵיהּ דְּרַב נָתָן לְרַב פַּפָּא: וְהָא תַּנְיָא, "פַּר יוֹם הַכִּפּוּרִים לְכָל מַה שֶּׁאָמַר בָּעִנְיָן" קָאָמַר! תַּנָּאֵי הִיא, תַּנָּא דְּבֵי רַב מְרַבֵּי הָכִי, תַּנָּא דְּבֵי רַבִּי יִשְׁמָעֵאל לָא מְרַבֵּי הָכִי.

Rav Huna, son of Rav Natan, said to Rav Pappa: But the *tanna* said: "With the bull"; this serves to include **the bull of Yom Kippur for all that is stated in this matter.**[N] This statement indicates that all the details applying to the bull for an unwitting communal sin are extended to the bull of Yom Kippur by means of a single derivation. Rav Pappa responded: This issue **is a** dispute between ***tanna'im*****,** as **the *tanna* of the school of Rav**[N] **amplifies** the *halakha* through **this** juxtaposition, whereas **the *tanna* of the school of Rabbi Yishmael does not amplify** the *halakha* through **this** juxtaposition, but maintains that an additional derivation is necessary with regard to the diaphragm and the two kidneys.

תָּנָא דְּבֵי רַבִּי יִשְׁמָעֵאל: מִפְּנֵי מָה נֶאֶמְרוּ יוֹתֶרֶת וּשְׁתֵּי כְלָיוֹת בְּפַר כֹּהֵן מָשִׁיחַ, וְלֹא נֶאֶמְרוּ בְּפַר הֶעְלֵם דָּבָר שֶׁל צִבּוּר? מָשָׁל לְמֶלֶךְ בָּשָׂר וָדָם שֶׁזָּעַם עַל אוֹהֲבוֹ, וּמִיעֵט בְּסִרְחוֹנוֹ מִפְּנֵי חִיבָּתוֹ.

§ The Gemara cites a statement that is related to the above *halakhot*. **The school of Rabbi Yishmael taught: For what** reason **are the diaphragm and the two kidneys stated with regard to the bull** for an unwitting sin **of the anointed priest, and they are not** explicitly **stated with regard to the bull for an unwitting communal sin?** This can be explained by **a parable:** It can be compared **to a flesh-and-blood king who grew angry with his beloved**[N] servant for his misdeeds, **but spoke little of** the servant's **offense due to his** great **affection** for him. Likewise, as the Jewish people are beloved by God, the Torah does not describe their sin offering in detail.

וְתָנָא דְּבֵי רַבִּי יִשְׁמָעֵאל: מִפְּנֵי מָה נֶאֶמְרָה "פָּרֹכֶת הַקֹּדֶשׁ" בְּפַר כֹּהֵן מָשִׁיחַ, וְלֹא נֶאֱמַר בְּפַר הֶעְלֵם דָּבָר שֶׁל צִבּוּר? מָשָׁל לְמֶלֶךְ בָּשָׂר וָדָם שֶׁסָּרְחָה עָלָיו מְדִינָה, אִם מִיעוּטָהּ סָרְחָה – פָּמַלְיָא שֶׁלּוֹ מִתְקַיֶּימֶת, אִם רוּבָּהּ סָרְחָה – אֵין פָּמַלְיָא שֶׁלּוֹ מִתְקַיֶּימֶת.

And the school of Rabbi Yishmael further **taught: For what** reason **is it stated:** "Before **the Curtain of the Sanctuary**" (Leviticus 4:6), **with regard to the bull** for an unwitting sin **of the anointed priest, and** this **is not stated with regard to the bull for an unwitting communal sin,** where it merely states: "Before the Curtain" (Leviticus 4:17)? This can be explained by **a parable:** It can be compared **to a flesh-and-blood king against whom a province sinned. If a minority of** that province **sinned,** his relationship with **his entourage** [*pamalya*][L] **remains,** i.e., the king continues to treat his loyal followers in the usual manner. But **if the majority of** the province **sinned,** his relationship with **his entourage does not remain,**[N] and he no longer meets even those who remained devoted to him. Similarly, when the entire people sins, God no longer has the same relationship with them, and it is as though the place where the priest sprinkles the blood is no longer sacred.

"לְפִיכָךְ אִם נָתַן כּוּלָּן כְּתִיקְנָן" כו׳. תְּנַן הָתָם: פִּיגֵּל בַּקּוֹמֶץ וְלֹא בַּלְּבוֹנָה, בַּלְּבוֹנָה וְלֹא בַּקּוֹמֶץ, רַבִּי מֵאִיר אוֹמֵר: פִּיגּוּל וְחַיָּיבִין עָלָיו כָּרֵת,

§ The mishna teaches that all the placements upon the inner altar are indispensable, and **therefore if** the High Priest **placed all** the placements **in their proper manner,** and one in an improper manner, i.e., with the intent to eat or burn the offering beyond its designated time, the offering is disqualified, but there is no liability for *karet* for one who partakes of the offering. The Gemara states that **we learned** in a mishna **there** (*Menaḥot* 16a), with regard to the burning of the handful of a meal offering and the frankincense, both of which render the meal offering permitted for eating: If the priest had an intention that can **render** the offering ***piggul*****,** and this occurred **during** the burning of **the handful but not during** the burning of **the frankincense,** or **during** the burning of **the frankincense but not during** the burning of **the handful,** i.e., he burned one of them with the intention of eating the remainder of the offering beyond its designated time, **Rabbi Meir says:** The offering is ***piggul*** **and one** who eats it is **liable** to receive ***karet*****.**

וַחֲכָמִים אוֹמְרִים: אֵין בּוֹ כָּרֵת עַד שֶׁיְּפַגֵּל בְּכָל הַמַּתִּיר.

And the Rabbis say: There is no liability for ***karet*** **in this** case **unless he renders** the offering ***piggul*** **during** the performance of **the entire permitting factor,**[H] i.e., the burning of both the handful and the frankincense.

NOTES

But the *tanna* said "with the bull"…for all that is stated in this matter – **וְהָא תַּנְיָא...לְכָל מַה שֶּׁאָמַר בָּעִנְיָן:** According to Rashi, the Gemara here returns to the earlier statement of Rav Pappa (40a), who maintains that the bull of Yom Kippur is alluded to in the phrase: "So shall he do" (Leviticus 4:20), to teach that the three *halakhot* of *et*, in the blood, and immersion, apply to the bull of Yom Kippur. Rav Huna, son of Rav Natan, rejects the proof from the *baraita* cited in support of this opinion, as he claims that the phrase: For all that is stated in this matter, indicates that the derivation applies to all the *halakhot*.

Others explain that this paragraph is a continuation of the discussion concerning the derivation from the bull for an unwitting communal sin, teaching the *halakha* of the goats for an unwitting communal sin of idol worship. Rav Huna, son of Rav Natan, claims that just as the derivation from the bull for an unwitting communal sin teaching the *halakha* of the bull of Yom Kippur is referring to all matters stated in the chapter, including the *halakha* of the diaphragm and the two kidneys, the same should apply to the derivation from the bull for an unwitting communal sin teaching the *halakha* of the goats for an unwitting communal sin of idol worship. If so, the question remains: What need is there for the juxtaposition of "their sin offering…for their error" (*Tosafot*, citing Rabbeinu Yitzḥak of Dampierre).

The *tanna* of the school of Rav [*devei Rav*] – **תַּנָּא דְּבֵי רַב:** This refers to the first *baraita*, cited at the beginning of this discussion (39a–b). Rashi explains that this does not mean that the *baraita* came from the school of the *amora* Rav. Rather, the phrase *devei Rav* means the school of a rabbi, i.e., a study hall. If so, the reference is to the *baraita* that was generally studied in the study halls, i.e., the Midrash of *Torat Kohanim*. This Midrash was called *Sifra devei Rav*, in contrast to the Midrash of the school of Rabbi Yishmael, which was taught only by Rabbi Yishmael's disciples (Rashi on *Ḥullin* 66a).

Who grew angry with his beloved – **שֶׁזָּעַם עַל אוֹהֲבוֹ:** Rashi maintains that the beloved is the Jewish people, as in the verse: "The seed of Abraham, My beloved" (Isaiah 41:8). When the entire Jewish people sins, the Torah prefers to describe in as brief a manner as possible the service of the offering that must be brought (see *Iyyun Ya'akov*). Others explain in the opposite manner, that the beloved is the High Priest. By describing in detail the remedy of his bringing an offering, the Torah indicates that it seeks to lessen the effect of his sin (Maharsha).

His entourage does not remain – **אֵין פָּמַלְיָא שֶׁלּוֹ מִתְקַיֶּימֶת:** It is as though all sanctity has left the Temple, and therefore the Curtain can no longer be called the Curtain of the Sanctuary.

LANGUAGE

Entourage [*pamalya*] – **פָּמַלְיָא:** From the Latin familia, which means the attendants and all those tied to a family estate. Accordingly, the *pamalya* of Heaven refers to all those who minister to God. Rashi maintains that in this context *pamalya* means the gathering together of the king with his entourage.

HALAKHA

Unless he renders it *piggul* during the performance of the entire permitting factor – **עַד שֶׁיְּפַגֵּל בְּכָל הַמַּתִּיר:** With regard to an offering for which there are two permitting factors, e.g., the handful and the frankincense in the case of a meal offering, it is rendered *piggul* only if the priest intended to eat or burn it beyond its designated time while performing the rites of both. If he had the intention that can render the offering *piggul* while performing the rites of only one of them, the offering is not *piggul* (Rambam *Sefer Avoda, Hilkhot Pesulei HaMukdashin* 16:7).

אָמַר רַבִּי שִׁמְעוֹן בֶּן לָקִישׁ: לָא תֵּימָא טַעְמָא דְּרַבִּי מֵאִיר דְּקָסָבַר מְפַגְּלִין בַּחֲצִי מַתִּיר, אֶלָּא הָכָא בְּמַאי עָסְקִינַן – כְּגוֹן שֶׁנָּתַן אֶת הַקּוֹמֶץ בְּמַחֲשָׁבָה, וְהַלְּבוֹנָה בִּשְׁתִיקָה; קָסָבַר: כָּל הָעוֹשֶׂה – עַל דַּעַת רִאשׁוֹנָה הוּא עוֹשֶׂה.

Rabbi Shimon ben Lakish said: Do not say that the **reason of Rabbi Meir,** who holds that the offering is *piggul,* is **that he holds** in general that **one renders** an offering ***piggul*** even if he intended to eat or burn the offering beyond its designated time **during** the performance of only **half a permitting factor. Rather, what are we dealing with here?** We are dealing with a case **where he** initially **placed the handful** of the meal offering on the altar, to burn it, **with** the improper **intention**[N] to eat the remainder beyond its designated time, **and** afterward he placed **the frankincense** on the altar **silently,** i.e., without any particular intent. Rabbi Meir **holds: Anyone who performs** an action **performs** it **with his initial intent.**[N] Therefore, his action with the frankincense is considered to have been performed with the same improper intention as his action with the handful.

מִמַּאי – מִדְּקָתָנֵי: לְפִיכָךְ אִם נָתַן כּוּלָּן כְּתִיקְנָן וְאַחַת שֶׁלֹּא כְּתִיקְנָהּ – פָּסוּל וְאֵין בּוֹ כָּרֵת; הָא אַחַת שֶׁלֹּא כְּתִיקְנָהּ וְכוּלָּן כְּתִיקְנָן – פִּיגּוּל.

The Gemara asks: **From where** does Rabbi Shimon ben Lakish learn that this is the case? He learns it **from** the fact **that** the mishna **teaches: Therefore, if he placed all** the placements **in their proper manner and one in an improper manner,** the offering is **disqualified, but there is no** liability for ***karet.* Consequently** it follows that if he initially placed **one** placement **in an improper manner,** with the intent to eat or burn the offering beyond its designated time, **and all** the other placements **in the proper manner,** the offering is ***piggul.***

מַנִּי? אִילֵימָא רַבָּנַן – הָא אָמְרִי רַבָּנַן: אֵין מְפַגְּלִין בַּחֲצִי מַתִּיר! אֶלָּא רַבִּי מֵאִיר;

The Gemara explains: **Whose** opinion is this? **If we say** it is the opinion of **the Rabbis, don't the Rabbis** explicitly **say** that **one cannot render** an offering ***piggul*** with an improper intention **in** the performance of only **half a permitting factor?** Here, the priest placed one placement in the proper manner. **Rather,** it must represent the opinion of **Rabbi Meir,** who says that if he had an improper intention with regard to the handful and not the frankincense the offering is *piggul.*

וְאִי טַעְמָא דְּרַבִּי מֵאִיר מִשּׁוּם דִּמְפַגְּלִין בַּחֲצִי מַתִּיר הוּא – אֲפִילּוּ כִּדְקָתָנֵי נָמֵי! לָאו מִשּׁוּם דְּקָסָבַר: כָּל הָעוֹשֶׂה – עַל דַּעַת רִאשׁוֹנָה הוּא עוֹשֶׂה?

And if Rabbi Meir's reason is that he holds in general that **one renders** an offering ***piggul*** even **during** the performance of only **half a permitting factor, even** if the priest acted **as it taught** in the mishna, the offering should **also** be *piggul,* as he had an improper intention during half the permitting **factor.** Rather, is Rabbi Meir's reason **not because he holds** that **anyone who performs** an action **performs** it **with** his **initial intent?** Consequently, if he placed the first placement with an improper intention, the offering is *piggul,* and if his intention during the first placement was proper, the offering is not *piggul.*

אָמַר רַבִּי שְׁמוּאֵל בַּר יִצְחָק: לְעוֹלָם רַבָּנַן הִיא, וּמַאי ״כְּתִיקְנָן״ – כְּתִיקְנָן לְפִיגּוּל.

Rabbi Shmuel bar Yitzḥak says: Actually, it is possible that the mishna **is** in accordance with the opinion of **the Rabbis,**[N] who maintain that one cannot render an offering *piggul* with an improper intention during half a permitting factor. **And what** is the meaning of the term: **In their proper manner,** in the context of the mishna? It means **in their proper manner with regard to *piggul,*** i.e., he placed the blood with an intention that renders the offering *piggul.* The mishna is teaching that although he placed the first placements with an improper intention, one does not say that the last placement, which was placed without any specific intention, was performed with his initial intent.

NOTES

Where he placed the handful with the intention – שֶׁנָּתַן אֶת הַקּוֹמֶץ בְּמַחֲשָׁבָה: This is not referring specifically to the handful, as the same applies if he had the improper intent when burning the frankincense if that was burned first. The important point is that he performed the first service with an intention that renders the offering *piggul,* while the second permitting factor was performed silently.

Performs it with his initial intent – עַל דַּעַת רִאשׁוֹנָה הוּא עוֹשֶׂה: According to this explanation, the Rabbis reject the opinion of Rabbi Meir and hold that one is not considered to have performed the second action with the same intention as the first. It should be noted that the Gemara in *Menahot* 16a states that there is an opinion that maintains that the Rabbis do not disagree with Rabbi Meir in this case.

Actually it is the opinion of the Rabbis – לְעוֹלָם רַבָּנַן הִיא: According to this interpretation, one should not infer from the mishna that if he placed one placement in the proper manner, i.e., silently, and the others in an improper manner, i.e., with the intent to eat it beyond its designated time, the offering is *piggul.* The reason this inference is not valid is that the case stated in the mishna itself teaches a novelty, namely, that the last placement is not considered to have been performed with his initial intent. When a clause of a mishna teaches a novelty, one cannot infer from it that the *halakha* is different in another case, as it is taught for the sake of its novelty, and not for the inference.

וְהָא מְדַקְתָּנֵי: לְפִיכָךְ, אִם נָתַן כּוּלָּן כְּתִיקְנָן וְאַחַת שֶׁלֹּא כְּתִיקְנָן – פָּסוּל וְאֵין בּוֹ כָּרֵת, מִכְּלָל דְּ״תִיקְנָהּ״ לְהֶכְשֵׁירָהּ הוּא דַּאֲתָא!

The Gemara raises a difficulty: **But from** the fact **that it teaches: Therefore, if he placed all** the placements **in their proper manner and one in an improper manner,** the offering is **disqualified but there is no** liability for ***karet,*** which indicates that the offering is disqualified due to the one placement performed improperly, one can learn **by inference that** the term: **In their proper manner, comes to** indicate an intention that **renders** the offering **fit,**[N] and not an intention that renders it *piggul.*

אָמַר רָבָא: מַאי ״שֶׁלֹּא כְּתִיקְנָהּ״ – חוּץ לִמְקוֹמוֹ. רַב אַשִׁי אָמַר: שֶׁלֹּא לִשְׁמוֹ.

Rava says: It can still be explained that the term: In their proper manner, is referring to an intention that renders the offering *piggul;* and **what** is the meaning of: **In an improper manner?** This is referring to the intent to eat the offering **outside its** designated **area.** This intention serves to disqualify the offering, which means that it is not *piggul,* as not all its rites have been performed in the proper manner. **Rav Ashi says:** The term: In an improper manner, in the mishna, means that he placed one placement **not for the sake of**[N] the offering being sacrificed, and in the case of a sin offering an intention of this kind disqualifies the offering; therefore, it is not *piggul.*

מִכְּלָל דְּכִי לָא עָבֵיד לָהּ חוּץ לִמְקוֹמוֹ וְשֶׁלֹּא לִשְׁמוֹ מִחַיַּיב!

The Gemara raises a difficulty: If so, one can learn **by inference that when** the priest **does not perform** the last placement with the intent to eat the offering **outside its** designated **area or not for the sake of** the offering, but silently, **he becomes liable,** as the offering is *piggul.* This is certainly not in accordance with the opinion of the Rabbis, as they maintain that one cannot render an offering *piggul* with an improper intention during half a permitting factor.

אַיְּידֵי דִּתְנָא רֵישָׁא: פִּיגּוּל וְחַיָּיבִין עָלָיו כָּרֵת – תְּנָא נַמִי סֵיפָא: פָּסוּל וְאֵין בּוֹ כָּרֵת.

The Gemara answers: The wording of the mishna is imprecise, as in fact, even if he placed the last placement silently the offering is not *piggul.* But **since the** *tanna* of the mishna **taught** in **the first clause,** with regard to an offering whose blood is placed on the external altar: If he placed the first placement with the intent to eat the offering beyond its designated time and the second placement with the intent to eat it outside its designated area, the offering is ***piggul*** **and one is liable** to receive ***karet*** **for** its consumption, **he likewise taught the latter clause,** with regard to a sin offering whose blood is placed on the inner altar, in a similar manner, that if he placed the last placement with the intent to eat it outside its designated area or not for the sake of the offering, the offering is **disqualified, but there is no** liability for ***karet*** **for** its consumption. One cannot infer from here that if he placed the last placement without intent the offering is *piggul.*

מֵיתִיבֵי: בַּמֶּה דְּבָרִים אֲמוּרִים – בְּדָמִים הַנִּיתָּנִין עַל מִזְבֵּחַ הַחִיצוֹן,

The Gemara **raises an objection** to the opinion of Rabbi Shimon ben Lakish from a *baraita*: **In what** case **is this statement,** that the offering is rendered *piggul* even when he intends to eat it beyond its designated time only in the first placement, **said? In** the case of **blood that is placed on the external altar,** where one placement renders the offering permitted.

NOTES

By inference that the term: In their proper manner, comes to indicate an intention that renders it fit – מִכְּלָל דְּתִיקְנָהּ לְהֶכְשֵׁירָה הוּא דַּאֲתָא: Rashi explains: One cannot say that the phrase: One in an improper manner, means that it was performed silently, without any intention. The reason is that the mere lack of intent does not disqualify an offering. Rather, it must be that the term: In their proper manner, should be interpreted in accordance with its straightforward meaning, i.e., to mean: With proper intention. Others question this explanation, as the Gemara emphasizes the term: In their proper manner, whereas according to Rashi the inference is from the term: In an improper manner. Instead, they propose that the proof is from the style of the mishna. After stating that all the placements are indispensable, the mishna states that if the priest placed all of them in their proper manner and one in an improper manner, the offering is disqualified. This indicates that even if he placed one placement improperly he has disqualified the offering, whereas if he had placed all the placements properly it would be valid. This certainly does not suit the interpretation that the term: In their proper manner, is referring to an intention that renders the offering *piggul* (Rabbeinu Peretz).

Not for the sake of – שֶׁלֹּא לִשְׁמוֹ: Rav Ashi infers this from the fact that in the previous case discussed by the mishna, with regard to the blood of a sin offering placed on the external altar, it is mentioned that the second placement was performed with the intention to eat it outside its designated area. The difference in wording in this clause of the mishna, which states that it was performed in an improper manner, indicates that the mishna is referring to a different intention (Netziv).

אבל דמים הניתנין על המזבח הפנימי, כגון ארבעים ושלש של יום הכיפורים, ואחד עשר של פר כהן משיח, ואחד עשר של פר העלם דבר של ציבור, פיגל בין בראשונה ובין בשניה ובין בשלישית – רבי מאיר אומר: פיגול, וחייבין עליו כרת, וחכמים אומרים: אין בו כרת עד שיפגל בכל המתיר;

But with regard to the **blood placed** inside, i.e., in the Holy of Holies, on the Curtain, and **on the inner altar, e.g.,** the **forty-three** presentations of the blood **of** the bull and goat of **Yom Kippur,**[N] **and the eleven** presentations of the blood **of the bull**[N] **for** an unwitting sin of the **anointed priest, and** the **eleven** presentations of the blood **of the bull for an unwitting communal sin,** if in those cases the priest had an intention that can **render** the offering ***piggul*****, whether during the first**[N] set of presentations, **whether during the second** set, **or whether during the third** set, i.e., in any of the requisite sets of presentations, **Rabbi Meir says:** The offering is ***piggul*** **and one is liable** to receive ***karet*** **for its** consumption. **And the Rabbis say: There is no** liability for ***karet*** **unless he** had an intention that can **render** the offering ***piggul*** **during** the performance of **the entire permitting factor.**[H]

קתני מיהא: פיגל בין בראשונה בין בשניה בין בשלישית, ופליג!

In any event, this *baraita* **teaches:** If the priest had an intention that can **render** the offering ***piggul*****, whether during the first** set of presentations, **whether during the second** set, or **whether during the third** set, **and** yet Rabbi Meir **disputes** the ruling of the Rabbis and says that the offering is *piggul.* If the priest's intent renders the offering *piggul* whether it was during the first, second, or third set of presentations, evidently Rabbi Meir's ruling must be based on the consideration that one can render an offering *piggul* during half a permitting factor. According to Rabbi Shimon ben Lakish's claim that Rabbi Meir's reason is that anyone who performs an action performs it with his initial intent, the offering shoud be *piggul* only if the first set of presentations was performed with an improper intention while the rest were performed silently.

אמר רב יצחק בר אבין: הכא במאי עסקינן – כגון שפיגל בשחיטה, דחד מתיר הוא. אי הכי, מאי טעמא דרבנן?

Rav Yitzḥak bar Avin says: What are we dealing with here? We are not dealing with a case of a priest who had improper intention in the presentations themselves, where the issue of half a permitting factor is relevent. Rather, we are dealing with a case **where** he had an improper intention that can **render** the offering ***piggul*** **during** the act of **slaughter.** In other words, after presenting the blood of the bull inside the Sanctuary, the rest of the blood spilled, and he had to slaughter another bull so that he could continue with the presentations, this time on the Curtain. The reason for Rabbi Meir's ruling is **that** the act of slaughter **is one permitting factor,** and therefore the priest's improper intent involved an entire service, not half a permitting factor. The Gemara asks: **If so, what is the reason for** the ruling of **the Rabbis?**

HALAKHA

Unless he had an intention that can render it *piggul* during the entire permitting factor – עד שיפגל בכל המתיר: With regard to all blood placed on the inner altar, if the priest intended to burn the offering beyond its designated time during the first placement and was silent during the rest, or if he performed all the placements in the proper manner apart from the last one, in which he intended to burn the offering beyond its designated time, the offering is disqualified but it is not *piggul*. It is *piggul* only if he performed all the placements with the intent to burn the offering beyond its designated time, in accordance with the opinion of the Rabbis (Rambam *Sefer Avoda, Hilkhot Pesulei HaMukdashin* 17:2).

NOTES

The forty-three presentations of Yom Kippur – ארבעים ושלש של יום הכפורים: As explained by Rashi, these forty-three are divided into four sets. The High Priest sprinkles once upward and seven times downward between the two staves of the Ark with the blood of the bull, and then does the same with the blood of the goat. Afterward, he sprinkles once upward and seven times downward on the Curtain with the blood of the bull, and again does the same with the blood of the goat. Next he mixes together the blood of the bull and the blood of the goat and places from this mixture four times, once on each of the corners of the inner altar. Finally, he sprinkles seven times from this mixture, on the top of the inner altar. These make a total of forty-three presentations.

The eleven of the bull – אחד עשר של פר: In the cases of both the bull for an unwitting sin of the anointed priest and the bull for an unwitting communal sin, the priest sprinkles seven times on the Curtain, followed by four placements, one on each of the corners of the inner altar, for a total of eleven presentations.

Render the offering *piggul,* whether during the first, etc. – פיגל בין בראשונה וכו׳: Rashi explains that the first means the first set of sprinklings, i.e., between the staves of the Ark, the second refers to the sprinklings on the Curtain, while the third refers to the sprinklings on the corners of the inner altar. Others maintain that this simply means the first or the second set of presentations, i.e., that of the forty-three or that of the eleven (*Keren Ora*).

אָמַר רָבָא: מַאן חֲכָמִים – רַבִּי אֱלִיעֶזֶר הִיא, דִּתְנַן: הַקּוֹמֶץ, וְהַלְּבוֹנָה, וְהַקְּטוֹרֶת, וּמִנְחַת כֹּהֲנִים, וּמִנְחַת כֹּהֵן מָשִׁיחַ, וּמִנְחַת נְסָכִים, שֶׁהִקְרִיב מֵאַחַת מֵהֶן כְּזַיִת בַּחוּץ – חַיָּיב, וְרַבִּי אֱלִיעֶזֶר פּוֹטֵר עַד שֶׁיַּקְרִיב אֶת כּוּלָּן.

Rava says: Who are these Rabbis? This is the opinion of **Rabbi Eliezer,**[N] **as we learned** in a mishna (109b): With regard to **the handful** of a meal offering, **and the frankincense, and the incense, and the meal offering of priests,**[B] **and the meal offering of** the **anointed priest,**[B] **and the meal offering** brought with the **libations**[B] that accompany animal offerings, in a case **where one sacrificed**[H] even **an olive-bulk from** any **one of these,** which should be sacrificed on the altar, **outside** the Temple, he is **liable,** as the burning of an olive-bulk is considered a proper burning. **And Rabbi Eliezer deems** him **exempt unless he sacrifices the whole of** any one of these items outside the Temple. This indicates that according to Rabbi Eliezer even when one performs a proper action he is not liable unless he completes the service. The same should apply to the slaughter of different bulls for different sets of presentations; one should be liable only if he rendered each of them *piggul.*

וְהָאָמַר רָבָא: וּמוֹדֶה רַבִּי אֱלִיעֶזֶר בְּדָמִים, דִּתְנַן: רַבִּי אֱלִיעֶזֶר וְרַבִּי שִׁמְעוֹן אוֹמְרִים: מִמָּקוֹם שֶׁפָּסַק מִשָּׁם הוּא מַתְחִיל!

The Gemara raises a difficulty: How can you explain Rabbi Eliezer's opinion with regard to the presentation of the blood in this manner? **But doesn't Rava say: And Rabbi Eliezer concedes with regard to blood** that even one who sacrifices part of the blood outside the Temple is liable? **As we learned** in a mishna (*Yoma* 60a) that **Rabbi Eliezer and Rabbi Shimon say:** If the blood of the bull or goat of Yom Kippur spilled, even if this occurred in the middle of one of the sets of sprinklings, and the High Priest slaughtered another animal, nevertheless, **from the place that he interrupted** that particular rite, when the blood spilled, **there he resumes**[HN] performance of that rite. In Rabbi Eliezer's opinion, each individual sprinkling in each of these rites is an act in and of itself, and therefore the offering can be rendered *piggul* through any one of them. This is certainly not the opinion of the Rabbis who disagree with Rabbi Meir in the *baraita.*

אֶלָּא אָמַר רָבָא: כְּגוֹן שֶׁפִּיגֵּל בָּרִאשׁוֹנָה וְשָׁתַק בַּשְּׁנִיָּה וְחָזַר וּפִיגֵּל בַּשְּׁלִישִׁית;

Rather, Rava says:[N] Rabbi Shimon ben Lakish would explain that the *baraita* does not mean that the priest had an improper intention either during the first set of sprinklings or the second or the third. Instead, this is referring to a case **where** the High Priest had an improper intention that can **render** the offering ***piggul*** **during the first** set of sprinklings, in the Holy of Holies, **and was silent during the second** set of sprinklings, on the Curtain, **and again** had an improper intention that can **render** the offering ***piggul*** **during the third** set of sprinklings, on the inner altar. There is a certain novelty in this case according to the opinion of Rabbi Meir, who maintains that anyone who performs an action performs it with his initial intent.

NOTES

This is Rabbi Eliezer – רַבִּי אֱלִיעֶזֶר הִיא: Rabbi Eliezer maintains that even with regard to a complete rite, e.g., the burning of an olive-bulk of a handful, if the rite is not completed by means of that action, one is not liable for it. Here too, since the service is completed only in conjunction with the first bull, whose blood was spilled, one cannot render the offering *piggul* solely by means of the slaughter of the second bull, although this is a full permitting factor (Rashi). Admittedly, Rabbi Eliezer was referring to the transgression of sacrificing offerings outside the Temple, and not to *piggul,* but one can claim *a fortiori* that if his ruling applies to sacrificing outside the Temple, which applies to the handful itself, it certainly applies to *piggul,* which must involve both the handful and the frankincense, the other permitting factor. In other words, if Rabbi Eliezer exempts one who sacrifices outside the Temple unless he burns the entire handful, the same certainly applies to *piggul* (*Tosafot*).

From the place that he interrupted, there he resumes – מִמָּקוֹם שֶׁפָּסַק מִשָּׁם הוּא מַתְחִיל: According to the first *tanna* in that mishna, if the blood was spilled in the middle of a set of sprinklings, the priest must slaughter another animal and start from the beginning. Rabbi Eliezer and Rabbi Shimon maintain that he continues from where he left off. This indicates that each part of the sprinkling is considered a separate unit, even if the service was not completed.

Rather, Rava says – אֶלָּא אָמַר רָבָא: Since Rabbi Yitzḥak bar Avin's interpretation of the *baraita,* that it is discussing improper intent in the slaughter, has been rejected, the difficulty raised against the opinion of Rabbi Shimon ben Lakish remains. Rabbi Shimon ben Lakish maintains that according to Rabbi Meir one cannot render an offering *piggul* by means of half a permitting factor, and yet the *baraita* explicitly states that if the improper intent was in the second or third sprinklings, Rabbi Meir says that the offering is *piggul.* His reasoning apparently cannot be based on the consideration that anyone who performs an action does so with his initial intent, as that applies only to the first sprinkling. Rava claims that this *baraita* is indeed taught in accordance with the principle that anyone who performs an action performs it with his initial intent, and it serves to teach a novelty with regard to this principle, as he proceeds to explain.

BACKGROUND

Meal offering of priests – מִנְחַת כֹּהֲנִים: This is any meal offering contributed and brought by a priest, whether voluntarily or as a sin offering. The same *halakhot* that apply to other meal offerings apply to meal offerings of priests, with one exception: A priest's meal offering is not eaten. Instead, the entire offering is burned on the altar (see Leviticus 6:16).

Meal offering of the anointed priest – מִנְחַת כֹּהֵן מָשִׁיחַ: This meal offering is brought daily by the High Priest, and its ingredients are acquired with his own money. Twelve loaves are prepared by being fried in a shallow pan. The dough, which is made of a tenth of an ephah of flour and oil, is also baked. Frankincense is then added to it. Ultimately, all these are burned on the altar: Half of the meal offering is burned in the morning in conjunction with the daily offering of the morning, and the other half in the evening with the day's second daily offering. There is a dispute as to whether the twelve loaves were broken into halves so that twelve parts were sacrificed each time, or whether they were sacrificed whole, i.e., six at each time. None of this meal offering was eaten by the priests.

Meal offering brought with the libations – מִנְחַת נְסָכִים: Meal offerings were brought together with all animal burnt offerings and all peace offerings, both individual and communal. These meal offerings were accompanied by libations of wine. Oil, but not frankincense, was added to the meal offering brought with the libations. No handful of flour was removed from this meal offering, nor was it waved or brought near to the altar, as were other types of meal offerings. The entire meal offering was burned on the altar, and none of it was eaten by the priests. The quantities of flour brought for the meal offering brought with libations are fixed by the Torah: Three-tenths of an ephah for a bull, two-tenths for a ram, and one-tenth for a lamb. A tenth of an ephah is the equivalent of approximately 3 ℓ. The animal offerings that were accompanied by a meal offering brought with libations were not rendered unfit if the meal offering was not sacrificed. Likewise, although the meal offering brought with libations was supposed to be sacrificed together with the animal sacrifice, it remained acceptable even if it was sacrificed later.

HALAKHA

The handful, and the frankincense…in a case where one sacrificed, etc. – הַקּוֹמֶץ וְהַלְּבוֹנָה...שֶׁהִקְרִיב וכו׳: With regard to any item that one is liable for sacrificing outside the Temple, as soon as he sacrifices an olive-bulk of it outside the Temple he is liable. This is the *halakha* whether he first sacrificed the other part inside and then the last olive-bulk outside, or whether he left all the rest inside and first took an olive-bulk and burned it outside. The *halakha* is in accordance with the opinion of the first *tanna* (Rambam *Sefer Avoda, Hilkhot Ma'aseh HaKorbanot* 19:8).

From the place that he interrupted, there he resumes – מִמָּקוֹם שֶׁפָּסַק מִשָּׁם הוּא מַתְחִיל: If the blood spilled before the High Priest finished the entire service in the Holy of Holies, he must bring other blood and start the sprinklings of the Holy of Holies from the beginning. The *halakha* is in accordance with the opinion of the first *tanna* in the mishna in *Yoma* 60a (Rambam *Sefer Avoda, Hilkhot Avodat Yom HaKippurim* 5:5).

מַהוּ דְּתֵימָא: אִי סָלְקָא דַּעְתָּךְ עַל דַּעַת רִאשׁוֹנָה הוּא, מִיהֲדַר פִּיגּוּלֵי בַּשְּׁלִישִׁית לָמָּה לִי? קָא מַשְׁמַע לָן. מַתְקִיף לָהּ רַב אַשִׁי: מִידֵי "שָׁתַק" קָתָנֵי?

Rava elaborates: **Lest you say** that **if** it **enters your mind** that when the priest performs the second set of sprinklings **he** does so **with** his **initial intent,** i.e., that which he had at the time of the first set of sprinklings, **why do I** need him once **again** to have an improper intention that can **render** the offering ***piggul* during the third** set of sprinklings? Doesn't his explicit intent during the third set of sprinklings indicate that he did not have this intent during the second set of sprinklings? Therefore, the *baraita* **teaches us** that this is not so, but rather his silence during the second set is considered a continuation of his initial intent. **Rav Ashi objects to this: Is** it **taught** that he was **silent** during the second set of sprinklings? According to Rava's interpretation this is the key detail of the case, and yet it is not mentioned in the *baraita*.

אֶלָּא אָמַר רַב אַשִׁי: הָכָא בְּמַאי עָסְקִינַן – כְּגוֹן שֶׁפִּיגֵּל בָּרִאשׁוֹנָה וּבַשְּׁנִיָּה וּבַשְּׁלִישִׁית; מַהוּ דְּתֵימָא: אִי סָלְקָא דַּעְתָּךְ כָּל הָעוֹשֶׂה עַל דַּעַת רִאשׁוֹנָה הוּא עוֹשֶׂה, מִהֲדַר פִּיגּוּלֵי בְּכָל חֲדָא וַחֲדָא לָמָּה לִי? קָא מַשְׁמַע לָן.

Rather, Rav Ashi said: What are we dealing with here? We are dealing with a case **where** the High Priest had an intention that can **render** the offering ***piggul* during the first** set of sprinklings, in the Holy of Holies, **and during the second** set,[N] on the Curtain, **and during the third,** on the corners of the inner altar. But during the fourth set, the sprinklings on the top of the inner altar, he was silent. **Lest you say** that **if** it **enters your mind** to say that **anyone who performs** an action **performs** it **with** his **initial intent, why do I** need him once **again** to have an improper intention that can **render** the offering ***piggul* during each and every** set of sprinklings? Therefore, the *baraita* **teaches us** that even so he is considered to have performed all the sprinklings with his initial intent.

NOTES

Where he had an intention that can render it *piggul* during the first and during the second set – כְּגוֹן שֶׁפִּיגֵּל בָּרִאשׁוֹנָה וּבַשְּׁנִיָּה: That is, in all the sprinklings he had an intention that can render the offering *piggul*. Rashi adds that the last service, the sprinkling on the top of the inner altar, was performed silently. This must be the case, as otherwise he had improper intention throughout the permitting factor, which everyone agrees renders the offering *piggul*. *Tosafot* cite the explanation of Rashi in *Menaḥot* 16a that the priest was silent during the third set of sprinklings. *Tosafot* further suggest that this *baraita* is in accordance with the opinion that the pouring of the remainder of the blood is indispensable, and that he was silent during the performance of this service.

Perek **IV**
Daf **42** Amud **b**

וְהָא "בֵּין" "בֵּין" קָתָנֵי! קַשְׁיָא.

The Gemara raises a difficulty: How can Rav Ashi explain the *baraita* as referring to a case where the High Priest had an improper intention during the first, second, and third sets of sprinklings? **But doesn't** the *baraita* **teach:** If the priest had an intention that can render the offering *piggul*, **whether** during the first set of presentations, **whether** during the second set, or whether during the third set? This indicates that he did not have improper intent during all the sprinklings but only in part of them. The Gemara comments: Indeed, this is **difficult,** as the wording of the *baraita* does not suit this interpretation.

אָמַר מָר: רַבִּי מֵאִיר אוֹמֵר: פִּיגּוּל וְחַיָּיבִין עָלָיו כָּרֵת. מִכְּדֵי, כָּרֵת לָא מִיחַיַּיב עַד שֶׁיִּקְרְבוּ כָּל מַתִּירָיו, דְּאָמַר מָר: כְּהַרְצָאַת כָּשֵׁר כָּךְ הַרְצָאַת פָּסוּל, מָה הַרְצָאַת כָּשֵׁר – עַד שֶׁיִּקְרְבוּ כָּל מַתִּירָיו, אַף הַרְצָאַת פָּסוּל – עַד שֶׁיִּקְרְבוּ כָּל מַתִּירָיו.

§ The Gemara returns to discuss the *baraita* that addresses the blood presented inside the Sanctuary. **The Master said** that if the High Priest had an improper intention in one of the sets of presentations, e.g., inside the Holy of Holies, **Rabbi Meir says:** The offering is ***piggul* and one is liable** to receive ***karet* for its** consumption, despite the fact that he performed the rest of the rite silently. The Gemara asks: **Now** consider, **one is not liable** to receive ***karet* unless all the permitting factors** of the offering **have been sacrificed,** i.e., if the whole service is completed, including the presentation of the blood. **As the Master said:** As is **the acceptance of a valid** offering, **so is the** lack of **acceptance of a disqualified** offering: **Just as** there is no **acceptance of a valid** offerning **unless all its permitting factors have been sacrificed, so too,** there is no lack of **acceptance of a disqualified** offering, i.e., it is not rendered *piggul*, **unless all its permitting factors have been sacrificed.** That is to say, in the absence of one of its permitting factors it does not become *piggul*.

וְהָא, כֵּיוָן דְּחָשֵׁיב בֵּיהּ בִּפְנִים פְּסוּלָה – כְּמַאן דְּלָא אַדֵּי דָּמֵי, כִּי הָדַר מַדֵּי בַּהֵיכָל – מַיָּא בְּעָלְמָא הוּא דְּקָא אַדֵּי!

But here, in the case of the bull or goat of Yom Kippur, **since he intended** to burn the offering beyond its designated time while he was sprinkling the blood **inside** the Holy of Holies, the sprinkling is **not valid,** and therefore the High Priest is **considered like one who did not sprinkle** the blood, as every one of the sprinklings of the blood of an inner sin offering is indispensable. If so, **when he sprinkles** the blood **again** later **in the Sanctuary,** on the Curtain and the inner altar, it is as though **he is merely sprinkling water,** and not the blood of the offering. Consequently, the permitting factors of the offering have not been sacrificed, and therefore the offering should not be rendered *piggul.*

אָמַר רַבָּה: מַשְׁכַּחַתְּ לָהּ בְּאַרְבָּעָה פָּרִים וּבְאַרְבָּעָה שְׂעִירִים.

Rabba says: You find it in a case **of four bulls and of four goats.**[N] After sprinkling blood inside the Holy of Holies with the intent to burn the offering beyond its designated time, the blood spilled. Since the priest did not use that blood again, the service inside the Holy of Holies was completed, and that permitting factor was performed properly. He then had to slaughter another bull and goat for the other sprinklings inside the Sanctuary, which he again performed with improper intent and again the blood spilled. The same sequence repeated itself in the sprinklings on the inner altar and on the top of the altar. In this manner each permitting factor was performed properly.

וְרָבָא אָמַר: אֲפִילּוּ תֵּימָא בְּפַר אֶחָד וְשָׂעִיר אֶחָד, לְפִיגּוּלוֹ מְרַצֶּה.

Rava said: You may **even say** that this is a case where there is only **one bull and one goat,** as the sprinkling **effects acceptance with regard to** the offering's status of ***piggul.***[N] In other words, even though the High Priest sprinkled the blood inside the Holy of Holies with an improper intention, and thereby disqualified the offering, nevertheless, since he completed the service, he is considered as having sacrificed all the permitting factors with regard to *piggul.*

״אַרְבָּעִים וְשָׁלֹשׁ״. וְהָא תַּנְיָא: אַרְבָּעִים וָשֶׁבַע! הָא כְּמַאן דְּאָמַר מְעָרְבִין לַקְּרָנוֹת, וְהָא כְּמַאן דְּאָמַר אֵין מְעָרְבִין לַקְּרָנוֹת.

§ The *baraita* mentioned that there are **forty-three**[H] presentations of the blood of the bull and the goat of Yom Kippur. The Gemara asks: **But isn't it taught** otherwise in a different *baraita,* that there are **forty-seven** presentations of that blood? The Gemara answers: **This** statement, that there are forty-three presentations, **is in accordance with** the opinion of **the one who says** that the High Priest **mixes** the blood of the bull and the goat before placing it **on the corners** of the inner altar, rather than placing the blood of each one separately. **And that** statement, that there are forty-seven presentations, **is in accordance with** the opinion of **the one who says** that the High Priest **does not mix** the two types of blood before placing them **on the corners,**[N] but sprinkles four times from the blood of the bull and another four times from the blood of the goat, and only afterward mixes the blood of the two animals for placement on the top of the altar.

וְהָא תַּנְיָא: אַרְבָּעִים וּשְׁמוֹנֶה! הָא כְּמַאן דְּאָמַר שִׁירַיִים מְעַכְּבִין, הָא כְּמַאן דְּאָמַר אֵין שִׁירַיִים מְעַכְּבִין.

The Gemara raises another difficulty: **But isn't it taught** in yet another *baraita* that there are **forty-eight** presentations? The Gemara answers: **This** statement, that there are forty-eight presentations, **is in accordance with** the opinion of **the one who says** that the pouring of the **remainder** of the blood on the base of the external altar **is indispensable,** and therefore this act is added to the total. **That** statement, that there are only forty-seven presentations, **is in accordance with** the opinion of **the one who says** that the pouring of the **remainder** of the blood **is not indispensable.**[H]

NOTES

You find it in a case of four bulls and of four goats – מַשְׁכַּחַתְּ לָהּ בְּאַרְבָּעָה פָּרִים וּבְאַרְבָּעָה שְׂעִירִים: The assumption is that each set of presentations is considered a separate unit, i.e., if the blood was sprinkled properly in the Holy of Holies and the rest of the blood spilled, the High Priest would not have to perform those sprinklings again, but would continue from where he left off (*Yoma* 60a). If so, this first service has been completed with regard to *piggul* as well, and the other permitting factors are performed properly afterward.

It effects acceptance with regard to its status of *piggul* – לְפִיגּוּלוֹ מְרַצֶּה: According to Rava, Rabbi Meir maintains that it is a Torah edict that after there has been intent that renders an offering *piggul,* if the rest of its service does not include any other disqualifying intent, whether to perform the service outside its designated area or not for the sake of that offering, the service is considered properly performed, and *piggul* status applies to that offering.

Does not mix them before placing them on the corners – אֵין מְעָרְבִין לַקְּרָנוֹת: With regard to the seven sprinklings on the top of the inner altar, everyone agrees that the High Priest first mixes the blood of the bull and the goat. Since the Torah explicitly states that there are seven sprinklings of this type, he may not add to this number (*Sefat Emet,* based on *Tosafot* on *Yoma* 57b).

HALAKHA

Forty-three – אַרְבָּעִים וְשָׁלֹשׁ: The blood of the bull and goat of Yom Kippur must each be sprinkled eight times between the staves of the Ark and eight times on the Curtain. The High Priest then mixes the blood of the bull and the blood of the goat together and sprinkles four times from the mixture, once on each of the four corners of the inner altar, and then he performs seven sprinklings upon this altar (Rambam *Sefer Avoda, Hilkhot Ma'aseh HaKorbanot* 5:12 and *Hilkhot Avodat Yom HaKippurim* 4:2).

The remainder of the blood is not indispensable – אֵין שִׁירַיִים מְעַכְּבִין: The pouring of the remainder of blood after the rest has been presented, including the blood of offerings whose main blood is sprinkled inside the Sanctuary, is not indispensable for atonement (Rambam *Sefer Avoda, Hilkhot Ma'aseh HaKorbanot* 19:4).

מֵיתִיבֵי: בַּמֶּה דְּבָרִים אֲמוּרִים – בִּקְמִיצָה, בְּמַתַּן כְּלִי, וּבְהִילּוּךְ.

The Gemara **raises an objection**[N] to Rabbi Shimon ben Lakish's understanding of Rabbi Meir's opinion, that one cannot render an offering *piggul* with an improper intention during the performance of half a permitting factor, from a *baraita* discussing *piggul* of a meal offering, which states: **In what** case **is this statement said,** i.e., that if the priest had an improper intention during the performance of one of its services, the offering is *piggul,* despite the fact that he performed the rest of the services silently? When he had the improper intention **in the removal of the handful,**[H] **or in the placement** of the handful **in** a service **vessel, or in the walking** with the handful to the altar.

אֲבָל בָּא לוֹ לְהַקְטָרָה, נָתַן אֶת הַקּוֹמֶץ בְּמַחֲשָׁבָה וְאֶת הַלְּבוֹנָה בִּשְׁתִיקָה, אוֹ שֶׁנָּתַן אֶת הַקּוֹמֶץ בִּשְׁתִיקָה וְאֶת הַלְּבוֹנָה בְּמַחֲשָׁבָה, רַבִּי מֵאִיר אוֹמֵר: פִּיגּוּל וְחַיָּיבִין עָלָיו כָּרֵת, וַחֲכָמִים אוֹמְרִים: אֵין בּוֹ כָּרֵת עַד שֶׁיְּפַגֵּל בְּכָל הַמַּתִּיר.

But if **he came to** perform **the burning** of the handful and the frankincense, and **he presented the handful** on the altar **with** an improper **intention and the frankincense** he presented **silently, or he presented the handful silently and the frankincense** he presented **with** an improper **intention, Rabbi Meir says:** The offering is ***piggul* and one is liable** to receive ***karet* for** consuming **it. And the Rabbis say: There is no** liablility to receive ***karet* unless** the priest had an improper intention that can **render** the offering ***piggul* during** the performance of **the entire permitting factor.**[H]

קָתָנֵי מִיהָא: אֶת הַקּוֹמֶץ בִּשְׁתִיקָה וְאֶת הַלְּבוֹנָה בְּמַחֲשָׁבָה, וּפָלֵיג! אֵימָא: כְּבָר נָתַן אֶת הַלְּבוֹנָה בְּמַחֲשָׁבָה.

In any event, this *baraita* **teaches:** Or he presented **the handful silently and the frankincense** he presented **with** an improper **intention, and** yet Rabbi Meir **disagrees** with the ruling of the Rabbis and says that the offering is *piggul.* This indicates that the decisive factor according to Rabbi Meir is not that the priest continues his initial intent, but that one can render an offering *piggul* during the performance of half a permitting factor. The Gemara answers: **Say** and explain the *baraita* as follows: Or he presented the handful silently after **he had already presented the frankincense with** an improper **intention.** In this case the offering is *piggul* because he performed the second action with his initial intent.

חֲדָא – דְּהַיְינוּ רֵישָׁא! וְעוֹד: הָא תַּנְיָא "וְאַחַר כָּךְ"! קַשְׁיָא.

The Gemara refutes this interpretation: **One** counterclaim is **that** if this is what the *baraita* is saying, **this is** exactly the same case as **the first clause. And furthermore, isn't it taught** explicitly in another *baraita*: **And afterward** he presented the frankincense with an improper intention. The Gemara states: Indeed, this is **difficult** for the opinion of Rabbi Shimon ben Lakish, who claims that according to Rabbi Meir one cannot render an offering *piggul* during the performance of half a permitting factor.

מתני׳ וְאֵלּוּ דְּבָרִים שֶׁאֵין חַיָּיבִין עֲלֵיהֶם מִשּׁוּם פִּיגּוּל: הַקּוֹמֶץ, וְהַקְּטֹרֶת, וְהַלְּבוֹנָה,

MISHNA **And these are** the **items for which one is not liable** to receive *karet* **due to** violation of the prohibition of ***piggul.***[H] One is liable to receive *karet* only if he partakes of an item that was permitted for consumption or for the altar by another item. As for the items listed here, either nothing else renders them permitted for consumption or for the altar, or they themselves render other items permitted. They are as follows: **The handful** of flour, which permits consumption of the meal offering; **the incense,** which is burned in its entirety, without another item rendering it permitted for the altar; **the frankincense,** which is burned together with the handful of the meal offering;

NOTES

Raises an objection – מֵיתִיבֵי: The Gemara here returns to the comment of Rabbi Shimon ben Lakish (41b) concerning the dispute between Rabbi Meir and the Rabbis in *Menaḥot* 16a with regard to one who had intent that renders an offering *piggul* during the rite of either the handful of a meal offering or the frankincense. Rabbi Meir states that the offering is *piggul.* Rabbi Shimon ben Lakish explained that Rabbi Meir's ruling applies only if the priest had the improper intent during the first rite he performed and was silent in the other. If it was the first rite that was performed silently the offering is not *piggul,* as one cannot render an offering *piggul* during the performance of half a permitting factor. The *baraita* cited by the Gemara here explicitly states the opposite.

HALAKHA

In the removal of the handful, etc. – בִּקְמִיצָה וכו׳: With regard to a meal offering from which a handful is taken, it can be rendered *piggul* during one of four rites: Taking the handful, placing the handful into a service vessel, walking with the handful to the altar, and throwing it onto the fire (Rambam *Sefer Avoda, Hilkhot Pesulei HaMukdashin* 13:6).

Unless he had an improper intention that can render it *piggul* during the entire permitting factor – עַד שֶׁיְּפַגֵּל בְּכָל הַמַּתִּיר: If the priest intended to burn a meal offering beyond its designated time during the taking of the handful but not during the collecting of the frankincense, or if he had this improper intent when collecting the frankincense but not when taking the handful, this meal offering is disqualified but it is not *piggul.* It is *piggul* only if he had this improper intent during the performance of the entire permitting factor, which includes both the handful and the frankincense. This intent can be either when taking the handful and collecting the frankincense, or when placing them both in a vessel, or when walking with them both to the altar, or when burning both of them. The *halakha* is in accordance with the opinion of the Rabbis (Rambam *Sefer Avoda, Hilkhot Pesulei HaMukdashin* 16:7).

Items for which one is not liable to receive *karet* due to *piggul* – דְּבָרִים שֶׁאֵין חַיָּיבִים עֲלֵיהֶם מִשּׁוּם פִּיגּוּל: One is liable to receive *karet* only for partaking of items that were rendered permitted either for human consumption or for the altar. If one ate from the permitting factor itself he is not liable to receive *karet* but is flogged, like one who eats other consecrated items that were disqualified but that do not have *piggul* status. How so? With regard to a meal offering that is *piggul,* one who eats an olive-bulk of its remainder is liable to receive *karet.* But if he ate from its handful or from its frankincense, he is not liable to receive *karet,* as they are the permitting factors that enable the offering to be eaten by the priests (Rambam *Sefer Avoda, Hilkhot Pesulei HaMukdashin* 18:7–8).

ומנחת כהנים, ומנחת כהן משיח, והדם. והנסכים הבאין בפני עצמן, דברי רבי מאיר, וחכמים אומרים: אף הבאין עם הבהמה.

the meal offering of priests,[H] from which no handful of flour is removed and which is burned in its entirety (see Leviticus 6:16); **the meal offering of the anointed priest,** which is sacrificed by the High Priest each day, half in the morning and half in the evening; **the blood,**[H] which permits all the offerings; **and the libations that are brought by themselves**[N] as a separate offering and do not accompany an animal offering; this is **the statement of Rabbi Meir. And the Rabbis say:** The same *halakha* applies **even** with regard to libations **that are brought with an animal** offering.[HN]

לוג שמן של מצורע, רבי שמעון אומר: אין חייבין עליו משום פיגול, ורבי מאיר אומר: חייבין עליו משום פיגול, שדם האשם מתירו. וכל שיש לו מתירין, בין לאדם בין למזבח – חייבין עליו משום פיגול;

With regard to **the** *log* **of oil** that accompanies the guilt offering of a recovered **leper,**[HN] **Rabbi Shimon says: One is not liable for** consuming **it due to** violation of the prohibition of ***piggul,*** because it is not permitted by any other item. **And Rabbi Meir says: One is liable for** consuming **it due to** violation of the prohibition of ***piggul,*** **as the blood of the guilt offering** of the leper **permits its** use,[N] as only after the blood's sacrifice is the oil sprinkled and given to the priests. **And** the principle is: With regard to **any** item **that has permitting factors, either** for consumption by **a person or** for burning on **the altar, one is liable for** eating **it due to** violation of the prohibition of ***piggul.***

העולה – דמה מתיר את בשרה למזבח, ועורה לכהנים. עולת העוף – דמה מתיר את בשרה למזבח. חטאת העוף – דמה מתיר את בשרה לכהנים. פרים הנשרפים ושעירים הנשרפים – דמן מתיר את אימוריהן ליקרב.

The mishna elaborates: **The burnt offering, its blood permits its flesh** to be burned on **the altar and its hide** to be used by **the priests. The bird burnt offering, its blood permits its flesh** and its skin to be burned on **the altar. The bird sin offering, its blood permits its meat** for consumption by **the priests. Bulls that are burned,**[H] e.g., the bull for an unwitting communal sin, **and goats that are burned,**[N] e.g., the goats sacrificed for an unwitting communal sin of idol worship, **their blood permits their sacrificial portions to be sacrificed** on the altar.

HALAKHA

The meal offering of priests, etc. – מנחת כהנים וכו׳: With regard to those meal offerings that are entirely burned, e.g., the meal offering of priests and the meal offering brought with libations, one cannot be liable for eating them in a status of *piggul*, as there is no handful that renders them permitted (Rambam *Sefer Avoda, Hilkhot Pesulei HaMukdashin* 18:8).

Blood – דם: One who consumed an olive-bulk of blood from a *piggul* offering is not liable, as the blood permits its sacrificial portions for the altar. Likewise, with regard to sin offerings brought inside the Sanctuary, their blood permits the sacrificial portions for the altar. In the case of a burnt offering, the blood permits all of its flesh for the altar (Rambam *Sefer Avoda, Hilkhot Pesulei HaMukdashin* 18:7).

Libations that are brought with an animal offering – נסכים הבאין עם הבהמה: One is not liable for consuming a *piggul* offering if he drinks wine, whether it is brought together with an offering or by itself, in accordance with the opinion of the Rabbis (Rambam *Sefer Avoda, Hilkhot Pesulei HaMukdashin* 18:8).

The *log* of oil of a leper – לוג שמן של מצורע: With regard to the *log* of oil used in the purification rites of the leper, one who consumes it is not liable for consuming *piggul*. The blood of the guilt offering is not considered to permit the oil, as one can bring the oil several days after the guilt offering, as stated by the Rabbis in the *baraita* on 44a (Rambam *Sefer Avoda, Hilkhot Pesulei HaMukdashin* 18:8 and *Kesef Mishne* there, and see *Tosefot Yom Tov*).

Bulls that are burned, etc. – פרים הנשרפים וכו׳: The presentation of the blood of the sin offerings inside the Sanctuary permits their sacrificial portions to be burned on the altar. Therefore, one who eats these portions is liable for consuming *piggul*. The rest of the flesh of these sin offerings can never attain *piggul* status (Rambam *Sefer Avoda, Hilkhot Pesulei HaMukdashin* 18:7).

NOTES

The libations that are brought by themselves – הנסכים הבאין בפני עצמן: According to Rashi, this is referring not only to the wine of libations, but also to the meal offering brought with the libations that accompany animal offerings (see Numbers 15:1–12). This meal offering does not have a permitting factor, as no handful is removed from it; rather, it is entirely burned upon the altar. When these libations are brought together with an offering they are fixed as the libations of that offering. Therefore, Rabbi Meir maintains that the presentation of the blood of that offering is considered the permitting factor for these libations, which means that if the priest rendered the offering *piggul* through the blood's presentation, the libations have *piggul* status as well, and similarly the libations are *piggul* if he slaughtered the animal with the intent to sacrifice its libations on the following day (see *Menaḥot* 15b).

It should be noted that there are two ways in which libations can be brought by themselves. One is the situation addressed by Rashi, in which the libations that accompany an offering are not brought on the same day as the offering but at a later stage (see *Menaḥot* 44b). It is also possible for an individual to donate a meal offering brought with libations.

Some commentaries have a version of the mishna that reads: The meal offering of the anointed priest, the meal offering brought with libations, and the blood (Rambam). Rashi rejects this version, as he maintains that this case of a meal offering brought with libations is subject to the dispute of Rabbi Meir and the Rabbis. *Tosafot* contend that the term: Meal offering brought with libations, is referring to the libations that accompany an offering but that are brought later, whereas when Rabbi Meir mentions libations that come to be sacrificed in and of themselves he is dealing with a meal offering brought with libations that is not connected to an offering at all (see *Tosefot Yom Tov*). Yet another possibility is that in the first clause the mishna is speaking of a meal offering brought with libations, and the case discussed by Rabbi Meir and the Rabbis concerns wine brought by itself, as one can donate wine alone, which is poured on the altar (Rambam; see *Menaḥot* 104b).

Even with regard to libations that are brought with an animal offering – אף הבאין עם הבהמה: Since they can be sacrificed by themselves at a later stage, the offering does not permit the libations at all (Rashi). The *Tosefta* (5:1) cites the continuation of the discussion between Rabbi Meir and the Rabbis. The Rabbis claim that as the libations can be changed from one offering to another even after they have been consecrated in a service vessel, it is clear that the libations do not depend on that offering at all (see *Tosafot* on *Menaḥot* 15b and *Ḥazon Yeḥezkel* on the *Tosefta*).

The *log* of oil of a leper – לוג שמן של מצורע: After sprinkling on the leper from the blood of the guilt offering, the priest takes the *log* of oil and sprinkles from it onto the tips of the right ear, thumb, and big toe of the leper (see Leviticus 14:15–17). The remainder of the oil is consumed by the priests.

As the blood of the guilt offering of the leper permits its use – שדם האשם מתירו: The oil is placed on the leper only if the blood of the guilt offering has already been placed upon him. Consequently, the blood of the guilt offering permits the oil. Rashi adds, citing a *baraita* on 44b, that Rabbi Meir disagrees only in a case where the *log* is brought together with the guilt offering, and not if it was brought at a later stage.

Bulls that are burned and goats that are burned – פרים הנשרפים ושעירים הנשרפים: This is a reference to sin offerings brought inside the Sanctuary, whose blood is presented on the Curtain and the inner altar, and, in the case of the bull and goat of Yom Kippur, inside the Holy of Holies, between the staves of the Ark. The flesh of these animals is not sacrificed at all, but is burned outside Jerusalem. The category of bulls that are burned includes the bull of Yom Kippur, the bull for an unwitting communal sin, and the bull for an unwitting sin of the anointed priest. The goats that are burned are the goat of Yom Kippur and the goat for an unwitting communal sin of idol worship. In all these cases, their sacrificial portions are burned upon the altar after the presentation of the blood, which is considered their permitting factor. Therefore, if the priest rendered the offering *piggul*, e.g., if he slaughtered it with the intent to present the blood the following day, and he ate from its sacrificial portions, he is liable to receive *karet*. But if he ate from the rest of the flesh, which was slated to be burned outside Jerusalem, he is not liable to receive *karet*, as the blood does not permit this flesh at all (*Tiferet Yisrael*). Furthermore, if he intended to burn the flesh the following day, the offering does not have *piggul* status, as *piggul* applies only if his intent is with regard to an item that is consumed by a person or burned on the altar (see 35a).

רַבִּי שִׁמְעוֹן אוֹמֵר: כֹּל שֶׁאֵינוֹ עַל הַמִּזְבֵּחַ הַחִיצוֹן כִּשְׁלָמִים – אֵין חַיָּיבִין עָלָיו מִשּׁוּם פִּיגּוּל.

Rabbi Shimon says: Those bulls and goats are not subject to *piggul* because their blood is presented in the Sanctuary, and in the case of **any** offering **whose** blood **is not** presented **on the external altar**[N] **like** that of **a peace offering,** with regard to which the *halakha* of *piggul* was stated in the Torah, **one is not liable for** eating **it due to** violation of the prohibition of ***piggul.***

גמ׳ אָמַר עוּלָּא: קוֹמֶץ פִּיגּוּל שֶׁהֶעֱלוֹ עַל גַּבֵּי הַמִּזְבֵּחַ – פָּקַע פִּיגּוּלוֹ מִמֶּנּוּ, אִם אֲחֵרִים מֵבִיא לִידֵי פִּיגּוּל – הוּא עַצְמוֹ לֹא כׇּל שֶׁכֵּן. מַאי קָאָמַר? הָכִי קָאָמַר: אִם אֵינוֹ מִתְקַבֵּל, הֵיאַךְ מֵבִיא אֲחֵרִים לִידֵי פִּיגּוּל?

GEMARA **Ulla says:** With regard to **a handful** of a meal offering that is ***piggul***[NH] **that was offered up on the altar, its *piggul* status has left it.** His reasoning is as follows: **If** this handful **brings other** items **to** a status of ***piggul,*** with regard to **itself** is it **not all the more so?** The Gemara asks: **What is** Ulla **saying?** This consideration does not explain why the status of *piggul* should leave the handful. The Gemara answers that **this** is what **he is saying: If** the handful **is not accepted,** i.e., if its sacrifice is disqualified, **how can it bring other** items[N] **to** a status of ***piggul?*** A meal offering is considered *piggul* only if its handful is properly sacrificed.

מַאי קָא מַשְׁמַע לַן? אִי דְּאֵין חַיָּיבִין עָלָיו מִשּׁוּם פִּיגּוּל – תְּנֵינָא: אֵלּוּ דְּבָרִים שֶׁאֵין חַיָּיבִין עֲלֵיהֶם מִשּׁוּם פִּיגּוּל: הַקּוֹמֶץ, וְהַקְּטֹרֶת, וְהַלְּבוֹנָה, וּמִנְחַת כֹּהֲנִים, וּמִנְחַת כֹּהֵן מָשִׁיחַ, וּמִנְחַת נְסָכִים, וְהַדָּם!

The Gemara asks: **What is** Ulla **teaching us? If** he is teaching us **that one is not liable for** eating the handful **due to** violation of the prohibition of ***piggul,* we learn** this in the mishna: **These are** the **items for which one is not liable due to *piggul*: The handful, the incense, the frankincense, the meal offering of priests, the meal offering of** the **anointed priest, the meal offering** brought with the **libations** that accompany animal offerings, **and the blood.** If so, one is not liable for eating the handful even if it was not offered up on the altar.

אֶלָּא, דְּאִם עָלוּ לֹא יֵרְדוּ – תְּנֵינָא: הַלָּן, וְהַיּוֹצֵא, וְהַטָּמֵא, וְשֶׁנִּשְׁחַט חוּץ לִזְמַנּוֹ וְחוּץ לִמְקוֹמוֹ – אִם עָלוּ לֹא יֵרְדוּ!

Rather, Ulla is teaching **that if** items with *piggul* status **ascended** the altar, **they shall not descend.** But this too, **we learn** in a mishna (84a): With regard to sacrificial flesh **that** is **left** overnight, **or that emerges** from the Temple courtyard, **or that is ritually impure, or** an offering **that was slaughtered** with the intention of eating the meat **beyond its** designated **time or outside its** designated **area,** thereby acquiring the status of *piggul,* **if** any one of these **ascended** the altar **they shall not descend.**

וְאֶלָּא, דְּאִם יָרְדוּ יַעֲלוּ – הָא נַמִי תְּנֵינָא: כְּשֵׁם שֶׁאִם עָלוּ לֹא יֵרְדוּ – כָּךְ אִם יָרְדוּ לֹא יַעֲלוּ! לָא צְרִיכָא, שֶׁמָּשְׁלָה בָּהֶן הָאוּר.

Rather, Ulla is teaching **that if** items with *piggul* status **descended** from the altar after having been brought up there, **they ascend** once again. But **we also learn** in that same mishna (84b) that **this** is not so: **Just as if they ascended** the altar, **they shall not descend, so** too, **if they descended** from the altar **they shall not ascend.** The Gemara answers: **No,** Ulla's ruling is **necessary** in a case **where the fire has** already **taken hold of it,**[NH] i.e., the handful began to burn before it came down from the altar. Ulla teaches that in such a case the priests should return the handful to the altar, as its *piggul* status has already left it.

הָא נַמִי אֲמָרָהּ עוּלָּא חֲדָא זִימְנָא. דְּאָמַר עוּלָּא: לֹא שָׁנוּ אֶלָּא שֶׁלֹּא מָשְׁלָה בָּהֶן הָאוּר, אֲבָל מָשְׁלָה בָּהֶן הָאוּר – יַעֲלוּ! מַהוּ דְּתֵימָא: הָנֵי מִילֵּי

The Gemara raises a difficulty: But **this** *halakha* **too, Ulla** already **said it** on **another occasion. As Ulla says:** The mishna **taught** that items that descended from the altar shall not ascend again **only where the fire has not taken hold of them, but where the fire has** already **taken hold of them, they shall ascend.** The Gemara explains: Even so, there is a novelty in Ulla's ruling: **Lest you say** that **this matter** applies only

NOTES

Any offering whose blood is not presented on the external altar – כֹּל שֶׁאֵינוֹ עַל הַמִּזְבֵּחַ הַחִיצוֹן: On 14a it is established that while Rabbi Shimon maintains that this offering is not *piggul*, he concedes that it is disqualified. This is derived by way of an *a fortiori* inference from the *halakha* of an intent to slaughter not for the sake of the offering being sacrificed.

A handful that is *piggul* – קוֹמֶץ פִּיגּוּל: For example, the priest took the handful with the intent to burn it beyond its designated time, or to eat its remainder beyond the designated time. An offering whose rites were performed with an improper intent to burn or eat it beyond its designated time or outside its designated area certainly may not be burned on the altar *ab initio*. The case here involves a priest who transgressed and brought it onto the altar.

How can it bring other items – הֵיאַךְ מֵבִיא אֲחֵרִים: If the sacrifice of the handful is not valid, how can a meal offering become *piggul* at all? *Piggul* status takes effect only if the rest of the service was performed properly, and a meal offering is accepted solely through the burning of its handful. Accordingly, Ulla's statement should be read as follows: If the burning of the handful must be considered an accepted act with regard to the remainder of the meal offering in order to bring it into a status of *piggul*, is it not all the more so that the handful itself is fit?

Where the fire has taken hold of it – שֶׁמָּשְׁלָה בָּהֶן הָאוּר: At this stage the handful is already considered the food of the altar, and therefore its burning must be completed.

HALAKHA

A handful that is *piggul*, etc. – קוֹמֶץ פִּיגּוּל וכו׳: With regard to *piggul* that ascended to the altar, once the fire has taken hold of most of it, the prohibition leaves it, as stated by Ulla, in accordance with the explanation of Rabbi Yoḥanan on the following *amud* (Rambam *Sefer Avoda, Hilkhot Pesulei HaMukdashin* 18:21; see *Mishne LaMelekh* on 3:9).

Where the fire has taken hold of it – שֶׁמָּשְׁלָה בָּהֶן הָאוּר: With regard to all items disqualified for the altar, if their disqualification occurred after they were brought inside the Temple, e.g., if they were left overnight or taken outside, just as if they ascended the altar they shall not descend, so too, if they descended they shall not ascend again. If the fire has already taken hold of them, then even if they descended they should be brought back up to the top of the altar for the completion of their burning, as stated by Ulla (Rambam *Sefer Avoda, Hilkhot Pesulei HaMukdashin* 3:8–9).

אֵבֶר דִּמְחַבַּר, אֲבָל קוֹמֶץ דִּמְיפָּרַת – אֵימָא לָא, קָא מַשְׁמַע לַן.

to a **limb** of an offering, **which is** all **connected** together so that it forms a single unit, and one can say that if fire took hold of part of it, all of it is considered the food of the altar, and therefore it is returned to the altar if it came down; **but** with regard to **a handful, which** consists of **separate** pieces, perhaps only the part that the fire took hold of is returned to the altar, but as for the rest you might **say** that it does **not** ascend again. Therefore, Ulla **teaches us**[N] that the same *halakha* applies to the handful as to a limb, i.e., if it descended from the altar after fire already took hold of any part of it, it ascends once again in its entirety to the altar.

אָמַר רַב אַחַאי: הִלְכָּךְ, הַאי קוֹמֶץ פִּיגּוּל דְּפַלְגֵיהּ מַחֵית אַאַרְעָא וּפַלְגֵיהּ אַסְקֵיהּ אַמַּעֲרָכָה, וּמָשְׁלָה בּוֹ הָאוּר – מַסֵּיקְנָא לֵיהּ לְכוּלֵּיהּ לְכַתְּחִלָּה.

Rav Aḥai says: Since the handful is considered one unit, **therefore,** in the case of **this handful of** ***piggul*****, half of which**[H] **lies on the ground and half of which was brought up to the** wood **arrangement** on the altar **and the fire took hold of it, one brings all of it up**[N] to the altar ***ab initio*****.**

אָמַר רַבִּי יִצְחָק אָמַר רַבִּי יוֹחָנָן: הַפִּיגּוּל וְהַנּוֹתָר וְהַטָּמֵא שֶׁהֶעֱלָן לְגַבֵּי מִזְבֵּחַ – פָּקַע אִיסּוּר מֵהֶן. אָמַר רַב חִסְדָּא: מָרֵי דִּיכִי! מִזְבֵּחַ מִקְוֶה טָהֳרָה?! אָמַר רַבִּי זֵירָא: שֶׁמָּשְׁלָה בָּהֶן הָאוּר.

Rabbi Yitzḥak says that **Rabbi Yoḥanan says:** With regard to ***piggul*****, *notar*,**[H] i.e., offerings that remain after the time allotted for their consumption, **and ritually impure** flesh, **where one brought them up to the altar, their prohibition has left them.**[N] **Rav Ḥisda said** in astonishment: **Teacher of this** ***halakha*****,**[N] is the **altar a bath of ritual purification** that can render an impure item pure? **Rabbi Zeira says:** This is referring to a case **where the fire took hold of them,** and therefore the item belongs to the altar and the prohibition lapses.

מֵתִיב רַבִּי יִצְחָק בַּר בִּיסְנָא: אֲחֵרִים אוֹמְרִים: ״וְטֻמְאָתוֹ עָלָיו״ – מִי שֶׁטּוּמְאָה פּוֹרַחַת מִמֶּנּוּ, יָצָא בָּשָׂר שֶׁאֵין טוּמְאָה פּוֹרַחַת מִמֶּנּוּ; וְאִם אִיתָא – הֲרֵי טוּמְאָה פּוֹרַחַת מִמֶּנּוּ עַל יְדֵי הָאוּר!

Rabbi Yitzḥak bar Bisna raises an objection from a *baraita*. **Others say:** The verse states: "But the soul that eats of the meat of the sacrifice of peace offerings, which pertain to the Lord, **having his impurity upon him,** that soul shall be cut off from his people" (Leviticus 7:20). Although this can also be read as: Having its impurity upon it, referring to the meat of the peace offerings, the verse in fact is referring to **one whose impurity can depart from him,**[N] i.e., a person who is currently impure, but can attain a state of ritual purity by immersing in a ritual bath. This serves to **exclude** the impure **flesh** of offerings, **as its impurity cannot depart from it,** since ritually impure flesh cannot be purified. **And if it is so** that Rabbi Yoḥanan's statement is correct, the **impurity** of flesh **can** in fact **depart from it by means of the fire** of the altar.

אָמַר רָבָא: עַל יְדֵי מִקְוֶה קָאָמְרִינַן. מִידֵּי מִקְוֶה כְּתִיב? אֶלָּא אָמַר רַב פָּפָּא: בִּבְשַׂר שְׁלָמִים עָסְקִינַן, דְּלָא חֲזֵי לְהַקְרָבָה.

Rava says: When the *baraita* speaks of an item whose impurity cannot depart from it, **we say** it is referring to purification **by means of a ritual bath,** not through any other means. The Gemara raises a difficulty: **Is** the term **ritual bath written** in the *baraita*? It speaks only in general terms about impurity that can or cannot depart from an item. **Rather, Rav Pappa says:** In that verse **we are dealing with the meat of peace offerings, which are not fit for sacrificing,** as the meat of a peace offering is eaten rather than being burned on the altar. Therefore, bringing it up to the altar does not remove its impurity from it.

רָבִינָא אָמַר: ״וְטֻמְאָתוֹ עָלָיו״ – מִי שֶׁטּוּמְאָה פּוֹרַחַת מִמֶּנּוּ כְּשֶׁהוּא שָׁלֵם; יָצָא בָּשָׂר, דָּבָר שֶׁאֵין טוּמְאָה פּוֹרַחַת כְּשֶׁהוּא שָׁלֵם, אֶלָּא כְּשֶׁהוּא חָסֵר.

Ravina says there is a different answer: Even if the impurity of flesh leaves it when it is brought up to the altar, this verse cannot be referring to the impure meat of peace offerings, as the phrase **"having his impurity upon him"** is referring to **one whose impurity departs from him when he is whole;** the term "upon him" indicates that he is in a state of wholeness. This serves to **exclude** sacrificial **flesh,** which is **an item whose impurity does not depart from it when it is whole, but** only **when it is deficient,** i.e., when fire takes hold of it on the altar.

NOTES

Teaches us – **קָא מַשְׁמַע לַן**: Although the handful is not a solid entity, since it is taken from the meal offering in one action it is halakhically considered a single unit. Consequently, once the fire has taken hold of it, the entire handful is brought back to the altar if it came down.

One brings all of it up – **מַסֵּיקְנָא לֵיהּ לְכוּלֵּיהּ**: According to Rashi, this is referring to a case where only half of the handful was brought up to the altar at the outset. Since the handful is considered a single unit it is brought up in its entirety. Others add that this follows Ulla's earlier reasoning: If the handful can cause other items to become *piggul* once the fire takes hold of most of it, certainly it renders the rest of the handful permitted for the altar (*Panim Meirot*). Some commentaries understand that this is referring to a case where the entire handful was brought up to the altar, and subsequently half of it came down (*Tosafot* on 42b).

Their prohibition has left them – **פָּקַע אִיסּוּר מֵהֶן**: As far as *piggul* is concerned, this means that if the flesh came down from the altar it is brought back up, as the Gemara stated earlier concerning the statement of Ulla. With regard to *notar* and impure flesh, they are no longer prohibited for consumption (Rashi).

Teacher [*marei*] of this *halakha* – **מָרֵי דִּיכִי**: Rashi explains this term literally as referring to the teacher of the *halakha* in question. An alternative version of the text reads: My teacher and Rabbi (*Arukh*). Some maintain that *marei* here means Master, i.e., God, and it is an exclamation similar to: Master of the Universe! (*Arukh HaShalem*).

One whose impurity can depart from him – **מִי שֶׁטּוּמְאָה פּוֹרַחַת מִמֶּנּוּ**: Admittedly, ritual impurity can also depart from flesh, when it is no longer fit to be eaten. In that case, the possibility of it being prohibited for consumption is no longer relevant, as it does not have the status of food.

HALAKHA

This handful of *piggul*, half of which – **הַאי קוֹמֶץ פִּיגּוּל דְּפַלְגֵיהּ**: If part of a *piggul* handful was left on the ground and the fire of the altar took hold of the other part, all of it shall ascend to the altar (Rambam *Sefer Avoda*, *Hilkhot Pesulei HaMukdashin* 3:10).

***Piggul*, *notar*, etc.** – **הַפִּיגּוּל וְהַנּוֹתָר וכו׳**: With regard to a piece of flesh that has the status of *piggul*, *notar*, or impure flesh, that ascended to the top of the altar, once the fire takes hold of most of the piece its prohibition departs from it, in accordance with the opinion of Rabbi Yitzḥak (Rambam *Sefer Avoda*, *Hilkhot Pesulei HaMukdashin* 18:21).

גופא: "וטמאתו עליו" – בטומאת הגוף הכתוב מדבר.

§ The Gemara proceeds to analyze **the** matter **itself.** In the *baraita* the Rabbis attempt to prove that the verse: "But the soul that eats of the meat of the sacrifice of peace offerings, which pertain to the Lord, having his impurity upon him, that soul shall be cut off from his people" (Leviticus 7:20), is referring to a ritually impure person, and not to impure flesh. The *baraita* states: **"Having his impurity upon him"; the verse speaks of impurity of the body** of the person, not the impurity of the flesh of the offering.

אתה אומר: בטומאת הגוף, או אינו אלא בטומאת בשר? נאמר כאן: "טמאתו" ונאמר להלן: "טמאתו (עליו) [בו]", מה להלן בטומאת הגוף הכתוב מדבר – אף כאן בטומאת הגוף הכתוב מדבר.

The question may be raised: **Do you say** that it is dealing **with impurity of the body? Or is it** speaking **only of impurity of the flesh,** as is suggested by the fact that the term for "meat" [*basar*] is masculine, matching the masculine pronominal suffix attached to the word "impurity," whereas the word for "soul" [*nefesh*] is feminine? The answer is that **here it is stated:** "Having **his impurity** upon him," **and there it is stated:** "Whoever touches the dead, the body of any man that has died, and does not purify himself, he has defiled the Tabernacle of the Lord; and that soul shall be cut off from Israel, because the water of sprinkling was not sprinkled upon him, he shall be impure, **his impurity** is yet **upon him"** (Numbers 19:13).[N] **Just as there, the verse is speaking of impurity of the body, so too here, the verse is speaking of impurity of the body.**

רבי יוסי אומר: הואיל ונאמרו קדשים בלשון רבים, ונאמרה טומאה בלשון יחיד – בטומאת הגוף הכתוב מדבר. רבי אומר: "ואכל" – בטומאת הגוף הכתוב מדבר. אחרים אמרו: "וטמאתו עליו" – מי שטומאה פורחת ממנו, יצא בשר שאין טומאה פורחת ממנו.

Rabbi Yosei says there is a different proof: **Since** in this verse (Leviticus 7:20) the **sacrificial** animals **are mentioned in the plural** form, i.e., "peace offerings," **but** the **impurity is mentioned in the singular:** "Upon him," evidently **the verse is speaking of impurity of the body,** and not impurity of the peace offerings. **Rabbi** Yehuda HaNasi **says** there is yet another proof: Since the next verse states: "And when anyone shall touch any impure item… **and eat** of the meat of the sacrifice of peace offerings" (Leviticus 7:21), this indicates that **the verse is speaking of impurity of the body,** as will be explained. **Others say** that the phrase **"having his impurity upon him"** proves that the reference here is to **one whose impurity can depart from him,** i.e., a person. This serves to **exclude** the impure **flesh** of offerings, **as its impurity cannot depart from it.** This concludes the *baraita*.

אמר מר: רבי אומר: "ואכל" – בטומאת הגוף הכתוב מדבר. מאי משמע? אמר רבא: כל קרא דלא מפרש ליה רב יצחק בר אבודימי, וכל מתניתא דלא מפרשא לה רב זעירי – לא מיפרשא.

The Gemara analyzes the *baraita*. **The Master said: Rabbi** Yehuda HaNasi **says** that the term **"and eat"** indicates that **the verse is speaking of impurity of the body.** The Gemara asks: **From where** is this **inferred?** How is the meaning of this verse derived from this term, which appears in a different verse? In this connection the Gemara notes that **Rava said: Any verse that was not explained by Rav Yitzḥak bar Avudimi,**[P] **and any *baraita* that was not explained by Rav Ze'eiri,**[P] **was not explained,** as these Sages are the most accomplished interpreters of verses and *baraitot*, respectively.

הכי אמר רב יצחק בר אבודימי: הואיל ופתח הכתוב בלשון נקבה וסיים בלשון נקבה, ולשון זכר באמצע – בטומאת הגוף הכתוב מדבר.

Rava cites the relevant explanation of the verse referred to by Rabbi Yehuda HaNasi: **This** is what **Rav Yitzḥak bar Avudimi says:** The next verse states: "And when anyone shall touch any impure item, whether it is the impurity of man, or an impure animal, or any impure detestable thing, and eat of the meat of the sacrifice of peace offerings, which pertain to the Lord, that soul shall be cut off from his people" (Leviticus 7:21). The beginning of that verse: "And when anyone shall touch," and the end of that verse: "That soul shall be cut off," are in the feminine form, whereas the middle of the verse: "And eat of the meat," is in the masculine form, and yet it is clear that the verse is speaking of impurity of the body. The same may be said about the previous verse: **Since the verse begins in the feminine** form **and ends in the feminine** form, **and the masculine** form is used **in the middle, the verse** must be **speaking of impurity of the body,**[NH] despite the change from the feminine to the masculine.

NOTES

And there it is stated, his impurity is yet upon him – ונאמר להלן טמאתו בו: According to an alternative reading of the text, which is rejected by Rashi, the reference is to the following verse: "Whoever he is of all your seed throughout your generations, who approaches to the sacred items, which the children of Israel consecrate to the Lord, having his impurity upon him" (Leviticus 22:3). That verse is clearly referring to the impurity of the person (see *Tosafot*).

The verse is speaking of impurity of the body – בטומאת הגוף הכתוב מדבר: As explained, the main difficulty with the claim that the verse: "But the soul that eats of the meat of the sacrifice of peace offerings, which pertain to the Lord, having his impurity upon him, that soul shall be cut off from his people" (Leviticus 7:20), is referring to impurity of the body is that the term "soul" is in the feminine form, whereas the phrase "having his impurity upon him" is in the masculine, an indication that this is referring to impurity of the meat, which is also in the masculine. Rav Yitzḥak bar Avudimi notes the subsequent verse in order to compare the stylistic forms of the two verses. Once it has been shown that the next verse starts in the feminine form before moving on to the masculine, it is evident that this shift is not an anomaly, and therefore it can be accepted that the first verse is written in a similar style.

PERSONALITIES

Rav Yitzḥak bar Avudimi – רב יצחק בר אבודימי: The Talmud mentions two Sages of this name. The first Sage lived in the transitional generation between the *tanna'im* and the *amora'im*, whereas the Rav Yitzḥak bar Avudimi mentioned here was a Babylonian *amora* from the third generation. He was probably a disciple and colleague of Rav Ḥisda, and was famous for his breadth of knowledge of the Bible, as well as his unique method of study, by which he would seek evidence and allusions to all statements of the Sages in the Bible itself. Numerous *halakhot* are stated in his name. Apparently, both Abaye and Rava were disciples of Rav Yitzḥak bar Avudimi with regard to matters of biblical explication, as they both attribute various traditions to him.

Ze'eiri – זעירי: Ze'eiri was a Babylonian *amora* of the second generation, and a student of Rav and Rav Kahana. At a young age, Ze'eiri emigrated to Eretz Yisrael where he studied under Ḥanina bar Ḥama, whom he often quoted. He subsequently enrolled as a student of Rabbi Yoḥanan, who so admired him that he desired him as a son-in-law, as the Gemara relates. Ze'eiri's refusal to the match stemmed from his sense that Babylonian scholars were superior to those of Eretz Yisrael. Ze'eiri eventually returned to Babylonia, where he was instrumental in transmitting the traditions of Eretz Yisrael to the students in the Neharde'a yeshiva. His departure from Eretz Yisrael was apparently the reason why Ze'eiri was never ordained. The generations that followed him held him in high esteem, to such an extent that Rava was confident in stating here that a *baraita* that had not been explicated by Ze'eiri remains unexplained. Ze'eiri's statements are exclusively concerned with the realm of *halakha*. His primary student was Rav Ḥiyya bar Ashi.

HALAKHA

The verse must be speaking of impurity of the body – בטומאת הגוף הכתוב מדבר: With regard to one who contracted a level of ritual impurity for which he would be liable to receive *karet* if he entered the Temple in that state, if he intentionally ate an olive-bulk of sacrificial food he is liable to receive *karet*, whether the food was impure or pure (Rambam *Sefer Avoda, Hilkhot Pesulei HaMukdashin* 18:13).

מַתְנִיתָא – דְּתַנְיָא: אִם נֶאֶמְרוּ קַלּוֹת לָמָּה נֶאֶמְרוּ חֲמוּרוֹת, וְאִם נֶאֱמַר חֲמוּרוֹת לָמָּה נֶאֱמַר קַלּוֹת? אִם נֶאֱמַר קַלּוֹת וְלֹא חֲמוּרוֹת, הָיִיתִי אוֹמֵר: עַל הַקַּלּוֹת בְּלָאו וְעַל הַחֲמוּרוֹת בְּמִיתָה – לְכָךְ נֶאֱמַר חֲמוּרוֹת. וְאִם נֶאֱמַר חֲמוּרוֹת וְלֹא נֶאֶמְרוּ קַלּוֹת, הָיִיתִי אוֹמֵר: עַל הַחֲמוּרוֹת יְהֵא חַיָּיב, וְעַל הַקַּלּוֹת יְהֵא פָּטוּר – לְכָךְ נֶאֱמַר קַלּוֹת.

The Gemara cites the *baraita*, alluded to by Rava, through which the interpretative prowess of Rav Ze'eiri is demonstrated. This *baraita* also discusses the topic of eating consecrated food while in a state of ritual impurity. **As it is taught** in a *baraita*: **If the lenient are stated, why are the stringent stated; and if the stringent** are **stated, why** are the **lenient stated? If the lenient were stated and not the stringent, I would say: For the lenient,** one is liable to receive lashes **for** violating **a prohibition, and for the stringent,** one is liable **to** be punished with **death** at the hand of Heaven. **Therefore,** the **stringent** are **stated. And if** the **stringent were stated and the lenient were not stated, I would say:** Only **for the stringent should one be liable** to receive a punishment; **but for the lenient, one should be** entirely **exempt. Therefore,** the **lenient** are **stated.** This concludes the *baraita*, the meaning of which is opaque.

מַאי "קַלּוֹת" וּמַאי "חֲמוּרוֹת"? אִילֵימָא "קַלּוֹת" – מַעֲשֵׂר, "חֲמוּרוֹת" – תְּרוּמָה; הָיִיתִי אוֹמֵר בְּמִיתָה? הָשְׁתָּא נַמִּי הָא בְּמִיתָה!

The Gemara asks: **What** are the **lenient, and what** are the **stringent?** It is known that the *baraita* is discussing the broad topic of eating consecrated food in a state of impurity, but its precise meaning requires elucidation. **If we say** that the **lenient** is referring to the consumption of second **tithe**[NB] while one is impure, and the **stringent** is referring to the partaking of ***teruma***, the portion of the produce designated for the priest, in a state of impurity, how can the *baraita* say that had the Torah stated only the prohibition against eating second tithe **I would** incorrectly **have said** that one who partakes of *teruma* is liable to be punished **with death** at the hand of Heaven? **Now too, this** is the *halakha*; one who partakes of *teruma* when he is in a state of impurity is indeed liable **to** be punished with **death** at the hand of Heaven.[H]

[וְתוּ], וְאִי לֹא נֶאֱמַר הָיִיתִי אוֹמֵר בְּמִיתָה? דַּיּוֹ לַבָּא מִן הַדִּין לִהְיוֹת כַּנִּדּוֹן!

And furthermore, is it correct to say: **And if** the Torah **had not stated** the stringent case of *teruma* but only the lenient case of second tithe, and I would learn the *halakha* in the stringent case from the *halakha* in the lenient case by way of an *a fortiori* inference, **I would** then **say** that the punishment in the stringent case is that **of death** at the hand of Heaven? This is impossible, as there is a principle with regard to *a fortiori* inferences that **it is sufficient for the** conclusion that **emerges from** an *a fortiori* **inference to be like** its **source.**[B] In other words, a *halakha* derived by means of an *a fortiori* inference can be no more stringent than the source from which it is derived. In this instance, if an impure person who eats second tithe is flogged for violating a prohibition, then the punishment for partaking of *teruma* in a state of impurity, were it not stated in the Torah, could be no more severe than that.

אֶלָּא: "קַלּוֹת" – טוּמְאַת שֶׁרֶץ, "חֲמוּרוֹת" – טוּמְאַת מֵת;

Rather, when the *baraita* refers to the **lenient** it is referring to **the impurity of** the carcass of **a creeping animal,** while the **stringent** is referring to **the impurity** imparted by **a corpse,** as the Torah discusses both these cases in the context of eating consecrated foods in a state of ritual impurity: "And whoever touches anything that is impure by the dead, or a man whose semen goes from him, or whoever touches any creeping animal" (Leviticus 22:4–5).

וּבְמַאי? אִי בִּתְרוּמָה – אִידֵי וְאִידֵי הוּא בְּמִיתָה! וְתוּ, לְכָךְ נֶאֶמְרוּ חֲמוּרוֹת דִּבְלָאו? הָא בְּמִיתָה הִיא! (וְאִי לֹא נֶאֱמַר הָיִיתִי אוֹמֵר בְּמִיתָה? דַּיּוֹ לַבָּא מִן הַדִּין לִהְיוֹת כַּנִּדּוֹן!)

The Gemara asks: **But** if so, **to what** food is this referring? **If** it is referring to the partaking **of *teruma***, both **this** one who was rendered impure by the dead **and that** one who was rendered impure by a creeping animal **are** liable to be punished **with death** at the hand of Heaven. No matter how he became impure, if he partakes of *teruma* in a state of ritual impurity he is liable to be punished with death. **And furthermore,** how can the *baraita* state: **Therefore, the stringent are stated,** i.e., to teach **that** one is liable only to be flogged **for** violating **a prohibition,** and not to be punished with death. After all, one who partakes of *teruma* when impure **is** in fact liable **to** be punished with **death**[N] at the hand of Heaven. Consequently, the reference to stringent and lenient cannot be referring to the partaking of *teruma*.

וְאִי בַּאֲכִילַת מַעֲשֵׂר,

And if the *baraita* is referring **to the eating of** second **tithe,** this too is difficult.

NOTES

If we say that the lenient is referring to the consumption of second tithe – אִילֵימָא קַלּוֹת מַעֲשֵׂר: The Gemara in *Yevamot* 74b discusses the following verses, which concern the prohibition against eating consecrated food in a state of ritual impurity: "And he shall not eat of the holy items, unless he has bathed his flesh in water. And when the sun has set, he shall be pure, and afterward he may eat from the holy items" (Leviticus 22:6–7). The Gemara explains that the first statement is referring to second tithe, which may be eaten as soon as one has immersed, while the second statement is referring to *teruma*, which may be partaken of only after sunset. With regard to second tithe the verse states only a prohibition: "And he shall not eat of the holy items," whereas concerning *teruma* it states: "And die therein if they profane it" (Leviticus 22:9).

Liable to be punished with death – בְּמִיתָה: There is a version of the text that adds here a reference to the principle that it is sufficient for the conclusion that emerges from an *a fortiori* inference to be like its source. Rashi on the following *amud* rejects this version as a scribal error that was included in the text merely because it appears in the preceding and subsequent discussions. Rashi's reasoning is clear; according to the interpretation that the *baraita* is referring solely to the partaking of *teruma* it makes no difference to one's punishment whether he contracted ritual impurity through contact with a corpse or through contact with the carcass of a creeping animal. Either way, he is liable to be punished with death at the hand of Heaven.

BACKGROUND

Second tithe – מַעֲשֵׂר שֵׁנִי: This is a tithe that is set aside after *teruma* is given to the priests and the first tithe is given to the Levites. Second tithe is separated during the first, second, fourth, and fifth years of the Sabbatical cycle. After second tithe is set aside, it is brought to Jerusalem to be eaten there by its owner. If the journey to Jerusalem is too long and it would be difficult to transport all the second tithe, or if the produce became ritually impure, it can be redeemed for an equivalent sum of money. If the owner redeems his own produce, he is required to add one-fifth of its value. This redemption money is brought to Jerusalem, where it is spent on food that must be consumed there. Second tithe can be redeemed only with minted coins bearing an imprint; blanks and promissory notes cannot be used. Today, second tithe is still redeemed, but for a nominal sum, as in the absence of the Temple it is no longer brought to Jerusalem. The *halakhot* of second tithe are discussed in tractate *Ma'aser Sheni*.

It is sufficient [*dayyo*] for the conclusion that emerges from an *a fortiori* inference to be like its source – דַּיּוֹ לַבָּא מִן הַדִּין לִהְיוֹת כַּנִּדּוֹן: This halakhic principle, referred to in shorthand as *dayyo*, restricts the conclusion that may be derived from an *a fortiori* inference. It prevents the implementation of limitless leniencies or stringencies from an *a fortiori* inference, by creating parameters for its implementation. The principle of *dayyo* establishes that an *a fortiori* inference teaches in the following manner: Just as X is more stringent than Y with regard to point A, X is no less stringent than Y with regard to point B. It does not teach: Just as X is more stringent than Y with regard to point A, X is similarly more stringent than Y with regard to point B. If that were the case, there would be no limits to the conclusion derived from the inference.

HALAKHA

An impure person with regard to *teruma* and tithe – טָמֵא בִּתְרוּמָה וּבְמַעֲשֵׂר: A ritually impure individual who partakes of *teruma* is liable to be punished with death at the hand of Heaven. If he was properly warned, he is flogged by the court. One who eats second tithe in a state of ritual impurity in the place where it is supposed to be eaten, i.e., Jerusalem, is flogged but is not liable to be punished with death (Rambam *Sefer Zera'im*, *Hilkhot Terumot* 7:1 and *Hilkhot Ma'aser Sheni* 3:1).

אִם לֹא נֶאֶמְרוּ חֲמוּרוֹת הָיִיתִי אוֹמֵר עַל הַחֲמוּרוֹת בְּמִיתָה? הָא מִטּוּמְאַת שֶׁרֶץ קָאָתְיָא, וְדַיּוֹ לַבָּא מִן הַדִּין לִהְיוֹת כַּנִּדּוֹן!

If the **stringent** case of impurity imparted by a corpse **were not stated,** but only the lenient case of the impurity of a creeping animal, **would I say** that the punishment in **the stringent** case is that **of death** at the hand of Heaven? **Rather,** the *halakha* in the case of impurity imparted by a corpse would be **derived from** the *halakha* in the case of **the impurity of a creeping animal** by means of an *a fortiori* inference, **and it is sufficient for** the conclusion **that emerges from** an *a fortiori* **inference to be like** its **source,** in this case that one is liable to be flogged for the violation of a prohibition, and no more.

אָמַר זְעֵירִי: ״קַלּוֹת״ – טוּמְאַת שֶׁרֶץ, ״חֲמוּרוֹת״ – טוּמְאַת מֵת. וְהָכִי קָאָמַר: אִילּוּ נֶאֱמַר טוּמְאַת שֶׁרֶץ וְנֶאֱמַר מַעֲשֵׂר וּתְרוּמָה, וְלֹא נֶאֶמְרָה טוּמְאַת מֵת – הָיִיתִי אוֹמֵר: [קַלּוֹת] – עַל הַקַּלּוֹת בְּלָאו, וְעַל הַחֲמוּרוֹת בְּמִיתָה.

Ze'eiri says: Indeed, the **lenient** case is referring to **the impurity of a creeping animal,**[N] and the **stringent** case is referring to **impurity** imparted by **a corpse. And this** is what the *baraita* **is saying: If the impurity of a creeping animal was stated, and it was stated** that one who eats second **tithe** while impure with such impurity has violated a prohibition **and** one who partakes of ***teruma*** in that state is liable to be punished with death at the hand of Heaven, **and the impurity** imparted by **a corpse was not stated** in this context, **I would say** as follows: The **lenient** level of impurity, that of a creeping animal, **with regard to** food with **lenient** *halakhot*, second tithe, **involves** the violation of **a prohibition, and with regard to** food with **stringent** *halakhot*, *teruma*, it involves liability to be punished **with death** at the hand of Heaven.

וּמִדְּקַלּוֹת עַל הַחֲמוּרוֹת בְּמִיתָה – חֲמוּרוֹת נַמִי עַל הַקַּלּוֹת בְּמִיתָה, לְכָךְ נֶאֶמְרוּ חֲמוּרוֹת.

Ze'eiri continues his explanation of the *baraita*: **And from** the fact **that** the **lenient** level of impurity, that of a creeping animal, **with regard to** food with **stringent** *halakhot*, *teruma*, involves liability to be punished **with death** at the hand of Heaven, it may be inferred that **also** in the analogous case of the **stringent** level of impurity, imparted by a corpse, **with regard to** food with **lenient** *halakhot*, there is liability to be punished **with death** at the hand of Heaven. **Therefore, the stringent** level of impurity, imparted by a corpse, **was stated** with regard to second tithe, which has lenient *halakhot*, to teach that even if one contracted impurity from a corpse, he has violated only a prohibition for eating second tithe, and is not liable to be punished with death at the hand of Heaven.

״כָּל שֶׁיֵּשׁ לוֹ מַתִּירִין בֵּין לָאָדָם בֵּין לַמִּזְבֵּחַ – חַיָּיבִין עָלָיו מִשּׁוּם פִּיגּוּל״.

§ The mishna teaches: With regard to **any** item **that has permitting factors, either for** consumption by **a person or for** burning on **the altar, one is liable for** eating **it due to** violation of the prohibition of ***piggul.*** The Gemara cites a verse and a related *baraita*. The verse states: "And if any be at all eaten of the flesh of the sacrifice of his peace offering on the third day, it shall not be accepted, neither shall it be imputed to him who sacrifices it; it shall be *piggul*, and the soul that eats of it shall bear his iniquity" (Leviticus 7:18). The *baraita* first demonstrates that the *halakha* of *piggul* applies not only to a peace offering, with regard to which it is stated in the Torah, but to all offerings.

תָּנוּ רַבָּנַן: אוֹ אֵינוֹ מֵבִיא אֶלָּא כַּיּוֹצֵא בִּשְׁלָמִים, מַה שְּׁלָמִים מְיוּחָדִים – נֶאֱכָלִין לִשְׁנֵי יָמִים וְלַיְלָה אֶחָד, אַף כָּל נֶאֱכָל לִשְׁנֵי יָמִים וְלַיְלָה אֶחָד.

The Sages taught in a *baraita*: **Or perhaps** the *halakha* of *piggul* **extends only**[N] **to** an offering that is **similar to peace offerings: Just as peace offerings are notable** in that **they are eaten for two days and one night, so too,** the *halakha* of *piggul* applies to **any** offering that is **eaten for two days and one night.**

NOTES

Lenient is referring to the impurity of a creeping animal – **קַלּוֹת טוּמְאַת שֶׁרֶץ**: The second part of the *baraita* is not cited as a difficulty for any of the interpretations, as it can be understood in a relatively straightforward manner according to each interpretation. According to the current explanation, the last clause of the *baraita* should be understood as follows: Had the Torah stated only that one who became impure through contact with a corpse is liable to be punished with death at the hand of Heaven for partaking of *teruma* and to be flogged for consuming second tithe, I would have said that if he was impure through contact with the carcass of a creeping animal he would be entirely exempt.

NOTES

Or perhaps the *halakha* of *piggul* extends only – **אוֹ אֵינוֹ מֵבִיא אֶלָּא**: This is a citation from the middle of a *baraita* in *Torat Kohanim* on Leviticus 7:18. The *baraita* starts with a question: From where is it derived that the punishment of *karet* stated with regard to *piggul* applies to all offerings? The *baraita* quotes the verse: "That they separate themselves from the sacred items of the children of Israel" (Leviticus 22:2), which indicates that the prohibition applies to all consecrated items. Admittedly, this verse is discussing ritual impurity; but it is derived by way of a verbal analogy that the same applies to *piggul*. The *baraita* proceeds with the sentence brought here, asking: How is it known that this prohibition is not referring only to what is stated in the immediate context, namely peace offerings?

נֶאֱכָל לְיוֹם וְלַיְלָה מִנַּיִן? תַּלְמוּד לוֹמַר: ״מִבְּשַׂר״ – כָּל שֶׁשִּׁירַיִן נֶאֱכָלִין. עוֹלָה שֶׁאֵין שְׁיָרֶיהָ נֶאֱכָלִין מִנַּיִן? תַּלְמוּד לוֹמַר: ״זֶבַח״.

But as for an offering that **is eaten** only **for one day,** i.e., the day the offering is sacrificed, **and** the following **night,** e.g., a sin offering, guilt offering, and firstborn offering, **from where** is it derived that the *halakha* of *piggul* applies to this offering as well? The verse states: **"Of the flesh** of the sacrifice of his peace offering," which teaches that the status of *piggul* can apply to **any** offering **whose remainder** of meat **is eaten** after its sacrificial portions have been offered on the altar. The *baraita* asks: With regard to **a burnt offering, whose remainder** of meat **is not eaten,** as it is burned in its entirety on the altar, **from where** is this *halakha* derived? **The verse states: "Sacrifice,"** which includes any offering that is slaughtered.

מִנַּיִן לְרַבּוֹת הָעוֹפוֹת וְהַמְּנָחוֹת, עַד שֶׁאֲנִי מְרַבֶּה לוֹג שֶׁמֶן שֶׁל מְצוֹרָע? תַּלְמוּד לוֹמַר: ״אֲשֶׁר הֵם מַקְדִּישִׁים לִי״;

The *baraita* asks: **From where** is it derived **to include bird** offerings, e.g., doves or pigeons, which are not slaughtered but whose napes of their necks are pinched, **and meal offerings, until I include** even the ***log*** **of oil** that accompanies the guilt offering **of** a recovered **leper? The verse states** with regard to the consumption of consecrated food in a state of ritual purity: "That they separate themselves from the sacred items of the children of Israel, **which they consecrate to Me,**[N] and that they do not profane My holy name" (Leviticus 22:2).

וְאָתֵי נוֹתָר – חִילּוּל חִילּוּל מִטּוּמְאָה, וְאָתֵי פִּיגּוּל – ״עָוֹן״ ״עָוֹן״ מִנּוֹתָר.

The *baraita* clarifies this derivation: The *halakha* that the prohibition of ***notar*** applies to all these offerings is **derived** through a verbal analogy of **profanation** in the context of *notar*: "And if anything remains until the third day, it shall be burned in fire… and anyone who eats it shall bear his iniquity, because he has profaned the sacred item of the Lord" (Leviticus 19:6–8), and **profanation** stated in the verse discussing **ritual impurity:** "And that they do not profane My holy name." **And** the *halakha* that ***piggul*** applies to all these offerings is subsequently **derived** through a verbal analogy of **"iniquity"** in the context of *piggul* and **"iniquity"** stated in the verse discussing ***notar.*** With regard to *piggul,* the verse states: "It shall be *piggul,* and the soul that eats of it shall bear his iniquity" (Leviticus 7:18), and with regard to *notar,* it is stated in the aforementioned verse: "And anyone who eats it shall bear his iniquity."

וּמֵאַחַר שֶׁסּוֹפוֹ לְרַבּוֹת כָּל דָּבָר, לָמָּה נֶאֱמַר שְׁלָמִים מֵעַתָּה? לוֹמַר לְךָ: מַה שְּׁלָמִים מְיוּחָדִים, שֶׁיֵּשׁ לָהֶן מַתִּירִין בֵּין לָאָדָם בֵּין לַמִּזְבֵּחַ, אַף כָּל שֶׁיֵּשׁ לוֹ מַתִּירִין, בֵּין לָאָדָם בֵּין לַמִּזְבֵּחַ – חַיָּיבִין עֲלֵיהֶן מִשּׁוּם פִּיגּוּל;

The *baraita* asks: **And since** the verse **eventually includes all items,** even meal offerings and the *log* of oil of a leper, **now** one can ask: **Why does** the verse **state** *piggul* specifically with regard to **peace offerings?** The *baraita* answers: This serves **to tell you** that the offering must be similar to peace offerings in the following way: **Just as peace offerings are notable** in **that they have permitting factors, either for** consumption by **a person or for** burning on **the altar, so too,** with regard to **any** item **that has permitting factors, either for a person or for the altar, one is liable for** eating **it due to** violation of the prohibition of ***piggul.***

הָעוֹלָה – דָּמָהּ מַתִּיר אֶת בְּשָׂרָהּ לַמִּזְבֵּחַ וְעוֹרָהּ לַכֹּהֲנִים, עוֹלַת הָעוֹף – דָּמָהּ מַתִּיר אֶת בְּשָׂרָהּ לַמִּזְבֵּחַ, חַטַּאת הָעוֹף – דָּמָהּ מַתִּיר אֶת בְּשָׂרָהּ לַכֹּהֲנִים, פָּרִים הַנִּשְׂרָפִים וּשְׂעִירִים הַנִּשְׂרָפִים – דָּמָם מַתִּיר אֶת אֵימוּרֵיהֶן לִיקָּרֵב.

The *baraita* specifies: With regard to **the burnt offering, its blood renders its flesh permitted to** be burned on **the altar and its hide** to be used **by the priests.** With regard to **the bird burnt offering, its blood renders its flesh** and its skin **permitted to** be burned on **the altar.** With regard to **the bird sin offering, its blood renders its flesh permitted for** consumption by **the priests.** With regard to **bulls that are burned,** e.g., the bull sacrificed for an unwitting communal transgression, **and goats that are burned,** e.g., the goat sacrificed for an unwitting communal sin of idol worship, **their blood renders their sacrificial portions permitted to be sacrificed** on the altar.

וּמוֹצִיא אֲנִי אֶת הַקּוֹמֶץ, וְאֶת הַלְּבוֹנָה, וְהַקְּטוֹרֶת, וּמִנְחַת כֹּהֲנִים, וּמִנְחַת כֹּהֵן מָשִׁיחַ, וּמִנְחַת נְסָכִים, וְהַדָּם.

And I exclude, via the analogy to peace offerings, **the handful** of a meal offering, **the frankincense, the incense, the meal offering of priests, the meal offering of** the **anointed priest, the meal offering** brought with the **libations** that accompany animal offerings, **and the blood.** All these do not have an item that renders them permitted either for a person or for the altar.

NOTES

Which they consecrate to Me – אֲשֶׁר הֵם מַקְדִּישִׁים לִי: This derivation involves two verbal analogies, as this verse, which is referring to ritual impurity, is first applied to *notar,* and from *notar* it is extended to *piggul.* The Gemara will discuss the possibility of deriving by way of a verbal analogy from a case that itself was derived only by verbal analogy (see *Tosafot*).

רַבִּי שִׁמְעוֹן אוֹמֵר: מַה שְּׁלָמִים מְיוּחָדִין – שֶׁיֵּשׁ בּוֹ עַל מִזְבֵּחַ הַחִיצוֹן, וְחַיָּיבִין עָלָיו, אַף כָּל שֶׁיֶּשְׁנָן עַל מִזְבֵּחַ הַחִיצוֹן חַיָּיבִין עָלָיו מִשּׁוּם פִּיגּוּל; יָצְאוּ פָּרִים הַנִּשְׂרָפִים וּשְׂעִירִים הַנִּשְׂרָפִים, הוֹאִיל שֶׁאֵין עַל מִזְבֵּחַ הַחִיצוֹן כִּשְׁלָמִים – אֵין חַיָּיבִין עָלָיו מִשּׁוּם פִּיגּוּל.

The *baraita* concludes: **Rabbi Shimon says** that the fact that the verse specifies peace offerings as the standard case of *piggul* teaches: **Just as peace offerings are notable** in **that they have** a permitting factor that is sacrificed **on the external altar,** i.e., their blood, **and one is liable for** eating **them** due to violation of the prohibition of *piggul*, **so too,** with regard to **any** item **that** has a permitting factor that **is** sacrificed **on the external altar, one is liable for** eating **it due to** violation of the prohibition of ***piggul***. This serves to **exclude bulls that are burned and goats that are burned: Since** their blood is **not** presented **on the external altar like peace offerings, one is not liable for** eating **them due to** violation of the prohibition of ***piggul***.

אָמַר [מָר]: כַּיּוֹצֵא בִּשְׁלָמִים. מַאי נִיהוּ – בְּכוֹר, דְּנֶאֱכָל לִשְׁנֵי יָמִים וְלַיְלָה אֶחָד. בְּמַאי אָתֵי? אִי בְּ״מַה מָּצִינוּ״ – אִיכָּא לְמִיפְרַךְ.

The Gemara analyzes the *baraita*. **The Master said:** Perhaps the *halakha* of *piggul* extends only to an offering that is **similar to peace offerings: What is this** offering that is similar to a peace offering but not included in the category of peace offerings? The Gemara answers: The reference is to **a firstborn**[B] offering, **which is eaten for two days and one night,** as is a peace offering. The Gemara raises a difficulty: **By what** hermeneutical principle **is** the *halakha* of the firstborn offering **derived? If** it is **by** the hermeneutical principle of: **What do we find** with regard to, a principle of inductive reasoning involving a comparison between cases that include similar details, i.e., since the peace offering and firstborn offering are similar with regard to the time designated for their eating, *piggul* status should apply to each, this **can be refuted.**

מַה לִּשְׁלָמִים, שֶׁהֵן טְעוּנִין סְמִיכָה, וּנְסָכִים, וּתְנוּפַת חָזֶה וְשׁוֹק!

The Gemara clarifies the refutation: **What** is notable **about peace offerings?** They are notable in **that they require placing hands** on the head of the offering, **libations, and waving**[B] **of the breast and thigh.** None of these apply in the case of a firstborn offering.

אֶלָּא: מֵ״אִם הֵאָכֹל יֵאָכֵל״

Rather, the *halakha* that *piggul* status applies to a firstborn offering is derived through the hermeneutical principle of a generalization and a detail and a generalization, **from** the following verse: **"And if any be at all eaten** of the flesh of the sacrifice of his peace offerings on the third day, it shall not be accepted" (Leviticus 7:18). The terms: "And if any" and "be at all eaten" are generalizations, while the words: "The flesh of the sacrifice of his peace offering" constitute a detail. According to the hermeneutical principle of a generalization and a detail and a generalization, in such a case one includes any item that is similar to the detail, and therefore one includes the firstborn offering.

הָנֵי תְּרֵי כְּלָלֵי דִּסְמִיכִי אַהֲדָדֵי נִינְהוּ! אָמַר רָבָא, כִּדְאָמְרִי בְּמַעְרְבָא: כָּל מָקוֹם שֶׁאַתָּה מוֹצֵא שְׁנֵי כְלָלוֹת הַסְּמוּכִים זֶה לָזֶה – הַטֵּל פְּרָט בֵּינֵיהֶם, וְדוּנֵם בִּכְלָל וּפְרָט.

The Gemara raises a difficulty: **These two** phrases **are generalizations that are adjacent to one another,** which means that this is not an instance of a generalization and a detail and a generalization, as they are not in that order. **Rava said:** The hermeneutical principle applies even in this case, **as they say in the West,** Eretz Yisrael: In **every place that you find two generalizations that are adjacent to one another, cast** the **detail** that is written afterward **between them, and interpret them in** the manner of **a generalization and a detail** and a generalization. Consequently, this verse is considered to state a generalization and a detail and a generalization.

BACKGROUND

Firstborn – בְּכוֹר: The male firstborn of cattle, sheep, or goats belonging to a Jew is consecrated from birth and must be given to a priest to be sacrificed on the altar in the Temple, with its meat eaten by the priests and their families (see Numbers 18:17–18). If a firstborn animal develops a physical blemish that disqualifies it from being sacrificed as an offering, it still is given to a priest, who may slaughter and eat it like any other non-sacred kosher animal.

Waving – תְּנוּפָה: A waving action is performed with peace offerings, thanks offerings, and the nazirite's ram. Following the slaughter of the animal and the sprinkling of its blood against the altar, its carcass is skinned, its fats, kidneys and tail are removed, and the breast and right hind leg are separated. These latter parts are grasped by the individual bringing the offering, and the officiating priest puts his hands beneath those of the owner. Together they wave the sacrificial parts in the four directions of the compass, and then up and down. In the case of a thanks offering, four bread loaves of different types are placed above the pile of animal parts before the waving commences. In two instances, a live animal is waved before it is slaughtered: The lambs sacrificed on *Shavuot* and the leper's guilt offering are both waved by the priest as an initial step in their sacrifice. Besides these animal offerings, there are several meal offerings that are also waved. The *omer* meal offering is brought on the sixteenth of Nisan and waved by the priest. The two loaves brought on *Shavuot* are waved. The meal offering of a *sota* is waved by a woman suspected of adultery. First fruits brought to the Temple by a farmer are also waved by him and the priest together. Finally, following the naziriteship term of a man or a woman, the right hind leg of the ram brought as a peace offering is waved by the nazirite, along with a wafer and a loaf of bread.

"עַד שֶׁאֲנִי מְרַבֶּה לוֹג שֶׁמֶן שֶׁל מְצוֹרָע". הָא מַנִּי? רַבִּי מֵאִיר הִיא. דְּתַנְיָא: לוֹג שֶׁמֶן שֶׁל מְצוֹרָע חַיָּיבִין עָלָיו מִשּׁוּם פִּיגּוּל, דִּבְרֵי רַבִּי מֵאִיר. אֵימָא סֵיפָא: וּמוֹצִיא אֲנִי מִנְחַת נְסָכִים וְהַדָּם – אֲתָאן לְרַבָּנַן,

§ The *baraita* teaches: **Until I include** even **the *log* of oil of a leper.** The Gemara asks: In accordance with **whose** opinion **is this** ruling? The Gemara answers that **it is** in accordance with the opinion of **Rabbi Meir, as it is taught** in a *baraita*: With regard to the ***log* of oil of the leper, one is liable for** consuming **it due to** violation of the prohibition of ***piggul***, if the guilt offering that this oil accompanied became *piggul*; this is **the statement of Rabbi Meir.** The Gemara raises a difficulty: **Say the latter clause: And I exclude the meal offering** brought with the **libations** that accompany animal offerings, **and the blood,** as they do not have a permitting factor. Here **we arrive at** the opinion of **the Rabbis,** who dispute the ruling of Rabbi Meir.

דְּתַנְיָא: נִסְכֵּי בְהֵמָה חַיָּיבִין עֲלֵיהֶן מִשּׁוּם פִּיגּוּל, מִפְּנֵי שֶׁדַּם הַזֶּבַח מַתִּירָן לִיקָּרֵב, דִּבְרֵי רַבִּי מֵאִיר. אָמְרוּ לוֹ: וַהֲלֹא אָדָם מֵבִיא אֶת זְבָחָיו הַיּוֹם וּנְסָכִין מִיכָּן עַד עֲשָׂרָה יָמִים! אָמַר לָהֶן: אַף אֲנִי לֹא אָמַרְתִּי אֶלָּא בַּבָּאִין עִם הַזֶּבַח!

The Gemara elaborates: **As it is taught** in another *baraita*: With regard to the **libations of an animal** offering, **one is liable for** consuming **them due to** violation of the prohibition of ***piggul***, as **the blood of the offering renders them permitted to be offered** on the altar; this is **the statement of Rabbi Meir.** The Rabbis **said to him: But a person** may **bring his offerings today**[H] **and** the accompanying **libations from now until** even **ten days** later. Evidently, then, the blood of the offering does not render the libations permitted. Rabbi Meir **said to them: I too spoke only about** libations that **come** to be sacrificed together **with the offering.** If so, the *baraita* under discussion represents two conflicting opinions.

אָמַר רַב יוֹסֵף: הָא מַנִּי – רַבִּי הִיא, דְּאָמַר: לוֹג שֶׁמֶן שֶׁל מְצוֹרָע מַתְּנוֹתָיו שָׁרוּ לֵיהּ, וּמִדְּמַתְּנוֹתָיו שָׁרוּ לֵיהּ – מַתְּנוֹתָיו מְפַגְּלֵי לֵיהּ.

Rav Yosef said: In accordance with **whose** opinion **is this** ruling, that even the *log* of oil of a leper is included in the prohibition of *piggul*? **It is** in accordance with the opinion of **Rabbi** Yehuda HaNasi, **who** agrees with the Rabbis that the libations of an animal offering are not permitted by the blood of the offering. And Rabbi Yehuda HaNasi **says** with regard to the ***log* of oil of a leper** that it is not the blood of the guilt offering that renders it permitted; rather, the **placements of its** oil "before the Lord" (Leviticus 14:16) **render** the remainder of the oil **permitted** to be eaten by the priests. **And from** the fact **that** the **placements of its** oil **render** the oil **permitted,** by the same token the **placements of its** oil **render it *piggul***, i.e., if the oil was placed with the intent that the priests should consume its remainder on the following day, one who consumes the oil is liable for consuming *piggul*.

דְּתַנְיָא: לוֹג שֶׁמֶן שֶׁל מְצוֹרָע – מוֹעֲלִין בּוֹ עַד שֶׁיִּזָּרוֹק הַדָּם, נִזְרַק הַדָּם – לֹא נֶהֱנִין וְלֹא מוֹעֲלִין.

The Gemara cites the source for Rabbi Yehuda HaNasi's opinion. **As it is taught** in a *baraita*: With regard to the ***log* of oil of a leper,** one who derives benefit **from it** is liable for **misusing** consecrated property[HB] if he derives benefit from it at any point after it has been consecrated in a service vessel, **until the blood** of the leper's guilt offering **is sprinkled.** At this stage the oil is permitted to the priests, and therefore the prohibition against misusing property consecrated to the Temple no longer applies to it. Once **the blood has been sprinkled, one may not derive benefit** from the oil *ab initio*, by rabbinic law, as it must still be placed on the leper's right ear, thumb, and big toe. **But** if one derived benefit from it, he is **not** liable for **misuse.**

רַבִּי אוֹמֵר: מוֹעֲלִין עַד שֶׁיִּתֵּן מַתְּנוֹתָיו. וְשָׁוִין, שֶׁאָסוּר בַּאֲכִילָה עַד שֶׁיִּתֵּן מַתַּן שֶׁבַע וּמַתַּן בְּהוֹנוֹת.

Rabbi Yehuda HaNasi **says:** One who derives benefit from the oil is liable for **misusing** consecrated property **until** the priest **places its own placements,**[N] i.e., until the oil is sprinkled seven times toward the Sanctuary, as these sprinklings render the remainder of the oil permitted to the priests. **And** the Rabbis and Rabbi Yehuda HaNasi **agree that consumption** of the *log* of oil is **prohibited**[NH] **until** the priest **places the seven placements,** i.e., sprinklings, of oil toward the Sanctuary, **and** performs the **placing** of the oil **on the** leper's **thumb and big toe.**[B]

אָמְרוּהָ קַמֵּיהּ דְּרַבִּי יִרְמְיָה, אֲמַר: גַּבְרָא רַבָּא כְּרַב יוֹסֵף לֵימָא כִּי הָא מִילְּתָא?

They said this statement **before Rabbi Yirmeya** in Eretz Yisrael, whereupon **he said:** Would **a great man such as Rav Yosef say such a matter,** that the sprinkling of the oil renders the rest of the oil *piggul*?

HALAKHA

A person may bring his offerings today, etc. – אָדָם מֵבִיא אֶת זְבָחָיו הַיּוֹם וכו׳: One may bring the guilt offering of a leper on one day and the *log* of oil even many days later, in accordance with the opinion of the Rabbis (Rambam *Sefer Korbanot*, *Hilkhot Meḥusrei Kappara* 5:4).

Liable for misusing consecrated property – מוֹעֲלִין בּוֹ: If one derives benefit from the leper's *log* of oil between the time it is consecrated in a service vessel and when the blood of the guilt offering is sprinkled, he has misused consecrated property. Once the blood has been sprinkled, one may not derive benefit from the oil *ab initio*, but if he did so, he is not liable for misuse. When the oil has been placed on the leper's right ear, thumb, and big toe, the remainder is permitted to the priests like the meat of a sin offering and a guilt offering, in accordance with the opinion of the Rabbis (Rambam *Sefer Avoda*, *Hilkhot Me'ila* 2:10).

And they agree that consumption of the oil is prohibited – וְשָׁוִין שֶׁאָסוּר בַּאֲכִילָה: One may not consume the *log* of oil employed in the purification rites of the leper until after it has been sprinkled seven times and placed on the leper's right ear, thumb, and big toe. One who consumes the oil before this stage is flogged, like one who eats sacrificial meat before the sprinkling of the blood, as stated in the *baraita* (Rambam *Sefer Korbanot*, *Hilkhot Meḥusrei Kappara* 4:3).

BACKGROUND

Misuse of consecrated property – מְעִילָה: The *halakhot* of misuse of consecrated property are stated in the Torah (Leviticus 5:14–16) and discussed in great detail in tractate *Me'ila*. The basic principle is that anyone who derives benefit from consecrated property unwittingly, i.e., without the knowledge that it was consecrated property, is obligated to bring an offering and to pay to the Temple the value of the item from which he benefited. Furthermore, he must pay an extra one-fifth of the value as a fine. After one uses such an item it loses its consecrated status, which is transferred to the money that he pays to the Temple. The Torah does not discuss the case of an individual who derives benefit from consecrated items intentionally. Therefore, such a person cannot atone for his act by bringing an offering or by paying the additional one-fifth of the value as a fine.

Thumb and big toe – בְּהוֹנוֹת: The purification process for lepers is detailed in the Torah (see Leviticus, chapter 14). This ritual includes the requirement that a priest apply oil that has been sanctified for this purpose, as well as blood from the guilt offering, upon the leper's right earlobe, right big toe, and right thumb.

NOTES

One is liable for misusing consecrated property until the priest places its placements – מוֹעֲלִין עַד שֶׁיִּתֵּן מַתְּנוֹתָיו: Rabbi Yehuda HaNasi maintains that the placements of the oil, not the blood of the guilt offering, render the remainder of the oil permitted. Rashi notes that Rabbi Yehuda HaNasi is referring only to the sprinkling of the oil toward the Sanctuary, although others understand this to be the sprinkling on the Curtain (see *Keneset HaRishonim*). Either way, he agrees that the placing of oil on the leper's thumb and big toe is not indispensable, and therefore this action does not affect the status of the oil with regard to misuse of consecrated property.

That consumption of the oil is prohibited – שֶׁאָסוּר בַּאֲכִילָה: By rabbinic law, the priests may not derive benefit from the oil until the entire service has been completed, including the placing of the oil on the leper's right ear, thumb, and big toe (Rashi). Some commentaries maintain that although consuming the oil before this time it is not considered misuse of consecrated property, a priest who does so has violated a Torah prohibition against the consumption of consecrated foods, even according to the opinion of the Rabbis. Therefore, he is punished with a flogging, like one who eats the meat of sacrificial food before the presentation of the blood (Rambam).

NOTES

To include the *log* of oil – לְרַבּוֹת לוֹג שֶׁמֶן: Rashi notes that this *log* of oil is called an offering, as it is stated: "And the priest shall take one of the lambs, and offer it for a guilt offering, and the *log* of oil" (Leviticus 14:12).

הֲרֵי לוֹג [הַבָּא] בִּפְנֵי עַצְמוֹ, דִּלְכוּלֵּי עָלְמָא מַתְּנוֹתָיו שָׁרוּ לֵיהּ – וְלָא מְפַגְּלִין לֵיהּ! דְּתַנְיָא: לוֹג שֶׁמֶן שֶׁל מְצוֹרָע – חַיָּיבִין עָלָיו מִשּׁוּם פִּיגּוּל, מִפְּנֵי שֶׁדָּם מַתִּירוֹ לִבְהוֹנוֹת, דִּבְרֵי רַבִּי מֵאִיר.

But there is the case of the *log* **of oil that is brought by itself,** i.e., where the leper brings it after he has sacrificed his offerings. There **everyone** agrees that **its placements render** the remainder of the oil **permitted to** the priests, **and** yet **they do not render** the oil *piggul*, **as it is taught** in a *baraita*: With regard to the *log* **of oil of a leper, one is liable for** consuming **it due to** violation of the prohibition of *piggul*, **as the blood** of the offering **renders it permitted to** be placed on **the thumb and big toe** of the leper. This is **the statement of Rabbi Meir.**

אָמְרוּ לוֹ לְרַבִּי מֵאִיר: וַהֲלֹא אָדָם מֵבִיא אֲשָׁמוֹ עַכְשָׁיו, וְלוֹג מִיכָּן וְעַד עֲשָׂרָה יָמִים! אָמַר לָהֶן: אַף אֲנִי לֹא אָמַרְתִּי אֶלָּא בַּבָּא עִם הָאָשָׁם.

The Rabbis **said to Rabbi Meir: But a person** may **bring his guilt offering today**[H] **and** the accompanying *log* of oil **from now until** even **ten days** later. Rabbi Meir **said to them: I too spoke only about** a *log* of oil that **comes with the guilt offering.** This indicates that even according to the opinion of Rabbi Meir, it is the blood of the offering that renders the oil *piggul*.

אֶלָּא אָמַר רַבִּי יִרְמְיָה: לְעוֹלָם רַבִּי מֵאִיר הִיא, וּסְמֵי מִיכָּן נְסָכִים. אָמַר אַבַּיֵּי: לְעוֹלָם לָא תִּסְמֵי, וְתָנָא לוֹג הַבָּא עִם הָאָשָׁם, וְהוּא הַדִּין לִנְסָכִים הַבָּאִין עִם הַזֶּבַח. וַהֲדַר תָּנָא נְסָכִים הַבָּאִין בִּפְנֵי עַצְמָן, וְהוּא הַדִּין לְלוֹג הַבָּא לִפְנֵי עַצְמוֹ.

Rather, Rabbi Yirmeya says: Actually, the aforementioned *baraita* **is** in accordance with the opinion of **Rabbi Meir, and omit** the case of the meal offering brought with the **libations** that accompany animal offerings **from** the list of items that are not subject to the *halakha* of *piggul*. **Abaye says: Actually, do not omit** this item from the list, and the *baraita* can be explained in accordance with the opinion of Rabbi Meir as follows: The *tanna* first **taught** the *halakha* with regard to the *log* of oil **that comes with the** leper's **guilt offering, and the same is true of libations that come with** an animal **offering,** as according to Rabbi Meir *piggul* status applies to both of these. **And then** the *tanna* **taught** that *piggul* does not apply to **libations that come by themselves, and the same is true of a** *log* of oil **that comes by itself.**

״חַטַּאת הָעוֹף – דָּמָהּ מַתִּיר אֶת בְּשָׂרָהּ לַכֹּהֲנִים״. מְנָא הָנֵי מִילֵּי? דְּתָנֵי לֵוִי.

§ The mishna teaches: With regard to **the bird burnt offering, its blood renders its meat** and its skin **permitted to** be eaten by **the priests.** The Gemara asks: **From where is this matter,** that the meat of a bird burnt offering is eaten by the priests, derived? The Gemara cites a *baraita* **that Levi teaches,** with regard to a verse that discusses the gifts that are to be presented to the priests: "This shall be yours of the most sacred items, from the fire: Every offering of theirs, every meal offering of theirs, and every sin offering of theirs, and every guilt offering of theirs, which they shall render to Me, shall be most sacred for you and for your sons" (Numbers 18:9).

״כׇּל קׇרְבָּנָם״ – לְרַבּוֹת לוֹג שֶׁמֶן שֶׁל מְצוֹרָע. סָלְקָא דַּעְתָּךְ אָמִינָא: ״מִן הָאֵשׁ״ כְּתַב רַחֲמָנָא, וְהַאי לָאו מוֹתָר מִן הָאֵשׁ הוּא – קָא מַשְׁמַע לָן.

The *baraita* clarifies what is included by the term "every" in each of these clauses. The verse states: **"Every offering of theirs,"** which serves **to include** the *log* **of oil**[N] **of a leper;**[H] it too is given to the priests. The Gemara explains why it is necessary to derive from the verse that the oil is a gift to the priesthood: It might **enter your mind to say** that the oil should not be included, as **the Merciful One writes** in this same verse: **"From the fire," and this** *log* of oil, notwithstanding its status as an offering, **is not reserved from the fire.** Only an item concerning which part of it is brought to the altar can be said to be reserved from the fire, and none of the oil is brought to the altar. Therefore, the verse **teaches us** by the phrase: "Every offering of theirs," that the oil goes to the priests.

HALAKHA

A person may bring his guilt offering today, etc. – אָדָם מֵבִיא אֲשָׁמוֹ עַכְשָׁיו וכו׳: The *log* of oil employed in the purification rites of the leper is not dependent upon the blood of the guilt offering, as it is permitted to bring one's guilt offering today and the *log* of oil several days later. Consequently, *piggul* status does not apply to the *log* of oil, in accordance with the opinion of the Rabbis (Rambam *Sefer Avoda, Hilkhot Pesulei HaMukdashin* 18:8).

To include the *log* of oil of a leper – לְרַבּוֹת לוֹג שֶׁמֶן שֶׁל מְצוֹרָע: After the priest has sprinkled from the *log* of oil and placed some of the oil on the leper's right ear, thumb, and big toe, the remainder of the oil is distributed between the priests and is eaten by priests (Rambam *Sefer Korbanot, Hilkhot Meḥusrei Kappara* 4:2–3).

״לְכָל מִנְחָתָם״ – לְרַבּוֹת מִנְחַת עוֹמֶר וּמִנְחַת הַקְּנָאוֹת. סָלְקָא דַּעְתָּךְ אָמִינָא: ״וְאָכְלוּ אוֹתָם אֲשֶׁר כֻּפַּר בָּהֶם״, וּמִנְחַת הָעוֹמֶר – לְהַתִּיר אָתְיָא, וּמִנְחַת קְנָאוֹת – לְבָרֵר עָוֹן קָאָתְיָא, קָא מַשְׁמַע לַן.

The phrase: **"Every meal offering of theirs,"** serves **to include** the ***omer***[B] **meal offering,**[H] brought as a communal offering on the sixteenth of Nisan, **and the meal offering of jealousy,**[HB] brought by a *sota*. The Gemara elaborates: It might **enter your mind to say** that as the verse states with regard to the consumption of sacrificial food by the priests: **"And they shall eat those items with which atonement is achieved"** (Exodus 29:33),[N] only those foods that facilitate atonement are given to the priests. **And** this would exclude the *omer* meal offering and the meal offering of jealousy, as **the *omer* meal offering comes to permit** the consumption of the new crop, **and the meal offering of jealousy comes to clarify** the **transgression** of the *sota*, as part of the ordeal undergone by the woman. Therefore, the verse **teaches us** by the phrase: "Every meal offering of theirs," that even these meal offerings are eaten by the priests.

״וּלְכָל חַטָּאתָם״ – לְרַבּוֹת חַטַּאת הָעוֹף. סָלְקָא דַּעְתָּךְ אָמִינָא: נְבֵילָה הִיא.

The phrase: **"And every sin offering of theirs,"** serves **to include the bird sin offering;**[H] its meat too is given to the priests. The Gemara explains: It might **enter your mind to say** that this meat should not be eaten at all, as **it is** an unslaughtered **animal carcass,**[B] since the bird is killed by pinching its nape (see Leviticus 5:8) rather than by slaughtering, which is the manner of ritual slaughter of non-sacred birds. Therefore, the phrase: "And every sin offering of theirs," teaches that the bird sin offering is eaten by the priests.

״לְכָל אֲשָׁמָם״ – לְרַבּוֹת אֲשַׁם נָזִיר וַאֲשַׁם מְצוֹרָע. סָלְקָא דַּעְתָּךְ אָמִינָא: לְהַכְשִׁיר קָאָתוּ, קָא מַשְׁמַע לַן.

The phrase: **"Every guilt offering of theirs,"** serves **to include the guilt offering of a nazirite**[HB] who contracted ritual impurity, **and the guilt offering of a leper.**[HB] The Gemara elaborates: It might **enter your mind to say** that these should not be given to the priests to eat, as **they come to qualify** these individuals, rather than to atone. The guilt offering of a nazirite renders him fit to restart his term of naziriteship, and the guilt offering of a leper qualifies him to eat sacrificial food, whereas the verse states: "And they shall eat those items with which atonement is achieved" (Exodus 29:33). Therefore, the verse **teaches us** by the phrase: "Every guilt offering of theirs," that these offerings as well are eaten by the priests.

אֲשַׁם מְצוֹרָע בְּהֶדְיָא כְּתִיב בֵּיהּ! אֶלָּא: לְרַבּוֹת אֲשַׁם נָזִיר כַּאֲשַׁם מְצוֹרָע.

The Gemara challenges: **It is explicitly written with regard to the guilt offering of a leper** that it is consumed by the priests: "For as the sin offering is the priest's, so is the guilt offering" (Leviticus 14:13). Why, then, is this derivation necessary? **Rather,** the *baraita* means to say that the phrase: "Every guilt offering of theirs," serves **to include the guilt offering of a nazirite,** teaching that it is **like the guilt offering of a leper,** in that both are eaten by the priests.

HALAKHA

To include the *omer* meal offering – לְרַבּוֹת מִנְחַת הָעוֹמֶר: The priest takes a handful from the *omer* meal offering and burns it on the altar. The rest is eaten by the priests, like the remainders of other meal offering (Rambam *Sefer Avoda, Hilkhot Temidin UMusafin* 7:12).

To include…the meal offering of jealousy – לְרַבּוֹת…מִנְחַת הַקְּנָאוֹת: After the *sota* drinks from the waters, she and the priest bring her meal offering. The priest takes a handful from the meal offering and burns it on the altar. The remainder of the meal offering is eaten by the priests (Rambam *Sefer Nashim, Hilkhot Sota* 3:15).

To include the bird sin offering – לְרַבּוֹת חַטַּאת הָעוֹף: After the priest drains out the blood of the bird sin offering, the rest of the sin offering is eaten by priests, like all other sin offerings (Rambam *Sefer Avoda, Hilkhot Ma'aseh HaKorbanot* 7:7).

To include the guilt offering of a nazirite – לְרַבּוֹת אֲשַׁם נָזִיר: With regard to all guilt offerings, after their blood has been presented and their portions burned, their meat is eaten by priests in the Temple courtyard (Rambam *Sefer Avoda, Hilkhot Ma'aseh HaKorbanot* 9:1).

To include…the guilt offering of a leper – לְרַבּוֹת…אֲשַׁם מְצוֹרָע: Although the sprinkling of the blood of the guilt offering of a leper differs from other guilt offerings, the rest of its service is performed like them, and its meat is eaten by the priests (Rambam *Sefer Avoda, Hilkhot Ma'aseh HaKorbanot* 9:2).

NOTES

With which atonement is achieved – אֲשֶׁר כֻּפַּר בָּהֶם: The Sages derived from this verse that the remainder of offerings is not merely a gift to the priests, but their consumption of these remainders actually constitutes part of the sacrificial rites, through which the owners of the offerings achieve atonement (see *Yoma* 68b). This is alluded to in the statement of Moses to Aaron: "Why have you not eaten the sin offering in the place of the Sanctuary, seeing it is most sacred, and He has given it you to bear the iniquity of the congregation, to make atonement for them before the Lord"? (Leviticus 10:17). Consequently, it is reasonable to suggest that an offering that does not come to facilitate atonement should not be eaten by the priests.

BACKGROUND

Omer – עוֹמֶר: Technically, an *omer* is a measure of grain, one-tenth of an ephah. The term is also used to refer to the measure of barley sacrificed in the Temple on the sixteenth of Nisan, the second day of Passover. The offering was brought irrespective of whether the sixteenth of Nisan was a Shabbat or a weekday. The *omer* consisted of newly ripe barley that was prepared as roasted flour. The barley was harvested on the night following the first day of Passover. A handful of the flour was burned on the altar while the rest was eaten by the priests. In addition to the flour offering, a male sheep was sacrificed as a burnt offering, together with a wine libation and two-tenths of an ephah of wheat flour as a meal offering. Once the *omer* had been sacrificed, grain from the new harvest could be eaten.

Meal offering of jealousy – מִנְחַת הַקְּנָאוֹת: This is a meal offering brought by a suspected adulteress (see Numbers 5:11–31). This woman, whose husband brings her to the Temple to undergo the biblical procedure to test her faithfulness to him, is required to bring a meal offering of barley flour. This is unlike most meal offerings, which are brought from wheat flour. Another difference from most meal offerings is that no oil or incense is added to it (see Numbers 5:15). A handful of flour is removed from this offering and burned on the altar, and the remainder of it is eaten by the priests (see Numbers 5:25–26).

Unslaughtered animal carcass – נְבֵילָה: Although *neveila* is translated as an animal carcass, not all animal carcasses are included in this halakhic category. Specifically, it refers to the carcasses of large mammals, whether or not they are kosher animals. Among kosher animals this includes an animal that died of natural causes or as a result of an improperly performed act of ritual slaughter. It is prohibited to eat an unslaughtered animal, and that animal is a primary source of ritual impurity. Although an unslaughtered kosher animal may not be eaten, one may derive benefit from it. Certain types of severe anatomical defects place an animal in this category even while alive, e.g., a completely broken neck.

Guilt offering of a nazirite – אֲשַׁם נָזִיר: If a nazirite becomes ritually impure by contact with a corpse, whether intentionally or not, he must first purify himself and then bring two pigeons to the Temple, one for a sin offering and the other for a burnt offering, as well as a lamb as a guilt offering. After this, he must start his term as of naziriteship afresh.

Guilt offering of a leper – אֲשַׁם מְצוֹרָע: An individual suffering from leprosy is ritually impure and sent of out of the camp or the city until he is cured of his condition. Once cured, he undergoes a special ceremony involving two birds and then waits seven days for purification. On the eighth day, he brings a female lamb for a sin offering, a male lamb for a burnt offering, and a second male lamb for a guilt offering. He also brings a meal offering. The blood of the guilt offering is used in a purification ritual: Blood from the animal and oil that the leper brings are dabbed on parts of his body.

NOTES

Item stolen from a convert – גֶּזֶל הַגֵּר: With regard to one who robs another and takes a false oath that he did not rob him, when he confesses his transgression he must bring a guilt offering and return the stolen item plus an additional one-fifth of its value (see Leviticus 5:20–26). If the robbery victim already died, he must give the stolen item and the one-fifth to his heirs. In Numbers 5:7 the Torah states that if the owner of the stolen item does not have an heir, the principal and the one-fifth are given to a priest. The Sages explain that this is referring to a convert, as there is no born Jew who does not have an heir, however distant.

With regard to a matter that is performed inside – בְּדָבָר הַנַּעֲשֶׂה בִּפְנִים: The first *tanna* of the mishna maintains that in the case of the bulls and goats that are burned, their blood renders their portions permitted to be sacrificed on the external altar, and therefore this service can render the offering *piggul*. Rabbi Shimon contends that *piggul* does not apply, as their blood is not presented on the external altar in the manner of peace offerings. The ruling of Rabbi Yosei HaGelili is somewhat of a compromise between these two opinions. He agrees with Rabbi Shimon that the *halakha* of *piggul* does not apply inside the Sanctuary, but he disputes his ruling that *piggul* does not apply to these offerings at all. Rabbi Yosei HaGelili's reasoning is that although their blood is presented inside, part of the service of these offerings is performed outside, and therefore he distinguishes between those acts that are performed inside the Sanctuary and those that are performed outside, in the Temple courtyard.

״אֲשֶׁר יָשִׁיבוּ״ – זֶה גֶּזֶל הַגֵּר, ״לְךָ הוּא״ – שֶׁלְּךָ יִהְיֶה, אֲפִילּוּ לְקַדֵּשׁ בּוֹ אֶת הָאִשָּׁה.

The *baraita* continues: With regard to the phrase **"which they shall render** to Me," **this is** referring to an item **stolen** from **a convert.**[NH] One who robs a convert who then dies with no heirs must give the stolen item and an additional one-fifth to the priests. Finally, the term **"for you"** teaches that **it shall be yours, even to betroth a woman with it,** i.e., these gifts are considered the priest's property in all regards.

תַּנְיָא, רַבִּי אֶלְעָזָר אוֹמֵר מִשּׁוּם רַבִּי יוֹסֵי הַגְּלִילִי: פִּיגֵּל בְּדָבָר הַנַּעֲשֶׂה בַּחוּץ – פִּיגֵּל, בְּדָבָר הַנַּעֲשֶׂה בִּפְנִים – לֹא פִּיגֵּל.

§ According to the first *tanna* of the mishna, the bulls that are burned and the goats that are burned, the blood of which is presented on the inner altar, are subject to *piggul*, whereas Rabbi Shimon rules that they are not subject to *piggul*. **It is taught** in a *baraita* that there is a third opinion concerning the matter: **Rabbi Elazar says in the name of Rabbi Yosei HaGelili:** If in his service of the bulls that are burned or the goats that are burned the priest had an intention that can **render** the offering ***piggul* with regard to a matter that is performed outside**[H] the Sanctuary, i.e., in the Temple courtyard, **he has rendered** the offering ***piggul***. If his intention was **with regard to a matter that is performed inside**[N] the Sanctuary or the Holy of Holies, **he has not rendered** the offering ***piggul***.

כֵּיצַד? הָיָה עוֹמֵד בַּחוּץ, וְאָמַר: ״הֲרֵינִי שׁוֹחֵט לְהַזּוֹת מִדָּמוֹ לְמָחָר״ – לֹא פִּיגֵּל, שֶׁמַּחְשָׁבָה בַּחוּץ בְּדָבָר הַנַּעֲשֶׂה בִּפְנִים לֹא פִּיגֵּל. הָיָה עוֹמֵד בִּפְנִים, וְאָמַר: ״הֲרֵינִי מַזֶּה עַל מְנָת לְהַקְטִיר אֵימוּרִים וְלִשְׁפּוֹךְ שִׁירַיִם לְמָחָר״ – לֹא פִּיגֵּל, שֶׁמַּחְשָׁבָה בִּפְנִים בְּדָבָר הַנַּעֲשֶׂה בַּחוּץ.

The *baraita* elaborates: **How so? If he was standing outside** when slaughtering the animal, **and said: I hereby slaughter** the animal with the intention of **sprinkling its blood tomorrow** inside the Sanctuary, **he has not rendered** the offering ***piggul***. The reason is **that** in the case of **an intention outside with regard to a matter that is performed inside, one has not rendered** the offering ***piggul***. Likewise, if **he was standing inside** when sprinkling, **and said: I hereby sprinkle** the blood of the sin offering **in order to burn** its **sacrificial portions** on the external altar **and to pour out** its **remainder** on the base of the altar **tomorrow, he has not rendered** the offering ***piggul***, as this is **an intention inside with regard to a matter that is performed outside.**

אֲבָל הָיָה עוֹמֵד בַּחוּץ, וְאָמַר: ״הֲרֵינִי שׁוֹחֵט לִשְׁפּוֹךְ שִׁירַיִם לְמָחָר״ אוֹ: ״לְהַקְטִיר אֵימוּרִים לְמָחָר״ – פִּיגֵּל, שֶׁמַּחְשָׁבָה בַּחוּץ בְּדָבָר הַנַּעֲשֶׂה בַּחוּץ.

But if **he was standing outside, and said: I hereby slaughter** the animal with the intention of **pouring out** the **remainder** of its blood **tomorrow, or to burn** its **sacrificial portions tomorrow, he has rendered** the offering ***piggul***, as this is **an intention outside with regard to a matter that is performed outside.**

אָמַר רַבִּי יְהוֹשֻׁעַ בֶּן לֵוִי: מַאי קְרָא? ״כַּאֲשֶׁר יוּרַם מִשּׁוֹר זֶבַח הַשְּׁלָמִים״, וְכִי מָה לָמַדְנוּ מִשּׁוֹר זֶבַח הַשְּׁלָמִים מֵעַתָּה?

Rabbi Yehoshua ben Levi says: What is the verse from which this is derived? The verse states with regard to the sacrificial portions of a bull for an unwitting sin of the anointed priest, which is one of the bulls that are burned: **"As it is taken off from the bull of the peace offering"** (Leviticus 4:10). **But what, then, do we learn from the bull of a peace offering?** Everything that is specified with regard to a peace offering is stated with regard to this bull as well.

HALAKHA

Stolen from a convert – גֶּזֶל הַגֵּר: If someone robbed a convert and took a false oath that he did not rob him, and the convert died without leaving any heirs, the robber must pay the principal and the one-fifth to the priests of the priestly watch serving when he brings his guilt offering. The sum that he pays is non-sacred in all regards (Rambam *Sefer Nezikin, Hilkhot Gezeila VaAveda* 8:5 and *Sefer Zera'im, Hilkhot Bikkurim* 1:7).

An intention that can render the offering *piggul* with regard to a matter that is performed outside – פִּיגֵּל בְּדָבָר הַנַּעֲשֶׂה בַּחוּץ: If a priest performing the service of those offerings brought inside the Sanctuary was in the courtyard and intended to perform a service inside beyond its designated time, the offering is not *piggul*. If his intention was concerning a service performed outside, it is *piggul*. How so? If during the slaughter of the animal he said: I am hereby slaughtering in order to sprinkle its blood tomorrow, it is not *piggul*, as its sprinkling is performed inside. Likewise, if he was standing inside the Sanctuary and said: I am hereby sprinkling its blood in order to sacrifice its portions tomorrow, it is not *piggul*, as his intent occurred during the performance of a service inside. If in the slaughter of the animal outside he intended to pour the remainder or burn its portions on the following day, the offering is *piggul*, as he had an improper intent with regard to a service outside during the performance of a service outside. The *halakha* is in accordance with the opinion of Rabbi Elazar citing Rabbi Yosei, following the ruling of Rav (Rambam *Sefer Avoda, Hilkhot Pesulei HaMukdashin* 17:4–6; see 17:2).

אֶלָּא: מַקִּישׁ פַּר כֹּהֵן מָשִׁיחַ לְשׁוֹר זֶבַח הַשְּׁלָמִים, מָה שׁוֹר זֶבַח הַשְּׁלָמִים – עַד שֶׁיְּהוּ מַעֲשָׂיו וּמַחְשְׁבוֹתָיו עַל מִזְבֵּחַ הַחִיצוֹן, אַף פַּר כֹּהֵן מָשִׁיחַ – עַד שֶׁיְּהוּ מַחְשְׁבוֹתָיו וּמַעֲשָׂיו עַל הַמִּזְבֵּחַ הַחִיצוֹן.

Rather, the verse **juxtaposes the bull** for an unwitting sin **of the anointed priest with the bull of the peace offering: Just as the bull of the peace offering** is not rendered *piggul* **unless** the priest's **actions and intentions** relate to the service performed **on the external altar,** as that is where it is offered, **so too, the bull** for an unwitting sin **of the anointed priest** is not rendered *piggul* **unless** the priest's **intentions and actions** relate to the service performed **on the external altar.**

אָמַר רַב נַחְמָן אָמַר רַבָּה בַּר אֲבוּהּ אָמַר רַב: הֲלָכָה כְּרַבִּי אֶלְעָזָר שֶׁאָמַר מִשּׁוּם רַבִּי יוֹסֵי.

Rav Naḥman says that **Rabba bar Avuh says** that **Rav says:** The *halakha* **is in accordance with** the opinion of **Rabbi Elazar, who says** his ruling **in the name of Rabbi Yosei.**

אֲמַר רָבָא:

Rava said:

Perek **IV**
Daf **45** Amud **a**

הִלְכְתָא לִמְשִׁיחָא? אֲמַר לֵיהּ אַבָּיֵי: אֶלָּא מֵעַתָּה, כָּל שְׁחִיטַת קָדָשִׁים לָא לִתְנֵי, הִלְכְתָא לִמְשִׁיחָא הוּא! אֶלָּא: דְּרוֹשׁ וְקַבֵּל שָׂכָר – הָכָא נַמִי דְּרוֹשׁ וְקַבֵּל שָׂכָר! הָכִי קָאָמִינָא לָךְ: הִלְכְתָא לָמָּה לִי? לִישָּׁנָא אַחֲרִינָא, אֲמַר לֵיהּ: הֲלָכָה קָאָמִינָא.

Does one issue **a *halakha* for the messianic** period, when the Temple will be rebuilt? **Abaye said to him: If that is so,** that such *halakhot* are not taught, **let** the *tanna* **not teach all** the *halakhot* of **the slaughter of sacrificial** animals, i.e., tractate *Zevaḥim*, as **it is** entirely **a *halakha* for the messianic** period. **Rather,** one studies these *halakhot* due to the principle of: **Study** Torah **and receive reward,** i.e., one is rewarded for the study of Torah regardless of its practical applicability. **Here too, study** Torah **and receive reward.** Rava said to him: **This is** what **I am saying to you: Why do I** need a practical ruling of ***halakha***? According to **another version,** which presents the same answer in different terms, Rava **said to him: I spoke** in reference to the ruling of ***halakha***, as it is puzzling that a halakhic ruling is given in this case.

מתני׳ קָדְשֵׁי גוֹיִם – אֵין חַיָּיבִין עֲלֵיהֶם מִשּׁוּם פִּיגּוּל נוֹתָר וְטָמֵא, וְהַשּׁוֹחֲטָן בַּחוּץ – פָּטוּר, דִּבְרֵי רַבִּי שִׁמְעוֹן, רַבִּי יוֹסֵי מְחַיֵּיב.

MISHNA With regard to **offerings** consecrated by **gentiles**[NH] for sacrifice to God, **one is not liable for** eating **them,** neither **due to** violation of the prohibition of ***piggul*** if the sacrificial rites were performed with the intent to eat the offering beyond its designated time, nor due to violation of the prohibition of ***notar,* nor** due to violation of the prohibition against eating the meat while **ritually impure. And one who slaughters them outside**[H] the Temple courtyard is **exempt;**[N] this is **the statement of Rabbi Shimon. And Rabbi Yosei deems** him **liable.**

גמ׳ תָּנוּ רַבָּנַן: קָדְשֵׁי גוֹיִם – לֹא נֶהֱנִין וְלֹא מוֹעֲלִין, וְאֵין חַיָּיבִין עֲלֵיהֶן מִשּׁוּם פִּיגּוּל נוֹתָר וְטָמֵא.

GEMARA The Sages taught in a *baraita*: With regard **to offerings** consecrated by **gentiles,** one **may not derive benefit** from them *ab initio*, **but** if one derived benefit from them, he is **not** liable after the fact for **misusing**[H] consecrated property. **And one is not liable for** eating **them,** neither **due to** violation of the prohibition of ***piggul*** if the sacrificial rites were performed with the intent to eat the offering beyond its designated time, nor due to violation of the prohibition of ***notar,* nor** due to violation of the prohibition against eating the meat while **ritually impure.**

NOTES

Offerings consecrated by gentiles – קָדְשֵׁי גוֹיִם: Although gentiles are not commanded to sacrifice offerings, and one may not accept from them any obligatory offerings, they may bring gift offerings, which are sacrificed in the Temple. In the Gemara in *Menaḥot* 73b, the Sages discuss whether only their burnt offerings are accepted, or if even their peace offerings are accepted.

One who slaughters them outside the Temple courtyard is exempt – הַשּׁוֹחֲטָן בַּחוּץ פָּטוּר: The Gemara does not provide a source for this *halakha*. In the *Sifrei* on Deuteronomy (12:13), Rabbi Shimon infers this ruling from the verse: "Take heed to yourself that you do not sacrifice your burnt offerings in every place that you see" (Deuteronomy 12:13), which indicates that this prohibition applies only to "your burnt offerings," but not those of gentiles. This is probably the source for the Rambam's ruling that the same exemption applies to the prohibition against burning the sacrificial portions of offerings outside the Temple.

Other commentaries cite different proof texts for this *halakha*. Some quote another verse that discusses the prohibition against slaughtering consecrated animals outside the Temple: "To the end that the children of Israel shall bring their offerings, which they sacrifice in the open field, even that they shall bring them to the Lord" (Leviticus 17:5). Again, this verse indicates that the prohibition applies only to offerings of the children of Israel, not those of gentiles (*Tosefot Yom Tov*). Alternatively, just as the prohibition not to sacrifice outside the Temple was given to Jews, not gentiles, likewise the prohibition against slaughtering outside does not apply to their offerings (*Shita Mekubbetzet*, citing Rabbeinu Peretz).

HALAKHA

Offerings consecrated by gentiles – קָדְשֵׁי גוֹיִם: With regard to the consecrations of gentiles, one is not liable for consuming *piggul* or *notar*, or for eating an offering in a state of ritual impurity. The *halakha* is in accordance with the opinion of Rabbi Shimon, as the discussion in the Gemara in tractate *Temura* (2b–3a) is in accordance with his opinion (*Kesef Mishne*; *Leḥem Mishne*). Some commentaries say that the dispute between Rabbi Shimon and Rabbi Yosei applies only to the last *halakha*, with regard to one who slaughters offerings outside the Sanctuary (Mahari Kurkus). If so, the rulings concerning *piggul*, *notar*, and eating in a state of ritual impurity are in accordance with the unattributed opinion in the mishna (Rambam *Sefer Avoda, Hilkhot Pesulei HaMukdashin* 18:24).

One who slaughters them outside – הַשּׁוֹחֲטָן בַּחוּץ: One who slaughters offerings of gentiles outside their designated area is liable, in accordance with the opinion of Rabbi Yosei (Rambam *Sefer Avoda, Hilkhot Ma'aseh HaKorbanot* 19:16).

One may not derive benefit but he is not liable for misusing – לֹא נֶהֱנִין וְלֹא מוֹעֲלִין: With regard to items consecrated by gentiles, if they were consecrated for Temple maintenance, one who derives benefit from them is liable for misuse of consecrated property. If they were consecrated for the altar, by Torah law the prohibition of misuse does not apply to them (Rambam *Sefer Avoda, Hilkhot Me'ila* 5:15).

וְאֵין עוֹשִׂין תְּמוּרָה, וְאֵין מְבִיאִין נְסָכִים, אֲבָל קׇרְבְּנָן טָעוּן נְסָכִים, דִּבְרֵי רַבִּי שִׁמְעוֹן.

And gentiles **cannot render** an animal **a substitute,**[H] i.e., if a gentile stated with regard to an animal that it should be the substitute of a consecrated animal, the substitution does not take effect. **And** gentiles **cannot bring libations**[HN] that are brought by themselves as a separate offering and do not accompany an animal offering, **but their** animal **offerings require libations.** This is **the statement of Rabbi Shimon.**

אָמַר רַבִּי יוֹסֵי: רוֹאֶה אֲנִי בְּכוּלָּן לְהַחְמִיר, שֶׁנֶּאֱמַר בָּהֶן: ״לַה׳״. בַּמֶּה דְּבָרִים אֲמוּרִים – בְּקׇדְשֵׁי מִזְבֵּחַ, אֲבָל בְּקׇדְשֵׁי בֶּדֶק הַבַּיִת – מוֹעֲלִין בָּהֶן.

Rabbi Yosei says: I see the logic of the opinion that **in all of** these cases it is correct **to be stringent** about the offerings of gentiles, **as it is stated with regard to them:** "Any man of the house of Israel, or of the strangers in Israel that will sacrifice his offering… **to the Lord**" (Leviticus 22:18). This indicates that all offerings, even those of gentiles, are fully consecrated to God; therefore, the *halakhot* of misuse, *piggul, notar,* and eating the meat while ritually impure should all apply to the offerings of gentiles. **In what** case **is this statement said?**[N] In the case of items **consecrated for the altar. But** with regard to items that are **consecrated** by gentiles **for Temple maintenance,**[B] one who derives benefit from them is liable for **misusing them.** This concludes the *baraita.*

״לֹא נֶהֱנִין וְלֹא מוֹעֲלִין״. לֹא נֶהֱנִין – מִדְּרַבָּנַן,

The Gemara begins to analyze this *baraita* in detail. The *baraita* taught that one **may not derive benefit** from items consecrated by gentiles *ab initio,* **but** if one derived benefit from them, he is **not** liable after the fact for **misusing** of consecrated property. The Gemara explains: **One may not** derive **benefit** from them **by rabbinic law,** as the Sages prohibited deriving benefit from any item that was consecrated to God.

וְלֹא מוֹעֲלִין – דְּגָמַר מְעִילָה ״חֵט״ ״חֵט״ מִתְּרוּמָה, דְּבִתְרוּמָה כְּתִיב ״בְּנֵי יִשְׂרָאֵל״ – וְלֹא גּוֹיִם.

The Gemara's explanation continues: **But** if one derived benefit from them, he is **not** liable after the fact for **misusing** consecrated property, **as the** *tanna* of the *baraita* **derives the** *halakha* of **misuse** of consecrated property through a verbal analogy between **"sin"** stated with regard to misuse of consecrated items and the word **"sin"** stated with regard to ***teruma.*** With regard to misuse of consecrated property, the verse states: "If any one commits a trespass, and sins through error, in the sacred items of the Lord" (Leviticus 5:15). In the case of *teruma,* the verse states: "Lest they bear sin for it, and die due to it, if they profane it" (Leviticus 22:9). And **with regard to *teruma,* it is written:** "And they shall not profane the sacred items of **the children of Israel"** (Leviticus 22:15), which indicates: **But not** the sacred items of **gentiles,** i.e., one is not liable for partaking of the *teruma* of gentiles while he is in a state of ritual impurity.

״וְאֵין חַיָּיבִין עָלָיו מִשּׁוּם פִּיגּוּל, נוֹתָר וְטָמֵא״. מַאי טַעְמָא? דְּאָתֵי פִּיגּוּל ״עָוֹן״ ״עָוֹן״ מִנּוֹתָר,

The *baraita* further taught: **And one is not liable for** eating the offerings of gentiles **due to** violation of the prohibition of ***piggul,*** or ***notar,* or** eating the meat while **ritually impure.** The Gemara asks: **What is the reason** for this? The Gemara explains that the *halakha* of ***piggul* is derived** through a verbal analogy between the word **"iniquity"** stated with regard to *piggul* and the word **"iniquity"** stated with regard to ***notar.*** With regard to *piggul,* the verse states: "It shall be *piggul,* and the soul that eats it shall bear his iniquity" (Leviticus 7:18), and with regard to leftover sacrificial meat the verse states: "Therefore anyone who eats it shall bear his iniquity" (Leviticus 19:8).

וְאָתֵי נוֹתָר ״חִילּוּל״ ״חִילּוּל״ מִטּוּמְאָה, וּבְטוּמְאָה כְּתִיב ״בְּנֵי יִשְׂרָאֵל״ – וְלֹא גּוֹיִם.

And the *halakha* of ***notar*** itself is **derived** through a verbal analogy between **profanation** stated with regard to *notar* and **profanation** stated with regard to **ritual impurity.** With regard to *notar* the verse states: "Because he has profaned the sacred item of the Lord" (Leviticus 19:8), and with regard to impurity the verse states: "And that they do not profane My holy name" (Leviticus 22:2). **And with regard to impurity it is written** in that same verse: "That they separate themselves from the sacred items of **the children of Israel,"** which indicates: **But not** the sacred items of **gentiles.**

HALAKHA

And gentiles cannot render an animal a substitute – וְאֵין עוֹשִׂין תְּמוּרָה: Gentiles cannot perform substitution by Torah law. Nevertheless, if a gentile substituted another animal for his offering it is considered a substitute by rabbinic law. The *halakha* is in accordance with the opinion of Rabbi Shimon, as the Gemara in tractate *Arakhin* (5b) follows his ruling (Rambam *Sefer Korbanot, Hilkhot Temura* 1:6, and see *Kesef Mishne, Leḥem Mishne,* and Mahari Kurkus there).

And gentiles cannot bring libations – וְאֵין מְבִיאִין נְסָכִים: Gentiles do not bring libations together with their burnt offerings. The libations are acquired with communal funds (Rambam *Sefer Avoda, Hilkhot Ma'aseh HaKorbanot* 3:5, and see *Leḥem Mishne* there).

NOTES

And gentiles cannot bring libations – וְאֵין מְבִיאִין נְסָכִים: Rashi explains that gentiles cannot bring a gift offering of libations by itself, an option available to Jews. Nevertheless, if they send an offering they must include the money for its libations *ab initio.* If they neglected to do so, the libations are supplied from communal funds, as stated in the mishna in tractate *Shekalim* (7:6). Some say that gentiles need not bring libations with their offerings even *ab initio,* and these are bought from communal funds, as every burnt offering requires libations (*Shita Mekubbetzet* on *Menaḥot* 73b; Rabbeinu Gershom Meor HaGola on *Temura* 2b).

In what case is this statement said – בַּמֶּה דְּבָרִים אֲמוּרִים: According to Rashi, this question refers back to the opinion of the first *tanna* that with regard to items consecrated by gentiles, one is not liable for misuse of consecrated property. The *baraita* adds that the dispute between the first *tanna* and Rabbi Yosei relates only to items consecrated for the altar, but as for items consecrated for Temple maintenance, everyone agrees that one is liable even for items consecrated by gentiles. Others maintain, in light of the discussion in the Gemara, that this clause is the continuation of the statement of Rabbi Yosei, who concedes to the first *tanna* with regard to items consecrated for the altar. If so, the first *tanna* holds that one is not liable for misuse in either case (Rabbeinu Yitzḥak of Dampierre, cited by *Tosafot*).

BACKGROUND

Items consecrated for Temple maintenance – קׇדְשֵׁי בֶּדֶק הַבַּיִת: A distinction is drawn between animals consecrated as sacrificial offerings and items donated to the Temple for other purposes. Items in the latter category are considered consecrated for Temple maintenance, and they are used, or sold for money that is used, to repair the Temple, to replace its utensils, or to beautify the structure. Anything of worth can be consecrated for Temple maintenance, but animals that are fit for use as offerings may be consecrated only as offerings.

״וְאֵין עוֹשִׂין תְּמוּרָה״. מַאי טַעְמָא? דְּאִיתְקַשׁ תְּמוּרָה לְמַעְשַׂר בְּהֵמָה, וּמַעְשַׂר בְּהֵמָה אִיתְקַשׁ לְמַעְשַׂר דָּגָן, וּבְמַעֲשַׂר דָּגָן כְּתִיב: ״בְּנֵי יִשְׂרָאֵל״ – וְלֹא גּוֹיִם.

The *baraita* also teaches: **And** gentiles **cannot render** an animal **a substitute.** The Gemara asks: **What is the reason** for this? The Gemara explains: It is **because substitution is juxtaposed** in the Torah **with animal tithe,**[B] as the verse states: "And concerning the tithe of the herd, or of the flock…the tenth shall be sacred to the Lord…neither shall he make a substitute for it" (Leviticus 27:32–33). **And animal tithe is juxtaposed with the tithe of grains,** as the verse states: "You shall tithe [*asser te'asser*] all the increase of your seed that the field brings forth year by year. And you shall eat before the Lord your God, in the place that He shall choose to place His name there, the tithe of your grain" (Deuteronomy 14:22–23). The doubled verb form, *asser te'asser*, is understood as an allusion to two tithes, grain tithe and animal tithe. **And with regard to the tithe of grains it is written:** "When you take of **the children of Israel** the tithes" (Numbers 18:24), which indicates: **But not of gentiles.**

וְכִי דָּבָר הַלָּמֵד בְּהֶיקֵּשׁ חוֹזֵר וּמְלַמֵּד בְּהֶיקֵּשׁ? מַעְשַׂר דָּגָן חוּלִּין הוּא.

The Gemara asks: **But does a matter derived via a juxtaposition**[N] **again teach via a juxtaposition?** There is a principle that in consecrated matters, a *halakha* derived via a juxtaposition cannot teach another *halakha* via a juxtaposition. The Gemara answers: This derivation is not relevant exclusively to consecrated matters, as the **tithe of grains is non-sacred** food.

הָנִיחָא לְמַאן דְּאָמַר: בָּתַר מְלַמֵּד אָזְלִינַן, אֶלָּא לְמַאן דְּאָמַר: בָּתַר לָמֵד אָזְלִינַן, מַאי אִיכָּא לְמֵימַר?

The Gemara raises a difficulty: **This works out well according to the one who says** that when implementing this principle **we follow** the source that **teaches** the *halakha*, i.e., if the matter that teaches the first juxtaposition involves non-sacred items, one can employ two juxtapositions even with regard to deriving the *halakha* for consecrated matters. **But according to the one who says** that **we follow** the matter that **is taught** the *halakha*, i.e., the case to which we wish to apply the *halakha*, and if that case involves offerings one cannot employ two juxtapositions, **what can be said?**

אֶלָּא: מַעְשַׂר בְּהֵמָה חוֹבָה שֶׁאֵין קָבוּעַ לָהּ זְמַן הוּא, וְחוֹבָה שֶׁאֵין לָהּ זְמַן קָבוּעַ – יִשְׂרָאֵל מַיְיתוּ, גּוֹיִם לָא מַיְיתוּ.

Rather, the reason why gentiles cannot bring an animal tithe offering is that **animal tithe is an obligation for which there is no fixed time,**[N] and with regard to any **obligation for which there is no fixed time, a Jew can bring** it but **gentiles cannot bring** it. And as stated, substitution is juxtaposed with the animal tithe, and therefore gentiles can also not render an animal a substitute.

״וְאֵין מְבִיאִין נְסָכִים״. תָּנוּ רַבָּנַן: ״אֶזְרָח״ – אֶזְרָח מֵבִיא נְסָכִים, וְאֵין הַגּוֹי מֵבִיא נְסָכִים. יָכוֹל לֹא תְּהֵא עוֹלָתוֹ טְעוּנָה נְסָכִים? תַּלְמוּד לוֹמַר: ״כָּכָה״.

§ The *baraita* teaches: **And** gentiles **cannot bring libations** that are brought by themselves as a separate offering and do not accompany an animal offering, but their animal offerings require libations. The Gemara cites the source of these *halakhot*. **The Sages taught** in a *baraita*: The verse states with regard to libations: "All who are **homeborn** shall do these things after this manner" (Numbers 15:13), which teaches that those who are **homeborn,** i.e., Jews, can **bring libations** as a separate offering, **but a gentile cannot bring** such **libations.** One **might** consequently have thought that a gentile's **burnt offering should not require** the standard accompanying **libations.** Therefore, **the verse states: "So**[N] it shall be done for each bull" (Numbers 15:11), which indicates that every offering requires libations.

״אָמַר רַבִּי יוֹסֵי: רוֹאֶה אֲנִי בְּכוּלָּן לְהַחְמִיר. בַּמֶּה דְּבָרִים אֲמוּרִים – בְּקָדְשֵׁי מִזְבֵּחַ״ כו׳. מַאי טַעְמָא?

The *baraita* continues: **Rabbi Yosei says: I see** that **in all of** these cases it is correct **to be stringent. In what** case **is this statement said? In** the case of items **consecrated for the altar.** But with regard to items that are consecrated by gentiles for Temple maintenance, one who derives benefit from them is liable for misusing them. The Gemara asks: **What is the reason** of Rabbi Yosei?

קָסָבַר: כִּי גָּמְרָה מְעִילָה ״חֵטְא״ ״חֵטְא״ מִתְּרוּמָה – דּוּמְיָא דִּתְרוּמָה דִּקְדִישָׁא קְדוּשַּׁת הַגּוּף, אֲבָל קְדוּשַּׁת בֶּדֶק הַבַּיִת, דִּקְדוּשַּׁת דָּמִים – לָא.

The Gemara answers that Rabbi Yosei **holds** that **when** the *halakha* of **misuse** of consecrated property **is derived** through a verbal analogy between **"sin"** stated with regard to misuse of consecrated property and **"sin"** stated with regard to *teruma*, this is referring to items that are **similar to *teruma*, which is sacred** with **inherent sanctity. But** with regard to an item **consecrated for Temple maintenance, which** has no inherent sanctity, but only **sanctity** that inheres in its **value,** this exemption of gentiles does not apply.

BACKGROUND

Animal tithe – מַעְשַׂר בְּהֵמָה: On three occasions each year (see *Bekhorot* 57b), the owner of a herd of kosher animals was required to gather all the animals born during the preceding period into an enclosure and to let them out one by one. These animals passed "under the rod" (Leviticus 27:32), and every tenth animal was marked with red paint, to indicate that it was animal tithe and sacred. If it was fit to be sacrificed, the animal was brought to the Temple and sacrificed in a manner similar to that of a peace offering. Its blood was sprinkled on the altar, and its meat was eaten by its owner but not by the priests. The details of the *halakhot* of animal tithe are elucidated in tractate *Bekhorot*.

NOTES

But does a matter derived via a juxtaposition – וְכִי דָּבָר הַלָּמֵד בְּהֶיקֵּשׁ: Although the Gemara previously accepted a two-tiered derivation, of *piggul* from *notar* and *notar* from impurity, that case was different, as it was derived via a verbal analogy. A *halakha* that is derived via a verbal analogy can again teach via a verbal analogy, even in the case of consecrated matters.

Obligation for which there is no fixed time – חוֹבָה שֶׁאֵין קָבוּעַ לָהּ זְמַן הוּא: Gentiles can bring only vow offerings or gift offerings, and these must be offered as burnt offerings or, according to one opinion, also as peace offerings (see *Menaḥot* 73b). They cannot sacrifice those offerings that are not brought as a result of a vow or one's own free will, e.g., sin offerings and guilt offerings.

The verse states, so – תַּלְמוּד לוֹמַר כָּכָה: The full verse reads as follows: "So it shall be done for each bull, or for each ram, or for each of the lambs, or of the kids" (Numbers 15:11). This indicates that the requirement of libations depends on the offering in question, regardless of who brings it. Therefore, if the gentile did not send money for the libations, they are supplied from communal funds. Others cite the following verse: "So you shall do for every one according to their number" (Numbers 15:12), which supports their opinion that the libations of a gentile's offering are bought with communal funds *ab initio* (Rambam).

תָּנוּ רַבָּנַן: דָּם שֶׁנִּטְמָא וּזְרָקוֹ, בְּשׁוֹגֵג – הוּרְצָה,

The Gemara continues to analyze the opinion of Rabbi Yosei. **The Sages taught** in a *baraita*: With regard to **blood that became impure and** a priest **sprinkled it** on the altar, if he did so **unwittingly,** the offering is **accepted.**

בְּמֵזִיד – לֹא הוּרְצָה. בַּמֶּה דְּבָרִים אֲמוּרִים – בְּיָחִיד, אֲבָל בְּצִיבּוּר – בֵּין בְּשׁוֹגֵג בֵּין בְּמֵזִיד הוּרְצָה. וּבְגוֹיִם – בֵּין בְּשׁוֹגֵג וּבֵין בְּמֵזִיד לֹא הוּרְצָה.

But if he sprinkled the blood **intentionally,** the offering is **not accepted.**[N] **In what** case **is this statement said?** It is **with regard to** the offering of **an individual. But with regard to** the offering of **the community, whether** the priest sprinkled the blood **unwittingly or** he did so **intentionally,** the offering is **accepted. And** in the case of the offerings **of gentiles, whether** he sprinkled the blood **unwittingly or** he did so **intentionally,** the offering is **not accepted.**[N]

אֲמַרוּהָ רַבָּנַן קַמֵּיהּ דְּרַב פָּפָּא: כְּמַאן – דְּלָא כְּרַבִּי יוֹסֵי, דְּאִי רַבִּי יוֹסֵי – הָאָמַר: בְּכוּלָּן אֲנִי רוֹאֶה לְהַחְמִיר.

The Sages said before Rav Pappa: In accordance with whose opinion was this *baraita* taught? Apparently, it was taught **not in accordance with** the opinion of **Rabbi Yosei, as if** it reflects the opinion of **Rabbi Yosei,** there is a difficulty: **Doesn't** Rabbi Yosei **say: I see** the logic of the opinion that **in all of** these cases it is correct **to be stringent** about the offerings of gentiles? This indicates that Rabbi Yosei equates the *halakhot* applying to the offerings of gentiles with those governing the offerings of Jews.

אֲמַר לְהוּ רַב פָּפָּא: אֲפִילּוּ תֵּימָא רַבִּי יוֹסֵי, שָׁאנֵי הָתָם דְּאָמַר קְרָא ״לָהֶם״, לָהֶם – וְלֹא לְגוֹיִם.

Rav Pappa said to them: You may **even say** that the *baraita* is in accordance with the opinion of **Rabbi Yosei,** and it **is different there, as the verse states** with regard to the High Priest's frontplate, which atones for ritual impurity contracted by offerings in the Temple without the knowledge of those offering them: "And it shall be always upon his forehead that it may be accepted **for them** before the Lord" (Exodus 28:38), which indicates that it is accepted **for them,** i.e., for Jews, **but not for gentiles.**

אֲמַר לֵיהּ רַב הוּנָא בְּרֵיהּ דְּרַב נָתָן לְרַב פָּפָּא: אֶלָּא מֵעַתָּה, ״אֲשֶׁר הֵם מַקְדִּישִׁים״, הָכִי נָמֵי: הֵם – וְלֹא גּוֹיִם?

Rav Huna, son of Rav Natan, said to Rav Pappa: If that is so, with regard to the verse discussing ritually impure priests and consecrated items: "That they separate themselves from the sacred items of the children of Israel, **which they consecrate to Me"** (Leviticus 22:2), **so too,** would Rabbi Yosei say that the prohibition against eating consecrated items in a state of ritual impurity applies only to offerings which **they,** the Jews, consecrate, **and not** to those of **gentiles?** This cannot be, as Rabbi Yosei explicitly states in the *baraita* that in this regard the offerings of gentiles are like those of Jews.

אֶלָּא אָמַר רַב אַשִׁי, אָמַר קְרָא: ״לְרָצוֹן לָהֶם״ – וְגוֹיִם לָאו בְּנֵי הַרְצָאָה נִינְהוּ.

Rather, Rav Ashi says that it is not from the words "for them" that one derives that the offering of a gentile is not accepted when the blood that was sprinkled had become impure. Rather, it is because the atonement achieved by way of the High Priest's frontplate does not apply to gentiles, as **the verse states: "That it may be accepted for them** before the Lord" (Exodus 28:38), **and gentiles are not subject to** the **acceptance** of offerings.[N]

NOTES

Intentionally, the offering is not accepted – בְּמֵזִיד לֹא הוּרְצָה: Rashi explains that this does not mean that the offering is not accepted at all, since by Torah law the frontplate renders the offering accepted. Rather, this is referring to a penalty imposed by rabbinic law, that the meat of this offering may not be eaten.

And in the case of gentiles…it is not accepted – וּבְגוֹיִם...לֹא הוּרְצָה: Consequently, this offering is not brought up to the altar, and the gentile must bring another offering to fulfill his vow (Rabbi Shimshon of Saens on *Torat Kohanim*; see *Tosafot* on *Avoda Zara* 5b).

Are not subject to the acceptance of offerings – לָאו בְּנֵי הַרְצָאָה נִינְהוּ: The term acceptance connotes atonement for sin, in the case of a sin offering and a guilt offering, or general acceptance before God in the case of a burnt offering, or establishment of peace with God in the case of a peace offering (see Rashi on 29b and on *Rosh HaShana* 5b). With regard to gentiles, although they may bring their vow offerings and gift offerings to the Temple, these offerings are merely an expression of goodwill on their part, and do not entail atonement and acceptance. The proof for this is that they cannot bring sin offerings or guilt offerings. It can be derived from here that the atonement of the frontplate, concerning which the verse states: "That they may be accepted before the Lord" (Exodus 28:38), applies only to those offerings that include an aspect of atonement or acceptance.

מתני׳ דְּבָרִים שֶׁאֵין חַיָּיבִים עֲלֵיהֶם מִשּׁוּם פִּיגּוּל – חַיָּיבִין עֲלֵיהֶן מִשּׁוּם נוֹתָר וּמִשּׁוּם טָמֵא, חוּץ מִן הַדָּם. רַבִּי שִׁמְעוֹן מְחַיֵּיב בְּדָבָר שֶׁדַּרְכָּן לֶאֱכוֹל, אֲבָל הָעֵצִים וְהַלְּבוֹנָה וְהַקְּטוֹרֶת – אֵין חַיָּיבִין עָלָיו מִשּׁוּם טוּמְאָה.

MISHNA Even with regard to those **items** enumerated in the previous mishna (42b) for **which one is not liable for** eating **them due to** violation of the prohibition of ***piggul***, e.g., the handful, the frankincense, and the incense, **one is,** nevertheless, **liable for** eating **them due to** violation of the prohibition of ***notar***,[H] **and due to** violation of the prohibition against eating consecrated food while **ritually impure, except for the blood. Rabbi Shimon deems one liable for an item whose** typical **manner** is such that one **eats** it. **But** with regard to **the wood, the frankincense, and the incense,**[H] **one is not liable for** eating **them due to** violation of the prohibition against eating a consecrated item while **ritually impure.**

גמ׳ תָּנוּ רַבָּנַן: יָכוֹל לֹא יְהוּ חַיָּיבִין מִשּׁוּם טוּמְאָה אֶלָּא עַל דָּבָר שֶׁיֵּשׁ לוֹ מַתִּירִין, בֵּין לָאָדָם בֵּין לַמִּזְבֵּחַ?

GEMARA **The Sages taught** in a *baraita*: It **might** have been thought that **one should be liable due to** violation of the prohibition against eating consecrated food while in a state of **ritual impurity only for an item that has permitting factors, either for** consumption by **a person or for** burning on **the altar.**

וְדִין הוּא: וּמָה פִּיגּוּל שֶׁהוּא בִּקְבִיעָה, וּבִידִיעָה אַחַת, וְלֹא הוּתַּר מִכְּלָלוֹ – אֵין חַיָּיבִין עָלָיו אֶלָּא עַל דָּבָר שֶׁיֵּשׁ לוֹ מַתִּירִין בֵּין לָאָדָם בֵּין לַמִּזְבֵּחַ.

The *baraita* explains: **And** this may be derived via **a logical derivation: Just as** with regard to ***piggul*****, which** renders one who unwittingly eats it liable to bring **a fixed** sin offering, **and** this liability is incurred **with one** change in his **awareness,** i.e., it suffices for the sinner to become aware after the fact that he had sinned unwittingly, **and** it has **no permitted** exceptions **from its general** prohibition, as there are no circumstances in which one is permitted to eat *piggul*, and yet **one is liable due to** violation of the prohibition against eating *piggul* **only for an item that has permitting factors, either for** consumption by **a person or for** burning on **the altar,** so too, the same should certainly apply to the more lenient case of ritual impurity.

טוּמְאָה שֶׁהִיא בְּעוֹלֶה וְיוֹרֵד, וּבִשְׁתֵּי יְדִיעוֹת, וְהוּתְּרָה מִכְּלָלָהּ – אֵינוֹ דִּין שֶׁאֵינוֹ חַיָּיב אֶלָּא עַל דָּבָר שֶׁיֵּשׁ לוֹ מַתִּירִין בֵּין לָאָדָם בֵּין לַמִּזְבֵּחַ?

The Gemara elaborates: **Impurity** is more lenient than *piggul*, **as** it renders the unwitting sinner liable only to bring **a sliding-scale offering,** which varies according to his financial circumstances: A poor person brings a bird offering or even a meal offering (see Leviticus 5:6–13). **And** liability is incurred only **with two** changes in his **awareness,** i.e., when the sinner was aware of his impurity beforehand, then forgot about it at the time of his sin, and then once again became aware of his impurity. **And** it has **permitted** exceptions **from its general** prohibition with regard to the community, as it is permitted to sacrifice communal offerings in the Temple in a state of impurity. With these leniencies in mind, **is it not right that one should be liable** due to violation of the prohibition against eating consecrated food while ritually impure **only for an item that has permitting factors, either for a person or for the altar.**

תַּלְמוּד לוֹמַר: ״אֲשֶׁר הֵם מַקְדִּשִׁים לִי״.

Therefore, **the verse states,** with regard to eating consecrated foods in a state of ritual impurity: "That they separate themselves from the sacred items of the children of Israel, **which they consecrate to Me,** and that they do not profane My holy name" (Leviticus 22:2). This teaches that a ritually impure person is liable for eating any item that has been consecrated.

יָכוֹל מִיָּד? תַּלְמוּד לוֹמַר: ״יִקְרַב״; אָמַר רַבִּי אֶלְעָזָר: וְכִי יֵשׁ נוֹגֵעַ שֶׁהוּא חַיָּיב?

One **might** have thought that one is liable for eating sacred items **immediately** after they have been consecrated. Therefore, **the verse states:** "Whoever he is of all your seed among your generations that **approaches** the sacred items" (Leviticus 22:3), and **Rabbi Elazar said,** in explanation of this verse: **But is there** one who merely **touches,** i.e., approaches, consecrated items, **who is liable?**[N] Only one who eats consecrated food while in a state of ritual impurity is liable.

HALAKHA

One is liable for them due to *notar* – חַיָּיבִין עֲלֵיהֶן מִשּׁוּם נוֹתָר: With regard to those items enumerated in the mishna (42b) for the consumption of which one is not liable to receive *karet* due to violation of the prohibition of *piggul*, e.g., the handful, the frankincense, and the incense; one is liable to receive *karet* due to violation of the prohibition of *notar*. The exception is blood, for which one is liable only for the prohibition against consuming blood (Rambam *Sefer Avoda, Hilkhot Pesulei HaMukdashin* 18:17).

The wood, the frankincense, and the incense – הָעֵצִים וְהַלְּבוֹנָה וְהַקְּטוֹרֶת: One is not liable to receive *karet* for the consumption of frankincense and incense, whether due to *piggul* or *notar*, or for consuming them in a state of ritual impurity. This is in accordance with the opinion of Rabbi Shimon; see 46b (Rambam *Sefer Avoda, Hilkhot Pesulei HaMukdashin* 18:24).

NOTES

But is there one who touches who is liable – וְכִי יֵשׁ נוֹגֵעַ שֶׁהוּא חַיָּיב: Rashi notes that it cannot be claimed that this very verse teaches that one is liable for mere touching, as the entire passage deals specifically with eating, as is explicitly stated in the next verse: "He shall not eat of the sacred items" (Leviticus 22:4). Others add that were one liable for simply touching consecrated items in a state of ritual impurity, there would be no need for the verse to state that one is also liable for eating (*Korban Aharon*).

אֶלָּא מַה תַּלְמוּד לוֹמַר "יִקְרַב" – בְּהוּכְשַׁר [בָּשָׂר] לִיקָּרֵב הַכָּתוּב מְדַבֵּר. הָא כֵּיצַד? יֵשׁ לוֹ מַתִּירִין – מִשֶּׁיִּקְרְבוּ מַתִּירִין, אֵין לוֹ מַתִּירִין – מִשֶּׁיִּקְדַּשׁ בִּכְלִי.

Rather, what is the meaning when **the verse states:** "Approaches [*yikrav*]"? This term alludes to sacrificing [*hakrava*], as though the verse has stated: Whoever sacrifices sacred items and eats them. This teaches that **the verse is speaking of flesh that has been rendered fit to be sacrificed. How so?**[N] With regard to an item **that has permitting factors,** one is liable **from when** the **permitting factors are sacrificed.** In the case of an item that **does not have permitting factors,** one is liable **from when it is sanctified in** a service **vessel** for the purpose of its sacrifice.

אַשְׁכַּחַן טוּמְאָה, נוֹתָר מְנָלַן? אָתֵי "חִילּוּל" "חִילּוּל" מִטּוּמְאָה.

The Gemara asks: **We have found** proof that the prohibition against eating consecrated food in a state of **ritual impurity** applies even to an item that does not have a permitting factor. **From where do we** derive that ***notar*** likewise applies to an item that does not have a permitting factor? The Gemara answers: This is **derived** through a verbal analogy between **profanation** stated in the context of *notar* and **profanation** stated in the context of **ritual impurity.** With regard to *notar* the verse states: "Because he has profaned the sacred item of the Lord" (Leviticus 19:8), and with regard to impurity the verse states: "And that they do not profane My holy name" (Leviticus 22:2).

וְלֵילַף "עָוֹן" "עָוֹן" מִפִּיגּוּל!

The Gemara challenges: **But let** the *halakha* of *notar* **be derived** through a verbal analogy between **"iniquity"** stated in the context of *notar* and **"iniquity"** stated in the context of ***piggul.*** With regard to *piggul,* the verse states: "It shall be *piggul,* and the soul that eats of it shall bear his iniquity" (Leviticus 7:18), and with regard to leftover sacrificial meat the verse states: "Therefore anyone who eats it shall bear his iniquity" (Leviticus 19:8). If so, the *halakha* of *notar* should be similar to that of *piggul,* for which one is liable only for an item that has a permitting factor.

מִסְתַּבְּרָא, מִטּוּמְאָה הֲוֵי לֵיהּ לְמֵילַף, שֶׁכֵּן גז"ל סִימָן.

The Gemara answers that **it is** more **reasonable to derive** *notar* **from ritual impurity, for** several reasons, as indicated by the **mnemonic: *Gimmel, zayin, lamed.***[N] Both *notar* and impurity are disqualifications that apply to the body [*guf*] of the offering itself, whereas *piggul* is caused by intent; unlike *piggul,* these two disqualifications are not determined by the sprinkling [*zerika*] of the blood, and in both cases the Torah uses the term profanation [*ḥillul*].

אַדְּרַבָּה, מִפִּיגּוּל הֲוָה לֵיהּ לְמֵילַף שֶׁכֵּן נוֹתָר, צִיץ, טָהוֹר, בִּזְמָן, קָרֵב, וְהָנֵי נְפִישָׁן!

The Gemara responds: **On the contrary, it is** more **reasonable to derive** *notar* **from** ***piggul,*** **as** like *piggul* it does not have **permitted** exceptions from its general prohibition, it has no atonement through the High Priest's **frontplate,** both *notar* and *piggul* apply **to a ritually pure** offering, these disqualifications are dependent **on time,** and both of them are disqualifications of the item being **sacrificed,** not the priest performing the service. None of these features are true of ritual impurity. **And these** reasons for comparing *notar* to *piggul* are more **numerous.**

אֶלָּא מִדְּתָנֵי לֵוִי, דְּתָנֵי לֵוִי: מִנַּיִן שֶׁאַף בִּפְסוּל זְמָן הַכָּתוּב מְדַבֵּר – תַּלְמוּד לוֹמַר: "וְלֹא יְחַלְּלוּ אֶת קָדְשֵׁי בְּנֵי יִשְׂרָאֵל",

Rather, the *halakha* of *notar* is derived **from that** which **Levi taught** with regard to the verse: "That they separate themselves from the sacred items of the children of Israel, which they consecrate to Me, and that they do not profane My holy name" (Leviticus 22:2), which is referring to the eating of consecrated food in a state of ritual impurity. **As Levi taught: From where** is it derived **that the verse is speaking even of a disqualification** caused by **time,** and not only ritual impurity? **The verse states** profanation elsewhere: **"And they shall not profane the sacred items of the children of Israel"** (Leviticus 22:15).

NOTES

How so – הָא כֵּיצַד: Some explain this passage as follows: How can you explain this apparent contradiction, as the phrase "which they consecrate to Me" teaches that the prohibition applies immediately upon their consecration, whereas the term *yikrav* indicates that the prohibition goes into effect only after it has been rendered fit to be sacrificed. The Gemara answers that with regard to an item that has a permitting factor, the prohibition applies from when it is rendered permitted to be sacrificed, whereas in the case of an item that does not have a permitting factor, one is liable from when it is sanctified in a service vessel (*Korban Aharon*).

Mnemonic *gimmel, zayin, lamed* – גז"ל סִימָן: The commentaries ask: If the *lamed* is a reference to the term profanation [*hillul*], which appears in the Torah with regard to both *notar* and impurity, when the Gemara listed the arguments in favor of a juxtaposition between *notar* and *piggul* it should have noted that the word sin is common to them both, as stated several times in this chapter (*Tosafot*). Therefore, *Tosafot* prefer the explanation of Rabbeinu Ḥananel, that the *lamed* is a reference to *kulo,* meaning: All of it. In other words, unlike *notar* and impurity, which apply only to that part of the offering that became impure or was left over, the prohibition of *piggul* applies to all of it.

בִּשְׁנֵי חִילּוּלִין הַכָּתוּב מְדַבֵּר, אֶחָד פְּסוּל נוֹתָר, וְאֶחָד פְּסוּל טוּמְאָה.

The verse is speaking here **of two profanations;**[N] **one is the disqualification of** ***notar***[N] **and one is the disqualification of ritual impurity.** This teaches that like impurity, *notar* applies even to an item that does not have a permitting factor.

״חוּץ מִן הַדָּם״ כו׳. מְנָא הָנֵי מִילֵּי? אָמַר עוּלָּא, אָמַר קְרָא: ״וַאֲנִי נְתַתִּיו לָכֶם״ – שֶׁלָּכֶם יְהֵא.

§ The mishna teaches: Even with regard to the items for which one is not liable for eating them due to violation of the prohibition of *piggul*, one is, nevertheless, liable for eating them due to violation of the prohibition of *notar*, and due to violation of the prohibition against eating consecrated food while ritually impure, **except for the blood.** The Gemara asks: **From where are these matters** derived? Before answering this question, the Gemara cites another discussion as to why the *halakha* of misuse of consecrated property does not apply to blood. **Ulla says: The verse states** with regard to blood: "For the life of the flesh is in the blood, **and I have given it to you** upon the altar to make atonement for your souls" (Leviticus 17:11). "To you" indicates that **it shall be yours;**[N] it is not the property of the Temple, so it is not subject to the prohibition of misuse of consecrated property.

דְּבֵי רַבִּי יִשְׁמָעֵאל תָּנָא, אָמַר קְרָא: ״לְכַפֵּר״ – לְכַפָּרָה נְתַתִּיו, וְלֹא לִמְעִילָה.

The school of Rabbi Yishmael similarly **taught: The verse states: "To make atonement,"** teaching that God is saying: **I gave it for atonement, and not for** the prohibition of **misuse** of consecrated property.

רַבִּי יוֹחָנָן אָמַר: אָמַר קְרָא ״הוּא״ – הוּא לִפְנֵי כַפָּרָה כִּלְאַחַר כַּפָּרָה, מָה אַחַר כַּפָּרָה אֵין בּוֹ מְעִילָה – אַף לִפְנֵי כַפָּרָה אֵין בּוֹ מְעִילָה.

Rabbi Yoḥanan says that this *halakha* is derived from the latter part of **the verse,** which **states:** "For **it is**[N] the blood that makes atonement for the soul" (Leviticus 17:11). The term "it is" teaches that the status of the blood remains as it is, i.e., **it is before atonement as** it is **after atonement.** As the Gemara will state, there is a principle that once the mitzva involving a consecrated item has been performed, the item is no longer subject to the prohibition of misuse of consecrated property. Accordingly, the term "it is" teaches that **just as after atonement,** i.e., after the blood has been presented on the altar, **it is not subject to** the prohibition of **misuse** of consecrated property, as the mitzva has already been performed, **so too, before atonement,** i.e., before the blood has been presented on the altar, **it is not subject to** the prohibition of **misuse** of consecrated property.[H]

אֵימָא: לְאַחַר כַּפָּרָה כִּלְפְנֵי כַפָּרָה, מָה לִפְנֵי כַפָּרָה יֵשׁ בּוֹ מְעִילָה – אַף לְאַחַר כַּפָּרָה יֵשׁ בּוֹ מְעִילָה! אֵין לְךָ דָּבָר שֶׁנַּעֲשֵׂית מִצְוָתוֹ וּמוֹעֲלִין בּוֹ.

The Gemara asks: But if the term "it is" teaches that the status of the blood remains the same before and after atonement, one can **say** just the opposite: It is **after atonement as** it is **before atonement. Just as before atonement** the blood **is subject to** the prohibition of **misuse** of consecrated property, **so too after atonement it is subject to** the prohibition of **misuse** of consecrated property. The Gemara rejects this: This cannot be the case, as there is a principle: **There is no item whose mitzva has been performed**[N] **that is** still **subject to** the prohibition of **misusing** consecrated property.

וְלָא? וַהֲרֵי תְּרוּמַת הַדֶּשֶׁן!

The Gemara asks: **And is there no** such case? **But there is** the mitzva of **the removal of the ashes**[HB] of offerings burned on the altar. Any benefit derived from them between their removal and their required burial constitutes misuse of consecrated property, despite the fact that their mitzva has already been performed.

BACKGROUND

The removal of the ashes – תְּרוּמַת הַדֶּשֶׁן: There is a positive mitzva to remove some of the ashes from the altar each morning and bring them to the floor of the courtyard. The verse states: "And he shall take up the ashes to which the fire has reduced the burnt offering on the altar, and place them beside the altar" (Leviticus 6:3). This was the first of the daily rites performed in the Temple. In addition, from time to time, when the ashes accumulated, they would be removed from the Temple to a place set aside outside Jerusalem called the Place of the Ashes. The fact that the ashes were placed in a designated spot indicates that they retained some measure of sanctity, and were therefore subject to misuse (Rabbeinu Gershom's commentary to *Me'ila* 11:2). Rashi explains that the purpose of storing the ashes away was to prevent people from benefiting from them. According to this interpretation as well, it follows that there exists a prohibition of misuse.

NOTES

Of two profanations – בִּשְׁנֵי חִילּוּלִין: According to the version of the text accepted by Rashi, the Gemara is referring to the verse that discusses eating consecrated foods in a state of ritual impurity: "That they separate themselves from the sacred items of the children of Israel, which they consecrate to Me, and that they do not profane My holy name" (Leviticus 22:2). The claim that the verse is referring to two profanations is based on the fact that the two clauses: "That they separate," and: "That they do not profane," are set apart from one another, an indication that the verse is speaking of two different disqualifications. Others maintain that the derivation is based on the plural form: "And that they do not profane" (*Tosafot*). Alternatively, the Gemara infers that there are two profanations from the use of the term *yeḥallelu*, they profane, rather than the shorter form *yeḥalu* (Rashi, according to *Shita Mekubbetzet*; see *Panim Meirot* on 15b).

One is the disqualification of ***notar*** **– אֶחָד פְּסוּל נוֹתָר:** The reason that *notar* is included is that the term profanation is stated with regard to *notar* as well (Rashi). Rashi is referring to the verse: "And they shall not profane the sacred items of the children of Israel" (Leviticus 22:15), which does not appear in the text of the Gemara, according to the version he accepts.

To you, indicates that it shall be yours – לָכֶם שֶׁלָּכֶם יְהֵא: Some commentaries claim, based on the *Torat Kohanim*, that this derivation is based on the fact that the verse does not state: Upon you, but: "To you," which indicates that it belongs to you, i.e., it is not subject to the prohibition of misuse (*Rosh HaMizbe'aḥ*).

It is – הוּא: Although the standard text of Rashi cites the verse: "For as to the life of all flesh, the blood, it is all one with its life" (Leviticus 17:14), that verse is referring to blood in general, not specifically the blood of offerings. Therefore, the commentaries explain that Rashi is actually referring to Leviticus 17:11, which discusses offerings: "For it is the blood that makes atonement for the soul" (*Ḥok Natan*).

Whose mitzva has been performed – שֶׁנַּעֲשֵׂית מִצְוָתוֹ: Since its mitzva has already been performed, it is no longer in the category of "the sacred items of the Lord" (Leviticus 5:15), which is stated with regard to the prohibition of misuse (Rashi).

HALAKHA

Misuse does not apply to blood – דָּם אֵין בּוֹ מְעִילָה: One is not liable for misuse of consecrated property from deriving benefit from blood of a slaughtered offering, either before or after atonement, until the remainder of blood flows to the Kidron River. Once that blood has reached the Kidron River, one is liable by rabbinic law for its misuse (Ra'avad). In Temple times, gardeners paid for this water for use as fertilizer and thereby redeemed the remainder of blood from its sanctity (see *Yoma* 58b). If one performs bloodletting on a consecrated animal, one is prohibited to derive benefit from the blood, and the prohibition of misuse applies. The reason is that as the animal cannot live without its blood, it is considered like its body (Rambam *Sefer Avoda, Hilkhot Me'ila* 2:11).

The removal of the ashes – תְּרוּמַת הַדֶּשֶׁן: Some of the ashes removed from the altar are deposited outside the city. It is prohibited to derive benefit from these ashes, whether before or after their removal (Rambam *Sefer Avoda, Hilkhot Me'ila* 2:14 and *Hilkhot Temidin UMusafin* 2:15).

מִשּׁוּם דְּהָוֵי תְּרוּמַת הַדֶּשֶׁן וּבִגְדֵי כְהוּנָּה שְׁנֵי כְתוּבִין הַבָּאִין כְּאֶחָד, וְכָל שְׁנֵי כְתוּבִים הַבָּאִין כְּאֶחָד אֵין מְלַמְּדִין.

The Gemara answers: The principle does not apply in that case, **because** the matter of **the removal of the ashes and** the matter of the **priestly vestments,** the four white garments worn by the High Priest on Yom Kippur, are both subject to the *halakha* that misuse of consecrated property applies to them even after their mitzva has been performed. Consequently, they **are two verses that come as one,** i.e., they share a unique *halakha* not found elsewhere. **And** there is a principle: **Any two verses that come as one do not teach** their common element to apply to other cases. Instead, they are considered exceptional instances that cannot serve as models for other cases.

הָנִיחָא לְרַבָּנַן דְּאָמְרִי: ״וְהִנִּיחָם שָׁם״ – מְלַמֵּד שֶׁטְּעוּנִין גְּנִיזָה.

The Gemara raises a further difficulty: **This works out well according to** the opinion of **the Rabbis, who say** that the verse: "And he shall take off the linen garments, which he wore when he went into the Sanctuary, **and shall leave them there**" (Leviticus 16:23), **teaches that** the four white garments worn by the High Priest on Yom Kippur are not fit for further use, and **they require interment.**[H]

אֶלָּא לְרַבִּי דּוֹסָא, דְּאָמַר: מוּתָּרוֹת הֵן לְכֹהֵן הֶדְיוֹט, וּבִלְבַד שֶׁלֹּא יִשְׁתַּמֵּשׁ בָּהֶן לְיוֹם הַכִּפּוּרִים אַחֵר, מַאי אִיכָּא לְמֵימַר?

But according to the opinion of **Rabbi Dosa, who says** that these priestly vestments **are fit for an ordinary priest** and do not require interment, **provided that** a High Priest **does not use them on Yom Kippur** in **a different** year, one does not misuse consecrated property by using them after their mitzva has been performed, and therefore **what is there to say?** In his opinion, the *halakha* of misuse of consecrated property after the performance of a mitzva applies only to the removal of ashes from the altar, not to the priestly vestments, which means it is stated in only a single case. Why, then, does this case not serve as a paradigm for other instances in the Torah?

מִשּׁוּם דְּהָוֵי תְּרוּמַת הַדֶּשֶׁן וְעֶגְלָה עֲרוּפָה שְׁנֵי כְתוּבִין הַבָּאִין כְּאֶחָד, וְכָל שְׁנֵי כְתוּבִין הַבָּאִין כְּאֶחָד אֵין מְלַמְּדִין.

The Gemara responds: It is **because** the cases of **the removal of the ashes and** the *halakha* of **the heifer whose neck is broken**[HBN] are **two verses that come as one,** as it is prohibited to derive benefit from either of them even after their mitzva is completed, **and any two verses that come as one do not teach** their common element to apply to other cases.

הָנִיחָא לְמַאן דְּאָמַר אֵין מְלַמְּדִין, אֶלָּא לְמַאן דְּאָמַר מְלַמְּדִין, מַאי אִיכָּא לְמֵימַר?

The Gemara challenges this from a different angle: **This works out well according to the one who says** that two verses that come as one **do not teach** their common element to apply to other cases, **but according to the one who says** that two verses that come as one do **teach** their common element to apply to other cases, **what is there to say?**

תְּרֵי מִיעוּטֵי כְּתִיבִי, הָכָא כְּתִיב: ״הָעֲרוּפָה״, וְהָתָם כְּתִיב: ״וְשָׂמוֹ״.

The Gemara answers: **Two exclusions are written** in these two cases, which indicate that this *halakha* applies to them alone. **Here,** with regard to the heifer whose neck is broken, **it is written: "Whose neck was broken"** (Deuteronomy 21:6),[N] and this superfluous description teaches that this *halakha,* that the prohibition of misuse of consecrated property is in effect even after the performance of a mitzva, applies solely to this case and should not be extended to others. **And there,** with regard to the removal of ashes, **it is written: "And he shall put it"** (Leviticus 6:3), indicating that this *halakha* applies to "it," and nothing else.

HALAKHA

Teaches that they require interment – מְלַמֵּד שֶׁטְּעוּנִין גְּנִיזָה: Worn-out garments of the High Priest must be buried. The same applies to the white garments in which he serves on Yom Kippur. It is prohibited to derive any benefit from them, in accordance with the opinion of the Rabbis (Rambam *Sefer Avoda, Hilkhot Kelei HaMikdash* 8:5).

Heifer whose neck is broken – עֶגְלָה עֲרוּפָה: It is prohibited to derive benefit from the heifer whose neck is broken. This prohibition begins from the moment the animal is led toward the forceful stream, and it continues to apply whether its neck is indeed broken or whether it dies or is slaughtered before its neck is broken. The carcass of the animal is buried (Rambam *Sefer Nezikin, Hilkhot Rotze'aḥ UShmirat HaNefesh* 10:6).

BACKGROUND

Heifer whose neck is broken – עֶגְלָה עֲרוּפָה: When a murder victim's corpse is found outside a town and it is not known who caused his death, the following procedure is observed (Deuteronomy 21:1–9): First, judges who are members of the Great Sanhedrin measure the distance between the corpse and the nearby towns, to determine which town is closest and must perform the rite. This measurement is performed even if it is clear which town is closest to the corpse. Afterward, the Elders of that town bring a heifer that has never been used for any labor, and break its neck in a forceful stream. The Elders wash their hands and make a statement absolving themselves of guilt. If the murderer is discovered before the heifer is killed, the rite is not performed.

NOTES

Heifer whose neck is broken – עֶגְלָה עֲרוּפָה: Rashi explains that the source of this *halakha* in the case of the heifer whose neck is broken is the term "there" in the verse: "And the Elders of that city shall bring down the heifer to a forceful stream, which may neither be plowed nor sown, and shall break the heifer's neck there" (Deuteronomy 21:4). This indicates that the heifer must be buried there, and it may not be used for any other purpose.

Whose neck was broken – הָעֲרוּפָה: Since this verse is stated after the heifer's neck has already been broken, it is unnecessary to describe the animal in this manner. The Gemara explains that this term serves to emphasize that this unusual ruling, that the prohibition of misuse is in effect even after the mitzva is completed, applies only to the heifer whose neck was broken, and that *halakha* is not extended other mitzvot.

וּתְלָתָא קְרָאֵי בְּדָם לָמָּה לִי?

The Gemara asks: **And why do I** need these **three verses** stated **with regard to blood,** from which it is derived that the prohibition of misuse of consecrated property does not apply to blood? The reference is to the three terms specified earlier, in the expositions of Ulla, the school of Rabbi Yishmael, and Rabbi Yoḥanan, from the verse: "I have given it to you upon the altar to make atonement for your souls, for it is the blood that makes atonement for the soul" (Leviticus 17:11).

לְמַעוּטֵי מִמְּעִילָה מִנּוֹתָר וּמִטּוּמְאָה.

The Gemara answers: One of those terms serves **to exclude** the blood **from** the prohibition of **misuse** of consecrated property. Another phrase serves to exclude blood **from** the prohibition of ***notar***. If one consumed leftover blood, he is not liable for consuming *notar*. Rather, he is liable for violating only the prohibition against consuming blood. **And** the last phrase serves to exclude it **from** the prohibition of **ritual impurity.** If one consumed this blood in a state of ritual impurity, he is liable only for consuming blood, but not on account of consuming consecrated food while ritually impure.

אֲבָל פִּיגּוּל לָא צְרִיךְ קְרָא, דִּתְנַן: כֹּל שֶׁיֵּשׁ לוֹ מַתִּירִין בֵּין לָאָדָם בֵּין לַמִּזְבֵּחַ – חַיָּיבִין עָלָיו מִשּׁוּם פִּיגּוּל, וְדָם גּוּפֵיהּ מַתִּיר הוּא.

But no verse is required to exclude this blood from the *halakha* of ***piggul***, because this is already derived from another source, **as we learned** in the mishna (43a): With regard to **any** item **that has permitting factors, either for** consumption by **a person or for** burning on **the altar, one is liable for** eating **it due to** violation of the prohibition of ***piggul***. The permitting factor itself is not subject to *piggul*. **And** consequently, *piggul* does not apply to **blood itself,** as **it** renders the offering **permitted** for human consumption or for the altar.

אָמַר רַבִּי יוֹחָנָן: שְׁלֹשָׁה כְּרֵיתוֹת בִּשְׁלָמִים לָמָּה?

§ **Rabbi Yoḥanan says: Why do I** need **three** mentions of ***karet*** **with regard to** one who eats **peace offerings** in a state of ritual impurity? The three verses are: "But the soul that eats of the flesh of the sacrifice of peace offerings, that pertain to the Lord, having his impurity upon him, that soul shall be cut off [*venikhreta*] from his people" (Leviticus 7:20); "And when anyone shall touch any impure item, whether it is the impurity of man, or an impure animal, or any unclean detestable thing, and eat of the flesh of the sacrifice of peace offerings, that pertain to the Lord, that soul shall be cut off from his people" (Leviticus 7:21); and: "Whoever he is of all your seed among your generations that approaches the sacred items, which the children of Israel consecrate to the Lord, having his impurity upon him, that soul shall be cut off from before Me; I am the Lord" (Leviticus 22:3).

אַחַת לִכְלָל, וְאַחַת לִפְרָט, וְאַחַת לִדְבָרִים שֶׁאֵינָן נֶאֱכָלִין.

One mention of *karet* in the verse: "That approaches the sacred items," is **for a generalization, and one** mention in the verse: "Of the flesh of the sacrifice of peace offerings," is **for a detail.**[N] This detail serves to include all items consecrated to the altar, in accordance with the hermeneutical principle that any matter that was included in a generalization but was explicitly specified to teach a certain *halakha* was intended to teach not just about itself but about the entire generalization. **And one** mention of *karet* in the verse: "And when anyone shall touch any impure item," serves **to include items whose** typical manner is such that they are **not to be eaten,** e.g., wood and frankincense, and teaches that one who eats even these items is liable to receive *karet*.

NOTES

One for a generalization and one for a detail – אַחַת לִכְלָל וְאַחַת לִפְרָט: This statement is based on the fact that one mention of *karet* appears with regard to offerings in general, while the other is referring to a specific type of offering, the peace offering. Some commentaries explain that this does not refer to the hermeneutical principle of a generalization and a detail. Rather, one mention of *karet* serves to exclude a specific detail, i.e., the blood, to which the *halakha* of ritual impurity does not apply (Ri Migash on *Shevuot* 7a; see Meiri there).

וּלְרַבִּי שִׁמְעוֹן, דְּאָמַר: דְּבָרִים שֶׁאֵין נֶאֱכָלִין – אֵין חַיָּיבִין עֲלֵיהֶם מִשּׁוּם טוּמְאָה, לְאִיתּוּיֵי מַאי? לְאִיתּוּיֵי חַטָּאוֹת הַפְּנִימִיּוֹת.

The Gemara asks: **And according to** the opinion of **Rabbi Shimon, who says** in the mishna with regard to **items whose** typical manner is such that they are **not to be eaten,** that one is **not liable for** eating **them due to** violation of the prohibition against eating consecrated items in a state of **ritual impurity, what** does this last mention of *karet* serve **to include?** The Gemara answers that it serves **to include the sin offerings** whose blood is presented **inside**[H] the Sanctuary.

סָלְקָא דַּעְתָּךְ אָמִינָא, הוֹאִיל וְאָמַר רַבִּי שִׁמְעוֹן: כָּל שֶׁאֵינוֹ עַל מִזְבֵּחַ הַחִיצוֹן כִּשְׁלָמִים אֵין חַיָּיבִין עָלָיו מִשּׁוּם פִּיגּוּל – מִשּׁוּם טוּמְאָה נַמִי לָא לִיחַיַּיב, קָא מַשְׁמַע לָן.

The Gemara explains why this inclusion is necessary. It might **enter your mind to say: Since Rabbi Shimon says** that concerning **any** offering **whose** blood **is not** presented **on the external altar like** that of **a peace offering, one is not liable for** eating **it due to** violation of the prohibition of ***piggul***, one should likewise **not be liable** for eating it **due to** violation of the prohibition of **ritual impurity.** Therefore, the additional mention of *karet* **teaches us** that one who is impure is in fact liable for eating these sin offerings brought inside the Sanctuary.

״נוֹמִי רַבִּי שִׁמְעוֹן מְחַיֵּיב אֶת שֶׁדַּרְכּוֹ לֶאֱכוֹל״ כו׳. אִיתְּמַר, רַבִּי יוֹחָנָן וְרֵישׁ לָקִישׁ, רַבִּי אֶלְעָזָר וְרַבִּי יוֹסֵי בְּרַבִּי חֲנִינָא, חַד מֵהַאי זוּזָא וְחַד מֵהַאי זוּזָא,

§ The mishna teaches that **Rabbi Shimon stated** a ruling in which he **deems** one **liable** for eating in a state of ritual impurity an item **whose** typical **manner** is such that one **eats it,** but not for eating the wood, the frankincense, or the incense, whose typical manner is such that one does not eat it. The Rabbis disagree and deem him liable in all these cases. **It was stated** that two pairs of *amora'im* disagreed with regard to this issue; one pair is **Rabbi Yoḥanan and Reish Lakish,** and the other pair is **Rabbi Elazar and Rabbi Yosei, son of Rabbi Ḥanina.** The two different opinions that follow were respectively stated by **one of this pair**[N] **and one of that pair.**

חַד אָמַר: מַחֲלוֹקֶת בְּטוּמְאַת בָּשָׂר, אֲבָל בְּטוּמְאַת הַגּוּף – דִּבְרֵי הַכֹּל אֵינוֹ לוֹקֶה.

One says: The **dispute** between the Rabbis and Rabbi Shimon is **with regard to the impurity of meat,**[H] i.e., the item that is eaten is impure. The Rabbis maintain that one who eats impure wood or frankincense is flogged, as derived from the two mentions of flesh in the verse: "And the meat that touches any impure item shall not be eaten; it shall be burned with fire. And as for the meat, everyone who is pure may eat of it" (Leviticus 7:19). **But** if one ate wood or frankincense **in** a state of **impurity of the body,**[H] **everyone agrees** that **he is not flogged.**[N]

וְחַד אָמַר: כְּמַחֲלוֹקֶת בָּזוֹ כָּךְ מַחֲלוֹקֶת בָּזוֹ, מַאי טַעְמָא? כֵּיוָן דְּקָרֵינָא בֵּיהּ: ״וְהַבָּשָׂר אֲשֶׁר יִגַּע בְּכָל טָמֵא״ – קָרֵינַן בֵּיהּ: ״וְטֻמְאָתוֹ עָלָיו״.

And one says: As there is **a dispute with regard to this** case, when the item eaten is impure, **so** is there **a dispute with regard to that** case, when the one eating the wood or frankincense is impure. **What is the reason** for this opinion? **Since one reads with regard to** these inedible items: **"And the flesh that touches any impure item"** (Leviticus 7:19), as this phrase serves to include even items such as wood and frankincense in the prohibition against eating them when they are impure, **one** likewise **reads with regard to** them the next verse: "But the person that eats of the flesh of the sacrifice of peace offerings… **having his impurity upon him,** that soul shall be cut off from his people" (Leviticus 7:20), which discusses one in a state of impurity who eats consecrated items.

רַב טַבְיוּמֵי מַתְנֵי הָכִי. רַב כָּהֲנָא מַתְנֵי הָכִי: חַד מֵהַאי זוּזָא וְחַד מֵהַאי זוּזָא אַסֵּיפָא, חַד אָמַר: מַחֲלוֹקֶת בְּטוּמְאַת הַגּוּף, אֲבָל בְּטוּמְאַת בָּשָׂר – דִּבְרֵי הַכֹּל לוֹקֶה. וְחַד אָמַר: כְּמַחֲלוֹקֶת בָּזוֹ כָּךְ מַחֲלוֹקֶת בָּזוֹ.

The Gemara notes: **Rav Tavyumei teaches** the discussion in **this** preceding manner, whereas **Rav Kahana teaches** it in **this** alternative manner: **One of this pair** of *amora'im* **and one of that pair** disagreed **with regard to the latter clause** in the mishna, i.e., the meaning of Rabbi Shimon's statement. **One says** that Rabbi Shimon's **dispute** with the Rabbis is **with regard to the impurity of the body,** as he maintains that an impure individual who eats wood or frankincense is exempt. **But with regard to the impurity of flesh,** i.e., these items themselves, **everyone agrees** that one is **flogged. And one says: As** there is **a dispute with regard to this** case, **so** is there **a dispute with regard to that** case, i.e., Rabbi Shimon holds that one is exempt in both cases.

HALAKHA

To include the sin offerings whose blood is presented inside – לְאִיתּוּיֵי חַטָּאוֹת הַפְּנִימִיּוֹת: If one eats from the flesh of sin offerings whose blood is presented inside the Sanctuary, after the blood has been presented, he is liable to receive *karet* (Rambam *Sefer Avoda, Hilkhot Pesulei HaMukdashin* 18:16).

Impurity of meat – טוּמְאַת בָּשָׂר: The Sages established a higher standard with regard to consecrated items, as despite the fact that wood and frankincense are inedible, they contract ritual impurity like food with regard to offerings. If they are rendered impure they are disqualified for use in the service. The Rambam rules in accordance with the opinion of Rabbi Shimon (Rambam *Sefer Avoda, Hilkhot Issurei Mizbe'aḥ* 6:8; see *Hilkhot Pesulei HaMukdashin* 18:12 and *Sefer Tahara, Hilkhot Tumat Okhalin* 8:9).

In a state of impurity of the body – בְּטוּמְאַת הַגּוּף: One who consumes frankincense, wood, or incense is not liable due to *notar* nor for consuming them in a state of ritual impurity, in accordance with the opinion of Rabbi Shimon. Apparently, the Ra'avad disagrees with the Rambam in this regard, and maintains that the *halakha* is in accordance with the majority opinion in the mishna, that of the Rabbis, who deem one liable for consuming these items when ritually impure. Nevertheless, even the Ra'avad agrees that this ruling applies only after they have been consecrated in a service vessel (Rambam *Sefer Avoda, Hilkhot Pesulei HaMukdashin* 18:24; see *Likkutei Halakhot*).

NOTES

One of this pair – חַד מֵהַאי זוּזָא: Rabbi Yoḥanan and Reish Lakish were a pair of contemporaries who often engaged in disputes. This was also true of Rabbi Elazar and Rabbi Yosei, son of Rabbi Ḥanina, both of whom were students of Rabbi Yoḥanan.

In a state of impurity of the body, everyone agrees that he is not flogged – בְּטוּמְאַת הַגּוּף דִּבְרֵי הַכֹּל אֵינוֹ לוֹקֶה: He is not flogged for violating the prohibition derived from the verse: "She shall touch no hallowed item" (Leviticus 12:4), that one may not eat consecrated food when ritually impure. He is all the more so not liable to receive *karet*.

אֲמַר רָבָא: מִסְתַּבְּרָא כְּמַאן דְּאָמַר כְּמַחֲלוֹקֶת בָּזוֹ כָּךְ מַחֲלוֹקֶת בָּזוֹ, מַאי טַעְמָא? כֵּיוָן דְּלָא קָרֵינָא בֵּיהּ: ״וְטֻמְאָתוֹ עָלָיו וְנִכְרְתָה״ – לָא קָרֵינַן בֵּיהּ: ״וְהַבָּשָׂר אֲשֶׁר יִגַּע בְּכָל טָמֵא לֹא יֵאָכֵל״.

Rava said: It **stands to reason** that the correct interpretation is **like the one who says: As** there **is a dispute with regard to this** case, **so** is there **a dispute with regard to that** case. **What is the reason? Since one does not read with regard to** these inedible items: **"Having his impurity upon him, that soul shall be cut off,"** as according to both alternative explanations Rabbi Shimon deems exempt one who eats these items when he is in a state of impurity, similarly **one does not read with regard to** them the previous verse: **"And the flesh that touches any impure item shall not be eaten."**

וְהָאָמַר מָר: ״וְהַבָּשָׂר״ – לְרַבּוֹת עֵצִים וּלְבוֹנָה! לְפוּסְלָהּ בְּעָלְמָא.

The Gemara raises a difficulty: **But doesn't the Master say** that the term: **"And as for the flesh,"** in the same verse, serves **to include wood and frankincense?** This indicates that even these items can become ritually impure, and the prohibition against eating consecrated items that are impure applies to them. The Gemara answers: This is referring **merely to disqualification,** i.e., this inclusion applies by rabbinic law, and the verse is cited in mere support.

מתני׳ לְשֵׁם שִׁשָּׁה דְּבָרִים הַזֶּבַח נִזְבָּח: לְשֵׁם זֶבַח, לְשֵׁם זוֹבֵחַ, לְשֵׁם הַשֵּׁם, לְשֵׁם אִשִּׁים, לְשֵׁם רֵיחַ, לְשֵׁם נִיחוֹחַ. וְהַחַטָּאת וְהָאָשָׁם – לְשֵׁם חֵטְא.

MISHNA The slaughtered offering is slaughtered[N] **for the sake of six matters,**[H] and one must have all of these matters in mind: **For the sake of** the particular type of **offering** being sacrificed; **for the sake of the one who sacrifices** the offering; **for the sake of God; for the sake of** consumption by **the fires** of the altar; **for the sake of** the **aroma; for the sake of** the **pleasing** of God, i.e., in fulfillment of God's will; **and,** in the cases **of a sin offering and a guilt offering, for the sake of** atonement for the **sin.**[N]

אָמַר רַבִּי יוֹסֵי: אַף מִי שֶׁלֹּא הָיָה בְּלִבּוֹ לְשֵׁם אֶחָד מִכָּל אֵלּוּ – כָּשֵׁר, שֶׁהוּא תְּנַאי בֵּית דִּין, שֶׁאֵין הַמַּחֲשָׁבָה הוֹלֶכֶת אֶלָּא אַחַר הָעוֹבֵד.

Rabbi Yosei says: Even in the case of **one who did not have in mind** to slaughter the offering **for the sake of any one of these,** the offering is **valid, as it is a stipulation of the court**[N] that he should not state any intent *ab initio*. This is necessary **because the intent follows only the one performing the** sacrificial **rite,** and therefore if the one who slaughters the animal is not careful and states the wrong intent, the offering would be disqualified through his improper intent.

גמ׳ אָמַר רַב יְהוּדָה אָמַר רַב: ״עוֹלָה״ – לְשֵׁם עוֹלָה, לְאַפּוֹקֵי לְשֵׁם שְׁלָמִים דְּלָא. ״אִשִּׁים״ – לְשֵׁם אִשִּׁים, לְאַפּוֹקֵי כְּבָבָא דְּלָא.

GEMARA Rav Yehuda says that **Rav says** with regard to the verse: "A burnt offering, an offering made by fire, of a pleasing aroma to the Lord" (Leviticus 1:9), the term **"a burnt offering"** means that one must intend that it be **for the sake of a burnt offering, to the exclusion of** one who sacrifices a burnt offering **for the sake of a peace offering, which** one may **not** do. The mention of **fires,** i.e., the term "an offering made by fire," teaches that the offering must be sacrificed **for the sake of** complete consumption by the **fires** of the altar, **to the exclusion of** one who intends that its portions should only be **roasted**[N] on the fire, as one may **not** do so.

״רֵיחַ״ – לְשֵׁם רֵיחַ, לְאַפּוֹקֵי אֵבָרִים שֶׁצְּלָאָן וְהֶעֱלָן, דְּלָא; דְּאָמַר רַב יְהוּדָה אָמַר רַב: אֵבָרִים שֶׁצְּלָאָן וְהֶעֱלָן – אֵין בָּהֶן מִשּׁוּם רֵיחַ.

Rav continues to expound the verse. The term **"aroma"** indicates that the offering must be sacrificed **for the sake of** the **aroma, to the exclusion of limbs that one** first **roasted and** afterward **took them up**[H] to the altar, **which** he may **not** do. **As Rav Yehuda says** that **Rav says:** With regard to **limbs that one** first **roasted and** afterward **took them up** to the altar, **they do not constitute** fulfillment of the requirement that the offering must be sacrificed for the sake of the **aroma.**

NOTES

The slaughtered offering is slaughtered – הַזֶּבַח נִזְבָּח: Some commentaries understand this mishna to be referring specifically to the act of slaughter (Rambam). Others explain that these requirements apply to the four sacrificial rites, i.e., slaughter, collecting the blood, conveying the blood to the altar, and presenting the blood upon the altar; and to the burning of the offering on the altar (*Tosafot* on 2a).

For the sake of atonement for the sin – לְשֵׁם חֵטְא: With regard to one who sacrifices a sin offering that was set aside for one sin for the sake of a different sin, e.g., a sin offering for eating forbidden fats that he sacrificed for the sake of the sin of eating blood, see 9a.

As it is a stipulation of the court – שֶׁהוּא תְּנַאי בֵּית דִּין: Rashi maintains that the court stipulated that one should not articulate the purpose for which he is sacrificing the offering, *ab initio*. The reason is that the intent follows the one performing the rite, and if he specifies his intent he might err in his wording and thereby disqualify the offering (see *Tosafot* on 2b). Some commentaries explain the mishna differently: According to the first *tanna* the owner must have these six matters in mind, whereas Rabbi Yosei maintains that it is a stipulation of the court that the intent of the owner of the offering should be entirely disregarded, and that the intent follows the one performing the rite (Rambam's Commentary on the Mishna).

To the exclusion of roasted [*kevava*] – לְאַפּוֹקֵי כְּבָבָא: One should not intend to roast the offering over coals (Rashi). Others understand that he should not intend to leave the flesh on the fire just a little until it is roasted, but should burn it entirely in the fire of the altar (Ramban on Leviticus 1:9). The Ramban there cites another version of the Gemara that reads *gevava*, rakings of wood, i.e., he should not intend to place the sacrificial portions of offerings that are to be consumed on the altar on straw or rakings, but only on the wood of the altar. Yet another interpretation is that *kevava* is related to *kibbui*, extinguishing. That is, he should not intend to place the offering on coals which are dying out (see Ra'avad on *Torat Kohanim*).

HALAKHA

The slaughtered offering is slaughtered for the sake of six matters – לְשֵׁם שִׁשָּׁה דְּבָרִים הַזֶּבַח נִזְבָּח: One must have the following six matters in mind at the time of the slaughter of a burnt offering: That it is for the sake of the particular type of offering; that it is for the sake of the one who sacrifices; that the sacrifice should be for the sake of God; that it should be burned for the sake of consumption by the fires of the altar; that it should be burned for the sake of the aroma; and that this aroma should be for the sake of pleasing God. If one slaughtered without any of these intents, the offering is valid. One who slaughters a sin offering and a guilt offering must also have in mind the specific sin for which the offering is brought (Rambam *Sefer Avoda*, *Hilkhot Ma'aseh HaKorbanot* 4:11).

Limbs that one roasted and took them up – אֵבָרִים שֶׁצְּלָאָן וְהֶעֱלָן: If one first roasted limbs and then took them up to the altar, this does not constitute fulfillment of the requirement that the offering be sacrificed for the sake of the pleasing aroma (Rambam *Sefer Avoda*, *Hilkhot Ma'aseh HaKorbanot* 6:4).

HALAKHA

Sin offering that one slaughtered for the sake of a burnt offering – חַטָּאת שֶׁשְּׁחָטָהּ לְשֵׁם עוֹלָה: If one slaughtered a sin offering for the sake of a different offering, it is disqualified. If he slaughtered it for the sake of a non-sacred animal, it is valid, although the owner has not fulfilled his obligation. The *halakha* is in accordance with the statement of Rav Yehuda (Rambam *Sefer Avoda*, *Hilkhot Pesulei HaMukdashin* 15:4).

NOTES

And they shall not profane – וְלֹא יְחַלְּלוּ: According to this interpretation, the verse is not understood as a command, but as a statement of fact: They cannot profane the sacred animals of the children of Israel and turn them into non-sacred animals, as this improper intent does not disqualify their offerings.

״נִיחוֹחַ״ – לְשֵׁם הֲנָחַת רוּחַ. ״לַה׳״ – לְשֵׁם מִי שֶׁאָמַר וְהָיָה הָעוֹלָם.

The term **"pleasing"** means **for the sake of pleasing** God's **spirit,** i.e., that the offering should be accepted by God. Finally, the expression **"to the Lord"** indicates that it should be **for the sake of the One Who spoke and the world came into being.**

אָמַר רַב יְהוּדָה אָמַר רַב: חַטָּאת שֶׁשְּׁחָטָהּ לְשֵׁם עוֹלָה – פְּסוּלָה, לְשֵׁם חוּלִּין – כְּשֵׁרָה. אָמַר רַבִּי אֶלְעָזָר: מַאי טַעְמָא דְּרַב? ״וְלֹא יְחַלְּלוּ אֶת קׇדְשֵׁי בְּנֵי יִשְׂרָאֵל״, קֳדָשִׁים מְחַלְּלִין קֳדָשִׁים, וְאֵין חוּלִּין מְחַלְּלִין קֳדָשִׁים.

Rav Yehuda says that **Rav says:** With regard to **a sin offering that one slaughtered** with intent that the slaughter be **for the sake of a burnt offering,**[H] it is **disqualified.** As explained (2a), a sin offering that was slaughtered for the sake of another offering is entirely disqualified. But if he intended the slaughter to be **for the sake of a non-sacred** animal, it is **valid. Rabbi Elazar says: What is the reason of Rav?** The verse states: **"And they shall not profane**[N] **the sacred items of the children of Israel"** (Leviticus 22:15). This teaches that **consecrated items,** i.e., the intent to slaughter an offering for the sake of another type of offering, **profane consecrated items, but** the intent to slaughter an offering for the sake of **a non-sacred** animal **does not profane consecrated items.**

מְתִיב רַבָּה: אָמַר רַבִּי יוֹסֵי: אַף מִי שֶׁלֹּא הָיָה בְּלִבּוֹ לְשֵׁם אֶחָד מִכׇּל אֵלּוּ – כָּשֵׁר, שֶׁהוּא תְּנַאי בֵּית דִּין; טַעְמָא שֶׁלֹּא הָיָה בְּלִבּוֹ כְּלָל, הָא הָיָה בְּלִבּוֹ לְשֵׁם חוּלִּין – פָּסוּל!

Rabba raises an objection from the mishna: **Rabbi Yosei says: Even** in the case of **one who did not have in mind** to slaughter the offering **for the sake of any one of these,** the offering is **fit, as it is a stipulation of the court** that one not state any intent *ab initio*. Rabba infers from this that **the reason** the offering is valid and it effects acceptance is that **he did not have in mind** any intent **at all. But** if **he had in mind** to slaughter the offering **for the sake of a non-sacred** animal, it is **disqualified.**

אֲמַר לֵיהּ אַבָּיֵי: דִּלְמָא, לֹא הָיָה כְּלָל – כָּשֵׁר וּמְרַצֶּה, הָא הָיָה בְּלִבּוֹ לְשֵׁם חוּלִּין – כָּשֵׁר וְאֵינוֹ מְרַצֶּה.

Abaye said to Rabba: **Perhaps** Rabbi Yosei means the following: If he **did not have** in mind any intent **at all,** the offering is **valid and** it **effects acceptance, but** if he **had in mind** to slaughter the offering **for the sake of a non-sacred** animal, the offering is **valid, but it does not effect acceptance,** as it is a flawed offering. Rav's statement can be understood in a similar fashion.

אָמַר רַבִּי אֶלְעָזָר: חַטָּאת שֶׁשְּׁחָטָהּ לְשֵׁם חוּלִּין – כְּשֵׁרָה, מִשּׁוּם חוּלִּין – פְּסוּלָה. כִּדְבְעָא מִינֵּיהּ שְׁמוּאֵל מֵרַב הוּנָא:

Rabbi Elazar says: Indeed, **a sin offering that one** intentionally **slaughtered for the sake of a non-sacred** animal **is valid,** as stated by Rav. But if he slaughtered it **as a non-sacred** animal, actually thinking that it was non-sacred, it is **disqualified,** as when he slaughtered it, he did not intend to perform a sacrificial rite. This is **like the dilemma that Shmuel raised before Rav Huna:**

Perek **IV**
Daf **47** Amud **a**

HALAKHA

To one who acts unawares in the case of consecrated items – לַמִּתְעַסֵּק בְּקָדָשִׁים: If when one slaughters an offering he acts unawares, rather than intending the act of slaughter, the offering is disqualified (Rambam *Sefer Avoda*, *Hilkhot Pesulei HaMukdashin* 1:3, and Mahari Kurkus there).

מִנַּיִן לַמִּתְעַסֵּק בְּקָדָשִׁים שֶׁהוּא פָּסוּל? שֶׁנֶּאֱמַר: ״וְשָׁחַט אֶת בֶּן הַבָּקָר לִפְנֵי ה׳״ – עַד שֶׁתְּהֵא שְׁחִיטָה לְשֵׁם בֶּן בָּקָר.

From where is it derived with regard **to one who acts unawares** in the case **of consecrated** items,[H] i.e., if one slaughtered an offering without intending to perform the act of slaughter at all, but rather like one occupied with other matters, **that** the offering **is disqualified?** Rav Huna said to Shmuel: It is derived from a verse, **as it is stated: "And he shall slaughter the young bull before the Lord"** (Leviticus 1:5), teaching that the mitzva is not performed properly **unless the slaughter is for the sake of a young bull,** i.e., knowing that he is performing an act of slaughter.

אֲמַר לֵיהּ: זוֹ בְּיָדֵינוּ הִיא, לְעַכֵּב מִנַּיִן? אֲמַר לֵיהּ: ״לִרְצֹנְכֶם תִּזְבָּחֻהוּ״ – לְדַעְתְּכֶם זְבִיחוּ.

Shmuel **said to** Rav Huna: **We have this** as an established *halakha* already, that it is a mitzva to slaughter the offering for the sake of a bull, but **from where** is it derived that this requirement is **indispensable?** Rav Huna **said to him** that the verse states: **"With your will you shall slaughter it"** (Leviticus 19:5),[N] i.e., **with your** full **awareness you shall slaughter** it, in the form of a purposeful action.

NOTES

With your will [*lirtzonkhem*] you shall slaughter it – לִרְצֹנְכֶם תִּזְבָּחֻהוּ: According to this interpretation, *lirtzonkhem*, which is generally translated as: That you may be accepted, is a reference to one's will [*ratzon*], i.e., an intentional, deliberate act, which excludes one who acts unawares. This expression appears twice, in Leviticus 19:5 and in 22:29, a repetition that indicates that not only is this intent required *ab initio*, but the offering is disqualified if it is lacking.

"שֶׁאֵין הַמַּחֲשָׁבָה הוֹלֶכֶת אֶלָּא אַחַר הָעוֹבֵד". מַתְנִיתִין דְּלָא כִּי הַאי תַּנָּא. דְּתַנְיָא, אָמַר רַבִּי אֶלְעָזָר בְּרַבִּי יוֹסֵי: שָׁמַעְתִּי שֶׁהַבְּעָלִים מְפַגְּלִין. אָמַר רָבָא: מַאי טַעְמָא דְּרַבִּי אֶלְעָזָר בְּרַבִּי יוֹסֵי? דְּאָמַר קְרָא: "וְהִקְרִיב הַמַּקְרִיב".

§ The mishna teaches: **Because the intent follows only the one performing the** sacrificial **rite.**[H] The Gemara comments: **The mishna is not in accordance with** the opinion of **this *tanna*, as it is taught** in a *baraita* that **Rabbi Elazar, son of Rabbi Yosei, says: I heard that** even **the owner** of an offering **can render it *piggul***[N] through improper intention. **Rava says: What is the reason of Rabbi Elazar, son of Rabbi Yosei? As the verse states: "Then he who sacrifices shall sacrifice**[N] his offering to the Lord" (Numbers 15:4). The term "he who sacrifices" is a reference to the owner; since the owner is considered one who sacrifices, he too can render his offering *piggul* with an improper intention.

אָמַר אַבַּיֵי: רַבִּי אֶלְעָזָר בְּרַבִּי יוֹסֵי, וְרַבִּי אֱלִיעֶזֶר, וְרַבִּי שִׁמְעוֹן בֶּן אֶלְעָזָר – כּוּלְּהוּ סְבִירָא לְהוּ: זֶה מְחַשֵּׁב וְזֶה עוֹבֵד – הָוְיָא מַחֲשָׁבָה; רַבִּי אֶלְעָזָר בְּרַבִּי יוֹסֵי – הָא דַּאֲמָרַן;

Abaye says: Rabbi Elazar, son of Rabbi Yosei, and Rabbi Eliezer, and Rabbi Shimon ben Elazar all hold that even in a case involving two people, where **this one has intention and that one performs the service, it is the intention** that is relevant, i.e., it is as though the one performing the service had the intention. The Gemara explains: The statement of **Rabbi Elazar, son of Rabbi Yosei, is that which we** just **said,** that the owner can render his offering *piggul* through improper intention despite the fact that it is the priest who performs the service.

רַבִּי אֱלִיעֶזֶר – דִּתְנַן: הַשּׁוֹחֵט לְגוֹי – שְׁחִיטָתוֹ כְּשֵׁרָה, וְרַבִּי אֱלִיעֶזֶר פּוֹסֵל;

The statement of **Rabbi Eliezer** is **as we learned** in a mishna (*Ḥullin* 38b): With regard to **one who slaughters** an animal on behalf **of a gentile,**[H] **his slaughter is valid** and a Jew may eat the meat of this animal. **But Rabbi Eliezer deems it unfit,** as the intention of the gentile, which is presumably to use the animal for idol worship, invalidates the act of slaughter performed by the Jew.

רַבִּי שִׁמְעוֹן בֶּן אֶלְעָזָר – דִּתְנַן, כְּלָל אָמַר רַבִּי שִׁמְעוֹן בֶּן אֶלְעָזָר: כָּל שֶׁאֵין כָּשֵׁר לְהַצְנִיעַ, וְאֵין מַצְנִיעִין כָּמוֹהוּ, הוּכְשַׁר לָזֶה וְהִצְנִיעוֹ, וּבָא אַחֵר וְהוֹצִיאוֹ – נִתְחַיֵּיב זֶה בְּמַחֲשָׁבָה שֶׁל זֶה.

The statement of **Rabbi Shimon ben Elazar is as we learned** in a *baraita*: **Rabbi Shimon ben Elazar stated a principle:** In the case of **any** item **that is not fit to be stored,**[H] **and** therefore people do **not** typically **store** items **like it,** but **it was deemed fit** for storage **by this** person **and he stored it, and another** person **came and carried out**[B] on Shabbat the item that was stored, **that** one who carried it out **is rendered liable by the thought of this** one who stored it.

תַּרְוַיְיהוּ אִית לְהוּ דְּרַבִּי אֶלְעָזָר בְּרַבִּי יוֹסֵי, הָשְׁתָּא בַּחוּץ אָמְרִינַן – בִּפְנִים מִיבַּעְיָא?

The Gemara notes: **These two** Sages, Rabbi Eliezer and Rabbi Shimon ben Elazar, although their rulings are stated in the context of entirely different matters, **accept** as *halakha* the ruling **of Rabbi Elazar, son of Rabbi Yosei.** The Gemara explains: **Now** that concerning matters **outside** the Temple, i.e., non-sacred slaughter and carrying on Shabbat, with regard to which the Torah makes no reference to intention, **we say** that the intention of one person is effective for the action of another, **is it necessary** to state that the same *halakha* applies to matters **inside** the Temple, i.e., offerings, with regard to which it is explicitly stated that intention is effective, as indicated by the verse: "With your will you shall slaughter it" (Leviticus 19:5)?

רַבִּי אֶלְעָזָר בְּרַבִּי יוֹסֵי לֵית לְהוּ דְּתַרְוַיְיהוּ, דִּלְמָא בִּפְנִים הוּא דְּאָמְרִינַן, בַּחוּץ לָא אָמְרִינַן.

But **Rabbi Elazar, son of Rabbi Yosei, does not** necessarily **accept** as *halakha* the rulings of **these two** Sages, Rabbi Eliezer and Rabbi Shimon ben Elazar. The Gemara explains: **Perhaps** it is only concerning **inside** the Temple **that we say** that one person's intention is effective for the action of another, whereas concerning **outside** the Temple, **we do not say** this.

HALAKHA

The intent follows…the one performing the rite – הַמַּחֲשָׁבָה הוֹלֶכֶת...אַחַר הָעוֹבֵד: The intent follows only the one who performs the sacrificial rite; the owner's intent is irrelevant. Even if it is known that the owner had an improper intent of the type that can render an offering *piggul*, if there was nothing amiss with the intent of the one performing the rite, the offering is valid, in accordance with the opinion of Rabbi Yosei in the mishna (Rambam *Sefer Avoda, Hilkhot Pesulei HaMukdashin* 14:1, and see *Kesef Mishne* there).

One who slaughters on behalf of a gentile – הַשּׁוֹחֵט לְגוֹי: If one slaughters an animal on behalf of a gentile the slaughter is valid, even if the gentile intends it to be for idol worship. The reason is that only the intent of the one performing the act of slaughter is taken into account. Consequently, if a gentile slaughters on behalf of a Jew the meat is non-kosher, even if the gentile is a minor. The *halakha* is not in accordance with the opinion of Rabbi Eliezer (Rambam *Sefer Kedusha, Hilkhot Sheḥita* 2:22 and *Kesef Mishne* there; *Shulḥan Arukh, Yoreh De'a* 4:3).

Any item that is not fit to be stored, etc. – כָּל שֶׁאֵין כָּשֵׁר לְהַצְנִיעַ וכו׳: In the case of an item that people generally do not store and that is not fit to be stored, but one nevertheless stored it, if he transferred it from one domain to another on Shabbat, he is liable, whereas all others who do so are exempt. The *halakha* is not in accordance with the opinion of Rabbi Shimon ben Elazar (Rambam *Sefer Zemanim, Hilkhot Shabbat* 18:22).

NOTES

That the owner can render it *piggul* – שֶׁהַבְּעָלִים מְפַגְּלִין: This is referring to a case where the priest performs the rite in silence, while the owner has an improper intention that renders the offering *piggul*.

Then he who sacrifices shall sacrifice – וְהִקְרִיב הַמַּקְרִיב: This is referring to the owner of the offering, not the priest who performs the rite. Consequently, the verse that discusses *piggul*: "Neither shall it be imputed to he who sacrifices it" (Leviticus 7:18), should be explained in the same manner, as referring to the owner.

BACKGROUND

Carrying out – הוֹצָאָה: One of the Torah's thirty-nine categories of labor prohibited on Shabbat is the act of carrying out items, which is treated in detail in a significant portion of tractate *Shabbat*. The labor of carrying out includes two different situations. First, the transfer of an item from a private to a public domain or vice versa, without regard to the distance the item was moved; second, carrying an item four cubits in the public domain. Despite the differences between these scenarios, they share several common elements. In both cases, the item in question is lifted from a significant surface of a minimum requisite measure, and then placed on another similar surface. If only one of the stages, lifting or placing, was performed by an individual or if each was performed by a different person, the act does not constitute labor prohibited on Shabbat by Torah law.

רַבִּי שִׁמְעוֹן בֶּן אֶלְעָזָר אִית לֵיהּ דְּרַבִּי אֱלִיעֶזֶר, הָשְׁתָּא בְּשַׁבָּת אָמְרִינַן, בַּעֲבוֹדָה זָרָה מִיבַּעְיָא?

The Gemara further differentiates between the opinions of those two Sages themselves. **Rabbi Shimon ben Elazar accepts** as *halakha* the ruling **of Rabbi Eliezer: Now** that **with regard to Shabbat we say** that the intention of one person is effective for the action of another, **is** it **necessary** to say that the same applies **concerning idol worship,** where the actions are somewhat similar to those performed in the Temple?

רַבִּי אֱלִיעֶזֶר לֵית לֵיהּ דְּרַבִּי שִׁמְעוֹן בֶּן אֶלְעָזָר, דִּלְמָא בַּעֲבוֹדָה זָרָה הוּא דְּאָמְרַתְּ כְּעֵין בִּפְנִים, אֲבָל שַׁבָּת – מְלֶאכֶת מַחֲשֶׁבֶת אָסְרָה תוֹרָה.

But **Rabbi Eliezer does not** necessarily **accept** as *halakha* the ruling **of Rabbi Shimon ben Elazar: Perhaps it is** only **with regard to idol worship that you say** that one person's intention is effective for the action of another, as idol worship is somewhat **similar to** service performed **inside**[N] the Temple. Consequently, it is reasonable that one person's intention is effective for the action of another in the case of idolatry, as it does for offerings. **But** with regard to **Shabbat, the Torah prohibited** only **planned,** constructive **labor,**[N] i.e., one is liable only for an action that includes the creative intent of the doer, and here the one who took the item out did not intend to perform a labor.

הדרן עלך בית שמאי

NOTES

Somewhat similar to service performed inside – **כְּעֵין בִּפְנִים**: There is a principle with regard to idol worship that one is liable whether he performs the particular service of that idol or worships it in a manner similar to the service in the Temple, even if the idol is not usually served in that fashion. Consequently, it is reasonable that the details of the service inside the Temple, e.g., intent, should equally apply to idol worship.

The Torah prohibited only planned labor – **מְלֶאכֶת מַחֲשֶׁבֶת אָסְרָה תוֹרָה**: A large proportion of the *halakhot* of Shabbat are derived by juxtaposition with the instructions of the building of the Tabernacle (see Exodus 35:1–3 and onward). This juxtaposition teaches that the various forms of labor performed in the Tabernacle are those that are prohibited on Shabbat. With regard to the labor of the Tabernacle it is stated: "Creative labor" (Exodus 35:33), from which it is derived that the labors prohibited on Shabbat must be purposeful and constructive. With regard to *piggul*, the *halakha* is that the one who slaughters must intend to perform that action, and one who by mistake has an improper thought has not rendered the offering *piggul*. Nevertheless, the disqualification of *piggul* refers to the offering, through the intent of the person. By contrast, in the case of Shabbat the liability is not applied to the item carried, but to the individual who performs the action. Consequently, if he himself does not have the improper intent, it cannot be ascribed to him through the intent of another, and therefore he is not deemed liable (see *Rosh HaMizbe'aḥ*).

Summary of **Perek IV**

Although different forms of presenting blood are prescribed for the various offerings, e.g., on all four corners of the altar, or on two diagonally opposite corners, a single presentation is sufficient after the fact. This *halakha* has ramifications for *piggul,* as it means that *piggul* status applies only if the improper intention was in the first presentation. This principle does not apply to those sin offerings whose blood is presented inside the Sanctuary, as all these presentations are indispensable and the set of presentations is considered a single unit. Therefore, *piggul* status takes effect only if the priest had the improper intention in the performance of all the presentations.

This ruling is connected to another *halakha,* that an item that has more than one permitting factor becomes *piggul* only if the improper intention occurred in the performance of all its permitting factors. Furthermore, in general *piggul* applies only if the permitting factor was sacrificed in accordance with its mitzva, and therefore a different improper intention in its performance, e.g., the intent to eat the offering outside its designated area, would prevent *piggul* status from taking effect. If that other intention occurred in the second presentation of the blood of an offering sacrificed outside the Sanctuary, the offering is *piggul,* as that presentation is not indispensable to the atonement.

Another principle with regard to *piggul* is that it is modeled on the example of peace offerings, in which the *halakha* of *piggul* is stated. Consequently, *piggul* status applies only if the intention to burn or eat the offering outside its designated time occurred in the performance of a service outside the Sanctuary, or when the intention referred to sacrificing or eating outside the Sanctuary, but not when one of these was inside.

It is further derived from the basic model of the peace offering that *piggul* applies only to an item that has a permitting factor, not to the permitting factor itself. Therefore, *piggul* status is not conferred on blood, in the case of an animal offering, or the handful or frankincense, which are the permitting factors of a meal offering.

Some offerings do not have permitting factors, e.g., the meal offering of priests, from which no handful is separated; libations, whether they are brought together with an offering or by themselves; and the oil employed in the purification rites of the leper. With regard to such offerings, one who eats them is not liable for consuming *piggul.* Even in those situations where one is not liable for *piggul,* one can be liable for eating sacrificial food in a state of ritual impurity and for eating *notar.*

Concerning gentiles who brought offerings to the Temple, although these offerings are sacrificed on their behalf, nevertheless the *halakhot* of the offerings of a Jew do not apply to these offerings. Accordingly, one is not liable for *piggul, notar,* or for eating them in a state of ritual impurity.

At the end of the chapter, a list is provided of matters for the sake of which an offering must be slaughtered, i.e., the proper intentions that must accompany the bringing of an offering. The Sages stated that it is preferable not to state these intentions explicitly, to avoid articulating improper intentions by mistake.

Introduction to **Perek V**

This is the law of the burnt offering, of the meal offering, and of the sin offering, and of the guilt offering, and of the consecration offering, and of the sacrifice of peace offerings; which the Lord commanded Moses on Mount Sinai, in the day that he commanded the children of Israel to present their offerings to the Lord, in the wilderness of Sinai.

(Leviticus 7:37–38)

This chapter is an overview of all of the animal offerings in the Temple. It does not address bird offerings, which are examined in the sixth and seventh chapters. It also does not address meal offerings or other items brought to the altar, which are described in tractate *Menaḥot*, although they are also discussed in passing in the next chapter (63a).

The offerings are mentioned in their order of sanctity. First the Gemara discusses offerings of the most sacred order, which must be slaughtered in the north of the Temple courtyard. Then it continues with an analysis of offerings of lesser sanctity, which may be slaughtered anywhere in the Temple courtyard. The next distinction between the offerings is where the blood is presented and how that presentation is performed. If the blood is presented closer to the innermost sanctum the offering has greater sanctity, and if more blood presentations are required it also has greater sanctity. An additional distinction is drawn on the basis of the time allotted for eating the offering. Generally, an offering that is permitted to be eaten for a shorter duration of time is discussed earlier in the chapter.

The order in which the various *halakhot* of offerings are detailed in the mishna is as follows: The location of slaughter, the location of the blood presentation, what is done with the flesh and sacrificial portions, and how the remainder of the blood is poured.

Another topic described in this chapter is the methodology of halakhic exposition in the realm of consecrated matters. The Sages had a tradition that not all of the hermeneutical principles may be used to derive a *halakha* and then be used again to apply that *halakha* to another matter in the realm of consecrated matters. This chapter clarifies which principles may be used in this way and which may not.

The details of these *halakhot* and hermeneutical principles are the main topic of this chapter.

מתני׳ אֵיזֶהוּ מְקוֹמָן שֶׁל זְבָחִים? קָדְשֵׁי קָדָשִׁים שְׁחִיטָתָן בַּצָּפוֹן.

MISHNA **What is the location** of the slaughtering and consumption **of offerings?**[N] The principle is that with regard to **offerings of the most sacred order,**[B] **their slaughter** is **in the north**[H] of the Temple courtyard.

פַּר וְשָׂעִיר שֶׁל יוֹם הַכִּפּוּרִים – שְׁחִיטָתָן בַּצָּפוֹן, וְקִיבּוּל דָּמָן בִּכְלִי שָׁרֵת בַּצָּפוֹן, וְדָמָן טָעוּן הַזָּיָה עַל בֵּין הַבַּדִּים וְעַל הַפָּרוֹכֶת וְעַל מִזְבַּח הַזָּהָב, מַתָּנָה אַחַת מֵהֶן מְעַכֶּבֶת. שְׁיָרֵי הַדָּם הָיָה שׁוֹפֵךְ עַל יְסוֹד מַעֲרָבִי שֶׁל מִזְבֵּחַ הַחִיצוֹן, וְאִם לֹא נָתַן – לֹא עִכֵּב.

Specifically, with regard to **the bull and the goat of Yom Kippur,**[HB] **their slaughter is in the north and the collection of their blood in a service vessel is in the north, and their blood requires sprinkling between the staves** of the Ark in the Holy of Holies, **and upon the Curtain** separating the Sanctuary and Holy of Holies, **and on the golden altar.**[B] Concerning all those sprinklings, failure to perform even **one placement of their** blood **disqualifies** the offering. As to **the remainder of the blood,** which is left after those sprinklings, a priest **would pour it onto the western base of the external altar.**[B] **But if he did not place** the remainder of the blood on the western base, it does **not disqualify** the offering.

פָּרִים הַנִּשְׂרָפִים וּשְׂעִירִים הַנִּשְׂרָפִים – שְׁחִיטָתָן בַּצָּפוֹן, וְקִיבּוּל דָּמָן בִּכְלִי שָׁרֵת בַּצָּפוֹן, וְדָמָן טָעוּן הַזָּיָה עַל הַפָּרוֹכֶת וְעַל מִזְבַּח הַזָּהָב,

With regard to **bulls that are burned and goats that are burned,**[H] **their slaughter** is **in the north** of the Temple courtyard, **and the collection of their blood in a service vessel** is **in the north, and their blood requires sprinkling upon the Curtain**[B] separating the Sanctuary and Holy of Holies, **and upon the golden altar,**

NOTES

Offerings [*zevaḥim*] – זְבָחִים: Even though the biblical term *zevaḥim* is used specifically in reference to peace offerings (see, e.g., Leviticus 3:1), the mishna uses the term in reference to all animals that are slaughtered, to exclude bird offerings, meal offerings, and incense (Rashbatz).

HALAKHA

Offerings of the most sacred order…in the north – קָדְשֵׁי קָדָשִׁים...בַּצָּפוֹן: Offerings of the most sacred order must be slaughtered in the north, and their blood must be collected in the north (Rambam *Sefer Avoda, Hilkhot Ma'aseh HaKorbanot* 5:2).

The bull and the goat of Yom Kippur – פַּר וְשָׂעִיר שֶׁל יוֹם הַכִּפּוּרִים: The blood of the bull and the blood of the goat of Yom Kippur each require eight sprinklings between the staves of the Ark and eight sprinklings on the Curtain. Afterward, the blood of the bull is mixed with the blood of the goat, and the mixture is sprinkled on the four corners of the golden altar and then sprinkled seven times on the top of that altar (Rambam *Sefer Avoda, Hilkhot Ma'aseh HaKorbanot* 5:12 and *Hilkhot Avodat Yom HaKippurim* 4:2).

Bulls that are burned and goats that are burned – פָּרִים הַנִּשְׂרָפִים וּשְׂעִירִים הַנִּשְׂרָפִים: The blood of bulls that are burned and goats that are burned is sprinkled seven times on the Curtain between the Holy of Holies and the Sanctuary, and four times on the golden altar, once on each of its four corners (Rambam *Sefer Avoda, Hilkhot Ma'aseh HaKorbanot* 5:13).

BACKGROUND

Offerings of the most sacred order – קָדְשֵׁי קָדָשִׁים: Burnt offerings, sin offerings, guilt offerings, and communal peace offerings are included in this category. The following *halakhot* apply specifically to these offerings: They are slaughtered only in the northern section of the Temple courtyard. Those offerings that are eaten may be eaten only on the day the animal is sacrificed and the following night, only by priests, and only within the Temple courtyard. The prohibition against misuse of Temple property applies to these offerings as soon as they are consecrated. Once their blood is presented on the altar, the prohibition against misuse continues to apply to portions of the offering consumed on the altar, but not to portions of the offering that are to be eaten.

Northern section of the Temple courtyard

The bull and goat of Yom Kippur – פַּר וְשָׂעִיר שֶׁל יוֹם הַכִּפּוּרִים: On Yom Kippur, the High Priest sacrifices a bull as a sin offering for himself, his family, and all the members of the priesthood (see Leviticus 16:3, 6). The bull's slaughter, the burning of its flesh, and the sprinkling of its blood resemble the procedures of the bulls that are burned outside Jerusalem. In contrast to those, its blood is also sprinkled between the staves of the Holy Ark in the Holy of Holies. The blood of this bull is first sprinkled on its own; afterward it is mixed with the blood of the goat sacrificed as a sin offering for the entire people, and the mixed blood is sprinkled on the golden incense altar.

Golden altar – מִזְבַּח הַזָּהָב: Also known as the incense altar and the inner altar, the golden altar stood in the middle of the Sanctuary. It was one cubit square along its entire height of two cubits. This altar was overlaid with gold, and it had four protrusions, one on each corner. Incense was sacrificed every day on the inner altar, and on Yom Kippur the blood of the special Yom Kippur offerings was sprinkled on its top and on its corners.

Golden altar

Base of the altar – יְסוֹד הַמִּזְבֵּחַ: This diagram shows the place where the offerings were burned, the corners of the altar, the ledge surrounding the altar, and the base on the north and west sides of the altar.

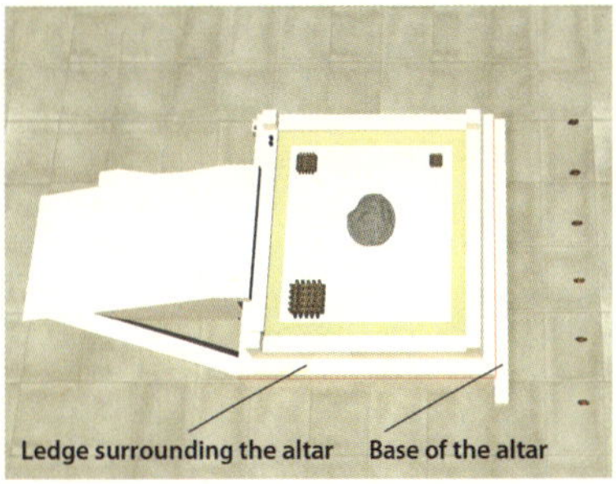

Aerial view of the altar

Curtain – פָּרוֹכֶת: The Curtain in the Tabernacle and the First Temple, or two Curtains in the Second Temple, divided the Sanctuary from the Holy of Holies. The blood of the bulls that are burned, as well as the blood of the offerings sacrificed by the High Priest on Yom Kippur was sprinkled on this curtain. This term can also refer to other curtains hung over certain gates in the Temple complex.

High Priest sprinkling blood on the Curtain on Yom Kippur

מַתָּנָה אַחַת מֵהֶן מְעַכֶּבֶת. שְׁיָרֵי הַדָּם הָיָה שׁוֹפֵךְ עַל יְסוֹד מַעֲרָבִי שֶׁל מִזְבֵּחַ הַחִיצוֹן, וְאִם לֹא נָתַן – לֹא עִיכֵּב. אֵלּוּ וָאֵלּוּ נִשְׂרָפִין אַבֵּית הַדֶּשֶׁן.

and failure to perform even **one placement of their** blood **disqualifies** the offering. As for **the remainder of the blood** that is left after those sprinklings, a priest **would pour** it **onto the western base of the external altar,**[B] **but if he did not pour** the remainder it does **not disqualify** the offering. **These,** the bull and the goat of Yom Kippur, **and those,** the bulls and the goats that are burned, **are** then **burned in the place of the ashes,**[NH] a place outside of Jerusalem where the priests would bring the ashes from the altar.

גמ׳ וְנִיתְנֵי נַמִי: וְקִיבּוּל דָּמָן בִּכְלִי שָׁרֵת בַּצָּפוֹן! כֵּיוָן דְּאִיכָּא אֲשַׁם מְצוֹרָע דְּקִיבּוּל דָּמוֹ בְּיָד הוּא – שַׁיְירֵיהּ.

GEMARA The mishna opens with a principle that the slaughter of offerings of the most sacred order is in the north of the Temple courtyard. The Gemara inquires: **And let** the mishna **also teach** as a principle: **And the collection of their blood in a service vessel** is **in the north** of the Temple courtyard. Since collecting the blood is an indispensable part of the service, why is it not listed in this clause of the mishna? The Gemara explains: **Since there is** among the offerings of the most sacred order **the guilt offering of a leper,** for **which the collection of its blood is in the hand,** the mishna could not state this as a principle. Therefore, the *tanna* **omitted** this from the requirements for offerings of the most sacred order.

וְלָא? וְהָא קָתָנֵי לַהּ לְקַמָּן: אֲשַׁם נָזִיר וַאֲשַׁם מְצוֹרָע – שְׁחִיטָתָן בַּצָּפוֹן, וְקִבּוּל דָּמָן בִּכְלִי שָׁרֵת בַּצָּפוֹן!

The Gemara challenges: **And** is the blood of the guilt offering of a leper **not** collected in a service vessel? **But** the mishna **teaches** this *halakha* **later** (54b): With regard to **the guilt offering of a nazirite** brought for his purification **and the guilt offering of a leper** brought for his purification, **their slaughter** is **in the north** of the Temple courtyard **and collection of their blood in a service vessel** is **in the north.** Apparently, the *tanna* maintains that the blood of the guilt offering of a leper must be collected in a service vessel.

מֵעִיקָּרָא סָבַר: קִיבּוּל דָּמוֹ בְּיָד הוּא, שַׁיְירֵיהּ. וְכֵיוָן דְּלָא סַגִּי לֵיהּ אֶלָּא בִּכְלִי – הֲדַר תַּנְיֵיהּ.

The Gemara answers: **Initially,** the *tanna* **held** that since **collection of the blood of** the guilt offering of a leper must also be **in the** priest's **hand,** not exclusively in a service vessel, **he omitted it. But since** it is the case **that it is possible for** one to collect some of the blood **only in** a service **vessel,** the *tanna* **subsequently taught it.**

דְּתַנְיָא: ״וְלָקַח״, יָכוֹל בִּכְלִי? תַּלְמוּד לוֹמַר: ״וְנָתַן״, מָה נְתִינָה בְּעַצְמוֹ שֶׁל כֹּהֵן – אַף לְקִיחָה בְּעַצְמוֹ שֶׁל כֹּהֵן.

This is **as it is taught** in a *baraita* (*Tosefta, Nega'im* 9:2): The Torah states with regard to the guilt offering of a leper: **"And** the priest **shall take** of the blood of the guilt offering, and the priest shall put it upon the tip of the right ear of him who is to be purified, and upon the thumb of his right hand, and upon the big toe of his right foot" (Leviticus 14:14). One **might** have thought that he should take it **in a vessel;** therefore, **the verse states: "And** the priest **shall put." Just as putting** the blood on the ear, thumb, and big toe must be performed **with the priest's own** body, **so too, taking** of the blood is performed **with the priest's own** body, not with a service vessel.

BACKGROUND

Western base of the external altar – יְסוֹד מַעֲרָבִי שֶׁל מִזְבֵּחַ הַחִיצוֹן: The image shows the place where the offerings were burned, the corners of the altar, the ledge surrounding the altar, and the base on the western and northern sides of the altar.

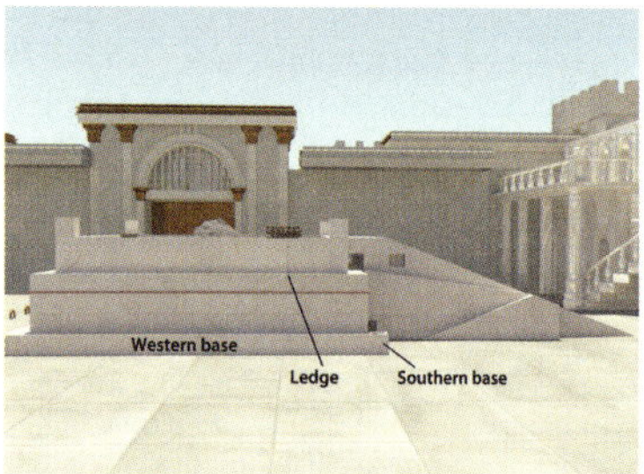

View of the altar from the west

HALAKHA

These and those are burned in the place of the ashes – אֵלּוּ וָאֵלּוּ נִשְׂרָפִין אַבֵּית הַדֶּשֶׁן: Sin offerings that are burned must be slaughtered and have their blood sprinkled in the Sanctuary. Afterward, the remainder of the blood is poured on the western base of the external altar, and then the portions for the altar are removed and thrown onto the fire. The remainder of the animal is taken outside Jerusalem and burned in the place of the ashes (Rambam *Sefer Avoda, Hilkhot Ma'aseh HaKorbanot* 5:11, 7:2 and *Hilkhot Avodat Yom HaKippurim* 4:2).

NOTES

Burned in the place of the ashes – נִשְׂרָפִין אַבֵּית הַדֶּשֶׁן: This is a specific place described in the Torah: "And he shall take off his garments, and put on other garments, and carry forth the ashes without the camp unto a pure place" (Leviticus 6:4). When the Jewish people were in the wilderness, the ashes were placed outside the entire camp. In the time of the Temple, the place of the ashes was outside the city of Jerusalem. The Torah states explicitly that the bull of the anointed priest must be burned in this place: "He shall carry forth, outside the camp, the whole bull, to a pure place, where the ashes are poured out, and burn it on wood with fire; where the ashes are poured out it shall be burned" (Leviticus 4:12). The place of the ashes is not mentioned explicitly with regard to the other offerings that are burned. Rashi explains that the derivation for this principle with regard to the bull for an unwitting communal sin is from the verse: "And he shall carry forth the bull outside the camp, and burn it as he burned the first bull; it is the sin offering for the assembly" (Leviticus 4:21). The term "first bull" is a reference to the bull of the anointed priest, to teach that the bull for an unwitting communal sin is burned in the same place. The requirement to burn the bull of Yom Kippur and the goat brought for communal idolatry in that same place is derived by the Talmud (39b) through juxtaposition of those verses with those concerning the bull of an anointed priest.

יָכוֹל אַף לַמִּזְבֵּחַ כֵּן? תַּלְמוּד לוֹמַר: "כִּי כַּחַטָּאת הָאָשָׁם הוּא", מָה חַטָּאת טְעוּנָה כְּלִי – אַף אָשָׁם טָעוּן כְּלִי. נִמְצֵאתָ אַתָּה אוֹמֵר: אֲשַׁם מְצוֹרָע שְׁנֵי כֹהֲנִים מְקַבְּלִין אֶת דָּמוֹ, אֶחָד בַּיָּד וְאֶחָד בִּכְלִי, זֶה שֶׁקִּיבְּלוֹ בִּכְלִי – בָּא לוֹ אֵצֶל מִזְבֵּחַ, וְזֶה שֶׁקִּיבְּלוֹ בַּיָּד – בָּא לוֹ אֵצֶל מְצוֹרָע.

The *baraita* continues: One **might** have thought that **even** with regard to the blood of the leper's guilt offering that he presents **on the altar,** like the blood of other guilt offerings, it is **so,** that he collects the blood in his hand rather than with a vessel. To counter this, **the verse states: "For as the sin offering is, so is the guilt offering"** (Leviticus 14:13).[N] This teaches that **just as a sin offering requires a vessel** for collection of its blood, **so too,** the blood of **a guilt offering requires a vessel** for collection of its blood. **You** consequently **say:** In the case of **a leper's guilt offering, two priests collect its blood;**[H] **one** collects the blood **by hand, and** the other **one** collects the blood **in a vessel.**[N] **This one, who collected** the blood **in a vessel, comes to the altar** and sprinkles some of the blood on it. **And that** one, **who collected** the blood **by hand, comes to** the **leper** and places some of the blood on his right ear, right thumb, and right big toe.

NOTES

As the sin offering is so is the guilt offering – כִּי כַּחַטָּאת הָאָשָׁם הוּא: The *halakha* of the sin offering is learned from the *halakha* of the burnt offering through a verbal analogy using the term "take." With regard to the burnt offering the verse states explicitly: "And Moses took half of the blood and put it in basins, and half of the blood he dashed against the altar" (Exodus 24:6).

One by hand and one in a vessel – אֶחָד בַּיָּד וְאֶחָד בִּכְלִי: The *baraita* states that the first priest collects the blood in a vessel and afterward the second priest collects it in his hand. The *Meshekh Ḥokhma* explains that whereas the order in the *baraita* is according to the order in which the service is performed, the Gemara here teaches the collection by hand first, because this is the unusual element of the service.

HALAKHA

A leper's guilt offering, two priests collect its blood – אֲשַׁם מְצוֹרָע שְׁנֵי כֹהֲנִים מְקַבְּלִין אֶת דָּמוֹ: After the leper's guilt offering is slaughtered, two priests collect the blood. One collects it in a vessel and sprinkles it on the altar, and the other collects it in his right hand, pours it into his left hand, and walks to the leper and places the blood from his hand onto the leper's right earlobe, right thumb, and right big toe (Rambam *Sefer Korbanot*, *Hilkhot Meḥusrei Kappara* 4:2).

Perek **V**
Daf **48** Amud **a**

"פַּר וְשָׂעִיר שֶׁל יוֹם הַכִּיפּוּרִים" כו׳. מִכְּדִי צָפוֹן בְּעוֹלָה כְּתִיב, נִיתְנֵי עוֹלָה בְּרֵישָׁא!

§ The mishna teaches: With regard to **the bull and the goat of Yom Kippur,** their slaughter is in the north and the collection of their blood in a service vessel is in the north. The Gemara asks: Why does the mishna list these sin offerings first? **After all,** while the *halakha* that slaughter must be in the **north** of the Temple courtyard **is written** in the Torah **with regard to a burnt offering** (Leviticus 1:11), the Torah does not explicitly state that the other offerings must be slaughtered in the north. Therefore, **let** the *tanna* of the mishna **teach** the *halakha* of **a burnt offering first.**

חַטָּאת, אַיְּידֵי דַּאֲתֵי מִדְּרָשָׁא חֲבִיבָא לֵיהּ.

The Gemara answers: **Since** the location for slaughtering the **sin offering is derived through interpretation, it is dear to** the *tanna*,[N] and he therefore he gives it precedence. The verse states: "Speak to Aaron and to his sons, saying: This is the law of the sin offering: In the place where the burnt offering is slaughtered shall the sin offering be slaughtered before the Lord; it is most holy" (Leviticus 6:18). The Gemara (55a) derives from this verse that the sin offering must be slaughtered in the same place as the burnt offering, i.e., in the north of the Temple courtyard.

וְנִיתְנֵי חַטָּאוֹת הַחִיצוֹנוֹת! אַיְּידֵי דְּנִכְנָס דָּמָן לִפְנַי וְלִפְנִים חֲבִיבָא לֵיהּ.

The Gemara challenges: **But let** the *tanna* of the mishna **teach** first the *halakha* of **the external sin offerings,** since those are the offerings to which the verse is referring. The Gemara explains: **Since** the **blood** of the Yom Kippur sin offerings **enters the innermost sanctum,** these offerings are **dear to** the *tanna*, and he taught them first.

וְ"צָפוֹנָה" בְּעוֹלָה הֵיכָא כְּתִיבָא? "וְשָׁחַט אֹתוֹ עַל יֶרֶךְ הַמִּזְבֵּחַ צָפֹנָה".

The Gemara asks: **And where** is it **written** that **a burnt offering** must be slaughtered in the **north** of the Temple courtyard? The Gemara answers that with regard to a sheep that is brought as a burnt offering the Torah states: **"And he shall slaughter it on the side of the altar northward** before the Lord; and Aaron's sons, the priests, shall dash its blood against the altar round about" (Leviticus 1:11).

NOTES

Since it…is derived through interpretation it is dear to him – אַיְּידֵי דַּאֲתֵי מִדְּרָשָׁא חֲבִיבָא לֵיהּ: This concept appears elsewhere in the Talmud to explain the order of a mishna. Usually it is in reference to an interpretation of the verse by the Sages, whereas in this case the Torah itself juxtaposes the sin offering to the burnt offering with regard to their place of slaughter. Nevertheless, the *halakha* derived from this juxtaposition is still considered dear, since the location for slaughtering a sin offering is not explicit in the verse and requires an interpretation to derive it.

HALAKHA

Uncertain misuse of consecrated property – סָפֵק מְעִילוֹת: If one is uncertain whether he has committed a sin for which he would be liable to bring a guilt offering, e.g., for misuse of consecrated property, he is exempt from bringing an offering (Rambam *Sefer Korbanot, Hilkhot Shegagot* 9:11).

אַשְׁכְּחַן בֶּן צֹאן, בֶּן בָּקָר מְנָא לַן? אָמַר קְרָא: "וְאִם מִן הַצֹּאן" – וי"ו מוֹסִיף עַל עִנְיָן רִאשׁוֹן, וְיִלָּמֵד עֶלְיוֹן מִתַּחְתּוֹן.

The Gemara clarifies: **We have found** that this verse provides a source that **a young sheep** burnt offering must be slaughtered in the north. **From where do we** derive that **a young bull** burnt offering must also be slaughtered in the north? The Gemara answers: **The verse states: "And if** his offering be **of the flock,** whether of the sheep, or of the goats, for a burnt offering, he shall offer it a male without blemish" (Leviticus 1:10). The conjunctive "and" represented by the letter ***vav* adds to the previous matter.** The previous passage addresses cattle offerings. **And let** the **upper** passage, the place of the slaughter of a bull, **be learned from** the **lower** passage, the place of slaughtering a sheep.

הָנִיחָא לְמַאן דְּאָמַר מְלַמְּדִין, אֶלָּא לְמַאן דְּאָמַר אֵין מְלַמְּדִין מַאי אִיכָּא לְמֵימַר?

The Gemara comments: **This works out well according to the one who says** that **we learn** *halakhot* in this manner. **But according to the one who says** that **we do not learn** *halakhot* in this manner, **what is there to say?**

דְּתַנְיָא: "וְאִם נֶפֶשׁ" וגו' – לְחַיֵּיב עַל סְפֵק מְעִילוֹת אָשָׁם תָּלוּי, דִּבְרֵי רַבִּי עֲקִיבָא, וַחֲכָמִים פּוֹטְרִין; מַאי לָאו בְּהָא קָא מִיפַּלְגִי, מָר סָבַר: לְמֵידִין, וּמָר סָבַר: אֵין לְמֵידִין?

As it is taught in a *baraita*: Immediately following the passage in the Torah addressing a guilt offering for misuse of consecrated property, the Torah discusses the *halakhot* of a provisional guilt offering, brought by one who is uncertain as to whether he committed a sin that requires a sin offering. The verse states: **"And if anyone** sin, and does any of the commandments which the Lord has commanded not to be done, though he did not know it, yet is he guilty, and shall bear his iniquity" (Leviticus 5:17). This serves **to render** him **liable** to bring **a provisional guilt offering**[N] **for uncertain misuse** of consecrated property;[H] this is **the statement of Rabbi Akiva. And the Rabbis deem** him **exempt** in such a case. The Gemara suggests: **What, is it not** that **they disagree with regard to this:** One **Sage,** Rabbi Akiva, **holds** that **we learn** *halakhot* of the upper passage from the lower passage, **and the** other **Sage,** i.e., the Rabbis, **holds** that **we do not learn** *halakhot* in this manner?

אָמַר רַב פַּפָּא: דְּכוּלֵּי עָלְמָא לְמֵידִין, וְהַיְינוּ טַעְמָא דְּרַבָּנַן: נֶאֱמַר כָּאן "מִצְוֹת" וְנֶאֱמַר בְּחַטַּאת חֵלֶב "מִצְוֹת",

Rav Pappa said: This is not correct, **as everyone** holds that **we learn** *halakhot* of the upper passage from the lower passage. **And this is** the **reason that the Rabbis** exempt from bringing an offering one who is uncertain whether he misused consecrated property: They learn a verbal analogy. **It is stated here:** "And if anyone sin, and does any of the **commandments** which the Lord has commanded not to be done" (Leviticus 5:17). **And it is stated with regard to the sin offering for** eating forbidden **fat:**[N] "And if any one of the common people sin through error, in doing any of the **commandments** which the Lord has commanded not to be done, and be guilty" (Leviticus 4:27).

מַה לְּהַלָּן דָּבָר שֶׁחַיָּיבִין עַל זְדוֹנוֹ כָּרֵת וְעַל שִׁגְגָתוֹ חַטָּאת – אַף כָּאן שֶׁחַיָּיבִין עַל זְדוֹנוֹ כָּרֵת וְעַל שִׁגְגָתוֹ חַטָּאת.

The verbal analogy teaches that **just as there,** the sin offering is brought only for an act **that for its intentional** violation **one is liable** to be punished with ***karet*, and for its unwitting** violation one is liable to bring **a sin offering, so too here,** one brings a provisional guilt offering only for an act **that for its intentional** violation **one is liable** to be punished with ***karet*, and for its unwitting** violation one is liable to bring **a sin offering,** which is not the case concerning misuse of consecrated property.

NOTES

Provisional guilt offering – אָשָׁם תָּלוּי: A sin offering is brought by one who unwittingly violates a prohibition that is punishable by *karet* if violated intentionally. A provisional guilt offering is brought for transgressions that require one to bring a sin offering, in a case where it is unclear whether one actually committed the transgression. For example, if one is not sure whether he consumed blood or not, he brings a provisional guilt offering until the facts are clarified. If he subsequently learns that he did sin, he brings a sin offering. Rabbi Akiva holds that even though the Torah in this passage makes reference only to transgressions for which one is liable to bring a sin offering, nevertheless, because of the placement of this passage it also applies to an uncertain case of misuse of consecrated property, which is a transgression for which one brings a guilt offering in cases of definite transgression. An example of this uncertainty would be if there were two pieces of meat, one consecrated and one unconsecrated, and he ate one of them, but does not know whether it was the consecrated one or not.

Sin offering for forbidden fat – חַטַּאת חֵלֶב: The term: Sin offering for forbidden fat, is used for any sin offering brought by one who unwittingly violates a prohibition whose intentional violation is punishable by *karet*. This is in contrast to communal sin offerings or the sin offering of a nazirite. Rashi explains that the name: Sin offering for forbidden fat, is used due to the fact that immediately after the Torah delineates the prohibition: "You shall eat neither fat nor blood" (Leviticus 3:17), it delineates the *halakhot* of sin offerings.

The Rosh explains that the source of the use of this term is the fact that this particular sin is common; when one slaughters an animal in order to eat its meat, it could easily happen that one would fail to remove all of the forbidden fat. Additionally, once the fat has been removed from the animal it is very difficult to distinguish between the permitted fat and the forbidden fat, as they appear very similar. Therefore, one is likely to eat the forbidden fat unwittingly and be required to bring a sin offering on its account.

וְרַבִּי עֲקִיבָא: מָה לְהַלָּן בִּקְבוּעָה – אַף כָּאן בִּקְבוּעָה, לְאַפּוֹקֵי חַטַּאת דְּטוּמְאַת מִקְדָּשׁ וְקָדָשָׁיו דְּעוֹלֶה וְיוֹרֵד הוּא.

The Gemara asks: **And** what does **Rabbi Akiva** derive from this verbal analogy? He learns that **just as there** the verse obligates one to bring **a fixed** sin offering, **so too here,** with regard to the provisional guilt offering, one brings it for a case of uncertain transgression of a prohibition for which one would be liable to bring **a fixed** sin offering, **to exclude a sin offering** brought for uncertain transgression **of** the **defiling of** the **Temple or sacrificial** foods, **as** the sin offering for that transgression is not fixed, but **is a sliding-scale** offering.[B] If the sinner is poor he brings a meal offering or a bird offering; if he is rich he brings an animal offering. In a case of uncertainty one does not bring a provisional guilt offering.

וְרַבָּנַן: אֵין גְּזֵירָה שָׁוָה לְמֶחֱצָה. וְרַבִּי עֲקִיבָא נַמִי, אֵין גְּזֵירָה שָׁוָה לְמֶחֱצָה!

And as for **the Rabbis,** who derived a different *halakha* from the verbal analogy, they hold that **there is no verbal analogy for half** of a matter. Once a provisional guilt offering is compared to a sin offering, it must be completely similar, and both matters are derived from the verbal analogy. The Gemara asks: **But Rabbi Akiva also** must hold that **there is no verbal analogy for half** of a matter, so why does he not agree with the derivation of the Rabbis?

אִין הָכִי נַמִי. וְהָכָא בְּהָא קָמִיפַּלְגִי, רַבִּי עֲקִיבָא סָבַר: "וְאִם נֶפֶשׁ" כְּתִיב, וי"ו מוֹסִיף עַל עִנְיָן רִאשׁוֹן.

The Gemara reconsiders: **Yes, this** is **indeed so. And here they disagree with regard to this: Rabbi Akiva holds** that **it is written** with regard to the provisional guilt offering: **"And if anyone** sin, and does any of the commandments which the Lord has commanded not to be done, though he did not know it, yet is he guilty, and shall bear his iniquity" (Leviticus 5:17). The word "and" represented by the letter ***vav*** **adds to the previous matter.** When a phrase begins with the conjunction *vav*, it is a continuation of the previous matter, and the *halakhot* of the previous passage can be learned from the subsequent passage. Therefore one brings a provisional guilt offering for uncertain misuse of consecrated property.

וְרַבָּנַן נַמִי, הָכְתִיב: "וְאִם נֶפֶשׁ"! לֵימָא בְּהָא קָמִיפַּלְגִי, דְּמָר סָבַר: הֶיקֵּשׁ עָדִיף, וּמָר סָבַר: גְּזֵירָה שָׁוָה עָדִיף?

The Gemara asks: **But** according to the opinion of **the Rabbis also, isn't it written: "And if anyone** sin"? **Let us say** that **they disagree about this: As one Sage,** Rabbi Akiva, **holds** that a derivation from **a juxtaposition is preferable,**[N] and derives from the juxtaposition of the *halakhot* of misuse of consecrated property to the *halakhot* of a provisional guilt offering that one is liable to bring a provisional guilt offering if he is not certain whether he misused consecrated property. **And** one **Sage,** i.e., the Rabbis, **holds** that a derivation from **a verbal analogy is preferable,** and therefore derive from a verbal analogy between the passage of misuse of consecrated property and the passage of a sin offering for eating forbidden fat that one is not liable to bring a provisional guilt offering if he is not certain whether he misused consecrated property.

לָא, דְּכוּלֵּי עָלְמָא דְּהֶיקֵּשׁ עָדִיף, וְאָמְרִי לָךְ רַבָּנַן: תַּחְתּוֹן הוּא דְּגָמַר מֵעֶלְיוֹן

The Gemara rejects this: **No,** it may be that **everyone** agrees **that** a derivation from **a juxtaposition is preferable. And the Rabbis would say to you** that the reason one is exempt from bringing a provisional guilt offering in a case of uncertain misuse of consecrated property is that the juxtaposition should be understood in the opposite manner. **It is the lower** passage **that** is **derived from** the **upper** passage.

לְאָשָׁם בְּכֶסֶף שְׁקָלִים, שֶׁלֹּא תֹּאמַר: לֹא יְהֵא סְפֵיקוֹ חָמוּר מִוַּדָּאוֹ, מָה וַדָּאוֹ חַטָּאת בַּת דַּנְקָא – אַף סְפֵיקוֹ אָשָׁם בַּר דַּנְקָא.

The juxtaposition teaches that a provisional **guilt offering** must be a ram **worth** a minimum of two **silver shekels,**[H] as is the *halakha* with regard to the offering brought for misuse of consecrated property. This derivation is needed **so that you should not say** that a provisional guilt offering, brought for **his uncertain** transgression, **should not be** more **stringent than** the offering one brings in a case of **his definite** transgression. According to that claim, one would say that **just as** for **his definite** transgression one may bring **a sin offering worth** only **one-sixth** [*danka*][NL] of a dinar, **so too,** for **his uncertain** transgression one may bring a provisional **guilt offering worth** only **one-sixth** of a dinar.

BACKGROUND

Sliding-scale offering – **קׇרְבָּן עוֹלֶה וְיוֹרֵד**: This type of sin offering is unique in that the offering which is brought depends on the financial circumstances of the sinner. One with sufficient means is required to bring a sin offering of a female lamb or goat. A poor person, who is unable to afford such an offering, brings a pair of birds instead, one as a burnt offering and one as a sin offering. One who cannot afford even a pair of birds brings a meal offering. The sliding-scale offering is brought for the violation of three sins: Violating an oath, taking a false oath to avoid giving testimony, and entering the Temple or partaking of sacrificial foods while ritually impure.

NOTES

A juxtaposition is preferable, etc. – **הֶיקֵּשׁ עָדִיף וכו׳**: Each type of derivation has its merits. A juxtaposition is more explicit in the verse, because the Torah equates two concepts by placing them next to each other, whereas a verbal analogy is based on identical words in two different places. Conversely, since a verbal analogy may be derived only on the basis of a tradition, and one may not create a new verbal analogy, it has greater strength.

Worth one-sixth [*danka*] – **בַּת דַּנְקָא**: A *danka* is equivalent to the Hebrew coin known as a *ma'a*. Rashi holds that in this case it does not refer to a specific minimum value, but means any small amount.

HALAKHA

Guilt offering worth two silver shekels – **אָשָׁם בְּכֶסֶף שְׁקָלִים**: A ram brought for a guilt offering, including a provisional guilt offering, must be worth at least two silver shekels. The exceptions are the guilt offerings of the nazirite and the leper, which have no minimum value (Rambam *Sefer Avoda, Hilkhot Pesulei HaMukdashin* 4:22).

LANGUAGE

One-sixth [*danka*] – **דַּנְקָא**: From the Middle Persian dāng, meaning particle, *danka* was the name of a Persian coin, called a *ma'a* in Aramaic. Since the *ma'a* was one-sixth of a dinar, the Sages used the word *danka* to refer to one-sixth in many contexts.

וְרַבִּי עֲקִיבָא, הָא סְבָרָא מְנָא לֵיהּ? נָפְקָא לֵיהּ מִ״זֹּאת תּוֹרַת הָאָשָׁם״ – תּוֹרָה אַחַת לְכׇל הָאֲשָׁמוֹת.

The Gemara asks: **And from where** does **Rabbi Akiva** derive **this conclusion?** The Gemara answers: **He derives** it **from** the verse that states: **"And this is the law of the guilt offering"** (Leviticus 7:1), which teaches that there is **one law for all of the guilt offerings**[N] and they must all be worth at least two shekels, provisional guilt offerings included.

תֵּינַח מַאן דְּאִית לֵיהּ ״תּוֹרַת״, מַאן דְּלֵית לֵיהּ ״תּוֹרַת״ מֵהֵיכָא גָּמַר? גָּמַר ״בְּעֶרְכְּךָ״ ״בְּעֶרְכְּךָ״.

The Gemara asks: This **works out well** according to **one who holds** that there is a derivation from the word **"law,"** but according to the **one who does not hold** that there is a derivation from the word **"law," from where does he learn** that all guilt offerings must have the same minimum value? The Gemara answers: **He learns** it from a verbal analogy between the term **"according to your valuation"** stated with regard to a guilt offering for misuse of consecrated property (Leviticus 5:15) and the term **"according to your valuation"** stated with regard to a provisional guilt offering (Leviticus 5:18) and a guilt offering for robbery (Leviticus 5:25).

תֵּינַח הֵיכָא דִּכְתִיב ״בְּעֶרְכְּךָ״, אֲשַׁם שִׁפְחָה חֲרוּפָה דְּלָא כְּתִיב בֵּיהּ ״בְּעֶרְכְּךָ״, מַאי אִיכָּא לְמֵימַר?

The Gemara asks: This **works out well** concerning guilt offerings **where it is written "according to your valuation,"** but with regard to **a guilt offering** brought for engaging in sexual intercourse with **an espoused maidservant, concerning which** it is **not written** in the Torah **"according to your valuation," what is there to say?** How does one derive that the guilt offering brought for engaging in sexual intercourse with an espoused maidservant must be worth a minimum of two silver shekels?

גָּמַר ״בְּאֵיל״ ״בְּאֵיל״.

The Gemara answers that it is **derived** from a verbal analogy between the term **"with the ram"** stated with regard to a guilt offering for misuse of consecrated property (Leviticus 5:16) and the term **"with the ram"** stated with regard to the guilt offering for engaging in sexual intercourse with an espoused maidservant (Leviticus 19:22).

חַטָּאת מְנָא לַן דְּבָעְיָא צָפוֹן – דִּכְתִיב: ״וְשָׁחַט אֶת הַחַטָּאת בִּמְקוֹם הָעוֹלָה״.

§ The Gemara returns to discuss the mishna. **From where do we** derive that **a sin offering requires** slaughter in the **north** of the Temple courtyard? The Gemara answers: **As it is written** with regard to an individual sin offering: "And he shall place his hand upon the head of the sin offering, **and slaughter the sin offering in the place of the burnt offering**" (Leviticus 4:29). Just as a burnt offering must be slaughtered in the north of the Temple courtyard, so too, a sin offering must also be slaughtered in the north.

אַשְׁכְּחַן שְׁחִיטָה, קַבָּלָה מְנָא לַן? דִּכְתִיב: ״וְלָקַח הַכֹּהֵן מִדַּם הַחַטָּאת״.

The Gemara asks: **We have found** from this verse that the **slaughter** must be in the north. **From where do we** derive that **collection** of the blood must also be in the north? The Gemara answers: **As it is written: "And the priest shall take of the blood of the sin offering** with his finger and place it upon the corners of the altar of burnt offering, and all its remaining blood he shall pour out at the base of the altar" (Leviticus 4:34). As this verse immediately follows the verse discussing the slaughter of a sin offering, evidently the taking of the blood is performed in the same place as the slaughter.

מְקַבֵּל עַצְמוֹ מְנָא לַן? אָמַר קְרָא ״וְלָקַח״ – לוֹ יִקַּח.

The Gemara asks: **From where do we** derive that **the one collecting** the blood must **himself** stand in the north of the Temple courtyard? Perhaps he may stand near the north and extend his arm to collect the blood. The Gemara answers that **the verse states: "And** the priest **shall take** [*velakaḥ*]" (Leviticus 4:34), which can be read, as: **He will take himself**[N] [*lo yikkaḥ*].

אַשְׁכְּחַן לְמִצְוָה, לְעַכֵּב מְנַיִן? קְרָא אַחֲרִינָא כְּתִיב: ״וְשָׁחַט אוֹתוֹ בִּמְקוֹם אֲשֶׁר יִשְׁחַט אֶת הָעוֹלָה״; וְתַנְיָא: הֵיכָן עוֹלָה נִשְׁחֶטֶת – בַּצָּפוֹן, אַף זֶה בַּצָּפוֹן.

The Gemara asks: **We have found** that the offering must be slaughtered in the north and the blood collected in the north **to** perform the **mitzva** in the optimal manner. **From where** is it derived that if one slaughters the offering or collects the blood anywhere else the offering is **disqualified?** The Gemara answers: **It is written** in **another verse**[N] which speaks of a goat sin offering brought by a king who sins: "And he shall place his hand upon the head of the goat **and slaughter it in the place where they slaughter the burnt offering** before the Lord; it is a sin offering" (Leviticus 4:24). **And it is taught** in a *baraita*: **Where is the burnt offering slaughtered? In the north. This** sin offering of a king must **also** be slaughtered **in the north** of the Temple courtyard.

NOTES

One law for all of the guilt offerings – תּוֹרָה אַחַת לְכׇל הָאֲשָׁמוֹת: This does not actually mean that all of the guilt offerings are identical, but rather applies only to all those for which one must bring a ram. The guilt offerings of a nazirite and of a leper are sheep, not rams, and therefore have lesser value.

And shall take, he will take himself – וְלָקַח לוֹ יִקַּח: Rashi explains that this is based on transposing the first two letters of the word, as if it were written: He will take himself. On the next *amud* the Gemara has another derivation from the extra letter *vav*, that the term could have been written simply as: Take, but instead it is written as "and take" (see Rid). Perhaps these two explanations complement each other, and it is because of the extra *vav* that the word can be interpreted as if the first two letters were reversed.

It is written in another verse – קְרָא אַחֲרִינָא כְּתִיב: Since it is written twice in the Torah it teaches that if not done in this manner it is disqualified.

וְכִי מִכָּאן אַתָּה לָמֵד? וַהֲלֹא כְּבָר נֶאֱמַר ״בִּמְקוֹם אֲשֶׁר תִּשָּׁחֵט הָעוֹלָה תִּשָּׁחֵט הַחַטָּאת״! הָא לָמָּה יָצָא – לִקְבּוֹעַ לוֹ מָקוֹם, שֶׁאִם לֹא שְׁחָטָהּ בַּצָּפוֹן – פָּסוּל.

The Gemara asks: **And do you learn** this *halakha* **from here? But isn't it already stated:** "Speak to Aaron and to his sons, saying: This is the law of the sin offering: **In the place where the burnt offering is slaughtered shall the sin offering be slaughtered** before the Lord; it is most holy" (Leviticus 6:18)? If so, **to what** purpose **was this singled out?** Why did the Torah state explicitly that the sin offering of the king requires slaughter in the north? The Gemara answers: **To fix a place for it,**[H] that this is the only place where a sin offering may be slaughtered, teaching **that if it was not slaughtered in the north** of the Temple courtyard, the offering is **disqualified** even after the fact.

אַתָּה אוֹמֵר לְכָךְ יָצָא, אוֹ אֵינוֹ אֶלָּא שֶׁזֶּה טָעוּן צָפוֹן וְאֵין אַחֵר טָעוּן צָפוֹן? תַּלְמוּד לוֹמַר: ״וְשָׁחַט אֶת הַחַטָּאת בִּמְקוֹם הָעוֹלָה״, זֶה בָּנָה אָב לְכָל חַטָּאוֹת שֶׁיְּהוּ טְעוּנוֹת צָפוֹן.

The Gemara asks: Do **you say** that it is **singled out for this** purpose, to teach that even after the fact a sin offering slaughtered anywhere other than in the north is disqualified? **Or** perhaps **it is only** to teach **that this** goat sin offering **requires** slaughter in the **north but no other** goat sin offering **requires** slaughter in the **north.** The Gemara answers: **The verse states:** "And he shall place his hand upon the head of the sin offering, **and slaughter the sin offering**[N] **in the place of the burnt offering**" (Leviticus 4:29). **This established a paradigm for all sin offerings,** teaching **that they require** slaughter in the **north.**

אַשְׁכְּחַן שְׂעִיר נָשִׂיא בֵּין לְמִצְוָה בֵּין לְעַכֵּב. שְׁאָר חַטָּאוֹת נַמִי אַשְׁכְּחַן לְמִצְוָה, לְעַכֵּב מְנָא לַן?

The Gemara continues its explanation: **We have found** that the Torah writes with regard to the **goat** sin offering **of a king** that it requires slaughter in the north **both to** perform the **mitzva** in the optimal manner and **to disqualify** the offering even after the fact. **We have also found** with regard to the **other sin offerings** that the Torah states that **to** perform the **mitzva**[N] in the optimal manner they must be slaughtered in the north of the Temple courtyard. **From where do we** derive the *halakha* **to disqualify** other sin offerings if they were not slaughtered in the north?

דִּכְתִיב בְּכִבְשָׂה וּכְתִיב בִּשְׂעִירָה.

The Gemara explains: **As it is written with regard to a lamb** sin offering that it must be slaughtered in the north: "And slaughter the sin offering in the place of the burnt offering" (Leviticus 4:33) **and** it is also **written with regard to a she-goat** sin offering: "And he shall place his hand upon the head of the sin offering, and slaughter it for a sin offering in the place of the burnt offering" (Leviticus 4:29). This repetition teaches that a sin offering is disqualified if it is not slaughtered in the north.

אֶלָּא ״אֹתוֹ״ לָמָּה לִי?

§ Having derived from these verses that all sin offerings are disqualified if they are slaughtered not in the north, the Gemara questions its earlier explanation. **Rather, why do I** need the term **"it"** stated with regard to the sin offering of a king in the verse: "And he shall place his hand upon the head of the goat, and slaughter it in the place where they slaughter the burnt offering before the Lord; it is a sin offering" (Leviticus 4:24)?

NOTES

And slaughter the sin offering – **וְשָׁחַט אֶת הַחַטָּאת**: Rashi explains that the paradigm is derived from the fact that the verse does not write: And slaughter it, but: "And slaughter the sin offering." This means that every offering that is called a sin offering has the same requirement to be slaughtered in the north, in the place that the burnt offering is slaughtered. In general, a paradigm can be used to derive that which is written explicitly to all similar cases, even without a deductive inference from the verse. In this case this paradigm would not have been used without the deductive inference, due to the exclusionary term "it" stated with regard to the sin offering of a king.

We have also found with other sin offerings that to perform the mitzva – **שְׁאָר חַטָּאוֹת נַמִי אַשְׁכְּחַן לְמִצְוָה**: Even though the Gemara has already cited two verses which refer to the other sin offerings: "In the place where the burnt offering is slaughtered shall the sin offering be slaughtered" (Leviticus 6:18), and: "And slaughter the sin offering in the place of the burnt offering" (Leviticus 4:29), the *baraita* explains that these verses are necessary to teach that all the sin offerings apart from the goat offering of a king also require slaughter in the north of the Temple courtyard.

HALAKHA

To fix a place for it – **לִקְבּוֹעַ לוֹ מָקוֹם**: Offerings of the most sacred order that are slaughtered in the south of the Temple courtyard or have their blood collected in the south are disqualified, in accordance with the conclusion of the Gemara (Rambam *Sefer Avoda, Hilkhot Pesulei HaMukdashin* 1:7).

NOTES

Derive placing hands itself via a paradigm – סְמִיכָה גּוּפַהּ תֵּיתֵי מִבִּנְיַן אָב: The verse states: "And he shall place his hand upon the head of the sin offering, and slaughter the sin offering in the place of the burnt offering" (Leviticus 4:29). One can learn from here that any offering described as a sin offering requires placing hands on the head of the offering.

We do not learn from sin offerings applicable to all generations – מִדּוֹרוֹת לָא גָּמְרִינַן: Any derivation through a paradigm is based on the principle that there is some commonality and comparison between the other cases and the paradigm. Since offerings that were brought only once in history are unique, their details cannot be derived from a paradigm. Details that can be derived from apparently superfluous words in the Torah are not dependent on comparison.

מִיבָּעֵי לֵיהּ לְכִדְתַנְיָא: אוֹתוֹ בַּצָּפוֹן, וְאֵין שְׂעִיר נַחְשׁוֹן בַּצָּפוֹן.

The Gemara answers: **It is required for that which is taught** in a *baraita*: **It,** the goat sin offering of a king, is slaughtered **in the north** of the Tabernacle, **but** the **goat** offered by **Nahshon** and the other princes was **not** slaughtered **in the north.** Nahshon was the prince of the tribe of Judah. He, along with all the other princes of the tribes, brought offerings to inaugurate the altar and the Tabernacle, as recorded in the Torah (Numbers, chapter 7). Although the offerings were classified as sin offerings because they shared some characteristics of sin offerings, they were not brought to atone for any particular sin. Therefore, the term "it" teaches that the offerings of the princes did not require slaughter in the north.

וְתַנְיָא: ״וְסָמַךְ יָדוֹ עַל רֹאשׁ הַשָּׂעִיר״ – לְרַבּוֹת שְׂעִיר נַחְשׁוֹן לִסְמִיכָה, דִּבְרֵי רַבִּי יְהוּדָה. רַבִּי שִׁמְעוֹן אוֹמֵר: לְרַבּוֹת שְׂעִירֵי עֲבוֹדָה זָרָה לִסְמִיכָה.

And the reason that it is necessary for the Torah to exclude Nahshon's sin offering from the requirement of slaughter in the north is because **it is taught** in a *baraita*: The verse states with regard to the sin offering of a king: **"And he shall place his hand upon the head of the goat,** and slaughter it in the place where they slaughter the burnt offering before the Lord; it is a sin offering" (Leviticus 4:24). The verse could have stated: Upon its head. The reason it adds "of the goat" is **to include** the **goat** brought as a sin offering by **Nahshon in** the requirement of **placing hands** on the head of an offering. This is **the statement of Rabbi Yehuda. Rabbi Shimon says:** The term "of the goat" serves **to include** the **goats** brought as sin offerings for communal **idol worship in** the requirement of **placing hands** on the head of an offering.

סָלְקָא דַעְתָּךְ אָמִינָא: הוֹאִיל וְאִיתְרַבּוּ לִסְמִיכָה – אִיתְרַבּוּ נַמִי לְצָפוֹן, קָא מַשְׁמַע לַן.

The Gemara explains: It might **enter your mind to say** that **since** the sin offerings of the princes **are included in** the requirement of **placing hands, they are also included in** the requirement of being slaughtered in the **north.** Therefore, the term "it" **teaches us** that for the goat brought as a sin offering by Nahshon and the other princes there was no requirement of slaughter in the north.

מַתְקִיף לַהּ רָבִינָא: הָנִיחָא לְרַבִּי יְהוּדָה, לְרַבִּי שִׁמְעוֹן מַאי אִיכָּא לְמֵימַר?

Ravina objects to this interpretation: **This works out well according to** the opinion of **Rabbi Yehuda,** who says that the offering of Nahshon required him to place his hands on the head of the animal. But **according to** the opinion of **Rabbi Shimon, what is there to say?** Why should the Torah write the term "it," since there is no reason to assume that it would require slaughter in the north?

אֲמַר לֵיהּ מָר זוּטְרָא בְּרֵיהּ דְּרַב טָבִי לְרָבִינָא: וּלְרַבִּי יְהוּדָה מִי נִיחָא? לְמַאי דְּאִיתְרַבֵּי – אִיתְרַבֵּי, וּמַאי דְּלָא אִיתְרַבֵּי – לָא אִיתְרַבֵּי!

Mar Zutra, son of Rav Tavi, said to Ravina: And according to the opinion of **Rabbi Yehuda, does it work out well?** Why is it necessary for the Torah to specifically exclude the offerings of the princes from the requirement of slaughter in the north? Why not say that **for that** for **which it was included,** i.e., placing hands on the head of an animal, **it was included, and** for **that which it was not included,** i.e., slaughter in the north, **it was not included.**

וְכִי תֵּימָא, אִי לָא מַעֲטֵיהּ קְרָא, הֲוָה אָמִינָא: תֵּיתֵי בְּבִנְיַן אָב – אִם כֵּן, סְמִיכָה גּוּפַהּ תֵּיתֵי מִבִּנְיַן אָב! אֶלָּא מִדּוֹרוֹת לָא גָּמְרִינַן – הָכִי נַמִי מִדּוֹרוֹת לָא גָּמְרִינַן!

And if you would say that **if the verse had not excluded** the offerings of the princes **I would say** that one could **derive** the requirement for slaughter in the north **via a paradigm**[B] from all other sin offerings, **if so,** one could also **derive** the requirement for **placing hands** on the head of an animal **itself via** the same **paradigm.**[N] **Rather,** the reason that the requirement of placing hands cannot be derived via a paradigm is that **we do not learn** the requirements of the sin offering of Nahshon, which was only for the time of the inauguration of the Tabernacle alone, **from** the requirement of sin offerings applicable to all **generations. So too,** the requirement of slaughter in the north cannot be derived via a paradigm because **we do not learn** the requirements of the sin offering of Nahshon **from** the requirement of sin offerings applicable to all **generations.**[N]

BACKGROUND

Paradigm – בִּנְיַן אָב: Paradigms are among the fundamental talmudic principles of biblical interpretation, and they appear in all the standard lists of hermeneutical principles. The simplest form of the analogy is: Just as a particular *halakha* applies in one case, it may be inferred that in another case that is similar to the first case, the same *halakha* applies.

וְאֶלָּא: אוֹתוֹ בַּצָּפוֹן, וְאֵין שׁוֹחֵט בַּצָּפוֹן.

Rather, the term "it" stated with regard to the sin offering of a king serves to teach that **it** must be slaughtered **in the north** of the Temple courtyard, **but the one who slaughters** it does **not** need to stand **in the north** when he slaughters it.

שׁוֹחֵט מִדְּרַבִּי אֲחִיָּא נָפְקָא. דְּתַנְיָא, רַבִּי אֲחִיָּא אוֹמֵר: "וְשָׁחַט אוֹתוֹ עַל יֶרֶךְ הַמִּזְבֵּחַ צָפֹנָה" מַה תַּלְמוּד לוֹמַר?

The Gemara challenges this: The *halakha* of the one who **slaughters** the offering has already been **derived from** the statement **of Rabbi Aḥiyya,**[N] **as it is taught** in a *baraita*: **Rabbi Aḥiyya says:** The verse states with regard to the burnt offering: **"And he shall slaughter it on the side of the altar northward** before the Lord" (Leviticus 1:11). **Why must the verse state** the exclusionary term "it"?

לְפִי שֶׁמָּצִינוּ עוֹמֵד בַּצָּפוֹן וּמְקַבֵּל בַּצָּפוֹן, וְאִם עָמַד בַּדָּרוֹם וְקִיבֵּל בַּצָּפוֹן פָּסוּל, יָכוֹל אַף זֶה כֵּן? תַּלְמוּד לוֹמַר: "אוֹתוֹ" – אוֹתוֹ בַּצָּפוֹן וְאֵין הַשּׁוֹחֵט בַּצָּפוֹן!

He explains: **Since we have found** that the priest **stands in the north and collects** the blood from the neck of the animal **in the north, and if he stood in the south and collected** the blood **in the north**[H] the offering is **disqualified,** one **might** have thought that this is **so also** with regard to **this** one who slaughters the offering. Therefore, **the verse states:** "And he shall slaughter **it,**" to teach that **it,** the animal, must be **in the north, but the one who slaughters** it is **not** required to be standing **in the north**[H] of the Temple courtyard when he slaughters the animal. Therefore, the question must be addressed: What is derived from the exclusionary term "it" stated with regard to the sin offering of a king?

אֶלָּא: אוֹתוֹ בַּצָּפוֹן וְאֵין בֶּן עוֹף בַּצָּפוֹן. דְּתַנְיָא: יָכוֹל יְהֵא בֶּן עוֹף טָעוּן צָפוֹן? וְדִין הוּא: וּמַה בֶּן צֹאן שֶׁלֹּא קָבַע לוֹ כֹּהֵן – קָבַע לוֹ צָפוֹן, בֶּן עוֹף שֶׁקָּבַע לוֹ כֹּהֵן – אֵינוֹ דִּין שֶׁיִּקְבַּע לוֹ צָפוֹן? תַּלְמוּד לוֹמַר: "אוֹתוֹ".

The Gemara explains: **Rather,** the term "it" stated with regard to the sin offering of a king serves to teach that **it,** a goat brought as a sin offering, must be slaughtered **in the north, but a young bird** brought as an offering does **not** need to be killed **in the north.** This is **as it is taught** in a *baraita*: One **might** have thought that **a male bird requires** pinching of the nape in the **north** of the Temple courtyard. **And this** can be derived through **a logical inference: Just as a young sheep** brought as a burnt offering is an offering for **which** the Torah **did not fix** that **its** slaughter must be performed by **a priest** but nevertheless **fixed** that **its** slaughter must be in the **north,** with regard to **a young bird** brought as an offering, for **which** the Torah **did fix** that **its** killing must be performed by **a priest, is it not logical that** the Torah **should** also **fix its** slaughter in the **north?** Therefore, **the verse states "it,"** to exclude a male bird from the requirement of being killed in the north.

מַה לְבֶן צֹאן שֶׁכֵּן קָבַע לוֹ כְּלִי!

The Gemara questions the logical inference. One cannot derive the *halakha* of a bird offering from the *halakha* of a sheep offering, as **what** is notable **about a young** sheep offering? It is notable **in that** the Torah **fixed** the requirement that **it** be slaughtered with **a utensil,** i.e., a knife. A bird, by contrast, is killed by the priest using his fingernail. Therefore, the term "it" cannot serve to counter this derivation.

אֶלָּא: אוֹתוֹ בַּצָּפוֹן וְאֵין פֶּסַח בַּצָּפוֹן.

The Gemara explains: **Rather,** the term "it" stated with regard to the sin offering of a king serves to teach that **it,** the goat of the king, is slaughtered **in the north, but** the **Paschal offering** is **not** slaughtered **in the north.**

דְּתַנְיָא, רַבִּי אֱלִיעֶזֶר בֶּן יַעֲקֹב אוֹמֵר: יָכוֹל יְהֵא פֶּסַח טָעוּן צָפוֹן? וְדִין הוּא: וּמָה עוֹלָה, שֶׁכֵּן לֹא קָבַע לוֹ זְמַן לִשְׁחִיטָתוֹ – קָבַע לוֹ צָפוֹן, פֶּסַח שֶׁקָּבַע לוֹ זְמַן לִשְׁחִיטָתוֹ – אֵינוֹ דִּין שֶׁיִּקְבַּע לוֹ צָפוֹן? תַּלְמוּד לוֹמַר: "אוֹתוֹ".

As it is taught in a *baraita*: **Rabbi Eliezer ben Yaakov says:** One **might** have thought that **a Paschal offering requires** slaughter in the **north. And this** can be derived through **a logical inference: Just as a burnt offering** is an offering for **which** the Torah **did not fix a time for its slaughter** but **fixed** that **it** requires slaughter in the **north,** with regard to **a Paschal offering,** for **which** the Torah **fixed a time for its slaughter,** as it must be slaughtered in the afternoon of the fourteenth day of Nisan, **is it not logical that** the Torah **would fix** that **it** must be slaughtered in the **north?** Therefore, **the verse states "it,"** to exclude the Paschal offering from the requirement of slaughter in the north.

מַה לְעוֹלָה שֶׁכֵּן כָּלִיל!

The Gemara questions the logical inference. One cannot derive the *halakha* of a Paschal offering from the *halakha* of a burnt offering, as **what** is notable **about a burnt offering?** It is notable **in that** the Torah teaches that **it is entirely** burned on the altar. This is not so with regard to a Paschal offering.

NOTES

Is derived from the statement of Rabbi Aḥiyya – מִדְּרַבִּי אֲחִיָּא נָפְקָא: Even though Rabbi Ahiyya's statement was in reference to a burnt offering and not a sin offering, it can be understood based on the words of the Gemara at the end of the *amud* that the derivation cannot be more stringent than the primary source. The requirement for slaughter in the north is stated with regard to a burnt offering. If one who slaughters a burnt offering is not required to stand in the north as he slaughters, certainly one who slaughters a sin offering is not required to stand in the north (see *Tosafot* on *Menaḥot* 56a).

HALAKHA

Stood in the south and collected the blood in the north – עָמַד בַּדָּרוֹם וְקִיבֵּל בַּצָּפוֹן: If a priest stands in the south of the Temple courtyard and reaches out to collect the blood in the north, the offering is disqualified, in accordance with the opinion of the *tanna* of the *baraita* (Rambam *Sefer Avoda, Hilkhot Pesulei HaMukdashin* 1:9).

But the one who slaughters is not in the north – וְאֵין הַשּׁוֹחֵט בַּצָּפוֹן: If one stands in the south and reaches out to slaughter an animal standing in the north of the Temple courtyard, the slaughter is valid, in accordance with the opinion of Rabbi Aḥiyya (Rambam *Sefer Avoda, Hilkhot Pesulei HaMukdashin* 1:8).

NOTES

Not to exclude one who slaughters – לָאו לְמַעוּטֵי שׁוֹחֵט: According to the text of the Gemara here, Rashi explains that this is referring to the term "it" stated with regard to the goat. According to the version that appears in the parallel discussion in tractate *Menaḥot* (56a) this phrase is explaining Rabbi Aḥiyya's interpretation.

מֵחַטָּאת. מָה לְחַטָּאת שֶׁכֵּן מְכַפֶּרֶת עַל חַיָּיבֵי כְּרֵיתוֹת!

The Gemara continues: If you would suggest a logical inference **from** the *halakha* of **a sin offering,** which is not entirely burned upon the altar but is slaughtered only in the north, this too can be refuted. As **what** is notable **about a sin offering?** It is notable **in that it atones for** those sins that render one **liable for** punishment by ***karet,*** which is not so with regard to a Paschal offering.

מֵאָשָׁם. מָה לְאָשָׁם שֶׁכֵּן קָדְשֵׁי קֳדָשִׁים! מִכּוּלָּן נַמִּי, שֶׁכֵּן קָדְשֵׁי קֳדָשִׁים!

The Gemara continues: If you would suggest a logical inference **from** the *halakha* of **a guilt offering,** which is not entirely burned, which does not atone for those sins punishable by *karet*, and which is slaughtered only in the north, this too can be refuted. As **what** is notable **about a guilt offering?** It is notable **in that** it has the status of **an offering of the most sacred order,** which is not so with regard to a Paschal offering. The Gemara adds: Having noted this distinction between a guilt offering and a Paschal offering, one can say that for **all of** the three offerings **as well,** the *halakha* of a Paschal offering cannot be derived **from them, since** they all have the status of **offerings of the most sacred order.**

לְעוֹלָם כְּדַאֲמָרַן מֵעִיקָּרָא: אוֹתוֹ בַּצָּפוֹן וְאֵין שׁוֹחֵט בַּצָּפוֹן. וּדְקַשְׁיָא לָךְ: מִדְּרַבִּי אַחְיָא נָפְקָא לָן – לָאו לְמַעוּטֵי שׁוֹחֵט בַּצָּפוֹן, אֶלָּא: אֵין שׁוֹחֵט בַּצָּפוֹן, אֲבָל מְקַבֵּל בַּצָּפוֹן.

The Gemara returns to the earlier inference: **Actually,** the term "it" teaches **as we said initially: It,** i.e., the animal, must be standing **in the north, but** the **one who slaughters** the animal does **not** have to stand **in the north. And that** which is **difficult for you,** that **we derive** this *halakha* **from** the statement **of Rabbi Aḥiyya,** is in fact not difficult. The derivation from the term "it" is **not to exclude** one who **slaughters**[N] from the requirement to slaughter **in the north,** since that *halakha* is known already from the statement of Rabbi Aḥiyya. **Rather,** the derivation is that it is only one who **slaughters** the animal who does **not** have to stand **in the north, but** by inference, the one who **collects** the blood from the neck of the animal must stand **in the north.**

מְקַבֵּל מִ״לָקַח״ ״וְלָקַח״ נָפְקָא! ״לָקַח״ ״וְלָקַח״ לָא מַשְׁמַע לֵיהּ.

The Gemara questions this inference: The *halakha* that the one who **collects** the blood from the neck of the animal must stand in the north is derived **from** the fact that the Torah could have written: The priest **shall take,** and instead writes: **"And** the priest **shall take"** [***velakaḥ***] (Leviticus 4:34), which may be read as: He will take himself [*lo yikaḥ*], as explained on the previous *amud*. The Gemara explains: This *tanna* **does not learn** anything from this distinction between: The priest **shall take,** and: **"And** the priest **shall take."** He does not agree with this derivation, and therefore he must derive the requirement to collect the blood while standing in the north from a different verse.

אַשְׁכְּחַן שְׁחִיטָה בְּעוֹלָה לְמִצְוָה, קַבָּלָה נַמִּי לְמִצְוָה אַשְׁכְּחַן, שְׁחִיטָה וְקַבָּלָה לְעַכֵּב מְנָלַן?

§ The Gemara asks: **We found** a source for the requirement of **slaughter** in the north **with regard to a burnt offering** in order **to** perform the **mitzva** in the optimal manner. **We also found** a source for the requirement of **collecting** the blood while standing in the north in order **to** perform the **mitzva** in the optimal manner. **From where do we** derive that **slaughter and collection** of the blood are **disqualified** if they are not performed in the north?

אָמַר רַב אַדָּא בַּר אַהֲבָה, וְאִיתֵימָא רַבָּה בַּר שֵׁילָא: קַל וָחוֹמֶר, וּמָה חַטָּאת הַבָּאָה מִכֹּחַ עוֹלָה – מְעַכֶּבֶת, עוֹלָה שֶׁבָּאָה חַטָּאת מִכֹּחָהּ – אֵינוֹ דִּין שֶׁמְּעַכֶּבֶת?

Rav Adda bar Ahava says, and some say it was **Rabba bar Sheila** who says: It is derived via **an *a fortiori*** inference: **Just as** the *halakha* that the slaughter and blood collection of **a sin offering** be performed in the north **comes by virtue of** a comparison to the *halakha* of **a burnt offering,** as the verse states: "And slaughter the sin offering in the place of the burnt offering" (Leviticus 4:29), yet if the animal was not slaughtered or its blood was not collected in the north it **disqualifies** the offering, with regard to the **burnt offering** itself, **as** the *halakha* that the slaughter and blood collection of **a sin offering** be in the north **comes by virtue of it, is it not logical that** if it was not slaughtered or its blood was not collected in the north, this should **disqualify** the offering?

מָה לְחַטָּאת שֶׁכֵּן מְכַפֶּרֶת עַל חַיָּיבֵי כְּרֵיתוֹת!

The Gemara rejects this logical inference: **What** is notable **about a sin offering?** It is notable **in that it atones for** those sins that render one **liable for** punishment by ***karet,*** which is not so with regard to a burnt offering.

אֲמַר רָבִינָא: הָא קַשְׁיָא לֵיהּ לְרַב אַדָּא בַּר אַהֲבָה: כְּלוּם מָצִינוּ טָפֵל חָמוּר מִן הָעִיקָּר?

Ravina said: This is what is **difficult for Rav Adda bar Ahava.** In other words, regardless of the notable characteristic of a sin offering, he still is of the opinion that his logical inference stands. **Have we ever found** that **a secondary** prohibition is more **stringent than a primary** prohibition?[N] Since the *halakha* of a sin offering is derived via a comparison to the *halakha* of a burnt offering, the former cannot have stringencies that the latter lacks.

אֲמַר לֵיהּ מָר זוּטְרָא בְּרֵיהּ דְּרַב מָרִי לְרָבִינָא: וְלָא?

Mar Zutra, son of Rav Mari, said to Ravina: But have we **not** found a secondary prohibition that is more stringent than the primary one?

NOTES

A secondary prohibition is more stringent than a primary prohibition – טָפֵל חָמוּר מִן הָעִיקָּר: The Torah could have written the requirement of slaughter in the north in the verses of the sin offering, instead of comparing it to the burnt offering. Since the Torah did not do so, this indicates that not only must the sin offering be slaughtered in the same place as the burnt offering, but that the requirement to slaughter it in the north stems from the requirement to slaughter the burnt offering there. The sin offering therefore cannot have stringencies that the burnt offering does not have.

Perek **V**
Daf **49** Amud **a**

וְהֲרֵי מַעֲשֵׂר, דְּהוּא נִפְדֶּה, וְאִילּוּ לָקוּחַ בְּכֶסֶף מַעֲשֵׂר אֵינוֹ נִפְדֶּה. דִּתְנַן: הַלָּקוּחַ בְּכֶסֶף מַעֲשֵׂר שֶׁנִּטְמָא – יִפָּדֶה, רַבִּי יְהוּדָה אוֹמֵר: יִקָּבֵר; נִטְמָא – אִין, לֹא נִטְמָא – לָא!

But there is the case of the second **tithe, which** may be **redeemed, whereas** food that is **purchased with** second-**tithe** redemption **money**[H] may **not** be **redeemed. As we learned** in a mishna (*Ma'aser Sheni* 10:10): With regard to food **that was purchased with** second-**tithe money** and **that** then **became ritually impure,** this ritually impure food **must be redeemed** with money, with which one must purchase other food. **Rabbi Yehuda says:** The food **must be buried.** The Gemara infers from the mishna: If the food purchased with the second-tithe money **became impure, yes,** it may be redeemed, but if it **did not become impure,** it may **not** be redeemed. If so, according to Rabbi Yehuda, the *halakha* that food purchased with second-tithe money must be buried if it becomes impure is more stringent than the *halakha* for second-tithe produce itself, which may be redeemed if it becomes impure.

הָתָם לָא אַלִּימָא קְדוּשָּׁתֵיהּ לְמִיתְפַּס פִּדְיוֹנֵיהּ.

The Gemara answers: **There,** the reason one may not redeem food that was purchased with second-tithe money and that then became ritually impure is not that the *halakha* is more stringent. Rather, there is a different reason. Since this food was merely purchased with second-tithe money, its **sanctity is not** as **strong** as the tithe itself and is unable **to grasp its redemption** money. Its status as second tithe is weak, and cannot be transferred to a third item. Consequently, if it becomes impure, according to Rabbi Yehuda it cannot be redeemed for money but must be buried, as an item that one is prohibited to derive benefit from.

וַהֲרֵי תְּמוּרָה, דְּאִילּוּ קָדָשִׁים לָא חָיְילִי עַל בַּעַל מוּם קָבוּעַ, וְאִילּוּ אִיהִי חָיְילָא!

Mar Zutra asks: **But there is** the case of **a substitution,**[HB] as the status of **an offering does not take effect**[N] **with regard to a permanently blemished** animal, **while** consecration performed via substitution does **take effect** with regard to an animal with a permanent blemish. Although the animal cannot be sacrificed as an offering and must be redeemed, even after its redemption it may not be used for labor and its wool may not be used.

תְּמוּרָה מִכֹּחַ קָדָשִׁים קָא אָתְיָא, וְקָדָשִׁים מִכֹּחַ חוּלִּין קָאָתֵי.

The Gemara answers: The sanctity of **a substitution comes by virtue of a consecrated** animal; therefore it has a stronger sanctity. **But** the sanctity of **a consecrated** animal itself **comes by virtue of a non-sacred** animal, as there was no consecrated animal by which the owner extended the sanctity to this animal.

הֲרֵי פֶּסַח, דְּהוּא אֵינוֹ טָעוּן סְמִיכָה וּנְסָכִים וּתְנוּפַת חָזֶה וָשׁוֹק, וְאִילּוּ מוֹתַר דִּידֵיהּ טָעוּן סְמִיכָה וּנְסָכִים וּתְנוּפַת חָזֶה וָשׁוֹק!

Mar Zutra asks: But **there is** the case of **a Paschal offering, as it does not require** the **placing** of **hands** on its head, **or** wine **libations** to accompany the offering, **or waving** of the **breast and thigh. While its remainder,** an animal that was designated as a Paschal offering but was not sacrificed at the right time, which is then sacrificed as a peace offering, has more stringent *halakhot*, because it **requires** the **placing** of **hands** on its head, **and** wine **libations** to accompany the offering, **and waving** of the **breast** and **thigh.**

HALAKHA

Food purchased with second-tithe money – הַלָּקוּחַ בְּכֶסֶף מַעֲשֵׂר: Food purchased with money of the second tithe may not be redeemed outside of Jerusalem unless it has become impure through contact with a primary source of impurity. It must be brought to and eaten in Jerusalem. In this way it is more stringent than the produce of the second tithe itself (Rambam *Sefer Zera'im, Hilkhot Ma'aser Sheni* 7:1–2).

But there is a substitution, etc. – וַהֲרֵי תְּמוּרָה וכו׳: A blemished animal that was substituted for an offering must be redeemed. Even after its redemption it does not become completely non-sacred, and it remains prohibited to shear the animal for its wool or to perform labor with it. Consecration performed via substitution takes effect even on an animal with a permanent blemish (Rambam *Sefer Korbanot, Hilkhot Temura* 3:5).

BACKGROUND

Substitution – תְּמוּרָה: Although it is prohibited to substitute one animal for an animal consecrated as an offering (see Leviticus 27:33), if one transgresses this prohibition, both the original animal and the substitute are consecrated. Substitution applies only to animals brought as offerings by individuals and not to those designated as communal offerings. Even an animal with a blemish that renders it unfit to be sacrificed can become consecrated if consecrated via substitution. The *halakhot* governing this subject are discussed in tractate *Temura*.

NOTES

An offering does not take effect – קָדָשִׁים לָא חָיְילִי: This does not mean that there is no sanctity at all. Rather it means that an animal with a permanent blemish cannot have inherent sanctity like an animal that will be offered on the altar. Rather, it is as though one sanctified an item, and its sanctity inheres only in its value. For example, if one says that a blemished animal should be set aside as a burnt offering, it is sold, its value is used to purchase another animal as a burnt offering, and the animal he consecrated reverts to its non-sacred status. By contrast, an animal substituted for an offering does gain inherent sanctity, and even once it has been redeemed, it retains a certain degree of sanctity. It may not be used for labor or shorn for its wool (see *Temura* 16b).

פֶּסַח בִּשְׁאָר יְמוֹת הַשָּׁנָה שְׁלָמִים הוּא.

The Gemara answers: **A Paschal offering on the rest of the days of the year is** the same as **a peace offering,**[NH] and the animal is no longer considered to be a Paschal offering. Since it is a peace offering, all the *halakhot* of a peace offering apply to it, and the fact that it was once designated as a Paschal offering is irrelevant. The conclusion of the Gemara is that there are no cases where a secondary status is more stringent than the corresponding primary status. Therefore, the derivation from the *halakha* of a sin offering to the *halakha* of a burnt offering, that the latter should be disqualified if it was not slaughtered in the north or if its blood was not collected in the north, remains.

וְאִיבָּעֵית אֵימָא: אָמַר קְרָא ״הָעוֹלָה״ – בִּמְקוֹמָהּ תְּהֵא.

And if you wish, say there is a different proof that even after the fact a burnt offering that was not slaughtered in the north is disqualified. **The verse states:** "And slaughter the sin offering in the place of **the burnt offering**" (Leviticus 4:29). Since the earlier verse (Leviticus 4:24) already stated: "In the place of the burnt offering," the repetition in this verse stresses that **it shall be in its place,** meaning that the offering is disqualified if it is slaughtered anywhere else.

אָשָׁם מִנַּלַּן דִּבְעֵי צָפוֹן? דִּכְתִיב: ״בִּמְקוֹם אֲשֶׁר יִשְׁחֲטוּ אֶת הָעֹלָה יִשְׁחֲטוּ אֶת הָאָשָׁם״.

§ The Gemara asks: **From where do we** derive **that a guilt offering,** which is an offering of the most sacred order, **requires** slaughter in the **north?**[H] The Gemara answers: **As it is written: "In the place where they slaughter the burnt offering they shall slaughter the guilt offering,** and its blood shall be sprinkled around the altar" (Leviticus 7:2). Since the burnt offering must be slaughtered in the north, the guilt offering must also be slaughtered in the north.

אַשְׁכַּחַן שְׁחִיטָה, קַבָּלָה מְנָא לַן? ״וְאֶת דָּמוֹ יִזְרוֹק״ – קִבּוּל דָּמוֹ נַמִי בַּצָּפוֹן.

The Gemara asks: **We have found** a source that the **slaughter** must be in the north. **From where do we** derive that the **collection** of the blood must also be in the north? The Gemara answers that the second half of the verse states: **"And its blood shall be sprinkled**[N] around the altar." Since the blood must be collected immediately after the slaughter and before the sprinkling, just as the slaughter must be in the north, so the **collection of its blood** must **also** be **in the north.**

מְקַבֵּל עַצְמוֹ מְנָא לַן? ״דָּמוֹ״ – ״וְאֶת דָּמוֹ״.

The Gemara asks: **From where do we** derive that the one who **collects** the blood must **himself** stand in the north? The Gemara answers: It is derived from the fact that the verse does not only state: **"Its blood** shall be sprinkled," but states: **"And its blood** shall be sprinkled" (Leviticus 7:2). The conjunction "and [*ve'et*]" serves to include the one who collects the blood.

אַשְׁכַּחַן לְמִצְוָה, לְעַכֵּב מְנָא לַן? קְרָא אַחֲרִינָא כְּתִיב: ״וְשָׁחַט אֶת הַכֶּבֶשׂ״.

The Gemara asks: **We have found** a verse teaching that in order **to** perform the **mitzva** in the optimal manner, the slaughtering of the guilt offering is in the north. **From where do we** derive **to disqualify** after the fact an offering slaughtered elsewhere, not in the north? The Gemara answers: **Another verse is written,** referring to a guilt offering, which states: **"And he shall slaughter the sheep** in the place where they slaughter the sin offering and the burnt offering, in the place of the Sanctuary; for as the sin offering, so is the guilt offering; to the priest, it is most holy" (Leviticus 14:13). This teaches that all guilt offerings are disqualified if they are not slaughtered in the north.

NOTES

A Paschal offering on the rest of the days of the year is a peace offering – פֶּסַח בִּשְׁאָר יְמוֹת הַשָּׁנָה שְׁלָמִים הוּא: The proper time for slaughtering the Paschal offering is from shortly after midday on the fourteenth of Nisan until sunset. After that time, an animal set aside as a Paschal offering has the status of a peace offering and is not considered to be a Paschal offering at all. Therefore, it is not an example of the *halakhot* of a secondary case being more stringent than those of the primary case.

And its blood shall be sprinkled – וְאֶת דָּמוֹ יִזְרוֹק: Rashi explains that the derivation is from the conjunction "and," which teaches that the sprinkling of the blood is also included in that which preceded it in the verse: "In the place where they slaughter the burnt offering" (Leviticus 7:2).

HALAKHA

A Paschal offering on the rest of the days of the year is a peace offering – פֶּסַח בִּשְׁאָר יְמוֹת הַשָּׁנָה שְׁלָמִים הוּא: An animal that was set aside as a Paschal offering but became too old, or a peace offering that was initially a Paschal offering, is considered a peace offering. It requires the placing of hands on the head of the offering, wine libations to accompany the offering, and waving of the breast and thigh (Rambam *Sefer Korbanot, Hilkhot Korban Pesaḥ* 4:7).

Guilt offering in the north – אָשָׁם בַּצָּפוֹן: A guilt offering must be slaughtered in the north of the Temple courtyard. This is derived from the verse: "In the place that they slaughter the burnt offering they shall slaughter the guilt offering" (Leviticus 7:2), and the fact that the Torah specifies that the burnt offering must be slaughtered in the north. If it is slaughtered in the south it is disqualified, even after the fact, like all offerings of the most sacred order (Rambam *Sefer Avoda, Hilkhot Ma'aseh HaKorbanot* 5:3 and *Hilkhot Pesulei HaMukdashin* 1:7).

וְהַאי לְהָכִי הוּא דַּאֲתָא? הַאי מִיבְּעֵי לֵיהּ לְכִדְתַנְיָא: דָּבָר שֶׁהָיָה בִּכְלָל וְיָצָא לִידּוֹן בְּדָבָר הֶחָדָשׁ – אִי אַתָּה רַשַּׁאי לְהַחֲזִירוֹ לִכְלָלוֹ עַד שֶׁיַּחֲזִירֶנּוּ הַכָּתוּב לִכְלָלוֹ בְּפֵירוּשׁ.

The Gemara asks: But **does this** verse **come to** teach **this** *halakha*? **This** verse **is necessary for that which is taught** in a *baraita*: With regard to **a matter that was included in a general** category **but left to discuss a new matter,** i.e., if a novel aspect or special ruling is taught with regard to a specific case within a broader general category, **you may not return it to its general** category even for other matters, and this case is understood to have been entirely removed from the general category, **until the verse explicitly returns it to its general** category.

כֵּיצַד? "וְשָׁחַט אֶת הַכֶּבֶשׂ בִּמְקוֹם אֲשֶׁר יִשְׁחַט אֶת הַחַטָּאת וְאֶת הָעוֹלָה בִּמְקוֹם הַקֹּדֶשׁ כִּי כַּחַטָּאת הָאָשָׁם הוּא" וגו׳, שֶׁאֵין תַּלְמוּד לוֹמַר "כַּחַטָּאת הָאָשָׁם". מָה תַּלְמוּד לוֹמַר "כַּחַטָּאת הָאָשָׁם"?

The Gemara explains: **How so?** The verse states: **"And he shall slaughter the sheep in the place where they slaughter the sin offering and the burnt offering, in the place of the Sanctuary; for as the sin offering, so is the guilt offering;** to the priest, it is most holy" (Leviticus 14:13). As there is **no** need for **the verse to state: "As the sin offering, so is the guilt offering,"** since the verse had already equated the guilt offering with the sin offering, **why** does the **verse state: "As the sin offering, so is the guilt offering"?** What does it serve to teach?

לְפִי שֶׁיָּצָא אֲשַׁם מְצוֹרָע לִידּוֹן בְּדָבָר הֶחָדָשׁ, בְּבוֹהֶן יָד וּבוֹהֶן רֶגֶל וְאוֹזֶן יְמָנִית, יָכוֹל לֹא יְהֵא טָעוּן מַתַּן דָּמִים וְאֵימוּרִין לְגַבֵּי מִזְבֵּחַ?

Since the guilt offering of a leper left the general category of guilt offerings **to teach a new matter,** as there is a *halakha* unique to the guilt offering of a leper in that blood of the offering is placed **on the** right **thumb of the hand and** the right **big toe of the foot and** the **right ear** of the leper, one **might** have thought that this guilt offering **does not require placement of blood or** the burning of **sacrificial portions on the altar,** as the *halakhot* of this guilt offering are unique.

תַּלְמוּד לוֹמַר: "כַּחַטָּאת הָאָשָׁם הוּא", מָה חַטָּאת טְעוּנָה מַתַּן דָּמִים וְאֵימוּרִין לְגַבֵּי מִזְבֵּחַ – אַף אֲשַׁם מְצוֹרָע טָעוּן מַתַּן דָּמִים וְאֵימוּרִין לְגַבֵּי מִזְבֵּחַ.

To counter this reasoning, **the verse states: "As the sin offering, so is the guilt offering." Just as the sin offering requires the placement of the blood and** the burning of **sacrificial portions on the altar,**[N] **so too, the guilt offering of a leper requires placement of the blood and** the burning of **sacrificial portions on** the **altar.** Similarly, just as the verse had to teach these two *halakhot*, so too, the verse had to state: "And he shall slaughter the sheep in the place where they slaughter the sin offering and the burnt offering," to teach that it requires slaughter in the north. It cannot serve as a source for the general *halakha* that a guilt offering slaughtered in a place other than in the north is disqualified.

אִם כֵּן, נִכְתּוֹב בְּהַאי וְלָא נִכְתּוֹב בְּהַאי.

The Gemara explains: **If so,** that the optimal manner to perform the mitzva is to slaughter a guilt offering in the north but failure to do so does not disqualify the offering, **let** the Torah **write** the requirement to slaughter in the north **in this** context, i.e., in the context of the guilt offering of a leper, **and not write it in that** context, i.e., that of the standard guilt offering. The requirement for slaughter in the north for all other guilt offerings could be derived from the guilt offering of the leper. The repetition of the requirement to slaughter in the north serves to disqualify a guilt offering whose slaughter is not in the north.

הָנִיחָא אִי סְבִירָא לַן: יָצָא לִידּוֹן בְּדָבָר הֶחָדָשׁ – אִיהוּ הוּא דְּלָא גָּמַר מִכְּלָלוֹ,

The Gemara comments: **This works out well if we hold** that with regard to a matter that **left** its category **to teach a new matter,** the following principle applies: That matter itself **does not learn** *halakhot* **from its general** category until the Torah explicitly returns it to that category,

NOTES

Just as the sin offering requires the placement of the blood and the burning of sacrificial portions on the altar, etc. – **מָה חַטָּאת טְעוּנָה מַתַּן דָּמִים וְאֵימוּרִין לְגַבֵּי מִזְבֵּחַ וכו׳:** This is not a proper juxtaposition and derivation from a sin offering, because if so, the guilt offering of a leper would also require that its blood be sprinkled on all four sides of the altar, like a sin offering. Rather it returns the guilt offering of a leper to its general category of other guilt offerings.

NOTES

Once the verse returned it, it returned it – **כֵּיוָן דְּאַהַדְרֵיהּ אַהַדְרֵיהּ**: In other words, the question is based on the assumption that the detail which left the general category is not returned to its general category. Once the Torah returns it explicitly to its general category, that the blood and sacrificial portions of a leper's guilt offering must be placed on the altar like all other guilt offerings, as learned on the previous *amud*, it is clear that the requirement to slaughter it in the north is also the same as for other guilt offerings. Therefore, the fact that the Torah explicitly writes the requirement to slaughter it in the north serves only to teach that even after the fact, if it was not slaughtered in the north, the offering is disqualified.

אֲבָל כְּלָלוֹ גָּמַר מִינֵּיהּ (לְצָפוֹן) – שַׁפִּיר, אֶלָּא אִי סְבִירָא לָן דְּלָא הוּא גָּמַר מִכְּלָלוֹ וְלָא כְּלָלוֹ גָּמַר מִינֵּיהּ, הַאי לְגוּפֵיהּ אִיצְטְרִיךְ!

but other matters in **its general** category **learn** *halakhot* **from it;** in this case **with regard to** the *halakha* of slaughtering a guilt offering in the **north,** it is **well.** Although some of the *halakhot* of the guilt offering of a leper do not apply to the category of guilt offerings in general, it can still serve as the source for the *halakha* that any guilt offering is disqualified if slaughtered not in the north. **But if we hold that** in the case of a matter that left its category to teach a new matter, **it,** the original matter, **does not learn** *halakhot* **from its general** category **and its general** category **does not learn** *halakhot* **from it,** then **this** verse **is necessary to** teach **its own** *halakha*.

כֵּיוָן דְּאַהַדְרֵיהּ אַהַדְרֵיהּ.

The Gemara answers: **Once** the verse **returned** the *halakha* of the guilt offering of a leper to the general category by stating "as the sin offering, so is the guilt offering," **it returned it**[N] completely. Therefore, when the verse states that it requires slaughter in the north of the Temple courtyard, the phrase is not needed to teach the *halakha* about the guilt offering of a leper, and it can be used to teach the *halakha* about guilt offerings in general.

אֲמַר לֵיהּ מָר זוּטְרָא בְּרֵיהּ דְּרַב מָרִי לְרָבִינָא: אֵימָא, כִּי אַהַדְרֵיהּ קְרָא לְגַבֵּי מַתַּן דָּמִים וְאֵימוּרִין דְּבָעֵי כְּהוּנָּה, אֲבָל שְׁחִיטָה דְּלָא בָּעֲיָא כְּהוּנָּה – לָא מִיבָּעֵי צָפוֹן!

Mar Zutra, son of Rav Mari, said to Ravina: Say that **when the verse returned** the guilt offering of a leper to the class of standard guilt offerings, that is only **with regard to placement of blood** on the altar **and** burning the **sacrificial portions, which require priesthood,** i.e., only a priest may perform those rites. As the verse states: "For as the sin offering, so is the guilt offering; to the priest" (Leviticus 14:13). **But** say that **slaughter, which does not require priesthood,** as even a non-priest may slaughter an offering, **does not require** that it be done in the **north** of the Temple courtyard.

אִם כֵּן, נֵימָא קְרָא: "כִּי כַּחַטָּאת הוּא", מַאי "כַּחַטָּאת הָאָשָׁם" – כִּשְׁאָר אֲשָׁמוֹת יִהְיֶה.

Ravina answered him: **If so, let the verse state: For as the sin offering, so is it. What** is added by the expanded phrase: "**For as the sin offering, so is the guilt offering**"? It teaches that the guilt offering of a leper **will be like the rest of** the **guilt offerings.**

לָמָּה לִי לְאַקְשׁוּיֵי לְחַטָּאת, לָמָּה לִי לְאַקְשׁוּיֵי לְעוֹלָה?

§ The Gemara asks: **Why do I** need **to juxtapose** the guilt offering of a leper **to a sin offering** to teach the *halakha* that it must be slaughtered in the north, and **why do I** need **to juxtapose** it **to a burnt offering** to teach the same *halakha*? The verse states: "And he shall slaughter the sheep in the place where they slaughter the sin offering and the burnt offering, in the place of the Sanctuary" (Leviticus 14:13).

אֲמַר רָבִינָא: אִיצְטְרִיךְ, אִי אַקְשֵׁיהּ לְחַטָּאת וְלָא אַקְשֵׁיהּ לְעוֹלָה, הֲוָה אָמִינָא: חַטָּאת מֵהֵיכָן לָמְדָה – מֵעוֹלָה, דָּבָר הַלָּמֵד בְּהֶיקֵּשׁ חוֹזֵר וּמְלַמֵּד בְּהֶיקֵּשׁ.

Ravina said: It **was necessary** to juxtapose the guilt offering to both of them, as, **if** the verse **had juxtaposed it** only **to a sin offering but had not juxtaposed it to a burnt offering, I would say: From where** is the requirement to slaughter **a sin offering** in the north **derived?** It is **from** the *halakha* of **a burnt offering,** as explained on 48a. I would then assume that **a matter derived via a juxtaposition,** i.e., the *halakha* of a sin offering, which was derived via a juxtaposition to the *halakha* of a burnt offering, **then teaches** that *halakha* to another case **via a juxtaposition.** But there is a principle that with regard to matters of consecration the *halakha* may not be derived via a juxtaposition from another *halakha* that was itself derived via a juxtaposition. To prevent this incorrect assumption, the verse had to specifically teach the juxtaposition to a burnt offering.

אֲמַר לֵיהּ מָר זוּטְרָא בְּרֵיהּ דְּרַב מָרִי לְרָבִינָא: וְנִיקְשֵׁיהּ לְעוֹלָה וְלָא נִיקְשֵׁיהּ לְחַטָּאת!

Mar Zutra, son of Rav Mari, said to Ravina: But let the verse **juxtapose** the guilt offering of a leper only **to a burnt offering and not juxtapose it to a sin offering.** The juxtaposition to a sin offering appears superfluous.

הֲוָה אָמִינָא: דָּבָר הַלָּמֵד בְּהֶיקֵּשׁ חוֹזֵר וּמְלַמֵּד בְּהֶיקֵּשׁ; וְכִי תֵּימָא נִיקְשֵׁי אַקּוֹשֵׁי לְחַטָּאת – נִיחָא לֵיהּ דְּמַקִּישׁ לֵיהּ לְעִיקָּר וְלָא נַקִּישׁ לֵיהּ לַטָּפֵל. לְהָכִי אַקְשֵׁיהּ לְחַטָּאת וְאַקְשֵׁיהּ לְעוֹלָה – לְמֵימַר: דָּבָר הַלָּמֵד בְּהֶיקֵּשׁ שֶׁאֵינוֹ חוֹזֵר וּמְלַמֵּד בְּהֶיקֵּשׁ.

Ravina answered: If that had been so, **I would** still **say** that **a matter derived via a juxtaposition then teaches** its *halakha* **via a juxtaposition. And if you would say** that if that were to be so, **let** the verse **juxtapose** the guilt offering of a leper only **to a sin offering,** one could answer that **it is preferable for** the Torah **that it juxtaposes** the guilt offering **to the primary** offering about which it states that it must be slaughtered in the north, i.e., the burnt offering, **and not juxtapose it to the secondary** offering, the sin offering. **For this** reason, i.e., to prevent the incorrect assumption that a matter derived via a juxtaposition then teaches its *halakha* via a juxtaposition, the verse **juxtaposed it to a sin offering and** also **juxtaposed it to a burnt offering, to say** that **a matter derived via a juxtaposition does not then teach** its *halakha* **via a juxtaposition.**

רָבָא אָמַר: מֵהָכָא, דִּכְתִיב: ״כַּאֲשֶׁר יוּרָם מִשּׁוֹר זֶבַח הַשְּׁלָמִים״, לְמַאי הִלְכְתָא? אִי לְיוֹתֶרֶת הַכָּבֵד וּשְׁתֵּי הַכְּלָיוֹת – בְּגוּפֵיהּ כְּתִיב.

Rava says: The principle that a matter derived via a juxtaposition cannot then teach its *halakha* via a juxtaposition is derived **from here, as it is written** with regard to the sin offering brought by the High Priest: "And the two kidneys, and the fat that is upon them, which is by the loins, and the diaphragm with the liver, which he shall take away by the kidneys. **As it is taken off from the ox of the sacrifice of peace offerings;** and the priest shall make them smoke upon the altar of burnt offering" (Leviticus 4:9–10). One can ask: **For what *halakha*** is this offering juxtaposed to that of a peace offering? **If** it is **to** teach that the priest must sacrifice **the diaphragm with the liver and the two kidneys** from the offering, that is **written with regard to** the offering **itself,** in the previous verse. This does not need to be derived via a juxtaposition.

מִשּׁוּם דְּבָעֵי אַגְמוּרֵי יוֹתֶרֶת הַכָּבֵד וּשְׁתֵּי הַכְּלָיוֹת מִפַּר הֶעְלֵם דָּבָר שֶׁל צִבּוּר לִשְׂעִירֵי עֲבוֹדָה זָרָה; בְּגוּפֵיהּ לָא כְּתִיב, וּמִפַּר כֹּהֵן מָשִׁיחַ הוּא דְּגָמַר

It is written **due to** the fact **that** the verse **wants to teach** the *halakha* of **the diaphragm with the liver and the two kidneys,** deriving it **from** the *halakha* of the offering of **the bull for an unwitting communal sin,** then teaching it **to** apply it to the *halakha* of the **goats** brought as sin offerings for communal **idol worship. It is not written** explicitly **in** the passage discussing the bull for an unwitting communal sin **itself, and it is derived from** the *halakha* of **the bull for** an unwitting sin of **an anointed priest,** i.e., the High Priest. The offering for an unwitting communal sin is juxtaposed to the sin offering brought by the High Priest in the verse: "So shall he do with the bull; as he did with the bull of the sin offering, so shall he do with this" (Leviticus 4:20).

לְהָכִי אִיצְטְרִיךְ ״כַּאֲשֶׁר יוּרָם״ דְּנֶיהֱוֵי כְּמַאן דִּכְתַב בְּגוּפֵיהּ, וְלָא נֶיהֱוֵי דָּבָר הַלָּמֵד בְּהֶיקֵּשׁ חוֹזֵר וּמְלַמֵּד בְּהֶיקֵּשׁ.

For this reason it **was necessary** for the verse to state: **"As it is taken off from the ox"** (Leviticus 4:10), so **that it is as though it wrote** explicitly **in** the passage discussing the bull for an unwitting communal sin **itself.** One of the hermeneutical principles applied to understanding verses in the Torah is: If the *halakha* stated is not required for the matter in which it is written, apply it to another matter. When this principle is employed, the *halakha* written in one context is viewed as if it were written elsewhere. In this case, as it was not necessary for the verse to write the juxtaposition to a peace offering in the context of the sin offering brought by the High Priest, it is applied to the case of the bull for an unwitting communal sin. **And** therefore it **will not be** a case of **a matter derived via a juxtaposition** that **then teaches** its *halakha* **via a juxtaposition.**

אֲמַר לֵיהּ רַב פַּפָּא לְרָבָא: וְלִיכְתְּבֵיהּ בְּגוּפֵיהּ וְלָא נַקִּישׁ!

Rav Pappa said to Rava: But why not **let** the Torah **write** explicitly **in** the passage discussing the bull for an unwitting communal sin **itself** that the diaphragm with the liver and two kidneys must be removed from the ox, **and not juxtapose** it to a peace offering in this convoluted manner?

אִי כָּתַב בְּגוּפֵיהּ וְלָא אַקִּישׁ – הֲוָה אָמִינָא: דָּבָר הַלָּמֵד בְּהֶיקֵּשׁ חוֹזֵר וּמְלַמֵּד בְּהֶיקֵּשׁ; וְכִי תֵּימָא נַקְשֵׁי אַקּוֹשֵׁי – נִיחָא לֵיהּ דְּכַתְבֵיהּ בְּגוּפֵיהּ מִדְּאַקִּישׁ לֵיהּ אַקּוֹשֵׁי. לְהָכִי כַּתְבֵיהּ וְאַקְשֵׁיהּ, לְמֵימְרָא: דָּבָר הַלָּמֵד בְּהֶיקֵּשׁ אֵין חוֹזֵר וּמְלַמֵּד בְּהֶיקֵּשׁ.

Rava answered: **If** the Torah **had written** it **in** that passage **itself, and not juxtaposed** it, **I would say** that in general **a matter derived via a juxtaposition then teaches via a juxtaposition,** as one would not have this instance to serve as a counterexample to that principle. **And if you would say:** If so, why not simply **juxtapose** the case of the bull for an unwitting communal sin to the case of the bull of the anointed priest, I would answer: **It is preferable for** the verse **that it writes it in** the passage **itself** rather **than to juxtapose it** alone. It is **for this** reason that **it wrote it and juxtaposed it, to say** that **a matter derived via a juxtaposition cannot then teach** its *halakha* **via a juxtaposition.**

§ Before beginning a lengthy discussion concerning derivations via compounded methodologies of the hermeneutical principles, the Gemara presents **a mnemonic** for its forthcoming discussion: **Juxtaposition, verbal analogy, an *a fortiori* inference.**

(הֶיקֵּשׁ, גְּזֵירָה שָׁוָה, קַל וָחוֹמֶר, סִימָן).

The principle that **a matter derived via a juxtaposition cannot then teach** its *halakha* **via a juxtaposition** is indicated **either from** the proof **of Rava or from** the proof **of Ravina,** both cited earlier. The Gemara asks: **What is** the *halakha* with regard to whether **a matter derived via a juxtaposition can** then **teach** its *halakha* to another matter **via a verbal analogy?**

דָּבָר הַלָּמֵד בְּהֶיקֵּשׁ אֵין חוֹזֵר וּמְלַמֵּד מֵהֶיקֵּשׁ, אִי מִדְּרָבָא, אִי מִדְּרָבִינָא. דָּבָר הַלָּמֵד בְּהֶיקֵּשׁ מַהוּ שֶׁיְּלַמֵּד בִּגְזֵירָה שָׁוָה?

The Gemara suggests: **Come** and **hear** a proof from a *baraita*: **Rabbi Natan ben Avtolemos says: From where** is it derived **that** if leprosy **of garments**[B] **spreads** throughout an entire garment **that it is pure?** It is derived via a verbal analogy: **A bareness within** [*karaḥat*] **and a bareness without** [*gabbaḥat*][B] are **stated with regard to** leprosy of **garments:** "And the priest shall look, after that the mark is washed; and behold, if the mark has not changed its color, and the mark has not spread, it is impure; you shall burn it in the fire; it is a fret, whether the bareness be within or without" (Leviticus 13:55); **and a bald head** [*karaḥat*] **and a bald forehead** [*gabbaḥat*] are **stated with regard to** leprosy of **a person:** "But if there be in the bald head, or the bald forehead, a reddish-white plague, it is leprosy breaking out in his bald head, or his bald forehead" (Leviticus 13:42).

תָּא שְׁמַע: רַבִּי נָתָן בֶּן אַבְטוֹלְמוֹס אוֹמֵר: מִנַּיִן לִפְרִיחָה בִּבְגָדִים שֶׁהִיא טְהוֹרָה? נֶאֱמַר קָרַחַת וְגַבַּחַת בִּבְגָדִים, וְנֶאֱמַר קָרַחַת וְגַבַּחַת בְּאָדָם,

Just as there, with regard to a person, if the leprosy **spread throughout him** entirely he is **pure,** as the verse states: "Then the priest shall look; and behold, if the leprosy has covered all of his flesh, he shall pronounce the one who has the mark pure; it is all turned white: He is pure" (Leviticus 13:13), **so too here** with regard to garments, if the leprosy **spread throughout the entire** garment it is **pure.**

מָה לְהַלָּן פָּרַח בְּכוּלּוֹ טָהוֹר – אַף כָּאן פָּרַח בְּכוּלּוֹ טָהוֹר.

The Gemara continues its proof: **But there,** with regard to the head, which serves as the source for this verbal analogy, **from where do we** derive that if the leprosy spreads throughout the head he is pure? **As it is written:** "And if the leprosy breaks out on the skin, and the leprosy covers all the skin of the one who has the mark, **from his head to his feet,** as far as it appears to the priest" (Leviticus 13:12). **And** the verse thereby **juxtaposes** leprosy on **his head to** leprosy on his **foot,** teaching the following *halakha*: **Just as there,** with regard to leprosy of the body and foot, if **its entirety turned white,** and it **spread all over him,** he is **pure, so too here,** in the case of leprosy of the head, if **its entirety turned white and it spread over all his** head, he is **pure.** Evidently, a matter derived via a juxtaposition can then teach its *halakha* to another matter via a verbal analogy.

וְהָתָם מְנָא לַן? דִּכְתִיב: "מֵרֹאשׁוֹ וְעַד רַגְלָיו", וְאִיתְקַשׁ רֹאשׁוֹ לְרֶגֶל, מָה לְהַלָּן כּוּלּוֹ הָפַךְ לָבָן פָּרַח בְּכוּלּוֹ – טָהוֹר, אַף כָּאן כּוּלּוֹ הָפַךְ לָבָן פָּרַח בְּכוּלּוֹ – טָהוֹר.

Rabbi Yoḥanan says: This cannot serve as a proof with regard to the *halakhot* of consecrated matters. **With regard to the entire Torah,** one **derives** a *halakha* **derived** via a verbal analogy **from** a *halakha* **derived** via a juxtaposition, **apart from** with regard to **consecrated** matters, **where** one **does not derive** a *halakha* **derived** via a verbal analogy **from** a *halakha* **derived** via a juxtaposition.

אָמַר רַבִּי יוֹחָנָן: בְּכָל הַתּוֹרָה כּוּלָּהּ לְמֵידִין לָמֵד מִלָּמֵד, חוּץ מִן הַקֳּדָשִׁים שֶׁאֵין דָּנִין לָמֵד מִלָּמֵד.

Rabbi Yoḥanan explains: **As if** it were to be **so** that one could derive a *halakha* in this manner even concerning consecrated matters, the verse **should not state** the requirement for slaughter in the **north with regard to a guilt offering,**[N] as stated from the explicit juxtaposition of a burnt offering and a sin offering, **and** instead **derive it through a verbal analogy.** The verse describes a guilt offering **as an offering of the most sacred order** (see Leviticus 7:1), and its *halakha* can be derived via a verbal analogy **from** that of **a sin offering,** which is described in the same manner (see Leviticus 6:18).

דְּאִם כֵּן, לֹא יֹאמַר צָפוֹנָה בְּאָשָׁם וְתֵיתֵי בִּגְזֵירָה שָׁוָה דְּקָדְשֵׁי קֳדָשִׁים מֵחַטָּאוֹת.

Rabbi Yoḥanan continues: Is this **not to say,** at least with regard to consecrated matters, **that a matter derived via a juxtaposition cannot then teach** its *halakha* to another matter **via a verbal analogy?**

לָאו לְמֵימְרָא, דְּדָבָר הַלָּמֵד בְּהֶיקֵּשׁ אֵין חוֹזֵר וּמְלַמֵּד בִּגְזֵירָה שָׁוָה?

BACKGROUND

Leprosy of garments – צָרַעַת בְּגָדִים: By Torah law, if bright red or green marks appear on clothing, the garment must be brought to a priest to determine whether or not the marks indicate leprosy of garments (see Leviticus 13:47–59). The affected garment is then put aside for a week, after which it is reexamined by the priest. If the marks have spread, the clothing is immediately declared ritually impure by the priest and burned. If the marks have not spread, the clothing is laundered and then put aside for another week, after which the priest reexamines it. If the marks have disappeared or become darker, the garment is laundered and immersed in a ritual bath, after which it is considered ritually pure. Otherwise, the affected part, and sometimes the entire garment, must be burned. A leprous garment may not be used, and it renders people and items that come in contact with it ritually impure, in the same way as a leprous person does. The *halakhot* of leprosy of clothing apply only to leather, wool, and linen garments.

***Karaḥat* and *gabbaḥat* – קָרַחַת וְגַבַּחַת:** The loss of half the hair on one's head is a symptom of a particular type of leprosy of the skin. Loss of hair in the front half of the head is called *gabbaḥat*; loss of hair in the back half of the head is called *karaḥat* (Leviticus 13:40–44). The halfway mark of the head is considered a line from one ear to the other. A man who has lost half his hair this way and who subsequently finds white discoloration in one of these areas is treated as having leprosy of the skin, and is sent to a priest. The person is checked for healthy skin within the white area [*miḥya*] which indicates leprosy, and later spread of the white spot [*pisyon*]. Subsequent treatment of the individual follows the standard procedures for leprosy found elsewhere on the body.

NOTES

Should not state the requirement for slaughter in the north with regard to a guilt offering – לֹא יֹאמַר צָפוֹנָה בְּאָשָׁם: The underlying assumption of the Gemara in this discussion is that there is not a single superfluous word in the Torah. Any matter which can be derived through interpretation of a verse does not need to be written separately. Accordingly, although the requirement to slaughter a guilt offering in the north is not written explicitly but is derived from its juxtaposition to a burnt offering and a sin offering, the juxtaposition is explicit: "In the place that he slaughters the sin offering and the burnt offering" (Leviticus 14:13). The Gemara assumes that if it were possible to derive this matter without writing it explicitly in the juxtaposition, it would not have been written in the Torah (see *Ḥok Natan*).

וְדִלְמָא מִשּׁוּם דְּאִיכָּא לְמִיפְרַךְ: מָה לְחַטָּאת שֶׁכֵּן מְכַפֶּרֶת עַל חַיָּיבֵי כְרֵיתוֹת!

The Gemara rejects Rabbi Yoḥanan's proof: **But perhaps** the requirement to slaughter a guilt offering in the north must be written explicitly **because** the verbal analogy **can be refuted** as follows: **What** is notable **about a sin offering?** It is notable **in that it atones for** those sins **liable for** punishment by ***karet***, which is not so with regard to a guilt offering.

קָדְשֵׁי קָדָשִׁים יְתֵירֵי כְּתִיבִי.

The Gemara rejects this claim: There are **additional** descriptions of a guilt offering and a sin offering as **offerings of the most sacred order written** in the verses: "This shall be yours of the most sacred items, reserved from the fire: Every offering of theirs, every meal offering of theirs, and every sin offering of theirs, and every guilt offering of theirs, which they may offer to Me, shall be most holy for you and for your sons" (Numbers 18:9). A verbal analogy derived from extra phrases in the verse cannot be refuted with a logical claim. Therefore, Rabbi Yoḥanan's claim stands, and, at least with regard to consecrated matters, a matter derived via a juxtaposition cannot then teach its *halakha* to another matter via a verbal analogy.

דָּבָר הַלָּמֵד מֵהֶיקֵּשׁ חוֹזֵר וּמְלַמֵּד בְּקַל וָחוֹמֶר,

The Gemara states: That **a matter derived via a juxtaposition then teaches** its *halakha* **via an *a fortiori*** inference[B]

BACKGROUND

An *a fortiori* inference – קַל וָחוֹמֶר: One of the fundamental principles of rabbinic exegesis, the *a fortiori* inference appears in all of the standard lists of hermeneutical principles. It is a principle of logical argumentation where a comparison is drawn between two cases, one more lenient and the other more stringent. The *a fortiori* inference asserts that if the *halakha* is stringent in a case where the ruling is usually lenient, then all the more so will it be stringent in a more severe case; likewise, if the *halakha* is lenient in a case where the ruling is not usually lenient, then it will certainly be lenient in a less stringent case. *A fortiori* argumentation appears in the Bible, and the Sages compiled lists of verses in which *a fortiori* inferences appear. For example: "If you have run with the foot soldiers, and they have wearied you, how can you contend with horses?" (Jeremiah 12:5).

Perek **V**
Daf **50** Amud **a**

מִדְּתָנָא דְּבֵי רַבִּי יִשְׁמָעֵאל.

is apparent **from that which the school of Rabbi Yishmael taught,** discussed in the previous chapter (41a).

דָּבָר הַלָּמֵד בְּהֶיקֵּשׁ מַהוּ שֶׁיְּלַמֵּד בְּבִנְיַן אָב? אָמַר רַבִּי יִרְמְיָה: לָא לִכְתּוֹב צָפוֹנָה בְּאָשָׁם וְתֵיתֵי מִבִּנְיַן אָב מֵחַטָּאת, לְמַאי הִלְכְתָא כְּתָבֵיהּ – לָאו לְמֵימְרָא, דְּדָבָר הַלָּמֵד בְּהֶיקֵּשׁ אֵין חוֹזֵר וּמְלַמֵּד בְּבִנְיַן אָב?

The Gemara asks: **What is** the *halakha* as to whether **a matter derived via a juxtaposition** can **teach** its *halakha* in another context **via a paradigm? Rabbi Yirmeya says:** It must be that it cannot, as, if it could, **let** the Torah **not write** the requirement to slaughter an offering in the **north** of the Temple courtyard **with regard to a guilt offering** (see Leviticus 14:13), **and** one can **derive** it **via a paradigm from** the *halakha* of **a sin offering,** since they are both offerings of the most sacred order. **For what** *halakha* **did** the verse **write it** with regard to a guilt offering as well? Is this **not to say that a matter derived via a juxtaposition cannot then teach** its *halakha* in another context **via a paradigm?**

וְלִיטַעְמִיךְ, תֵּיתֵי מִבִּנְיַן אָב מֵעוֹלָה! מַאי טַעְמָא לָא אָתֵי – מִשּׁוּם דְּאִיכָּא לְמִיפְרַךְ: מָה לְעוֹלָה שֶׁכֵּן כָּלִיל – חַטָּאת נַמִי אִיכָּא לְמִיפְרַךְ: מָה לְחַטָּאת שֶׁכֵּן מְכַפֶּרֶת עַל חַיָּיבֵי כְרֵיתוֹת.

The Gemara questions this proof: **But according to your reasoning,** why not **derive** the *halakha* that a guilt offering must be slaughtered in the north **from** the *halakha* of **a burnt offering, via a paradigm? What is the reason** that this *halakha* **is not derived** from there? It must be **because it can be refuted**[N] with the following claim: **What** is notable **about a burnt offering?** It is notable **in that** the Torah teaches that **it is entirely** burned on the altar, which is not so with regard to a guilt offering. The Gemara now states its objection: In that case, the derivation from **a sin offering** via a paradigm **can also be refuted: What** is notable **about a sin offering?** It is notable **in that it atones for** those sins **liable for** punishment by ***karet***, which is not so with regard to a guilt offering. If so, there is no proof from here.

חֲדָא מֵחֲדָא לָא אָתְיָא, תֵּיתֵי חֲדָא מִתַּרְתֵּי!

The Gemara suggests an alternative paradigm: Although the requirement to slaughter **one** of these three offerings, i.e., a burnt offering, sin offering, or guilt offering, in the north **cannot be derived from** any **one** of the others, one can **derive** the *halakha* concerning **one** of them **from** the other **two.**

מֵהֵי תֵּיתֵי? לָא נִכְתּוֹב רַחֲמָנָא עוֹלָה וְתֵיתֵי מֵחַטָּאת וְאָשָׁם – מָה לְהָנָךְ שֶׁכֵּן מְכַפְּרִין;

The Gemara clarifies: **From which** two could one **derive** the third? **Let the Merciful One not write** the requirement to slaughter the offering in the north with regard to **a burnt offering, and derive** this *halakha* **from** the *halakhot* of **a sin offering and a guilt offering.** The Gemara refutes this derivation: **What** is notable **about these** two offerings? They are notable **in that they atone** for transgressions, whereas a burnt offering does not atone for any sin.

NOTES

Because it can be refuted, etc. – דְּאִיכָּא לְמִיפְרַךְ וכו׳: Only those principles based on logic, i.e., a paradigm and an *a fortiori* inference, can be refuted by logic. Juxtaposition is not based on logic or comparison, but is a Torah edict equating the *halakha* of two matters, and therefore it cannot be refuted.

HALAKHA

A thanks offering can come from the second tithe – תּוֹדָה שֶׁבָּא מִן הַמַּעֲשֵׂר: If one specified in his vow that he wished to use the money with which he redeemed his second tithe to purchase a thanks offering, he may do as he had vowed, in accordance with the mishna in *Menaḥot* 81b (Rambam *Sefer Avoda, Hilkhot Ma'aseh HaKorbanot* 16:17).

A peace offering can come from the second tithe – שְׁלָמִים דְּאָתוּ מִמַּעֲשֵׂר: One may purchase an animal for a peace offering with money from the redemption of the second tithe, because peace offerings may be eaten by non-priests (Rambam *Sefer Zera'im, Hilkhot Ma'aser Sheni* 7:12).

לָא נִכְתּוֹב רַחֲמָנָא בְּחַטָּאת וְתֵיתֵי מֵהָנָךְ – מַה לְּהָנָךְ שֶׁכֵּן זְכָרִים;

The Gemara suggests: **Let the Merciful One not write** the requirement to slaughter an offering in the north **with regard to a sin offering, and derive** this *halakha* **from** the *halakhot* of **these** others, the burnt offering and the guilt offering. The Gemara refutes this derivation: **What** is notable **about these** two offerings? They are notable **in that** they are brought only from **male** animals, whereas an individual's sin offering is a female animal.

לָא נִכְתּוֹב בְּאָשָׁם וְתֵיתֵי מֵהָנָךְ – מַה לְּהָנָךְ שֶׁכֵּן יֶשְׁנָן בְּצִיבּוּר כְּבְיָחִיד.

The Gemara suggests: **Let the Merciful One not write** the requirement to slaughter an offering in the north **with regard to a guilt offering, and derive** this *halakha* **from** the *halakhot* of **these** other two. The Gemara refutes this derivation: **What** is notable **about these** two offerings? They are notable **in that they are** brought **by a community just as** they are brought **by an individual,** whereas a guilt offering can be brought only by an individual.

דָּבָר הַלָּמֵד בִּגְזֵירָה שָׁוָה מַהוּ שֶׁיְּלַמֵּד בְּהֶיקֵּשׁ? אָמַר רַב פַּפָּא: ״וְזֹאת תּוֹרַת זֶבַח הַשְּׁלָמִים [וגו׳] אִם עַל תּוֹדָה״ – לָמַדְנוּ לְתוֹדָה שֶׁבָּא מִן הַמַּעֲשֵׂר, מִדְּאַשְׁכְּחַן שְׁלָמִים דְּאָתוּ מִמַּעֲשֵׂר;

The Gemara returns to its discussion of hermeneutical principles. **What is** the *halakha* as to whether **a matter derived via a verbal analogy** can **teach** its *halakha* to another matter **via a juxtaposition? Rav Pappa says:** The verse states: **"And this is the law of the sacrifice of peace offerings,** which one may offer to the Lord. **If** he sacrifices it **for a thanks offering,** then he shall offer with the thanks offering unleavened cakes mingled with oil, and unleavened wafers spread with oil, and cakes mingled with oil, of fine flour soaked" (Leviticus 7:11–12). From this juxtaposition **we have learned that** the money to purchase **a thanks offering** can **come from** money used to redeem **the** second **tithe,**[H] **since we find that** the money to purchase **a peace offering** can **come from** money used to redeem the second **tithe.**[H]

שְׁלָמִים גּוּפַיְיהוּ מְנָא לַן – דִּכְתִיב: ״שָׁם״ ״שָׁם״.

The Gemara asks: **From where do we** derive that the money to purchase **peace offerings themselves** can come from money used to redeem the second tithe? **As it is written** with regard to peace offerings: "And you shall sacrifice peace offerings and shall eat **there**" (Deuteronomy 27:7). And it is written with regard to second tithe: "And you shall eat before the Lord your God, in the place which He shall choose to cause His name to dwell **there**" (Deuteronomy 14:23). The usage of the term "there" in both passages serves as a verbal analogy, and demonstrates that a *halakha* derived via a verbal analogy, that of a peace offering, can then teach a *halakha* via its juxtaposition to a thanks offering.

אֲמַר לֵיהּ מָר זוּטְרָא בְּרֵיהּ דְּרַב מָרִי לְרָבִינָא: מַעְשַׂר דָּגָן חוּלִּין בְּעָלְמָא הוּא!

Mar Zutra, son of Rav Mari, said to Ravina: This is not a proof, because the **tithe of grain,** including the second tithe, **is merely non-sacred.** Therefore, it cannot be used to prove that in the realm of consecrated matters a *halakha* derived via a verbal analogy can teach a *halakha* via a juxtaposition.

אֲמַר לֵיהּ: אֲמַר אֲמָרָהּ לָמֵד קֹדֶשׁ וּמְלַמֵּד קֹדֶשׁ?

Ravina **said to him:** Does the one who **said** that in the realm of consecrated matters a *halakha* derived via one of the hermeneutical principles cannot teach via another of those principles **say this**[N] only when the *halakha* that is **derived** is in the realm of **consecrated** matters **and** the *halakha* that **teaches** is in the realm of **consecrated** matters as well? He holds that even if that which is derived is in the realm of consecrated matters it cannot teach its *halakha* via one of the hermeneutical principles. Therefore, since peace offerings are in the realm of consecrated matters, the *halakha* derived from the juxtaposition of thanks offerings to peace offerings serves as a source that a matter derived via a verbal analogy can teach its *halakha* to another matter via a juxtaposition.

NOTES

Said, say this – אֲמַר אֲמָרָהּ: The commentary of Rashi as printed in the standard version of the Talmud does not explain this obscure phrasing. The *Shita Mekubbetzet* cites a different version of Rashi's commentary, which explains: The one who said it said it. In other words, this anonymous Sage said it. The Rashbam had a different version of the text which read: Did you really say this? Rabbeinu Tam had a version of the text which read: Ami said this.

דָּבָר הַלָּמֵד בִּגְזֵירָה שָׁוָה מַהוּ שֶׁיְּלַמֵּד בִּגְזֵירָה שָׁוָה? אָמַר רָמִי בַּר חָמָא: תַּנְיָא "סֹלֶת מֻרְבֶּכֶת" – לָמַדְנוּ לִרְבוּכָה שֶׁבָּאָה סוֹלֶת.

§ The Gemara asks: **What is the** *halakha* as to whether **a matter derived via a verbal analogy** can **teach** its *halakha* to another matter **via** another **verbal analogy? Rami bar Ḥama says: It is taught** in a *baraita* with regard to the types of bread that accompany a thanks offering: "If he sacrifices it for a thanks offering, then he shall sacrifice with the thanks offering unleavened loaves mingled with oil, and unleavened wafers spread with oil, and loaves mingled with oil, of **fine flour cooked** with oil" (Leviticus 7:12). **We have derived** from here **that** the **poached** breads[HB] accompanying the thanks offering **come from fine flour.**

חַלּוֹת מִנַּיִן? תַּלְמוּד לוֹמַר: "חַלּוֹת" "חַלּוֹת". רְקִיקִין מִנַּיִן? תַּלְמוּד לוֹמַר: "מַצּוֹת" "מַצּוֹת".

The *baraita* continues: **From where** is it derived that the **loaves** accompanying a thanks offering are also prepared with fine flour? **The verse states: "Loaves** mingled with oil, of fine flour cooked with oil" (Leviticus 7:12), and it also states in the same verse: "Unleavened **loaves** mingled with oil." **From where** is it derived that the unleavened **wafers** accompanying a thanks offering are also prepared with fine flour? **The verse states: "Unleavened** cakes mingled with oil" (Leviticus 7:12), and the verse also states: **"Unleavened** wafers spread with oil." The *baraita* derives via a verbal analogy that the unleavened loaves mingled with oil are prepared with fine flour, and then teaches the *halakha* concerning unleavened wafers using a verbal analogy from the *halakha* of unleavened loaves.

אֲמַר לֵיהּ רָבִינָא: מִמַּאי דְּ"מַצּוֹת" "מַצּוֹת" מֵחַלּוֹת גָּמַר? דִּלְמָא מִמַּאֲפֵה תַנּוּר גָּמַר!

Ravina said to Rami bar Ḥama: **From where** do you know **that** the *tanna* of the *baraita* **learns** the verbal analogy of **"unleavened"** and **"unleavened" from loaves** of the thanks offering? **Perhaps** the *tanna* **learns** the verbal analogy **from** the word "unleavened" stated with regard to meal offerings **baked in an oven,** about which the verse states explicitly that they are prepared with fine flour: "And when you bring a meal offering baked in the oven, it shall be unleavened cakes of fine flour mingled with oil, or unleavened wafers spread with oil" (Leviticus 2:4). If so, there is no source that a *halakha* derived via a verbal analogy can teach a *halakha* via a verbal analogy.

אֶלָּא אָמַר רָבָא, תַּנְיָא: "וְקִרְבּוֹ וּפִרְשׁוֹ וְהוֹצִיא" – מְלַמֵּד שֶׁמּוֹצִיאוֹ שָׁלֵם.

Rather, Rava says that the source is from a different *baraita*, as **it is taught** in a *baraita* with regard to the bull offering of a High Priest: "And the skin of the bull and all its flesh, with its head and with its legs, **and its innards, and its dung,** the whole bull **shall he carry out** of the camp to a pure place, where the ashes are poured out, and burn it on wood with fire" (Leviticus 4:11–12). This **teaches that he brings** the offering **out whole.**

יָכוֹל יִשְׂרְפֶנּוּ שָׁלֵם? נֶאֱמַר כָּאן: "רֹאשׁוֹ וּכְרָעָיו", וְנֶאֱמַר לְהַלָּן: "רֹאשׁוֹ וּכְרָעָיו", מַה לְּהַלָּן עַל יְדֵי נִיתּוּחַ – אַף כָּאן עַל יְדֵי נִיתּוּחַ.

The *baraita* continues: One **might** have thought **that he should burn it whole** as well. **It is stated here: "Its head and its legs,"**[N] **and it is stated there,** with regard to a burnt offering: "And he shall cut it into its pieces; and the priest shall lay them, with **its head** and its fats, in order on the wood that is on the fire which is upon the altar. But the innards **and the legs** shall he wash with water" (Leviticus 1:12–13). **Just as there,** the burnt offering is burned **by means of cutting** the offering into pieces, as explicitly stated in the verse, **so too here,** it is burned **by means of cutting**[H] the offering into pieces.

אִי מַה לְּהַלָּן בְּהֶפְשֵׁט – אַף כָּאן נַמִי בְּהֶפְשֵׁט! תַּלְמוּד לוֹמַר: "וְקִרְבּוֹ וּפִרְשׁוֹ". מַאי תַּלְמוּדָא? אָמַר רַב פַּפָּא: כְּשֵׁם שֶׁפִּרְשׁוֹ בְּקִרְבּוֹ – כָּךְ בְּשָׂרוֹ בְּעוֹרוֹ.

The Gemara clarifies: **If** these are compared, one could say that **just as there,** the burnt offering is prepared for being burned **by** first **flaying** it, **so too here,** the bull offering of a High Priest should **also** be prepared for being burned **by** first **flaying** it. To counter this reasoning, **the verse states: "And its innards and its dung"** (Leviticus 4:11). The Gemara asks: **What is the** biblical **derivation?** How do these words teach that there is no requirement to flay the animal? **Rav Pappa says: Just as the dung** remains **inside** the animal[N] when the animal is burned, **so** the animal's **flesh** remains **inside its skin.** In any event, the *halakha* that the bull offering of a High Priest is cut into pieces before it is burned is derived via a verbal analogy.

HALAKHA

We have derived from here that the poached breads, etc. – לָמַדְנוּ לִרְבוּכָה וכו׳: All meal offerings were made from fine wheat flour, apart from the meal offering brought by a woman suspected by her husband of having been unfaithful and the *omer* offering, which are made from barley (Rambam *Sefer Avoda, Hilkhot Ma'aseh HaKorbanot* 12:2).

By means of cutting – עַל יְדֵי נִיתּוּחַ: With regard to sin offerings that are burned, after removing those sacrificial portions that will be offered on the altar, the animal is taken outside of the Temple and dissected in the same way that the burnt offering is dissected, with its skin. They are burned there in the place of the ashes, in accordance with the opinion of the *tanna* of the *baraita* (Rambam *Sefer Avoda, Hilkhot Ma'aseh HaKorbanot* 7:2, and see Mahari Kurkus there).

BACKGROUND

Loaves of a thanks offering – חַלּוֹת הַתּוֹדָה: Four types of bread are brought with a thanks offering, three of which are types of unleavened bread, namely, wafers, loaves, and poached breads. The fourth type consists of loaves of leavened bread.

NOTES

It is stated here, its head and its legs – נֶאֱמַר כָּאן רֹאשׁוֹ וּכְרָעָיו: The correct version of this text should be: Head and legs, since the Torah does not actually use identical words in both places, but does mention the head and the legs in both places (see Rashi).

Just as the dung remains inside the animal – כְּשֵׁם שֶׁפִּרְשׁוֹ בְּקִרְבּוֹ: Rashi explains that it is inconceivable that the dung should be removed from the animal before it is burned, because that is disgusting and not appropriate for a sacrificial rite. Therefore, it must remain within the animal. Then the juxtaposition teaches that the flesh should also remain within the skin of the animal.

ותניא, רבי אומר: נאמר כאן עור ובשר [ופרש],

Rava continues: **And it is taught** in a *baraita* that **Rabbi** Yehuda HaNasi **says:** It **is stated here,** with regard to the bull and goat offered by the High Priest on Yom Kippur, the terms **skin, flesh, and dung,** in the verse: "And the bull of the sin offering, and the goat of the sin offering, whose blood was brought in to make atonement in the Sanctuary, shall be carried out of the camp; and they shall burn in the fire their skin, and their flesh, and their dung" (Leviticus 16:27).

Perek **V**
Daf **50** Amud **b**

ונאמר להלן עור ובשר ופרש, מה להלן על ידי ניתוח שלא בהפשט – אף כאן על ידי ניתוח שלא בהפשט.

And it is stated below, with regard to the bull sin offerings that are burned, the terms **skin, flesh, and dung,** in the verse: "But the skin of the bull, and all its flesh, with its head, and with its legs, and its innards, and its dung" (Leviticus 4:11). **Just as below** it is prepared for burning **by means of cutting** it into pieces but **not by means of flaying,** as derived by the verbal analogy, **so too here** it is prepared for burning **by means of cutting** it into pieces but **not by means of flaying.** Evidently, a *halakha* derived via a verbal analogy can then teach another *halakha* via a verbal analogy.

דבר הלמד בגזירה שוה מהו שילמד בקל וחומר? קל וחומר: ומה היקש שאינו מלמד בהיקש, אי מדרבא אי מדרבינא – מלמד בקל וחומר, מדתנא דבי רבי ישמעאל; גזירה שוה המלמדת בהיקש, מדרב פפא – אינו דין שתלמד בקל וחומר?

§ The Gemara asks: **What is** the *halakha* as to whether **a matter derived via a verbal analogy** can **teach** its *halakha* to another matter **via an *a fortiori*** inference? The Gemara answers: That question itself can be answered with **an *a fortiori*** inference: **And just as** a matter derived via **a juxtaposition, which cannot** then **teach** its *halakha* **via a juxtaposition,** as proven **either from** the statement **of Rava or from** the statement **of Ravina** (49b), can nevertheless **teach** its *halakha* **via an *a fortiori*** inference, as proven **from** the statement **that the school of Rabbi Yishmael taught** (50a), with regard to a matter derived via **a verbal analogy, which** can **teach** its *halakha* **via a juxtaposition,** as proven **from** the statement **of Rav Pappa** (50a), **is it not logical that it should teach** its *halakha* **via an *a fortiori*** inference?

הניחא למאן דאית ליה דרב פפא, אלא למאן דלית ליה דרב פפא מאי איכא למימר?

The Gemara clarifies: **This works out well according to the one who accepts** the statement **of Rav Pappa. But according to the one who does not accept** the statement **of Rav Pappa,** i.e., Mar Zutra, son of Rav Mari, **what is there to say?**

אלא קל וחומר: ומה היקש שאין מלמד בהיקש, אי מדרבא אי מדרבינא – מלמד בקל וחומר, מדתנא דבי רבי ישמעאל; גזירה שוה המלמדת בגזירה שוה חבירתה, מדרמי בר חמא – אינו דין שתלמד בקל וחומר?

Rather, this can be derived through a different ***a fortiori*** inference: **And just as** a matter derived via **a juxtaposition, which cannot** then **teach** its *halakha* **via a juxtaposition,** as proven **either from** the statement **of Rava or from** the statement **of Ravina** (49b), can nevertheless **teach** its *halakha* **via an *a fortiori*** inference, as proven **from** the statement **that the school of Rabbi Yishmael taught** (50a), with regard to a matter derived via **a verbal analogy, which** can **teach** its *halakha* **via another verbal analogy,** as proven **from** the statement **of Rami bar Ḥama** (50a), **is it not logical that it should teach** its *halakha* **via an *a fortiori*** inference?

דבר הלמד בגזירה שוה מהו שילמד בבנין אב? תיקו.

The Gemara asks: **What is** the *halakha* as to whether **a matter derived via a verbal analogy** can **teach** its *halakha* to another matter **via a paradigm?** The question **shall stand** unresolved.

דבר הלמד בקל וחומר מהו שילמד בהיקש? קל וחומר: ומה גזירה שוה שאינה למדה בהיקשא, מדרבי יוחנן – מלמד בהיקש, מדרב פפא; קל וחומר הלמד מהיקש, מדתנא דבי רבי ישמעאל – אינו דין שילמד בהיקש?

§ The Gemara asks: **What is** the *halakha* as to whether **a matter derived via an *a fortiori*** inference can **teach** its *halakha* to another matter **via a juxtaposition?** The Gemara answers that this itself can be derived via **an *a fortiori*** inference: **And just as** a *halakha* derived via **a verbal analogy, which cannot be derived** from another *halakha* derived **via a juxtaposition,** as proven **from** the statement **of Rabbi Yoḥanan** (49b), can nevertheless **teach** its *halakha* to another matter **via a juxtaposition,** as proven **from** the statement **of Rav Pappa** (50a), with regard to a *halakha* derived via **an *a fortiori*** inference, which **can be derived** from another *halakha* derived **via a juxtaposition,** as proven **from** the statement **that the school of Rabbi Yishmael taught** (50a), **is it not logical that it should teach** its *halakha* **via a juxtaposition?**

הָנִיחָא לְמַאן דְּאִית לֵיהּ דְּרַב פַּפָּא, אֶלָּא לְמַאן דְּלֵית לֵיהּ דְּרַב פַּפָּא מַאי אִיכָּא לְמֵימַר? תֵּיקוּ.

The Gemara clarifies: **This works out well according to the one who accepts** the statement **of Rav Pappa. But according to the one who does not accept** the statement **of Rav Pappa,** i.e., Mar Zutra, son of Rav Mari, **what is there to say?** The Gemara comments: The question **shall stand** unresolved.

דָּבָר הַלָּמֵד בְּקַל וָחוֹמֶר מַהוּ שֶׁיְּלַמֵּד בִּגְזֵירָה שָׁוָה? קַל וָחוֹמֶר: וּמַה גְּזֵירָה שָׁוָה שֶׁאֵינָהּ לְמֵידָה בְּהֶיקֵּשָׁא, מִדְּרַבִּי יוֹחָנָן – מְלַמֵּד בִּגְזֵירָה שָׁוָה, מִדְּרָמִי בַּר חָמָא; קַל וָחוֹמֶר הַלָּמֵד בְּהֶיקֵּשׁ, מִדְּתָנָא דְּבֵי רַבִּי יִשְׁמָעֵאל – אֵינוֹ דִּין שֶׁתְּלַמֵּד בִּגְזֵירָה שָׁוָה?

The Gemara asks: **What is** the *halakha* as to whether **a matter derived via an *a fortiori*** inference can **teach** its *halakha* to another matter **via a verbal analogy?** The Gemara answers that this itself can be derived via **an *a fortiori*** inference. **And just as** a *halakha* derived via **a verbal analogy, which cannot be derived** from another *halakha* derived **via a juxtaposition,** as proven **from** the statement **of Rabbi Yoḥanan** (49b), can nevertheless **teach** its *halakha* to another matter **via a verbal analogy,** as proven **from** the statement **of Rami bar Ḥama** (50a), with regard to a *halakha* derived via **an *a fortiori*** inference, which **can be derived** from another *halakha* derived **via a juxtaposition,** as proven **from** the statement **that the school of Rabbi Yishmael taught** (50a), **is it not logical that it should teach** its *halakha* **via a verbal analogy?**

דָּבָר הַלָּמֵד בְּקַל וָחוֹמֶר מַהוּ שֶׁיְּלַמֵּד בְּקַל וָחוֹמֶר? קַל וָחוֹמֶר: וּמַה גְּזֵירָה שָׁוָה שֶׁאֵינָהּ לְמֵידָה בְּהֶיקֵּשׁ, מִדְּרַבִּי יוֹחָנָן – מְלַמֵּד בְּקַל וָחוֹמֶר, כִּדַאֲמַרַן; קַל וָחוֹמֶר הַלָּמֵד מֵהֶיקֵּשׁ, מִדְּתָנָא דְּבֵי רַבִּי יִשְׁמָעֵאל – אֵינוֹ דִּין שֶׁיְּלַמֵּד בְּקַל וָחוֹמֶר?

The Gemara asks: **What is** the *halakha* as to whether **a matter derived via an *a fortiori*** inference can **teach** its *halakha* to another matter **via an *a fortiori*** inference? The Gemara answers that this itself can be derived via **an *a fortiori*** inference. **And just as** a *halakha* derived via **a verbal analogy, which cannot be derived** from another *halakha* derived **via a juxtaposition,** as proven **from** the statement **of Rabbi Yoḥanan** (49b), can nevertheless **teach** its *halakha* to another matter **via an *a fortiori*** inference, **as we have said,**[N] with regard to a *halakha* derived via **an *a fortiori*** inference, which **can be derived** from another *halakha* derived **via a juxtaposition,** as proven **from** the statement **that the school of Rabbi Yishmael taught** (50a), **is it not logical that it should teach** its *halakha* **via an *a fortiori*** inference?

וְזֶהוּ קַל וָחוֹמֶר בֶּן קַל וָחוֹמֶר. בֶּן בְּנוֹ שֶׁל קַל וָחוֹמֶר הוּא!

The Gemara comments: **And this is an *a fortiori*** inference that is the **son of,** i.e., is derived from, another ***a fortiori*** inference. The Gemara challenges this last statement: **It is** not the son of an *a fortiori* inference, but the **grandson of an *a fortiori*** inference,[N] which cannot be used. The very fact that a matter derived via a verbal analogy can then teach its *halakha* via an *a fortiori* inference is itself derived from an *a fortiori* inference, as the Gemara stated.

אֶלָּא קַל וָחוֹמֶר: וּמָה הֶיקֵּשׁ שֶׁאֵינוֹ לָמֵד בְּהֶיקֵּשׁ, אִי מִדְּרָבָא אִי מִדְּרָבִינָא – מְלַמֵּד בְּקַל וָחוֹמֶר, מִדְּתָנָא דְּבֵי רַבִּי יִשְׁמָעֵאל; קַל וָחוֹמֶר הַלָּמֵד מֵהֶיקֵּשׁ, מִדְּתָנֵי דְּבֵי רַבִּי יִשְׁמָעֵאל – אֵינוֹ דִּין שֶׁיְּלַמֵּד בְּקַל וָחוֹמֶר? וְזֶהוּ קַל וָחוֹמֶר בֶּן קַל וָחוֹמֶר.

Rather, the *halakha* as to whether a matter derived via an *a fortiori* inference can teach its *halakha* to another matter via an *a fortiori* inference can be derived via another ***a fortiori*** inference. **And just as** a matter derived via **a juxtaposition, which cannot be derived via a juxtaposition,** as proven **either from** the statement **of Rava or from** the statement **of Ravina** (49b), can nevertheless **teach** its *halakha* **via an *a fortiori*** inference, as proven **from** the statement **that the school of Rabbi Yishmael taught** (50a), with regard to a *halakha* derived via **an *a fortiori*** inference, which **can be derived** from another *halakha* derived **via a juxtaposition,** as proven **from** the statement **that the school of Rabbi Yishmael taught** (50a), **is it not logical that it should teach** its *halakha* **via an *a fortiori*** inference? The Gemara comments: **And this is an *a fortiori*** inference that is the **son of** another ***a fortiori*** inference.

NOTES

Teach via an *a fortiori* inference, as we have said – מְלַמֵּד בְּקַל וָחוֹמֶר כְּדַאֲמַרַן: The *Shita Mekubbetzet* writes that the correct version of the text here should read: Teach through an *a fortiori* inference from the statement of the cultivated garden. He explains that the term cultivated garden is a reference to the study hall. In other words, this statement was not made by an individual Sage, but was the conclusion of the general discussion in the study hall.

Grandson of an *a fortiori* inference – בֶּן בְּנוֹ שֶׁל קַל וָחוֹמֶר: Rashi explains that since there is a chain of *a fortiori* inferences, perhaps it cannot be utilized to teach a *halakha*. *Tosafot* reject this explanation, explaining they know of no reason why a chain of inferences should be less able to teach a *halakha* than a single inference. They explain that it is circular reasoning to prove that a matter derived though an *a fortiori* inference can teach another matter through an *a fortiori* inference by using two *a fortiori* inferences to do so.

דָּבָר הַלָּמֵד בְּקַל וָחוֹמֶר מַהוּ שֶׁיְּלַמֵּד בְּבִנְיַן אָב? אָמַר רַבִּי יִרְמְיָה, תָּא שְׁמַע: מָלַק וְנִמְצֵאת טְרֵיפָה, רַבִּי מֵאִיר אוֹמֵר: אֵינָהּ מְטַמְּאָה בְּבֵית הַבְּלִיעָה, רַבִּי יְהוּדָה אוֹמֵר: מְטַמְּאָה בְּבֵית הַבְּלִיעָה.

The Gemara asks: **What is** the *halakha* as to whether **a matter derived via an** ***a fortiori*** **inference can teach** its *halakha* to another matter **via a paradigm? Rabbi Yirmeya says: Come** and **hear** a proof from a mishna (69a–b): If a priest **pinched** the nape of a bird offering properly **and it was** then **found** to be a bird **with a wound that would have caused it to die within twelve months** [***tereifa***],[N] which disqualifies it from being used as an offering and renders it prohibited for consumption by the priests, **Rabbi Meir says:** An olive-bulk of its meat **does not render** one who swallows it **ritually impure** when it is **in the throat,** as is the *halakha* concerning a bird carcass, as the fact that it underwent pinching means that it is not in the category of a carcass. **Rabbi Yehuda says:** Its status is like that of any other carcass of a kosher bird, and its meat **renders** one who swallows it **ritually impure** when it is **in the throat.**

אָמַר רַבִּי מֵאִיר: קַל וָחוֹמֶר, וּמָה נִבְלַת בְּהֵמָה שֶׁמְּטַמְּאָה בְּמַגָּע וּבְמַשָּׂא – שְׁחִיטָתָהּ מְטַהֶרֶת טְרֵיפָתָהּ מִטּוּמְאָתָהּ, נִבְלַת עוֹף שֶׁאֵין מְטַמָּא בְּמַגָּע וּבְמַשָּׂא – אֵינוֹ דִּין שֶׁתְּהֵא שְׁחִיטָתָהּ מְטַהֶרֶת טְרֵיפָתָהּ מִטּוּמְאָתָהּ? מָה מָצִינוּ בִּשְׁחִיטָה שֶׁמַּכְשַׁרְתָּהּ בַּאֲכִילָה

The mishna continues: **Rabbi Meir said:** My opinion can be proved via **an** ***a fortiori*** inference. **And just as** with regard to **the carcass of an animal, which transmits impurity** to a person **through touching** it **and carrying** it, **its slaughter** nevertheless **purifies its** ***tereifa*** **from its impurity,** with regard to **the carcass of a bird,** which possesses less severe impurity, **as it does not transmit impurity through touching** it **and carrying** it, but only when it is in the throat, **is it not logical that its slaughter purifies its** ***tereifa*** **from its impurity?** And once it is established that slaughter purifies a bird that is a *tereifa*, it can be derived: **Just as we found with regard to** a bird's **slaughter that it permits it for consumption**

Perek **V**
Daf **51** Amud **a**

מְטַהֶרֶת טְרֵיפָתָהּ מִטּוּמְאָתָהּ, אַף מְלִיקָה שֶׁמַּכְשַׁרְתָּהּ בַּאֲכִילָה – תְּטַהֵר טְרֵיפָתָהּ מִטּוּמְאָתָהּ.

and it purifies its ***tereifa*** **from its impurity, so too its pinching, which permits** bird offerings **with regard to consumption, should purify its** ***tereifa*** **from its impurity.**

רַבִּי יוֹסֵי אוֹמֵר: דַּיָּהּ כְּנִבְלַת בְּהֵמָה טְהוֹרָה, שֶׁשְּׁחִיטָתָהּ מְטַהַרְתָּהּ וְלֹא מְלִיקָתָהּ.

Rabbi Yosei says: Although one can derive from the case of an animal that slaughter purifies the *tereifa* of a bird from its impurity, that derivation cannot be extended to pinching. The same restriction that applies to every *a fortiori* inference, namely, that a *halakha* derived by means of an *a fortiori* inference is no more stringent than the source from which it is derived, applies here: **It is sufficient** for the halakhic status of the carcass of a bird that is a *tereifa* to be **like** that of **the carcass of an animal** of **a kosher** species that is a *tereifa*; i.e., **that** only **its slaughter purifies it, but not its pinching.**[H]

NOTES

Pinched and it was found to be a ***tereifa*** **– מָלַק וְנִמְצֵאת טְרֵיפָה:** There are two ways of killing a bird such that it remains ritually pure. A non-sacred bird is slaughtered with a knife, and offerings are pinched from the nape of the neck. A bird that dies in any other way is a carcass [*neveila*]. A bird that is a *neveila* is different from an animal that is a *neveila* in that it does not impart ritual impurity to a person through contact, but only if he eats it. Once it reaches his throat, the person becomes impure. The Sages disagreed with regard to the status of a bird that was either slaughtered or pinched in the correct way but then is found to have been a *tereifa*. The slaughter or pinching in such a case is not sufficient to render the bird permitted to be eaten. The dispute is whether the slaughter or pinching is sufficient to remove the bird from the category of a *neveila*, just as slaughter does for an animal (see *Ḥullin* 128b). As explained in a mishna (*Teharot* 1:1), there are three opinions. Rabbi Meir holds that either slaughter or pinching removes the bird from the category of *neveila*. Rabbi Yehuda holds that neither slaughter nor pinching removes the bird from the category of *neveila*. Rabbi Yosei holds that slaughter does remove it from the category of *neveila* but pinching does not.

HALAKHA

Its slaughter purifies it but not its pinching – שֶׁשְּׁחִיטָתָהּ מְטַהַרְתָּהּ וְלֹא מְלִיקָתָהּ: A bird of a kosher species which became a *tereifa* and was then slaughtered with a valid slaughter is thereby removed from becoming impure as a bird carcass. This is the *halakha* even if it was slaughtered in the Temple courtyard. If this bird had its nape pinched, the pinching does not render it pure. This is in accordance with the opinion of Rabbi Yosei (Rambam *Sefer Tahara, Hilkhot She'ar Avot HaTumot* 3:12 and *Sefer Avoda, Hilkhot Pesulei HaMukdashin* 7:3).

וְלָא הִיא, הָתָם תִּיהֱוֵי הִיא, מִשְּׁחִיטָה דְּחוּלִּין קָאָתְיָין.

The Gemara rejects this proof: **And that is not so. Let it remain there,**[N] i.e., one cannot learn from it, as that is a case that **comes from the slaughter of non-sacred** animals. The *halakha* of the pinching of a consecrated bird is derived through a paradigm from the *halakha* of the slaughter of a non-sacred bird, and the *halakha* of the slaughter of a non-sacred bird is derived through an *a fortiori* inference from the *halakha* of the slaughter of a non-sacred animal. Outside of the realm of consecrated matters there is no question that a matter derived via one of the hermeneutical principles can then teach its *halakha* via another principle. The entire question under discussion is only with regard to the realm of consecrated matters.[B]

NOTES

Let it remain there, etc. – הָתָם תִּיהֱוֵי וכו׳: This text is Rashi's version of the text. It seems that he divides this sentence into two: There, i.e., from there the matter can be derived. The Gemara means that the main derivation is in fact from a juxtaposition, as explained later (62b). Furthermore: Let it remain [*tehevei*], as it is derived from the slaughter of non-sacred animals. In other words, even if this were to be a proof, it would not answer the Gemara's question, since it is not in the realm of consecrated matters. See *Tosafot*, whose version of the text reads: They are both learned [*tarvaihu*] from the slaughter of non-sacred animals. In other words, in this case, both of the matters that are learned are learned from non-sacred matters. The slaughter of the bird is learned from the slaughter of a non-sacred animal, and the pinching of the nape of the neck of a bird is learned from the slaughter of a non-sacred bird.

BACKGROUND

A matter derived – דָּבָר הַלָּמֵד: Can a matter derived through a hermeneutical principle then teach through a hermeneutical principle? See table below.

Principle	Conclusion	Source	Notes
Derived via a juxtaposition; teach via a juxtaposition	No	Statement of Rava or Ravina (49b)	If the *halakha* is derived from two juxtapositions it is as if it is written explicitly, and may teach via another juxtaposition (41a)
Derived via a juxtaposition; teach via a verbal analogy	No	Statement of Rabbi Yoḥanan (49b)	Some hold the conclusion remains uncertain (*Tosafot* on 63b)
Derived via a juxtaposition; teach via an *a fortiori* inference	Yes	School of Rabbi Yishmael (50a)	
Derived via a juxtaposition; teach via a paradigm	Unresolved	Rabbi Yirmeya's claim that it may not teach is rejected (50a)	*Tosafot* bring proof that it can teach
Derived via a verbal analogy; teach via a juxtaposition	Unresolved	Statement of Rav Pappa (50a)	
Derived via a verbal analogy; teach via a verbal analogy	Yes	Statement of Rami bar Ḥama or Rava (50a)	
Derived via a verbal analogy; teach via an *a fortiori* inference	Yes	An *a fortiori* inference based on the fact that a verbal analogy teaches via juxtaposition, according to Rav Pappa, or an *a fortiori* inference based on the fact that a verbal analogy teaches via another verbal analogy (50b)	
Derived via a verbal analogy; teach via a paradigm	Unresolved	50b	
Derived via an *a fortiori* inference; teach via a juxtaposition	Unresolved	An *a fortiori* inference based on the fact that a verbal analogy teaches via a juxtaposition (50b)	This depends on whether the conclusion is in accordance with the opinion of Rav Pappa that a matter derived via a verbal analogy may teach via a juxtaposition
Derived via an *a fortiori* inference; teach via a verbal analogy	Yes	An *a fortiori* inference based on the fact that a verbal analogy teaches via a verbal analogy (50b)	
Derived via an *a fortiori* inference; teach via an *a fortiori* inference	Yes	An *a fortiori* inference based on the fact that a juxtaposition teaches via an *a fortiori* inference (50b)	
Derived via an *a fortiori* inference; teach via a paradigm	Unresolved	51a	Rashi apparently holds that according to Rav Pappa this can be done; others explain that even Rav Pappa concedes that this cannot be done (*Shita Mekubbetzet*)
Derived via a paradigm; teach via a juxtaposition	Unresolved	51a	
Derived via a paradigm; teach via a verbal analogy	Unresolved	51a	
Derived via a paradigm; teach via an *a fortiori* inference	Unresolved	51a	Some hold that this case is resolved and this can be done (*Tzon Kedoshim*), but *Tosefot Rabbeinu Peretz* disagrees
Derived via a paradigm; teach via a paradigm	Yes	51a	According to Rashi this remains unresolved

דָּבָר הַלָּמֵד בְּבִנְיַן אָב מַהוּ שֶׁיְּלַמֵּד בְּהֶיקֵּשׁ וּבִגְזֵירָה שָׁוָה וּבְקַל וָחוֹמֶר וּבְבִנְיַן אָב?

§ The Gemara asks: **What is** the *halakha* as to whether **a matter derived via a paradigm** can **teach** its *halakha* to another matter **via a juxtaposition or via a verbal analogy or via an** ***a fortiori*** inference **or via a paradigm?**

פְּשׁוֹט מִיהָא חֲדָא: מִפְּנֵי מָה אָמְרוּ: לָן בְּדָם כָּשֵׁר – שֶׁהֲרֵי לָן בְּאֵימוּרִין כָּשֵׁר, לָן בְּאֵימוּרִין כָּשֵׁר – שֶׁהֲרֵי לָן בְּבָשָׂר כָּשֵׁר.

The Gemara states: **Resolve at least one** of those questions. The Gemara cites a lengthy *baraita* before stating the resolution inferred from that *baraita*. **For what** reason **did** the Sages **say** that **in** the case of **blood left overnight**[N] it is **fit,** i.e., if blood of an offering had been left overnight and was then placed on the altar it need not be removed? This is **as** it is **in** the case of **sacrificial portions,**[B] where if they are **left overnight** they are **fit.** From where is it derived that **in** the case of **sacrificial portions** which are **left overnight,** they are **fit?** This is **as** it is **in** the case of **meat,** where if it is **left overnight** it is **fit,** because the meat of a peace offering may be eaten for two days and one night.

יוֹצֵא – הוֹאִיל וְיוֹצֵא כָּשֵׁר בְּבָמָה,

From where is it derived that if an offering that has **left** the Temple courtyard is then placed on the altar it need not be removed? This is derived by a paradigm, **since** an offering that **leaves** its area is **fit in** the case of an offering brought on a private **altar.**

טָמֵא – הוֹאִיל וְהוּתַּר בַּעֲבוֹדַת צִיבּוּר.

From where is it derived that if an offering that has become **ritually impure** is placed on the altar it need not be removed? This is derived by a paradigm, **since** one is **permitted** to offer an impure offering **in** the case of **communal rites,** i.e., communal offerings. In cases of necessity, the communal offerings may be sacrificed even if they are ritually impure.

חוּץ לִזְמַנּוֹ – הוֹאִיל וּמְרַצֶּה לְפִיגּוּלוֹ.

From where is it derived that in the case of an offering that was disqualified due to the intention of the priest who slaughtered it to consume it **beyond its** designated **time** [***piggul***], if it was placed on the altar it need not be removed? The *halakha* applies there **since** the sprinkling of its blood **effects acceptance** of the offering notwithstanding **its** status of ***piggul.*** The status of *piggul* takes effect only if the sacrificial rites involving that offering were otherwise performed properly. This indicates that it still has the status of an offering, so it need not be removed from the altar.

חוּץ לִמְקוֹמוֹ – הוֹאִיל וְהוּקַּשׁ לְחוּץ לִזְמַנּוֹ.

From where is it derived that in the case of an offering that was disqualified due to the intention of the priest who slaughtered it to consume it **outside its** designated **area,** if it was placed on the altar it need not be removed? This is derived by a paradigm, **since** it is **juxtaposed to** an offering that was slaughtered with intent to consume it **beyond its** designated **time.**

שֶׁקִּיבְּלוּ פְּסוּלִין וְזָרְקוּ דָּמָן – בְּהָנָךְ פְּסוּלִין דַּחֲזוּ לַעֲבוֹדַת צִיבּוּר.

From where is it derived that in the case of an offering for **which** priests who are **disqualified collected and sprinkled its blood,** if it was placed on the altar it need not be removed? This is derived **from** the *halakha* of **these** priests who are generally **disqualified** because they are impure, yet **who are fit to** perform the **communal rites,** i.e., to sacrifice communal offerings, when all the priests or the majority of the Jewish people are impure. In any event, the *halakha* of the sacrificial portions was derived via a paradigm from the *halakha* of meat that was left overnight, and then the *halakha* of blood was derived via a paradigm from the *halakha* of the sacrificial portions. Evidently, a matter derived via a paradigm can teach its *halakha* to another matter via a paradigm.

וְכִי דָּנִין דָּבָר שֶׁלֹּא בְּהֶכְשֵׁירוֹ מִדָּבָר שֶׁבְּהֶכְשֵׁירוֹ?

The Gemara questions the derivations of the *baraita*: **But can one deduce** the *halakha* of **a matter that is not fit,** i.e., sacrificial portions that are disqualified due to having been left overnight, **from** the *halakha* of **a matter that is fit,** i.e., the peace offering, which is permitted to be eaten for two days and one night? Similarly, how can the *baraita* derive the *halakha* of meat that was removed from the Temple courtyard from the *halakha* of a private altar, which has no sacred area surrounding it?

NOTES

Left overnight, etc. – **לָן וכו׳**: The Torah states: "Command Aaron and his sons, saying: This is the law of the burnt offering: It is that which goes up on its firewood upon the altar all night until the morning; and the fire of the altar shall be kept burning thereby" (Leviticus 6:2). The Sages derived from the phrase "law of the burnt offering," which is an amplification, that any offering that ascends to the altar does not descend from it. This includes offerings that were disqualified from the outset. Rabbi Yehuda derives from three restrictions in the verse that there are three categories that do descend again, even if they ascended to the altar: An offering that was slaughtered at night, an offering whose blood was spilled, and an offering whose blood has been taken outside the Temple courtyard. The *baraita* here is based on the disqualified offerings listed in the mishna (84a). Even according to Rabbi Yehuda's opinion, if these disqualified offerings ascend to the altar they do not descend from it. The Gemara explains the source that they are included in this amplification.

BACKGROUND

Sacrificial portions – **אֵימוּרִין**: This term is a reference to the portions of sin offerings, guilt offerings, and peace offerings that are consumed on the altar, among them the fats, kidneys, and sheep tail. Occasionally, the sacrificial portions of the burnt offering are also included in this expression.

תַּנָּא, מִ״זֹּאת תּוֹרַת הָעוֹלָה״ רִיבָּה, סָמֵיךְ לֵיהּ.

The Gemara answers: The *tanna* **relied on** the verse: "Command Aaron and his sons, saying: **This is the law of the burnt offering**: It is that which goes up on its firewood upon the altar all night until the morning; and the fire of the altar shall thereby be kept burning" (Leviticus 6:2), which **amplified it**,[N] teaching that many types of disqualified offerings may be left upon the altar. The derivations written in the *baraita* are mere supports for those *halakhot*.

״שְׁיָרֵי הַדָּם״ כּו׳. מַאי טַעְמָא? אָמַר קְרָא: ״אֶל יְסוֹד מִזְבַּח הָעֹלָה אֲשֶׁר פֶּתַח אֹהֶל מוֹעֵד״ – הַהוּא דְּפָגַע בְּרֵישָׁא.

§ The mishna teaches with regard to the sin offerings whose blood is presented inside the Sanctuary: As to **the remainder of the blood** which is left after the sprinklings, a priest would pour it onto the western base of the external altar. But if he did not place the remainder of the blood on the western base, it does not disqualify the offering. The Gemara asks: **What is the reason** that it must be poured on the western base? The Gemara answers: **The verse states** with regard to the bull offering of the High Priest: "And the priest shall sprinkle the blood upon the corners of the altar of sweet incense before the Lord, which is in the Tent of Meeting; and all the remaining blood of the bull he shall pour out **at the base of the altar of burnt offering, which is at the entrance of the Tent of Meeting**" (Leviticus 4:7). This means that he must pour it on **that** base **which he encounters first**[H] when he leaves the Tent of Meeting, which is the western base.

תָּנוּ רַבָּנַן: ״אֶל יְסוֹד מִזְבַּח הָעֹלָה״ – וְלֹא יְסוֹד מִזְבֵּחַ הַפְּנִימִי,

The Sages taught in a *baraita*: There are three verses that contain the same phrase. With regard to pouring the remainder of the blood of a bull offering of the High Priest, the verse states: "All the remaining blood of the bull he shall pour out **at the base of the altar of burnt offering**" (Leviticus 4:7). This teaches that it must be on the base of the external altar, **but not on the base of the inner altar,** where he had sprinkled the blood.

״אֶל יְסוֹד מִזְבַּח הָעֹלָה״ – אֵין לוֹ יְסוֹד לִפְנִימִי עַצְמוֹ,

The *baraita* continues: With regard to the bull sacrificed for an unwitting communal sin the verse states: "And he shall sprinkle the blood upon the corners of the altar which is before the Lord, that is in the Tent of Meeting, and all the remaining blood shall he pour out **at the base of the altar of burnt offering,** which is at the entrance of the Tent of Meeting" (Leviticus 4:18). This teaches that the **inner altar itself has no base** at all.

״אֶל יְסוֹד מִזְבַּח הָעֹלָה״ – תֵּן יְסוֹד לַמִּזְבֵּחַ שֶׁל עוֹלָה.

Finally, the verse states with regard to the sin offering of a king: "And the priest shall take of the blood of the sin offering with his finger and place it upon the corners of the altar of burnt offering, and the remaining blood thereof shall he pour out **at the base of the altar of the burnt offering**" (Leviticus 4:25). This teaches that you must **give a base to the altar of** the **burnt offering,**[N] i.e., that the remainder of any blood placed on the altar must be poured on the base.

אוֹ אֵינוֹ אֶלָּא: מִזְבְּחָהּ שֶׁל עוֹלָה יְהֵא לִיסוֹד? אָמַר רַבִּי יִשְׁמָעֵאל: קַל וָחוֹמֶר, מָה שִׁירַיִים שֶׁאֵין מְכַפְּרִין – טְעוּנִין יְסוֹד, תְּחִלַּת עוֹלָה שֶׁמְּכַפֶּרֶת – אֵינוֹ דִּין שֶׁטְּעוּנָה יְסוֹד?

The *baraita* continues: **Or** perhaps it **is not** so, but **rather** the verse serves to teach that any sprinkling of blood on the corners of the **altar of** the **burnt offering will be** done on a part of the altar where there is **a base.**[N] **Rabbi Yishmael said:** There is no need for the verse to teach that *halakha*, because it can be derived via **an *a fortiori*** inference: **Just as** the **remainder** of the blood, **which does not effect atonement, requires** pouring on the **base** of the altar, with regard to **the initial** sprinkling of the blood **of a burnt offering, which effects atonement, is it not logical that it requires** a part of the altar where there is **a base?**

אָמַר רַבִּי עֲקִיבָא: מָה שִׁירַיִים שֶׁאֵין מְכַפְּרִין, וְאֵין בָּאִין לְכַפָּרָה – טְעוּנָה יְסוֹד, תְּחִלַּת עוֹלָה שֶׁמְּכַפֶּרֶת וּבָאָה לְכַפָּרָה – אֵינוֹ דִּין שֶׁטְּעוּנָה יְסוֹד?

Similarly, **Rabbi Akiva said: Just as** the **remainder** of the blood, **which does not effect atonement and does not come for atonement,** nevertheless **requires** pouring on the **base** of the altar, with regard to **the initial** sprinkling of the blood **of a burnt offering, which effects atonement and comes for atonement, is it not logical that it requires** a part of the altar where there is **a base?**

NOTES

Relied on: This is the law of the burnt offering, which amplified it – מִזֹּאת תּוֹרַת הָעוֹלָה רִיבָּה סָמֵיךְ לֵיהּ: The main source that any offering that ascends to the altar does not descend from it is from the phrase: "The law of the burnt offering." The *halakhot* of offerings left overnight, those that are impure or taken out of the area in which they must be consumed, are derived from there (Rashi; see *Birkat HaZevaḥ*).

Give a base to the altar of the burnt offering – תֵּן יְסוֹד לַמִּזְבֵּחַ שֶׁל עוֹלָה: There are many explanations of this statement. Rashi explains that the verse teaches that the remainder of any blood which is placed on the external altar is poured on the base of the external altar. *Tosafot* challenge Rashi's explanation, because the Gemara (37a) provided different sources for that *halakha*. They cite Rabbeinu Ḥayyim, explaining that the expression: To the altar of the burnt offering, refers only to the remainder of the blood of a burnt offering, which requires pouring on the base. There are other verses that teach about the remainder of blood of other offerings. They also offer another explanation, which is also suggested by the Ra'avad, that this is not referring to the remainder of the blood, but to the placement of blood. It teaches that all placement of blood on the external altar must be above the base, with the exception of a sin offering, about which the Torah states "around" (see Leviticus 8:15), to teach that it must be placed on all four corners of the altar.

Altar of the burnt offering will be on a base – מִזְבְּחָהּ שֶׁל עוֹלָה יְהֵא לִיסוֹד: In other words, that place which is considered an altar for the burnt offering, the place where the blood is sprinkled, will be in a place which has a base, and the blood shall be sprinkled there. The southeast corner of the altar did not have a base (see 52b). Since the blood of the burnt offering was sprinkled on two diagonal corners of the altar, the priest had to sprinkle it on the southwest corner and the northeast corner.

This is according to Rashi's explanation, and that of Rabbeinu Ḥayyim, cited by *Tosafot*. According to the Ra'avad and the second explanation of *Tosafot*, who say that this itself is the explanation of the phrase: Give a base to the altar of the burnt offering, here the *baraita* suggests that the sprinkling of the blood of the burnt offering should be identical to that of the remainder, i.e., on the base itself. Alternatively, perhaps this is referring only to the burnt offering, not to any other offerings.

HALAKHA

That which he encounters first – הַהוּא דְּפָגַע בְּרֵישָׁא: The remainder of the blood of all sin offerings that are burned is poured on the western base of the external altar, which is the first one the priest encounters when he leaves the Sanctuary (Rambam *Sefer Avoda*, *Hilkhot Ma'aseh HaKorbanot* 5:11).

אִם כֵּן, מָה תַּלְמוּד לוֹמַר ״אֶל יְסוֹד מִזְבַּח הָעֹלָה״ – תֵּן יְסוֹד לְמִזְבְּחָה שֶׁל עוֹלָה.

The *baraita* concludes: **If so, why** must **the verse state: "At the base of the altar of burnt offering"** (Leviticus 4:25)? It is to teach that you must **give a base to the altar of** the **burnt offering,** i.e., that the remainder of the blood of the offering must be poured on the base.

אָמַר מָר: ״אֶל יְסוֹד מִזְבַּח״ – וְלֹא יְסוֹד מִזְבַּח הַפְּנִימִי. הָא מִיבְּעֵי לֵיהּ לְגוּפֵיהּ! מֵ״אֲשֶׁר פֶּתַח אֹהֶל מוֹעֵד״ נָפְקָא.

The Gemara discusses this *baraita.* **The Master says:** The verse states: **"At the base of the altar** of burnt offering, which is at the entrance of the Tent of Meeting" (Leviticus 4:18). This teaches that it must be on the base of the external altar, **but not the base of the inner altar.** The Gemara asks: **Isn't that necessary for the matter itself,** to teach that the remainder of the blood must be poured onto the base of the external altar? The Gemara answers: That *halakha* is **derived from: "Which is at the entrance of the Tent of Meeting"** (Leviticus 4:18), referring to the external altar. Therefore, the verse mentions the altar of burnt offering to exclude the base of the inner altar.

״אֶל יְסוֹד מִזְבַּח הָעוֹלָה״,

The *baraita* teaches with regard to the sin offering of a king: The verse states: "And the priest shall take of the blood of the sin offering with his finger, and place it upon the corners of the altar of burnt offering, and the remaining blood thereof shall he pour out **at the base of the altar of burnt offering"** (Leviticus 4:25).

Perek **V**
Daf **51** Amud **b**

תֵּן יְסוֹד לְמִזְבֵּחַ שֶׁל עוֹלָה.

This teaches that you must **give a base to the altar of** the **burnt offering,** i.e., that the remainder of any blood placed on the altar must be poured on the base.

דְּאִי סָלְקָא דַּעְתָּךְ כִּדְכְתִיב, הָנֵי לָמָּה לִי קְרָא – לְשִׁירַיִם, שִׁירַיִם? הָא בָּרַאי עָבֵיד לְהוּ!

The Gemara explains: **Because if it enters your mind** that the verse states this simply to teach **as it is written,** concerning this offering alone, **why do I** need **these verses** with regard to the sin offering of a king? If you would answer: The verses are needed **to** teach the *halakha* that the **remainder** of the blood must be poured on the external altar rather than on the inner altar, then the question remains: Is there any need for the Torah to teach this about the **remainder? But** the sprinklings of blood themselves are **performed** on the **external** altar, so why would one think that the remainder of the blood should be poured on the inner altar?

וְכִי תֵּימָא, דְּאַפֵּיךְ מֵיפַּךְ,

And if you would say that one might mistakenly say **that** the priest **reverses** the sprinklings,

Perek **V**
Daf **52** Amud **a**

דְּבָרַאי לְגַוַּאי וּדְגַוַּאי לְבָרַאי – הָא אֵין לוֹ יְסוֹד לִפְנִימִי עַצְמוֹ.

such that with regard to an offering for **which** he sprinkles the blood on the **external** altar he should pour the remainder of the blood **on** the **inner** altar, **and** this is analogous to the *halakha* that he pours the remainder **of** the blood sprinkled on the **inner** altar **on** the base of the **external** altar, this is not possible. **But the inner** altar **itself does not have a base,** and therefore it is not possible to pour the remainder of the blood on the base of the inner altar. Therefore, the verse must teach that the remainder of the blood of the burnt offering is poured on the base of the external altar.

״אוֹ אֵינוֹ אֶלָּא מִזְבֵּחַ שֶׁל עוֹלָה יְהֵא לִיסוֹד״. מִי כְּתִיב ״אֶל יְסוֹד הָעוֹלָה״? ״אֶל יְסוֹד מִזְבַּח הָעוֹלָה״ כְּתִיב!

The Gemara analyzes the next clause of the *baraita*: **Or** perhaps it is **not** so, but **rather** the verse serves to teach that any sprinkling of blood on the corners of the **altar of** the **burnt offering will be** done on a part of the altar where there is **a base.** The Gemara asks: How can the verse mean that? **Is it written: At the base of the burnt offering?** This would indicate that the blood of the burnt offering must be placed where there is a base. **It is written** in the verse: **"At the base of the altar of burnt offering"** (Leviticus 4:25).

אִי הֲוָה כְּתִיב ״אֶל יְסוֹד הָעוֹלָה״ – הֲוָה אָמִינָא בִּזְקִיפָה אֶל יְסוֹד, הָשְׁתָּא דִּכְתִיב ״אֶל יְסוֹד מִזְבַּח הָעוֹלָה״ – אַגַּגּוֹ דִּיסוֹד.

The Gemara answers: Even if the verse were to be speaking about sprinkling the blood of the burnt offering and is not referring to pouring the remainder of the blood, the term "altar of" is necessary, because **if it were written: At the base of the burnt offering, I would say** that the priest must sprinkle the blood **on the upright** wall **of the base** of the altar, i.e., the side of the base, rather than on the upper surface of the base. **Now that it is written: "At the base of the altar of the burnt offering,"** it means that the blood must be sprinkled **on the upper surface of the base.**[NH]

אָמַר רַבִּי יִשְׁמָעֵאל: גַּג יְסוֹד לָמָּה לִי קְרָא? קַל וָחוֹמֶר הוּא: וּמַה שְּׁיָרֵי חַטָּאת שֶׁאֵינָהּ מְכַפֶּרֶת – טְעוּנָה גַּג יְסוֹד, תְּחִלַּת עוֹלָה שֶׁמְּכַפֶּרֶת – אֵינוֹ דִּין שֶׁטְּעוּנָה גַּג יְסוֹד?

The Gemara explains the next clause of the *baraita* based on this understanding: **Rabbi Yishmael said: Why do I** need **a verse** to teach that the blood must be sprinkled on the **upper surface of** the **base** of the altar? **It** can be derived via **an *a fortiori*** inference: **Just as the remainder** of the blood **of a sin offering, which does not effect atonement,** nevertheless **requires** that it must be poured on the **upper surface of** the **base** of the altar, with regard to **the initial** sprinkling of the blood **of a burnt offering, which effects atonement, is it not logical that it requires** the **upper surface of** the **base** of the altar?

אָמַר רַבִּי עֲקִיבָא: וּמַה שְּׁיָרֵי חַטָּאת שֶׁאֵין מְכַפְּרִין וְאֵין בָּאִין לְכַפֵּר – טְעוּנָה גַּג יְסוֹד, תְּחִלַּת עוֹלָה שֶׁמְּכַפֶּרֶת וּבָאָה לְכַפֵּר – אֵינוֹ דִּין שֶׁטְּעוּנָה גַּג יְסוֹד? אִם כֵּן, מַה תַּלְמוּד לוֹמַר ״אֶל יְסוֹד מִזְבַּח הָעוֹלָה״ – תֵּן יְסוֹד לַמִּזְבֵּחַ שֶׁל עוֹלָה.

Rabbi Akiva explained similarly and **said: And just as the remainder** of the blood **of a sin offering, which does not effect atonement and does not come for atonement,** nevertheless **requires** that it must be poured on the **upper surface of the base,**[N] with regard to **the initial** sprinkling of the blood **of a burnt offering, which effects atonement and comes for atonement, is it not logical that it requires** the **upper surface of** the **base** of the altar? The *baraita* concludes: **If so, why must the verse state: "At the base of the altar of burnt offering"** (Leviticus 4:25)? It is to teach that you must **give a base to the altar of** the **burnt offering,** i.e., that the remainder of any blood sprinkled on the altar must be poured on the base.

מַאי בֵּינַיְיהוּ? אָמַר רַב אַדָּא בַּר אַהֲבָה: שִׁירַיִם מְעַכְּבִים אִיכָּא בֵּינַיְיהוּ, מָר סָבַר: מְעַכְּבִי, וּמָר סָבַר: לָא מְעַכְּבִי.

The Gemara asks: **What is** the difference **between** the explanations of Rabbi Yishmael and Rabbi Akiva? **Rav Adda bar Ahava says:** The difference **between them** is whether failure to pour the **remainder** of the blood **disqualifies** the offering, so that all the sprinklings must be done again. One **Sage,** Rabbi Yishmael, **holds** that failure to pour the remainder of the blood does **disqualify** the offering. **And** one **Sage,** Rabbi Akiva, who adds the words: Which does not come for atonement, **holds** that failure to pour the remainder of the blood does **not disqualify** the offering.[H]

רַב פַּפָּא אָמַר: דְּכוּלֵּי עָלְמָא שִׁירַיִם אֵין מְעַכְּבִים, וְהָכָא בְּמִיצּוּי חַטַּאת הָעוֹף מְעַכֵּב קָא מִיפַּלְגִי, מָר סָבַר: מְעַכֵּב, וּמָר סָבַר: לָא מְעַכֵּב.

Rav Pappa says: Everyone agrees that failure to pour the **remainder** of the blood on the base does **not disqualify** the offering. **But here they disagree with regard to** the issue of whether failure to **squeeze** the blood from **a bird sin offering**[NH] after sprinkling the blood **disqualifies** the offering or not. One **Sage,** Rabbi Yishmael, **holds** that it does **disqualify** the offering, **and** one **Sage,** Rabbi Akiva, **holds** that it does **not disqualify** the offering.

NOTES

On the upper surface of the base – **אַגַּגּוֹ דִּיסוֹד**: Rashi explains that this is derived from the combination of the words: "Base of the altar." It refers to that part of the base which is similar to the altar, i.e., the flat surface on top. Others explain that the term: "At the base," indicates a part of the base that can have items placed on it, which does not apply to the sides of the altar in any case. *Tosafot* explain that it does not mean that the blood of the burnt offering must be sprinkled on the base itself, because the blood must be sprinkled on the wall of the altar. Rather, it means that the blood must be sprinkled above the upper surface of the base, rather than on the side of the base.

Sprinkling blood on the base of the altar

And just as the remainder of the blood of a sin offering…requires pouring on the upper surface of the base – **וּמַה שְּׁיָרֵי חַטָּאת...טְעוּנָה גַּג יְסוֹד**: There is no dispute about this matter, because it is the straightforward meaning of the verse: "And all the remaining blood of the bull shall he pour out at the base of the altar of burnt offering, which is at the entrance of the Tent of Meeting" (Leviticus 4:7). There are some who have a version of the text that reads simply: Remainder of the blood, and does not specify: Of the sin offering, which is similar to the *baraita* on the previous *amud*. This would be referring to the remainder of the burnt offering itself (see *Tosafot*, citing Rabbeinu Ḥayyim, and *Shita Mekubbetzet*).

Squeeze the blood from a bird sin offering – **מִיצּוּי חַטַּאת הָעוֹף**: The Torah states with regard to the bird sin offering: "And he shall sprinkle of the blood of the sin offering upon the side of the altar, and the remainder of the blood shall be squeezed out at the base of the altar; it is a sin offering" (Leviticus 5:9). See 64b for a further discussion of this matter.

HALAKHA

Remainders of the blood require the upper surface – **שִׁירַיִם טְעוּנִים גַּג**: The remainder of the blood of a burnt offering, guilt offering, and peace offering is poured on the top of the base of the external altar (Rambam *Sefer Avoda, Hilkhot Ma'aseh HaKorbanot* 5:6, and see *Kesef Mishne* and Mahari Kurkus there).

Failure to pour the remainder of the blood does not disqualify the offering – **שִׁירַיִם אֵין מְעַכְּבִים**: If a priest does not pour the remainder of the blood on the external altar it does not disqualify the offering. Even for offerings whose blood is sprinkled on the inner altar, if the priest did not pour the remainder of the blood on the external altar they are not disqualified, because the *halakha* is ruled in accordance with the opinion of Rabbi Akiva in his disputes with a single colleague. Furthermore, according to Rav Pappa's explanation, Rabbi Yishmael does not disagree with regard to this matter (Rambam *Sefer Avoda, Hilkhot Avodat Yom HaKippurim* 5:8 and *Hilkhot Ma'aseh HaKorbanot* 19:4 and *Kesef Mishne* there).

Squeeze the blood from a bird sin offering – **מִיצּוּי חַטַּאת הָעוֹף**: Failure to squeeze the blood from a bird sin offering onto the side of the altar disqualifies the offering, in accordance with the discussion in tractate *Me'ila* 8b (Rambam *Sefer Avoda, Hilkhot Ma'aseh HaKorbanot* 7:7 and *Kesef Mishne* there).

תַּנְיָא כְּוָותֵיהּ דְּרַב פַּפָּא: "וְאֵת כׇּל הַדָּם יִשְׁפֹּךְ", מַה תַּלְמוּד לוֹמַר "הַפָּר" – לִימֵּד עַל פַּר יוֹם הַכִּיפּוּרִים שֶׁטָּעוּן מַתַּן דָּמִים לַיְּסוֹד, דִּבְרֵי רַבִּי.

It is taught in a *baraita* **in accordance with** the opinion **of Rav Pappa** that even Rabbi Yishmael agrees that failure to pour the remainder of the blood on the base does not disqualify the offering. The verse states: "And the priest shall sprinkle the blood upon the corners of the altar of sweet incense before the Lord, which is in the Tent of Meeting; **and all the remaining blood** of the bull **he shall pour out** at the base of the altar of burnt offering, which is at the entrance of the Tent of Meeting" (Leviticus 4:7). **What** is the meaning when **the verse states "of the bull"?** This seems superfluous, as the entire passage is referring to the bull. This serves to **teach** the *halakha* of another bull, i.e., **the bull of Yom Kippur, which** also **requires placement of blood on the base** of the external altar.[H] This is **the statement of Rabbi** Yehuda HaNasi.

אָמַר רַבִּי יִשְׁמָעֵאל: קַל וָחוֹמֶר, וּמָה אִם מִי שֶׁאֵין נִכְנָס דָּמוֹ לִפְנִים חוֹבָה – טָעוּן יְסוֹד, מִי שֶׁנִּכְנָס דָּמוֹ לִפְנִים חוֹבָה – אֵינוֹ דִּין שֶׁטָּעוּן יְסוֹד?

The *baraita* continues: **Rabbi Yishmael said:** It is not necessary for the Torah to write that the blood of the bull of Yom Kippur requires placement of blood on the base of the external altar. This is because it can be derived via **an *a fortiori*** inference: **And just as if** the bull of the anointed priest, i.e., the sin offering of a High Priest, with regard to **which it is not obligatory to bring its blood inside** the Sanctuary, i.e., it is not an obligatory offering, as he brings it only if he sins, nevertheless **requires** sprinkling blood on the **base** of the altar; with regard to the bull of Yom Kippur, with regard to **which it is obligatory to bring its blood inside** the Sanctuary, i.e., it must be brought every year, **is it not logical that it requires** sprinkling of its blood on the **base** of the altar?

אָמַר רַבִּי עֲקִיבָא: וּמַה מִּי שֶׁאֵין דָּמוֹ נִכְנָס לִפְנַי וְלִפְנִים בֵּין לְחוֹבָה בֵּין לְמִצְוָה – טָעוּן יְסוֹד, מִי שֶׁנִּכְנָס דָּמוֹ חוֹבָה לִפְנַי וְלִפְנִים – אֵינוֹ דִּין שֶׁטָּעוּן יְסוֹד?

Rabbi Akiva said: Just as the bull of a High Priest, with regard to **which its blood does not enter the innermost sanctum,**[N] **whether** as a fixed **obligation or as a mitzva,** nevertheless **requires** pouring of blood on the **base** of the altar, concerning the bull of Yom Kippur, with regard to **which its blood enters the innermost sanctum** as **an obligation, is it not logical that it requires** pouring of blood on the **base** of the altar?

יָכוֹל יְעַכְּבֶנּוּ – תַּלְמוּד לוֹמַר: "וְכִלָּה מִכַּפֵּר אֶת הַקֹּדֶשׁ" שֶׁלָּמוּ כׇּל הַכַּפָּרוֹת כּוּלָּן, דִּבְרֵי רַבִּי יִשְׁמָעֵאל.

The *baraita* continues: One **might** have thought that the reason the Torah writes the phrase "of the bull" is to teach that failure to place the blood on the base of the external altar **disqualifies** the offering. Therefore, **the verse states** with regard to the service of Yom Kippur, after sprinkling the blood in the Sanctuary: **"And when he has made an end of atoning for the Sanctuary,** and the Tent of Meeting, and the altar, he shall present the live goat" (Leviticus 16:20). This teaches that once he has sprinkled the blood in the innermost sanctum **all the atonements are completed.** This is **the statement of Rabbi Yishmael.**

קַל וָחוֹמֶר לְפַר כֹּהֵן מָשִׁיחַ מִשְּׂעִיר נָשִׂיא מֵעַתָּה: וּמַה מִּי שֶׁאֵין נִכְנָס דָּמוֹ לִפְנִים לֹא חוֹבָה וְלֹא מִצְוָה – טָעוּן יְסוֹד, מִי שֶׁנִּכְנָס דָּמוֹ לִפְנִים בֵּין לְחוֹבָה בֵּין לְמִצְוָה – אֵינוֹ דִּין שֶׁטָּעוּן יְסוֹד?

The *baraita* continues: **From now,** i.e., based on this, one can state **an *a fortiori*** inference **to** derive the *halakha* of **the bull of** the **anointed priest from** the *halakha* of **the goat of** the **king. Just as** the goat sin offering of a king, with regard to **which its blood does not enter inside** the Sanctuary, **whether** as a fixed **obligation or** as **a mitzva,** but is sprinkled, like other individual sin offerings, on the external altar, **requires** that the blood be poured on the **base** of the altar (see Leviticus 4:25); with regard to the sin offering of a High Priest, the blood of **which enters inside** the Sanctuary, **whether as** a fixed **obligation or as a mitzva, is it not logical that it should require** pouring on the **base** of the altar?

יָכוֹל יְעַכְּבֶנּוּ – תַּלְמוּד לוֹמַר: "וְאֵת כׇּל (הַדָּם) [דַּם הַפָּר] יִשְׁפֹּךְ",

If so, the verse that states that there is a requirement that the blood of the sin offering of a High Priest is poured on the base of the altar is apparently superfluous. One **might** have thought that the reason the Torah writes it is to teach that failure to pour the blood there **disqualifies** the offering. Therefore, **the verse states:** "And the priest shall sprinkle of the blood upon the corners of the altar of sweet incense before the Lord, which is in the Tent of Meeting, **and all the remaining blood of the bull he shall pour**[N] out at the base of the altar of burnt offering, which is at the entrance of the Tent of Meeting" (Leviticus 4:7).

HALAKHA

The bull of Yom Kippur which requires placement of blood on the base of the external altar – פַּר יוֹם הַכִּפּוּרִים שֶׁטָּעוּן מַתַּן דָּמִים לַיְּסוֹד: After the High Priest has completed placing the blood of the bull on the golden altar, he pours the remainder of the blood on the western base of the external altar (Rambam *Sefer Avoda, Hilkhot Avodat Yom HaKippurim* 4:2).

NOTES

With regard to which its blood does not enter the innermost sanctum – שֶׁאֵין דָּמוֹ נִכְנָס לִפְנַי וְלִפְנִים: Rather than derive the *halakha* from the difference between an offering that is a fixed obligation, i.e., the bull of Yom Kippur, and an offering that is brought only when necessary, i.e., the bull of an High Priest, which is brought only if he happens to sin, Rabbi Akiva prefers to derive the *halakha* from the more fundamental difference, between the blood of the bull of Yom Kippur, which is brought into the innermost chamber, and the blood of the bull of the High Priest, whose blood is not brought into the innermost chamber but is sprinkled on the golden altar.

And all the remaining blood of the bull he shall pour – וְאֵת כׇּל הַדָּם יִשְׁפֹּךְ: This directive is in the future tense, as opposed to the previous directives, which are in the past tense (Rashi).

נִתְּקוֹ הַכָּתוּב לַעֲשֵׂה, וַעֲשָׂאוֹ שְׁיָרֵי מִצְוָה, לוֹמַר לָךְ: שִׁירַיִם אֵין מְעַכְּבִין.

The *baraita* explains: Since the verse inverted the terms in the clause, writing: "And all the remaining blood of the bull he shall pour out," and not: He shall pour out all the remaining blood of the bull, the **verse detaches this positive** mitzva[N] of pouring the remaining blood from the other mitzvot in the verse. **And** the verse thereby **made this a non-essential mitzva, to tell you** that failure to pour the **remainder** of the blood on the base of the altar does **not disqualify** the offering. This *baraita* supports Rav Pappa's interpretation, that Rabbi Yishmael agrees that failure to pour the remainder of the blood on the base of the altar does not disqualify the offering.

וְסָבַר רַבִּי יִשְׁמָעֵאל מִיצּוּי חַטַּאת הָעוֹף מְעַכֵּב? וְהָתָנָא דְּבֵי רַבִּי יִשְׁמָעֵאל: "וְהַנִּשְׁאָר בַּדָּם יִמָּצֵה" – וְהַנִּשְׁאָר יִמָּצֶה,

The Gemara asks: **But** does **Rabbi Yishmael hold** that failure to **squeeze out** the blood of **a bird sin offering disqualifies** the offering, as Rav Pappa explained? **But the school of Rabbi Yishmael taught:** The verse states: "And he shall sprinkle of the blood of the sin offering upon the side of the altar; **and the remainder of the blood shall be squeezed out** at the base of the altar; it is a sin offering" (Leviticus 5:9). This means: **And the remainder shall be squeezed out,** i.e., it needs to be squeezed out only if some blood remains.

וְשֶׁאֵינוֹ נִשְׁאָר – לֹא יִמָּצֶה! תְּרֵי תַּנָּאֵי וְאַלִּיבָּא דְּרַבִּי יִשְׁמָעֵאל.

And that which does not remain, i.e., if there is no blood remaining, **he shall not squeeze** it **out.** This indicates that failure to squeeze the blood does not disqualify the offering. The Gemara answers: There are **two** *tanna'im*, **and** they disagree **with regard to** the opinion **of Rabbi Yishmael.**

אָמַר רָמִי בַּר חָמָא: הַאי תַּנָּא סָבַר: שִׁירַיִם מְעַכְּבִי. דְּתַנְיָא: "הַכֹּהֵן הַמְחַטֵּא אֹתָהּ", אוֹתָהּ שֶׁנִּיתַּן דָּמָהּ לְמַעְלָה, וְלֹא אוֹתָהּ שֶׁנִּיתַּן דָּמָהּ לְמַטָּה.

The Gemara continues its discussion of the remainder of the blood. **Rami bar Ḥama says: This** following *tanna* **holds** that failure to pour the **remainder** of the blood of offerings whose blood is sprinkled inside the Sanctuary **disqualifies** the offering, **as it is taught** in a *baraita*: **"The priest that sacrifices it for sin**[N] shall eat it" (Leviticus 6:19). The verse states the word "it" to teach that **it,** the offering **whose blood was sprinkled** correctly, **above** the red line of the altar, is valid, and the priest may eat the meat. **But** this is **not** so for an offering **whose blood was sprinkled below** the red line, which is disqualified.

אָמַרְתָּ: וְכִי מֵאַיִן בָּאתָה? מִכְּלָל שֶׁנֶּאֱמַר: "וְדַם זְבָחֶיךָ יִשָּׁפֵךְ עַל מִזְבַּח" וגו' לָמַדְנוּ לַנִּיתָּנִין בְּמַתַּן אַרְבַּע, שֶׁאִם נְתָנָן בְּמַתָּנָה אַחַת – כִּיפֵּר, יָכוֹל אַף הַנִּיתָּנִין לְמַעְלָה שֶׁנְּתָנָן לְמַטָּה כִּיפֵּר?

The *baraita* continues: **You said** this, **but from where did you come?** In other words, why would one think that such an offering is valid, so that the verse needs to teach that it is not? The *baraita* explains: **From the fact that it is stated:** "And you shall offer your burnt offerings, the flesh and the blood, upon the altar of the Lord your God; **and the blood of your offerings shall be poured out**[N] **against the altar** of the Lord your God, and you shall eat the flesh" (Deuteronomy 12:27), **we learned** that **with regard to** those offerings whose blood is **placed with four placements** on the corners[H] of the altar, **that if** the priest **placed them with** only **one placement, he has effected atonement.** Therefore, since it is derived that if the priest does not present the blood on the specified corners of the altar, the offering is nevertheless valid, one **might** have thought that blood **that** should have been **placed above** the red line but **that one placed below**[H] the red line **effects atonement as well,** and the offering is valid.

NOTES

The verse detaches this positive mitzva – נִתְּקוֹ הַכָּתוּב לַעֲשֵׂה: There are other versions of this text that read only: The verse detaches it. In other words, the verse removed it from the category of a mitzva related to the blood of the bull of the High Priest, and labeled it a mitzva in its own right.

The priest that sacrifices it for sin – הַכֹּהֵן הַמְחַטֵּא אֹתָהּ: The phrase "that offers it for sin" refers to the priest who sprinkles the blood, as sprinkling the blood effects atonement for the sin. That priest may eat the meat of the sin offering (see *Targum Onkelos* and Rashi's commentary on the verse). The additional emphasis provided by the superfluous word "it" teaches that a priest may eat a sin offering only if he performs its sprinkling correctly. Otherwise the offering is disqualified and the meat may not be eaten.

And the blood of your offerings shall be poured out – וְדַם זְבָחֶיךָ יִשָּׁפֵךְ: The term "shall be poured out" indicates that even if the priest performed only one of the blood placements the offering is nevertheless valid. When the Torah states at the end of the verse: "And you shall eat the flesh," it indicates that the atonement has been completed, and the offering was accepted. This teaches that even if the priest did not place the blood correctly it does not disqualify the offering.

HALAKHA

Placed with four placements on the corners, etc. – נִיתָּנִין בְּמַתַּן אַרְבַּע וכו׳: With regard to all of the offerings whose blood is placed on the external altar, if the priest placed blood only once, he has effected atonement. Even with a sin offering it is only the first blood placement that is indispensable. This is in accordance with the opinion of Beit Hillel in the mishna on 36b (Rambam *Sefer Avoda, Hilkhot Pesulei HaMukdashin* 2:1).

Blood that should have been placed above but that one placed below, etc. – הַנִּיתָּנִין לְמַעְלָה שֶׁנְּתָנָן לְמַטָּה וכו׳: With regard to blood that is to be placed on the upper half of the altar but that was placed on the lower half, or vice versa, or blood that is to be placed inside the Sanctuary but that was placed on the external altar, in all these cases the flesh of the offering is disqualified. Even so, the owner achieved atonement through his offering, since the blood was placed on the altar. This is in accordance with the statement of Shmuel on 26b (Rambam *Sefer Avoda, Hilkhot Pesulei HaMukdashin* 2:10, and see *Hilkhot Ma'aseh HaKorbanot* 7:9).

וְדִין הוּא: נֶאֶמְרוּ דָּמִים לְמַעְלָה וְנֶאֶמְרוּ דָּמִים לְמַטָּן, מַה דָּמִים הָאֲמוּרִים לְמַטָּן שֶׁנְּתָנָן לְמַעְלָן – לֹא כִּיפֵּר, אַף דָּמִים הָאֲמוּרִים לְמַעְלָן אִם נְתָנָן לְמַטָּה – לֹא כִּיפֵּר!

The *baraita* continues: **And** it would seem there **is a logical inference** to counter this logic. **It is stated** that **blood** is to be sprinkled **above**[N] the red line, referring to the blood of an animal sin offering, which is to be sprinkled on the corners on the upper half of the altar, **and it is stated** that **blood** is to be sprinkled **below** the red line, referring to the blood of a bird sin offering, which is to be sprinkled on the lower half of the altar. **Just as** with regard to the **blood** about **which** it **is stated** that it is to be **below** the red line, if it is a case **where one placed** it **above** the red line, it does **not effect atonement,**[N] as the Sages derived from the verse: "And he shall sprinkle of the blood of the sin offering upon the side of the altar, and the remainder of the blood shall be squeezed out at the base of the altar; it is a sin offering" (Leviticus 5:9), **so too,** with regard to the **blood,** about **which** it **is stated** that it is to be **above** the red line, if it is a case **where one placed** it **below** the red line, it does **not effect atonement.**

לֹא, אִם אָמַרְתָּ בַּתַּחְתּוֹנִים שֶׁנִּיתָּנִין בִּנְתִינָה לְמַעְלָה – שֶׁאֵין סוֹפָן לְמַעְלָן, לֹא כִּיפֵּר, תֹּאמַר בָּעֶלְיוֹנִים שֶׁנְּתָנָן לְמַטָּה, שֶׁיֵּשׁ מֵהֶן קָרֵב לְמַטָּה?

This logical inference is rejected: **No, if you said** that this is the *halakha* **with regard to** the blood of a bird sin offering, which is to be sprinkled **below** the red line **that was placed with a placement above** the red line, that may be **because they will not ultimately** be sprinkled **above.** For this reason it does **not effect atonement. Shall you** also **say** that this is the *halakha* **with regard to** the blood that is to be sprinkled **above** the red line, i.e., the blood of an animal sin offering, but **which one placed below** the red line, that it will not effect atonement? The blood that is to be sprinkled above the red line is different, **as** some **of it is sacrificed below** the red line, when the remainder of the blood is poured on the base of the altar.

דָּמִים (שִׁירַיִים) הַפְּנִימִיִּים יוֹכִיחוּ, שֶׁיֵּשׁ מֵהֶן קָרֵב בַּחוּץ, וְאִם נְתָנָן בַּתְּחִלָּה בַּחוּץ – לֹא כִּיפֵּר!

The *baraita* responds: The **blood** that is placed **inside** the Sanctuary **will prove** it, **as** some **of it is sacrificed outside, but if** the priest **initially placed** the blood on the altar **outside** the Sanctuary it does **not effect atonement.**[N]

לֹא, אִם אָמַרְתָּ בְּדָמִים הַפְּנִימִיִּים – שֶׁאֵין מִזְבֵּחַ הַפְּנִימִי מְמָרְקָן, תֹּאמַר בָּעֶלְיוֹנִים – שֶׁהֲרֵי קְרָנוֹת מְמָרְקוֹת אוֹתָן, אִם נְתָנָן לְמַטָּה כְּשֵׁרִים!

The *baraita* rejects this proof: **No, if you said** that this is the *halakha* **with regard to** the **blood** that is placed **inside** the Sanctuary, concerning **which the inner altar does not complete** the atonement, as they require additional blood placements, **shall you** also **say** that this is the *halakha* **with regard to** the blood offered **above** the red line, i.e., the blood of an animal sin offering, concerning **which** the **corners** of the altar **complete** the atonement? Accordingly, it is possible to say that **if one placed them below** the red line **they are valid.**

תַּלְמוּד לוֹמַר: "אוֹתָהּ" – אוֹתָהּ שֶׁנִּיתַּן דָּמִים לְמַעְלָה, וְלֹא שֶׁנִּיתַּן דָּמָהּ לְמַטָּה.

The *baraita* concludes: To counter this reasoning, **the verse states** with regard to an animal sin offering that is sacrificed outside: "The priest that sacrifices **it** for sin shall eat it" (Leviticus 6:19), to emphasize that **it,** the offering **whose blood was placed** correctly, **above** the red line of the altar, is valid, and the priest may eat the meat. **But** this is **not** so for an offering **whose blood was placed below** the red line, which is disqualified.

מַאי "שֶׁאֵין מִזְבֵּחַ הַפְּנִימִי מְמָרְקָן"? לָאו אֵלּוּ שִׁירַיִים?

Rami bar Ḥama proves his point: **What** does the *baraita* mean when it says: If you said that this is the *halakha* with regard to the blood that is placed inside the Sanctuary, concerning **which the inner altar does not complete** the atonement? What is required to complete the atonement? Is it **not** referring to **this remainder** of the blood and is teaching that failure to pour the remainder of the blood on the base of the altar disqualifies the offering?

אֲמַר לֵיהּ רָבָא: אִי הָכִי, תֵּיתֵי בְּקַל וָחוֹמֶר.

Rava said to Rami bar Ḥama: **If so,** that the *tanna* of the *baraita* holds that failure to pour the remainder of the blood of the offerings whose blood is sprinkled inside the Sanctuary disqualifies the offering, you could **derive** the *halakha* that if the priest sprinkled the blood below the red line the offering is disqualified **via an *a fortiori*** inference.

NOTES

It is stated: Blood, above, etc. – **נֶאֶמְרוּ דָּמִים לְמַעְלָה וכו׳**: This is explained later in the Gemara (53a). The verse states with regard to an animal brought as a sin offering: "And the priest shall take of the blood of the sin offering with his finger and place it upon the corners of the altar of burnt offering, and all its remaining blood he shall pour out at the base of the altar" (Leviticus 4:34). This indicates that it should be placed above the red line. Some explain that it means on the actual corners of the altar.

With regard to the bird sin offering the verse states: "And he shall sprinkle of the blood of the sin offering upon the side of the altar, and the remainder of the blood shall be squeezed out at the base of the altar; it is a sin offering" (Leviticus 5:9). The Sages derived from here that the blood must be placed on the wall of the altar and from there drip down onto the base, which indicates that it must be done on the lower half of the altar (see 64b).

Where one placed it above the red line it does not effect atonement – **שֶׁנְּתָנָן לְמַעְלָן לֹא כִּיפֵּר**: Rashi writes that the source for this is from that which is written with regard to the bird sin offering: "And he shall sprinkle of the blood of the sin offering upon the side of the altar; and the remainder of the blood shall be squeezed out at the base of the altar; it is a sin offering" (Leviticus 5:9). The closing phrase of the verse stresses that the offering is valid only if the rite was performed correctly, and the blood was not placed anywhere else.

If he initially placed the blood on the altar outside the Sanctuary it does not effect atonement – **אִם נְתָנָן בַּתְּחִלָּה בַּחוּץ לֹא כִּיפֵּר**: The Sages derived this *halakha* (see 39a) from the verse: "So shall he do with the bull; as he did with the bull of the sin offering, so shall he do with this; and the priest shall make atonement for them, and they shall be forgiven" (Leviticus 4:20).

מַה שִּׁירַיִים הַפְּנִימִיִּים שֶׁסּוֹפָן חוֹבָה בַּחוּץ, עֲשָׂאָן בַּתְּחִלָּה בַּחוּץ – לֹא כִּיפֵּר, הַנִּיתָּנִין לְמַעְלָה שֶׁאֵין סוֹפָן חוֹבָה לְמַטָּה, וַעֲשָׂאָן בַּתְּחִלָּה לְמַטָּה – אֵינוֹ דִּין שֶׁלֹּא כִּיפֵּר?

Just as it is with regard to **the remainder** of the blood of the offerings **of the inner** altar, concerning **which their ultimate** rite, pouring on the base of the altar, is **obligatory on the external** altar, but if the priest **initially performed** the rite of placing the blood **on the external** altar, it does **not effect atonement,** with regard to those offerings whose blood **is placed above** the red line, concerning **which their ultimate** rite, pouring on the base of the altar, is **not obligatory below** the red line of the altar, **and** the priest **initially performed** the rite of placing the blood **below** the red line, **is it not logical that** it does **not effect atonement?** Since the *baraita* does not advance this claim, but derived the *halakha* from a verse, this indicates that pouring the remainder of the blood is not obligatory.

אֶלָּא, אֵין מִזְבֵּחַ הַפְּנִימִי מְמָרְקָן בִּלְבַד, אֶלָּא פָּרוֹכֶת.

Rava continues: **Rather,** when the *baraita* states that the blood of the offerings offered inside the Sanctuary are those concerning which the inner altar does not complete the atonement it means that **the inner altar does not complete** the atonement **alone,** but **rather** requires that blood also be sprinkled inside the Sanctuary on the **Curtain**[N] separating the Sanctuary and Holy of Holies.

תָּנוּ רַבָּנַן: "וְכִלָּה מִכַּפֵּר", אִם כִּיפֵּר – כִּלָּה, וְאִם לֹא כִּיפֵּר – לֹא כִּלָּה, דִּבְרֵי רַבִּי עֲקִיבָא. אָמַר לוֹ רַבִּי יְהוּדָה: מִפְּנֵי מָה לֹא נֹאמַר: אִם כִּלָּה – כִּיפֵּר, אִם לֹא כִּלָּה – לֹא כִּיפֵּר, שֶׁאִם חִיסֵּר אַחַת מִכׇּל הַמַּתָּנוֹת לֹא עָשָׂה וְלֹא כְּלוּם?

§ **The Sages taught** in a *baraita*: The verse states concerning the sacrificial rite performed by the High Priest on Yom Kippur: **"And when he has finished atoning**[N] for the Sanctuary, and the Tent of Meeting, and the altar, he shall present the live goat" (Leviticus 16:20). This verse indicates that **if he performed** the **atonement, he has finished** the service, **but if he did not perform** the **atonement, he has not finished.** This is **the statement of Rabbi Akiva. Rabbi Yehuda said to him: For what** reason **do we not say:**[N] **If he finished, he has performed atonement,** but **if he did not finish, he has not performed atonement?** This derivation would indicate **that if one of any of the** blood **placements is lacking**[H] it is as though **he did nothing.**

מַאי בֵּינַיְיהוּ? רַבִּי יוֹחָנָן וְרַבִּי יְהוֹשֻׁעַ בֶּן לֵוִי, חַד אָמַר: מַשְׁמָעוּת דּוֹרְשִׁין אִיכָּא בֵּינַיְיהוּ. וְחַד אָמַר: שִׁירַיִים מְעַכְּבִין אִיכָּא בֵּינַיְיהוּ.

The Gemara clarifies the two opinions: **What** is the difference **between them? Rabbi Yoḥanan and Rabbi Yehoshua ben Levi** engaged in a dispute concerning this. **One says** that **interpretation of the meaning** of the verse **is** the difference **between them,** i.e., there is no halakhic difference between them but only a dispute as to how to interpret the verses. **And one says** that **there is** a difference **between them** with regard to whether failure to pour the **remainder** of the blood at the base of the altar **disqualifies**[N] the offering. According to Rabbi Akiva, it does not disqualify the offering, whereas Rabbi Yehuda maintains that it does disqualify the offering.

תִּסְתַּיֵּים דְּרַבִּי יְהוֹשֻׁעַ בֶּן לֵוִי הוּא דְּאָמַר שִׁירַיִים מְעַכְּבִי, דְּאָמַר רַבִּי יְהוֹשֻׁעַ בֶּן לֵוִי: לְדִבְרֵי הָאוֹמֵר שִׁירַיִים מְעַכְּבִין, מֵבִיא פַּר אֶחָד וּמַתְחִיל בַּתְּחִלָּה בִּפְנִים.

The Gemara suggests: **It may be concluded that Rabbi Yehoshua ben Levi is** the one **who says** that Rabbi Akiva and Rabbi Yehuda disagree as to whether or not failure to pour the **remainder** of the blood on the altar **disqualifies** the offering. **As Rabbi Yehoshua ben Levi says: According to the statement of the one who says** that failure to pour the **remainder** of the blood on the base of the altar **disqualifies** the offering, if the priest finished placing the blood on the inner altar and the blood was spilled before he poured the remainder on the external altar, he must **bring one bull**[N] and slaughter it, **and begin** the sprinkling of the blood as he did **initially on the inner** altar, so that there will be blood remaining from the sprinkling, and then he pours the remainder of the blood on the external altar. Rabbi Yehoshua ben Levi discusses the opinion that failure to pour the remainder of the blood on the base of the altar disqualifies the offering, apparently in reference to the *baraita* cited here.

NOTES

Rather on the Curtain – אֶלָּא פָּרוֹכֶת: Since there are two parts of the service performed with this blood, its *halakhot* are more stringent, and one cannot derive the *halakha* from here to the sin offerings brought outside, whose service is completed once the blood is placed on the corners of the altar.

And when he has finished atoning – וְכִלָּה מִכַּפֵּר: This phrase does not seem to add anything, and the Torah could have continued with its description of the service: "He shall present the live goat" (Leviticus 16:20). Therefore, it is understood to emphasize that only after the High Priest has completed the atonement does he continue with the rest of the service (see Rashi on 40a).

For what reason do we not say – מִפְּנֵי מָה לֹא נֹאמַר: The derivation suggested by Rabbi Yehuda has an advantage, because Rabbi Akiva interprets the verse out of order, whereas Rabbi Yehuda's interpretation is in the order of the verse (Rashi).

There is a difference between them with regard to whether the remainder of the blood disqualifies – שִׁירַיִים מְעַכְּבִין אִיכָּא בֵּינַיְיהוּ: Rashi explains that Rabbi Akiva holds that failure to pour the remainder of the blood does not disqualify the offering. When the verse states: "And when he has finished atoning," it means that he completes the service as described in the preceding verses, and the remainder of the blood is not mentioned there. Others explain that the phrase "and when he has finished atoning" teaches that if he completes that part of the service which effects atonement, which is the sprinkling of the blood, then he has completed the offering. The remainder of the blood does not serve to effect atonement but to complete the rite (*Sefat Emet*, based on Rashi on 52a; *Ḥiddushei Rabbeinu Ḥayyim HaLevi al HaRambam*). Both explanations understand the opinion of Rabbi Yehuda to be that the verse means that the priest must complete the entire service, including pouring the remainder of the blood, to effect atonement, and if not he does not effect atonement.

The Ra'avya challenges this interpretation, based the words of Rabbi Yehuda: If one of any of the placements is lacking. This indicates that only sprinkling is indispensable, and pouring the remainder is not. Therefore, the Ra'avya explains the entire discussion as the reverse of Rashi's explanation, and it is Rabbi Yehuda who holds that failure to pour the remainder of the blood does not disqualify the offering. He brings support for his opinion from the Jerusalem Talmud (see *Keneset HaRishonim* on 40a).

According to the statement of the one who says…he must bring one bull – לְדִבְרֵי הָאוֹמֵר...מֵבִיא פַּר אֶחָד: Rashi explains that the priest does not have to perform again all the sprinklings that were done inside, because the actual atonement is complete. Nevertheless, although pouring the remainder of the blood is not part of the atonement, it is an indispensable part of the service. Therefore he must again put blood on the golden altar, even though he already placed blood from the initial bull there, so that the blood that he pours on the external altar will be a remainder.

HALAKHA

If one of any of the blood placements is lacking, etc. – חִיסֵּר אַחַת מִכׇּל הַמַּתָּנוֹת וכו׳: With regard to all the placement of blood on the inner altar, if a single placement is lacking the offering does not effect atonement, in accordance with the opinion of the *tanna* in the mishna on 36b (Rambam *Sefer Avoda*, *Hilkhot Pesulei HaMukdashin* 2:3).

אִטּוּ רַבִּי יוֹחָנָן לֵית לֵיהּ הָא סְבָרָא? וְהָאָמַר רַבִּי יוֹחָנָן: תָּנָא רַבִּי נְחֶמְיָה כְּדִבְרֵי הָאוֹמֵר שִׁירַיִם מְעַכְּבִין!

The Gemara asks: **Is that to say** that **Rabbi Yoḥanan does not** agree with **this reasoning? But doesn't Rabbi Yoḥanan** himself **say** (111a): **Rabbi Neḥemya taught** a *halakha* **in accordance with the statement of the one who says** that failure to pour the **remainder** of blood **disqualifies** the offering? Rabbi Yoḥanan also discusses the opinion of a *tanna* who holds that failure to pour the remainder of blood disqualifies the offering, apparently in reference to the *baraita* cited here.

אֶלָּא כְּדִבְרֵי הָאוֹמֵר וְלָאו לְהָנֵי תַּנָּאֵי, הָכָא נָמֵי כְּדִבְרֵי הָאוֹמֵר וְלָאו לְהָנֵי תַּנָּאֵי.

Rather, there is no proof that Rabbi Yoḥanan is referring to the dispute between Rabbi Akiva and Rabbi Yehuda. He is stating a *halakha* **in accordance with the statement of the one who says** that it disqualifies the offering, whichever *tanna* that may be, **but** he is **not** referring **to** the dispute between **these** ***tanna'im***. **Here too,** Rabbi Yehoshua ben Levi is stating a *halakha* **in accordance with the statement of the one who says** that it disqualifies the offering, whichever *tanna* that may be, **but** he is **not** referring **to** the dispute between **these** ***tanna'im***.

מתני׳ חַטֹּאות הַצִּבּוּר וְהַיָּחִיד; אֵלּוּ הֵן חַטֹּאות הַצִּבּוּר: שְׂעִירֵי רָאשֵׁי חֳדָשִׁים וְשֶׁל מוֹעֲדוֹת; שְׁחִיטָתָן בַּצָּפוֹן, וְקִיבּוּל דָּמָן בִּכְלִי שָׁרֵת בַּצָּפוֹן, וְדָמָן טָעוּן אַרְבַּע מַתָּנוֹת עַל אַרְבַּע קְרָנוֹת. כֵּיצַד?

MISHNA These are the *halakhot* of **the communal and the individual sin offerings. These are the communal sin offerings: Goats of the New Moon**[B] **and of the Festivals.**[B] **Their slaughter** is **in the north** of the Temple courtyard, and the **collection of their blood in a service vessel** is **in the north, and their blood requires four placements**[H] **on the four corners of the altar. How** did the priest do so?

BACKGROUND

Goats of the New Moon – שְׂעִירֵי רָאשֵׁי חֳדָשִׁים: The Torah (Numbers 28:15) requires a goat to be sacrificed on the New Moon as a communal sin offering, and it follows the same procedure as that of an individual sin offering. It atones for certain transgressions involving the defiling of the Temple by entering it while ritually impure, or defiling its sacrificial foods by partaking of them while ritually impure.

Goats of the Festivals – שְׂעִירֵי מוֹעֲדוֹת: The Torah (Numbers, chapter 28) requires a goat to be sacrificed on each day of every Festival as a communal sin offering, with a procedure identical to that of individual sin offerings. These goats were intended to atone for transgressions involving the defiling of the Temple and its sacred foods.

HALAKHA

And their blood requires four placements, etc. – וְדָמָן טָעוּן אַרְבַּע מַתָּנוֹת וכו׳: Sin offerings that are eaten require that their blood be placed on all four corners of the external altar on the upper half of the altar (Rambam *Sefer Avoda, Hilkhot Ma'aseh HaKorbanot* 5:7).

Perek **V**
Daf **53** Amud **a**

עָלָה בַכֶּבֶשׁ, וּפָנָה לַסּוֹבֵב, וּבָא לוֹ לְקֶרֶן דְּרוֹמִית מִזְרָחִית, מִזְרָחִית צְפוֹנִית, צְפוֹנִית מַעֲרָבִית, מַעֲרָבִית דְּרוֹמִית. שְׁיָרֵי הַדָּם הָיָה שׁוֹפֵךְ עַל יְסוֹד דְּרוֹמִית. וְנֶאֱכָלִין לִפְנִים מִן הַקְּלָעִים, לְזִכְרֵי כְהוּנָּה, בְּכׇל מַאֲכָל, לְיוֹם וָלַיְלָה עַד חֲצוֹת.

He ascended the ramp[HN] of the altar **and turned** right **to the surrounding ledge**[N] and he continued east, **and he came to the southeast corner** and sprinkled the blood of the sin offering there and then to the **northeast** corner and sprinkled the blood there, and then to the **northwest** corner and sprinkled the blood there, and the **southwest** corner, where he performed the fourth sprinkling and descended from the altar. **He would pour the remainder of the blood on the southern base**[N] of the altar. **And** the meat portions of the offering **are eaten within the curtains,**[HN] i.e., in the Temple courtyard, **by the males of the priesthood.** And they are eaten prepared **in any** form of **food**[N] preparation, **on the day** the offering is sacrificed **and** during the **night** that follows, **until midnight.**[N]

HALAKHA

He ascended the ramp, etc. – עָלָה בַכֶּבֶשׁ וכו׳: From where does a priest begin to sprinkle the blood of a sin offering? He ascends the ramp and turns right. He walks along the surrounding ledge and sprinkles blood on the southeast corner first. Afterward he sprinkles on the next corner that he arrives at, which is the northeastern one. He continues to the northwest corner and sprinkles there, and finally to the southwest corner, and sprinkles there. Then he pours the remainder of the blood on the base in the southwest corner, where he finishes his sprinkling (Rambam *Sefer Avoda, Hilkhot Ma'aseh HaKorbanot* 5:10).

And are eaten within the curtains – וְנֶאֱכָלִין לִפְנִים מִן הַקְּלָעִים: After a sin offering is slaughtered, and the blood has been placed on the altar, and the sacrificial portions have been burned, the remainder is eaten within the Temple courtyard, by males of the priestly families, within one day and one night. By Torah law, they may eat it until dawn, but in order to distance them from sin the Sages decreed that it must be eaten by midnight. The priests may eat it prepared in any manner. They may roast, boil, or bake it, and they may flavor it with non-sacred spices (Rambam *Sefer Avoda, Hilkhot Ma'aseh HaKorbanot* 7:1, 10:3, 7, 10).

NOTES

Ascended the ramp – עָלָה בַכֶּבֶשׁ: The altar was ten cubits high. The base was one cubit high. The body of the altar was one cubit narrower and five cubits high. Above this the altar became one cubit narrower again, which created a walkway around the altar at the height of six cubits from the ground. This was called the surrounding ledge. The priests would walk around this to sprinkle the blood of the sin offerings. The blood of most offerings was presented on the lower part of the altar, but the blood of the sin offering was sprinkled on the upper half, i.e., at least five cubits, or approximately 2.5 m, above the ground. Therefore, the priests were unable to sprinkle the blood while standing on the ground and had to stand on the surrounding ledge in order to sprinkle the blood. The Gemara (62b) will explain that the ramp mentioned in this mishna is not the main ramp that led to the top of the altar, but a smaller ramp on the southern side adjacent to the main ramp.

And turned to the surrounding ledge – וּפָנָה לַסּוֹבֵב: He turned toward the east, which is to the right of one who ascends from the south. The reason for this is that all the turns in the Temple, and for mitzvot in general, should be to the right (see 62b).

On the southern base – עַל יְסוֹד דְּרוֹמִית: There were two openings on the base of the southwest corner of the altar. The western one was where they poured the remainder of the blood from the offerings whose blood was sprinkled inside the Sanctuary. The southern one was designated for pouring the remainder of the blood of offerings whose blood had been sprinkled on the external altar.

Within the curtains – לִפְנִים מִן הַקְּלָעִים: The term curtains is precise only with regard to the Tabernacle, which was surrounded by woven curtains. The equivalent of this part of the Tabernacle in the Temple was the Temple courtyard.

In any form of food – בְּכׇל מַאֲכָל: They were no restrictions on how the food was to be prepared. Rashi explains that the mishna has to teach this because the Paschal offering must be eaten roasted.

Until midnight – עַד חֲצוֹת: By Torah law the offering may be eaten all night long, as the verse states: "And the flesh of the sacrifice of his peace offerings for thanksgiving shall be eaten on the day of his offering; he shall not leave any of it until the morning" (Leviticus 7:15). The Sages decreed that one may eat it only until midnight, so that one would not inadvertently eat of the offering after the permitted time (see *Berakhot* 2a).

גמ׳ הֵיכִי עָבֵיד? רַבִּי יוֹחָנָן וְרַבִּי אֶלְעָזָר, חַד אָמַר: נוֹתֵן אַמָּה אֵילָךְ וְאַמָּה אֵילָךְ, וְחַד אָמַר: מְחַטֵּא וְיוֹרֵד כְּנֶגֶד חוּדּוֹ שֶׁל קֶרֶן.

GEMARA

How does the priest **perform** the rite of sprinkling the blood on the corners of the altar? There is a dispute between **Rabbi Yoḥanan and Rabbi Elazar. One says** that the priest **places** the blood within **a cubit on this side**[N] **or a cubit on that** side. He places the blood wherever he wants, provided that it is within one cubit of the corner of the altar. **And one says** that **he sprinkles** the blood **on the** outer **edge of** the **corner** of the altar, **and** it flows **down** on both sides of the altar.

אַלִּיבָּא דְּרַבִּי אֶלְעָזָר בְּרַבִּי שִׁמְעוֹן, דְּאָמַר: הִיא עַצְמָהּ אֵינָהּ נַעֲשֵׂית אֶלָּא בְּגוּפָהּ שֶׁל קֶרֶן – דְּכוּלֵּי עָלְמָא לָא פְּלִיגִי. כִּי פְּלִיגִי – אַלִּיבָּא דְּרַבִּי, מָר סָבַר: אַמָּה אֵילָךְ וְאַמָּה אֵילָךְ כְּנֶגֶד קֶרֶן הוּא, וּמָר סָבַר: כְּנֶגֶד חוּדָּהּ – אִין, טְפֵי – לָא.

The Gemara comments: **According to** the opinion **of Rabbi Elazar, son of Rabbi Shimon, who says** that the sprinkling of the blood of a sin offering **itself is performed only on the actual corner,**[B] the one-by-one-cubit projection above each corner of the altar, **everyone agrees** that the blood may be sprinkled anywhere on the corner, and this will be a fulfillment of the verse: "And put it upon the corners of the altar of burnt offering" (Leviticus 4:25). **When they disagree** is only **according to** the opinion **of Rabbi** Yehuda HaNasi, who holds that the blood may be sprinkled anywhere above the red line on the edge of the altar. One **Sage holds** that the blood may be sprinkled on the cubit on either side of the edge, because **a cubit on this side and a cubit on that** side **is** still considered to be **on the corner. And** one **Sage holds** that **on its edge, yes,** it is fit, but any **further** on either side is **not.**

מֵיתִיבִי: חַטַּאת הַצִּיבּוּר וְהַיָּחִיד כֵּיצַד מַתַּן דָּמָן? הָיָה עוֹלֶה לַכֶּבֶשׁ, וּפָנָה לַסּוֹבֵב וּבָא לוֹ לְקֶרֶן דְּרוֹמִית מִזְרָחִית, וְטוֹבֵל בְּאֶצְבָּעוֹ הַיְמָנִית הַמְיוּמֶּנֶת שֶׁבְּיָמִין, מִן הַדָּם שֶׁבַּמִּזְרָק, וְחוֹמֵר בְּגוּדָלוֹ מִלְמַעְלָה וּבְאֶצְבָּעוֹ קְטַנָּה מִלְּמַטָּה, וּמְחַטֵּא וְיוֹרֵד כְּנֶגֶד חוּדָּהּ שֶׁל קֶרֶן עַד שֶׁמְּכַלֶּה כׇּל הַדָּם שֶׁבְּאֶצְבַּע וְכֵן כׇּל קֶרֶן וְקֶרֶן!

The Gemara **raises an objection** to the opinion that one cubit on either side of the edge is still considered on the edge, from a *baraita*: With regard to **communal sin offerings and individual** sin offerings, **how is the placement of their blood**[H] on the altar performed? The priest **would ascend the ramp** of the altar **and turn** right **to the surrounding ledge** and he continued east, **and** he would **come to the southeast corner. And** he would then **dip with his right** [*haymanit*] **finger, the** most **dexterous** [*hamyumenet*][L] **of the right** hand, i.e., the index finger, **of the blood that is in the bowl, and** would **gather** the blood **with his thumb**[N] **above and his smallest finger below,** so that it would remain on his finger. **And** he would **sprinkle** the blood **and** move his hand **down on the** outer **edge of the corner, until** he would **finish** sprinkling **all the blood that** was **on his finger. And** he would act **similarly** at **each and every corner.** This *baraita* states explicitly that the blood must be sprinkled on the actual edge.

הָכִי קָאָמַר: מִצְוָה בְּחוּדָּהּ, אִי עֲבַד אַמָּה אֵילָךְ וְאַמָּה אֵילָךְ לֵית לַן בַּהּ.

The Gemara answers: **This** is what the *baraita* **is saying:** The optimal manner to perform the **mitzva** is to sprinkle the blood **on the edge of** the corner. But **if he did** the sprinkling on the **cubit on this** side, **or** the **cubit on that** side, **we have no** problem **with it,** and he has still fulfilled the mitzva.

מַאי רַבִּי, וּמַאי רַבִּי אֶלְעָזָר בְּרַבִּי שִׁמְעוֹן? דְּתַנְיָא: דָּמִים הָעֶלְיוֹנִים נִיתָּנִין מֵחוּט הַסִּיקְרָא וּלְמַעְלָה, דָּמִים הַתַּחְתּוֹנִים נִיתָּנִין מֵחוּט הַסִּיקְרָא וּלְמַטָּן, דִּבְרֵי רַבִּי.

The Gemara discusses the aforementioned dispute. **What** is the opinion of **Rabbi** Yehuda HaNasi, **and what** is the opinion of **Rabbi Elazar, son of Rabbi Shimon?** This is **as it is taught** in a *baraita* (*Tosefta* 6:11): The **blood** that must be placed on **the upper** half of the altar, e.g., the blood of a sin offering, **is placed** anywhere **from the red line**[H] that circumscribed the middle of the altar **and above.** The **blood** that must be placed on **the lower** half of the altar **is placed** anywhere **from the red line or below it.** This is **the statement of Rabbi** Yehuda HaNasi.

רַבִּי אֶלְעָזָר בְּרַבִּי שִׁמְעוֹן אוֹמֵר: בַּמֶּה דְּבָרִים אֲמוּרִין – בְּעוֹלַת הָעוֹף, אֲבָל בְּחַטַּאת בְּהֵמָה – הִיא עַצְמָהּ אֵין נַעֲשֵׂית אֶלָּא עַל גּוּפָהּ שֶׁל קֶרֶן.

The *baraita* continues: **Rabbi Elazar, son of Rabbi Shimon says: In what case is this statement said?** It is said **with regard to a bird burnt offering,** as its blood may be placed anywhere above the red line. **But with regard to an animal sin offering,** the placement **itself may be performed only on the actual corner** of the altar. This is based on the verse that states: "And the priest shall take of the blood of the sin offering with his finger, and put it upon the corners of the altar of burnt offering" (Leviticus 4:25).

NOTES

Places the blood within a cubit on this side – נוֹתֵן אַמָּה אֵילָךְ: In other words, the priest is not required to sprinkle the blood specifically on the edge of the corner, but anywhere near it, within one cubit. The *Zevaḥ Toda* says that since the Torah states that the blood must be presented around the altar, if one presents the blood on only one side of the corner, e.g., on the southern side of the southeast corner, he must ensure that he presents some blood on the eastern side of the northeast corner, so that the blood will be on all four sides of the altar.

Would gather with his thumb – חוֹמֵר בְּגוּדָלוֹ: Rashi indicates that the priest must scrape and clean the blood from his index finger with his thumb and his little finger. In this way all the blood that is on the finger will be sprinkled on the altar. It appears that the Rambam had a different version of the text, and writes that the thumb and middle finger support the index finger as the priest performs the sprinkling.

BACKGROUND

Actual corner – גּוּפָהּ שֶׁל קֶרֶן:

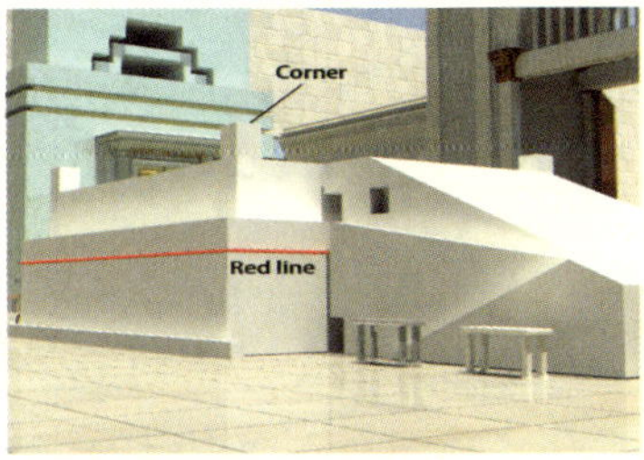

Area of sprinkling of the blood of a sin offering

HALAKHA

How is the placement of their blood – כֵּיצַד מַתַּן דָּמָן: The blood of sin offerings must be presented on all four corners on the upper half of the external altar. How did the priest perform this? He collected the blood in a basin and took it to the altar. He dipped his right index finger into the blood and supported it with his thumb and middle finger. He sprinkled the blood in a downward movement toward the edge of the corner of the altar until he sprinkled all the blood on his finger. If he presented the blood within a cubit of the corner he effected atonement and the offering was valid. This is in accordance with the opinion of Rabbi Yehuda HaNasi, since the *halakha* is in accordance with his opinion in his disputes with any single *tanna* (Rambam *Sefer Avoda*, *Hilkhot Ma'aseh HaKorbanot* 5:7, and see *Kesef Mishne* and Mahari Kurkus there).

Red line – חוּט הַסִּיקְרָא: A red line marked the midpoint of the height of the altar, one cubit below the surrounding ledge. This separated between the area for the blood that had to be presented on the upper half of the altar and the area for the blood that had to be presented on the lower half of the altar (Rambam *Sefer Avoda*, *Hilkhot Beit HaBeḥira* 2:9).

LANGUAGE

Dexterous [*meyumenet*] – מְיוּמֶּנֶת: The root *yod*, *mem*, *nun* is used in several ways. In addition to referring to the right side or to dexterity, it can also refer in general to something important or unique.

אָמַר רַבִּי אַבָּהוּ: מַאי טַעְמָא דְּרַבִּי – דִּכְתִיב: ״וְהַהַרְאֵל אַרְבַּע אַמּוֹת וּמֵהָ־אֲרָאֵיל וּלְמַעְלָה״ וגו׳; אַרְבַּע אַמּוֹת הוּא דְּהָוְיָא? אֲמַר רַב אַדָּא בַּר אַהֲבָה: וּמְקוֹם קְרָנוֹת אַרְבַּע. מְקוֹם קְרָנוֹת אַרְבַּע הָוְיָא?! אֶלָּא אֵימָא: רְשׁוּת קְרָנוֹת אַרְבַּע.

Rabbi Abbahu says: What is the reason for the opinion **of Rabbi** Yehuda HaNasi? **As it is written: "And the altar shall be four cubits; and from the altar and above** there shall be four corners" (Ezekiel 43:15). The Gemara asks: **Was** the altar only **four cubits** wide? **Rav Adda bar Ahava said: And** the total **area** of the four **corners,** which were each one square cubit, was **four** cubits. The Gemara asks: **Was the area of** the **corners four** square cubits? If the four corners would be placed together the area would be only two square cubits. **Rather, say** that the **domain** of the **corners** is **four** cubits. In other words, the verse means that the blood may be sprinkled up to four cubits beneath the actual corners of the altar.

תְּנַן הָתָם: חוּט שֶׁל סִיקְרָא חוֹגְרוֹ בָּאֶמְצַע, לְהַבְדִּיל בֵּין דָּמִים הָעֶלְיוֹנִים לְדָמִים הַתַּחְתּוֹנִים. מְנָא הָנֵי מִילֵּי? אֲמַר רַב אַחָא בַּר רַב קְטִינָא: שֶׁנֶּאֱמַר ״וְהָיְתָה הָרֶשֶׁת עַד חֲצִי הַמִּזְבֵּחַ״ – הַתּוֹרָה נָתְנָה מְחִיצָה לְהַבְדִּיל בֵּין דָּמִים הָעֶלְיוֹנִים לְדָמִים הַתַּחְתּוֹנִים.

We learned in a mishna **there** (*Middot* 35b): **A red line circumscribed** the altar **in the middle, to separate between** the area for the **blood** that must be placed on **the upper** part of the altar **and** the area for the **blood** that must be placed on **the lower** part of the altar. The Gemara asks: **From where is this matter** derived? **Rav Aḥa bar Rav Ketina said** it is derived from a verse, **as it is stated:** "And you shall put it under the ledge round the altar beneath, **and the net will reach halfway up the altar"** (Exodus 27:5). **The Torah provided** for **a separation** on the altar, **to separate between** the area for the **blood** placed on **the upper** part of the altar **and** the area for the **blood** placed on **the lower** part of the altar.

״שְׁיָרֵי הַדָּם״ כו׳. תָּנוּ רַבָּנַן: ״אֶל יְסוֹד מִזְבַּח״ – זֶה יְסוֹד דְּרוֹמִי. אַתָּה אוֹמֵר: זֶה יְסוֹד דְּרוֹמִי, אוֹ אֵינוֹ אֶלָּא יְסוֹד מַעֲרָבִי?

§ The mishna teaches: He would pour **the remainder of the blood** on the southern base of the altar. **The Sages taught** in a *baraita*: Concerning the phrase: **"At the base of the altar"** (Leviticus 4:30), mentioned with regard to pouring the remainder of the blood of the sin offering of a king, **this** is referring to the **southern base** of the altar. The *baraita* challenges: **Do you say** that **this** is referring to the **southern base, or is it** referring **only** to the **western base?**

וְיִלְמַד סָתוּם מִן הַמְפוֹרָשׁ! אָמַרְתָּ: יִלְמַד יְרִידָתוֹ מִן הַכֶּבֶשׁ לִיצִיאָתוֹ מִן הַהֵיכָל, מַה יְּצִיאָתוֹ מִן הַהֵיכָל – בְּסָמוּךְ לוֹ, אַף יְרִידָתוֹ מִן הַכֶּבֶשׁ – בְּסָמוּךְ לוֹ.

The *baraita* suggests: **And** one can **derive** the meaning of this **unspecified** phrase **from** the meaning of **the explicit** phrase, as follows: **You said** that one can **derive** the location of the priest's **descent from the ramp** of the external altar after sprinkling blood of the sin offering by comparing it **to his exit from the Sanctuary** with the blood that remained after having sprinkled blood inside the Sanctuary. The verse states with regard to the bull offering of the High Priest: "And all the remaining blood of the bull he shall pour out at the base of the altar of burnt offering, which is at the entrance of the Tent of Meeting" (Leviticus 4:7). **Just as** upon **his exit from the Sanctuary** the priest pours the remainder of the blood **on** the side **closest to him,** the western side, **so too,** upon **his descent from the ramp** of the external altar after sprinkling blood from the sin offering, he pours the blood **on** the side **closest to him,** which is the southern side.

תַּנְיָא, רַבִּי יִשְׁמָעֵאל אוֹמֵר: זֶה וָזֶה יְסוֹד מַעֲרָבִי. רַבִּי שִׁמְעוֹן בֶּן יוֹחַאי אוֹמֵר: זֶה וָזֶה יְסוֹד דְּרוֹמִי.

It is taught in another *baraita*: **Rabbi Yishmael says: This and that,** both the remainder of the blood sprinkled inside the Sanctuary and the remainder of the blood sprinkled on the external altar, are poured on the **western base** of the altar. **Rabbi Shimon ben Yoḥai says: This and that** are poured on the **southern base** of the altar.

בִּשְׁלָמָא לְמַאן דְּאָמַר יְסוֹד מַעֲרָבִי – קָסָבַר: יִלְמַד סָתוּם מִן הַמְפוֹרָשׁ.

The Gemara clarifies: **Granted, according to the one who says** that the blood is poured on the **western base** of the altar, it is clear how he derived his *halakha*. He **holds** that one can **derive** the meaning of **an unspecified** phrase **from** the meaning of **the explicit** phrase. Therefore, just as the remainder of the blood sprinkled inside the Sanctuary is poured on the western base of the external altar, the same is done with the remainder of the blood sprinkled on the external altar.

אֶלָּא לְמַאן דְּאָמַר יְסוֹד דְּרוֹמִי, מַאי טַעְמָא? אֲמַר רַבִּי אַסִּי, קָסָבַר הַאי תַּנָּא: כּוּלֵּיהּ מִזְבֵּחַ בַּצָּפוֹן קָאֵי. לִישָּׁנָא אַחֲרִינָא: כּוּלֵּיהּ פֶּתַח בַּדָּרוֹם קָאֵי.

But according to the one who says that the blood is poured on the **southern base** of the altar, **what is the reason? Rabbi Asi said: This *tanna* holds** that **the entire** external **altar stands in the north**[N] of the Temple courtyard. Therefore, the southern base is in the center of the courtyard, opposite the entrance to the Sanctuary. This is what the verse is referring to when it states: "At the entrance of the Tent of Meeting" (Leviticus 4:7). The Gemara presents **another formulation** of Rabbi Asi's explanation: **The entire entrance** of the Sanctuary **stands in the south** of the altar. Accordingly, when the priest exits the Sanctuary the southern base is the first one he encounters.

NOTES

The entire altar stands in the north – כּוּלֵּיהּ מִזְבֵּחַ בַּצָּפוֹן קָאֵי: Rashi provides two explanations, which are contingent on the discussion at the beginning of the next chapter. According to the first explanation the entire altar was to the north of the entrance of the Sanctuary, apart from one cubit of the southern base. This is where the priest came when he left the Sanctuary. According to the second explanation, it does not mean that the entire altar was to the north of the entrance of the Sanctuary, but that all of it is in the northern half of the Temple courtyard. When the priest left the entrance of the Sanctuary, if he exited in the middle of the doorway he would be closest to the southern edge of the altar. See *Tosafot*, who are inclined to follow Rashi's second explanation.

תַּנָא דְּבֵי רַבִּי יִשְׁמָעֵאל כְּרַבִּי שִׁמְעוֹן בֶּן יוֹחַי אוֹמְרִים: זֶה וָזֶה יְסוֹד מַעֲרָבִי, וְסִימָנֵיךְ: מְשַׁכוּ גַּבְרֵי לְגַבְרָא.

The school of Rabbi Yishmael, in accordance with the opinion of **Rabbi Shimon ben Yoḥai, says:** Both **this and that,** i.e., the blood of an inner sin offering and that of an external sin offering, were poured at the **western base** of the altar. According to this version, Rabbi Shimon ben Yoḥai agrees with the opinion of Rabbi Yishmael. The Gemara comments: **And your mnemonic** to remember this change in opinion is: **The men pulled the man.**[N] In this case, the numerous students of Rabbi Yishmael claim that Rabbi Shimon ben Yoḥai agrees with their teacher.

מתני׳ הָעוֹלָה קָדְשֵׁי קֳדָשִׁים, שְׁחִיטָתָהּ בַּצָּפוֹן, וְקִיבּוּל דָּמָהּ בִּכְלִי שָׁרֵת בַּצָּפוֹן, וְדָמָהּ טָעוּן שְׁתֵּי מַתָּנוֹת שֶׁהֵן אַרְבַּע, וּטְעוּנָה הֶפְשֵׁט וְנִיתּוּחַ וְכָלִיל לָאִשִּׁים.

MISHNA **The burnt offering is an offering of the most sacred order.**[N] **Its slaughter** is **in the north** of the Temple courtyard **and the collection of its blood in a service vessel** is **in the north, and its blood requires two placements**[H] **that are four,**[N] **and it requires flaying**[H] of its carcass **and the cutting** of the sacrificial animal into pieces, **and** it is consumed **in its entirety,** with the exception of its hide, **by the fire** of the altar.

גמ׳ עוֹלָה מַאי טַעְמָא תָּנֵי לֵיהּ קָדְשֵׁי קֳדָשִׁים? מִשּׁוּם דְּלָא כְּתִיב בָּהּ (לַה׳) ״קָדְשֵׁי קֳדָשִׁים הִיא״.

GEMARA **What is the reason** that the *tanna* **taught** that **a burnt offering** is **an offering of the most sacred order,** when the mishna earlier (52b) did not mention that a sin offering is of the most sacred order? The Gemara answers: It is **because** in the Torah **it is not written** explicitly **with regard to** the burnt offering: **It is most sacred,** as it states concerning the sin offering and the guilt offering in a verse concerning a meal offering: "It shall not be baked with leaven. I have given it as their portion of My offerings made by fire; it is most sacred, as the sin offering, and as the guilt offering" (Leviticus 6:10). Consequently, the *tanna* explicitly states that a burnt offering is likewise of the most sacred order.

״וְדָמָהּ טָעוּן שְׁתֵּי מַתָּנוֹת״. הֵיכִי עָבֵיד? אָמַר רַב: נוֹתֵן וְחוֹזֵר וְנוֹתֵן. וּשְׁמוּאֵל אָמַר: מַתָּנָה אַחַת כְּמִין גַּמָּא נוֹתֵן.

The mishna teaches: **And its blood requires two placements** that are four. **How does** the priest **perform** the placements? **Rav says: He places** the blood on one side of the corner of the altar, **and places** it **again** on the other side of the corner of the altar. He repeats this on the diagonally opposite corner, so that he places on two corners but on all four sides of the altar. **And Shmuel says:** He **places one placement** on each of the two diagonally opposite corners, so that each placement is **similar to** the shape of the Greek letter **gamma,**[HL] which is bent at a right angle.

NOTES

The men pulled the man – מְשַׁכוּ גַּבְרֵי לְגַבְרָא: Rashi explains that the men who were the majority, i.e., the students of Rabbi Yishmael, pulled the single man, i.e., Rabbi Shimon, and stated their opinion in his name. *Tosafot* had a different version of the text, which read: This and that are the southern base, which is the opinion of Rabbi Shimon in the *baraita*. They explain that the term: The men, is referring to Rabbi Shimon ben Yoḥai, whose name consists of the names of two men, Shimon and his father Yoḥai. He pulled Rabbi Yishmael, whose name consists of a single appellation. The Gemara on 119b and *Yoma* 59a have slightly different versions of this phrase.

The burnt offering is an offering of the most sacred order – הָעוֹלָה קָדְשֵׁי קֳדָשִׁים: The prohibition against the misuse of consecrated property applies even before the blood has been sprinkled (see *Me'ila* 7b). The offering is disqualified if it is removed from the Temple courtyard (see *Tosafot*).

Two placements that are four – שְׁתֵּי מַתָּנוֹת שֶׁהֵן אַרְבַּע: The priest stands on the floor of the courtyard and does not ascend to the surrounding ledge, since the blood of the burnt offering must be placed below the red line. He takes the blood of the burnt offering in a vessel and sprinkles it on two corners of the altar that are diagonally opposite each other so that the blood reaches all four sides of the altar, as explained in the Gemara. The mishna (*Tamid* 30b) explains that it must be specifically the northeast corner and the southwest corner.

LANGUAGE

Gamma – גַּמָּא: This is the third letter of the Greek alphabet. Greek script was well known in the talmudic era, and the form of its letters served as an example for various shapes. The form of the capital letter gamma depicts a right angle.

Γ

Gamma

HALAKHA

And its blood requires two placements, etc. – וְדָמָהּ טָעוּן שְׁתֵּי מַתָּנוֹת וכו׳: How is the blood of a burnt offering sprinkled? The priest takes the blood in a vessel and sprinkles some of the blood from the container twice on the lower half of the altar. He does this in the northeast corner and the southwest corner. The remainder of the blood is poured onto the southern base of the altar. This is in accordance with the mishna here and on *Tamid* 30b (Rambam *Sefer Avoda, Hilkhot Ma'aseh HaKorbanot* 5:6).

Requires flaying, etc. – טְעוּנָה הֶפְשֵׁט וכו׳: How are the rites of a burnt offering performed? One slaughters the animal, and a priest presents the blood; he then flays the skin and cuts the animal into pieces. He then burns the pieces on the top of the altar (Rambam *Sefer Avoda, Hilkhot Ma'aseh HaKorbanot* 6:1).

Similar to the letter gamma – כְּמִין גַּמָּא: When the priest sprinkles the blood of the burnt offering on the northeast and southwest corners of the altar he does so in such a way that the blood will be on two sides of the altar, like the Greek letter gamma, so that there is blood placed on all four sides of the altar. This is in accordance with the opinion of Shmuel. Even though in general the *halakha* is in accordance with the opinion of Rav in ritual matters, nevertheless, the unattributed mishna accords with the opinion of Shmuel, as does the first *tanna* of the *baraita* (Rambam *Sefer Avoda, Hilkhot Ma'aseh HaKorbanot* 5:6, and see Radbaz there).

כְּתַנָּאֵי: יָכוֹל יִזְרְקֶנּוּ זְרִיקָה אַחַת? תַּלְמוּד לוֹמַר: "סָבִיב". אִי סָבִיב, יָכוֹל יַקִּיפֶנּוּ כְּחוּט? תַּלְמוּד לוֹמַר: "וְזָרְקוּ"; הָא כֵּיצַד – כְּמִין גַּמָּא, וְדָמָהּ טָעוּן שְׁתֵּי מַתָּנוֹת שֶׁהֵן אַרְבַּע.

The Gemara comments: This dispute between Rav and Shmuel is **like** a dispute between *tanna'im*: One **might** have thought that a priest **should sprinkle one sprinkling** with the blood of a burnt offering. To counter this possibility, **the verse states:** "And sprinkle the blood **around** against the altar that is at the entrance of the Tent of Meeting" (Leviticus 1:5). **If** the blood must be sprinkled **around** the altar, one **might** have thought that **he should circumscribe** the altar **as** one would do with **a thread,** and sprinkle the blood all around. To counter this possibility, **the verse states:** "Shall present the blood, **and sprinkle** the blood around against the altar" (Leviticus 1:5), and one cannot have the blood circumscribe the altar as a thread would without directly applying it with a finger. **How** can **these** verses be reconciled? He applies the blood in a shape that is **similar to** that of the Greek letter **gamma, and its blood requires two sprinklings that are four.** This opinion accords with the opinion of Shmuel.

רַבִּי יִשְׁמָעֵאל אוֹמֵר: נֶאֱמַר כָּאן "סָבִיב" וְנֶאֱמַר לְהַלָּן "סָבִיב", מַה לְּהַלָּן – פִּיסּוּק וְאַרְבַּע מַתָּנוֹת, אַף כָּאן – פִּיסּוּק וְאַרְבַּע מַתָּנוֹת.

The *baraita* continues: **Rabbi Yishmael says: It is stated here:** "Shall present the blood, and sprinkle the blood **around** against the altar" (Leviticus 1:5), **and it is stated there,** with regard to the sin offering sacrificed at the inauguration of the Tabernacle: "And when it was slain, Moses took the blood, and put it upon the corners of the altar **around** with his finger" (Leviticus 8:15). **Just as there,** with regard to the sin offering, the blood was placed **discretely and** with **four placements,** one on each corner, **so too here,** with regard to a burnt offering, it must be placed **discretely and** with **four placements.** This opinion accords with the opinion of Rav.

אִי מַה לְּהַלָּן אַרְבַּע מַתָּנוֹת עַל אַרְבַּע קְרָנוֹת, אַף כָּאן אַרְבַּע מַתָּנוֹת עַל אַרְבַּע קְרָנוֹת? אָמַרְתָּ: עוֹלָה טְעוּנָה יְסוֹד, וְקֶרֶן מִזְרָחִית דְּרוֹמִית לֹא הָיָה לָהּ יְסוֹד.

If these offerings are compared to each other, why not say that **just as there,** the blood of the sin offering must have **four placements on** the **four corners, so too here,** the blood of the burnt offering requires **four placements on** the **four corners? You said** that **a burnt offering requires** that the blood be placed on a part of the altar that has **a base,**[N] **and** the **southeast corner** of the altar **had no base**[H] beneath it. Therefore, the blood had to be placed on the northeast corner and the southwest corner.

מַאי טַעְמָא? אָמַר רַבִּי אֶלְעָזָר: לְפִי שֶׁלֹּא הָיְתָה בְּחֶלְקוֹ שֶׁל טוֹרֵף. דְּאָמַר רַב שְׁמוּאֵל בַּר רַב יִצְחָק: מִזְבֵּחַ אוֹכֵל בְּחֶלְקוֹ שֶׁל יְהוּדָה אַמָּה.

The Gemara asks: **What is the reason** that there was no base on the southeast corner of the altar? **Rabbi Elazar says: Because it was not in the portion** of land **of the one who tears,**[N] i.e., the tribe of Benjamin, as he is described in the following manner: "Benjamin is a wolf that tears apart; in the morning he devours the prey, and in the evening he divides the spoil" (Genesis 49:27). **As Rav Shmuel, son of Rav Yitzḥak, says:** The **altar** would **consume,** i.e., occupy, **one cubit of the portion of Judah.**[NB] The part of the altar in Judah's portion was the southeast corner of the base, and therefore there was no base on that corner.

אָמַר רַבִּי לֵוִי בַּר חָמָא אָמַר רַבִּי חָמָא בְּרַבִּי חֲנִינָא: רְצוּעָה הָיְתָה יוֹצְאָה מֵחֶלְקוֹ שֶׁל יְהוּדָה וְנִכְנֶסֶת בְּחֶלְקוֹ שֶׁל בִּנְיָמִין, וְהָיָה בִּנְיָמִין הַצַּדִּיק מִצְטַעֵר עָלֶיהָ בְּכָל יוֹם לְנוֹטְלָהּ, שֶׁנֶּאֱמַר:

Rabbi Levi bar Ḥama says that **Rabbi Ḥama, son of Rabbi Ḥanina, says: A strip** of land **emerged from the portion of Judah and entered into the portion of Benjamin,** and the southeast corner of the base was on that strip. **And** the tribe of **Benjamin the righteous would agonize over it every day,** desiring **to take it** into its portion, due to its unique sanctity. **As it is stated** in Moses' blessing to the tribe of Benjamin:

NOTES

A burnt offering requires a base – עוֹלָה טְעוּנָה יְסוֹד: Rabbi Yishmael himself taught this (51a) based on an *a fortiori* inference from the remainder of the blood of a sin offering. Pouring the remainder of the blood and sprinkling the blood both require a base.

In the portion of the one who tears – בְּחֶלְקוֹ שֶׁל טוֹרֵף: Jacob prophetically blessed Benjamin: "Benjamin is a wolf that tears apart; in the morning he devours the prey, and in the evening he divides the spoil" (Genesis 49:27). This blessing means that the altar upon which the offerings would be burned was to be built in the portion of Benjamin. The altar is like a wolf, which devours everything. Onkelos interprets the continuation of this verse to mean: In the morning the priests will present the offerings.

Consume one cubit of the portion of Judah – אוֹכֵל בְּחֶלְקוֹ שֶׁל יְהוּדָה אַמָּה: Rashi explains that this cubit was the same strip referred to by Rabbi Levi bar Ḥama. As explained in a *baraita* in tractate *Yoma* (12a), the eastern side of the Temple courtyard until the altar was in the portion of Judah, and a strip extended into the portion of Benjamin from the southeast corner in two directions, along the east side of the altar until one cubit from the north side, and along the south until one cubit from the west side. In tractate *Middot* (35b) it is explained that the base extended along the entire northern and western sides of the altar, but extended along only one cubit on each of the southern and eastern sides, as these two cubits were part of the portion of Benjamin.

Based on Rashi's explanation, several commentaries drew a picture of the base as it appears in most printed editions of tractate *Middot*, with one cubit of base extending along both the eastern and southern walls of the altar (*Birkat HaZevaḥ*; *Tzon Kodashim*). The *Panim Meirot* claims that the cubits being discussed are in fact the end face of the northern and western bases, and there was no base at all on the eastern or southern walls. The Rambam and others also explain the mishna in tractate *Middot* in this manner.

HALAKHA

The southeast corner had no base – קֶרֶן מִזְרָחִית דְּרוֹמִית לֹא הָיָה לָהּ יְסוֹד: The base of the altar did not surround all four sides. Rather, it circumscribed the entire north and west sides of the altar, and extended a single cubit into the south and east sides. The southeast corner did not have a base (Rambam *Sefer Avoda*, *Hilkhot Beit HaBeḥira* 2:10).

BACKGROUND

The altar would consume one cubit in the portion of Judah – מִזְבֵּחַ אוֹכֵל בְּחֶלְקוֹ שֶׁל יְהוּדָה אַמָּה: The base of the altar protruded one cubit to the east and one cubit to the south.

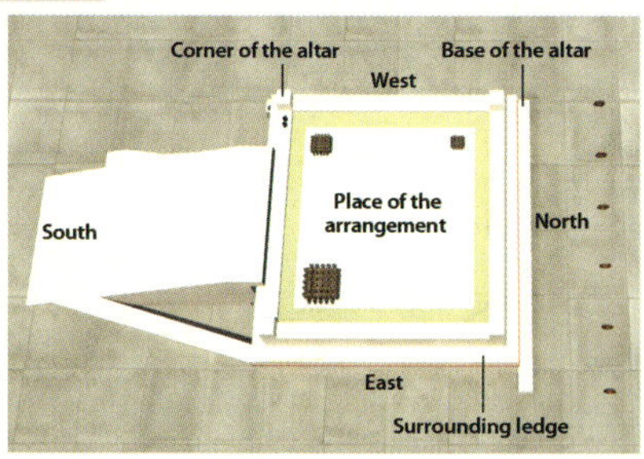

Aerial view of the altar

״חֹפֵף עָלָיו כׇּל הַיּוֹם״, לְפִיכָךְ זָכָה בִּנְיָמִין הַצַּדִּיק וְנַעֲשָׂה אוּשְׁפִּיזְכָן לְהַקָּדוֹשׁ בָּרוּךְ הוּא, שֶׁנֶּאֱמַר: ״וּבֵין כְּתֵפָיו שָׁכֵן״.

"He covers it throughout the day,[N] and He dwells between his shoulders" (Deuteronomy 33:12). The term "covers it" is understood to mean that Benjamin is continually focused upon that site. **Therefore, Benjamin the righteous was privileged and became the host of the Holy One, Blessed be He,** as the Holy of Holies was built in his portion. **As it is stated: "And He dwells between his shoulders."**

מֵיתִיבֵי: עוֹלַת הָעוֹף כֵּיצַד הָיְתָה נַעֲשֵׂית? הָיָה מוֹלֵק אֶת רֹאשָׁהּ מִמּוּל עׇרְפָּהּ וּמַבְדִּיל, וּמְמַצֶּה דָּמָהּ עַל קִיר הַמִּזְבֵּחַ.

The Gemara **raises an objection** from a *baraita*: **How** was the rite **of a bird burnt offering performed?** The priest ascended the ramp and turned to the surrounding ledge. When he arrived at the southeast corner, the priest **would pinch** the bird's **head**[H] by pinching **at its nape** with his thumbnail **and sever** the bird's head from its body, **and** would **squeeze out its blood on the wall of the altar.**

וְאִי אָמְרַתְּ לֹא הָיָה לָהּ יְסוֹד – בַּאֲוִירָא בְּעָלְמָא הוּא דְּקָא עָבֵיד? אָמַר רַב נַחְמָן בַּר יִצְחָק: אֵימַר כָּךְ הִתְנוּ, אֲוִירָא דְּבִנְיָמִין, קַרְקַע דִּיהוּדָה.

The Gemara states its objection: **And if you say** that the southeast corner of the altar **had no base, is he merely performing** the rite **in the air,**[N] i.e., not within the domain of the altar? **Rav Naḥman bar Yitzḥak said: Say** that when Eretz Yisrael was apportioned, they **made this condition: The airspace** of what would become the southeast part of the altar is in the portion of the tribe **of Benjamin,** so the pinching of the bird offering was performed within the domain of the altar. But the **land** was in the portion of the tribe **of Judah.**

מַאי לֹא הֲוָה לָהּ יְסוֹד? רַב אָמַר: בְּבִנְיָן, לֵוִי אָמַר: בְּדָמִים. רַב מְתַרְגֵּם: ״בְּאַחְסַנְתֵּיהּ יִתְבְּנֵי מַדְבְּחָא״, לֵוִי מְתַרְגֵּם: ״בְּאַחְסַנְתֵּיהּ יִתְבְּנֵי מַקְדְּשָׁא״, מָקוֹם מְקוּדָּשׁ לְדָמִים.

§ The Gemara asks: **What** does the *baraita* mean when it states that the southeast corner of the altar **had no base? Rav says:** It is **with regard to** the fact that it had no base **built** on those sides. **Levi says:** It is **with regard to** the fact that no **blood** was sprinkled on that side, as the blood was not permitted to be presented there, even though there was a physical base. Based on this dispute, each of them disagreed as to the correct Aramaic translation of the verse: "Benjamin is a wolf that tears apart; in the morning he devours the prey, and in the evening he divides the spoil" (Genesis 49:27). **Rav translates** this as: **In his portion will the altar be built. Levi translates** this as: **In his portion will the Sanctuary be built,** which means: **A place sanctified for blood.**

תָּא שְׁמַע: הַיְסוֹד הָיָה מְהַלֵּךְ עַל פְּנֵי כׇּל הַצָּפוֹן וְעַל פְּנֵי כׇּל הַמַּעֲרָב, אוֹכֵל בַּדָּרוֹם אַמָּה אַחַת וּבַמִּזְרָח אַמָּה אַחַת! מַאי אוֹכֵל? נַמִי בְּדָמִים.

The Gemara brings proof for each opinion: **Come** and **hear** a proof for the explanation of Rav from a mishna (*Middot* 35b): **The base** of the altar **would extend along all of the northern** side **and along all of the western** side. **It consumed one cubit on the southern** side **and one cubit on the eastern** side. This indicates that there was no base on most of the southern or eastern sides of the altar. The Gemara comments: Levi would explain: **What** is the meaning of the term: **Consume?** The *baraita*, **as well,** is stated **with regard** to consuming **blood** of the offerings.

תָּא שְׁמַע: הַמִּזְבֵּחַ הָיָה שְׁלֹשִׁים וּשְׁתַּיִם עַל שְׁלֹשִׁים וּשְׁתַּיִם! הָכָא בְּמַאי עָסְקִינַן – מִן הַצַּד.

The Gemara suggests: **Come** and **hear** a proof for the explanation of Levi from that same mishna: **The altar was thirty-two**[H] cubits **by thirty-two** cubits. This indicates that there was a base on all four sides, in accordance with the opinion of Levi. Rav could answer: **Here we are dealing with** the measurement **from the side.** In other words, only the northern and western sides were thirty-two cubits in length.

תָּא שְׁמַע: נִמְצָא פּוֹרֵחַ אַמָּה עַל יְסוֹד וְאַמָּה עַל סוֹבֵב! אֵימָא: כְּנֶגֶד אַמָּה יְסוֹד וְעַל אַמָּה סוֹבֵב.

The Gemara suggests: **Come** and **hear** a proof for the explanation of Levi from a *baraita*: **It turns out** the top of the ramp of the altar would **overhang** one **cubit** in the air **over the base** of the altar **and** one **cubit over the surrounding ledge.** This indicates that it had a base on all four sides, as the ramp was on the southern side. Rav could answer: **Say** that the *baraita* means it would overhang **toward** the place where the **base** of a **cubit** would have been, **and one cubit over** the **surrounding ledge.**

NOTES

He covers [*hofef*] it throughout the day – חֹפֵף עָלָיו כׇּל הַיּוֹם: The straightforward meaning of the verse is that God covers and protects the tribe of Benjamin. The Sages interpret the word *ḥofef* to mean rubbing or scratching. Just as one may scratch one's hair in thought, it is as if to say that Benjamin's thoughts were constantly conscious of the location of the altar.

Is he merely performing the rite in the air – בַּאֲוִירָא בְּעָלְמָא הוּא דְּקָא עָבֵיד: Although the priest would be standing on the surrounding ledge, it seems that it is accurate to state that the pinching was performed in the air and not over the ledge. This is because the surrounding ledge was only one cubit wide, and the priest would pinch the nape of the neck of the bird with his right hand, which was further from the altar. There was no requirement that the priest ensure that the bird be directly above the ledge. In addition, Rashi explains that a bird sin offering could be pinched anywhere above the red line, including beneath the surrounding ledge.

Rashi explains that the Gemara's question is not with regard to pinching the nape of the bird in the air of the courtyard, but with regard to the blood, which falls on the ground and goes to waste instead of reaching the base. Alternatively, *Ḥok Natan* explains Rashi's opinion that the concern is with regard to the blood that is squeezed onto the side of the altar, which should reach the base of the altar and not the floor. Rashi is forced to explain that the Gemara's answer is that the air where the base should have been is in the portion of Benjamin, and that there must have been some kind of protrusion there onto which the blood should fall.

Rabbeinu Tam rejects Rashi's explanation. He explains that the issue is not the blood that falls on the ground and goes to waste, but the actual pinching of the nape itself. According to the *baraita* (64b), the pinching must be done on the top of the altar, like the burning of the offerings. Failing that, it must be done in the air above the altar. The Gemara's answer is that the air is part of the tribal portion of Benjamin, and therefore it is considered to be the air of the altar.

Tosafot cite an alternative explanation from Rabbeinu Ḥayyim, based on a version of the *baraita* that makes reference to pouring the remainder of the blood of a bird burnt offering on the base of the altar. If so, the Gemara's question is straightforward: If you claim that there was no base there, it turns out that he is pouring the blood into the air. According to this explanation of the question, the Gemara's answer is very difficult to understand, because not only does one have to posit that there was a protrusion from the wall of the altar to collect the blood, but also this protrusion must have the status of the base of the altar. *Tosafot* raise additional difficulties with this explanation.

HALAKHA

He would pinch the bird's head – הָיָה מוֹלֵק אֶת רֹאשָׁהּ: What is the rite of the bird burnt offering? The priest would ascend the ramp to the southeast corner of the surrounding ledge of the altar. He then pinched the nape of the bird with his fingernail, completely detaching its head from its body. Next, he squeezed out the blood of the head and of the body on the upper half of the altar, i.e., above the red line (Rambam *Sefer Avoda*, *Hilkhot Ma'aseh HaKorbanot* 6:20).

The altar was thirty-two, etc. – הַמִּזְבֵּחַ הָיָה שְׁלֹשִׁים וּשְׁתַּיִם וכו׳: The altar that was constructed by those who returned from the Babylonian exile, and the altar that will be built in the future, have the dimensions of thirty-two cubits by thirty-two cubits (Rambam *Sefer Avoda*, *Hilkhot Beit HaBeḥira* 2:5).

תָּא שְׁמַע, דְּתָנֵי לֵוִי: כֵּיצַד בּוֹנִין אֶת הַמִּזְבֵּחַ? מְבִיאִין מַלְבֵּן שֶׁהוּא שְׁלֹשִׁים וּשְׁתַּיִם עַל שְׁלֹשִׁים וּשְׁתַּיִם וְגוֹבְהוֹ אַמָּה, וּמֵבִיא חֲלוּקֵי אֲבָנִים מְפוּלָּמוֹת, בֵּין גְּדוֹלוֹת בֵּין קְטַנּוֹת, וּמֵבִיא סִיד וְקוּנְיָא וְזֶפֶת וּמְמַחֶה וְשׁוֹפֵךְ, וְזֶה הוּא מְקוֹם יְסוֹד.

The Gemara suggests: **Come and hear** a proof, **as Levi teaches** in a *baraita*: **How does one build the altar?**[H] He **brings a square** wooden frame, **which is thirty-two** cubits **by thirty-two** cubits, **and its height is one cubit. And he brings pieces of** damp [*mefulamot*][L] **stone,**[N] **both large and small,** which are the main components of the altar, which is described as: "An altar of stone" (Exodus 20:22). **And he brings plaster and molten lead and tar, and melts** them **and pours** the mixture into the gaps between the stones. **And this is the place of** the **base** of the altar.

וְחוֹזֵר וּמֵבִיא מַלְבֵּן שֶׁהוּא שְׁלֹשִׁים אַמָּה עַל שְׁלֹשִׁים אַמָּה וְגוֹבְהוֹ חָמֵשׁ אַמּוֹת, וּמֵבִיא חֲלוּקֵי אֲבָנִים כו׳. וְחוֹזֵר וּמֵבִיא מַלְבֵּן שֶׁהוּא עֶשְׂרִים וּשְׁמוֹנֶה עַל עֶשְׂרִים וּשְׁמוֹנֶה אַמּוֹת וְגוֹבְהוֹ שָׁלֹשׁ אַמּוֹת, וּמֵבִיא חֲלוּקֵי כו׳, וְהוּא מְקוֹם הַמַּעֲרָכָה.

And then he brings a square wooden frame, **which is thirty cubits by thirty cubits, and its height is five cubits. And he brings pieces of** damp **stone,** both large and small. And he brings plaster and molten lead and tar, and melts them and pours the mixture into the gaps between the stones. **And then he brings a square** wooden frame, **which is twenty-eight** cubits **by twenty-eight cubits, and its height is three cubits. And he brings pieces of** damp stone, both large and small. And he brings plaster and molten lead and tar, and melts them and pours the mixture into the gaps between the stones. **And this is the place of the arrangement** of wood on the altar.

וְחוֹזֵר וּמֵבִיא מַלְבֵּן שֶׁהוּא אַמָּה עַל אַמָּה, וּמֵבִיא חֲלוּקֵי אֲבָנִים מְפוּלָּמוֹת בֵּין גְּדוֹלוֹת בֵּין קְטַנּוֹת, וּמֵבִיא זֶפֶת וְקוּנְיָא, וּמְמַחֶה וְשׁוֹפֵךְ, וְזֶהוּ קֶרֶן, וְכֵן לְכׇל קֶרֶן וְקֶרֶן!

And then he brings a square wooden frame, **which is** one **cubit by** one **cubit. And he brings pieces of damp stone, both large and small. And he brings plaster and molten lead and tar, and melts** them **and pours** the mixture into the frame. **And this is** the **corner** of the altar. **And so** he does this **for each and every corner.** This *baraita* indicates that the altar had a base around all four sides.

וְכִי תֵּימָא

The Gemara comments: **And if you would say**

דְּגָייז לֵיהּ – "אֲבָנִים שְׁלֵמוֹת" כְּתִיב!

that he cuts the base on the southern and western sides after he has poured the mixture for the altar and it has dried, **it is written** concerning the altar: "You shall build the altar of the Lord your God of **unhewn stones;** and you shall offer burnt offerings on it to the Lord your God" (Deuteronomy 27:6), so it cannot be cut.

דְּמָחֵית מִידֵּי מִתּוּתֵיהּ וְשָׁקֵיל לֵיהּ. דְּאִי לָא תֵּימָא הָכִי, הָא דְּאָמַר רַב כָּהֲנָא: אֲבָנִים שֶׁל קְרָנוֹת חֲלוּלוֹת הָיוּ, דִּכְתִיב: "וּמָלְאוּ כַּמִּזְרָק כְּזָוִיּוֹת מִזְבֵּחַ", הָכָא נַמִי – "אֲבָנִים שְׁלֵמוֹת" אָמַר רַחֲמָנָא! אֶלָּא: דְּמָחֵית מִידֵּי מִתּוּתֵיהּ וְשָׁקֵיל לֵיהּ, הָכָא נַמִי, דְּמָחֵית מִידֵּי מִתּוּתֵיהּ וְשָׁקֵיל לֵיהּ.

Rav could answer: This means **that he places something under** the frame, in the place where there is to be no base, **and** after the poured mixture has dried he **removes it,** leaving the space empty. **As if you do not say so,** how will you explain **that which Rav Kahana says: The stone** interiors **of the corners were hollow,**[N] i.e., there were gaps between the stones, **as it is written: "And they shall be filled like the basins, like the corners of the altar"** (Zechariah 9:15)? The verse compares the corners to hollow basins. **Here too,** doesn't **the Merciful One state** that the altar must be made of **"unhewn stones"**? If so, how could the corners be hollow? **Rather,** it must be **that he places something,** e.g., sticks and twigs, **under** the frame and pours the mixture for the corners over it, **and** when it has hardened, **removes** the sticks and twigs, leaving the corners somewhat hollow. **Here too, he places something under**[H] the frame **and** later **removes it.**

דָּרַשׁ רָבָא: מַאי דִּכְתִיב: "וַיֵּלֶךְ דָּוִד וּשְׁמוּאֵל וַיֵּשְׁבוּ בְּנָוֹית בָּרָמָה", וְכִי מָה עִנְיַן נָוִיוֹת אֵצֶל רָמָה? אֶלָּא, שֶׁהָיוּ יוֹשְׁבִין בְּרָמָה, וְעוֹסְקִין בְּנוֹיוֹ שֶׁל עוֹלָם;

§ Apropos the altar and the Temple, the Gemara relates that **Rava taught: What** is the meaning of that **which is written** concerning David: **"And he and Samuel**[N] **went and dwelt in Naioth.** And it was told Saul, saying: Behold, David is at Naioth [*beNayot*] **in Ramah"** (1 Samuel 19:18–19)? **But what does Naioth have to do with Ramah?** They are in two distinct places. **Rather,** this means **that they were sitting in Ramah and** were **involved in** discussing **the beauty** [*benoyo*] **of the world,**[N] i.e., the Temple.

HALAKHA

How does one build the altar – כֵּיצַד בּוֹנִין אֶת הַמִּזְבֵּחַ: The altar is constructed as a solid block with no hollow spaces. Large and small stones are placed in a frame, and lime, tar, and molten lead are poured into it. The stones for the altar were brought from virgin ground or from the Mediterranean Sea (Rambam *Sefer Avoda, Hilkhot Beit HaBeḥira* 1:14, 2:16).

LANGUAGE

Damp [*mefulamot*] – מְפוּלָּמוֹת: From the Greek πήλωμα, *pēloma*, meaning mud or moisture. In this context, it is referring to moist, muddy stones.

NOTES

Pieces of damp [*mefulamot*] stone – חֲלוּקֵי אֲבָנִים מְפוּלָּמוֹת: The stones of the altar must be whole stones, without any blemish or scratch. They could not be hewn with a chisel, as the verse states: "And there you shall build an altar to the Lord your God, an altar of stones; you may not lift up any iron tool on them" (Deuteronomy 27:5). Therefore, they would take stones that were naturally smooth. In order to ensure that no human hand would shape the stones, they would bring damp stones, i.e., freshly quarried stone from virgin ground (see *Middot* 36a). The *Arukh* explains that *mefulamot* refers to strong pieces of stone. He understands that the issue is that the altar must be built in a way that ensures its strength and sustainability. Tractate *Ḥagiga* (12a) discusses damp stone that was found at the bottom of the sea. Apparently, this is the source for the Rambam's claim that they would bring stones from the sea to build the altar.

NOTES

Were hollow – חֲלוּלוֹת הָיוּ: The Rambam understands that the interiors of the corners were completely hollow. Rashi explains that each corner had holes in it where the blood of sin offerings would be absorbed, according to the opinion of Rabbi Elazar, son of Rabbi Shimon (53a). The mishna in tractate *Sukka* (48a) states explicitly that the southwest corner had holes in it into which they would pour the wine and water libations.

David and Samuel – דָּוִד וּשְׁמוּאֵל: There is support to the claim that it was David and Samuel who selected the site and plan of the Temple, as the verse states: "All these that were chosen to be porters in the gates were two hundred and twelve. These were reckoned by genealogy in their villages, whom David and Samuel the seer did ordain in their set office" (1 Chronicles 9:22).

Beauty of the world – נוֹיוֹ שֶׁל עוֹלָם: The Temple is referred to by this name because it embodies the splendor and beauty of the world. Furthermore, the Sages said concerning the Temple built by Herod: One who has not seen Herod's building has never seen a beautiful building in his life (*Bava Batra* 4a).

HALAKHA

He places something under – דְּמָחֵית מִידֵּי מִתּוּתֵיהּ: When constructing the altar, stone, lime, and plaster are poured into a frame. A block of wood or stone is placed on the southeast base and similarly inside each of the corners of the altar. Once the stone has hardened and the frame is removed, these blocks are removed so that the southeast corner has no base, and the corners are hollow (Rambam *Sefer Avoda, Hilkhot Beit HaBeḥira* 2:16).

אָמְרִי: כְּתִיב ״וְקַמְתָּ וְעָלִיתָ אֶל הַמָּקוֹם״ – מְלַמֵּד שֶׁבֵּית הַמִּקְדָּשׁ גָּבוֹהַּ מִכָּל אֶרֶץ יִשְׂרָאֵל, וְאֶרֶץ יִשְׂרָאֵל גְּבוֹהָה מִכָּל אֲרָצוֹת. לָא הֲווּ יָדְעִי דּוּכְתֵּיהּ הֵיכָא,

David and Samuel **said: It is written: "Then you shall arise, and get you up unto the place** which the Lord your God shall choose" (Deuteronomy 17:8). This **teaches that the Temple is higher than all** places in **Eretz Yisrael. And Eretz Yisrael is higher than all countries. They did not know where** the highest **place** in Eretz Yisrael was.

אַיְיתוּ סֵפֶר יְהוֹשֻׁעַ, בְּכוּלְּהוּ כְּתִיב: ״וְיָרַד״ ״וְעָלָה הַגְּבוּל״ ״וְתָאַר הַגְּבוּל״, בְּשֵׁבֶט בִּנְיָמִין ״וְעָלָה״ כְּתִיב, ״וְיָרַד״ לָא כְּתִיב. אָמְרִי: שְׁמַע מִינָּהּ הָכָא הוּא מְקוֹמוֹ.

They brought the book of Joshua. With regard to all of the borders of the tribes **it is written: "And went down"** (see Joshua 15:10, 16:3, 17:9),[N] and it is written: **"And the border went up** to Beth Hoglah." (Joshua 15:6), and: **"And the border was drawn** from the top of the mountain to the fountain of the waters of Nephtoah" (Joshua 15:9). The verse uses different terms to describe the borders of the portion of each tribe. And **with regard to** the borders of **the tribe of Benjamin it is written** only: **"And went up"** (Joshua 18:11), but **it is not written: "And went down." They said: Conclude from** the verses that the Temple's **place is here,** in the portion of Benjamin.

סְבוּר לְמִבְנְיֵיהּ בְּעֵין עֵיטָם דְּמִדְלֵי, אָמְרִי: נֵיתַתֵּי בֵּיהּ קַלִּיל, כְּדִכְתִיב: ״וּבֵין כְּתֵפָיו שָׁכֵן״.

They thought to build it at Ein Eitam,[B] **which is higher**[N] than any other place in the portion of Benjamin. **They said: Let us lower it a bit, as it is written:** "He covers it throughout the day, **and He dwells between his shoulders"** (Deuteronomy 33:12). This indicates that the Temple is situated slightly lower, between two peaks.

וְאִיבָּעֵית אֵימָא: גְּמִירִי דְּסַנְהֶדְרִין בְּחֶלְקוֹ דִּיהוּדָה, וּשְׁכִינָה בְּחֶלְקוֹ דְּבִנְיָמִין, וְאִי מַדְלִינַן לֵיהּ – מִתְפְּלֵיג טוּבָא, מוּטָב דְּנִיתַתֵּי בֵּיהּ פּוּרְתָּא, כְּדִכְתִיב: ״וּבֵין כְּתֵפָיו שָׁכֵן״.

And if you wish, say instead that **it is learned** as a tradition **that the Sanhedrin** is to be located **in the portion of Judah,**[N] and the place of the **Divine Presence** is to be located **in the portion of Benjamin.** They said: **And if we raise it** and place it near Ein Eitam **it** will be **too distant** from the portion of Judah. They said: It is **preferable that we lower it a bit, as it is written:** "He covers it throughout the day, **and He dwells between his shoulders"** (Deuteronomy 33:12).

וְעַל דָּבָר זֶה נִתְקַנֵּא דּוֹאֵג הָאֲדוֹמִי בְּדָוִד, כְּדִכְתִיב: ״כִּי קִנְאַת בֵּיתְךָ אֲכָלָתְנִי״, וּכְתִיב: ״זְכוֹר ה׳ לְדָוִד אֵת כׇּל עֻנּוֹתוֹ אֲשֶׁר נִשְׁבַּע לַה׳ וגו׳ אִם אָבֹא בְּאֹהֶל בֵּיתִי וגו׳ אִם אֶתֵּן שְׁנַת לְעֵינָי לְעַפְעַפַּי תְּנוּמָה עַד אֶמְצָא מָקוֹם לַה׳״ וגו׳.

And with regard to this matter, that David and Samuel discovered the location of the Temple, **Doeg the Edomite was jealous**[N] **of David, as it is written: "Because jealousy for Your House has eaten me up"** (Psalms 69:10), **and it is written: "Lord, remember for David all his affliction; how he swore to the Lord,** and vowed unto the Mighty One of Jacob: **I will not come into the tent of my house,** nor go up into the bed that is spread for me; **if I will give sleep to my eyes, or slumber to my eyelids; until I find a place for the Lord,** a dwelling place for the Mighty One of Jacob" (Psalms 132:1–5).

NOTES

With regard to all of them it is written: And went down, etc. – **בְּכוּלְּהוּ כְּתִיב וְיָרַד וכו׳:** The commentaries have struggled to explain this passage, since it seems at odds with the biblical text, which uses the term "went down" in describing the borders of Benjamin but not those of some other tribes. Some have explained that this statement refers not to the full description of the borders of each tribe, but rather specifically to the southern border of the portion of Judah. Where Judah borders the portion of Benjamin, the term "went down" is not used. Where Judah borders other tribes, the term is used (see Rashi and *Shita Mekubbetzet*).

At Ein Eitam which is higher – **בְּעֵין עֵיטָם דְּמִדְלֵי:** According to the Sages (*Yoma* 31a and Jerusalem Talmud, *Yoma* 3:8) this was higher than the Temple, and from there an aqueduct brought the water to the Temple.

The Sanhedrin is in the portion of Judah – **סַנְהֶדְרִין בְּחֶלְקוֹ דִּיהוּדָה:** Rashi explains, citing the *Sifrei*, that this is based on the verse: "The scepter shall not depart from Judah, nor the ruler's staff from between his feet, as long as men come to Shiloh; and the obedience of the peoples shall be to him" (Genesis 49:10). The ruler's staff refers to the Sanhedrin. Since the Sanhedrin sat in the Temple in the Chamber of Hewn Stone, the Temple had to be adjacent to the portion of Judah.

And with regard to this matter Doeg the Edomite was jealous – **וְעַל דָּבָר זֶה נִתְקַנֵּא דּוֹאֵג הָאֲדוֹמִי:** The verse states: "Now a certain man of the servants of Saul was there that day, detained before the Lord; and his name was Doeg the Edomite, the most important of the herdsmen that belonged to Saul" (I Samuel 21:8). He spoke against the priests of Nov, who helped David as he fled from Saul, and he killed them all. According to the Sages he was a great Torah scholar, but his jealousy led him to attempt to disqualify David not only from becoming king but also from being part of the Jewish people (see *Yevamot* 76b).

BACKGROUND

Ein Eitam – **עֵין עֵיטָם:** Ein Eitam is identified by some as the Atan Spring alongside the third of Solomon's pools, approximately 3 km southwest of Bethlehem. A long aqueduct, the lower aqueduct, flows from this and other springs for roughly 20 km, winding between the mountains and passing through tunnels until it reaches the Temple Mount. The present-day Atan Spring is located at an altitude of 760 m above sea level, approximately 25 m higher than the Temple Mount. This aqueduct was destroyed at the time of the destruction of the Temple, but it was later restored and carried water to Jerusalem over the course of many generations. The lower aqueduct was Hasmonean while the upper one was built later, to the west, during the Roman era.

Section of the lower aqueduct in Armon Hanatziv, Jerusalem

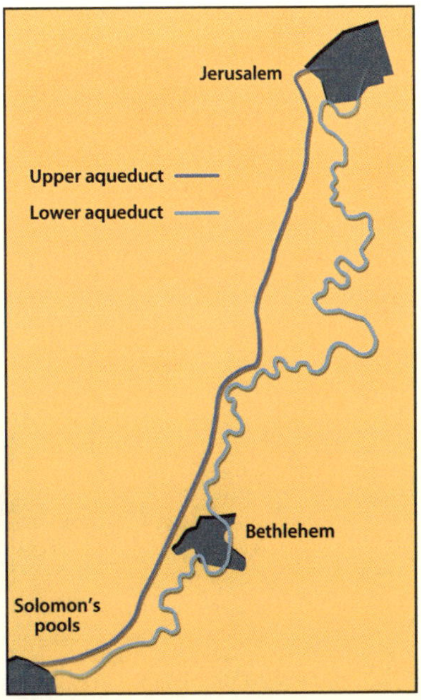

Map of the aqueducts to Jerusalem

״הִנֵּה שְׁמַעֲנוּהָ בְאֶפְרָתָה מְצָאנוּהָ בִּשְׂדֵה יָעַר״, ״בְּאֶפְרָתָה״ – זֶה יְהוֹשֻׁעַ דְּקָאָתֵי מֵאֶפְרַיִם, ״מְצָאנוּהָ בִּשְׂדֵה יָעַר״ – זֶה בִּנְיָמִין, דִּכְתִיב: ״בִּנְיָמִין זְאֵב יִטְרָף״.

The verse following those verses states: **"We heard of it as being in Ephrath; we found it in the field of the wood"** (Psalms 132:6). Rava explains the meaning of these words: **"In Ephrath"; this** is a reference to **Joshua, who came from** the tribe of **Ephraim.** This alludes to the fact that David and Samuel were able to locate the highest place in Eretz Yisrael based on the book of Joshua. **"We found it in the field of the wood"; this** is a reference to **Benjamin, as it is written** concerning him: **"Benjamin is a wolf that tears apart;** in the morning he devours the prey, and in the evening he divides the spoil" (Genesis 49:27). A wolf is a wild animal living in the field, and David and Samuel found the location of the Temple in the portion of Benjamin.

מתני׳ זִבְחֵי שַׁלְמֵי צִבּוּר וַאֲשָׁמוֹת; אֵלּוּ הֵן אֲשָׁמוֹת: אֲשַׁם גְּזֵילוֹת, אֲשַׁם מְעִילוֹת, אֲשַׁם שִׁפְחָה חֲרוּפָה, אֲשַׁם נָזִיר, אֲשַׁם מְצוֹרָע, אָשָׁם תָּלוּי;

MISHNA These are the *halakhot* of **communal peace offerings**[N] **and guilt offerings.**[H] **These are guilt offerings: The guilt offering for robbery,** brought by one from whom another demanded payment of a debt and he denied it and took a false oath (see Leviticus 5:20–26); **the guilt offering for** unwitting **misuse** of consecrated property (see Leviticus 5:14–16); **the guilt offering of an espoused maidservant,**[N] brought by one who engaged in sexual intercourse with a Canaanite maidservant betrothed to a Hebrew slave (see Leviticus 19:20–22); **the guilt offering of a nazirite** who became impure via contact with a corpse (see Numbers 6:12); **the guilt offering of a leper,** brought for his purification (see Leviticus 14:12); and **the provisional guilt offering,** brought by one who is uncertain as to whether he committed a sin that requires a sin offering (see Leviticus 5:17–18).

שְׁחִיטָתָן בַּצָּפוֹן, וְקִיבּוּל דָּמָן בִּכְלִי שָׁרֵת בַּצָּפוֹן, וְדָמָן טָעוּן שְׁתֵּי מַתָּנוֹת שֶׁהֵן אַרְבַּע, וְנֶאֱכָלִין לִפְנִים מִן הַקְּלָעִים, לְזִכְרֵי כְהוּנָּה, לְכָל מַאֲכָל, לְיוֹם וְלַיְלָה עַד חֲצוֹת.

Concerning all of these, **their slaughter** is **in the north** of the Temple courtyard **and collection of their blood in a service vessel is in the north, and their blood requires two placements that are four.**[H] **And** the meat portions of the offering **are eaten within the curtains,**[H] i.e., in the Temple courtyard, **by male priests.** And they are eaten prepared **in any** manner of **food**[H] preparation, **on the day** the offering was sacrificed **and** during the **night** that follows, **until midnight.**[H]

NOTES

Communal peace offerings – זִבְחֵי שַׁלְמֵי צִבּוּר: This refers to the two sheep brought on the festival of *Shavuot* along with the two loaves. The Torah states concerning them: "And you shall offer one he-goat for a sin offering, and two he-lambs in their first year for a sacrifice of peace offerings" (Leviticus 23:19). There are no other communal peace offerings.

Espoused maidservant – שִׁפְחָה חֲרוּפָה: The *halakha* of the espoused maidservant appears in Leviticus (19:20–22), but the depiction in the Torah is somewhat vague. The mishna in tractate *Karetot* (11a) presents a dispute between *tanna'im* as to whether this refers to a Canaanite maidservant, or a woman who is a half-slave half-free woman. According to accepted explanation, an espoused maidservant is a woman who is a half-slave half-free woman, e.g., she was owned by two partners and one of them freed her. She was subsequently betrothed to a Hebrew slave. Since she does not have the same status as a betrothed Jewish woman, if someone other than the maidservant's betrothed engages in sexual intercourse with her, he is liable to bring a guilt offering whether he acted intentionally or unwittingly.

HALAKHA

Communal peace offerings and guilt offerings – זִבְחֵי שַׁלְמֵי צִבּוּר וַאֲשָׁמוֹת: All offerings of the most sacred order, including guilt offerings and communal peace offerings, must be slaughtered in the Temple courtyard, north of the altar (Rambam *Sefer Avoda, Hilkhot Ma'aseh HaKorbanot* 5:3).

Their blood requires two placements that are four – דָּמָן טָעוּן שְׁתֵּי מַתָּנוֹת שֶׁהֵן אַרְבַּע: The blood of a guilt offering and a communal or individual peace offering must be placed on two diagonally opposite corners of the altar, similar to the placement of the blood of a burnt offering (Rambam *Sefer Avoda, Hilkhot Ma'aseh HaKorbanot* 5:6).

And they are eaten within the curtains – וְנֶאֱכָלִין לִפְנִים מִן הַקְּלָעִים: Once the sacrificial portions that must be burned have been placed on the altar, the meat of a guilt offering or a communal peace offering may be eaten only by male priests in the Temple courtyard (Rambam *Sefer Avoda, Hilkhot Ma'aseh HaKorbanot* 9:1, 10:3).

In any manner of food – לְכָל מַאֲכָל: It is permitted to eat the meat of offerings with any other food, and to eat it cooked or roasted in any manner. It may be seasoned with non- sacred spices (Rambam *Sefer Avoda, Hilkhot Ma'aseh HaKorbanot* 10:10).

On the day it was sacrificed and during the night until midnight – לְיוֹם וְלַיְלָה עַד חֲצוֹת: Guilt offerings and communal peace offerings may be eaten on the day they are slaughtered and on the following night, until dawn. The Sages decreed that it must be eaten before midnight, in order to distance oneself from sin (Rambam *Sefer Avoda, Hilkhot Ma'aseh HaKorbanot* 10:7–8).

גמ׳ מנא לן דבעי צפון? דתני רבה בר רב חנן קמיה דרבא: "ועשיתם שעיר עזים אחד לחטאת", מה חטאת בצפון – אף שלמי צבור בצפון.

GEMARA **From where do we derive that** the communal peace offerings, i.e., the two sheep brought on *Shavuot*, **require** slaughter in the **north**[N] of the Temple courtyard? The Gemara answers: **As Rabba bar Rav Ḥanan taught before Rava:** The passage in the Torah discussing the offerings of *Shavuot* states: **"And you shall offer one he-goat for a sin offering,** and two male sheep in their first year for a sacrifice of peace offerings" (Leviticus 23:19). The peace offerings are juxtaposed with the sin offering. **Just as the sin offering** must be slaughtered **in the north** of the Temple courtyard, **so too, communal peace offerings** must be slaughtered **in the north** of the Temple courtyard.

אמר ליה רבא: וכי חטאת מהיכן למדה – מעולה, דבר הלמד בהיקש חוזר ומלמד בהיקש?

Rava said to him: But from where is the requirement to slaughter **a sin offering** in the north of the Temple courtyard **derived?** It is derived **from** its juxtaposition with **a burnt offering,** as the verse states: "Speak to Aaron and to his sons, saying: This is the law of the sin offering: In the place where the burnt offering is slaughtered shall the sin offering be slaughtered before the Lord; it is most holy" (Leviticus 6:18). In the realm of consecrated matters, can **a matter derived via a juxtaposition then teach its** ***halakha*** **via a juxtaposition!** The Gemara (49b) demonstrates that it cannot.

אלא, מדתני רב מרי בריה דרב כהנא: "על עלתיכם ועל זבחי שלמיכם", מה עולה קדשי קדשים – אף זבחי שלמי צבור קדשי קדשים, מה עולה בצפון – אף זבחי שלמי צבור בצפון.

Rava explains: **Rather,** the source that communal peace offerings must be slaughtered in the north of the Temple courtyard is derived **from** that **which Rav Mari, son of Rav Kahana, teaches:** The verse states: "Also in the day of your gladness, and in your appointed seasons, and in your New Moons, you shall blow with the trumpets **over your burnt offerings, and over your peace offerings;** and they shall be to you for a memorial before your God: I am the Lord your God" (Numbers 10:10). This verse directly juxtaposes burnt offerings with communal peace offerings. **Just as burnt offerings** are **offerings of the most sacred order, so too, communal peace offerings** are **offerings of the most sacred order.**[N] Furthermore, **just as a burnt offering** must be slaughtered **in the north** of the Temple courtyard, **so too, communal peace offerings** must be slaughtered **in the north** of the Temple courtyard.

אלא היקשא קמא למאי אתא? כי חטאת, מה חטאת אינה נאכלת אלא לזכרי כהונה – אף זבחי שלמי צבור לזכרי כהונה.

The Gemara asks: **Rather, what** *halakha* does **the first juxtaposition** between communal peace offerings and the he-goat sin offering **come to** teach? The Gemara answers: It teaches that the *halakhot* of communal peace offerings are **like** the *halakhot* of **a sin offering. Just as a sin offering is eaten only by male priests, so too, communal peace offerings** are eaten only **by male priests.**

אמר ליה אביי: אי הכי, גבי איל נזיר, דכתיב: "והקריב את קרבנו לה׳ כבש בן שנתו תמים אחד לעלה וכבשה אחת בת שנתה [תמימה] לחטאת ואיל אחד [תמים] לשלמים", הכי נמי נימא דהקיש הכתוב לחטאת: מה חטאת אינה נאכלת אלא לזכרי כהונה – אף איל נזיר נמי אינו נאכל אלא לזכרי כהונה?

Abaye said to Rava: **If so,** then **with regard to a nazirite's ram,** concerning **which it is written** in the verse: **"And he shall present his offering to the Lord, one he-lamb in its first year without blemish for a burnt offering, and one ewe-lamb in its first year without blemish for a sin offering, and one ram without blemish for a peace offering"** (Numbers 6:14), **so too shall we say that the Torah juxtaposed** the nazirite's ram **with a sin offering** of a nazirite to teach that **just as a sin offering is eaten only by male priests, so too, a nazirite's ram is eaten only by male priests?** As the next mishna states, a nazirite's ram may be eaten by every ritually pure Jew.

הכי השתא?! התם, כיון דכתיב: "ולקח הכהן את הזרע בשלה מן האיל" – מכלל דכוליה בעלים אכלי ליה.

Rava answers: **How can** these cases **be compared?**[B] **There,** with regard to the nazirite's ram, **since it is written: "And the priest shall take the foreleg of the ram when it is cooked"** (Numbers 6:19), **by inference** one can deduce **that the owner may eat all of** the remaining portions of the animal.

BACKGROUND

How can these cases be compared – הכי השתא: The Gemara uses this expression to reject a proposed comparison between two cases. How can you compare case A, which has one set of circumstances, with case B, which has a different set of circumstances?

NOTES

From where do we derive that they require slaughter in the north – מנא לן דבעי צפון: This discussion is referring specifically to communal peace offerings. With regard to guilt offerings the Torah states explicitly that they are offerings of the most sacred order, and they must be slaughtered in the same place as the burnt offering and may be eaten only by male priests (see Leviticus 7:1–6).

So too communal peace offerings are offerings of the most sacred order – אף זבחי שלמי צבור קדשי קדשים: Rashi writes that even though the Torah does not state specifically that this refers to communal peace offerings, nevertheless, since it speaks of blowing the trumpets while the offering is being sacrificed, it must be referring to a communal offering, as explained in tractate *Arakhin* (11b). Some question Rashi's explanation because this principle itself is derived from the juxtaposition stated here. Some suggest emending the text here to match the text in *Arakhin* so that it reads: So too peace offerings are offerings of the most sacred order. In other words, the juxtaposition teaches that the peace offerings referred to here are those of the most sacred order, which can be referring only to the communal peace offerings. Individual peace offerings are offerings of lesser sanctity (*Heshek Shlomo*).

זְרוֹעַ בְּשֵׁלָה מִיהָא לָא לִיתְאֲכִיל אֶלָּא לְזִכְרֵי כְהוּנָּה! קַשְׁיָא.

The Gemara asks: If so, **in any event,** the **cooked foreleg** of the nazirite's ram **should be eaten only by male priests.** The mishna states that the cooked foreleg may be eaten by priests, their wives, and their slaves. The Gemara concedes: This is **difficult.** Based on its juxtaposition with the sin offering of a nazirite, the *halakha* should be that only the male priests may eat it, yet that is not the case.

וְאִיבָּעֵית אֵימָא: קׇדָשִׁים אִיקְרִי, קׇדְשֵׁי קֳדָשִׁים לָא אִיקְרוּ. וְאֶלָּא לְמַאי הִלְכְתָא אִיתַּקַּשׁ? אָמַר רָבָא: שֶׁאִם גִּלַּח עַל אֶחָד מִשְּׁלׇשְׁתָּן – יָצָא.

The Gemara offers another explanation: **And if you wish, say** that the foreleg of the nazirite's ram **is called sacred,**[N] **but it is not called an offering of the most sacred order.** Therefore, it cannot be juxtaposed with the sin offering of a nazirite in this regard. The Gemara asks: **But rather, with regard to what *halakha* is** the nazirite's ram **juxtaposed** with the sin offering of a nazirite? **Rava says:** It is juxtaposed to teach **that if** the nazirite **shaved after** the sacrifice of any **one of the three** offerings,[NH] he has **fulfilled** his obligation after the fact.

מתני׳ הַתּוֹדָה וְאֵיל נָזִיר קׇדָשִׁים קַלִּים; שְׁחִיטָתָן בְּכׇל מָקוֹם בָּעֲזָרָה, וְדָמָן טָעוּן שְׁתֵּי מַתָּנוֹת שֶׁהֵן אַרְבַּע, וְנֶאֱכָלִין בְּכׇל הָעִיר, לְכׇל אָדָם, בְּכׇל מַאֲכָל, לְיוֹם וְלַיְלָה עַד חֲצוֹת. הַמּוּרָם מֵהֶם כַּיּוֹצֵא בָּהֶן, אֶלָּא שֶׁהַמּוּרָם נֶאֱכָל לַכֹּהֲנִים, לִנְשֵׁיהֶם וְלִבְנֵיהֶם וּלְעַבְדֵיהֶם.

MISHNA **The thanks offering and nazirite's ram**[NH] **are offerings of lesser sanctity.**[B] **Their slaughter** is **anywhere in the** Temple **courtyard, and their blood requires two placements that are four, and they are eaten throughout the city**[H] of Jerusalem, **by every person,** i.e., any ritually pure Jew, prepared **in any** manner of **food** preparation, **on the day** the offering was sacrificed **and** during the **night** that follows, **until midnight.** The status of the portion **that is separated from them**[H] and given to the priests **is similar to theirs; but** the portion **that is separated is eaten by the priests, by their wives,**[N] **and by their children, and by their slaves.**

גמ׳ תָּנוּ רַבָּנַן: ״אֵת חֲזֵה הַתְּנוּפָה וְאֵת שׁוֹק הַתְּרוּמָה תֹּאכְלוּ בְּמָקוֹם טָהוֹר״, אָמַר רַבִּי נְחֶמְיָה: וְכִי רִאשׁוֹנִים בְּטוּמְאָה אֲכָלוּם?

GEMARA **The Sages taught** in a *baraita*: The verse states with regard to the priests: **"And the breast of waving and the thigh of heaving you shall eat in a pure place;** you, and your sons, and your daughters with you; for they are given as your due, and your sons' due, out of the peace offerings of the children of Israel" (Leviticus 10:14). **Rabbi Neḥemya said: But did they eat** the **first** offerings, mentioned in the previous two verses, **in a place of impurity?**[N] The previous verses make reference to the remainder of the meal offering, which also had to be eaten in a pure place.

NOTES

Is called sacred, etc. – קָדָשִׁים אִיקְרִי וכו׳: Rashi explains that the fact that they are not referred to explicitly as offerings of the most sacred order is not sufficient to teach that they are merely sacred, since they are juxtaposed with sin offerings, which are offerings of the most sacred order. This means that although they are juxtaposed with sin offerings, they are nevertheless called only "sacred" to teach that they do not have the same status as sin offerings.

Any one of the three offerings – אֶחָד מִשְּׁלׇשְׁתָּן: The nazirite would shave even after having brought only his peace offering (see *Nazir* 45a and Rashi here).

Thanks offering and nazirite's ram – תּוֹדָה וְאֵיל נָזִיר: These two offerings are types of peace offerings, as is explicitly stated in the Torah. A priest receives the breast and thigh as a gift, as with all other peace offerings (see Leviticus 7:11–12 and Numbers 6:14, 20). They are different from the other portions of peace offerings in that they may be eaten only for one day and one night, and each has additional gifts to the priests. For a thanks offering, the priests receive one of each type of loaf that is brought with the offering. For a nazirite's ram, the priest also receives the right foreleg of the ram, and one loaf and one wafer of the loaves that are brought with the ram.

By the priests, by their wives, etc. – לַכֹּהֲנִים לִנְשֵׁיהֶם וכו׳: Rashi cites the source for this from the verse: "And the breast of waving and the thigh of heaving you shall eat in a pure place; you, and your sons, and your daughters with you; for they are given as your due, and your sons' due, out of the peace offerings of the children of Israel" (Leviticus 10:14). The source that the wife of a priest and his slaves may also eat these portions is derived from the juxtaposition of these offerings with *teruma*, and therefore like *teruma* they may be eaten by the priest and his entire household. The *Tosefta* states explicitly that anyone who may partake of *teruma* may partake of these offerings (Mahari Kurkus).

But did they eat the first offerings in a place of impurity – וְכִי רִאשׁוֹנִים בְּטוּמְאָה אֲכָלוּם: It is obvious that these were not eaten in an impure place, because it is prohibited for one to render offerings impure. Therefore, the word "pure" must mean that it has a certain degree of purity but is not entirely pure. Rashi understands that the derivation is from the use of the word "pure" as opposed to the term "sacred place," which is written in the previous verse with regard to the remainders of the meal offering. There it indicates that the remainders of the meal offering are eaten in a place that is entirely sacred, i.e., the Temple courtyard.

HALAKHA

That if the nazirite shaved after the sacrifice of any one of the three offerings – שֶׁאִם גִּלַּח עַל אֶחָד מִשְּׁלׇשְׁתָּן: A nazirite first slaughters his sin offering, then his burnt offering, and finally his peace offering. Then, he shaves his hair. If he shaves his hair after he slaughters either the burnt offering or the sin offering he fulfills his obligation (Rambam *Sefer Hafla'a, Hilkhot Nezirut* 8:2).

Thanks offering and nazirite's ram – תּוֹדָה וְאֵיל נָזִיר: The thanks offering and the nazirite's ram are types of peace offerings. Just like other offerings of lesser sanctity they may be slaughtered and their blood collected anywhere in the Temple courtyard. The blood requires two placements that are four (Rambam *Sefer Avoda, Hilkhot Ma'aseh HaKorbanot* 5:2, 6, 9:5).

Eaten throughout the city – נֶאֱכָלִין בְּכׇל הָעִיר: The thanks offering and the nazirite's ram may be eaten anywhere in the Israelite camp, which in later generations meant anywhere in the city of Jerusalem. They may be eaten only on the day they were slaughtered and the following night. The Sages decreed that they must be eaten before midnight (Rambam *Sefer Avoda, Hilkhot Ma'aseh HaKorbanot* 10:5, 7).

That is separated from them – הַמּוּרָם מֵהֶם: The bread that a priest waves from the loaves accompanying a thanks offering, and similarly the breast and thigh, are called that which is elevated from the thanks offering. The cooked leg, along with the breast, thigh, and the bread that a priest waves, are called that which is elevated from the nazirite's ram. These are eaten by male priests or unmarried daughters of priests, the wives of priests, and the slaves of priests, anywhere in the city of Jerusalem, on the day of slaughter and the following night, just like the portion eaten by the owners (Rambam *Sefer Avoda, Hilkhot Ma'aseh HaKorbanot* 9:12, 10:4–5, 7).

BACKGROUND

Offerings of lesser sanctity – קׇדָשִׁים קַלִּים: This category includes individual peace offerings, the thanks offering, the nazirite's ram, the firstborn male of a kosher animal, the animal tithes, and the Paschal offering. These offerings may be slaughtered anywhere in the Temple courtyard. With the exception of the thanks offering, the nazirite's ram, and the Paschal offering, they may be eaten until, but not including, the night following the day after they were sacrificed. They may be eaten by the priests and their wives, children, and slaves, and, with the exception of the offering of a firstborn animal, by the people who bring them and anyone they invite who is ritually pure, and if male, circumcised. There is no need to consume these offerings within the Temple premises, but they must be consumed within the walls of Jerusalem. The prohibition against the misuse of consecrated property with regard to offerings of lesser sanctity applies only to the portions consumed on the altar and only after the blood has been presented on the altar.

אֶלָּא, טָהוֹר מִכְּלָל שֶׁהוּא טָמֵא, טָהוֹר – מְטוּמְאַת מְצוֹרָע, וְטָמֵא – מְטוּמְאַת זָב, וְאֵיזֶה זֶה – זֶה מַחֲנֵה יִשְׂרָאֵל.

Rather, by inference, the word **"pure"** in this context is referring to a place **that is** to some degree **ritually impure,** but pure in some respects. The priest must eat in a place that is **pure due to the impurity of a leper, but** it may be a place that is **impure due to the impurity of a man who experiences a gonorrhea-like discharge [*zav*]. And which place is this? This is the Israelites' camp** in the wilderness, and, once the Temple was built in Jerusalem, the entire city of Jerusalem. A *zav* could remain in these places, but not a leper. This is the source for the *halakha* in the mishna that these offerings may be eaten anywhere in Jerusalem.

וְאֵימָא: טָהוֹר – מְטוּמְאַת זָב, וְטָמֵא – מְטוּמְאַת מֵת, וְאֵיזֶה זֶה – זֶה מַחֲנֵה לְוִיָּה!

The Gemara asks: **But** why not **say** that the word "pure" is referring to a place which is **pure from the impurity of a *zav* and impure due to ritual impurity** imparted **by a corpse? And which** place **is this? This is the Levites' camp** in the wilderness, and, once the Temple was built in Jerusalem, the Temple Mount.

אָמַר אַבַּיֵי: אָמַר קְרָא "וַאֲכַלְתֶּם אֹתָהּ בְּמָקוֹם קָדוֹשׁ" – אוֹתָהּ בְּמָקוֹם קָדוֹשׁ, וְלֹא אַחֶרֶת בְּמָקוֹם קָדוֹשׁ, אַפְּקַהּ לְמַחֲנֵה לְוִיָּה; הֲדַר כְּתִיב: "בְּמָקוֹם טָהוֹר" – אַפְּקַהּ לְמַחֲנֵה יִשְׂרָאֵל.

Abaye says that **the verse states** with regard to the meal offering: **"And you shall eat it in a sacred place"** (Leviticus 10:13). The word "it" is a restriction, teaching that one must eat **"it,"** i.e., the meal offering, **in a sacred place,** i.e., in the camp of the Divine Presence, **but** one is **not** required to eat **another** offering, i.e., the breast of waving and the thigh of heaving, **in a sacred place.** This **removes** the portions from the camp of the Divine Presence, **to** be eaten in **the Levites' camp. Then it is written:** "You shall eat **in a pure place,"** which **removes** the portions from the Levites' camp, **to** be eaten in **the Israelites' camp.**

רָבָא אָמַר: אוֹתָהּ בְּמָקוֹם קָדוֹשׁ וְלֹא אַחֶרֶת בְּמָקוֹם קָדוֹשׁ – אַפְּקַהּ לְגַמְרֵי; הֲדַר כְּתַב רַחֲמָנָא: "תֹּאכְלוּ בְּמָקוֹם טָהוֹר" – עַיְּילָא לְמַחֲנֵה יִשְׂרָאֵל.

Rava says a different explanation: **"It,"** i.e., the meal offering, must be eaten **in a sacred place, but** one is **not** required to eat **another** offering, i.e., the breast of waving and the thigh of heaving, **in a sacred place.** This verse **removes** the portions **completely** from any pure place, and according to this stage of Rava's interpretation, these portions may be eaten anywhere. **Then the Merciful One wrote: "You shall eat in a pure place,"** which **brings it into the Israelites' camp,** which is a pure place, relative to everywhere outside it.

וְאֵימָא: עַיְּילָא לְמַחֲנֵה לְוִיָּה! לַחֲדָא מְעַיְּילִינַן, לְתַרְתֵּי לָא מְעַיְּילִינַן.

The Gemara asks: **But** why not **say** that the verse **brings it into the Levites' camp,** which is also referred to as pure? The Gemara answers: **We bring it into one** camp, adjacent to the area outside the encampment of the Jewish people, but **we do not bring it into two** camps.

אִי הָכִי, אַפּוֹקֵי נַמִי, לַחֲדָא מַפְּקִינַן, מִתַּרְתֵּי לָא מַפְּקִינַן! וְעוֹד, "לֹא תוּכַל לֶאֱכוֹל בִּשְׁעָרֶיךָ" כְּתִיב! אֶלָּא, מְחַוַּורְתָּא כְּדְאַבַּיֵי.

The Gemara asks: **If so, also** with regard to **removing it,** why not say that **we remove it to one** place, but **we do not remove it from two** places? Accordingly, the initial derivation should be to eat it in the Israelites' camp. **And furthermore, it is written: "You may not eat within your gates** the tithe of your grain, or of your wine, or of your oil, or the firstborn of your herd or of your flock, nor any of your vows which you vow, nor your gift offerings, nor the offering of your hand" (Deuteronomy 12:17). This verse negates the possibility that an offering may be eaten "in your gates," i.e., outside of Jerusalem. **Rather, it is clear** that the source for the ruling of the *baraita* is **in accordance with** the explanation **of Abaye.**

מתני׳ שְׁלָמִים קָדָשִׁים קַלִּים; שְׁחִיטָתָן בְּכָל מָקוֹם בַּעֲזָרָה, וְדָמָן טָעוּן שְׁתֵּי מַתָּנוֹת שֶׁהֵן אַרְבַּע, וְנֶאֱכָלִין בְּכָל הָעִיר, לְכָל אָדָם, בְּכָל מַאֲכָל, לִשְׁנֵי יָמִים וְלַיְלָה אֶחָד. הַמּוּרָם מֵהֶם כַּיּוֹצֵא בָּהֶם, אֶלָּא שֶׁהַמּוּרָם נֶאֱכָל לַכֹּהֲנִים, לִנְשֵׁיהֶם וְלִבְנֵיהֶם וּלְעַבְדֵיהֶם.

MISHNA **Peace offerings**[H] are **offerings of lesser sanctity. Their slaughter is anywhere in** the Temple **courtyard,**[N] **and their blood requires two placements that are four, and they are eaten throughout the city** of Jerusalem, **by every person,** i.e., any ritually pure Jew, prepared **in any** manner of **food** preparation, **for two days and one night,** i.e., the day on which they are slaughtered, the following day, and the intervening night. The status of the portion **that is separated from them** and given to the priests **is similar to theirs; but the** portion **that is separated is eaten by the priests, by their wives, and by their children, and by their slaves.**

HALAKHA

Peace offerings – שְׁלָמִים: Peace offerings may be slaughtered anywhere in the Temple courtyard. Their blood must be sprinkled on the two diagonally opposite corners of the altar. They may be eaten anywhere in the city of Jerusalem on the day they were slaughtered, the following night, and the next day until sunset. This time restriction applies both to the parts eaten by the owner of the offering, and the parts eaten by the priests, i.e., the breast and the thigh. The priests' portion may be eaten by male priests or unmarried daughters of priests, the wives of priests, and their slaves (Rambam *Sefer Avoda*, *Hilkhot Ma'aseh HaKorbanot* 5:4, 6, 10:4–6).

NOTES

Their slaughter is anywhere in the Temple courtyard, etc. – שְׁחִיטָתָן בְּכָל מָקוֹם בַּעֲזָרָה וכו׳: The Torah does not require that they be slaughtered in the north of the courtyard in the place of the burnt offering. Their blood requires two placements on two diagonal corners of the altar, like a burnt offering, since the Torah uses the term "around" (see 53b). They may be eaten anywhere in the city of Jerusalem, as the Gemara derives with regard to the thanks offering. They may be eaten for two days and one night, as the Torah states explicitly: "But if the sacrifice of his offering be a vow, or a gift offering, it shall be eaten on the day that he offers his sacrifice; and on the morrow that which remains of it may be eaten" (Leviticus 7:16).

גמ׳ תָּנוּ רַבָּנַן: ״וּשְׁחָטוֹ פֶּתַח אֹהֶל מוֹעֵד״, ״וְשָׁחַט אֹתוֹ לִפְנֵי אֹהֶל מוֹעֵד״, ״וְשָׁחַט אוֹתוֹ לִפְנֵי אֹהֶל מוֹעֵד״.

GEMARA **The Sages taught** in a *baraita*: With regard to cattle peace offerings, the verse states: "And he shall lay his hand upon the head of his offering, **and slaughter it at the entrance of the Tent of Meeting**" (Leviticus 3:2). With regard to sheep peace offerings the verse states: "And he shall lay his hand upon the head of his offering, **and slaughter it before the Tent of Meeting**" (Leviticus 3:8). With regard to goat peace offerings the verse states: "And he shall lay his hand upon the head of it, **and slaughter it before the Tent of Meeting**" (Leviticus 3:13).

לְהַכְשִׁיר אֶת כָּל הָרוּחוֹת בְּקָדָשִׁים קַלִּים. קַל וָחוֹמֶר לַצָּפוֹן: וּמָה קָדְשֵׁי קָדָשִׁים שֶׁלֹּא הוּכְשְׁרוּ בְּכָל הָרוּחוֹת – הוּכְשְׁרוּ בַּצָּפוֹן, קָדָשִׁים קַלִּים שֶׁהוּכְשְׁרוּ בְּכָל הָרוּחוֹת – אֵינוֹ דִּין שֶׁהוּכְשְׁרוּ בַּצָּפוֹן?

This repetition serves **to render fit all directions** of the Temple courtyard **for** the slaughter of **offerings of lesser sanctity.** From here one can derive **an *a fortiori*** inference **to** permit slaughter in **the north** of the Temple courtyard: **Just as** the rites of slaughtering **offerings of the most sacred order, which are not rendered fit in all directions, are rendered fit in the north,** with regard to the rites of slaughtering **offerings of lesser sanctity, which are rendered fit in all directions, is it not logical that they are rendered fit in the north?**

רַבִּי אֱלִיעֶזֶר אוֹמֵר: לֹא נֶאֱמַר הַכָּתוּב אֶלָּא לְהַכְשִׁיר צָפוֹן. שֶׁיָּכוֹל, וַהֲלֹא דִּין הוּא: וּמָה קָדָשִׁים קַלִּים שֶׁהוּכְשְׁרוּ בְּכָל הָרוּחוֹת – לֹא הוּכְשַׁר מְקוֹמָן אֵצֶל קָדְשֵׁי קָדָשִׁים, קָדְשֵׁי קָדָשִׁים שֶׁלֹּא הוּכְשְׁרוּ אֶלָּא בַּצָּפוֹן – אֵינוֹ דִּין שֶׁלֹּא הוּכְשַׁר מְקוֹמָן אֵצֶל קָדָשִׁים קַלִּים? תַּלְמוּד לוֹמַר: ״אֹהֶל מוֹעֵד״.

Rabbi Eliezer says: The repetition of **the verse is stated only to render fit** slaughter in the **north. As** one **might** have thought: **And could this not** be derived through **logical inference? Just as** with regard to **offerings of lesser sanctity, whose** slaughter is **rendered fit in any direction,** nevertheless **their place is not rendered fit for** the slaughter of **offerings of the most sacred order,** with regard to **offerings of the most sacred order, whose** slaughter is **rendered fit only in the north, is it not logical that their place should not be rendered fit for** the slaughter of **offerings of lesser sanctity?** Therefore, **the verse states: "Tent of Meeting,"** to teach that offerings of lesser sanctity may be slaughtered in the north.

Perek **V**
Daf **55** Amud **b**

בְּמַאי קָא מִיפַּלְגִי? תַּנָּא קַמָּא סָבַר: תְּלָתָא קְרָאֵי כְּתִיבִי, חַד – לְגוּפֵיהּ, דְּנִיבְעֵי פֶּתַח אֹהֶל מוֹעֵד, וְחַד – לְהַכְשִׁיר צְדָדִין, וְחַד – לִפְסוֹל צִידֵּי צְדָדִין; וְצָפוֹן לָא אִיצְטְרִיךְ קְרָא.

The Gemara clarifies: **With regard to what do they disagree? The first *tanna* holds** that **three verses are written. One** verse serves to teach the *halakha* **itself, that we require** that the slaughter take place at the **entrance of the Tent of Meeting.**[N] **And one** verse serves **to render fit** slaughter at the **sides,** i.e., the entire length of the Temple courtyard eastward from the entrance, and not only that part which is directly in front of the entrance. **And one** verse serves **to disqualify the sides of the sides,**[N] i.e., those parts of the courtyard that are not in front of the entrance at all. **And it was not necessary** to have **a verse** teach the fitness of slaughtering in the **north,** as it can be derived via an *a fortiori* inference.

וְרַבִּי אֱלִיעֶזֶר סָבַר: חַד – לְגוּפֵיהּ, דְּנִיבְעֵי פֶּתַח אֹהֶל מוֹעֵד, וְחַד – לְהַכְשִׁיר צָפוֹן, וְחַד – לְהַכְשִׁיר צְדָדִין; וְצִידֵּי צְדָדִין לָא אִיצְטְרִיךְ קְרָא.

And Rabbi Eliezer holds that **one** verse is necessary **to** teach the *halakha* **itself, that we require** slaughter at the **entrance of the Tent of Meeting. And one** verse serves **to render fit** slaughter in the **north** of the courtyard. **And one** verse serves **to render fit** slaughter at the **sides** of the courtyard. **But** according to him, **it was not necessary** to have **a verse** teach that the **sides of the sides** are not fit for the slaughter of the offering.

NOTES

That we require slaughter at the entrance of the Tent of Meeting – דְּנִיבְעֵי פֶּתַח אֹהֶל מוֹעֵד: The Gemara subsequently explains that if the entrance to the Sanctuary is not open, one may not slaughter peace offerings (Rashi). The Ra'avad suggests that the intent is merely that the offering must be slaughtered in the Temple courtyard.

To disqualify the sides of the sides – לִפְסוֹל צִידֵּי צְדָדִין: Rashi explains that this refers to the chambers which were in the Temple courtyard, as explained in the Gemara (56a). Although they are built in the sacred area and open into the sacred area, they are still not considered part of the Temple courtyard itself. *Tosafot*, cited in the *Shita Mekubbetzet*, write that even according to this opinion there is no need to exclude the chambers, because they are not part of the courtyard. Rather, the term: Sides of the sides, should be understood as it is explained, i.e., as referring to any part of the courtyard that is not to the east of the entrance of the Sanctuary, but rather to the west.

מַאי שְׁנָא הָכָא דִּכְתִיב: "פֶּתַח אֹהֶל מוֹעֵד", וּמַאי שְׁנָא הָתָם דִּכְתִיב: "לִפְנֵי אֹהֶל מוֹעֵד"? קָא מַשְׁמַע לָן כִּדְרַב יְהוּדָה אָמַר שְׁמוּאֵל. דְּאָמַר רַב יְהוּדָה אָמַר שְׁמוּאֵל: שְׁלָמִים שֶׁשְּׁחָטָן קוֹדֶם שֶׁיִּפָּתְחוּ דַּלְתוֹת הַהֵיכָל – פְּסוּלִין, שֶׁנֶּאֱמַר: "וּשְׁחָטוֹ פֶּתַח אֹהֶל מוֹעֵד" – בִּזְמַן שֶׁהוּא פָּתוּחַ, וְלֹא בִּזְמַן שֶׁהוּא נָעוּל.

§ The Gemara asks: **What is different here that it is written: "At the entrance to the Tent of Meeting"** (Leviticus 3:2), **and what is different there that it is written: "Before the Tent of Meeting"** (Leviticus 3:8, 13)? The Gemara answers: This **teaches us** a matter **in accordance with that** which **Rav Yehuda** says that **Shmuel says. As Rav Yehuda says** that **Shmuel says: Peace offerings that one slaughtered** in the Temple **before the doors of the Sanctuary were opened**[H] **are disqualified, as it is stated** with regard to peace offerings: **"And he shall slaughter it at the entrance to the Tent of Meeting"** (Leviticus 3:2), which teaches that it must be slaughtered **when** the entrance **is open** and serves as an actual entrance, **and not when it is locked.** As long as the entrance to the Tent of Meeting, or in the Temple the doors to the Sanctuary, remain closed, one may not sacrifice the peace offerings, and if they are sacrificed, they are disqualified.

אִיתְּמַר נַמִי, אָמַר מָר עוּקְבָא בַּר חָמָא אָמַר רַבִּי יוֹסֵי בְּרַבִּי חֲנִינָא: שְׁלָמִים שֶׁשְּׁחָטָן קוֹדֶם שֶׁיִּפָּתְחוּ דַּלְתוֹת הַהֵיכָל – פְּסוּלִין, שֶׁנֶּאֱמַר: "וּשְׁחָטוֹ פֶּתַח אֹהֶל מוֹעֵד" – בִּזְמַן שֶׁפֶּתַח הַהֵיכָל פָּתוּחַ, וְלֹא בִּזְמַן שֶׁהוּא נָעוּל.

It was also stated: Mar Ukva bar Ḥama says that **Rabbi Yosei, son of Rabbi Ḥanina, says: Peace offerings that one slaughtered before the doors of the Sanctuary were opened are disqualified, as it is stated** in the verse: **"He shall slaughter it at the entrance to the Tent of Meeting"** (Leviticus 3:2). This means **when the entrance of the Sanctuary is open, and not when it is locked.**

בְּמַעֲרָבָא מַתְנֵי הָכִי, אָמַר רַב יַעֲקֹב בַּר אַחָא אָמַר רַב אַשִׁי: שְׁלָמִים שֶׁשְּׁחָטָן קוֹדֶם שֶׁיִּפָּתְחוּ דַּלְתוֹת הַהֵיכָל – פְּסוּלִים. וּבַמִּשְׁכָּן – קוֹדֶם שֶׁיַּעֲמִידוּ לְוִיִּם אֶת הַמִּשְׁכָּן, וּלְאַחַר שֶׁיְּפָרְקוּ לְוִיִּם אֶת הַמִּשְׁכָּן – פְּסוּלִים.

In the West,[B] Eretz Yisrael, **they teach** this *halakha* **like this: Rav Ya'akov bar Aḥa says** that **Rav Ashi says: Peace offerings that one slaughtered before the doors of the Sanctuary were opened are disqualified. And in the Tabernacle,** which had no doors, peace offerings that were slaughtered **before the Levites erected the Tabernacle or after** the **Levites dismantled the Tabernacle are disqualified.**

פְּשִׁיטָא: מוּגָּף – כְּנָעוּל דָּמֵי, וִילוֹן מַאי? אָמַר רַבִּי זֵירָא: הוּא עַצְמוֹ אֵין נַעֲשֶׂה אֶלָּא כְּפֶתַח פָּתוּחַ.

The Gemara comments: It is **obvious** that if the door is **closed** but not locked it has the same status **as if it were locked.**[H] The Gemara asks: If there is **a curtain** covering the entrance, **what is** the *halakha*? **Rabbi Zeira says:** A curtain **itself is made only** to be used **like an open entrance,**[N] and therefore it is not considered as if the entrance is closed.

גּוֹבְהָה מַאי? תָּא שְׁמַע, דְּתַנְיָא, רַבִּי יוֹסֵי בְּרַבִּי יְהוּדָה אוֹמֵר: שְׁנֵי פִשְׁפָּשִׁין הָיוּ בְּבֵית הַחֲלִיפוֹת וְגוֹבְהָן שְׁמֹנֶה, כְּדֵי לְהַכְשִׁיר אֶת הָעֲזָרָה כּוּלָּהּ לַאֲכִילַת קָדְשֵׁי קָדָשִׁים, וְלִשְׁחִיטַת קֳדָשִׁים קַלִּים;

The Gemara asks: **What** is the *halakha* if **a tall** item is blocking the entrance? The Gemara suggests: **Come and hear** a proof that a tall item does not render an entrance as closed, **as it is taught** in a *baraita*: **Rabbi Yosei, son of Rabbi Yehuda, says: There were two wickets,** i.e., openings, **in the Chamber of Knives,**[NB] **and their height** was **eight** cubits. The function of these openings was **in order to render fit the entire** Temple **courtyard for the eating of offerings of the most sacred order, and** to render fit all of the Temple courtyard **for the slaughter of offerings of lesser sanctity.** Due to the openings, the western area of the courtyard was considered to be "before the Tent of Meeting."

HALAKHA

Peace offerings that one slaughtered in the Temple before the doors of the Sanctuary were opened – שְׁלָמִים שֶׁשְּׁחָטָן קוֹדֶם שֶׁיִּפָּתְחוּ דַּלְתוֹת הַהֵיכָל: Peace offerings that were slaughtered before the doors of the Temple courtyard were opened are disqualified. This is in accordance with the statement of Rav Yehuda, citing Shmuel (Rambam *Sefer Avoda, Hilkhot Ma'aseh HaKorbanot* 5:5).

Closed as if it were locked – מוּגָּף כְּנָעוּל דָּמֵי: If the doors of the Temple courtyard were closed but not locked, it is nevertheless considered as if they are locked. A curtain over the door does not disqualify the offering (Rambam *Sefer Avoda, Hilkhot Ma'aseh HaKorbanot* 5:5).

NOTES

It is made only like an open entrance – אֵין נַעֲשֶׂה אֶלָּא כְּפֶתַח פָּתוּחַ: In other words, a curtain is only for purposes of modesty, yet the entrance remains open (Rashi).

The Chamber of Knives – בֵּית הַחֲלִיפוֹת: The Entrance Hall of the Sanctuary was fifteen cubits wider than the Sanctuary to the north and the south. This was known as the Chamber of Knives because the knives for slaughtering were stored there. Each priestly watch had its own compartment in which it stored its knives (see *Middot* 37a). According to Rashi, the *Tosefta* explains that the two wickets were on the western side, i.e., the back of these two wings, one to the northwest and one to the southwest. In this way the entire Temple courtyard was considered to be "before the Tent of Meeting," i.e., in front of one of the entrances. The entire courtyard was therefore fit for the slaughter of offerings of lesser sanctity, and for the eating of offerings of the most sacred order.

BACKGROUND

The West – מַעֲרָבָא: In the Babylonian Talmud, Eretz Yisrael is referred to as the West, since it is southwest of Babylonia. In later periods, the customs in Eretz Yisrael were referred to as western customs, as opposed to the eastern customs of Babylonia.

The Chamber of Knives – בֵּית הַחֲלִיפוֹת: Initially the Gemara assumes that the wickets were in the western wall of the Chamber of Knives; see the two places where the number 1 appears in the image. The conclusion of the Gemara is that they were in the corners; see number 2.

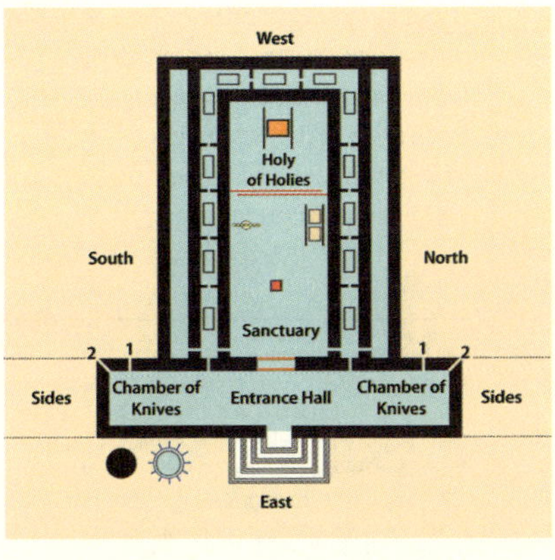

Wickets in the Chamber of Knives

מַאי לָאו דְּאִיכָּא קַמַּיְיהוּ שְׁמוֹנֶה? לָא, דְּגָבְהוּ נִינְהוּ שְׁמוֹנֶה.

The Gemara explains the inference: **What, is** the reference to eight cubits **not** referring to the fact **that in front of** the wickets there was an obstruction **eight** cubits high? Nevertheless, the area outside of it is considered open to the Chamber of Knives. The Gemara answers: **No, their height** was **eight** cubits, i.e., the wickets themselves were eight cubits high.

מֵיתִיבֵי: כׇּל הַשְּׁעָרִים שֶׁהָיוּ שָׁם, גּוֹבְהָן עֶשְׂרִים אַמָּה וְרוֹחְבָּן עֶשֶׂר אַמָּה! פִּשְׁפָּשִׁין שָׁאנֵי.

The Gemara **raises an objection** to this explanation from a mishna (*Middot* 35a), which teaches: **All the gates**[H] **that were there,** in the Temple, were **twenty cubits high and ten cubits wide.** If so, how could these wickets be only eight cubits high? The Gemara answers: The **wickets are different,** and they are not considered gates.

וְהָאִיכָּא צְדָדִין! דִּמְעַיֵּיל לְהוּ בְּקֶרֶן זָוִית.

The Gemara questions the ruling of the *baraita*. How did the wickets render fit the entire Temple courtyard? **But there are the sides,** i.e., to the north and south of the Chamber of Knives, and the wickets faced only to the west. The Gemara answers **that they inserted** the wickets **in the corner**[N] of the Chamber, so that one opened to the northwest, and one to the northeast.

אֲחוֹרֵי בֵּית הַכַּפּוֹרֶת מַאי? תָּא שְׁמַע, דְּאָמַר רָמִי בַּר רַב יְהוּדָה אָמַר רַב: לוּל קָטָן הָיָה אֲחוֹרֵי בֵּית הַכַּפּוֹרֶת גָּבוֹהַּ שְׁמוֹנֶה אַמּוֹת, כְּדֵי לְהַכְשִׁיר אֶת הָעֲזָרָה לַאֲכִילַת קׇדְשֵׁי קֳדָשִׁים וְלִשְׁחִיטַת קֳדָשִׁים קַלִּים. וְהַיְינוּ דִּכְתִיב: ״שְׁנַיִם לַפַּרְבָּר״. מַאי ״לַפַּרְבָּר״? אָמַר רַבָּה בַּר רַב שֵׁילָא: כְּמַאן דְּאָמַר: ״כְּלַפֵּי בַּר״.

The Gemara asks: **What** is the *halakha* with regard to the area **behind the Hall of the Ark Cover,**[H] i.e., behind the Sanctuary, from where one could not see the entrance of the Temple courtyard or the two wickets? The Gemara answers: **Come** and **hear, as Rami bar Rav Yehuda says** that **Rav says: There was a small niche behind the Hall of the Ark Cover,** which was **eight cubits high.** The function of this niche was **in order to render fit the entire** Temple **courtyard for the eating of offerings of the most sacred order, and** to render fit all of the Temple courtyard **for the slaughter of offerings of lesser sanctity. And this is as it is written:** "For the precinct westward, four at the causeway, and **two at the precinct**" (1 Chronicles 26:18). **What** is the meaning of the term: **"For the precinct [*laparbar*]"? Rabba bar Rav Sheila said:** It is **like one who says: Facing outward [*kelappei bar*].**

אָמַר רַב יְהוּדָה אָמַר שְׁמוּאֵל: אֵין חַיָּיבִין מִשּׁוּם טוּמְאָה אֶלָּא עַל

§ **Rav Yehuda says** that **Shmuel says:** One is **liable for** entering the Temple courtyard in a state of **ritual impurity only**[B] **with regard to**

HALAKHA

All the gates – כׇּל הַשְּׁעָרִים: All the gates of the Temple courtyard were twenty cubits high and ten cubits wide (Rambam *Sefer Avoda, Hilkhot Beit HaBeḥira* 5:5).

Behind the Hall of the Ark Cover – אֲחוֹרֵי בֵּית הַכַּפּוֹרֶת: From where is it derived that offerings of lesser sanctity may be slaughtered even behind the Sanctuary? The verse states with regard to peace offerings: "And he shall lay his hand upon the head of his offering, and slaughter it at the entrance of the Tent of Meeting" (Leviticus 3:2). This teaches that it may be slaughtered in any direction, as the verse did not specify a direction. The *halakha* is the same concerning all other offerings of lesser sanctity, in accordance with the conclusion of the discussion of the Gemara here (Rambam *Sefer Avoda, Hilkhot Ma'aseh HaKorbanot* 5:4, and see *Kesef Mishne* and Radbaz there).

NOTES

That they inserted the wickets in the corner – דִּמְעַיֵּיל לְהוּ בְּקֶרֶן זָוִית: Some explain that this means that they would slaughter the offerings in the corner so that they could see the opening of the wickets. In the version of the Gemara text as presented by Rashi and the *Shita Mekubbetzet*, both commentaries understand that this means that the wickets themselves were in the corners so that they also opened to the sides.

BACKGROUND

One is liable for impurity only – אֵין חַיָּיבִין מִשּׁוּם טוּמְאָה אֶלָּא: The Torah renders it prohibited for one who is ritually impure to eat consecrated food (see Leviticus 7:19–20), and to enter the Temple (see Numbers 19:20). If one intentionally transgresses either of these prohibitions, he is liable to receive *karet*. If he transgresses these prohibitions unwittingly, he must bring an offering as atonement. This offering is brought on a sliding scale, depending on the financial state of the one bringing it. There is a unique aspect to the unwitting transgression of these mitzvot: For one to be obligated to bring an offering he must have been aware both of his personal status and of the sanctity of the Temple or of the consecrated foods involved from the outset, prior to transgressing. He must then have forgotten one of the factors while transgressing, and must remember it afterward. If he was unaware of both factors before transgressing, even if he became aware of them afterward, he does not bring an offering.

Perek **V**
Daf **56** Amud **a**

אוֹרֶךְ מֵאָה וּשְׁמוֹנִים וְשֶׁבַע עַל רוֹחַב מֵאָה וּשְׁלֹשִׁים וְחָמֵשׁ.

an area whose **length** is 187 cubits **by** 135 cubits in **width.**

תָּנֵי תַּנָּא קַמֵּיהּ דְּרַב נַחְמָן: כׇּל הָעֲזָרָה הָיְתָה מֵאָה שְׁמוֹנִים וְשֶׁבַע עַל רוֹחַב מֵאָה שְׁלֹשִׁים וְחָמֵשׁ. אֲמַר לֵיהּ: הָכִי אֲמַר לִי אַבָּא: כְּגוֹן זֶה, כֹּהֲנִים נִכְנָסִין לְשָׁם וְאוֹכְלִין שָׁם קׇדְשֵׁי קֳדָשִׁים, וְשׁוֹחֲטִין שָׁם קֳדָשִׁים קַלִּים, וְחַיָּיבִין מִשּׁוּם טוּמְאָה.

A *tanna* **taught** a *baraita* **before Rav Naḥman: The entire** Temple **courtyard**[H] **was** 187 cubits in length **by** 135 cubits in **width.** Rav Naḥman **said to the** *tanna*: **My father**[P] **said this to me:** In an area **such as this,** the **priests enter there and eat offerings of the most sacred order there, and slaughter offerings of lesser sanctity there, and are liable due to** entering in a state of **ritual impurity.**

HALAKHA

The entire Temple courtyard, etc. – כׇּל הָעֲזָרָה וכו׳: The total length of the Temple courtyard was 187 cubits, and the width was 135 cubits (Rambam *Sefer Avoda, Hilkhot Beit HaBeḥira* 5:4).

PERSONALITIES

The father of Rav Naḥman – אָבִיו שֶׁל רַב נַחְמָן: Rav Naḥman's father was named Ya'akov, and the Jerusalem Talmud always refers to Rav Naḥman as Rav Naḥman bar Ya'akov. The Babylonian Talmud simply calls him Rav Naḥman (see *Ketubot* 104b). The Talmud (*Bava Metzia* 16b) relates that Rav Naḥman's father was a scribe in the court of Shmuel, and he would often take Rav Naḥman with him when he was a child. It appears that Rav Naḥman's father taught him most of the Torah that he learned as a child, and Rav Naḥman would cite his father as an authority (see *Beitza* 24b). Although there are no explicit statements in the Talmud from Rav Naḥman's father, it appears from this story and others that he was one of the leading Sages of his generation. He would teach his son not only Mishna but also other Torah subjects.

לְמַעוּטֵי מַאי? אִילֵימָא לְמַעוּטֵי חַלּוֹנוֹת דְּלָתוֹת וְעוֹבִי הַחוֹמָה – תְּנֵינָא: הַחַלּוֹנוֹת וְעוֹבִי הַחוֹמָה כְּלִפְנִים!

The Gemara asks: These specific dimensions serve **to exclude what? If we say** they are stated **to exclude** the **windows, doors, and thickness of the wall, we learn** the opposite in a mishna (*Pesaḥim* 85b): **The windows** in the wall **and the thickness of the wall**[N] are considered **as though** they are **inside**[H] the Temple courtyard.

וְאֶלָּא לְמַעוּטֵי לְשָׁכוֹת; וְאִי בְּנוּיוֹת בַּחוֹל וּפְתוּחוֹת לַקֹּדֶשׁ – וְהָתְנַן: תּוֹכָן קוֹדֶשׁ! מִדְּרַבָּנַן.

But rather, they are stated **to exclude** the **chambers**[N] in the Temple courtyard. The Gemara asks: **And if** it is referring to chambers that are **built in the non-sacred** area, which is outside this designated space, **and open to the sacred** area, **but didn't we learn** in a mishna (*Ma'aser Sheni* 3:8): The inside of chambers that are built in the sacred area but are open to the non-sacred area is non-sacred, but their roofs are sacred. If they are built in a non-sacred area and open to a sacred area, **their interior is sacred**[H] and their roofs are non-sacred? The Gemara answers: They have sanctity **by rabbinic law.**[N]

וּדְאוֹרָיְיתָא לָא? וְהָתַנְיָא: לְשָׁכוֹת בְּנוּיוֹת בַּחוֹל וּפְתוּחוֹת לַקֹּדֶשׁ, מִנַּיִן שֶׁהַכֹּהֲנִים נִכְנָסִין לְשָׁם וְאוֹכְלִים שָׁם קׇדְשֵׁי קֳדָשִׁים וּשְׁיָרֵי מְנָחָה – תַּלְמוּד לוֹמַר: ״בַּחֲצַר אֹהֶל מוֹעֵד יֹאכְלוּהָ״, הַתּוֹרָה רִיבְּתָה חֲצֵירוֹת הַרְבֵּה אֵצֶל אֲכִילָה אַחַת!

The Gemara asks: **And do** they **not** have sanctity **by Torah law? But isn't it taught** in a *baraita*: With regard to the **chambers** that are **built in the non-sacred** area of the Temple Mount **and open to the sacred** area, **from where** is it derived **that the priests enter there and eat there offerings of the most sacred order and the remainders of meal offerings? The verse states** with regard to a meal offering: "It shall be eaten without leaven in a holy place; **in the courtyard of the Tent of Meeting they shall eat it."** (Leviticus 6:9). The verse could have simply stated: "In a holy place," which indicates the courtyard. By also stating: "In the courtyard of the Tent of Meeting," **the Torah amplified many courtyards with one** type of **eating,** i.e., of the meal offering. If the chambers do not have sanctity by Torah law, the Sages would not have permitted the priests to eat offerings of the most sacred order there.

אֲמַר רָבָא: לַאֲכִילָה שָׁאנֵי.

Rava said: The *halakha* **concerning eating is different.** The Torah specifically includes these chambers in addition to the Temple courtyard itself for eating offerings of the most sacred order. By contrast, with regard to slaughtering offerings of lesser sanctity and the punishment for entering the courtyard in a state of ritual impurity, these chambers are not considered sacred by Torah law.

אֲבָל לְעִנְיַן טוּמְאָה לָא? וְהָתַנְיָא: לְשָׁכוֹת הַבְּנוּיוֹת לַחוֹל וּפְתוּחוֹת לַקּוֹדֶשׁ – כֹּהֲנִים נִכְנָסִין לְשָׁם וְאוֹכְלִין שָׁם קׇדְשֵׁי קֳדָשִׁים, וְאֵין שׁוֹחֲטִין שָׁם קֳדָשִׁים קַלִּים, וְחַיָּיבִין מִשּׁוּם טוּמְאָה!

The Gemara asks: **But with regard to ritual impurity,** is one **not** liable to receive *karet* for entering these chambers? **But isn't it taught** in a *baraita*: With regard to the **chambers that are built in the non-sacred** area **and** that **open to the sacred** area, **priests enter there and eat offerings of the most sacred order there, but may not slaughter offerings of lesser sanctity there, and are liable** to receive *karet* **due to ritual impurity** if they enter there while ritually impure?

לָאו אָמְרַתְּ: אֵין שׁוֹחֲטִין? תְּנֵי נַמִי: אֵין חַיָּיבִין.

Rava could answer: **Did you not say** in the *baraita* that **they may not slaughter** offerings of lesser sanctity in those chambers? If so, emend the text of the *baraita* and **teach also: They are not liable** to receive *karet* for entering in a state of ritual impurity.

בִּשְׁלָמָא אֵין שׁוֹחֲטִין – בָּעֵינָא נֶגֶד הַפֶּתַח, וְלֵיכָּא. אֶלָּא אֵין חַיָּיבִין אַמַּאי?

The Gemara challenges: **Granted,** the priests **may not slaughter** there, because slaughtering an offering **requires** that it be performed **before the entrance** of the Temple courtyard, **and** if he slaughters it inside a chamber, it **is not. But why** would they **not** be **liable** for entering there in a state of ritual impurity?

NOTES

The windows and the thickness of the wall – הַחַלּוֹנוֹת וְעוֹבִי הַחוֹמָה: This refers to the thickness of the opening of the window space, and similarly the thickness of the wall above (Rashi).

Chambers – לְשָׁכוֹת: There were many chambers in the Temple with many different uses. Among them were six chambers on the sides of the Sanctuary described in the mishna in tractate *Middot* (37b). The principle is that the status of the chamber is based on the location of its entrance. If it opens into the sacred part of the Temple, the chamber is sacred. If it opens into a non-sacred part, the chamber is not sacred. If it has two openings, one to a sacred part and one to a non-sacred part, the part of the chamber that is built within the boundary of the sacred area is sacred, and the part which is outside has the status of the rest of the Temple Mount.

By rabbinic law – מִדְּרַבָּנַן: Rashi explains that this sanctity is with regard to ritual impurity. Although the Sages prohibited one from entering there in a state of ritual impurity so as to prevent one from entering from there into the Temple courtyard, nevertheless, they were not sanctified with the sanctity of the Temple Mount such that one would be liable to receive *karet* for entering there while impure. The Torah prohibits slaughtering offerings of lesser sanctity there, as explained in the Gemara.

HALAKHA

The windows and the thickness of the wall are as though they are inside – הַחַלּוֹנוֹת וְעוֹבִי הַחוֹמָה כְּלִפְנִים: The windows and width of the walls are considered as if they are inside the Temple courtyard both with regard to eating offerings of the most sacred order and with regard to ritual impurity. The Ra'avad points out, based on the discussion in *Pesaḥim* (86a), that this is the *halakha* only when they are level with the ground of the courtyard. Some write that the Rambam agrees with this (Rambam *Sefer Avoda*, *Ma'aseh HaKorbanot* 10:5 and *Hilkhot Beit HaBeḥira* 6:9, and see *Kesef Mishne* and Mahari Kurkus there).

Their interior is sacred, etc. – תּוֹכָן קוֹדֶשׁ וכו׳: The chambers that were built in the non-sacred part of the Temple Mount but that opened into the sacred part are considered to be sacred with regard to eating offerings of the most sacred order. Despite this, one may not slaughter offerings of lesser sanctity there. One who enters there in a state of ritual impurity is exempt. This is in accordance with the opinion expressed in the *baraita*, based on Rava's explanation and in accordance with the conclusion of the Gemara (Rambam *Sefer Avoda*, *Hilkhot Beit HaBeḥira* 6:8).

NOTES

And for eating do we not require before the entrance – **וְלַאֲכִילָה לָא בָּעֵינַן כְּנֶגֶד הַפֶּתַח**: Based on this explanation of the *baraita*, that it applies whether it is before the entrance or not, it can be inferred that with regard to eating the offerings the same *halakha* should apply. In other words, the offerings may be eaten in any place, even not before the entrance. Accordingly, a challenge to this ruling can be raised from another *baraita* (*Tzon Kodashim*; see *Ḥok Natan*).

HALAKHA

From where is it derived that the blood of offerings becomes disqualified at sunset – **מִנַּיִן לַדָּם שֶׁנִּפְסָל בִּשְׁקִיעַת הַחַמָּה**: The blood of an offering may be presented only on the day of the slaughter, as the verse states: "It shall be eaten on the day that he offers his sacrifice; and on the morrow that which remains of it may be eaten" (Leviticus 7:16). Once the sun has set, the blood is disqualified and the offering is disqualified (Rambam *Sefer Avoda*, *Hilkhot Ma'aseh HaKorbanot* 4:1 and *Hilkhot Pesulei HaMukdashin* 1:37).

וְלִיטַעֲמֵיךְ, אֵין שׁוֹחֲטִין, מִי לָא עָסְקִינַן דְּאִיכָּא שְׁחִיטָה כְּנֶגֶד הַפֶּתַח? דְּאִי לֵיכָּא – לְמַאי אִיצְטְרִיךְ? אֶלָּא אַף עַל גַּב דְּקָא שָׁחֵיט כְּנֶגֶד הַפֶּתַח תָּנֵי אֵין שׁוֹחֲטִין, מִשּׁוּם דְּלָא קַדִּישׁ; תְּנֵי נַמִּי: אֵין חַיָּיבִין.

The Gemara answers: **And according to your reasoning,** when it teaches that they **may not slaughter** there, **are we not dealing** even with a case in **which there is** an act of **slaughter** performed **before the entrance,** i.e., the entrance to the chamber directly faced the entrance of the Temple? **As if not, for what** purpose was it **necessary** to teach this at all? **Rather, even though he slaughters** the offering **before the entrance,** the *baraita* **teaches** that a priest **may not slaughter** offerings in the chambers **because** that area **is not sacred.** If so, **teach also** that they **are not liable** to receive *karet* for entering the chambers in a state of ritual impurity, as they are not sacred.

וְלַאֲכִילָה לָא בָּעֵינַן כְּנֶגֶד הַפֶּתַח? וְהָתַנְיָא, רַבִּי יוֹסֵי בְּרַבִּי יְהוּדָה אוֹמֵר: שְׁנֵי פִשְׁפָּשִׁין הָיוּ בְּבֵית הַחֲלִיפוֹת גּוֹבְהָן שְׁמוֹנֶה, כְּדֵי לְהַכְשִׁיר אֶת הָעֲזָרָה לַאֲכִילַת קָדְשֵׁי קָדָשִׁים וְלִשְׁחִיטַת קָדָשִׁים קַלִּים! אֲמַר רָבִינָא: סְמִי מִכָּאן אֲכִילָה.

The Gemara asks: **And for eating** an offering, **do we not require** that this take place **before the entrance**[N] of the Temple courtyard? **But isn't it taught** in a *baraita*: **Rabbi Yosei, son of Rabbi Yehuda, says: There were two wickets in the Chamber of Knives,** and **their height** was **eight** cubits; the function of these openings was **in order to render fit the** entire Temple **courtyard for the eating of offerings of the most sacred order, and** to render fit all of the Temple courtyard **for the slaughter of offerings of lesser sanctity? Ravina said: Remove from here** the clause concerning **eating.** The eating of offerings does not have to take place before the entrance of the Temple courtyard.

וְהָכְתִיב: "בַּשְּׁלוּ אֶת הַבָּשָׂר פֶּתַח אֹהֶל מוֹעֵד וְשָׁם תֹּאכְלוּ אוֹתוֹ"! קָדְשֵׁי שָׁעָה שָׁאנֵי.

The Gemara asks: **But isn't it written** with regard to the offerings brought at the inauguration of the Tabernacle: "And Moses said to Aaron and to his sons: **Cook the meat at the entrance of the Tent of Meeting; and eat it there**" (Leviticus 8:31). This indicates that the eating of offerings had to be at the entrance of the Tent of Meeting. The Gemara answers: **Offerings** that were sacrificed only one **time are different.** Since they were specifically commanded for just that time, one cannot derive from there any *halakhot* with regard to offerings in general.

אָמַר רַב יִצְחָק בַּר אֲבוּדִימִי: מִנַּיִן לַדָּם שֶׁנִּפְסָל בִּשְׁקִיעַת הַחַמָּה – שֶׁנֶּאֱמַר: "בְּיוֹם הַקְרִיבוֹ אֶת זִבְחוֹ יֵאָכֵל", בְּיוֹם שֶׁאַתָּה זוֹבֵחַ אַתָּה מַקְרִיב, בְּיוֹם שֶׁאִי אַתָּה זוֹבֵחַ – אִי אַתָּה מַקְרִיב.

§ **Rav Yitzḥak bar Avudimi says: From where** is it derived **that the blood** of offerings **becomes disqualified at sunset**[H] and can no longer be presented on the altar? This is **as it is stated** in the verse: "But if the sacrifice of his offering be a vow, or a gift offering, **it shall be eaten on the day that he sacrifices his offering** [*zivḥo*], and on the morrow" (Leviticus 7:16). This means that **on the day that you slaughter** [*zove'aḥ*] the offering **you sacrifice** it on the altar and present its blood. But **on the day that you do not slaughter** the offering **you may not sacrifice** it and present its blood.

הַאי מִיבָּעֵי לֵיהּ

The Gemara challenges: But **he requires this** verse

Perek **V**
Daf **56** Amud **b**

לְגוּפֵיהּ! אִם כֵּן, נֵימָא קְרָא: "בְּיוֹם זִבְחוֹ יֵאָכֵל", "הַקְרִיבוֹ" לָמָּה לִי? שְׁמַע מִינָּהּ: בְּיוֹם שֶׁאַתָּה זוֹבֵחַ אַתָּה מַקְרִיב, בְּיוֹם שֶׁאִי אַתָּה זוֹבֵחַ – אִי אַתָּה מַקְרִיב.

for the matter **itself,** to teach that a peace offering may be eaten for only two days? The Gemara answers: **If so, let the verse state: On the day he slaughters it shall it be eaten,** and the following day. **Why do I** need the verse to add the term **"that he sacrifices it"? Conclude from** the wording of the verse that **on the day that you slaughter** the offering **you sacrifice** the blood on the altar, but **on a day that you do not slaughter** the offering **you do not sacrifice** the blood on the altar.

וְדִילְמָא הָכִי קָאָמַר רַחֲמָנָא: אִי קָרֵיב דָּם הָאִידָּנָא – נִיתְאֲכֵיל בָּשָׂר הָאִידָּנָא וּלְמָחָר, אִי קָרֵיב דָּם לְמָחָר – נִיתְאֲכֵיל בָּשָׂר לְמָחָר וּלְיוֹמָא אוֹחֲרָא! אִם כֵּן, נֵימָא קְרָא: "בְּיוֹם הַקְרִיבוֹ יֵאָכֵל", "זִבְחוֹ" לָמָּה לִי? שְׁמַע מִינָּהּ: בְּיוֹם שֶׁאַתָּה זוֹבֵחַ אַתָּה מַקְרִיבוֹ, בְּיוֹם שֶׁאִי אַתָּה זוֹבֵחַ – אִי אַתָּה מַקְרִיבוֹ.

The Gemara questions this proof: **But perhaps this** is what **the Merciful One is saying: If** the **blood is sacrificed today,** i.e., the day the offering was slaughtered, the **meat** may **be eaten today and tomorrow. If** the **blood is sacrificed tomorrow,** the **meat may be eaten tomorrow and the following day.** The Gemara answers: **If so, let the verse state: On the day it is sacrificed it shall be eaten,** and the following day. **Why do I** need the verse to state: "That he sacrifices **his offering**"? **Conclude from** the wording of the verse that **on the day that you slaughter** the offering **you sacrifice** the blood on the altar, but **on a day that you do not slaughter** the offering **you do not sacrifice** the blood on the altar.

אִיתְּמַר: הַמְחַשֵּׁב לְאוֹר שְׁלִישִׁי, חִזְקִיָּה אָמַר: כָּשֵׁר, רַבִּי יוֹחָנָן אָמַר: פָּסוּל. חִזְקִיָּה אָמַר כָּשֵׁר – דְּהָא לָא אִינְתִּיק לִשְׂרֵיפָה, רַבִּי יוֹחָנָן אָמַר: פָּסוּל – דְּהָא אִידְּחֵי לֵיהּ מֵאֲכִילָה.

§ **It was stated:** With regard to **one who** slaughters a peace offering and **intends** to eat it **on the evening** preceding the **third** day,[H] **Ḥizkiyya says:** The offering is **valid**, and it is not disqualified due to his intention to eat it after its designated time [*piggul*]. And **Rabbi Yoḥanan says:** It is **disqualified.**[N] The Gemara explains: **Ḥizkiyya says** that the offering is **valid because** on the evening preceding the third day, the peace offering has **not** yet **been removed** from its previous status and designated **for burning.**[N] A peace offering is not burned until the third morning, as the verse states: "It shall be eaten the same day you offer it, and on the following day; and if anything remain until the third day, it shall be burned with fire" (Leviticus 19:6). **Rabbi Yoḥanan says** it is **disqualified, because it has been rejected from** being **eaten.**

הָאוֹכֵל לְאוֹר שְׁלִישִׁי, חִזְקִיָּה אָמַר: פָּטוּר – דְּלָא אִינְתִּיק לִשְׂרֵיפָה, רַבִּי יוֹחָנָן אָמַר: חַיָּיב – דְּהָא אִידְּחֵי לֵיהּ מֵאֲכִילָה.

These two *amora'im* have the same dispute concerning a similar matter: With regard to **one who eats** a peace offering **on the evening** preceding the **third** day,[H] **Ḥizkiyya says:** He is **exempt** from *karet*, **because** the offering has **not** yet **been removed** from its previous status and designated **for burning.** And **Rabbi Yoḥanan says:** He is **liable** to receive *karet*, **because it has been rejected from** being **eaten.**

תַּנְיָא כְּווֹתֵיהּ דְּרַבִּי יוֹחָנָן: קֳדָשִׁים הַנֶּאֱכָלִין לְיוֹם אֶחָד – מְחַשְּׁבִין בְּדָמָן מִשֶּׁתִּשְׁקַע הַחַמָּה, וּבִבְשָׂרָן וּבְאֵימוּרֵיהֶן – מִשֶּׁיַּעֲלֶה עַמּוּד הַשַּׁחַר. קֳדָשִׁים הַנֶּאֱכָלִין לִשְׁנֵי יָמִים וְלַיְלָה אַחַת – מְחַשְּׁבִין בְּדָמָן מִשֶּׁתִּשְׁקַע הַחַמָּה, וּבְאֵימוּרֵיהֶן מִשֶּׁיַּעֲלֶה עַמּוּד הַשַּׁחַר, וּבִבְשָׂרָן מִשֶּׁתִּשְׁקַע הַחַמָּה שֶׁל שְׁנֵי יָמִים.

It is taught in a *baraita* **in accordance with** the opinion **of Rabbi Yoḥanan:** With regard to **sacrificial** animals **that may be eaten for one day,** if one **intends to** present **their blood after sunset, or** if one intends **to eat their meat or to** sacrifice **their sacrificial portions after the first rays of dawn,** the offering is considered to be *piggul* and is disqualified. With regard to **sacrificial** animals **that may be eaten for two days and one night,** if one **intends to** present **their blood after sunset, or** if one intends **to** sacrifice **their sacrificial portions after the first rays of dawn, or** if one intends **to eat their meat after sunset** following the second **of the two days,** the offering is considered to be *piggul* and is disqualified.

תָּנוּ רַבָּנַן: יָכוֹל יְהוּ נֶאֱכָלִין לְאוֹר שְׁלִישִׁי. וְדִין הוּא: זְבָחִים נֶאֱכָלִין לְיוֹם אֶחָד וּזְבָחִים נֶאֱכָלִין לִשְׁנֵי יָמִים, מָה זְבָחִים הַנֶּאֱכָלִין לְיוֹם אֶחָד – לַיְלָה אַחֲרֵיהֶן, אַף זְבָחִים הַנֶּאֱכָלִין לִשְׁנֵי יָמִים – לַיְלָה אַחֲרֵיהֶן!

The Gemara cites another *baraita* on this topic. **The Sages taught:** One **might** have thought that peace offerings, which may be eaten for two days, **may** also **be eaten on the evening** preceding the **third** day. **And this is** the conclusion of **a logical inference:** Other **offerings,** e.g., thanks offerings, **are eaten for one day, and** peace **offerings are eaten for two days. Just as** with regard to **offerings that are eaten for one day,** the **night follows** the previous day, i.e., the offering may be eaten during the day and the subsequent night, **so too,** with regard to peace **offerings that are eaten for two days,** say that the **night follows** the day, and rule that they may be eaten on the night after the second day.

תַּלְמוּד לוֹמַר: "וְהַנּוֹתָר עַד יוֹם" – בְּעוֹד יוֹם הוּא נֶאֱכָל, וְאֵינוֹ נֶאֱכָל לְאוֹר שְׁלִישִׁי.

To counter this logic, **the verse states:** "And when you sacrifice a peace offering to God, you shall sacrifice it of your own will. It shall be eaten the same day you sacrifice it, and on the next day; **and if any remains until** the third **day,**[N] it shall be burned with fire" (Leviticus 19:5–6). This teaches that **it may be eaten while** it is still **daytime,** i.e., during the second day, **but it may not be eaten on the evening** preceding the **third** day.

יָכוֹל יִשָּׂרֵף מִיָּד? וְדִין הוּא: זְבָחִים נֶאֱכָלִין לְיוֹם אֶחָד, וּזְבָחִים נֶאֱכָלִין לִשְׁנֵי יָמִים, מָה זְבָחִים הַנֶּאֱכָלִין לְיוֹם אֶחָד – תֵּיכֶף לַאֲכִילָה שְׂרֵיפָה, אַף זְבָחִים הַנֶּאֱכָלִין לִשְׁנֵי יָמִים – תֵּיכֶף לַאֲכִילָה שְׂרֵיפָה!

The *baraita* continues: If a peace offering may not be eaten beyond the second day, one **might** have thought that it should **be burned immediately** after the conclusion of the second day, **and this** too is the conclusion of **a logical inference:** Other **offerings are eaten for one day, and** peace **offerings are eaten for two days. Just as** with regard to **offerings that are eaten for one day, immediately** after the conclusion of their permitted time **for eating** should their **burning**[N] commence, on the morning of the second day, **so too,** with regard to peace **offerings that are eaten for two days** say that **immediately** after the conclusion of their permitted time **for eating** should their **burning** commence, at night after the second day.

תַּלְמוּד לוֹמַר: "בַּיּוֹם הַשְּׁלִישִׁי בָּאֵשׁ יִשָּׂרֵף", בַּיּוֹם אַתָּה שׂוֹרְפוֹ, וְאִי אַתָּה שׂוֹרְפוֹ בַּלַּיְלָה.

To counter this logic, **the verse states:** "And if any remains of the flesh of the sacrifice **on the third day, it shall be burned with fire**" (Leviticus 7:17), meaning: **You must burn it during the day,**[H] **but you may not burn it during the night.**

HALAKHA

One who intends to eat it on the evening preceding the third day, etc. – הַמְחַשֵּׁב לְאוֹר שְׁלִישִׁי וכו׳: If one slaughters an offering with the intent of presenting the blood after sunset, which is not the correct time for this rite, or with the intent of burning a part of it the following day, after dawn, which is not the appropriate time for that rite, or to eat a part of it after its designated time, the offering is *piggul*. This is in accordance with the opinion of Rabbi Yoḥanan, who holds that *piggul* follows the time of eating. What is the appropriate time for eating peace offerings? It is the day that the offering is sacrificed, that night, and the following day until sunset. This applies both to the portions eaten by the priests and the portions eaten by the one who brings the offering. This is also the *halakha* for animal tithe offerings and a firstborn offering, which, like peace offerings, are offerings of lesser sanctity (Rambam *Sefer Avoda, Hilkhot Pesulei HaMukdashin* 13:1 and *Hilkhot Ma'aseh HaKorbanot* 10:6).

One who eats it on the evening preceding the third day – הָאוֹכֵל לְאוֹר שְׁלִישִׁי: One who intentionally eats meat that is *notar* is liable to receive *karet*. If he ate it unwittingly he must bring a sin offering. From when is one liable for eating *notar*? For offerings of the most sacred order, one is liable immediately after dawn on the day after the offering was sacrificed. For offerings of lesser sanctity, one is liable from sunset on the second day, which is the beginning of the night of the third day. This is in accordance with the opinion of Rabbi Yoḥanan (Rambam *Sefer Avoda, Hilkhot Pesulei HaMukdashin* 18:10).

You burn it during the day – בַּיּוֹם אַתָּה שׂוֹרְפוֹ: *Notar* may be burned only during the day (Rambam *Sefer Avoda, Hilkhot Pesulei HaMukdashin* 19:4).

NOTES

Disqualified – פָּסוּל: The offering is disqualified. To be more specific, it is *piggul*, like any offering slaughtered with intent to eat it beyond its designated time. One who eats such an offering intentionally is liable to receive *karet*. One who eats it unwittingly brings a sin offering.

Because it has not yet been removed from its previous status and designated for burning – דְּהָא לָא אִינְתִּיק לִשְׂרֵיפָה: According to Ḥizkiyya, even though the meat of the peace offering is no longer permitted to be eaten, nevertheless, it is rendered *piggul* only if one intends to eat it beyond the time that the meat becomes *notar*, i.e., leftover. As long as the mitzva to burn the remaining flesh does not take effect, it does not have the status of *notar*.

The verse states: And if any remains until the third day – תַּלְמוּד לוֹמַר וְהַנּוֹתָר עַד יוֹם: Rashi explains that it is as if the verse had stated: On the day that you slaughter it you may eat it, and the following day, and any that remains until the day. This means that it must be eaten while it is still daylight and not afterward. *Tosafot* understand that it means until the third day, i.e., up to, but not including. This teaches that it may not be eaten at all on the third day.

Immediately after their time for eating is their burning – תֵּיכֶף לַאֲכִילָה שְׂרֵיפָה: Rashi writes that this is derived from the verse stated with regard to the inauguration of the Tabernacle: "And if any of the flesh of the consecration, or of the bread, remain until the morning, then you shall burn the remainder with fire; it shall not be eaten, because it is holy" (Exodus 29:34). This means that immediately after the designated time for eating has concluded, the leftover flesh must be burned.

מתני׳ הַבְּכוֹר וְהַמַּעֲשֵׂר וְהַפֶּסַח קָדָשִׁים קַלִּים; שְׁחִיטָתָן בְּכָל מָקוֹם בָּעֲזָרָה, וְדָמָן טָעוּן מַתָּנָה אַחַת, וּבִלְבַד שֶׁיִּתֵּן כְּנֶגֶד הַיְסוֹד.

MISHNA The **firstborn** offering, **the** animal **tithe** offering, **and the Paschal offering**[N] **are offerings of lesser sanctity. Their slaughter is anywhere in the** Temple **courtyard,**[H] **and their blood requires one placement,**[NH] **provided that** the priest **places it** so that the blood goes **on the base** of the altar.

שִׁינָּה בַּאֲכִילָתָן: הַבְּכוֹר נֶאֱכָל לַכֹּהֲנִים, וְהַמַּעֲשֵׂר לְכָל אָדָם, וְנֶאֱכָלִין בְּכָל הָעִיר, בְּכָל מַאֲכָל, לִשְׁנֵי יָמִים וְלַיְלָה אֶחָד. הַפֶּסַח אֵינוֹ נֶאֱכָל אֶלָּא בַּלַּיְלָה, וְאֵינוֹ נֶאֱכָל אֶלָּא עַד חֲצוֹת, וְאֵינוֹ נֶאֱכָל אֶלָּא לִמְנוּיָו, וְאֵינוֹ נֶאֱכָל אֶלָּא צָלִי.

The *halakha* **differs with regard to their consumption. The firstborn** offering **is eaten by the priests, and the** animal **tithe** offering is eaten **by any person,**[NH] i.e., any ritually pure Jew. **And they are eaten throughout the city**[NH] of Jerusalem, prepared **in any** manner of **food** preparation, **for two days**[N] **and one night. The Paschal offering is eaten only at night,**[H] **and it is eaten only until midnight,**[NH] **and it is eaten only by its registrants,**[H] i.e., those who registered in advance to partake of the offering, **and it is eaten only roasted,**[NH] not prepared in any other manner.

NOTES

The firstborn offering, the animal tithe offering, and the Paschal offering – הַבְּכוֹר וְהַמַּעֲשֵׂר וְהַפֶּסַח: In Rambam's Commentary on the Mishna it is explained that these three offerings are included in the category of peace offerings. The verse states: "This is the law of the burnt offering, of the meal offering, and of the sin offering, and of the guilt offering, and of the consecration offering, and of the sacrifice of peace offerings" (Leviticus 7:37). Since the firstborn offering, animal tithe offering, and Paschal offering are not listed separately, they must be included within the general category of peace offerings. This explanation also provides a source for many of the *halakhot* of these offerings that are not discussed by the Gemara. Rashi and *Tosafot* attempt to find the sources for these *halakhot*.

Requires one placement – טָעוּן מַתָּנָה אַחַת: Unlike with regard to peace offerings, the Torah does not state "around" with regard to the placement of the blood of these three offerings, and therefore they require only a single placement of blood.

And the animal tithe offering by any person – וְהַמַּעֲשֵׂר לְכָל אָדָם: The Torah does not mention that the animal tithe offering must be given to the priests. With regard to a firstborn offering the Torah does specify that it belongs to the priests.

Throughout the city – בְּכָל הָעִיר: Rashi explains that the source for this *halakha* is the verse: "And you shall bring there your burnt offerings, and your offerings, and your tithes, and the offering of your hand, and your vows, and your gift offerings, and the firstborn of your herd and of your flock" (Deuteronomy 12:6). Rabbi Akiva understands that the verse is referring to both the second tithe and the animal tithe. Firstborn animals are also mentioned in that same verse. Since the Torah does not specify that they may be eaten only in the Temple, it is permitted to eat them throughout Jerusalem.

For two days, etc. – לִשְׁנֵי יָמִים וכו׳: Rashi writes that the Gemara derives this *halakha* with regard to a firstborn offering, but he is not aware of any source that states that an animal tithe offering must be eaten within this time frame. *Tosafot* claim that Rashi subsequently revises his commentary, and holds that there is a verbal analogy to be made between a firstborn offering and an animal tithe offering.

Only at night…only until midnight – אֶלָּא בַּלַּיְלָה...אֶלָּא עַד חֲצוֹת: The Paschal offering must be eaten at night, as the verse states explicitly: "And they shall eat the meat on that night, roasted with fire, and *matza*; with bitter herbs they shall eat it" (Exodus 12:8).

Only by its registrants…only roasted – אֶלָּא לִמְנוּיָו...אֶלָּא צָלִי: These specifications are both stated explicitly in the Torah: "And if the household be too little for a lamb, then shall he and his neighbor next to his house take one according to the number of the souls; according to every man's eating you shall make your count for the lamb" (Exodus 12:4), and: "Do not eat it raw, nor cooked at all with water, but roasted with fire; its head with its legs and with its innards" (Exodus 12:9).

HALAKHA

Their slaughter is anywhere in the Temple courtyard – שְׁחִיטָתָן בְּכָל מָקוֹם בָּעֲזָרָה: Offerings of lesser sanctity may be slaughtered anywhere in the Temple courtyard (Rambam *Sefer Avoda*, *Hilkhot Ma'aseh HaKorbanot* 5:4).

Their blood requires one placement – דָּמָן טָעוּן מַתָּנָה אַחַת: The blood of an animal tithe offering or a Paschal offering requires one pouring toward the base of the altar. This can be on any of the three sides of the altar that have a base. From where is it derived that they require only one pouring? The verse states: "Sprinkle their blood on the altar" (Numbers 18:17), with regard to firstborn offerings. The Sages had a tradition that the *halakha* is the same for animal tithe offerings and Paschal offerings (Rambam *Sefer Korbanot*, *Hilkhot Korban Pesaḥ* 1:6).

The firstborn offering is eaten by the priests and the animal tithe offering is eaten by any person – הַבְּכוֹר נֶאֱכָל לַכֹּהֲנִים וְהַמַּעֲשֵׂר לְכָל אָדָם: After the blood of a firstborn animal or animal tithe has been sprinkled, the skin is flayed, the inner portions that are to be burned on the altar are removed, and they are salted and burned on the altar. The remainder of the meat of a firstborn animal is eaten by priests. The remainder of the meat of animal tithe offering is eaten by the owners (Rambam *Sefer Avoda*, *Hilkhot Ma'aseh HaKorbanot* 9:25).

Eaten throughout the city – נֶאֱכָלִין בְּכָל הָעִיר: Meat from a peace offering, an animal tithe offering, or a Paschal offering may be eaten throughout the city of Jerusalem, as they are all offerings of lesser sanctity (Rambam *Sefer Avoda*, *Hilkhot Ma'aseh HaKorbanot* 10:5).

The Paschal offering is eaten only at night – הַפֶּסַח אֵינוֹ נֶאֱכָל אֶלָּא בַּלַּיְלָה: It is a positive mitzva to eat the meat of the Paschal offering on the night of the fifteenth of Nisan (Rambam *Sefer Korbanot*, *Hilkhot Korban Pesaḥ* 8:1).

And it is eaten only until midnight – וְאֵינוֹ נֶאֱכָל אֶלָּא עַד חֲצוֹת: It is a positive mitzva to eat the meat of the Paschal offering on the night of the fifteenth of Nisan. By Torah law, it may be eaten until sunrise. The Sages decreed that it must be eaten before midnight, in order to distance one from sin (Rambam *Sefer Korbanot*, *Hilkhot Korban Pesaḥ* 8:1, 15).

And it is eaten only by its registrants – וְאֵינוֹ נֶאֱכָל אֶלָּא לִמְנוּיָו: The Paschal offering is slaughtered with the intent that it will be eaten only by those who registered, while it was alive, to eat it (Rambam *Sefer Korbanot*, *Hilkhot Korban Pesaḥ* 2:1).

And it is eaten only roasted – וְאֵינוֹ נֶאֱכָל אֶלָּא צָלִי: The Paschal offering may be eaten only roasted. One who eats an olive-bulk of it raw or boiled on the first night of Passover is flogged (Rambam *Sefer Korbanot*, *Hilkhot Korban Pesaḥ* 8:4).

גמ׳ מַאן תְּנָא? אָמַר רַב חִסְדָּא: רַבִּי יוֹסֵי הַגְּלִילִי הִיא, דְּתַנְיָא, רַבִּי יוֹסֵי הַגְּלִילִי אוֹמֵר: "חֶלְבּוֹ" לֹא נֶאֱמַר, אֶלָּא: "חֶלְבָּם", "דָּמוֹ" לֹא נֶאֱמַר, אֶלָּא: "דָּמָם", לִימֵּד עַל בְּכוֹר וּמַעֲשֵׂר וּפֶסַח שֶׁטְּעוּנִין מַתַּן דָּמִים וְאֵימוּרִין לְגַבֵּי מִזְבֵּחַ.

GEMARA Who is the *tanna* who **taught**[N] that the blood of these offerings is placed, not poured, so that it goes on the base of the altar? **Rav Ḥisda says** that **it is Rabbi Yosei HaGelili, as it is taught** in a *baraita*: **Rabbi Yosei HaGelili says:** The verse states: "But the firstborn of an ox, or the firstborn of a sheep, or the firstborn of a goat, you shall not redeem; they are sacred; you shall sprinkle their blood upon the altar and you shall burn their fat for an offering made by fire, for a pleasing aroma to the Lord" (Numbers 18:17). **It is not stated: Its fat, but** rather: **"Their fat."** Similarly, **it is not stated: Its blood,**[N] **but** rather: **"Their blood."** This **teaches with regard to a firstborn** offering, which is mentioned explicitly in the verse, **and** an animal **tithe** offering, **and a Paschal offering,** which are similar in their sanctity to a firstborn offering, **that they** all **require placement of their blood and** the burning of their **sacrificial portions on the altar.**

כְּנֶגֶד הַיְסוֹד מְנָא לַן? אָמַר רַבִּי אֱלִיעֶזֶר: אָתְיָא זְרִיקָה זְרִיקָה מֵעוֹלָה,

The Gemara asks: **From where do we** derive that their blood must be placed so that it goes **on the base** of the altar? **Rabbi Eliezer says:** This is **derived** by way of a verbal analogy, with the meaning of the word **"sprinkling"** stated here derived **from** the meaning of the word **"sprinkling"** stated with regard to **a burnt offering.**

וְעוֹלָה גּוּפַהּ מְנָלַן – דִּכְתִיב: "אֶל יְסוֹד מִזְבַּח הָעוֹלָה", לִמֵּד עַל עוֹלַת חוֹבָה שֶׁטְּעוּנָה יְסוֹד.

The Gemara asks: **And from where do we** derive the *halakha* that **a burnt offering itself** has its blood presented on the altar in a place where there is a base? The Gemara answers: We derive it from a verse, **as it is written:** "And he shall pour all the blood of the bull **at the base of the altar of the burnt offering**" (Leviticus 4:7). This **teaches that** the blood of **an obligatory burnt offering requires** presentation at the **base** of the altar, as the verse specifically describes the base of the altar as connected to the burnt offering.

אִי מָה לְהַלָּן שְׁתֵּי מַתָּנוֹת שֶׁהֵן אַרְבַּע – אַף כָּאן שְׁתֵּי מַתָּנוֹת שֶׁהֵן אַרְבַּע!

The Gemara asks: **If** it is derived from a burnt offering via a verbal analogy, one might think that **just as there,** a burnt offering requires **two placements that are four, so too here,** a firstborn offering, an animal tithe offering, and a Paschal offering should also require **two placements that are four,** and not just a single placement.

אָמַר אַבָּיֵי: לָמָּה לִי לְמִכְתַּב "סָבִיב" בְּעוֹלָה, "סָבִיב" בְּחַטָּאת? הָווּ שְׁנֵי כְתוּבִין הַבָּאִין כְּאֶחָד, וְכׇל שְׁנֵי כְתוּבִין הַבָּאִין כְּאֶחָד אֵין מְלַמְּדִין.

Abaye says: Why do I need the Torah **to write:** "And Aaron's sons, the priests, shall present the blood, and sprinkle the blood **around** against the altar" (Leviticus 1:5), **with regard to a burnt offering,** to teach that the blood must be placed on all four sides of the altar, in addition to writing: "And Moses took the blood, and put it upon the corners of the altar **around** with his finger" (Leviticus 8:15), **with regard to a sin offering? They are two verses that come as one,** i.e., they teach the same matter; **and any two verses that come as one do not teach** their common aspect to apply to other cases. Therefore, a firstborn offering, an animal tithe offering, and a Paschal offering do not require two placements that are four.

NOTES

Who is the *tanna* who taught – מַאן תְּנָא: Rashi explains as follows: Since the mishna equates all three offerings with regard to placing their blood on the altar, it is understood that the sprinkling of the blood is required not only for the firstborn, where it is stated explicitly in the verse, but also for animal tithe and the Paschal offering, about which the Torah does not state it explicitly. They all require that the blood be placed in a vessel and sprinkled on the wall of the altar, as opposed to being poured on the base of the altar. Rabbi Yishmael is of the opinion that the Paschal offering does require the pouring of its blood on the base of the altar (see 37a).

Other *tanna'im* similarly hold that since the blood rites of the animal tithe and Paschal offering are not stated explicitly in the Torah, they are included within the general requirement of pouring the blood, as stated in the Torah: "And you shall offer your burnt offerings, the flesh and the blood, upon the altar of the Lord your God; and the blood of your offerings shall be poured out against the altar of the Lord your God, and you shall eat the meat" (Deuteronomy 12:27). From the Rambam, it seems that the discussion here is with regard to all three of the offerings and why they require only one placement of the blood on the altar, as stated explicitly with regard to a firstborn offering (see *Kesef Mishne*).

It is not stated: Its blood – דָּמוֹ לֹא נֶאֱמַר: The plural alludes to the fact that there are other similar offerings. These are the animal tithe offering and the Paschal offering, the *halakhot* of which are not stated explicitly in the Torah. This teaches that they also require their blood to be sprinkled on the altar, and their sacrificial portions to be offered on the altar. Rabbi Yishmael holds that the verse simply uses plural language because it is referring to the various types of firstborn animals mentioned there.

הָנִיחָא לְמַאן דְּאָמַר אֵין מְלַמְּדִין, אֶלָּא לְמַאן דְּאָמַר מְלַמְּדִין מַאי אִיכָּא לְמֵימַר? הָוֵי אָשָׁם שְׁלֹשָׁה, וּשְׁלֹשָׁה וַדַּאי אֵין מְלַמְּדִין.

The Gemara asks: **This works out well according to the one who says** that two verses that come as one **do not teach** their common aspect with regard to other cases. **But according to the one who says** that two verses that come as one do **teach** their common aspect with regard to other cases, **what is there to say?** The Gemara answers: Together with the verse stated with regard to **a guilt offering, there are three** verses, as it is written: "And its blood shall be sprinkled around the altar" (Leviticus 7:2), **and three** verses which come as one **certainly do not teach** their common aspect with regard to other cases.

״הַבְּכוֹר נֶאֱכָל לַכֹּהֲנִים״. תָּנוּ רַבָּנַן: מִנַּיִן לִבְכוֹר שֶׁנֶּאֱכָל לִשְׁנֵי יָמִים וְלַיְלָה – שֶׁנֶּאֱמַר: ״וּבְשָׂרָם יִהְיֶה לָּךְ כַּחֲזֵה הַתְּנוּפָה וּכְשׁוֹק הַיָּמִין״, הִקִּישׁוֹ הַכָּתוּב לְחָזֶה וְשׁוֹק שֶׁל שְׁלָמִים: מַה שְּׁלָמִים נֶאֱכָלִין לִשְׁנֵי יָמִים וְלַיְלָה אֶחָד – אַף בְּכוֹר נֶאֱכָל לִשְׁנֵי יָמִים וְלַיְלָה אֶחָד.

§ The mishna teaches: **The firstborn** offering is **eaten by the priests,** throughout the city of Jerusalem, prepared in any manner of food preparation, for two days and one night. **The Sages taught** in a *baraita*: **From where** is it derived **with regard to a firstborn** offering **that** it is **eaten for two days and** the intervening **night?** It is derived from a verse, **as it is stated** with regard to a firstborn offering: **"And their flesh shall be yours, as the breast of waving and as the right thigh"** (Numbers 18:18). **The verse juxtaposes** the firstborn offering **with the breast and thigh of peace offerings. Just as peace offerings are eaten for two days and one night, so too, a firstborn** offering is **eaten for two days and one night.**

וְזוֹ שְׁאֵלָה נִשְׁאֲלָה לִפְנֵי חֲכָמִים בְּכֶרֶם בְּיַבְנֶה: בְּכוֹר לְכַמָּה נֶאֱכָל? נַעֲנָה רַבִּי טַרְפוֹן וְאָמַר: לִשְׁנֵי יָמִים וְלַיְלָה אֶחָד.

The *baraita* relates: **And this question was asked before the Sages in the vineyard,** i.e., the academy, **in Yavne:**[B] **For how many** days and nights is **a firstborn** offering **eaten? Rabbi Tarfon responded and said: For two days and one night.**

הָיָה שָׁם תַּלְמִיד אֶחָד שֶׁבָּא לְבֵית הַמִּדְרָשׁ לִפְנֵי חֲכָמִים תְּחִלָּה, וְרַבִּי יוֹסֵי הַגְּלִילִי שְׁמוֹ. אָמַר לוֹ: רַבִּי, מִנַּיִן לְךָ? אָמַר לוֹ: בְּנִי, שְׁלָמִים קָדָשִׁים קַלִּים וּבְכוֹר קָדָשִׁים קַלִּים, מַה שְּׁלָמִים נֶאֱכָלִין לִשְׁנֵי יָמִים וְלַיְלָה אֶחָד – אַף בְּכוֹר נֶאֱכָל לִשְׁנֵי יָמִים וְלַיְלָה אֶחָד.

There was one student there who came to the study hall before the Sages for the **first** time, **and his name** was **Rabbi Yosei HaGelili.**[P] **He said to** Rabbi Tarfon: **My teacher, from where do you** derive this? Rabbi Tarfon **said to him: My son, peace offerings** are **offerings of lesser sanctity, and a firstborn** offering is **an offering of lesser sanctity. Just as peace offerings are eaten for two days and one night, so too, a firstborn** offering is **eaten for two days and one night.**

אָמַר לוֹ: רַבִּי, בְּכוֹר – מַתָּנָה לַכֹּהֵן, וְחַטָּאת וְאָשָׁם מַתָּנָה לַכֹּהֵן, מָה חַטָּאת וְאָשָׁם לְיוֹם וְלַיְלָה – אַף בְּכוֹר לְיוֹם וְלַיְלָה!

Rabbi Yosei HaGelili **said to him: My teacher,** there is a different comparison that can be made: **A firstborn** offering is given as **a gift to the priest, and a sin offering and a guilt offering** are each given as **a gift to the priest. Just as a sin offering and a guilt offering** are eaten **for** one **day and** one **night, so too, a firstborn** offering should be eaten **for** one **day and** one **night.**

אָמַר לוֹ: נָדוֹן דָּבָר מִתּוֹךְ דָּבָר וְנִלְמַד דָּבָר מִתּוֹךְ דָּבָר: מַה שְּׁלָמִים אֵין בָּאִין עַל חֵטְא – אַף בְּכוֹר אֵינוֹ בָּא עַל חֵטְא, מַה שְּׁלָמִים נֶאֱכָלִים לִשְׁנֵי יָמִים וְלַיְלָה אֶחָד – אַף בְּכוֹר נֶאֱכָל לִשְׁנֵי יָמִים וְלַיְלָה אֶחָד.

Rabbi Tarfon **said to him: Let us judge a matter from a matter** to which it is most similar, i.e., a firstborn offering is an offering of lesser sanctity, as are peace offerings, **and learn a matter from a matter,** i.e., there is another comparison to be made: **Just as peace offerings do not come** as atonement **for a sin, so too, a firstborn** offering **does not come** as atonement **for a sin. Just as peace offerings are eaten for two days and one night, so too, a firstborn** offering is **eaten for two days and one night.**

אָמַר לוֹ: רַבִּי, נָדוֹן דָּבָר מִדָּבָר יִלְמַד דָּבָר מִדָּבָר: חַטָּאת וְאָשָׁם מַתָּנָה לַכֹּהֵן, וּבְכוֹר מַתָּנָה לַכֹּהֵן, מָה חַטָּאת וְאָשָׁם אֵין בָּאִין בְּנֶדֶר וּנְדָבָה – אַף בְּכוֹר אֵינוֹ בְּנֶדֶר וּנְדָבָה, מָה חַטָּאת וְאָשָׁם נֶאֱכָלִין לְיוֹם אֶחָד – אַף בְּכוֹר נֶאֱכָל לְיוֹם אֶחָד!

Rabbi Yosei HaGelili **said to him: My teacher,** I can answer you in a similar way. **Let us judge a matter from a matter** to which it is most similar, i.e., a firstborn offering is more similar to a sin offering and a guilt offering, and **learn a matter from a matter,** i.e., there is another comparison to be made: **A sin offering and a guilt offering** are each given as **a gift to the priest, and a firstborn** offering is given as **a gift to the priest. Just as a sin offering and a guilt offering do not come as a vow** offering **or as a gift** offering,[B] i.e., they are brought only by one obligated to bring them, **so too, a firstborn** offering **does not** come **as a vow** offering **or as a gift** offering. **Just as a sin offering and a guilt offering are eaten for one day** and one night, **so too, a firstborn** offering should be **eaten for one day** and one night.

BACKGROUND

The vineyard in Yavne – כֶּרֶם בְּיַבְנֶה: The seat of the Sanhedrin in Yavne after the destruction of the Second Temple was called the vineyard in Yavne. According to an ancient tradition, the Sanhedrin was called a vineyard because when it was in session, the Sages themselves, along with their students, would sit in rows, like the rows of a vineyard. There was not an actual vineyard nearby (Jerusalem Talmud). Since most of the prominent Sages of that generation assembled there and their decisions were especially significant for the future existence of the Jewish people, the academy located at the seat of the Sanhedrin in the vineyard in Yavne was held in high regard. The *halakhot* taught there are extremely authoritative.

Vow offering and gift offering – נֶדֶר וּנְדָבָה: The difference between vow offerings and gift offerings is that one takes a vow as a personal obligation. In the case of a vow, one states, for example: I accept upon myself to bring a burnt offering. He is obligated to bring a burnt offering even if the animal he intended to bring dies or is lost. Conversely, with regard to gift offerings, a specific animal is designated as an offering. If one states, for example: This animal will be a burnt offering, and subsequently the animal dies or is lost, no replacement is necessary.

PERSONALITIES

Rabbi Yosei HaGelili – רַבִּי יוֹסֵי הַגְּלִילִי: Rabbi Yosei was known as HaGelili, from the Galilee, to distinguish him from Rabbi Yosei ben Ḥalafta, who was also known as simply Rabbi Yosei. Rabbi Yosei HaGelili was a *tanna* in the first generation after the destruction of the Second Temple. It is not known who his initial teachers in the Galilee were, but from the story here it seems that he was already a respected Torah scholar even before his arrival in Yavne. Elsewhere the Gemara describes other disputes that he had with Rabbi Tarfon and Rabbi Akiva, who accorded him special honor. It appears that he received the title of Rabbi very soon after arriving in Yavne and was counted among the elders. Rabbi Akiva's students often taught his statements.

Rabbi Yosei HaGelili's statements appear dozens of times in the Mishna, where he engages in disputes with the greatest scholars of the generation on various subjects. Even though his opinion was not accepted by all, there were places that followed his rulings. While it seems that his primary area of expertise was in the realm of *halakha*, there are also several aggadic statements in his name.

Rabbi Yosei HaGelili was famous for his piety. He was also known as one who was humble and whose prayers were accepted.

His wife was ill-tempered, and he divorced her, although he required financial assistance to do so. Nevertheless, when he later discovered that she and her new husband were poor, he provided for them financially for the remainder of their lives. One of his sons died young. Two of his sons, Rabbi Eliezer and Rabbi Ḥanina, were among the great Torah scholars of the next generation. Rabbi Eliezer was famous as a master of aggadic statements.

קָפַץ רַבִּי עֲקִיבָא, וְנִסְתַּלֵּק רַבִּי טַרְפוֹן. אָמַר לוֹ: הֲרֵי הוּא אוֹמֵר: ״וּבְשָׂרָם יִהְיֶה לָּךְ״ – הִקִּישָׁן הַכָּתוּב לְחָזֶה וְשׁוֹק שֶׁל שְׁלָמִים, מַה שְּׁלָמִים נֶאֱכָלִין לִשְׁנֵי יָמִים וְלַיְלָה אֶחָד – אַף בְּכוֹר נֶאֱכָל לִשְׁנֵי יָמִים וְלַיְלָה אֶחָד.

Rabbi Akiva jumped into the discussion, **and Rabbi Tarfon left.**[N] Rabbi Akiva **said to** Rabbi Yosei HaGelili: **But the verse states: "And their flesh shall be yours,** as the breast of waving and as the right thigh" (Numbers 18:18). **The verse juxtaposes** firstborn offerings **with a breast and thigh of peace offerings. Just as peace offerings are eaten for two days and one night, so too, a firstborn** offering **is eaten for two days and one night.**

אָמַר לוֹ: הִיקַּשְׁתּוֹ לְחָזֶה וְשׁוֹק שֶׁל שְׁלָמִים, וַאֲנִי מַקִּישׁוֹ לְחָזֶה וְשׁוֹק שֶׁל תּוֹדָה: מַה תּוֹדָה נֶאֱכֶלֶת לְיוֹם וְלַיְלָה – אַף בְּכוֹר נֶאֱכָל לְיוֹם וְלַיְלָה!

Rabbi Yosei HaGelili **said to** Rabbi Akiva: **You juxtaposed it with a breast and thigh of peace offerings. But** since the Torah does not specify with which offering the firstborn is juxtaposed, **I juxtapose it with a breast and thigh of a thanks offering,**[N] which are also given to a priest. **Just as a thanks offering is eaten for** one **day and** one **night, so too, a firstborn** offering should **be eaten for** one **day and** one **night.**

אָמַר לוֹ: הֲרֵי הוּא אוֹמֵר: ״וּבְשָׂרָם יִהְיֶה לָּךְ״, שֶׁאֵין תַּלְמוּד לוֹמַר ״לְךָ יִהְיֶה״, וּמַה תַּלְמוּד לוֹמַר ״לְךָ יִהְיֶה״ – הוֹסִיף הַכָּתוּב הֲוָיָה אַחֶרֶת בִּבְכוֹר.

Rabbi Akiva **said to** Rabbi Yosei HaGelili: I concede that it is possible to juxtapose a firstborn offering with a thanks offering, **but** the verse **states: "And their flesh shall be yours,** as the breast of waving and as the right thigh, it shall be yours" (Numbers 18:18). **Since** there is **no** need for **the verse to state** a second time: **"It shall be yours," what** is the meaning when **the verse states** a second time: **"It shall be yours"? The verse adds another** day on which it is permitted **for a firstborn** offering to **be** eaten, i.e., a second day.

וּכְשֶׁנֶּאֶמְרוּ דְּבָרִים לִפְנֵי רַבִּי יִשְׁמָעֵאל, אָמַר לָהֶן: צְאוּ וְאִמְרוּ לוֹ לְרַבִּי עֲקִיבָא: טָעִיתָ, תּוֹדָה מֵהֵיכָן לְמֵדָה – מִשְּׁלָמִים, [וְכִי] דָּבָר הַלָּמֵד בְּהֶיקֵּשׁ חוֹזֵר וּמְלַמֵּד בְּהֶיקֵּשׁ? הָא אֵין עָלֶיךָ לִידּוֹן בְּלָשׁוֹן אַחֲרוֹן אֶלָּא בְּלָשׁוֹן רִאשׁוֹן.

The Gemara relates: **And when these matters were said before Rabbi Yishmael, he said to** his students: **Go out and tell Rabbi Akiva: You were mistaken** when you conceded to Rabbi Yosei HaGelili that the allotted time for eating a firstborn offering could have been derived from the allotted time for eating a thanks offering. Why? **From where is** it **derived** that the breast and thigh of **a thanks offering** are eaten by priests? It is derived **from** a juxtaposition with **a peace offering.** Nowhere is it stated explicitly that the breast and thigh of a thanks offering are eaten only by priests. **And** in the realm of consecrated matters, **can a matter derived via a juxtaposition then teach** its *halakha* **via a juxtaposition?** The Gemara (49b) demonstrated that it cannot. **Consequently, you should not infer from the latter formulation** of the verse, from the words "It shall be yours," **but** rather, **from the first formulation** of the verse, as you claimed that the Torah juxtaposes a firstborn offering with the breast and thigh of a peace offering.

וְרַבִּי יִשְׁמָעֵאל, הַאי ״לְךָ יִהְיֶה״ מַאי עָבֵיד לֵיהּ? לִימֵּד עַל בְּכוֹר בַּעַל מוּם שֶׁהוּא מַתָּנָה לַכֹּהֵן, שֶׁלֹּא מָצִינוּ בְּכָל הַתּוֹרָה.

The Gemara asks: **And what does Rabbi Yishmael do with this** extra phrase: **"It shall be yours"?** This **teaches about a blemished firstborn**[H] offering, **that it is** also given as **a gift to the priest, as we have not found** it written explicitly anywhere **in the entire Torah** what should be done with a blemished firstborn.

וְרַבִּי עֲקִיבָא? יָלֵיף לֵיהּ מִ״בְּשָׂרָם״ – חַד תָּם, וְחַד בַּעַל מוּם. וְרַבִּי יִשְׁמָעֵאל? מִבְּשָׂרָם דְּהָנָךְ בְּכוֹרוֹת קָאָמַר.

The Gemara asks: **And** from where does **Rabbi Akiva** derive that a blemished firstborn offering is also given as a gift to the priest? **He derives it from** the term **"their flesh,"** which is written in the plural. This teaches that **both an unblemished** firstborn offering **and a blemished** firstborn offering are given as gifts to the priest. The Gemara asks: **And** how does **Rabbi Yishmael** understand the plural term? The Gemara answers that he understands it to be **saying** that the priest receives gifts **from the flesh of** all **these firstborn** offerings mentioned in the verse, i.e., the firstborn of cattle, sheep, and goats.

NOTES

And Rabbi Tarfon left – וְנִסְתַּלֵּק רַבִּי טַרְפוֹן: In other words, he left the discussion and remained quiet, and had no reply. He felt that the two opinions carried equal weight, and if so, perhaps one should act stringently.

But I juxtapose it with a breast and thigh of a thanks offering – וַאֲנִי מַקִּישׁוֹ לְחָזֶה וְשׁוֹק שֶׁל תּוֹדָה: He prefers the juxtaposition with a thanks offering because of the principle that it is preferable to grasp less, in this case one day and one night, rather than attempt to grasp more, i.e., two days and one night (Rashi). *Tosafot* explain that there is a principle that a juxtaposition should be used to teach a stringency rather than a leniency.

HALAKHA

A blemished firstborn – בְּכוֹר בַּעַל מוּם: A male firstborn of a kosher animal that has a blemish, whether it was born with that blemish or developed it later, is the property of the priest. If the priest wishes, he may eat it anywhere, or he may sell it, or he may feed it to whomever he wishes, even to a gentile, because it is non-sacred (Rambam *Sefer Korbanot*, *Hilkhot Bekhorot* 1:3).

NOTES

Just as the High Priest sprinkles in the innermost sanctum – כְּשֵׁם שֶׁמַּזֶּה לִפְנַי וְלִפְנִים: The sprinklings of the blood of a bull and a goat in the innermost sanctum are derived from a juxtaposition and another principle. With regard to the bull the Torah states that the blood must be sprinkled seven times below but does not mention how many times it must be sprinkled above. With regard to the goat the Torah mentions a single sprinkling above, but does not mention how many times the blood must be sprinkled below. The Torah connects the two via a juxtaposition. The actual requirement of sprinkling is not derived from the juxtaposition; only its details are derived. Therefore, it is derived from a juxtaposition and another principle.

HALAKHA

Just as the High Priest sprinkles in the innermost sanctum, etc. – כְּשֵׁם שֶׁמַּזֶּה לִפְנַי וְלִפְנִים וכו׳: The blood of the bull and goat offered on Yom Kippur must be sprinkled eight times between the staves and eight times on the Curtain separating the Sanctuary from the Holy of Holies (Rambam *Sefer Avoda, Hilkhot Ma'aseh HaKorbanot* 5:12 and *Hilkhot Avodat Yom HaKippurim* 3:5).

בְּמַאי קָמִיפַּלְגִי? מָר סָבַר: הֵימֶנּוּ וְדָבָר אַחֵר – הָוֵי הֶיקֵּשׁ, וּמָר סָבַר: לָא הָוֵי הֶיקֵּשׁ.

The Gemara asks: Since Rabbi Akiva and Rabbi Yishmael both agree that a matter derived via a juxtaposition cannot then teach its *halakha* via a juxtaposition, **with regard to what** principle **do they disagree?** The Gemara answers: One **Sage,** Rabbi Yishmael, **holds** that a *halakha* derived both **from that** juxtaposition **and** from **another** principle **is** considered **a juxtaposition.** In this case, the specific detail that the breast and thigh of a thanks offering are given to a priest is derived from a juxtaposition with peace offerings. The length of time in which it may be eaten, one day and one night, is written explicitly. Since it is nevertheless considered a juxtaposition, it cannot be used to teach the *halakha* with regard to a firstborn offering. **And** one **Sage,** Rabbi Akiva, **holds** that such a case **is not** considered to be **a juxtaposition,** and therefore it can be used to teach another *halakha* via a juxtaposition.

בִּשְׁלָמָא לְמַאן דְּאָמַר לָא הָוֵי הֶיקֵּשׁ – הַיְינוּ דִּכְתִיב: ״וְכֵן יַעֲשֶׂה לְאֹהֶל מוֹעֵד״,

The Gemara comments: **Granted, according to the one who says** that a matter derived via a juxtaposition and another principle **is not** considered **a juxtaposition, this is** the reason **that it is written** with regard to the rites performed by the High Priest on Yom Kippur: **"And so shall he do for the Tent of Meeting** that dwells with them in the midst of their impurity" (Leviticus 16:16).

כְּשֵׁם שֶׁמַּזֶּה לִפְנַי וְלִפְנִים אַחַת לְמַעְלָה וְשֶׁבַע לְמַטָּה מִדַּם הַפָּר – כָּךְ מַזֶּה בַּהֵיכָל,

The High Priest sprinkles the blood of two offerings, the bull and the goat. He sprinkles their blood between the staves of the Ark and on the Curtain separating the Sanctuary and Holy of Holies. In each location he sprinkles their blood once above and seven times below. The verse does not write all of the details of these sprinklings with regard to each offering, and the details of each are derived from what is written explicitly in the other, as follows: **Just as** the High Priest **sprinkles in the innermost sanctum,**[NH] between the staves of the Ark, **once above and seven** times **below, with the blood of the bull, so he sprinkles** on the Curtain **in the Sanctuary.**

וּכְשֵׁם שֶׁלִּפְנַי וְלִפְנִים אַחַת לְמַעְלָה וְשֶׁבַע לְמַטָּה מִדַּם הַשָּׂעִיר – כָּךְ מַזֶּה בַּהֵיכָל.

And just as in the innermost sanctum he sprinkles **once above and seven** times **below, with the blood of the goat, so he sprinkles** on the Curtain **in the Sanctuary.** This is an instance of a *halakha* derived both from a juxtaposition and from another principle, and the stringency that a matter derived via a juxtaposition cannot also teach its *halakha* via a juxtaposition is not applied in this case.

אֶלָּא לְמַאן דְּאָמַר הָוֵי הֶיקֵּשׁ מַאי אִיכָּא לְמֵימַר? מְקוֹמוֹת הוּא דְּגָמְרִי מֵהֲדָדֵי.

But according to the one who says that this too **is** considered **a juxtaposition, what can be said?** How can these *halakhot* be derived? The Gemara answers: **It is the locations** where the blood is sprinkled **that are derived from one another** in the second juxtaposition. The first juxtaposition teaches one *halakha*, namely, that the blood of the bull and the blood of the goat are to be compared to one another. The second juxtaposition does not teach a *halakha* with regard to the blood of the bull and the blood of the goat per se; rather it teaches a comparison between the sprinkling performed in the Holy of Holies and the sprinkling performed in the Sanctuary. These are two unconnected juxtapositions.

וְאִיבָּעֵית אֵימָא: חוּץ מִפְּנִים בְּחַד זִימְנָא גָּמֵיר.

The Gemara suggests: **And if you wish, say**[N] there is a different resolution: The sprinkling **outside is derived from** the sprinkling **inside, all at once.** There are not two comparisons here, one derived from the other, but rather a single, complex juxtaposition, from which all of the relevant *halakhot* are derived.

NOTES

And if you wish, say – וְאִיבָּעֵית אֵימָא: In other words, the service of Yom Kippur has a general juxtaposition connecting its service performed in the inner sanctum to its service performed in the Sanctuary. This includes several of the *halakhot* mentioned explicitly in the context of the service of the inner sanctum, as well as those *halakhot* derived through juxtaposition. By contrast, with regard to the derivation of the *halakhot* concerning a thanks offering from those concerning a firstborn, the only *halakha* learned is that the priests have one day and one night to eat their portion, and the fact they receive a portion is derived via a juxtaposition (Rashi; see *Tosafot*). Rabbeinu Yitzḥak of Dampierre explains that the Gemara means that there are not two separate juxtapositions, but it is all a single derivation, that the service of the goat offered outside has the same *halakhot* as the bull offered inside and the goat offered inside. Rabbeinu Ḥananel has a different version of the text and explains that the juxtaposition between the goat and the bull teaches that they should be the same in every way, one sprinkling upward and seven downward, both inside and out.

בִּשְׁלָמָא לְמַאן דְּאָמַר [לָא] הָוֵי הֶיקֵּשׁ – הַיְינוּ דִּכְתִיב: ״מִמּוֹשְׁבֹתֵיכֶם תָּבִיאוּ לֶחֶם תְּנוּפָה״,

The Gemara comments: **Granted, according to the one who says** that a matter derived via a juxtaposition and another principle **is not a juxtaposition, this is the reason that it is written** with regard to the offering brought on *Shavuot*: **"You shall bring out of your dwellings two wave loaves**[H] of two-tenths of an ephah; they shall be of fine flour" (Leviticus 23:17).

שֶׁאֵין תַּלְמוּד לוֹמַר ״תָּבִיאוּ״, מַה תַּלְמוּד לוֹמַר ״תָּבִיאוּ״? כׇּל שֶׁאַתָּה מֵבִיא מִמָּקוֹם (לְמָקוֹם) אַחֵר הֲרֵי הוּא כָּזֶה, מַה לְּהַלָּן עִשָּׂרוֹן לְחַלָּה – אַף כָּאן עִשָּׂרוֹן לְחַלָּה.

Since apparently there is **no** need for **the verse to state: "You shall bring,"** as it already states: "And you shall present a new meal offering to the Lord" (Leviticus 23:16), **why** must **the verse state: "You shall bring"?** It states this to teach that **anything that you bring from another place**[N] that is similar to this offering, i.e., the leavened bread that accompanies a thanks offering, **shall be** prepared **like this. Just as there,** with regard to the two loaves, they must be prepared from **a tenth** of an ephah[NB] of flour **for** each **loaf, so too here,** each of the ten loaves of leavened bread that accompany a thanks offering must be prepared from **a tenth** of an ephah of flour **for** each **loaf.**

אִי מַה לְּהַלָּן שְׁנֵי עֶשְׂרוֹנִים, אַף כָּאן שְׁנֵי עֶשְׂרוֹנִים! תַּלְמוּד לוֹמַר: ״תִּהְיֶינָה״.

If they are compared, why not say that **just as there,** with regard to the two loaves, the total amount of flour is **two-tenths** of an ephah, **so too here,** with regard to the ten loaves that accompany a thanks offering, the total amount of flour for all ten should be **two-tenths** of an ephah? To counter this comparison, **the verse states: "They shall be,"**[N] to serve as a restriction and teach that only these two loaves amount to a total of two-tenths of an ephah, but the bread accompanying the thanks offering does not amount to two-tenths of an ephah.

וְלָמַדְנוּ עֲשָׂרָה לְחָמֵץ, עֲשָׂרָה לְמַצָּה מִנַּיִן? תַּלְמוּד לוֹמַר: ״עַל חַלֹּת לֶחֶם חָמֵץ״ – נֶגֶד חָמֵץ הָבֵא מַצָּה;

The Gemara continues: The ten loaves accompanying a thanks offering must each be a tenth of an ephah, and this has been derived from two sources: A juxtaposition with the offering of *Shavuot* and another principle, which is that which the verse states concerning the thanks offering, that there must be ten leavened loaves. **And we have learned** that **ten**-tenths of an ephah is required **for** the ten loaves of **leavened bread. From where** is it derived that **ten**-tenths of an ephah are required **for the *matza***[NH] which also accompanies a thanks offering? After stating that thirty *matzot* accompany a thanks offering, **the verse states: "With cakes of leavened bread"** (Leviticus 7:13), to juxtapose the *matza* with the leavened bread. This teaches that one must **bring *matza*** of an amount **corresponding to the leavened bread.**[N] In any event, this derivation can be employed according to the one who says that a matter derived via a juxtaposition and another principle is not a juxtaposition.

אֶלָּא לְמַאן דְּאָמַר (לָא) הָוֵי הֶיקֵּשׁ, מַאי אִיכָּא לְמֵימַר? ״תָּבִיאוּ״ יְתֵירָא הִיא.

But according to the one who says that a matter derived via a juxtaposition and another principle **is a juxtaposition,** and therefore it cannot then teach its *halakha* via another juxtaposition, **what is there to say?** How can the measure of flour for the *matza* be derived from the measure of flour for the leavened bread? The Gemara answers: The first *halakha,* connecting the two loaves of *Shavuot* to the bread accompanying a thanks offering, is not derived via a juxtaposition, but rather via a superfluous word. The term **"You shall bring,"** written with regard to the two loaves, **is extra,** and is therefore considered as if it were written explicitly with regard to the leavened bread accompanying the thanks offering. Therefore, it is possible to derive the *halakha* concerning matza from the *halakha* concerning leavened bread via a juxtaposition.

HALAKHA

Wave loaves – לֶחֶם תְּנוּפָה: The offering of the two loaves from the new wheat on *Shavuot* is brought from two-tenths of an ephah of fine flour (Rambam *Sefer Avoda, Hilkhot Temidin UMusafin* 8:3).

Ten-tenths for leavened bread…ten-tenths for *matza* – עֲשָׂרָה לְחָמֵץ עֲשָׂרָה לְמַצָּה: How does one prepare the bread that accompanies a thanks offering? One takes twenty-tenths of an ephah of fine flour and separates them into ten-tenths of an ephah for leavened bread and ten-tenths of an ephah for unleavened bread. The ten-tenths of an ephah for the leavened bread are made into ten loaves. The ten-tenths of an ephah for the unleavened bread are made into thirty equal loaves. Ten are baked in an oven, ten are wafers, and ten are boiled (Rambam *Sefer Avoda, Hilkhot Ma'aseh HaKorbanot* 9:17–18).

NOTES

Anything that you bring from another place – כׇּל שֶׁאַתָּה מֵבִיא מִמָּקוֹם אַחֵר: This means all the leavened bread that you bring. All of the other meal offerings were *matza*, and the only two types of leavened bread brought were the two loaves on *Shavuot* and the leavened bread accompanying the thanks offering.

Just as there they must be prepared from a tenth of an ephah – מַה לְּהַלָּן עִשָּׂרוֹן: The Torah states: "You shall bring out of your dwellings two wave loaves of two-tenths of an ephah; they shall be of fine flour; they shall be baked with leaven, for first fruits to the Lord" (Leviticus 23:17). Since the verse states that the two loaves were two-tenths of an ephah, it indicates that each one was a tenth of an ephah. In addition, it is known that ten loaves of leavened bread must be brought to accompany a thanks offering. If so, the ten loaves must be made from ten-tenths of an ephah.

The fact that ten loaves are required is derived via a verbal analogy from the *halakha* of *teruma* of the tithe, about which the Torah states: "Moreover you shall speak to the Levites, and say to them: When you take of the children of Israel the tithe which I have given you from them for your inheritance, then you shall set apart of it a gift for the Lord, a tithe of the tithe" (Numbers 18:26). The phrase "gift for the Lord" also appears in the context of the loaves accompanying the thanks offering: "And of it he shall present one out of each offering for a gift to the Lord; it shall be the priest's that sprinkles the blood of the peace offerings against the altar" (Leviticus 7:14). This teaches that the priest receives one-tenth of each of the four types of bread. It also indicates that in total there are ten loaves of leavened bread.

The verse states: They shall be – תַּלְמוּד לוֹמַר תִּהְיֶינָה: There are various explanations as to how this exclusion is derived. The explanations are contingent upon the version of the text in *Menaḥot* (77b–78a). According to Rashi the term "They shall be" is written with an extra letter *yod*, which has the numerical value of ten. Since that letter is not needed to teach the *halakha* of the two loaves, it is applied to teach the *halakha* concerning the leavened bread accompanying the thanks offering. *Tosafot* claim that the letter *yod* is not redundant. Therefore, they explain that the word itself indicates a limitation. It is as if the verse is stating that the two-tenths of an ephah is only for the two loaves, but not for any other loaves. This is also how it is explained in a *baraita* in *Torat Kohanim*. *Korban Aharon* explains that even according to Rashi the derivation from the letter *yod* is a mere support and not the actual source.

From where is it derived that ten-tenths of an ephah are for *matza* – עֲשָׂרָה לְמַצָּה מִנַּיִן: The Torah states that one must bring with a thanks offering three types of *matza* and one type of leavened bread. The Torah does not specify their weight. This juxtaposition teaches that they must be made from ten-tenths of an ephah of fine flour. This ten-tenths of an ephah is divided between all thirty *matzot*, and another ten-tenths of an ephah is used for the ten leavened loaves.

Bring *matza* corresponding to the leavened bread – נֶגֶד חָמֵץ הָבֵא מַצָּה: The juxtaposition between *matza* and leavened bread is based on the juxtaposition with the two loaves concerning a tenth of an ephah for each loaf, and also that ten loaves of leavened bread accompany a thanks offering. For this reason it is a case of a derivation via a juxtaposition and another principle.

BACKGROUND

A tenth of an ephah – עִשָּׂרוֹן: The ephah is a biblical measure of volume. There is much discussion between later authorities as to how much a tenth of an ephah of flour would weigh; opinions range from 1.6 to 2.25 kg.

"הַפֶּסַח אֵינוֹ נֶאֱכָל". מַאן תַּנָּא? אֲמַר רַב יוֹסֵף: רַבִּי אֶלְעָזָר בֶּן עֲזַרְיָה הִיא. דְּתַנְיָא, רַבִּי אֶלְעָזָר [בֶּן עֲזַרְיָה] אוֹמֵר: נֶאֱמַר כָּאן: "בַּלַּיְלָה [הַזֶּה]", וְנֶאֱמַר לְהַלָּן: "וְעָבַרְתִּי בְאֶרֶץ מִצְרַיִם בַּלַּיְלָה הַזֶּה",

§ The mishna teaches: **The Paschal offering is eaten only** at night and it is eaten only until midnight. The Gemara asks: **Who is the *tanna*** who taught this mishna? **Rav Yosef said** that **it is Rabbi Elazar ben Azarya. As it is taught** in a *baraita*: The verse states: "And they shall eat of the flesh on that night" (Exodus 12:8). **Rabbi Elazar ben Azarya says: It is stated here: "On that night,"** without stating when the night ends. **And it is stated there,** with regard to the plague that afflicted the firstborn Egyptians: **"And I will pass through the land of Egypt on that night** and I will strike every firstborn in the land of Egypt" (Exodus 12:12). With regard to the death of the firstborns the Torah states: "So said the Lord: At about midnight, I will go out into the midst of Egypt and every firstborn in Egypt shall die" (Exodus 11:4–5).

מַה לְּהַלָּן עַד חֲצוֹת – אַף כָּאן עַד חֲצוֹת.

Rabbi Elazar ben Azarya continues: **Just as** in the verse **there,** the death of the firstborns occurred **until midnight,** as stated explicitly in the verse, **so too,** in the verse **here,** the mitzva to eat the Paschal offering continues **until midnight** but not beyond.

אָמַר לוֹ רַבִּי עֲקִיבָא: וַהֲלֹא כְּבָר נֶאֱמַר: "וַאֲכַלְתֶּם אוֹתוֹ בְּחִפָּזוֹן" – עַד שְׁעַת חִפָּזוֹן!

Rabbi Akiva said to Rabbi Elazar ben Azarya: **But isn't it** already **stated:** "And so you shall eat it, with your loins girded, your shoes on your feet, your staffs in your hands, **and you will eat it in haste,** for it is the Paschal offering for the Lord" (Exodus 12:11)? This verse indicates that the Paschal offering may be eaten **until the time of haste,** i.e., until dawn, as the Jewish people left Egypt hastily the next morning.

אִם כֵּן, מַה תַּלְמוּד לוֹמַר "בַּלַּיְלָה הַזֶּה"? שֶׁיָּכוֹל יְהֵא כְּכָל הַקֳּדָשִׁים הַנֶּאֱכָלִים בַּיּוֹם? תַּלְמוּד לוֹמַר: "בַּלַּיְלָה", בַּלַּיְלָה יְהֵא נֶאֱכָל וְאֵינוֹ נֶאֱכָל בַּיּוֹם.

The Gemara asks: **If so, why** must **the verse state: "On that night,"** with regard to eating the Paschal offering? The Gemara explains: This phrase is necessary, as one **might** have thought that the Paschal offering is **like all the** other **offerings** in **that it should be eaten during the day,** on the day it is sacrificed. To counter this reasoning, **the verse states: "On** that **night,"** to emphasize that this particular offering **shall be eaten at night,**[H] **but it shall not be eaten during the day.**

אֲמַר לֵיהּ אַבַּיֵי: וּמִמַּאי דְּרַבִּי אֶלְעָזָר בֶּן עֲזַרְיָה, וּדְאוֹרַיְיתָא? דִּלְמָא דְּרַבָּנַן, וּלְהַרְחִיק מִן הָעֲבֵירָה! אִם כֵּן, מַאי "אֶלָּא עַד חֲצוֹת"? [אֶלָּא] כִּי הָתָם, מָה הָתָם דְּאוֹרַיְיתָא – אַף כָּאן נַמִי דְּאוֹרַיְיתָא.

Abaye said to Rav Yosef: **And from where** do you know **that** the mishna represents the opinion **of Rabbi Elazar ben Azarya, and** is stating that the Paschal offering must be eaten by midnight **by Torah law? Perhaps** the mishna is in accordance with the opinion of Rabbi Akiva, and is stating that the Paschal offering must be eaten by midnight **by rabbinic law, and** the reason for the rabbinic decree was **to distance** one **from a sin.**[N] Rav Yosef replied: **If so, what** does the mishna mean when it says: It is eaten **only until midnight?** With regard to the other offerings the mishna teaches: Until midnight, without specifying: Only. **Rather,** one must say that it is **like there,** with regard to the other *halakhot* of the Paschal offering stated in the mishna. **Just as there,** the requirements are **by Torah law, so too here,** with regard to the final time for eating the meat, the requirement is **also by Torah law.**

הדרן עלך איזהו מקומן

HALAKHA

Shall be eaten at night, etc. – בַּלַּיְלָה יְהֵא נֶאֱכָל וכו׳: The Rambam writes that by Torah law the Paschal offering may be eaten all night until dawn. The Sages ruled that it must be eaten before midnight, to distance one from a sin. This is in accordance with the opinion of Rabbi Akiva, based on the principle that the *halakha* is in accordance with his opinion when he engages in a dispute with one of his colleagues. Many of the early commentaries rule that the *halakha* is in accordance with the opinion of Rabbi Elazar ben Azaria, as there is an unattributed mishna in accordance with his opinion (Rabbeinu Ḥananel; *Tosafot*). They hold that one does not fulfill one's obligation by eating the Paschal offering after midnight. Therefore, the *Shulḥan Arukh* rules that the *matza* that is eaten toward the end of the Passover seder as a reminder of the Paschal offering must be eaten before midnight. The later authorities rule that if one did not eat an olive-bulk of *matza* on the first night of Passover before midnight, one must eat it after midnight without reciting a blessing (Rambam *Sefer Korbanot, Hilkhot Korban Pesaḥ* 8:15; *Shulḥan Arukh, Oraḥ Ḥayyim* 477:1, and see *Mishna Berura* there).

NOTES

To distance one from a sin – לְהַרְחִיק מִן הָעֲבֵירָה: The mishna in tractate *Berakhot* (2a) states similarly with regard to offerings that are eaten for one day and one night. Even though by Torah law they may be eaten all night long, the Sages decreed that they must be eaten before midnight in order to distance one from sin.

Summary of **Perek V**

This chapter began with a discussion of offerings of the most sacred order. It described their slaughter and the collection of their blood in the north of the Temple courtyard, and noted that Israelites have no portion in these offerings. The *halakhot* of misuse of consecrated property apply to them even before the blood has been sprinkled on the altar. These offerings include sin offerings brought inside, i.e., bulls and goats that are burned, burnt offerings, sin offerings brought outside, guilt offerings, and communal peace offerings.

The chapter began by describing the offerings whose blood is sprinkled inside the Sanctuary. First it discussed the bull and goat of Yom Kippur, whose blood is brought to the Holy of Holies. Afterward it examined those offerings whose blood is sprinkled in two locations within the Sanctuary, i.e., on the Curtain and on the golden altar. The flesh of these offerings is not placed on the altar but burned outside of Jerusalem.

Next the chapter described those offerings whose blood is presented on the external altar, the altar of the burnt offering. First it discussed communal and individual sin offerings, whose blood must be placed on the four corners of the altar. Parts of these offerings are placed on the altar, and the remainder is eaten by priests within the Temple courtyard within one day and one night.

The next offering mentioned is the burnt offering, which also has a unique aspect of sanctity in that it is entirely burned on the altar. Its blood requires only two placements, on the two diagonal corners of the altar.

The chapter continued by elaborating on the communal peace offerings that are brought on *Shavuot* with the two loaves, and guilt offerings. Their blood is presented in the same way as is the blood of a burnt offering, but they are eaten in the same way as are sin offerings, by male priests within the Temple courtyard.

Then the chapter examined offerings of lesser sanctity. These may be slaughtered anywhere within the Temple courtyard, and they may be eaten throughout Jerusalem by any ritually pure Jew. There is no liability for misuse of consecrated property concerning an offering of lesser sanctity except on that portion which is placed on the altar. Included within the category of offerings of lesser sanctity are thanks offerings, the nazirite's ram, peace offerings, firstborn offerings, animal tithe offerings, and Paschal offerings.

The blood of a thanks offering and of a nazirite's ram is presented on the two diagonal corners of the altar. Their sacrificial portions are offered on the altar, and the rest of the meat is eaten by any ritually pure Jew throughout Jerusalem. Certain parts of these offerings belong to the priests, and they, their families, and their slaves may eat the meat anywhere in the city. These offerings are mentioned first because their meat must be eaten within one day and one night.

Peace offerings are identical to thanks offerings except that they may be eaten within two days and the intervening night.

Firstborn offerings, animal tithe offerings, and Paschal offerings have their own *hala-khot*. They are mentioned last because their blood requires only a single presentation on the altar. Certain sacrificial portions of these offerings are burned on the altar, in the same way as those of peace offerings, thanks offerings, and the nazirite's ram. The differences between them are with regard to how they are eaten. A firstborn offering belongs to the priests. An animal tithe offering is eaten by the owners, and both are eaten within two days and a night, like peace offerings. The Paschal offering is unique in that it must be eaten before midnight of the night of Passover, it may be partaken of only by those who are registered for it, and it may be consumed only roasted.

With regard to the hermeneutical principles, there are some that may be used both to derive and teach in the realm of consecrated matters, and some that may not. In certain cases the Gemara does not reach a clear conclusion.

Introduction to **Perek VI**

And if his offering to the Lord be a burnt offering of birds, then he shall bring his offering of doves, or of pigeons. And the priest shall bring it to the altar, and pinch off its head, and make it smoke on the altar; and its blood shall be drained out on the side of the altar. And he shall take away its crop with its feathers, and toss it beside the altar on the east part, in the place of the ashes. And he shall rend it by its wings but shall not separate it; and the priest shall make it smoke upon the altar, upon the wood that is upon the fire; it is a burnt offering, an offering made by fire, of a sweet savor unto the Lord.

(Leviticus 1:14–17)

And he shall bring them unto the priest, who shall offer that which is for the sin offering first, and pinch off its head opposite its nape, but shall not separate it. And he shall sprinkle of the blood of the sin offering upon the side of the altar; and the rest of the blood shall be drained out at the base of the altar; it is a sin offering. And he shall prepare the second for a burnt offering, according to the ordinance; and the priest shall make atonement for him as concerning his sin which he has sinned, and he shall be forgiven

(Leviticus 5:8–10)

This chapter is a continuation of the previous one, which detailed the proper location for the slaughter and other sacrificial rites of animal offerings. It continues by discussing whether offerings may be slaughtered on top of the altar and then digresses to examine other *halakhot* pertaining to the altar. Following that, the chapter briefly addresses the location for the rites of the meal offering, a topic that is explored more fully in tractate *Menaḥot*.

The chapter then discusses the proper location for sacrificing bird offerings, and engages in a detailed explication of the sacrificial rites of bird offerings. Whereas animal offerings are slaughtered with a knife, an act that may be carried out even by a non-priest, bird offerings are slaughtered differently: A priest cuts the bird's nape, starting from the back, with his thumbnail, before placing some of the blood on the side of the altar. There are differences between the sacrificial rites of bird burnt offerings and bird sin offerings, some of which are described in this chapter and some in the following chapter.

There are a number of *halakhot* with regard to which bird burnt offerings and bird sin offerings are similar to animal burnt offerings and animal sin offerings, e.g., improper intention that disqualifies the offerings and the manner in which the offerings are eaten. But since the sacrificial rites are different, the Gemara specifies how these *halakhot* apply to bird offerings. The main topic of this chapter is the explanation of these *halakhot* and how they are derived from the Torah.

מתני׳ קָדְשֵׁי קֳדָשִׁים שֶׁשְּׁחָטָן בְּרֹאשׁ הַמִּזְבֵּחַ, רַבִּי יוֹסֵי אוֹמֵר: כְּאִילּוּ נִשְׁחֲטוּ בַּצָּפוֹן. רַבִּי יוֹסֵי בְּרַבִּי יְהוּדָה אוֹמֵר: מֵחֲצִי הַמִּזְבֵּחַ וּלְדָרוֹם – כַּדָּרוֹם, מֵחֲצִי הַמִּזְבֵּחַ וְלַצָּפוֹן – כַּצָּפוֹן.

MISHNA It was taught in the previous chapter that offerings of the most sacred order are to be slaughtered in the northern section of the Temple courtyard. With regard to **offerings of the most sacred order that one slaughtered atop the altar,**[H] **Rabbi Yosei says:** Their status is **as though they were slaughtered in the north,** and the offerings are therefore valid. **Rabbi Yosei, son of Rabbi Yehuda, says:** The status of the area **from the halfway point of the altar and to the south is like** that of **the south,** and offerings of the most sacred order slaughtered in that area are therefore disqualified. The status of the area **from the halfway point of the altar and to the north** is like that of **the north.**

גמ׳ אָמַר רַב אַסִּי אָמַר רַבִּי יוֹחָנָן, אוֹמֵר הָיָה ר׳ יוֹסֵי: כּוּלֵּיהּ מִזְבֵּחַ בַּצָּפוֹן קָאֵי. וּמַאי כְּאִילּוּ? מַהוּ דְּתֵימָא בָּעֵינַן יֶרֶךְ וְלֵיכָּא, קָא מַשְׁמַע לָן.

GEMARA Rav Asi says that **Rabbi Yoḥanan says: Rabbi Yosei used to say: The entire altar stands in the north** section of the Temple courtyard. The Gemara asks: **And what** is the meaning of Rabbi Yosei's statement that if one slaughtered offerings of the most sacred order atop the altar it is **as though** they were slaughtered in the north, which indicates that they were not actually slaughtered in the north? The Gemara answers: Rabbi Yosei said this **lest you say** that **we require** that the offering be slaughtered **"on the side** of the altar northward" (Leviticus 1:11), i.e., on the ground beside the altar, **and** that requirement **is not** fulfilled when it is slaughtered on top of the altar. Therefore, Rabbi Yosei **teaches us** that the offering is still valid.

אֲמַר לֵיהּ רַבִּי זֵירָא לְרַב אַסִּי: אֶלָּא מֵעַתָּה, לְרַבִּי יוֹסֵי בְּרַבִּי יְהוּדָה הָכִי נַמִּי דְּחֶצְיוֹ בַּצָּפוֹן וְחֶצְיוֹ בַּדָּרוֹם?

Rabbi Zeira said to Rav Asi: Rabbi Yoḥanan apparently understands that the reason Rabbi Yosei holds that an offering of the most sacred order slaughtered on the altar is valid is because the entire altar is in the northern section of the Temple courtyard. **If that is so,** shall one **also** say **that according to Rabbi Yosei, son of Rabbi Yehuda, half of** the altar was situated **in the north** of the Temple courtyard **and half of it** was situated **in the south?**

וְכִי תֵּימָא הָכִי נַמִּי – וְהָא אַתְּ הוּא דַּאֲמַרְתְּ מִשְּׁמֵיהּ דְּרַבִּי יוֹחָנָן: מוֹדֵי רַבִּי יוֹסֵי בְּרַבִּי יְהוּדָה שֶׁאִם שְׁחָטָן כְּנֶגְדָּן בַּקַּרְקַע פְּסוּלָה!

And if you would say that **indeed** that is so, **wasn't it you who said in the name of Rabbi Yoḥanan** that **Rabbi Yosei, son of Rabbi Yehuda, concedes that if one slaughtered** offerings of the most sacred order **on the ground opposite** the northern half of the altar, the offering is **disqualified?** Accordingly, Rabbi Yosei, son of Rabbi Yehuda, apparently maintains that the altar is not located in the north at all.

אֲמַר לֵיהּ: הָכִי קָאָמַר רַבִּי יוֹחָנָן: שְׁנֵיהֶם מִקְּרָא אֶחָד דָּרְשׁוּ: ״וְזָבַחְתָּ עָלָיו אֶת עֹלֹתֶיךָ וְאֶת שְׁלָמֶיךָ״.

Rav Asi **said to** Rabbi Zeira: Rabbi Yoḥanan's statement with regard to Rabbi Yosei's opinion is an independent statement rather than an inference from the mishna. And with regard to the dispute in the mishna, **this is what Rabbi Yoḥanan says: Both of them derived** their opinions **from one verse:** "An altar of earth you shall make for Me, **and you shall slaughter upon it your burnt offerings and your peace offerings"** (Exodus 20:21).

רַבִּי יוֹסֵי סָבַר: כּוּלּוֹ לְעוֹלָה וְכוּלּוֹ לִשְׁלָמִים, וְרַבִּי יוֹסֵי בְּרַבִּי יְהוּדָה סָבַר: חֶצְיוֹ לְעוֹלָה וְחֶצְיוֹ לִשְׁלָמִים;

Rabbi Yosei maintains that the verse teaches that **all of it,** i.e., the entire altar, is fit **for** slaughtering **a burnt offering, and all of it** is also fit **for** slaughtering **a peace offering. And Rabbi Yosei, son of Rabbi Yehuda, maintains** that the verse teaches that **half of it** is fit **for** slaughtering **a burnt offering and half of it** is fit **for** slaughtering **a peace offering.**[N]

HALAKHA

Offerings of the most sacred order that one slaughtered atop the altar – קָדְשֵׁי קֳדָשִׁים שֶׁשְּׁחָטָן בְּרֹאשׁ הַמִּזְבֵּחַ: Offerings of the most sacred order that were slaughtered atop the altar are considered as having been slaughtered in the north side of the Temple courtyard and are therefore valid, in accordance with the opinion of Rabbi Yosei. Commentaries on the Rambam question how the Rambam rules in accordance with this mishna, which maintains that the entire altar stood in the northern section of the Temple courtyard, while at the same time ruling in accordance with the mishna in *Middot* that maintains that the altar stood primarily in the southern section (Rambam *Sefer Avoda, Hilkhot Pesulei HaMukdashin* 3:1 and *Kesef Mishne* there).

NOTES

Half of it is fit for slaughtering a burnt offering and half of it is fit for slaughtering a peace offering – חֶצְיוֹ לְעוֹלָה וְחֶצְיוֹ לִשְׁלָמִים: As stated later in the Gemara, Rabbi Yosei, son of Rabbi Yehuda, holds that the entire altar was located in the southern section of the Temple courtyard. Nevertheless, he derived from this verse that the northern half of the altar is a valid location for slaughtering offerings of the most sacred order (*Sefat Emet*).

HALAKHA

That the altar must be attached to the earth – שֶׁיְּהֵא מְחוּבָּר מֵאֲדָמָה: The altar must be attached to the ground, and not built upon arches or tunnels (Rambam *Sefer Avoda, Hilkhot Beit HaBeḥira* 1:13, 2:16).

דְּאִי סָלְקָא דַּעְתָּךְ כּוּלּוֹ לְעוֹלָה כָּשֵׁר, הַשְׁתָּא כּוּלּוֹ לְעוֹלָה כָּשֵׁר – כּוּלּוֹ לִשְׁלָמִים מִיבַּעְיָא?

The Gemara explains the reasoning of Rabbi Yosei, son of Rabbi Yehuda: **As if** it **enters your mind** that **all of it is fit for** slaughtering **a burnt offering, now** that **all of it is fit for** slaughtering **a burnt offering,** which must be slaughtered in the northern section of the Temple courtyard (see 53b), **is it necessary** to teach that it is also fit **for** slaughtering **a peace offering,** which may be slaughtered anywhere in the Temple courtyard (see 55a)? The verse therefore must be understood as teaching that half the altar is fit for slaughtering burnt offerings and half is fit for slaughtering peace offerings.

וְאִידָּךְ: אִיצְטְרִיךְ, סָלְקָא דַּעְתָּךְ אָמִינָא: עוֹלָה הוּא דִּדְחִיק לֵיהּ מָקוֹם, אֲבָל שְׁלָמִים דְּלָא דְּחִיק לֵיהּ מָקוֹם – אֵימָא לָא, קָא מַשְׁמַע לַן.

The Gemara asks: **And** how does **the other** Sage, Rabbi Yosei, respond to this reasoning? The Gemara answers: It **was necessary** for the verse to mention peace offerings. Otherwise, it could **enter your mind to say** that the verse allows one to slaughter only **a burnt offering** atop the altar, **as the location** where **it** may be slaughtered on the ground is **narrow. But** with regard to **peace offerings, whose location** for slaughter on the ground is **not narrow, say** that **no,** one may not slaughter them atop the altar. Therefore, the verse **teaches us** that peace offerings as well may be slaughtered atop the altar.

גּוּפָא, אָמַר רַב אַסִי אָמַר רַבִּי יוֹחָנָן: מוֹדֵי רַבִּי יוֹסֵי בְּרַבִּי יְהוּדָה שֶׁאִם שְׁחָטָן כְּנֶגְדָּן בַּקַּרְקַע פְּסוּלוֹת. אֲמַר לֵיהּ רַב אַחָא מִדִּיפְתִּי לְרָבִינָא: מַאי "כְּנֶגְדָּן בַּקַּרְקַע"? אִילֵימָא אַמָּה יְסוֹד אַמָּה סוֹבֵב – הַאי גּוּפֵיהּ מִזְבֵּחַ הוּא! וְעוֹד, מַאי "כְּנֶגְדָּן בַּקַּרְקַע"?

§ The Gemara discusses **the** matter **itself: Rav Asi says** that **Rabbi Yoḥanan says: Rabbi Yosei, son of Rabbi Yehuda, concedes that if one slaughtered** offerings of the most sacred order **on the ground opposite** the northern half of the altar, the offering is **disqualified. Rav Aḥa of Difti said to Ravina: What** is the meaning of the phrase: **On the ground opposite**[N] the northern half of the altar? **If we say** it means that the offering was sacrificed upon the **cubit**-wide **base** of the altar or upon the **cubit**-wide **surrounding ledge** of the altar, **this itself is** part of the **altar. And furthermore, what** is the meaning of the phrase: **On the ground opposite** the northern half of the altar? The base and ledge are not on the ground.

וְכִי תֵּימָא, דַּעֲבִיד מְחִילּוֹת בַּקַּרְקַע וְשָׁחֵיט בְּהוּ – וְכִי הַאי גַּוְונָא מִי הָוֵי מִזְבֵּחַ? וְהָתַנְיָא: "מִזְבַּח אֲדָמָה תַּעֲשֶׂה לִּי" – שֶׁיְּהֵא מְחוּבָּר מֵאֲדָמָה, שֶׁלֹּא יִבְנֶנּוּ לֹא עַל גַּבֵּי מְחִילּוֹת וְלֹא עַל גַּבֵּי כִּיפִּין!

And if you would say that the case is **where one dug tunnels in the ground** beneath the altar, **and slaughtered** the offerings **in them, in a case like this would** the **altar** itself **be** fit for use so that according to Rabbi Yosei, son of Rabbi Yehuda, one may slaughter the offerings of the most sacred order on the altar but not on the ground? **But isn't it taught** in a *baraita*: The verse states: **"An altar of earth you shall make for Me"** (Exodus 20:21)? This verse indicates **that** the altar **must be attached to the earth,**[H] so **that one may not build it on top of tunnels nor on top of arches.**

לָא צְרִיכָא, דְּבַצְרֵיהּ בְּצוּרֵי.

The Gemara answers: **No,** it is **necessary** to have the phrase: On the ground opposite the northern half of the altar, in order to teach the *halakha* in a case **where one minimized** the dimensions of the altar[N] and slaughtered the offerings on the ground where the northern half of the altar had previously stood.

NOTES

What is the meaning of on the ground opposite – מַאי כְּנֶגְדָּן בַּקַּרְקַע: Rashi points out that the Gemara's question is not referring to the ground to the east and west of the altar, parallel to its northern section, as neither fulfills the requirement of "on the side of the altar northward." Rather, a careful reading of the expression: On the ground opposite the northern half of the altar, makes it clear that this is a reference to the ground beneath the altar.

Where one minimized the dimensions of the altar – דְּבַצְרֵיהּ בְּצוּרֵי: The case is where one minimized the altar's dimensions, thereby leaving earth in place of where that part of the altar previously stood. It is permitted to do this, as the Gemara states (62a) that the measurements of the length and width of the altar are not critical, so long as they are the same (see Ya'avetz). It is evident from here that there is a unique condition that offerings of the most sacred order must be sacrificed atop the altar, and not merely in the altar's space. One can also conclude from here that Rabbi Yosei, son of Rabbi Yehuda, maintains that the altar was located in the southern section of the Temple courtyard (Rashi).

אֲמַר רַבִּי זֵירָא: אֶפְשָׁר אִיתָא לְהָא דְּרַבִּי יוֹחָנָן וְלָא תָּנֵינָא לָהּ בְּמַתְנִיתִין?

§ The Gemara returns to discuss Rabbi Yoḥanan's statement that according to Rabbi Yosei the entire altar was located in the northern section of the Temple courtyard. The Gemara had mentioned that Rabbi Yoḥanan's statement is an independent statement, not based on the mishna. **Rabbi Zeira said:** Is it **possible** that **this** statement **of Rabbi Yoḥanan** is correct **and we did not learn it in** any **mishna?**

נְפַק, דַּק וְאַשְׁכַּח, דִּתְנַן: בֵּירְרוּ מִשָּׁם עֲצֵי תְאֵינָה יָפִים לְסַדֵּר מַעֲרָכָה שְׁנִיָּה שֶׁל קְטֹרֶת, כְּנֶגֶד קֶרֶן מַעֲרָבִית דְּרוֹמִית, מָשׁוּךְ מִן הַקֶּרֶן כְּלַפֵּי צָפוֹן אַרְבַּע אַמּוֹת; בְּאוֹמֶד חָמֵשׁ סְאִין גֶּחָלִים, וּבְשַׁבָּת בְּאוֹמֶד שְׁמוֹנֶה סְאִין גֶּחָלִים; שֶׁשָּׁם הָיוּ נוֹתְנִין שְׁנֵי בְזִיכֵי לְבוֹנָה שֶׁל לֶחֶם הַפָּנִים.

Rabbi Zeira **went out, examined** the matter, **and discovered** a mishna that alludes to Rabbi Yoḥanan's statement, **as we learned** in a mishna (*Tamid* 2:5): The priests **selected fine wood of a fig tree**[N] **from** the chamber of firewood,[H] with which **to lay out a second arrangement** of wood[B] on the altar so that coals from this arrangement could be used **for** burning the **incense.**[N] This second arrangement was located **opposite** the **southwest corner** of the altar, **distanced from** the **corner northward** by **four cubits.** They would arrange enough wood which, when burned, would produce **approximately five** *se'a* of coals. **And on Shabbat,** there was enough wood to produce **approximately eight** *se'a* of coals, **as they would place there the two bowls of frankincense of the shewbread.**

וּמַאי סִימָנָא? רַבִּי יוֹסֵי הִיא, דְּתַנְיָא:

The Gemara asks: **And what is the** significance of the mishna's **defining** the precise location of the arrangement and the fact that this is where the frankincense is burned? The Gemara embarks on a lengthy discussion to answer this question: This mishna **is** in accordance with the opinion of **Rabbi Yosei,** who holds that this arrangement of wood and the burning of the frankincense must be in that precise location, **as it is taught** in a *baraita*:

NOTES

Wood of a fig tree – עֲצֵי תְאֵינָה: The simple reason for using such wood is that it produced high-quality coals, which were used in burning the incense. Rashi explains homiletically that the tree from which Adam sinned was a fig tree (see *Berakhot* 40a). Therefore, it was befitting that atonement in the Temple be effected with wood of that tree.

A second arrangement for incense – מַעֲרָכָה שְׁנִיָּה שֶׁל קְטֹרֶת: Atop the altar there was a large pyre. It was a structure-like arrangement of logs upon which burnt offerings and portions of offerings were burned. An additional pyre was arranged next to it, whose purpose was to provide coals for the burning of the incense upon the golden altar. The logs from the large pyre were not used for that purpose, as they were covered in ashes of burned offerings.

HALAKHA

They selected fine wood of a fig tree from the chamber of firewood – בֵּירְרוּ מִשָּׁם עֲצֵי תְאֵינָה יָפִים: After the priests arranged the large pyre, they would select fine wood of a fig tree and arrange the second pyre for the incense. This second pyre was located on top of the altar, four cubits to the north of its southwest corner. The second pyre produced roughly five *se'a* of coals, and on Shabbat it produced roughly eight *se'a*, as the additional two bowls of frankincense of the shewbread were burned there on Shabbat (Rambam *Sefer Avoda*, *Hilkhot Temidin UMusafin* 2:8).

BACKGROUND

Location of the second arrangement of wood – מְקוֹם הַמַּעֲרָכָה הַשְּׁנִיָּה: The adjacent diagrams depict the possible locations of the second arrangement opposite the entrance to the Sanctuary (A) and the entrance to the Entrance Hall (B), according to the opinion that the sanctity of the Sanctuary and that of the Entrance Hall are equivalent. The Gemara concludes that the altar must be located wholly in the north courtyard for the arrangement to be positioned at a distance of exactly four cubits from the southern edge of the altar, so that its southern edge is opposite the northern end of the Sanctuary entrance.

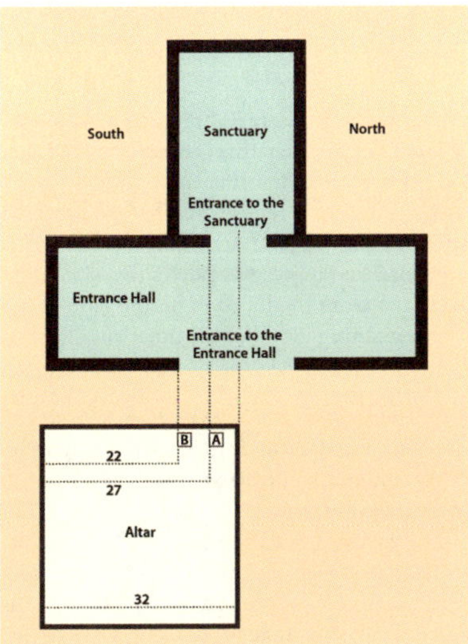

Possible locations of the arrangement, with the altar situated wholly in the south

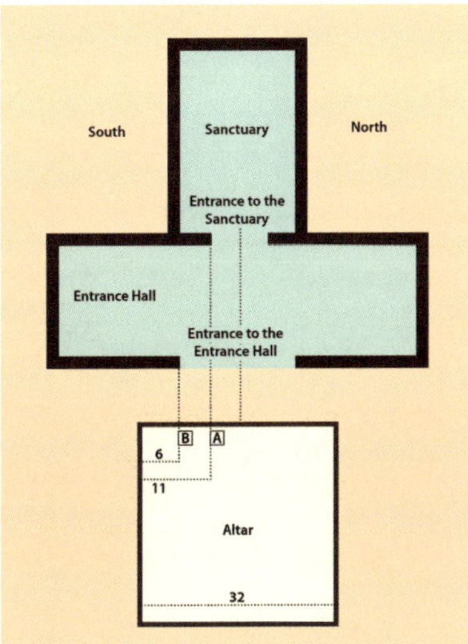

Possible locations of the arrangement, with the altar aligned in the center of the courtyard

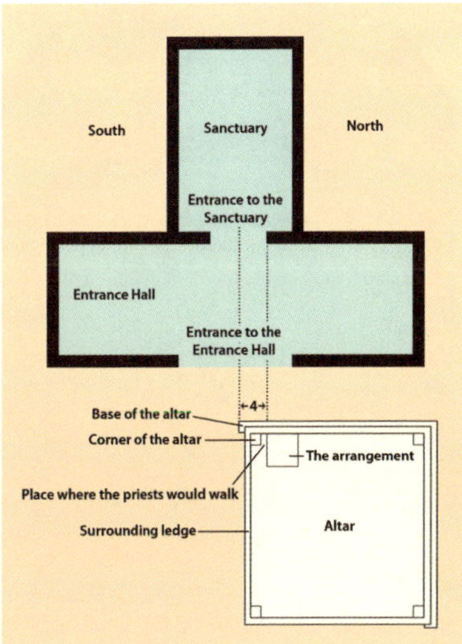

Location of the arrangement, with the altar wholly in the north

BACKGROUND

Two bowls of frankincense – שְׁנֵי בְזִיכֵי לְבוֹנָה: When the priests arranged the shewbread on the Temple table on Shabbat, they would place two bowls of frankincense on it as well. The following Shabbat, when they removed the bread, they sacrificed the frankincense and divided the shewbread among the priests.

There are many disputes as to the components of the incense, yet there are some elements about which there is almost no disagreement. One of these is the *levona*, frankincense, also used with most of the meal offerings. This is identified as the sap derived from *Boswellia sacra*, the frankincense tree.

Reproduction of vessels used for frankincense in the Temple

Shewbread – לֶחֶם הַפָּנִים: The Torah (Leviticus 24:5–9) describes the offering of the twelve loaves of shewbread that were placed on the table in the Sanctuary each Shabbat. The shewbread was unleavened and placed on the table in two arrangements of six loaves each. Two bowls of frankincense were placed between them, or on top of them according to other opinions.

Modern rendering of the shewbread

רַבִּי יוֹסֵי אוֹמֵר: זֶה סִימָן, כׇּל הַנִּיטָּל בִּפְנִים לִינָּתֵן בַּחוּץ – אֵינוֹ נוֹתֵן אֶלָּא בְּסָמוּךְ שֶׁאֵין לִפְנִים,

Rabbi Yosei says: This is the **principle** of where sacrificial items are placed on the inner and outer altars: **Any** sacrificial item **that is taken** from the altar located **inside** the Sanctuary in order **to be placed** on the altar **outside** the Sanctuary, in the Temple courtyard, **may be placed only on** the area of that altar that is **near** the Sanctuary, so **that there is no** area closer to the **inside** of the Sanctuary. It must therefore be placed on the part of the external altar closest to the entrance to the Sanctuary.

וְכׇל הַנִּיטָּל בַּחוּץ לִינָּתֵן לִפְנִים – אֵינוֹ נִיטָּל אֶלָּא בְּסָמוּךְ שֶׁאֵין לִפְנִים;

And any sacrificial item **that is taken** from the altar **outside** the Sanctuary, in the Temple courtyard, in order **to be placed** on the altar located **inside** the Sanctuary, **may be taken only from** the area of the external altar that is **near** the Sanctuary, so **that there is no** area closer to the **inside** of the Sanctuary, i.e., from the part of the external altar closest to the entrance to the Sanctuary.

״כׇּל הַנִּיטָּל בִּפְנִים לִינָּתֵן בַּחוּץ״. מַאי נִיהוּ? אִילֵּימָא שִׁירַיִם – בְּהֶדְיָא כְּתִיב בְּהוּ: ״אֶל יְסוֹד מִזְבַּח הָעוֹלָה אֲשֶׁר פֶּתַח אֹהֶל מוֹעֵד״!

The Gemara clarifies: With regard to the statement concerning **any** sacrificial item **that is taken** from the altar located **inside** the Sanctuary in order **to be placed** on the altar **outside** the Sanctuary, **what are these** items? **If we say** they are the **remaining** blood of the sin offerings whose blood is presented on the inner altar, there is no reason for Rabbi Yosei to formulate his principle, as **it is explicitly written concerning them:** "And all the remaining blood of the bull he shall pour out **at the base of the altar of the burnt offering, which is at the entrance to the Tent of Meeting**" (Leviticus 4:7). This verse describes how the blood of the inner sin offerings that remained after the sprinkling was to be poured out on the base of the west side of the altar, which is the side closest to the entrance to the Sanctuary.

וְתוּ: ״כׇּל הַנִּיטָּל בַּחוּץ לִינָּתֵן בִּפְנִים״ מַאי נִיהוּ? אִילֵּימָא גֶּחָלִים שֶׁל יוֹם הַכִּיפּוּרִים – בְּהֶדְיָא כְּתִיב בְּהוּ: ״וְלָקַח מְלֹא הַמַּחְתָּה גַּחֲלֵי אֵשׁ״ וגו׳!

And furthermore, with regard to the statement about **any** sacrificial item **that is taken** from the altar **outside** the Sanctuary, in the Temple courtyard, in order **to be placed** on the altar located **inside** the Sanctuary, **what are these** items? **If we say** these are the **coals of** the **Yom Kippur** service, which must be taken from the western side of the altar, **it is explicitly written concerning them: "And he shall take a coal pan full of coals of fire** from off the altar before the Lord" (Leviticus 16:12). The expression "before the Lord" is a reference to the western side of the altar, which is the side closest to the Sanctuary.

אֶלָּא: כׇּל הַנִּיטָּל בִּפְנִים לִינָּתֵן בַּחוּץ – שְׁנֵי בְזִיכֵי לְבוֹנָה שֶׁל לֶחֶם הַפָּנִים, דְּגָמְרִי מִשִּׁירַיִם.

The Gemara continues: **Rather,** Rabbi Yosei's statement with regard to **any** sacrificial item **that is taken** from the altar located **inside** the Sanctuary in order **to be placed** on the altar **outside** the Sanctuary is referring to the **two bowls of frankincense**[B] **of the shewbread.**[B] According to Rabbi Yosei, they must be burned on the western side of the altar, **as he derives** this *halakha* **from** the location on the base of the altar where the **remaining** blood of the inner sin offerings is poured.

הַנִּיטָּל בַּחוּץ לִינָּתֵן בִּפְנִים – גֶּחָלִים דְּכׇל יוֹמָא וְיוֹמָא, דְּגָמְרָן מִגֶּחָלִים שֶׁל יוֹם הַכִּפּוּרִים;

Rabbi Yosei's next statement, that any sacrificial item **that is taken** from **the** altar **outside** the Sanctuary in order **to be placed on** the altar located **inside** the Sanctuary may be taken only from the area of the external altar that is near the Sanctuary, is referring to the **coals that** are taken from the external altar **each and every day** and placed on the inner altar in order to burn the incense. According to Rabbi Yosei these coals must be taken from the western side of the altar, **as we derive** this *halakha* **from** the location on the altar from where the **coals of** the **Yom Kippur** service must be taken.

וּמַאי קָסָבַר? אִי קָסָבַר כּוּלֵּיהּ מִזְבֵּחַ בַּדָּרוֹם קָאֵי – עֶשְׂרִים וְשֶׁבַע בָּעֵי לְמֵיתֵי,

The Gemara discusses Rabbi Yosei's opinion that the second arrangement of wood was placed four cubits[B] north of the southwest corner of the altar: **And what does** Rabbi Yosei **hold** about the placement of the altar in the Temple courtyard? **If he holds** that **the entire altar stands in the south** side of the Temple courtyard, then only the five northernmost cubits of the altar are opposite the entrance to the Sanctuary. Accordingly, in order for the arrangement of wood to be opposite the entrance to the Sanctuary, one is **required to move** it **twenty-seven** cubits north of the southwest corner of the altar.

וְאִי נַמִי קָסָבַר קְדוּשַּׁת הֵיכָל וְאוּלָם חֲדָא הִיא – עֶשְׂרִים וְתַרְתֵּי בָּעֵי מֵיתֵי!

The Gemara continues: **And even if** Rabbi Yosei **holds** that the level of **sanctity of the Sanctuary and** the **Entrance Hall is the same,**[N] so that the arrangement of wood can be opposite the Entrance Hall, which is ten cubits wider than the Sanctuary, his opinion is still difficult. In order for the arrangement of wood to be opposite the Entrance Hall, one is **required to move** it **twenty-two** cubits north of the southwest corner of the altar.

וְאִי קָסָבַר חֶצְיוֹ בַּצָּפוֹן וְחֶצְיוֹ בַּדָּרוֹם – חַד סְרֵי בָּעֵי לְמֵיתֵי, וְאֶלָּא קָסָבַר: קְדוּשַּׁת הֵיכָל וְאוּלָם חֲדָא מִילְּתָא הִיא – שִׁית בָּעֵי לְמֵיתֵי!

The Gemara continues: **And** even **if** Rabbi Yosei **holds** that **half of** the altar was located **in the north** side of the Temple courtyard **and half in the south,** in order for the arrangement of wood to be opposite the entrance to the Sanctuary one is still **required to move** it **eleven** cubits to the north of the southwest corner of the altar. **And** if one suggests that, **rather, he holds that the sanctity of the Sanctuary and the Entrance Hall is one matter,** i.e., equal, one is still **required to move** the arrangement of wood **six** cubits from the southwest corner in order to be opposite the Entrance Hall.

אֶלָּא לָאו מִשּׁוּם דְּקָסָבַר כּוּלֵּיהּ מִזְבֵּחַ בַּצָּפוֹן קָאֵי,

Rather, is it **not** that Rabbi Yosei's opinion that the arrangement of wood was located four cubits from the altar's southwest corner is **due to** the fact **that he holds** that **the entire altar stands in the north** side of the Temple courtyard? Accordingly, only the five southernmost cubits of the altar were opposite the entrance to the Sanctuary.

וְהָנֵי אַרְבַּע אַמּוֹת – אַמָּה יְסוֹד, וְאַמָּה סוֹבֵב, וְאַמָּה מְקוֹם קְרָנוֹת, וְאַמָּה מְקוֹם רַגְלֵי הַכֹּהֲנִים, דְּכִי מְסַגּוּ לְקַמֵּיהּ טְפֵי – תּוּ לֵיכָּא פֶּתַח.

And of **these four cubits** from which the arrangement of wood was distanced from the southwest corner of the altar, one **cubit** was the **base** of the altar; **and** one **cubit** was **the surrounding ledge** of the altar; **and** one **cubit** was the **place** where the **corners** of the altar were located; **and** another **cubit** was **the place of the feet of the priests,** i.e., space for the priests to walk around the perimeter of the surface of the altar in order to perform the sacrificial rites. The arrangement of wood was located specifically in that location, **as if** one were to **move** it **farther away** from the southwest corner of the altar, it would **no longer** be opposite the **entrance** to the Sanctuary.[N] This proves that according to Rabbi Yosei, the entire altar was located in the northern side of the Temple courtyard, as stated by Rabbi Yoḥanan.

BACKGROUND

Cubit [*amma*] – **אַמָּה**: Several different lengths are referred to by this name. The physical origin of the measure is the distance from the elbow to the end of the middle finger, which is called *amma* in Hebrew. The common cubit is six handbreadths long, equal to 48 cm according to one opinion and 57.6 cm according to another. In the Talmud one also finds mention of a short cubit, which is five handbreadths long. Four cubits would be between 1.92 and 2.3 m. Two other cubits of different sizes were used for measuring in the Temple.

NOTES

The level of sanctity of the Sanctuary and the Entrance Hall is the same – **קְדוּשַּׁת הֵיכָל וְאוּלָם חֲדָא הִיא**: This means that the Entrance Hall, located in front of the Sanctuary, is considered a part of the Sanctuary.

It would no longer be opposite the entrance to the Sanctuary – **תּוּ לֵיכָּא פֶּתַח**: One can infer from here that Rabbi Yosei maintains that the level of sanctity of the Entrance Hall is a separate, lesser sanctity than that of the Sanctuary.

NOTES

Let him interpret it in accordance with the opinion of Rabbi Yosei, etc. – **נוֹקְמַהּ כְּרַבִּי יוֹסֵי וכו׳**: The point of Rav Adda bar Ahava's statement is to demonstrate that it cannot be proven from the mishna in *Tamid* that Rabbi Yosei holds that the entire altar was located in the north side of the Temple courtyard. This goal could also have been accomplished by stating that the mishna in *Tamid* is in accordance with the opinion of Rabbi Yosei, that Rabbi Yosei holds that the altar was located in the middle of the Temple courtyard, and that the four cubits mentioned in the mishna do not include the cubit of the altar's base and the cubit of the surrounding ledge.

It is in accordance with the opinion of Rabbi Yosei HaGelili – **רַבִּי יוֹסֵי הַגְּלִילִי הִיא**: Rav Sherevya is also attempting to reject Rabbi Zeira's proof from the mishna. He differs from Rav Adda bar Ahava in that the latter suggested the mishna in *Tamid* can be understood only if it is referring to a case where the altar was located in the center of the Temple courtyard, not in accordance with the opinion of Rabbi Yosei. By contrast, Rav Sherevya agrees that the case of the mishna is where the altar stood completely in the north, but suggests the *tanna* of the mishna is not Rabbi Yosei but Rabbi Yosei HaGelili.

אֲמַר רַב אַדָּא בַּר אַהֲבָה: הָא מַנִּי – רַבִּי יְהוּדָה הִיא. דְּתַנְיָא, רַבִּי יְהוּדָה אוֹמֵר: מִזְבֵּחַ מְמוּצָּע וְעוֹמֵד בְּאֶמְצַע הָעֲזָרָה, וּשְׁלֹשִׁים וּשְׁתַּיִם אַמּוֹת הָיוּ לוֹ, עֶשֶׂר אַמּוֹת כְּנֶגֶד פִּתְחוֹ שֶׁל הֵיכָל, אַחַת עֶשְׂרֵה אַמָּה מִיכָּן וְאַחַת עֶשְׂרֵה אַמָּה מִיכָּן, נִמְצָא מִזְבֵּחַ מְכוּוָּן כְּנֶגֶד הֵיכָל.

The Gemara challenges this proof by suggesting an alternative explanation of the mishna in *Tamid*: **Rav Adda bar Ahava said:** In accordance with **whose** opinion **is this** mishna? **It is** in accordance with the opinion of **Rabbi Yehuda, as it is taught** in a *baraita*: **Rabbi Yehuda says: The altar was centered and standing** precisely **in the middle of the** Temple **courtyard, and it was thirty-two cubits** wide. **Ten cubits** were **opposite the entrance to** the **Sanctuary, eleven cubits** were **to this** side of the entrance to the Sanctuary, **and eleven cubits** were **to that** side of the entrance to the Sanctuary. It **turns out** that the length of the **altar was aligned opposite** the width of the **Sanctuary,** which itself was thirty-two cubits wide.

סוֹף סוֹף לְרַבִּי יְהוּדָה חַד סְרֵי בָּעֵי לְמֵיתֵי! וְאִי קָסָבַר: קְדוּשַּׁת הֵיכָל וְאוּלָם חֲדָא מִילְּתָא הִיא – שִׁית בָּעֵי לְמֵיתֵי!

The Gemara asks: **Ultimately, according to Rabbi Yehuda,** one is still **required to move** the arrangement of wood **eleven** cubits from the southwest corner in order for it to be opposite the entrance to the Sanctuary. **And** even **if he holds** that **the sanctity of** the **Sanctuary and** the **Entrance Hall is one matter,** i.e., equal, one is still **required to move** the arrangement of wood **six** cubits in order to be opposite the Entrance Hall. Therefore, the mishna, which states that the arrangement of wood is four cubits north of the southwest corner, cannot be in accordance with the opinion of Rabbi Yehuda.

מִי סָבְרַתְּ הָנֵי אַרְבַּע אַמּוֹת בַּהֲדֵי אַמָּה יְסוֹד וְאַמָּה סוֹבֵב? אַרְבַּע אַמּוֹת בַּר מֵאַמָּה יְסוֹד וְאַמָּה סוֹבֵב.

The Gemara responds: **Do you hold** that **these four cubits include** the **cubit** of the **base** of the altar **and** the **cubit** of the **surrounding ledge** of the altar? Actually, the **four cubits** are **aside from** the **cubit** of the **base** of the altar **and** the **cubit** of the **surrounding ledge** of the altar. Accordingly, the arrangement of wood was actually a total of six cubits from the southwest corner of the altar, and the mishna can be in accordance with the opinion of Rabbi Yehuda.

וְנוֹקְמַהּ כְּרַבִּי יוֹסֵי, וּבִמְמוּצָּע! מִשּׁוּם דְּרַבִּי יְהוּדָה שְׁמַעֲנָא לֵיהּ מְמוּצָּע בְּהֶדְיָא.

The Gemara asks why Rav Adda bar Ahava interpreted the mishna to be in accordance with the opinion of Rabbi Yehuda: **But let him interpret it** to be **in accordance with** the opinion of **Rabbi Yosei**[N] **and** explain that the altar is located **in the center** of the Temple courtyard. The Gemara explains: Rav Adda bar Ahava interpreted the mishna to be in accordance with the opinion of Rabbi Yehuda **because we heard that Rabbi Yehuda explicitly** said that the altar was positioned **in the center** of the Temple courtyard, whereas we did not hear that Rabbi Yosei maintains such an opinion.

וְרַב שֵׁרֵבְיָא אֲמַר: הָא מַנִּי – רַבִּי יוֹסֵי הַגְּלִילִי הִיא, דְּתַנְיָא, רַבִּי יוֹסֵי הַגְּלִילִי אוֹמֵר: מִתּוֹךְ שֶׁנֶּאֱמַר ״וְנָתַתָּ אֶת הַכִּיּוֹר בֵּין אֹהֶל מוֹעֵד״ וְגוֹמֵר, ״וְאֵת

And Rav Sherevya said: In accordance with **whose** opinion **is this** mishna in *Tamid*, which holds that the entire altar was located in the northern part of the Temple courtyard? **It is** in accordance with the opinion of **Rabbi Yosei HaGelili,**[N] **as it is taught** in a *baraita*: **Rabbi Yosei HaGelili says: Since it is stated: "And you shall set the Basin**[B] **between the Tent of Meeting** and the altar" (Exodus 40:7), and another verse states: **"And**

BACKGROUND

Basin – **כִּיּוֹר**: A large, bronze basin of water stood in the Temple courtyard, placed between the altar and the Sanctuary (see Exodus 30:18–21). The Basin had twelve taps from which the priests would wash their hands and feet before beginning their service in the Temple.

Modern reconstruction of the Basin

מִזְבַּח הָעוֹלָה״ וגו׳ – מִזְבֵּחַ בְּפֶתַח אֹהֶל מוֹעֵד, וְלֹא כִּיּוֹר בְּפֶתַח אֹהֶל מוֹעֵד; הֵיכָן הָיָה נוֹתְנוֹ – בֵּין הָאוּלָם וְלַמִּזְבֵּחַ, מָשׁוּךְ קִימְעָא כְּלַפֵּי הַדָּרוֹם.

the altar of the burnt offering he set at the entrance to the Tabernacle of the Tent of Meeting." (Exodus 40:29), indicating that no object was allowed to be located between the altar and the Tent of Meeting, whose parallel, in the Temple, was the Sanctuary. Rabbi Yosei HaGelili derives from these verses that only the **altar** stood **at the entrance to the Tent of Meeting, but the Basin** did **not** stand **at the entrance to the Tent of Meeting. Where would** they **place** the Basin? It was placed **between the Entrance Hall and the altar, extended slightly toward the south.**[HN] Therefore, although the Basin was closer to the Sanctuary than the altar was, it did not actually stand between the altar and the Sanctuary.

מַאי קָסָבַר? אִי קָסָבַר כּוּלֵּיהּ מִזְבֵּחַ בַּדָּרוֹם קָאֵי – נוֹקְמֵיהּ מִכּוֹתֶל הֵיכָל וְלַדָּרוֹם בֵּין אוּלָם לַמִּזְבֵּחַ.

The Gemara seeks to clarify: **What does** Rabbi Yosei HaGelili **hold? If he holds** that **the entire altar stands in the south** section of the Temple courtyard, **let him stand** the Basin anywhere **from** where **the wall of the Sanctuary** begins **and southward,** so that it is not opposite the entrance to the Sanctuary but it is **between the Entrance Hall and the altar.** This would allow for the optimal fulfillment of both verses (Exodus 40:29; Leviticus 4:7), as the Basin would be located between the altar and the Sanctuary without interposing between the altar and the entrance to the Sanctuary.

וְאִי נַמִּי קָסָבַר: קְדוּשַּׁת הֵיכָל וְאוּלָם חֲדָא הִיא – נוֹקְמֵיהּ מִכּוֹתֶל אוּלָם וְלַדָּרוֹם בְּבֵין אוּלָם לַמִּזְבֵּחַ.

The Gemara continues: **And even if he holds** that **the** level of **sanctity of the Sanctuary and the Entrance Hall is the same,** in which case the Basin could not be located opposite the entrance to the Entrance Hall as this too would be considered a violation of the second verse, **let him stand** the Basin anywhere **from** where **the wall of the Entrance Hall** begins **and southward,** so that it is not opposite the entrance to the Entrance Hall but is **in between** the **Entrance Hall and the altar.** From the fact that Rabbi Yosei HaGelili did not say that, it is clear he held that the altar was not located in the southern section of the Temple courtyard.

HALAKHA

The Basin's placement between the Entrance Hall and the altar – כִּיּוֹר בֵּין הָאוּלָם וְלַמִּזְבֵּחַ: The Basin stood between the Entrance Hall and the altar, extending slightly to the south, i.e., to the left of one entering the Temple. This ruling is in accordance with the mishna in Tractate *Middot*, according to Rabbi Yosei HaGelili's opinion (Rambam *Sefer Avoda, Hilkhot Beit HaBeḥira* 1:6, 5:15, and see *Hilkhot Temidin UMusafin* 2:8 and *Leḥem Mishne* there).

NOTES

Extended slightly toward the south – מָשׁוּךְ קִימְעָא כְּלַפֵּי הַדָּרוֹם: As the Gemara proceeds to demonstrate, according to Rabbi Yosei HaGelili it was not possible to fulfill both requirements of the verses, i.e., that the Basin should be placed between the Tent of Meeting and the altar, and that it should not interpose between the altar and the entrance to the Sanctuary. This is so because the south side of the altar was aligned with the entrance to the Sanctuary, which required that the Basin be placed south of the altar in order not to interpose between it and the entrance to the Sanctuary, thereby fulfilling only the second condition in the verses.

According to the Ra'avad, in his commentary to *Torat Kohanim*, most of the Basin in fact did interpose between the altar and the wall of the Sanctuary. It was only a small section of the Basin that jutted slightly beyond the altar, southward. See *Shita Mekubbetzet*, who cites an opinion that suggests that the phrase: Extended slightly toward the south, means that the Basin was extended south from the entrance to the Sanctuary, not the altar.

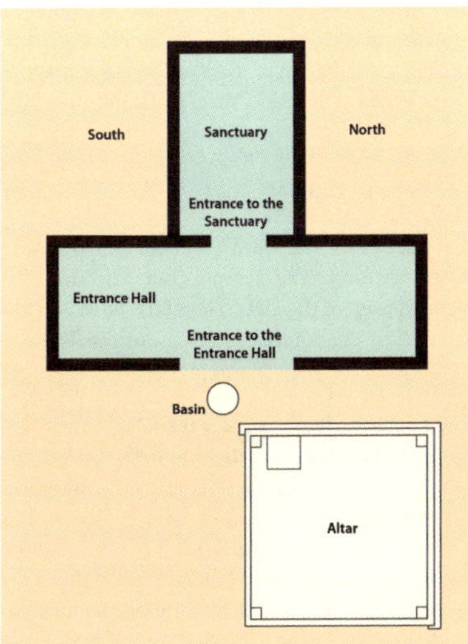

Location of the Basin according to Rabbi Yosei HaGelili

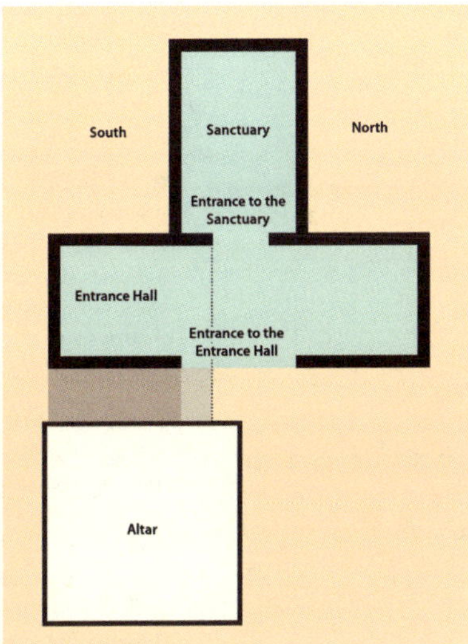

Area available for the Basin when the altar is situated wholly in the south

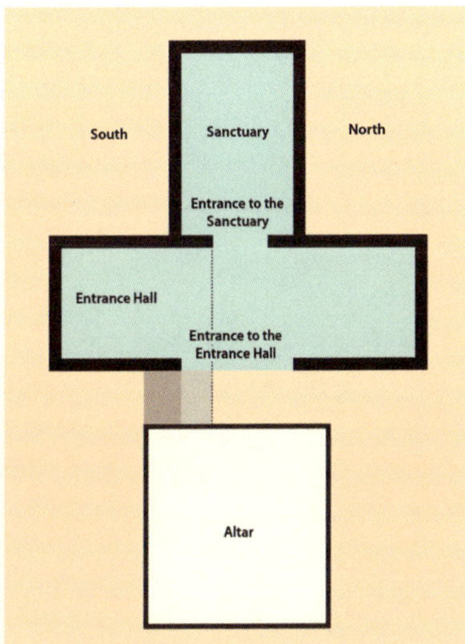

Area available for the Basin when the altar is aligned in the center of the courtyard

NOTES

The verse states northward – אָמַר קְרָא צָפוֹנָה: Had the verse simply stated the word north [*tzafon*], this would have indicated only on which side of the Temple courtyard the offering must be slaughtered. The word "northward [*tzafona*]" includes the entire north side onward as a valid area in which to slaughter the offerings, and it also indicates that the entire north side should be vacant of any vessels so as to allow for slaughtering anywhere in that area.

The north must be vacant of everything – צָפוֹן פָּנוּי מִכְּלוּם: Rashi explains that the homiletic derivation is from the extra *heh* at the end of the word *tzafona*. From the parallel *baraita* in *Torat Kohanim*, it emerges that the emphasis here is on the fact that the verse states: "Northward before the Lord," indicating that only the north of the Temple courtyard, and nothing else, is to be before the Lord. Otherwise, the verse could have been written as: And he shall slaughter it northward, on the side of the altar, before the Lord (*Korban Aharon*). See the Ra'avad's commentary on *Torat Kohanim*, where he suggests that the verse means that the side of the altar of the north should be before the Lord, i.e., that only the northern edge should be opposite the entrance to the Sanctuary, and nothing else.

That were slaughtered there – שֶׁנִּשְׁחֲטוּ שָׁם: The later commentaries disagree with regard to the precise meaning of this phrase. Some explain that this is referring to a case where the offerings were slaughtered while the altar was still whole, yet became damaged prior to the presentation of the blood (*Birkat HaZevaḥ*; *Sefat Emet*). It seems that the Rambam also understands the disqualification here to be the inability to present the blood on the altar. The question is raised: Why was this *halakha* taught here, when it was already taught on 54a? Some, citing Rashi, suggest the Gemara is referring to a case where the offerings were slaughtered in the Temple courtyard when the altar was already damaged. In such a case, since the blood would not be disqualified, as it assumes the status of being initially deferred, the Gemara is therefore discussing a novel *halakha* not included in the earlier Gemara (*Panim Meirot*).

HALAKHA

An altar that was damaged – מִזְבֵּחַ שֶׁנִּפְגַּם: In a case where the altar became damaged, all of the sacrificial animals that were slaughtered without yet having their blood presented are disqualified. This is due to the fact that the altar was not qualified to receive their blood at the time of slaughter, and the verse states: "And you shall slaughter upon it" (Exodus 20:21), which indicates that the altar must be qualified at the time of the slaughtering. Sacrificial animals that were present while the altar was damaged are not disqualified, as live animals are not permanently deferred. The *halakha* is in accordance with Rav's ruling (Rambam *Sefer Avoda*, *Hilkhot Pesulei HaMukdashin* 3:22–23).

אִי נַמִּי קָסָבַר: חֶצְיוֹ בַּצָּפוֹן וְחֶצְיוֹ בַּדָּרוֹם – נוֹקְמֵיהּ מִכּוֹתֶל הֵיכָל וְלַדָּרוֹם בֵּין אוּלָם וְלַמִּזְבֵּחַ.

Alternatively, if Rabbi Yosei HaGelili **holds** that **half of** the altar was located **in the north** section of the Temple courtyard **and half of it** was located **in the south, let him stand** the Basin anywhere **from** where **the wall of** the **Sanctuary** begins **and southward,** so that it is not opposite the entrance to the Sanctuary but **between** the **Entrance Hall and the altar.** Since the entrance to the Sanctuary was five cubits wide and stood in the middle of the courtyard, and the altar was thirty-two cubits long, there would have been eleven cubits to both the north and the south of the entrance to the Sanctuary where the Basin could be placed in order to be located between the altar and the Sanctuary without interposing between the altar and the entrance to the Sanctuary.

וְאִי נַמִּי קָסָבַר: קְדוּשַּׁת הָאוּלָם וְהֵיכָל חֲדָא הִיא – נוֹקְמֵיהּ מִכּוֹתֶל אוּלָם וְלַדָּרוֹם בֵּין אוּלָם וְלַמִּזְבֵּחַ! אֶלָּא לָאו מִשּׁוּם דְּקָסָבַר: כּוּלֵּיהּ מִזְבֵּחַ בַּצָּפוֹן.

And even if Rabbi Yosei HaGelili **holds** that **the** level of **sanctity** of the **Entrance Hall and** that of the **Sanctuary is the same,** in which case the Basin could not be located opposite the entrance to the Entrance Hall because this too would be considered a violation of the second verse, **let him stand** the Basin anywhere **from** where **the wall of** the **Entrance Hall** begins **and southward,** so that it is not opposite the entrance to the Entrance Hall but **in between** the **Entrance Hall and the altar.** Why does Rabbi Yosei HaGelili require that the Basin be placed south of the altar? The Gemara concludes: **Rather, is it not due to** the fact **that** Rabbi Yosei HaGelili **holds** that **the entire altar** stood **in the north** section of the Temple courtyard?

כִּי נַמִּי מוֹקְמַתְּ לָהּ מִכּוֹתֶל הֵיכָל וְלַצָּפוֹן, הָוֵה לֵיהּ בֵּין אוּלָם וְלַמִּזְבֵּחַ;

The Gemara asks: Even if this is the case, why does Rabbi Yosei HaGelili require that the Basin be located to the south of the altar so that it is not actually in between the altar and the Sanctuary? **Even if you stand it** anywhere **from** where **the wall of** the **Sanctuary** begins **and northward,** it would not interpose between the altar and the entrance to the Sanctuary but **it would** actually **be** located in **between** the **Entrance Hall and the altar.**

וְנוֹקְמָהּ מִכּוֹתֶל אוּלָם וְלַצָּפוֹן בְּבֵין אוּלָם וְלַמִּזְבֵּחַ!

And even if Rabbi Yosei HaGelili holds that the sanctity of the Entrance Hall is equal to that of the Sanctuary, and that the Basin cannot interpose between the altar and the entrance to the Entrance Hall, **stand** the Basin anywhere **from** where **the wall of** the **Entrance Hall** begins **and northward,** so that it is not opposite the entrance to the Entrance Hall but it is located **in between** the **Entrance Hall and the altar.**

אָמַר קְרָא: "צָפוֹנָה" – שֶׁיְּהֵא צָפוֹן פָּנוּי מִכֵּלִים.

The Gemara answers: That suggestion is technically not feasible, as **the verse states:** "And he shall slaughter it on the side of the altar **northward** [*tzafona*]" (Leviticus 1:11).[N] This verse indicates **that the north** section of the Temple courtyard must **be vacant of** all **vessels,** including the Basin. This concludes the Gemara's explanation of Rav Sherevya's assertion that the mishna in *Tamid*, which holds that the altar was located in the northern part of the Temple courtyard, is in accordance with the opinion of Rabbi Yosei HaGelili.

מַאן תַּנָּא דִּפְלִיג עֲלֵיהּ דְּרַבִּי יוֹסֵי הַגְּלִילִי? רַבִּי אֱלִיעֶזֶר בֶּן יַעֲקֹב הִיא. דְּתַנְיָא, רַבִּי אֱלִיעֶזֶר בֶּן יַעֲקֹב אוֹמֵר: "צָפוֹנָה" – שֶׁיְּהֵא צָפוֹן פָּנוּי מִכְּלוּם, וַאֲפִילּוּ מִן הַמִּזְבֵּחַ.

The Gemara asks: **Who is the *tanna* who disagrees with Rabbi Yosei HaGelili?** The Gemara answers: **It is Rabbi Eliezer ben Yaakov, as it is taught** in a *baraita* that **Rabbi Eliezer ben Yaakov says:** The verse states: **"Northward** before the Lord" (Leviticus 1:11). This indicates **that the north** section of the Temple courtyard must **be vacant of everything,**[N] **and even of the altar.** Therefore, he maintains that the entire altar stood in the southern section of the Temple courtyard.

אָמַר רַב: מִזְבֵּחַ שֶׁנִּפְגַּם – כָּל הַקֳּדָשִׁים שֶׁנִּשְׁחֲטוּ שָׁם פְּסוּלִין, מִקְרָא הוּא בְּיָדֵינוּ וּשְׁכַחְנוּהוּ. כִּי סְלֵיק רַב כָּהֲנָא, אַשְׁכְּחֵיהּ לְרַבִּי שִׁמְעוֹן בְּרַבִּי דְּקָאָמַר מִשּׁוּם רַבִּי יִשְׁמָעֵאל בְּרַבִּי יוֹסֵי: מִנַּיִן לְמִזְבֵּחַ שֶׁנִּפְגַּם שֶׁכָּל הַקֳּדָשִׁים שֶׁנִּשְׁחֲטוּ שָׁם פְּסוּלִין?

§ **Rav says:** In a case of **an altar that was damaged,**[H] **all sacrificial** animals **that were slaughtered there**[N] are **disqualified.** Rav continues: **We have a verse** as the source for this *halakha* **but we have forgotten** which one **it** is. **When Rav Kahana,** Rav's disciple, **ascended** from Babylonia to Eretz Yisrael, **he found Rabbi Shimon, son of** Rabbi Yehuda HaNasi, **saying in the name of Rabbi Yishmael, son of Rabbi Yosei: From where** is it derived that in the case of **an altar that was damaged, that all sacrificial** animals **that were slaughtered there** are **disqualified?**

שֶׁנֶּאֱמַר: ״וְזָבַחְתָּ עָלָיו אֶת עֹלֹתֶיךָ וְאֶת שְׁלָמֶיךָ״; וְכִי עָלָיו אַתָּה זוֹבֵחַ? אֶלָּא, כְּשֶׁהוּא שָׁלֵם וְלֹא כְּשֶׁהוּא חָסֵר. אָמַר: הַיְינוּ קְרָא דְּאִישְׁתְּמִיט לֵיהּ לְרַב.

It is derived from a verse, **as it is stated** in the verse with regard to the altar: "An altar of earth you shall make for Me, **and you shall slaughter upon it your burnt offerings and your peace offerings** [*shelamekha*]" (Exodus 20:21). **Is it** true that **you slaughter** sacrificial animals **on** the altar itself? They are slaughtered on the ground near the altar. No, **rather,** the verse indicates that one is able to slaughter the sacrificial animals on account of the altar, i.e., **when** the altar **is complete** [*shalem*], **but not when it is lacking,** i.e., damaged. Rav Kahana **said: This is the verse that eluded Rav.**

וְרַבִּי יוֹחָנָן אָמַר: אֶחָד זֶה וְאֶחָד זֶה פְּסוּלִין. בְּמַאי פְּלִיגִי? רַב סָבַר: בַּעֲלֵי חַיִּים אֵינָן נִדְחִים, וְרַבִּי יוֹחָנָן סָבַר: בַּעֲלֵי חַיִּים נִידְחִין

And Rabbi Yoḥanan says: Both this one **and that** one **are disqualified,** i.e., all animals that were designated as offerings when the altar was in a damaged state are disqualified, even if they were not yet slaughtered. The Gemara asks: **With regard to what** issue do Rav and Rabbi Yoḥanan **disagree?** The Gemara answers: **Rav holds** that **living** animals **are not** permanently **deferred, and Rabbi Yoḥanan holds** that **living** animals are permanently **deferred.** If the altar is damaged and it is therefore impossible to sacrifice offerings, Rav holds that only offerings that were already slaughtered become permanently deferred, whereas Rabbi Yoḥanan holds that even those that were not yet slaughtered become permanently deferred.

מֵיתִיבֵי: כָּל הַקֳּדָשִׁים שֶׁהָיוּ עַד שֶׁלֹּא נִבְנָה הַמִּזְבֵּחַ, וְאַחַר כָּךְ נִבְנָה הַמִּזְבֵּחַ – פְּסוּלִין; נִבְנָה? דְּחוּיִין מֵעִיקָּרָא נִינְהוּ!

The Gemara **raises an objection** to Rav's opinion, based on a *baraita*: In the case of **all sacrificial animals that were** consecrated **before the altar was built,**[H] **and then the altar was** subsequently **built,** the animals are **disqualified.** The Gemara assumes that this *baraita* is referring to animals that were consecrated before the building of the altar in the Second Temple. The Gemara responds: In a case where the animals were consecrated before the altar **was built,** the animals are considered **initially deferred,** i.e., deferred from the time they were initially consecrated. In this case all agree they are not permanently deferred and they can be sacrificed when the altar is built.

אֶלָּא: עַד שֶׁלֹּא נֶהֱרַס הַמִּזְבֵּחַ; נֶהֱרַס? הָא אִיזְקִין לְהוּ!

Rather, explain the *baraita* as follows: If the animals were consecrated **before the altar was destroyed** in the First Temple, and then the altar was destroyed and rebuilt, the animals are still disqualified. The Gemara questions this reading: Can the *baraita* be referring to a case where the altar was **destroyed** in the First Temple? **Didn't** the animals **become** too **old** for sacrifice by the time the altar was constructed in the Second Temple?

אֶלָּא, עַד שֶׁלֹּא נִפְגַּם הַמִּזְבֵּחַ, וְאַחַר כָּךְ נִפְגַּם הַמִּזְבֵּחַ – פְּסוּלִין! וְלָא תְּרוּצֵי קָא מְתָרְצַתְּ? אֵימָא: שֶׁנִּשְׁחֲטוּ.

The Gemara emends the *baraita* yet again: **Rather,** the *baraita* is referring to a case where one consecrated the animals **before the altar was damaged, and subsequently the altar was damaged.** The *halakha* is that the animals are **disqualified.** It seems from this *baraita* that even sacrificial animals that were not yet slaughtered when the altar became damaged are nevertheless permanently disqualified, in contrast to the opinion of Rav. The Gemara rejects this proof: **But did you not** already have to **emend** the text of the *baraita*? Emend it differently and **say that** the case is where the animals **were slaughtered** before the altar became damaged. Accordingly, there is no proof from this *baraita* with regard to the deferral of living animals.

וְהָאָמַר רַב גִּידֵּל אָמַר רַב: מִזְבֵּחַ שֶׁנֶּעֱקַר – מַקְטִירִין קְטֹרֶת בִּמְקוֹמוֹ.

Rav said that sacrificial animals that were slaughtered in the Temple courtyard when the altar was in a damaged state are disqualified. The Gemara asks: **But doesn't Rav Giddel say** that **Rav says:** In a case **where** the golden **altar became uprooted**[H] from its location in the Sanctuary, **one may burn** the **incense in its place?** Apparently, it is not essential to have the altar in order to sacrifice offerings.

כִּדְאָמַר רָבָא: מוֹדֶה הָיָה רַבִּי יְהוּדָה בְּדָמִים. הָכָא נַמִי, מוֹדֶה רַב בְּדָמִים.

The Gemara answers: It is **like that which Rava says** (60a): Although Rabbi Yehuda maintains that the entire Temple courtyard is fit for burning the sacrificial portions of offerings, **Rabbi Yehuda would concede with regard to** the presenting of the **blood** that it must be performed specifically on the altar. **Here too,** the Gemara says, **Rav concedes with regard to** the **blood** that an altar is required. Consequently, if consecrated offerings were slaughtered when the altar was in a damaged state, since the blood may not be presented, the offering is disqualified.

HALAKHA

Before the altar was built – **עַד שֶׁלֹּא נִבְנָה הַמִּזְבֵּחַ:** If before the altar was built one consecrated animals to be sacrificed, they may be sacrificed once the altar is built, as a case where an animal was initially deferred is not considered as having the status of deferment (Rambam *Sefer Avoda, Hilkhot Pesulei HaMukdashin* 3:24).

Where the altar became uprooted – **מִזְבֵּחַ שֶׁנֶּעֱקַר:** In a case where the altar became entirely uprooted, one is able to burn the incense it its original location, in accordance with the ruling of Rav (Rambam *Sefer Avoda, Hilkhot Temidin UMusafin* 3:2).

NOTES

The copper altar, etc. – מִזְבַּח וכו׳: The standard text of the verse, as well as the text in all versions of the Gemara, is: "The copper altar that was before the Lord." It seems from 60a that the Gemara initially understood that according to Rabbi Yehuda, the copper altar mentioned in the verse was that which was built by Moses. This presumably is the source for the parenthetical text referring to Moses in the *baraita*. In any event, it is clear that the altar discussed was actually built by Solomon in place of Moses' altar, in accordance with Rashi's commentary here (see notes to 60a).

מַאי רַבִּי יְהוּדָה? דְּתַנְיָא: ״בַּיּוֹם הַהוּא קִידֵּשׁ הַמֶּלֶךְ תּוֹךְ הֶחָצֵר וגו׳ כִּי מִזְבַּח (שֶׁעָשָׂה מֹשֶׁה) קָטֹן מֵהָכִיל״. דְּבָרִים כִּכְתָבָן, דִּבְרֵי רַבִּי יְהוּדָה.

Having briefly mentioned Rabbi Yehuda's opinion, the Gemara asks: **What** is the context of the statement of **Rabbi Yehuda?** The Gemara answers: **As it is taught** in a *baraita*: The verse states with regard to the inauguration of the Temple in the time of King Solomon: **"On that day the king sanctified the middle of the court** that was before the House of the Lord; as there he offered the burnt offering, and the meal offering, and the fat of the peace offerings; **because the copper altar**[N] **that was before the Lord was too small to receive** the burnt offering, and the meal offering, and the fat of the peace offerings" (I Kings 8:64). **The matters** in the verse **are** to be understood **as they** are **written,** i.e., that the altar in the Temple was too small to receive all of the offerings that Solomon sacrificed, and Solomon therefore sanctified the Temple courtyard so that it, too, could function as an altar; this is **the statement of Rabbi Yehuda.**

אָמַר לוֹ רַבִּי יוֹסֵי:

Rabbi Yosei said to him:

Perek **VI**
Daf **59** Amud **b**

NOTES

A thousand burnt offerings did Solomon offer, etc. – אֶלֶף עֹלוֹת יַעֲלֶה שְׁלֹמֹה וכו׳: The area of the pyre on this altar was quite small, as the Gemara proceeds to demonstrate. Therefore, a significant amount of time was needed for the burning of the one thousand burnt offerings. Rashi adds that a fire descended from Heaven to hasten this process.

This was greater than that – זֶה גָּדוֹל מִזֶּה: The area of the pyre on Moses' altar was one square cubit, while the area of the pyre on Solomon's altar in the Temple was four hundred square cubits (see *Middot* 35b). If Solomon sacrificed one thousand offerings on Moses' altar, he could have sacrificed 400,000 on his altar, which is far more than the 142,000 offerings he sacrificed.

What is, was too small to receive – מַהוּ קָטֹן מֵהָכִיל: The verse does not mean that the purpose for Solomon's consecration of the floor of the Temple courtyard was to use it as the area in which to burn the offerings. Rather, it is teaching that Solomon consecrated it for the purpose of the large altar that he was to build (see 60a). Accordingly, the phrase "too small to receive" is referring not to the copper altar of Solomon but to the altar constructed by Moses. As the Gemara will explain, this phrase is a euphemism alluding to the reason for discontinuing the use of Moses' altar.

Was large – גָּדוֹל הָיָה: Moses' altar measured ten cubits by ten cubits. The area of the pyre was six cubits by six cubits, a total of thirty-six square cubits, while the area of the pyre on Solomon's altar was four hundred square cubits, i.e., approximately eleven times larger. According to the ratio of one thousand offerings to thirty-six square cubits, only eleven thousand sacrifices should have been able to fit on Solomon's altar, significantly less than his 142,000. Therefore, Rabbi Yehuda maintains that the verse is to be understood literally.

LANGUAGE

Dwarf [*nanas*] – נַנָּס: From the Greek νᾶνος, *nanos*, meaning dwarf.

וַהֲלֹא כְּבָר נֶאֱמַר: ״אֶלֶף עֹלוֹת יַעֲלֶה שְׁלֹמֹה עַל הַמִּזְבֵּחַ הַהוּא״, וְאִילּוּ בְּבֵית עוֹלָמִים הוּא אוֹמֵר: ״וַיִּזְבַּח שְׁלֹמֹה אֵת זֶבַח הַשְּׁלָמִים אֲשֶׁר זָבַח לַה׳ בָּקָר עֶשְׂרִים וּשְׁנַיִם אֶלֶף״,

But isn't it already stated with regard to the altar that Moses built: **"A thousand burnt offerings did Solomon offer**[N] **upon that altar"** (I Kings 3:4), **while with regard to the Eternal House,** i.e., the Temple, **it states: "And Solomon offered for the sacrifice of peace offerings, which he offered to the Lord, two and twenty thousand cattle** and one hundred and twenty thousand sheep" (I Kings 8:63)?

וּכְשֶׁאַתָּה מַגִּיעַ לְחֶשְׁבּוֹן עוֹלוֹת וּלְמִנְיַן אַמּוֹת – זֶה גָּדוֹל מִזֶּה!

And when you arrive at the calculation of burnt offerings and the number of cubits for each altar, **this** was **greater than that,**[N] i.e., Solomon sacrificed more offerings per square cubit on Moses' altar than he did on the altar in the Temple upon its inauguration. Therefore, it is difficult to suggest that the altar in the Temple was not large enough to accommodate the number of offerings that Solomon sacrificed.

אֶלָּא מַהוּ ״קָטֹן מֵהָכִיל״ – כְּאָדָם הָאוֹמֵר לַחֲבֵירוֹ: ״פְּלוֹנִי נַנָּס הוּא״, וּפָסוּל לַעֲבוֹדָה.

Rabbi Yosei presents an alternative understanding of the verse: **Rather, what is** the meaning of the phrase "because the copper altar… was **too small to receive**"?[N] It is not referring to the altar built by Solomon, but rather to the copper altar built in the time of Moses, which was disqualified from use from the day of the Temple's inauguration on. Rather than stating outright that the altar became disqualified, the verse employed a euphemism, **like a person who says to his friend: So-and-so is a dwarf** [*nanas*],[L] **and** what he really means to say is that he is **disqualified from** performing the Temple **service.** Similarly, rather than stating outright that the altar built in the time of Moses became disqualified, the verse states that it was too small to accommodate the offerings sacrificed in the Temple.

וְרַבִּי יְהוּדָה, שַׁפִּיר קָאָמַר רַבִּי יוֹסֵי! רַבִּי יְהוּדָה לְטַעְמֵיהּ, דְּאָמַר: מִזְבֵּחַ שֶׁעָשָׂה מֹשֶׁה גָּדוֹל הָיָה. דְּתַנְיָא: ״חָמֵשׁ אַמּוֹת אֹרֶךְ וְחָמֵשׁ אַמּוֹת רֹחַב״ – דְּבָרִים כִּכְתָבָן, דִּבְרֵי רַבִּי יוֹסֵי.

The Gemara asks: **And** how does **Rabbi Yehuda** respond to this claim? **Rabbi Yosei is saying well,** i.e., his claim is persuasive. The Gemara explains: **Rabbi Yehuda** conforms **to his** standard line of **reasoning, as he says** that **the altar that Moses built was large.**[N] **As it is taught** in a *baraita*: The verse states that the altar built in the time of Moses was: **"Five cubits long and five cubits wide"** (Exodus 27:1). **The matters** in the verse are to be understood **as they are written;** this is **the statement of Rabbi Yosei.**

רַבִּי יְהוּדָה אוֹמֵר: נֶאֱמַר כָּאן ״רָבוּעַ״ וְנֶאֱמַר לְהַלָּן ״רָבוּעַ״, מָה לְהַלָּן – מֵאֶמְצָעִיתוֹ הָיָה מוֹדֵד, אַף כָּאן – מֵאֶמְצָעִיתוֹ הָיָה מוֹדֵד.

Rabbi Yehuda says: It is stated here that the altar built in the time of Moses was: **"Square"** (Exodus 27:1), **and it is stated there,** in Ezekiel's prophetic description of the altar, that it is: **"Square"** (Ezekiel 43:16). **Just as there,** in Ezekiel's vision, **he was measuring** the distance in each direction **from its center, so too here,** the verse **was measuring** the altar that Moses built **from its center.** Accordingly, the altar built by Moses was ten cubits by ten cubits. As a result, Solomon sacrificed more offerings per square cubit of space on the altar in the Temple than he did on the altar built by Moses. It is therefore possible that the altar in the Temple was not sufficient to accommodate the offerings, and Solomon consecrated the Temple courtyard to serve as an altar.

וְהָתָם מְנָלַן? דִּכְתִיב: "וְהָאֲרִיאֵל שְׁתֵּים עֶשְׂרֵה אַמָּה" – לְכָל רוּחַ, אוֹ אֵינוֹ אֶלָּא שְׁתֵּים עֶשְׂרֵה עַל שְׁתֵּים עֶשְׂרֵה? כְּשֶׁהוּא אוֹמֵר: "אֶל אַרְבַּעַת רְבָעָיו" – מְלַמֵּד שֶׁמֵּאֶמְצַע הוּא מוֹדֵד.

The Gemara asks: **And from where do we** derive that the altar mentioned **there,** in Ezekiel, was measured from its center? The Gemara answers: **As it is written: "And the hearth shall be twelve cubits** long by twelve wide, square, to its four sides" (Ezekiel 43:16). The Gemara asks: Does the verse mean twelve cubits **in each direction** from the center of the altar, so that in total it was twenty-four by twenty-four cubits? **Or** perhaps the altar was **only** a total of **twelve by twelve** cubits. The Gemara answers: **When** the verse **states: "To its four sides," it teaches that** Ezekiel was **measuring from the center** of the altar.

וְרַבִּי יוֹסֵי: כִּי גָּמַר גְּזֵירָה שָׁוָה – בְּגוֹבְהָהּ הוּא דְּגָמֵיר. דְּתַנְיָא: "וְשָׁלֹשׁ אַמּוֹת קוֹמָתוֹ" – דְּבָרִים כִּכְתָבָן, דִּבְרֵי רַבִּי יְהוּדָה.

The Gemara asks: **And** how does **Rabbi Yosei** respond to Rabbi Yehuda's claim? The Gemara answers: **When he learns the verbal analogy, he learns it with regard to** the altar's **height.**[H] **As it is taught** in a *baraita*: The verse states with regard to the altar built in the time of Moses: **"And its height shall be three cubits"** (Exodus 27:1). The **matters** in the verse are to be understood **as they are written,** i.e., that the height of the altar was three cubits. This is **the statement of Rabbi Yehuda.**

רַבִּי יוֹסֵי אוֹמֵר: נֶאֱמַר כָּאן: "רָבוּעַ" וְנֶאֱמַר לְהַלָּן: "רָבוּעַ", מַה לְּהַלָּן גּוֹבְהוֹ פִּי שְׁנַיִם כְּאׇרְכּוֹ – אַף כָּאן פִּי שְׁנַיִם כְּאׇרְכּוֹ.

Rabbi Yosei says: It is stated here that the altar built in the time of Moses was: **"Square"** (Exodus 27:1), **and it is stated there** that the incense altar was: **"Square"** (Exodus 30:2). The verbal analogy indicates that **just as there,** with regard to the incense altar, **its height** was **twice its length, so too here,** the height of the altar built in the time of Moses was **twice its length,** i.e., ten cubits.

אָמַר לֵיהּ רַבִּי יְהוּדָה: וַהֲלֹא כְּבָר נֶאֱמַר: "וְאֶת הֶחָצֵר מֵאָה אַמָּה...וְקוֹמָה חָמֵשׁ אַמּוֹת" וגו', אֶפְשָׁר כֹּהֵן עוֹמֵד עַל גַּבֵּי הַמִּזְבֵּחַ וַעֲבוֹדָה בְּיָדוֹ, וְכׇל הָעָם רוֹאִין אוֹתוֹ מִבַּחוּץ?

Rabbi Yehuda said to Rabbi Yosei: **But isn't it already stated:** "The length of **the court shall be a hundred cubits... and the height five cubits"** (Exodus 27:18)? Is it **possible** that the **priest** would **stand atop the altar and** hold the items with which he would perform the sacrificial **service in his hand, and the whole nation** could **see him from outside** the courtyard? That would constitute a lack of respect for the service in the Tabernacle.

אָמַר לוֹ רַבִּי יוֹסֵי: וַהֲלֹא כְּבָר נֶאֱמַר: "וְאֵת קַלְעֵי הֶחָצֵר וְאֶת מָסַךְ שַׁעַר הֶחָצֵר אֲשֶׁר עַל הַמִּשְׁכָּן וְעַל הַמִּזְבֵּחַ", מַה מִּשְׁכָּן עֶשֶׂר אַמּוֹת – אַף מִזְבֵּחַ עֶשֶׂר אַמּוֹת. וְאוֹמֵר: "קְלָעִים חֲמֵשׁ עֶשְׂרֵה

Rabbi Yosei said back **to him: But isn't it already stated: "And the curtains of the court, and the screen for** the door of the **gate of the court which is by the Tabernacle and by the altar"** (Numbers 4:26)? This verse juxtaposes the Tabernacle with the altar to teach that **just as** the **Tabernacle** was **ten cubits** high, **so too,** the **altar** was **ten cubits** high. **And** another verse **states: "The curtains were fifteen**

Perek **VI**
Daf **60** Amud **a**

אַמָּה אֶל הַכָּתֵף". וּמַה תַּלְמוּד לוֹמַר: "חָמֵשׁ אַמּוֹת" – מִשְּׂפַת מִזְבֵּחַ וּלְמַעְלָה,

cubits[N] **for the one side"** (Exodus 38:14), which indicates that the height of the curtains surrounding the courtyard of the Tabernacle was fifteen cubits. **And what** is the meaning when **the verse states:** "And the height **five cubits"** (Exodus 27:18)? It is referring to the height of the curtains **from the** upper **edge of the altar and above;** the curtains surrounding the courtyard were five cubits higher than the altar.

וּמַה תַּלְמוּד לוֹמַר: "וְשָׁלֹשׁ אַמּוֹת קוֹמָתוֹ" – מִשְּׂפַת סוֹבֵב וּלְמַעְלָה.

Rabbi Yosei continues: **And what** is the meaning when **the verse states:** "And you shall make the altar... **and its height shall be three cubits"** (Exodus 27:1)? The verse means that the altar measures three cubits **from the edge of the surrounding ledge and above.**[N]

HALAKHA

The altar's height – גֹּבַהּ הַמִּזְבֵּחַ: All of the altars, including the altar Moses built in the wilderness, the altar Solomon built, those built by the Jews in exile, and the altar destined to be built, are ten cubits high, in accordance with the opinion of Rabbi Yosei (Rambam *Sefer Avoda, Hilkhot Beit HaBeḥira* 2:5).

NOTES

And another verse states, the curtains were fifteen cubits – וְאוֹמֵר קְלָעִים חֲמֵשׁ עֶשְׂרֵה אַמָּה: It seems that Rashi understands this as a source that Rabbi Yosei cites to prove the height of the curtains at the entrance to the Tabernacle courtyard. *Tosafot* disagree with this understanding, as it is clear from the verse's context that it is referring to the curtains' width on either side of the entrance to the Tabernacle. *Tosafot* conclude, therefore, that the term: And it states, should be removed from the Gemara's text. They explain that Rabbi Yosei is not citing a verse, but rather he is stating his opinion based on logic, and, if anything, he is using the verse in a stylistic manner (see Rabbeinu Tam, *Sefer HaYashar* 319).

NOTES

From the edge of the surrounding ledge and above – מִשְּׂפַת סוֹבֵב וּלְמַעְלָה: Moses' altar did not have a surrounding ledge. Instead, it had a copper meshwork one cubit high, which was located at the midpoint of the altar. Consequently, according to Rabbi Yosei, this meshwork reached the height of six cubits, plus an additional three cubits until the top of the altar, and one more cubit for the corners of the altar.

NOTES

The stone altar that Solomon built, etc. – מִזְבַּח אֲבָנִים שֶׁעָשָׂה שְׁלֹמֹה וכו׳: Although Solomon's altar was made of stone, the relevant verse refers to it as the copper altar (1 Kings 8:64). This is because it served the same function as Moses' copper altar in the Tabernacle, i.e., it was the external altar for animal offerings.

וְרַבִּי יְהוּדָה, כִּי גָּמֵיר גְּזֵירָה שָׁוָה – בְּרׇחְבָּהּ הוּא דְּגָמֵיר.

The Gemara asks: **And** how does **Rabbi Yehuda,** who understands that the copper altar built in the time of Moses was actually three cubits high, interpret the verbal analogy based upon the word "square," from which Rabbi Yosei derived that the height of the copper altar was ten cubits? The Gemara answers: **When he learns** the **verbal analogy, he learns it with regard to the** altar's **width,** not its height. This is based on the verse in Ezekiel (see 59b). Accordingly, it teaches that the altar built in the time of Moses was ten cubits by ten cubits.

וּלְרַבִּי יְהוּדָה, הָא קָא מִיתְחֲזֵי כֹּהֵן! נְהִי דְּכֹהֵן מִיתְחֲזֵי, עֲבוֹדָה דְּבִידוֹ לָא מִיתְחֲזֵי.

The Gemara asks: **And according to Rabbi Yehuda,** who maintains that the altar was three cubits high and the curtains surrounding the courtyard of the Tabernacle were five cubits high, **isn't the priest visible** while performing the service atop the altar? The Gemara answers: **Granted, the priest is visible,** but the items with which he performs the sacrificial **service that** are **in his hand** are **not visible.**

בִּשְׁלָמָא לְרַבִּי יְהוּדָה – הַיְינוּ דִּכְתִיב: "קִידַּשׁ", אֶלָּא לְרַבִּי יוֹסֵי מַאי "קִידַּשׁ"? לְהַעֲמִיד בָּהּ מִזְבֵּחַ.

The Gemara returns to the original dispute between Rabbi Yehuda and Rabbi Yosei with regard to whether or not Solomon consecrated the floor of the Temple courtyard. **Granted, according to Rabbi Yehuda,** who maintains that the floor of the Temple courtyard was consecrated so that it could serve as an altar, **this is** the meaning of that **which is written:** "The king **sanctified** the middle of the court" (1 Kings 8:64). **But according to Rabbi Yosei, what** is the meaning of the phrase "the king **sanctified**"? The Gemara answers: It means that Solomon sanctified the courtyard in order **to stand the altar in it.**

בִּשְׁלָמָא לְרַבִּי יוֹסֵי – הַיְינוּ דִּכְתִיב "קָטֹן", אֶלָּא לְרַבִּי יְהוּדָה מַאי "קָטֹן"? הָכִי קָאָמַר: מִזְבַּח אֲבָנִים שֶׁעָשָׂה שְׁלֹמֹה תַּחַת מִזְבַּח הַנְּחֹשֶׁת – קָטָן הֲוָה.

The Gemara continues: **Granted, according to Rabbi Yosei,** who maintains that the surface of the altar built in the time of Moses was five cubits by five cubits, **this is** the meaning of that **which is written** in the continuation of that verse: "Because the copper altar that was before the Lord was **too small** to receive." **But according to Rabbi Yehuda,** who maintains that its surface area was ten cubits by ten cubits, **what** is the meaning of the phrase "**too small**"? The Gemara answers: The verse is referring to the altar built by Solomon, and **this** is what it **is saying: The stone altar that Solomon built**[N] **in place of the copper altar** built in the time of Moses **was** too **small** to accommodate the large quantity of offerings.

בְּמַאי פְּלִיגִי? מָר סָבַר: דָּנִין חוּץ מֵחוּץ, וְאֵין דָּנִין חוּץ מִפְּנִים.

The Gemara asks: **With regard to what** principle do Rabbi Yehuda and Rabbi Yosei **disagree** that causes them to interpret differently the verbal analogy based on the word "square"? The Gemara answers: One **Sage,** Rabbi Yehuda, **holds** that **we derive** the dimensions of the **external** altar built in the time of Moses **from** the **external** altar described in Ezekiel; **but we do not derive** the dimensions of the **external** altar **from** the dimensions of the **inner** altar, used for burning the incense.

וּמָר סָבַר: דָּנִין כְּלִי מִכְּלִי, וְאֵין דָּנִין כְּלִי מִבִּנְיָן.

And one **Sage,** Rabbi Yosei, **holds** that **we derive** the dimensions of a portable **vessel,** i.e., the copper altar built in the time of Moses, **from** the dimensions of another portable **vessel,** i.e., the golden incense altar built at that time; **but we do not derive** the dimensions of a portable **vessel from** the dimensions of **an edifice,** i.e., the stone altar in the Temple.

אָמַר רָבָא: מוֹדֶה רַבִּי יְהוּדָה בְּדָמִים. דְּתַנְיָא, רַבִּי יְהוּדָה אוֹמֵר: כּוֹס אֶחָד הָיָה מְמַלֵּא מִדַּם הַתַּעֲרוֹבוֹת וְשׁוֹפְכוֹ עַל גַּבֵּי מִזְבֵּחַ, שֶׁאִם יִשָּׁפֵךְ דָּמוֹ שֶׁל אַחַת מֵהֶן – נִמְצָא זֶה מַכְשִׁירוֹ;

§ **Rava says:** Although **Rabbi Yehuda** maintains that the entire Temple courtyard is fit for burning the sacrificial portions of offerings, he **concedes with regard to** the **blood** and holds that it must be presented on the altar, **as it is taught** in a *baraita*: **Rabbi Yehuda says:** On Passover eve, a priest **would fill one cup with the blood of the** many offerings brought that day and that was now **mixed** together on the floor. **And** then he would **pour it on the altar, so that if** all of **the blood of one of the** offerings had been **spilled** and was never presented on the altar, **this** cup would contain a small amount of that blood and pouring it on the altar **would render** the offering **fit.**

וְאִי סָלְקָא דַּעְתָּךְ סָבַר רַבִּי יְהוּדָה כּוּלָּהּ עֲזָרָה מִיקַּדְשָׁא, הָא אִיתְעֲבִידָא לֵיהּ מִצְוָותֵיהּ.

Rava explains his proof: **And if** it **enters your mind** that **Rabbi Yehuda maintains the entire Temple courtyard was consecrated** so that it had the status of the altar, then **the mitzva of** sacrificing the Paschal offering **was performed** even if the blood spilled on the ground of the courtyard and was never presented on the altar.

וְדִלְמָא מִשּׁוּם דְּקָסָבַר: שְׁפִיכָה מִכֹּחַ הָאָדָם בָּעֵינַן! אִם כֵּן, נִשְׁקְלֵיהּ וְנִשְׁפְּיךְ לֵיהּ אַדּוּכְתֵּיהּ.

The Gemara attempts to reject this proof: **Perhaps** Rabbi Yehuda requires pouring a cup of the mixture of blood on the altar **due to** the fact **that he holds we require pouring** of the blood of the Paschal offering **by human force.** Since the blood on the floor of the courtyard was not poured there by a person, the mitzva has not yet been fulfilled despite the fact that the floor has the same status as the altar. The Gemara responds: **If so, let** the priest **take** the cup of the mixture of blood **and pour it in its place** on the floor rather than on the altar.

וְדִלְמָא מִשּׁוּם דְּבָעֵינַן מִצְוָה מִן הַמּוּבְחָר.

The Gemara rejects Rava's proof: **But perhaps** Rabbi Yehuda requires the blood to be poured on the altar only **due to** the fact **that we require** the **mitzva** to be performed in **the optimal** manner. Even if Rabbi Yehuda holds that the floor of the courtyard has the same status as the altar, he would agree that it is preferable for the blood to be poured on the altar itself.

אָמַר רַבִּי אֶלְעָזָר: מִזְבֵּחַ שֶׁנִּפְגַּם – אֵין אוֹכְלִים בִּגְינוֹ שְׁיָרֵי מִנְחָה, שֶׁנֶּאֱמַר: "וְאִכְלוּהָ מַצּוֹת אֵצֶל הַמִּזְבֵּחַ", וְכִי אֵצֶל הַמִּזְבֵּחַ אֲכָלוּהָ? אֶלָּא, בִּזְמַן שֶׁהוּא שָׁלֵם וְלֹא בִּזְמַן שֶׁהוּא חָסֵר.

§ **Rabbi Elazar says:** In the case of **an altar that was damaged,**[H] **one may not eat the remainder of a meal offering on its account, as it is stated:** "Take the meal offering… **and eat it without leaven beside the altar;** for it is most holy" (Leviticus 10:12). The verse is difficult: **But did** the priests have to **eat** the meal offering **beside the altar?**[N] A priest may eat sacrificial items even of the most sacred order anywhere in the Temple courtyard. **Rather,** the verse means that one may eat the meal offering only **at a time when** the altar **is complete, but not at a time when it is lacking.**

אַשְׁכַּחַן שְׁיָרֵי מִנְחָה, קָדְשֵׁי קָדָשִׁים מְנָלַן? תַּלְמוּד לוֹמַר: "קֹדֶשׁ קָדָשִׁים".

The Gemara continues: **We found** a source for this *halakha* with regard to the **remainder of a meal offering; from where do we** derive that this *halakha* applies to all **offerings of the most sacred order?** The Gemara answers: The end of **the verse states:** "For it is **most holy.**" Since this term is also used with regard to the other offerings of the most sacred order, it is derived through verbal analogy that these offerings may not be eaten if the altar is damaged.

קָדָשִׁים קַלִּים מִנַּיִן? אָמַר אַבָּיֵי: אָתְיָא מִדְּרָשָׁא דְּרַבִּי יוֹסֵי. דְּתַנְיָא, רַבִּי יוֹסֵי אוֹמֵר שְׁלֹשָׁה דְּבָרִים מִשּׁוּם

The Gemara continues: **From where** is it derived that this *halakha* also applies to **offerings of lesser sanctity? Abaye said:** It is **derived from the exposition of Rabbi Yosei, as it is taught** in a *baraita*: **Rabbi Yosei says three** halakhic **matters in the name of**

HALAKHA

An altar that was damaged, etc. – מִזְבֵּחַ שֶׁנִּפְגַּם וכו׳: It is prohibited to eat offerings of the most sacred order or offerings of lesser sanctity while the altar is damaged, as the verse states: "And eat it without leaven beside the altar" (Leviticus 10:12). Offerings of lesser sanctity may not be consumed in Jerusalem until the altar is repaired, in accordance with the opinions of Rabbi Elazar and Abaye (Rambam *Sefer Avoda, Hilkhot Pesulei HaMukdashin* 3:25).

NOTES

But did the priests have to eat it beside the altar – וְכִי אֵצֶל הַמִּזְבֵּחַ אֲכָלוּהָ: According to *halakha*, a priest may partake of meal offerings anywhere in the Temple courtyard, in which case the verse cannot be taken literally. Therefore, Rabbi Elazar explains that the word: Beside, is to be understood as having an existential, rather than a spatial, connotation.

Perek **VI**
Daf **60** Amud **b**

שְׁלֹשָׁה זְקֵנִים, וְזֶה אֶחָד מֵהֶן: רַבִּי יִשְׁמָעֵאל אוֹמֵר: יָכוֹל יַעֲלֶה אָדָם מַעֲשֵׂר שֵׁנִי לִירוּשָׁלַיִם וְיֹאכְלֶנּוּ בִּזְמַן הַזֶּה? וְדִין הוּא: בְּכוֹר טָעוּן הֲבָאַת מָקוֹם וּמַעֲשֵׂר טָעוּן הֲבָאַת מָקוֹם, מַה בְּכוֹר אֵינוֹ אֶלָּא בִּפְנֵי הַבַּיִת – אַף מַעֲשֵׂר אֵינוֹ אֶלָּא בִּפְנֵי הַבַּיִת.

three elders, and this is one of them: Rabbi Yishmael says: One **might** have thought that **a person would bring second-tithe**[N] produce **up to Jerusalem in the present,**[H] after the destruction of the Temple, **and eat it. And** ostensibly, **it** could be derived by means of **a logical inference** that one may not do so: **A firstborn** offering **requires bringing** it **to the place,** to Jerusalem, and eating it there, **and second-tithe** produce **requires bringing** it **to the place** (see Deuteronomy 12:17–18); **just as the firstborn** offering may be eaten there **only in the presence of the Temple,**[N] **so too,** second-**tithe** produce may be eaten there **only in the presence of the Temple.**

HALAKHA

Second tithe in the present day – מַעֲשֵׂר שֵׁנִי...בִּזְמַן הַזֶּה: The mitzva of second tithe is applicable even nowadays, in the absence of the Temple. It may be eaten only while the Temple exists, as the verse juxtaposes second tithe with a firstborn, in accordance with Rabbi Yishmael's statement. The *Mishne LaMelekh* adds that the second tithe may be eaten in the event that the altar is constructed (Rambam *Sefer Zera'im, Hilkhot Ma'aser Sheni* 2:1).

NOTES

Second tithe – מַעֲשֵׂר שֵׁנִי: This is the tithe one separates from his produce after giving *teruma* to the priest and the first tithe to the Levite. The Torah states that one is obligated to bring the second tithe and consume it: "Before the Lord, in the place that He shall choose" (Deuteronomy 14:23). If the distance is too great for one to bring his produce to Jerusalem, he must redeem it where he lives and bring the money to Jerusalem, where he purchases food with the second-tithe money and consumes the food.

Just as the firstborn offering may be eaten only in the presence of the Temple – מַה בְּכוֹר אֵינוֹ אֶלָּא בִּפְנֵי הַבַּיִת: According to *halakha*, a firstborn male animal is given to the priest. In the absence of the Temple, however, he may not partake of it until it develops a blemish, thereby becoming disqualified from being fit for sacrifice.

מַה לִּבְכוֹר שֶׁכֵּן טָעוּן מַתַּן דָּמִים וְאֵימוּרִים לְגַבֵּי מִזְבֵּחַ!

Rabbi Yishmael notes that this derivation can be challenged: **What** is notable **about a firstborn?** Bringing the firstborn to Jerusalem is required only in the presence of the Temple, because it is notable **in that it requires placement of** its **blood and** its **sacrificial portions upon** the **altar;** will you say the same with regard to second-tithe produce, which requires only that it be consumed in Jerusalem?

בִּיכּוּרִים יוֹכִיחוּ. מַה לְּבִיכּוּרִים שֶׁכֵּן טְעוּנִין הֲנָחָה!

He continues: **First fruits will prove** that placement of blood upon the altar is not a factor, as they do not require placement of blood upon the altar, and yet they are brought to Jerusalem only in the presence of the Temple. Rabbi Yishmael counters: **What** is notable **about first fruits?** They are notable **in that they require placement** alongside the altar. Perhaps, since second-tithe produce does not require placement at all, even in the present one must bring it to Jerusalem and eat it there.

תַּלְמוּד לוֹמַר: ״וַהֲבֵאתֶם שָׁמָּה עֹלֹתֵיכֶם״ וגו׳, מַקִּישׁ מַעֲשֵׂר לִבְכוֹר, מַה בְּכוֹר אֵינוֹ אֶלָּא בִּפְנֵי הַבַּיִת – אַף מַעֲשֵׂר אֵינוֹ אֶלָּא בִּפְנֵי הַבַּיִת.

Rabbi Yishmael concludes: Therefore, **the verse states: "And there you shall bring your burnt offerings,** and your sacrifices, and your tithes…and the firstborns of your herd and of your flock" (Deuteronomy 12:6); the Torah **juxtaposes** second-**tithe** produce **with** the **firstborn. Just as** the **firstborn** offering may be eaten there **only in the presence of the Temple, so too,** second-**tithe** produce may be eaten there **only in the presence of the Temple.**

וְנִיהֲדַר דִּינָא, וְנֵיתֵי בְּ״מַה הַצַּד״!

The Gemara questions why a verse was needed to teach that second-tithe produce may not be consumed nowadays: **But let the logical derivation return and** the *halakha* **will be derived from the common element** between the *halakhot* of firstborn animals and first fruits. Although each has a unique factor, they share a common element: They must be brought to Jerusalem and that they may be eaten only in the presence of the Temple. So too, second-tithe produce, which also must be brought to Jerusalem, should be permitted for consumption only in the presence of the Temple.

מִשּׁוּם דְּאִיכָּא לְמִיפְרַךְ: מַה לְּהַצַּד הַשָּׁוֶה שֶׁבָּהֶן – שֶׁכֵּן יֵשׁ בָּהֶן צַד מִזְבֵּחַ.

The Gemara answers: Rabbi Yishmael did not present this derivation **because** it **can be refuted** in the following manner: **What** is notable **about** the two sources that share **a common element?** Both firstborn animals and first fruits are notable **in that they possess an aspect** of being offered upon the **altar.** Since second-tithe produce does not share this characteristic, its *halakhot* cannot be derived from those pertaining to firstborn animals and first fruits.

מַאי קָסָבַר? אִי קָסָבַר קְדוּשָּׁה רִאשׁוֹנָה קִידְּשָׁה לִשְׁעָתָהּ וְקִידְּשָׁה לֶעָתִיד לָבֹא – אֲפִילּוּ בְּכוֹר נַמִי, וְאִי קָסָבַר: לֹא קִידְּשָׁה לֶעָתִיד לָבֹא – אֲפִילּוּ בְּכוֹר נַמִי תִּיבָּעֵי!

The Gemara asks: **What does** Rabbi Yishmael **hold? If he holds** that the **initial consecration**[H] of the Temple **sanctified it for its time and sanctified it forever,** then it should be permitted to build an altar and sacrifice offerings even nowadays, and therefore **even a firstborn** animal may be eaten. **And if he holds** that the initial consecration of the Temple area **did not sanctify it forever, let the dilemma be raised** with regard to **a firstborn as well.**[N]

אֲמַר רָבִינָא: לְעוֹלָם קָסָבַר לֹא קִידְּשָׁה. וְהָכָא בְּמַאי עָסְקִינַן – בִּבְכוֹר שֶׁנִּזְרַק דָּמוֹ קוֹדֶם חוּרְבַּן הַבַּיִת, וְחָרַב הַבַּיִת, וַעֲדַיִין בְּשָׂרוֹ קַיָּים;

Ravina said: Actually, Rabbi Yishmael **holds** that that the initial consecration of the Temple **did not sanctify it** forever. **And** although one cannot slaughter the firstborn to begin with, **here we are dealing with a firstborn** that was slaughtered and **whose blood was sprinkled** on the altar **before the destruction of the Temple, and** then **the Temple was destroyed, and the meat of** the firstborn **still exists.**

וְאִיתַּקַּשׁ בְּשָׂרוֹ לְדָמוֹ, מַה דָּמוֹ בְּמִזְבֵּחַ – אַף בְּשָׂרוֹ בְּמִזְבֵּחַ; וְאָתֵי מַעֲשֵׂר וְיָלֵיף מִבְּכוֹר.

It is prohibited to eat the meat of the firstborn in this case because **its meat was juxtaposed with its blood,** which is mentioned in the previous verse, as it is stated: "You shall sprinkle their blood… and you shall burn their fats…and their flesh shall be yours" (Numbers 18:17–18). The juxtaposition teaches that **just as its blood** is sprinkled only **on the altar, so too, its meat** may be consumed only **in** a time when there is **an altar. And** the case of second-**tithe** produce **comes and is derived from** the case of **a firstborn.** Consequently, second-tithe produce may not be consumed unless there is an altar.

HALAKHA

Initial consecration – **קְדוּשָּׁה רִאשׁוֹנָה**: The sanctity that David and Solomon conferred upon the Temple area and Jerusalem has not ceased, as it is a consequence of the Divine Presence resting there. Therefore, sacrifices may be offered despite the fact that the Temple is not yet rebuilt, and one may consume the meat of offerings of the most sacred order in the Temple courtyard, even though there are no walls delineating the area. One may consume offerings of lesser sanctity and the second tithe in Jerusalem, even though it is not walled, provided that the altar is built (*Mishne LaMelekh*).

By contrast, the sanctity of Eretz Yisrael with regard to the land-dependent mitzvot ceased with the destruction of the First Temple, except for the parts of Eretz Yisrael that were seized by those who returned from Babylonia in the times of Ezra (Rambam *Sefer Avoda, Hilkhot Beit HaBeḥira* 6:15–16, and see Ra'avad, Radbaz, and *Kesef Mishne* there).

NOTES

Let the dilemma be raised with regard to a firstborn as well – **אֲפִילּוּ בְּכוֹר נַמִי תִּיבָּעֵי**: In other words, if the Gemara questions whether or not the second tithe may be eaten nowadays, despite the condition that it must be eaten "before the Lord," it seems that the Temple's existence is not a critical factor in fulfilling this condition. If so, one could present a dilemma with regard to a firstborn, as Ravina proceeds to describe, in which its blood was presented upon the altar while the Temple stood, and then the Temple was destroyed before the firstborn offering was consumed. This explanation follows Rashi's commentary.

Tosafot disagree with this explanation for many reasons. They point out that if Rabbi Yishmael maintains the initial consecration did not sanctify the Temple forever, it follows that, upon the Temple's destruction, neither the second-tithe produce nor a firstborn offering may be eaten there; the reason being that the consecration of Jerusalem is dependent on the consecration of the Temple. Accordingly, there is no dilemma with regard to a firstborn, and therefore no reason to derive the *halakha* of second tithe from that of the firstborn. Instead, *Tosafot* suggest that the Gemara's text reads: And if he holds that the initial consecration did not sanctify, even the second tithe as well may not be consumed in Jerusalem. Ravina's answer that follows is also emended to explain that Rabbi Yishmael maintains the initial consecration did sanctify Jerusalem forever. See the discussion in the early commentaries to *Makkot* 19a.

וְכִי דָּבָר הַלָּמֵד בְּהֶיקֵּשׁ חוֹזֵר וּמְלַמֵּד בְּהֶיקֵּשׁ? מַעְשַׂר דָּגָן חוּלִּין הוּא.

The Gemara asks: **But does a matter derived via a juxtaposition** with another case **then teach** that the *halakha* applies to a third case **via a juxtaposition** between the second and third cases? There is a principle that this is not a valid method of deriving *halakhot* pertaining to consecrated matters. Since the *halakha* with regard to the meat of the firstborn offering is derived from the juxtaposition of the meat with the blood of the firstborn, one cannot then prove that the same *halakha* applies to second-tithe produce simply because it is juxtaposed in a verse with the meat of the firstborn. The Gemara answers: Second-**tithe grain is non-sacred,** and therefore the acceptable methods for deriving its *halakhot* are not limited in this manner.

הָנִיחָא לְמַאן דְּאָמַר בָּתַר לָמֵד אָזְלִינַן, אֶלָּא לְמַאן דְּאָמַר בָּתַר מְלַמֵּד אָזְלִינַן, מַאי אִיכָּא לְמֵימַר?

The Gemara asks: **This works out well according to the one who says:** In determining whether the derivation involves consecrated matters or whether it involves non-sacred matters, **we follow** the matter that **is derived** from a matter derived from a juxtaposition. Since in this case the matter derived is second-tithe produce, which for these purposes is non-sacred, its legal status may be derived from juxtaposition with the *halakhot* of sacrificial matters. **But according to the one who says: We follow** the matter that **teaches,** i.e., from which the *halakha* is derived, **what is there to say?** The status of second-tithe produce may not be derived by means of juxtaposition with the status of the firstborn offering, which itself was derived from the blood of the offering, because the firstborn offering is a sacrificial matter.

דָּם וּבָשָׂר חֲדָא מִילְּתָא הִיא.

The Gemara answers: This is not a matter derived from a matter derived from a juxtaposition, as the status of the firstborn offering is not derived from the status of blood; **blood and meat are one matter.** There is only one derivation in this case, which is that the status of second-tithe produce is derived from the status of the blood and the meat of the firstborn. In any event, Abaye has proven, quoting Rabbi Yishmael's statement cited by Rabbi Yosei, that even sacrificial items of lesser sanctity may not be eaten if the altar is missing or damaged.

כִּי סְלֵיק רָבִין אֲמָרָהּ לִשְׁמַעֲתָא קַמֵּיהּ דְּרַבִּי יִרְמְיָה. אֲמַר: בַּבְלָאֵי טִפְּשָׁאֵי, אַמְּטוּל דְּיָתְבִי בְּאַרְעָא חֲשׁוּכָא אָמְרִי שְׁמַעֲתָא דְּמַחְשְׁכָא! לָא שְׁמִיעַ לְהוּ הָא דְּתַנְיָא: בִּשְׁעַת סִילּוּק מַסָּעוֹת קָדָשִׁים נִפְסָלִין, וְזָבִים וּמְצוֹרָעִים מִשְׁתַּלְּחִים חוּץ לִמְחִיצָה;

The Gemara relates: **When Ravin**[P] **ascended** from Babylonia to Eretz Yisrael, **he stated this *halakha*,** that even items of lesser sanctity are disqualified if the altar is damaged or missing, **in the presence of Rabbi Yirmeya.** Rabbi Yirmeya **said: Foolish Babylonians! Because they dwell in a dark land, they state *halakhot* that are dim. Have they not heard that which is taught** in a *baraita*: **At the time** when the Jewish people would dismantle the Tabernacle in order to **depart** on their **journeys** in the wilderness, **sacrificial** food was **disqualified** from being consumed, since the altar was not in place. Nevertheless, ***zavim* and lepers** were **sent out of** the relevant **partition;** a *zav* was sent out of the Levite camp and a leper was sent out of the Israelite camp.

וְתַנְיָא אִידָךְ: בִּשְׁנֵי מְקוֹמוֹת קָדָשִׁים נֶאֱכָלִים; מַאי לָאו – הָא בְּקָדְשֵׁי קָדָשִׁים, הָא – בְּקָדָשִׁים קַלִּים?

And it is taught in **another** *baraita*: **Sacrificial** food could be **consumed in two locations,** i.e., one could eat it while the Tabernacle was in place and one could continue eating it after the Tabernacle had been disassembled and transported. **What, is it not** that **this** first *baraita* is referring **to offerings of the most sacred order,** and **that** second *baraita* is referring **to offerings of lesser sanctity?** Accordingly, Abaye's statement that offerings of lesser sanctity may not be consumed if the altar is damaged is incorrect.

אֲמַר רָבִינָא: אִידִי וְאִידִי בְּקָדָשִׁים קַלִּים, וְלָא קַשְׁיָא:

Ravina said that there is an alternative reconciliation of the two *baraitot*: Both **this** *baraita* **and that** *baraita* are referring **to offerings of lesser sanctity, and** it is **not difficult:**

PERSONALITIES

Ravin – רָבִין: Ravin's name is an abbreviation of Rabbi Avin. He is called Rabbi Bon in the Jerusalem Talmud. He was the most important of those who descended, i.e., who went from Eretz Yisrael to Babylonia, in the third and fourth generations of the Babylonian *amora'im*.

Rabbi Avin was born in Babylonia and immigrated to Eretz Yisrael at an early age. There he was fortunate to study Torah from Rabbi Yoḥanan, who lived to be an old man. After Rabbi Yoḥanan's death, Ravin studied from his many students. Rabbi Avin was appointed an emissary to Babylonia to disseminate innovative Torah insights from Eretz Yisrael, as well as various Eretz Yisrael traditions that were unknown in other lands. He succeeded Rav Dimi as the emissary from Eretz Yisrael. Ravin transmitted new and revised formulations of the *halakhot*. Therefore, he is considered an authority and, in general, the *halakha* was decided in accordance with his opinions. Ravin returned to Eretz Yisrael several times. There he served as the transmitter of the Torah studied in Babylonia. His statements are often cited in the Jerusalem Talmud.

Perek **VI**
Daf **61** Amud **a**

NOTES

Before the Levites erect – קוֹדֶם שֶׁיַּעֲמִידוּ: Rashi holds that this statement cannot be understood literally, as it is clear from the verses (see Numbers 10:11–28) that the altar was not placed in its location until after the Tabernacle was erected, and one was certainly not permitted to consume offerings of the most sacred order before the altar was placed in its location. Therefore, the Gemara must mean that the case in which the offerings may be consumed is when the Tabernacle and altar are properly erected.

Alternatively, this statement can be understood literally, and the case involves a situation where the Levites erroneously switched the correct order of the assembly procedure; first the altar and only then the Tabernacle around it (see *Tosafot*).

הָא רַבִּי יִשְׁמָעֵאל, הָא רַבָּנַן.

This first *baraita* is in accordance with the opinion of **Rabbi Yishmael,** who derives that meat of a firstborn offering, which is an offering of lesser sanctity, cannot be consumed if the altar is damaged or absent, based upon the *halakha* pertaining to the blood of the firstborn. **That** second *baraita* is in accordance with the opinion of **the Sages,** who disagree with Rabbi Yishmael.

וְאִיבָּעֵית אֵימָא: הָא וְהָא בְּקָדְשֵׁי קָדָשִׁים, וּמַאי ״בִּשְׁנֵי מְקוֹמוֹת״ – קוֹדֶם שֶׁיַּעֲמִידוּ לְוִיִּם אֶת הַמִּשְׁכָּן,

And if you wish, say there is a different resolution of the two *baraitot*: Both **this** *baraita* **and that** *baraita* are referring **to offerings of the most sacred order. And what** does the second *baraita* mean when it says the food may be consumed **in two locations?** It is referring to when the Israelites arrive at a new camp, **before the Levites erect**[N] **the Tabernacle,**

Perek **VI**
Daf **61** Amud **b**

NOTES

The altar in Shiloh – מִזְבֵּחַ שֶׁל שִׁילֹה: It is recorded in the book of Joshua (18:1) that after the Jewish people finished conquering Eretz Yisrael and divided it among the tribes, Joshua, along with the rest of the nation, established the Tabernacle of God in Shiloh. It remained there until the Ark was taken from there during the Philistine war in the time of the High Priest Eli (see I Samuel, chapter 4). The mishna (112b) teaches that this structure was not like the Tabernacle in the wilderness, but rather was a permanent structure built of stone and covered with curtains.

And one in Nov and Gibeon – וְאֶחָד שֶׁל נוֹב וְגִבְעוֹן: The reference to the shewbread in Nov, city of priests, in I Samuel 21:7, proves that the Tabernacle was once situated there. At a later point, during the time of Solomon, the verse mentions a great public altar located in Gibeon, where the king went to sacrifice offerings prior to the construction of the Temple (see I Kings 3:4). Although these are two distinct locations, the Gemara counts them as one because the great public altars located there were of lesser sanctity than the altars in Shiloh and the Temple (see Rashi).

Until Manasseh came and removed it – עַד שֶׁבָּא מְנַשֶּׁה וְסִילְּקָהּ: II Chronicles 33:16 states that Manasseh rebuilt the altar when he repented from his sinful ways. It can be deduced from this that he had previously destroyed it (Ra'avad in his commentary to *Torat Kohanim*).

וּלְאַחַר שֶׁיְּפָרְקוּ הַלְוִיִּם אֶת הַמִּשְׁכָּן;

and, when they are leaving the camp, **after the Levites dismantle the Tabernacle** but before they remove the altar. Since the altar has not yet been moved, it is still permitted to consume the sacrificial food.

מַהוּ דְּתֵימָא אִיפְּסִיל לְהוּ בְּיוֹצֵא – קָא מַשְׁמַע לַן.

The Gemara continues: It was necessary to state this *halakha* **lest you say** that once the partitions surrounding the courtyard have been taken down, the sacrificial food **has been disqualified because** it is considered to have **left** the courtyard of the Tabernacle. Therefore, the *baraita* **teaches us** that the food is permitted for consumption as long as the altar remains in place.

וְאֵימָא הָכִי נַמִי! אָמַר קְרָא: ״וְנָסַע אֹהֶל מוֹעֵד״, אַף עַל פִּי שֶׁנָּסַע – אֹהֶל מוֹעֵד הוּא.

The Gemara challenges: **And say** it is **indeed** so, that the sacrificial food should be disqualified because it is no longer within the partitions surrounding the courtyard. The Gemara explains: **The verse states: "Then the Tent of Meeting shall travel"** (Numbers 2:17). This verse indicates that **even though it traveled it is** still considered **the Tent of Meeting.** Therefore, the sacrificial food is not considered to have left its designated area.

אָמַר רַב הוּנָא אָמַר רַב: מִזְבֵּחַ שֶׁל שִׁילֹה שֶׁל אֲבָנִים הָיָה. דְּתַנְיָא: רַבִּי אֱלִיעֶזֶר בֶּן יַעֲקֹב אוֹמֵר: מָה תַּלְמוּד לוֹמַר: ״אֲבָנִים״ ״אֲבָנִים״ ״אֲבָנִים״ שָׁלֹשׁ פְּעָמִים? אֶחָד שֶׁל שִׁילֹה, וְאֶחָד שֶׁל נוֹב וְגִבְעוֹן, וּבֵית עוֹלָמִים.

§ The Gemara raises another discussion concerning the altar: **Rav Huna says** that **Rav says: The altar in Shiloh**[N] **was** fashioned **of stones,** unlike the portable altar constructed in the time of Moses, which was fashioned from copper. This is **as it is taught** in a *baraita*: **Rabbi Eliezer ben Yaakov says: Why** must **the verses state** that the altar must be fashioned from **stones** (Exodus 20:22), and state again that the altar must be fashioned from **stones** (Deuteronomy 27:5), and mention yet again the word **stones** (Deuteronomy 27:6), with regard to the altar, for a total of **three times?** These allude to three different stone altars: **One in Shiloh, and one in Nov and Gibeon,**[N] **and** one in the **Eternal House,** i.e., the Temple.

מְתִיב רַב אַחָא בַּר אַמֵּי: אֵשׁ שֶׁיָּרְדָה מִן הַשָּׁמַיִם בִּימֵי מֹשֶׁה – לֹא נִסְתַּלְּקָה מֵעַל מִזְבַּח הַנְּחוֹשֶׁת אֶלָּא בִּימֵי שְׁלֹמֹה, וְאֵשׁ שֶׁיָּרְדָה בִּימֵי שְׁלֹמֹה – לֹא נִסְתַּלְּקָה עַד שֶׁבָּא מְנַשֶּׁה וְסִילְּקָהּ; וְאִם אִיתָא – מֵעִיקָּרָא הוּא דְּאִיסְתַּלַּק לֵיהּ!

Rav Aḥa bar Ami raises an objection based on a *baraita*: The **fire that descended from Heaven** upon the altar **in the days of Moses** (see Leviticus 9:24) **departed from atop the copper altar only in the days of Solomon,** when he replaced the copper altar with a stone altar, **and the fire that descended** upon the altar **in the days of Solomon did not depart until Manasseh came and removed it**[N] by destroying the altar. **And if it is so** that the altar in Shiloh was fashioned of stones, **it** emerges **that** the fire **departed** the copper altar **earlier,** when the stone altar in Shiloh replaced the copper altar of Moses, many years before King Solomon.

הוּא דַּאֲמַר כְּרַבִּי נָתָן. דְּתַנְיָא, רַבִּי נָתָן אוֹמֵר: מִזְבַּח שֶׁל שִׁילֹה שֶׁל נְחוֹשֶׁת הָיָה, חָלוּל וּמָלֵא אֲבָנִים.

The Gemara explains: Rav Huna **stated** his opinion **in accordance with** the statement of **Rabbi Natan, as it is taught** in a *baraita* that **Rabbi Natan says: The altar in Shiloh was** fashioned **of copper**; it was **hollow and full of stones.**

רַב נַחְמָן בַּר יִצְחָק אָמַר: מַאי ״לֹא נִסְתַּלְּקָה״ – לֹא נִסְתַּלְּקָה לְבַטָּלָה. מַאי הִיא? רַבָּנַן אָמְרִי: שְׁבִיבָא הֲוָה מַשְׁדְּרָא. רַב פָּפָּא אָמַר: אוּשְׁפִּיזָא הֲוָה נָקֵט, וְזִימְנִין הָכָא וְזִימְנִין הָכָא.

Rav Naḥman bar Yitzḥak says there is an alternative answer: **What** is the meaning of the statement in the *baraita* that the fire **did not depart** until the days of Solomon? It means that **it did not depart** in a manner in which it was **nullified;** it was still somewhat present in Shiloh on the copper altar, which stood together with the stone altar. The Gemara asks: **What is it,** i.e., what does it mean that the fire did not depart a manner in which it was nullified? The Gemara answers: **The Rabbis say:** The fire on the copper altar **would emit sparks** toward the stone altar when the priests would sacrifice offerings on the stone altar. **Rav Pappa says:** The fire **was as a guest; sometimes** it was **here,** on the copper altar, **and sometimes** it was **there,** on the stone altar.

תְּנַן הָתָם: וּכְשֶׁעָלוּ בְּנֵי הַגּוֹלָה, הוֹסִיפוּ עָלָיו אַרְבַּע אַמּוֹת מִן הַדָּרוֹם וְאַרְבַּע אַמּוֹת מִן הַמַּעֲרָב כְּמִין גַּמָּא. מַאי טַעְמָא? אָמַר רַב יוֹסֵף: מִשּׁוּם דְּלָא סָפַק.

§ The Gemara continues discussing the altar: **We learned** in a mishna **there** (*Middot* 35b): The altar in the First Temple was twenty-eight by twenty-eight cubits. **When the members of the exile ascended** to Jerusalem in the beginning of the Second Temple period, **they added four cubits to it**[H] **on the south and four cubits on the west** sides of the altar, **like** the shape of the Greek letter **gamma,**[L] i.e., the additions made a right angle. As a result, the altar in the Second Temple was thirty-two by thirty-two cubits. The Gemara asks: **What was the reason** for this expansion? **Rav Yosef said: Because** the size of the altar from the First Temple **was not sufficient.**

אֲמַר לֵיהּ אַבָּיֵי: הַשְׁתָּא מִקְדָּשׁ רִאשׁוֹן, דִּכְתִיב בֵּיהּ: ״יְהוּדָה וְיִשְׂרָאֵל רַבִּים כַּחוֹל אֲשֶׁר עַל שְׂפַת הַיָּם״ – סָפַק, מִקְדָּשׁ שֵׁנִי דִּכְתִיב בֵּיהּ: ״כׇּל הַקָּהָל כְּאֶחָד אַרְבַּע רִבּוֹא״ לֹא סָפַק?! אֲמַר לֵיהּ: הָתָם – אֵשׁ שֶׁל שָׁמַיִם מְסַיַּיעְתָּן, הָכָא – אֵין אֵשׁ שֶׁל שָׁמַיִם מְסַיַּיעְתָּן.

Abaye said to him: Now, if in **the First Temple** era, **about which it is written: "Judah and Israel were many as the sand that is by the sea"** (I Kings 4:20), the altar **was sufficient,** how could it be that in **the Second Temple** era, **about which it is written: "The whole congregation together was forty** and two **thousand** three hundred and sixty" (Ezra 2:64), the altar **was not sufficient?** Rav Yosef **said to** Abaye: **There,** in the First Temple, a **heavenly fire** would **assist them** and consume the offerings. **Here,** in the Second Temple, there was **no heavenly fire**[N] that would **assist them.** Therefore, they needed a larger area in which to burn the offerings.

כִּי אֲתָא רָבִין אָמַר רַבִּי שִׁמְעוֹן בֶּן פָּזִי מִשּׁוּם בַּר קַפָּרָא: שִׁיתִין הוֹסִיפוּ. מֵעִיקָּרָא סְבוּר: ״מִזְבַּח אֲדָמָה״ – שֶׁהוּא אָטוּם בַּאֲדָמָה.

When Ravin came from Eretz Yisrael to Babylonia, he reported that which **Rabbi Shimon ben Pazi says in the name of Bar Kappara** with regard to the expansion of the altar: **They expanded** the altar to extend over the underground **cavities**[N] into which the libations flowed. **Initially,** in the First Temple era, **they held** that when the verse states: **"An altar of earth** you shall make for Me" (Exodus 20:21), it means **that it** should be completely **filled with earth.**

וּלְבַסּוֹף סְבוּר: שְׁתִיָּה כַּאֲכִילָה. וּמַאי ״מִזְבַּח אֲדָמָה״ – שֶׁהוּא מְחוּבָּר בַּאֲדָמָה; שֶׁלֹּא יִבְנֶנּוּ לֹא עַל גַּבֵּי כִּיפִּים,

But ultimately, in the Second Temple era, **they maintained** that the altar's **drinking is like** its **eating,** i.e., just as the offerings are burned upon the altar, so too, the libations must be poured onto the altar itself and not down its side. Consequently, they expanded the altar to cover the underground cavities, and created holes in the altar so that the libations could be poured on top of the altar and flow into the underground cavities. **And** according to this, **what** is the meaning of the phrase **"an altar of earth"?** It teaches **that** the altar must **be attached to the earth, so that one may not build it on top of arches**[H]

HALAKHA

They added four cubits to it – הוֹסִיפוּ עָלָיו אַרְבַּע אַמּוֹת: The area of the altar constructed by the people who returned from exile, which will also be the area of the altar constructed in the Third Temple, was thirty-two square cubits (Rambam *Sefer Avoda, Hilkhot Beit HaBeḥira* 2:5).

May not build it on top of arches – שֶׁלֹּא יִבְנֶנּוּ לֹא עַל גַּבֵּי כִּיפִּים: The altar must be constructed in such a way that it is attached to the ground and is built neither upon arches nor caverns (Rambam *Sefer Avoda, Hilkhot Beit HaBeḥira* 1:13).

LANGUAGE

Gamma – גַּמָּא: This is the third letter of the Greek alphabet. Greek script was well known in the talmudic era and the forms of its letters served as examples for various shapes. The form of the letter gamma, Γ, depicts a right angle, which serves as an example of the altar's expansion.

NOTES

There was no heavenly fire – אֵין אֵשׁ שֶׁל שָׁמַיִם: The Gemara in tractate *Yoma* (21b) explains that either there was no heavenly fire at all upon the altar during the Second Temple era, or that even if the fire was present, it was not strong enough to consume the offerings. Rather, it appeared as being crouched atop the altar.

They expanded over the underground cavities – שִׁיתִין הוֹסִיפוּ: In the First Temple era there was a hole in the ground next to the southwest corner of the altar, from where the water and wine of the libations would flow into deep underground cavities. During the Second Temple era, those who returned from exile expanded that corner of the altar to cover the hole. They made two separate holes atop the altar through which the water and wine libations would be poured into the ground.

וְלֹא עַל גַּבֵּי מְחִילּוֹת.

and one may **not** build it **on top of tunnels.**[N]

אָמַר רַב יוֹסֵף, לָאו הַיְינוּ דְּתַנְיָא: ״וַיָּכִינוּ אֶת הַמִּזְבֵּחַ עַל מְכוֹנָתוֹ״ – שֶׁהִגִּיעוּ לְסוֹף מִדּוֹתָיו? וְהָכְתִיב: ״הַכֹּל בִּכְתָב מִיַּד ה׳ עָלַי הִשְׂכִּיל״!

The Gemara relates that after reconsidering the reason for the expansion of the altar, **Rav Yosef said: Is this not as it is taught**[N] in a *baraita* with regard to the verse: **"And they set the altar upon its bases"** (Ezra 3:3), which teaches **that** in the Second Temple the size of the altar **reached its full measure,** i.e., that it was the ideal size, whereas in the First Temple it was not the ideal size? The Gemara asks: **But isn't it written** with regard to the instructions David gave Solomon about how to build the Temple: **"All this in writing, as the Lord has made me wise by His hand upon me,** even all the works of this pattern" (I Chronicles 28:19), indicating that the design of the First Temple was dictated by God?

אֶלָּא אָמַר רַב יוֹסֵף, קְרָא אַשְׁכַּח וְדָרַשׁ: ״וַיֹּאמֶר דָּוִיד זֶה הוּא בֵּית ה׳ הָאֱלֹהִים וְזֶה מִזְבֵּחַ לְעֹלָה לְיִשְׂרָאֵל״, כִּי בַּיִת: מָה בַּיִת שִׁשִּׁים אַמָּה – אַף מִזְבֵּחַ שִׁשִּׁים אַמָּה.

Rather, Rav Yosef said: The size of the altar in the First Temple was ideal, but in the Second Temple era there was a need to expand the altar, and they **found a verse and interpreted** it as follows. The verse states: **"Then David said: This is the House of the Lord God, and this is the altar of burnt offering for Israel"** (I Chronicles 22:1). The verse juxtaposes the House, i.e., the Temple, with the altar, which indicates that the altar is **like the Temple: Just as** the **House** was **sixty cubits**[N] (see I Kings 6:2), **so too,** the **altar** may be extended up to a length of **sixty cubits.**

בִּשְׁלָמָא בַּיִת – מִינְכְּרָא צוּרָתוֹ, אֶלָּא מִזְבֵּחַ מְנָא יָדְעִי?

§ The Gemara discusses the construction of the altar in the Second Temple. The Gemara asks: **Granted,** with regard to the location of the **House, its shape** was **discernable** from the vestiges of its foundations; **but how did they know** the proper location of the **altar?**

אָמַר רַבִּי אֶלְעָזָר: רָאוּ מִזְבֵּחַ בָּנוּי וּמִיכָאֵל הַשַּׂר הַגָּדוֹל עוֹמֵד וּמַקְרִיב עָלָיו. וְרַבִּי יִצְחָק נַפָּחָא אָמַר: אֶפְרוֹ שֶׁל יִצְחָק רָאוּ שֶׁמּוּנָּח בְּאוֹתוֹ מָקוֹם. וְרַבִּי שְׁמוּאֵל בַּר נַחְמָנִי אָמַר: מִכָּל הַבַּיִת כּוּלּוֹ הֵרִיחוּ רֵיחַ קְטֹרֶת, מִשָּׁם הֵרִיחוּ רֵיחַ אֵבָרִים.

The Gemara answers that **Rabbi Elazar says: They saw** a vision of the **altar** already **built and Michael**[B] **the** archangel **standing and sacrificing** offerings **upon it. And Rabbi Yitzhak Nappaha says: They saw** a vision **of the ashes of Isaac**[N] that were **placed in that location. And Rabbi Shmuel bar Nahmani says: From the entire House they smelled the scent of incense,** yet **from there,** the location of the altar, **they smelled a scent of** burned animal **limbs.**

אָמַר רַבָּה בַּר בַּר חָנָה אָמַר רַבִּי יוֹחָנָן: שְׁלֹשָׁה נְבִיאִים עָלוּ עִמָּהֶם מִן הַגּוֹלָה, אֶחָד שֶׁהֵעִיד לָהֶם עַל הַמִּזְבֵּחַ, וְאֶחָד שֶׁהֵעִיד לָהֶם עַל מְקוֹם הַמִּזְבֵּחַ, וְאֶחָד שֶׁהֵעִיד לָהֶם שֶׁמַּקְרִיבִין אַף עַל פִּי שֶׁאֵין בַּיִת.

Rabba bar bar Hana says that **Rabbi Yohanan says: Three prophets**[H] **ascended with them from the exile: One who testified to them about** the size and shape **of the altar, and one who testified to them about the** proper **location of the altar, and one who testified to them that one sacrifices** offerings **even if there is no Temple,** provided that there is a proper altar.

בְּמַתְנִיתָא תָּנָא, רַבִּי אֱלִיעֶזֶר בֶּן יַעֲקֹב אוֹמֵר: שְׁלֹשָׁה נְבִיאִים עָלוּ עִמָּהֶן מִן הַגּוֹלָה; אֶחָד שֶׁהֵעִיד לָהֶם עַל הַמִּזְבֵּחַ וְעַל מְקוֹם הַמִּזְבֵּחַ, וְאֶחָד שֶׁהֵעִיד לָהֶם שֶׁמַּקְרִיבִין אַף עַל פִּי שֶׁאֵין בַּיִת, וְאֶחָד שֶׁהֵעִיד לָהֶם עַל הַתּוֹרָה שֶׁתִּכָּתֵב אַשּׁוּרִית.

It was taught in a *baraita* that **Rabbi Eliezer ben Yaakov says: Three prophets ascended with** the Jewish people **from the exile: One who testified to them about** the size and shape of **the altar and about the** proper **location of the altar, and one who testified to them that one sacrifices** offerings **even if there is no Temple, and one who testified to them about the Torah** and instructed **that it be written** in **Assyrian script** [*Ashurit*][B] rather than the ancient Hebrew script used in the times of Moses.

NOTES

And not on top of tunnels – וְלֹא עַל גַּבֵּי מְחִילּוֹת: It would seem that these underground cavities are in direct contradiction to this condition. *Tosafot* explain that they pose no contradiction, as they are actually considered part and parcel of the altar.

Is this not as it is taught – לָאו הַיְינוּ דְּתַנְיָא: Rashi, citing *Nedarim* 41a, explains that Rav Yosef fell ill toward the end of his life and, as a result, would sometimes forget his Torah scholarship. That is why here he asks if the reason for the altar's expansion in the Second Temple era is based on a particular *baraita*, whereupon he realizes that he was mistaken and then remembers the correct source.

Just as the House was sixty cubits, etc. – מָה בַּיִת שִׁשִּׁים וכו׳: Rashi explains that just as the Temple that Solomon built was sixty cubits long, so too, the altar could be expanded up to a length of sixty cubits. It seems the verse is not stating an imperative; rather, it is granting the option should the need arise. It is stated in the *Sefat Emet* that were it not for Rashi's explanation, it would be possible to explain the sixty cubits as referring to the aggregate length of both the altar and its ramp.

The ashes of Isaac – אֶפְרוֹ שֶׁל יִצְחָק: This expression is mentioned multiple times throughout the Talmud and Midrash. Its meaning is that although Isaac was not actually sacrificed, the ram sacrificed in Isaac's stead is considered as Isaac himself, and therefore the ashes of the ram are considered to be his own (see Genesis 22:12, which alludes to this point). These ashes were placed at the base of the altar, which, according to tradition, was in the same location that the binding occurred.

HALAKHA

Three prophets, etc. – שְׁלֹשָׁה נְבִיאִים וכו׳: Three prophets ascended with the returnees from the Babylonian exile. One verified to them the precise location of the altar; one verified to them the size and structure of the altar; and one verified to them that all of the offerings were to be sacrificed even though the Temple was not yet built (Rambam *Sefer Avoda*, *Hilkhot Beit HaBehira* 2:4).

BACKGROUND

Michael – מִיכָאֵל: Of the many named angels listed in rabbinic literature, just two, Michael and Gabriel, have their origins in the Bible. The former is a protector of the Jewish people who contends with the princes of Persia and Greece, as reported in Daniel, chapter 10. The latter assists Daniel (in Daniel, chapter 8) in understanding a prediction of those empires' fates. According to Midrash, these two angels join Raphael and Uriel in surrounding God's throne (*Bemidbar Rabba* 2:10).

Ashurit – אַשּׁוּרִית: The Hebrew script currently in use is called *Ashurit* by the Sages, in contrast to the ancient Hebrew [*Ivri*] script used by the Samaritans. The Sages disagree as to why the script is called *Ashurit*. Some explain that the Jews adopted it during the Babylonian exile, when the Jews lived in an area that included Assyria [*Ashur*]. Others explain that it derives from the word happiness [*osher*] or the word directness [*yosher*], which indicates an aesthetic, straightforward script.

תָּנוּ רַבָּנַן: קֶרֶן וְכֶבֶשׁ וִיסוֹד וְרִיבּוּעַ – מְעַכְּבִין, מִדַּת אָרְכּוֹ וּמִדַּת רׇחְבּוֹ וּמִדַּת קוֹמָתוֹ אֵין מְעַכְּבִין. מְנָא הָנֵי מִילֵּי? אָמַר רַב הוּנָא, אָמַר קְרָא: ״הַמִּזְבֵּחַ״, כׇּל מָקוֹם שֶׁנֶּאֱמַר ״הַמִּזְבֵּחַ״ – לְעַכֵּב.

§ **The Sages taught** in a *baraita*: The **corner** built at each point where the edges of the altar meet, the **ramp** upon which the priests ascended the altar, the **base** of the altar, **and** the requirement that the altar must be exactly **square, are all indispensable**[H] in order for the altar to be fit for use. But **the measurement of its length, and the measurement of its width, and the measurement of its height are not indispensable.** The Gemara asks: **From where are these matters** derived? **Rav Huna says:** In reference to each of these characteristics **the verse states** the term **"the altar,"**[N] and there is a principle that **wherever** the term **"the altar" is stated,** it serves **to** indicate that the halakhic detail mentioned is **indispensable.**

אֶלָּא מֵעַתָּה, כִּיּוּר לְרַבִּי, וְסוֹבֵב לְרַבִּי יוֹסֵי בְּרַבִּי יְהוּדָה, הָכִי נַמִי דִּמְעַכֵּב? דִּכְתִיב: ״וְנָתַתָּה אֹתָהּ תַּחַת כַּרְכֹּב הַמִּזְבֵּחַ מִלְּמָטָּה״; וְתַנְיָא: אֵיזֶהוּ כַּרְכּוֹב? רַבִּי אוֹמֵר: זֶה כִּיּוּר, רַבִּי יוֹסֵי בְּרַבִּי יְהוּדָה אוֹמֵר: זֶה הַסּוֹבֵב!

The Gemara asks: **If that is so,** then the **engraving** [*kiyyur*][L] that was on the altar **according to Rabbi** Yehuda HaNasi, **or the surrounding ledge** of the altar **according to Rabbi Yosei, son of Rabbi Yehuda,** should **also be indispensable, as it is written: "And you shall put it under the *karkov* of the altar beneath"** (Exodus 27:5). **And it is taught** in a *baraita*: **What is the *karkov*?**[N] **Rabbi** Yehuda HaNasi **says: This is the engraving** on the altar. **Rabbi Yosei, son of Rabbi Yehuda, says: This is the surrounding ledge.**

אִין, דְּתַנְיָא: אוֹתוֹ הַיּוֹם נִפְגְּמָה קֶרֶן מִזְבֵּחַ, וְהֵבִיאוּ בּוּל שֶׁל מֶלַח וּסְתָמוּהוּ. וְלֹא מִפְּנֵי שֶׁכָּשֵׁר לַעֲבוֹדָה, אֶלָּא שֶׁלֹּא יֵרָאֶה מִזְבֵּחַ פָּגוּם. שֶׁכׇּל מִזְבֵּחַ שֶׁאֵין לוֹ קֶרֶן וְכֶבֶשׁ וִיסוֹד וְרִיבּוּעַ – פָּסוּל. רַבִּי יוֹסֵי בְּרַבִּי יְהוּדָה אוֹמֵר: אַף הַסּוֹבֵב.

The Gemara answers: **Yes,** the *karkov* is also indispensable, **as it is taught** in a *baraita*: On **that day** when *etrogim* were pelted at a Sadducee priest who poured the water libation of *Sukkot* on his feet rather than on the altar (see *Sukka* 48b), **the corner of the altar was damaged** as a result of the pelting and the ensuing chaos. **They brought a fistful of salt and sealed** the damaged section. They did this **not because** it rendered the altar **fit for the Temple service, but** in deference to the altar, **so that the altar would not be seen** in its **damaged** state. The reason the altar is disqualified is **because any altar that does not have a corner, a ramp, and a base, and** any altar that is not **square,** is **disqualified. Rabbi Yosei, son of Rabbi Yehuda, says: Even the surrounding ledge** is indispensable.

תָּנוּ רַבָּנַן: אֵיזֶהוּ כַּרְכּוֹב – בֵּין קֶרֶן לְקֶרֶן מְקוֹם הִילּוּךְ רַגְלֵי הַכֹּהֲנִים אַמָּה. אַטּוּ הַכֹּהֲנִים בֵּין קֶרֶן לְקֶרֶן הֲווּ אָזְלִי? אֶלָּא אֵימָא: וּמְקוֹם הִילּוּךְ רַגְלֵי הַכֹּהֲנִים אַמָּה.

§ **The Sages taught** in a *baraita*: **What is the *karkov*** of the altar? It is the area **between one corner and** the next **corner,** which is the **cubit**-wide **place** on top of the altar where **the priests** would **walk.** The Gemara asks: **Is that to say** that **the priests would walk between** one **corner and the next corner?** The Gemara answers: **Rather, say:** The *karkov* is the cubit-wide area between one corner and the other, **and** there was an additional **cubit** that was **the place** where **the priests** would **walk.**

וְהָכְתִיב: ״תַּחַת כַּרְכֻּבּוֹ מִלְּמַטָּה עַד חֶצְיוֹ״! אָמַר רַב נַחְמָן בַּר יִצְחָק: תְּרֵי הָווּ, חַד לְנוֹי, וְחַד לַכֹּהֲנִים דְּלָא נִשְׁתָּרְקוּ.

The Gemara asks: **But isn't it written:** "And he made for the altar a grating of network of brass, **under the *karkov* beneath, reaching halfway up"** (Exodus 38:4), which indicates that the *karkov* was on the side of the altar and not on top of it? The Gemara answers: **Rav Naḥman bar Yitzḥak said: There were two**[N] entities called *karkov*. **One** was a slight protrusion above the midway point of the altar **for aesthetic** purposes, **and one** was an indentation on top of the altar **for** the benefit of **the priests,** to ensure **that they** would **not slip** off the top of the altar.

״מִדַּת אָרְכּוֹ וּמִדַּת רׇחְבּוֹ וּמִדַּת קוֹמָתוֹ אֵין מְעַכְּבִין״. אָמַר רַבִּי מָנִי: וּבִלְבַד שֶׁלֹּא יִפְחָתֶנּוּ מִמִּזְבֵּחַ שֶׁעָשָׂה מֹשֶׁה. וְכַמָּה? אָמַר רַב יוֹסֵף: אַמָּה. מְחַכוּ עֲלֵיהּ: ״חָמֵשׁ אַמּוֹת אֹרֶךְ וְחָמֵשׁ אַמּוֹת רֹחַב רָבוּעַ יִהְיֶה הַמִּזְבֵּחַ״!

It was taught in a *baraita* cited above that **the measurement of** the altar's **length, and the measurement of its width, and the measurement of its height are not indispensable. Rabbi Mani says:** This is the *halakha* **provided that one does not decrease its** size so that it is smaller **than the altar constructed by Moses.**[H] The Gemara asks: **And how** large was the altar constructed by Moses? **Rav Yosef says:** One **cubit.** Those in the study hall **mocked** Rav Yosef, as it is written explicitly: **"Five cubits long and five cubits wide; the altar shall be square"** (Exodus 27:1).

אֲמַר לֵיהּ אַבַּיֵי: דִּלְמָא מְקוֹם מַעֲרָכָה קָאָמַר מָר? אֲמַר לֵיהּ: מָר דְּגַבְרָא רַבָּה הוּא יָדַע מַאי קָאָמִינָא. קָרֵי עֲלַיְיהוּ.

Abaye said to Rav Yosef: **Perhaps the Master is speaking** about **the area of the arrangement** of wood? Since the corners took up one cubit on each side and there was an additional cubit on each side for the priests to walk, only one cubit was left for the arrangement of wood. Rav Yosef **said to** Abaye: **The Master,** i.e., Abaye, **who is a great man, knows what I** mean to **say.** Rav Yosef **read,** i.e., applied, the following verse **to those** who mocked him:

HALAKHA

The corner, the ramp, the base, and the square are indispensable – קֶרֶן וְכֶבֶשׁ וִיסוֹד וְרִיבּוּעַ מְעַכְּבִין: The four corners of the altar, its base, its square shape, and its ramp are indispensable. The measurements of its length, width, and height are not. This is in accordance with the opinion of the *tanna* in the *baraita* (Rambam *Sefer Avoda*, *Hilkhot Beit HaBeḥira* 2:17).

Provided that one does not decrease its size smaller than the altar constructed by Moses – וּבִלְבַד שֶׁלֹּא יִפְחָתֶנּוּ מִמִּזְבֵּחַ שֶׁעָשָׂה מֹשֶׁה: The minimum dimensions of the altar are one cubit wide, one cubit long, and three cubits high. This is in accordance with the opinion of Rabbi Mani (Rambam *Sefer Avoda*, *Hilkhot Beit HaBeḥira* 2:17).

NOTES

The altar – הַמִּזְבֵּחַ: In reference to the requirement that the altar be square, the verse states: "The altar shall be square" (Exodus 27:1), and with regard to both the base and the corners, the verse states: "The corners of the altar…the base of the altar" (see Exodus 29:12). It should be pointed out that the ramp is not mentioned explicitly in the Torah; the Sages in the *Mekhilta* derive its source from the Torah prohibition against ascending the altar by way of steps (see Exodus 20:22). Nevertheless, Rashi does cite a Torah source from the verse that states: "In front of the altar" (Leviticus 6:7), which indicates the area where the priests ascend the altar.

What is the *karkov* – אֵיזֶהוּ כַּרְכּוֹב: As Rashi explains further on, the Gemara is discussing the *karkov* that is mentioned in the context of Moses' altar. Rashi understands *karkov* as being a slight groove around the altar's perimeter, generally made for aesthetic purposes. It seems from Rashi's commentary on the Torah that Rabbi Yosei, son of Rabbi Yehuda, maintains the *karkov* was a one-cubit-high groove, and below it there was a one-cubit-high meshwork netting that reached the midpoint of the altar. Rabbi Yehuda HaNasi maintains that the *karkov* refers to a design made along the altar's perimeter, in that same location. Some explain that according to Rabbi Yosei, son of Rabbi Yehuda, the *karkov* was a slight groove along the top of the altar, beside the place the priests would walk.

There were two – תְּרֵי הָווּ: One is mentioned in the verse, and was for aesthetic purposes. It is with regard to this that Rabbi Yosei, son of Rabbi Yehuda, and Rabbi Yehuda HaNasi disagree. The second one, not mentioned in the verse, was located atop the altar (Rashi). It is significant to note that this Gemara refers only to Moses' altar, as no aesthetic *karkov* is mentioned in reference to the altar in the Temple. Although *Shekalim* 8:8 mentions the *karkov* in reference to the altar in the Temple, Rashi (*Sukkah* 54b) explains that it is referring to the surrounding ledge of the altar, which was in the precise location of the *karkov* on Moses' altar, according to the opinion that the two altars were of equal height.

LANGUAGE

Engraving [*kiyyur*] – כִּיּוּר: This means embossed, and refers to engravings, generally made in clay. The verb *kiyyar* also appears in other sources as *kiyyad*. It is unclear which is the original form.

NOTES

Before Rabbi Tarfon…the children of Keturah – קַמֵּיהּ דְּרַבִּי טַרְפוֹן...בְּנֵי קְטוּרָה: In this context, Rashi explains the connotation of this term differently, intimating that Rabbi Tarfon's nephews were not capable of engaging in a halakhic discussion.

With a shortened cubit [*amah geduma*] – בְּאַמָּה גְּדוּמָה: This follows Rashi's version of the text and means that this *amah* is slightly shorter than the standard length. According to Rashi's explanation, Rav Yosef was challenging Rabbi Yirmeya's statement by citing a *baraita*, from which it seems that the standard-sized cubit was used. Others suggest that Rav Yosef was citing a *baraita* that supports Rabbi Yirmeya's statement (*Shita Mekubbetzet*, citing *Tosefot Rabbeinu Peretz*). *Tosafot* cite the version of the text of the Gemara found in the *Arukh*, which reads: *Amah geruma*, meaning an extended cubit. According to this, Rav Yosef's challenge from the *baraita*, which indicates that the wood may not extend beyond the pyre, is readily understood.

It is written in a verse that the altar must be square [*ravua*] – רָבוּעַ כְּתִיב: Since the letters *ayin* and *tzadi* may be interchanged, the word may be read as though it says *ravutz*, which means lying down or crouching.

HALAKHA

The logs that Moses prepared – גְּזִירִין שֶׁעָשָׂה מֹשֶׁה: The logs that Moses prepared were one cubit long by one cubit wide, and their thickness was that of a level used for smoothing out a pile of grain in a container the size of one *se'a*. All subsequent logs followed these dimensions (Rambam *Sefer Avoda*, *Hilkhot Issurei Mizbe'aḥ* 7:3).

There was a ramp on the south side of the altar – כֶּבֶשׁ הָיָה לִדְרוֹמָהּ שֶׁל מִזְבֵּחַ: A ramp was attached to the south side of the altar. Its length was thirty-two cubits and its width was sixteen cubits (Rambam *Sefer Avoda*, *Hilkhot Beit HaBeḥira* 2:13).

"בְּנֵי קְטוּרָה". בְּנֵי אַחְתֵיהּ דְּרַבִּי טַרְפוֹן הָווּ יָתְבִי קַמֵּיהּ דְּרַבִּי טַרְפוֹן, פְּתַח וַאֲמַר: "וַיֹּסֶף אַבְרָהָם וַיִּקַּח אִשָּׁה וּשְׁמָהּ יוֹחָנִי". אָמְרִי לֵיהּ: "קְטוּרָה" כְּתִיב! קָרֵי עֲלֵיהֶם: "בְּנֵי קְטוּרָה".

"**The children of Keturah**" (Genesis 25:4). Although Keturah's children were children of Abraham, they were not of the same caliber as Isaac. Similarly, Rav Yosef was saying that his other students were not of the caliber of Abaye. Having mentioned this term, the Gemara relates: **The sons of Rabbi Tarfon's sister were sitting** silently **before Rabbi Tarfon.** In an attempt to encourage them to say something, **he began and said:** The verse states: **And Abraham took another wife, and her name was Yoḥani. They said to** Rabbi Tarfon: **It is written: "Keturah"** (Genesis 25:1), not Yoḥani. Rabbi Tarfon **read,** i.e., said, **about them** the phrase **"the children of Keturah"**[N] as they were able to contribute only this small piece of information.

אָמַר אַבַּיֵי בַּר הוּנָא אָמַר רַב חָמָא בַּר גּוּרְיָא: גְּזִירִין שֶׁעָשָׂה מֹשֶׁה, אוֹרְכָּן אַמָּה וְרוֹחְבָּן אַמָּה, וְעוֹבְיָין כְּמַחַק גּוֹדֶשׁ סְאָה.

§ **Abaye bar Huna says** that **Rav Ḥama bar Gurya says:** With regard to the **logs that Moses prepared**[H] for the mitzva of burning wood upon the altar, **their length** was **a cubit and their width** was **a cubit, and their thickness** was **like** that of **a leveler,** a kind of flat stick used to remove the excess grain **heaped** on top of a container that holds one ***se'a*.**

אָמַר רַבִּי יִרְמְיָה: בְּאַמָּה גְּדוּמָה. אֲמַר רַב יוֹסֵף, וְלָאו הַיְינוּ דְּתַנְיָא: "עַל הָעֵצִים אֲשֶׁר עַל הָאֵשׁ אֲשֶׁר עַל הַמִּזְבֵּחַ" – שֶׁלֹּא יְהוּ עֵצִים יוֹצְאִין מִן הַמִּזְבֵּחַ כְּלוּם.

Rabbi Yirmeya says: The length and width of the logs mentioned were measured **with a shortened cubit.**[N] **Rav Yosef said: Is this not as it is taught** in a *baraita*: The verse states: **"Upon the wood that is on the fire that is upon the altar"** (Leviticus 1:8). The seemingly superfluous phrase "that is upon the altar" teaches **that the wood should not extend at all beyond** the area of **the altar** designated for the arrangement of wood. Since this area was one square cubit, the logs were exactly one cubit as well.

תְּנַן הָתָם: כֶּבֶשׁ הָיָה לִדְרוֹמָהּ שֶׁל מִזְבֵּחַ, אוֹרֶךְ שְׁלֹשִׁים וּשְׁתַּיִם עַל רוֹחַב שֵׁשׁ עֶשְׂרֵה. מְנָא הָנֵי מִילֵּי? אֲמַר רַב הוּנָא, אָמַר קְרָא: "וְשָׁחַט אוֹתוֹ עַל יֶרֶךְ הַמִּזְבֵּחַ צָפוֹנָה" – שֶׁיְּהֵא יָרֵךְ בַּצָּפוֹן וּפָנָיו בַּדָּרוֹם.

§ The Gemara discusses the ramp of the altar: **We learned** in a mishna **there** (*Middot* 36a): **There was a ramp** that was located **on the south side of the altar,**[H] whose size was **a length of thirty-two** cubits **by a width of sixteen** cubits. The Gemara asks: **From where are these matters** derived, i.e., from where is it derived that the ramp is on the south side of the altar? **Rav Huna said: The verse states: "And he shall slaughter it on the side [*yerekh*] of the altar northward"** (Leviticus 1:11), which teaches **that** the altar's **thigh [*yarekh*] should be** located **in the north, and its face,** i.e., the front of the altar where the priests ascend to it, should be **in the south.** The verse likens the positioning of the altar to a person who is lying down flat, in which case if his legs are to the north, his face is to the south.

אֵימָא: יָרֵךְ בַּצָּפוֹן וּפָנָיו בַּצָּפוֹן! אֲמַר רָבָא: רְמִי גַּבְרָא אַאַפֵּיהּ. אֲמַר לֵיהּ אַבַּיֵי: אַדְּרַבָּה, תָּרֵיץ וְאוֹתֵיב גַּבְרָא!

The Gemara asks: Why not **say** that its **thigh** should be **in the north and its face** should also be **in the north?** Perhaps the verse is referring to a person sitting with both his face and feet in the north. **Rava said** in response: **Place the man on his face,** i.e., the analogy is to a man who is lying down. **Abaye said to him: On the contrary, sit the man straight up** so that his face and his legs are facing the same direction.

אֲמַר לֵיהּ: "רָבוּעַ" כְּתִיב. וְהָא מִיבָּעֵי לֵיהּ דִּמְרַבַּע רַבּוּעֵי! מִי כְּתִיב "מְרוּבָּע"? וְלִיטַעֲמֵיךְ, מִי כְּתִיב "רָבוּץ"? אֲמַר לֵיהּ: "רָבוּעַ" כְּתִיב, דְּמַשְׁמַע הָכִי וּמַשְׁמַע הָכִי.

Rava **said** back **to him: It is written** in a verse that the altar must be "**square [*ravua*]**" (Exodus 27:1),[N] which indicates lying down or crouching, as it is similar to the term *ravutz*, meaning crouching. Abaye challenges Rava: **But** this word is **necessary to** teach **that** the altar must be **square.** Rava responds: **Is it written** in the verse that the altar must be **square [*merubba*]?** The verse specifically uses the form *ravua* in order to allude to the word *ravutz*, crouching. Abaye counters: **According to your reasoning, is it written** in the verse that the altar must be ***ravutz*?** Rava answers: It **is written** in the verse that the altar must be ***ravua*, which** is a term that **indicates this,** i.e., that the altar must be square, **and indicates that,** i.e., that its positioning is comparable to that of a person who is lying down.

וְתַנָּא מַיְיתֵי לַהּ מֵהָכָא, דְּתַנְיָא, רַבִּי יְהוּדָה אוֹמֵר: ״וּמַעֲלֹתֵהוּ פְּנוֹת קָדִים״ כׇּל פִּינּוֹת שֶׁאַתָּה פּוֹנֶה – לֹא יְהוּ אֶלָּא דֶּרֶךְ יָמִין, לַמִּזְרָח.

The Gemara adds: **And another *tanna* cites** the source for the ramp's positioning **from here, as it is taught** in a *baraita* that **Rabbi Yehuda says:** The verse states with regard to the future altar: **"And its steps shall look [*penot*] toward the east"** (Ezekiel 43:17), which indicates that **all the turns [*pinot*] that you turn**[H] **should be only to the right** and you should turn **to the east.**[N] Only if the ramp is in the south can one turn to the right and be facing eastward.

וְאֵימָא: שְׂמֹאל לַמִּזְרָח? לֹא סָלְקָא דַּעְתָּךְ, דְּתָנֵי רָמֵי בַּר (יְחִזְקִיָּה): יָם שֶׁעָשָׂה שְׁלֹמֹה, ״עֹמֵד עַל שְׁנֵים עָשָׂר (עֲמוּדִים) בָּקָר שְׁלֹשָׁה פֹנִים צָפוֹנָה וּשְׁלֹשָׁה פֹנִים יָמָּה וּשְׁלֹשָׁה פֹּנִים נֶגְבָּה וּשְׁלֹשָׁה פֹּנִים מִזְרָחָה״, כׇּל פִּינּוֹת שֶׁאַתָּה פּוֹנֶה – לֹא יְהוּ אֶלָּא דֶּרֶךְ יָמִין, לַמִּזְרָח.

The Gemara challenges: The verse indicates only that after a person turns he is facing eastward. Why not **say** that the ramp was located in the north and the priest turns **left** and faces **eastward?** The Gemara answers: This possibility should **not enter your mind, as Rami bar Yeḥizkiya**[N] **teaches:** A verse describes the **sea,** i.e., the Basin, **that Solomon built,** in the following terms: **"It stood upon twelve oxen, three looking toward [*ponim*] the north, and three looking toward [*ponim*] the west, and three looking toward [*ponim*] the south, and three looking toward [*ponim*] the east"** (II Chronicles 4:4). From the order of the directions in which the verse lists the groups of oxen under the Basin, it can be derived that **all the turns that you turn should be only to the right** and **to the east.**

הַהוּא מִיבְּעֵי לֵיהּ לְגוּפֵיהּ! אִם כֵּן, ״פֹּנִים״ ״פֹּנִים״ לָמָּה לִי?

The Gemara challenges: **That** verse **is necessary to** teach **its own** information describing the Basin. The Gemara explains: **If so, why do I need** the verse to repeat the term ***ponim*, *ponim*?** It must be in order to teach how one turns while performing the sacrificial rite upon the altar, which, in turn, teaches the location of the ramp.

שָׁאַל רַבִּי שִׁמְעוֹן בֶּן יוֹסֵי בֶּן לָקוֹנְיָא אֶת רַבִּי יוֹסֵי: אוֹמֵר הָיָה רַבִּי שִׁמְעוֹן בֶּן יוֹחַי, אֲוִיר יֵשׁ בֵּין כֶּבֶשׁ לַמִּזְבֵּחַ? אָמַר לוֹ: וְאַתָּה אִי אַתָּה אוֹמֵר כֵּן? וַהֲלֹא כְּבָר נֶאֱמַר: ״וְעָשִׂיתָ עֹלֹתֶיךָ הַבָּשָׂר וְהַדָּם״, מָה דָּם בִּזְרִיקָה – אַף בָּשָׂר בִּזְרִיקָה!

§ **Rabbi Shimon ben Yosei ben Lakonya asked Rabbi Yosei:** Is it so that **Rabbi Shimon ben Yoḥai used to say** that **there is airspace,** i.e., a gap, **between the ramp and the altar?**[H] Rabbi Yosei **said to him: And you, don't you say so** as well? **But isn't it already stated: "And you shall offer your burnt offerings, the flesh and the blood"** (Deuteronomy 12:27)? The verse juxtaposes the flesh of the burnt offering with its blood to teach that **just as** the **blood** is presented upon the altar **via tossing**[H] while the priest stands on the ground next to the altar (see Leviticus 1:5), **so too,** the **flesh** of the burnt offering is presented **via tossing.** In order to fulfill this requirement, the priest stands on the ramp and tosses the flesh over the gap between the ramp and the altar, so that it lands on the arrangement of wood.

אָמַר לוֹ: שֶׁאֲנִי אוֹמֵר, עוֹמֵד בְּצַד מַעֲרָכָה וְזוֹרֵק.

Rabbi Shimon ben Yosei ben Lakonya **said to him:** If the verse simply teaches that the flesh must be tossed onto the arrangement of wood, it does not prove that there must be a gap between the ramp and the altar, **as I say** that the priest should **stand next to** the **arrangement** of wood **and toss** the flesh onto it.

אָמַר לוֹ: כְּשֶׁהוּא זוֹרֵק, לְמַעֲרָכָה דְּלוּקָה הוּא זוֹרֵק אוֹ לְמַעֲרָכָה שֶׁאֵינָהּ דְּלוּקָה הוּא זוֹרֵק? הֱוֵי אוֹמֵר: לְמַעֲרָכָה דְּלוּקָה הוּא זוֹרֵק; הָתָם מִשּׁוּם דְּלָא אֶפְשָׁר!

Rabbi Yosei **said to him: When he tosses** the flesh, **does he toss** it **onto** a part of the **arrangement** of wood that is **burning or does he toss** it **onto** a part of the **arrangement** of wood **that is not burning? You must say** that **he tosses** it **onto** a part of the **arrangement** of wood that is **burning.** And **there,** according to your suggestion that the priest is standing next to the arrangement of wood, he would have to toss the flesh, **because it is impossible** to place the flesh directly into the fire without the priest getting burned. It would be unnecessary for the verse to teach that the priest tosses the flesh while standing next to the arrangement. Consequently, when the verse juxtaposed the blood with the flesh, it must be teaching that the flesh must be tossed over a gap between the ramp and the altar.

רַב פַּפָּא אָמַר: כִּי דָם, מָה דָּם אֲוִיר קַרְקַע מַפְסִיקוֹ – אַף בָּשָׂר אֲוִיר קַרְקַע מַפְסִיקוֹ.

Rav Pappa says: The requirement that there be a gap between the ramp and the altar can be derived from this verse, because the juxtaposition teaches that the flesh is **like blood** in the manner in which it is tossed: **Just as** with regard to the **blood** there is **space** on the **ground** that **interposes** between the priest and the altar, **so too** with regard to the **flesh,** there is **space** on the **ground** that **interposes** between the priest and the altar, i.e., he stands on the ground next to the altar and tosses the flesh onto the altar.

HALAKHA

All the turns that you turn – כׇּל פִּינּוֹת שֶׁאַתָּה פּוֹנֶה: All of the priests who ascended the altar would turn and walk to the right and descend the ramp via the left side, after circling the altar (Rambam *Sefer Avoda, Hilkhot Ma'aseh HaKorbanot* 7:11).

Airspace between the ramp and the altar – אֲוִיר...בֵּין כֶּבֶשׁ לַמִּזְבֵּחַ: There was a slight gap between the ramp and the altar to allow for the tossing of the sacrificial parts upon the altar pyre. This is in accordance with the opinion of Rabbi Shimon (Rambam *Sefer Avoda, Hilkhot Beit HaBeḥira* 2:13).

Blood via tossing – דָּם בִּזְרִיקָה: The sacrificial parts are tossed atop the altar, just as the blood is (Rambam *Sefer Avoda, Hilkhot Ma'aseh HaKorbanot* 6:4).

NOTES

To the right, to the east – דֶּרֶךְ יָמִין לַמִּזְרָח: The Gemara interprets the verse to mean that when the priest circles the top of the altar, he must walk toward the right side, i.e., the east. The only way to reach the east by turning right is if the ramp is located in the south.

Rami bar Yeḥizkiya – רָמֵי בַּר יְחִזְקִיָּה: The text should in fact read Rami bar Yeḥezkel.

BACKGROUND

Two small ramps – שְׁנֵי כְּבָשִׁים קְטַנִּים:

Small ramp on the western side of the large ramp

Small ramp on the eastern side of the large ramp

אָמַר רַב יְהוּדָה: שְׁנֵי כְּבָשִׁים קְטַנִּים יוֹצְאִין מִן הַכֶּבֶשׁ, שֶׁבָּהֶן פּוֹנִים לַיְּסוֹד וְלַסּוֹבֵב, וּמוּבְדָּלִין מִן הַמִּזְבֵּחַ מְלֹא נִימָא, מִשּׁוּם שֶׁנֶּאֱמַר: ״סָבִיב״. וְרַבִּי אַבָּהוּ אָמַר: ״רָבוּעַ״.

§ The Gemara continues discussing the ramp: **Rav Yehuda says:** There were **two small ramps**[BH] **protruding from the** main **ramp** that led to the altar, **on which** the priests could **turn to the base** of the altar **and to the surrounding ledge** of the altar. They were **separated from the altar** by **a hairbreadth, because it is stated: "Roundabout"** (Leviticus 1:5), with regard to the altar. This indicates that nothing is attached to the entire perimeter of the altar. **And Rabbi Abbahu says** there is a different source, as it states: **"Square"** (Exodus 27:1), and if the ramps would be connected to the altar it would no longer be square.

וְאִיצְטְרִיךְ לְמִכְתַּב ״סָבִיב״ וְאִיצְטְרִיךְ לְמִכְתַּב ״רָבוּעַ״, דְּאִי כָּתַב רַחֲמָנָא ״סָבִיב״ הֲוָה אָמִינָא דְּעָגֵיל מְעַגָּל – כָּתַב רַחֲמָנָא ״רָבוּעַ״, וְאִי כָּתַב רַחֲמָנָא ״רָבוּעַ״ הֲוָה אָמִינָא דַּאֲרִיךְ וְקָטִין – כָּתַב רַחֲמָנָא ״סָבִיב״.

The Gemara continues: **And it was necessary** for the verse **to write: "Roundabout," and it was necessary** for the verse **to write: "Square," as, had the Merciful One written** only: **"Roundabout," I would say that** the altar **can be circular.** Therefore, **the Merciful One wrote** that the altar must be **"square." And had the Merciful One written** only that the altar must be **"square** [*ravua*]**," I would say that** the word *ravua* simply means rectangular and the altar can be **long and narrow.** Therefore, **the Merciful One wrote** the term **"roundabout,"** which teaches that the altar must not have some sides that are longer than others.

תְּנַן הָתָם: הַכֶּבֶשׁ וְהַמִּזְבֵּחַ שִׁשִּׁים וּשְׁתַּיִם. הָנֵי שִׁיתִּין וְאַרְבְּעָה הָווּ! נִמְצָא פּוֹרֵחַ אַמָּה עַל יְסוֹד וְאַמָּה עַל סוֹבֵב.

§ **We learned** in a mishna **elsewhere** (*Middot* 37b): **The ramp and the altar** together were **sixty-two** cubits long. The Gemara challenges: The dimensions of **these are sixty-four** cubits, as the altar and the ramp were each thirty-two cubits long (*Middot* 36a). The Gemara explains: The thirty-two-cubit measurement of the ramp is explained by a *baraita* that states: It **is found** that the ramp of the altar **overhung** the **base** of the altar by one **cubit**[H] **and the surrounding ledge** by one **cubit,** resulting in an aggregate length of thirty-two cubits.

HALAKHA

Two small ramps – שְׁנֵי כְּבָשִׁים קְטַנִּים: Two minor ramps protruded from the large ramp of the altar, from which the priests could walk onto the altar base and the surrounding ledge. They were distanced from the altar by a hairbreadth (Rambam *Sefer Avoda, Hilkhot Beit HaBeḥira* 2:14).

The ramp overhung the base by one cubit, etc. – פּוֹרֵחַ אַמָּה וכו׳: The large ramp of the altar was thirty cubits long upon the ground. An additional cubit extended above the altar's base and another cubit above the surrounding ledge, bringing it to a total of thirty-two cubits long (Rambam *Sefer Avoda, Hilkhot Beit HaBeḥira* 2:13).

Perek **VI**
Daf **63** Amud **a**

אָמַר רָמִי בַּר חָמָא: כׇּל כִּבְשֵׁי כְּבָשִׁים שָׁלֹשׁ אַמּוֹת לְאַמָּה, חוּץ מִכִּבְשׁוֹ שֶׁל מִזְבֵּחַ שֶׁהָיָה שָׁלֹשׁ אַמּוֹת וּמֶחֱצָה וְאֶצְבַּע וּשְׁלִישׁ אֶצְבַּע בְּזַכְרוּתָא.

Rami bar Ḥama says: The slope of **each of the minor ramps,**[N] was **one cubit** of rise **per three cubits** of run; this was true **aside from the** main **ramp of the altar, which** rose one cubit in **three and a half cubits**[N] **and one fingerbreadth and one-third of a fingerbreadth,** measured **by the tip**[N] of the thumb. The slope of the main ramp of the altar was slightly less than that of the minor ramps in order to make it easier for the priests to ascend the ramp while holding the sacrificial portions.

NOTES

Each of the minor ramps, etc. – כׇּל כִּבְשֵׁי כְּבָשִׁים וכו׳: Literally: All of the ramps' ramps. Some explain that this expression refers specifically to the two minor ramps protruding from the altar's main ramp (see *Ḥavvot Ya'ir*). It seems from Rashi that this is an inclusive expression alluding to all ramps located in the Temple.

Three and a half cubits, etc. – שָׁלֹשׁ אַמּוֹת וּמֶחֱצָה וכו׳: The calculation is as follows: The altar ramp was 32 cubits long and reached the top of the altar at a height of 9 cubits, 1 cubit for the base of the altar plus 5 cubits until the surrounding ledge, an additional 3 cubits until the altar top, and the tenth cubit occupied by the corners. One cubit comprises 24 fingerbreadths, or 6 handbreadths, as 1 handbreadth comprises 4 fingerbreadths. In other words, the ramp extended 32/9 cubits, or 3⁵⁄₉ cubits, horizontally, for every 1 cubit it rose vertically. The measurement of 3⁵⁄₉ cubits can also be expressed as 3½ cubits plus 1/18 cubits. The measurement of 1/18 is equivalent to 1⅓ fingerbreadths. Therefore, the Gemara refers to the gradient of the main ramp, 3⁵⁄₉, as a run of 3½ cubits plus 1 fingerbreadth plus 1/3 fingerbreadth, for every 1 cubit of rise.

Tosafot cite Rashi as presenting a different opinion in the name of his teacher, who maintains that for every 1 cubit of rise the ramp actually extended 3½ cubits plus 1 handbreadth plus 1/3 of a fingerbreadth, a lower gradient than the one according to Rashi. Rashi himself disagrees with this opinion, as it would mean that the top of the ramp did not reach the top of the altar. This would be problematic, since the Torah renders forbidden steps leading up to the altar (see Exodus 20:22). See *Tosafot* for a possible resolution to Rashi's question.

By the tip – בְּזַכְרוּתָא: Rashi does not have this term in his version of the text. Some explain that this refers to the knuckle of the thumb (see *Tosafot* on *Menaḥot* 41b). Some explain that it refers to the tip of the thumb, which is a smaller size than the knuckle (see Maharam of Rothenburg). The *Arukh* has a different version of the term, which apparently refers to the pinky.

מתני׳ מְנָחוֹת הָיוּ נִקְמָצוֹת בְּכָל מָקוֹם בָּעֲזָרָה, וְנֶאֱכָלוֹת לִפְנִים מִן הַקְּלָעִים, לְזִכְרֵי כְהוּנָּה, בְּכָל מַאֲכָל, לְיוֹם וָלַיְלָה עַד חֲצוֹת.

MISHNA **Handfuls were removed**[B] **from the meal offerings in any place**[H] **in the** Temple **courtyard and were consumed within** the area enclosed by **the curtains by males of the priesthood,** prepared **in any** form of **food** preparation that he chooses, e.g., roasted or boiled, **for one day and night, until midnight.**

גמ׳ אָמַר רַבִּי אֶלְעָזָר: מִנְחָה שֶׁנִּקְמְצָה בַּהֵיכָל – כְּשֵׁירָה, שֶׁכֵּן מָצִינוּ בְּסִילּוּק בָּזִיכִין.

GEMARA **Rabbi Elazar says: A meal offering that had its handful removed in the Sanctuary**[H] **is valid, as we found with regard to the removal** of the two **bowls** of frankincense that were placed beside the shewbread on the Table, which was located in the Sanctuary. On Shabbat, these bowls of frankincense were removed and burned on the altar, which allowed the shewbread to be eaten. Removal of the bowls of frankincense paralleled the process of removing a handful from a meal offering; just as the removal of the bowls took place in the Sanctuary, so could the removal of a handful of the meal offering be done in the Sanctuary.

מְתִיב רַבִּי יִרְמְיָה: "וְקָמַץ מִשָּׁם" – מִמָּקוֹם שֶׁרַגְלֵי הַזָּר עוֹמְדוֹת!

Rabbi Yirmeya raises an objection from a *baraita*: The verse states with regard to the meal offerings: "And he shall bring it to Aaron's sons, the priests; **and he shall take from there** his handful" (Leviticus 2:2). The term "from there" indicates that the handful must be taken **from a place where the feet of the non-priest** who brought the meal offering may **stand,** i.e., the Temple courtyard, but not the Sanctuary, in direct contradiction to the opinion of Rabbi Elazar.

בֶּן בְּתֵירָא אוֹמֵר: מִנַּיִן שֶׁאִם קָמַץ בִּשְׂמֹאל, שֶׁיַּחֲזִיר וְיִקְמוֹץ בְּיָמִין – תַּלְמוּד לוֹמַר: "מִשָּׁם", מִמָּקוֹם שֶׁקָּמַץ כְּבָר.

The *baraita* continues: **Ben Beteira says** there is a different explanation of the verse. **From where** is it derived **that if** the priest **removed a handful with** his **left** hand, **that he should return** the handful to the vessel **and** then **remove** another **handful with** his **right** hand? **The verse states:** "And he shall take **from there** his handful," indicating that he may take it **from the place where he already removed a handful.**

אִיכָּא דְּאָמְרִי: הוּא מוֹתִיב לַהּ וְהוּא מְפָרֵק לַהּ, אִיכָּא דְּאָמְרִי: אֲמַר לֵיהּ רַבִּי עֲקִיבָא לְרַבִּי יִרְמְיָה בַּר תַּחְלִיפָא: אַסְבְּרָא לָךְ, לָא נִצְרְכָא אֶלָּא לְהַכְשִׁיר כָּל הָעֲזָרָה כּוּלָּהּ;

The Gemara answers: **There are** those **who say** that Rabbi Yirmeya **raises the objection and he resolves it,** and **there are** those **who say** that **Rabbi Akiva said to Rabbi Yirmeya bar Taḥlifa: I will explain to you** the solution. The verse that indicates that the handful is taken from a place where non-priests may stand **is necessary only to render the entire** Temple **courtyard valid** for removing the handful, but not to indicate that one may not take the handful in the Sanctuary.

סָלְקָא דַּעְתָּךְ אָמֵינָא: הוֹאִיל וְעוֹלָה קׇדְשֵׁי קָדָשִׁים וּמִנְחָה קׇדְשֵׁי קָדָשִׁים, מָה עוֹלָה טְעוּנָה צָפוֹן – אַף מִנְחָה טְעוּנָה צָפוֹן.

This was necessary because it might **enter your mind to say** that **since a burnt offering** is one of the **offerings of the most sacred order, and a meal offering** is also one of the **offerings of the most sacred order, just as a burnt offering requires** slaughter specifically in the **north** side of the Temple courtyard, **so too, a meal offering requires** the taking of the handful specifically in the **north** side of the Temple courtyard.

מָה לְעוֹלָה, שֶׁכֵּן כָּלִיל!

The Gemara responds: **What** is notable **about a burnt offering?** It is notable **in that** it is **completely** burned upon the altar. Therefore, one would not have derived that just as a burnt offering must be slaughtered in the north side of the Temple courtyard, the handful must be taken from a meal offering in the north side of the Temple courtyard.

מֵחַטָּאת. מָה לְחַטָּאת, שֶׁכֵּן מְכַפֶּרֶת עַל חַיָּיבֵי כְרֵיתוֹת!

And if one would attempt to derive that the handful of a meal offering must be taken in the north side of the Temple courtyard **from** the *halakha* pertaining to **a sin offering,** which is an offering of the most sacred order whose slaughtering must take place in the north side, yet is not completely consumed upon the altar, this too can be refuted: **What** is notable **about a sin offering?** It is notable **in that it atones for those liable to** receive *karet*.

BACKGROUND

Handfuls were removed – נִקְמָצוֹת: For most meal offerings a priest takes a handful and burns it on the altar; see, e.g., Leviticus 2:2. This rite, which parallels the slaughtering of an animal sacrifice, may be performed only by a priest. According to many authorities, the priest scooped out the flour with the three middle fingers of his right hand, using his thumb and little finger to remove any surplus flour. He then consecrated the flour by placing it in a service vessel. Since the priest had to scoop out a precise handful of flour, no more and no less, the scooping of the handful was considered one of the more difficult services in the Temple to perform correctly.

HALAKHA

Handfuls were removed from the meal offerings in any place, etc. – מְנָחוֹת נִקְמָצוֹת בְּכָל מָקוֹם וכו׳: It is permitted for the priest to remove the handful of the meal offering anywhere in the Temple courtyard. The removed part of the meal offering may be consumed anywhere in the Temple courtyard by male priests alone. The meal offering may be consumed with any type of food preparation, provided it is not consumed in a leavened form. By Torah law, it may be consumed until daybreak, but the Sages, as a preventative measure, dictated that it may be consumed until midnight. This is in accordance with the mishna (Rambam *Sefer Avoda, Hilkhot Ma'aseh HaKorbanot* 10:3, 8; 12:12, 14).

Had its handful removed in the Sanctuary – נִקְמְצָה בַּהֵיכָל: The handful of a meal offering that was removed in the Sanctuary is valid. This is in accordance with the opinion of Rabbi Elazar and the conclusion of the Gemara (Rambam *Sefer Avoda, Hilkhot Ma'aseh HaKorbanot* 12:12).

מֵאָשָׁם. מָה לְאָשָׁם שֶׁכֵּן מִינֵי דָמִים!

And if one would attempt to derive that the handful of a meal-offering must be taken in the north side of the Temple courtyard **from** the *halakha* pertaining to **a guilt offering,** which is an offering of the most sacred order that must be slaughtered in the north, and that does not share the unique characteristics of the burnt offering or sin offering, this too can be refuted: **What** is notable **about a guilt offering?** It is notable **in that** it is one of the **types of** offerings whose sacrificial rites are performed with their **blood,** which is not so with regard to a meal offering.

מִכּוּלְּהוּ. מָה לְכוּלְּהוּ שֶׁכֵּן מִינֵי דָמִים!

The Gemara adds: It also cannot be suggested to draw an analogy **from** the common element shared by **all of the** offerings mentioned above. **What** is notable **about all of them?** They are notable **in that** they are all **types of** offerings whose sacrificial rites are performed with their **blood.**

אֶלָּא אִיצְטְרִיךְ, סָלְקָא דַעְתָּךְ אָמֵינָא: הוֹאִיל וּכְתִיב ״וְהִגִּישָׁהּ אֶל הַמִּזְבֵּחַ״, ״וְהֵרִים מִמֶּנּוּ בְּקֻמְצוֹ״,

The Gemara presents a different answer: **Rather, it was necessary** for the *baraita* to teach that the handful may be taken from the meal offering anywhere in the Temple courtyard because it may **enter your mind to say** that **since it is written: "And he shall bring it to the altar"** (Leviticus 2:8), and then it states: **"And he shall take up from there his handful"** (Leviticus 6:8), indicating that the handful must be taken from the vessel in which the meal offering was brought near the altar, that the verses also indicate that the handful must be taken in the place where the vessel is brought near the altar.

מָה הַגָּשָׁה בְּקֶרֶן מַעֲרָבִית דְּרוֹמִית – אַף קְמִיצָה בְּקֶרֶן מַעֲרָבִית דְּרוֹמִית, קָא מַשְׁמַע לַן.

Therefore, **just as** one must **bring** the meal offering **to** the **southwest corner**[H] of the altar, **so too,** the **removal of** its **handful** must take place **at** the **southwest corner** of the altar. To counter this, the *baraita* **teaches us** that the removal of the handful may take place anywhere in the Temple courtyard.

אָמַר רַבִּי יוֹחָנָן: שְׁלָמִים שֶׁשְּׁחָטָן בַּהֵיכָל כְּשֵׁרִים, שֶׁנֶּאֱמַר: ״וּשְׁחָטוֹ (אותו) פֶּתַח אֹהֶל מוֹעֵד״, וְלֹא יְהֵא טָפֵל חָמוּר מִן הָעִיקָּר.

§ **Rabbi Yoḥanan says: Peace offerings that one slaughtered in the Sanctuary**[HN] **are valid, as it is stated: "And he shall slaughter it at the entrance of the Tent of Meeting"** (Leviticus 3:2), i.e., in the courtyard; **and** the courtyard, which is of **secondary** sanctity, **should not be weightier than the** place of **primary** sanctity. Accordingly, as the offering is valid if it was slaughtered in the courtyard, it is certainly valid if it was slaughtered in the Sanctuary.

מֵיתִיבִי, רַבִּי יוֹחָנָן בֶּן בְּתֵירָה אוֹמֵר: מִנַּיִן שֶׁאִם הִקִּיפוּ גּוֹיִם אֶת כָּל הָעֲזָרָה, שֶׁהַכֹּהֲנִים נִכְנָסִין לְשָׁם וְאוֹכְלִין שָׁם קָדְשֵׁי קֳדָשִׁים – תַּלְמוּד לוֹמַר: ״בְּקֹדֶשׁ הַקֳּדָשִׁים תֹּאכְלֶנּוּ״;

The Gemara **raises an objection** to Rabbi Yoḥanan's statement from a *baraita*: **Rabbi Yoḥanan ben Beteira says: From where** is it derived **that if gentiles surrounded the entire** Temple **courtyard**[H] and were attacking, making it impossible for the priests to remain there, **the priests may enter that area,** i.e., the Sanctuary, **and eat the offerings of the most sacred order there? The verse states: "In a most holy place shall you eat it"** (Numbers 18:10).

וְאַמַּאי? נֵימָא ״בַּחֲצַר אֹהֶל מוֹעֵד יֹאכְלוּהָ״, וְלֹא יְהֵא טָפֵל חָמוּר מִן הָעִיקָּר!

The Gemara asks: **But why** is there a need to derive the *halakha* from this source? **Let us say** that it can be derived from the verse: **"In the court of the Tent of Meeting they shall eat it"** (Leviticus 6:9), **and** the place of **secondary** sanctity **should not be weightier than the** place of **primary** sanctity. Therefore, similar to Rabbi Yoḥanan's statement, if the sacrificial food can be eaten in the courtyard, it can certainly be eaten in the Sanctuary. The fact that the *baraita* requires another source indicates that Rabbi Yoḥanan's method of derivation is not valid.

הָכִי הָשְׁתָּא?! הָתָם, עֲבוֹדָה דְּאָדָם עוֹבֵד בִּמְקוֹם רַבּוֹ – אָמְרִינַן לֹא יְהֵא טָפֵל חָמוּר מִן הָעִיקָּר. אֲכִילָה, דְּאֵין אָדָם אוֹכֵל בִּמְקוֹם רַבּוֹ – לֹא יְהֵא טָפֵל חָמוּר מִן הָעִיקָּר לָא אָמְרִינַן.

The Gemara answers: **How can these cases be compared? There,** with regard to slaughtering offerings, the act of slaughter is a sacrificial **rite,** and **a person serves in the presence of his master.** Therefore, **we say** that the place of **secondary** sanctity **should not be weightier than the** place of **primary** sanctity, and if one can slaughter an offering in the courtyard, he can certainly do so in the Sanctuary. By contrast, in the case of **eating** sacrificial food, **which** is different because **a person does not eat in the presence of his master, we do not say** the rationale that the place of **secondary** sanctity **should not be weightier than the** place of **primary** sanctity. Therefore, a verse was required to teach that the priest may partake of the offerings in the Sanctuary.

HALAKHA

One must bring the meal offering to the southwest corner – **הַגָּשָׁה בְּקֶרֶן מַעֲרָבִית דְּרוֹמִית**: All meal offerings offered upon the altar require being brought near the tip of its southwest corner (Rambam *Sefer Avoda, Hilkhot Ma'aseh HaKorbanot* 12:6, 13:12).

Peace offerings that one slaughtered in the Sanctuary – **שְׁלָמִים שֶׁשְּׁחָטָן בַּהֵיכָל**: Offerings of lesser sanctity, such as peace offerings, may be slaughtered in any location in the Temple courtyard. Even if they are slaughtered within the Sanctuary, they are valid (Rambam *Sefer Avoda, Hilkhot Ma'aseh HaKorbanot* 5:4).

That if gentiles surrounded the entire courtyard, etc. – **שֶׁאִם הִקִּיפוּ גּוֹיִם אֶת כָּל הָעֲזָרָה וכו׳**: Sin offerings, guilt offerings, and meal offerings are consumed by male priests in the Temple courtyard. In extenuating circumstances they may be consumed in the Sanctuary. This is in accordance with the opinion of Rabbi Yehuda ben Beteira (Rambam *Sefer Avoda, Hilkhot Ma'aseh HaKorbanot* 10:3 and *Kesef Mishne* there).

NOTES

Peace offerings that one slaughtered in the Sanctuary – **שְׁלָמִים שֶׁשְּׁחָטָן בַּהֵיכָל**: Some point out that this logical conclusion can be drawn only with regard to peace offerings. By contrast, offerings of the most sacred order may not be slaughtered in the Sanctuary. This is presumably due to the fact that offerings of the most sacred order must be slaughtered in the north, and the Sanctuary is not considered to be in the north (Radbaz; *Keren Ora*; *Shita Mekubbetzet* 14a).

מתני׳ חַטַּאת הָעוֹף הָיְתָה נַעֲשֵׂית עַל קֶרֶן דְּרוֹמִית מַעֲרָבִית. וּבְכָל מָקוֹם הָיְתָה כְּשֵׁירָה, אֶלָּא זֶה הָיְתָה מְקוֹמָהּ. וּשְׁלֹשָׁה דְּבָרִים הָיְתָה אוֹתָהּ קֶרֶן מְשַׁמֶּשֶׁת מִלְּמַטָּה, וּשְׁלֹשָׁה מִלְּמַעְלָה, מִלְּמַטָּה: חַטַּאת הָעוֹף, וְהַגָּשׁוֹת, וּשְׁיָרֵי הַדָּם.

MISHNA The sacrificial rite of **a bird sin offering**[H] **would be performed at the southwest corner** of the altar. **And** if its sacrificial rite was performed **in any place** on the altar, the offering **was** deemed **valid; but that** corner **was its** designated **place. And** there were **three matters**[H] for which the portion of **that corner below** the red line that served as the demarcation between the upper and lower portions of the altar **served** as the proper location, **and** there were **three** matters for which the portion of that corner **above** the red line served as their proper location. The following rites were performed **below** the red line: Sacrificing **a bird sin offering, and bringing** meal offerings **near** the altar before removal of the handful, **and** pouring out **the remaining blood.**[N]

וּמִלְּמַעְלָן: נִיסּוּךְ הַיַּיִן, וְהַמַּיִם, וְעוֹלַת הָעוֹף כְּשֶׁהִיא רַבָּה בַּמִּזְרָח.

And the following rites were performed **above** the red line: **The wine libation**[B] that is brought together with animal offerings or as an offering by itself, **and the water** libation[NB] on the festival of *Sukkot*, **and** sacrificing **a bird burnt offering when** they were **numerous** and it was impossible to perform the rite **in the east,** i.e., the southeastern corner where the bird burnt offering was sacrificed.

כָּל הָעוֹלִין לַמִּזְבֵּחַ – עוֹלִין דֶּרֶךְ יָמִין

All those **who ascend** the ramp **to the altar ascend via** the **right**[H] side of the ramp toward the southeast corner

HALAKHA

A bird sin offering, etc. – חַטַּאת הָעוֹף וכו׳: The bird sin offering was pinched at the nape of the neck in the southwest corner of the altar. Strictly speaking, it is permitted to pinch the nape at any location on the altar, provided that its blood is sprinkled on the lower half of the altar's wall (Rambam *Sefer Avoda, Hilkhot Ma'aseh HaKorbanot* 7:6, 9).

There were three matters for which…served – שְׁלוֹשָׁה דְּבָרִים הָיְתָה...מְשַׁמֶּשֶׁת: The following three matters were performed in the southwest corner of the altar below the red line: The rite of a bird sin offering; the bringing near of the meal offering; and the rite of the remaining blood of burnt offerings, consumed sin offerings, guilt offerings, and peace offerings. The following three matters were performed in that same corner above the red line: The water libations on the festival of *Sukkot*, the wine libations, and the rite of a bird burnt offering when there was a lack of space in the southeast corner. This is in accordance with the mishna (Rambam *Sefer Avoda, Hilkhot Ma'aseh HaKorbanot* 7:10).

Ascend via the right – עוֹלִין דֶּרֶךְ יָמִין: Everyone who ascends the altar does so via the right side of the ramp, circles the altar counterclockwise, and descends via the left side of the ramp. This is the *halakha* with the exception of one ascending for one of three matters that are performed atop the altar on its southwest corner. In these instances, one ascends via the left side of the ramp, immediately turns left to the southwest corner, and, upon completing the rite, retraces his steps and descends the ramp. This is in accordance with the mishna (Rambam *Sefer Avoda, Hilkhot Ma'aseh HaKorbanot* 7:11).

NOTES

And the remaining blood – וּשְׁיָרֵי הַדָּם: Rashi notes that this is referring specifically to the blood of sin offerings whose rites are performed on the outer altar. This is in contrast to sin offerings whose rites are performed on the inner altar, whose remaining blood was poured on the entire western base of the altar; not necessarily on its southern corner (see *Shita Mekubbetzet* on 64a). According to this explanation, the mishna can also be referring to the blood remaining from burnt offerings, guilt offerings, and peace offerings. This, in fact, is the opinion of the Rambam. It is possible that Rashi mentioned only sin offerings whose rites are performed on the outer altar since remaining blood was mentioned only in their context in the previous chapter.

The mishna (*Tamid* 30a) mentions the existence of two holes in the southwest corner of the altar into which the blood, applied to the western and southern sides of the base of the altar, descended. It seems, therefore, that the southwest corner was also the location of the presenting of the remaining blood of sin offerings whose rites are performed on the inner altar (see 64a). *Tiferet Yisrael* suggests that the blood poured on the western base drained into the southwest corner via a pipe. It should be noted that the mishna here refers to the one cubit of the altar's base that juts out into the south side of the Temple courtyard.

The wine libation and the water libation – נִיסּוּךְ הַיַּיִן וְהַמַּיִם: The water libation and the wine libation were performed in the southwest corner. There were two underground cavities beneath this corner into which the libations drained. There were two small openings in this corner into which the libations were poured, and from there they descended through drainpipes into the underground cavities below. According to one tradition, these cavities were in existence from the time of the world's creation, while according to another tradition, King David was the one who excavated the cavities (see *Sukka* 49a and 53a).

BACKGROUND

Wine libation – נִיסּוּךְ הַיַּיִן: Wine sacrificed on the altar is referred to as a libation. Wine libations were brought together with burnt offerings of animals and peace offerings, as well as with the leper's sin offering and guilt offering. Different quantities of wine were required depending on the animal that was sacrificed: One-fourth of a *hin*, i.e., three *log*, accompanied any sheep sacrifices other than a ram; one-third of a *hin*, or four *log*, was brought with a ram; and half a *hin*, or six *log*, was brought with a bull. A *log* is equivalent to between 300 and 600 ml. Libations of wine could also be brought as independent, voluntary offerings. The wine was brought to the top of the altar where it was poured into a receptacle. From there it flowed through a spigot onto the altar and through a hole in the top of the structure. A drainage channel carried the wine to the Kidron River.

Water libation – נִיסּוּךְ הַמַּיִם: During the festival of *Sukkot*, in addition to the other offerings sacrificed in the Temple, a water libation was poured over the altar. This libation is not mentioned explicitly in the Torah, and its source is an oral tradition transmitted to Moses from Sinai. The water libation was accompanied by great festivity and ceremony, from the time that the water was drawn from the Siloam pool until it was poured over the altar. The water libation was performed on all seven days of *Sukkot*, including Shabbat, although it was not permitted to draw water for this offering on Shabbat.

ומקיפין ויורדין דרך שמאל, חוץ מן העולה לשלשה אלו, שהיו עולין ויורדין על העקב.

and circle the altar until reaching the southwest corner **and descend via** the **left** side of the ramp, **except for one who ascends** for one of **these three matters, where they would ascend** directly to the southwest corner of the altar, **and descend** by turning **on** their **heels**[N] and retracing the path by which they ascended rather than circling the altar.

גמ׳ מנא הני מילי? אמר רבי יהושע: אמר קרא: ״לא ישים עליה שמן ולא יתן עליה לבנה כי חטאת היא״, חטאת קרויה מנחה, ומנחה קרויה חטאת;

GEMARA The Gemara asks a question about the mishna's statement that the sacrificial rite of a bird sin offering is performed at the southwest corner of the altar: **From where are these matters** derived? **Rabbi Yehoshua says: The verse states** with regard to the sin offering of a destitute sinner, which is a meal offering brought in lieu of an animal or bird: **"He shall put no oil upon it, neither shall he put any frankincense on it; for it is a sin offering"** (Leviticus 5:11). From this verse it is evident that **a sin offering is called a meal offering and a meal offering is called a sin offering,** so that their *halakhot* may be compared.

מה חטאת טעונה צפון – אף מנחה טעונה צפון, ומה מנחה בקרן מערבית דרומית – אף חטאת בקרן מערבית דרומית.

Just as a sin offering requires slaughtering in the **north**[N] section of the Temple courtyard, **so too,** the handful of **a meal offering requires** sanctification in a service vessel in the **north. And just as a meal offering** is brought near **to the southwest corner** of the altar, **so too,** the blood of **a sin offering** is sprinkled **on** the **southwest corner**[N] of the altar.

ומנחה גופה מנלן? דתניא: ״לפני ה׳״, יכול במערב? תלמוד לומר: ״אל פני המזבח״;

The Gemara asks: **And** with regard to **a meal offering itself, from where do we** derive that it must be brought near the altar at the southwest corner? **As it is taught** in a *baraita* with regard to the verse: "And this is the law of the meal offering… **before the Lord,** in front of the altar" (Leviticus 6:7). From the phrase: "Before the Lord," one **might** have thought that the rite of bringing the meal offering near the altar must be performed **at the west** side of the altar, which faces the Sanctuary. Therefore, **the verse states: "In front of the altar,"** which is its south side, from where the priests ascend the ramp.

אי ״אל פני המזבח״, יכול בדרום? תלמוד לומר: ״לפני ה׳״; הא כיצד? מגישה בקרן מערבית דרומית כנגד חודה של קרן, ודיו.

The *baraita* continues: **If** the verse merely stated: **"In front of the altar,"** one **might** have thought that the practice of bringing the meal offering near the altar must be performed **at the south** side of the altar. Therefore, **the verse states: "Before the Lord,"** which indicates the west side. **How** can **these** texts be reconciled? The priest **brings it near at** the **southwest corner**[H] of the altar, **opposite the edge of** the **corner** of the altar, **and** that is **sufficient.**[N]

רבי אליעזר אומר: יכול יגישנה למערבה של קרן או לדרומה של קרן? אמרת: כל מקום שאתה מוצא שני מקראות, אחד מקיים עצמו ומקיים חבירו, ואחד מקיים עצמו ומבטל חבירו – מניחין זה שמקיים עצמו ומבטל חבירו, ותופשין את שמקיים עצמו ומקיים חבירו.

The *baraita* continues: **Rabbi Eliezer says:** One **might** have thought that the priest may **bring it near** the altar **to the west of** the southwest **corner or to the south of** the southwest **corner. You must say: Anywhere you find two verses,** and acting in accordance with **one** of them **fulfills itself,** i.e., the requirement stated in that verse, **and fulfills the** requirement stated in the **other** verse, whereas acting in accordance with the other **one** of them **fulfills itself and negates the** requirement stated in the **other** verse, **one leaves the** verse **that fulfills itself and negates the other, and seizes** the verse **that fulfills itself and fulfills the other** verse as well.

כשאתה אומר ״אל פני ה׳״ במערב, היכן קיימת ״אל פני המזבח״? וכשאתה אומר ״אל פני המזבח״ בדרום – קיימת ״לפני ה׳״.

The Gemara explains: In this context, **when you say: "Before the Lord,"** which indicates that the meal offering should be brought near the altar **at the west** side of the altar, **how have you fulfilled** the other part of the verse: **"In front of the altar,"** which indicates the south side? **But when you say: "In front of the altar,"** and bring it near the altar **at the south** side, **you have** also **fulfilled** the phrase: **"Before the Lord."** Consequently, the meal offering must be brought near the south side of the altar.

NOTES

They would ascend and descend on their heels – שהיו עולין ויורדין על העקב: When a priest would complete the rite at the southwest corner, he would be facing the north of the altar. In order to descend the ramp, he needed to turn right, to the south of the altar, toward the ramp.

Just as a sin offering requires the north, etc. – מה חטאת טעונה צפון וכו׳: Rashi asserts that this version of the text is clearly problematic, since neither the removal of the handful of the meal offering nor a bird sin offering are performed in the north (see 63a). In its stead, he suggests an alternative text, found in *Menaḥot* (4a), which reads: Just as a sin offering is disqualified if offered not for its own sake, so too, a meal offering is disqualified if offered not for its own sake. See the first chapter of *Zevaḥim* for a lengthy discussion with regard to the meaning of an offering's own sake.

Tosefot Rabbeinu Peretz explains that the text that appears in the Gemara is that of Rabbeinu Gershom Meor HaGola. According to that version, the Gemara is drawing an analogy between an animal sin offering, whose blood must be received in the northern section of the Temple courtyard, and the rite parallel to that in the case of a meal offering; namely, the sanctification of the handful in a service vessel, and not the removal of the handful.

Alternatively, Rabbeinu Tam suggests that the correct version of the text reads: Just as the service of a sin offering requires the right hand, so too, the service of a meal offering requires the right hand. It should be noted that this version is not in accordance with the opinion of Rabbi Shimon, who permits performance of the service of the meal offering with the left hand (see 25a).

Tosafot, citing Rabbi Ḥayyim, suggest an alternative version of the text, based on *Menaḥot* 61a: Just as the remaining blood of the sin offering is poured on the base of the altar, so too, the meal offering must be brought near the corner above the base of the altar.

So too a sin offering is on the southwest corner – אף חטאת בקרן מערבית דרומית: This is referring specifically to the sprinkling of its blood, since the act of pinching its nape is not limited to one location. The rationale behind this comparison is that the sprinkling of blood is the only act that is analogous to the sacrificing of the meal offering, as both rites are performed directly upon the altar (Rashi). Additionally, logic dictates that one derive the *halakha* of the sin offering's primary rite of sprinkling the blood from the primary rite of the meal offering.

And that is sufficient – ודיו: Rashi, citing the Gemara in *Sota* (14b), explains that the term sufficient is a reference to the fact that the priest does not need to have the actual meal offering touch the altar. Instead, having the vessel in which it is contained touch the altar is sufficient.

HALAKHA

He brings it near at the southwest corner – מגישה בקרן מערבית דרומית: The ritual of carrying the offering to the altar is required for all meal offerings, and must be performed at the southwest corner of the altar, opposite its edge. This is in accordance with the opinion of the first *tanna* (Rambam *Sefer Avoda, Hilkhot Ma'aseh HaKorbanot* 13:12).

בִּדְרוֹם הֵיכָן קַיֵּימְתָּ? אָמַר רַב אַשִׁי, קָסָבַר הַאי תַּנָּא: כּוּלֵּיהּ מִזְבֵּחַ בַּצָּפוֹן קָאֵי.

The Gemara asks: If one brought the meal offering near the altar **at the south** side, **how have you fulfilled** the phrase: "Before the Lord"? **Rav Ashi says: This *tanna* holds** that **the entire altar stood in the north** section of the Temple courtyard. The southern side of the altar was directly aligned with the midpoint of the Temple courtyard, directly opposite the entrance of the Sanctuary, and therefore it is considered "before the Lord."

"בְּכָל מָקוֹם הָיְתָה כְּשֵׁירָה" [וכו']. מַאי קָאָמַר? אָמַר רַב אַשִׁי, הָכִי קָאָמַר: בְּכָל מָקוֹם הָיְתָה כְּשֵׁירָה לִמְלִיקָתָהּ, אֶלָּא זֶה הָיָה מְקוֹמָהּ לְהַזָּאָתָהּ.

§ The mishna teaches that if the sacrificial rite of a bird sin offering was performed **in any place** on the altar, the offering is **valid**, but the southwest corner was its designated place. The Gemara asks: **What is** the mishna **saying** when it states that the southwest corner was its designated place? The mishna already stated that the sacrificial rite of a bird sin offering should be performed at the southwest corner. **Rav Ashi said: This** is what the mishna **is saying: Any place was valid for its pinching, but** the southwest corner **was the place for** the **sprinkling** of its blood.

תְּנֵינָא לְהָא דְּתָנוּ רַבָּנַן: מְלָקָהּ בְּכָל מָקוֹם בַּמִּזְבֵּחַ – כְּשֵׁירָה, הִיזָּה דָּמָהּ בְּכָל מָקוֹם – כְּשֵׁירָה, הִיזָּה וְלֹא מִיצָּה – כְּשֵׁירָה, וּבִלְבַד שֶׁיִּתֵּן מֵחוּט הַסִּיקְרָא וּלְמַטָּה מִדַּם הַנֶּפֶשׁ.

The Gemara notes: **We learn** in this mishna **that which the Sages taught** explicitly in a *baraita* with regard to a bird sin offering: If the priest **pinched its** nape **in any place on the altar,** it is **valid.**[H] If **he sprinkled its blood in any place**[H] on the altar, it is **valid.**[N] If **he sprinkled** the blood, **but did not squeeze out**[H] the remaining blood upon the lower part of the wall of the altar, in accordance with the verse: "And he shall sprinkle of the blood of the sin offering upon the side of the altar; and the rest of the blood shall be squeezed out at the base of the altar" (Leviticus 5:9), it is nevertheless **valid,**[N] **provided that he places** some **of the blood of the soul**[N] anywhere on the altar **from the red line and below.**

מַאי קָאָמַר? הָכִי קָאָמַר: מְלָקָהּ בְּכָל מָקוֹם בַּמִּזְבֵּחַ – כְּשֵׁירָה, מִיצָּה דָּמָהּ בְּכָל מָקוֹם בַּמִּזְבֵּחַ – כְּשֵׁירָה,

The Gemara asks: **What is** the *baraita* **saying?** It first states that the offering is valid no matter where on the altar its blood is sprinkled, and it then states that blood must be placed specifically below the red line. The Gemara answers: **This** is what the *baraita* **is saying:** If **he pinched its** nape **in any place on the altar,** it is **valid.** If **he squeezed out its blood in any place on the altar,** it is **valid,**

Perek **VI**
Daf **64** Amud **a**

שֶׁאִם הִיזָּה וְלֹא מִיצָּה כְּשֵׁירָה, וּבִלְבַד שֶׁיִּתֵּן מֵחוּט הַסִּיקְרָא וּלְמַטָּה מִדַּם הַנֶּפֶשׁ.

because if he sprinkled the blood **but did not squeeze out** the rest of it, it is still **valid, provided that he places** some **of the blood of the soul** anywhere on the altar **from the red line and below.** This version of the *baraita* states that the offering is valid no matter where on the altar its blood was squeezed out; but it is essential that blood is sprinkled on the lower half of the altar.

"שְׁלֹשָׁה דְּבָרִים" כו'. חַטַּאת הָעוֹף – הָא דַּאֲמַרַן,

§ The mishna teaches that there were **three matters** for which the portion of the southwest corner below the red line served as the proper location: The sacrificing of a bird sin offering, and the bringing of the meal offerings near the altar, and pouring the remaining blood. The Gemara cites sources to prove that each of these three matters was performed at the southwest corner: The source with regard to **the bird sin offering** is **that which we said** earlier (63b), that it is derived from a comparison to meal offerings.

הַגָּשׁוֹת – דִּכְתִיב: "וְהִגִּישָׁהּ אֶל פְּנֵי הַמִּזְבֵּחַ". שְׁיָרֵי הַדָּם – דִּכְתִיב "וְאֵת כָּל דַּם הַפָּר יִשְׁפֹּךְ אֶל יְסוֹד הַמִּזְבֵּחַ".

The source for **bringing** meal offerings **near** the altar at the southwest corner is derived from that **which is written: "And he shall bring it to the front of the altar."**[N] The source for pouring **the remaining blood** at the southwest corner of the altar is **as it is written: "And all the remaining blood of the bull he shall pour out at the base of the altar"** (Leviticus 4:7), which the Gemara derives to be referring to the southwest corner (see 53a).

HALAKHA

If the priest pinched its nape in any place…it is valid – מְלָקָהּ בְּכָל מָקוֹם...כְּשֵׁירָה: It is preferable to pinch the nape of a bird sin offering at the southwest corner of the altar. If it was pinched anywhere on the altar, it is valid, provided its blood was sprinkled below the red line (Rambam *Sefer Avoda, Hilkhot Ma'aseh HaKorbanot* 7:6, 7).

If he sprinkled its blood in any place – הִיזָּה דָּמָהּ בְּכָל מָקוֹם: If the priest sprinkled the blood of a bird sin offering in any place on the altar, it is valid, provided some of the blood of the soul was applied below the red line. Significantly, this follows the initial version of the *baraita*, even though it does not accord with the Gemara's final reading (Rambam *Sefer Avoda, Hilkhot Ma'aseh HaKorbanot* 7:9, and see Mahari Kurkus there).

If he sprinkled but did not squeeze out – הִיזָּה וְלֹא מִיצָּה: The squeezing out of the blood of a bird sin offering is indispensable. This is in accordance with the Gemara's conclusion in *Me'ila* (8b), in contrast to this *baraita* (Mahari Kurkus). Ra'avad, in his commentary to *Kinnim* 1:1, maintains that it is not indispensable (Rambam *Sefer Avoda, Hilkhot Ma'aseh HaKorbanot* 7:7).

NOTES

If he sprinkled its blood in any place it is valid – הִיזָּה דָּמָהּ בְּכָל מָקוֹם כְּשֵׁירָה: Rashi is careful to note that the term any place includes above the red line, provided it is near the southwest corner, a condition clearly mentioned in the mishna.

If he sprinkled but did not squeeze out it is valid – הִיזָּה וְלֹא מִיצָּה כְּשֵׁירָה: This is in accordance with the opinion cited earlier (52a) in the name of Rabbi Yishmael, which states that the intention of the verse is that the blood must be squeezed out only if some remains. If none remains, the absence of squeezing does not disqualify the offering. Others maintain that the squeezing is indeed indispensable for the validity of the offering (see *Me'ila* 8b). According to this opinion, attributed by some to Rabbi Yishmael as well, the squeezing of the blood has equal status to that of the sprinkling.

The blood of the soul – דַּם הַנֶּפֶשׁ: This is a reference to the blood that spurts from the bird when its nape is pinched, i.e., the blood with which the soul leaves the body. This excludes both blood of exudate, i.e., blood that exudes from the bird after the initial spurt of its slaughter concludes, as well as blood located in the limbs.

NOTES

And he shall bring it to the front of the altar – וְהִגִּישָׁהּ אֶל פְּנֵי הַמִּזְבֵּחַ: There is no single verse that contains this precise phrase. Rashi's version of the Gemara cites the verse: "The sons of Aaron shall offer it before the Lord, in front of the altar" (Leviticus 6:7). That verse was cited on 63b as the source for the *halakha* that the meal offering is brought near the altar at the southwest corner. *Tosafot* note that the Gemara should have simply stated that the source for this *halakha* was mentioned earlier, as it does with regard to the bird sin offering. The *Shita Mekubbetzet*, citing the Riva, explains that the Gemara here is referring to the verse: "And he shall bring it to the altar" (Leviticus 2:8), because that is the source of the very requirement to bring the meal offering near the altar before the handful is taken. The fact that this is performed at the southwest corner is derived from the other verse, as stated on 63b.

מִלְמַעְלָה: נִיסּוּךְ הַמַּיִם וְהַיַּיִן, וְעוֹלַת הָעוֹף כְּשֶׁהִיא רַבָּה בַּמִּזְרָח". מַאי טַעְמָא? רַבִּי יוֹחָנָן אָמַר: מִפְּנֵי שֶׁקְּרוֹבָה מִבֵּית הַדֶּשֶׁן."

§ The mishna teaches that there were three matters for which the portion of the southwest corner **above** the red line served as the proper location: **The water and wine libations, and** sacrificing **a bird burnt offering when** they were **numerous in the east,** i.e., the southeast corner. The Gemara asks: **What is the reason** the sacrificial rites of a bird burnt offering were ideally supposed to be performed at the southeast corner of the altar? **Rabbi Yoḥanan says: Because it is the closest** of all the corners **to the place of the ashes,** i.e., the place where the ashes from the altar are placed every morning. The crop and feathers of a bird burnt offering are placed there as well.

אָמַר רַבִּי יוֹחָנָן: בֹּא וּרְאֵה כַּמָּה גָּדוֹל כֹּחָן שֶׁל כֹּהֲנִים, שֶׁאֵין לְךָ קַל בָּעוֹפוֹת יוֹתֵר מִמּוּרְאָה וְנוֹצָה, פְּעָמִים שֶׁהַכֹּהֵן זוֹרְקָן יוֹתֵר מִבִּשְׁלֹשִׁים אַמָּה.

The Gemara cites a comment pertaining to the mishna's statement that when the southeast corner of the altar is too crowded, the sacrificial rites of a bird burnt offering can be performed at the southwest corner: **Rabbi Yoḥanan says: Come and see how great** was **the strength of the priests, as you have no** parts **of birds lighter**[N] **than the crop and feathers,** and there were **times when the priest would toss them**[B] **more than thirty cubits**[N] from the southwest corner of the altar to the place of the ashes.

דִּתְנַן: נָטַל מַחְתָּה שֶׁל כֶּסֶף וְעָלָה לְרֹאשׁ הַמִּזְבֵּחַ, וּפִינָּה אֶת הַגֶּחָלִים אֵילָךְ וָאֵילָךְ, וְחָתָה מִן הַמְאוּכָּלוֹת הַפְּנִימִיּוֹת וְיוֹרֵד. הִגִּיעַ לָרִצְפָּה, מַחֲזִיר פָּנָיו כְּלַפֵּי צָפוֹן וְהוֹלֵךְ לְמִזְרָחוֹ שֶׁל כֶּבֶשׁ כְּעֶשֶׂר אַמּוֹת, צָבַר אֶת הַגֶּחָלִים עַל גַּבֵּי הָרִצְפָּה, רָחוֹק מִן הַכֶּבֶשׁ שְׁלֹשָׁה טְפָחִים, מָקוֹם שֶׁנּוֹתְנִין מוּרְאָה וְנוֹצָה וְדִישּׁוּן מִזְבֵּחַ הַפְּנִימִי וְהַמְּנוֹרָה.

This is **as we learned** in a mishna (*Tamid* 28b) describing the procedure of separating the ashes: The priest **would take a coal pan of silver**[H] **and ascend to the top of the altar and clear the** upper layer of **coals to this side and to** that **side, and,** using the coal pan, **scoop up** coals **from** among **the inner, consumed** coals **and descend** the ramp. When he **reached the floor** of the Temple courtyard, he would **turn his face** to the left, **toward the north, and walk about ten cubits along the eastern** side of the ramp. There, he would **heap the coals upon the floor** at **a distance** of **three handbreadths from the ramp.** This was **the location where one places** the **crop and feathers, and the ashes removed from the inner altar and the Candelabrum.**

הָנֵי טְפֵי מִתְּלָתִין וְחַד הָוְיָין! מְקוֹם גַּבְרֵי לָא חָשֵׁיב.

The Gemara challenges: The distance from the southwest corner to the location described in that mishna **is more than thirty-one cubits.**[N] The Gemara answers: Rabbi Yoḥanan **did not consider the space** taken up by **people,** i.e., the priest performing the service, in his calculation.

"כָּל הָעוֹלִים לַמִּזְבֵּחַ". מַאי טַעְמָא? אָמַר רַבִּי יוֹחָנָן: נְסָכִים – שֶׁמָּא יִתְעַשְּׁנוּ, וְעוֹלַת הָעוֹף – שֶׁמָּא תָּמוּת בֶּעָשָׁן.

§ The mishna teaches that **everyone who ascends** the ramp **to the altar** ascends via the right side of the ramp, circles the altar until reaching the southwest corner, and descends via the left side of the ramp, with the exception of one ascending in order to perform the wine or water libations, or to sacrifice a bird burnt offering on the southwest corner of the altar. In those cases the priest would ascend directly to the southwest corner. The Gemara asks: **What is the reason** for these exceptions to the standard practice? **Rabbi Yoḥanan says:** With regard to the **libations,** the priest would not walk all the way around the altar **lest** the wine or water **absorb** the **smoke**[NH] of the altar fire. **And** with regard to **a bird burnt offering** he would not walk all the way around **lest** the bird **die from** inhaling **the smoke.**

NOTES

As you have no parts of birds lighter – שֶׁאֵין לְךָ קַל בָּעוֹף: The lighter the material, the more difficult it is to toss it long distances (Rashi).

More than thirty cubits – יוֹתֵר מִבִּשְׁלֹשִׁים אַמָּה: Rabbi Yoḥanan is discussing a scenario where the priest performs the rite of a bird burnt offering on the southwest corner. As part of the rite, he must toss the crop and feathers a distance of more than 30 cubits to the place of the ashes. How so? The length of the top of the altar was 28 cubits. The ramp was 16 cubits wide, and its top was located at the center of the altar top, leaving a space of 6 cubits from the altar corners on either side. Consequently, there was a distance of 22 cubits from the southwest corner to the northern edge of the ramp. As the Gemara proceeds to explain, the place of the ashes was a distance of 22 cubits south of the edge of the altar. It emerges that the priest had to toss the crop and feathers the distance of the diagonal of a square whose sides are 22 cubits long. Assuming the diagonal of a square is 1⅖ cubits, if one would multiply this number by 22, the result is 30⅘ cubits.

It is more than thirty-one cubits – הָנֵי טְפֵי מִתְּלָתִין וְחַד הָוְיָין: As the mishna stated, the place of the ashes was a distance of three handbreadths eastward from the altar ramp. And if, as demonstrated, the distance from the southwest corner to the edge of the ramp adjacent to the place of ashes was 30⅘ cubits, it emerges that the additional three handbreadths brings the number to greater than 31 cubits (Rashi).

Libations, lest they absorb the smoke – נְסָכִים שֶׁמָּא יִתְעַשְּׁנוּ: The mishna in tractate *Menaḥot* (86b) explains that wine that absorbed smoke is disqualified from being used for libations, even after the fact. The Rambam explains that the wine is disqualified since the smoke ruins its taste.

BACKGROUND

There were times when the priest would toss them, etc. – פְּעָמִים שֶׁהַכֹּהֵן זוֹרְקָן וכו׳: In the image below, the dotted triangle depicts Rashi's understanding of how to calculate the distance between the priest and the place of ashes as he performs the rite of a bird burnt offering.

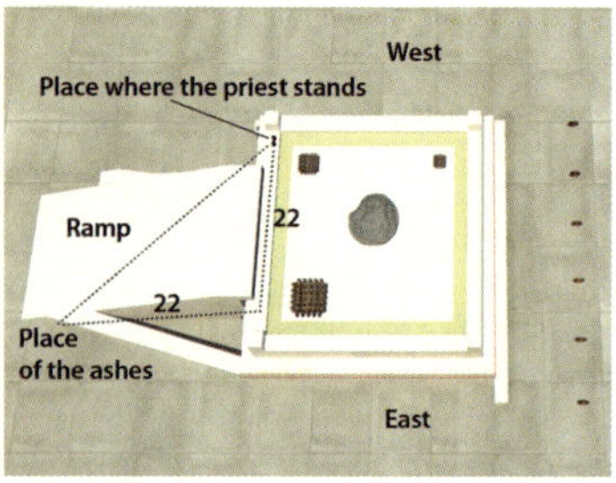

Aerial view of the altar

HALAKHA

Would take a coal pan of silver, etc. – נָטַל מַחְתָּה שֶׁל כֶּסֶף וכו׳: There is a positive mitzva to separate the ashes from the altar every day. How so? The priest who was assigned the rite to separate the ashes would take the coal pan designated for the task and ascend the altar. There, he would clear the upper layer of coals to the side and scoop up coals from the inner, consumed coals, and descend the ramp to the floor of the Temple courtyard. Upon descending, he would turn his face back toward the north and walk approximately ten cubits. There, approximately three handbreadths from the ramp, he would heap the ashes from the coals he scooped up. This was also the location where the crop of a bird burnt offering, and the ashes removed from the inner altar and the Candelabrum, were placed (Rambam *Sefer Avoda*, *Hilkhot Temidin UMusafin* 2:10).

Lest they absorb the smoke – שֶׁמָּא יִתְעַשְּׁנוּ: All priests who ascend the altar do so via the right side of the ramp, except for those who perform the following three rites: The water libations on the festival of *Sukkot*, the wine libations, and the rite of a bird burnt offering when it was too crowded on the southeast corner. In these instances, the priests would turn left at the top of the ramp to the southwest corner, instead of circling its entirety. The reason for this was to prevent the water and wine of the libations from absorbing smoke emitting from the altar pyre, and to prevent a bird burnt offering from dying due to the excessive smoke (Rambam *Sefer Avoda*, *Hilkhot Ma'aseh HaKorbanot* 7:11).

וּרְמִינְהוּ: בָּא לוֹ לְהַקִּיף אֶת הַמִּזְבֵּחַ, מֵאַיִן הוּא מַתְחִיל? מִקֶּרֶן דְּרוֹמִית מִזְרָחִית, מִזְרָחִית צְפוֹנִית, צְפוֹנִית מַעֲרָבִית, מַעֲרָבִית דְּרוֹמִית, וְנוֹתְנִין לוֹ יַיִן לְנַסֵּךְ!

The Gemara **raises a contradiction** from the following mishna (*Tamid* 33b): If the High Priest was performing the sacrificial rites of the daily offering, after he would place the limbs on the fire on top of the altar and **he would come to circle the altar, from where does he start** walking? He starts **from** the **southeast corner,** continues to the **northeast** corner, then to the **northwest** corner, and finally arrives at the **southwest** corner. **And he is given wine to pour** on the altar. This indicates that the High Priest circles the altar while holding the wine for the libation, and there is no concern that it will absorb too much smoke.

אָמַר רַבִּי יוֹחָנָן:

Rabbi Yoḥanan says:

Perek **VI**
Daf **64** Amud **b**

הַקָּפָה בָּרֶגֶל. אֲמַר רָבָא: דַּיְקָא נַמִי, דְּקָתָנֵי: נוֹתְנִין לוֹ יַיִן לְנַסֵּךְ, וְלָא קָתָנֵי: אוֹמֵר לוֹ ״נַסֵּךְ״, שְׁמַע מִינָּהּ.

The **circling** around the altar by the High Priest is done **on foot,**[H] i.e., empty-handed, as he was given the wine to pour only once he arrived at the southwest corner. **Rava said:** The language of the mishna **is also precise, as it teaches** that **he is given wine to pour, and** the mishna **does not teach** that **one tells him** to **pour** the wine, which would have indicated that the High Priest was already holding the wine as he circled the altar. The Gemara comments: **Conclude from** the language of the mishna that the High Priest was given the wine only once he arrived at the southwest corner of the altar.

תָּנוּ רַבָּנַן: כָּל הָעוֹלִין לַמִּזְבֵּחַ – עוֹלִין דֶּרֶךְ יָמִין וְיוֹרְדִין דֶּרֶךְ שְׂמֹאל, עוֹלִין דֶּרֶךְ מִזְרָח וְיוֹרְדִין דֶּרֶךְ מַעֲרָב, חוּץ מִן הָעוֹלֶה לִשְׁלֹשָׁה דְּבָרִים הַלָּלוּ, שֶׁעוֹלִים דֶּרֶךְ מַעֲרָב וְיוֹרְדִין דֶּרֶךְ מַעֲרָב, עוֹלִין דֶּרֶךְ יָמִין וְיוֹרְדִין דֶּרֶךְ יָמִין.

§ **The Sages taught** in a *baraita*: **All** those **who ascend** the ramp to **the altar ascend via** the **right**[N] side of the ramp **and descend via** the **left** side; they **ascend via** the **east** side of the ramp **and descend via** the **west** side, **except for one who ascends for** one of **these three matters:** The wine libation, the water libation, and the sacrificial rite of a bird burnt offering. In these cases, one **ascends via** the **west** side of the ramp **and descends via** the **west** side; one **ascends via** the **right** side **and descends via** the **right** side.

דֶּרֶךְ יָמִין?! דֶּרֶךְ שְׂמֹאל הוּא! אָמַר רָבִינָא: תְּנֵי שְׂמֹאל. רָבָא אָמַר: מַאי יָמִין – יָמִין דְּמִזְבֵּחַ, וּמַאי שְׂמֹאל – שְׂמֹאל דְּגַבְרָא.

The Gemara asks: Does one who ascends via the west side of the ramp do so **via** the **right** side? Ascending via the west side of the ramp **is** the same as ascending **via** the **left. Ravina says:** Emend the *baraita* so that it **teaches** that he ascends via the **left** side. **Rava says: What** is the meaning of the **right** side mentioned in the latter clause of the *baraita*? It is the **right** side from the standpoint **of** the **altar,** facing south, in which case the altar's west side is synonymous with its right side. **And what** is the meaning of the **left** side mentioned in the first clause of the *baraita*? It is the **left** side from the standpoint **of a person** facing the altar.

וְנִיתְנֵי אוֹ אִידִי וְאִידִי דְּמִזְבֵּחַ, אוֹ אִידִי וְאִידִי דְּגַבְרָא! קַשְׁיָא.

The Gemara objects: **But let** the *baraita* be consistent and **teach** both **this** case **and that** case, i.e., the first clause and latter clause, from the standpoint **of the altar, or** let it teach both **this** case **and that** case from the standpoint **of a person** facing the altar. The Gemara concedes: This is **difficult.**

NOTES

Ascend via the right, etc. – עוֹלִין דֶּרֶךְ יָמִין וכו׳: Rashi explains that since the priests would need to turn right upon reaching the top of the ramp, they would ascend the ramp as far to the right as possible, in order to minimize unnecessary walking.

HALAKHA

Circling on foot – הַקָּפָה בָּרֶגֶל: Out of concern that the libation water and wine would become disqualified by absorbing smoke while the priest circled the altar while performing their rites, it was not permitted for the priest to hold the contents while circling. Instead, he would circle the altar counterclockwise beginning in the southeast corner. Only upon reaching the southwest corner was he given the contents for libation. If the priest did not circle the altar, he would turn left immediately upon reaching the altar's top, and perform the necessary rite. This ruling follows the mishna in *Tamid* 33b and the opinion of Rabbi Yoḥanan (Rambam *Sefer Avoda*, *Hilkhot Ma'aseh HaKorbanot* 7:12).

מתני׳ חטאת העוף כיצד היה נעשית? (עלה לכבש ופנה לסובב, בא לו לקרן דרומית מזרחית) היה מולק את ראשה ממול ערפה ואינו מבדיל, ומזה מדמה על קיר המזבח. שירי הדם היה מתמצה על היסוד, ואין למזבח אלא דמה, וכולה לכהנים.

MISHNA The sacrifice of **the bird sin offering, how was it performed?**[NH] The priest **would pinch** off **the** bird's **head** by cutting **opposite its nape**[N] with his thumbnail **and** would **not separate**[N] the bird's head from its body. **And he sprinkles from its blood on the wall of the altar** below the red line. **The remaining blood would be squeezed out** from the body of the bird **on the base**[N] of the altar. **The altar has only its blood**[H] **and the entire** bird goes **to the priests** for consumption.

גמ׳ תנו רבנן: "והזה מדם החטאת" – מגוף החטאת. הא כיצד? אוחז בראש ובגוף ומזה על קיר המזבח, ולא על קיר הכבש, ולא על קיר היכל, ולא על קיר אולם. ואיזה – זה קיר התחתון.

GEMARA **The Sages taught** in a *baraita*: The verse states with regard to the bird sin offering: **"And he shall sprinkle of the blood of the sin offering** upon the side of the altar" (Leviticus 5:9). This teaches that the blood is sprinkled directly **from the body of the sin offering,**[N] not with the priest's finger or from a vessel. **How so?** The priest **holds the head and the body and sprinkles** its blood **on the wall of the altar. And** he does **not** sprinkle it **on the wall of the ramp, and not on the wall of** the **Sanctuary, and not on the wall of** the **Entrance Hall. And which** is this wall of the altar that the blood is sprinkled on? **This is the lower wall,** below the red line.

או אינו אלא קיר העליון? ודין הוא: ומה בהמה שעולתה למטה – חטאתה למעלה, עוף שעולתו למעלה – אינו דין שחטאתו למעלה?

The *baraita* suggests: **Or** perhaps the verse is referring **only** to **the upper wall,** above the red line. **And** this should be **a logical inference: Just as** with regard to **an animal** offering, **where** the blood of **a burnt offering** is applied **below** the red line (see 10b), nevertheless, the blood of **the sin offering** is applied **above** the red line (see Leviticus 4:30), with regard to **a bird** offering, **where** the blood of **the burnt offering** is sprinkled **above** the red line (see 65a), **is it not logical that** the blood of **its sin offering** is sprinkled **above** the red line?

תלמוד לומר: "והנשאר בדם ימצה אל יסוד המזבח" – קיר שהשירין שלו מתמצים ליסוד, ואיזה זה – קיר התחתון.

Therefore, **the verse states: "And the rest of the blood shall be squeezed out** [*yimmatze*] **at the base of the altar"** (Leviticus 5:9), which teaches that the priest sprinkles the blood on the **wall where its remaining** blood **drains to the base** of the altar. **And which** wall is this? **This is the lower wall.** The surrounding ledge of the altar is located one cubit above the red line, and any blood sprinkled above this ledge will not drip down to the base of the altar. The verse teaches that the blood is sprinkled on the wall of the altar from which it would drip down to the altar's base unimpeded.

ונעביד מעילאי והדר נעביד מתתאי! אמר רבא: מי כתיב "ימצה"? "ימצה" כתיב, דממילא משמע.

The Gemara suggests: **Let** the priest **perform** the sprinkling of the blood **above,** as the *baraita* logically deduced, **and then perform** the squeezing **below** in fulfillment of the aforementioned verse. **Rava said: Is it written: He shall drain** [*yematze*]? **It is written: It shall be drained** [*yimmatze*],[N] **which indicates** that the blood trickles down to the base of the altar **by itself.** Accordingly, the blood must be sprinkled on a part of the altar wall from which it can trickle down to the base of the altar.

NOTES

How was it performed – כיצד היה נעשית: There is a sentence that appears here in the Hebrew text, which reads: The priest would ascend the ramp and turn onto the surrounding ledge of the altar, and arrive at the southeast corner of the altar. It is clear that this sentence, which appears in the Vilna Talmud in parentheses, does not belong here. The bird sin offering was sacrificed at the bottom part of the wall of the altar, so that there was no need for the priest to ascend the ramp. Additionally, the sacrificial rite was performed at the southwest corner, not the southeast corner.

Opposite its nape – ממול ערפה: The mishna here adopts the phraseology used by the verse (see Leviticus 5:8). As Rashi explains, opposite in this context is not to be understood literally, as that would indicate the priest pinches the throat, which is clearly incorrect. Rather, the verse means that pinching may performed anywhere along the entire nape of the bird, and opposite indicates the entire area of the nape of the bird that can be seen, which reaches the wings.

And would not separate – ואינו מבדיל: As the Torah states: "And he shall pinch its head opposite its nape, but shall not separate it" (Leviticus 5:8). The Rambam understands this literally, that the head may not be separated from the body. Rashi, by contrast, apparently based on the Gemara in *Ḥullin* 20a, explains that the prohibition against separating the head is not literal, but rather, it is referring to the cutting of both the gullet and the windpipe. Therefore, with regard to a bird burnt offering, in which the bird's head is separated, the priest merely needs to cut the gullet and the windpipe, but not literally detach its head. With regard to a bird sin offering, it is sufficient for the priest to cut only one of the two *simanim*, and that is enough for the slaughtering of a bird, unlike an animal, whose slaughter requires the cutting of both *simanim*.

Squeezed out on the base – מתמצה על היסוד: Here Rashi explains that the priest would press against the altar wall the area on the nape of the bird that was pinched, thereby squeezing out the blood. See *Menaḥot* 2b, where he explains that the priest squeezed the neck of the bird, spraying the blood on the altar wall.

From the body of the sin offering – מגוף החטאת: Rashi, along with most commentaries, explains that the priest sprinkles the blood directly from the sin offering's body to the altar, and does not do so using his finger or by receiving the blood in a vessel and then sprinkling it on to the wall. The Ra'avad, in his commentary to *Torat Kohanim*, suggests that the Gemara means that the primary mitzva is to sprinkle the blood of the body and not the blood of the head, though the latter would not disqualify the offering.

It is written: It shall be drained [*yimmatze*] – ימצה כתיב: The word *yimmatze* indicates that the blood of the bird should be squeezed out at the base of the altar in addition to having been sprinkled upon the altar. It can also be translated to mean that the blood shall be drained. Had the verse been referring only to the action of squeezing out the blood it would have used the active verb *yematze*, he shall squeeze. Since it uses the passive term *yimmatze*, it is derived that in addition to mandating that the priest must squeeze out the blood of the bird on the wall of the altar, the verse also means to indicate the other meaning of the term, which is that the blood shall drain out to the base of the altar. Based upon this meaning of the term *yimmatze*, the verse is stating that the priest must sprinkle the blood on a part of the altar from which it can drain on its own to the base of the altar, i.e., the wall of the altar below the red line.

HALAKHA

Rite of the bird sin offering – מעשה חטאת העוף: The priest would pinch the nape of a bird sin offering in the southwest corner of the altar, by cutting the majority of either the windpipe or gullet with his fingernail, yet he would not completely detach the head from the body. He would then sprinkle some of its blood on the lower half of the altar, i.e., below the red line, and then squeeze out the remaining blood on the base of the altar (Rambam *Sefer Avoda, Hilkhot Ma'aseh HaKorbanot* 7:6).

The altar has only its blood – ואין למזבח אלא דמה: Only the blood of a bird sin offering goes upon the altar; the rest of it is consumed by a male priest (Rambam *Sefer Avoda, Hilkhot Ma'aseh HaKorbanot* 7:7).

אָמַר רַב זוּטְרָא בַּר טוֹבִיָּה אָמַר רַב: כֵּיצַד מוֹלְקִין חַטַּאת הָעוֹף? אוֹחֵז גַּפָּיו בִּשְׁתֵּי אֶצְבָּעוֹת, וּשְׁתֵּי רַגְלַיִם בִּשְׁתֵּי אֶצְבָּעוֹת, וּמוֹתֵחַ צַוָּארָהּ עַל רוֹחַב גּוּדָלוֹ, וּמוֹלְקָהּ.

§ **Rav Zutra bar Toviyya says that Rav says: How** does the priest **pinch**[N] the nape of **a bird sin offering?**[B] He holds the bird by its back in the palm of his hand and **holds its wings with two fingers,**[H] i.e., the middle and index fingers, **and its two legs with** his next **two fingers,** i.e., the ring finger and pinky, leaving the head resting between his index finger and thumb, **and he stretches its neck over the width of his thumb and pinches** its nape with his thumbnail.

בְּמַתְנִיתָא תָּנָא צִיפְּרָא מִלְּבָר: אוֹחֵז גַּפָּיו בִּשְׁתֵּי אֶצְבָּעוֹת, וּשְׁנֵי רַגְלַיִם בִּשְׁתֵּי אֶצְבָּעוֹת, וּמוֹתֵחַ צַוָּארוֹ עַל רוֹחַב שְׁתֵּי אֶצְבְּעוֹתָיו, וּמוֹלֵק. וְזוֹ עֲבוֹדָה קָשָׁה שֶׁבַּמִּקְדָּשׁ.

The Gemara cites a varying opinion: **It was taught in a *baraita*: The bird** is not in the priest's palm, but rather **on the outside** of his hand. The priest **holds its wings with two fingers and its two legs with two fingers.** Using his thumb, the priest bends its head into his palm **and stretches its neck over the width of his two fingers, and pinches** its nape. **And this is the** most **difficult** sacrificial **rite in the Temple** to perform.

זוֹ הִיא וְתוּ לָא? וְהָאִיכָּא: קְמִיצָה וַחֲפִינָה! אֶלָּא אֵימָא: זוֹ עֲבוֹדָה קָשָׁה מֵעֲבוֹדוֹת קָשׁוֹת שֶׁבַּמִּקְדָּשׁ.

The Gemara asks: **This is** the most difficult rite to perform, **and no other? But isn't there** also the **removal of the handful** of the meal offering **and the handful** of the incense[N] on Yom Kippur? The Gemara answers: **Rather, say** that the pinching procedure was **a difficult** sacrificial **rite,** one **of the** most **difficult** sacrificial **rites in the Temple** to perform.

מתני׳ עוֹלַת הָעוֹף כֵּיצַד נַעֲשֵׂית? עָלָה לַכֶּבֶשׁ, וּפָנָה לַסּוֹבֵב, בָּא לוֹ לְקֶרֶן דְּרוֹמִית מִזְרָחִית. הָיָה מוֹלֵק אֶת רֹאשָׁהּ מִמּוּל עָרְפָּהּ וּמַבְדִּיל, וּמִיצָּה אֶת דָּמָהּ עַל קִיר הַמִּזְבֵּחַ. נָטַל אֶת הָרֹאשׁ וְהִקִּיף בֵּית מְלִיקָתוֹ לַמִּזְבֵּחַ, סְפָגוֹ בְּמֶלַח, וּזְרָקוֹ עַל גַּבֵּי הָאִשִּׁים.

MISHNA The sacrifice of **the bird burnt offering, how was it performed?**[H] The priest **ascended the ramp and turned to the surrounding ledge and came to the southeast corner** of the altar. He **would** then **pinch** off **the** bird's **head** by cutting **at its nape** with his thumbnail **and separate** the bird's head from its body, **and** would **squeeze out its blood on the wall of the altar. He took the head and neared the place of its pinching,** i.e., its nape, **to the altar** in order to squeeze the blood from the head. **He would** then **absorb** the remaining blood **with salt**[N] **and throw** the head **onto the fire** on the altar.

בָּא לוֹ לַגּוּף, וְהֵסִיר אֶת הַמּוּרְאָה וְאֶת הַנּוֹצָה וְאֶת בְּנֵי הַמֵּעַיִם הַיּוֹצְאִין עִמָּהּ וְהִשְׁלִיכָן לְבֵית הַדֶּשֶׁן. שִׁיסַּע וְלֹא הִבְדִּיל, וְאִם הִבְדִּיל – כָּשֵׁר. סוֹפְגוֹ בְּמֶלַח, וּזְרָקוֹ עַל גַּבֵּי הָאִשִּׁים.

He then **arrived at the body and removed the crop and the feather** attached to it **and the innards that emerge with them and he tossed them to the place of the ashes. He** then **ripped** the bird lengthwise **and did not separate**[N] the two halves of the bird; **but if he separated** them, the offering **is valid.** He would then **absorb** the remaining blood **with salt and throw** the body of the bird **onto the fire** on the altar.

NOTES

How does the priest pinch, etc. – כֵּיצַד מוֹלְקִין וכו׳: Some commentaries explain that, similar to other sacrificial rites, the priest would hold the bird in his left hand and, using his right thumb, perform the pinching (Rav Ovadya Bartenura; Rambam; see Rashi). The *Shita Mekubbetzet*, citing *Tosafot*, maintains that the entire pinching procedure was performed with the priest's right hand. This accords with the Gemara's statement that this was one of the most difficult of the sacrificial rites in the Temple to perform.

Removal of the handful of the meal offering and the handful of the incense – קְמִיצָה וַחֲפִינָה: With regard to the removal of the handful of the meal offering, the priest would scoop the flour out with the three middle fingers of his right hand, using his thumb and pinky to remove any surplus flour. He would then place the flour in a service vessel to consecrate it. Its difficulty lay in the fact that he had to scoop out a precise handful of flour, being careful not to drop any flour (see *Yoma* 47b). With regard to the removal of the incense on Yom Kippur, the High Priest had to pour the incense from its receptacle, which he was holding, into his cupped hands, without the aid of another priest (see *Yoma* 49a).

He would absorb with salt – סְפָגוֹ בְּמֶלַח: It is apparent from Rashi that there is no mitzva to absorb the blood with salt, as the blood of the bird's head was already squeezed out. Rather, this follows the general mitzva of salting any item before it is burned on the altar, as the verse states: "On all your offerings you shall offer salt" (Leviticus 2:13). In this context, the priest would place salt on the area of the pinching, thereby absorbing any remaining blood. Rabbi Ovadya Bartenura understands this clause to mean that the priest would fill the head with salt.

He ripped it and did not separate – שִׁיסַּע וְלֹא הִבְדִּיל: The verse states: "And he shall rend it by its wings but shall not separate it" (Leviticus 1:17). According to its straightforward meaning, the verse indicates that it is forbidden to separate the body. In fact, the *Halakhot Gedolot* counts this as a prohibition. The Rambam, by contrast, maintains that the Torah does not mean to prohibit separating. Nevertheless, since there is a mitzva to dismember the limbs of an animal burnt offering (see Leviticus 1:6), the Torah makes it clear in this context that no such mitzva exists, but if the priest does separate the body, it is a valid offering.

HALAKHA

He holds its wings with two fingers, etc. – אוֹחֵז גַּפָּיו בִּשְׁתֵּי אֶצְבָּעוֹת וכו׳: How does the priest hold the bird while pinching its nape? He holds its two legs between his two fingers, i.e., the pinky and ring fingers, and its two wings between his two fingers, i.e., the index and middle fingers, stretches its throat over the inner width of those two fingers, and pinches its nape. This is in accordance with the *baraita*. This was one of the most difficult rites performed in the Temple. If the priest deviated from this exact method and held the bird in any other way, it is still valid (Rambam *Sefer Avoda*, *Hilkhot Ma'aseh HaKorbanot* 7:8).

Rite of the bird burnt offering – מַעֲשֵׂה עוֹלַת הָעוֹף: What is the rite of a bird burnt offering? The priest would ascend the ramp to the southeast corner of surrounding ledge of the altar. He then pinched the nape of the bird with his fingernail, completely detaching its head from its body. Next, he squeezed out the blood of the head and of the body on the upper wall of the altar, i.e., above the red line. He then applied salt upon the head and threw it to the fire atop the altar. Next, he came to the body and, using his hand, removed the crop and skin over it, along with the feathers and innards that emerged with it and tossed them onto the place of the ashes, and ripped the body lengthwise with his hand, not a knife. He was not required to separate the two halves of the body, but if he did so, it is valid. Finally, he applied salt to the body and threw it into the fire atop the altar (Rambam *Sefer Avoda*, *Hilkhot Ma'aseh HaKorbanot* 6:20–22).

BACKGROUND

How does the priest pinch the nape of a bird sin offering – כֵּיצַד מוֹלְקִין חַטַּאת הָעוֹף: The first illustration depicts the pinching procedure of a bird sin offering according to Rav, where the priest both holds and pinches the bird with his right hand. The second depicts the pinching of a bird sin offering according to the *baraita* where the bird is located on the back of the priest's hand. This is also in accordance with the opinion that the pinching was performed with the right hand.

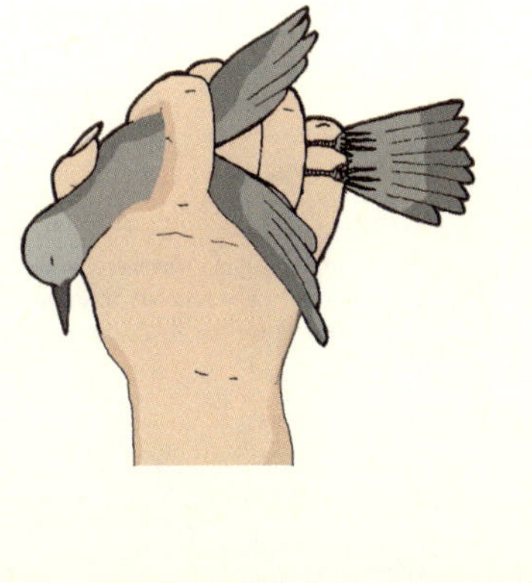

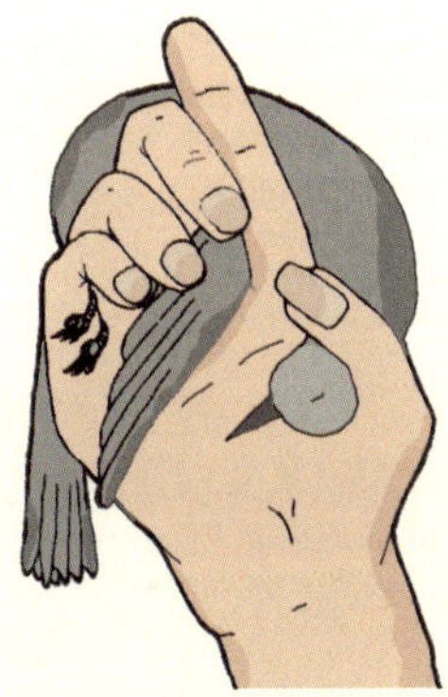

Above: Pinching of a bird sin offering according to the *baraita*

Left: Pinching of a bird sin offering according to Rav

לֹא הֵסִיר הַמּוּרְאָה וְלֹא הַנּוֹצָה וְאֶת בְּנֵי מֵעַיִם הַיּוֹצְאִין עִמָּם, וְלֹא סְפָגוֹ בְּמֶלַח, כׇּל שֶׁשִּׁינָּה בָּהּ מֵאַחַר שֶׁמִּיצָּה אֶת דָּמָהּ – כְּשֵׁירָה. הִבְדִּיל בַּחַטָּאת וְלֹא הִבְדִּיל בָּעוֹלָה – פָּסוּל. מִיצָּה אֶת דַּם הָרֹאשׁ וְלֹא מִיצָּה דַּם הַגּוּף – פְּסוּלָה. דַּם הַגּוּף וְלֹא מִיצָּה דַּם הָרֹאשׁ – כְּשֵׁירָה.

If he neither removed the crop,[H] **nor the feather and the innards that emerge with them, nor absorbed** the blood **with salt,** with regard to **any** detail **that he changed in** the sacrificial rites **after he squeezed out its blood,** the offering is **valid. If he separated** the head from the body **in** sacrificing **the sin offering,**[H] **or** if **he did not separate** the head from the body **in** sacrificing **the burnt offering,** the offering is **disqualified.** In a case where **he squeezed out the blood of the head**[H] **and did not squeeze out the blood of the body, it is disqualified.** If he squeezed out the **blood of the body and did not squeeze out the blood of the head,** the offering is **valid.**

חַטַּאת הָעוֹף שֶׁמְּלָקָהּ שֶׁלֹּא לִשְׁמָהּ, מִיצָּה דָּמָהּ שֶׁלֹּא לִשְׁמָהּ, לִשְׁמָהּ וְשֶׁלֹּא לִשְׁמָהּ, אוֹ שֶׁלֹּא לִשְׁמָהּ וְלִשְׁמָהּ – פָּסוּל. עוֹלַת הָעוֹף – כְּשֵׁירָה, וּבִלְבַד שֶׁלֹּא עָלְתָה לַבְּעָלִים לְשֵׁם חוֹבָה.

In the case of **a bird sin offering that** the priest **pinched not for its sake,**[H] or if **he squeezed out its blood not for its sake,**[N] or if he did so **for its sake** and then **not for its sake, or not for its sake** and then **for its sake,** it is **disqualified,** like all other sin offerings that are disqualified when performed not for their sake (see 2a). **A bird burnt offering** sacrificed not for its sake is **valid;**[H] it is **just that it did not satisfy the obligation of the owner.**

אֶחָד חַטַּאת הָעוֹף וְאֶחָד עוֹלַת הָעוֹף, שֶׁמְּלָקָן וְשֶׁמִּיצָּה אֶת דָּמָן לֶאֱכוֹל דָּבָר שֶׁדַּרְכּוֹ לֶאֱכוֹל, וּלְהַקְטִיר דָּבָר שֶׁדַּרְכּוֹ לְהַקְטִיר, חוּץ לִמְקוֹמוֹ – פָּסוּל וְאֵין בּוֹ כָּרֵת. חוּץ לִזְמַנּוֹ – פִּיגּוּל וְחַיָּיבִין עָלָיו כָּרֵת, וּבִלְבַד שֶׁיַּקְרִיב הַמַּתִּיר כְּמִצְוָתוֹ.

With regard to **both a bird sin offering and a bird burnt offering where** the priest **pinched its nape or squeezed out its blood** with the intent **to partake of an item whose** typical **manner** is such that one **partakes** of it,[HN] **or to burn an item whose** typical **manner** is such that one **burns** it on the altar, **outside its** designated **area,**[H] the offering is **disqualified. But there is no** liability to receive ***karet*** for one who partakes of the offering. If his intent was to eat it or burn it **beyond its** designated **time,** the offering is ***piggul*** and one is **liable** to receive ***karet*** **for** partaking of the offering, **provided that the permitting factor,** the blood, **was sacrificed in accordance with its mitzva.**

כֵּיצַד קָרֵב הַמַּתִּיר כְּמִצְוָתוֹ? מָלַק בִּשְׁתִיקָה וּמִיצָּה הַדָּם חוּץ לִזְמַנּוֹ, אוֹ שֶׁמָּלַק חוּץ לִזְמַנּוֹ וּמִיצָּה הַדָּם בִּשְׁתִיקָה, אוֹ שֶׁמָּלַק וּמִיצָּה הַדָּם חוּץ לִזְמַנּוֹ – זֶהוּ שֶׁקָּרֵב הַמַּתִּיר כְּמִצְוָתוֹ.

How is **the permitting factor sacrificed in accordance with its mitzva?** If one **pinched** the nape **in silence,** i.e., with no disqualifying intent, **and squeezed out** its **blood** with the intent to partake of the parts typically eaten or to burn the portions that are to be burned on the altar, **beyond its** designated **time; or** in the case of one **who pinched** with the intent to partake of the offering or burn it on the altar **beyond its** designated **time, and squeezed out** its **blood in silence; or** in the case of one **who pinched and squeezed out the blood** with the intent to partake of the offering or burn it on the altar **beyond its** designated **time, that is** the case of a bird offering **where** the **permitting factor is sacrificed in accordance with its mitzva.**

כֵּיצַד לֹא קָרֵב הַמַּתִּיר כְּמִצְוָתוֹ? מָלַק חוּץ לִמְקוֹמוֹ מִיצָּה הַדָּם חוּץ לִזְמַנּוֹ, אוֹ שֶׁמָּלַק חוּץ לִזְמַנּוֹ וּמִיצָּה הַדָּם חוּץ לִמְקוֹמוֹ, אוֹ שֶׁמָּלַק וּמִיצָּה הַדָּם חוּץ לִמְקוֹמוֹ;

How is **the permitting factor not sacrificed in accordance with its mitzva?** If the priest **pinched** the nape of the bird with the intent to partake of it or burn it **outside its** designated **area** and **squeezed out** its **blood** with the intent to partake of it or burn it **beyond its** designated **time, or** he **pinched** with the intent to partake of it or burn it **beyond its** designated **time and squeezed out** its **blood** with the intent to partake of it or burn it **outside its** designated **area, or** if the priest **pinched and squeezed out the blood** with the intent to partake of it or burn it **outside its** designated **area,**

HALAKHA

He neither removed the crop – לֹא הֵסִיר אֶת הַמּוּרְאָה: In the event the priest did not remove the crop, the feathers, the innards, or did not apply salt to the bird, it is still a valid offering, since these deviations occurred after the blood was squeezed out (Rambam *Sefer Avoda, Hilkhot Ma'aseh HaKorbanot* 6:22).

He separated in the sin offering, etc. – הִבְדִּיל בַּחַטָּאת וכו׳: If, while pinching the nape of a bird sin offering, the priest separated its head from its body, or while pinching the nape of a bird burnt offering, the priest did not separate its head from its body, in either instance, the offering is disqualified (Rambam *Sefer Avoda, Hilkhot Ma'aseh HaKorbanot* 7:6, 6:20).

He squeezed out the blood of the head, etc. – מִיצָּה דַּם הָרֹאשׁ וכו׳: With regard to a bird burnt offering, if the priest squeezed out the blood of the head only, and not the blood of the body, it is disqualified. If he squeezed out the blood of the body and not the blood of the head, it is valid (Rambam *Sefer Avoda, Hilkhot Ma'aseh HaKorbanot* 6:20).

A bird sin offering that he pinched not for its sake – חַטַּאת הָעוֹף שֶׁמְּלָקָהּ שֶׁלֹּא לִשְׁמָהּ: Bird offerings are disqualified by improper intent with regard to two of their sacrificial rites: Pinching the nape and sprinkling or squeezing out its blood. The rite of a bird sin offering that was performed not for its sake is disqualified (Rambam *Sefer Avoda, Hilkhot Pesulei HaMukdashin* 13:5, 15:1).

A bird burnt offering that was pinched not for its sake – עוֹלַת הָעוֹף שֶׁמְּלָקָהּ שֶׁלֹּא לִשְׁמָהּ: A bird burnt offering that was either pinched not for its sake or whose blood was squeezed out not for its sake is valid, yet it does not satisfy the obligation of the owner (Rambam *Sefer Avoda, Hilkhot Pesulei HaMukdashin* 15:1).

To partake of an item whose typical manner is such that one partakes of it, etc. – לֶאֱכוֹל דָּבָר שֶׁדַּרְכּוֹ לֶאֱכוֹל וכו׳: If, during one of the sacrificial rites, one has an improper intent to eat or burn an item either beyond its designated time or outside its designated area, if it is an item whose typical manner is such that one does not eat it or an item whose typical manner is such that one does not burn it, respectively, the offering is valid (Rambam *Sefer Avoda, Hilkhot Pesulei HaMukdashin* 14:8).

Outside its designated area, etc. – חוּץ לִמְקוֹמוֹ וכו׳: If, during either the pinching or squeezing out of the blood of the bird offerings, one had improper intent to sacrifice it or eat it outside its designated area, it is disqualified, but the one who partakes of it is not liable to receive *karet*. If the improper intent was to sacrifice or eat it beyond its designated time, the offering is *piggul*. This is the *halakha* provided there was no other disqualifying intention. If there was another disqualifying intention, the offering is disqualified, but is not *piggul*. If the improper intent occurred during the sacrificing or eating, it is disqualified but it is not *piggul* (Rambam *Sefer Avoda, Hilkhot Pesulei HaMukdashin* 16:1).

NOTES

He squeezed out its blood not for its own sake – מִיצָּה דָּמָהּ שֶׁלֹּא לִשְׁמָהּ: This is certainly the *halakha* if its blood was sprinkled not for its sake, as that is its primary rite (*Tiferet Yisrael*; *Minḥat Ḥinnukh*). It seems from the wording of this mishna that squeezing out the blood is an indispensable action. It should be noted that this is in contrast to the opinion of other *tanna'im* and *amora'im* (see 52a and 65a; *Me'ila* 8b).

To partake of an item whose typical manner is such that one partakes of it, etc. – לֶאֱכוֹל דָּבָר שֶׁדַּרְכּוֹ לֶאֱכוֹל וכו׳: For a list of these items see 35a. See also Rambam *Sefer Avoda, Hilkhot Pesulei HaMukdashin* 14:5, 7.

חַטַּאת הָעוֹף שֶׁמְּלָקוֹ שֶׁלֹּא לִשְׁמָהּ וּמִיצָּה הַדָּם חוּץ לִזְמַנּוֹ, אוֹ שֶׁמָּלַק חוּץ לִזְמַנּוֹ וּמִיצָּה דָּמוֹ שֶׁלֹּא לִשְׁמָהּ, אוֹ שֶׁמָּלַק וּמִיצָּה הַדָּם שֶׁלֹּא לִשְׁמָהּ – זֶהוּ שֶׁלֹּא קָרַב הַמַּתִּיר כְּמִצְוָתוֹ.

or in the case of **a bird sin offering where one pinched** its nape **not for its sake and squeezed out** its **blood** with the intent of consuming it or burning it **beyond its** designated **time, or** in a case **where he pinched** its nape with the intent to consume it or burn it **beyond its** designated **time and squeezed out** its **blood not for its sake, or** in a case **where he pinched** its nape **and squeezed out its blood not for its sake, that is** a case of a bird offering **whose permitting factor is not sacrificed in accordance with its mitzva.**

לֶאֱכוֹל כְּזַיִת בַּחוּץ כְּזַיִת לְמָחָר, כְּזַיִת לְמָחָר כְּזַיִת בַּחוּץ, כַּחֲצִי זַיִת בַּחוּץ כַּחֲצִי זַיִת לְמָחָר, כַּחֲצִי זַיִת לְמָחָר כַּחֲצִי זַיִת בַּחוּץ – פָּסוּל, וְאֵין בּוֹ כָּרֵת.

If one pinched the nape of the bird and squeezed out its blood with the intent **to eat an olive-bulk** of the offering **outside** its designated area and **an olive-bulk the next day,**[H] or **an olive-bulk the next day** and **an olive-bulk outside** its designated area, or **half an olive-bulk outside** its designated area and **half an olive-bulk the next day,** or **half an olive-bulk the next day** and **half an olive-bulk outside** its designated area, the offering is **disqualified and** it **does not include** liability to receive ***karet.***

אָמַר רַבִּי יְהוּדָה: זֶה הַכְּלָל, אִם מַחְשֶׁבֶת הַזְּמַן קָדְמָה לְמַחְשֶׁבֶת הַמָּקוֹם – פִּיגּוּל וְחַיָּיבִין עָלָיו כָּרֵת, וְאִם מַחְשֶׁבֶת הַמָּקוֹם קָדְמָה לְמַחְשֶׁבֶת הַזְּמַן – פָּסוּל וְאֵין בּוֹ כָּרֵת. [וַחֲכָמִים אוֹמְרִים: זֶה וָזֶה פָּסוּל וְאֵין בּוֹ כָּרֵת].

Rabbi Yehuda disagreed and **said**[N] that **this is the principle: If the** improper **intent** with regard to **the time preceded the intent** with regard to **the area,** the offering is ***piggul*** **and one is liable** to receive ***karet*** **for** eating **it. And if the intent** with regard to **the area preceded the intent** with regard to **the time,** the offering is **disqualified and** it **does not include** liability to receive ***karet.*** **And the Rabbis say:**[N] In both **this** case where the intent with regard to time came first **and that** case where the intent with regard to area came first, the offering is **disqualified and** it **does not include** liability to receive ***karet.***

לֶאֱכוֹל כַּחֲצִי זַיִת וּלְהַקְטִיר כַּחֲצִי זַיִת – כָּשֵׁר, שֶׁאֵין אֲכִילָה וְהַקְטָרָה מִצְטָרְפִין.

If his intent was **to eat half an olive-bulk and to burn**[H] half an **olive-bulk** not at the appropriate time or in the appropriate area, the offering is **valid, because eating and burning do not join together.**

גמ׳ תָּנוּ רַבָּנַן: ״וְהִקְרִיבוֹ״, מַה תַּלְמוּד לוֹמַר?

GEMARA **The Sages taught** a *baraita* with regard to the verse pertaining to a bird burnt offering: "And the priest shall bring it to the altar, and pinch off its head, and make it smoke on the altar" (Leviticus 1:15). **What** is the meaning when **the verse states: And** the priest **shall bring it** to the altar? Since the previous verse states that "he shall bring his offering," this verse should have started with the phrase "And he shall pinch off its head."

לְפִי שֶׁנֶּאֱמַר: ״וְהִקְרִיב מִן הַתּוֹרִים אוֹ מִן בְּנֵי הַיּוֹנָה״, יָכוֹל הַמִּתְנַדֵּב עוֹף לֹא יִפְחוֹת מִשְּׁנֵי פְרִידִין? תַּלְמוּד לוֹמַר ״וְהִקְרִיבוֹ״ – אֲפִילּוּ פְּרִידָה אַחַת יָבִיא אֶל הַמִּזְבֵּחַ.

Since it is stated in the preceding verse: "And if his offering to the Lord be a burnt offering of birds, **then he shall bring** his offering **of doves, or of pigeons**" (Leviticus 1:14), one **might** have thought that **one who donates a bird** as an offering **may not** donate **fewer than two birds.** Therefore, **the verse states: "And** the priest **shall bring it,"** indicating that **one may bring even one bird**[H] **to** be sacrificed on **the altar.**

מַה תַּלְמוּד לוֹמַר ״הַכֹּהֵן״ – לִקְבּוֹעַ לוֹ כֹּהֵן. שֶׁיָּכוֹל, וַהֲלֹא דִּין הוּא: וּמָה בֶּן צֹאן שֶׁקָּבַע לוֹ צָפוֹן – לֹא קָבַע לוֹ כֹּהֵן, עוֹף שֶׁלֹּא קָבַע לוֹ צָפוֹן – אֵינוֹ דִּין שֶׁלֹּא יִקְבַּע לוֹ כֹּהֵן? תַּלְמוּד לוֹמַר: ״(אֶל) הַכֹּהֵן״, לִקְבּוֹעַ לוֹ כֹּהֵן.

The *baraita* continues analyzing the verse: **What** is the meaning when **the verse states** that **"the priest** shall bring it to the altar" (Leviticus 1:15)? It is **to establish** that only **a priest** may pinch its nape, as one **might** have thought that even a non-priest may perform this procedure. **Could this not** be derived through **logical inference: And if** with regard to **a sheep** burnt offering, with regard **to which** the verse **established** that **it** must be slaughtered in the **north** (see Leviticus 1:11), it did **not establish** that **it** must be slaughtered by a **priest** (see 32a), then in the case of **a bird** burnt offering, with regard to **which** the verse **did not establish** that its nape must be pinched in the **north, is it not logical that** the verse does **not establish** that its nape must be pinched by **a priest?** To counter this, **the verse states** that **"the priest** shall bring it to the altar," in order **to establish** that its nape must be pinched specifically by **a priest.**

HALAKHA

An olive-bulk outside and an olive-bulk the next day – **כְּזַיִת בַּחוּץ כְּזַיִת לְמָחָר**: If, during one of the four sacrificial rites, one intended to either eat an olive-bulk of the permitted parts of the sacrifice outside its designated area and to eat an olive-bulk the next day, or vice versa, the offering is disqualified. Similarly, if one intended to either eat half an olive-bulk outside its designated area and another half the next day, or vice versa, the offering is disqualified. In all these instances, the offering is disqualified and not considered *piggul*. This is in accordance with the opinion of the Rabbis (Rambam *Sefer Avoda, Hilkhot Pesulei HaMukdashin* 16:2).

To eat half an olive-bulk and to burn, etc. – **לֶאֱכוֹל כַּחֲצִי זַיִת וּלְהַקְטִיר וכו׳**: If, during one of the four sacrificial rites, one intended to either eat half an olive-bulk outside its designated area and to burn half an olive-bulk outside its designated area, or to burn half an olive-bulk beyond its designated time and to eat half an olive-bulk beyond its designated time, the offering is valid, because eating and burning do not join together (Rambam *Sefer Avoda, Hilkhot Pesulei HaMukdashin* 14:10).

Even one bird – **אֲפִילּוּ פְּרִידָה אַחַת**: One who vows to offer a bird burnt offering may bring either a dove or a pigeon, in accordance with the ruling of the *baraita* (Rambam *Sefer Avoda, Hilkhot Ma'aseh HaKorbanot* 16:10).

NOTES

Rabbi Yehuda said, etc. – **אָמַר רַבִּי יְהוּדָה וכו׳**: There are two opinions as to what Rabbi Yehuda means, as discussed on 29b.

And the Rabbis say – **וַחֲכָמִים אוֹמְרִים**: See the Notes section on 29b, which discuss what this statement is meant to add.

יָכוֹל יִמְלְקֶנּוּ בְּסַכִּין? וְדִין הוּא: וּמָה אִם שְׁחִיטָה שֶׁלֹּא קָבַע לָהּ כֹּהֵן – קָבַע לָהּ כְּלִי, מְלִיקָה שֶׁקָּבַע לָהּ כֹּהֵן – אֵינוֹ דִּין שֶׁיִּקְבַּע לָהּ כְּלִי?

The *baraita* continues: One **might** have thought that the priest should **pinch its** nape **with a knife. And** one could derive this through **a logical inference: And if** with regard to **slaughtering,** with regard to **which** the verse **did not establish** that **it** must be performed by **a priest,** it **established** that **it** must be performed with **an instrument,** i.e., a knife (see 97b); then in the case of **pinching, which** the verse **established** must be performed by **a priest, is it not logical that** the verse **establishes** that **it** must be performed with **an instrument?**

תַּלְמוּד לוֹמַר: ״כֹּהֵן וּמָלַק״. אָמַר רַבִּי עֲקִיבָא: וְכִי תַּעֲלֶה עַל דַּעְתְּךָ שֶׁזָּר קָרֵב לְגַבֵּי מִזְבֵּחַ? אֶלָּא מַה תַּלְמוּד לוֹמַר ״כֹּהֵן״ – שֶׁתְּהֵא מְלִיקָה בְּעַצְמוֹ שֶׁל כֹּהֵן.

To counter this, **the verse states:** "And the **priest** shall bring it near the altar **and pinch off** its head." In explanation of this verse, **Rabbi Akiva said:**[N] **Could it enter your mind that a non-priest may approach**[N] the **altar** in order to sacrifice an offering? Since this is impossible, the verse does not need to state that the sacrificial rite is performed by a priest. **Rather, what** is the meaning when **the verse states:** "The **priest**"? It means **that the pinching must be** performed **with the very** body of the **priest.**[H]

יָכוֹל יִמְלְקֶנָּה בֵּין מִלְמַעְלָה בֵּין מִלְּמַטָּה – תַּלְמוּד לוֹמַר: ״וּמָלַק וְהִקְטִיר״, מָה הַקְטָרָה בְּרֹאשׁ הַמִּזְבֵּחַ – אַף מְלִיקָה בְּרֹאשׁ הַמִּזְבֵּחַ.

The *baraita* continues to analyze the verse: One **might** have thought that the priest **may pinch** the bird's nape **whether above** the red line of the altar **or below** it. To counter this, **the verse states:** "And the priest shall bring it unto the altar **and pinch off** its head, **and make it smoke** on the altar." The verse juxtaposes the pinching to the burning of the bird on the altar to teach that **just as the burning** occurs **atop the altar, so too,** the **pinching** occurs **on the top** part of the wall of **the altar.**[H]

״וּמָלַק״ – מִמּוּל עוֹרֶף. אַתָּה אוֹמֵר מִמּוּל עוֹרֶף, אוֹ אֵינוֹ אֶלָּא מִן הַצַּוָּאר? וְדִין הוּא: נֶאֱמַר כָּאן ״וּמָלַק״ וְנֶאֱמַר לְהַלָּן ״וּמָלַק״, מַה לְּהַלָּן מִמּוּל עוֹרֶף – אַף כָּאן מִמּוּל עוֹרֶף.

The *baraita* continues: The verse states that the priest shall **"pinch off** its head," which must be performed **at the nape. Do you say** that the pinching occurs **at the nape, or** is it **only at the throat? It** can be derived through **a logical inference:** It **is stated here,** with regard to a bird burnt offering: **"And pinch off** its head" (Leviticus 1:15), **and** it **is stated there,** with regard to a bird sin offering: **"And pinch off** its head opposite its nape, but shall not separate it" (Leviticus 5:8). **Just as there,** the head is pinched **at the nape, so too here,** the head is pinched **at the nape.**

אִי מַה לְּהַלָּן מוֹלֵק וְאֵינוֹ מַבְדִּיל, אַף כָּאן מוֹלֵק וְאֵינוֹ מַבְדִּיל! תַּלְמוּד לוֹמַר: ״וּמָלַק וְהִקְטִיר״, מָה הַקְטָרָה – הָרֹאשׁ לְעַצְמוֹ וְהַגּוּף לְעַצְמוֹ, אַף מְלִיקָה – הָרֹאשׁ לְעַצְמוֹ וְהַגּוּף לְעַצְמוֹ.

If the *halakha* of a bird burnt offering is derived from that of a bird sin offering, perhaps it should also be derived that **just as there,** the priest **pinches** off the head **but does not separate** it completely from the body, **so too here,** with regard to a bird burnt offering, he **pinches** off the head **but does not separate** it from the body. To counter this, **the verse states** with regard to a bird burnt offering: **"And pinch off** its head, **and make it smoke** on the altar" (Leviticus 1:15). This indicates that **just as** with regard to the **burning** of the bird burnt offering, **the head** is burned **by itself and the body** is burned **by itself, so too** with regard to the **pinching, the head** is **by itself and the body** is **by itself,** i.e., the head is completely detached from the body.

וּמִנַּיִן שֶׁהַקְטָרַת הָרֹאשׁ בְּעַצְמוֹ וְהַגּוּף בְּעַצְמוֹ? שֶׁנֶּאֱמַר: ״וְהִקְטִיר אוֹתוֹ״ – הֲרֵי הַקְטָרַת הַגּוּף אֲמוּרָה, הָא מָה אֲנִי מְקַיֵּים ״וְהִקְטִיר הַמִּזְבֵּחָה״ – בְּהַקְטָרַת הָרֹאשׁ הַכָּתוּב מְדַבֵּר.

The *baraita* continues: **And from where** is it derived **that the burning of the head** is **by itself**[H] **and the body** is burned **by itself? As it is stated:** "And he shall rend it by its wings… **and** the priest **shall make it smoke** upon the altar" (Leviticus 1:17). Since **the burning of the body is stated** in this verse, **how do I realize** the meaning of the earlier phrase: **"And make it smoke on the altar"** (Leviticus 1:15)? One must conclude that **the verse is speaking about the burning of the head.**

״וְנִמְצָה דָמוֹ״ – כּוּלּוֹ, ״אֶל קִיר הַמִּזְבֵּחַ״ – וְלֹא עַל קִיר הַכֶּבֶשׁ, וְלֹא עַל קִיר הַהֵיכָל. וְאֵיזֶה זֶה – זֶה קִיר הָעֶלְיוֹן.

The *baraita* continues to expound the verse stated with regard to a bird burnt offering: "And its blood shall be drained out on the wall of the altar" (Leviticus 1:15). When the verse states: **"And its blood shall be drained out,"** it means that **all of it**[N] must be drained out. The continuation of the verse indicates that it must be drained out **"on the wall of the altar," and not on the wall of the ramp, nor on the wall of the Sanctuary. And which** wall of the altar **is this? This is the upper wall,** i.e., above the red line.

NOTES

Rabbi Akiva said, etc. – אָמַר רַבִּי עֲקִיבָא וכו׳: The commentary follows the explanation of Rashi, who maintains that Rabbi Akiva is not disagreeing with the first *tanna*. Rather, he is explaining what the verse is adding with the word "priest." Others maintain that there is in fact a dispute between Rabbi Akiva and the first *tanna*. According to the first *tanna*, the word "priest" teaches both that only a priest may perform the pinching and that he must do so with his body, i.e., his finger. Rabbi Akiva claims that the first *halakha* is obvious even without the verse, and the verse is needed only to teach the second *halakha* (*Shita Mekubbetzet*).

That a non-priest may approach, etc. – שֶׁזָּר קָרֵב וכו׳: The verse in Numbers (18:3) states with regard to the Levites, and it is certainly applicable to Israelites as well, that: "Only they shall not come near the holy vessels and to the altar and they shall not die" (Rabbi Shimshon of Saens, in his commentary to *Torat Kohanim*).

And its blood shall be drained out, all of it – וְנִמְצָה דָמוֹ כּוּלּוֹ: The inference is from the expression "its blood" as opposed to: Of its blood. Alternatively, according to a variant reading of Rashi, the verse could have simply said: And the blood shall be squeezed out.

HALAKHA

Pinching must be with the very body of the priest – מְלִיקָה בְּעַצְמוֹ שֶׁל כֹּהֵן: How is the pinching procedure performed? The priest, using his fingernail, slits the bird at its nape and cuts in a downward motion (Rambam *Sefer Avoda*, *Hilkhot Ma'aseh HaKorbanot* 6:23).

Pinching occurs on the top of the altar – מְלִיקָה בְּרֹאשׁוֹ שֶׁל מִזְבֵּחַ: The rite of a bird burnt offering was as follows: The priest would ascend the ramp of the altar and turn onto the surrounding ledge and reach the southeast corner. There, he would pinch the nape of the bird and separate its head from its body (Rambam *Sefer Avoda*, *Hilkhot Ma'aseh HaKorbanot* 6:20).

The burning of the head is by itself – הַקְטָרַת הָרֹאשׁ לְעַצְמוֹ: After having separated the head from the body of a bird burnt offering, the priest presses its head to the altar, squeezing out its blood. He then salts it and throws it into the fire atop the altar. After the rite of the head, the priest returns to the body and performs its rite (Rambam *Sefer Avoda*, *Hilkhot Ma'aseh HaKorbanot* 6:21, 22).

אוֹ אֵינוֹ אֶלָּא קִיר הַתַּחְתּוֹן! וְדִין הוּא: מָה בְּהֵמָה שֶׁחַטָּאתָהּ לְמַעְלָה – עוֹלָתָהּ לְמַטָּה, עוֹף שֶׁחַטָּאתוֹ לְמַטָּה – אֵינוֹ דִּין שֶׁעוֹלָתוֹ לְמַטָּה?

Or perhaps the verse is referring **only to the lower wall,** i.e., below the red line; **and this** can be supported by **a logical inference:** And if with regard to **an animal** offering, **where** the blood of **its sin offering** is applied **above** the red line, the blood of **its burnt offering** is applied **below** the red line, then with regard to **a bird** offering, **where** the blood of **its sin offering** is sprinkled **below** the red line, **is it not logical that** the blood of **its burnt offering** is sprinkled **below** the red line?

תַּלְמוּד לוֹמַר: ״וּמָלַק וְהִקְטִיר וְנִמְצָה דָמוֹ״, וְכִי תַּעֲלֶה עַל דַּעְתְּךָ לְאַחַר שֶׁהִקְטִיר חוֹזֵר וּמְמַצֶּה? אֶלָּא לוֹמַר לָךְ: מָה הַקְטָרָה בְּרֹאשׁ הַמִּזְבֵּחַ – אַף מִיצּוּי בְּרֹאשׁ הַמִּזְבֵּחַ. הָא כֵּיצַד? הָיָה עוֹלֶה בַּכֶּבֶשׁ וּפוֹנֶה לַסּוֹבֵב, וּבָא לוֹ לְקֶרֶן דְּרוֹמִית מִזְרָחִית, הָיָה מוֹלֵק אֶת רֹאשָׁהּ מִמּוּל עָרְפָּהּ וּמַבְדִּיל, וּמְמַצֶּה מִדָּמָהּ עַל קִיר הַמִּזְבֵּחַ. אִם עֲשָׂאָהּ לְמַטָּה מֵרַגְלָיו אֲפִילּוּ אַמָּה – כְּשֵׁירָה.

To counter this, **the verse states: "And pinch off** its head, **and make it smoke** on the altar; **and its blood shall be drained out." Could it enter your mind that after he has burned** the bird, the priest **goes back and drains out** its blood? **Rather,** the verse serves **to tell you: Just as the burning** occurs **atop the altar, so too,** the **draining** occurs **atop the altar. How so?** The priest **would ascend the ramp and turn to the surrounding ledge and arrive at the southeast corner. He would pinch off the** bird's **head at its nape, and separate** it from its body. **He would** then **squeeze out its blood on the wall of the altar** beside him. Nevertheless, **if** the priest **performed** the squeezing **below his feet,**[H] i.e., below the surrounding ledge, **even** one **cubit**[N] beneath the ledge, it is **valid.**

רַבִּי נְחֶמְיָה וְרַבִּי אֱלִיעֶזֶר בֶּן יַעֲקֹב אוֹמְרִים: כָּל עַצְמָהּ אֵין נַעֲשֵׂית אֶלָּא בְּרֹאשׁ הַמִּזְבֵּחַ. מַאי בֵּינַיְיהוּ?

The *baraita* concludes by citing a dissenting opinion: **Rabbi Neḥemya and Rabbi Eliezer ben Ya'akov say: The entire** rite of a bird burnt offering **is performed only atop the altar.**[N] The Gemara asks: Since the first *tanna* and Rabbi Neḥemya and Rabbi Eliezer ben Ya'akov agree that the bird must be burned atop the altar and its blood must be squeezed on the top part of the wall of the altar, **what is the difference between them?**

אַבַּיֵי וְרָבָא דְּאָמְרִי תַּרְוַיְיהוּ: עוֹשֶׂה מַעֲרָכָה עַל גַּבֵּי סוֹבֵב אִיכָּא בֵּינַיְיהוּ.

Abaye and Rava both say: There is a difference **between them** with regard to whether one may **form an arrangement** of wood **on** the **surrounding ledge** and burn the bird there. According to the first *tanna*, this is permitted when needed, and therefore it is valid if the priest squeezes out the blood on the wall up to a cubit below the surrounding ledge. According the Rabbi Neḥemya and Rabbi Eliezer ben Ya'akov, one may never burn the bird on the surrounding ledge, and therefore it is not valid if the priest squeezed out the blood below the surrounding ledge.

״בָּא לוֹ לַגּוּף״ כו׳. תָּנוּ רַבָּנַן: ״וְהֵסִיר אֶת מֻרְאָתוֹ בְּנֹצָתָהּ״ – זוֹ זֶפֶק.

§ The mishna teaches that after the priest throws the bird's head onto the fire on the altar, **he arrives at the body** and removes the crop and the feathers attached to it and the innards that emerge with them, and tosses them to the place of the ashes. **The Sages taught** in a *baraita* with regard to the verse pertaining to a bird burnt offering: **"And he shall take away** ***murato*** **with its feathers"** (Leviticus 1:16). **This** word, *murato*, is referring to the **crop.**[B]

יָכוֹל יַקְדִּיר בְּסַכִּין וְיִטְּלֶנּוּ? תַּלְמוּד לוֹמַר: ״בְּנֹצָתָהּ״ – נוֹטֵל אֶת הַנּוֹצָה עִמָּהּ. אַבָּא יוֹסֵי בֶּן חָנָן אוֹמֵר: נוֹטְלָהּ וְנוֹטֵל קוּרְקְבָנָהּ עִמָּהּ.

Had the verse written only "its crop," one **might** have thought that the priest may **cut** the skin **with a knife and take** the crop without any other part of the bird. Therefore, **the verse states: "With its feathers** [***benotzatah***]," which teaches that **he takes the feathers**[H] **with it,**[N] i.e., he must remove the skin with the feathers still attached. The Gemara presents another opinion: **Abba Yosei ben Ḥanan says: He takes** the crop **and he** also **takes its gizzard**[N] **with it.**

NOTES

Below his feet even one cubit – לְמַטָּה מֵרַגְלָיו אֲפִילּוּ אַמָּה: Rashi explains that this is valid because the squeezing is performed above the red line. It seems that he holds that the term: Atop the altar, refers to any point on the altar above the red line. Based on the Gemara's following discussion, this *tanna* deems valid squeezing out the blood above the surrounding ledge because the surrounding ledge is actually atop the altar, as it is a valid location for burning. Apparently, he deems valid squeezing performed one cubit below the surrounding ledge, because as long as the squeezing is done near the top of the altar it is still valid.

Performed only atop the altar – אֵין נַעֲשֵׂית אֶלָּא בְּרֹאשׁ הַמִּזְבֵּחַ: It stands to reason that just as the first *tanna* maintains that the squeezing may be performed even one cubit below the ledge, which, according to him, is a valid location for burning, similarly, Rabbi Neḥemya and Rabbi Elazar ben Yaakov would agree that the squeezing need not take place literally atop the altar; even near it is valid. The Ra'avad, in his commentary to tractate *Kinnim*, writes that the latter two maintain that the squeezing must take place on the wall of the corner atop the altar, since the top of the corner is a valid location for burning in exigent circumstances.

He takes the feathers with it – נוֹטֵל אֶת הַנּוֹצָה עִמָּהּ: Rashi explains this to mean the skin and the feathers that are on it. The Ra'avad contends that the priest only tosses the feathers and the innards to the place of ashes. That patch of skin is burned atop the altar along with the rest of the skin.

He takes its gizzard – נוֹטֵל קוּרְקְבָנָהּ: Rashi explains that Abba Yosei ben Ḥanan interprets the word *notza* as meaning something repulsive. According to this interpretation, none of the feathers at all are taken. The Ramban, in his commentary on the Torah, disagrees with this explanation and maintains that the gizzard, being part of the bird's digestive system, has status equal to the crop and is therefore included in the term *murato*. Accordingly, Abba Yosei ben Ḥanan agrees with the *tanna* of the *baraita* that the feathers are removed as well.

Some of the early commentaries maintain that Abba Yosei ben Ḥanan concurs with the *tanna* in the mishna (Ramban; Mahari Kurkus). The Ra'avad, in his commentary to *Torat Kohanim*, contends that the *tanna* in the mishna requires only the removal of innards that are cut out with the crop, and nothing else. Abba Yosei ben Ḥanan, by contrast, maintains that the crop, down to the gizzard, is removed and tossed on the place of the ashes.

HALAKHA

If he performed it below his feet, etc. – עֲשָׂאָהּ לְמַטָּה מֵרַגְלָיו וכו׳: The blood of a bird burnt offering is squeezed out on the upper part of the altar wall, i.e., above the red line, in accordance with the opinion of the first *tanna* (Rambam *Sefer Avoda, Hilkhot Ma'aseh HaKorbanot* 6:20).

He takes the feathers – נוֹטֵל אֶת הַנּוֹצָה: After having separated the head from the body of a bird burnt offering, the priest returns to its body, from which he removes the crop, along with the skin and feathers covering it. He also removes the innards that emerge with the crop upon its removal, and tosses them to the place of the ashes (Rambam *Sefer Avoda, Hilkhot Ma'aseh HaKorbanot* 6:21 and Mahari Kurkus there).

BACKGROUND

Crop and gizzard – זֶפֶק וְקֻרְקְבָן: During a bird's digestive process, the food first reaches the crop, which stores excess food prior to digestion. The food then travels to the gizzard, a specialized stomach constructed of thick, muscular walls, which grinds up the food, often aided by particles of stone and grit swallowed by the bird. Once sufficiently broken down, the remains of the food move through the small intestines and into the large intestine.

דְּבֵי רַבִּי יִשְׁמָעֵאל תָּנָא: ״בְּנֹצָתָהּ״ – בְּנוֹצָה שֶׁלָּהּ, קוֹדְרָהּ בְּסַכִּין כְּמִין אֲרוּבָּה.

A Sage **from the school of Rabbi Yishmael taught:** The word ***benotzatah*** is a contraction of the words ***benotza shelah***, meaning its feathers. This teaches that the priest **cuts it with a knife,** creating an opening **like a window** opposite the crop. This allows him to remove the crop with only the feathers and skin directly opposite it, and that is what he brings to the place of the ashes.

Perek **VI**
Daf **65** Amud **b**

״שִׁיסַּע וְלֹא הִבְדִּיל״. תָּנוּ רַבָּנַן: ״וְשִׁסַּע״ – אֵין שִׁיסַּע אֶלָּא בַּיָּד, וְכֵן הוּא אוֹמֵר: ״וַיְשַׁסְּעֵהוּ כְּשַׁסַּע הַגְּדִי״.

§ The mishna teaches that after removing the crop and the feathers and innards that emerged with it, the priest **ripped** the bird lengthwise **and did not separate** the two halves of the bird. In this regard **the Sages taught** in a *baraita*: The verse states: **"And he shall rend"** (Leviticus 1:17). The act of **rending is** performed **only by hand,**[H] **and so too,** the verse **states** with regard to Samson: **"And he rent it as one would have rent a kid,** and he had nothing in his hand" (Judges 14:6).

״לֹא הֵסִיר אֶת הַמּוּרְאָה״ כו׳. מַתְנִיתִין דְּלָא כְּרַבִּי אֶלְעָזָר בְּרַבִּי שִׁמְעוֹן. דְּתַנְיָא, אָמַר רַבִּי אֶלְעָזָר בְּרַבִּי שִׁמְעוֹן: שָׁמַעְתִּי שֶׁמַּבְדִּילִין בְּחַטַּאת הָעוֹף.

§ The mishna teaches that if the priest **did not remove the crop,** or he changed any detail of the sacrificial rite after he squeezed out the blood, the offering is valid. If he separated the head from the body of a bird sin offering, it is disqualified. The Gemara says: **The mishna is not in accordance with** the opinion of **Rabbi Elazar, son of Rabbi Shimon, as it is taught** in a *baraita* that **Rabbi Elazar, son of Rabbi Shimon, said: I heard that one may separate** the head from the body **of a bird sin offering.**

מַאי בֵּינַיְיהוּ? אָמַר רַב חִסְדָּא: מִיצּוּי חַטַּאת הָעוֹף מְעַכֵּב אִיכָּא בֵּינַיְיהוּ. תַּנָּא קַמָּא סָבַר: מִיצּוּי חַטַּאת הָעוֹף מְעַכֵּב, וְכֵיוָן דְּמִיצּוּי דָּם – קָעָבֵיד מַעֲשֵׂה עוֹלָה בְּחַטַּאת הָעוֹף.

The Gemara asks: **What** is the reason for the difference **between them,** i.e., what is the basis of the disagreement? **Rav Ḥisda says:** The difference **between them** concerns the question of whether **squeezing out** the blood of **a bird sin offering** after its blood has been sprinkled is **indispensable. The first *tanna*,** whose opinion is cited in the mishna, **holds** that **squeezing out** the blood of **a bird sin offering**[H] is **indispensable. And since squeezing out** the **blood** is indispensable, the priest will have to squeeze out the blood after separating the head from the body, and he will have **performed the rite of** a bird **burnt offering on a bird sin offering,** which disqualifies the offering (see 66a).

וְרַבִּי אֶלְעָזָר בְּרַבִּי שִׁמְעוֹן סָבַר: מִיצּוּי חַטַּאת הָעוֹף לָא מְעַכֵּב, וּמְחַתֵּךְ בָּשָׂר בְּעָלְמָא הוּא.

And Rabbi Elazar, son of Rabbi Shimon, holds that **squeezing out** the blood of **a bird sin offering is not indispensable.** Consequently, if the priest would separate the bird's head from its body, he would refrain from squeezing out the blood, in which case the rite is dissimilar to that of a bird burnt offering. **And** the separation of the head **is** considered as though the priest was **merely cutting flesh,** and the offering is valid.

רָבָא אָמַר: שְׁהִיָּיה בְּסִימָן שֵׁנִי בְּעוֹלַת הָעוֹף מְעַכֵּב אִיכָּא בֵּינַיְיהוּ; תַּנָּא קַמָּא סָבַר: שְׁהִיָּיה בְּסִימָן שֵׁנִי בְּעוֹלַת הָעוֹף – לָא מְעַכֵּב, וְאַף עַל גַּב דְּשַׁהְיָיהּ – קָא עָבֵיד מַעֲשֵׂה עוֹלָה בְּחַטָּאת.

Rava says there is an alternative explanation of the dispute: It is possible that all agree that squeezing the blood of a bird sin offering is indispensable, and **there is** a difference **between them** with regard to whether **interrupting** the pinching before severing the **second *siman*,**[N] i.e., the gullet or windpipe, one of the organs that must be cut in the ritual slaughter, **of a bird burnt offering disqualifies** the offering. **The first *tanna* holds** that **interrupting** the pinching before severing the **second *siman* of a bird burnt offering does not disqualify** the offering, **and** therefore, if the priest separates the head of a bird sin offering from its body, **even though he interrupted** the pinching before severing the second *siman*, **he has performed the rite of** a bird **burnt offering on** a bird **sin offering,** which disqualifies it.

HALAKHA

Rending is only by hand – אֵין שִׁיסַּע אֶלָּא בַּיָּד: The priest rips the bird burnt offering lengthwise at its wings. He must do so only with his hand and not with an instrument such as a knife, in accordance with the *baraita* (Rambam *Sefer Avoda, Hilkhot Ma'aseh HaKorbanot* 6:22).

Squeezing out the blood of a bird sin offering – מִיצּוּי חַטַּאת הָעוֹף: Squeezing out the blood of a bird sin offering is an indispensable element of its sacrificial rite, in accordance with the opinion of the first *tanna* (Rambam *Sefer Avoda, Hilkhot Ma'aseh HaKorbanot* 7:7).

NOTES

Interrupting before severing the second *siman* – שְׁהִיָּיה בְּסִימָן שֵׁנִי: Interrupting refers to an instance where an amount of time elapses between the severing of the first *siman* that must be severed during ritual slaughter and the second, and is a disqualifying factor with regard to slaughter of an animal offering or non-sacred animal. Rashi notes a distinction between interrupting with regard to an animal offering and a bird offering: With regard to an animal offering, the slaughtering is not valid unless both the gullet and the windpipe have been severed. Therefore, a delay in severing the second *siman* disqualifies the offering, since the animal is considered a *tereifa* once its first *siman* has been severed.

By contrast, with regard to a bird offering, the act of severing the nape, analogous to the slaughtering of a non-consecrated bird, is considered complete upon the cutting of the first *siman*. The purpose of cutting the second *siman* in a bird burnt offering is to fulfill only the additional mitzva of separating. One could, therefore, suggest that delaying is not a disqualifying factor in its sacrificial rite. One could also suggest that although the requirement to cut the second *siman* is only because of the additional mitzva of separating, since the offering is nevertheless not valid without it, perhaps the cutting of the second *siman* is viewed as an indispensable part of the pinching process and a delay would disqualify it.

וְרַבִּי אֶלְעָזָר בְּרַבִּי שִׁמְעוֹן סָבַר: מְעַכֵּב, וְכֵיוָן דְּשַׁהְיָיה – מְחַתֵּךְ בָּשָׂר בְּעָלְמָא הוּא.

And Rabbi Elazar, son of Rabbi Shimon, holds that interrupting the pinching of a bird burnt offering **disqualifies** the offering. Therefore, in the case of a bird sin offering, **since** the priest **interrupted** the pinching before severing the second *siman*, even if he separates the head from the body **he is merely cutting flesh,** i.e., it is an insignificant act because he is not performing the rite of a burnt offering on a sin offering, and the offering is not disqualified.

אַבַּיֵי אָמַר: רוֹב בָּשָׂר מְעַכֵּב אִיכָּא בֵּינַיְיהוּ.

Abaye says there is a third explanation of the dispute between the *tanna'im*: It is possible that all agree that interrupting the pinching before severing the second *siman* disqualifies a bird burnt offering, and **there is** a difference **between them** with regard to whether cutting the **majority of** the **flesh** of the nape of a bird sin offering is **indispensable.**[N]

וּבִפְלוּגְתָּא דְּרַבִּי זֵירָא וְרַבִּי שְׁמוּאֵל בַּר רַב יִצְחָק, חַד אָמַר: שְׁהִיָּיה בְּסִימָן שֵׁנִי בְּעוֹלַת הָעוֹף מְעַכֵּב אִיכָּא בֵּינַיְיהוּ, וְחַד אָמַר: רוֹב בָּשָׂר מְעַכֵּב אִיכָּא בֵּינַיְיהוּ.

The Gemara points out: **And** Rava and Abaye disagree **with regard to** the issue that is the subject of **the dispute**[N] **between Rabbi Zeira and Rabbi Shmuel bar Rav Yitzḥak. One says** that the difference **between** the first *tanna* and Rabbi Elazar, son of Rabbi Shimon, concerns whether **interrupting** the pinching before severing the **second *siman* of a bird burnt offering disqualifies** the offering. **And one says** that the difference **between them** concerns whether cutting the **majority of** the **flesh** of the nape of a bird sin offering is **indispensable.**

מִכְּלָל דְּבָעֵינַן דְּרוֹב בָּשָׂר בִּתְחִילָּה? אִין, וְהָתַנְיָא: כֵּיצַד מוֹלְקִין חַטַּאת הָעוֹף? חוֹתֵךְ שִׁדְרָה וּמַפְרֶקֶת בְּלֹא רוֹב בָּשָׂר, עַד שֶׁמַּגִּיעַ לַוֶּושֶׁט אוֹ לַקָּנֶה. הִגִּיעַ לַוֶּושֶׁט אוֹ לַקָּנֶה – חוֹתֵךְ סִימָן אֶחָד אוֹ רוּבּוֹ, וְרוֹב בָּשָׂר עִמּוֹ. וּבְעוֹלָה – שְׁנַיִם אוֹ רוֹב שְׁנַיִם.

The Gemara asks: Since there is a dispute concerning whether cutting the majority of the flesh of the nape of a bird sin offering is indispensable, can it be deduced **by inference** that all agree **that we require** the priest to cut **the majority of the flesh *ab initio*?** The Gemara responds: **Yes; and** similarly **it was taught** in *baraita*: **How does one pinch**[H] the nape of **a bird sin offering?** Using his thumbnail, the priest **cuts** the **spine and nape, without** cutting through the **majority of the flesh,**[N] **until he reaches** either **the gullet or the windpipe.** Upon **reaching the gullet or the windpipe, he cuts one *siman*** entirely, **or** at least **the majority of it, and** he cuts **the majority of the flesh with it. And in** the case of a bird **burnt offering,** he cuts the **two** *simanim* **or the majority of the two**[N] *simanim*.

HALAKHA

How does one pinch – כֵּיצַד מוֹלְקִין: The procedure for the pinching of a bird offering is as follows: The priest cuts the nape and drags his thumbnail down opposite the nape. He can either cut the nape in a back-and-forth motion, or he can simply press his nail down into the nape. If either the gullet or the windpipe becomes dislodged, it is still valid. The priest then cuts the spinal cord and the nape without cutting the greater part of the flesh, as otherwise this would render the bird a corpse before reaching the *simanim*. With regard to a bird burnt offering, the priest must sever both the gullet and the windpipe with the downward motion of his finger, while with regard to a bird sin offering, he may sever both or only one (Rambam *Sefer Avoda, Hilkhot Ma'aseh HaKorbanot* 6:23, 7:6).

NOTES

Cutting the majority of the flesh of the nape of a bird sin offering is indispensable – רוֹב בָּשָׂר מְעַכֵּב: According to the first *tanna*, cutting the majority of the flesh is not indispensable, and therefore when the priest pinches the nape of a bird sin offering, it is possible that he will immediately sever the second *siman*. If he would do so and then separate the head from the body, he has performed the rite of a burnt offering on a sin offering and thereby disqualified it. Rabbi Elazar, son of Rabbi Shimon, holds that when pinching the nape of a sin offering, the priest must sever one of the organs, then cut the majority of the flesh of the nape, and then sever the second organ. Consequently, there will always be an interruption between severing the first and second *simanim*. Even if the priest would then separate the head of the offering, he would not be performing the rite of a burnt offering on a sin offering, and the offering would remain valid.

Preparing for pinching the nape by grasping the bird's legs and wings

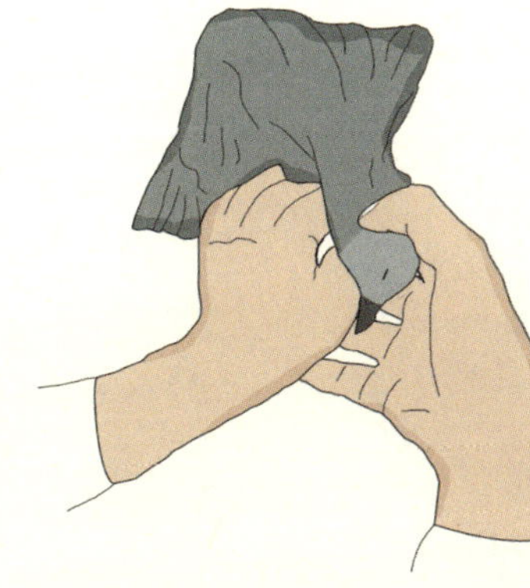

Position of hands just before pinching the bird's nape

And with regard to the dispute – וּבִפְלוּגְתָּא: According to this version of the text, Abaye and Rava engage in the same dispute as Rabbi Zeira and Rabbi Shmuel bar Rav Yitzḥak. According to other versions, Rabbi Zeira and Rabbi Shmuel bar Rav Yitzḥak do not represent the two respective opinions presented by Abaye and Rava. Rather, they disagree only with regard to whether or not cutting through the greater part of the flesh is indispensable.

Cuts the spine and nape without the majority of the flesh – חוֹתֵךְ שִׁדְרָה וּמַפְרֶקֶת בְּלֹא רוֹב בָּשָׂר: The reason for this particular order is that were the priest to sever the nape and cut through the greater part of the flesh before severing the necessary *simanim*, the bird would be considered dead before the act of severing took place.

He cuts two or the majority of the two – שְׁנַיִם אוֹ רוֹב שְׁנַיִם: These two options reflect two opinions cited in tractate *Ḥullin* (21a): Two *simanim* reflects the opinion of the Rabbis, and the greater part of two *simanim* reflects the opinion of Rabbi Elazar, son of Rabbi Shimon.

NOTES

They said this before, etc. – **אמרוה קמיה וכו׳**: The Sages related the explanations of the various *amora'im* with regard to the opinion of Rabbi Elazar, son of Rabbi Shimon. Genealogically, it is likely that they were referring specifically to Rabbi Zeira and Rabbi Shmuel bar Rav Yitzhak, as they were contemporaries of Rabbi Yirmeya.

אמרוה קמיה דרבי ירמיה, אמר: לא שמיע להו הא דאמר רבי שמעון בן אליקים משום רבי אלעזר בן פדת משום רבי אלעזר בן שמוע: אומר היה רבי אלעזר ברבי שמעון: שמעתי בחטאת העוף שמבדילין, ומאי "לא יבדיל"

The Gemara relates that the Rabbis **said this** dispute between the *amora'im* concerning the reason for the opinion of Rabbi Elazar, son of Rabbi Shimon, **before**[N] **Rabbi Yirmeya.** Rabbi Yirmeya **said: Have they not heard that which Rabbi Shimon ben Elyakim said in the name of Rabbi Elazar ben Pedat, in the name of Rabbi Elazar ben Shammua: Rabbi Elazar, son of Rabbi Shimon, used to say: I heard that one may** completely **separate** the head of **a bird sin offering** from its body. **And what** is the meaning of the verse that states: "But **shall not separate it**" (Leviticus 5:8)?

Perek **VI**
Daf **66** Amud **a**

NOTES

Does not have to separate it – **אין צריך להבדיל**: The distinction between Rabbi Yirmeya and the other *amora'im* is as follows: According to the other *amora'im*, Rabbi Elazar, son of Rabbi Shimon, agrees with the first *tanna* in that it is prohibited to separate the head of a bird sin offering. But he holds that if, after the fact, it was separated, the offering is still valid. From the statement of Rabbi Yirmeya, it is clear that Rabbi Elazar, son of Rabbi Shimon, disagrees entirely with the first *tanna* and maintains that it is permitted to separate the head even *ab initio*. According to him, the verse is merely teaching that one is not obligated to separate it.

Tosafot, citing Rabbeinu Tam, suggests an alternative understanding. He maintains that Rabbi Elazar agrees that it is prohibited to separate the head. But this prohibition is in effect only before the sprinkling of the blood, not afterward. Consequently, the verse indicates two *halakhot*: First, the prohibition to separate before the sprinkling, and second, that after the sprinkling one may choose not to separate the head. It should be noted that if the priest accidentally separated the head before the sprinkling, the offering is not disqualified.

Since it is written: And the priest shall bring it, etc. – **מכדי כתיב והקריבו וכו׳**: Rashi explains that Rabbi Elazar, son of Rabbi Shimon, derives from this verse that there is a distinction between the rite of the bird burnt offering and the bird sin offering. Accordingly, the phrase: He does not separate, in the context of a bird burnt offering, must mean that one is not obligated to separate the head, as, if it were meant as a prohibition, then it could be inferred only with regard to a bird burnt offering that it is optional to separate the head, but not a mitzva. The only way to infer that there is an obligation to separate the head of a bird burnt offering is if the phrase: And he does not separate, is not a prohibition but an option.

A more straightforward understanding of this Gemara is that it is derived on 66b from another verse that the head of a bird burnt offering must be completely detached. If so, the term: "He shall bring it," which alludes to the distinction between the bird burnt offering and bird sin offering, already teaches that the head of the bird sin offering must not be separated. According to this, the Gemara questions the purpose of: And he does not separate, stated in the context of the bird sin offering. The Gemara answers that it teaches that the separating of its head is optional. It should be noted that even according to this more straightforward understanding, there are several difficulties (see Maharam and Malbim on Leviticus 5:8).

A burnt offering – **עולה**: After describing the rite of the bird burnt offering, the verse states: "It is a burnt offering," which appears to be an unnecessary phrase. The *baraita* derives from the term "burnt offering" that the offering maintains this status even if it is missing something that one might have thought would be essential to this status. Yet, the expression "it is" teaches that the offering is valid only if the rite was performed as described in the verses. The *baraita* therefore seeks to determine which aspect of the sacrificial rite is deemed indispensable and which is deemed non-essential (*Korban Aharon*).

אין צריך להבדיל. אמר ליה רב אחא בריה דרבא לרב אשי: אלא מעתה, גבי בור דכתיב: "ולא יכסנו", הכי נמי דאין צריך לכסות?

It means that the priest **does not have to separate** it,[N] but not that it is prohibited to do so. **Rav Aha, son of Rava, said to Rav Ashi: If that is so,** then **with regard to a pit** in the public domain, **where it is written:** "And if a man shall open a pit…**and does not cover it**" (Exodus 21:33), can one claim that this verse **also** means **that he does not have to cover** it?

הכי השתא?! התם, כיון דכתיב: "בעל הבור ישלם" – עלויה הוא דרמי לכסויי. אבל הכא, מכדי כתיב: "והקריבו", חלק הכתוב בין חטאת העוף לעולת העוף,

The Gemara responds: **How can** these cases **be compared? There,** with regard to a pit, **since it is written** in the following verse: **"The owner of the pit shall pay"** (Exodus 21:34), it is evident that **it is incumbent upon him to cover** the pit. **But here, since it is written** with regard to a bird burnt offering: **"And** the priest **shall bring it**[N] to the altar" (Leviticus 1:15), the term "it" indicates that the verse is referring only to a burnt offering, and **the verse** has thereby **differentiated between a bird sin offering and a bird burnt offering.**

"לא יבדיל" למה לי? שמע מינה: אין צריך להבדיל.

Consequently, it is obvious that whereas the priest must completely separate the head of a bird burnt offering, this is not the *halakha* with regard to a sin offering. **Why do I** need the verse to state with regard to a bird sin offering: "But **shall not separate it**" (Leviticus 5:8)? **Conclude from** this verse that it is not forbidden to separate the head of a bird sin offering from the body, but rather **one does not have to separate** it.

"מיצה דם הגוף". תנו רבנן: "עולה" – אף על פי שמיצה דם הגוף ולא מיצה דם הראש. יכול מיצה דם הראש ולא מיצה דם הגוף? תלמוד לומר: "הוא".

§ The mishna teaches that if the priest squeezed out the blood of the head and did not squeeze out the blood of the body, it is disqualified. If he **squeezed out** the **blood of the body** and did not squeeze out the blood of the head, the offering is valid. **The Sages taught** in a *baraita*: In reference to a bird burnt offering, the verse states, seemingly unnecessarily: "It is **a burnt offering**" (Leviticus 1:17).[N] This teaches **that even though** the priest **squeezed out the blood of the body and did not squeeze out the blood of the head,** it is valid. One **might** have thought that if the priest **squeezed out the blood of the head and did not squeeze out the blood of the body** the offering is still valid. Therefore, **the verse states: "It is."**

מאי תלמודא? אמר רבינא: מסתברא, דרוב דמים בגוף שכיחי.

The Gemara asks: **What is the** biblical **derivation** for the opinion that the offering is valid if the priest squeezed out only the blood of the body but not if he squeezed out only the blood of the head? **Ravina said:** There is no conclusive proof from the language of the verse itself, but it **stands to reason** that this is the case, **as most of the blood is found in the body,** not the head.

הדרן עלך קדשי קדשים

Summary of **Perek VI**

It was stated in this chapter that the status of the altar itself is like that of the northern part of the Temple courtyard in that it is a valid location for the slaughter of offerings of the most sacred order. Apropos the altar's status with regard to sacrificial slaughter, the Gemara discussed the position of the altar relative to the entrance to the Sanctuary, in addition to other details of the altar's size and structure, as well as the minor ramps that protruded from it.

Meal offerings belong to the category of offerings of the most sacred order. The parts of meal offerings that are consumed must be eaten in the Temple courtyard by male priests during the day of the slaughter and the following night.

Bird offerings are brought exclusively from mature doves and pigeons. Birds may be sacrificed as burnt offerings or sin offerings. There are several distinctions between the rites of these two types of offerings, e.g., the sacrificial rite of a bird burnt offering is performed at the southeast corner of the altar, whereas the rite of a bird sin offering is performed at its southwest corner.

The sacrificial rite of bird offerings differs from that of animal offerings. Whereas animal offerings must be slaughtered at the throat using a knife, in the case of bird offerings, a priest pinches their napes from the back using his thumbnail. This procedure is carried out differently for a burnt offering and a sin offering. In the case of a burnt offering, the priest separates the head from the body, or, according to a different opinion, he entirely cuts through both the gullet and windpipe. In the case of a sin offering, the priest does not separate the head from the body and cuts either the gullet or the windpipe.

An additional distinction between the bird burnt offering and sin offering is that the blood of a sin offering is sprinkled on the lower half of the wall of the altar, below the red line, while the blood of a burnt offering is squeezed out on the upper half of the wall of the altar.

Bird burnt offerings and bird sin offerings share some common characteristics with their animal counterparts. Like the animal sin offering, a bird sin offering is disqualified if the priest intends its sacrifice to be for the sake of a different offering or a different individual. Conversely, an animal or bird burnt offering would not be disqualified, but the owner would not fulfill his obligation to bring the offering and would have to bring another one. Whereas sin offerings are consumed by male priests in the Temple courtyard, burnt offerings are consumed by the fire on the altar.

Bird offerings are similar to animal offerings with regard to cases where the priest intended to perform one of its rites or eat the offering beyond the designated time or outside the designated area. They differ in that animal offerings have four essential rites whereas bird offerings have only two, the pinching of the nape and the presenting of the blood on the altar.

Image **Credits**

All images are copyright © Koren Publishers Jerusalem Ltd., except:

pp205–207 all images © **courtesy of the Temple Institute**; **p212** © Israel Krul; **pp214–16** all images © **courtesy of the Temple Institute**; **p218** © brightasafig; **pp224–26** all images © **courtesy of the Temple Institute**; **p269** left image and upper right image © HaRav Menachem Makover, courtesy of *Harenu Bevinyano*; **p269** center image and bottom right image © **courtesy of the Temple Institute**; **p270** © HaRav Menachem Makover, courtesy of *Harenu Bevinyano*; **p295** © **courtesy of the Temple Institute**; **p301** © HaRav Menachem Makover, courtesy of *Harenu Bevinyano*; **p304** © HaRav Menachem Makover, courtesy of *Harenu Bevinyano*; **p307** left image © Deror avi; **p313** © HaRav Menachem Makover, courtesy of *Harenu Bevinyano*; **p332** top image© **courtesy of the Temple Institute**; **p332** bottom image © Professor Zohar Amar: recreated by Professor Zohar Amar of Bar Ilan University; **p334** © **courtesy of the Temple Institute**: vessels recreated by the Temple Institute; **p350** both images © HaRav Menachem Makover, courtesy of *Harenu Bevinyano*; **p356** © HaRav Menachem Makover, courtesy of *Harenu Bevinyano*; **p7** © HaRav Menachem Makover, courtesy of *Harenu Bevinyano*.

My Notes

My Notes

My Notes

תלמוד בבלי

— מהדורת נאה —

זבחים חלק ג

Steinsaltz Center

KOREN

Please note that the number ranges that appear at the bottom of each daf of the Vilna pages indicate the corresponding pages of the Koren Talmud Bavli translation and commentary.

תלמוד בבלי

הוצאת קורן ירושלים

— מהדורת נאה —

מסכת זבחים
דף לו: עד דף סו.

COMMENTARY BY

Rabbi Adin Even-Israel Steinsaltz

EDITOR-IN-CHIEF

Rabbi Dr Tzvi Hersh Weinreb

EXECUTIVE EDITOR

Rabbi Joshua Schreier

•

STEINSALTZ CENTER
KOREN PUBLISHERS JERUSALEM

מז א מיי' פי"ד מהל' פסה"מ הלכה ט:
מח ב מיי' פי"ח מהל' פסה"מ הלכה יט:
מט ג מיי' שם הל' יח:
א ד ה מיי' פ"ב מהל' פסה"מ הלכה א:
ב ו מיי' פי"ז מהלכות פסה"מ הל' א:
ג ז מיי' פ"ב שם הל' ג:
ד ח מיי' פי"ז שם הל' א:

[לעיל לא.] [נ"ל מחשבת אכילה]

תורה אור

יהא חייב? א] והתניא, רבי יהודה אומר: יכול חטאת ששחטה בדרום יהא חייב? ת"ל: "לא תזבח לה' אלהיך שור ושה וגו' כל דבר רע" — על ב] דבר רע אתה מחייבו, ואי אתה מחייבו על חטאת ששחטה בדרום! תרי תנאי אליבא דרבי יהודה. אמר ג] רבי אבא: ומודה רבי יהודה, שחוזר וקובעו לפיגול. ד] אמר רבא: תדע, דפיגול לפני זריקה לא כלום הוא, ואתיא זריקה וקבעה לה בפיגול. ולא היא, התם הוא חדא מחשבה היא, הכא — תרי מחשבות. איתיביה רב הונא ה] לרבי אבא: *ליתן את הניתנין למעלה למטה, למטה למעלה, לאלתר — כשר; חזר וחישב חוץ למקומו — פסול ואין בו כרת, חוץ לזמנו — פיגול וחייבין עליו כרת. למחר — פסול; חזר וחישב, בין חוץ לזמנו בין חוץ למקומו — פסול, ואין בו כרת. תיובתא ו] דרבי אבא! תיובתא. אמר רב חסדא אמר רבינא בר סילא: חישב שיאכלוהו טמאים למחר — חייב. אמר רבא: תדע, דבשר לפני זריקה לא חזי, וכי מחשב ביה — מיפסיל. ולא היא, התם — זריק ומיחזי, הכא — לא מיחזי כלל. אמר רב חסדא, *מרגלא בפומיה דרב דימי בר חיננא: בשר פסח שלא הוצלה, ולחמי תודה שלא הורמו — חייבין עליהן משום טומאה. אמר רבא: תדע, *דתניא: "אשר לה'" — לרבות אימורי קדשים קלים לטומאה; אלמא, אע"ג דלאו בני אכילה נינהו — חייבין עליהן משום טומאה. הכא נמי — אע"ג דלאו בני אכילה נינהו — חייבין עליהן משום טומאה. ולא היא, התם — אימורי קדשים קלים חזו לגבוה, לאפוקי בשר פסח שלא הוצלה ולחמי תודה שלא הורמו, דלא חזו לא לגבוה ולא להדיוט. (א) ז] (לישנא אחרינא: הא אימורין לא חזו. ולא היא, הנך חזו למילתייהו, והני לא חזו כלל).§

הדרן עלך כל הפסולין

סנהדרין ד. פסחים פט:

בית שמאי אומרים: *כל הניתנין על מזבח החיצון, שנתן ח] במתנה אחת — כיפר, ובחטאת — שתי מתנות. ובית הלל אומרים: אף חטאת שנתנה מתנה אחת — כיפר. לפיכך, אם נתן את הראשונה כתיקנה ואת השניה חוץ לזמנה — כיפר, ואם נתן את הראשונה חוץ לזמנה ואת השניה חוץ למקומה — פיגול וחייבין עליו כרת. כל הניתנין על המזבח הפנימי ט] שאם חיסר אחת מן המתנות — כאילו לא כיפר. לפיכך, נתן כולן כתיקנן ואחת שלא כתיקנה — פסולה ואין בו כרת.§

גמ' תנו רבנן: *מנין לניתנין על מזבח החיצון שנתנן י] במתנה אחת, שכיפר? תלמוד לומר: "ודם זבחיך ישפך". (דברים יב) והאי להכי הוא דאתא? האי מיבעי ליה לכדתניא: מנין

שיאכלוהו טמאים. לא דמי לאכילת כלבים. *דבטמאים מיפסיל קודם אכילה משעת נגיעה. ואפי' תחב לו חבירו, מ"מ בהך כב] *(מחשבה אכילת) דבר אחר גורס לו, שבלא אכילה יכול לפוסלו בנגיעה. **בשר** פסח שלא הוצלה. הא דתניא ב"הקומץ רבה" (מנחות דף כה:) דשאין ניתר לטהורים אין חייבין עליו משום טומאה — היינו בדבר שצריך היתר מזבח, כגון בשר שנטמא לפני זריקה. ולא דמי לבשר פסח שלא הוצלה, ולחמי תודה שלא הורמו. וצריך לדקדק: דהכא דרשינן "אשר לה'" לרבות אימורי קדשים קלים לטומאה, והתם מוקמינן ליה לרבות לן ויולא.

יהא חייב. מלקות. דבר רע. מום בגלוי שהוא מגונה קרי "דבר רע", בבכורות בפרק "על אלו מומין" (דף לז.). ומודה רבי יהודה. בחישב על מנת יא] להניח — (ב) שחוזר וקובעו לפיגול אם חזר וחישב בעבודה שניה על מנת לאכול חוץ לזמנו, ולא אמרי' כבר נפסל במחשבת הינוח. אמר רבא תדע. דמחשבת הינוח לרבי יהודה לאו כמחשבת חוץ למקומו ושלא לשמו היא, לאפוקי מידי פיגול. דהא פיגול, דשוחטו על מנת לזרוק את דמו למחר — לפני זריקה לאו כלום היא, ואין המחשבה מועלת עד שיזרק הדם היום, דבעינן יב] קרב כל מתיריו. ומיהו, מחשבה קמייתא מחשבת הינוח הוי, וכי זריק ליה — אתיא זריקה יג] וקבעי ליה, (ג) ולא אמרי': הואיל ומעיקרא פיגול לא הוילא — איפסיל ליה במחשבת הינוח, וכי זריק ליה או בפיגול או בשתיקה לא ליחול פיגול. התם חד מחשבה. דלא שינה יד] מחשבתו הראשונה, והיא היתה לשם פיגול. תרי מחשבות. והאחד שם פסול לה ולא שם פיגול. כשר. כדאמרינן במתני' לדברי הכל. למחר פסול. חישב ליתן למחר את הניתנין למטה למעלן. ואוקי בפרק שני משום מחשבת הינוח, כרבי יהודה, ולא משום מחשבת נתינת מחר, דא"כ — פיגול מיבעיא ליה. טו] אלמא לא הוי פיגול, דזריקה דלא כשר באכילה לא אתיא לידי פיגול. וקתני: חזר וחישב בו, אלמא לא מיקבע תו טז] פיגול. חישב שיאכלוהו טמאים למחר. פיגול. ולא אמרינן לאו מחשבה היא, דאכילת טמאים לא חזיא, והוי כמחשב מחשבת פסול. תדע. דמחשבת אכילת פסול לא מפקא מידי פגול, בר יז] מחשבת חוץ למקומו (ולזמנו). דהא בשר לפני זריקה לא חזי לאכילה, וכי מחשב ביה בשחיטה ע"מ לאוכלה למחר — מפגיל, יח] דהשתא אכילה פסולה היא בלא שום פיגול. התם זריק ומיחזי. ואשמעינן דלמחר, אי לאו משום פיגול, הוה יט] חזיא לאכילה. שלא הורמה. ד' חלות הנתרמות לכהן מארבעה מינין שבה, דכתיב: "והקריב ממנו אחד מכל קרבן תרומה" וגו' (ויקרא ז). משום טומאה. אם אכלן בטומאת הגוף. ואע"ג דקי"ל* כ] שאין ניתר לטהורים אין חייבין עליו משום טומאה, האי כיון דאיזרק דם — ניתר לטהורין קרינן ביה, ואע"ג דאין פסח נאכל אלא צלי, וחלות התודה עד שיורמו. ה"ג אשר לה' לרבות אימורי קדשים קלים לטומאה. "והנפש אשר תאכל" מבשר זבח השלמים אשר לה'". לטומאה. להתחייב כרת האוכלן בטומאת הגוף. ד"אשר לה'" יתירא הוא, למידרש ביה דבר שהוא עולה לגבוה.

הדרן עלך כל הפסולין

[מנחות מז:]

הדרן עלך כל הפסולין

מנין לניתנין על מזבח החיצון שנתנן מתנה אחת כיפר כו'. לכאורה אתיא כבית שמאי. דבית הלל, כג] *כיון דמכשרי בחטאת לקמן: "וכפר" אע"פ שלא נתן אלא אחד — לא צריך קרא לשאר קרבנות. וכן משמע בסוף שמעתין, דקאמר: וכל הנך תנאי דמפקי ליה להאי "ודם זבחיך ישפך" לדרשא אחרינא, כל הניתנין על מזבח החיצון שנתנן במתנה אחת שכיפר מנא להו? סברי לה כבית הלל, דאמרי: אף חטאת שנתנה במתנה אחת כיפר, וילפי כולהו מחטאת. ונראה דאתיא אפי' כב"ה, וקסבר האי תנא דלא ילפינן מחטאת, משום דשתי מתנות שהן ארבע דשאר קרבנות ילפי' בפ' "איזהו מקומן" (לקמן דף נג:) מדכתיב "סביב", כד] *והוה אמינא שתים עשאן הכתוב כמתנה אחת ולא כיפר, אי נמי: משום דטובא "סביב" כתיבי, כה] ושנה לעכב. ולקמן נמי אמרי' "וכפר" ו"כפר" מפני הדין כו', מה דמים האמורים למטה שנתן מתנה אחת — כיפר, אף דמים שלמעלה כן

נ"א כיון דמכשרי אף בחטאת ויליף לקמן מוכפר אע"פ כו'. ל"ק

גי' ל"ק וכו"א שעשאן הכתוב כו'

בית שמאי אומרים. מתנה אחת. זריקה אחת — כיפר, אע"פ שרוצה טעונים שתי מתנות שהן ארבע. ובחטאת שתי מתנות. מתנות ארבע ממש. ובגמרא יליף טעמא. לפיכך. חטאת וכל הזבחים לבית הלל, ולבית שמאי שאר זבחים חוץ מחטאת. נתן את הראשונה כתקנה. בשתיקה, ואת השניה במחשבת אכילת בשר חוץ לזמנו — כיפר, וכשר הקרבן. שכבר ניתר הקרבן ליקרב על ידי מתנה ראשונה, ואין השניה מעורת את הבשר — לפיכך אינה מפגלת. פיגול וחייבין עליו כרת. שאין מחשבת חוץ למקומו דשניה מוציאתו מידי פיגול, שכבר הוקבע בראשונה, שכבר קרבו כל מתיריו. שחיסר אחת מכל המתנות לא כיפר. כדיליף בברייתא בגמרא. לפיכך. הואיל וכולן מתירות אין זו מעורת בלא זו, ואין זו מפגלת בלא זו. ואם נתן כולן כתקנן בשתיקה, ואחת שלא כתקנה, כגון שנתנה במחשבת חוץ למקומו או חוץ לזמנו — פסול, שלא ניתר בראשונות, ואין בו כרת — שאין האחרונה מפגלתו, דקסבר: אין מפגלין בחצי מתיר. **גמ'** ישפך. שפיכה אחת משמע, כא] דלא כתיב "סביב" דילפינן מיניה שתי מתנות שהן ארבע בפרק "איזהו מקומן".

מנין

שיטה מקובצת

א] והתניא בספרי בפרשת שופטים מייתי קצת בע"א (ותיבת הי' נמחק): ב] על כל דבר: ג] אמר רבא ומודה ר"י: ד] אמר רבא תדע כו'. תימה א"כ אפי' במחשבת חוץ למקומו ושלא לשמו בפסח וחטאת לא תוציא מפיגול מטעמיה דרבא ואי משום דגלי קרא לא יערב בו מחשבות אחרות א"כ אפי' מחשבת הינוח נמי וי"ל דהא דקאמר הכא שהוקבעו לפיגול לא קאי לכולהו מחשבות דלעיל במתני' אלא אלהניח דמו למחר כיון שחזר וחשב לזרקו למחר אין זה עירוב מחשבות אלא עירוב מחשבתו ראשונה דלהניח ולזרוק דמו קאמר וקצת קשה דמשמע דקאי אכוליה מתני' גם אלהוציאו [לחוץ או להניחו] למחר (בחוץ) כמו שהזכיר בקונטרס לכך נראה למהר"פ דהא דגלי דעירוב מחשבות מוציא מידי פיגול היינו דוקא במחשבות הכתובות בפסוק דהיינו חוץ למקומו או שלא לשמו אבל מחשבת הינוח דמיפסלא מסברא לא וא"ת א"כ אמאי איצטריך להאי תדע דקאמר רבא וי"ל שלא תלמוד אותו פסול מחשבת הינוח משאר עבודות דכתיב בקראי ועוד שלא תאמר כהרצאת כשר: ה] הונא לרבא: ו] תיובתא דרבא: ז] מכאן ועד סוף הפרק נמחק: ח] החיצון שנתן מתנה: ט] הפנימי שחיסר אחת מן המתנות לא כפר: י] שנתנן מתנה אחת: יא] מנת להוציאו לחוץ או להניחו למחר שחוזר: יב] דבעינן קרבו כל: יג] זריקה וקבעא: יד] שינה ממחשבתו: טו] ליה אלא לא הוי פיגול דזריקה דלא שריא בשר באכילה לא מייתי לידי: טז] תו בפיגול הס"ד: יז] בר ממחשבת חוץ למקומו: יח] מפגיל אע"ג דהשתא: יט] הוה חזי לאכילה: כ] שאם אין ניתר: כא] משמע מדלא כתיב: כב] בהך מחשבת אכילה דבר: כג] כיון דמכשרי בחטאת ומכפר אע"פ ומתיבת ומכפר עד תיבת לא בס"א אינו: כד] והו"א שעשאן מתנה אחת לא כיפר: כה] כתיבי דשנה לעכב ולקמן נמי אמרי' לב"ה וכפר:

הגהות הב"ח

(א) גמ' לישנא אחרינא ולא היא הני אימורים חזו למילתייהו הני לא חזו כלל כל"ל: (ב) רש"י ד"ה ומודה וכו' על מנת להניח את דמו או אבריו שחוזר וקובעו: (ג) ד"ה אמר רבא וכו' וקבעי ליה בפיגול ולא:

מנין. שכל הדמים של כל הקרבנות שטעונים מתן דם ליסוד אם נשאר מן הדם בכלי לאחר שזרק שתי מתנותיו, שצריך לשופכו ליסוד, ואע"פ שלא נאמר שפיכת שיריים אלא בחטאת. והנשאר בדם וגו'. בחטאת העוף כתיב, "והנשאר ימצה" הוה ליה למכתב. ומה תלמוד לומר בדם כו' אלא על הניתנין מתן ארבע. היינו חטאת, שטעונה ארבע מתנות על ארבע קרנות, ובחטאת כתיבי שיריים לשפיכה. לימד על כל הדמים. שנשאר בהן כלום לאחר עיקר זריקתן, שישפך הנשאר ליסוד. מנין לניתנין בזריקה. כל הדמים ח] שכתב בהן זריקה, כגון עולה ושלמים ואשם דכתיב בהו "וזרקו", ובכור דכתיב ביה "ואת דמם תזרוק" (במדבר יח). וכל זריקה מרחוק משמע, שזורק מן הכלי למזבח למרחוק. שפיכה. עומד אצל היסוד ושופך. ודם זבחיך ישפך. כל זבחים במשמע. בירך ברכת הפסח פטר את של זבח. חגיגת ארבעה עשר שבאה עם הפסח כשהחבורה מרובה. ושנינו בתוספתא דפסחים: על הפסח הוא אומר "ברוך אשר קדשנו במצותיו וצונו לאכול ט] הפסח", ועל הזבח הוא אומר "אשר קדשנו במצותיו וצונו לאכול את הזבח". ואם בירך על הפסח – פטר את הזבח. י] על הזבח לא פטר את הפסח. וקס"ד, ובפסחים נמי הכי מפרש, דקסבר רבי ישמעאל זריקה בכלל שפיכה, יא] כדאמר לעיל: מנין לניתנין בזריקה *הניתנין בשפיכה יצא. הלכך, מתן דם שלמים שכתב בה זריקה – בכלל מתן דם פסח שכתב בה שפיכה כדאמרינן לקמן, וכי בירך על הפסח – פטר את הזבח, שהזבח בכלל פסח. אבל בירך על הזבח – לא פטר את הפסח, שלא מצינו לניתנין בשפיכה שכשרין בזריקה, הלכך אין פסח בכלל שלמים. ר' עקיבא אומר אין זו פוטרת את זו. דלית ליה יב] לניתנין בזריקה שנתנן בשפיכה יצא, דהא דפסח בשפיכה מ"ודם זבחיך ישפך" נפקא לן לקמן, ואתרי לא דרשת מיניה. ולקמן פריך לרבי ישמעאל: היכי יג] דרשת ליה להכי ולהכי? ותנא דברייתא קמייתא סבר לה כרבי עקיבא בהא דאין זריקה בכלל שפיכה, אבל בפסח בשפיכה לא סבירא ליה כוותיה, דהא לא מייתר ליה קרא, דמיבעיא ליה לכל הניתנין יד] במזבח החיצון שנתנן במתנה אחת כיפר. והכי אמרינן בשמעתין. סבר לה כרבי יוסי הגלילי. דאמר: פסח בזריקה ונפקא ליה (ב) מ"ואת דמם", טו] דלא כתיב "דמו" דליקו אבכור לחודיה. ור' ישמעאל האי קרא. ד"ודם זבחיך ישפך". מפיק ליה להכי ולהכי. בתמיה. דריש ליה לניתנין בזריקה שנתנן בשפיכה. דעל כרחך כר"ע לא אתיא, דאם כן – אמאי אין פסח פוטר את הזבח, הואיל ושלמים בכלל פסח? ואי נמי סבירא ליה לר' עקיבא פסח בזריקה כר' יוסי הגלילי – כל שכן דשניהם פוטרין זה את זה. וקדריש טז] להו תו לפסח דבשפיכה. תרי תנאי אליבא דר' ישמעאל. דמאן דיליף ליה לפסח בשפיכה – לית ליה פסח פוטר את הזבח. ולא פליג רבי ישמעאל אדר' עקיבא בהאי, יז] כיון דפסח בשפיכה מהאי קרא יליף – תו לית לן למילף מיניה ניתנין בזריקה כשרים בשפיכה. ומאן דאית ליה פלוגתא – לית ליה פסח בשפיכה, אלא בזריקה כשלמים. ומיהו פסח עיקר וזבח טפל לו, הלכך אין זבח פוטרו לפסח, אבל פסח פוטר את הזבח. ובפסחים ירושלמי האי טעמא יח] אמר בה. בשלמא רבי ישמעאל. דמפיק מתן פסח מ"דם זבחיך ישפך", והאי לשון רבים ד"דמם וחלבם" – כוליה בבכור מוקי לה, יט] ובשור וכשב ועז הוא דנקט לשון רבים. *והאי נמי דקאי לשון רבים ד"בשרם יהיה לך" דסמיך ליה – אבכור שור ובכור כשב ובכור עז. אלא לרבי יוסי הגלילי. דאית ליה כ] בכור לשון יחיד, וקרא דנקט לשון רבים – משום מעשר ופסח נקט לה, ומעשר ופסח פשיטא לן שאינה מתנה לכהן, אלא בעלים אכלי ליה. מאי ובשרם. דקא"ל רחמנא לאהרן? ומשני: אחד תם ואחד בעל מום. כלומר, לעולם לשון רבים דנקט קרא קמא – לאו אמיני כא] דבכורות קאי, דכולן בלשון חד בכור מפיק להו. ו"דמם כב] וחלבם" – לרבות מעשר ופסח. ולשון רבים ד"בשרם" – אבכור קאי. ולא אשלשת מיני בכור דקרא, דתימא ד"חלבם ודמם" נמי עלייהו קאי, אלא אבכור דחד מינא נמי שייך למימר ו"בשרם" – אתם ובעל מום.

מנין לכל הדמים שטעונים א] מתן דם ליסוד? ת"ל: "ודם זבחיך ישפך"! נפקא ליה מדרבי. דתניא, רבי אומר: °"והנשאר בדם ימצה" (ויקרא ה), שאין ת"ל "בדם", ב] ומה ת"ל "בדם"? לפי שלא למדנו אלא לניתנין מתן ד' שטעונין מתן דמים ליסוד, שאר דמים מנין? ת"ל: ג] "והנשאר בדם ימצה", שאין ת"ל "בדם", ומה ת"ל "בדם"? לימד על כל הדמים שטעונין מתן דמים ליסוד. ואכתי, להכי הוא דאתא? מיבעי ליה *לכדתניא: מנין לניתנין בזריקה שנתנן ד] בשפיכה [א]יצא – ת"ל: "ודם זבחיך ישפך"! סבר לה כר' עקיבא, דאמר: *לא זריקה בכלל שפיכה, ולא שפיכה בכלל זריקה. דתנן: *בירך ברכת הפסח – פטר את של זבח, של זבח – לא פטר את הפסח, דברי רבי ישמעאל. רבי עקיבא אומר: [א] לא זו פוטרת זו, ולא זו פוטרת זו. אכתי להכי הוא דאתא? מיבעי ליה לכדתניא: ר' ישמעאל אומר: מתוך שנאמר: °"אך בכור שור או בכור כשב או בכור עז" וגו' (במדבר יח), למדנו לבכור שטעון מתן דמים ואימורים לגבי מזבח, מעשר ופסח מנין? תלמוד לומר: "ודם זבחיך ישפך"! סבר לה כר' יוסי הגלילי; *דתניא, רבי יוסי הגלילי אומר: "דמו" לא נאמר אלא "דמם", "חלבו" לא נאמר אלא "חלבם" – לימד על [ב]בכור מעשר ופסח ה] שטעון מתן דמים [ג]ואימורין לגבי מזבח. ו] ורבי ישמעאל, האי קרא מפיק ליה להכי ומפיק ליה להכי? תרי תנאי אליבא דרבי ישמעאל. בשלמא לרבי ישמעאל דמוקים ז] לה כוליה בבכור – היינו דכתיב: °"ובשרם יהיה לך" (שם), אלא לרבי יוסי (א) דמוקי ליה נמי במעשר ופסח – מעשר ופסח בעלים אכלי ליה, מאי "ובשרם יהיה לך"? אחד תם ואחד בעל מום, לימד

כן. ולמטה מנא לן, אם לא מ"ודם זבחיך ישפך"? אלמא דבית הלל נמי דרשי ליה. ומיהו, יש לדחות. כג] ונראה לי (תוספת) דשאר זבחים כד] ידע מדלא שנה בהן לעכב, אבל חטאת לא נכשיר מטעמא דלא שנה, אלא פשיטא ליה כה] דגמר חטאת חילון מחטאת פנימי לעכב, אי לא אשכחן בעלמא דמלינן למיגמר מיניה כו] דמתנה אחת כיפר. א"כ על כרחיך לב"ש בעי הכא: מנין? דנגמר מחטאת דבעי שתי מתנות! אע"ג דחטאת חמירא – גילוי מילתא היא ללמוד סתום מן המפורש. דאי לבית הלל מאי בעי "מנין"? הא לא שנה לעכב. ומהאי טעמא לא מצי למיבעי: יהא כז] כשרה בדיעבד בולא כלום, דכפרה בכדי לא אשכחן*. ברו"ך. ע"כ.

מתן דם ליסוד ת"ל ודם זבחיך ישפך. אע"ג דלא כתיב יסוד, מצינו שירים שנשפכין ליסוד, דכתיב בחטאת: "ואת דמה ישפך אל יסוד המזבח". **תרי** תנאי ואליבא דרבי ישמעאל. דמאן דיליף ליה לפסח בשפיכה – לית ליה פסח פוטר את הזבח. ולא פליג ר' ישמעאל אדרבי עקיבא, כח] דכיון דפסח בשפיכה מהאי קרא – תו לית לן למילף מיניה כט] ניתנין בזריקה כשרין בשפיכה. ומאן דאית ליה פלוגתא – לית ליה פסח בשפיכה, אלא בזריקה כשלמים. ומיהו, פסח עיקר וזבח טפל לו, הלכך אין זבח פוטר לפסח אבל פסח פוטר זבח. ובפסחים ירושלמי האי טעמא ל] אמר בה, כך פי' בקונט'. ויש תימה מסוגיא דסוף "ע"פ" (פסחים קכא.) גבי בירך ברכת הפסח פטר את של זבח. דקאמר עלה: כשתימצי לומר לדברי ר' ישמעאל זריקה בכלל שפיכה ולא שפיכה בכלל זריקה, ולדברי ר' עקיבא לא שפיכה בכלל זריקה ולא זריקה בכלל שפיכה. אלמא ר' ישמעאל אית ליה תרתי, דפסח לא] בשפיכה, וזריקה בכלל שפיכה! ועוד קשה לפירוש הקונטרס לב] מסוגיא דשמעתין, דקאמר לעיל: סבר לה כר' עקיבא. ולא סבר לה כוותיה לגמרי, דרבי עקיבא סבירא ליה דפסח בשפיכה, ותנא דברייתא סבר לג] בזריקה! [א] ועוד, מאי לד] האי דפריך: סבר כר"ע דאמר פסח בשפיכה? הלא מאן דאמר פסח בשפיכה – היינו מ"דם זבחיך ישפך", דתניא, ר' ישמעאל אומר כו', אם כן לא אייתר קרא למתנה אחת כיפר! ע"כ. לה] ועוד קשה: דאמר בפסחים פרק "האשה" (דף פח:) גבי חמשה שנתערבו עורות פסחיהם: והא שלמים בזריקה ופסח בשפיכה! ומשני: מאי נפקא מינה, והתניא: מנין לניתנין בזריקה שנתנן בשפיכה שילא. אלמא אית ליה תרתי: דפסח בשפיכה, וניתנין בזריקה שנתנן בשפיכה שילא! ועוד: מדקתני בברייתא: מנין לניתנין בזריקה כו' – מכלל דאיכא שפיכה. ואי פסח בזריקה – אם כן כולהו בזריקה לו] [ב] נינהו! לז] [ועוד קשה: הא אמרי' בספרי, ר' יאשיה אומר "קודש הם" למה נאמר – להביא את המעשר ואת הפסח שיטענו שפיכה אחת, שלא שמענו להם בכל התורה כולה]. ורבי יצחק אומר: אין צריך, שהרי כבר נאמר "ודם זבחיך ישפך" – להביא את המעשר ואת הפסח שיטענו שפיכה. ומה תלמוד לומר "קודש הם" – להביא את המעשר לח] שיטעון הקטר חלבים, שלא מצינו בכל התורה כולה. משמע דרבי יאשיה שפיכה לט] דרבי יצחק קאמר. ואע"ג דדריש ליה מקרא דכתיב גבי בכור מ] בזריקה – דלמא מדאתו מריבויא ולא כתבינהו בהדיא מא] קדריש. וכי פריך [התם אבא חנן: למה נאמר, ומה שאר קדשים שלא הושוו במתן דמים – היינו] דאתא למעוטי חטאת דבאצבע. ונראה דרבי ישמעאל (דפסחים) קסבר דפסח בשפיכה מקרא אחרינא, ולא מ"דם זבחיך". וכי פריך הכא: [ג] האי מיבעי ליה לכדתניא, רבי ישמעאל אומר: מתוך – מב] הוה מצי למימר דקסבר פסח בשפיכה מקרא אחרינא, ולא מ"דם זבחיך", אלא משום דאשכח ברייתא דרבי יוסי הגלילי נקטה. ורבינו שמואל בשם רבינו שלמה פי' בענין אחר: האי ד"ערבי פסחים" (דף קכא.) כשתימצי לומר לדברי רבי ישמעאל זריקה בכלל שפיכה. כלומר, מתוך דברי רבי ישמעאל תוכל

מסורת הש"ס: תורה אור | ויקרא ה | פסחים פט. | [פסחים קכא.] | שם | במדבר יח | פסחים סד: לקמן נו: | [נ"ל שנתנן] | שם

עין משפט נר מצוה:
ה א מיי' פ"ב מהלכות פסה"מ הלכה ב:
[א מיי' פ"ח מהלכות חמץ ומצה הלכה ז]:
ו ב מיי' פ"ה מהלכות מעה"ק הלכה יז:
ז ג מיי' שם הלכה יח:

[וע"ע תוספות סנהדרין ד. ד"ה כל]

הגהות הב"ח
(א) גמ' אלא לרבי יוסי הגלילי דמוקי: (ב) רש"י ד"ה סבר וכו' מאת דמם:

שיטה מקובצת
א] מתן. עיין תוס' ד"ה [תן יסוד למזבח של עולה] (דף נ"א ע"ב): ב] ת"ל בדם אלא והנשאר ימצה: ג] שאר דמים מנין ת"ל בדם לימד (והשאר ל"ש): ד] בשפיכה שיצא ת"ל כו' ישפך עיין [תוס'] סנהדרין (דף ד ע"א) [ד"ה כל]: ה] שטעונין מתן: ו] ורבי ישמעאל האי קרא כו' פי' הקונטרס ר"י דריש מיניה לניתנים בזריקה שניתנין בשפיכה כדאיתא בברייתא דלעיל דע"כ כר"י אתיא דאל"כ אמאן תרמיה דע"כ כר"ע כו' ולא נהירא משום דלא אתיא כר"ע נימא דאתיא כר"י דלמא לא אתיא לא כמר ולא כמר אלא תנא אחרינא הוא לכך נראה דהכי פריך כיון דדריש פסח בשפיכה מדם זבחיך ישפך ושמעינן ליה לר"י דאמר בירך על של פסח פטר של זבח וא"כ סבר דניתנין בזריקה שנתנן בשפיכה יצא דאם לא יצא היכא פטר את הזבח והלא פסח בשפיכה וזבח בזריקה אלא ודאי ס"ל דיצא וא"כ היכא מפיק תרוייהו מדם זבחיך: ז] דמוקי' ליה: ח] הדמים שכתוב: ט] לאכול את הפסח: י] מה"ד ואם בירך על הזבח: יא] כדאמרינן לעיל מנין לניתנין בזריקה שנתנן בשפיכה שיצא הלכך מתן דם זבח שהוא שלמים שכתוב בו זריקה בכלל מתן דם פסח שכתוב בו שפיכה: יב] ניתנין בזריקה: יג] היכי דריש ליה להכי ולהכי כו' סבר ליה כר"ע כו' אבל בפסח. ס"א פליג עליה דר"ע דשפיכה לר"ע בפסח נפקא ליה מדם זבחיך ישפך ותנא דברייתא מפיק ליה מדם זבחיך לכל הניתנין כו': יד] הניתנין על מזבח החיצון שנתנן מתנה אחת: טו] דמם תורק דלא: טז] וקדריש ליה: יז] בהאי קרא דכתיב דפסח: יח] טעמא אמרי בה: יט] לה ואשור וכשב ועז קאי נמי לשון רבים: כ] ליה לבכור לשון: כא] אמיני בכורות דקרא קאי: כב] וחלבם לעולם לרבות: כג] מתיבות ונראה לי עד סוף הדבור מוקף בחצי לבנה ותיבת

שיטה מקובצת
ותיבת תוספות נמחק: כד] זבחים ידענו ממילא: כה] ליה דנגמר חטאת: כו] מיניה דכמתנה אחת: כז] יהא כשר בדיעבד: כח] עקיבא בהא דכיון: כט] מיניה דניתנין: ל] טעמא אמרי בה כך פירש בקונטרס משמע דמאן דאית ליה הפסח פוטר של זבח לית ליה דפסח בשפיכה ומאן דאית ליה פסח בשפיכה לית ליה שניתנים בזריקה שניתנים בשפיכה יצא ויש: לא] בשפיכה ס"א וניתנים בזריקה שנתנם בשפיכה יצא ועוד דוחק לפ"ה דפי' דתנא דברייתא דלעיל ס"ל כר"ע כו': לב] מסוגיא ס"א דמסוגיא דשמעתין וכו' לגמרי כר"ע משמע דסבירא ליה דפסח בשפיכה הלא מ"ד פסח כו': לג] ע' בהשמטות בסוף המסכת: לד] מאי סבר הא דפריך דאי סבר וכו' ומתיבת ועוד כו' עד תיבות אחת כיפר בס"א אינו: לה] ע"כ הגה: לו] נינהו אם לא נאמר דאתי למעוטי חטאת דבאצבע לכך נראה דודאי מאן דאית ליה פסח בשפיכה סבר שפיר בניתנין בזריקה שנתנן בשפיכה יצא ופסח בשפיכה לאו מודם זבחיך מפיק ליה אלא מקודש הם מפיק ליה כדדרש בספרי ר' יאשיה אומר קודש הם למה נאמר להביא את המעשר ואת הפסח שטעונין שפיכה אחת שלא שמענו להן בכל התורה כולה: ס"א אם לא נאמר דאתאי למעוטי חטאת דבאצבע ונראה דרבי ישמעאל דפסחים כו' עד זבחיך. הגה ואיכא מאן דדריש מקודש הם דאמרינן בספרי ר' יאשיה כו' עד כל התורה כולה ר"י אומר כו' עד בהדיא קדריש עכ"ה וכי פריך הכא האי מבעיא ליה כו': לז] מתיבת ועוד קשה עד תיבת ור' יצחק אומר ל"ש: לח] להביא את המעשר ואת הפסח הקטר: לט] שפיכה קאמר דומיא: מ] בכור דהוי בזריקה: מא] קדריש א"נ בכור נמי בשפיכה חוץ האמורה בבכור למעוטי שלא יהא כחטאת דבאצבע והכי נמי איתא בתוספתא דזבחים דבכור נמי בשפיכה ואין נראה זה הפירוש ודוחק גדול הוא לומר דפסח בשפיכה מדרשה שלא הביאו התלמוד ומתיבת וכי עד תיבת וכו' נראה נמחק (והגה שהגיה מרש"ק ל"ש): מב] מתוך והו' הוה: קריבה

הגהות צ"ק [א] נ"א וא"כ מאי סבר לה דפריך דאי כר"ע וכו' וגו' נ"ק בזריקה דאי כר"ע וכו': [ב] נ"ל ניכנסו ודוחק לומר דאתא למעוטי חטאת דבאצבע. תורת חיים: [ג] ור"י האי קרא מפיק ליה כו' הוי מצי למימר:

ח א מיי' פ"א מהלכות בכורות הלכה ג:
ט ב מיי' פ"ג מהלכות תמורה הלכה ב:
י ג מיי' פ"ד שם הלכה ו:
[לקמן נז. בכורות כח.]
יא ד מיי' פ"ד מהלכות קרבן פסח הלכה ו:

תורה אור

*לִימֵּד אעַל בְּכוֹר בַּעַל מוּם שֶׁנִּיתָּן לַכֹּהֵן, *שֶׁלֹּא מָצִינוּ לוֹ בְּכָל הַתּוֹרָה כּוּלָּהּ. וְרַבִּי יִשְׁמָעֵאל? נָפְקָא לֵיהּ מִ"לְּךָ יִהְיֶה" דְּסֵיפָא. בִּשְׁלָמָא לְר' יוֹסֵי הַגְּלִילִי דְּמוֹקֵי לֵיהּ נַמִי בְּמַעֲשֵׂר וּפֶסַח – הַיְינוּ דִּכְתִיב: °"לֹא תִפְדֶּה (כִּי) קֹדֶשׁ הֵם" – הֵם קְרֵיבִין, (במדבר יח) וְאֵין תְּמוּרָתָן קְרֵיבָה, (א) א] דִּתְנַן: *תְּמוּרַת בבְּכוֹר וּמַעֲשֵׂר – הֵן גוּוְלָדָן וּוְלַד וְלָדָן עַד סוֹף כָּל הָעוֹלָם – הֲרֵי הֵן כִּבְכוֹר וּמַעֲשֵׂר, וְיֵאָכְלוּ בְּמוּמָן לַבְּעָלִים; וּתְנַן, *אָמַר רַבִּי יְהוֹשֻׁעַ: שָׁמַעְתִּי שֶׁתְּמוּרַת פֶּסַח קְרֵיבָה, וּתְמוּרַת פֶּסַח אֵינָהּ קְרֵיבָה, וְאֵין לִי לְפָרֵשׁ. אֶלָּא לְרַבִּי יִשְׁמָעֵאל דְּמוֹקֵי לֵיהּ כּוּלֵּיהּ בִּבְכוֹר, מַעֲשֵׂר וּפֶסַח דְּלָא קְרֵיבָה תְּמוּרָתָן מְנָא לֵיהּ? מַעֲשֵׂר גָּמַר *עֲבָרָה עֲבָרָה מִבְּכוֹר. פֶּסַח – בְּהֶדְיָא כָּתַב בֵּיהּ: "כֶּשֶׂב", מַה ת"ל: "אִם כֶּשֶׂב" – דלְרַבּוֹת תְּמוּרַת הַפֶּסַח אַחַר הַפֶּסַח, שֶׁתִּקְרַב שְׁלָמִים. יָכוֹל אַף לִפְנֵי הַפֶּסַח כֵּן? ב] ת"ל: "הוּא". וְכָל הָנָךְ תַּנָּאֵי דְּמַפְּקִי לֵיהּ לְהַאי "דַּם זְבָחֶיךָ יִשָּׁפֵךְ" לִדְרָשָׁא אַחֲרִינָא, הַאי כָּל הַנִּיתָּנִין עַל מִזְבֵּחַ הַחִיצוֹן שֶׁנְּתָנָן מַתָּנָה אַחַת שֶׁכִּיפֵּר, מְנָא לְהוּ? ג] סָבְרִי לְהוּ כְּבֵית הִלֵּל, דְּאָמְרִי: אַף חַטָּאת שֶׁנְּתָנָהּ מַתָּנָה אַחַת כִּיפֵּר, וְיָלְפִינַן כּוּלְּהוּ מֵחַטָּאת.§ "וְהַחַטָּאת – שְׁתֵּי מַתָּנוֹת".§ *אָמַר רַב הוּנָא: מ"ט דְּב"ש? °"קַרְנֹת" "קַרְנֹת" "קַרְנוֹת" (ויקרא ד) – הֲרֵי כָּאן שֵׁשׁ, אַרְבָּעָה לְמִצְוָה וּשְׁתַּיִם לְעַכֵּב. וּבֵית הִלֵּל: "קַרְנֹת" "קַרְנֹת" "קַרְנוֹת" – הֲרֵי כָּאן אַרְבַּע, שָׁלֹשׁ לְמִצְוָה וְאַחַת לְעַכֵּב. וְאֵימָא: כּוּלְּהוּ לְמִצְוָה! כַּפָּרָה בְּכְדִי לָא אַשְׁכַּחַן. וְאִיבָּעֵית אֵימָא, הַיְינוּ טַעְמָא דְּבֵית הִלֵּל: אַהֲנֵי מִקְרָא – וְאַהֲנֵי מָסוֹרֶת, אַהֲנֵי מִקְרָא – לְטַפּוּיֵי חֲדָא, וְאַהֲנֵי מָסוֹרֶת – לְבַצּוּרֵי חֲדָא. אֶלָּא מֵעַתָּה, °"לְטֹטָפֹת" °"לְטֹטָפֹת" °"לְטוֹטָפוֹת" (דברים ו, שם יא, שמות יג) *הֲרֵי כָּאן אַרְבַּע, אַהֲנֵי (ג) קְרָא וְאַהֲנֵי מָסוֹרֶת – חֲמִשָּׁה בָּתֵּי בָּעֵי לְמֶיעֱבַד! סָבַר לָהּ כְּר' עֲקִיבָא, דְּאָמַר: "טט" בְּכַתְפֵּי שְׁתַּיִם, "פת" בְּאַפְרִיקִי שְׁתַּיִם. אֶלָּא מֵעַתָּה, °"בַּסֻּכֹּת" "בַּסֻּכֹּת" "בַּסּוּכּוֹת" (ויקרא כג) – אַהֲנֵי מִקְרָא וְאַהֲנֵי מָסוֹרֶת, חַמְשָׁה דַּפְנָתָא בָּעֵי לְמֶיעֱבַד! הָתָם

לִימֵּד עַל בְּכוֹר בַּעַל מוּם שֶׁנִּיתָּן לַכֹּהֵן שֶׁלֹּא מָצִינוּ לוֹ ד] מָקוֹם אַחֵר בְּכָל הַתּוֹרָה כּוּלָּהּ. וְ"דָמָן וְחֶלְבָּן" לֵיכָּא לְאוֹקוּמֵי בְּחַד בְּכוֹר, דְּבַעַל מוּם לֹא קָרֵב. דְּסֵיפֵיהּ. "וּכְשׁוֹק הַיָּמִין לְךָ יִהְיֶה". הַיְינוּ דִּכְתִיב קֹדֶשׁ הֵם כו' וּתְנַן כו'. כְּלוֹמַר, הַיְינוּ דְּ"קוֹדֶשׁ הֵם" מְמַעֵט נַמִי תְּמוּרַת מַעֲשֵׂר וּפֶסַח מֵהַקְרָבָה, וְגָמִיר ה] מִינָּהּ טַעְמָא דְּהָנָךְ ג' מִשְׁנָיוֹת דִּתְנַן בְּהוּ דְּלָא קָרְבִי (וּוְלָדָן). כִּבְכוֹר וּמַעֲשֵׂר. דְּאֵין נִפְדִּין בְּמוּם לָחוּל קְדוּשָּׁה עַל הַמָּעוֹת. וּמִיהוּ, ו] לֹא כִּבְכוֹר וּמַעֲשֵׂר לִקְרַב, אֶלָּא יֹאכְלוּ בְּעָלִים בְּמוּם. וּתְנַן נַמִי. בִּפְסָחִים דִּתְמוּרַת פֶּסַח לֹא קְרֵבָה. וְאֵין לִי לְפָרֵשׁ. הֵי קְרֵיבָה וְהֵי לֹא קְרֵיבָה. וְקַיְימָא לָן דִּתְמוּרָה שֶׁהֵמִיר בּוֹ אַחַר הַפֶּסַח – קְרֵיבָה, דִּתְמוּרַת שְׁלָמִים הִיא. וְשֶׁהֵמִיר בּוֹ קוֹדֶם זְמַנּוֹ – לֹא קְרֵבָה, דִּתְמוּרַת הַפֶּסַח הִיא. עֲבָרָה עֲבָרָה. "כֹּל אֲשֶׁר יַעֲבוֹר תַּחַת הַשָּׁבֶט" בְּמַעֲשֵׂר, "וְהַעֲבַרְתָּ כָל פֶּטֶר" בִּבְכוֹר. **אִם כֶּשֶׂב.** בִּשְׁלָמִים כְּתִיב. שֶׁקְּרֵיבָה שְׁלָמִים. שֶׁהֲרֵי מוּתָּר ז] נַעֲשֶׂה שְׁלָמִים מִשֶּׁעָבַר זְמַנּוֹ. **הוּא.** "זֶבַח פֶּסַח הוּא" – הוּא קָרֵב וְאֵין תְּמוּרָתוֹ קְרֵיבָה. **אַף חַטָּאת כו'.** וְיָלְפִינַן לָהּ מִקְּרָאֵי בִּשְׁמַעְתִּין, ח] וַהֲדַר יָלְפִינַן כּוּלְּהוּ זְבָחִים מֵחַטָּאת. קַרְנֹת קַרְנֹת קַרְנוֹת. שָׁלֹשׁ פָּרָשִׁיּוֹת נֶאֶמְרוּ בְּחַטָּאוֹת הַחִיצוֹנוֹת בְּוַיִּקְרָא, אַחַת בִּשְׂעִיר נָשִׂיא, וּב' בְּחַטַּאת יָחִיד – אַחַת בְּכִשְׂבָּה וְאַחַת בִּשְׂעִירָה, בִּשְׁתַּיִם כְּתִיב "עַל קַרְנֹת" חָסֵר, וְהָאַחַת מָלֵא. וּב"ש אִית לְהוּ יֵשׁ אֵם לַמִּקְרָא – הֲרֵי כָּאן שֵׁשׁ, וְאֵין בַּמִּזְבֵּחַ אֶלָּא אַרְבַּע, ט] וְהַשְּׁתַּיִם יְתֵירוֹת לֹא נֶאֶמְרוּ אֶלָּא שֶׁשָּׁנָה עָלֶיהָ הַכָּתוּב לְעַכֵּב. אַרְבַּע נֶאֶמְרוּ לְמִצְוָה, שֶׁמִּצְוָה בְּאַרְבַּע מַתָּנוֹת, וּשְׁתַּיִם נִשְׁנוּ מֵהֶן לְעַכֵּב. וּב"ה. סָבְרִי: יֵשׁ אֵם לַמָּסוֹרֶת. הִלְכָּךְ, הֲרֵי י] ד', ג' מֵהֶן לְמִצְוָה נֶאֶמְרוּ, שֶׁמִּצְוָה לְכַתְּחִילָּה לִיתֵּן אַף עֲלֵיהֶן, וְהָאַחַת מְעַכֶּבֶת, כִּדְמְפָרֵשׁ וְאָזֵיל. **וְאֵימָא כּוּלְּהוּ** לְמִצְוָה. וְאֵין כָּאן יא] אַחַת לְעַכֵּב, שֶׁהֲרֵי לֹא שָׁנָה בְּאַחַת מֵהֶן. **בִּכְדִי.** בְּלֹא מַתַּן דָּמִים. **אַהֲנֵי** יב] **קְרָא.** דְּמַשְׁמַע שֵׁשׁ. **וְאַהֲנֵי מָסוֹרֶת.** דְּמַשְׁמַע אַרְבַּע. הִלְכָּךְ טְפֵי חֲדָא אַמָּסוֹרֶת וּבְצִיר חֲדָא מִמִּקְרָא, וְהָווּ לְהוּ חָמֵשׁ, נִמְצָא שֶׁשָּׁנָה בְּאַחַת. לְטֹטָפֹת לְטֹטָפֹת לְטוֹטָפוֹת. דְּיָלְפִינַן מִינָּהּ אַרְבַּע בָּתִּים לִתְפִילִּין, וַאֲנַן בְּכוּלְּהוּ "לְטוֹטָפוֹת" קָרֵינַן, יג] נַמִי אַהֲנֵי קְרָא כו'. סָבְרִי לָהּ כְּרַבִּי עֲקִיבָא. דְּיָלֵיף לָהּ מִקְּרָא אַחֲרִינָא. **כַּתְפֵּי.** שֵׁם מָקוֹם. הָתָם

[שבת פג: וש"נ]
תמורה כא.
פסחים לו:
[לעיל ט. מעילה יג: תמורה ה:]
סנהדרין ד.
סנהדרין ד: מנחות לד:

הגהות הב"ח
(א) גמ' ואין תמורתן קריבה ותנן: (ב) שם אהני מקרא:

תוכל לדקדק דזריקה בכלל שפיכה, דכיון דקאמר דבירך על הפסח פטר את הזבח – אם כן סבירא ליה דמתנותיהם שוין, ואף פסח בזריקה. והא דזבח לא פטר פסח – משום יד] דזבח טפל לו. וכיון דפסח בזריקה, אם כן אייתר ליה "דם זבחיך ישפך" טו] ומצי למידרש מיניה לומר דזריקה בכלל שפיכה. ולא גרים "ולא שפיכה בכלל זריקה", דלהאי תנא דרבי ישמעאל כולהו בזריקה. ולדברי ר"ע טז] דלא זה פוטר את זה – אם כן אין מתנותיהם שוות, דפסח בשפיכה מקרא: "ודם זבחיך ישפך", ואם כן לא זריקה בכלל שפיכה ולא שפיכה בכלל זריקה, דהא "ודם זבחיך" איצטריך ליה לדידיה לומר דפסח בשפיכה. ולהאי פירושא קשה מכל מקום מההיא ד"האשה" (פסחים דף פט.). ועוד: מנא ליה לרבי ישמעאל דזריקה בכלל שפיכה משום דמייתר "ודם זבחיך ישפך"? דלמא אתא לכל הניתנין על מזבח החיצון שנתנן במתנה אחת כיפר! וה"ר חיים אומ"ר דבספרי"ם ישני"ם גרסינן: כשתימצי לומר לדברי רבי ישמעאל זריקה בכלל שפיכה ושפיכה בכלל זריקה. דהכל אחד, דכל הקרבנות בזריקה לרבי ישמעאל, ואין לחוש אם בזריקה אם בשפיכה, והיינו כשיטת רבינו שמואל. וכל מה שהקשיתי עליו קשה גם לפי' זה. ולכולהו לישני קשה: אי פסח בשפיכה (לרבי עקיבא) אם כן דריש לקרא יז] ד"דמו" כרבי ישמעאל, *"ובשרם" דהנך (קאמר) כרבי ישמעאל, ואחד תם ואחד בעל מום נפקא ליה יח] מ"יהיה לך". ולקמן בסוף "איזהו מקומן" (דף נז.) פליג רבי עקיבא ארבי ישמעאל, ומוקי לה לקרא ד"ובשרם" אחד תם ואחד בעל מום, כרבי יוסי הגלילי דהכא! **אחד** תם ואחד בעל מום. אע"ג יט] ד"יהיו לך כחזה התנופה וכשוק התרומה" מוקמינן ליה בסוף "איזהו מקומן" (שם) ובבכורות (כז:) בבכור תם, רישיה דקרא ד"בשרם" לשון רבים נקט משום בעל מום. **שלא** מצינו כ] לו בכל התורה כולה. פירש בקונט': שלא מצינו לו קרא אחר בכל התורה כולה. ונראה לפרש: שלא מצינו בכל התורה כענין זה, דשאר פסולי המוקדשין אינו מתנה לכהן, אלא פודהו ומקריב אחר תחתיו, וזה מתנה לכהן ואוכלו במומו. כא] כי האי גוונא בפ' "שתי מדות" (מנחות נא.): שלא מצינו בכל התורה שיהא טפל חמור מן העיקר, גבי כב] "את הכבש" – זו עולת יולדת, "האחד" – זו אחד עשר של מעשר א). **קודש** הם הם קריבין ואין תמורתן קריבה. תימה: דבפ"ק דתמורה (דף ה:) בין אביי ורבא מוקמי "הם" *לבכור ומעשר שנתערבו כג] בכל העולין, שקריבין לגבי מזבח. ואין תמורתן קריבה נפקא להו מדכתיב "לה'" – הוא קרב ואין תמורתו קריבה. ועוד קשה: דאביי גופיה דריש ליה התם בפרק "אלו קדשים" (תמורה כא.) מקרא דהכא, מדכתיב "קודש הם"! **שמעתי** שתמורת פסח קריבה ותמורת פסח אינה קריבה. מפרש התם: כד] בפסח שנמצא קודם שחיטה ירעה, וכן תמורתו, *משום פסח עצמו דלא קרב – לא קרבה תמורתו. ועוד איכא כה] למאן דאמר התם דנמצא קודם שחיטה והמיר בו אחר שחיטה – תמורתו קריבה שלמים, אע"פ שהפסח רועה. ואע"ג דדרשינן: הוא קרב ואין תמורתו קריבה – הכי קאמר: הוא קרב, כלומר פסח כו] קרב, ואין תמורתו קריבה – כשהוא מימר בפסח, *דחזי, ללישנא קמא דרבה דבפרק "מי שהיה טמא" (פסחים צו:) אפילו המיר בו לאחר שחיטה, וללישנא בתרא היכא דהמיר קודם שחיטה. וההוא לישנא לא קאי, דאיתותב התם. וקצת קשה: הא דדרשינן "קודש הם" אבכור מעשר ופסח הם קריבים ואין תמורתן קריבה, דלא הוי מעין אחד, דגבי פסח אם המיר בפסח עצמו שקרב לשם פסח – תמורתו נמי קריבה, דאם איתא דלא קרב – אמאי איתותב התם לשון שני של רבה? לימא דברייתא בהכי מיירי! ועוד דרשינן התם: "אם כשב" – לרבות פסח שעברה שנתו, ושלמים הבאים מחמת פסח לכל מצות שלמים. ופירש התם בקונט': שלמים הבאין מחמת פסח – דהיינו תמורת הפסח עצמו. ובענין אחר לא מיתוקם, כדפרישית לעיל פ"ק (דף ט.) ובכל מקום שהפסח קרב, או לשם פסח או לשם שלמים – גם התמורה קריבה, כיון דלא אתיא מכח קדושה דחויה. ול"ע אם יכול להקריב התמורה לשם פסח קודם שחיטה, דשמא יש לדרוש: הוא קרב לשם פסח, ואין תמורתו קריבה לשם פסח, אבל לשם שלמים קריבה כשקרב הוא לשם פסח. **הרי** כאן שש. וא"ת: בחמש סגי, דלאחת לא איצטריך, דכפרה בכדי לא אשכחן! וי"ל: דדילמא ב"ש לית ליה האי טעמא. **לטוטפות**. ואמר רבינו תם: דבספרים מדוייקים לא כתיב "לטוטפות" כלל בוי"ו לבסוף, כז] אלא וי"ו ד"ולטטפת" דריש. ואפילו למאן דלא דריש וי"ו – וי"ו למ"ד דריש, כדאמר גבי "והנותר" פ' "הערל" (יבמות עב:). ויש מפרשים ד"לטוטפת" דריש, דכתיב "לטוטפת" מלא בוי"ו, דוי"ו דבין שני הטיתין דריש, וקסבר: גורעין ומוסיפין ודורשין. ואומר רבינו תם: דלא אמרינן גורעין ומוסיפין ודורשין באמצע התיבה, אלא בתחלת התיבה או בסוף, כדאשכחן בפרק "הזהב" (ב"מ דף נד:) גבי "וחמישיתו", וגבי "דם מהפר" יקבלנו, ב) וגבי "ונתתם את נחלתו לשארו" ב"ש נוחלין" (ב"ב דף קיא*:)*. **טט** בכתפי שתים. וא"ת: א"כ ליבעי תרי סרי בתי! כח] וי"ל: כיון דמנין הוא – איך הוו להו כפרשה שנאמרה ונשנית. ולא דמו לקרנות, שאין המנין כתוב בפירוש. וה"ר יהודה מקורבי"ל מפרש: דחד "טטפת" לגופיה, ואיך תרתי אתו ג) למנין כט] בתים, בלשון כתפי ובל' אפריקי*. **אלא** מעתה בסכת כו'. ל] במס' סוכה (דף ו:) דדרשינן לדפנות, וכן בפ' "המביא" (ביצה ל:) גבי אין נוטלים עצים מן הסוכה אסרינן נמי מן הדפנות, מדכתיב "חג הסוכות", דכשם שחל שם שמים על לא] החגיגה כך חל על הסוכה. ותימה: דגבי אין מסככין בדבר המקבל טומאה, וגבי תעשה ולא מן העשוי, לא לב] דרשינן לדפנות. התם

א) [וע"ע תוס' בכורות כח. ד"ה שלא] ב) [לעיל כה.] ג) נ"א למנין ד' בתים נ"ק

ס"א לכ"ע

נ"א ובשרם עליהו דהנך בכורות קאמר כר"י וכו'

נ"א לדרשא אחריתי אביי מוקי הם בהוייתן יהו ורבא מוקי לבכור כו' ועיין נ"ק

ע' נ"ק שמהפך הגירס' של תוס' בשם ס"י וע' בסוגיא דהתם בפסחים שם

נ"א מיהו

[וע"ע תוס' סנהדרין ד: ותוס' מנחות לד: ד"ה לטוטפת]

[וע"ע שם בסנהדרין ובמנחות לד: בתוס' ד"ה טוטי]

שיטה מקובצת

א] קריבה ותנן אות ד' נמחק: ב] ת"ל הוא האי דרשא גמורה היא אבל אם כבש לרבות תמורת פסח אחר הפסח שקרב שלמים אסמכתא בעלמא היא כדאמרינן בפ' מי שהיה טמא דאם כבש בא לרבות שעברה שנתו: ג] סברי להו כב"ה וקשה דאטו אותם תנאי דנפקי ניתנים במתנה אחת כיפר מודם זבחיך שבקי ב"ה ועבדי כב"ש וי"ל דאתיא שפיר כב"ה נמי למידרש מודם זבחיך [כל הניתנין על מזבח החיצון] שנתנן מתנה אחת כיפר בשאר קרבנות דהוי שונה הכתוב לעכב הלכך הו"א אע"ג דבחטאת במתנה אחת כיפר מ"מ שאר קרבנות דכתיב טובא סביב בפרשה ליבעי שתי מתנות שהן ד' לעכב לכך איצטריך ודם זבחיך ישפך. ת' מהר"פ והן כתובין בדפוס [בד"ה מנין למעלה דף לו ע"ב בריש הפרק]: ד] לו מקרא אחר בכל התורה כולה שבכור בעל מום לא קרב ודמן וחלבן ליכא לאוקמי אלא אחד בכור דבעל: ה] מיניה טעמא דהנך כו' קרב תמורתן וולדן הס"ד: ו] ומיהו לאו כבכור: ז] מותר הפסח נעשה: ח] והדר ילפי כולהו מקראי: ט] ארבע קרנות והשתים: י] הרי זו ד': יא] כאן אפילו אחת: יב] אהני מקרא. דמשמע: יג] קרינן נימא נמי כו' סברי לה ב"ה: יד] משום דפסח עיקר והזבח טפל: טו] תיבות ומצי למידרש מיניה נמחק: טז] מתיבות דלא זה כו' עד תיבת לא זריקה בס"א אינו: יז] דקרא דדמם ובשרם דהנך בבכורות כר"י: יח] ליה מלך יהיה ולקמן כו' פליג ר"ע אדרבי ישמעאל: יט] אע"ג דכחזה התנופה ושוק הימין מוקמינן: כ] מקרא אחר בכל התורה וקשה דהא בכל התלמוד לא אשכחן כי האי לישנא ובכל מקום שמרבינן שום דבר מקרא יכול לומר שלא מצינו כו' לכך נראה לפרש: כא] במומו וכי האי גוונא אשכחן בפ': כב] גבי לכבש זו שנתערבו דמן בכל העולין הקריבין לגבי מזבח כו' נפקא להו מדכתיב לה': כד] התם בפסחים הפסח שנמצא כו' ירעה כו' וכן תמורתו משום דהואיל והוא עצמו לא קרב לא: כה] איכא לישנא דאמר ותיבת למאן ל"ש: כו] פסח כשר קרב ואין כו' בפסח דחוי ללישנא קמא: כז] לבסוף בין פא לתיו: כח] בתי דשלשה טוטפת כתיבי: כט] למנין ד' בתים: ל] כו' הכא דרשינן ותיבות במס' סוכה ואות ד' נמחק: לא] דכשם שחל שם שמים על [סככו] כך חל על הדפנות ותימה: לב] דרשינן ס"א לא חיישינן:

הָתָם (א) חַד קְרָא א] כּוּלֵּיהּ לְגוּפֵיהּ, וְחַד לִסְכָכָה, אֲתַאי הִלְכְתָא וּגְרַעְתָּהּ לַשְּׁלִישִׁית וְאוֹקִימְתָּהּ אַטֶּפַח. אֶלָּא מֵעַתָּה, °"וְטָמְאָה שְׁבוּעַיִם" – שִׁבְעִים, אַהֲנֵי קְרָא וְאַהֲנֵי מָסוֹרֶת – אַרְבָּעִים וּתְרֵין בָּעֲיָא לְמֵיתַב! שָׁאנֵי הָתָם, דִּכְתִי': °"כְּנִדָּתָהּ". וְתַנָּא מַיְיתֵי לַהּ מֵהָכָא: *°"וְכִפֶּר" "וְכִפֶּר" "וְכִפֶּר" – מִפְּנֵי הַדִּין. ב] שֶׁיָּכוֹל, וַהֲלֹא דִּין הוּא: נֶאֶמְרוּ דָּמִים לְמַטָּה וְנֶאֶמְרוּ דָּמִים לְמַעְלָה, מַה ג] מַתַּן דָּמִים הָאֲמוּרִים לְמַטָּה שֶׁנְּתָנָן בְּמַתָּנָה אַחַת כִּיפֵּר – אַף דָּמִים הָאֲמוּרִים לְמַעְלָה שֶׁנְּתָנָן בְּמַתָּנָה אַחַת כִּיפֵּר. אוֹ כְּלָךְ לְדֶרֶךְ זוֹ: נֶאֶמְרוּ דָּמִים בִּפְנִים וְנֶאֶמְרוּ דָּמִים בַּחוּץ, מַה דָּמִים הָאֲמוּרִים בִּפְנִים – חִיסֵּר אַחַת מִן הַמַּתָּנוֹת לֹא עָשָׂה וְלֹא כְּלוּם, אַף דָּמִים הָאֲמוּרִין בַּחוּץ – חִיסֵּר אַחַת מִן הַמַּתָּנוֹת לֹא עָשָׂה וְלֹא כְּלוּם! נִרְאֶה לְמִי דּוֹמֶה, דָּנִין חוּץ מֵחוּץ, וְאֵין דָּנִין חוּץ ד] מִבִּפְנִים. אוֹ כְּלָךְ לְדֶרֶךְ זוֹ: דָּנִין חַטָּאת וְאַרְבַּע קְרָנוֹת מֵחַטָּאת וְאַרְבַּע קְרָנוֹת, וְאַל יוֹכִיחַ חוּץ, שֶׁאֵין חַטָּאת וְאַרְבַּע קְרָנוֹת! תַּלְמוּד לוֹמַר: "וְכִפֶּר" "וְכִפֶּר" "וְכִפֶּר" (מִפְּנֵי הַדִּין) "וְכִפֶּר" – אע"פ שֶׁלֹּא נָתַן אֶלָּא שָׁלֹשׁ, "וְכִפֶּר" – אע"פ שֶׁלֹּא נָתַן אֶלָּא שְׁתַּיִם, "וְכִפֶּר" – אע"פ שֶׁלֹּא נָתַן אֶלָּא אַחַת. וְהַאי מִיבָּעֵי לֵיהּ לְגוּפֵיהּ! אָמַר רָבָא: בַּר אַדָּא מָרִי אַסְבְּרָהּ לִי, אָמַר קְרָא: "וְכִפֶּר וְנִסְלַח" – זוֹ הִיא כַּפָּרָה זוֹ הִיא סְלִיחָה. אֵימָא: "וְכִפֶּר" – אע"פ שֶׁלֹּא נָתַן אֶלָּא שָׁלֹשׁ לְמַעְלָה וְאַחַת לְמַטָּה, "וְכִפֶּר" – אע"פ שֶׁלֹּא נָתַן אֶלָּא שְׁתַּיִם לְמַטָּה וּשְׁתַּיִם לְמַעְלָה, "וְכִפֶּר" – אע"פ שֶׁלֹּא נָתַן לְמַעְלָה אֶלָּא לְמַטָּה! אָמַר רַב אַדָּא בַּר יִצְחָק: א"כ, בִּיטַּלְתָּ תּוֹרַת אַרְבַּע קְרָנוֹת. וְאִי רַחֲמָנָא אָמַר – לִיבַּטְּלוּן! אָמַר *רָבָא: אֵיזֶהוּ דָּבָר שֶׁצָּרִיךְ שָׁלֹשׁ – הֱוֵי אוֹמֵר: אֵלּוּ קְרָנוֹת. ה] אֵימָא: "וְכִפֶּר" – אע"פ שֶׁלֹּא נָתַן אֶלָּא ו] אַחַת לְמַעְלָה וְשָׁלֹשׁ לְמַטָּה! לֹא מָצִינוּ דָּמִים שֶׁחֶצְיָין לְמַעְלָה וְחֶצְיָין לְמַטָּה. וְלָא? וְהָתְנַן: *א"הִזָּה מִמֶּנּוּ אַחַת לְמַעְלָה וְשֶׁבַע לְמַטָּה! (ב) ז] "כְּמַצְלִיף". מַאי "כְּמַצְלִיף"? מַחֲוֵי רַב יְהוּדָה: כְּמַנְגְּדָנָא. *ב"הִזָּה עַל טָהֳרוֹ שֶׁל מִזְבֵּחַ שֶׁבַע פְּעָמִים"; מַאי

ויקרא יב | שם | שם ד | ל"ג | יומא נח:

רש"י

הָתָם דַּל חַד (ג) לְגוּפֵיהּ. פָּשׁוּ לְהוּ אַרְבַּע. וְחַד לִסְכָךְ. מֵאַחַר שֶׁהִתְחִיל לְפָרֵשׁ ח] תַּבְנִיתָהּ פֵּירֵשׁ סְכָךְ עִם דְּפָנוֹתֶיהָ – פָּשׁוּ תְּלָת. אֲתַאי הִילְכְתָא. שֶׁנֶּאֶמְרָה לְמֹשֶׁה מִסִּינַי וּגְרַעְתָּהּ לַשְּׁלִישִׁית – כָּךְ נֶאֶמְרָה הֲלָכָה שֶׁהַשְּׁלִישִׁית דַּיָּיהּ בְּטֶפַח, הַיְינוּ דִּתְנַן: שְׁתַּיִם כְּהִלְכָתָן, שְׁלִישִׁית אֲפִי' טֶפַח. וְטָמְאָה שְׁבוּעַיִם שִׁבְעִים. כְּתִיב, נֵימָא נַמִי: אַהֲנֵי מָסוֹרֶת לְטַפּוּיֵי פַּלְגָּא דְּתוֹסֶפְ' שִׁבְעִים *עַל שְׁבוּעַיִם, וְאַהֲנֵי מִקְרָא לְגַלּוּיֵי פַּלְגָּא – נִמְצֵאתָ מוֹסִיף עַל שְׁבוּעַי' כ"ח, חֶצְיוֹ שֶׁל נ"ו. ט] בָּעֲיָ' לְמֵיתַב. יְמֵי טוּמְאָה יוֹלֶדֶת נְקֵבָה. שָׁאנֵי הָתָם דִּכְתִיב כְּנִדָּתָהּ. מַשְׁמַע שֶׁלֹּא יָרַד הַכָּתוּב לְמִנְיַן יָמִים אֶלָּא לְמִנְיַן שָׁבוּעוֹת, שֶׁהַנִּדָּה שָׁבוּעַ אַחַת וְהַיּוֹלֶדֶת שְׁבוּעַיִם. שֶׁאִם אַתָּה אוֹמֵר שִׁבְעִים – הִפְלַגְתָּ מִתּוֹרַת נִדָּה הַרְבֵּה, אֲבָל כְּשֶׁאַתָּה אוֹמֵר שְׁבוּעַיִם – קֵרַבְתָּ' לְתוֹרַת נִדָּה. וְתַנָּא. י] דְּמַתְנִי', לָא מַיְיתֵי לְהָא דְּב"ה כְּרַב הוּנָא, אֶלָּא מֵהָכָא. וְכִפֶּר וְכִפֶּר וְכִפֶּר. בִּשְׂעִיר נָשִׂיא וּשְׂעִירָה יא] וְכִשְׂבָּה, שֶׁכּוּלָּן עַל הַמִּזְבֵּחַ הַחִיצוֹן. מִפְּנֵי הַדִּין. יב] שֶׁחָזַר חֲלִילָה, וּמְלַמֵּד עַל הַחַטָּאת הַחִיצוֹנָה שֶׁכָּל מַתְּנוֹתֶיהָ מְעַכְּבוֹת – לְכָךְ נֶאֶמְרוּ אֵלּוּ, לְהַכְשִׁיר אִם חִיסֵּר. וַהֲלֹא דִּין הוּא. יג] לְהַכְשִׁירָהּ בְּמַתָּנָה אַחַת, וּקְרָא לָמָּה לִי? נֶאֶמְרוּ דָּמִים לְמַטָּה. מִחוּט הַסִּיקְרָא, כָּל הַדָּמִים חוּץ מֵחַטָּאת. וְנֶאֶמְרוּ דָּמִים לְמַעְלָה מִחוּט הַסִּיקְרָא – חַטָּאת. מַה יד] תַּחְתּוֹנִים כִּפֵּר בְּמַתָּנָה אַחַת, •דִּכְתִיב: "וְדַם זְבָחֶיךָ יִשָּׁפֵךְ". וּמִיהוּ, חַטָּאת מֵהַאי קְרָא לָא יָלֵיף, דְּלָא טו] שַׁיְיכֵי בֵּיהּ לְשׁוֹן שְׁפִיכָה כִּי אִם זְרִיקָה, שֶׁהִיא בְּמַתְּנַת אֶצְבַּע. אֶלָּא בְּבִנְיַן אָב לָמֵד מִן הַתַּחְתּוֹנִים, דְּאַף הוּא כִּפֵּר בְּמַתָּנָה אַחַת. בִּפְנִים. בַּחַטָּאוֹת הַפְּנִימִיּוֹת. בַּחוּץ. בַּחַטָּאוֹת הַחִיצוֹנוֹת. לֹא עָשָׂה וְלֹא כְלוּם. בְּפִירְקִין יָלְפִינַן לָהּ. חוּץ מֵחוּץ. חַטָּאת מֵעוֹלָה. דָּנִין חַטָּאת. הַחִיצוֹנָה, שֶׁהִיא חַטָּאת וּכְתִיב בָּהּ אַרְבַּע קְרָנוֹת, כְּמוֹ שֶׁאָמַרְנוּ לְמַעְלָה "קַרְנֹת" "קַרְנֹת" "קְרָנוֹת", מֵחַטָּאת הַפְּנִימִית, שֶׁהִיא חַטָּאת וְנֶאֶמְרוּ בָּהּ אַרְבַּע קְרָנוֹת, כִּדִלְקַמָּן: לְמַעְלָה הוּא אוֹמֵר "קֶרֶן" "קַרְנוֹת" בְּפַר כֹּהֵן מָשִׁיחַ – הֲרֵי שְׁתַּיִם, לְמַטָּה הוּא אוֹמֵר בְּפַר הָעֵדָה "קֶרֶן" "קַרְנוֹת" – טז] אַרְבַּע. וְלֹא יוֹכִיחַ חוּץ. דִּשְׁאָר *דָּמִים יז] חוּץ, וְלֹא נֶאֱמַר בָּהֶן קְרָנוֹת. מִיבָּעֵי לֵיהּ לְגוּפֵיהּ. בְּכָל חַד וְחַד, לְלַמֶּדְךָ שֶׁכִּפֵּר עַל הַחֵטְא. אֵימָא וְכִפֶּר כו'. אֲבָל לְמֵיעַקְרִינְהוּ לְגַמְרֵי לָא! א"כ. דְּדָרְשִׁינַן: כִּפֵּר אע"פ שֶׁנְּתָנָן כּוּלָּן לְמַטָּה מִן הַחוּט. בִּטַּלְתָּ תּוֹרַת קְרָנוֹת. הַכְּתוּבִים בְּחַטָּאת, וְעַל חִנָּם כְּתִיב בָּהּ קְרָנוֹת, דְּהַיְינוּ לְמַעְלָה. וּפָרְכִינַן: וְאִי יח] דְּרַחֲמָנָא אָמַר. דְּלִיבַּטְּלוּן בְּדִיעֲבַד מִ"וְּכִפֶּר" – לִיבַּטְּלוּן, וְכִי כְּתָבִינְהוּ – לְמִצְוָה כְּתָבִינְהוּ! אֵיזֶהוּ דָּבָר שֶׁצָּרִיךְ שְׁלֹשָׁה. "וְכִפֶּר", הֱוֵי אוֹמֵר אֵלּוּ קְרָנוֹת, וּכְדְאָמְרִינַן דְּכָל חַד וְחַד מִיעֵט יט] חֲדָא קֶרֶן, וְקָם לֵיהּ אַקֶּרֶן אַחַת לְעַכֵּב. דְּאִי כִּדְקָאָמְרַתְּ, לְאַשְׁמוּעִינַן דְּאִי יָהֵיב כּוּלְּהוּ לְמַטָּה כָּשֵׁר כ] (לְמַטָּה) – אַרְבַּע "וְכִפֶּר" הֲוָה לֵיהּ לְמִיכְתַּב, לְהַכְשִׁיר אַרְבַּע הַמַּתָּנוֹת לְמַטָּה. וְאֵימָא וְכִפֶּר אַף ע"פ שֶׁלֹּא נָתַן אֶלָּא אַחַת לְמַעְלָה וְשָׁלֹשׁ לְמַטָּן. וּלְהָכִי לָא כְּתִיבֵי אַרְבָּעָה, מִשּׁוּם דַּחֲדָא מִיהָא כא] (לָא) מְעַכְּבָא בִּלְמַעְלָה, וּתְלָת אִיתַּכְשְׁרֵי לְמַטָּה. אֲבָל לְמֵיעַקְרִינְהוּ – לָא! הִזָּה מִמֶּנּוּ. מִדַּם פַּר יוֹם הַכִּפּוּרִים, בְּסֵדֶר יוֹמָא. אַחַת לְמַעְלָה וְשֶׁבַע לְמַטָּה. כְּדִכְתִיב: "עַל פְּנֵי הַכַּפֹּרֶת קֵדְמָה וְלִפְנֵי הַכַּפֹּרֶת יַזֶּה שֶׁבַע פְּעָמִים" (ויקרא טז), וְקָא ס"ד: אַחַת מֵחֲלִי עָבְיוֹ שֶׁל כַּפֹּרֶת וּלְמַעְלָה, וְשֶׁבַע מֵחֶצְיָהּ וּלְמַטָּה. וּמְשַׁנֵּי: הַהוּא כְּמַצְלִיף. כִּדְמְפָרֵשׁ וְאָזֵיל. כְּמַנְגְּדָנָא. כְּאָדָם הַמַּכֶּה מַלְקוּת אַרְבָּעִים בִּרְצוּעָה, כב] זוֹ לְמַטָּה מִזּוֹ בְּסָמוּךְ, וְלֹא שֶׁכִּיוֵּן אַחַת מֶחֶצְיוֹ וּלְמַעְלָה וְהַשְּׁאָר מֶחֶצְיוֹ וּלְמַטָּה. וְהָא דְּקָתָנֵי הָאַחַת חֲלוּקָה מֵהַשֶּׁבַע – כג] לְעִנְיַן לִידּוּד יָדוֹ קָתָנֵי, כִּדְמְפָרֵשׁ הָתָם: כְּשֶׁהוּא מַזֶּה לְמַעְלָה – מְגַדֵּד יָדוֹ לְמַטָּה, וּכְשֶׁהוּא מַזֶּה לְמַטָּה – מְגַדֵּד יָדוֹ לְמַעְלָה. הִזָּה עַל טָהֳרוֹ. וְהָתְנַן הָתָם: הִזָּה עַל טָהֳרוֹ שֶׁל מִזְבֵּחַ הַפְּנִימִי, כְּדִכְתִיב: "וְהִזָּה עָלָיו מִן הַדָּם" וגו' (גם זה שם). מַאי

[סנהדרין ד: כל הענין] | סנהדרין ד: | ס"א רב | יומא טו. נג:

תוספות

התם כד] חד קרא כוליה לגופיה. לא דמי ל"קרנות" דדרשינן תחילות. ד"קרנות" משמע מניינא, אבל "סוכות" לא משמע מניין דפנות, אלא משמע שתי סוכות, הלכך אין לנו לדרוש תחילות. וא"ע גבי "אלהים" (סנהדרין דף ג:) דמשמע נמי מניין, ולא דרשינן תחילות.

ארבעין ותרתין. חלי שבעים וחלי ארבעה עשר.

כה] דכתיב כנדתה. פי': כשיעור נדתה יש לך להוסיף אנקבה יותר מן הזכר. כו] ובפ' קמא דסנהדרין (דף ד.) לא מייתי ליה להאי "כנדתה".

דנין חטאת וארבע קרנות. תימה: דאפילו חוץ מפנים בעי למילף משום חטאת וארבע קרנות – כל שכן פנים מבפנים. ולקמן מצריך קרא לכל הפנימים דמעכבי, ולא ילפי מהדדי. *דדריש: "לפר" – זה כז] הפר כהן המשיח, להקישו לפר העלם דבר של ציבור, לומר דמעכבי, וביום הכפורים צריך קרא! וכפר אע"פ שלא נתן למעלה אלא למטה. תימה: אמאי איפסיק מסדר שהתחיל לדרוש, דהוה ליה למימר: "וכפר" – אע"פ שלא נתן כח] למעלה אלא אחת ושלש למטה! וי"ל: דלא משמע ליה לדרוש שיעשה למטה אלא בהכשר דמים הניתנין למטה. ושתים למעלה וב' למטה דקאמר – היינו שיעשה למטה כט] אחת שהיא שתים, וכן "וכפר" אע"פ שנתן כולן למטה – היינו כדין שאר דמים הניתנין *למטה. אבל אי אמרת אחת למעלה ושלש למטה – הוי למטה אחת שהיא שתים, ואחת שהיא אחת – ל] פוסל. והיינו תרי שינויי, שרובה למטה, וגם האחת אינו כמשפט דמים של מטה. אבל שלש למעלה ואחת למטה, אע"פ שאותה אחת אינו כמשפט – אין קפידא, כיון שהרוב למעלה, ע"כ. ומשני רבא: איזהו דבר שצריך שלש "וכפר" – הוי אומר לא] זה קרנות. פירוש: דלדידך בתרי "וכפר" סגי, דכיון דלא בעינן קרא לאחת למעלה ושלש למטה, לפי שאינו כדין דמים הניתנין למטה – אם כן שלש למעלה ואחת למטה נמי, אע"ג דרובן למעלה – לא ליבעי קרא, דאין זה כדין לב] הניתנין למטה, שכל הניתנין למטה ממתנות ארבע הויא אחת שהיא שתים. ופריך: ואימא "וכפר" אע"פ שלא נתן אלא אחת למעלה ושלש למטה, לג] ולא כולן למטה. ולא אחוש בסברא זו, דטוב להכשיר אחת למעלה לד] מכולן למטה! (הגה"ה תוספת. ודברי רש"י יש לה] לפרש דסבירא ליה כיון ד"וכפר" שלישי אתי לשלש למטה, כיון דהרוב למטה כשר – הוא הדין כולן למטה. ומשני: איזהו דבר שצריך שלש "וכפר", כו' ולדבריך ארבע "וכפר" היה לו ליכתוב, והוא הדין שלך אינו טוב. והדר פריך: ודילמא שלש למטה דוקא כשר, ולא כולן. מיהו לישנא דצריך שלש, דמשמע ולדבריך אינו צריך שלש – לו] משמע כפי' התוס'. ע"כ הגה"ה). וצריך לדקדק: אמאי לא דרשינן להני לז] "וכפר" – אע"פ שלא נתן לקרנות כלומר בחודה, "וכפר" – אע"פ שלא נתן באצבע, "וכפר" – אע"פ שלא נתן ארבע מתנות אלא שתים שהן ד'? לח] וזה אין להקשות, דהכא דרשינן "וכפר" לגמרי ואפילו בשר שרי באכילה, ולעיל בפרק שני (דף כו:) דרשינן: לכפרה נתתיו ולא לדבר אחר. דיש לחלק בין "לכפר" בין ל"וכפר".

לט] כמצליף. תימה: ומאי ס"ד דמקשה? הא בהדיא קתני הכי בסיפא ביומא פ' "הוציאו לו" (דף נג:) דתנן: לא היה מתכוין להזות לא למעלה ולא למטה אלא כמצליף! וי"ל: שבא לתרץ דהאי כמצליף – כמנגדנא, והכל במקום אחד. וכמו שמפורש בערוך: מ] כמנגדנא – שמריס ידו ואינו מכה עד שיורד. ירושלמי: מצליף – מא] *כמטברר. פי' בערוך: שמטה ידו עד טיבורו. מאי לאו אפלגיה דמזבח. ואם כן מצינו דמים חציין למעלה וחציין למטה, דמתחלה נתן מב] אקרנות ואחר כך לחצי המזבח. תוספות. ורש"י מפרש בע"א.

וליתניה

ס"א מא] מצליף

עין משפט נר מצוה

יב א ב מיי' פ"ה מהל' עבודת יוה"כ הל' ה:

מסורת הש"ס — גליונות

גי' הג"ק על שבועים דהוי נ"ו ואהני מ'

גי' הג"ק דדריש לפר זה פר יוה"כ כלומר עשה לפר זה פר כהן משוח להקישו כו' לומר למה דמעכבי ולמה צריך קרא הס"ד. ועיין סנהדרין דף ד ע"ב ד"ה דנין דמתרצו קושיא זו

למטה שנים שהן ד' אבל כו' נ"ק

הגהות הב"ח

(א) גמ' התם דל חד קרא כוליה לגופיה וחד לסכך פשו תלת אתאי הלכתא וכו' אהני מקרא: (ב) שם ובשבע למטה הוא דהוי כמצליף: (ג) רש"י ד"ה התם דל חד קרא לגופיה:

נ"ל דמים שאינם חטאת ולא נאמר כו' נ"ק

גליון הש"ס

רש"י ד"ה נאמרו דמים וכו' דכתיב ודם זבחיך. עיין לעיל דף לו ע"ב תוס' ד"ה מנין:

שיטה מקובצת

א] התם דל חד קרא לגופיה וחד לסכך אתאי: ב] תיבת שיכול נמחק: ג] תיבת מתן נמחק: ד] חוץ מפנים אות ב' נמחק: ה] ואימא וכפר וכו'. וא"ת לעיל מעיקרא נמי למה לא קאמר כמו שאמר השתא ודילג באמצע שהיה לו לפרש ולדרוש וכפר אע"פ שלא נתן אלא אחת למעלה וכו' וי"ל דאין סברא שיכפר אלא בהכשר דמים הניתנים למטה ובכאן נמי אם נתנם למטה אחת שהן שתים כיפר אבל ג' למטה דהיינו אחת שהיא אחת ואחת שהיא שתים לא כיפר שלא מצינו בזה הכשר דמים וקאמר א"כ בטלת ד' קרנות כך כתוב בכל הספרים ונראה דה"פ כיון שבאת לדרוש כך אע"פ שלא נתן כולן אלא למטה א"כ על חנם כתיב ד' מתנות על ד' קרנות שהרי אינו נותן אפי' אחת על הקרנות רק כולו למטה אבל למאי דדרשינן אע"פ שלא נתן אלא אחת למעלה לא ביטלת תורת ד' קרנות שהרי צריך מתנה אחת בדיעבד על א' מד' קרנות ועל איזה מד' קרנות שיתן מתנה אחת כיפר ומשני איזה דבר שצריך ג' ופ"ה כדפי' דאי אתא לומר שאם נתנן כולן למטה כשר א"כ ארבע וכפר [הוה ליה למכתב] כו' וקשה דא"כ הול"ל איזה דבר שאינו צריך אלא ג' ועוד דהא לא שייך לדרוש קרא להכשיר אחת למעלה וג' למטה כדפי' ולהכי לא כתיב ד' וכפר א) וכו' עד מכולן למטה לבטל כל הקרנות והשתא צריכי ג' וכפר כי טוב יותר לומר כן מלמטה ג' מתנות משלא יעשה כלל מיהו קשה קצת מאי ס"ד סברת המקשה שלא היה מצריך קרא למעט אחת למעלה וג' למטה והיה מצריך קרא למעט ג' למעלה ואחת למטה הלא לא מצינו אחת למטה בהכשר דמים כמו ג' למטה ואמר מורי ש' דהוי סובר דאחת למטה הוי שפיר בהכשר דמים הניתנים למטה כגון בכור ומעשר ופסח שניתנים במתנה אחת למטה ומ"מ שפיר קאמר רבא איזה דבר הצריך ג' כדפי' דלדידך לא איצטריך כי אם שתים דמהאי טעמא דלא איצטריך קרא למעט ג' למטה לא יצטרך קרא למעט אחת למטה ואע"ג דאשכחן בבכור ומעשר ופסח שניתנים במתנה אחת למטה מ"מ לא דמי דהתם ליכא בשום מקום רק מתנה אחת למטה אבל כה"ג שטעונין ד' מתנות דג' למעלה ואחת למטה לא אשכחן ועי"ל דסברת המקשה בג' למעלה ואחת למטה כיון שרובן למעלה שפיר טפי: ו] אלא ג' למעלה ואחת למטה וכפר אע"פ שלא נתן אלא שתים למעלה ושתים למטה וכפר אע"פ שלא נתן אלא אחת: ז] למטה ההוא כמצליף ותיבות מאי כמצליף בס"א אינו: ח] לפרש בתבניתה כו' פשו להו תלת הס"ד כו' מסיני ע"פ במחיצות דקי"ל שיעורין חציצין ומחיצות הל"מ וגרעתה: ט] ארבעים ושתים בעינן למיתב: י] ותנא דמתניתא לא: יא] וכבשה שכולן: יב] הדין שחוזר כו' החטאות החיצונות שכל: יג] הוא. להכשיר: יד] מה דמים התחתונים כפר: טו] דלא שייכא: טז] קרנות הרי כאן ארבע: יז] דמים שאינן חטאת ולא נאמר: יח] רחמנא אמר: יט] מיעט חד קרן: כ] תיבת למטה נמחק: כא] מיהא מעכבא בלמעלה ותלת מיתכשרי למטה: כב] ברצועה עד טבורו זו למטה כו' מחציו עובי הכפורת ולמעלה: כג] מהשבע לא קאי אענין מקום הזאות אלא קאי אאצבע לענין: כד] התם דל חד [קרא] לגופיה: כה] מה"ד שאני התם דכתיב כנדתה פ"ה משמע כו' ודוחק אלא ה"פ פי' כשיעור: כו] הזכר דהיינו ז' ימים: כז] זה פר כהן כו' דמעכבי ופר יום הכפורים נמי צריך קרא: כח] נתן אלא אחת למעלה ושלש: כט] למטה שתי מתנות שהן ארבע א"נ א': ל] אחת תוס' ותיבת פוסל ל"ש ונמחק: לא] אומר אלו קרנות: לב] כדין דמים הניתנין: לג] ושלש למטה כלומר ולא אחוש לסברא ותיבות ולא כולן למטה נמחק: לד] למעלה ושלש למטה מכולן: לה] יש לתרץ אמאי הפסיק מסדר שהתחיל דס"ל: לו] שלשה כי אם שתים משמע כפי' ראשון ס"א התוס': לז] וכפר הכי וכפר אע"פ: לח] תיבת וזה נמחק: לט] מה"ד ההוא כמצליף: מ] בערוך וזה לשונו כמנגדנא: מא] ג) כמטבריה פי' מטה ותיבות (כמטברר) בערוך ל"ש: מב] נתן ד' מתנות על ארבע קרנות ואח"כ נתן שבע על חצי המזבח:

א) [נראה דחסר כאן וצ"ל לכן נראה לפרש דרבא ה"ק דלדידך בתרי וכפר סגי וכו' (וכמ"ש בתוס' ד"ה וכפר) עד וכולן למטה והשתא צריכי כו' משלא יעשה כלל לבטל כל הקרנות. מיהו כו']: ב) לפנינו בירושלמי איתא כמטורר וע"ש בפ"מ שהוא שני תיבות כמטווה וכך [וכ"ה בכתובות קף עב: בטווה וכך וע"ש ברש"י]

א] מַאי לָאו אַפַּלְגֵיהּ דְּמִזְבֵּחַ, כִּדְאָמְרִי אֱנָשֵׁי "טְהַר טִיהֲרָא (א) דְּיוֹמָא"? ב] אָמַר רָבָא בַּר שֵׁילָא: לָא, אַגִּילּוּיֵיהּ, דִּכְתִיב: °"וּכְעֶצֶם הַשָּׁמַיִם לָטוֹהַר". וְהָאִיכָּא שִׁירַיִם! שִׁירַיִם לָא מְעַכְּבִי. וְהָאִיכָּא שִׁירַיִם הַפְּנִימִים, דְּאִיכָּא ג] דְּמ"ד מְעַכְּבִי! בְּחַד מָקוֹם קָאָמְרִינַן.§ תַּנְיָא, רַבִּי אֱלִיעֶזֶר בֶּן יַעֲקֹב אוֹמֵר, בֵּית שַׁמַּאי אוֹמְרִים: שְׁתֵּי מַתָּנוֹת שֶׁבְּחַטָּאת, וְאַחַת שֶׁבְּכׇל הַזְּבָחִים — מַתִּירוֹת וּמְפַגְּלוֹת. בֵּית הִלֵּל אוֹמְרִים: אַחַת שֶׁבְּחַטָּאת, וְאַחַת שֶׁבְּכׇל הַזְּבָחִים אמַתֶּרֶת בוּמְפַגֶּלֶת. *מַתְקִיף לָהּ רַב אוֹשַׁעְיָא: אִם כֵּן, לִיתְנְיֵיהּ גַּבֵּי קוּלֵּי בֵּית שַׁמַּאי וְחוּמְרֵי בֵּית הִלֵּל! אֲמַר לֵיהּ רָבָא: כִּי אִיתְשִׁיל — לְהֶתֵּירָא אִיתְשִׁיל, דְּהָווּ לְהוּ בֵּית שַׁמַּאי לְחוּמְרָא.§ אָמַר רַבִּי יוֹחָנָן: שָׁלֹשׁ מַתָּנוֹת שֶׁבְּחַטָּאוֹת גאֵינָן בָּאוֹת בַּלַּיְלָה, וּבָאוֹת לְאַחַר מִיתָה, דוְהַמַּעֲלֶה מֵהֶן בַּחוּץ חַיָּיב. אָמַר רַב פָּפָּא: יֵשׁ מֵהֶן ד] כִּתְחִלָּתוֹ, וְיֵשׁ מֵהֶן כְּסוֹפוֹ; חוּץ, וְלַיְלָה, זָרוּת, וּכְלִי שָׁרֵת, קֶרֶן, וְאֶצְבַּע, כִּיבּוּס, וְשִׁירַיִם — כִּתְחִלָּתָן. מִיתָה, לָא שָׁרְיָא, וְלָא מְפַגְּלָא, וְלָא עַיְילָא לְגַוַּאי — כְּסוֹפָן. אָמַר רַב פָּפָּא: מְנָא אָמֵינָא לָהּ? *דִּתְנַן: הנִיתַּז מִן הַצַּוָּאר עַל הַבֶּגֶד — אֵינוֹ טָעוּן כִּיבּוּס, מִן הַקֶּרֶן וּמִן הַיְסוֹד — אֵינוֹ טָעוּן כִּיבּוּס; הָא מִן הָרָאוּי לַקֶּרֶן — טָעוּן כִּיבּוּס! וְלִיטַעֲמִיךְ, מִן הַיְסוֹד ה] אֵינוֹ טָעוּן כִּיבּוּס, הָא מִן הָרָאוּי לַיְסוֹד טָעוּן כִּיבּוּס? °"אֲשֶׁר יַזֶּה" כְּתִיב, *ופְּרָט לָזֶה שֶׁכְּבָר הוּזָּה! הָא מַנִּי? רַבִּי נְחֶמְיָה; *דִּתְנַן, רַבִּי נְחֶמְיָה אוֹמֵר: שְׁיָרֵי הַדָּם שֶׁהִקְרִיבָן בַּחוּץ — חַיָּיב. אֵימַר דְּשָׁמְעַתְּ לֵיהּ לְר' נְחֶמְיָה לְעִנְיַן הַעֲלָאָה, מִידֵּי דַּהֲוֵי אַאֵיבָרִים וּפְדָרִים, לְעִנְיַן כִּיבּוּס מִי שָׁמְעַתְּ לֵיהּ? אִין, וְהָתַנְיָא

מַאי לָאו אַפַּלְגֵיהּ דְּמִזְבֵּחַ. כְּנֶגֶד חֲצִי גּוֹבְהוֹ? וְאִי אֶפְשָׁר לְהַכְנִיס שֶׁלֹּא יְהֵא מְקַנְּחָם לְמַעְלָה וּמְקַנְּחָם לְמַטָּה! טִיהֲרָא = צָהֳרַיִם ו]. לָא, אַגִּילּוּיֵיהּ דְּמִזְבֵּחַ. עַל ז] גַּגּוֹ שֶׁל מִזְבֵּחַ, שֶׁהָיָה מְטַהֲרוֹ תְּחִלָּה מִדֶּשֶׁן שֶׁעָלָיו וּמְגַלֶּה אֶת גַּגּוֹ, וְעַל ח] שֶׁמְּטַהֲרוֹ וּמְיַיפֵּהוּ קָרֵי לֵיהּ "טָהֳרוֹ", כִּדְכְתִיב: *וְטִהֲרוֹ. וְהָא אִיכָּא שִׁירַיִם. שֶׁנִּשְׁפָּכִים לַיְסוֹד, וְעִיקַּר הַמַּתָּנוֹת לְמַעְלָה. שִׁירַיִם לָא מְעַכְּבִי. כַּפָּרָה, וְתַנַּן בְּדָמִים הַמְעַכְּבִים קָאָמְרִינַן, דְּלָא מָלֵינוּ חֶצְיָין לְמַעְלָה וְחֶצְיָין לְמַטָּה. דְּאִיכָּא לְמ"ד מְעַכְּבִי. לְקַמָּן בְּ"אֵיזֶהוּ מְקוֹמָן" (דף נב.). וְעִיקַּר הַמַּתָּנוֹת בַּקְּרָנוֹת הַפְּנִימִי דְּהַיְינוּ לְמַעְלָה, וְהַשִּׁירַיִם בִּיסוֹד מִזְבֵּחַ הַחִיצוֹן דְּהַיְינוּ לְמַטָּה! בְּחַד מָקוֹם. בְּמִזְבֵּחַ אֶחָד. שְׁתֵּי מַתָּנוֹת שֶׁבְּחַטָּאת מַתִּירוֹת. כׇּל זְמַן שֶׁלֹּא ט] נִיתַּן שְׁתַּיִם — לֹא הוּתְּרוּ אֵימוּרִין לְהַקְטָרָה, וְלֹא הַבָּשָׂר לַאֲכִילָה. וּמְפַגְּלוֹת. אִם נָתַן שְׁתֵּיהֶן בְּמַחֲשֶׁבֶת פִּיגּוּל. אֲבָל אַחַת בִּשְׁתִיקָה וְאַחַת בְּמַחֲשָׁבָה — לֹא פִּיגֵּל, שֶׁאֵין מְפַגְּלִין בַּחֲצִי מַתִּיר. לִתְנְיֵיהּ. לְהָךְ פְּלוּגְתָּא בְּעֵדִיּוֹת גַּבֵּי קוּלֵּי בֵּית שַׁמַּאי, שֶׁכּוּלָּן נִסְדְּרוּ בְּמִשְׁנַת עֵדִיּוֹת. וְהָא נַמִי קוּלֵּי ב"ש הוּא, דִּלְב"ש לֹא פִּיגֵּל אֶלָּא אִם כֵּן חִישֵּׁב בִּשְׁתֵּיהֶן, וּלְבֵית הִלֵּל פִּיגֵּל בְּאַחַת מֵהֶן. כִּי אִיתְשִׁיל. י] מִשְׁנָה (ב) בְּבֵית הַמִּדְרָשׁ תְּחִלָּה, וְנֶחְלְקוּ עָלֶיהָ בֵּית שַׁמַּאי וּב"ה. לְהֶיתֵּירָא אִיתְשִׁיל. לְעִנְיַן הֶיתֵּר הַבָּשָׂר וְהָאֵימוּרִין נִשְׁאֲלָה. שֶׁעָמַד הַשּׁוֹאֵל וְשָׁאַל: נָתַן מַתָּנָה אַחַת בְּחַטָּאת וְנִשְׁפַּךְ הַדָּם, הוּתְּרוּ הָאֵימוּרִין וְהַבָּשָׂר אוֹ לֹא הוּתְּרוּ? עָמְדוּ בֵּית שַׁמַּאי וּפְסָלוּ, עָמְדוּ ב"ה וְהִכְשִׁירוּ, דְּהָווּ לְהוּ ב"ש (ג) חוּמְרָא. וּמִינָּהּ גָּמְרִינַן, דְּכֵיוָן דְּאֵינָהּ מַתֶּרֶת לְבַדָּהּ — אֵינָהּ מְפַגֶּלֶת. אָמַר רַבִּי יוֹחָנָן שָׁלֹשׁ מַתָּנוֹת. יא] אַחֲרוֹנוֹת שֶׁבְּחַטָּאת אֵין בָּאוֹת בַּלַּיְלָה. וְאע"פ שֶׁאֵינָן מְעַכְּבִים וְלָאו זְרִיקָה גְּמוּרָה הִיא, מִיהוּ דָּם נִפְסָל בִּשְׁקִיעַת הַחַמָּה כִּדְלְקַמָּן,* וְאֵין מַעֲלִין יב] לְגַבֵּי מִזְבֵּחַ לְכַתְּחִילָּה. בָּאוֹת לְאַחַר מִיתָה. אִם נָתַן מַתָּנָה רִאשׁוֹנָה וּמֵתוּ בְּעָלֶיהָ — כְּבָר כִּפֵּר בָּרִאשׁוֹנָה, וְאֵין שֵׁם חַטָּאת גְּמוּרָה עַל הַדָּם עוֹד, לִפְסוֹל מִשּׁוּם חַטָּאת שֶׁמֵּתוּ בְּעָלֶיהָ. יֵשׁ מֵהֶן כִּתְחִלָּתוֹ יג]. יֵשׁ מִדְּבָרִים שֶׁבְּתוֹרַת דָּמִים שֶׁהַשָּׁלֹשׁ מַתָּנוֹת כְּמַתָּנָה *רִאשׁוֹנָה, וְיֵשׁ דְּבָרִים שֶׁהֵן בְּתוֹרַת שְׁיָרֵי הַדָּם. חוּץ. *)הַזּוֹרֵק אוֹתָן בַּחוּץ חַיָּיב, שֶׁהֲרֵי רְאוּיִים לִפְנִים בְּתוֹרַת זְרִיקָה גְּמוּרָה. וְאָסוּר לִיתְּנָן בַּלַּיְלָה, דְּנִפְסְלוּ מִלִּזְרוֹק, וְהָא זְרִיקָה הִיא. וְזָר חַיָּיב עֲלֵיהֶן מִיתָה בִּפְנִים. וּטְעוּנוֹת כְּלִי שָׁרֵת, יד] וּמַתָּנָה (ד) אֶצְבַּע. וְכִיבּוּס — אִם נִיתַּז מִדַּם הַחַטָּאת עַל הַבֶּגֶד לְאַחַר שֶׁנָּתַן טו] בְּמַתָּנָה אַחַת — טָעוּן כִּיבּוּס, כִּדְכְתִיב: "וַאֲשֶׁר יִזֶּה מִדָּמָהּ" וגו', כְּאִילּוּ נִיתַּז קוֹדֶם לָכֵן. אֲבָל אִם נָתַן כׇּל מַתְּנוֹתֶיהָ, וְאַחַר כָּךְ נִיתַּז מִן הַשִּׁירַיִם — אֵין טָעוּן כִּיבּוּס, כִּדְאָמְרִינַן בִּשְׁמַעְתִּין: "אֲשֶׁר יִזֶּה" — פְּרָט לָזֶה שֶׁכְּבָר הוּזָּה. שִׁירַיִם. חַטָּאת שֶׁקִּיבֵּל דָּמָהּ בְּאַרְבַּע כּוֹסוֹת וְנָתַן מַתָּנָה אַחַת *מִכׇּל אֶחָד — כּוּלָּן נַעֲשׂוּ שִׁירַיִם לִישָּׁפֵךְ לַיְסוֹד, אַף הַג' כּוֹסוֹת טז] שִׁירַיִם שֶׁלָּהֶן כְּמוֹ *הָרִאשׁוֹנִים. כְּתְחִלָּתוֹ. כְּמַתָּנָה הָרִאשׁוֹנָה. מִיתָה. בָּאוֹת לְאַחַר מִיתָה, כִּדְאָמַר לְעֵיל. לָא שָׁרְיָא. בָּשָׂר, שֶׁכְּבָר הוּתַּר. וְלָא מְפַגְּלָא. אִם נָתַן הָרִאשׁוֹנָה בִּשְׁתִיקָה וְהַשָּׁלֹשׁ בְּמַחֲשָׁבָה — לֹא פִּיגֵּל, וְכָשֵׁר, כִּדְתְנַן בְּמַתְנִי'. וְלָא עַיְילָא יז]. אֵין לָהֶם תּוֹרַת פְּסוּל כְּנִיסַת פְּנִים, שֶׁאִם נָתַן מַתָּנָה אַחַת בַּחוּץ וְהִכְנִיס הַשְּׁאָר יח] לַהֵיכָל — לֹא נִפְסַל מִשּׁוּם חַטָּאת שֶׁנִּכְנַס דָּמָהּ לִפְנִים, דִּכְתִיב: "לְכַפֵּר בַּקּוֹדֶשׁ" (ויקרא ו) — בְּרָאוּי לְכַפָּרָה הַכָּתוּב מְדַבֵּר. כְּסוֹפָן. יט] כְּשִׁירַיִם. מְנָא אָמֵינָא לָהּ. דִּטְעוּנָה כִּיבּוּס. נִיתַּז מִן הַצַּוָּאר עַל הַבֶּגֶד אֵין טָעוּן כִּיבּוּס. כִּדְאָמְרִינַן בְּפֶרֶק "דַּם חַטָּאת" (לקמן דף צג.): "אֲשֶׁר יִזֶּה" — בְּרָאוּי לְהַזָּאָה, יָצָא זֶה שֶׁלֹּא נִתְקַבֵּל בִּכְלִי. מִן הַקֶּרֶן. מִשֶּׁנָּגַע בְּקֶרֶן הַמִּזְבֵּחַ נִיתַּז עַל הַבֶּגֶד. אוֹ מִן הַיְסוֹד. מִשֶּׁנִּשְׁפְּכוּ שִׁירַיִם לַיְסוֹד נִיתַּז מִן הַיְסוֹד לַבֶּגֶד. אֵין טָעוּן כִּיבּוּס. כִּדְאָמְרִינַן: "אֲשֶׁר יִזֶּה" — פְּרָט לָזֶה שֶׁכְּבָר הוּזָּה. הָא מִן הָרָאוּי לַקֶּרֶן. כׇּל דְּהוּ, וַאֲפִילּוּ שָׁלֹשׁ מַתָּנוֹת שֶׁבְּחַטָּאוֹת טָעוּן כִּיבּוּס. הָא מִן הָרָאוּי לַיְסוֹד. כְּגוֹן שְׁיָרֵי הַדָּם הָרְאוּיִין לִישָּׁפֵךְ לַיְסוֹד. טָעוּן כִּיבּוּס. בִּתְמִיָּה. הָא מַנִּי ר' נְחֶמְיָה הִיא כ] כו'. הָא מִילְּתָא הַתַּלְמוּד קָאָמַר לָהּ, וּמַסְקָנָא דְּקוּשְׁיָין הִיא, לְאַפּוּקֵי מִדְּרַב פָּפָּא. כְּלוֹמַר, מֵהָא לָא אִירְיָא טַעְמָא דִּידָךְ, דְּהָא כא] רַבִּי נְחֶמְיָה הִיא, דַּאֲפִילּוּ בְּשִׁירַיִם נַמִי טָעוּן כִּיבּוּס. שְׁיָרֵי הַדָּם. אַף שֶׁל חַטָּאוֹת הַחִיצוֹנוֹת שֶׁהִקְרִיבָן בַּחוּץ חַיָּיב. אַלְמָא דָּם כב] קָחָשֵׁיב לְהוּ. מִידֵּי דַּהֲוֵי אַאֵיבָרִים. דְּלָאו דָּמִים נִינְהוּ, כג] הַמַּעֲלָן בַּחוּץ חַיָּיב מִשּׁוּם דְּחָזוּ לִפְנִים.

דָּמִים

*) אחד מהן הזורק אותה כו' כצ"ל נ"ק

וליתנייה גבי קולי בית שמאי. פי' רש"י: דסבר דשתי מתנות מפגלות ולא אחת, דאין מפגלים בחצי מתיר. כד] וא"ת, אימא: מפגלות — היינו באחת מהן, ולבית הלל בראשונה דווקא, ולכולהו מפגלין בחצי מתיר. כה] וא"כ אף בפיגול זימנין דהוי חומרא לב"ש, אם נתן ראשונה כתיקנה ושניה חוץ לזמנה — הוי פיגול, ולב"ה אינו פיגול כדאמר במתני'! כו] *וי"ל: מדקאמרי בית הלל ראשונה מפגלת — מכלל דלב"ש לא מפגלא, כז] *דהוה ליה למימר: בראשונה ולא בשניה. ותו י"ל: דומיא דמתירות, דהיינו דשתיהן דווקא הוי מפגלות. וה"ר יצחק כח] כתב דכן מוכח בתוספתא בהדיא: א"ר אלעזר בן יעקב: דבר זה כט] מקולי בית שמאי ומחומרי בית הלל, שתי מתנות שבחטאת מכשירות ומפגלות. כיצד? אחת שלא ל] בזמנה ונשפך הדם — פסול ואין בו כרת, דברי ב"ש. ובית הלל אומרים: פיגול, ויש בו כרת. אלמא באחת אין בו פיגול לב"ש, לא] ומשמע — משום דנשפך הדם ולא קרבו כל מתיריו, אבל אם לא נשפך הדם ונתן השניה כתיקנה — הוי פיגול, דמפגלי' בחצי מתיר, ולא כפי' רש"י, ולבית הלל פיגל — דקרבו כל מתיריו. או שמא אפי' לא נשפך, ונתן השני' כתיקנה — נמי אינו פיגול לב"ש, דאין מפגלין בחצי מתיר. ונשפך דקתני — משום בית הלל אשמועינן, דהיינו קרבו כל מתיריו. השתא ממה נפשך, *בין סברי בית שמאי מפגלין בחצי מתיר לב] הוו לקולא, אכתי קשיא לי, למה תירץ: כי איתשיל בהתירא איתשל? אפי' אי איתשיל בפיגול הוי בית שמאי לחומרא, היכא דלא נשפך, ונתן לג] ראשונה כתיקנה והשניה בפיגול, דמפגלין בחצי מתיר! *וליכא למימר דנשפך דווקא הוי מקולי ב"ש, דלמה ליה למימר בעדיות קולא דנשפך, כיון דבלא נשפך הוי חומרא? ויש לומר: דהאי גוונא אינו שנוי לא במשנה ולא בברייתא בפירוש, אבל לישנא דברייתא בנשפך — הוי לקולא לבית שמאי, לכך פריך: ליתני' בעדיות לד].

הגה"ה: הא מני רבי נחמיה היא דאמר שירים. לה] ולפירוש הקונטרס שנדחה סייעתה דרב פפא, לו] קשה: דהוה ליה למימר "אלא" ולפום ריהטא שינויא הוא אליבא דרב פפא. והיינו טעמא: דכיון דאשכחן לרבי נחמיה דטעון כיבוס היכא דחייב בחוץ, לז] לרב פפא נמי, כיון דחייב בחוץ בג' מתנות שבחטאת — הוא הדין דטעון כיבוס, לח] *דכיבוס וחיוב חוץ חדא מילתא היא, *)דפשיטא שעל זה לא הוצרך ראייה. לט] ופריך: אימר דשמעת ליה לר' נחמיה לענין העלאה כו' לענין כיבוס מי שמעת ליה? ואם כן לא דייקינן: הא מן הראוי ליסוד, והוא הדין דלא תידוק: הא מן הראוי לקרן! ומשני: אין, והתניא כו'. וכולה סוגיא לקיומי סייעתא דרב פפא, עד לבסוף, דמשני: אלא כי תניא ההיא בדמים הפנימים, דנדחו דבריו. (תוספות) ומיהו, מ] כל זה אמר רב פפא לקיים דבריו — בחטאות הפנימיות, ולהכי מחשבה מועלת בהן. ומיירי בשירים, כלמשמע לישנא דברייתא דנשפכים ליסוד, ולא בשלש מתנות. דכיון דאיירי בפנימיות — כך שוה כמו מתנה ראשונה, כיון דכל ארבע מעכבות לכולי עלמא, ולא הוי קרי להו נשפכין ליסוד. ובסיפא לא מלי לפלוגי בדמים החיצונים, דרבי נחמיה היא דחייב בשיריהם בחוץ, ואם כן לא מלי למיתני תלתא פטור מא].

הגה"ה: ויש מב] מפרש: הא מני רבי נחמיה היא כו'. ואתיא סיפא ד"הא מן הראוי ליסוד" כמו רבי נחמיה, ורישא ד"הא מן הראוי לקרן" כרבנן. ואשכחן כי האי גוונא בפ' "שתי הלחם" (מנחות דף צה.), מג] דתנא: ואפייתו בפנים — אלמא תנור מקדש, ואין דוחות את השבת איפסלי להו בלינה. וכן ברייתא דריש "טבול יום" (לקמן דף ק:) דיום שמועה כיום קבורה וכו'. ושקיל וטרי עד: אלא כי תניא ההיא בשלש מתנות שבחטאת. מד] וגרס "אלא" בספרים מדוייקים, והוי סייעתא דרב פפא מהך בתרייתא, ולא מקמייתא. ולפי שיטה זו יש ליישב כולה סוגיא. ובקונטרס פירש כולה שמעתא בע"א.

הא

*) נ"א דפשיטא שחייב בחוץ על זה כו'

עין משפט נר מצוה

יג א מיי' פ"ב מהלכות פסולי המוקדשין הלכה ח:
יד ב מיי' פי"ח שם ה"א:
טו ג מיי' פ"ד מהלכות מעשה הקרבנות הלכה ה:
טז ד מיי' פי"ז שם ה"ג:
יז ה מיי' פ"ח מהלכות מעשה הקרבנות ה"ו:
יח ו מיי' שם הלכה ז:

נ"א וצ"ל מדקאמרי נ"ק

לא"כ הו"ל למימר נ"ק

נ"א אפי'

גי' נ"ק ולימא דנשפך כו' ולמה ליה למימר

וחיוב חוץ וטעון כיבוס לחדא הוא מלתא דפשיטא היא ועי"ז כו' נ"ק

מסורת הש"ס

לטוהר נ"ק

יומא טו. נג.

שמות כד

[יומא פ. חולין נב: קה. בכורות לג: ערכין כז:]

לקמן נג.

ויקרא ו

[לקמן נג. מעילה ה.]

לקמן קי: קיב.

[דף טו:]

נ"א ראשונה ויש מהן כסופו ויש דברים כו'

נ"ל מאחד

הראשונה נ"ק

הגהות הב"ח

(א) גמ' טהר טיהרא והוי פלגיה דיומא: (ב) רש"י ד"ה כי איתשיל משנה זו בבהמ"ד: (ג) ד"ה להיתירא וכו' לחומרא: (ד) ד"ה חוץ וכו' ומתנת קרן ואצבע כיבוס:

שיטה מקובצת

א] מאי לאו אפלגיה דמזבח. פ"ה כנגד כו' וקשה כיון דאינו מכוין היינו כמנגדנא לכך נראה לר' חיים כהן דפריך משום שכבר נתן ד' מתנות על ד' קרנות למעלה ואח"כ נתן שבע על חצי המזבח דהיינו למטה ומשני לא אטיהרו ר"ל על נילוייא והכל היה למעלה על הקרנות ועל גב מזבח וקרו ליה טהרו על שהיה מטהרו ומייפהו תחלה מהדשן שעליו: ב] דיומא והוי פלגא: ג] דאיכא למ"ד: ד] מהן כתחלתן ויש מהן כסופן: ה] היסוד נמי מן היסוד הוא דאינו טעון כיבוס: ו] צהרים דהוא חצי היום הס"ד: ז] על גילוי גגו: ח] ועל שם שמטהרו: ט] שלא נתן שתים: י] איתשיל מתנה אחת בבהמ"ד: יא] מתנות אחרונות שבחטאת: יב] מעלין פסולין לגבי מזבח: יג] כתחלתן. יש דברים: יד] ומתנת אצבע: טו] שנתן מתנה: טז] כוסות של שלש מתנות אחרונות יש להן שיריים כמו הראשונים הס"ד ומה"ד כתחלתן. כלומר דינן כמתנה: יז] עיילי לגואי: יח] השאר בהיכל: יט] כסופן דינן כשיריים: כ] היא. כולה הא מלתא: כא] דהא מני ר' נחמיה כו' נמי אית ליה כיבוס הס"ד: כב] דם גמור קחשיב: כג] נינהו והמעלן כו' לפנים הס"ד ומה"ד אין והתניא: כד] מתיר וב"ה סברי דקמייתא חשיבא שפיר מתיר שלם: כה] מתיר ס"א והוי נמי ב"ש לחומרא דלב"ש ב' מתנות מפגלות זו או זו ולב"ה כו': כו] במתני' ונ"ל מדקאמרי ב"ה אחת שבחטאת מפגלת דהיינו ראשונה: כז] מפגלא אותה אחת דאל"כ הוה ליה למימר אין מתיר ומפגל אלא בראשונה: כח] יצחק מצא בתוספתא ותיבות כתב דכן מוכח ל"ש: כט] זה אחד מקולי: ל] שלא לזמנו: לא] הוי משום תיבת ומשמע ל"ש: לב] מתיר בין לא סברי הוו: לג] ונתן מתן ראשונה כו' בחצי מתיר ולימא דנשפך: לד] בעדיות ע"כ: לה] שיריים פי' הקונטרס: לו] פפא ומסקנא דקושיא היא לאפוקי מדרב פפא וה"ק אלא כלומר לא איירי בטעמא דידך דהא מני ר' נחמיה היא כלומר דמחייב בחוץ בשיריים וה"ה נמי בג' מתנות שבחטאת שטעון כבוס אבל לרבנן דלא מחייב בשיריים משום חוץ ה"ה נמי דאינו טעון כבוס בג' מתנות ולא תפשוט מידי לרבנן ולא נהירא דא"כ הל"ל אלא ועוד דבסמוך מייתי למלתיה לרב פפא דקאמר לא שריא ולא מפגלא כסופן ועוד דלפום רהיטא משמע דשנויא הוא לרב פפא לכך נראה דשנויא הוא וה"ק הא מני ר' נחמיה היא וכי היכא דאשכחן כיבוס כו': לז] בחוץ לרבנן נמי ותיבת לרב פפא ל"ש ונמחק: לח] כיבוס דטעון כיבוס וחיוב: לט] ראייה דמהא לא פליגי רבנן עליה דר' נחמיה: מ] ומיהו נ"ל דגם זה אמר ר"פ לקיים דבריו בדמים הפנימים ולהכי מחשבה מועלת כו' דברייתא טעונין יסוד ולא: מא] פטור ע"כ: מב] ויש מפרשי': מג] מדרתנא ואפייתו: מד] שבחטאת וגרסי' אלא:

והתניא: דמים הטעונין יסוד — טעונין כיבוס, ומחשבה מועלת בהן, והמעלה מהן בחוץ חייב. ודמים הנשפכין לאמה — אין טעונין כיבוס, ואין מחשבה מועלת בהן, והמעלה מהן בחוץ פטור; מאן שמעת ליה דאמר: מעלה מהן בחוץ חייב — רבי נחמיה א] היא, וקאמר: טעון כיבוס. ומחשבה מועלת בהן? והתניא: °יצאו שירים והקטרת אימורין שאין מעכבין את הכפרה, שאין מחשבה מועלת בהן! ב] כי תניא ההיא — בשלש מתנות שבחטאת. אי הכי, טעונין יסוד? לקרן אזלי! אימא: ניטענין יסוד. ומחשבה מועלת בהן? האמרת: לא שרי' ולא מפגלא ולא עיילא לגואי, כסופן! אלא, ג] כי תניא ההיא — בדמים [דף לח.] הפנימים. אבל בדמים החיצונים מאי, פטור? אדתני: דמים הנשפכין לאמה, ליפלוג וליתני בדידה: במה דברים אמורים — בדמים הפנימים, אבל בדמים החיצונים — פטור! ד] הא מני *רבי נחמיה היא, דאמר: שירי הדם שהקריבן בחוץ חייב, ולא מתני ליה תלתא פטורי לבהדי תלתא חיובי. רבינא אמר: מן הקרן — ה] ממש, מן היסוד — מן הראוי ליסוד. אמר ליה רב תחליפא בר גזא לרבינא: אימא אידי ואידי ראוי ו] הוא? האי מאי? השתא ראוי לקרן אמרת לא, ראוי ליסוד מיבעיא? אלא מן הקרן — מן הקרן ממש, מן היסוד — מן הראוי ליסוד.§ "כל הניתנין על מזבח הפנימי" כו'.§ ת"ר: ז] *°"ועשה כאשר עשה" — מה ח] [ויקרא ד] בא ללמוד? לכפול בהזאתו. ולמד שאם חיסר אחת מכל המתנות — לא עשה ולא כלום. אין לי אלא מתן שבע ט] שמעכבות בכל מקום, מתן ד' מניין? ת"ל: "כן יעשה", "לפר" — זה פר יום הכפורים, כאשר

ס"י *[והתניא. בניחותא]. דמים הטעונין יסוד. היינו שירים, י] שטעון שפיכת יסוד. יא] מחשבה מועלת בהן. אם חישב בשפיכתן על מנת לאכול בשר למחר. ולקמן רמינן עלה. ודמים הנשפכין לאמה. שנפסלו, ושופכין אותו לסילון שבעזרה יב] המוליא לנחל קדרון. כי תניא ההיא. דמחשבה מועלת בהן. בשלש מתנות כו'. וכולה חדא מלתא היא, דמסקנא דקושיא היא ולאו שינויא. יג] כלומר: לא תשמע מינה דשירים טעון כיבוס ואפי' לר' נחמיה, דהך ברייתא יד] בשלשה מתנות שבחטאות. נטענין יסוד. מצות טעינת יסוד עליהם, ששופך שיריהם ליסוד. ה"ג: אלא כי תניא ההיא בדמים הפנימיים. ולעולם בשירים, וכמ"ד לקמן שירים הפנימיים מעכבי, הילכך חשיבי לפגל טו] לענין חוץ ולענין כיבוס. ור' נחמיה היא דאמר. אף שירים החיצונים שהקריבן בחוץ חייב, ומשום הכי לא מצי לפלוגי בדידה. דלא מתני ליה תלתא פטורי. בחיצונים. לבהדי תלתא חיובי. דתנא בפנימיות. דבשלמא בכיבוס ובמחשבה מצי לפלוגי, אבל בהעלאת חוץ לא מצי למיתנייה. רבינא אמר. הא דפרכת לעיל: וליטעמיך מן היסוד [לעיל לח:] הוא דאין טעון כיבוס, הא מן הראוי ליסוד כו' — לאו פירכא היא. ד"מן הקרן" — מן הקרן ממש קאמר. הא מן הראוי לקרן, כגון טז] שלש מתנות שבחטאות — טעון כיבוס, כדרב פפא. והא דתנן בהו "מן היסוד" — לאו מן היסוד ממש, דתידוק מינה: הא מן הראוי ליסוד טעון כיבוס, ותקשה לך. אלא מן הראוי ליסוד קאמר, ואשמעינן דמשכלתה זריקה אין השירים טעון כיבוס. דאילו מן היסוד ממש לא איצטריכא ליה, [מנחות כז.] דהשתא מן הקרן אמרת לא, מן היסוד מיבעי? ואימא אידי ואידי ראוי. וקמ"ל דיש לך ראוי לקרן ואין טעון כיבוס, ואיזה זה — יז] שלשה מתנות שבחטאות! ראוי לקרן אמרת לא. משנתן מתנה ראשונה ממעטת לכוליה דם מכיבוס. ראוי ליסוד. דכבר נגמרו מתנותיו, מיבעיא ליה למיתני? בתמיה, הא מקמייתא אידחי ליה מכיבוס! אלא ודאי מן הקרן קרן ממש. אבל הראוי לקרן, כל זמן שלא גמר מתנותיו — טעון כיבוס. והדר אשמעינן דמן הראוי ליסוד אין טעון כיבוס, ולמעוטי שירים. דאי מן היסוד ממש — לא איצטריכא ליה. ועשה כאשר עשה. בפר העלם דבר, (א) לאחר שפי' בו כל מתנות דמו, שנה לכתוב "ועשה לפר כאשר עשה לפר החטאת" וגו'. ומקרא שאינו צריך הוא, שהרי כל עבודותיו נתפרשו, יח] חוץ מיותרת הכבד ושתי הכליות, שהוא צריך ללמוד מפר כהן משיח האמור למעלה הימנו, והא ליכא למימר דלהכי הדר ואקשינהו להא מלתא, דהאי קרא כתיב ביה כפרה, "וכפר עליהם" וגו', ואימורין לא מעכבי כפרה. אלא כולה לדרשא, וסרסהו, יט] דע"כ לא מצי למימר כדכתיב: "כאשר עשה לדם הפר" דמשמע מאחרינא יליף, דלא חסר מידי דניבעי למילפיה. אלא: "ועשה כאשר עשה" — לכפול באזהרת הזאות שלו. והכי משמע כ] "כאשר עשה" (לו) — כאשר כתבתי לך כל עשיותיו, ושנה עליהם לעכב, שאם חיסר כו'. כן שמעתי במנחות. מתן שבע. על הפרכת, שמעכבות בכל מקום. לקמן מפרש. מתן ארבע. שאין מעכבות בחטאת החיצונה, כדאמרינן לעיל, מניין שמעכבות בקרנות הפנימי? ולקמן פריך: למה לי קרא? (ב) האי כפילא כא] "ועשה כאשר עשה" נמי עלייהו קאי, דהא אינהו נמי בהדיא כתיבו. תלמוד לומר כן יעשה לו. חזר וכפל, ואם אינו לענין מתן שבע — תנהו לענין מתן ארבע. לפר זה פר יום הכפורים. להשוותו לפר העלם דבר. ולקמיה מפרש למאי הילכתא. כאשר

הא מני רבי נחמיה היא. דאמר: שירי הדם שהקריבן בחוץ חייב, ולא מיתני כב] תלתא פטורי בהדי תלתא חיובי. כולה סוגיא דשמעתא משמע דרבי נחמיה איירי בדמים החיצונים. כג] והקשה הרב רבי יעקב מאורלינ"ש: דלקמן בסוף "השוחט והמעלה" (דף קיא.) אמרינן: והשתא דאמר רב אדא בר אהבה מחלוקת בשירים הפנימים, אבל בשירים החיצוני' — דברי הכל אין מעכבין, כד] וכי קאמר ר' נחמיה — בשירים הפנימים! ועוד קשה: דקאמר *)[א"ר יוחנן:] ר' נחמיה כדברי האומר שירים מעכבין. והכא אשכחן כה] חיצונים דמקריבן בחוץ חייב ואינן מעכבין, דקאמר הכא לר' נחמיה בדמים החיצונים תרי פטורי וחד חיובא, וכיון דאין מחשבה מועלת בהן ואין טעונין כיבוס — א"כ לא מעכבי! ועוד: דאי שירים הניתנין ליסוד בדמים החיצונים מעכבי — א"כ מצינו דמים חציין למטה וחציין למעלה, ובחד מקום לא אשכחן, כדאמר לעיל!* ועוד: מי עדיפי משלש מתנות שבחטאת? ועוד: אמרינן בסוף "השוחט והמעלה" (לקמן דף קיב.) גבי חטאת שקיבל דמה בשתי כוסות דמוקי לה כר' נחמיה: מסל למה"ד כו', ומוקי לה בשעיר נשיא, אלמא: כו] ר"נ בחיצונות איירי דומיא דשעיר נשיא! מיהו, הא לא קשיא: אע"ג דהמשל איירי בשעיר נשיא — מ"מ רישא לא הוי בשעיר נשיא. כז] ונ"ל: סוגיא דשמעתא אתיא דלא כר' יוחנן. וברייתא לא קשיא לר' יוחנן, דהא דלא מפליג כח] בדידיה — משום דכולה בפנימים קמיירי. (תוס') ויש לפרש: א"ר יוחנן: ר' נחמיה כמ"ד שירים הפנימיים מעכבי, ואילו היה עושה אותה בחוץ חייב — א"כ יש לחייב אף בחיצונים אע"ג דלא מעכבי, דגמרי' מאיברים ופדרים. ואי פרכת: מה לאיברים ופדרים שכן תחילת עבודה — שיריים כט] פנימיים יוכיחו. ואי פרכת: מה לשיריים הפנימיים שכן מעכבין — איברים ופדרים יוכיחו. ונ"ע: דהא שיריים הפנימיים קורא אותן תחילת עבודה לקמן. ל] (הגהה) ר"ת השיב לו: לא] דאמת הוא דר' נחמיה אף בשירים (ג) החיצונים מיירי, מדקתני שירי הדם סתמא, ל"ש פנימים ול"ש חיצונים. והכי פי' דשמעתא דסוף "השוחט והמעלה" (ג"ז שם): והשתא דא"ר אדא בר אהבה מחלוקת בשירים הפנימים אבל חיצונים דברי הכל לא מעכבי, וכי קאמר ר' לב] *יהודה בשירים הפנימים, פירוש: כי קאמר דשירים מעכבי לג] מ"וכלה מכפר" — היינו בשירים הפנימים. וכי תניא ההיא — בשירים החיצונים, פי': ההיא דר' נחמיה ור' עקיבא בשירים החיצונים. כל זה מדברי רב אדא, ולדבריו דרבי עקיבא לד] התלמוד קאמר, דמה שאמר ר"ע שירי הדם שירי מצוה הן — משמע ל"ש פנימים ולא שנא חיצונים — לא קשיא לרב אדא, דר"ע לדברי עצמו השיב לה] לך, דפליג אדר' *יהודה, ואית ליה שירים אין מעכבים אפי' בפנימים. ורבי נחמיה ס"ל לעולם דפנימים מעכבין ושירים חיצונים אין מעכבין — לו] אפ"ה חייבין בחוץ. ור' יוחנן היה סובר דאף חיצונים מעכבין לר' נחמיה. ובזה לא היה מוקשה דמלא שום תנא דסבר חיצונים מעכבים, דודאי איכא שום תנא דאית לז] ליה האי סברא דחיצונים מעכבין. אלא בזה איתותב, לח] דרבי נחמיה הוה ס"ל דחיצונים מעכבין, וטעמא דר' נחמיה דמחייב בחוץ משום עיכובא הוא — דהא ודאי ליתיה. וק' לפר"ת: דע"כ ליכא שום תנא שיאמר שירים החיצונים מעכבין כדפרישי', דלא מצינו דמים שחציין למטה וחציין למעלה. ועוד: דלא אפשר לומר לט] כן לר' נחמיה שירים החיצונים מעכבין, כדמוכח בסוף "הוציאו לו" (יומא דף ס.) דפליגי ר' יהודה ור' נחמיה בדברים הנעשין בבגדי לבן בחוץ, דלרבי יהודה לא מעכבי ולרבי נחמיה מעכבי, דמפרש ר' יוחנן דשניהם מקרא אחד דרשו: "והיתה זאת לכם" וגו', וכתיב "זאת" וכתיב "אחת", לר' יהודה חד למעוטי בגדי לבן בחוץ, וחד למעוטי בגדי זהב בחוץ. ולרבי נחמיה חד למעוטי בגדי זהב, וחד למעוטי שירים דלא מעכבי. מ] והתם פריך [שפיר] דרבי יוחנן אדרבי יוחנן מההיא דלקמן, דקאמר ר' יוחנן דתני ר' נחמיה לדברי האומר שירים מעכבין, מא] קשיא. ועשה מב] לפר כאשר עשה. פי' בקונט': בפר העלם דבר של צבור כתיב, ומקרא שאינו צריך הוא, שהרי כל עבודותיו נתפרשו בו חוץ מיותרת הכבד ושתי הכליות, שהוא צריך ללמוד מפר כהן המשיח האמור למעלה

*) דקאמר ר' יוחנן התם ר' נחמיה כו'. נ"ק

סימנו

א] תיבת היא נמחק: ב] כי תניא ההיא. פי' דמחשבה מועלת בהן בג' מתנות ואפי' כרבנן אתיא וסייעתא היא לרב פפא דלדברי הכל מוכח בהדיא דבג' מתנות טעון כיבוס (כי תניא ההיא בדמים הפנימים) כו': ג] כי תניא ההיא בדמים הפנימים. ולעולם אימא לך בשיריים כמאן דאמר לקמן שיריים הפנימים מעכבין הלכך חשיבי לפגל ולענין חוץ ולענין כיבוס אבל לעולם לא איפשיטא ליה כרב פפא בדמים החיצונים: ד] הא מני ר' נחמיה היא. והשתא ניחא דראוי ליסוד טעון כיבוס ומ"מ מן הקרן אין טעון כיבוס אפי' לר' נחמיה שכבר נעשה מצותו אבל שיריים אין מצותו נעשית עד שישפכנו ליסוד. מהר"פ: ה] הקרן מן הקרן ממש: ו] תיבת הוא נמחק: ז] ועשה כאשר עשה. פ"ה דמקרא שאינו צריך עד דהא כפרה כתיב בהאי קרא ואימורים לא מעכבי כפרה ואע"ג דמוכח לקמן דיותרת הכבד ושתי הכליות אתיא מהך היקשא מ"מ ע"כ לאו לענין יותרת הכבד ושתי הכליות לחוד אתא כיון דוכפר כתיב משמע דאיתקש גם לענין כפרה והיינו דקאמר מה ת"ל לענין כפרה אלא ש"מ לכפול בהזאות לומר שאם [חיסר] אחת מן כולם לא עשה ולא כלום. לפום רהיטא משמע דה"פ להכי אקשי לפר כהן משיח לכולהו עשיות ועבודות שכתובות בהדיא בפר העלם גופיה לכפול בהזאות שהרי שינה הכתוב בהן וה"ק קרא ועשה לפר זה דהעלם כאשר עשה לפר דכהן משיח וכן משמע קצת בפ"ג דמנחות [אבל קשה] דא"כ איצטריך לפר שני דכתיב כאשר עשה לפר להאי היקשא דלכפול בהזאות ובסמוך מפרש תלמודא לפר זה פר כהן המשיח למאי הלכתא לעכב ונראה לעכב כפרה [יליף] מדאיתקש לפר העלם כדפי' בקונטרס בסמוך וגם דומיא דלעכב דיוה"כ והשתא בלאו עיכובא בגופיה דפר כהן משיח איצטריך לפר [זה] הפר כהן משיח כדי לכפול בהזאות בפר העלם דבר כדפי' לכך נראה כדפ"ה דועשה כאשר עשה לחוד (בא) [בלא] שום לפר ילפינן לכפול בהזאות דכוליה קרא אפר העלם קאי וה"ק ועשה לפר כלומר ועשה לו להאי פר העלם כאשר כתבתי כבר עשיותיו הרי שכפל בהזאות בפר העלם בלא שום היקש דפר כהן [משיח] והלכך אייתרי להו תרי לפר פר ראשון ליוה"כ ופר שני דכאשר לפר זה פר כהן המשיח לעכב בפר כהן משיח גופיה מהיקשא דפר העלם דהא להיקש ולכפול בהזאות לא איצטריך כדפי' וכן לפר ראשון לא איצטריך לגופיה דפר העלם דהא בפר העלם איירי קרא ומועשה לחוד ידעינן דאפר העלם קאי הלכך אייתר ליה לפר הראשון לפר יוה"כ. מ"מ קשה לפ"ה דמפירושו משמע מדבעי תלמודא כאשר עשה מה ת"ל דאי מצינא לאוקמי הך היקשא גופיה לעבודת הדם לא הוי מוקמינן ליה לכפול בהזאות וקשה דהא לר"ש איצטריך בסמוך הך היקשא לעבודת הדם למתן ארבע וא"כ לדידיה מנ"ל לכפול בהזאות לכך נראה דועשה כאשר עשה משמע דלכפול כל מה שבענין כי נמי איצטריך לעבודת הדם נמי משמע ועשה כאשר עשה דקאמר אכולהו עשיות ועבודות שנאמרו בפר כהן משיח והוי כאילו כתוב בהדיא ועשה ככל עשיותיו ולהכי קאמר מה ת"ל הרי עיקר העבודות מפורשות בהדיא א לפר העלם. ויש לקיים פ"ה מ"מ ולא קשה מההיא דר"ש בסמוך משום דגבי מתן ארבע כי היכי דצריך ללמוד מפר כהן משיח ה"נ צריך ללמוד פר כהן משיח מפר העלם לגבי מתן ארבע דאידי ואידי קרנות כתיב בהו דלא משמע כי אם שתי קרנות הלכך ליכא [לאוקמי הך] היקשא דועשה כאשר עשה לגבי האי מלתא דמתן ד' לחוד דהאי לישנא דועשה כאשר עשה משמע שעיקר היקשא ללמוד פר העלם מפר כהן משיח ולא ללמוד פר כהן משיח מפר העלם אבל לגבי יותרת ושתי הכליות שפר העלם למד מפר כהן משיח ואינו מלמד הוי משמע שפיר היקשא להכי אי לאו דבהאי קרא כתיב כפרה ואימורים לא מעכבא כפרה [אלא] אכתי אימא דהיקשא דועשה כאשר עשה לאת בדם וטבילה אתיא שפר העלם למד מפר כהן המשיח ואינו מלמד כדפי' בקונטרס לקמן בסוף שמעתין ומידי דכפרה הוא שפיר בשלמא לפיר"ת דלקמן ניחא שפי' דאת בדם וטבילה כתיבי בפר העלם כמו בפר כהן משיח אבל לפ"ה דלקמן קשה לפי שיטת הקונטרס דהכא וי"ל דמ"מ ליכא לאוקמי היקשא דועשה כאשר עשה לדאת בדם וטבילה שהרי ועשה כאשר עשה משמע עיקר עשיה ואת בדם וטבילה אינו עיקר עשיה כי אם פירוש ההזאות איך יעשה אותם: ח] מה תלמוד לומר לכפול בהזאות ללמד שאם: ט] שבע שמעכבת: י] שיריים שטעונין: יא] מה"ד ומחשבה: יב] שבעזרה המוציאן: יג] שנויא היא כלומר לא תשמע מינה: יד] ברייתא בשלש: טו] לפגל ולענין חוץ: טז] כגון שלש מתנות כו' כיבוס כרב פפא והא דתנן בהו ומן: יז] שלש מתנות: יח] נתפרשו בפר העלם כמו בפר כהן משיח חוץ: יט] וסרסהו על כרחך דלא מצי כו' עשה לפר דמשמע דמאחרינא יליף הוא דלא: כ] משמע ועשה לו כאשר כתבתי כו': כא] כפילא דועשה: כב] מיתני ליה תלתא פטורי כו' דשמעתא מוכחא דר"נ: כג] והקשה. עיין בתוס' יומא (דף ס' ע"ב): כד] מעכבין כי קאמר כו' דקאמר ר' יוחנן דקסבר ר' נחמיה: כה] אשכחן דמקריב בחוץ: כו] אלמא בחיצונים מיירי ואפ"ה מוקי לה כר' נחמיה. ס"א כרבנן אע"ג כו' ומתיבת בחיצוניות עד תיבת אע"ג ל"ש: כז] נשיא וסוגיא דשמעתין צ"ל דאתיא: כח] בדידה משום כו' תוס' ובשם רבינו יצחק מצאתי כתוב ויש לפרש כו' נחמיה כדברי האומר שיריים מעכבי וכיון דפנימים מעכבי ואלו כו': כט] שיריים הפנימים: ל] לקמן בפ' השוחט והמעלה: לא] לו בסגנון [זה] והא לך פירושו דאמת: לב] ר' נחמיה דשיריים הפנימים: לג] דוכלה כפר: לד] עקיבא קאמר תלמודא דמה שאמר כו' מצוה הם דמשמע: לה] חשיב לו: לו] ואפ"ה חייב אכולן בחוץ כו' לא היה מוקשה דמצי לאשכוחי שום תנא: לז] ליה. עיין בתוס' ע"ב בדף זה: לח] איתותב דהוא סבר דרבי נחמיה: לט] לר' נחמיה דשיריים תיבת כן נמחק: מ] מעכבי ואע"ג דהתם: מא] מעכבין ומסיק קשיא מ"מ רב אדא שלא היה צריך לכך מי ידחקנו לומר דשיריים הפנימים מעכבי לר' נחמיה: מב] ועשה כאשר עשה ותיבת לפר נמחק:

הגהות הב"ח

(א) רש"י ד"ה ועשה וכו' דבר כתיב לאחר: (ב) ד"ה מתן ד' וכו' למה לי קרא הא האי: (ג) תוס' ד"ה הא מני וכו' ור"ת השיב וכו' החיצונים מיירי. נ"ב ועי' בפירש"י בע"ב ד"ה שפיכת שיריים:

גליון הש"ס

גמ' יצאו שירים והקטרת אימורין. לעיל דף יג ע"א:

°"כַּאֲשֶׁר עָשָׂה לְפַר" — זֶה פַּר כֹּהֵן מָשִׁיחַ, "הַחַטָּאת" — א] אֵלּוּ שְׂעִירֵי עֲבוֹדָה זָרָה. ב] יָכוֹל שֶׁאֲנִי מְרַבֶּה אַף שְׂעִירֵי הָרְגָלִים וּשְׂעִירֵי רָאשֵׁי חֳדָשִׁים? תַּלְמוּד לוֹמַר: "לוֹ". וּמָה רָאִיתָ לְרַבּוֹת אֶת אֵלּוּ וּלְהוֹצִיא אֶת אֵלּוּ? אַחַר שֶׁרִיבָּה הַכָּתוּב וּמִיעֵט, מְרַבֶּה אֲנִי אֶת אֵלּוּ שֶׁמְּכַפְּרִין עַל עֲבֵירַת מִצְוָה יְדוּעָה, וּמוֹצִיא אֲנִי אֵלּוּ שֶׁאֵין מְכַפְּרִין עַל עֲבֵירַת מִצְוָה יְדוּעָה. "וְכִפֶּר" — אַף עַל פִּי שֶׁלֹּא סָמַךְ, ג] "וְנִסְלַח" — אַף עַל פִּי שֶׁלֹּא נָתַן שִׁירַיִם. וּמָה רָאִיתָ לִפְסוֹל בְּהַזָּאוֹת וּלְהַכְשִׁיר בִּסְמִיכָה וְשִׁירַיִם? אָמַרְתָּ, פּוֹסֵל ד] בְּהַזָּאוֹת שֶׁמְּעַכְּבוֹת בְּכָל מָקוֹם, וּמַכְשִׁיר אֲנִי בִּסְמִיכָה וְשִׁירַיִם שֶׁאֵין מְעַכְּבוֹת בְּכָל מָקוֹם.
אָמַר

תורה אור ויקרא ד

כַּאֲשֶׁר עָשָׂה ה] (לְדַם) לַפָּר. לָאו "כַּאֲשֶׁר עָשָׂה" קָדָרֵישׁ, שֶׁהֲרֵי כְּבָר סֵירְסוֹ וְדָרְשׁוֹ, אֶלָּא "לַפָּר" קָדָרֵישׁ. **זֶה פַּר כֹּהֵן מָשִׁיחַ.** הָאָמוּר בַּפָּרָשָׁה הָעֶלְיוֹנָה וְלֹא נִכְפַּל, לְכָךְ חָזַר וְהִקִּישָׁן יַחַד (א) ו] שֶׁלִּימֵּד עִיכּוּב חִיסּוּר מַתְּנוֹתָיו מִזֶּה. **אֵלּוּ שְׂעִירֵי עֲבוֹדָה זָרָה.** לַהֲבִיאָן בְּדִין פַּר הֶעְלֵם דָּבָר, לִיטְעוֹן הַזָּיָה עַל הַפָּרוֹכֶת וְעַל מִזְבַּח הַזָּהָב, וְלִישָּׂרֵף חוּץ לְשָׁלֹשׁ מַחֲנוֹת. לְפִי שֶׁבִּמְקוֹמוֹ לֹא נִתְפָּרְשׁוּ הִלְכוֹתָיו בְּפָרָשַׁת "שְׁלַח לְךָ". **יָכוֹל שֶׁאֲנִי מְרַבֶּה שְׂעִירֵי הָרְגָלִים וְרָאשֵׁי חֳדָשִׁים.** לִהְיוֹת פְּנִימִים וְנִשְׂרָפִין. ת"ל כֵּן יֵעָשֶׂה לוֹ. לָזֶה וְלֹא לְאַחֵר. **מְרַבֶּה אֲנִי שְׂעִירֵי עֲבוֹדָה זָרָה.** לְתוֹרַת פַּר הֶעְלֵם דָּבָר. **שֶׁמְּכַפְּרִין עַל עֲבֵירַת מִצְוָה יְדוּעָה.** כְּמוֹתוֹ, שֶׁשְּׁנֵיהֶם בָּאִין עַל חֵטְא ז] הַיָּדוּעַ. **וּמוֹצִיא אֲנִי** שֶׁל רְגָלִים שֶׁלֹּא הָיוּ שָׁוִין לוֹ, שֶׁהֲרֵי אֵין דּוֹמִין לוֹ בְּכַפָּרָתוֹ, שֶׁאֵלּוּ בָּאִין עַל טוּמְאַת מִקְדָּשׁ וְקָדָשָׁיו שֶׁאֵין בָּהּ יְדִיעָה לֹא בַּתְּחִלָּה וְלֹא בַּסּוֹף, שֶׁנִּטְמָא וְנִכְנַס לַמִּקְדָּשׁ וְאֵינוֹ מַכִּיר וְלֹא הוֹדַע לוֹ לֹא טוּמְאָתוֹ וְלֹא כְּנִיסָתוֹ, כִּדְאָמְרִינַן בִּשְׁבוּעוֹת (דף ב.). **וְכִפֶּר.** וְכִפֶּר מִכָּל מָקוֹם. **אע"פ שֶׁלֹּא סְמָכוֹ.** עָלָיו זְקֵנִים. **וְנִסְלַח אע"פ שֶׁלֹּא נָתַן שִׁירַיִם.** לִיסוֹד מִזְבַּח הַחִיצוֹן. דְּלָא תֵּימָא: הוֹאִיל וּכְתִיבָא ח] בָּהּ בְּהֶדְיָא כְּפִילָה דִּ"וְעָשָׂה כַּאֲשֶׁר עָשָׂה" – נַמִּי עֲלַיְיהוּ קָאֵי, הִילְכָּךְ מַעַטִינְהוּ קְרָא. **שֶׁמְּעַכְּבוֹת בְּכָל מָקוֹם.** כִּדְמְפָרֵשׁ לְקַמֵּיהּ: בְּפָרָה וּבִנְגָעִים. **סְמִיכָה לֹא מְעַכֶּבֶת בְּעָלְמָא.** כִּדְאָמְרִינַן בְּפֶרֶק קַמָּא: "וְסָמַךְ וְנִרְצָה" וְכִי סְמִיכָה מְכַפֶּרֶת וכו'? **שְׁפִיכַת שִׁירַיִם לָא מְעַכְּבָא.** בְּחַטָּאת הַחִיצוֹנָה (ב) לְדִבְרֵי הַכֹּל.
בְּפָרָה

הימנו. והא ליכא למימר דלהכי הדר ואקשינהו להא מילתא – דהא קרא כפרה כתיב ביה "וכפר עליהם", ואימורין לא מעכבי כפרה. משמע לפי' דאי הוה מצינו לאוקומי לעבודת דם – לא הוה ט] מוקמינא ליה לכפול בהזאות. וקשה: לר' שמעון בסמוך קמיבעי למימר דאיצטריך י] "כן יעשה" למתן ארבע (אפ"ה מצי נמי לכפול בהזאה ד"ועשה" לכפול כל מה דאמר בענין אתא) דלא כתב מתן ד' בהעלם דבר, ומקרנות דכהן משיח למד. ואם כן, אימא: איצטריך "ועשה כאשר עשה" למתן ד', *וא"כ מנא ליה לכפול בהזאות? לכך נראה ד"ועשה" יא] לכפול לכל מה שאמור בענין אתיא. וא"ת: א"כ מצי נמי קאי אמתן ד' לכפול בהזאות, ד"ועשה" לכפול כל מה דאמר בענין אתיא! וי"ל: יב] ד"ועשה" לא משמע להוסיף בפר העלם שתי מתנות הכתובות בכהן משיח, דאין ניכר שיהא חסר שום הזאה, אלא הנך שתים דפר העלם היינו אותן שתים דמשיח. וקשה: דילמא "ועשה כאשר עשה" אתי ל"את בדם וטבילה", דלא כתיב בפר העלם וכתיב בפר כהן, לפירוש רש"י, יג] ולא לכפול בהזאות! י"ל: ד"את בדם וטבילה" אין זה חסרון עבודה אלא תיקון עבודה, ולא שייך בהו "ועשה כאשר עשה". ברו"ך. **לפר*** זה פר יום הכפורים. יד] לקמן אמר: לא נצרכא אלא ל"את בדם וטבילה", אבל לעכב לא איצטריך, ד"חוקה" כתיבא ביה. טו] וגם "וכלה וכפר" דרשינן מיניה: אם כלה – כפר. ותימה: ולמה ליה "ועשה" לכפול בהזאות? תיפוק לי מדאיתקש לפר יום הכפורים! טז] ועוד קשה: דלרבי יהודה דריש לקמן: "וכלה מכפר", אם כלה – כיפר, ואם לא כלה – לא כיפר, לומר דמתנות יום הכפורים מעכבות. תיפוק לי מהיקישא דפר העלם דבר! ומיהו, להאי לישנא דאמר בפרק "איזהו מקומן" (לקמן דף נב:) ופרק "הוציאו לו" (יומא דף ס:) דלרבי יהודה שירים מעכבים – ניחא. אבל יז] להאי דאמר משמעות דורשין איכא בינייהו, ושירים לא מעכבי לרבי יהודה – קשה: דלעכב בהזאות לא צריך "וכלה מכפר", דמפר העלם נפקא! ויש לומר: דאיצטריך "וכלה" לשבע הזאות שעל טהרו, דליתנהו בפר העלם. יח] (תוספות עד ושעירי ראשי חדשים) ואם תאמר: היא גופה נילף בפר העלם דבר בהיקישא! וכ"ת דפר יום הכפורים הוא דאיתקש לפר העלם דבר, ולא פר העלם לפר יום הכפורים – הא ליתא, יט] דהא ילפינן יותרת ושתי הכליות בפר העלם מפר כהן משיח דאתו מייתורא דהאי קרא, וכן לר"ש בסמוך ילפינן ארבע מתנות בהעלם מכהן משיח – הכי נמי נילף עיכובא בהעלם מפר יום הכפורים! כ] הילכך נראה לי: "ועשה" דאתי לעיכובא ללמד בכהן משיח ושעירי עבודה זרה דכתיבי בהאי קרא מייתורא, לומר דמתנותיהם מעכבי, דקרבנות דאתי מריבויא דהאי קרא לא כא] ילפינן זה מזה. אבל לפירוש רש"י דלקמן אינו יכול להיות תירוץ זה, דפירש: "את בדם" לא כתב בהעלם כי אם בכהן משיח, וילפינן יום הכפורים ממשיח. וכיון דקרבנות דאתו מריבויא כב] גמרינן מהדדי, אם כן לישתוק מ"ועשה" וניגמר עיכובא *מכולהו מפר יום הכפורים. °מיהו פרש"י אין נראה לר"ת, כדמפרש לקמן. ברו"ך. ועוד נ"ל: דודאי פר העלם לא ילפינן עיכובא מפר יום הכפורים, שהרי אותן פרשיות רחוקות זו מזו, אבל פר העלם מפר כהן משיח – ילפינן שפיר ליותרת ולשתי הכליות למתן ארבע, שסמוכות הפרשיות זו אצל זו. ברוך. לפירוש זה ניחא, דלהכי לא ילפינן שבע על טהרו מפר יום הכפורים – לפי שהפרשיות רחוקות זו מזו. אבל להכי מהני "לפר" דמיותר – למידרש כג] יום הכפורים דילפינן ביה דינין של העלם. ולפירוש רש"י נמי, דילפינן פר העלם שפיר מפר כהן משיח, הא דלא ילפינן שבע דעל טהרו ושמונה דעל הפרכת בפר העלם מפר יום הכפורים – היינו טעמא: כיון דכתיב ביה "והזה שבע כד] על הפרכת" וגם "ונתן על קרנות", אם הוספת לא נתקיים הפסוק, ונראה הפסוק שקר. אבל ארבע דילפינן בקרנות ממשיח, משום דקרנות משמע שפיר טובא לכל הקרנות אחת, דהיינו ארבע. ובשעירי עבודה זרה דיליף משל העלם, ויהבינן שבע דעל הפרכת מהיקשא, וכן שעירי הרגלים אי לאו מיעוטא – משום דלא נכתב בהו כלל עבודת דם אלא כתובין סתם, וא"כ אין זה סתירת פסוק. ובאימורין דכתיב "כל חלבו" ואנן מוסיפין יותרת ושתי כליות – משום דליכא שום הקטרה בלא יותרת ושתי הכליות. ברו"ך. **ושעירי** ראשי חדשים. ואם תאמר: והיאך יכול לרבותו? והלא חטאת דראש חדש נאכל היה, כדכתיב: "דרש דרש משה והנה שורף"! ויש לומר: שעל זה הוא בא לדקדק, דנידרוש מ"שה" מהכא שיהא בשריפה כפנימים. **וכפר אע"פ שלא סמך.** אע"ג דלא מעכבא בעלמא הוה אמינא דמעכבא הכא, כדפי' בקונטרס משום ד"ועשה כאשר עשה" עלייהו כה] קאי. ומיהו, להקטרת אימורים לא איצטריך, דלא מעכבי בשום מקום, דאחר שהוכשר יחזור ויפסל. ולא דמי לסמיכה דהויא קודם עבודת הדם. ושיריים נמי עבודת הדם נינהו, ומעכבי לכמה תנאי. **ונסלח אע"פ שלא נתן שירים.** וא"ת: תיפוק לי מהא דדרשינן בפרק "איזהו מקומן" (לקמן דף נב:) בפר כהן משיח: "ואת כל הדם ישפך" – נתקו הכתוב ועשאו שירי מצוה, לומר שירים אין מעכבין. וה"נ נדרוש "ישפך" דפר העלם! ויש לומר: דהני מילי בפר כהן משיח, כו] כדפרישית לקמן בקונטרס דדריש מדשינה בהילוך לשונו, שבכל העבודות של כהן משיח כתיב "ולקח" "והזה" "ונתן", וכאן לא כתיב "ושפך את דמו (על) [אל] יסוד", אלא כז] בסתם "ישפך" – שינה במשמעו לנתקן. אבל הכא בפר העלם לא שינה הכתוב, דהא כתב נמי "יתן" – להכי איצטריך "ונסלח". מדאיתקש פר כהן משיח לפר העלם לא מצי למילף התם דלא מעכבי, כיון דשינה עליו הכתוב כדקאמרת התם ק"ו לפר כהן משיח מעתה, יכול יעכבנו. דמאי דכתב בגופיה הוי כאילו שנה לעכב, כיון דאפילו לא הוה כתב אתי מק"ו. כח] וקשיא לי: ד"ונסלח" בפר העלם למה לי? נילף מכהן משיח דשירים לא מעכבי! וכי תימא לא ילפינן קולות – הא ילפינן קולות בסמוך אמין דלא חייך. ברו"ך. **ומכשיר** אני בסמיכה ושירים שאין מעכבין בכל מקום. דלכל הפחות כט] חטאות החיצונות מודו כולי עלמא דשירים לא מעכבי. אבל להזאות לא אשכחן בשום מקום שלא יעכבו. ולפירוש רבינו תם, דאיכא תנא דאמר שירים החיצונים מעכבי – קשה: להאי תנא מנא לן לפסול בהזאות ולהכשיר בשירים? ושמא לא דריש "ונסלח". תדע, דלמאן דאמר נמי שירים הפנימים מעכבי – על כרחין בכל פנימים קאמר, מדקאמר: מחלוקת בשירים הפנימים אבל בשירים החיצונים כו'. ולא קאמר: מחלוקת בשירים דיוה"כ, אבל בשאר פנימים לא מעכבי.
מתן

רש"ק מ"ז

ומנ"ל לכפול בהזאות וי"ל דמסתברא דועשה לכפול בהזאות אתי ומצי נמי קאי אמתן ארבע לכפול בהזאות דועשה לכפול כל מה דאמור בענין אתי אבל [אין] לומר דועשה למתן ד' (אפי') [אתי] דועשה לא משמע להוסיף בפר העלם על ב' המתנות הכתובות כו' כצ"ל וכ"ה בס"י נ"ק

שייך לע"א

בכולהו נ"ק

שיטה מקובצת

א] החטאת אלו שעירי עבודה זרה. פי' שיהיו פנימים ונשרפים דחטאת בא לרבות חטאות אחרות של צבור שיהו כאלו: ב] יכול שאני מרבה כו'. דכיון שבא לרבות נרבה אף את אלו דנרבה כל חטאות צבור. ותימה היכי ס"ד לרבות שעירי ר"ח הא כתיב ואת שעיר החטאת דרוש דרש משה וגו' מדוע לא אכלתם אלמא שעירי ר"ח נאכלים דבשעירי ר"ח מיירי מדהשיב לו אהרן אם שמעת בקדשי שעה לא שמעת בקדשי דורות וי"ל דעל [זה] בא לדקדק הכא שהיה לו למשה לדרוש (מחטאות) [מהחטאת] שיהו שעירי ר"ח נשרפים ולמה כעם אשר שרפוה ודוחק הוא ונראה דעיקר קושיא דהכא אשעירי רגלים הוא ושעירי ר"ח אגב גררא נקטי ומיהו קשה לרבינו נתנאל דאכתי קשה דהיכי מצינו לרבויי שיהו פנימיים הא כתיב גבי מזבח הפנימי וכפר אהרן על קרנותיו אחת בשנה כלומר כפרה זו לא תהא אלא אחת בשנה ואילו שעירי רגלים שיהו פנימיים נמצא מזבח הפנימי מכפר כמה פעמים בשנה דנהי דבלאו הכי איכא פר כהן משיח ופר העלם ושעירי עבודת כוכבים התם על חטא באים ואינם קבועים אבל שעירי הרגלים קבועים הן. לכך נראה להר"ר נתנאל דה"ק יכול שאני מרבה אף שעירי הרגלים ושעירי ר"ח שיהו מתנותיו מעכבות ולעולם לא יהו פנימים ונשרפים אלא על מזבח החיצון ונאכלים. ומיהו קשה דא"כ אמאי איצטריך לומר בסמוך מרבה אני את אלו שהן מכפרים על עבירות מצות ידועות כו' לימא מרבה אני את אלו שכן פנימים ונשרפים כמו פר כהן ומשיח ופר העלם משא"כ בשעירי הרגלים ובשעירי ר"ח וי"מ דעדיפא מיניה פריך וגם זה דוחק. לכך נראה דלעולם לענין (שהיו) [שיהו] פנימים ונשרפין בעי לרבויינהו ומ"מ לא קשה אחת בשנה דכתיב גבי מזבח הפנימי דהתם לא בעי למעט שאר קרבנות ממזבח הפנימי אלא בא להשמיענו דשעיר הפנימי דיוה"כ כפרה אחד מכפר ואינו מכפר ב' כפרות כדדריש מיניה בפ"ק דשבועות גבי טומאת מקדש וקדשיו ותדע דאחת בשנה לא בא למעט קרבנות אחרים דהא למ"ד אין מערבין לקרנות אלא נותן מדם הפר לבדו על הקרנות וכן מדם השעיר לבדו א"כ שתים בשנה הן אלא ע"כ כדפי': ג] ונסלח אע"פ שלא נתן שירים. תימה היכי

הגהות הב"ח

(א) רש"י ד"ה זה פר וכו' יחד ללמד עיכוב: (ב) ד"ה שפיכת וכו' לדברי הכל. נ"ב עיין בתוס' בע"א ד"ה הא מני בקושי' מהר"י מאורלייניש וכאן בד"ה ומכשיר אני בסמיכה ושירים:

גליון הש"ס

תוס' ד"ה לפר וכו' ומיהו פירש"י אין נראה לר"ת. עיין לקמן דף מז ע"ב תוס' ד"ה אלו ואלו:

דריש מונסלח הא מבעיא ליה לגופיה דכה"ג אמר לעיל גבי חטאות חיצונות דדריש מתנה אחת מוכפר ונסלח מוקי ליה לגופיה ואומר הר"ר חיים בר שניאור דאה"נ דונסלח לגופיה ומכיפר דרשינן ב' דרשות אע"פ שלא סמך ואע"פ שלא נתן שירים כיון דלא מעכבי כפרה תרוייהו מחד קרא נפקא וכן משמע בסמוך דקאמר סד"א מידי דהוי אסמיכה ושירי הדם כו' והשתא אי לא נפקא לן מחד קרא אלא חדא דרשא א"כ מתן ד' מגילה דלא מעכבי הא ליכא אלא תרי קראי וכיפר ונסלח חד לסמיכה וחד לשיריים אלא ודאי דמחד קרא ילפינן שפיר תרתי או תלתא דרשות כדפי': ד] פוסל אני: ה] תיבת לדם נמחק: ו] יחד שילמד: ז] ידוע ומוציא אני של כו' שלא יהו שוין: ח] וכתיבא ביה בהדיא: ט] הוה מוקמינן: י] דאיצטריך ועשה כאשר עשה למתן ארבע א"כ מנ"ל לכפול בהזאות הא לא כתיב מתן ארבע בפר העלם ומקרנות דפר כהן משיח כו' והשאר נמחק: יא] דועשה משמע לכפול לכל מה שאמור בענין אתא הלכך כי נמי איצטריך לעבודת דם מ"מ משמע ועשה כאשר עשה דקאי נמי אכולהו עשיות ועבודות שנאמרו בפר כהן משיח והוי כאילו כתיב בהדיא ועשה בכל עשיות והלכי קאמר מה ת"ל הרי עיקר העבודות מפורשות בהדיא בפר העלם דבר מתו' מהר"פ ז"ל. מתיבת וא"ת עד תיבת וי"ל נמחק: יב] וי"ל לפי' רש"י דועשה: יג] רש"י אבל לפי' ר"ת דלקמן ניחא שפי' דאת בדם וטבילה כתיבי בפר העלם כמו בפר כהן משיח. מהר"פ ז"ל: יד] לקמן מפרש לא: טו] תיבות וגם כלה וכפר דרשינן מיניה אם כלה כפר נמחק: טז] הכפורים דכתיב ביה חוקה ועוד: יז] אבל למאן דאמר משמעות: יח] העלם מיהו אכתי קשה היא גופה כו' והשאר נמחק: יט] ליתא. [תוס' עד ושעירי ראשי חדשים] דהא: כ] הלכך נ"ל דועשה אתי. ומתיבת הלכך כו' עד תיבת הא דלא מוקף חצי לבנה: כא] לא ילפי זה מזה: כב] דקרבנות דאתו מריבויא גמרי: כג] למדרש זה פר יוה"כ: כד] שבע פעמים לפני ה' את פני הפרכת גם ויתן על קרנות כו' לא תקיים הפסוק: כה] עליהו נמי קאי ומיהו כו' מקום דכי לאחר שהוכשר: כו] כדפריש לקמן: כז] אל יסוד אלא הדם ישפך: כח] מתיבת וקשיא עד סוף הדבור מוקף חצי לבנה: כט] הפחות בחטאות:

אָמַר מָר: אֵין לִי אֶלָּא מַתַּן שֶׁבַע שֶׁמְּעַכְּבוֹת בְּכָל מָקוֹם. הֵיכָא? אָמַר רַב פַּפָּא: בְּפָרָה וּבִנְגָעִים. מַתַּן אַרְבַּע מִנַּיִן? ת"ל: "כֵּן יַעֲשֶׂה". מ"ש מַתַּן ז' – דִּכְתִיבָן וּכְפִילָן, מַתַּן ד' נַמִי כְּתִיבָן וּכְפִילָן! א"ר יִרְמְיָה: לָא נִצְרְכָא אֶלָּא לְר"ש; דְּתַנְיָא, לְמַעְלָה אוֹמֵר: א] "קֶרֶן קְרָנוֹת" – שְׁתַּיִם, לְמַטָּה הוּא אוֹמֵר: "קֶרֶן קְרָנוֹת" – אַרְבַּע, דִּבְרֵי ר"ש; ר' יְהוּדָה אוֹמֵר: אֵינוֹ צָרִיךְ, הֲרֵי הוּא אוֹמֵר "בְּאֹהֶל מוֹעֵד" – עַל כָּל הָאָמוּר בְּאֹהֶל מוֹעֵד. וְרַבִּי יְהוּדָה, "כֵּן יַעֲשֶׂה" מַאי עָבֵיד לֵיהּ? מִיבָּעֵי לֵיהּ לְכִדְתַנְיָא: לְפִי שֶׁלֹּא לָמַדְנוּ לְפַר יוה"כ לִסְמִיכָה וּשְׁיָרֵי הַדָּם, מִנַּיִן? ת"ל: "כֵּן יַעֲשֶׂה". וּלְפַר יוה"כ לֹא לָמַדְנוּ? הָא אָמְרַתְּ: "לַפָּר" – זֶה ב] *יוה"כ! אִיצְטְרִיךְ, סד"א: הָנֵי מִילֵּי עֲבוֹדָה דִּמְעַכְּבָא כַּפָּרָה, אֲבָל עֲבוֹדָה דְּלָא מְעַכְּבָא כַּפָּרָה אֵימָא לָא, קמ"ל. וְר"ש, הַאי "בְּאֹהֶל מוֹעֵד" מַאי עָבֵיד לֵיהּ? ג] "בְּאֹהֶל מוֹעֵד" מִבָּעֵי לֵיהּ, שֶׁאִם א נִפְחֲתָה ד] תִּקְרָה שֶׁל הֵיכָל – לֹא הָיָה מַזֶּה. וְאִידָךְ? מֵ"אֲשֶׁר". *וְאִידָךְ? "אֲשֶׁר" לֹא דָּרֵישׁ. אַבַּיֵי אָמַר: לְר' יְהוּדָה נַמִי אִיצְטְרִיךְ, סד"א: מִידֵּי דַּהֲוָה אַסְּמִיכָה וּשְׁיָרֵי הַדָּם, דְּאע"ג דִּכְתִיבָן וּכְפִילָן לָא מְעַכְּבָא – מַתַּן אַרְבַּע נַמִי לָא ה] תִּתְעַכֵּב, קמ"ל. "לַפָּר" – זֶה פַּר יוֹם הַכִּפּוּרִים. לְמַאי הִילְכְתָא? אִי לְעַכֵּב – פְּשִׁיטָא, "חוּקָּה" – כְּתִיבָה בֵּיהּ! אָמַר רַב נַחְמָן בַּר יִצְחָק: לָא נִצְרְכָא אֶלָּא לְרַבִּי יְהוּדָה, *דְּאָמַר: כִּי כְּתִיבָה °"חוּקָּה" – אַדְּבָרִים ב הַנַּעֲשִׂים בְּבִגְדֵי לָבָן בִּפְנִים, שֶׁאִם הִקְדִּים מַעֲשֶׂה לַחֲבֵירוֹ – לֹא עָשָׂה וְלֹא כְלוּם. אֲבָל דְּבָרִים הַנַּעֲשִׂים בְּבִגְדֵי לָבָן בַּחוּץ, הִקְדִּים מַעֲשֶׂה לַחֲבֵירוֹ – מַה שֶּׁעָשָׂה עָשׂוּי, אֵימָא מִדִּכְסִידְרָן לָא מְעַכְּבִי – הַזָּאוֹת נַמִי לָא מְעַכְּבִי, קמ"ל. מַתְקִיף לָהּ רַב פַּפָּא: וּמִי מָצֵית אָמְרַתְּ הָכִי? *וְהַתַנְיָא: °"וְכִלָּה מִכַּפֵּר אֶת הַקֹּדֶשׁ", ו] אִם כִּיפֵּר – כִּילָּה, וְאִם לֹא כִּיפֵּר – לֹא כִּילָּה, דִּבְרֵי *ר"ע; א"ל רַבִּי יְהוּדָה: מִפְּנֵי מָה לֹא נֹאמַר: אִם כִּילָּה – כִּיפֵּר, וְאִם לֹא כִּילָּה – לֹא כִּיפֵּר! ז] אָמַר רַב פַּפָּא: לָא נִצְרְכָא, אֶלָּא לְ"אֵת *דָּם וּבִטְבִילָה"; "אֵת" – אָמַר רַב אַחָא בַּר יַעֲקֹב: לָא נִצְרְכָא, ח] *לְהַכְשִׁיר

אמין

ויקרא טז | שם

רש"י

בְּפָרָה. "וְהִזָּה אֶל נֹכַח פְּנֵי אֹהֶל מוֹעֵד" וגו', וְכָתַב "חוּקָּה" לְעִיכּוּבָא. בִּנְגָעִים. בְּלוֹג שֶׁמֶן שֶׁל מְצוֹרָע: "וְהִזָּה מִן הַשֶּׁמֶן בְּאֶצְבָּעוֹ" וגו', וּכְתִיב: "זֹאת תִּהְיֶה תּוֹרַת הַמְּצוֹרָע" (ויקרא יד), וְכָל הֲוָיָה טו] עִיכּוּבָא. דִּכְתִיבָן. בְּהֶדְיָא. וּכְפִילָן. "וְעָשָׂה כַּאֲשֶׁר עָשָׂה". מַתַּן אַרְבַּע נַמִי כְּתִיבָן בְּהֶדְיָא וּכְפִילָן. ד"וְעָשָׂה כַּאֲשֶׁר עָשָׂה" אַכּוּלָּהּ מִילְּתָא קָאֵי, וּמֵהֵיכָא תֵּיתֵי לְמַעוּטִינְהוּ? לָא נִצְרְכָא אֶלָּא לְר"ש. יז] דְּאָמַר: לָא כְּתִיב יח] בֵּיהּ אֶלָּא שְׁתַּיִם, וּשְׁתַּיִם אֲחֵרוֹת בְּהֶיקֵּשָׁא דְּהַאי קְרָא אִיתְקוּשׁ פַּר כֹּהֵן מָשִׁיחַ וּפַר הֶעְלֵם דָּבָר, כִּדְאָמְרַן: "לַפָּר" – זֶה פַּר כֹּהֵן מָשִׁיחַ. הִילְכָּךְ, אִי לָא דַּהֲדַר כַּפְלִינְהוּ – לָא הָווּ כְּפוּלִין. לְמַעְלָה. בְּפַר כֹּהֵן מָשִׁיחַ. לְמַטָּה. בְּפַר הֶעְלֵם. קֶרֶן קְרָנוֹת. מִדְּמָצֵי לְמִיכְתַּב "קֶרֶן" וְכָתַב "קְרָנוֹת" – יב] הָוְיָא שְׁתַּיִם. דְּאִית לֵיהּ לְר"ש יֵשׁ אֵם לַמִּקְרָא, וְחוֹזְרִים וּמְלַמְּדִים זֶה מִזֶּה בְּהֶיקֵּשׁ. הֲרֵי הוּא יג] אוֹמֵר. בִּשְׁנֵיהֶם: "עַל קַרְנוֹת מִזְבַּח קְטֹרֶת סַמִּים אֲשֶׁר לִפְנֵי ה' אֲשֶׁר בְּאֹהֶל מוֹעֵד", וְהַאי "בְּאֹהֶל מוֹעֵד" יְתֵירָא הוּא, דְּהָא כְּתִיב "אֲשֶׁר לִפְנֵי ה'", יד] וּלְמֵדְךָ: עַל כָּל הַקְּרָנוֹת שֶׁבְּתוֹךְ הַהֵיכָל צָרִיךְ לִיתֵּן. סְמִיכָה וּשְׁפִיכַת שִׁירַיִם לֹא נֶאֶמְרוּ בְּפָרָשַׁת "אַחֲרֵי מוֹת". ת"ל כֵּן יַעֲשֶׂה. לְרַבּוֹת פַּר יוה"כ לִסְמִיכָה וְשִׁירַיִם. דְּהָא פַּר יוה"כ בְּהַאי קְרָא כְּתִיב, כִּדְאָמַר: "לַפָּר" – זֶה טו] *יוה"כ. וְהָאָמַרְתְּ לַפָּר כו'. וְכֵיוָן דְּאִיתְקַשׁ לְהַאי אִיתְרַבּוּ לְהוּ סְמִיכָה וְשִׁירַיִם בְּהֶיקֵּשָׁא, וְלָמָּה לִי תּוּ "כֵּן יַעֲשֶׂה"? ס"ד אָמִינָא. כִּי אִיתְקַשׁ, לַעֲבוֹדָה דִּמְעַכְּבָא כַּפָּרָה הוּא דְּאִיתְקַשׁ, כִּדְכְתִיב "וְכִפֶּר" בְּהַאי קְרָא, וּלְרַבּוּיֵי בֵּי' "אֵת בַּדָּם וּטְבִילָה", כִּדְמְפָרֵשׁ לְקַמָּן. נִפְחֲתָה. תִּקְרַת עֲלִיָּיתוֹ וְגַגּוֹ, תּוּ לָאו אֹהֶל הוּא. מֵאֲשֶׁר. נָפְקָא לֵיהּ אַרְבַּע קְרָנוֹת מֵ"אֲשֶׁר". דְּמָצֵי לְמִכְתַּב "אֲשֶׁר לִפְנֵי ה' בְּאֹהֶל מוֹעֵד", לָמָּה לִי טז] [לְמֵיהְדַּר] לְמִיכְתַּב "אֲשֶׁר"? אֶלָּא עַל כָּל הַקְּרָנוֹת אֲשֶׁר בָּאֹהֶל.* דְּהַאי "אֲשֶׁר" בַּתְרָא מִשּׁוּם מִזְבֵּחַ לָא אִיצְטְרִיךְ לְמִיכְתְּבֵיהּ. לְר' יְהוּדָה נַמִי. אע"ג דִּכְתִיבִי מַתַּן אַרְבַּע בְּהֶדְיָא, וּכְפִילָן בְּ"וְעָשָׂה כַּאֲשֶׁר עָשָׂה". אִיצְטְרִיךְ. "כֵּן יַעֲשֶׂה" לְרַבּוּיִינְהוּ יז] שֶׁיְּעַכְּבוּ. סד"א מִידֵּי דַּהֲוָה אַסְּמִיכָה וּשְׁיָרֵי הַדָּם. דְּפַר הֶעְלֵם גּוּפֵיהּ, דִּכְתִיבָן וּכְפִילָן וְלָא מְעַכְּבִי, כִּדְאוֹקִימְנָא עִילָוַיְיהוּ מִיעוּטָא ד"וְכִפֶּר וְנִסְלַח" מִשּׁוּם טַעַם דְּאֵין מְעַכְּבוֹת בְּכ"מ. מַתַּן אַרְבַּע. שֶׁאֵין מְעַכְּבוֹת בְּחַטָּאת הַחִיצוֹנָה נַמִי לָא לִיעַכְּבוּ, דְּנִימְעֲטוּ נַמִי מִ"וְכִפֶּר וְנִסְלַח"! קמ"ל. יח] (דִּלְעִנְיַן סְמִיכָה וְשִׁירַיִם שֶׁאֵין מְעַכְּבִין בְּכ"מ קָא חָשֵׁיב לְהוּ כַּפָּרָה) דְּאִילּוּ סְמִיכָה וְשִׁירַיִם אֲפִילּוּ עִקְּרִינְהוּ לְגַמְרֵי לָא מְעַכְּבֵי, וְאִילּוּ מַתַּן אַרְבַּע חֲדָא מִינַּיְיהוּ יט] מְעַכֵּב בְּחַטָּאת הַחִיצוֹנָה. הִילְכָּךְ מַיְיתִינַן לְכוּלְּהוּ לְעִיכּוּבָא מִ"וְכֵן יַעֲשֶׂה". לְמַאי הִילְכְתָא לְעַכֵּב. דְּהָא לָא כְּתִיבָן וּכְפִילָן בֵּיהּ, וְאִיצְטְרִיךְ כ] לְאַקְשׁוּיֵי. פְּשִׁיטָא. [לָא] גָּרְסִינַן גַּבֵּי פַּר יוה"כ. לְעַכֵּב. שֶׁיְּהוּ כָּל הַמַּתָּנוֹת מְעַכְּבוֹת. חוּקָּה כְּתִיב. בְּסוֹף פָּרָשַׁת "אַחֲרֵי מוֹת", "וְהָיְתָה זֹאת לָכֶם לְחוּקַּת עוֹלָם" וגו'. לְרַבִּי יְהוּדָה. בְּפ' "הוֹצִיאוּ לוֹ" (יומא דף ס.). דְּאָמַר דְּבָרִים הַנַּעֲשִׂין בְּבִגְדֵי לָבָן מִבִּפְנִים. כא] מַתָּנוֹת וּקְטֹרֶת שֶׁעַל בֵּין הַבַּדִּים. הִקְדִּים מַעֲשֶׂה כב] לַחֲבֵירוֹ לֹא עָשָׂה וְלֹא כְלוּם. ד"חוּקָּה" עֲלַיְיהוּ כְּתִיב. אֲבָל דְּבָרִים הַנַּעֲשִׂין בְּבִגְדֵי לָבָן מִבַּחוּץ. כְּגוֹן מַתְּנוֹת פַּר וְשָׂעִיר שֶׁעַל הַפָּרֹכֶת. הִקְדִּים שָׂעִיר לַפָּר מַה שֶּׁעָשָׂה עָשׂוּי. ד"חוּקָּה" לָאו עֲלַיְיהוּ כְּתִיב וְהָתָם מְפָרֵשׁ כג] טַעֲמַיְיהוּ. אֵימָא מִדִּכְסִידְרָן לָא מְעַכְּבִי. אַלְמָא "חוּקָּה" לָאו עֲלַיְיהוּ קַיְימָא, מִגּוֹ הַזָּאוֹת גּוּפַיְיהוּ נַמִי לָא לִיעַכֵּב אִם חִסֵּר מֵהֶן. קמ"ל. הֶיקֵּשָׁא דְּהָכָא. וּמִי מָצֵית אָמְרַתְּ הָכִי. דִּלְר' יְהוּדָה עִיכּוּבָא מֵהָכָא יָלֵיף. וְכִלָּה מְכַפֵּר. קְרָא יְתֵירָא הוּא, דְּלָא הֲוָה לֵיהּ לְמִיכְתַּב אֶלָּא "וְהִקְרִיב אֶת הַשָּׂעִיר הֶחָי". אִם כִּיפֵּר. כַּפָּרָה הַמְעַכֶּבֶת בִּשְׁאָר מְקוֹמוֹת, כְּגוֹן כד] מַתְּנַת דָּמִים, מַתַּן שֶׁבַע וּמַתַּן ד'. כִּילָּה. אע"פ שֶׁלֹּא שָׁפַךְ שִׁירַיִם לִיסוֹד מִזְבַּח חִיצוֹן. מִפְּנֵי מָה לֹא נִדְרוֹשׁ. הַמִּקְרָא כְּסֵדֶר מִכְתָּבוֹ, וְנֹאמַר: אִם כִּילָּה הַכֹּל, אֲפִילּוּ שְׁפִיכַת שִׁירַיִם – כִּיפֵּר. וְאִם לֹא כִּילָּה לֹא כִּיפֵּר. וְהָכִי מְפָרֵשׁ בְּסֵדֶר יוֹמָא דְּשִׁירַיִים מְעַכְּבִין אִיכָּא בֵּינַיְיהוּ. אַלְמָא, עִיכּוּב לְר' יְהוּדָה מֵהָכָא נָפְקָא! לָא נִצְרְכָא. הַאי דְּמַקִּישׁ פַּר יוה"כ לְפַר הֶעְלֵם דָּבָר וּלְפַר כֹּהֵן מָשִׁיחַ. אֶלָּא לְאֵת בְּדָם וּטְבִילָה. דִּבְפַר כֹּהֵן מָשִׁיחַ כְּתִיב: "וְטָבַל הַכֹּהֵן אֶת אֶצְבָּעוֹ בַּדָּם". וְאִי קַשְׁיָא: בְּהַאי קְרָא

תוספות

מתן ארבע נמי כתיבן וכפילן אמר רבי ירמיה לא נצרכה כו'. תימה: כיון דבכתיבן וכפילן תליא מילתא, אמאי תלי כה] רבי טעמא דברייתא במה שמעכבות בכל מקום? ויש לומר: דלא תימא דנילף מתן ארבע ממתן שבע. וא"ת: מתן שתים לכל הפחות כתיבן וכפילן ואפילו לר"ש, ואם כן נילף אינך שתים מינייהו! כו] (תוספת) נראה לי: דאחת *דכתיבה בעלמא כז] ומינה לא נילף, ומן השניה דכתיבה לא נילף השתים הנוספות, דתרתי מחדא לא ילפינן ע"כ. לא נצרכה אלא לר"ש דתניא כו'. פירש בקונטרס: דר"ש אית ליה יש אם למקרא. וכן ודאי שמעינן ליה בפ"ק דסנהדרין (דף ד.) גבי "בסכת" "בסכת". והא דשמעינן כח] בפ"ק דקדושין (דף יח:) דדריש תרוייהו יש אם למקרא ולמסורת גבי "בבגדו בה" – משום דהתם אפשר לקיים שניהם, אבל כאן אי אפשר לדרוש שניהם. אבל לר"ע קשה: דלא דריש התם תרוייהו, ובפ' "כל שעה" (פסחים דף לו.) גבי "על לחם עוני" דריש מקרא ומסורת. ובפ' לולב הגזול (סוכה דף לד:) תנן נמי, ר"ע אומר: כשם שלולב אחד ואתרוג אחד כו', ודריש בגמ'* לולב אחד מדכתיב "כפת"! וי"ל: דנהי דר"ע ס"ל מקרא כט] (ומסורת) עיקר, מ"מ לדרשא פורתא דרשינן ליה למסורת. ומיהו קשה מר"ש: דהכא סבירא ליה יש אם למקרא, ובסוף "כילד צולין" (פסחים דף פו:) גבי "בבית אחד יאכל" קסבר יש אם למסורת. והיא *ד"יותן" דומיא ד"כי יתן", *ו"עובד" דומיא ד"עבד", *"ישמע" "ישמיע", *ו"לא תשא" ו"לא תשיא". אומר ר"ת: דבהנהו כ"ע מודו שהמקרא והמסורת שניהם ל] משמעותם א', ולא שייכי לפלוגתא לא] (בין מקרא למסורת דשניהם משמעות אחד ולא שייכי לפלגותא) דמקרא ומסורת*. למטה הוא אומר קרן קרנות ארבע דברי ר"ש. וא"ת: כיון לב] דהוקשו בזו ובזו גבי הזאות נמי, א"כ ניבעי ארביסר! לג] וי"ל: דלא דמי, דמתן ד' אשכחן, אבל הזאות ארביסר לא אשכחן בשום מקום. לד] (תוספת) ועוד י"ל: ד"קרנות" טובא נמי משמע, ואם נאמר ארבע – אין זה סתירת הפסוק. אבל גבי הזאות כתיב והזה שבע ולא יותר. לסמיכה ושירי הדם. בפ' "איזהו מקומן" (לקמן דף נג.) דריש מדכתיב "הפר" – [לימד] על פר יוה"כ שטעון מתן דמים ליסוד. ותימה: להוא תנא, סמיכה מנא ליה? וי"ל: דבתורת כהנים דריש מדכתיב: "וסמך על ראש הפר" – לרבות פר יוה"כ לסמיכה. *) ואפי' נפקא ליה להוא תנא מהיקשא דהכא יותרת ושתי הכליות, אע"ג דלא מעכבי כפרה – מ"מ שירים לא נפקי, דגריעי, כדאמר בסוף "השוחט והמעלה" (לקמן דף קיא.) דאימורים תחילת עבודה, ושיריים סוף עבודה. אשר לא דריש. לעיל פירשתי, בריש פ"ב (דף יח: ד"ה ואידך). אביי אמר לרבי יהודה נמי איצטריך. תימה: הא שמעינן ליה לרבי יהודה דשיריים הפנימים מעכבי לה] לחד אמורא בפרק "איזהו מקומן" (לקמן דף נב:) ובפרק "הוציאו לו" (יומא דף ס:). והך ברייתא קתני: "ונסלח" אע"פ שלא נתן שיריים – לו] על כרחין דלא כוותיה, וכיון דשיריים מעכבין – כל שכן מתן ארבע! וכי תימא דהני מילי בשיריים דיוה"כ דגלי קרא: "וכלה מכפר" – לא משמע הכי כדפרישית, לז] מדלא קאמר מחלוקת בשיריים של יוה"כ, אלא מפליג בין פנימים לחיצונים, ובשום מקום לא מצינו שמחלק בפנימים. ועוד קשה הא דקאמר לעיל: סד"א הני מילי עבודה דמעכבא כפרה כו' – הא על כרחין שיריים לרבי יהודה מעכבי כפרה! ונראה דהך סוגיא אתא כריב"ל, דאמר: משמעות דורשין איכא בינייהו, ולית ליה לר' יהודה שיריים מעכבין. ור' יוחנן דאית ליה לר' יהודה שיריים מעכבי – איצטריך "וכן יעשה" לסמיכה לבד. אמר רב נחמן בר יצחק לא נצרכה אלא לרבי יהודה. כאביי ס"ל. דלר' ירמיה לח] לעיל לא מיתוקמא כר' יהודה, דר' יהודה דריש "כן יעשה" לסמיכה ושיריים, והך ברייתא מוקמא ליה למתן ארבע. לא נצרכה אלא לאת בדם ובטבילה. פי' בקונטרס: דלא כתיב "בדם" בפר העלם אלא בפר כהן משיח כתיב, וילפינן מיניה פר יוה"כ, לט] דאיתקש בהאי

*) גי' הצ"ק לסמיכה הס"ד ואח"כ מה"ד ה"מ עבודה כו' אע"ג דנפקא ליה להוא תנא כו'

שיטה מקובצת

א] קרן קרנות כו'. וא"ת כיון דהטעם משום דלא כפילן א"כ אמאי תלי טעמא בברייתא משום דמתן ד' אינו מעכב בשום מקום וי"ל דאיצטריך ההוא טעמא דלא תימא דנילף מתן ד' ממתן ז'. [אא"ה הוא לשון התוס' ד"ה מתן ד']: ב] זה פר יוה"כ: ג] ליה מבע"ל ותיבות באהל מועד נמחק: ד] תקרה ס"א א) תקרי: ה] לא תעכב קמ"ל אמר מר לפר זה פר כהן משיח למאי הלכתא לעכב. לפר: ו] הקודש את אהל מועד ואת המזבח אם: ז] כיפר שאם חיסר אחת מכל המתנות לא עשה ולא כלום אלא אמר ר"פ ל"נ אלא לאת בדם וטבילה: ח] נצרכא אלא להכשיר: ט] הוויה לעיכובא: י] לר"ש דלדידיה לא כפילן כדמסיק ואזיל דלא כתיב ביה אלא קרנות דהוו שתים ושתים אחרות בהיקשא קא אתי דאיתקש פר כהן משיח לפר העלם דבר כו'. כך היא נוסחת רש"י של הר"פ: יא] כתיב בהדיא ביה אלא כו' דהאי קרא אתי דאיתקש פר: יב] קרנות הרי שתים: יג] הוא אמור בשניהם: יד] ה' אלא ללמדך על כל: טו] זה פר יוה"פ: טז] למהדר ולמכתב: יז] שיעכבו הס"ד: יח] קמ"ל דמתן ד' לגבי סמיכה ושיריים מעכבות בכל מקום ותיבות דלענין סמיכה ושיריים שאין מעכבין קא חשיב להו כפרה נמחק: יט] מיניהו מיהת מעכבא: כ] ואיצטריך לאקושי הס"ד ומה"ד פשיטא לא: כא] מבפנים. כגון קטורת ומתנות שעל: כב] הקדים מעשה שעיר: כג] מפרש טעמיה הס"ד: כד] מתנת הדמים: כה] תיבת רבי נמחק: כו] מתיבת תוספת עד סוף הדבור מוקף בחצי לבנה: כז] בעלמא מינה: כח] דשמעינן ליה בפ"ק: כט] תיבת ומסורת נמחק: ל] שניהם שוים משמעותם: לא] מתיבת בין עד תיבת לפלוגתא נמחק: לב] כיון דמוקמי שבזו בזו גבי הזאות נמי נימא הכי [א"כ]: לג] ארביסר הזיות וי"ל: לד] מקום. לשון מהר"פ וא"ת לר"ש מתן ארבע לשעירי עכו"ם [illegible] הוא גופיה למד בהיקש מפר כהן משיח ואינו חוזר ומלמד בהיקש וי"ל דלמד לענין שתי קרנות דכתיב בגופיה דפר העלם למד נמי גם לענין ד' דהוי הימנו ודבר אחר דלא הוי היקש וא"ת התינח למ"ד לא הוי היקש אלא למ"ד הוי היקש מאי איכא למימר וי"ל דלמ"ד דהוי היקש יליף ליה מלפר זה פר העלם דקאמר ת"ק דתנא דבי ר' ישמעאל לענין יותרת ושתי כליות למהוי כמאי דכתיב בגופיה וה"ה לענין [מתן] ד' מיהו קשה דא"כ אמר רב פפא לקמן משום דבעי אגמורי פר העלם לשעירי עכו"ם לענין קרנות וי"ל משום דיותרת ושתי כליות פסיקא ליה גם לר' יהודה אבל קרן קרנות לא איצטריך לר' יהודה: לה] תיבות לחד אמורא נמחק: לו] שיריים ואיצטריך כן יעשה למתן ארבע על כרחין דלא כוותי' דכיון: לז] כדפרישית לעיל: לח] ירמיה דלעיל: לט] יוה"כ דאיתקש:

עין משפט נר מצוה

יט א מיי' פ"ה מהל' יוה"כ הל' כג:
כ ב מיי' שם הל"ח:

מסורת הש"ס / הגהות

נ"ל פר יוה"כ
[ע' תוס' לעיל יח: ד"ה ואידך]
פר יוה"כ נ"ק
תוספתא דיומא פ"ג [יומא נט: ס.]
מועד אתי אשר בתרא דמשום מזבח לא נ"ק יומא ס: לקמן נב:
[בילקוט אי' דברי רבי יהודה אמר לו ר' נחמיה מפני מה כו']
[נ"ל בדם ובטבילה]
[נ"ל אלא להכשיר]
רש"ק מ"ז
רש"ק
כתיבה בעלמא ומינה לא נילף למתן השתים הנוספות כצ"ל נ"ק
[סוכה לד.]
[לעיל יח: מנחות מג:]
קדושין נט: *פסחים כו. סנהדרין ז: *פעו.
[וע' היטב תוס' סנהדרין ד. ד"ה כולהו ותוס' סוכה ו: ד"ה ור"ש]

א) אולי נ"ל ס"א הקירוי.

כא א מיי' פ"ה מהל' מעשה קרבנות הל"ט:
כב ב מיי' פ"ה מהל' עבודת יוה"כ הל' כד:

א] אמין שבאצבע. "בדם" – *שיהא אבדם שיעור טבילה מעיקרא, "וטבל" – ולא מספג. *ואיצטריך למכתב ב] "בדם", דאי כתב רחמנא "וטבל", הוה אמינא: אע"ג דליכא שיעור טבילה מעיקרא – כתב רחמנא: "בדם"; ואי כתב רחמנא "בדם", ה"א: אפי' מספג – כתב רחמנא: "וטבל". "מזבח קטרת ג] סמים" למה לי? בשאם לא נתחנך המזבח בקטורת הסמים – לא היה מזה. תניא כוותיה דרב פפא: ועשה כאשר עשה", מה ת"ל "לפר"? לרבות פר יום הכפורים לכל ד] מה שאמור בענין, דברי *רבי. (א) א"ר ישמעאל: ק"ו, ומה במקום שלא ה] הושוה קרבן לקרבן – השוה מעשים למעשים, מקום שהשוה קרבן לקרבן – אינו דין שישוה מעשה למעשה? ו] אלא מה ת"ל "לפר" – זה פר העלם דבר של צבור, "לפר" – זה פר כהן משיח. אמר מר: ומה במקום שלא הושוה קרבן לקרבן. מאי "לא הושוה קרבן לקרבן"? אילימא פר יוה"כ ושעיר יום הכפורים – איכא למיפרך: מה להנך שכן נכנס דמם לפני ולפנים! אלא פר העלם דבר של צבור ושעירי עבודה זרה – איכא למיפרך: ז] מה להנך שכן מכפרין על עבירות מצוה ידועה! אלא פר העלם דבר של צבור ושעיר של יום הכפורים. והכי קאמר: ח] ומה במקום שלא הושוו קרבן לקרבן, דהאי פר והאי שעיר – ט] הושוו מעשים למאי דכתב בהו, מקום שהושוה קרבן לקרבן, דהאי פר והאי פר – אינו דין שהושוו

רש"י

קרא פר יום הכפורים לפר העלם הוא דאיתקש, דבדידיה קא מישתעי קרא, ובפר העלם לא כתיב את בדם וטבילה! י] הא אמרן: "כאשר עשה לפר" – זה פר כהן משיח, אלמא לפר כהן משיח נמי איתקוש. ובפר יום הכפורים לא כתיב "את" ולא כתיב טבילה ולא כתיב "בדם", דהכי כתיב: "ולקח מדם הפר יא] באצבעו". ואקשינ' להאי, ללמד הימנו הילכות ריבוייא של "את", והילכות "בדם" וטבילה כדמפרש. [להכשיר אמין]. תמן תנינן (חולין נה:): היא האם, היא טרפחת, היא שלפוחית. וכל שלפוחית היא *ווסיא"ה, כעין אותה של דג, כדאמרינן במסכת ע"ז:* "בשליפוחה" גבי עוברי דגים. ואם של בהמה כולה עשויה חבעבועות. תשובת מורי. את להכשיר אמין שבאצבע. שאם עלתה לו אם באצבע, שקורין *ווסיא"ה, כמו ניטלה האם ד"אלו טריפות" (חולין ד' נד.) – לא הויא חציצה, דאיתרבי מ"את אצבעו" – את הטפל לאצבעו. בדם שיהא בדם שיעור טבילה מעיקרא גרסינן. משעת קבלה ראשונה, למעוטי קבל פחות מכדי טבילה (ג) יב] בכלי זה ופחות מכדי טבילה בכלי זה ועירבן. והכי מפרש לה במנחות (דף ז:) ולקמן בפרק "דם חטאת" (דף צג:) ויליף מ"בדם" מדקרינן "וטבל יג] בדם" ולא קרינן בדם, משמע בדם שהיה כבר משעה ראשונה. מספג. מקנח בדופני הכלי. כן שמעתי במנחות. הכי גרסינן: הוה אמינא אף על גב דליכא שיעור טבילה מעיקרא. אלא שיהא בו עכשיו. אפילו מספג. דאשיעורא בעלמא הוא דקפיד קרא. מזבח קטרת הסמים למה לי. השתא דדרשת "אשר באהל מועד" על כל האמור כו'. "מזבח קטרת הסמים" מאי דרשת ביה? יד] דהאי יתירא, דהא כתיב "אשר לפני ה'". שאם לא נתחנך כו'. אם אירע פר העלם בעוד המזבח חדש, שלא הקטירו עליו קטרת מעולם. תניא כוותיה דרב פפא. דהיקשא ל"את בדם וטבילה" אתא טו]. לכל האמור בענין. הכל בכלל טז] "את בדם וטבילה". קל וחומר. כלומר, אין צריך להביא פר יום הכפורים לכאן, דמקל וחומר נפקא שכל דרכי פר יז] העלם בו. ומה במקום שלא הושוה קרבן לקרבן. שאין הבהמות ממין אחד. ולקמן מפרש מאי היא. הושוו מעשים למעשים. מעשה עבודותיהן שוין של זה לשל זה. מקום שהשוה קרבן לקרבן. כגון פר יום הכפורים ופר העלם, ששניהם מין אחד – אינו דין שיהא עבודותיהן שוות לעבודות שהצריך הכתוב לשניהן? כגון הזאות שבהיכל ושבמזבח יח] יהו מעשי עבודותיהן שוין ל"את בדם וטבילה". אלא מה תלמוד לומר לפר זה פר העלם. ולקמן פריך: מאי קאמר? הא קרא בדידיה קאי! לפר. "כאשר עשה לפר" – זה פר כהן משיח, בא להקישו לזה יט] לפוסלו בחיסור מתנות, כדפרישית לעיל, דבפר כהן משיח לא נכפלו וצריך ללמוד מזה. אילימא דפר ושעיר של יום הכפורים. שלא הושוו הבהמות, שזה פר וזה שעיר – הושוו מעשים של זה למעשים של זה, שכל עבודותיהן שוות. מקום שהושוו קרבן לקרבן, כגון פר כ] כהן משיח ופר יוה"כ, דשניהן מין אחד – אינו דין כו'. מה לפר ושעיר של יוה"כ. דין הוא שיושוו מעשה עבודותיהן, שהרי נכנס דם שניהם לפני ולפנים ואין חילוק ביניהם. תאמר שיושוו פר[א] העלם ופר יום הכפורים בעבודות האמורות בהן, שלא הושוו בכניסה לפני ולפנים, שזה נכנס וזה לא נכנס. אלא פר העלם ושעירי עבודה זרה. שהושוו מעשיהם, דאמרן לעיל: "החטאת" – לרבות שעירי עבודה זרה, ואף על פי שלא הושוו קרבן לקרבן, דהאי פר והאי שעיר. שכן שניהם מכפרין על עבירות מצוה ידועה. לפיכך הושוו מעשיהם. תאמר שיושוו כא] מעשה פר[ב] העלם ומעשה פר יום הכפורים – שכן לא הושוו בכפרתן, שזה מכפר על עבירת מצוה שאינה ידועה וזה מכפר על ידועה. כדאמר בשבועות (דף ב:): על שיש בה ידיעה בתחילה ואין בה ידיעה בסוף, שכשנטמא ידע שנטמא, ונעלמה ממנו טומאה ונכנס למקדש, ושוב לא נודעה לו כניסתו – שעיר הנעשה בפנים על ישראל, ופר על כהנים – תולה, עד שיוודע לו ויביא בעולה ויורד.

הושוו

תוספות

קרא. וקשה לרבינו תם: דאמר בשמעתא דאיצטריך "לפר" זה פר העלם דבר לאגמורי יותרת הכבד ושתי הכליות לשעירי עבודה זרה, דלא ליהוי דבר הבא מן ההיקש חוזר ומלמד בהיקש. ואי כב] איתקש כל הנהו דכתיבי בהאי קרא אהדדי, אם כן שעירי כג] עבודה זרה גופייהו דדרשינן מ"החטאת" – נילף מפר כהן משיח גופיה, דמפורשים בגופיה יותרת הכבד ושתי כליות, כד] [ג] וגם תרווייהו, שעירי עבודה זרה וכהן משיח, דכתיבי בהאי קרא מריבויא! וכן בפרק "איזהו מקומן" (לקמן דף מט:) דאיצטריך "כאשר יורם" למילף יותרת בשעירי עבודה זרה, שלא תאמר דפר העלם הוי דבר הבא מן ההיקש. וכן נמי אמרינן בשמעתין: סד"א הני מילי הזאות דכתיבי בגופיה, אבל יותרת ושתי הכליות דלא כתיבן בגופיה אימא לא. ואי הוקשו לפר כהן משיח – הא כתיבי בגופיה כמו בפר יום הכפורים בדם כה] וטבילה! כן פי' רבינו יצחק בר' אברהם ז"ל. ומיהו יש ליישב לפירוש הקונטרס: דלא דמי, דפשטא דקרא "ועשה לפר כאשר עשה לפר החטאת" – מקיש פר ראשון לפר אחרון, דהיינו פר יום הכפורים לפר כהן משיח. אבל "לפר החטאת" כו] דמוקמה בפר כהן משיח ובשעירי עבודה זרה – אין נחשב היקש כלל. ומיהו קשה: "את בדם וטבילה" בשעירי עבודה זרה[ד] מנין? דמפר העלם לא הוי כמאן דכתיב בגופיה, כמו ביותרת דבסמוך. הניחא לרבי ישמעאל, אלא לרבי דדריש "לפר" זה פר יוה"כ, מנא ליה? דבשלמא יותרת לא קשיא, דנפקא ליה מ"כאשר יורם" כדאיתא בפ' "איזהו מקומן" (ג"ז שם) דאייתר בפר כהן משיח למיהוי כמאן דכתיב בגופיה דפר העלם. אבל בדם וטבילה לא שייך ביה! ונראה לר"ת: כז] דלא איתקוש כולהו אהדדי, אלא כולהו איתקש לפר העלם, ופר העלם הוקש לפר כהן משיח. ובפר העלם דלא כתיב ביה "בדם" – הא כתיב ביה "וטבל אצבעו מן הדם", דמשמע שפיר שיהא בו שיעור טבילה מעיקרא, כמו "בדם", והא דנקט "בדם" – לפי שהוא תחילה בפרשה בפר כהן משיח. וכי תימא: הא איצטריך להא דמסקינן בפ"ק דמנחות (דף ז:) ולקמן בפרק "דם חטאת" (דף צג:): כח] מן הדם שבענין – לא[ה] מ"וטבל בדם" דריש, אלא מן "והזה מן הדם כט] באצבעו" דכתיב בפר כהן משיח בתר "וטבל". תדע, דהא מפרש ל] למעוטי משיריים שבאצבע שלא יזה פעם שניה, ומה ענין זה גבי "וטבל"? ואם תאמר: ובחטאות החיצונות מנא לן "את בדם וטבילה"? הלא אפילו פנימי מפנימי לא יליף אלא בהיקש. ובפ"ק דמנחות (דף ז:) משמע דאיתיה בכל חטאות, דקאמר דקומץ אינו קדוש לחלאין משום דילפינן מדם, כל שכן דאית לן למילף דם מדם! ולפי' רבינו תם ניחא, דבחטאות החיצונות כתיב "מן הדם" דהוי כמו "בדם", וכתיב בהו "ולקח" דדרשינן שיעור לקיחה כי היכי דדרשינן "וטבל" שיעור טבילה, ו"את" להכשיר אמין שבאצבע ילפינן מקל וחומר חיצונות מפנימיות. ומיהו, צריך לדקדק: מכל מקום היכי ילפינן קומץ מדם, דאפילו דם מדם לא יליף?. (תוספת) וקשה: דבפר העלם לא כתיב "את", וא"כ להכשיר אמין מנא ליה בפר יום הכפורים? ובמסורת כתב: קדמאה לא] את, תניינא לא כתב את. וכן כתב רבינו סעדיה בקרא ד"מן הדם" לא כתיב את. *לאת בדם וטבילה. הוה מצי למימר נמי ל"אהל מועד", לכדאמרן לעיל: שאם נפחתה תקרה כו', ול"קטורת סמים" – לכדאמר בסמוך: שאם לא נתחנך המזבח כו'. תניא כוותיה דרב פפא כו'. משמע ליה דהא דקתני בברייתא לכל מה שאמור בענין דל"את בדם וטבילה" קאמר. דאי לא אתיא אלא לעכב – לא הוה ליה למימר "לכל מה שאמור בענין". וליותרת ושתי הכליות ליכא למימר, דהא בעבודת דם הוקשו. ולשירים נמי לא קאמר,[ו] דרבי נפקא ליה מקרא אחרינא לקמן בפרק "איזהו מקומן" (דף נב.). ועוד: ק"ו דרבי ישמעאל "ומה במקום שלא הושוו" לא שייך אלא גבי "את בדם וטבילה". ומה במקום שלא הושוה קרבן לקרבן כו'. ולקמן בפרק "איזהו מקומן" (גם זה שם) יליף רבי ישמעאל מתן דם ליסוד בפר יום הכפורים מקל וחומר: ומה אם מי שאין נכנס דמו לפנים טובה טעון יסוד. ההוא ק"ו לא הוה מצי למימר הכא, משום "את" דהוי קולא, להכשיר אמין שבאצבע. והאי ק"ו דהכא לא מצי למימר התם, דלא ילפינן מהאי ק"ו דבר חדש ליתן האמור של זה בזה, דהא חזינן דמלוקין בכמה דברים. ולא ילפינן מהאי דינא אלא דלמאי דכתב בהו צריך שיהא זה כזה, דבאותו ענין שיעשה הזאות של זה יעשה הזאות של זה, והיינו ל"את בדם וטבילה". תדע, מדלא פליג רבי ישמעאל א"לפר" זה פר כהן משיח לעכב. דלמה לי? תיפוק לי מהאי קל וחומר: ומה במקום שלא הושוה קרבן לקרבן, כפר העלם ושעירי עבודה זרה – הושוו מעשים למעשים למעכבי, מקום שהושוה קרבן לקרבן לא כל שכן למעכבי? ומיהו יש לדחות: דמה להנך – שכן הושוו בציבור.

[לקמן נג. מנחות ז:]

נ"א ואיצטרך למיכתב וטבל ואיצטרך וכו'

[דף מ:]

[גי' הילקוט ר"ע]

שיטה מקובצת

א] אמין: ב] למכתב וטבל ואיצטריך למכתב בדם: ג] קטרת הסמים: ד] לכל (האמור) [מה שאמור] בענין. היינו תניא כוותיה דרב פפא דלכל האמור בענין משמע לענין דברים שלא נאמרו בהדיא בי"כ ונאמרו בפר העלם ואי לענין לעכב הא עיקר ההזאות כתיבי בגופיה דיוה"כ אלא ודאי לענין את בדם וטבילה קאמר שלא נאמרו ביוה"כ וא"ת והא לקמן מוכח גבי הא דפריך והא תנא לכל האמורים בענין קאמר דיותרת ושתי הכליות בפר יוה"כ נפקא לן מהך דרשא וא"כ היכי מייתי מינה סייעתא לרב פפא דלענין את בדם וטבילה אימא דאיירי דוקא לענין יותרת ושתי הכליו' שלא נאמרו כלל בפר יוה"כ מיהו י"ל מדקא מהדר ליה רבי ישמעאל ק"ו ומה במקום שלא השוה כו' דאיירי ע"כ לענין את בדם וטבילה כדמוכח לקמן דלא ילפינן מהאי ק"ח דלא השוה כו' שום דבר חדש רק תקון הזאות ופירושו מכלל דשמיע ליה מת"ק דהיינו רבי דלכל האמור דקאמר לענין את בדם וטבילה נמי קאמר וא"ת היא גופיה תיקשי מנליה לר' ישמעאל נמי דרבי איירי נמי לענין את בדם וטבילה אימא דדוקא איירי ביותרת ושתי הכליות וי"ל מדקאמר לכל האמור בענין משמע דאתי לכל הדברים שנאמרו בזה יותר מבזה. מהר"פ ז"ל: ה] שלא השוה: ו] ע' בהשמטות בסוף המסכת: ז] מה להנך שכן (מתכפרים) [מכפרים] כו' פ"ה שכן הושוו לדבר זה לענין מצוה ידועה ולכך דין הוא שיושוו בהם מעשים למעשים תאמר בפר העלם ופר יוה"כ שלא הושוו למצוה ידועה שהרי פר העלם על ידוע ובפר יוה"כ על אינו ידוע אבל לא רצה לפרש דמכח חומרא וקולא פריך מה להנך שכן יפה כחו במה שכן מכפרים על הידועה דא"כ התינח לענין בדם וטבילה דלא תילוף מינה דהוו חומרות אבל את (כל) [דבא] להכשיר אמין דהוי קולא כ"ש דאיכא למילף מקו"ח: ח] ומה במקום שלא הושוו קרבן לקרבן. מצאתי בס"א כגון פר יוה"כ ושעירי עבודה זרה הושוו מעשים המפורשים בשניהם שלא שינה בהם במתנות השוות בשניהם כגון הזאות שבהיכל מקום שהושוו קרבן לקרבן כגון שעיר יוה"כ ושעירי עבודה זרה אינו דין שישוו מעשים למעשים וילמוד סתום מן המפורש שעיר יוה"כ משעירי עבודה זרה וא"ת נימא דיו לבא מן הדין להיות כנדון דהא שעיר יוה"כ אכתי לא קמא לו ביה את בדם וטבילה וי"ל דקו"ח זה אינו בא ללמד דבר חדש אלא לפרש דין העבודה שתהא זו כזו וגילויא מילתא בעלמא. ע"כ: ט] הושוו מעשים למעשים דכתיב בהם. כלומר אע"ג דריבה הזאות בשעיר יוה"כ יותר מפר העלם בין הבדים ואף בפרוכת איכא ריבוי שהרי יש שמנה הזאות בשעיר יוה"כ ובפר העלם

שיטה מקובצת

ז' וכן במזבח הזהב איכא ריבויא דביוה"כ איכא נמי שבע על טהרו של מזבח ובפר העלם ליכא כי אם בקרנות מ"מ מה שהוצרך בשניהם בזה כמו בזה דהיינו שבע דפרכת וד' דקרנות השוה זה לזה שאלו על הפרכת כו' אלו על קרנות דפנימי ואלו על קרנות דפנימי אלו באצבע [כו'] וא"ת אכתי את בדם וטבילה שאנו דנין עליה והיא גופיה אנו באים ללמוד מקו"ח זה בזה לא הושוה מעשים דשעיר יוה"כ לפר העלם דהא את בדם וטבילה לא כתיב בשעיר יוה"כ וא"כ היאך בא הוא ללמוד מקו"ח זה השוואת [את] בדם טבילה בלמדים (את השוואת) כיון שאינה במלמדים וי"ל דודאי יש במלמדין (את) השוואת את בדם וטבילה דכיון שאנו רואין דלענין מאי דכתיב בהו דהיינו מה שהוצרך בשניהן שהן הזאות שבע ומתן ד' שהשוה זה לזה מעתה נאמר ילמוד סתום מן המפורש לענין את בדם וטבילה וגלי בפר העלם את בדם וטבילה וה"ה לשעיר יוה"כ וכן משמע מתוך פ"ה וז"ל אע"ג דאת בדם וטבילה כו' משמע קצת דמטעם ילמוד סתום מן המפורש: מהר"פ ז"ל: י] וטבילה. אלא מהיקשא דפר כהן משיח א"כ היכי הדר ולמד פר יוה"כ מיניה הא הוי היקש מן ההיקש תרי"ץ דכיון דפר כהן משיח כתיב בהאי קרא מקשינן פר יוה"כ לפר כהן משיח. מתו' מהר"פ: יא] הפר והזה באצבעו: יב] מכדי טבילת אצבע בכלי זה ופחות מכדי טבילת אצבע בכלי זה: יג] בדם ולא קרינן בדם: יד] ביה. דהא יתירא הוא דהא: טו] אתא ולא לענין לעכב הס"ד: טז] בכלל דאפי' את: יז] העלם ס"א כהן משיח: יח] ושבמזבח שיהו מעשי העבודות שוין: יט] לזה. לפסלו: כ] כהן משיח ס"א העלם: כא] שיושוו פר העלם ופר יוה"כ: כב] ואי כשיטת הקונטר' דאיתקש כל: כג] עכו"ם נמי גילף מפר כהן משיח דכתיב בהאי קרא מיהו יש ליישב כו' ת' מהר"פ: כד] מתיבת וגם עד תיבת ובכן הם: כה] ע' בהשמטות בסוף המסכת: כו] החטאת דמוקמינן: כז] לר"ת דלעולם לא איתקש: כח] תיבת באצבעו נמחק:

כח] הדם מן הדם שבענין התם לא מוטבל הכהן אצבעו מן הדם דרש: ל] מפרש התם במעוטי שיריים: לא] קדמאה כתיב את:

הגהות צ"ק [א] צ"ל משום: [ב] צ"ל משום: [ג] דגם כו' כתיבי בהאי קרא כו': [ד] מנין למילף מפר העלם וליהוי כמאן דכתיב כו' כצ"ל: [ה] מוטבל אצבעו מן הדם דריש אלא מן והזה מן הדם דכתיב בפר כו': [ו] צ"ל דרמי עקיצה:

הגהות הב"ח [illegible]

שהושוו מעשים למעשים? א] ואתא ליה פר יוה"כ (נמי) ל"את בדם וטבילה" מפר כהן משיח, ב] ואתי ליה שעיר יוה"כ *משעירי עבודה זרה מק"ו. וכי דבר הלמד בהיקש חוזר ומלמד בק"ו? אמר רב פפא: קסבר תנא דבי רבי ישמעאל: *דבר הלמד בהיקש חוזר ומלמד בק"ו. "לפר" — זה פר העלם דבר של צבור. הא ג] בציבור גופיה כתיב! אמר רב פפא: משום דבעי אגמורי פר העלם דבר של צבור ביותרת ושתי כליות לשעירי עבודה זרה, ופר העלם דבר של צבור בגופיה לא כתיב, בהיקשא אתי — *איצטריך ד] "לפר" למיהוי כמאן דכתיב ביה בגופיה, ולא ליהוי דבר הלמד בהיקש חוזר ומלמד בהיקש. תניא כוותיה דרב פפא: "ועשה כאשר עשה" — מה ת"ל "לפר"? לפי שנאמר: °"והם הביאו את קרבנם אשה לה'" ה] וגו', "חטאתם" — אלו שעירי עבודה זרה, "שגגתם" — זה פר העלם דבר של צבור, "חטאתם על שגגתם" — אמרה תורה: חטאתם הרי היא לך כשגגתם. ו] שגגתם מהיכן למדת — לא בהיקשא? וכי *דבר הלמד בהיקש חוזר ומלמד בהיקש? ז] ת"ל: "לפר" — זה פר העלם דבר של צבור, "לפר" — זה פר כהן משיח. אמר מר: "חטאתם" — אלו שעירי עבודה זרה. תיפוק ליה מקרא קמא, דאמר מר: "החטאת" — ח] לרבות שעירי עבודה זרה! אמר רב פפא: איצטריך, סלקא דעתך אמינא: ט] הני מילי הזאות דכתיבן בגופיה, אבל

במדבר טו

[לקמן מט:]

תורה אור

הושוו מעשים למאי דכתיב בהו. י] [א] שפירש הכתוב בהזאות הכתובות בהן לא שינה את זו מזו – אלו על הפרכת ואלו על הפרכת, אלו על הקרנות ואלו על הקרנות, אלו באצבע ואלו באצבע. ואע"ג דלא כתיב ביה בשעיר "את בדם וטבילה" – אין זה שינוי, דאיכא למימר לא פירש את הכל, דהא יא] במה דפריש לא שני. ואם זה נכנס לפנים וזה לא נכנס לפנים, וזה טעון שמנה הזאות וזה טעון שבע – מיהו למאי דכתיב בהו לא שינה, אם ריבה עבודות בזה יותר מזה, מכל מקום מעשה יב] עבודות שהצריך לשניהם לא שינה. מקום שהושווה קרבן לקרבן דהאי פר והאי פר אינו דין. שיושוו מעשה עבודות השוות בשניהם, כגון הזאות דפרכת ושל מזבח הזהב?* ה"ג: ואתא ליה פר יוה"כ לאת בדם וטבילה מפר יג] משיח. בהאי ק"ו כדאמרן. ואתי ליה שעיר יוה"כ נמי. ל"את בדם וטבילה" משעירי עבודה זרה בק"ו: מה במקום שלא הושווה קרבן לקרבן, דפר העלם ושעיר של יוה"כ – הושוו מעשים המפורשים בשניהם, שלא שינה בפי' עבודות השוות בהם כגון הזאות דהיכל. מקום שהושוה קרבן לקרבן, כגון שעיר יוה"כ ושעירי עבודה זרה – אינו דין שיושוו מעשים למעשים, וילמד סתום מן המפורש, שעיר של יוה"כ משעירי עבודה זרה? וכי דבר הלמד בהיקש. כגון שעירי עבודה זרה, לא למדנו בהן "את בדם וטבילה" אלא בהיקשא שהוקשו לפר *כהן משיח, וחוזרין ומלמדין "את בדם וטבילה" על שעיר יוה"כ כדאמר בק"ו? אמר רב פפא. האי "לפר" דמוקי רבי ישמעאל בפר העלם – משום דלקמן בעינן אגמורי פר העלם ביותרת הכבד ושתי הכליות לשעירי עבודה זרה בהיקשא ד"חטאתם על שגגתם". ופר העלם דבר בגופיה לא כתיב יותרת ושתי כליות, אלא "ואת כל חלבו יד] *ירים ממנו", [ב] ובהיקשא (להאי קרא) גמר להו מפר כהן משיח דכתיבי ביה. להכי אילטריך "לפר" יתירה טו] לפר העלם – לכפול בהיקשא שנייה, דהא בלאו הכי איתקש, דהאי קרא ביה קאי. וכתיב "כאשר עשה לפר" זה פר כהן משיח, וחזר וכפל "ועשה לפר" זה פר העלם – לכפול בהיקשו, ללמד ממנו יותרת, דליהוי האי היקש שני במקום כתיבה בגופו, דלא ניהוי דבר הלמד בהיקש חוזר ומלמד בהיקשא, דקיימא לן לקמן ב"איזהו מקומן" (דף מט:) דאין למדין בקדשים למד בהיקשא מן הלמד בהיקש. והם הביאו את קרבנם וגו'. בפרשת קרבנות עבודה זרה כתיב ב"שלח לך". ומקרא יתירא הוא לדרשא, דמה לו לכתוב זאת: "ונסלח להם כי שגגה היא והם הביאו את קרבנם"? לכתוב "ונסלח להם" ונשתוק! אלא משום דבעי לאקושי שעירי עבודה זרה דמשתעי ביה קרא לפר העלם להקטרת אימורים, טז] כדכתיב: "קרבנם אשה לה'" – היינו אימוריהם, ואקיש חטאתם לשגגה. חטאתם אלו שעירי עבודה זרה. דעלייהו קאי. שגגתם זה פר העלם. דכתיב ביה (ויקרא ד): "ואם כל עדת ישראל ישגו", אמרה תורה: חטאת דעבודה זרה זו הרי היא יז] כשאר שגגתם דשאר עבירות לענין אישים. ושגגתם מהיכן למד. הקטרת האישים שלה, לא בהיקש מפר כהן משיח? בתמיה, והיאך חוזר יח] ולמד בהיקש? ת"ל: "ועשה לפר" – זה פר העלם, חזר וכפל בהיקשן כדאמרן לעיל, למיהוי כמאן דכתיב בגופו. תיפוק ליה. יותרת הכבד לשעירי עבודה זרה. מקרא קמא. דאקשינן לעיל לפר העלם. דאמר מר החטאת אלו שעירי עבודה זרה. למה לי תו הך יט] ד"חטאתם על שגגתם"? סד"א הני מילי. דאיתרבו שעירי עבודה זרה לדין פר העלם – להזאות דכתיבן בגופיה בהדיא, אבל ליותרת וכליות לא. קמ"ל

נ"א נמי

[לקמן מט: נ.]

ע"כ שייך לעמוד הקודם

ב"מ ...

הושוו מעשים למעשים למאי דכתיב בהו. פי' בקונטרס: מה שפירש הכתוב בהזאות הכתובות בהן – לא שינה את זו מזו, אלו כ] [ואלו] על הפרכת, ואלו [ואלו] על הקרנות, ואלו [ואלו] באלבעות. ואע"ג דלא כתיב בשעיר "את בדם וטבילה" – אין זה שינוי, דאיכא למימר לא פירש הכל, דהא במאי דפריש לא שני. ואם זה נכנס לפנים וזה לא נכנס, וזה טעון שמונה הזאות וזה טעון שבע, מיהו למאי דכתיב בהו לא שני, ואם ריבה עבודות בזה יותר מבזה – מ"מ מעשה עבודות שהצריך לשניהם לא שינה. והגיה רבינו שמואל: דכל זה לא יתכן, דא"כ למה לנו ללמוד פר יוה"כ (הא) משעיר יוה"כ? [הא] מההוא טעמא כא] דנפיק שעיר ליפוק פר! ותו: מאי האי דאמרינן לקמן: ואתא ליה שעיר יוה"כ? מה צריך תו בהאי ק"ו? הרי כבר למד מפר העלם. כב] וגם לא הוזכר בברייתא דלעיל שנצטרך ללומדו! אלא הכי פירושו: ומה במקום שלא הושוו קרבן לקרבן, דהאי פר העלם והאי שעיר יוה"כ, דשני מיני בהמות הן – אפילו הכי הושוו מעשים למעשים ל"את בדם וטבילה" למאי דכתיב בהו, כלומר, אותן עבודות שכתובות בהן. אע"פ שאינן שוות בחשבון, דבשעיר יש לפני ולפנים ובהיכל אחת למעלה ושבע למטה, מיהו ל"את בדם וטבילה" הושוו, כדיליף לקמן שעיר יוה"כ משעירי עבודה זרה בק"ו, מקום שהושוו קרבן לקרבן, דהאי פר והאי פר כו'. וקיימא לן ב"איזהו מקומן" (לקמן דף נ:) דדבר הלמד בקל וחומר חוזר ומלמד בק"ו. והיינו דמפרש לקמיה: ואתא ליה שעיר יוה"כ משעירי עבודה זרה. כלומר, וכבר אתא ליה שעיר יוה"כ ויכול ללמד על פר יוה"כ כג] כדאמרינן. עד כאן לשונו כד][ג]. **וקשיא** היכי אתי שעיר יוה"כ משעירי עבודה זרה ופר העלם? מה להנך שכן מכפרין על כה] מלוה ידועה! ועוד, שכתוב בספרים: מפר יוה"כ ושעירי עבודה זרה. כו] ועל זה קשה: היכי אתי בק"ו ראשון פר יוה"כ משעיר יוה"כ ל"את בדם וטבילה"? הלא שעיר יוה"כ[ד] גופיה לא כז] קמה לו ל"את בדם וטבילה" בק"ו אחרון אלא מפר יוה"כ, והוא גופיה מנא ליה! כח] ונראה לפרש ק"ו ראשון כמו רש"י: ומה במקום שלא הושוו קרבן לקרבן, פר העלם ושעיר יוה"כ – הושוו מעשים למאי דכתיב בהו. השתא לא קאמר דהושוו ל"את בדם וטבילה" דהכתי לא קמה לו בשעיר יוה"כ, אלא הושוו שניהם על הפרכת ועל מזבח הזהב. מקום שהושוו קרבן לקרבן – אינו דין שיושוו למאי דכתיב בהו, אפילו ל"את בדם וטבילה"? וכן הוי ק"ו דשעיר יוה"כ. וצריך לדקדק אי שייך למימר "דיו" בהאי ק"ו, דמה בפר העלם לא הוי "את בדם וטבילה" אלא בשבע הזאות – אף פר יוה"כ כן, אבל הזאה שמינית – לא. ולהאי פירושא אתי שפיר דרבי חולק על קל וחומר זה שאינו פשוט, דתחילת דינו, דפר העלם דבר ושעיר יוה"כ בק"ו ראשון, דהושוו מעשים – לא הוי מ"את בדם וטבילה". ולא תיקשי לרבי: שעיר יוה"כ מנא ליה "את בדם וטבילה", כיון דלית ליה האי קל וחומר? כט] כיון דלרבי כתיב "לפר" [למידרש ביה] פר יוה"כ ל"את בדם וטבילה", א"כ אתיא ליה שעיר יוה"כ בק"ו גמור מפר יוה"כ ושעירי עבודה זרה, דלא הושווה קרבן לקרבן והושוו מעשים למעשים ל"את בדם וטבילה" – כל שכן שעירי[ה] (עבודה זרה ושעירי) יוה"כ. ע"כ. ברו"ך. **ואתא** ליה פר של יום הכפורים לאת בדם וטבילה מפר העלם של צבור. בקונטרס גריס: מפר כהן משיח, כי היכי דלא ליהוי למד מלמד. **ואתא** ליה שעיר של יוה"כ משעירי עבודה זרה מק"ו. ואם תאמר: א) רבי דלית ליה האי ק"ו, מהיכא יליף ל] ליה. וכי תימא, משום דאיתקש פר ושעיר של יוה"כ אהדדי – לא] דבקרא לא אשכחן הך היקשא! ותו: דא"כ לר' ישמעאל נמי תיפוק לי מהיקשא דהכא![ו] ותו: מנא ליה הכא וב"איזהו מקומן" (לקמן ד' נ.) לר' ישמעאל דדבר הלמד בהיקש חוזר ומלמד בקל וחומר? אימא איפכא, דדבר הלמד בקל וחומר חוזר ומלמד בהיקשא, דפר של יום הכפורים דאתי בק"ו מפר כהן משיח, חוזר ומלמד על שעיר בהיקש. ובפרק "איזהו מקומן" (גם זה שם:) משמע דקודם יש לנו לומר דדבר הלמד בקל וחומר חוזר ומלמד בהיקש, ממה שנאמר דבר הלמד בהיקש חוזר ומלמד בקל וחומר! לב] שעיר של יום הכפורים משעירי עבודה זרה, דלעיל דרשינן "החטאת" – אלו שעירי עבודה זרה, אבל שעיר של יום הכפורים לא אתיא מ"החטאת", כי היכי דלא מוקמי ליה בשעירי רגלים כדאמר לעיל. אבל

גליון הש"ס

גמ' איצטריך לפר למהוי כמאן דכתיב. עי' יומא דף מד ע"ב תוס' ד"ה אתיא כפרה.

שיטה מקובצת

א] (אלא מפר העלם ופר יוה"כ) [ואתי ליה פר יוה"כ מפר העלם] בקונטרס גרים מפר כהן משיח דאי מפר העלם הוא גופיה אתיא מהקיש' מפר כהן משיח והוי דבר הלמד בהיקש חוזר ומלמד בקו"ח וא"כ מיד היה לו להוכיח מכאן דדבר הלמד בהיקש חוזר ומלמד בקו"ח מהאי קו"ח ראשון ולמה המתין עד בסמוך בק"ו שני ולפי' ר"ת ניחא שפיר גירסא דפר העלם דבפר העלם גופיה כתיב את בדם וטבילה: ב] עיין בהשמטות בסוף המסכת: ג] הא בגופיה כתיב ותיבת בצבור נמחק: ד] איצטריך לפר למהוי כו' וא"ת ורבי דדריש לפר זה פר יוה"כ א"כ יותרת הכבד וב' הכליות למהוי כמאי דכתיב בגופיה בפר העלם לאגמורי מיניה לשעירי עבודה זרה מנליה וי"ל דנפקא ליה מאשר יורם דכתיב לגבי פר כהן משיח דמיותר ואם אינו ענין לפר כהן משיח תנהו לענין פר העלם למהוי כמאי דכתיב בגופיה כדאיתא באיזהו מקומן וא"ת ור"י דדריש לפר זה פר העלם למהוי כמאי דכתי' בגופיה כאשר יורם למה לי וי"ל דאיבעיא ליה כדדריש בפ' כל הבשר מה פר כהן משיח יש בו מעילה אף זבח שלמים יש בו מעילה לאימורים ואידך מכל חלב לרבות אימורי קדשים קלים למעילה: ה] לה' וחטאתם לפני ה' על שגגתם חטאתם אלו: ו] כשגגתם. ושגגתם: ז] בהיקש אלא מה ת"ל: ח] החטאת אלו שעירי ותיבת לרבות נמחק: ט] הני מילי הזאות דכתיבן בגופיה הוא דיליף שעירי עבודה זרה מריבויי דהחטאת וא"ת והא לענין את בדם וטבילה נמי ילפינן בשעירי עבודה זרה מפר העלם בהך היקשא דהחטאת ואת בדם וטבילה לא כתיב בגופיה דפר העלם לפי' רש"י כי אם מהיקש דפר כהן משיח וי"ל דשאני את בדם וטבילה דאינו ריבויי חדש כי אם דין הזאות ופירושן ולכך אתי מהחטאת אע"ג דלא כתיב בגופיה ומהאי טעמא נמי לא חשיב היקש מן ההיקש אף למ"ד הימנו ודבר אחר הוי היקש כדפי' לעיל אבל יותרת וב' הכליות תוספת דבר חדש ולכך לא יליף מהחטאת כיון דלא כתיב בגופיה וא"ת אמאי לא קאמר טעמא אחרינא דאי מהחטאת הו"א ה"מ לענין עבודות מעכבות הכפרה אבל עבודות דלא מעכבות הכפרה כגון (הקטרה) [הקטרת יותרת] וב' הכליות לא דכל הקטרה אינה מעכבת וכה"ג אמרינן לעיל גבי סמיכה ושיריים ביוה"כ דנפיק מוכן יעשה ולא נפיק מהיקשא קמא דלפר זה פר יוה"כ אע"ג דסמיכה ושיריים כתיב בגופיה ותירץ בקונטרס לקמן דדוקא שיריים דהוי סוף העבודה וסמיכה דאינה עבודה לא נפיק מהיקש קמייתא אבל הקטרת יותרת וב' הכליות דהקטרה חשיבא תחלת עבודה כדאיתא בפ' השוחט והמעלה אתיא שפיר מהיקש קמייתא אי לאו משום דלא כתיב בגופיה ועוד י"ל דהכא לר"ש איצטריך לומר טעמא דלא כתיב בגופיה ולא טעמא דמעכב כפרה דר"ש מוקי לוכן יעשה למתן ד' ולא לסמיכה ושיריים כדאיתא לעיל ואיכא למימר דהיינו משום דלר"ש אתו סמיכה ושיריים מהיקשא קמייתא ואע"ג דלא מעכבא כפרה אך קצת קשה ולר"ש נמי [י"ל] דמפיק סמיכה מוסמך ידו על ראש הפר ושיריים מואת כל הדם הפר ישפך כמו ההוא תנא דפרק איזהו מקומן מיהו איכא למימר לר"ש דכולה מילתא מהיקשא קמייתא נפקא: י] בהו מה שפירש: יא] דהא במאי דפריש: יב] מעשה העבודות שהצריך: יג] מפר כהן משיח: יד] חלבו ירים ממנו ובהיקשא דהאי קרא: טו] יתירה בפר העלם כו' דהא קרא ביה קאי: טז] אימורים. דיותרת וב' הכליות דבהקטרה ע"כ איירי קרא כדכתיב קרבנם אשה לה' דהיינו אימוריהם: יז] כשגגתם דשאר: יח] חוזר ומלמד: יט] הך היקשא: כ] אלו על הפרכת ואלו על הפרכת אלו על הקרנות ואלו על הקרנות אלו באצבעו ואלו באצבעו: כא] עי' בהשמטות בסוף המסכת: כב] העלם שעירי יוה"כ: כג] יוה"כ משעירי עבודה זרה: כד] עכ"ל לשון הר"פ וקשיא לפרשב"ם א"כ בפ' איזהו מקומן דמבעיא לן מעיקרא אי דבר הלמד בקו"ח (אי) חוזר ומלמד בקו"ח אי לא ופשיט ליה התם מכח סברא היה לו לפשוט האבעיא מברייתא' זו כי היכא דפשיט התם מכח ברייתא דדבר הלמד בהיקש חוזר ומלמד בק"ו וע"ק דע"כ צ"ל לפי שיטתו דקו"ח שני דגבי שעיר יוה"כ פשוט יותר מקו"ח ראשון מדסמיך בקו"ח ראשון על קו"ח שני כדפי' ואמאי הא בקו"ח שני איכא לאקשויי כמו בקו"ח ראשון דהיכא פשיט ליה במלמדין השוואת את בדם וטבילה דליכא למימר דשני המלמדין דקו"ח שני הוי שעירי עבודה זרה ופר העלם דכתיב בהו את בדם וטבילה דהא איכא למיפרך שכן מכפרין על מצות ידועה כמו גבי קו"ח ראשון אלא ע"כ היינו משעיר עבודה זרה ופר יוה"כ ואימא היא גופיה (קשה) [היקשא] כמו גבי קו"ח ראשון שהרי בפר יוה"כ גופיה לא כתיב את בדם וטבילה וליכא למימר דמ"מ פשיט ליה את בדם וטבילה בפר יוה"כ מכח קו"ח ראשון א"א לומר כן לפרשב"ם דאדרבה קו"ח ראשון נאמר מכח קו"ח שני כדפי' לכך נראה לפרש ההשוה מעשים למעשים דקאמר בתחילת דינא לגבי המלמדים דהיינו פר העלם ושעירי יוה"כ לעולם לאו לענין את בדם וטבילה קאמר דהא אכתי לא קיימא לן בשעיר יוה"כ עד קו"ח אחרון אלא השוה מעשים למעשים ממה שהשוה הכתוב בפירוש קאמר דהיינו לענין פרכת ומתן קרנות ואצבע כדפי' הקונטרס אלו בפרכת ואלו בפרכת ומ"מ שפיר קאמר בסוף דינא מקום שהשוה קרבן לקרבן דהאי פר והאי פר אינו דין שהשוה מעשים למעשים לגמרי גם לענין את בדם וטבילה אע"ג דההשוואה זו אינו במלמדים דתחילת דינא ודכוותיה אשכחן בפ' כיצד הרגל במילתיה דר' טרפון דיליף קרן בחצר הניזק להשוותם לשן בחצר הניזק לענין נזק שלם אע"ג דתחילת דינא במלמד היינו קרן ברה"ר ליכא נזק שלם כי אם חצי נזק וא"ת א"כ נימא דיו ולתחילת דינא מה תחילת דינא פר העלם ושעיר לא השוה מעשים למעשים כי אם פרכת ואצבע אותה השואה דוקא שישנו במלמדים בתחילת דינא וי"ל דא"כ הוי מיפרך קו"ח דהא לענין פרכת ואצבע לא מצטרך פר יוה"כ ללמוד מפר העלם דהא בגופיה דיוה"כ כתיב וא"ת התינח לר' טרפון דלית ליה דיו היכא דמיפרך קו"ח גבי קו"ח דשן וקרן בפ' כיצד הרגל אלא לרבנן דאית להו דיו היכא דמיפרך קו"ח א"כ הכא נמי נימא דיו כדפי' וי"ל דשאני הכא דאין קו"ח זה לרבות שום דבר חדש כי אם לפרש דין העבודות שיעשה העבודות בזה באותו ענין שעושה בזה הילכך אפי' רבנן מודו דלא אמרינן דיו כיון דמיפרך קו"ח כדפי' ר"ש מקוצי בפ"ק דקדושין ובפ"ק דפסחים ולא דמי להההיא קו"ח דשן ורגל דבפ' כיצד הרגל דהתם בעי למילף נזק שלם בקרן בחצר הניזק דהיינו דבר חדש דהא ברה"ר קרן חצי נזק הוא דמשלם וא"ת אכתי קשה קושיא דאמאי הוצרך להזכיר בסמוך ואתי ליה שעיר יוה"כ והלא לא החזכר בברייתא כלל ואמר מורי דנהי דקו"ח ראשון אינו בא מכח קו"ח שני מ"מ אם לא הייתי יכול ללמוד את בדם וטבילה בשעיר יוה"כ תו ליכא למילף את בדם וטבילה בפר יוה"כ מקו"ח קמא משום דאיכא למימר שעיר יוה"כ יוכיח שהשווה קרבן לקרבן לשעירי עבודה זרה דזה שעיר וזה שעיר ולא השוה מעשים למעשים לאת בדם וטבילה אם לא היינו דנין קו"ח שני וה"ק ואתי ליה שעיר יוה"כ כלומר דליכא למיפרך על קו"ח דפר יוה"כ ולומר דשעיר יוה"כ יוכיח כדפי' משום דשעיר יוה"כ גופיה ילפינן לאת בדם וטבילה להאי דינא דינא נמי כמו שמפרש והולך. כך נראה למורי ז"ל: כה] על עבירת מצוה: כו] עבודה זרה ס"א אתי שפיר: כז] קמא לן: כח] מתיבת ונראה עד סוף הדבור מוקף בחצאי לבנה: כט] וחומר די"ל כיון כו' למידרש ביה פר יוה"כ: ל] יליף הא ותיבת ליה ל"ש ונמחק: לא] אהדדי הא קרא לא אשכחן אלא הך היקשא: לב] וחומר וי"ל דנפקא ליה לרבי שעיר:

א) [עמ"ש בה"ז ונ"ק אולם לע דכה"ג כתבו תוס' לעיל ה. ד"ה הא שאר כו' ועוד ז: ד"ה מה שלמים וכו' וא"ת בלי שום תירוץ והגה עוד רבות כאשר רשמתי בלד תוס' ב"מ סא. ד"ה אלא ע"ש]:

הגהות צ"ק [א] דהא במה דפריש: [ב] ובהיקשא גמר להו מפר כהן משיח דכתיבי ביה בהאי קרא להכי איצטריך כו': [ג] הד"א: [ד] נ"א גופיה לא קאתי לאת כו': [ה] ג' תיבות אלו נמחק: [ו] ומנ"ל הכא ובאיזהו מקומן כו' כצ"ל:

נ"ל מייתר

כג א מיי' פט"ז מהל' פסה"מ הל"ז:

ה] אֲבָל יוֹתֶרֶת וּשְׁתֵּי כְלָיוֹת, דְּלָא כְּתִיבָן בְּגוּפֵיהּ – אֵימָא לָא, קָא מַשְׁמַע לָן.§ אֲמַר לֵיהּ רַב הוּנָא בְּרֵיהּ דְּרַב נָתָן לְרַב פַּפָּא: וְהָא תַּנָּא, ב] "פַּר יוה"כ לְכָל מַה שֶּׁאָמַר בָּעִנְיָן" קָאָמַר! תַּנָּאֵי הִיא, תַּנָּא דְּבֵי רַב מְרַבֵּי הָכִי, תַּנָּא דְּבֵי רַבִּי יִשְׁמָעֵאל לָא מְרַבֵּי הָכִי. תַּנָּא דְּבֵי רַבִּי יִשְׁמָעֵאל: מִפְּנֵי מָה נֶאֶמְרוּ יוֹתֶרֶת וּשְׁתֵּי כְלָיוֹת בְּפַר כֹּהֵן מָשִׁיחַ, וְלֹא נֶאֶמְרוּ בְּפַר הֶעְלֵם דָּבָר שֶׁל צִבּוּר? מָשָׁל לְמֶלֶךְ בָּשָׂר וָדָם ג] שֶׁזָּעַם עַל אוֹהֲבוֹ, וּמִיעֵט בְּסִרְחוֹנוֹ מִפְּנֵי חִיבָּתוֹ. וְתַנָּא דְּבֵי רַבִּי יִשְׁמָעֵאל: מִפְּנֵי מָה נֶאֶמְרָה °"פָּרֹכֶת הַקֹּדֶשׁ" ויקרא ד' בְּפַר כֹּהֵן מָשִׁיחַ, וְלֹא נֶאֱמַר בְּפַר הֶעְלֵם דָּבָר שֶׁל צִבּוּר? מָשָׁל לְמֶלֶךְ בָּשָׂר וָדָם שֶׁסָּרְחָה עָלָיו מְדִינָה, אִם מִיעוּטָהּ סָרְחָה – פַּמַּלְיָא שֶׁלּוֹ מִתְקַיֶּימֶת, אִם רוּבָּהּ סָרְחָה – אֵין פַּמַּלְיָא שֶׁלּוֹ מִתְקַיֶּימֶת.§ "לְפִיכָךְ אִם נָתַן כּוּלָּן כְּתִיקְנָן" כו'.§ תְּנַן הָתָם: *פִּיגֵּל בַּקּוֹמֶץ וְלֹא בַלְּבוֹנָה, בַּלְּבוֹנָה וְלֹא בַקּוֹמֶץ, רַבִּי מֵאִיר אוֹמֵר: פִּיגּוּל וְחַיָּיבִין עָלָיו כָּרֵת, וַחֲכָמִים אוֹמְרִים: אאֵין בּוֹ כָּרֵת עַד שֶׁיְּפַגֵּל בְּכָל הַמַּתִּיר. א"ר שִׁמְעוֹן בֶּן לָקִישׁ: לָא תֵּימָא טַעְמָא דְּר' מֵאִיר ד] דְּקָסָבַר מְפַגְּלִין בַּחֲצִי מַתִּיר, אֶלָּא הָכָא בְּמַאי עָסְקִינַן – כְּגוֹן שֶׁנָּתַן אֶת הַקּוֹמֶץ בְּמַחֲשָׁבָה, וְהַלְּבוֹנָה בִּשְׁתִיקָה; קָסָבַר: כָּל הָעוֹשֶׂה – עַל דַּעַת רִאשׁוֹנָה הוּא עוֹשֶׂה. מִמַּאי – ה] מִדְּקָתָנֵי: לְפִיכָךְ אִם נָתַן כּוּלָּן כְּתִיקְנָן וְאַחַת שֶׁלֹּא כְּתִיקְנָהּ – פָּסוּל וְאֵין בּוֹ כָּרֵת; הָא אַחַת שֶׁלֹּא כְּתִיקְנָהּ וְכוּלָּן כְּתִיקְנָן – פִּיגּוּל. מַנִּי? אִילֵימָא רַבָּנַן – הָא אָמְרִי רַבָּנַן: אֵין מְפַגְּלִין בַּחֲצִי מַתִּיר! אֶלָּא רַבִּי מֵאִיר; וְאִי טַעְמָא דְּרַבִּי מֵאִיר מִשּׁוּם דִּמְפַגְּלִין בַּחֲצִי מַתִּיר הוּא – אֲפִילּוּ כִּדְקָתָנֵי נַמִּי! ו] לָאו מִשּׁוּם דְּקָסָבַר: בכָּל הָעוֹשֶׂה – עַל דַּעַת רִאשׁוֹנָה הוּא עוֹשֶׂה? אָמַר רַבִּי שְׁמוּאֵל בַּר יִצְחָק: לְעוֹלָם רַבָּנַן הִיא, וּמַאי "כְּתִיקְנָן" – כְּתִיקְנָן לְפִיגּוּל. וְהָא מִדְּקָתָנֵי: לְפִיכָךְ, אִם נָתַן כּוּלָּן כְּתִיקְנָן וְאַחַת שֶׁלֹּא *כְּתִיקְנָן – פָּסוּל וְאֵין בּוֹ כָּרֵת, מִכְּלָל דְּ"תִיקְנָהּ" לְהֶכְשֵׁירָהּ הוּא דַּאֲתָא! אָמַר רָבָא: מַאי "שֶׁלֹּא כְּתִיקְנָהּ" – חוּץ לִמְקוֹמוֹ. רַב אַשִׁי אָמַר: שֶׁלֹּא לִשְׁמוֹ. מִכְּלָל דְּכִי לָא עָבֵיד לָהּ חוּץ לִמְקוֹמוֹ וְשֶׁלֹּא לִשְׁמוֹ מְחַיֵּיב! אַיְּידֵי דִּתְנָא רֵישָׁא: פִּיגּוּל וְחַיָּיבִין עָלָיו כָּרֵת – תְּנָא נַמִּי סֵיפָא: פָּסוּל וְאֵין בּוֹ כָּרֵת. מֵיתִיבִי: *)בַּמֶּה דְּבָרִים אֲמוּרִים – בְּדָמִים הַנִּיתָּנִין עַל מִזְבֵּחַ הַחִיצוֹן, אֲבָל

נ"ל כתיקנה

*) שם טז. [תוספתא דזבחים פ"ד]

תורה אור

קמ"ל. ז] דְּ"חַטָּאתָם עַל שִׁגְגָתָם" דִּלְעִנְיַן "אִשֶּׁה לַה'" נַמִּי אִיתְקוּשׁ. **וְהָא** **תַּנָּא** לְרַבּוֹת פַּר יוה"כ לְכָל ח] הָעִנְיָן קָאָמַר. אַלְמָא כּוּלָּהּ מִילְּתָא יָלֵיף מִינָּהּ, וַאֲפִילּוּ עִיכּוּבָא, וְאַתְּ אָמְרַתְּ לְ"אֶת בְּדָם וּטְבִילָה"! **תַּנָּאֵי הִיא** ט] **תַּנָּא** דְּבֵי רַב מְרַבֵּי הָכִי. כָּל א) "ת"ר" קָרֵי "תַּנָּא דְּבֵי רַב". הַהִיא מַתְנִי' קַמַּיְיתָא לָא מְרַבֵּי לֵיהּ אֶלָּא לְ"אֶת בְּדָם וּטְבִילָה". וְעִיכּוּבָא נָפְקָא לֵיהּ מֵ"חוּקָּה", וּלְרַבִּי יְהוּדָה מֵ"אִם כִּלָּה כִּפֵּר". **וְתַנָּא** דְּבֵי רַבִּי יִשְׁמָעֵאל. הַךְ תַּנָּא בַּתְרָא דְּאָמַר: לְכָל הָאָמוּר בָּעִנְיָן – י] מַתְנִיתִין דְּבֵי רַבִּי יִשְׁמָעֵאל הִיא, שֶׁנִּשְׁנֵית וְנִסְדְּרָה בְּבֵית מִדְרָשׁוֹ שֶׁל ר' יִשְׁמָעֵאל, וְסִידְּרוּ בָּהּ יא] תַּנָּאִים הַרְבֵּה כְּמוֹ שֶׁסִּידְּרוֹ רַבִּי חִיָּיא וְר' אוֹשַׁעְיָא. **עַל אוֹהֲבוֹ.** לִיבּוּר. מִיעֵט בְּסִרְחוֹנוֹ. קִילֵּר בִּדְבָרִים. מִפְּנֵי מָה נֶאֶמְרָה פָּרֹכֶת הַקֹּדֶשׁ. גָּרַס. יב] בְּפַר כֹּהֵן מָשִׁיחַ כְּתִיב: "אֶת פְּנֵי פָּרֹכֶת הַקֹּדֶשׁ" וּבְפַר הָעֵדָה כְּתִיב: "אֶת פְּנֵי הַפָּרֹכֶת". **פַּמַּלְיָא** שֶׁלּוֹ. כְּנִיסַת חֲבוּרַת עֲצָתוֹ יג] וּמֵהַמַּסְכִּימִים לְדַעְתּוֹ אֲשֶׁר דִּבְרֵי סִתְרוֹ אֲלֵיהֶם. וְאִם רוּבָּהּ סָרְחָה אֵין פַּמַּלְיָא שֶׁלּוֹ קַיֶּימֶת – הֲרֵי הוּא מְסוּלָּק מֵחִיבָּתָם וּמַכְנִיסָתָם בְּמִקְלָט, וְאֵין לִבּוֹ גַּם בָּהֶן כְּבָרִאשׁוֹנָה. ה"נ, כֵּיוָן דְּרוֹב לִיבּוּר יד] [סָרְחָה] – כִּבְיָכוֹל אֵין כָּאן קְדוּשָּׁה. **פִּיגֵּל בַּקּוֹמֶץ וְלֹא בַלְּבוֹנָה.** בְּהַקְטָרַת הַמִּנְחָה שְׁנֵי מַתִּירִין יֵשׁ, הַקּוֹמֶץ וְהַלְּבוֹנָה. וְאִם הִקְטִיר אֶת הָאֶחָד בְּמַחֲשֶׁבֶת פִּיגּוּל וְהָאֶחָד בִּשְׁתִיקָה. ר"מ **אוֹמֵר פִּיגּוּל.** כִּדְמְפָרֵשׁ טַעְמָא לְקַמָּן. כְּגוֹן שֶׁנָּתַן **אֶת** הַקּוֹמֶץ בְּמַחֲשָׁבָה. תְּחִילָּה, וְאַחַר כָּךְ הַלְּבוֹנָה בִּשְׁתִיקָה. וְה"ה אִם נָתַן לְבוֹנָה בְּמַחֲשָׁבָה תְּחִילָּה וְאַחַר כָּךְ קוֹמֶץ בִּשְׁתִיקָה. וְטַעְמָא – מִשּׁוּם דְּעַל דַּעַת רִאשׁוֹנָה עָשָׂה, וְנִמְצָא מְפַגֵּל בְּכָל הַמַּתִּיר. וְרַבָּנַן סָבְרֵי: עַל דַּעַת רִאשׁוֹנָה לָא אָמְרִינַן, אֶלָּא אִם כֵּן אָמַר אַף בַּשֵּׁנִי. וְכָל מַחֲשָׁבָה דְּקָדָשִׁים מוֹצִיא בַּפֶּה טו] הוּא. אֲבָל רִאשׁוֹנָה בִּשְׁתִיקָה וּשְׁנִיָּה בְּמַחֲשָׁבָה, דְּאֵין כָּאן אֶלָּא מַחֲשֶׁבֶת חֲצִי מַתִּיר – טז] [מוֹדֶה ר"מ] דְּלָא פִּיגֵּל אֶלָּא פָּסַל. מִדְּקָתָנֵי. מַתְנִיתִין. **לְפִיכָךְ אִם נָתַן** כּוּלָּן כְּתִקְנָן. וְקס"ד יז] הַיְינוּ שְׁתִיקָה. **וְאַחַת שֶׁלֹּא כְּתִקְנָהּ.** בְּמַחֲשֶׁבֶת חוּץ לִזְמַנּוֹ. **פָּסוּל** וְאֵין בּוֹ כָּרֵת. שֶׁלֹּא חִישֵּׁב אֶלָּא בַּחֲצִי מַתִּיר. דְּכוּלָּן מְעַכְּבוֹת בּוֹ וְכוּלָּן מַתִּירוֹת, וְאֵין פִּיגּוּל עַד שֶׁיְּפַגֵּל בְּכוּלָּן. **הָא אַחַת שֶׁלֹּא כְּתִיקְנָהּ.** הָרִאשׁוֹנָה בְּמַחֲשָׁבָה וְהַשְּׁאָר בִּשְׁתִיקָה – פִּיגּוּל, דְּאָמְרִינַן: עַל דַּעַת הָרִאשׁוֹנָה עָשָׂה, וַהֲוָה לֵי' מַחֲשָׁבָה בְּכוּלֵּיהּ מַתִּיר. **הָא אָמְרִינַן** אֵין מְפַגְּלִין בַּחֲצִי מַתִּיר. כִּדְקָתָנֵי בְּהֶדְיָא: עַד שֶׁיְּפַגֵּל בְּכָל הַמַּתִּיר, וַאֲפִי' רִאשׁוֹנָה בְּמַחֲשָׁבָה וּשְׁנִיָּה בִּשְׁתִיקָה מַשְׁמַע. אַלְמָא לֵית לְהוּ עַל דַּעַת יח] רִאשׁוֹנָה עָשָׂה. **אֲפִילּוּ כִּדְקָתָנֵי** נַמִּי. רִאשׁוֹנָה בִּשְׁתִיקָה וְאַחֲרוֹנָה בְּמַחֲשָׁבָה לֶיהֱוֵי פִּיגּוּל. יט] ב) אַלְמָא מִדְּשָׁנֵי לֵיהּ בֵּין רִאשׁוֹנָה בִּשְׁתִיקָה לְרִאשׁוֹנָה בְּמַחֲשָׁבָה – שְׁמַע מִינָּהּ טַעְמָא מִשּׁוּם דְּעָשָׂה עַל דַּעַת הָרִאשׁוֹנָה הוּא. כְּתִיקְנָהּ לְפִיגּוּל. הָרִאשׁוֹנוֹת כ] בְּמַחֲשָׁבוֹת דְּחוּץ לִזְמַנּוֹ. וְאַשְׁמְעִינַן דְּלָא אָמְרִינַן עַל דַּעַת הָרִאשׁוֹנָה עָשָׂה. **וְהָא מִדְּקָתָנֵי וְאַחַת שֶׁלֹּא כְּתִקְנָהּ.** וְלָא קָתָנֵי: כּוּלָּן כְּתִיקְנָן חוּץ מֵאַחַת מֵהֶן, אוֹ: וְאַחַת בִּשְׁתִיקָה – שְׁמַע מִינָּהּ: "כְּתִקְנָן" דְּאָמַר – כא] לְהֶכְשֵׁירוֹ הוּא. דְּאִי בְּמַחֲשָׁבָה וּלְפִיגּוּל – הֵיכִי מִקְרֵי לָהּ לְהָךְ דִּשְׁתִיקָה "שֶׁלֹּא כְּתִיקְנָהּ"? הָא לָא חָשֵׁיב בָּהּ מִידֵי, וְלָא קִילְקֵל מַחֲשַׁבְתּוֹ רִאשׁוֹנָה, דְּנִיקְרְיֵיהּ שֶׁלֹּא כְּתִיקְנָהּ לְפִיגּוּל! **אָמַר רָבָא.** לְעוֹלָם כְּתִקְנָהּ לְפִיגּוּל, וְרַבָּנַן הִיא. וּלְר"מ לָא תִּשְׁמַע מִינָּהּ מִידֵי. וְ"שֶׁלֹּא כְּתִקְנָהּ" דְּאַחֲרוֹנָה נַמִּי – שֶׁלֹּא כְּתִקְנָהּ לְפִיגּוּל קָאָמַר, וּכְגוֹן שֶׁנָּתַן בְּמַחֲשֶׁבֶת חוּץ לִמְקוֹמוֹ, הַמּוֹצִיאָהּ מִידֵי פִּיגּוּל, דְּהָא חַטָּאת הִיא, וּמַחֲשָׁבָה שֶׁלֹּא לִשְׁמוֹ פּוֹסֶלֶת בָּהּ וּמוֹצִיאָהּ מִידֵי פִּיגּוּל. **וְרַב אַשִׁי אָמַר** מַחֲשָׁבָה שֶׁלֹּא לִשְׁמוֹ. נַמִּי קָרֵי שֶׁלֹּא כְּתִקְנָהּ לְפִיגּוּל. ה"ג: **מִכְּלָל דְּכִי לָא עָבֵיד** לָהּ חוּץ לִמְקוֹמוֹ וְשֶׁלֹּא לִשְׁמוֹ מִיחַיֵּיב. מִדְּלָא קָרֵי לָהּ תַּנָּא פָּסוּל אֶלָּא בְּשֶׁחִישֵּׁב שֶׁלֹּא כְּתִיקְנָהּ, וְאוֹקִימְנָא בְּשֶׁלֹּא לִשְׁמוֹ אוֹ חוּץ לִמְקוֹמוֹ, מִכְּלָל דְּכִי לָא עָבֵיד לָהּ הָכִי אֶלָּא בִּשְׁתִיקָה – דְּחַיָּיב, כְּלוֹמַר, הָוֵי פִּיגּוּל לְחַיֵּיב עַל אֲכִילָתוֹ כָּרֵת. אַלְמָא עַל דַּעַת רִאשׁוֹנָה כב] עָשָׂה א"כ לָאו כְּרַבָּנַן מָצֵית לְאוֹקְמֵי! ה"ג: **אַיְּידֵי דִּתְנֵי רֵישָׁא פִּיגּוּל** וְחַיָּיבִין עָלָיו כָּרֵת **תְּנָא סֵיפָא** כג] **פָּסוּל וְאֵין בּוֹ כָּרֵת.** וְלָא גָּרְסִינַן "אֶלָּא". כְּלוֹמַר, לְעוֹלָם כְּתִקְנָן לְפִיגּוּל, וְשֶׁלֹּא כְּתִיקְנָהּ – חוּץ לִמְקוֹמוֹ, וְה"ה נַמִּי דְּאִם נָתַן בִּשְׁתִיקָה לָא פִּיגֵּל. וְהַאי דְּנָקַט שֶׁלֹּא כְּתִקְנָהּ – אַיְּידֵי דִּתְנָא רֵישָׁא בַּחִילּוּקוֹת: נָתַן אֶת הָרִאשׁוֹנָה חוּץ לִזְמַנָּהּ וְאֶת הַשְּׁנִיָּה חוּץ לִמְקוֹמוֹ פִּיגּוּל וְחַיָּיבִין עָלָיו כָּרֵת, כד] וְדַוְקָא נָקַט חוּץ לִמְקוֹמוֹ, לְאַשְׁמוֹעִינַן רְבוּתָא, דְּלָא אָתְיָא מַחֲשֶׁבֶת חוּץ לִמְקוֹמוֹ דִּשְׁנִיָּה וּמַפְקָא לָהּ מִידֵי פִּיגּוּל מִשּׁוּם דְּהוּקְבַּע בְּפִיגּוּל רִאשׁוֹנָה, שֶׁמַּתָּנָה אַחַת מַתֶּרֶת וּמְפַגֶּלֶת בָּהֶן – תָּנֵי נַמִּי סֵיפָא בִּפְנִימִיּוֹת, דְּכה"ג אָתְיָא מַחֲשָׁבָה שְׁנִיָּה וּמַפְקָא לֵיהּ מִידֵי פִּיגּוּל, אע"ג דְּלָא צָרִיךְ לְמִתְנְיֵיהּ, דְּהָא בְּלָאו הָכִי נַמִּי לָא הֲוָה מִיקְבַּע כה]. **בד"א כו'.** בַּתּוֹסֶפְתָּא דִּזְבָחִים הִיא. בד"א דְּבְמַתָּנָה אַחַת פִּיגֵּל. בְּדָמִים. הַחִיצוֹנִים, שֶׁמַּתָּנָה אַחַת מַתֶּרֶת וּמְפַגֶּלֶת בָּהֶן. אֲבָל

א) נ"ל ת"כ ב) נ"א אלא לאו מדשני כו' נ"ק

אבל יותרת ושתי הכליות דלא כתיבן בגופיה אימא לא. תימה: הא אמרת "לפר" *מייתי להכי למיהוי כמאן דכתב בגופיה, לאגמורי לשעירי עבודה זרה! ושמא אי לאו הך היקשא ד"חטאתם על שגגתם" – לא הוה דרישנא ליה הכי. **והא** תנא לרבות פר יוה"כ לכל האמור בענין קאמר. פירש בקונטרס: אלמא כולה מילתא יליף מיניה ואפילו עיכובא, ואת אמרת ל"את בדם וטבילה" כו] גרידא. וקשה לרב פפא דלעיל, דלא פי' דאתא לעיכובא! ומשני: תנאי היא. וא"ת: ולהאי תנא דיליף עיכובא בהיקשא, שבע על טהרו כז] ביוה"כ מנא ליה עיכובא? דליתנהו בפר העלם ובפר כהן משיח! וי"ל: דהיא גופיה ילפינן בהיקש, מה התם לא חלקת בהזאותיה – אף ביוה"כ לא תחלוק. (תוספת) ותימה: דלעיל הביא הברייתא לסיועיה לרב פפא, והשתא פריך מינה! ותו: מאי פריך על רב פפא דלא מוקי לה לעיכובא, כח] אלא עיכובא ביוה"כ מ"חוקה" נפקא או מ"וכלה מכפר" כדפריך לעיל! כט] וי"ל דפריך הכי: "לכל האמור בענין" משמע אפי' ליותרת ושתי הכליות, משום דכתיב "כאשר יורם" בפר כהן משיח, דאם אינו ענין לגופיה – תנהו ענין בפר העלם, כדדרשינן בפרק "איזהו מקומן" (לקמן דף מט:). ודרשינן: "לפר" – זה פר של יוה"כ, בין ל"את בדם וטבילה" בין ליותרת ושתי הכליות מחד היקשא. ל] הוא הדין לרבי ישמעאל דדריש "לפר" – זה פר העלם ליותרת [ושתי] כליות, ולא דריש "כאשר יורם" – דלא צריך אלא חד היקשא לא] ד"חטאת" לרבות שעירי עבודה זרה, וא"כ "חטאתם על שגגתם" למה לי? לב] א) וגבי שעירי עבודה זרה אמאי מצרכי תרי היקישי? ומשני: תנאי היא. והשתא להאי תנא לג] אתא ליה יותרת ושתי הכליות בפר יוה"כ מדתניא בתורת כהנים: "כל חלב לד] פר החטאת", "פר" – לרבות פר יום הכפורים ליותרת ושתי הכליות. יש לתמוה: דבכוליה התלמוד לה] נקיט "שעירי עבודה זרה" בלשון רבים, ו"פר העלם" בלשון יחיד. דמאי שנא? והא מאן דאית ליה בהוריות (דף ה.) שעיר לכל שבט ושבט אית ליה נמי פר לכל שבט ושבט!

ממאי מדקתני כו'. בכוליה שמעתא משמע דאע"ג דאין מפגלין בחצי מתיר – פסול מיהא הוי. ותימה: דבפ' "תמיד נשחט" (פסחים דף סא.) גבי: שחטו למולים ולערלים כו' ומוקי לה (שם סג.) בשוחט סימן ראשון למולים כו', ור"מ לטעמיה דאמר מפגלין בחצי מתיר, משמע התם דלרבנן הוי כשר גמור! ויש לומר: דהא דפסלי הכא – היינו משום דאיכא למיגזר, לו] כדאי' בפ"ב דמנחות (דף יד:) דרבנן גזרי קומץ אטו קומץ דמנחת חוטא, לבונה אטו לבונה הבאה בבזיכין. אבל התם לא שייך למיגזר סימן א' אטו שני סימנין. כגון

א) גי' נ"ק גבי שעירי עבודה זרה ואמאי מצרכי

שיטה מקובצת

א] אבל יותרת ושתי כליות כו' וא"ת והא דרשינן לפר זה פר העלם למהוי כמאן דכתי' בגופיה וי"ל דנהי דהוי כמאי דכתיב בגופיה לענין דלא הוי היקש מן ההיקש מ"מ אמת הוא דלא כתיב בגופיה בהדיא מידי דהוי לאידך תנא דנפיק ליה מכאשר יורם באם אינו ענין כו' למהוי כמאי דכתיב בגופיה דלא להוי היקש מן ההיקש ואעפ"כ חשיב ליה לא כתיב בגופיה לענין דלא אתי מהחטאת כדפי' בסמוך והא תנא לפר לכל האמור בענין וכדמפורש בתוס' מיהו מ"מ קשה דהיכא קאמר אבל יותרת ושתי הכליות דלא כתיב בגופיה אימא דלא יליף שעירי עבודה זרה מפר העלם מהיקשה קמייתא דחטאת א"כ לפר זה פר העלם למה לי הא כל עיקר לא בא אלא משום יותרת וב' הכליות למהוי כמאי דכתיב בגופיה לאגמורי לשעירי עבודה זרה וכיון דסוף סוף לא יליף משום דלא כתיב בגופיה בהדיא א"כ לפר זה פר העלם למה לי וי"ל דאה"נ קאמר דאי לאו היקשא שניה דחטאתם על שגגתם הו"א כיון דלא כתיב בגופיה לא יליף מהיקשא קמייתא ולפר זה פר העלם לא הוי דרשינן ליה אלא הוי דרשינן לפר זה פר יוה"כ: [illegible] הא ואי לרבות פר כו' פ"ה אלמא כו' (דבר רבי) [דבי רב מרבי] ולפי שיטתו צריך לומר דההוא תנא דיליף גם עיכובא מלפר לכל האמור בענין מ"ל כרבי יהודה דחוקה לא נאמרה אלא בדברים הנעשים בבגדי לבן לפני ולפנים הילכך לא יליף עיכובא מחוקה (מדברים) [בדברים] הנעשים בהיכל וכ"ת תיפוק ליה עיכובא מהיכא דנפקא ליה לר' יהודה דהיינו מכלה מכפר וי"ל דבההוא לא ס"ל כר"י אלא סבר לה כר"י בחדא דאם כיפר כילה ואיכא למימר אם כיפר מה שקרוי כפרה במקום אחר בחיצוניות היינו מתנה אחת הילכך לא שמעינן מינה עיכובא לכולהו מתנות כדפי' בקונטרס לקמן גבי מילתיה דרבא בפרק איזהו מקומן כך שיטת הקונטרס. וקשה חדא דלא לישתמש בעלמא שום תנא שיאמר דלא בין מחוקה ביוה"כ יליף עיכובא ומוכלה וכיפר. ועוד קשה דלעיל מדקדק לרב פפא לעיל לאוקמי דרשה דלפר זה פר יוה"כ ולענין את בדם וטבילה ולא לענין לעכב מחמת הברייתא שהביא דר"י דריש עיכובא מוכלה וכיפר ומה בכך אכתי יכול להעמידה עדיין לענין לעכב ובאותו

קאמר דהיינו לענין יותרת וב' הכליות ואע"ג דלא כתיב בגופיה דפר העלם בהדיא דנהי דמכאשר יורם איתרבי באם אינו ענין כדפי' לעיל כי היכי דלא להוי היקש מן ההיקש מ"מ הא לא כתיב בהדיא בגופיה דיותר אין לו להחשיבו כתוב בגופו מייתור דכאשר יורם טפי מייתור דלפר זה פר העלם אלמא הדא היקשא דלפר זה פר יוה"כ ילפינן פר יוה"כ מפר העלם אף מידי דלא כתיב בהדיא ומינה נשמע לאידך תנא דדריש לפר זה פר העלם דשמעינן (יותר) [יותרת ושתי הכליות] בשעירי עכו"ם מחדא היקשא מהיקשא קמייתא דחטאת והדרי קושיא לדוכתיה למה לי שגגתם על חטאתם דנהי דהוי מוקמינן דפליגי (מדרשה) [בדרשה] דלפר דמר מוקי בפר יוה"כ ומכאשר יורם דריש דלא להוי היקש מן ההיקש ומר דריש לפר זה פר העלם דלא להוי היקש מן ההיקש מ"מ (מסברא) [בסברא] זו אי מהניא היקשא קמייתא גם במידי דלא כתיב בגופיה בהדיא מסתמא לא פליגי אהדדי כך סובר המקשה ומשני תנאי היא ובהא גופיה פליגי ותנא דבי רב קורא תנא דספרי דחטאתם על שגגתם וא"ת ולתנא דלפר זה פר העלם מגליה בפר יוה"כ ליותרת וב' הכליות וי"ל מדרשה דת"כ ואת כל חלב פר החטאת גבי פר כהן משיח לרבות פר יוה"כ ליותרת ושתי הכליות מייתורא דפר ובמקום אחר הארכתי והר"ם פי' דקאי למיפרך אהא דקאמר דאיצטריך לפר זה פר העלם למהוי כמאי דכתיב בגופיה והיינו הקושיא שהקשו בתוס' לעיל ולרבי דדריש לפר זה פר יוה"כ א"כ יותרת וב' הכליות למהוי כמאי דכתיב בגופיה מגליה ומשני תנאי היא והאי תנא מפיק ליה מכאשר יורם ובתוס' רבינו אלידו נמצא גירסא וזה הוא החטאת אלו שעירי עכו"ם לרבות לכל האמור בענין המשמע דאף ליותרת וב' הכליות והשתא ניחא. מהר"פ: ג] ודם שבעים על אוהבו: ד] מאיר משום דקסבר: ה] עיין בהשמטות בסוף המסכת: ו] נמי אלא לאו משום: ז] קמ"ל חטאתם: ח] לכל האמור בענין: ט] היא האי תנא: י] בענין מתניתא דבי רבי: יא] בה דבריו: יב] דבפר כהן: יג] עצתו המסכימים לדעתו אשר דברי סתריו: יד] צבור חטאו: טו] בפה עי' תו' ב' ע"א [ד"ה כל בכספו ודף ד' ע"ב ד"ה מחשבה] (כ"א א' ד"ה ט"ם): טז] מתיר לא פיגל לר"מ אלא פסול: יז] וקס"ד דהיינו: יח] ראשונה עושה: יט] פיגול אלא לאו מדשני ליה כו' שמע מינה טעמיה משום דעושה ע"ד הראשונה עושה: כ] הראשונות במחשבת דחוץ לזמנו ואחת שלא כתקנה לפיגול אלא בשתיקה פסול ואין בו כרת: כא] דאמר להכשיר הוא: כב] ראשונ' עושה א"כ כו' לאוקמי גליון אלא כר"מ ותפשוט מינה דטעמא דר"א משום דעל דעת ראשונה הוא עושה: כג] סיפא נמי פסול כו' פיגול ולא אמרינן על דעת הראשונה עושה דרבנן הוא [והאי דנקיט]: כד] דדוקא נקט חוץ למקומו כו' דהוקבע פיגול בראשונה שמתנה: כה] מיקבע אפילו בשתיקה משום דלא אמרינן על דעת ראשונה עושה לרבנן: כו] גרידא ומקשי לרב פפא דאמר לעיל לאת בדם וטבילה אתא היקשא ומשני תנאי היא תנא דבי רב היינו [ההיא מתניתא] כו' ותנא דבי ר"י היינו אותה ברייתא דדריש לכל האמור בענין שבירכוה התלמידים מבית ר"י ושנו בה התלמידים דברי ר"י ודברי רבי: [illegible] לג] הא לעיל כו' ע"כ דבר עשירי: לד] תנא לדפר זה פר העלם אתא: לה] כל חלב לרבות פר יוה"כ והשאר נמחק: לו] הש"ס עי' תו' מנחות (דף נב ע"א) ד"ה פר העלם: לז] למיגזר כדאמרי' בפ"ב ד'

תנא שלישי דהך בריתא דלכל האמור בענין דלא דריש עיכובא לא [מחוקה ולא] מוכלה מכפר כדפ"ה ועוד קשה דלעיל מאות' בריתא עצמה דלכל האמור בענין מייתי סייעתא לרב פפא והשתא מקשי מינה ועוד דלמה המתין מלהקשות הך קושיא עד השתא הוה לעיל כיון (דלעיל) [דאדלעיל] קאי כרפ"ה לכן נראה לר"י דאדסליק מינה קאי שאמר רב פפא בסמוך לעיל דמהיקשא קמייתא דועשה לפר כאשר עשה לפר החטאת אלו שעירי עבודה זרה ולא נפקא לן יותרת וב' הכליות משום דלא כתיב בגופיה בהדיא ואע"ג דלא הוי היקש מן ההיקש [illegible] דאוקמנא לענין את בדם וטבילה מדמהדר ליה קו"ח [מתמהון] שלא הושוה [קרבן לקרבן השוה] מעשים למעשים כו' כרפ"י מ"מ לישנא דלכל האמור בענין משמע לכולה מילתא הנאמר בכאן ולא נאמרה כו' ביוה"כ

גליון הש"ס גמ' כל העושה ע"ד הראשונה. לעיל דף ב ע"ב שבת דף ק"ג:

אֲבָל דָּמִים הַנִּיתָּנִין עַל הַמִּזְבֵּחַ הַפְּנִימִי, כְּגוֹן אַרְבָּעִים וְשָׁלֹשׁ שֶׁל יוֹם הַכִּיפּוּרִים, וְאַחַד עָשָׂר שֶׁל פַּר כֹּהֵן מָשִׁיחַ, וְאַחַד עָשָׂר שֶׁל פַּר הֶעְלֵם דָּבָר שֶׁל צִיבּוּר, פִּיגֵּל בֵּין בָּרִאשׁוֹנָה וּבֵין בַּשְּׁנִיָּה וּבֵין בַּשְּׁלִישִׁית – רַבִּי מֵאִיר אוֹמֵר: פִּיגּוּל, וְחַיָּיבִין עָלָיו כָּרֵת, וַחֲכָמִים אוֹמְרִים: אאֵין בּוֹ כָּרֵת עַד שֶׁיְּפַגֵּל בְּכָל הַמַּתִּיר; קָתָנֵי מִיהָא: פִּיגֵּל בֵּין בָּרִאשׁוֹנָה בֵּין בַּשְּׁנִיָּה בֵּין בַּשְּׁלִישִׁית, וּפָלֵיג! אָמַר רַב יִצְחָק בַּר אָבִין: הָכָא בְּמַאי עָסְקִינַן – כְּגוֹן שֶׁפִּיגֵּל בִּשְׁחִיטָה, דְּחַד מַתִּיר הוּא. אִי הָכִי, מַאי טַעְמָא דְּרַבָּנַן? אָמַר רָבָא: *מַאן חֲכָמִים – רַבִּי א] אֱלִיעֶזֶר הִיא, *דִּתְנַן: בהַקּוֹמֶץ, וְהַלְּבוֹנָה, וְהַקְּטוֹרֶת, וּמִנְחַת כֹּהֲנִים, וּמִנְחַת כֹּהֵן מָשִׁיחַ, וּמִנְחַת נְסָכִים, שֶׁהִקְרִיב מֵאַחַת מֵהֶן כַּזַּיִת בַּחוּץ – חַיָּיב, וְר' אֱלִיעֶזֶר פּוֹטֵר עַד שֶׁיַּקְרִיב אֶת כּוּלָּן. וְהָאָמַר רָבָא: *וּמוֹדֶה רַבִּי אֱלִיעֶזֶר בְּדָמִים, דִּתְנַן: *גרַבִּי אֱלִיעֶזֶר וְר' שִׁמְעוֹן אוֹמְרִים: מִמָּקוֹם שֶׁפָּסַק מִשָּׁם הוּא מַתְחִיל! אֶלָּא *אָמַר רָבָא: כְּגוֹן שֶׁפִּיגֵּל בָּרִאשׁוֹנָה וְשָׁתַק בַּשְּׁנִיָּה וְחָזַר וּפִיגֵּל בַּשְּׁלִישִׁית; מה"ד: ב] אִי ס"ד עַל דַּעַת רִאשׁוֹנָה הוּא, ג] מִיהֲדַר פִּיגּוּלֵי בַּשְּׁלִישִׁית לָמָּה לִי? קמ"ל. מַתְקִיף לָהּ רַב אַשִׁי: מִידֵי "שָׁתַק" קָתָנֵי? אֶלָּא אָמַר רַב אַשִׁי: הָכָא בְּמַאי עָסְקִינַן – כְּגוֹן שֶׁפִּיגֵּל בָּרִאשׁוֹנָה וּבַשְּׁנִיָּה וּבַשְּׁלִישִׁית; מַהוּ דְּתֵימָא: אִי ס"ד כָּל הָעוֹשֶׂה עַל דַּעַת רִאשׁוֹנָה הוּא עוֹשֶׂה, מִהֲדַר פִּיגּוּלֵי בְּכָל חֲדָא וַחֲדָא לָמָּה לִי? קָא מַשְׁמַע לָן. וְהָא

רש"י

אֲבָל בְּדָמִים הַפְּנִימִים כְּגוֹן אַרְבָּעִים וְשָׁלֹשׁ שֶׁל יוֹם הַכִּיפּוּרִים. אַחַת לְמַעְלָה וְשֶׁבַע לְמַטָּה עַל בֵּין הַבַּדִּים מִדַּם הַפָּר, וּכְנֶגְדָּן מִדַּם הַשָּׂעִיר – הֲרֵי ט"ז, וּכְנֶגְדָּן עַל הַפָּרֹכֶת – הֲרֵי ל"ב, וְאַרְבַּע עַל קַרְנוֹת מִזְבַּח הַפְּנִימִי מִשְּׁנֵיהֶם כְּאֶחָד מְעוֹרָבִין, כְּדִכְתִיב: (וְנָתַן) "[וְלָקַח] מִדַּם הַפָּר וּמִדַּם הַשָּׂעִיר" (ויקרא טז) שֶׁיְּהוּ מְעוֹרָבִין – הֲרֵי ל"ו, וְשֶׁבַע הַזָּאוֹת עַל טָהֳרוֹ – הֲרֵי מ"ג. ד] פִּיגֵּל בֵּין בָּרִאשׁוֹנָה. בַּמַּתָּנוֹת שֶׁלִּפְנַי וְלִפְנִים. בֵּין בַּשְּׁנִיָּה. עַל הַפָּרֹכֶת. בֵּין בַּשְּׁלִישִׁית. עַל מִזְבַּח הַזָּהָב. קָתָנֵי מִיהַת בֵּין בַּשְּׁנִיָּה. דְּמַשְׁמַע לֹא בָּרִאשׁוֹנָה. וּפָלֵיג. ה] וְקָאָמַר ר"מ: פִּיגּוּל, וְאֵין כָּאן מִשּׁוּם דַּעַת רִאשׁוֹנָה, אֶלָּא דְּקָסָבַר מְפַגְּלִין בַּחֲצִי מַתִּיר. וּתְיוּבְתָּא דר"ל! כְּגוֹן שֶׁפִּיגֵּל בִּשְׁחִיטָה. הָא דְּקָאָמַר ר"מ: פִּיגֵּל בַּשְּׁנִיָּה פִּיגּוּל – כְּגוֹן שֶׁנִּשְׁפַּךְ הַדָּם לְאַחַר שֶׁגָּמַר מַתָּנוֹת שֶׁבִּפְנִים, וְקי"ל בְּסֵדֶר יוֹמָא (דף ס.): יָבִיא אַחֵר וְיַתְחִיל ו] בַּהֵיכָל, וּכְשֶׁשָּׁחַט אֶת הַשֵּׁנִי פִּיגֵּל בִּשְׁחִיטָתוֹ. וְקָאָמַר ר"מ דְּהַהוּא פַּר הָוֵי פִּיגּוּל, שֶׁהֲרֵי פִּיגֵּל בּוֹ בַּעֲבוֹדָה שְׁלֵמָה ז]. רַבִּי ח] אֱלִיעֶזֶר הִיא. דַּאֲפִילּוּ בְּהַעֲלָאַת חוּץ פּוֹטֵר ט] *בִּשְׁנֵי מַתִּירִין, אַלְמָא לָאו עֲבוֹדָה הִיא כְּלָל עַד שֶׁיִּגְמוֹר כָּל הָעֲבוֹדָה. וְאַע"ג דְּהַקְטָרַת כְּזַיִת הָוְיָא הַקְטָרָה, כִּדְקָתָנֵי הָתָם: וְכוּלָּן שֶׁהִקְרִיבָן בִּפְנִים וְשִׁייֵּר מֵהֶן כְּזַיִת וְהִקְרִיבוֹ בַּחוּץ – חַיָּיב אֲפִילּוּ לְר' אֱלִיעֶזֶר, מִיהוּ הֵיכָא דְּלָא גָּמַר עֲבוֹדָה הוּא – לָא חֲשִׁיב לָהּ לְחַיּוּבֵי עֲלֵיהּ בַּחוּץ. י] ה"נ, אַע"ג דִּשְׁחִיטָה עֲבוֹדָה שְׁלֵמָה הִיא, כֵּיוָן שֶׁאֵין הָעֲבוֹדָה נִגְמֶרֶת יא] בְּשָׂעִיר זֶה לְבַדּוֹ, שֶׁאֵינוֹ בָּא אֶלָּא לְהַשְׁלִים, יב] וַעֲבוֹדָה אַחַת הִיא שֶׁנַּעֲשֵׂית בִּשְׁתַּיִם וְשָׁלֹשׁ שְׁחִיטוֹת – אֵין הַשְּׁחִיטָה יג] חֲשׁוּבוֹת לְפַגֵּל. וְהָא אָמַר רָבָא. לְקַמָּן בְּפֶ' "הַשּׁוֹחֵט" (דף קי.) דְּקָתָנֵי: הַזּוֹרֵק מִקְצָת דָּמִים בַּחוּץ חַיָּיב, וְלָא פָּלֵיג רַבִּי אֱלִיעֶזֶר. וְאָמַר רָבָא עֲלָהּ בַּגְּמָרָא: מוֹדֶה רַבִּי אֱלִיעֶזֶר בְּדָמִים, שֶׁאִם יד] נוֹתֵן בְּמַתָּנָה אַחַת מֵחַטָּאוֹת הַפְּנִימִיּוֹת חוּץ לָעֲזָרָה – חַיָּיב. וְאַע"פ שֶׁכּוּלָּן עֲבוֹדָה אַחַת הֵן לְעַכֵּב, וְאִיכָּא לְמֵימַר דְּאֵין כָּאן אֶלָּא חֲצִי הָעֲבוֹדָה, דּוּמְיָא דְּקוֹמֶץ אוֹ לְבוֹנָה – חַיָּיב, הוֹאִיל וּכְנֶגְדָּהּ לִפְנַי וְלִפְנִים מִתְקַבֶּלֶת הִיא, שֶׁאִם נָתַן מַתָּנָה אַחַת בִּפְנִים וְנִשְׁפַּךְ הַדָּם – מֵבִיא דָּם אַחֵר וּמַתְחִיל מִמָּקוֹם שֶׁפָּסַק, לְר' אֱלִיעֶזֶר. דִּתְנַן ר' אֱלִיעֶזֶר וְר' שִׁמְעוֹן. טו] פְּלִיגֵי אַתַּנָּא קַמָּא, דְּאָמַר: נָתַן מִקְצָת מַתָּנוֹת שֶׁבִּפְנִים וְנִשְׁפַּךְ הַדָּם – יָבִיא דָּם אַחֵר וְיַתְחִיל בַּתְּחִלָּה, הוֹאִיל וְלֹא גָּמַר אוֹתָהּ כַּפָּרָה. ר' אֱלִיעֶזֶר וְר' שִׁמְעוֹן [אוֹמְרִים] כו' – אַלְמָא עֲבוֹדָה הִיא. וְאִי פִּיגּוּל לְחִיּוּב חוּץ קָא מְדַמֵּית, לָא מִיבַּעְיָא בִּשְׁחִיטָה טז] דַּהֲוָה פִּיגּוּל, אֶלָּא אֲפִילּוּ פִּיגֵּל בְּמַתָּנָה אַחַת לְר' אֱלִיעֶזֶר פִּיגּוּל הִיא!. אֶלָּא אָמַר רָבָא. לְעוֹלָם כְּשֶׁפִּיגֵּל בַּהַזָּאוֹת. וּדְקַשְׁיָא לָךְ: קָתָנֵי פִּיגֵּל בַּשְּׁנִיָּה אוֹ בַּשְּׁלִישִׁית, וְקס"ד דְּבָרִאשׁוֹנָה שָׁתַק, וְקָאָמַר ר' מֵאִיר פִּיגּוּל יז] *הוּא! דְּהָכָא בְּמַאי עָסְקִינַן – כְּגוֹן שֶׁפִּיגֵּל בָּרִאשׁוֹנָה וְשָׁתַק בַּשְּׁנִיָּה, וְחָזַר וּפִיגֵּל בַּשְּׁלִישִׁית. וּלְעוֹלָם טַעְמָא דר"מ מִשּׁוּם דְּקָסָבַר שְׁתִיקָה הַשְּׁנִיָּה עַל דַּעַת מַחֲשָׁבָה הָרִאשׁוֹנָה נַעֲשֵׂית, כר"ל. ה"ג: מה"ד אָמְרִינַן אִי ס"ד כָּל הָעוֹשֶׂה עַל דַּעַת הָרִאשׁוֹנָה עוֹשֶׂה מִיהֲדַר פִּיגּוּלֵי בַּשְּׁלִישִׁית לָמָּה לִי קמ"ל. כְּלוֹמַר, יח] וְהַאי דְּנָקַט חָזַר וּפִיגֵּל בַּשְּׁלִישִׁית – רְבוּתָא אַשְׁמְעִינַן, דְּאַע"ג דְּחָזַר וּפִיגֵּל בַּשְּׁלִישִׁית אָמְרִינַן דִּשְׁתִיקָה שְׁנִיָּה נַמִּי עַל דַּעַת מַחֲשָׁבָה קַמַּיְיתָא יְהָבָהּ. דְּמַהוּ דְּתֵימָא. אִי עַל דַּעַת רִאשׁוֹנָה הֲוַאי שְׁתִיקָה שְׁנִיָּה, אַמַּאי לֹא עָבַד נַמִּי שְׁלִישִׁית בִּשְׁתִיקָה? קמ"ל. דְּלָא אָמְרִינַן הָכִי. וְגִירְסָא הַכָּתוּב בַּסְּפָרִים יט] (וְאִי) "אָמְרִינַן אִי ס"ד" כו' – לָא שַׁיָּיךְ לְמִיגְרַס הָכָא הָכִי, דְּהָא מְהַדְּרִינַן לְתָרוֹצַהּ אַלִּיבָּא דְּרֵישׁ לָקִישׁ דְּאָמַר טַעַם דר"מ מִשּׁוּם דַּעַת רִאשׁוֹנָה הוּא. וְאִם תֹּאמַר: הַאי כ] "אִם ס"ד" אַלִּיבָּא דְּרַבָּנַן נָקַט, לְמֵימַר טַעְמָא דְּרַבָּנַן מִשּׁוּם הָכִי הוּא – לָאו מִילְּתָא הוּא, דְּהָא לְרֵישׁ לָקִישׁ אַלִּיבָּא *(דְּרַב) אֲפִילּוּ לֹא חָזַר וּפִיגֵּל בַּשְּׁלִישִׁית לֵית לְהוּ לְרַבָּנַן עַל דַּעַת רִאשׁוֹנָה עוֹשֶׂה. וּבִמְנָחוֹת (דף טז.) הוּא דְּגָרְסִינַן לַהּ הָכִי, דְּהָתָם לְרַב אוֹתִיבְנָא מֵהָא מַתְנִי', דְּאוֹקֵי פְּלוּגְתַּיְיהוּ בְּנוֹתֵן רִאשׁוֹנָה בִּשְׁתִיקָה וּשְׁנִיָּה בְּמַחֲשָׁבָה, וּבִמְפַגְּלִים בַּחֲצִי מַתִּיר פְּלִיגֵי, אֲבָל בְּנוֹתֵן רִאשׁוֹנָה בְּמַחֲשָׁבָה וּשְׁנִיָּה בִּשְׁתִיקָה – אֲפִילּוּ רַבָּנַן מוֹדוּ דְּפִיגֵּל, דְּאָמְרִינַן עַל דַּעַת רִאשׁוֹנָה עָשָׂה. וְאוֹתִיבְנָא מֵהָא דְּקָתָנֵי בֵּין בָּרִאשׁוֹנָה, וּמַשְׁמַע לֹא בַּשְּׁנִיָּה, וְקָאָמְרֵי רַבָּנַן לֹא פִּיגֵּל. וְשַׁנֵּי רַבָּה כא] *אַלִּיבַּיְיהוּ: כְּגוֹן שֶׁחָזַר וּפִיגֵּל בַּשְּׁלִישִׁית, דְּאָמְרִינַן אִי ס"ד עַל דַּעַת רִאשׁוֹנָה. בְּהָא נַמִּי גָּרַס: מַהוּ דְּתֵימָא כב] אִי ס"ד כו' קמ"ל. וְגִירְסָא שֶׁבַּסְּפָרִים דְּלָא גָּרְסִינַן "מַהוּ דְּתֵימָא" – בִּמְנָחוֹת (שם) אִיתָא, וְלָא שַׁיָּיךְ לְמִיגְרַס הָכָא הָכִי. אֶלָּא אָמַר רַב אַשִׁי. כְּגוֹן שֶׁפִּיגֵּל וְהוֹצִיא פִּיגּוּל בִּשְׂפָתָיו בָּרִאשׁוֹנָה וּבַשְּׁנִיָּה וּבַשְּׁלִישִׁית, כג] וּבָרְבִיעִית לֹא פִּיגֵּל, כִּדְקָתָנֵי בְּהֶדְיָא: כד] בֵּין בָּרִאשׁוֹנָה כו', וְלָא קָתָנֵי רְבִיעִית. וּבַהַזָּאוֹת שֶׁל טִיהֲרוֹ שָׁתֵיק. וּלְעוֹלָם טַעְמָא דר"מ מִשּׁוּם כה] דַּעַת רִאשׁוֹנָה הוּא, וּרְבוּתָא אַשְׁמְעִינַן, דְּאַע"פ שֶׁלֹּא שָׁתַק אֶלָּא בְּזוֹ – אָמְרִינַן עַל דַּעַת רִאשׁוֹנָה עֲשָׂאָהּ. דְּמַהוּ דְּתֵימָא: אִי ס"ד עַל דַּעַת הָרִאשׁוֹנָה עוֹשֶׂה – לָמָּה לֹא שָׁתַק בַּשְּׁנִיָּה וּבַשְּׁלִישִׁית, וְיַעֲשֶׂה עַל דַּעַת רִאשׁוֹנָה, קָא מַשְׁמַע לָן דְּלָא אָמְרִינַן הָכִי. "וְעוֹד" לָא גָּרְסִינַן. וְהָא

תוספות

כגון שפיגל בשחיטה דהוי מתיר אחד. פירש רבינו שמואל: בשעת שחיטה חישב ע"מ ליתן מתנות שבפנים חוץ לזמנו, או מתנות ההיכל, או מתנות דמזבח. והיינו פיגל בין בראשונה בין בשניה בין בשלישית, כמו שוחט שלמים ע"מ לזרוק חוץ לזמנו, או ע"מ להקטיר גרידא, דהוי פיגול לכ"ע כיון דכל השחיטה הויא בפיגול. [ופריך]: א"ה מאי טעמא דרבנן, דאפילו לשפוך שירים למחר קיימא לן (לקמן דף מד:) דהוי פיגול! *מאן חכמים – ר' כו] אליעזר היא, דכיון דלר' אליעזר *לא מיחייב במתנה אחת בחוץ – הכי נמי אי פיגל לא הוי פיגול. כז] ומיהו, לא יתכן לפרש כן, דלפירוש זה אי אפשר ליישב כלל "במה דברים אמורים בדמים הנתנין על כח] המזבח". ופירוש הקונטרס עיקר.

מאן חכמים רבי אליעזר היא. *ואמרינן דבעי עבודה טפי לפיגול. דנימא כט] כמ"ד דמחייב לא הוי, דהא מחייב כזית קומץ בחוץ. ואילו פיגול – אפילו בקומץ שלם לא הוי פיגול אם לא פיגל בלבונה. ומדרבי אליעזר לחודיה מייתי ראיה [דפוטר] גבי חוץ – כ"ש דלא הוי פיגול. ולמאי דמסיק דמודה ר' אליעזר בדמים – לא כמו שפי' בקונטרס דמחייב במקצת דמים בחוץ מכלל דהוי פיגול, דאין זה ראיה כדפרישית. ולא אתי אלא לדחות הא דשנינו: הא מני רבי אליעזר היא.

כגון שפיגל בראשונה ובשניה ובשלישית. פירש בקונטרס: וברביעית לא פיגל. וקשה: רביעית מאן דכר שמיה? ובפ' שני דמנחות (דף טז.*) פי' בקונטרס: שפיגל בראשונה ובשניה, ושתק בשלישית. וא"ת: א"כ קשיא, מידי "שתק" קתני? כדאקשי לעיל! ושמא לעיל, דשתק באמצעית הוה ליה לפרושי טפי, כיון דראשונה ושלישית במחשבה ושניה בשתיקה. ולהאי פירושא חשיב כל הזאות דמזבח הזהב אחת – שבע דטהרו, וארבע דקרנות. וכן משמע בפרק "הוציאו לו" (יומא דף סא.) דתניא: "וכפר את ל] הקודש" – זו לפני ולפנים, "ואת אהל מועד" – זה היכל, "ואת המזבח" – כמשמעו. ולא קתני כלל על טהרו. משמע, דחשיב דמזבח לא] כפרה אחת. *כדקאמר: מיכן אמרו עד גמר מתנות שבהיכל ונשפך הדם – יביא אחר ויתחיל לב] בתחילה. אבל לא קתני: גמר לקרנות ונשפך הדם שיביא אחריו ויתחיל בטהרו, *דכולהו חשיבי כאחת. וקשה: דלקמן [קאמר] משכחת לה בד' פרים וד' שעירים. פירוש: חד אהזאות דבין הבדים, וחד אהזאות דפרכת, וחד אהזאות דקרנות, וחד אטהרו. אלמא לא חשיבי לג] כחדא הזאות דקרנות ודטהרו! ושמא פר רביעי דלקמן – לאו משום דעל טהרו, אלא סבירא ליה דשירים מעכבין, והוי חד בשביל שירים. ולפירוש זה נוכל לגרוס: לד] כגון שפיגל בראשונה ובשניה ובשלישית. וכן בספר רבינו גרשום כאן. וב"הקומץ זוטא" (מנחות דף טז.) חשיב חצי מתיר, משום דאיכא עדיין שירים דמעכבי. וא"ת: והא בעל כרחין סבר האי תנא שיריים לא מעכבי, מדלא חשיב אלא מ"ג. דההוא דסבר שיריים מעכבי חשיב חדא טפי, כדמוכח בסמוך! וי"ל: דאע"ג דשיריים מעכבי – לא חשיב האי תנא אלא הזאות. כי

עין משפט נר מצוה

כד א מיי' פט"ז מהל' פסה"מ הלכה ו:
כה ב מיי' פי"ט מהל' מעה"ק הלכה ח ט:
כו ג מיי' פ"ה מהלכות יוה"כ הל' ה וכת"ק דפליג עליה שם:

מסורת הש"ס והגהות

[ערכין פג. וש"נ]
מנחות יב: לקמן קט:
נ"א כתני מתיר נ"ק
[לקמן קי:]
[יומא ס. לקמן קי: ושם איתא אלעזר וכצ"ל גם ברש"י]
כס"י לא היה כו'
גי' הג"ה אליבא דרבנן
נ"ל אליביה
נ"ל ומשני מאן נ"ק
נ"א לא מחייב בכזית אחת בחוץ הכי נמי לענין פיגול לא כו' נ"ק
נ"א ומדמינן פיגול לחוץ דנימא למ"ד חייב בכזית לא הוי דמי לפיגול דהא מחייב כזית קומץ וגי' הנ"ק ומקילינן טפי לענין פיגול דהא אפילו למ"ד דמחייב אכזית קומץ בחוץ ואילו פיגול וכו'
[מנחות טז. כל הענין]
[שם ד"ה כגון]
נ"א ועוד דקאמר התם
משמע נ"ק

שיטה מקובצת

א] ר' אלעזר וכן צ"ל לקמן: ב] מה"ד אמרינן אי: ג] הוא עושה מיהדר על פיגול בשלישית: ד] מ"ג הס"ד ומה"ד ואחד עשר של פר כהן משוח כו' היינו ז' הזאות שעל הפרכת וארבע על קרנות מזבח הזהב הס"ד: ה] ופליג ר"מ וקאמר פיגול: ו] בהיכל. מה שפ"ה מתחיל בתחילה בהיכל לכך פי' [כן] שאם היה מתחיל בתחילה פר קמא כמאן דליתא דמי ולמה הזכיר ראשונה ושניה ושלישית. ומיהו קשה לפי' הקונטרס שפי' פיגל בשחיטה דפר שהרי פיגל בראשון משמע דפיגל בהזאות ולא בשחיטה ועוד מאי קמדמי לקומץ שאני קומץ דמיעוטו מעכב רובו אבל כל שחיטה ושחיטה הוי דבר בפני עצמו ופרשב"ם פיגל בשחיטה על מנת שיזה דמו הראשונים או השניים למחר דהוי ליה מפגל בעסק שלם וה"ק הא מני ר"א היא דפטר א) בהקומץ בחוץ עד שהקטיר את כולן משום דמיעוטו מעכב את רובו וה"ה אם פיגל בעסק מתיר שלם כמו בקמיצה ע"מ להקטיר כזית מן הקומץ דלא פיגל עד שיחשוב בכולן ומייתי הר"ם ראיה במנחות [דף יג:] דמייתי מילתיה דר' אלעזר על משנה דהקומץ ע"מ להקטיר כזית חוץ לזמנו וקאמר דלר' אלעזר לא פיגל עד שיפגל בכולן וה"נ במחשב ע"מ לזרוק אחד מן הדמים למחר דאין זה פיגול כיון דמעכבות זו את זו ואי לא דחשיב (בהו) [בכולהו] לא מהניא מחשבה: ז] שלימה ס"א ולהכי פריך נשפך דאם לא נשפך למה יביא אחר: ח] ר' אלעזר וכצ"ל בכל העמוד: ט] פוטר בחצי מתיר ותיבת בשני ל"ש: י] בחוץ עד שיגמור כל העבודה: יא] בשעיר. ס"א בפר: יב] להשלים עבודה: יג] חשובה לפגל הס"ד: יד] שאם נתן מתנה: טו] ופליגי את"ק: טז] דהוי פיגול: יז] הוא היא: יח] כלומר האי: יט] בספרים דאמרינן אי ס"ד: כ] כי האי אי ס"ד אליבא דרבנן: כא] רבא אליבא דרב כבנן: כב] דתימא אמרינן אי: כג] וברביעית: כד] בהדיא בין בראשונה: כה] משום דעל דעת ראשונה הוא עושה: כו] ר' אלעזר וכצ"ל בכל העמוד: כז] פיגול תוספת: כח] על מזבח החיצון ופי' הקונטרס עיקר ע"כ תוספת: כט] דנימא לר"א תוספת: ל] ס"א מתנה אחת מיכן אמרו עד כו': לא] כפרה. ס"א מקדש הקודש: לב] ויתחיל במתנות המזבח נתן מקצת מתנות מזבח ונשפך הדם מביא אחר ויתחיל בתחילה אבל לא קתני גמר לקרנות ונשפך כו' ויתחיל מטהרו דכלהו כו' קאמר משכחת לה: לג] לגרוס בכאן כגון כו' ולא כתוב בספר רבינו גרשום כו' וחשיב חצי מתיר:

א) נראה דצ"ל דפטר גבי קומץ אם הקטיר כזית ממנו בחוץ עד שהקטיר וכו'.

עין משפט נר מצוה

ושוחט או מקבל נמי נימא כו' דכי חשיב בשחיטה או בקבלה כו' נ"ק

כז א מיי' פ"ה מהל' מעה"ק הל' יב ופ"ד מהלכות עבודת יוה"כ הלכה ב:

כח ב מיי' פי"ג מהל' פסה"מ הלכה ו:

כט ג מיי' פט"ז מהל' פסה"מ הלכה ז:

ל ד מיי' פי"ח מהלכות פסה"מ הלכה ח:

גמרא

וְהָא "בֵּין" "בֵּין" קָתָנֵי! קַשְׁיָא. *אָמַר מָר, רַבִּי מֵאִיר אוֹמֵר: פִּיגּוּל וְחַיָּיבִין עָלָיו כָּרֵת. מִכְּדֵי, כָּרֵת לָא מִיחַיַּיב עַד שֶׁיִּקְרְבוּ כָּל מַתִּירָיו, דְּאָמַר מָר: *כְּהַרְצָאַת כָּשֵׁר כָּךְ הַרְצָאַת פָּסוּל, מַה הַרְצָאַת כָּשֵׁר — עַד שֶׁיִּקְרְבוּ כָּל מַתִּירָיו, אַף הַרְצָאַת פָּסוּל — עַד שֶׁיִּקְרְבוּ כָּל מַתִּירָיו. וְהָא, כֵּיוָן דְּחָשֵׁיב בֵּיהּ א] בִּפְנִים פְּסוּלָה — כְּמַאן דְּלָא אַדֵּי דָּמֵי, כִּי הָדַר מַדֵּי בַּהֵיכָל — ב] מַיָּא בְּעָלְמָא הוּא דְּקָא אַדֵּי! אָמַר רַבָּה: מַשְׁכַּחַתְּ לָהּ ג] בְּאַרְבָּעָה פָּרִים וּבְד' שְׂעִירִים. ד] רָבָא אָמַר: אֲפִילּוּ תֵּימָא בְּפַר אֶחָד וְשָׂעִיר אֶחָד, לְפִיגּוּלוֹ מְרַצֶּה. "אַרְבָּעִים וְשָׁלֹשׁ". וְהָא תַּנְיָא: אַרְבָּעִים וְשֶׁבַע! הָא כְּמַאן דְּאָמַר *מְעָרְבִין לַקְּרָנוֹת, וְהָא כְּמַאן דְּאָמַר אֵין מְעָרְבִין לַקְּרָנוֹת. וְהָא תַּנְיָא: אאַרְבָּעִים וּשְׁמוֹנֶה! הָא כְּמַאן דְּאָמַר *שִׁירַיִים מְעַכְּבִין, הָא כְּמַאן דְּאָמַר אֵין שִׁירַיִים מְעַכְּבִין.§ מֵיתִיבֵי: *בַּמֶּה דְּבָרִים אֲמוּרִים — בבִּקְמִיצָה, בְּמַתַּן כְּלִי, וּבְהִילּוּךְ. אֲבָל בָּא לוֹ לְהַקְטָרָה, נָתַן אֶת הַקּוֹמֶץ בְּמַחֲשָׁבָה וְאֶת הַלְּבוֹנָה בִּשְׁתִיקָה, אוֹ שֶׁנָּתַן אֶת הַקּוֹמֶץ בִּשְׁתִיקָה וְאֶת הַלְּבוֹנָה בְּמַחֲשָׁבָה, רַבִּי מֵאִיר אוֹמֵר: פִּיגּוּל וְחַיָּיבִין עָלָיו כָּרֵת, וַחֲכָמִים אוֹמְרִים: גאֵין בּוֹ כָּרֵת עַד שֶׁיְּפַגֵּל בְּכָל הַמַּתִּיר. קָתָנֵי מִיהָא: אֶת הַקּוֹמֶץ בִּשְׁתִיקָה וְאֶת הַלְּבוֹנָה בְּמַחֲשָׁבָה, ה] וּפָלֵיג! אֵימָא: כְּבָר נָתַן אֶת הַלְּבוֹנָה בְּמַחֲשָׁבָה. חֲדָא — דְּהַיְינוּ (א)רֵישָׁא! וְעוֹד: הָא תַּנְיָא "וְאַחַר כָּךְ"! קַשְׁיָא.§

מתני' דא) וְאֵלּוּ *דְּבָרִים שֶׁאֵין חַיָּיבִין עֲלֵיהֶם מִשּׁוּם פִּיגּוּל: ו] הַקּוֹמֶץ, ז] וְהַקְּטֹרֶת, וְהַלְּבוֹנָה,

א) [במשנה שבמשניות איתא אלו]

[מנחות יז.]

רש"י

וְהָא בֵּין בֵּין קָתָנֵי. דְּמַשְׁמַע אוֹ בָּזוֹ אוֹ בָּזוֹ. אָמַר מָר כו'. אַמַּאן דִּמְהַדַּר לְאוֹקוּמֵי טַעְמָא דְּר"מ מִשּׁוּם מְפַגְּלִין בַּחֲצִי מַתִּיר קָפָרֵיךְ: נְהִי נַמִּי דִּבְעָלְמָא בְּקוֹמֶץ וּלְבוֹנָה אִיכָּא לְמֵימַר מְפַגְּלִין בַּחֲצִי מַתִּיר, אֶלָּא בַּחֲצִי זְרִיקָה הֵיכִי אָמַר ר' מֵאִיר פִּיגֵּל? מִכְּדֵי כָּרֵת לָא מִיחַיַּיב ח] (הָא וכו') עַד שֶׁיִּקְרְבוּ כָּל מַתִּירָיו. שֶׁתִּיכְלֶינָה עֲבוֹדוֹתָיו. דְּאָמַר מָר. בְּפ' שֵׁנִי (לעיל דף כח:). כִּי הָדַר מַדֵּי בַּהֵיכָל מַיָּא בְּעָלְמָא קָא מַדֵּי. וְנִמְצָא שֶׁלֹּא ט] זָרַק דָּמוֹ, דְּהָא מַתָּנָה אַחַת מֵהֶן מְעַכֶּבֶת. דְּבִשְׁלָמָא מְפַגֵּל בִּשְׁחִיטָה, אע"ג דְּפַסְלֵיהּ וַהֲדַר זָרַק לֵיהּ אוֹ בְּמַחֲשָׁבָה אוֹ בִּשְׁתִיקָה, כֵּיוָן דְּפִיגֵּל י] *בַּעֲבוֹדָה וְשׁוּב לֹא הוֹצִיא בּוֹ מַחֲשֶׁבֶת פְּסוּל אַחֵר, אע"פ שֶׁזְּרִיקַת דָּמוֹ יא] דַּם פָּסוּל הוּא, כֵּיוָן דְּרַבִּי רַחֲמָנָא פִּיגּוּל בִּשְׁחִיטָה כְּדַאֲמָרַן בְּפֶרֶק רִאשׁוֹן (לעיל יג.): בִּדְבָרִים הַמְּבִיאִים לִידֵי אֲכִילָה הַכָּתוּב מְדַבֵּר — ע"כ בְּהָכִי אָמַר רַחֲמָנָא יב] לְפִגּוּל, וּזְרִיקָה זוֹ כְּמוֹ שֶׁהִיא מְרַצָּה לְפִיגּוּלוֹ. וְכֵן לְרַבָּנַן דְּבָעוּ מַחֲשָׁבָה בְּכוּלֵּיהּ זְרִיקָה, וּלְמַאן דְּמוֹקֵי נַמִּי יג] טַעַם דְּר"מ מִשּׁוּם דַּעַת רִאשׁוֹנָה וּפִיגֵּל בְּכָל הָעֲבוֹדָה — בְּכֹה"ג אָמַר רַחֲמָנָא לְפִגּוּל, דְּלָא מַשְׁכַּחַתְּ יד] לְפִגּוּל בִּזְרִיקָה אֶלָּא בְּהָכִי. אֶלָּא לְמ"ד טַעְמָא מִשּׁוּם חֲצִי מַתִּיר — אֵין כָּאן זְרִיקָה, כֵּיוָן דְּלֹא גְּמָרָהּ טו] מַחֲשֶׁבֶת פִּיגּוּל וְעָשָׂה סוֹפָהּ לְדַעַת כְּשֵׁרָה, זִיל הָכָא חֲצִי עֲבוֹדָה הִיא, וְזִיל הָכָא חֲצִי עֲבוֹדָה הִיא! מַשְׁכַּחַתְּ לָהּ. הָא דְּקָאָמַר ר"מ פִּיגּוּל. בְּאַרְבָּעָה פָּרִים. פִּיגֵּל בֵּין הַבַּדִּים בְּכָל מַתְּנוֹתָיו, וְנִשְׁפַּךְ הַדָּם, וְשָׁחַט אַחֵר וְהִזָּה עַל הַפָּרֹכֶת, וְאֶחָד טז] עַל הַקְּרָנוֹת, וְאֶחָד לִטְיהֲרוֹ שֶׁל מִזְבֵּחַ. וְכֵיוָן דְּקַיְימָא לָן בְּסֵדֶר יוֹמָא (דף ס.) יז] כּוּלְּהוּ כַּפָּרָה בִּפְנֵי עַצְמוֹ, וְאִי עָבְדִינְהוּ כְּהִלְכָתָן מִתְכַּשְּׁרָה עֲבוֹדָה בְּהָכִי. אֲפִילּוּ לְרַבָּנַן דִּפְלִיגִי עֲלַיְיהוּ דְּר' שִׁמְעוֹן וְר' אֶלְעָזָר בְּנִשְׁפַּךְ הַדָּם בְּאֶמְצַע מַתָּנוֹת — בְּהָא מוֹדוּ דְּאֵין צָרִיךְ לַחֲזוֹר וּלְהַזּוֹת בַּמָּקוֹם שֶׁגָּמַר כָּל הַזָּאוֹתָיו, כִּדְאָמְרִינַן הָתָם — הִלְכָּךְ הָכָא נַמִּי פִּיגֵּל, שֶׁהֲרֵי קָרְבוּ מַתִּירָיו שֶׁל כָּל אֶחָד וְנִגְמְרָה הָעֲבוֹדָה בַּחֲבֵירוֹ. אֲבָל בְּפַר אֶחָד — מוֹדֶה ר"מ דְּלֹא פִּיגֵּל, מִשּׁוּם דְּלֹא גָּמַר זְרִיקָה מֵעוֹלָם. לְפִיגּוּלוֹ מְרַצֶּה. כִּי הֵיכִי דְּאִם חָשַׁב בִּשְׁחִיטָה קָרֵי לָהּ יח] לִזְרִיקָה דַּם הַפָּסוּל הַזֶּה קָרְבוּ מַתִּירָיו לְרַצּוֹת לְפִיגּוּלוֹ, כִּי חָשֵׁיב לֵיהּ (ב) בַּחֲצִי זְרִיקָה נַמִּי וְשָׁתַק בְּחֶלְיָהּ, כָּל זְמַן שֶׁלֹּא עֵירֵב בְּמַחֲשָׁבָה אַחֶרֶת — הָוֵי רִיצּוּי (ג) לְפִיגּוּל. הָא כְּמ"ד כו'. פְּלוּגְתָּא דְּר' יֹאשִׁיָּה וְר' יוֹנָתָן הִיא (יומא דף נז:) בְּמַתַּן הַקְּרָנוֹת יט] "וְלָקַח מִדַּם הַפָּר וּמִדַּם הַשָּׂעִיר", חַד אוֹמֵר: שֶׁיְּהוּ מְעוֹרָבִין, וְחַד אוֹמֵר: מַזֶּה בִּפְנֵי עַצְמוֹ וּמַזֶּה בִּפְנֵי עַצְמוֹ. וְהָא. דְּקָתָנֵי אַרְבָּעִים וְשֶׁבַע, כְּמ"ד אֵין מְעָרְבִין אֶת הַדָּמִים *לְמַתַּן כ] קְרָנוֹת (וְהָווּ תַּמְנֵי). שִׁירַיִם. שְׁפִיכַת שִׁירַיִם. וּפְלוּגְתָּא דְּר' עֲקִיבָא וְר' יְהוּדָה הִיא לְעֵיל (דף מ.) כא] אִם כִּלָּה כִּפֵּר כו'. בד"א כו'. בַּתּוֹסֶפְתָּא דִּמְנָחוֹת קָתָנֵי לָהּ: בד"א שֶׁהַמִּנְחָה נִפְגְּלָה בַּעֲבוֹדָה אַחַת — בִּקְמִיצָה אוֹ בְּמַתַּן כְּלִי וּבְהִילּוּךְ, שֶׁאֵין שָׁם אֶלָּא עֲבוֹדַת מַתִּיר אֶחָד, שֶׁאֵין קְמִיצָה וּמַתַּן כְּלִי *בִּלְבוֹנָה, וְהִילּוּךְ — בִּמְנָחוֹת (דף טז.) מְפָרֵשׁ לֵיהּ דְּלָא שַׁיָּיךְ בִּלְבוֹנָה. בָּא לוֹ לְהַקְטָרָה. שֶׁהִיא עֲבוֹדַת שְׁנֵי מַתִּירָיו, נָתַן כו'. אַלְמָא אֲפִילּוּ רִאשׁוֹנָה בִּשְׁתִיקָה וּשְׁנִיָּה בְּמַחֲשָׁבָה קָאָמַר ר' מֵאִיר פִּיגֵּל, אַלְמָא כב] מְפַגְּלִין בַּחֲצִי מַתִּיר, וּתְיוּבְתָּא דְּר"ל! אֵימָא וּכְבָר נָתַן לְבוֹנָה בְּמַחֲשָׁבָה. הִלְכָּךְ, שְׁנִיָּה שֶׁבִּשְׁתִיקָה עַל דַּעַת רִאשׁוֹנָה עוֹשֶׂה. כג] דְּהַיְינוּ קַמַּיְיתָא. דְּרִאשׁוֹן בְּמַחֲשָׁבָה הָא תָּנָא לֵיהּ: נָתַן אֶת הַקּוֹמֶץ בְּמַחֲשָׁבָה וְאֶת הַלְּבוֹנָה בִּשְׁתִיקָה. לָמָּה לִי לְמִיהְדַּר לְמִיתְנֵי: כד] אוֹ אֶת הַקּוֹמֶץ בִּשְׁתִיקָה, וּכְבָר נִתְּנָה לְבוֹנָה בְּמַחֲשָׁבָה? מַה לִּי לְהַקְדִּים קוֹמֶץ מַה לִּי לְבוֹנָה? וְעוֹד הָא תַּנְיָא. בְּבָרַיְיתָא אַחֲרִיתֵי: אוֹ שֶׁנָּתַן אֶת הַקּוֹמֶץ בִּשְׁתִיקָה וְאַחַר כָּךְ נָתַן לְבוֹנָה בְּמַחֲשָׁבָה. קַשְׁיָא. **מתני'** אֵלּוּ דְּבָרִים שֶׁאֵין חַיָּיבִין עֲלֵיהֶן. כָּרֵת בַּאֲכִילָתָן מִשּׁוּם פִּיגּוּל. הַקּוֹמֶץ. אִם קָמַץ לֶאֱכוֹל שִׁירַיִם לְמָחָר וְנִתְפַּגְּלָה הַמִּנְחָה — אֵין הָאוֹכֵל אֶת הַקּוֹמֶץ בְּכָרֵת. שֶׁאֵין הַפִּיגּוּל חָל אֶלָּא עַל דָּבָר שֶׁיֵּשׁ לוֹ מַתִּירִין אֲחֵרִים, וְהַקּוֹמֶץ אֵין אַחֵר מַתִּירוֹ, כִּי הוּא מַתִּיר אֶת הַמִּנְחָה. וְכֵן לְבוֹנָה, וְכֵן כּוּלָּם. מִנְחַת

[מנחות טז:] | לעיל כח: [מנחות טז:] | בעבודה אחת נ"ק | [מנחות טז: לקמן פא: יומא נז:] | [לקמן נב: קיא. מנחות טז: יומא ס:] | תוספתא דמנחות פ"ה [מנחות טז. ע"ש בתוס'] | ע' נ"ק | נ"ל והילוך בלבונה נ"ק

תוספות

כי מדי בהיכל מיא בעלמא קמדי. הקשה בקונטרס: כה] בהקומץ *ושוחט נמי נימא דלא מיפגל, דכי חשיב בקבלה – איפסיל, וכי זריק – מיא בעלמא זריק! ותירץ: דהתם גזירת הכתוב הוא. וב"הקומץ זוטא" (מנחות דף טז:) תירץ דאותה עבודה שפיגל בה נעשית כולה בקדושתה – שוחט ע"מ לזרוק או להקטיר, וכן מקבל ע"מ לזרוק או להקטיר. אבל הנך הזאות – כולהו חדא עבודה היא, ולא קרבו כו] מתירין העבודה בקדושתן. כז] וקשה: דכי פיגל בהזאות של בין הבדים – אינך דהיכל מים נינהו, אבל בהזאה ראשונה של בדים לא פריך דשאר הזאות של בדים מיא! כח] דיש לומר: יפגל באחרונה. או כיון דחד מקום הוי – אין בכך כלום, [כמו שאפרש] בסמוך. אי נמי, י"ל: דניחא ליה דלא הוו של בין הבדים מיא, משום דלא נגמר הפיגול עד שיזרוק כל הזאות של בין הבדים. אבל אותן של היכל לא תליא בהו גמר הפיגול, כיון שאם נשפך הדם – מביא פר אחר ויתחיל בהיכל ולא בין הבדים. וכן ההזאות של מזבח הזהב לא תלו בהזאות של היכל למימר בהו פיגול של היכל. ולרבנן לא פריך, דכיון דאין מפגלין בחצי מתיר, וצריך לפגל כל ההזאות – אם כן לא נגמר הפיגול עד שפיגל בכולן מתחילת בין הבדים עד גמר של טהרו. ומשני: בד' פרים. כדי לחשב ולפגל בכל המקומות קאמר ארבעה. וה"ה בפר ראשון של בין הבדים ונשפך הדם והביא פר שני ועשה כט] (פר שני) ממנו של היכל ושל מזבח בשתיקה, דהוי פיגול לר' מאיר. ברוך. וקשה: דאם כן פיגל בקומץ ולא בלבונה לרבי מאיר, ליפרוך: אמאי הוי פיגול בחצי מתיר? ל] *)והך עבודה לא נעשית בקדושתה, וכי מקטר ללבונה – עפרא בעלמא מקטר! וכי תימא משום דהוו שני מינים – אכתי קשה משני בזיכין, אם לא נחלק לא] כיון דבעו שני כלים דהוו כשני מינים, והוי פיגול. ורבינו תם מפרש: דבחד מקום פשיטא ליה דלא אמרינן מיא בעלמא הוא, דקמדי לב] תחילת עבודה בגמר עבודה, והכי גזירת הכתוב. אבל בשני מקומות – בהכי לא איירי קרא, ומיא בעלמא קמדי. **משכחת** לה בד' פרים. וא"ת: אכתי הזאות שבפנים היכי משכחת ליה פיגול בפר אחד? מכיון שהזה לג] בראשונה במחשבה – אידך מיא בעלמא קמדי! ולרבינו תם אתי שפיר, דחד מקום הוא. ויש לומר: כגון שפיגל בהזאה אחרונה של בין הבדים. **הא** כמאן דאמר שיריים מעכבין. ל"ע פ' "איזהו מקומן" (לקמן דף נב:) דקאמר רמי בר חמא: האי תנא סבר שיריים מעכבי, ומיירי מברייתא, ודחי לה. והוה מצי לאתויי הך! ועוד: מברייתא דלעיל (דף לט.) דדמים הטעונין יסוד טעונין כיבוס ומחשבה פוסלת בהן, ומוקמינן לה בשירים, וכמאן דאמר דמעכבי.

הקומץ. הקשה בקונטרס ב"הקומץ זוטא" (מנחות דף יד.): למה לי לד] דאין לו מתירין אלא הוא עצמו מתיר אחרים, כדאיתא בגמ'? תיפוק לי דבלאו הכי נמי פשיטא דקומץ לא מיחייב עליה משום פיגול, דהא אי אכיל מיניה – פקע פיגולו ממנו, שהרי לא קרב מתיר כמלותו! ותירץ: כגון שהוצתה האור ברובו, דחשיב כמאן דקרב המתיר, כדקאמר ב"הקומץ רבה" (שם דף כו:): מאימתי מתיר שירים באכילה – משהוצת האור ברובו. וקשה לפירושו: דאי הוצת האור ברובו – א"כ פקע פיגולו ממנו, כדאמר עולא בגמ' (דף מג.): דאם ירדו נמי יעלו. והוא הדין אפילו מאכילה, כדמשמע בכריתות פרק "אמרו לו" (דף יד. ושם)! וי"ל: לה] דמיירי שאליו העלה ע"ג מזבח ואליה לא העלה, דעל ההוא דאארעא לא פקע פיגולו ממנו וחייב עליו, אי לאו משום דהוא גופיה מתיר הוא. דהא דאמר בגמ' לגבי קומץ לו] דפיגול שהעלהו, דפלגא מחית אארעא ופלגיה מסקיה אמערכה ומשלה בו האור פקע פיגולו ומסקינן ליה לכתחילה, ובפ' "אמרו לו" (גם זה שם) מתירו ליה לאכילה – לז] מיירי כשהיה כבר על המזבח ההוא פלגא דמחית אארעא, אבל היכי דלא עלה למזבח מעולם – לא. כדמוכח בכריתות (גם זה שם) דאותו קלת לח] דחוץ למזבח לא מסקינן ליה, והוה ליה פיגול אע"ג דרובא דאבר אמזבח, אם איתא דלא הלכו באברים אחר הרוב, וכל שכן קומץ דמיפרת, דלא מסקינן. לט] ומיהו, *) פי' בקונטרס *דבגמרא משמע דאפילו לא עלה אמזבח מסקינן ליה לכתחילה, ולא דמיא להיא דכריתות, כמו שמפרש ר"ת, שהקומץ כולו חשוב אזכרה אחת וההוא פלגא דעל המזבח משיך ליה לפלגא דאארעא, דאי לאו הכי – הוה ההוא דעל המזבח קומץ שחסר וירד, וא"כ כיון דמשיך ליה – פקע פיגולו ממנו. אבל פלגא דאבר לא משיך אידך פלגא, דהוא עצמו שלא הוקטרו אימוריו כשר. אע"ג דמעיקרא סלקא דעתך דקומץ מ] גרע משום דמיפרת. ומפרש ר"ת: דטעמא דקומץ – לאו משום דהוא מתיר, אלא משום דלא שייך ביה הרצאה, מא] דאי אכלו ולא העלהו – אם כן לא קרבו מתיריו, ואי העלה אליו – פקע פיגולו מכוליה, אפילו מההוא דאארעא. והא דקאמר בגמרא: ומוציא אני את הקומץ בהדי הנהו

*) לפי' הקונטרס כו' כצ"ל נ"ק

נ"ב מג ע"ב נ"ק

הגהות הב"ח

(א) גמ' חדא דהיינו קמייתא ועוד: (ב) רש"י ד"ה לפיגולו מרצה וכו' כי חשיב ליה נמי בחצי זריקה ושתק וכו' לפיגול הס"ד ואח"כ מ"ה והא דקתני וכו' תמניא הס"ד ואחר כך ד"ה הא כמ"ד:

*)הא חד עבודה כו' ור"מ מפרש כו' הוא דקמדי כמו מתחלת עבודה לגמר עבודה דמהני כו' נ"ק

שיטה מקובצת

א] בפנים פסליה ותיבות כמאן דלא אדי דמי בס"א אינו אבל בספרים ישנים ישנם: ב] מיא בעלמא כו'. פ"ה בשלמא מפגל בשחיטה כו' עד מרצה לפיגולו וכן לרבנן ניחא דאינו מפגל עד לבסוף א"כ בשעת הזאה לא הוי פיגול אלא לר"מ דאמר מפגלין בחצי מתיר א"כ מיד כשפיגל גמר פיגולו והשאר מיא בעלמא קא מדי דבשלמא (כמו כן לר"מ) אי טעמא [לר"מ] משום עושה על דעת הראשונה ופיגל בכל העבודה בכה"ג אמר רחמנא ליפגל דלא משכחת פיגול אלא בהכי אלא למ"ד טעמא משום חצי מתיד מיא בעלמא קא מדי כך היא שיטת הקונטרס וא"ת כל פיגול הכי הוי א"כ לא נמצא פיגול לר"מ דכי השיב בהו נפגל אף בשחיטה או בקומץ וכי הדר זריק מיא בעלמא קא מדי וי"ל דלא אמרינן מיא בעלמא קא מדי אלא בעבודה אחת הואיל ואירע בו פסול אבל בשתי עבודות לא אמרי' מיא בעלמא קא מדי והזאות כולהו עבודה אחת נינהו מיהו קשה דאמרינן לעיל בפרק ב' וכן בפ"ק דמעילה גבי פלוגתא דר"י דאמר אם מחשבת הזמן קודם למחשבת המקום ומפרש אילפא מחלוקת בעבודה אחת כעין שתי עבודות כגון ששחט סימן אחד בחוץ לזמנו ושני בחוץ למקומו כו' ותירץ הר"מ דסבר אילפא דפיגול הוא מרצה כרבא ור"ת פי' דלא אמרינן מיא בעלמא מדי אלא בשתי מקומות כגון שחשב בפנים ומזה בהיכל דכיון שנסתלק מבפנים נגמרה מחשבתו והשתא ניחא דבשחיטה לא גמר עד לבסוף: ג] בארבעה פרים כו'. פ"ה ששוחט פר או שעיר והזה בפנים ופיגל באחרונה ונשפך הדם ומביא אחר ופיגל נמי באחרונה דהיכל ונשפך ושחט שלישית. והזה על הקרנות בשתיקה. והאי דנקט הקונטרס טהרו קודם לקרנות לא דק

...ב שבבי פי' שהולך בדרכי לבו עיין ערוך ערך שב] עסקינן דפיגל הרבה פעמים: ד] רבא. ס"א אביי: ה] במחשבה ופליגי: ו] הקומץ. וא"ת האי קומץ היכי מיירי אי קודם הקטרה אכתי לא קרבו מתיריו ... עד שיקרבו מתיריו אפילו שיריים ואי לאחר הקטרה ג) הלא הוא עצמו הוא המתיר ובקונטרס תירץ [וכו'] וקשה כו' וי"ל דלעולם איירי קודם הקטרה וכגון שנתקדשה בכלי כדאמרינן במנחות דהדבר שאין ... בכלי הלכך אי לאו דהוא עצמו המתיר הו"א דהוא פיגול משקדשו בכלי: ז] והלבונה והקטרת: ח] האוכלו עד שיקרבו כל מתיריו שתכלנה כל הוריקה הס"ד: ט] שלא נזרק דמו כו' אחת מעכבת בה...

ומנחת כהנים, ומנחת כהן משיח, והדם. והנסכים הבאין בפני עצמן, דברי רבי מאיר, וחכמים אומרים: [א]אף הבאין עם הבהמה. לוג שמן של מצורע, ר' שמעון אומר: [ב]אין חייבין עליו משום פיגול, ורבי מאיר אומר: חייבין עליו משום פיגול, שדם האשם מתירו. *וכל שיש לו מתירין, בין לאדם בין למזבח — חייבין עליו משום פיגול; העולה — [ג]דמה מתיר את בשרה למזבח, ועורה לכהנים. עולת העוף — דמה מתיר את בשרה למזבח. חטאת העוף — דמה מתיר את בשרה לכהנים. פרים הנשרפים ושעירים הנשרפים — דמן מתיר את אימוריהן ליקרב. **ר' שמעון אומר: כל שאינו על המזבח החיצון כשלמים — אין חייבין עליו משום פיגול.§

גמ' אמר עולא: *קומץ פיגול שהעלו על גבי המזבח — פקע פיגולו ממנו, אם אחרים מביא לידי פיגול — הוא עצמו לא כל שכן. מאי קאמר? הכי קאמר: אם אינו מתקבל, היאך מביא אחרים לידי פיגול? מאי קא משמע לן? אי דאין חייבין עליו משום פיגול — תנינא: אלו דברים שאין חייבין עליהם משום פיגול: הקומץ, א] והקטרת, והלבונה, ומנחת כהנים, ומנחת כהן משיח, ב] ומנחת נסכים, והדם! אלא, דאם עלו לא ירדו — תנינא: ג] *הלן, והיוצא, והטמא, ושנשחט חוץ לזמנו וחוץ למקומו — ד] אם עלו לא ירדו! ואלא, דאם ירדו ה] יעלו — הא נמי תנינא: *כשם שאם עלו לא ירדו — כך אם ירדו לא יעלו! לא צריכא, שמשלה בהן ו] האור. הא נמי אמרה עולא חדא זימנא. *דאמר עולא: לא שנו אלא שלא משלה בהן ז] האור, אבל משלה בהן האור — יעלו! מהו דתימא: הני מילי אבר

רש"י

מנחת נדבת כהנים. כולה כליל ואינה נקמצת, הלכך אין אחר מתירה. וכן מנחת כהן משיח. חביתי כהן גדול שמקריב בכל יום מחציתה בבקר ומחציתה בערב (ויקרא ו). ומנחת נסכים לא גרסי', דהא מיפלג פליגי בה, ח] ונתן חילוק בין באה עם הזבח לבאה לפני עצמו. והדם. הוא המתיר. והנסכים הבאין בפני עצמן. בין ט] שהתנדבן בפני עצמן, כדאמר במנחות (דף קד:): מתנדב אדם מנחת נסכים בין שבאו בגלל זבח, אלא שהביא י] היום זבחו ונסכיו למחר, דאמר מר: "מנחתם ונסכיהם" — אף למחר. אבל אם הביאן עם זבחו ופיגל בזבח — נתפגלו הנסכים. וחכמים אומרים אף הבאים עם הבהמה. דכיון דיכול להקריב נסכים למחר, נמצא שאין הזבח מתירן ליקרב, אלא הן מתירין את עצמן. לוג שמן של מצורע. שייריו נאכלין, כדיליף בפירקין לקמן (דף מד:). אין חייבין עליו משום פיגול. אם פיגל באשם לא יא] נפגל הלוג. ואע"פ שהלוג תלוי באשם, כדכתיב: "על מקום דם האשם" (ויקרא יד), ואם לא נתן מדם האשם תחילה אין נתינת השמן כלום, אפילו הכי, כיון דאדם מביא אשמו עכשיו ולוגו עד עשרה ימים — נמצא שאין האשם מתירו, וכיון דאין לו מתירין — אין חייבין עליו משום פיגול. ר"מ אומר. לוג הבא עם האשם בו ביום — חייבין עליו משום פיגול, אם פיגל באשם. בין לאדם בין למזבח. או לזה או לזה. דמה מתיר בשרה למזבח. דכתיב (שם א): "וזרקו" והדר "וערכו". ועורה לכהנים. יב] עור העולה אשר הקריבו אין לו אלא לאחר זריקה. חטאת העוף כו'. בגמ' מפרש מנין דנאכל לכהנים. דמן מתיר יג] אימוריהן ליקרב. לפיכך, פיגל באימורים בשעת עבודת הדם — נתפגלו *פרים. ר' שמעון. אפרים הנשרפין פליג. כל שאין מתן דמו על המזבח החיצון כשלמים. יד] שפיגול כתיב בהו (ויקרא ז) — אין חייבין עליו משום פיגול. **גמ'** פקע פיגולו ממנו. לקמן מפרש למאי הלכתא פקע. מאי קאמר. טו] קבעי למימר פקע פיגולו ממנו, ונסיב טעמא דבא לידי פיגול. אם אינו מתקבל. בהקטרה. היאך מביא אחרים לידי פיגול. טז] המקטיר קומץ על מנת שיאכל שיריים למחר, היאך מנחה מתפגלת אם אין יז] הקטרתו הקטרה? והכי קאמר: הוא עצמו לא כל שכן שיתקבל אחרי שמתקבל לרצות אחרים לפיגולו? מאי קא משמע לן. למאי מיבעי ליה הא יח] פקע פיגולו? אי. למימרא דאם אכל ממנו יט] אחרי שעלה אין חייבין עליו כרת. כ] תנינן. דבלאו עלה נמי אין חייבין עליו. אלא. להכי אהני פקיעה, דכיון שעלה לא ירד. תנינא ושנשחט חוץ לזמנו. דהיינו פיגול. הלן. בשר הלן. אלא. אהני פקיעה שאם ירד לאחר שהעלוהו (לא) יחזור ויעלה. תנינא. כא] *בלאו הכי! לא צריכא. הא דעולא, אלא שמשלה בו האור. ואשמעינן דנעשה לחמו של מזבח, ואפי' כב] ירדו — יעלו. וההיא דקתני לא יעלו — בשלא משלה בו האור. לא שנו. דאם ירדו הנך פסולין משעלו — לא יעלה. (בחד) אבר

תוספות

הנהו דאין לו כג] מתירין — כדי נסבה. וקשה: התינח קומץ, אלא לבונה ומנחת כהנים, תיפוק לי משום דאין בהם הרצאה! ועוד: דגבי דם כד] קאמר בפירוש משום מתיר, והיכי משכחת לה דמחייב משום פיגול? דאי אכיל ליה קודם שעשה מתנות — אם כן ליכא הרצאה, ואי מן הדם הנשאר במזרק לאחר שעשה מתנות — ההוא לאו מתיר הוא. ואם מאותו *שזרק על המזבח — הא פקע פיגול ממנו! ושמא לא שייך למימר גבי דם פקע פיגולו, כי אם גבי הקטרה דוקא, שנעשה לחמו של מזבח. ותימה הוא: כה] אם לא יתחייב בשירי הדם משום פיגול — הא יש להם מתירין, שהמתנות מתירות לשפיכות שיריים *למזבח, כמו שמתירות את האימורים! ושמא כו] *כמו מתחילה כל טיפה וטיפה ראויה לזריקה — חשיב כוליה דם מתיר. ונראה לפרש, דהיינו טעמא דקומץ וכולהו, דאי הוי בני חיובא — הוי דינן משקדש בכלי, וקידוש כלי היינו ההרצאה כז] דידיה, *כיון דאינהו גופייהו מתיר אחד, כדאמר לעיל (דף לד.) גבי טומאה: יש לו מתירין — משיקרבו מתירין, אין לו מתירין — משיקדש בכלי. **והלבונה**. ואם תאמר: והרי לבונה — הקומץ מתירה. כח] ואף על פי שיכול להקטירה קודם הקומץ כדאמר ב"הקומץ זוטא" (מנחות טז:) — מכל מקום קודם הקמילה ודאי נראה דאין להקטירה! ויש לומר: דמכל מקום לא הויא לבונה דומיא דשלמים, דלבונה היא גופה מתיר שמתרת שירים לאכילה, ועיקר פיגול ילפינן כט] משלמים. ואע"ג דשייך פיגול באימורים, וכמה דלא מיקטרי אימורים כהנים לא מצי אכלי — מכל מקום לא חשיבי מתיר, כיון דאם נטמאו או אבדו שרי בשר באכילה. ועוד יש לומר: דלבונה אין לה מתיר בעבודת המזבח, ולא הויא דומיא דשלמים שעבודת המזבח מתירן כגון זריקת הדם. *ואם תאמר: אמאי לא חשיב הכא עצים, כי היכי דחשיב לבונה אע"ג דלא חזיא לאכילה? דאי הוה להו מתירין — היה חייב עליהם משום פיגול כמו שחייבין עליהם משום טומאה, אבל אין להם מתירין, והן עצמן מתירין! ויש לומר: דלא שייך למיתני עצים, דהיכי דמי? אי כגון מתנדב עצים ל] לרבי דאמר ב"הקומץ רבה" (מנחות כ:) דטעונים קמיצה והגשה — הוי דינם כמנחה, ופטור על הקומץ וחייב על השירים. ואי בעצים דמערכה — לא שייך בהו מחשבה, דאי במחשב בשעת הולכה ע"מ להקטירו למחר — לא] *היו הולכת עצים למערכה לכולי עלמא לאו עבודה היא! ומיהו, לחריפי דפומבדיתא בסוף "הקומץ זוטא" (שם דף יז.) משכחת לה בהקטיר שומשום על מנת להקטיר שומשום למחר, דהקטרה מפגלת הקטרה. ושמא, אע"ג דחייבין על העצים משום טומאה — אין חייבין עליהם משום פיגול, דלאו קרבן גמור הם, לרבנן דפליגי עליה דרבי בפרק "הקומץ רבה" (שם כ:) דלא בעו מליחה, דמכשירי קרבן הם לב]* דלא קרבן. ומיהו קשה: דמאי שנא פיגול מטומאה? דאי משום דילפינן (לעיל דף כח:) פיגול משלמים — טומאה נמי כתיב בשלמים (ויקרא ז). ועוד: דפיגול אתי לקמן (דף מה.) "עון" "עון" מנותר, ונותר "חילול" "חילול" מטומאה! **מנחת** נסכים. פי' בקונטרס: דלא גרסינן מנחת נסכים, משום דפליגי בה בסיפא דהך משנה, דקתני: והנסכים הבאים בפני עצמן דברי רבי מאיר, וחכמים אומרים: אף הבאין עם הבהמה. ובפני עצמן דקאמר — היינו *כגון שהתנדב נסכים, לג] כדאמר גבי מתנדב אדם מנחת נסכים בכל יום, בין הבאין עם הבהמה, כגון שהביא זבחו היום ונסכים מכאן ועד עשרה ימים. ומיהו, יש ליישב גירסת הספרים: דמנחת נסכים מיירי במתנדב מנחת נסכים בכל יום, וההיא דבאין בפני עצמן — מיירי במביא זבחו היום ונסכים ביום מחר. אבל קשה: שלא היה לו להפסיק בדם, והוה ליה למיתני הכי: והדם ומנחת נסכים ונסכים הבאין בפני עצמם! ושמא איידי דתנא מנחת כהנים ומנחת כהן משיח — תנא נמי מנחת נסכים. ולוג שמן של מצורע — נראה דרבי שמעון דהכא הוא רבנן דלעיל גבי נסכים. וקשה: אמאי לא עירב? דתרווייהו חד טעמא הוא!* נאמר

שיטה מקובצת

א] הקומץ והלבונה והקטרת: ב] תיבות ומנחת נסכים נמחק: ג] תנינא ואלו אם עלו לא ירדו הלן: ד] תיבות אם עלו לא ירדו נמחק: ה] ירדו דלא יעלו תנינא ותיבות הא נמי נמחק ובס"י איתא תיבת נמי: ו] בהן את האור: ז] בהן את האור אבל משלה בהן את האור: ח] בה ונותן חילוק: ט] שהתנדבו: י] זבחו היום ונסכיו למחר כו' ונסכיהם אפילו למחר: יא] לא נתפגל: יב] לכהנים דכתיב עור העולה אשר הקריב: יג] דמן מתיר את אימוריהן ליקרב לפיכך כו' בשעת זריקת הדם נתפגלו: יד] בשלמים. שהפיגול כתוב בהן: טו] קאמר דבעי למימר: טז] פיגול והמקטיר: יז] אם אין הקטרתו של קומץ הקטרה והא בעינן קרבו מתירין אלא ודאי קרבו מתירין קרינן ביה דפקע פיגולא ממנו ולכן קבע השירים בפיגול והכי קאמר: יח] הא פקיעת פיגול הס"ד: יט] ממנו אחר שעלה: כ] מה"ד תנינא: כא] תנינא דלאו: כב] ואפילו ירד יעלה וההיא כו' משעלו לא יעלו הס"ד ותיבת בחד נמחק: כג] מתירין א] ס"א לא גרסינן ובת"כ ליתא א"נ כדי: כד] דקאמר בפירוש משום כו' שעשה המתנות א"כ: כה] אמאי לא יתחייב: כו] כיון שמתחלה: כז] הרצאה דידהו כיון דאינהו גופייהו אין להם מתיר אחר כדאמר לעיל ולהלן (דף מה ע"ב) גבי: כח] מתירה להקטרה: כט] ילפינן מבשר שלמים והתם לא הוי מתיר לאחר ואע"ג כו' באימורים ואע"ג דמתיר הבשר דכל כמה דלא מצי אכלי כשר מכל מקום: ל] עצים ולרבי: לא] למחר הא הולכת עצים: לב] הם ולא קרבן: לג] נסכים כדאמרינן מתנדב אדם:

א] ר"ל דהס"א גרסי בתוס' אחר תיבת מתירין לא גרסינן ובתו"כ ליתא א"נ כדי נסבה [ומיהו בתו"כ שלפנינו בפ' ט איתא את הקומץ וצ"ע].

גליון הש"ס

מתני' רש"א כל שאינו. עיין לקמן דף מה ע"ב תוספות ד"ה אבל:

עין משפט נר מצוה

לא א ב מיי' פי"ח מהלכות פסה"מ הל' ח:
לב ג מיי' שם הלכה ז:

מסורת הש"ס / הגהות

[יומא ס. לקמן מו. חולין קיז:]
לעיל יז. לקמן מו: שבועות ז.
מעילה ג: [כריתות יז.]
לקמן פד.
לקמן פד.
האימורין נ"ק
לקמן פה:
רש"ק מ"ז
בין נ"ק
שנעשה נ"ק
ליסוד נ"ק
כיון שמתחלה כו' נ"ק
וכיון דאינהו גופייהו מתירין אחרים לא מהני קידוש בכלי כדאמרינן גבי טומאה כו' נ"ק
[ועי' תוס' מנחות יב. ד"ה והלבונה]
נ"ל הא נ"ק
נ"ל ולא נ"ק
[התי"ט כתב ישוב על זה]

לג א מיי' פ"ג מהל' פסולי המוקדשין הלכה י:
לד ב ג מיי' פי"ח מהלכות פסה"מ הלכה כא:
[עיין לעיל טו: תוספות ד"ה אלא למעוטי]
לה ד מיי' שם הלכה יג:

אֵבֶר דִּמְחַבַּר, אֲבָל קוֹמֶץ דְּמִיפְּרַת — אֵימָא לָא, קמ"ל. אָמַר רַב אַחַאי: הִלְכָּךְ, אהַאי קוֹמֶץ פִּיגּוּל דְּפַלְגֵיהּ מָחֵית אַאַרְעָא וּפַלְגֵיהּ אַסְקֵיהּ אַמַּעֲרָכָה, וּמָשְׁלָה בּוֹ א] הָאוּר — מַסִּיקְנָא לֵיהּ לְכוּלֵּיהּ לְכַתְחִלָּה.§ אָמַר רַבִּי יִצְחָק אָמַר רַבִּי יוֹחָנָן: ב] בהַפִּיגּוּל וְהַנּוֹתָר וְהַטָּמֵא שֶׁהֶעֱלָן לְגַבֵּי מִזְבֵּחַ — פָּקַע אִיסּוּר מֵהֶן. אָמַר רַב חִסְדָּא: מָרֵי דִיכִי! ג] מִזְבֵּחַ מִקְוֶה טָהֳרָה?! אָמַר רַבִּי זֵירָא: גשֶׁמָּשְׁלָה בָּהֶן הָאוּר. מְתִיב ר' יִצְחָק בַּר בִּיסְנָא: אֲחֵרִים אוֹמְרִים: °"וְטוּמְאָתוֹ עָלָיו" (ויקרא ז) — מִי שֶׁטּוּמְאָה פּוֹרַחַת מִמֶּנּוּ, יָצָא בָּשָׂר שֶׁאֵין טוּמְאָה פּוֹרַחַת מִמֶּנּוּ; וְאִם אִיתָא — הֲרֵי טוּמְאָה פּוֹרַחַת מִמֶּנּוּ עַל יְדֵי הָאוּר! אָמַר רָבָא: עַל יְדֵי מִקְוֶה קָאָמְרִינַן. מִידֵי מִקְוֶה כְּתִיב? אֶלָּא אָמַר רַב פַּפָּא: בִּבְשַׂר שְׁלָמִים עָסְקִינַן, דְּלָא חֲזֵי לְהַקְרָבָה. רָבִינָא אָמַר: ד] "וְטוּמְאָתוֹ עָלָיו" — מִי שֶׁטּוּמְאָה פּוֹרַחַת מִמֶּנּוּ כְּשֶׁהוּא שָׁלֵם; יָצָא בָּשָׂר, ה] דָּבָר שֶׁאֵין טוּמְאָה פּוֹרַחַת כְּשֶׁהוּא שָׁלֵם, אֶלָּא כְּשֶׁהוּא חָסֵר.§ גּוּפָא: ד"וְטוּמְאָתוֹ עָלָיו" — בְּטוּמְאַת הַגּוּף הַכָּתוּב מְדַבֵּר. ו] אַתָּה אוֹמֵר: בְּטוּמְאַת הַגּוּף, אוֹ אֵינוֹ אֶלָּא בְּטוּמְאַת בָּשָׂר? נֶאֱמַר כָּאן: ז] "טוּמְאָתוֹ" וְנֶאֱמַר לְהַלָּן: "טוּמְאָתוֹ (עָלָיו) [*בּוֹ]", מַה לְּהַלָּן בְּטוּמְאַת הַגּוּף הַכָּתוּב מְדַבֵּר — אַף כָּאן בְּטוּמְאַת הַגּוּף הַכָּתוּב מְדַבֵּר. ר' ח] יוֹסֵי אוֹמֵר: הוֹאִיל וְנֶאֶמְרוּ קָדָשִׁים בִּלְשׁוֹן רַבִּים, וְנֶאֶמְרָה טוּמְאָה בִּלְשׁוֹן יָחִיד — בְּטוּמְאַת הַגּוּף הַכָּתוּב מְדַבֵּר. רַבִּי אוֹמֵר: "וְאָכַל" — בְּטוּמְאַת הַגּוּף הַכָּתוּב מְדַבֵּר. אֲחֵרִים ט] אָמְרוּ: "וְטוּמְאָתוֹ עָלָיו" — מִי שֶׁטּוּמְאָה פּוֹרַחַת מִמֶּנּוּ, יָצָא בָּשָׂר שֶׁאֵין טוּמְאָה פּוֹרַחַת מִמֶּנּוּ. אָמַר מָר, רַבִּי אוֹמֵר: "וְאָכַל" — בְּטוּמְאַת הַגּוּף הַכָּתוּב מְדַבֵּר. מַאי מַשְׁמַע? אָמַר רָבָא: כָּל קְרָא דְּלָא מְפָרֵשׁ לֵיהּ רַב יִצְחָק בַּר אֲבוּדִימִי, וְכָל מַתְנִיתָא דְּלָא מְפָרְשָׁא לָהּ י] רַב זְעִירִי — לָא מִיפַּרְשָׁא. הָכִי אָמַר ר' יִצְחָק בַּר אֲבוּדִימִי: הוֹאִיל וּפָתַח הַכָּתוּב בִּלְשׁוֹן נְקֵבָה וְסִיֵּים בִּלְשׁוֹן נְקֵבָה, וּלְשׁוֹן זָכָר בָּאֶמְצַע — בְּטוּמְאַת הַגּוּף הַכָּתוּב מְדַבֵּר. מַתְנִיתָא — דְּתַנְיָא: אִם נֶאֶמְרוּ קַלּוֹת לָמָּה נֶאֶמְרוּ חֲמוּרוֹת, וְאִם נֶאֱמַר חֲמוּרוֹת לָמָּה נֶאֱמַר קַלּוֹת? אִם נֶאֱמַר קַלּוֹת וְלֹא חֲמוּרוֹת, הָיִיתִי אוֹמֵר: עַל הַקַּלּוֹת בְּלָאו וְעַל הַחֲמוּרוֹת בְּמִיתָה — לְכָךְ נֶאֱמַר חֲמוּרוֹת. וְאִם נֶאֱמַר חֲמוּרוֹת וְלֹא נֶאֶמְרוּ קַלּוֹת, הָיִיתִי אוֹמֵר: עַל הַחֲמוּרוֹת יְהֵא חַיָּיב, וְעַל הַקַּלּוֹת יְהֵא פָּטוּר — לְכָךְ נֶאֱמַר קַלּוֹת. מַאי "קַלּוֹת" וּמַאי "חֲמוּרוֹת"? אִילֵימָא "קַלּוֹת" — מַעֲשֵׂר, "חֲמוּרוֹת" — תְּרוּמָה; הָיִיתִי אוֹמֵר בְּמִיתָה? הַשְׁתָּא נַמִי הָא בְּמִיתָה! יא] [וְתוּ] וְאִי לֹא נֶאֱמַר הָיִיתִי אוֹמֵר בְּמִיתָה? דַּיּוֹ לַבָּא מִן הַדִּין לִהְיוֹת כַּנִּדּוֹן! אֶלָּא: "קַלּוֹת" — טוּמְאַת שֶׁרֶץ, "חֲמוּרוֹת" — טוּמְאַת מֵת; וּבְמַאי? אִי בִּתְרוּמָה — אִידִי וְאִידִי יב] הוּא בְּמִיתָה! וְתוּ, לְכָךְ נֶאֶמְרוּ חֲמוּרוֹת דִּבְלָאו? הָא בְּמִיתָה הִיא! (וְאִי לֹא נֶאֱמַר הָיִיתִי אוֹמֵר בְּמִיתָה? דַּיּוֹ לַבָּא מִן הַדִּין לִהְיוֹת כַּנִּדּוֹן!) וְאִי בַּאֲכִילַת מַעֲשֵׂר,

אִם

אבר דמחבר. איכא יג] למ"ד כיון דמשלה האור במקצתו נקלט כולו בקדושה. **אבל קומץ דמיפרת.** אימא: במאי יד] דמשלה מקומץ — משלה, אידך כדקאי קאי, קמ"ל דכוליה כחד אבר דמי. **הלכך.** כיון טו] דמחשבת ליה מחובר, אפי' לא העלהו אלא חציו ומשלה בו האור — נקלט אף זה שעל הקרקע טז] ומעלה. דהא כי אסקיה לכוליה נמי לא היה לו להעלותו אם ירד, אלא משום ההוא שמשלה בו האור, וקאמרת דאם ירד השאר יעלה — אלמא אהני לכוליה, ואע"ג דמיפרת. הלכך לא שנא עלה כולו ולא שנא לא עלה אלא מקצתו. **פקע איסורן מהן.** איסור פיגול — לכדאמרן, שאם (א) ירד יעלה. ואיסור נותר וטמא נמי להכי יז] [פקע], שלא יתחייב האוכלו מידי. **מרי דיכי.** בעל השמועה יח] הזאת. **מזבח מקוה טהרה הוא.** לטהר את הטומאה משום דהעלוהו? **וטומאתו עליו כו'.** לקמן מייתינן לה בשמעתין (ב) למימרא דבטומאת הגוף יט] מדבר. ואהאי קרא קאי (ויקרא ז): "והנפש אשר תאכל בשר מזבח השלמים אשר לה' וטומאתו עליו", יכול טומאת הבשר, דנימא דהאי "עליו" אבשר קאי, ונימא דטהור שאכל את הטמא חייב? ת"ל: "וטומאתו עליו", משמע שעדיין היא עליו — ביכולין ליטהר הכתוב מדבר, וזהו הגוף, שטומאה פורחת ממנו על ידי טבילה. ואם איתא דבשר קדשים יכול ליטהר על ידי מזבח — מהיכא ילפי אחרים כ] דלא בבשר משתעי קרא? הרי טומאה פורחת ממנו! **בבשר שלמים עסקינן.** דקרא בשלמים כתיב, דאינו ראוי למזבח ואין מפריח כא] מטומאתו. **רבינא אמר.** אף כב] אברין הראויין למזבח כתיבי הכא, דכתיב (שם): "אשר לה'" — לרבות האימורים. ואפילו הכי לא תקשה, דשפיר ילפינן מיניה דטומאה לאו עלייהו קאי, מדכתיב: "וטומאתו עליו", דמשמע: בראוי להפריח טומאתו כשהוא שלם כעין שקיבלה, כג] "עליו" — בעיניה משמע. **בטומאת הגוף הכתוב מדבר.** שהרי עוסק בה והולך, דכתיב (שם): "כל טהור יאכל בשר", וסמיך ליה: "והנפש אשר תאכל בשר" וגו'. אע"פ שהתחיל להזכיר הגוף בלשון נקבה "והנפש אשר תאכל", וכתיב "וטומאתו עליו" לשון זכר, דמשמע דקאי אבשר — כד] בטומאת הגוף דבר ולא בטומאת בשר. **או אינו אלא בטומאת בשר.** דהא "עליו" לשון זכר הוא, והגוף הוזכר בלשון נקבה. הכי גרסינן: כה] טומאתו טומאתו לג"ש. ויליף מביאת מקדש דכתיב ביה: "עוד טומאתו בו" (במדבר יט). הכי גרסי': נאמר כאן טומאתו ונאמר להלן טומאתו. **הואיל ונאמרו קדשים בלשון רבים.** "שלמים" לשון רבים הן, וטומאה בלשון יחיד — דכתיב "וטומאתו עליו", ולא כתיב "וטומאתם עליהם". **רבי אומר ואכל בטומאת הגוף הכתוב מדבר.** מקרא שלאחריו יוכיח על זה, דכתיב בתריה (ויקרא ז): "נפש כי תגע בכל טמא וגו' ואכל מבשר זבח השלמים" וגו'. ולקמיה מפרש היכי משמע ליה מ"ואכל" דקרא בתרא הוכחה על כו] ראשון שבטומאת הגוף הכתוב מדבר. **וטומאתו עליו.** משמע שעדיין לא נטהר ממנו, במי שטומאתו פורחת ממנו הכתוב מדבר, דאי בבשר — לעולם כז] הוא עליו. **מאי משמע.** מקרא דבתריה דקמא בטומאת הגוף? דלמא בתרא בטומאת הגוף, כח] כדכתיב: "נפש אשר תגע בכל טמא", וקמא בטומאת בשר, מדלא כתיב "וטומאתה עליה" דמישתמע דא"והנפש אשר תאכל בשר" קאי! וכל מתניתא דלא מפרש לה זעירי. לקמיה מפרש מאי היא. הואיל ופתח הכתוב השני בלשון נקבה וסיים בלשון נקבה ולשון זכר באמצע. דכתיב (שם): "נפש כי תגע בכל טמא ואכל מבשר זבח השלמים ונכרתה הנפש" וגו' ולא כתיב "ואכלה מבשר זבח", כט] הוי אף הראשון אל תתמה עליו אם פתח וסיים בלשון נקבה ולשון זכר באמצע, אף [על פי כן] בטומאת הגוף הכתוב מדבר. ומסתברא הכי, שהרי בטומאת הגוף היה עוסק והולך, וכבר פסק מלדבר בטומאת בשר. דהכי כתיב קרא (שם): "והבשר אשר יגע בכל טמא לא יאכל" — הרי טומאת בשר, "והבשר כל טהור יאכל בשר" — פסק מטומאת בשר והתחיל בטומאת הגוף, וסמיך ליה "והנפש אשר תאכל" וגו'. ומשום דהזכיר הכתוב את האוכלו בלשון נקבה, וכתב "וטומאתו עליו" בלשון זכר — הייתי סבורים שבטומאת בשר מדבר, עכשיו ל] מקרא השני יוכיח שאף הוא בלשון הזה מדבר. ואי קשיא: שני כריתות בטומאת הגוף למה? שלש כריתות הן בטומאת הגוף, לא] ולקמיה מפרש בהאי פירקין (דף מו.) למאי איצטריכו. **מתניתא.** לב] דלא מפרש לה זעירי, מאי היא? איזה *משנה לא פירש יפה? אם נאמרו קלות. לענין אכילת קדשים בטומאת הגוף שנויה בת"כ. לקמיה מפרש לג] ואזיל מאי קלות ומאי חמורות, ומאי הייתי אומר. **אי נימא קלות מעשר חמורות תרומה.** שנאמרו שניהם בפרשה אחת (ויקרא כב): "ולא יאכל מן הקדשים כי אם רחץ בשרו במים", ואוקימנא ליה במעשר במסכת יבמות (דף עד:) דכתיב: "כי אם רחץ", הא אם רחץ — יאכל ואף על פי שלא העריב שמשו, הרי טמא שאכל מעשר בלאו. וכתיב: "ובא השמש וטהר ואחר יאכל מן הקדשים" ואוקימנא בתרומה, וכתיב בההוא ענינא אכל תרומה: "ומתו בו כי" וגו'. וקאמר התנא: *אם נאמר מעשר לד] מה שאמור בו, ולא נאמר תרומה, הייתי אומר במיתה. אבל השתא דנאמרו אינו במיתה? בתמיה, והא מיתה כתיבא ביה! ותו אם לא נאמרו הייתי אומר במיתה. בתמיה, מהיכא תיתי לי לה] בה מיתה? הא לא מייתינן לה אלא בקל וחומר ממעשר, ודיו לבא מן הדין להיות כנדון: מה מעשר בלאו ולא במיתה — אף תרומה בלאו ולא במיתה! **אלא קלות וחמורות דקאמר.** אטומאה קאי, דכתיב התם טומאת מת וטומאת שרץ, דכתיב (ויקרא כב): "והנוגע בכל טמא נפש" [וגו'] לו] "או איש אשר יגע בכל שרץ", דכתיב בתרווייהו אכילת מעשר ותרומה ועונשן. וקאמר: אם נאמרה טמא שרץ ולא נאמרה טומאת מת כו'. ובמאי, לז] ועל איזה אכילה? אי בתרומה — על שתיהן הטומאות הוא באכילת תרומה במיתה, ומאי "על הקלות בלאו" דקתני? ואם

תורה אור

*נאמר כאן וטומאתו עליו ונאמר להלן בביאת מקדש עוד טומאתו בו. כך גירסת הקונטרס ובתורת כהנים. ואית ספרים דגרסי: ונאמר להלן "כל איש אשר יקרב מכל זרעכם אל הקדשים אשר יקדישו בני ישראל לה' וטומאתו עליו" (ויקרא כב). ויש לפרש דפשיטא ליה דאיירי בטומאת הגוף, דאי בטומאת בשר — הוה ליה למיכתב "וטומאתם עליהן" לשון רבים, כדכתיב "אל הקדשים" לשון רבים. דאף על גב דלא מסיק השתא אדעתיה חילוק לשון רבים — היינו דליהוי "שלמים" לשון רבים, אבל "קדשים" פשיטא ליה דלשון רבים.

נאכל

שיטה מקובצת

א] בו את האור מסקינא: ב] הפיגול והנותר והטמא כו'. וא"ת טעמא מאי בנותר וטמא בשלמא בקומץ דהוי מתיר משום (דעולה) [טעמא דעולא] דלעיל דאם אחרים כו' אבל האי טעמא לא שייך בנותר וטמא [אפי' אי אמרינן] דמשמע אף באימורים וי"ל משום דנעשו לחמו של מזבח ולא נהירא דא"כ לעיל אמאי קאמר עולא בקומץ (נמי) דטעמא משום דאחרים מביא כו' (אבל האי) [דהאי] טעמא לא שייך בנותר וטמא דמשמע דמיירי אף באברים וי"ל (הכא) [דאין הכי] נמי [דקאי] האי [טעמא] משום אם אחרים כו' מיהו כיון דגלי בקומץ מהאי [טעם דאם משלה בו את] האור מפקיע הפיגול גלי בכל שאר איסורים: ג] דיכי וכי מזבח מקוה טהרה הוא אר"ז שמשלה בהן את האור: ד] אמר אף אימורים במשמע וטומאתו: ה] יצא בשר שאין טומאה פורחת ממנו כשהוא שלם: ו] הגוף הכתוב מדבר אי אתה: ז] כאן. ס"י וטומאתו עליו ונאמר להלן עוד טומאתו בו אמור עליהם לדורותיכם כל איש אשר יקריב מכל זרעכם אל (הקודש) [הקדשים] אשר (יקריבו) [יקדישו] בני ישראל (אל ה') [לה'] וטומאתו עליו: ח] ר' אחיא אומר הואיל ונאמרו קדשים בלשון רבים פ"ה שלמים וקשה דהוי ליה למימר הואיל ונאמרו שלמים בלשון רבים. ועוד קשה דבלשון יחיד לא היה יכול לומר אלא בלשון שלמים וא"כ משמע דאף שלמים הוא לשון יחיד ועוד קשה דמאי קאמר וכתיב וטומאתו עליו בלשון יחיד עליהם מבעיא ליה היאך יכול לומר עליהם הא אבשר זבח קאי דבלשון יחיד משמע לכך נראה כגי' הספרים ונאמר להלן כל איש אשר (יקריב) [יקרב] כו' והתם ע"כ בטומאת הגוף איירי דאי אבשר הוי ליה למימר עליהם כי היכי דכתיב קדשים והשתא שפיר יליף ר' אחיא מדכתיב אל הקדשים ולא כתיב אל הקודש אשר יקדישו אלא [לשון רבים] וסיפא לא נקט עליהם ש"מ בטומאת הגוף מיירי וכמו דכאן קאי אטומאת הגוף ה"נ בשלמים קאי אטומאת הגוף: ט] אחרים אומרים: י] לה זעירא ותיבת רב נמחק:

[כ"ה בנ"א וכצ"ל כנראה מפרש"י]

הגהות הב"ח

(א) רש"י ד"ה פקע איסורן וכו' ירד יעלה. נ"ב פי' אבל לענין זה לא פקע איסורו [שאם אכלו לאחר] שהעלו חייב וראיה לדבר מדפי' במתניתין דחשיב דם וקומץ שאין בהם משום פיגול משום דאיהו גופיה מתיר תיפוק ליה דלא שייך [ביה פיגול דאי] אכלן קודם שהעלו הרי לא קרב המתיר כמצותו ואי לאחר [שהעלו הרי פקע] איסורו מהן אלא ודאי דלהא פקע איסורו מהן שאם ירדו יעלו וזה הכריחו לרש"י לפרש כן: (ב) ד"ה וטומאתו וכו' בשמעתין ובעינן למימרא:

נ"ל ברייתא

נ"א אם שאמור כו' נ"ק

יא] בבמיתה והתם וס"י א) ותו לכך נאמרו חמורות דבלאו הא במיתה הוא: נאמר חמורות הייתי אומר: יב] אידי ואידי הא במיתה הוא [ותו] לכך נאמרו חמורות כו' הוא ואי מעשר והשאר נמחק: יג] איכא למימר כיון דמשלה האור במקצתו נקלט כולה בקדושה: יד] דמשלה משלה תיבת מקומץ נמחק: טו] כיון דחשבת ליה: טז] הקרקע ויעלה דהא: יז] וטמא להכי נמי ושלא: יח] השמועה הלזו הס"ד: יט] הגוף הכתוב מדבר ואהא: כ] דלאו בבשר: כא] ואין מפריח טומאתו: כב] אף אאברין: כג] שקיבלה דעליו: כד] אבשר אפ"ה בטומאת: כה] גרסינן ת"ל טומאתו: כו] על הראשון לעולם היא: כח] קאי כדכתיב נפש כי תגע בכל טמא וכו' דמשתמע מיניה דאו הנפש אשר: כט] זבח א"כ לא חש הכתוב לשונו אף על הראשון אל תתמה כו' באמצע דאף הוא בטומאת הגוף: ל] עכשיו המקרא: לא] הגוף ולקמן בפירקין מפרש ותיבת בהאי נמחק: לב] מתניתא דמפרש ליה זעירי מאי היא איזה ברייתא פירש יפה הס"ד: לג] מפרש לה ואזיל: לד] מעשר כמה שאמור בו ולא כו': לה] תיבת בה נמחק: לו] נפש וגו' או איש אשר יגע בכל שרץ כתיב בתרייהו אכילת מעשר: לז] ובמאי על איזו אכילה אי בתרומה על שתי הטומאות:

א) נראה דל"ל לכך נאמרו חמורות דבלאו הא במיתה הוא ותו ואי לא נאמרו חמורות הייתי אומר ור"ל דהס"י לא גרסי כלל בתחלה להשתא נמי הא במיתה.

אם לא נאמרו חמורות הייתי אומר על החמורות במיתה? הא מטומאת שרץ קאתיא, ודיו לבא מן הדין להיות כנדון! אמר זעירי: "קלות" – טומאת שרץ, "חמורות" – טומאת מת. והכי קאמר: אילו נאמר טומאת שרץ ונאמר מעשר ותרומה, ולא נאמרה טומאת מת – הייתי אומר: א] [קלות] – על הקלות בלאו, ועל החמורות במיתה. ומדקלות על החמורות במיתה – חמורות ב] נמי על הקלות במיתה, לכך נאמרו חמורות.§ "כל שיש לו מתירין בין לאדם בין למזבח – חייבין עליו משום פיגול".§ תנו רבנן: או אינו מביא אלא כיוצא בשלמים, מה שלמים מיוחדים – נאכלין לשני ימים ולילה אחד, אף כל נאכל לשני ימים ולילה אחד. נאכל ליום ולילה מנין? תלמוד לומר: "מבשר" – כל ג] ששיריו נאכלין. עולה שאין שיריה נאכלין מנין? תלמוד לומר: "זבח". מנין לרבות העופות והמנחות, עד שאני מרבה לוג שמן של מצורע? תלמוד לומר: °"אשר הם מקדישים לי"; ואתי נותר – חילול חילול מטומאה, ואתי פיגול – "עון" "עון" מנותר. ומאחר שסופו לרבות כל דבר, למה נאמר שלמים מעתה? לומר לך: מה שלמים מיוחדים, שיש להן מתירין בין לאדם בין למזבח, ד] אף כל שיש לו מתירין, בין לאדם בין למזבח – חייבין עליהן משום ה] פיגול.§ העולה – דמה מתיר את בשרה למזבח ועורה לכהנים, עולת העוף – דמה מתיר את בשרה למזבח, חטאת העוף – דמה מתיר את בשרה לכהנים, פרים הנשרפים ושעירים הנשרפים – דמם מתיר את אימוריהן ליקרב.§ ומוציא אני את הקומץ, ואת הלבונה, והקטרת, ו] ומנחת כהנים, ומנחת כהן משיח, ומנחת נסכים, והדם. ר"ש אומר: מה שלמים מיוחדין – ז] *שיש בו על מזבח החיצון, וחייבין עליו, אף כל שישנן על מזבח החיצון חייבין עליו משום פיגול; יצאו פרים הנשרפים ושעירים הנשרפים, הואיל ח] שאין על מזבח החיצון כשלמים – אין חייבין עליו משום פיגול. [אמר מר:] כיוצא בשלמים. מאי ניהו – בכור, דנאכל לשני ימים ולילה אחד. במאי אתי? אי ב"מה מצינו" – איכא למיפרך: מה לשלמים, ט] שהן טעונין סמיכה, ונסכים, ותנופת חזה ושוק! אלא: °מ"אם האכל יאכל" – הני תרי כללי דסמיכי אהדדי נינהו! אמר *רבא, *כדאמרי במערבא: כל מקום שאתה מוצא שני כללות הסמוכים זה לזה – הטל פרט ביניהם, ודונם בכלל ופרט.§ "עד שאני מרבה לוג שמן של מצורע".§ הא מני? רבי מאיר היא. דתניא: *לוג שמן של מצורע חייבין עליו משום פיגול, דברי רבי מאיר. אימא סיפא: ומוציא אני מנחת נסכים והדם – אתאן לרבנן, *דתניא: נסכי בהמה חייבין עליהן משום פיגול, מפני שדם הזבח מתירן ליקרב, דברי רבי מאיר. אמרו לו: והלא [א]אדם מביא י] את זבחיו היום א) ונסכין מיכן עד עשרה ימים! אמר להן: אף אני לא אמרתי אלא בבאין עם הזבח! אמר רב יוסף: הא מני – רבי היא, דאמר: לוג שמן של מצורע מתנותיו שרו ליה, ומדמתנותיו שרו ליה – מתנותיו מפגלי ליה. דתניא: [ב]לוג שמן של מצורע – מועלין בו עד שיזרוק הדם, נזרק הדם – לא נהנין ולא מועלין. רבי אומר: מועלין יא] עד שיתן מתנותיו. ושוין, [ג]שאסור באכילה עד שיתן מתן שבע ומתן בהונות. אמרוה קמיה דרבי ירמיה, אמר: ב) גברא רבא כרב יוסף לימא כי הא מילתא? הרי

א) [ע' תוס' ר"ה ל: ד"ה ונתקלקלו] ב) [לקמן ק: כתובות מג.]

רש"י

ואם לא נאמרו הייתי אומר כו' ל"ג הכא. דליכא למיפרך "דיו", דהא קלות נמי במיתה. ואי באכילת מעשר. קאמר, דאם לא נאמרו חמורות הייתי אומר: על טומאת שרץ בלאו, יב] על טומאת מת במיתה. לכך נאמרו טומאת מת חמורות ונאמר בהו לאו, דלא תימא בהו מיתה (א) במעשר. ואם לא נאמרו יג] *קלות הייתי אומר: על החמורות במיתה? הא מטומאת שרץ הוא דאתיא בק"ו. ודיו לבא מן הדין להיות כנדון. ולא אמינא בה מיתה אלא לאו! והכי קאמר אילו נאמר טומאת שרץ ונאמר מעשר. בלאו כדאיתא, ותרומה במיתה כדאיתא, ולא נאמר טומאת מת – הייתי אומר: קלות על הקלות בלאו – יד] בטומאה קלה דשרץ על אכילת קלות כגון מעשר – יהא בלאו, כדאיתא. וקלות על החמורות במיתה – וטומאת שרץ על אכילות החמורות כגון תרומה – במיתה, כדאיתא. ומינה הוה גמרינן דמה שרץ קלות על החמורות במיתה – אף חמורות טו] *על קלות נמי במיתה, דמה לי טומאה חמורה ואכילה קלה, מה לי אכילה חמורה וטומאה קלה. טז] (וטומאת המת על אכילת מעשר תהא במיתה). לכך נאמרו חמורות – טומאת המת – יז] על אכילת מעשר שלא תהא במיתה, ופירש בה לאו ולא במיתה, לומר לך שהיא באזהרה. או אינו מביא כו'. רישא דברייתא בת"כ לענין פיגול קתני: יכול לא יהא חייב אלא על השלמים בלבד? ת"ל לענין טומאה: "וינזרו מקדשי". ולקמן יליף נותר "חילול" "חילול" מטומאה, ופיגול ב"עון" "עון" מנותר. או אינו. מרבה אלא כיוצא בשלמים, שהרי כלל ופרט יח] אמור כאן, כדמפרש לקמן, ונימא: מה הפרט מפורש נאכלין לשני ימים כו'. ת"ל מבשר. ריבויא הוא, דכתיב גבי פיגול (ויקרא ז) "מבשר זבח השלמים", ועלה קאי "והנפש האוכלת ממנו עונה תשא". עד שאני מרבה. כלומר, אחרי יט] שאני מרבה – ארבה עמהם אף לוג שמן של מצורע, אם פיגל בדם האשם – נתפגל הלוג. תלמוד לומר. לענין טומאה: "אשר הם מקדישים", גבי "וינזרו" כתיב. ואתי נותר חילול חילול מטומאה: מה טומאה הכל בכלל – אף נותר הכל בכלל, בנותר כתיב: "כי את קודש ה' חילל" (ויקרא יט), ובטומאה כתיב: "וינזרו ולא יחללו" (שם כב). והדר אתי פיגול "עון" "עון" מנותר. אף כל שיש לו מתירין. או לאדם או למזבח. ועולה ילפא *)מאימורי שלמים, וכן אימורי כל הקדשים. כ] ובשר כל הקדשים הנאכלין ילפי מבשר שלמים, שאין לו מתירין אלא לאדם, וחייבין עליו. כיוצא בשלמים מאי ניהו. דקתני לעיל: או אינו מביא כו' אלא כא] (ג) כיוצא. האכל. כלל, "מבשר שלמים" – פרט, "יאכל" – חזר וכלל. הני תרי כללי דסמיכי כב] נינהו. שלא נכתב הפרט אלא בסוף. הטל פרט ביניהם. כג] הכתוב אחריהם הטל ביניהם, ודונם כו'. הלכך, אי לאו דרבי רחמנא "מבשר" כד] תחילה הוה דיינינן ליה במה הפרט מפורש כו'. חייבין עליו משום פיגול. אם בא עם האשם ופיגל באשם. ואף על גב שאם כה] היה רוצה יכול להביאו מכאן ועד עשרה ימים כדלקמן, אית ליה לרבי מאיר דכי הביאו עם האשם – דם האשם הוא המתירו למתן בהונות ושיריו לאכילה, ששירי הלוג נאכלין, כדאמרינן בשמעתא דלקמן. אמר רב יוסף כו] רבי היא כו'. וסבר לה כרבנן, דהואיל ואפשר להביא נסכים לאחר זמן – אין דם הזבח מפגלן, ואפילו הביאן עמו. ולוג שמן נמי, הא דקתני כז] נמי פיגול – לא שיהא דם האשם מפגלו, אלא מתנות שמן עצמו, שמזה ממנו שבע הזאות בפנים – הם מפגלין אותו, אם הזה על מנת לאכול שיריו חוץ לזמנו. והוא נאכל ליום ולילה, כדמרבינן ליה לקמן עם שאר קדשי קדשים. ומדשמעינן ליה לרבי כח] דאמר לוג שמן של מצורע מתנותיו שרו ליה. לכהנים, דקאמר: אף על פי שנזרק דם האשם יש מעילה בשמן עד שיתן שבע הזאות של צרכי גבוה – הלכך מתנותיו מפגלין ליה, שהן כט] מתירין. ולא נהנין. מדרבנן, עד שיתן מתנותיו ל]. ולא מועלין. דקסבר: דם האשם מתירו לכהנים, וכל שיש בו שעת היתר לכהנים – אין בו מעילה. רבי לא] אומר מועלין בו עד שיתן שבע הזאות של גבוה. אבל מתן בהונות דלאו צורך גבוה הוא – ודאי לא פליג רבי. ושוין. שאפילו נתן מתנות גבוה, אסור הוא לב] מדרבנן עד שיתן אף מתן בהונות. אמרוה. רבנן להא דרב יוסף.

*) [נ"א מאימורי שלמים לפי שאין להם מתירין אלא למזבח]

תוספות

נאכל ליום ולילה מנין. לקמן בסוף "דם חטאת" (דף נז.) דרשינן מהיקישא ד"זאת התורה": מה שלמים מפגלין כו'. ונראה דהאי תנא לית ליה ההוא היקישא, דאי אית ליה – לא היה צריך לכל הנך ייתורים. **ואתי** נותר חילול מטומאה ואתי פיגול עון עון מנותר. מכאן לג] הוה מצי למידק לקמן (דף נ:) דדבר הלמד בגזירה שוה חוזר ומלמד בגזירה שוה.

כיוצא בשלמים מאי ניהו בכור. משמע דבכור דמי לשלמים טפי משאר קדשים. ובעלמא אינו כן, לד] דאמר מנחות (דף נא:): מה שלמים באין בנדר ונדבה – אף כל בא בנדר ונדבה לה]. **אלא** מאם האכל יאכל. ואע"ג דאמרינן לעיל בסוף פרק שני (דף כח:): בשתי אכילות הכתוב מדבר – תרתי שמע מינה, מדלא כתיב "האכל האכל" או "יאכל יאכל", כדאמר בריש "הקומץ רבה" (מנחות דף יז:). ומיהו, רבי אליעזר דמוקי לה התם בדרשא אחרינא, נפקא ליה הך דרשא מקרא אחרינא *וכרבא דמפרש לעיל בסוף פרק שני (דף כח:) כולהו מקרא לו] (אחרינא) [אריכא], ודריש "מבשר זבח שלמיו" מה שלמים מפגלין ומתפגלין כו'. לא כמו שפירש שם בקונטרס מדכתיב "זבח שלמים" לז] דמשמע דמקיש זבח לשלמים, אלא אהך ברייתא סמיך. והקשה ה"ר חיים: אמאי שביק לשון הברייתא? דהוה ליה למימר: מה שלמים מיוחדים שיש להם מתירין בין לאדם בין למזבח! ועוד: דמלישנא דמפגל ומתפגלין לא *ממעיט דם, דדם מפגל ומתפגל, כדתניא בתוספתא דזריקה מפגלת ומתפגלת, שהדם מפגל הבשר, ומתפגלת על ידי זריקה – אם זרק על מנת לשפוך שיריים למחר. **ודונם** בכלל ופרט. ומ"מ צריכי ייתורי דלעיל. דמכלל ופרט לא מרבי אלא הדומה לפרט בכל צדדין.

סד"א

עין משפט נר מצוה

לו א מיי' פ"ה מהלכות מחוסרי כפרה הל' ז:

לז ב מיי' פ"ב מהלכות מעילה הלכה י:

לח ג מיי' פ"ד מהל' מחוסרי כפרה הל' ג:

שיטה מקובצת

א] אומר קלות על הקלות בלאו וקלות על החמורו': ב] חמורות על הקלות נמי במיתה לכך: ג] כל ששיריו נאכלין: ד] למזבח. ס"י וחייבין עליהן משום פיגול אף: ה] פיגול מרבה אני חטאת חעוף שיש לו מתירין לאדם מרבה אני פרים הנשרפים ושעירים הנשרפים שיש להם מתירין למזבח ומוציא כו' כל זה מצאתי בס"י והיא נוסחא אמתית ולא כלל העולה כו': ו] והקטרת ומנחת נסכים ומנחת כהנים ומנחת כהן משיח ונסכים ותיבת ומנחת נמחק: ז] מיוחדין שישנו על מזבח החיצון וחייבין עליהן אף כל שישנו: ח] הואיל שאינן על מזבח כו' אין חייבין עליהן משום פגול ס"א אמר מר כיוצא: ט] לשלמים שכן טעונין סמיכה: י] מביא זבחו היום ונסכיו מיכן עד י' ימים: יא] מועלין בו עד: יב] בלאו ועל טומאת: יג] כלום הייתי אומר כו' הוא דהוה אתי' בק"ו: יד] בלאו טומאת קלה: טו] חמורות דהיינו טומאת מת על מעשר קלות: טז] וטומאה קלה לכך נאמרו כו' והשאר נמחק: יז] המת חמורות על אכילת מעשר ופירש בה לאו ולא מיתה לומר לך שהיא באזהרה בלבד הס"ד: יח] ופרט וכלל אמור: יט] אחרי. ס"י שהתחלתי לרבות ארבה כו': כ] הקדשים מאימורי שלמים ילפי שאין להם מתירין אלא למזבח ואתרבו בשר כל הקדשים שהן הנאכלים: כא] אלא מאם האכל ותיבת כיוצא נמחק: כב] דסמיכי אהדדי נינהו: כג] ביניהם הפרט הכתוב: כד] מבשר הוה דיינינן ליה כו' מפורש כו' ולא הוי אתי אלא בכור הס"ד: כה] שאם רצה היה יכול להביא כו' דם האשם מתירו למתן בהונות ושיריו לאכילה דשירי הלוג נאכלין: כו] יוסף הא מני רבי: כז] דקתני פיגול: כח] לרבי לוג ותיבת דאמר נמחק: כט] שהן מתירין הס"ד: ל] שיתן מתנותיו שבע הס"ד: לא] רבי. גליון דמודה הוא דכיון שניתנו ממנו המתנות שהן צורך גבוה שוב אין מועלין בהן אע"פ שלא ניתן ממנו לבהונות. ע"כ: לב] הוא באכילה מדרבנן: לג] מכאן הוי מצי למיפרך לקמן כן הוא בס"א: לד] כן וי"ל דהכא איירי לגבי אכילה להכי מרבינן (הדמים) [הדומים] לאכילה. ת' מהר"פ ז"ל: לה] ונדבה לאפוקי בכור: לו] מקרא אריכא ודריש מבשר זבח: לז] שלמים דריש משמע דמקיש:

הגהות הב"ח

(א) רש"י ד"ה ולא אכלות וכו' דלא תימא בהו מיתה אף במעשר ואם לא נאמרו כלום הייתי: (ב) ד"ה כיוצא וכו' כיוצא הס"ד ואח"כ מ"ה הכי קרי וכו' בכור הס"ד ואח"כ מ"ה הכלל וכו' וכלל הס"ד ואח"כ מ"ה הכלל כלל וכו' ודונם כו' הולכך:

גליון הש"ס

גמ' ואתי נותר חילול. ע"ל דף מו ע"א תוס' ד"ה ג:

נ"ל אלא קלות וכו' הג"ה כלום במקום תיבת קלות | חולין קיז: | טומאת מת על קלות מעשר נמי נ"ק | נ"ק מ"ז | ויקרא כב | שם | נ"ל רבינא | נ"ל שישנו על כו' | נ"ק | חולין סו: כ"ק סד: בכורות נא. ע"ש שבועות ה. | תוספתא רפ"ה מנחות טו: | ורבא נ"ק | ממעטין נ"ק

הֲרֵי לוֹג א] [הַבָּא] בִּפְנֵי עַצְמוֹ, דִּלְכ"ע מַתְּנוֹתָיו שָׁרוּ לֵיהּ – וְלָא מְפַגְּלִין לֵיהּ! דְּתַנְיָא: *לוֹג שֶׁמֶן שֶׁל מְצוֹרָע – חַיָּיבִין עָלָיו מִשּׁוּם פִּיגּוּל, מִפְּנֵי שֶׁדָּם מַתִּירוֹ לִבְהוֹנוֹת, דִּבְרֵי ר"מ. אָמְרוּ לוֹ לְר"מ: וַהֲלֹא אאָדָם מֵבִיא אֲשָׁמוֹ עַכְשָׁיו, ב] וְלוֹג מִיכָּן וְעַד עֲשָׂרָה יָמִים! אָמַר לָהֶן: אַף אֲנִי לֹא אָמַרְתִּי אֶלָּא בַּבָּא עִם הָאָשָׁם. אֶלָּא א"ר יִרְמְיָה: לְעוֹלָם ר"מ הִיא, וּסְמֵי מִיכָּן נְסָכִים. ג] אָמַר אַבַּיֵי: לְעוֹלָם לָא תִּסְמֵי, וְתָנָא לוֹג הַבָּא עִם הָאָשָׁם, וְהוּא הַדִּין לִנְסָכִים הַבָּאִין עִם הַזֶּבַח. וַהֲדַר תָּנָא נְסָכִים הַבָּאִין בִּפְנֵי עַצְמָן, וְהוּא הַדִּין לְלוֹג הַבָּא בִּפְנֵי עַצְמוֹ.§ "חַטַּאת הָעוֹף – דָּמָהּ מַתִּיר אֶת בְּשָׂרָהּ לַכֹּהֲנִים".§ מְנָא הָנֵי מִילֵּי? *דְּתָנֵי לֵוִי: °"כָּל קָרְבָּנָם" – בלְרַבּוֹת לוֹג שֶׁמֶן שֶׁל מְצוֹרָע. סָלְקָא דַּעְתָּךְ אָמִינָא: "מִן הָאֵשׁ" ד] כָּתַב רַחֲמָנָא, וְהַאי לָאו מוּתָּר מִן הָאֵשׁ הוּא – קמ"ל.§ °"לְכָל מִנְחָתָם" – *גלְרַבּוֹת מִנְחַת עוֹמֶר דוּמִנְחַת הַקְּנָאוֹת. סָלְקָא דַּעְתָּךְ אָמִינָא: °"וְאָכְלוּ אוֹתָם אֲשֶׁר כֻּפַּר בָּהֶם", וּמִנְחַת הָעוֹמֶר – לְהַתִּיר אָתְיָא, וּמִנְחַת קְנָאוֹת – לְבָרֵר עָוֹן קָאָתְיָא, קמ"ל.§ "וּלְכָל חַטָּאתָם" – לְרַבּוֹת *החַטַּאת הָעוֹף. סָלְקָא דַּעְתָּךְ אָמִינָא: נְבֵילָה הִיא.§ ה] "לְכָל אֲשָׁמָם" – לְרַבּוֹת ואֲשַׁם נָזִיר זוַאֲשַׁם מְצוֹרָע. סָלְקָא דַּעְתָּךְ אָמִינָא: לְהַכְשִׁיר קָאָתוּ, קמ"ל. אֲשַׁם מְצוֹרָע בְּהֶדְיָא כְּתִיב בֵּיהּ! ו] אֶלָּא: לְרַבּוֹת אֲשַׁם נָזִיר כַּאֲשַׁם מְצוֹרָע.§ "אֲשֶׁר יָשִׁיבוּ" – *זֶה גֶּזֶל הַגֵּר, "לְךָ הוּא" – ז] חשֶׁלְּךָ יִהְיֶה, אֲפִילּוּ לְקַדֵּשׁ בּוֹ אֶת הָאִשָּׁה. *תַּנְיָא, ר' אֱלִיעֶזֶר אוֹמֵר מִשּׁוּם רַבִּי יוֹסֵי ח] *הַגְּלִילִי: טפִּיגֵּל בְּדָבָר הַנַּעֲשֶׂה בַּחוּץ – פִּיגֵּל, בְּדָבָר הַנַּעֲשֶׂה בִּפְנִים – לֹא פִּיגֵּל. כֵּיצַד? הָיָה עוֹמֵד בַּחוּץ, וְאָמַר: "הֲרֵינִי שׁוֹחֵט לְהַזּוֹת מִדָּמוֹ לְמָחָר" – לֹא פִּיגֵּל, שֶׁמַּחֲשָׁבָה בַּחוּץ בְּדָבָר הַנַּעֲשֶׂה בִּפְנִים ט] לֹא פִּיגֵּל. הָיָה עוֹמֵד בִּפְנִים, וְאָמַר: "הֲרֵינִי מַזֶּה עַל מְנָת י] לְהַקְטִיר אֵימוּרִים וְלִשְׁפּוֹךְ שִׁירַיִם לְמָחָר" – לֹא פִּיגֵּל, שֶׁמַּחֲשָׁבָה בִּפְנִים בְּדָבָר הַנַּעֲשֶׂה בַּחוּץ. יא] אֲבָל הָיָה עוֹמֵד בַּחוּץ, וְאָמַר: "הֲרֵינִי שׁוֹחֵט לִשְׁפּוֹךְ שִׁירַיִם לְמָחָר" אוֹ: "לְהַקְטִיר אֵימוּרִים לְמָחָר" – פִּיגֵּל, שֶׁמַּחֲשָׁבָה בַּחוּץ בְּדָבָר הַנַּעֲשֶׂה בַּחוּץ. א"ר יְהוֹשֻׁעַ בֶּן לֵוִי: מַאי קְרָא? °"כַּאֲשֶׁר יוּרַם מִשּׁוֹר זֶבַח הַשְּׁלָמִים", *"וְכִי מַה לָּמַדְנוּ יב] מִשּׁוֹר זֶבַח הַשְּׁלָמִים מֵעַתָּה? אֶלָּא: מַקִּישׁ פַּר כֹּהֵן מָשִׁיחַ לְשׁוֹר זֶבַח הַשְּׁלָמִים, מַה שּׁוֹר זֶבַח הַשְּׁלָמִים – עַד שֶׁיְּהוּ יג] מַעֲשָׂיו וּמַחְשְׁבוֹתָיו עַל מִזְבֵּחַ הַחִיצוֹן, אַף פַּר כֹּהֵן מָשִׁיחַ – עַד שֶׁיְּהוּ מַחְשְׁבוֹתָיו וּמַעֲשָׂיו עַל הַמִּזְבֵּחַ הַחִיצוֹן. אָמַר רַב נַחְמָן אָמַר רַבָּה בַּר אֲבוּהּ אָמַר רַב: הֲלָכָה כְּרַבִּי אֱלִיעֶזֶר שֶׁאָמַר מִשּׁוּם רַבִּי יוֹסֵי. אָמַר יד] *רָבָא: הִלְכְתָא

רש"י

הַבָּא בִּפְנֵי עַצְמוֹ. מְצוֹרָע שֶׁהֵבִיא אֲשָׁמוֹ הַיּוֹם וְלוֹגוֹ לְאַחַר עֲשָׂרָה יָמִים, דִּלְכ"ע מַתְּנוֹתָיו שַׁרְיָין לֵיהּ בַּאֲכִילָה, דְּהוֹאִיל וְלֹא קָדַשׁ בִּכְלִי כְּשֶׁנִּזְרַק דַּם הָאָשָׁם – לָאו שִׁירַיִם דִּידֵיהּ הוּא טו] וְלָא שָׁרֵי לֵיהּ, וַאֲפ"ה לָא מְפַגְּלִין לֵיהּ לְדִבְרֵי הַכֹּל, דְּאֵין בּוֹ מִשּׁוּם פִּיגּוּל, כִּדְקָתָנֵי: אַף אֲנִי לֹא אָמַרְתִּי כו'. הִלְכָּךְ, בָּא עִם הָאָשָׁם נַמִי, אע"ג דִּלְרַבִּי מַתְּנוֹתָיו שַׁרְיָין לֵיהּ – לָא מְפַגְּלִים לֵיהּ, שֶׁאֵין מְפַגֵּל אֶלָּא דָּם, אוֹ קוֹמֶץ אֶת שְׁיָרָיו, מִשּׁוּם דְּאִיתַּקַּשׁ מִנְחָה לִזְבָחִים. וְתָנָא. רֵישָׁא. לוֹג הַבָּא עִם הָאָשָׁם. שֶׁדַּם הָאָשָׁם מְפַגְּלוֹ וְאַע"פ שֶׁהָיָה טז] לוֹ לַהֲבִיאוֹ לְאַחַר עֲשָׂרָה יָמִים, וּמִמֶּנּוּ אַתָּה לָמֵד דְּה"ה לִנְסָכִים הַבָּאִים עִם הַזֶּבַח שֶׁדַּם הַזֶּבַח מְפַגְּלָן, וְאַע"פ שֶׁבְּיָדוֹ לַהֲבִיאָן לְאַחַר זְמַן. וְתָנָא סֵיפָא נְסָכִים הַבָּאִים בִּפְנֵי עַצְמָן. כִּדְקָתָנֵי לָהּ דּוּמְיָא דִּקְטֹרֶת וּלְבוֹנָה וּמִנְחַת כֹּהֲנִים שֶׁאֵין לָהֶן מַתִּירִין, וְקָאָמַר דְּאֵין מִתְפַּגְּלִין אִם הִקְרִיב מִקְצָתָן ע"מ פִּיגּוּל. וְה"ה לְלוֹג הַבָּא בִּפְנֵי עַצְמוֹ. מְנָהָנֵי מִילֵּי. דְּחַטַּאת הָעוֹף נֶאֱכֶלֶת יז]. כָּל קָרְבָּנָם. גַּבֵּי סֵדֶר מַתְּנוֹת כְּהוּנָּה יח] שֶׁנֶּאֱמַר לְאַהֲרֹן עַל הַסֵּדֶר בְּפָרָשַׁת קֹרַח: "וְזֶה יִהְיֶה לְךָ מִקֹּדֶשׁ הַקֳּדָשִׁים מִן הָאֵשׁ" וגו', וּכְתִיב בַּתְרֵיהּ: "בְּקֹדֶשׁ הַקֳּדָשִׁים תֹּאכְלֶנּוּ", וְקָדָרֵישׁ לְהוּ הָכָא כָּל "כָּל" דְּכוּלְּהוּ. לְרַבּוֹת לוֹג שֶׁמֶן. שֶׁאַף הוּא נֶאֱכָל, שֶׁהֲרֵי קָרוּי קָרְבָּן, דִּכְתִיב (ויקרא יד): "וְהִקְרִיב אוֹתוֹ לְאָשָׁם וְאֶת לוֹג הַשָּׁמֶן" – אַלְמָא הוּא נַמִי בִּכְלַל "וְהִקְרִיב", וְהַיְינוּ קָרְבָּן, כ"ש בִּמְנָחוֹת (דף עג.). ס"ד (א) כו'. כְּלוֹמַר, הַאי דְּאִיצְטְרִיךְ "כָּל" יט] קְרָא לְרַבּוּיֵי, וְלָא נָפְקָא לֵיהּ מִ"קָּרְבָּנוֹ". סד"א מִן הָאֵשׁ כְּתִיב. כ] "הַנּוֹתָר מִן הָאֵשׁ", וּמִזֶּה לֹא עָלָה לָאִשִּׁים כְּלָל. וְאָכְלוּ אוֹתָם אֲשֶׁר כּוּפַּר בָּהֶם. דָּבָר שֶׁיֵּשׁ בּוֹ כַּפָּרָה נֶאֱכָל, וְשֶׁאֵין בּוֹ כַּפָּרָה אֵינוֹ נֶאֱכָל. לְהַתִּיר אָתְיָא. חָדָשׁ בַּמְּדִינָה. נְבֵילָה הִיא. לְפִי שֶׁנִּמְלְקָה. לְרַבּוֹת אֲשַׁם נָזִיר. נָזִיר שֶׁנִּטְמָא בְּמֵת מֵבִיא אָשָׁם כְּשֶׁטָּהַר מִטּוּמְאָתוֹ, וּמַכְשִׁירוֹ לְהַתְחִיל וְלִמְנוֹת נְזִירוּת טָהֳרָה, וְהַיָּמִים הָרִאשׁוֹנִים (ב) יִפְּלוּ. *וּלְרַבּוֹת שֶׁיְּהֵא נֶאֱכָל. דְּאִי לָא כא] כְּתִיב "לְכָל" – לָא מְרַבֵּינַן לְהוּ, דִּכְתִיב: "אֲשֶׁר כּוּפַּר בָּהֶם", וְהָנֵי לְהַכְשִׁיר אָתוּ, זֶה לְהַכְשִׁירוֹ בְּקָדָשִׁים, וְזֶה לְהַתְחִיל נְזִירוּת כב] טָהֳרָה. אֲשַׁם מְצוֹרָע בְּהֶדְיָא כְּתִיב בֵּיהּ. דְּנֶאֱכָל, כג] "כִּי כַּחַטָּאת הָאָשָׁם הוּא" (ויקרא יד). וּמִיהוּ, נְהִי דַּ"אֲשָׁמָם" כְּתִיב הָכָא לְסַדֵּר בַּפָּרָשָׁה כָּל עֶשְׂרִים וְאַרְבַּע מַתְּנוֹת כְּהוּנָּה, אֶלָּא "כָּל" לָמָּה? אֲשֶׁר יָשִׁיבוּ זֶה גֶּזֶל הַגֵּר. דִּכְתִיב כד] (במדבר ה): "הָאָשָׁם הַמּוּשָׁב לַה' לַכֹּהֵן" וְתַנְיָא (ב"ק דף קי.): "אָשָׁם" – זֶה קֶרֶן, "הַמּוּשָׁב" – זֶה חוֹמֶשׁ. אוֹ אֵינוֹ אֶלָּא זֶה אָשָׁם מַמָּשׁ! כְּשֶׁהוּא אוֹמֵר "מִלְּבַד אֵיל הַכִּפּוּרִים" כה] (*הֲרֵי אָמוּר, אֶלָּא) "אָשָׁם" זֶה קֶרֶן. שֶׁהַגּוֹזֵל אֶת חֲבֵירוֹ וְנִשְׁבַּע לוֹ וְאַח"כ הוֹדָה – מְשַׁלֵּם קֶרֶן וְחוֹמֶשׁ לַבְּעָלִים, וְאָשָׁם לַמִּזְבֵּחַ, כִּדְכְתִיב בְּפָרָשַׁת וַיִּקְרָא: "וְהָיָה כִּי יֶחֱטָא וְאָשֵׁם" וגו'. וְאִם מֵת – נוֹתֵן לְיוֹרְשָׁיו. וְאִם גֵּר הָיָה וּמֵת, כו] וְאֵין לוֹ יוֹרְשִׁין לְהַחֲזִירוֹ לָהֶם – נְתָנָן הַכָּתוּב לַכֹּהֵן. וּפָרָשַׁת גֶּזֶל הַגֵּר אֲמוּרָה בְּפָרָשַׁת נָשֹׂא: "אִם אֵין לָאִישׁ גּוֹאֵל לְהָשִׁיב הָאָשָׁם" וגו', וְכִי יֵשׁ לְךָ אָדָם בְּיִשְׂרָאֵל שֶׁאֵין לוֹ גּוֹאֵל? אֶלָּא כז] זֶה גֶּזֶל הַגֵּר. "גֶּזֶל הַגֵּר בְּהֶדְיָא כְּתִיב בֵּיהּ" לָא גָּרְסִינַן, דְּהָא חַטָּאוֹת וַאֲשָׁמוֹת וּשְׁאָר הָאֲמוּרִים בַּפָּרָשָׁה בְּהֶדְיָא כְּתִיב כָּל אֶחָד וְאֶחָד בִּמְקוֹמוֹ, וְסִידְּרָן לוֹ הַכָּתוּב לְאַהֲרֹן כָּאן מִפְּנֵי מַחְלוֹקְתּוֹ שֶׁל קֹרַח שֶׁעִרְעֵר עָלָיו עַל הַכְּהוּנָּה. מְשַׁל הֶדְיוֹט אָמַר: כח] לְטוֹבָתוֹ נִשְׁבְּרָה רֶגֶל פָּרָתוֹ. *לְךָ הוּא וּלְבָנֶיךָ. שֶׁיְּהוּ כִּנְכָסִים שֶׁל חוּלִּין שֶׁאֵין בּוֹ שׁוּם קְדוּשָּׁה, דְּמָמוֹן בְּעָלִים הוּא. וְאַגֶּזֶל לְחוּדֵיהּ קָאֵי הַאי "לְךָ הוּא". וְהַאי דִּכְתִיב בַּתְרֵיהּ "בְּקֹדֶשׁ הַקֳּדָשִׁים תֹּאכְלֶנּוּ" – אַשְּׁאָרָא קָאֵי, דְּהָווּ מִידֵי דַּאֲכִילָה. תַּנְיָא אָמַר ר' אֶלְעָזָר כו'. אֵבָרִים הַנִּשְׂרָפִים דְּאִיפְלִיגוּ בָּהּ בְּמַתְנִי' קָאֵי. פִּיגֵּל בְּדָבָר הַנַּעֲשֶׂה בָּהֶן בַּחוּץ. הָעֲבוֹדָה שֶׁהָיָה עוֹבֵד בְּמַחֲשָׁבָה, וְהָאֲכִילָה שֶׁחִישֵּׁב עָלֶיהָ, אִם מַעֲשֵׂה עֲזָרָה הֵם – פִּיגֵּל, וְאִם מַעֲשֵׂה הֵיכָל הֵם – לֹא פִּיגֵּל. וּלְקַמָּן יָלֵיף טַעְמָא מִקְּרָאֵי. כט] שׁוֹחֵט. שֶׁהֲרֵי שְׁחִיטָתָהּ בָּעֲזָרָה הוּא. וְכָל "חוּץ" דְּהָכָא – עֲזָרָה הוּא. לְהַזּוֹת דָּמוֹ לְמָחָר. הֲרֵי חִישֵּׁב עַל אֲכִילַת מִזְבֵּחַ *שֶׁל פְּנִים "הֲרֵינִי מַזֶּה עַל הַפָּרֹכֶת אוֹ עַל הַמִּזְבֵּחַ הַפְּנִימִי" – שֶׁזּוֹ הִיא זְרִיקָתָן ל] הַמְּפַגֵּל. עַל מְנָת לִשְׁפּוֹךְ שִׁירַיִם. שֶׁהֲרֵי זוֹ אֲכִילַת מִזְבֵּחַ הַחִיצוֹן, דִּמְהַנְיָא בֵּיהּ מַחֲשָׁבָה. (ג) לֹא פִּיגֵּל. מִפְּנֵי שֶׁמַּחֲשָׁבָה הָיְתָה בִּשְׁעַת עֲבוֹדַת פְּנִים. כַּאֲשֶׁר יוּרַם. בְּפַר כֹּהֵן מָשִׁיחַ כְּתִיב, בְּהַפְרָשַׁת אֵימוּרָיו. *מַה לָּמַדְנוּ לוֹ. מִשְּׁלָמִים לְעִנְיַן אֵימוּרִים? הֲרֵי אַף לא] בָּזֶה כּוּלָּן מְפוֹרָשִׁים? חֵלֶב וּכְלָיוֹת וְיוֹתֶרֶת! אֶלָּא לֹא בָּא הֶיקֵּשׁ הַזֶּה אֶלָּא לְלַמֵּד עַל הַפִּיגּוּל שֶׁהוּא לָמֵד בְּכָל הַקֳּדָשִׁים מִשְּׁלָמִים, וּבָא לְלַמֶּדְךָ עַל אֵלּוּ שֶׁאֵין פִּיגּוּל נוֹהֵג בָּהֶן אֶלָּא כִּשְׁלָמִים: מַה שְּׁלָמִים אֵין פִּיגּוּלָן אֶלָּא עַל לב] מַעֲשֵׂי עֲבוֹדָה חִיצוֹנִית וּמַחֲשֶׁבֶת אֲכִילוֹת חִיצוֹנוֹת – שׁוֹחֵט אוֹ מְקַבֵּל אוֹ מוֹלִיךְ אוֹ זוֹרֵק, ע"מ לֶאֱכוֹל בָּשָׂר לג] לִשְׁפּוֹךְ שִׁירַיִם אוֹ לְהַקְטִיר אֵימוּרָיו חוּץ לִזְמַנּוֹ, אַף כָּאן – עַד שֶׁיְּחַשֵּׁב בַּעֲבוֹדוֹת *עַל אֲכִילַת חוּץ. מַחְשְׁבוֹתָיו. מַחֲשֶׁבֶת אֲכִילָתוֹ. וּמַעֲשָׂיו. עֲבוֹדָה שֶׁהוּא עוֹבֵד וּמְחַשֵּׁב.

הִלְכְתָא

תוספות

סד"א מן האש כו'. תימה: לד] לא לכתוב "מן האש", ולא בעי "לכל"! **זה** גזל הגר. דאע"ג דמכפר, לא הוה אמינא דליהוי לכהן אלא מידי לה] דמותר למזבח, ולא ממונא. ובספרים ישנים גרים: גזל הגר בהדיא כתיב ביה, בפרשת "נשא", דכתיב: "לכהן לו יהיה". ובקונטרס לא גריס ליה, משום דחטאות ואשמות ושאר לו] אימורים בפרשה בהדיא כתיבי כל אחד ואחד במקומו, וסדרן לו הכתוב לאהרן כאן מפני מחלוקתו *של קרח לז].

ואפילו לקדש בו את האשה. בפ' "התכלת" (מנחות דף מה:) אמרינן גבי שתי הלחם דעצרת: ורבי עקיבא מי כתיב "קודש יהיו לה' ולכהן"? "לה' לכהן" כתיב, כדרב הונא, דאמר רב הונא: קנאו השם ונתנו לכהן. ופי' שם בקונטרס: דמשלחן גבוה קא זכו. ועיקר מילתיה דרב הונא אגזל הגר איתמר בפ' "הגוזל עצים" (ב"ק דף קט:). לח] ולא מצינו דברי רב הונא לשם, אלא ברייתא היא התם בשילהי פירקין ובמסכת ערכין בשילהי "המקדיש שדהו" (דף כח:): "האשם המושב לה' לכהן" – קנאו השם ונתנו לכהן שבאותו המשמר. *ונראה דלא גרסינן לט] פרק "התכלת" – "כדרב הונא". אלא הכי גרסינן: "לה' לכהן" – קנאו השם ונתנו לכהן. ומיהו לא מצי לפרש לכהן שבאותו משמר, כי ההיא דגזל הגר דהתם, שהרי ברגל היו כל המשמרות שוות כדדרשינן בפ' בתרא דסוכה (דף נה:) מדכתיב: "ובא בכל אות נפשו ושרת", אלא כמו שפי' בקונטרס לענין דמשלחן גבוה קא זכו. ומיהו, מ] משמע מתוך דבריו דגזל הגר משלחן גבוה קא זכו – *אי אפשר לומר כן, דהא אמרינן הכא: "לך הוא ולבניך" – אפילו לקדש בו את האשה, ובקדושין (דף נב:) אמר במקדש בחלקו, בין בקדשי קדשים בין בקדשים קלים – אינה מקודשת, משום דמשלחן גבוה קא זכו! וצ"ל, דשאני הכא דגלי קרא "לך ולבניך". ויש תימה מא] (לך) "לה'" בגזל הגר למה לי? *דלגבי מאי נפקא מינה דקנאו השם למימר דמשלחן גבוה קא זכו?

בדבר הנעשה בפנים לא פיגל. והא דאמר ב"הניזקין" (גיטין דף נד:): כהן גדול ביום הכיפורים יוכיח, דכי אמר פיגול – מהימן. נהי דפיגול לא הוי – פסול מיהא הוי מק"ו, וכדאמר לעיל ספ"ק (דף יד.): מודה היה רבי שמעון לפסול מק"ו: ומה שלא לשמו כו'. וה"ר חיים מפ': דההוא פיגול – מיירי בפסול שלא לשמו. ולא משמע כן, דשלא לשמן לא קרי ליה "פיגול", כדאמר לעיל ספ"ק (דף יג.): דיקא נמי דקתני "שהזבח נפסל", ולא קתני "שהזבח מתפגל".

וכי מה למדנו משור זבח השלמים מעתה. נראה דלית ליה הא דדרשינן בפרק "איזהו מקומן" (לקמן דף מט:) מ"כאשר יורם" דאיצטריך ליותרת ושתי הכליות *)לפר יום הכיפורים, ומקרא אחרינא נפקא ליה להאי תנא.

הלכתא

*) נ"א לפר העלם דבר של צבור ומקרא כו' נ"ק

עין משפט נר מצוה

לט א מיי' פי"ח מהל' פסה"מ הלכה ח:
מ ב מיי' פ"ד מהלכות מחוסרי כפרה הל' ב:
[ועי' בתוס' דמנחות שהקשו דלפ"ז מאי פריך אשם מצורע בהדיא כתיב ביה וע"ש וברש"י כאן]
מא ג מיי' פ"ז מהלכות תמידין ומוספין הלכה יב:
מב ד מיי' פ"ג מהלכות סוטה הלכה טו:
מג ה מיי' פ"ז מהלכות מעה"ק הלכה ז:
מד ו מיי' פ"ט מהלכות מעה"ק הלכה ח:
מה ז מיי' שם הל' ב:
מו ח מיי' פ"ח מהלכות גזילה הלכה ה:
[וע"ש בתוס' מנחות שכתבו בענין אחר]
מז ט מיי' פי"ח מהל' פסה"מ הלכה ז:

שיטה מקובצת

א] לוג הבא בפני: ב] עכשיו ולוגו: ג] נסכים אביי אמר: ד] האש אמר רחמנא: ה] היא ולכל: ו] ביה. ס"י כי כחטאת האשם הוא לכם אלא: ז] הוא ולבניך שלך ולבניך יהיה (תיבת שלך נמחק) לקדש בו את האשה וא"ת והא כתיב בתריה בקודש קדשים תאכלנו וי"ל דאשאר מתנות קאי דהוי מידי דאכילה: ח] תיבת הגלילי נמחק: ט] תיבות לא פיגל נמחק: י] על מנת לשפוך שירים למחר כו' והשאר נמחק: יא] תיבת אבל נמחק: יב] למדנו. ס"י לפר כהן משיח משור: יג] שיהו מחשבותיו ומעשיו על מזבח החיצון: יד] אמר רב יוסף ותיבת רבא נמחק: טו] הוא. ס"א ולא שרי הדם לשיריים אלא מתנותיו שרו ליה: טז] שהיה יכול להביאו: יז] נאכלת לאחר שנמלקה ואינו נבילה: יח] כהונה שנאמרו לאהרן על הסדר בפרשת ויקח קרח: יט] כל לרבויי ולא נפקא ליה מקרבנם הס"ד: כ] כתיב דמשמע הנותר מן האשים ומזה לא עלה לאשים כלום הס"ד: כא] לא הוה כתיב לכל לא הוה מרבינן להו: כב] נזירות בטהרה הס"ד: כג] דנאכל דכתיב כי כחטאת האשם הוא לכהן ומיהו נהי דאשמם דכתיב הכא לסדר כו' למה לי הס"ד: כד] דכתיב ביה האשם: כה] הכפורים הוי אשם זה (ותיבות הרי אמור אלא ל"ש) קרן וכך הוא הענין שהגוזל את חבירו: כו] ומת שאין לו: כז] זה הגר תיבת גזל נמחק: כח] לטובתי נשברה רגל פרתי: כט] מה"ד הריני שוחט ששחיטתן בעזרה: ל] זריקתן המפגלת: לא] אף ביה נמחק: לב] על ידי מעשה: לג] בשר או לשפוך שיריים כו' בעבודות חוץ על אכילת חוץ: לד] כו' תימה דלא מייתי מתניתא מן האש כתיב כ"כ בס"י: לה] *)מיד דנותר למזבח: לו] ושאר האמורים מאי קאמר לעיל לכל חטאתם לרבות כו' נימא דנשנית מפני מחלוקתו של קרח אע"פ שאינו צריך וי"ל דנהי דנתפרשה פעם אחרת מ"מ איצטריך לומר מה היה צריך לומר ייתור דנאכל מאחר שאני יכול לשמוע ממקום אחר. ת' מהר"פ: לז] עצים ע"ב ולא: לט] גרסינן בפרק: מ] ומיהו מה שמשמע: מא] תימה לה' לכהן בגזל הגר ותיבת לך נמחק:

מסורת הש"ס

[מנחות עו: תוספתא פ"ה] [מנחות עג.] [שם ע"ש] מנחות נח. עג. [ע"ש כמה שינויים] מנחות יד. [תוספתא פ"ה] ע"ש מתוס' דזבחים יד. ד"ה מודה וכו' ותוס' מנחות יח. ד"ה פיגל כו' ותוס' גיטין נד: ד"ה דכי מוכח דל"ג הגלילי וכן במנחות ליתא וכן לקמן בסמוך הלכה כר"א משום רבי יוסי ליתא הגלילי חולין קיז. ע"ש

הגהות הב"ח

(א) רש"י ד"ה ס"ד כלומר כו' נ"ל ותיבת כו' נמחק: (ב) ד"ה לרבות אשם נזיר וכו' יפלו הס"ד ואח"כ מ"ה אשם מצורע בהדיא וכו' אלא כל למה לרבות שיהא נאכל דאי לא כו' נזירות בטהרה הס"ד ואח"כ מ"ה אשר ישיבו: (ג) ד"ה לא פיגל קודש ד"ה (המפגל) על מנת:

*הלכתא למשיחא? א"ל אביי: אלא מעתה, כל שחיטת קדשים לא לתני, הלכתא למשיחא הוא! אלא: *דרוש וקבל שכר – ה"נ דרוש וקבל שכר! הכי קאמינא לך: הלכתא למה לי? לישנא אחרינא, א"ל: הלכה קאמינא.§ **מתני'** [א]קדשי גוים – אין חייבין עליהן משום פיגול נותר וטמא, והשוחטן א] בחוץ – פטור, דברי *רבי שמעון, [ב]רבי יוסי מחייב.§ **גמ'** *ת"ר: קדשי גוים – [ג]לא נהנין ולא מועלין, ואין חייבין עליהן משום פיגול נותר וטמא, [ד]ואין עושין תמורה, [ה]ואין מביאין נסכים, אבל ב] קרבנן [ו]טעון נסכים, דברי רבי שמעון. ג] אמר רבי יוסי: רואה אני בכולן להחמיר, שנאמר בהן: "לה'". בד"א – בקדשי מזבח, אבל בקדשי בדק הבית – ד] מועלין בהן.§ "לא נהנין ולא מועלין".§ לא נהנין – מדרבנן, ולא מועלין – *דגמר מעילה "חטא" "חטא" מתרומה, (א) ה] ודבתרומה כתיב "בני ישראל" – ולא גוים.§ "ואין חייבין ו] עליו משום פיגול, נותר וטמא".§ מ"ט? דאתי פיגול "עון" "עון" מנותר, ואתי נותר "חילול" "חילול" מטומאה, ובטומאה כתיב (ב) ז] "בני ישראל" – ולא גוים.§ "ואין עושין תמורה".§ מאי טעמא? דאיתקש תמורה למעשר בהמה, ומעשר בהמה איתקש למעשר דגן, ובמעשר דגן כתיב: "בני ישראל" – ולא גוים. *וכי דבר הלמד בהיקש חוזר ומלמד בהיקש? *מעשר דגן חולין הוא. הניחא למאן דאמר: *בתר מלמד אזלינן, אלא למ"ד: בתר למד אזלינן, מאי איכא למימר? אלא: מעשר בהמה חובה שאין ח] קבוע לה זמן הוא, וחובה שאין ט] לה זמן קבוע – ישראל מייתו, גוים לא מייתו.§ "ואין מביאין נסכים".§ *תנו רבנן: °"אזרח" – אזרח י] *מביא נסכים, ואין הגוי מביא נסכים. יכול לא תהא עולתו טעונה נסכים? ת"ל: "ככה".§ "אמר רבי יוסי: רואה אני בכולן יא] להחמיר. בד"א – בקדשי מזבח" כו'.§ מ"ט? קסבר: כי גמרה מעילה "חטא" "חטא" מתרומה – דומיא דתרומה דקדישא קדושת הגוף, אבל קדושת בדק הבית, דקדושת דמים – לא. *ת"ר: [ז]דם שנטמא וזרקו, בשוגג – הורצה,

במזיד

תורה אור: במדבר טו

רש"י

הלכתא למשיחא. הרי קבע לנו הלכה המצריכה לנו לימות המשיח, כשיבנה בית המקדש, ועכשיו לא הוצרכנו לה! **א"ל** הלכה קאמינא. האי דמיתמהנא, יב] קביעות הלכה הוא דמיתמהנא. דמיגרס בעינן מיתני משניות ומחלוקת הלכות עבודה, לפי שתורה היא ודרוש וקבל שכר. אבל קיבוע הלכה אינה אלא להורות הלכה למעשה, ועכשיו אינו נוהג. **מתני'** קדשי גוים כו'. מפרש בגמ', וכשהתנדבום לגבוה קאמר. **גמ'** ת"ר כו'. מפרשה לקמיה. **ואין** מביאין נסכים. בפני עצמם בלא זבח, כישראל שמתנדבין יין, כדתנן במנחות (דף קד:). **בכולן אני רואה.** בכל הדברים הללו אני רואה בקדשי גוים להחמיר כבקדשי ישראל. **שנאמר בהם לה'.** דכתיב: "איש איש מבית ישראל" וגו' (ויקרא כב), ודרשינן ב"הכל שוחטין" (חולין יג:): "איש", מה ת"ל "איש איש" – לרבות את הגוים שנודרים נדרים ונדבות כישראל. **במה דברים אמורים.** דאין מועלין בהן. אתאן לת"ק. **אבל בקדשי בדק הבית.** גוי שהתפיס יג] לבדק הבית. **מועלין בו.** ולקמן מפרש טעמא. **דגמרינן מעילה חטא חטא מתרומה.** כתיב במעילה: "וחטאה בשגגה" (ויקרא ה), וכתיב בתרומה: "ולא ישאו עליו חטא" (שם כב), ובתרומה כתיב בתריה דהאי קרא: "ולא יחללו את קדשי בני ישראל". יד] *דבתרומה כתיב בני ישראל. "וינזרו מקדשי בני ישראל" (שם כב). **תמורה.** בהמה. **למעשר בהמה.** דכתיב במעשר: "והיה הוא ותמורתו" (שם כז). **ומעשר בהמה למעשר דגן.** "עשר תעשר", ואמר מר בבכורות (דף נג:): בשני מעשרות הכתוב מדבר, אחד מעשר בהמה ואחד מעשר דגן. **דבר הלמד.** טו] מעשר בהמה, הלמוד בהיקש שלא יהא נוהג בגוים, חוזר ומלמד על התמורה בהיקש? **מעשר דגן חולין הוא.** ובכל התורה למדין למד מן הלמד חוץ מן הקדשים, כדאמר ב"איזהו מקומן" (לקמן מט:). **הניחא** למאן דאמר בתר מלמד אזלינן. דאי מלמד חולין, אף על גב דלמד קדש – למדים בו הלמד מן הלמד. ופלוגתייהו ב"איזהו מקומן" (שם). **גוים לא מייתו.** דלא איתרבו גוים אלא לנדרים ונדבות, כדכתיב בקרא: "לכל נדריהם" וגו' (ויקרא כב). וה"ה נמי דלא מייתו חובה הקבוע טז] להם זמן כגון עולת ראייה ושלמי חגיגה, אלא לא פסיקא ליה, הואיל ומביאין עולה ושלמי נדבה. אבל מעשר יז] חטאת ואשם – לא שייך בהו כלל. **אזרח.** בפרשת נסכים כתיב ב"שלח לך" – "כל האזרח יעשה ככה", ומינה ילפינן לקמן בפרק "כל התדיר" (דף נא:): "האזרח" – מלמד שמתנדבים נסכים, יח] ומביא בפני עצמן נדבה. **ת"ל ככה.** יעשה לשור, יט] שאחר שחובה תלויה בקרבן – ל"ש ישראל ול"ש גוי. הלכך, שלח דמי נסכיה – יקרבו משלו, ואם לאו – כ] מקריבים משל ציבור, שתנאי ב"ד הוא, במסכת שקלים (דף יח:). **מ"ט כו'.** אמילתיה דר"ש קאי, אמעילה דקאמר: אבל קדשי בדק הבית דגוים מועלין. **וכי גמרה מעילה מתרומה.** למעוטי גוים, דומיא דתרומה – קדשי מזבח הוא כא] דגמרה, דקדיש גופייהו כתרומה, שאינן נפדין.

במזיד

תוספות

הלכתא למשיחא. כי האי גוונא פריך בריש "ד' מיתות" (סנהדרין נא:). ותימה: דבריש "עשרה יוחסין" (קדושין עב:) *א"ר יהודה אמר רב: הלכה כרבי יוסי דעתידין ממזרין ליטהר! כב] ושמא נפקא מינה עכשיו שלא להרחיק משפחות שאינן ידועות. ובקדושין (שם) פירשתי *במאי פליגי רבי יוסי ורבנן, בממזר ידוע או בשאין ידוע. ובפ"ק דיומא (דף יג.) דפסיק כר' יוסי כג] ראשון חוזר לעבודתו ושני אינו ראוי כו' – נפקא מינה עכשיו בנשיא או ראש ישיבה או פרנס שנתמנה על הציבור ועבר מחמת אונס, ועבר האונס. ובפרק "אלו דברים" (פסחים סט:) דפסיק הלכה כר"ע דכל מלאכה שאפשר לעשותה מערב שבת אינה דוחה את השבת לענין פסח – נפקא מינה בזמן הזה לענין מילה. ואע"ג דגבי מילה נמי פסיק הכי בהדיא (בשבת קלג.), מ"מ לאלומי פסקא דמילה פסק נמי גבי פסח הכי. ובפ"ק דתענית (דף ד:) דפסיק רבי אלעזר הלכה כר"ג דאמר: בשבעה במרחשון, ומוקי לה התם בזמן שבית המקדש קיים – נפקא מינה גם בזמן הזה לבני בבל דאית להו פירי בדברא, כדקאמר התם: הא לן והא להו. ומיהו בסוף "התכלת" (מנחות נב:) קשה, דפסיק רבי יוחנן כאבא יוסי בן דוסתאי גבי חביתי כ"ג! ונראה דרב יוסף דוקא, כד] דאית ליה הכא ובסנהדרין (דף נא:) דאין לפסוק הלכתא למשיחא. וה"ר חיים מפרש: דלא פריך "הלכתא למשיחא" אלא היכא דאיכא תרתי, שהוא למשיחא וגם עושה איסור. כה] דליכא נפקותא בהלכתא אלא על ידי איסור, לא שייך לפסוק למשיחא*.

והשוחטן בחוץ פטור דברי ר' שמעון. בגמרא לא תני בברייתא שוחט בחוץ, והכא לא תני תמורה ונסכים דתני בברייתא, וזה תימה. וא"ת: אי ר"ש ס"ל *כרבי כו] אליעזר דאמר פרק "ואלו מנחות" (דף עג:) דאין גוים מביאין אלא עולות – א"כ מאי איריא קדשי גוים דאין חייבין עליהם משום פיגול נותר וטמא? אפי' דישראל נמי, דהא שמעינן ליה לר"ש בסוף "דם שחיטה" (כריתות כג:) דאין פיגול בעולין, ואין נותר בעולין! וי"ל: דסבר לה כר' יוסי הגלילי, דמביאין אפילו שלמים. ועוד י"ל: דבכריתות (דף יג: ודף כג:) מוכח דטעמא דר"ש משום דאין איסור חל על איסור, וקדשי גוים שרו מדאורייתא, כדתניא בגמרא: לא נהנין – מדרבנן, ולא מועילין – דגמר "חטא" "חטא" מתרומה כז].

רואה אני בכולן להחמיר שנאמר בהן לה'. פי': בקרא ד"איש איש" דמרבינן גוים שנודרין, כתיב "לה'" למימר *שגוים הם בכלל קדשי ה'. משמע הכא דאיכא מעילה דאורייתא בקדשי מזבח. וקשה: דלא כח] איפריך מהכא לר' ינאי דאמר בפ' "קדשי מזבח" (דף טו.) במעילה, דאין חייבין מעילה אלא על קדשי בדק הבית, כדפריך התם,כט] ומשני: כולהו מדרבנן. ועוד תנן פ' "אמרו לו" (כריתות יג:): יש אוכל אכילה אחת וחייב עליה ארבע חטאות ואשם אחד. ותו: דשילהי "כל הבשר" (חולין דף קיז.) אמר ר' ינאי גופיה: "כאשר יורם" וגו', מה פר כהן משיח יש בו מעילה – אף שלמים יש בהן מעילה. ותו, דשילהי תמורה (דף לג:) א"ר ינאי גופיה: אין מעילה מפורשת מן התורה אלא בעולה בלבד, שנאמר: "לה'" – קדשים המיוחדים לה'! וי"ל: אסמכתא ניהו. ועוד י"ל: דר' ינאי לא איירי אלא בדבר הניתר לטהורים, אבל באימורים ועולה, דהמעילה לא פקעה – פשיטא דאיכא מעילה דאורייתא. וקשה לי על זה: אמאי לא משני במעילה הכי, דהי פריך מטובא, ל] וליטני באימורים!

ואין עושין תמורה דאיתקש למעשר בהמה. בפרק קמא דתמורה (דף ג.) דריש מדכתיב בריש ענינא: "דבר אל בני ישראל איש כי יפליא" וגו'*.

ומעשר בהמה למעשר דגן. בבכורות לא] (דף נג:) אמרינן לא איתקש אלא לענין שנה.

דומיא דתרומה דקדישא קדושת הגוף. וא"ת: אזהרה לנהנה מקדשי בדק הבית מנין? דתנן: "אלו הן הלוקין" (מכות יג.) וחשיב הקדש שלא נפדה, משמע דבר שיש לו פדיון, והיינו קדשי בדה"ב. הא לא ידעינן אזהרה במעילה אלא מגזריה שוה ד"חטא" "חטא" מתרומה פ' "הנשרפין" (סנהדרין פד.), והאי תנא לא יליף אלא דומיא דתרומה! וי"ל: דהקדש שלא נפדה לא מיירי בבדק הבית, אלא בקדשי המזבח שהוממו, דכיון דמעיקרא הוה בהו מעילה – בשביל שהוממו לא פקעה המעילה. ואכתי

קשה

מסורת הש"ס

סנהדרין נא:
[סוטה מד. סנהדרין שם ועת.]
תמורה ב: ערכין ה: [תוספתא פ"ה]
[תמורה ג.]
[פסחים לג. קדושין מב: סנהדרין פד. תמורה שם מעילה יח:]
נ"א ובטומאה ל"ק
[לקמן ס: מכות יט.]
[לקמן נ. תמורה כא:]
[מכות יט: ע"ש לקמן ס: תמורה כב: ע"ש]
[נ"ל דתניא]
[תמורה ג. מנחות עג:]
יומא ז. מנחות כה. יבמות נ. גיטין נד. פסחים עז: פ:
[ועי' היטב תוס' תמורה ג. ד"ה ומעשר דגן]

[שם איתא אמר ר"י אמר שמואל]
[לא נמצא שם בקדושין]
[בקצת נוסחאות ובמשנה שבמשניות איתא רבי מאיר]
[לאו יהיו כולם לדיקים כ"א בת"י ביומא וע"ע תוספות יומא יג. ד"ה הלכה וכו' ומה שנרשם שם בגליון]
נ"א רבי עקיבא
[נ"ל שקדשי גוים כו']

עין משפט נר מצוה

מח א מיי' פי"ח מהל' פסה"מ הלכה כד:
מט ב מיי' פי"ט מהל' מעה"ק הלכה טז:
נ ג מיי' פ"ה מהלכות מעילה הלכה טו:
נא ד מיי' פ"א מהלכות תמורה הלכה ו:
נב ה מיי' פ"ג מהלכות מעשה הקרבנות הל' ה ועיין רש"ק:
נג ו מיי' פ"א מהלכות פסה"מ הלכה לד:

גליון הש"ס

מתני' ר"י מחייב. עיין לקמן דף קטז ע"ב תוס' ד"ה אסור ומנחות דף קט ע"ב תוס' ד"ה והעלה: **גמ'** טעון נסכים דר"ש. בתשובת מוה' בצלאל אשכנזי סימן א' דף ט ע"ג כתב בכל ספרי עתיקי ודוקני אשר נמצאו בידי ל"ג דר"ש וכ"נ מדברי תוספות עכ"ל: **שם** דבתרומה כתיב בני ישראל. עיין קדושין דף מח ע"ב תוספות ד"ה והנכרי:

הגהות הב"ח

(א) גמ' ובתרומה כתיב וכו' ובטומאה כתיב בני ישראל ולא עובדי כוכבים. נ"ב עי' לעיל דף טו ע"ב בתוספות ד"ה אלא למעוטי כו':

שיטה מקובצת

א] בחוץ פטור. אמר הר"ם דכי היכי דדרשינן בשחוטי חוץ בני ישראל מצוין על שחוטי חוץ ולא גוים ה"נ נדרוש גבי הקרבן דדוקא קרבן של בני ישראל חייבין על שחוטי חוץ ולא בקרבן של גוים. מהר"פ: ב] אבל קרבנן טעון נסכים ואם שלח הנסכים יהיה משלו ואם לאו משל צבור. מהר"פ: ג] דברי רבי שמעון. בספרי כת"י אין כתוב בברייתא זו דברי ר' שמעון וכן נראה מדברי התוס' ד"ה דומיא דתרומה דקאמרי שם ועי"ל דלרבנן אפילו בדק הבית כו' ובזה יתיישב מה שפסק הרמב"ם בספי"ח מהל' פה"מ קדשי גוים אין חייבין עליהן משום פיגול נותר וטמא דלא כרבי יוסי ובהל' מעה"ק פסק כר' יוסי בשחטן בחוץ א) אבל ברש"י גרים דברי ר"ש: ד] הבית מודה ר"ש שמועלין בהן כך יש בס"י ורש"י לא גרים כן: ה] ובתרומה: ו] חייבין עליהן: ז] בני ישראל ולא גוים. וא"ת (משמע הכא) [הכא משמע] דדרשינן ולא יחללו אטומאת הגוף והא דרשינן לעיל בפרק קבלה אזרות או אטמא ששימש וי"ל דנפקא לן חילול חילול שיש בסיפא דקרא [בני ישראל] דכתיב [אשר יקדישו] בני ישראל וא"ת והלא לא כתיב שם חילול וי"ל דקרא (נמי קאי) [דחילול קאי נמי] אסיפא דקרא דבני ישראל. מהר"פ ז"ל: ח] שאין לו זמן קבוע וא"ת אמאי צריך להזכיר משום דאין קבוע להם זמן הלא הם אין מביאין [אפילו] קרבן הקבוע להם זמן כגון עולת ראייה ושלמי חגיגה וי"ל דמ"מ מביאין הדומה להם בשמייהו כגון שלמי נדבה או עולת נדבה משא"כ בשאר שאין קבוע להם זמן ולכך הזכיר משום דאין קבוע להם זמן משום דפסיקא ליה. מהר"פ ז"ל: ט] שאין לו אות ה' נמחק: י] אזרח מביא נסכים (עיין מנחות דף עג ע"ב) בחידושי שכתבתי: יא] להחמיר כו' בר"א בס"י יש אמר ר' יוסי כו' מ"ט לה' כתיב בהו במד"א בקדשי כו' קסבר כו' ורש"י לא גרים כן: יב] דמיתמהנא אקביעות הלכה: יג] שהתפים מנה לבדק: יד] ישראל ובטומאה כתיב: טו] הלמד בהיקש מעשר בהמה הלמוד בהיקש מדגן שלא יהא: טז] הקבוע לה זמן: יז] מעשר חטאת: יח] נסכים בכל יום ודוקא אזרח ולא גוי הס"ד ומה"ד ומביא נסכים: יט] לשור מאחר שחובה: כ] לאו קרבים משל: כא] הוא דקדיש תיבת דגמרה נמחק: כב] ליטהר ולא פריך הלכתא למשיחא: כג] יוסי דאמר: כד] דוקא הוא דאית: כה] איסור כיון דליכא: כו] עקיבא תיבת אליעזר נמחק: כז] מתרומה וא"ת הא דתנן לקמן נומא ר' שמעון בדבר שדרכו לאכול חייב אבל העצים והלבונה [כו'] [אא"ה בדפוס נדפס [סוף דברי התוס'] מתיבת אבל בע"ב לדבור בפ"ע שלא במקומו והוא שייך לכאן כי הוא דבור אחד עכ"ה]: כח] דלא פריך מהכא: כט] התם טובא ומשני: ל] מטובא לישני ואות ו' נמחק: לא] בבכורות (עי' תוס' בכורות לג ע"א נט ע"א):

ובעובדי

א) נ"ל דלפי גי' הנ"ל א"ש דברי הרמב"ם דגבי פיגול נותר וטמא פסק דלא כר"י משום דהתם פליג עליה ת"ק והלכה כת"ק נגד ר"י משא"כ בשחוטי חוץ דפליג עם ר"ש פסק כר"ע.

בְּמֵזִיד — לֹא הוּרְצָה. בד"א — בְּיָחִיד, אֲבָל בְּצִיבּוּר — בֵּין בְּשׁוֹגֵג בֵּין בְּמֵזִיד הוּרְצָה. א] *וּבְגוֹיִם — בֵּין בְּשׁוֹגֵג וּבֵין בְּמֵזִיד לֹא הוּרְצָה. אֲמַרוּהָ רַבָּנַן קַמֵּיהּ דְּרַב פַּפָּא: ב] כְּמַאן — דְּלָא כְּרַבִּי יוֹסֵי, דְּאִי רַבִּי יוֹסֵי — הָאָמַר: בְּכוּלָּן אֲנִי רוֹאֶה לְהַחְמִיר. אֲמַר לְהוּ רַב פַּפָּא: אֲפִי' תֵּימָא רַבִּי יוֹסֵי, שָׁאנֵי הָתָם דְּאָמַר קְרָא "לָהֶם", לָהֶם — וְלֹא לְגוֹיִם. אֲמַר לֵיהּ רַב הוּנָא בְּרֵיהּ דְּרַב נָתָן לְרַב פַּפָּא: אֶלָּא מֵעַתָּה, °"אֲשֶׁר הֵם מַקְדִּישִׁים", ה"נ: הֵם — וְלֹא גּוֹיִם? אֶלָּא אָמַר רַב אַשִׁי, אָמַר קְרָא: °"לְרָצוֹן לָהֶם" — וְגוֹיִם לָאו בְּנֵי הַרְצָאָה נִינְהוּ.§ **מתני'** ג] דְּבָרִים שֶׁאֵין חַיָּיבִים עֲלֵיהֶם מִשּׁוּם פִּיגּוּל — אחַיָּיבִין עֲלֵיהֶן מִשּׁוּם נוֹתָר וּמִשּׁוּם טָמֵא, חוּץ מִן הַדָּם. ד] ר' שִׁמְעוֹן מְחַיֵּיב *בְּדָבָר שֶׁדַּרְכָּן לֶאֱכוֹל, באֲבָל הָעֵצִים וְהַלְּבוֹנָה וְהַקְּטוֹרֶת — אֵין חַיָּיבִין עָלָיו מִשּׁוּם טוּמְאָה.§ **גמ'** ת"ר: *יָכוֹל לֹא יְהוּ חַיָּיבִין מִשּׁוּם טוּמְאָה אֶלָּא עַל דָּבָר שֶׁיֵּשׁ לוֹ מַתִּירִין, בֵּין לְאָדָם בֵּין לַמִּזְבֵּחַ? וְדִין הוּא: וּמַה פִּיגּוּל שֶׁהוּא בִּקְבִיעָה, וּבִידִיעָה אַחַת, וְלֹא הוּתַּר מִכְּלָלוֹ — אֵין חַיָּיבִין עָלָיו אֶלָּא עַל דָּבָר שֶׁיֵּשׁ לוֹ מַתִּירִין בֵּין לְאָדָם בֵּין לַמִּזְבֵּחַ. טוּמְאָה שֶׁהִיא בְּעוֹלֶה וְיוֹרֵד, וּבִשְׁתֵּי יְדִיעוֹת, וְהוּתְּרָה מִכְּלָלָהּ — אֵינוֹ דִּין שֶׁאֵינוֹ חַיָּיב אֶלָּא עַל דָּבָר שֶׁיֵּשׁ לוֹ מַתִּירִין בֵּין לְאָדָם בֵּין לַמִּזְבֵּחַ? ה] ת"ל: °"אֲשֶׁר הֵם מַקְדִּישִׁים לִי". יָכוֹל מִיָּד? ת"ל: °"יִקְרַב"; ו] אָמַר ר"א: וְכִי יֵשׁ נוֹגֵעַ שֶׁהוּא חַיָּיב? אֶלָּא מַה ת"ל "יִקְרַב" — בְּהוּכְשַׁר [בָּשָׂר] לִיקָּרֵב הַכָּתוּב מְדַבֵּר. הָא כֵּיצַד? יֵשׁ לוֹ מַתִּירִין — מִשֶּׁיִּקְרְבוּ מַתִּירִין, ז] אֵין לוֹ מַתִּירִין — מִשֶּׁיִּקְדַּשׁ בִּכְלִי. אַשְׁכַּחַן טוּמְאָה, נוֹתָר מְנָלַן? אָתֵי "חִילּוּל" "חִילּוּל" מִטּוּמְאָה. ח] וְלֵילַף "עָוֹן" "עָוֹן" מִפִּיגּוּל! מִסְתַּבְּרָא, מִטּוּמְאָה הֲוֵי לֵיהּ לְמֵילַף, ט] שֶׁכֵּן גז"ל סִימָן. אַדְּרַבָּה, מִפִּיגּוּל הֲוָה לֵיהּ לְמֵילַף שֶׁכֵּן *נוֹתָר, צִיץ, טָהוֹר, בִּזְמַן, קָרֵב, וְהָנֵי נְפִישָׁן! אֶלָּא מִדְּתָנֵי לֵוִי, דְּתָנֵי לֵוִי: מִנַּיִן שֶׁאַף בִּפְסוּל זְמַן הַכָּתוּב מְדַבֵּר — ת"ל: *°"וְלֹא יְחַלְּלוּ אֶת *(קָדְשֵׁי בְּנֵי יִשְׂרָאֵל",) בִּשְׁנֵי

ויקרא כב | שמות כח | ויקרא כב | שם | שם

תורה אור: אֶלָּא מֵעַתָּה אֲשֶׁר הֵם מַקְדִּישִׁים לִי.

בְּמֵזִיד לֹא הוּרְצָה. קְנָסָא דְּרַבָּנַן הוּא. וְלָא שֶׁיָּבִיא אַחֵר, דְּא"כ נִמְצְאוּ ב"ד מַתְנִין לַעֲקוֹר דָּבָר מִן הַתּוֹרָה וּלְהָבִיא חוּלִּין לָעֲזָרָה. אֶלָּא לֹא הוּרְצָה לְהַתִּיר בָּשָׂר בַּאֲכִילָה, י] אֲבָל בְּעָלִים נִתְכַּפְּרוּ. וְהָכִי אָמַר לָהּ *שְׁמוּאֵל בְּמַסֶּ' יְבָמוֹת (דף צ.). יא] [כְּמַאן]. הָא דְּקָתָנֵי דְּגוֹיִם לֹא הוּרְצָה — דְּלָא כְּר' יוֹסֵי. אֶלָּא מֵעַתָּה אֲשֶׁר הֵם מַקְדִּישִׁים לִי. דִּכְתִיב גַּבֵּי "וְיִנָּזְרוּ". הָכִי נַמִי הֵם וְלֹא גּוֹיִם. וְתֵימָה: דְּקָדְשֵׁי גוֹיִם אֵין חַיָּיבִין עֲלֵיהֶם מִשּׁוּם טוּמְאָה לְר' יוֹסֵי? וְהָא (א) קָאָמַר: בְּכוּלָּן אֲנִי רוֹאֶה לְהַחְמִיר! לְרָצוֹן לָהֶם. גַּבֵּי צִיץ כְּתִיב. לָאו בְּנֵי הַרְצָאָה. לְהַקב"ה הֵם, שֶׁאֵינוֹ מִתְרַצֶּה לָהֶם. **מתני'** דְּבָרִים שֶׁאֵין חַיָּיבִין עֲלֵיהֶם מִשּׁוּם פִּיגּוּל. כְּגוֹן הַקּוֹמֶץ וְהַקְּטֹרֶת, וְכָל הַשְּׁנוּיִים בְּמִשְׁנָתֵינוּ. חַיָּיבִין עֲלֵיהֶן מִשּׁוּם טוּמְאָה. כָּרֵת, הָאוֹכְלָן בְּטוּמְאַת הַגּוּף. וְעַל שִׁגְגָתָם חַטָּאת, כִּדְיָלֵיף בַּגְּמָרָא. חוּץ מִן הַדָּם. דְּאִימְעוּט בְּהֶדְיָא, כִּדְאָמַר בַּגְּמָ'. ה"ג: נוֹמִי ר"ש בְּדָבָר שֶׁדַּרְכּוֹ לֶאֱכוֹל חַיָּיב וְכָךְ שָׁמַעְתִּי מִבֵּית יב] מִדְרָשׁוֹ שֶׁל רַבֵּינוּ יַעֲקֹב. וְל"נ שֶׁכָּךְ פֵּירֵשׁ ר' מְשׁוּלָּם בַּר קְלוֹנִימוּס גָּאוֹן *בִּשְׁעַת מִיתָתוֹ: נוֹמִי ר"ש — כְּמוֹ אָמַר (ב) ר"ש. וּבִסְפָרִים הָיָה כָּתוּב הַדָּם יג] *וְעִמּוֹ. בְּדָבָר שֶׁדַּרְכּוֹ לֶאֱכוֹל. שֶׁדֶּרֶךְ בְּנֵי אָדָם יד] לֶאֱכוֹל, וְאַף עַל פִּי שֶׁזֶּה מִן [illegible] וְדוֹמִין לָהּ. אֲבָל לְבוֹנָה וְעֵצִים וּקְטֹרֶת אֵין חַיָּיבִין עֲלֵיהֶם מִשּׁוּם טוּמְאָה. וְרַבָּנַן פְּלִיגִי עֲלָהּ, כִּדְמְרַבִּינַן לְהוּ טו] "מִכָּל הַבָּשָׂר" יְתֵירָא לְרַבּוֹת עֵצִים וּלְבוֹנָה. **גמ'** וּמַה פִּיגּוּל. *הָאוֹכֵל פִּיגּוּל בְּשׁוֹגֵג. שֶׁהוּא בְּקָבוּעַ. חַטָּאתוֹ קָבוּעַ לְעָנִי כְּלֶעָשִׁיר, כִּשְׂבָּה אוֹ שְׂעִירָה. וּבִידִיעָה אַחַת. שֶׁאֵינוֹ צָרִיךְ יְדִיעָה בַּתְּחִלָּה, טז] שֶׁאָכַל בְּשׁוֹגֵג וְיָדַע שֶׁאָכַל. וְלֹא הוּתַּר מִכְּלָלוֹ. אֵצֶל צִיבּוּר. שֶׁהִיא בְּעוֹלֶה וְיוֹרֵד. לְעָשִׁיר בְּהֵמָה, וּבְדַלּוּת שְׁתֵּי תוֹרִים, וּבְדַלֵּי דַלּוּת עֲשִׂירִית הָאֵיפָה, גַּבֵּי שְׁמִיעַת קוֹל בְּ"וַיִּקְרָא" (ה). וּבִשְׁתֵּי יְדִיעוֹת. נִטְמָא וְיָדַע שֶׁנִּטְמָא, וְנֶעֶלְמָה מִמֶּנּוּ טוּמְאָה, וְאָכַל אֶת הַקּוֹדֶשׁ וְלֹא יָדַע, וּמִשֶּׁאָכַל יָדַע. אֲבָל יז] שֶׁיֵּשׁ בָּהּ יְדִיעָה בַּסּוֹף וְאֵין בָּהּ יְדִיעָה בַּתְּחִלָּה, שֶׁלִּפְנֵי אֲכִילָתוֹ לֹא יָדַע מֵעוֹלָם בְּטוּמְאָה זוֹ — פָּטוּר. וְהָכִי גָּמְרִי' לָהּ בִּשְׁבוּעוֹת (דף ז.). וְהוּתְּרָה מִכְּלָלָהּ. טוּמְאַת הַגּוּף הוּתְּרָה אֵצֶל צִיבּוּר בְּפֶסַח, דִּתְנַן (פסחים דף עו:): הַפֶּסַח שֶׁבָּא בְּטוּמְאָה נֶאֱכָל בְּטוּמְאָה. ת"ל אֲשֶׁר הֵם מַקְדִּישִׁים. רִיבָּה כָּל הַמּוּקְדָּשִׁים. וְגַבֵּי "וְיִנָּזְרוּ" כְּתִיב. יָכוֹל מִיָּד. יח] מִשֶּׁהוּקְדְּשׁוּ מִתְחַיֵּיב עָלָיו מִיָּד, אִם אֲכָלוֹ בְּטוּמְאָה? ת"ל אֲשֶׁר יִקְרַב. מִכָּל זַרְעֲכֶם. ר"א מְפָרֵשׁ לָהּ וְאָזֵיל. וְכִי יֵשׁ נוֹגֵעַ חַיָּיב. וַהֲלֹא אֵינוֹ חַיָּיב אֶלָּא אִם כֵּן אָכַל, כִּדְכְתִיב יט] (ויקרא כב): "אִישׁ אִישׁ מִזֶּרַע אַהֲרֹן" וגו'! בְּהוּכְשַׁר לִיקָּרֵב. וְאַקֳּדָשִׁים קָאֵי. וְהָכִי קָאָמַר: אֲשֶׁר יַקְרִיב קָדָשִׁים וְאח"כ יֹאכְלֵם כ] וְטוּמְאָה עָלָיו, כִּדְמְפָרֵשׁ אֲכִילָה בִּקְרָא דְּבַתְרֵיהּ. יֵשׁ לוֹ מַתִּירִין. כְּגוֹן אֵימוּרִים וּבָשָׂר שֶׁהַדָּם מַתִּירָן, וּשְׁיָרֵי מְנָחוֹת שֶׁהַקּוֹמֶץ מַתִּירָן — מִשֶּׁיִּקְרְבוּ מַתִּירָיו. וְשֶׁאֵין לוֹ מַתִּירִין, כְּגוֹן מִנְחַת כֹּהֲנִים וְלֹהֶן מָשִׁיחַ וּנְסָכִים — מִשֶּׁיִּקְדְּשׁוּ בִּכְלִי, שֶׁהוּא הַמַּכְשִׁירָן לַאֲכִילָה הָאֲמוּרָה בָּהֶן. נוֹתָר מְנָלַן. דְּחַיָּיב כא] (כֹּהֵן) עָלָיו אַף עַל דָּבָר שֶׁאֵין לוֹ מַתִּירִין, כִּדְקָתָנֵי מַתְנִי': דְּבָרִים שֶׁאֵין חַיָּיבִין עֲלֵיהֶן מִשּׁוּם פִּיגּוּל חַיָּיבִין עֲלֵיהֶן מִשּׁוּם נוֹתָר. שֶׁבֵּן גז"ל כב] סִימָן. נוֹתָר וְטוּמְאָה פְּסוּל הַגּוּף, וּפִיגּוּל פְּסוּל מַחֲשָׁבָה. כג] נוֹתָר וְטוּמְאָה אֵין זְרִיקַת הַדָּם מְבִיאָתָן לִידֵי כד] פִּסּוּלָן, וּפִיגּוּל זְרִיקַת הַדָּם קוֹבַעְתּוֹ בִּפְסוּל. נוֹתָר וְטָמֵא נֶאֱמַר בָּהֶן חִילּוּל*. שֶׁבֵּן הוּתַּר צִיץ טָהוֹר בִּזְמַן קָרֵב וְהָנֵי נְפִישָׁן. נוֹתָר וּפִיגּוּל לֹא הוּתְּרוּ מִכְּלָלָן כְּטוּמְאָה. וְאֵין הַצִּיץ מְרַצֶּה עֲלֵיהוּ כְּטוּמְאָה. וְאע"ג דִּבְטוּמְאַת הַגּוּף כה] קָאָמֵינָא, שֶׁאֵין הַצִּיץ מְרַצֶּה עָלֶיהָ — שֵׁם טוּמְאָה מִיהָא נִקְלֵית בַּצִּיץ. טָהוֹר. שְׁנֵיהֶן טְהוֹרִין. וּשְׁנֵיהֶן נִפְסָלִין בִּזְמַן, זֶה בְּנוֹתָר חוּץ לִזְמַנּוֹ וְזֶה בְּמַחְשֶׁבֶת זְמַן. וּשְׁנֵיהֶן פְּסוּלִין בְּקָרֵב, לְמַעוּטֵי טוּמְאַת הַגּוּף שֶׁפְּסוּלָהּ *בְּמַקְרִיב. מִנַּיִן שֶׁאַף בִּפְסוּל זְמַן הַכָּתוּב מְדַבֵּר. הַאי קְרָא דְ"וְיִנָּזְרוּ". וְלֹא יְחַלְּלוּ. דִּכְתִיב גַּבֵּי טוּמְאָה. בִּשְׁנֵי

קשה מהא דילפינן בפרק כו] בתרא דמעילה (דף יח:) "חטא" "חטא" מתרומה לענין פגם ונהנה כז] *במעילה במחובר לקרקע, ומחובר היינו קדושת דמים, ולא גמרי מתרומה! וי"ל: דהכא דוקא הוא דבעינן דומיא דתרומה, משום דכתיב "לה'" לרבויי, כח] דלא גמרינן אלא דומיא דתרומה דקדושת הגוף. כט] עוד יש לומר: דלרבנן אפי' בדק הבית גמרינן מתרומה למעט גוים, ל] *"בד"א" ר' יוסי קאמר ליה, ולא גמר בדק הבית מתרומה. וכן נראה, מדמייתי התלמוד: ר' יוסי אומר בכולן אני רואה להחמיר וכו'. ומפרש: מ"ט — דומיא דתרומה דקדושת הגוף. וה"ק: שכל קדשי גוים אני רואה להחמיר משום פיגול נותר וטמא. אבל מאי דאמריתו אין מועלין — הני מילי בקדשי המזבח דגמרינן מתרומה, לא] *(ואהני לינא) דלא גמרינן מתרומה אלא מידי דדמיא לה, אבל בדק הבית דלא דמי לה — מועלין. כך פירש רבינו. והקשה לו בנו ה"ר אלחנן: דבפ"ק דערכין (דף ה:) אמר *אביי: וערכו נגנז. ופריך: א"כ לא ימעלו בו, אלמה תניא: אבל קדשי בדק הבית מועלין? ולישני: ההיא ר' יוסי, אבל לרבנן אין מועלין! וי"ל: דשפיר משני התם. וכ"ז הגיה רבינו. **אבל** העצים והלבונה והקטרת אין בהם משום טומאה. לב] ואת תאמר: מאי איריא מחוח דאין נאכלין? תיפוק ליה דאין איסור טומאה חל עליהם, דהא יש בהן מעילה, ורבי שמעון היא, דאמר (כריתות כג:): אין פיגול בעולין ואין נותר בעולין, לפי שאין איסור חל על איסור! ועוד: חטאות הפנימיות אמאי צריך למעוטינהו מפיגול לר' שמעון, ואמאי חייבין עליהם משום נותר וטמא? והא אית בהו מעילה, ואין איסור חל על איסור! ומיהו, בזה יש לומר דמשכחת לה לאחר שניתך הבשר ועדיין ראויה לאכילה, דתנן במעילה (דף ט.) דמועלין בהן עד שיתוך הבשר. לג] ומ"מ קשה מפיגול, שהרי פקע פיגולו מכי משלה בו האור. אבל מעלים קשה, דיש בהן מעילה לעולים! וי"ל: דתנא דר' שמעון דהכא סבר ליה כההוא תנא דרבי שמעון דאמר התם: יש פיגול בעולין, ויש נותר בעולין. ועוד י"ל: דמשכחת לה בבת אחת, כגון שהביא שתי שערות אחר כך, לד] כדאשכחן ביבמות פרק "ד' אחין" (דף לג.). וקשה קצת הא דאמר פ' "דם שחיטה" (כריתות כג:): למאן דאמר אין איסור חל על איסור, "כל חלב" מאי עביד ליה? ומוקי לה בוולדי קדשים — לוקמי בהביא שתי שערות אחר כך, דהוה ליה בת אחת! ומיהו, בלאו הכי שפיר קמשני. וזה אין להקשות למ"ד אין איסור חל על איסור בקדשים: ◐ל"ל קרא בדם למעוטי מנותר וטמא? דהא איצטריך להביא שתי שערות אחר כך, דהוי כבת אחת, כדפרישנא. ומיהו, למאי דבעי למימרא בפ' "ד' אחין" (יבמות לג.) דר' שמעון אפי' בת אחת לית ליה — קשה. **תלמוד** לומר אשר הם מקדישים לי. גבי טמא כתיב, ומרבי הכא מיניה כל דבר. והא דמייתי ליה בברייתא דלעיל גבי פיגול, *היינו לה] דשייך טומאה בעופות ומנחות, והדר אתי נותר חילול חילול מטומאה, ופיגול עון עון מנותר. לו] ולאחר שריבה הכתוב כל דבר מטומאה — חוזר וממעט בפיגול מכלל ופרט וכלל. **יש** לו מתירין משיקרבו מתירין. מ"כל טהור יאכל בשר" דרשינן ליה ב"הקומץ רבה" (מנחות כה:) ◐ובסמוך* לז]. **שבן** גזל. פירש"י: למ"ד *היינו "חילול" "חילול". וקשה על זה: בתר הכי, דפריך: אדרבה מפיגול נילף שכן הותר וכו', אמאי לא אמר גם כן שכן עון מעון? ופר"ח: למ"ד דגזל היינו "כולו", פיגול שייך בכל הקרבן, אבל נותר וטומאה שייכי בחתיכה אחת. הכי

בכלילה וממעט מחובר לקרקע ומחובר היינו קדושת דמים וגמרינן מתרומה נ"ק

ובד"א נ"ק

נד א מיי' פי"ח מהל' פסה"מ הלכה יז:
נה ב מיי' שם הל' כד:

נ"א ואהני לי וגי' נ"ק ואהני לה'

נ"ל אבימי

[מעילה י: ע"ש]

גליון הש"ס

תוס' ד"ה אבל וכו' ומ"ל קרא בדם למעוטי מנותר וטמא וכו'. ק"ל הא תוספות כתבו כמה פעמים דדם שבבשלו אינו עובר עליו עיין חולין דף קט ע"א וכו' **ד"ה** יש לו מתירין וכו' ובסמוך דף מו ע"ב ד"ה אחת פירשתי כנ"ל:

נ"א כיון דשייך כו' הדר אתי נ"ק

אפרש הס"ד נ"ק
*דגזל היינו נ"ק

נ"ל ר' יוסי כ"ה נ"ק

[לעיל טו: מנחות כה.]

שבועות ז.

[וכ"כ תוס' במנחות קטו: ד"ה בתחלה ע"ש]

וטמי נ"ק

שהוא בקביעה האוכל פיגול בשוגג שהוא בקבוע חטאתו כו' כצ"ל נ"ק וכ"ה בס"י

נ"א הותר הגוף נ"ק

[נ"ל שם קדשי אשר הם מקדישים לי]

הגהות הב"ח

(א) רש"י ד"ה ה"ג הם ולא גוים וכו' והא קאמר נ"ב ע"ל ר"פ כל הזבחים דף טו ע"ב דגמ' מוכיח להדיא באופן אחר וע"ש בתוס' ד"ה אלא למעוטי וכו': (ב) ד"ה ה"ג נומי ר"ש וכו' כמו אמר ר"ש נ"ב וכ"כ בחולין דף ע ע"ב להדיא:

ופיגול לא נאמר בו חילול הס"ד נ"ק

במקריבו נ"ק

שיטה מקובצת

א] ובעובדי כוכבים. ע' רש"י לעיל (דף טו ע"ב): ב] כמאן דלא כרבי יוסי כו' האמר בכולן אני רואה אני: ג] אף דברים:

ד] הדם נומי ר"ש בדבר שדרכו לאכול חייב אבל העצים והלבונה כו' אין חייבין עליהן משום: ה] תלמוד לומר אשר הם מקדישים לי [illegible]

לכם

בשני חילולין הכתוב מדבר, אחד פסול נותר, ואחד פסול טומאה.§ "חוץ מן הדם" כו'.§ מנא הני מילי? *אמר עולא, אמר קרא: °"ואני נתתיו לכם" – א] שלכם יהא. דבי רבי ישמעאל תנא, אמר קרא: °"לכפר" – לכפרה נתתיו, ולא למעילה. רבי יוחנן אמר: אמר קרא °"הוא" – הוא לפני כפרה כלאחר כפרה, מה אחר כפרה אין בו מעילה – אף לפני כפרה אין בו מעילה. אימא: לאחר כפרה כלפני כפרה, מה לפני כפרה יש בו מעילה – אף לאחר כפרה יש בו מעילה! אין לך דבר שנעשית מצותו ומועלין בו. ולא? והרי תרומת הדשן! משום דהוי תרומת הדשן ובגדי כהונה שני כתובין הבאין כאחד, *וכל שני כתובים הבאין כאחד אין מלמדין. הניחא *לרבנן דאמרי: °"והניחם שם" – מלמד אשטעונין גניזה. אלא לרבי דוסא, דאמר: מותרות הן לכהן הדיוט, ובלבד שלא ישתמש בהן ליה"כ אחר, מאי איכא למימר? משום דהוי תרומת הדשן ועגלה ערופה שני כתובין הבאין כאחד, וכל שני כתובין הבאין כאחד אין מלמדין. הניחא למאן דאמר אין מלמדין, אלא למאן דאמר מלמדין, מאי איכא למימר? ב] תרי מיעוטי כתיבי, הכא כתיב: °"הערופה", והתם כתיב: °"ושמו". ותלתא קראי בדם למה לי? ג] למעוטי ממעילה מנותר ומטומאה. אבל פיגול לא צריך קרא, דתנן: *כל שיש לו מתירין בין לאדם בין למזבח – חייבין עליו משום פיגול, ודם ד] גופיה מתיר הוא. אמר רבי יוחנן: *שלשה כריתות בשלמים למה?

אחת

רש"י

בשני חילולים. מדלא כתיב "וינזרו ולא ה] יחללו". אחד פסול נותר. דאשכחן ביה חילול, דכתיב (ויקרא יט): "כי את קדש ה' חילל". ואתרוייהו קאי "אשר הם מקדישים", דמרבינן מיניה כל המוקדשים. מנא הני מילי. דדם אין חייבין עליו משום נותר, אם שגג בו בדם ונותר – אינו חייב שתים אלא אחת, וכן אם ו] אכלן בטומאת הגוף – אינו חייב שתים? אמר עולא אמר קרא כו'. הא דעולא לאו הכא איתמר, אלא גבי מעילה איתמר במס' מעילה (דף יא.), דקתני: אין מועלין בדמים. והכא ז] ה"ק: מנא הני מילי דמתניתין? אמר עולא: גבי מעילה אמר קרא "לכם", ותנא דבי רבי ישמעאל: "לכפר" כו', ור' יוחנן אמר: "הוא". ומסקנא: תלתא קראי, חד למעוטי מנותר, וחד למעוטי ח] ממעילה, וחד למעוטי מטומאה. ואני נתתיו לכם שלכם יהא. כחולין שלכם, שאין בהן מעילה. לכפר. "ואני נתתיו לכם על המזבח לכפר" (ויקרא יז) – לכפרה נתתיו בתורת קדשים ולא למעול בו, לענין מעילה אין בו דין קדשים. הוא. *"דמו בנפשו הוא" – בהווייתו יהא. הוא לפני כפרה כו' מה לאחר כפרה אין בו מעילה. דפשיטא לן כיון שנעשית מצותו אין מועלין בו, דכיון דלית ביה תו צורך גבוה – לא קרינן ביה "קדשי ה'". אין לך דבר כו'. הלכך ע"כ לא תדרשיה הכי, אלא איפכא. והרי תרומת הדשן. בכל יום חותה במחתה, ותורם את הדשן מלא המחתה ממנה ונותן במזרחו של כבש, כדכתיב "ושמו", משמע – ט] שם גניזתן ושם נבלע במקומן, אלמא אסור בהנאה! ובגדי כהונה. ארבעה בגדים שכהן גדול נכנס בהן לפני ולפנים ביוה"כ, שאסור להשתמש י] בו עוד, דכתיב: "ופשט את בגדי הבד וגו' והניחם שם", ודרשינן: מלמד שטעונין גניזה. פלוגתא דרבנן ורבי דוסא במס' יומא מייתי לה. לרבי דוסא דאמר כשרין הן לכהן [הדיוט]. לעבוד *כהן במקדש כל ימות השנה. ועגלה ערופה. דכתיב: "וערפו שם" (דברים כא), והאי "שם" קרא יתירא הוא, לומר יא] שתהא שם קבורתה. אין מלמדין. וכיון דלא ילפינן יב] ולא מייתי ראיה מינייהו – האי קרא נמי, הואיל ואיכא למדרשיה איפכא לא תדרשיה הכי. *מיעוטי כתיבי. לומר שאין למדין מהן. הערופה. זו ולא אחרת כזו. ושמו. מדהוה ליה למכתב "ושם" וכתיב "ושמו" – לזה ולא לאחר. תלתא קראי. "לכם", "לכפר", "הוא". למעוטי מנותר. "לכם" – יג] כשאר חולין ולא כקדשים, "לכפר" – לכפרה נתתיו כקדשים ולא לדבר אחר כקדשים, אלא כחולין, ולא יד] יתחייבו עליו משום טומאה. *"והוא" – למעוטי ממעילה, כדאמרן. שלשה כריתות. "אמור אליהם לדורותיכם" וגו' (ויקרא כב), "והנפש אשר תאכל בשר" וגו' (שם ז), "נפש כי תגע בכל טו] טומאת אדם" וגו' (שם).

אחת

תוספות

טו] **הכי** גרסינן: בשני חילולין הכתוב מדבר אחד פסול נותר. תימה לי: לעיל גבי קדשי גוים אתי נותר חילול חילול מטומאה, הלא חילול יז] טומאה נמי בנותר איירי! ועוד תימה: דבפ' "הנשרפין" (סנהדרין דף פג.) משמע דלא כתיב בנותר חילול דרבים, והכא משכחת לה מדתני! יח] ולעיל בריש פרק שני (דף טו:) פירשתי.

הוא לפני כפרה כלאחר כפרה. הקשה ר"ת: דבמעילה פרק יט] "[ולד] חטאת" (דף יב:) אמרינן: המקיז דם לבהמת קדשים – מועלין בו. אלמא יש מעילה בדם! ותירץ: דהתם כ] מחיים דלא שייכא כפרה, אבל לאחר שחיטה – אף לפני כפרה אין מועלין. וא"ת: דהתם כא] תני (דף יב.), ומייתי בפרק "כל שעה": דם בתחילה אין מועלין בו, יצא לנחל קדרון – מועלין! וי"ל: דמעילה דהתם דרבנן. וא"ת: א"כ, בריש מעילה (דף ג:) דדחיק לאשכוחי מי איכא מעילה דרבנן – לייתי מהך משנה! ועוד קשה: בסוף תמורה (דף לג:) גבי מקדיש עולה לבדק הבית, דקאמר שמועלין בה שתי מעילות, ופריך: אי מדרבנן אמאי ב' מעילות? כב] מאי קשה? הא איכא מעילה דדם שהיא דרבנן, וכן בקדשים שמתו בריש מעילה (דף ג.)! וי"ל: דהתם שיש מעילה דאורייתא משום כג] עולה – בדילי מיניה, ובדם דליכא מעילה דאורייתא כד] לא בדילי מיניה – תקינו רבנן מעילה. ובריש מעילה אקדשים ששחטן בדרום כה] קאי, דכמאן דחנקינון דמי, ועל כה"ג דחיק לאתויי ראיה דתקון רבנן מעילה אע"ג דבדילי מינייהו (כמו במתו, ומייתי כו] מרבי יוחנן דקדשים שמתו. וה"ר חיים היה מפרש: דיוצא לנחל קדרון – מועלין כז] דאורייתא, שב"ד מקדשין אותו שלא יהנו ממנו בלא פדיון. ודוחק הוא. ועוד: אכתי אמאי לא מייתי כח] בריש מעילה מההיא דסוף "התכלת" (מנחות דף נב.) גבי אפר פרה, דאמר: שתי תקנות הוו, מעיקרא תקינו בה מעילה? ואין לומר דמעיקרא נמי היתה מעילה דאורייתא, דתקון שיהיו ב"ד מקדשין אותו – א"כ היאך היו מזין? ועוד: דבמעילה בריש "ולד חטאת" (דף יב.) דאמר רבי יוחנן: קדשים שמתו יצאו מידי מעילה דבר תורה, אבל מדרבנן איכא מעילה. ופריך: מי איכא מידי דמעיקרא לית ביה מעילה, ולבסוף אית ביה מעילה? *ולא? והרי דם, דתנן בתחילתו כו'. ואי מעילה דנחל קדרון שבית דין מקדשין אותו – מאי קושיא? **אין** לך דבר שנעשית מצותו ומועלין בו. וא"ת: אדרבה, לא נמעט לפני כפרה, דאין לך [דבר] שלא נעשית מצותו שלא ימעלו. ואע"ג דאיכא קדשים קלים – היינו משום דלא איקרו "קדשי ה'"! וי"ל: דאשכחן טובא כט] דכותה דאין מועלין עד שעת מצותן, תרומת הדשן ועגלה ערופה עד אחר ירידתה. **ולא** והרי תרומת הדשן. והא דתנן במעילה פ' "ולד חטאת" (דף יא:): דישון מזבח הפנימי והמנורה לא נהנין ולא מועלין – היינו ל] מזבח הזהב מן הקטרת שנשרף עליו. והכא מזבח החיצון, שהיה חותה מלא המחתה מן המאוכלות הפנימיות ונותן במזרחו של כבש. ומיהו, בגמ' משמע התם דאף בחיצון אין מועלין, דקאמר: בשלמא מזבח החיצון דכתיב ביה "ושמו", אלא פנימי מנא לן? משמע דמ"ושמו" דריש דאין מועלין. ובשמעתא אדרבה, מ"ושמו" משמע ליה דמועלין! וי"ל: דמתני' דהתם משמע לא] דלא מועלין בדישון הפנימי – שהדישון מוציאו מידי מעילה, אבל קודם דישון מועלין, א"כ איכא מצוה לדשן. ועל זה קאמר: בשלמא חיצון דכתיב "ושמו" ולכך מצוה לדשן, לב] *מ"מ אף לאחר הרמה איכא מעילה כדדרשינן בסוף תמורה (דף לג.): "ושמו" – בנחת, "ושמו" – כולו, "ושמו" – שלא יפזר. אלא פנימי מנא לן דמצוה לדשן, שאתה אומר לג] שהדשן מוציאו מידי מעילה? ומשני: דאמר קרא "והסיר את מוראתו והשליך אל מקום הדשן". ובפ' שני *דיומא בירושלמי משמע כן קצת, דבעי ברישא: מנלן דעבדינן דישון כלל בפנימי? והדר בעי: מנלן שהדישון לד] אסור בהנאה? ואם תאמר: מוראה ונוצה ימעלו עד שיעשו מצותן שיושלכו אצל מזבח, כדישון מזבח הפנימי. ובתמורה (גז"ס) אמרינן: עולת העוף שנתמצה דמה, מוראה ונוצה – יצאו מידי מעילה! *וי"ל: שאני דישון מזבח הפנימי – דהיינו מצותו, אבל עולת העוף – עבודת דם מתיר מוראה ונוצה. וא"ת: *בקדושין (דף נה.) דאמר אין מועל אחר מועל אלא בהמה וכלי שרת – הא איכא תרומת הדשן דלא נפיק לחולין ע"י מעילה, כדמוכח בסוף תמורה! וי"ל: דהוי בכלל בהמה, דהיינו כמו אימורים דלא נפיק לחולין. **משום** דהוי תרומת הדשן ובגדי כהונה שני כתובין הבאין כאחד. במעילה פ' "ולד חטאת" (דף יא:) מאריך יותר, ומסקנא כדהכא. **עגלה** ערופה. פי' רש"י: מ"וערפו שם" כ"ל בפ"ק דכריתות (דף ו.). והאי דנ"ל בפ' "אין מעמידין" (ע"ז דף כט:) לה] מדכתיב בה כפרה כקדשים, י"ל: דשם צריך לאסור לאחר עריפה, שלא לומר: אין לך דבר שנעשית מצותו ומועלין בו*. **תרי** מיעוטי כתיבי. קשיא: דבחד סגי. וכן גבי "העוזים" בפרק "כל הבשר" (חולין דף קיג:)*. **חד** למעוטי מנותר וחד למעוטי מטומאה. תימה: לנותר וטומאה סגי בחד מיעוט, דילפינן מהדדי "חילול" "חילול". *ואף לקולא, כדלעיל גבי קדשי גוים! וי"ל: לו] דמוקמינא מיעוטא בנותר דוקא, אבל משום טומאה – הוה חייב, כי היכי דאין לו מתירין. כגון קומץ ומנחת כהנים, אע"ג דאין בהן פיגול יש בהן איסור טומאה, דמרבינן מ"אשר הם מקדישים", הכי הוה מרבינן נמי לגבי דם.

אחת

עין משפט נר מצוה

נו א מיי' פ"ח מהל' כלי המקדש הל' ה:

מסורת הש"ס

יומא נט: [מעילה יא. חולין קיז.]

[קדושין כד. וש"נ]

[נ"ל כי הדם הוא בנפש יכפר]

פסחים כו. יומא יב: כד. ס. כריתות ו. חולין קיז. מעילה יא:

לעיל מג. וש"נ

שבועות ז. [וכס איתא ר' אבהו]

(כהן נ"ק)

תרי מיעוטי נ"ק

הוא נ"ק

ומ"מ נ"ק

נ"א דתמורה

ועי' בתוספות דיומא נט ע"ב דמתלי בענין אחר

*משנה במעילה יט:

[ועי' תוספות קדושין נז. ד"ה כפרה]

[ועיין תוספות פסחים כו. ד"ה כתיב ותוס' מעילה יא. ד"ה תרי וביתר ביאור תילנו ביומא ס. ד"ה תרי ע"ש אבל בחולין קיג: ד"ה עזים ודף קיז: ד"ה תרי הניחו בתימה]

גליון הש"ס

תוס' ד"ה חד וכו' ואף לקולא וכו'. עי' קדושין ג ע"א תוס' ד"ה ואמא וכו'.

תורה אור

(ויקרא יז) (שם) (שם) (שם טז) (דברים כא) (ויקרא ו)

שיטה מקובצת

א] לכם לכם שלכם: ב] למימר מעוטי ותיבת תרי נמחק: ג] לי חד למעוטי מנותר וחד למעוטי מטומאה וחד למעוטי ממעילה. תימה למה לי תרי מיעוטא [בנותר וטומאה] בחדא סגי דילפינן מהדדי בג"ש חילול חילול אף לקולא כדלעיל וי"ל דאי (לאו) [לא] כתיב אלא חדא מיעוטא הוי מוקמינן ליה אנותר וטומאה לא הוי ילפינן מיניה דהוי מרבינן ליה מאשר הם מקדישים לי. מהר"פ: ד] ודם הוא גופיה: ה] ולא יחללו הס"ד: ו] אכלו בטומאת: ז] והכא ס"א נמי אמרי' מנא הני מילי כו': ח] למעוטי מטומאה וחד למעוטי ממעילה: ט] משמע ששם גניזתו ושם נבלע במקומו אלמא: י] בהן עוד: יא] שם תהא קבורתה: יב] ילפינן מינייהו ולא: יג] כשאר. ס"א בשר חולין: יד] ולא שיתחייבו עליו: טו] בכל טמא בטומאת אדם: טז] מה"ד הג"ה בשני ותיבות הכי גרסינן נמחק: יז] חילול דטומאה נמי: יח] מדתני לוי: יט] פרק ולד חטאת: כ] דהתם מיירי מחיים: כא] דהתם תנן ומייתי לה בפ' כל שעה: כב] מאי קושיא הא: כג] עולה בדילי אינשי מיניה כבר אבל (הני) בעוד דליכא. ס"א עולה אין לחכמים לתקן מעילה כיון דבלאו הכי בדילי ומשני ראוי למעול שתי מעילות (בבשר אינה מעילה דאורייתא משום עולה) [דתקון רבנן מעילה אעור משום דליכא מעילה מדאורייתא אלא בבשר א"כ לא] ותיבת ובדם ל"ש ונמחק: כד] דאורייתא א"כ לא: כה] קאמר דכמאן דחנקינו דמי: כו] ומייתי מדר' יוחנן: כז] מועלין בו מדאורייתא: כח] מייתי ראיה בריש: כט] טובא [דכוותה] הוא דאין מועלין: ל] היינו דמזבח הזהב כו' והכא במזבח החיצון שהיה כו' דאף בדחיצון אין מועלין כו': לא] משמע דאין מועלין תיבת דלא נמחק: לב] לדשן ומ"מ אף: לג] שהדישון מוציאו: לד] שהדישון בפנימי אסור. וא"ת א"כ מוראה ונוצה ימעלו בהם עד שיעשו כו' הפנימי ובסוף תמורה אמרי' דעולת העוף שנתמצה כו' עבודת הדם מתיר מוראה ונוצה וא"ת כו' דלא נפקי לחולין הס"ד: לה] אין מעמידין כפרה כתיב בה בקדשים י"ל כו' לאחר עריפה דלא נימא אין לך דבר: לו] וי"ל דהוה מוקמינא מיעוטא כו' הוה אמינא חייב כי היכי:

משום

נז א מיי' פי"ח מהל' פסה"מ הל' טז:
נח ב מיי' פ"ח מהל' טומאת אוכלין הל"ט ופ"ו מהלכות אסורי מזבח הלכה ח:
נט ג מיי' פ"ד מהל' מעה"ק הל' יח:
ס ד מיי' פט"ו מהלכות מעה"ק הלכה ד:
סא ה מיי' פט"ו מהל' פסה"מ הל' ז:

[לעיל מג. ושנ"ן]

אחת לכלל ואחת פרט. לאו כלל ופרט ממש, כד] דמרוחקים זה מזה הן. אלא, דבר שהיה בכלל ויצא מן הכלל – ללמד על הכלל כולו יצא, כדדרשינן כה] עולה בפ"ק דיבמות (דף ז.), וממעטינן קדשי בדק הבית. וא"ת: כו] קדשי בדק הבית נמי תיפוק לי מ"יקרב", דדרשי' בכשר ליקרב! וי"ל: דהוה אמינא כי בעינן כז] כשר ליקרב – הני מילי בקדשי מזבח. וא"ת: הא דאמר ב"הקומץ רבה" (מנחות דף כה:): "כל טהור יאכל בשר" – הניתר לטהורים חייבין עליו משום טומאה כו', למעוטי בשר לפני זריקה. תיפוק ליה מ"יקרב" דדרשינן לעיל: כח] בכשר ליקרב, הא כיצד? יש לו מתירין – משיקרבו מתירין כו'! וי"ל: דצריכי, דאי כתב רחמנא "כל טהור" ולא כתב "יקרב" הוה אמינא דקודם זריקה חשיב ניתר לטהורים, כיון דיכול לזרוק לכתחילה, ולא הוה ממעטי' אלא טמא לפני זריקה, *לן ויולא. ועוד: איצטריך "יקרב" לאין לו מתירין משיקדש בכלי. ואי כתב רחמנא "יקרב" ולא כתב "כל טהור", הוה אמינא: אפילו פיגולין ונותרות. ולא הוה אמינא "מזבח השלמים" מיעוט, אי לאו קרא דניתר לטהורים. **אבל** בטומאת הגוף דברי הכל אינו לוקה. וא"ת: והא אמינן לעיל: שלש כריתות בשלמים, חד לדברים שאינן נאכלין. כט] לכל הפחות תפשוט דר' יוחנן דאמר כמחלוקת בזו כך מחלוקת בזו! ל] ועוד תניא במעילה (דף י.) גבי לבונה: וחייבים עליה משום פיגול ונותר וטמא! וי"ל: דדוקא מלקות קאמר, דאינו לוקה, דלא איתרבו אלא לענין כרת. ומיהו, לא משמע הכי, מדקאמר: כיון דקרינן ביה "והבשר אשר יגע" קרינן ביה "וטומאתו עליו", משמע דאיירי נמי לענין כרת.

מחלוקת בטומאת בשר. הך פלוגתא דהכא, בין ללישנא קמא בין ללישנא בתרא – לא שייכא לפלוגתא דרבי יוחנן ור"ל דטמא שאכל בשר קדש לפני זריקה בפ' "כל הפסולין" (לעיל דף לד.), ובין לאביי ובין לרבא דהתם יש ליישב. וק"ל.

מנין

אַחַת לִכְלָל, וְאַחַת לִפְרָט, וְאַחַת לִדְבָרִים שֶׁאֵינָן נֶאֱכָלִין. וּלְרַבִּי שִׁמְעוֹן, דְּאָמַר: דְּבָרִים שֶׁאֵין נֶאֱכָלִין – אֵין חַיָּיבִין עֲלֵיהֶם מִשּׁוּם טוּמְאָה, לְאִיתוּיֵי מַאי? לְאִיתוּיֵי אחַטָּאוֹת הַפְּנִימִיּוֹת. ס"ד אָמִינָא, הוֹאִיל *וְאָמַר רַבִּי שִׁמְעוֹן: כָּל שֶׁאֵינוֹ עַל מִזְבֵּחַ הַחִיצוֹן כִּשְׁלָמִים אֵין חַיָּיבִין עָלָיו מִשּׁוּם פִּיגּוּל – א] מִשּׁוּם טוּמְאָה נַמִי לָא לִיחַיֵּיב, קמ"ל.§ "נוֹמִי ר' שִׁמְעוֹן ב] מְחַיֵּיב אֶת שֶׁדַּרְכּוֹ לֶאֱכוֹל" כו'.§ אִיתְּמַר, רַבִּי יוֹחָנָן וְרֵישׁ לָקִישׁ, רַבִּי אֶלְעָזָר וְרַבִּי יוֹסֵי בְּרַבִּי חֲנִינָא, חַד מֵהַאי ג] זוּזָא וְחַד מֵהַאי זוּזָא, חַד אָמַר: מַחֲלוֹקֶת בְּטוּמְאַת בָּשָׂר, אֲבָל בְּטוּמְאַת הַגּוּף – דִּבְרֵי הַכֹּל אֵינוֹ לוֹקֶה. וְחַד אָמַר: כְּמַחֲלוֹקֶת בָּזוֹ כָּךְ מַחֲלוֹקֶת בָּזוֹ, ד] מַאי טַעְמָא? כֵּיוָן דְּקָרֵינָא בֵּיהּ: °"וְהַבָּשָׂר אֲשֶׁר יִגַּע בְּכָל טָמֵא" (ויקרא ז) – קָרֵינַן בֵּיהּ: °"וְטוּמְאָתוֹ עָלָיו". רַב טַבְיוּמֵי מַתְנֵי (שם) הָכִי. רַב כָּהֲנָא מַתְנֵי ה] הָכִי: חַד מֵהַאי זוּזָא וְחַד מֵהַאי זוּזָא אַסֵּיפָא, חַד אָמַר: מַחֲלוֹקֶת בְּטוּמְאַת הַגּוּף, אֲבָל בְּטוּמְאַת בָּשָׂר – דִּבְרֵי הַכֹּל לוֹקֶה. וְחַד אָמַר: כְּמַחֲלוֹקֶת בָּזוֹ כָּךְ מַחֲלוֹקֶת בָּזוֹ. אָמַר רָבָא: מִסְתַּבְּרָא כְּמ"ד כְּמַחֲלוֹקֶת בָּזוֹ כָּךְ מַחֲלוֹקֶת בָּזוֹ, מַאי טַעְמָא? כֵּיוָן דְּלָא קָרֵינָא בֵּיהּ: "וְטוּמְאָתוֹ עָלָיו וְנִכְרְתָה" – לָא קָרֵינַן בֵּיהּ: "וְהַבָּשָׂר אֲשֶׁר יִגַּע בְּכָל טָמֵא לֹא יֵאָכֵל". *וְהָאָמַר מָר: וְהַבָּשָׂר" – בלְרַבּוֹת עֵצִים ו] וּלְבוֹנָה! לְפוֹסְלָהּ בְּעָלְמָא.§

מתני' *לְשֵׁם שִׁשָּׁה דְּבָרִים הַזֶּבַח נִזְבָּח: גלְשֵׁם זֶבַח, לְשֵׁם זוֹבֵחַ, לְשֵׁם הַשֵּׁם, לְשֵׁם אִשִּׁים, לְשֵׁם רֵיחַ, לְשֵׁם נִיחוֹחַ. וְהַחַטָּאת וְהָאָשָׁם – לְשֵׁם חֵטְא. אָמַר רַבִּי יוֹסֵי: ז] אַף מִי שֶׁלֹּא הָיָה בְּלִבּוֹ לְשֵׁם אֶחָד מִכָּל אֵלּוּ – כָּשֵׁר, שֶׁהוּא תְּנַאי בֵּית דִּין, שֶׁאֵין הַמַּחֲשָׁבָה הוֹלֶכֶת אֶלָּא אַחַר הָעוֹבֵד.§ **גמ'** אָמַר רַב יְהוּדָה אָמַר רַב: "עוֹלָה" – לְשֵׁם עוֹלָה, לְאַפּוּקֵי לְשֵׁם שְׁלָמִים דְּלָא. "אִשִּׁים" – לְשֵׁם אִשִּׁים, לְאַפּוּקֵי כְּבָבָא דְּלָא. "רֵיחַ" – לְשֵׁם רֵיחַ, לְאַפּוּקֵי אֵבָרִים שֶׁצְּלָאָן וְהֶעֱלָן, דְּלָא;* דְּאָמַר רַב יְהוּדָה אָמַר רַב: דאֵבָרִים שֶׁצְּלָאָן וְהֶעֱלָן – אֵין בָּהֶן מִשּׁוּם רֵיחַ. "נִיחוֹחַ" – לְשֵׁם הֲנָחַת רוּחַ. "לַה'" – לְשֵׁם מִי שֶׁאָמַר וְהָיָה הָעוֹלָם. *אָמַר רַב יְהוּדָה אָמַר רַב: החַטָּאת שֶׁשְּׁחָטָהּ לְשֵׁם עוֹלָה – פְּסוּלָה, לְשֵׁם חוּלִּין – כְּשֵׁרָה. אָמַר ר' ח] אֶלְעָזָר: מ"ט דְּרַב? °"וְלֹא יְחַלְּלוּ אֶת קָדְשֵׁי בְּנֵי יִשְׂרָאֵל" (שם כב), קָדָשִׁים מְחַלְּלִין קָדָשִׁים, וְאֵין חוּלִּין מְחַלְּלִין קָדָשִׁים.§ מְתִיב רַבָּה: אָמַר רַבִּי יוֹסֵי: ט] אַף מִי שֶׁלֹּא הָיָה בְּלִבּוֹ לְשֵׁם אֶחָד מִכָּל אֵלּוּ – כָּשֵׁר, שֶׁהוּא תְּנַאי ב"ד; טַעְמָא שֶׁלֹּא הָיָה בְּלִבּוֹ כְּלָל, הָא הָיָה בְּלִבּוֹ לְשֵׁם חוּלִּין – פָּסוּל! א"ל אַבַּיֵי: י] דִּלְמָא, לֹא הָיָה כְּלָל – כָּשֵׁר וּמְרַצֶּה, הָא הָיָה בְּלִבּוֹ לְשֵׁם חוּלִּין – כָּשֵׁר וְאֵינוֹ מְרַצֶּה. א"ר יא] אֶלְעָזָר: חַטָּאת שֶׁשְּׁחָטָהּ לְשֵׁם חוּלִּין – כְּשֵׁרָה, מִשּׁוּם חוּלִּין – פְּסוּלָה. כִּדְבָעָא מִינֵּיהּ שְׁמוּאֵל מֵרַב הוּנָא:

מִנַּיִן

אַחַת לִכְלָל וְאַחַת לִפְרָט. לִדְרוֹשׁ: דָּבָר שֶׁהָיָה בִּכְלָל וְיָצָא מִן הַכְּלָל לְלַמֵּד, לֹא לְלַמֵּד עַל עַצְמוֹ יָצָא אֶלָּא לְלַמֵּד עַל הַכְּלָל כּוּלּוֹ יָצָא. יב] "וְהַנֶּפֶשׁ אֲשֶׁר תֹּאכַל בָּשָׂר [מִזֶּבַח הַשְּׁלָמִים]" (ויקרא ז), וַהֲלֹא שְׁלָמִים בִּכְלַל כָּל *הַקֳּדָשִׁים הָיוּ, וְלָמָּה יָצְאוּ – לְהַקִּישׁ אֲלֵיהֶם, וְלוֹמַר לְךָ: מַה שְּׁלָמִים מְיוּחָדִים קָדְשֵׁי מִזְבֵּחַ – תורה אור אַף כָּל קָדְשֵׁי מִזְבֵּחַ. (בִּכְלַל כָּל הַקֳּדָשִׁים – "אֶל הַקֳּדָשִׁים אֲשֶׁר יַקְדִּישׁוּ בְנֵי יִשְׂרָאֵל יג] וְטוּמְאָתוֹ עָלָיו" (שם כב) כָּל הַקֳּדָשִׁים בִּכְלָל). לִדְבָרִים שֶׁאֵינָן נֶאֱכָלִין. כְּגוֹן עֵצִים וּלְבוֹנָה שֶׁאֵינָן רְאוּיִם לַאֲכִילָה, אִם אָכַל מֵהֶם בְּטוּמְאַת הַגּוּף – חַיָּיב, כְּרַבָּנַן דְּמַתְנִיתִין. וּלְר"שׁ. דְּמַתְנִי'. חַד מֵהַאי יד] זוּזָא. אָמְרֵי חֲדָא מִילְּתָא, וְאִיכָּא תְּרֵי חֲדָא מִילְּתָא. חַד אָמַר. חַד מֵהַאי טו] זוּזָא אָמַר: מַחֲלוֹקֶת שֶׁנֶּחְלְקוּ חֲכָמִים עַל רַבִּי שִׁמְעוֹן שֶׁחִיֵּיב. בְּטוּמְאַת בָּשָׂר. אִם אֲכָלָן לָעֵצִים וּלְבוֹנָה טְמֵאִין – לוֹקֶה מִשּׁוּם לָאו דְּ"וְהַבָּשָׂר אֲשֶׁר יִגַּע בְּכָל טָמֵא" וגו' (ויקרא ז), דְּאָמַר מָר (חולין דף לו:): "וְהַבָּשָׂר" יְתֵירָא – לְרַבּוֹת עֵצִים וּלְבוֹנָה. אֲבָל בְּטוּמְאַת הַגּוּף. וְהֵן טְהוֹרִים – דִּבְרֵי הַכֹּל אֵינוֹ לוֹקֶה, דְּלָא אִיתְרַבּוּ בָּהּ. הָכִי גָּרְסִינַן: כֵּיוָן דְּקָרֵינַן בֵּיהּ וְהַבָּשָׂר אֲשֶׁר יִגַּע וגו' קָרֵינָא בֵּיהּ וְטוּמְאָתוֹ עָלָיו וְנִכְרְתָה. כְּלוֹמַר, כֵּיוָן דִּבְטוּמְאַת בָּשָׂר אָמְרֵי רַבָּנַן לוֹקֶה – הָעֵצִים וּלְבוֹנָה בְּטוּמְאַת הַגּוּף נַמִי אִית לְהוּ דְּלוֹקֶה, דְּהָא גַּבֵּי הֲדָדֵי כְּתִיבִי. אַסֵּיפָא. אַמִּילְּתֵיהּ דְּר"שׁ. וְהָכִי אָמְרִינַן: מַחֲלוֹקֶת דְּרַבִּי שִׁמְעוֹן אַדְּרַבָּנַן דְּלָא לָקֵי – בְּטוּמְאַת הַגּוּף, דְּלָא רַבִּי רַחֲמָנָא. אֲבָל בְּטוּמְאַת עַצְמָן, דְּרַבִּינְהוּ קְרָא – דִּבְרֵי הַכֹּל לוֹקֶה. כֵּיוָן דְּלָא קָרֵינַן בְּהוּ. בְּעֵצִים וּלְבוֹנָה לְרַבִּי שִׁמְעוֹן "וְטוּמְאָתוֹ עָלָיו" דְּטוּמְאַת הַגּוּף – לָא קָרֵינַן בְּהוּ "וְהַבָּשָׂר אֲשֶׁר יִגַּע" וגו'. לְפוֹסְלָא בְּעָלְמָא. וּמַעֲלָה דְּרַבָּנַן הִיא, וּקְרָא אַסְמַכְתָּא טז] בְּעָלְמָא הוּא. וְהָכִי אָמְרִי' בִּפְסָחִים (דף כד:) וְאֵין לוֹקִין עָלָיו. **מתני'** לְשֵׁם זֶבַח. לְאַפּוּקֵי שִׁנּוּי קֹדֶשׁ, כְּגוֹן לְשֵׁם זֶבַח אַחֵר. לְשֵׁם זוֹבֵחַ. לְאַפּוּקֵי שִׁנּוּי בְּעָלִים. וְהָא יָלְפִינַן לְהוּ מִקְּרָאֵי בְּפ"ק (לעיל ד:). לְשֵׁם אִשִּׁים לְשֵׁם רֵיחַ. בַּגְּמָרָא מְפָרֵשׁ לְאַפּוּקֵי מַאי, וְיָלֵיף לָהּ מִקְּרָא. לְשֵׁם חֵטְא. לְשֵׁם חֶטְאוֹ שֶׁהוּא מְבִיאוֹ עָלָיו. אַף מִי שֶׁלֹּא הָיָה בְּלִבּוֹ כו'. שֶׁשָּׁחַט סְתָם כָּשֵׁר. שֶׁהוּא תְּנַאי בֵּית דִּין. יז] שֶׁיִּשָּׁחֵט סְתָם, כִּדְאָמְרַן בְּפ"ק (לעיל ב:): יח] הִתְנוּ בֵּית דִּין דְּלָא לֵימָא לִשְׁמוֹ, דִּלְמָא אָתֵי לְמֵימַר שֶׁלֹּא לִשְׁמוֹ. שֶׁאֵין הַמַּחֲשָׁבָה הוֹלֶכֶת אֶלָּא אַחַר הָעוֹבֵד. הִלְכָּךְ, אִי הֲוָה יט] שֶׁלֹּא לִשְׁמוֹ, אַע"ג דִּבְעָלִים אָמְרֵי לִשְׁמוֹ – לָאו מִידֵּי הוּא, דְּלָאו בְּדִידְהוּ תַּלְיָא מִילְּתָא, דִּכְתִיב: "הַמַּקְרִיב אוֹתוֹ לֹא יֵחָשֵׁב" (ויקרא ז). **גמ'** עוֹלָה לְשֵׁם עוֹלָה כו'. קְרָא קָדָרֵישׁ, "עוֹלָה אִשֵּׁה רֵיחַ נִיחוֹחַ לַה'" (ויקרא א). וְאַע"ג דְּלָאו בִּשְׁחִיטָה כְּתִיב – אַשְׁכְּחַן לֵיהּ בִּשְׁלָמִים גַּבֵּי זְבִיחָה "וְהִקְרִיב מִזֶּבַח הַשְּׁלָמִים אִשֶּׁה לַה'" (שם ג) – שְׁמַעְנָא זְבִיחָה לְשֵׁם שְׁלָמִים, לְשֵׁם אִשִּׁים, לְשֵׁם כ] שֵׁם. וְהַאי דִּנְקַט הָכָא קְרָא דְעוֹלָה – מִשּׁוּם דִּכְתִיבִי כּוּלְּהוּ גַּבֵּיהּ, וְגַבֵּי שְׁלָמִים לָא כְּתִיב בְּהַהוּא קְרָא "לְרֵיחַ נִיחוֹחַ". לְאַפּוּקֵי כְּבָבָא. ע"מ לַעֲשׂוֹתוֹ חֲתִיכוֹת לְצְלוֹיוֹת בְּגֶחָלִים, *קרבוניא"ש בְּלַעַ"ז. וְדוּגְמָתוֹ בְּעֵירוּבִין כא] (דף כט:): וְנַיְיתֵי *הוּגְנָא דַּעֲרָבְתָּא וְנִכְבֵּיב וְנֵיכוּל. כב] אֵין בָּהֶם מִשּׁוּם רֵיחַ. דְּכֵיוָן דִּצְלָאָן תְּחִילָּה חוּץ לַמַּעֲרָכָה – תּוּ לָא מַסְּקֵי רֵיחָא. הֲנָחַת רוּחַ. נַחַת רוּחַ לִפְנֵי הַקָּדוֹשׁ בָּרוּךְ הוּא, שֶׁאָמַר וְנַעֲשָׂה רְצוֹנוֹ. וְלֹא יְחַלְּלוּ. אֵין דָּבָר אַחֵר מְחַלֵּל אֶת קָדָשִׁים, אֶלָּא מִי מְחַלְּלוֹ – קָדָשִׁים מְחַלְּלִין קָדָשִׁים, כִּדְנָפְקָא לָן (לעיל ה.) דְּמַחֲשָׁבָה שֶׁלֹּא לִשְׁמוֹ מִתְחַלְּלִים, מִ"וְשָׁחַט אוֹתָהּ לְחַטָּאת". טַעְמָא דְּלֹא הָיָה בְּלִבּוֹ כְּלָל. שֶׁשְּׁחָטוֹ סְתָם, וּמִמֵּילָא קָרֵב לִשְׁמוֹ. הָא לְשֵׁם חוּלִּין כָּשֵׁר וְאֵינוֹ מְרַצֶּה. וְכִי אָמַר רַב נַמִי כְּשֵׁרָה – וְאֵינָהּ מְרַצָּה קָאָמַר. לְשֵׁם חוּלִּין. שֶׁיּוֹדֵעַ שֶׁהִיא חַטָּאת וְשָׁחַט לְשֵׁם חוּלִּין – כְּשֵׁרָה, כִּדַאֲמָרַן שֶׁאֵין חוּלִּין מְחַלְּלִין קָדָשִׁים. מִשּׁוּם חוּלִּין. כְּסָבוּר כג] שֶׁהֵם חוּלִּין – פְּסוּלָה, דְּהַיְינוּ מִתְעַסֵּק בִּדְבָרִים אֲחֵרִים, וְאֵינוֹ עָסוּק בְּקָדָשִׁים.

לַמִּתְעַסֵּק

גי' נ"ק לן ויולא להכי איצטריך יקרב לאין לו מתירין משיקרבו מתירין ועוד איצטריך כו'

גי' נ"ק הקדשים היו אלו הקדשים אשר יקדישו בני ישראל וטומאתו עליו כל הקדשים בכלל ולמה יצאו כו' נ"ק בשם ס"ו ונמחק מן בכלל עד הקדשים בכלל

חולין לו: ושנ"נ

לעיל ב:

מנחות כה.

לעיל ג.

שם איתא לייתי סוגיינא

שיטה מקובצת

א] משום טומאה נמי לא ליחייב וקשה דמשמע דהא בהא תליא והרי מנחת נסכים וכו' דאין חייב (עליו) [עליהן] משום פיגול וחייב עליו משום טומאה לכך נראה (דפריך) [דה"פ] משום דאמר שלמים יצא מן הכלל ללמד על טומאה וסד"א דכי היכי דלר"ש דריש משלמים דלגבי פיגול דוקא בדבר שהוא על מזבח החיצון כשלמים חייבין עליו משום פיגול ה"נ נימא דר"ש דריש משלמים דגבי טומאה דוקא דבר שהוא על מזבח החיצון כשלמים חייבין עליו משום טומאה קמ"ל. מהר"פ ז"ל: ב] תיבת מחייב נמחק: ג] מהאי זווא וחד מהאי זווא: ד] מחלוקת בזו אמר רבא מסתברא כמ"ד כמחלוקת בזו כך מחלוקת בזו מאי: ה] כהנא מתני חד ותיבת הכי נמחק: ו] ולבונה לפסולא בעלמא פ"ה ומעלה דרבנן הוא וקרא אסמכתא בעלמא הוא וקשה דבחולין מוכח דעושה שני ואם כן דאורייתא הוא וי"ל לפסולא בעלמא ולא ללקות עליו ולעולם דאורייתא הוא. מהר"פ ז"ל: ז] יוסי שמעתי שאף מי: ח] אלעאי תיבת אלעזר נמחק: ט] יוסי שמעתי שאף מי: י] דילמא לא היה בלבו כלל כשר ומרצה תימה מנ"ל למידק הכי הא איכא מחשבות כמו לשם ריח ניחוח לא מצינא למידק הכי הא לשם חולין אינה מרצה דפשיטא דמחשבת חולין לא פסלא באימורין דהן עצמן שלא הקטירו אימוריו כשר וי"ל דמ"מ משמע ליה מדנקט שלא היה בלבו דלגבי היכא דמצינו למידק דייקינן וא"ת מנ"ל למידק הכי ממילתיה דר"י אדרבה לישנא דר"י משמע לא מבעיא היה בלבו לשם אלו דכשר [אבל] למידק הא היה בלבו לשם חולין כשר היכי משמע כלל וצ"ע: יא] אלעאי תיבת אלעזר נמחק: יב] יצא כיצד והנפש אשר תאכל בשר וגו' והלא: יג] ישראל לה' וטומאתו: יד] חד מהאי זווא וחד מהאי זווא: טו] זווא אמר כו' שמעון לומר שחייב הס"ד: טז] אסמכתא עיין לעיל (דף לד ע"א) בתוס' ד"ה ואפי': יז] דין שישחטו ב"ד: יט] הוה אמר שלא: כ] לשם השם והאי דנקט כו' קרא ריח ניחוח הס"ד: כא] בעירובין בבבל מערבין (דף כט ע"ב) ונייתי סווינא דערבתא: כב] וניכול הס"ד מה"ד דלא כלומר שצריך שיהא שיצלאנו האש לגמרי ולא יורידנו משנצלה מעט הס"ד: כג] כסבור שהיא חולין פסולה: כד] ממש דהא הפרט בשלמים כתיב וכלל בפרשת אמור וא"כ הוי פרט וכלל ואיתרבי כל מילי אלא כיון דמרוחקים זה מזה הן אין דנין אותו בפרט וכלל אלא דרשינן בדבר שהיה: כה] כדדרשינן בפ"ק דיבמות שלמים בכלל כל הקדשים היו ולמה יצאו לומר לך מה שלמים קדשי מזבח אף כל קדשי: כו] וא"ת למה לי למעוטי קדשי בדק הבית תיפוק לי מדכתיב כל איש אשר יקרב דדרשינן לעיל בהוכשר ליקרב: כז] הוכשר ליקרב ה"מ בקדשי מזבח וכן הא דדרשינן לעיל באינו ניתר לטהורים אינו חייבין עליו משום טומאה והר"ר יעקב מקינון פי' דה"פ (דכאשר) [דאשר] יקרב בהוכשר ליקרב קאמר ולא בנוגע ממש היינו מכח האי פרט דשלמים שיצא מן הכלל ללמד כו' ובשלמים כתיב בהדיא אכילה ומיניהו שמעינן דבכל הקדשים נמי לא מיחייב אלא באכילה והלכך ע"כ אשר יקרב לאו בנוגע קאמר אבל בקונטרס פי' [illegible] לשון מהר"פ: כח] לעיל בהוכשר: כט] נאכלין וטומאת הגוף הוא לכל הפחות תפשוט דר' יוחנן הוא דאמר: ל] בזו [illegible] הגוף וי"ל דדוקא למלקות קאמר דאינו לוקה [illegible] אינו חייב ומיהו [illegible] עד כרת [illegible] ביה והבשר [אשר יגע בכל טמא] קרינן ביה וטומאתו עליו [illegible] לשון הר"פ:

לדעתכם

מנין למתעסק בקדשים שהוא פסול? שנאמר: "ושחט את בן הבקר לפני ה'" — עד שתהא שחיטה לשם בן בקר. א"ל: זו בידינו היא, לעכב מנין? א"ל: "לרצונכם תזבחהו" — לדעתכם [א] זביחו.§ ב"שאין המחשבה הולכת אלא אחר העובד".§ מתני' דלא כי האי תנא. דתניא, *א"ר אלעזר ברבי יוסי: שמעתי שהבעלים מפגלין. אמר רבא: מ"ט דרבי אלעזר ברבי יוסי? דאמר קרא: "והקריב המקריב". אמר אביי: רבי אלעזר ברבי יוסי, ורבי אליעזר, ור"ש בן אלעזר — כולהו סבירא להו: זה מחשב וזה עובד — הויא מחשבה; רבי אלעזר ברבי יוסי — הא דאמרן; רבי אליעזר — דתנן: *גהשוחט לגוי — שחיטתו כשרה, ורבי אליעזר פוסל; ר"ש בן אלעזר — [ב] *דתנן, *כלל אמר רבי שמעון בן אלעזר: כל שאין כשר להצניע, ואין מצניעין כמוהו, הוכשר לזה והצניעו, ובא אחר והוציאו — נתחייב זה במחשבה של זה. [ג] תרווייהו אית להו דרבי אלעזר ברבי יוסי, השתא בחוץ אמרינן — בפנים מיבעיא? רבי אלעזר ברבי יוסי לית [ד] להו דתרווייהו, דלמא בפנים הוא (א) דאמרינן, בחוץ לא אמרינן. ר"ש בן אלעזר אית ליה דר' אליעזר, השתא בשבת אמרינן, בעבודה זרה מיבעיא? רבי אליעזר לית ליה דרבי שמעון בן אלעזר, דלמא בעבודה זרה הוא דאמרת כעין [ה] בפנים, אבל *שבת — מלאכת מחשבת אסרה תורה.§

הדרן עלך בית שמאי

איזהו מקומן של זבחים? קדשי קדשים דשחיטתן בצפון. פר ושעיר של יום הכיפורים — שחיטתן בצפון, הוקיבול דמן בכלי שרת בצפון, ודמן טעון הזיה על בין הבדים ועל הפרוכת ועל מזבח הזהב, [ו] מתנה אחת מהן מעכבת. שירי הדם היה שופך על יסוד מערבי של מזבח החיצון, ואם לא נתן — לא עכב.§ זפרים הנשרפים ושעירים הנשרפים — שחיטתן בצפון, וקיבול דמן בכלי שרת בצפון, ודמן טעון הזיה על הפרוכת ועל מזבח הזהב, מתנה

תורה אור: ויקרא א — שם יט

רש"י

למתעסק בקדשים. שוחט קדשים ולא בכוונה, אלא כמתעסק בדברים אחרים. בידינו הוא. ראיה [ז] זאת כבר ידענו אותה. ומיהו, מצוה הוא דנפקא לן ולא עיכוב. שמעתי שהבעלים מפגלין. בעבודת הכהן, אם קיבל הכהן בשתיקה וחישבו הבעלים עליה על פיגול — הוי פיגול. והקריב המקריב. קרבנו. בפרשת נסכים כתיב: "והקריב המקריב קרבנו לה'" (במדבר טו), אלמא [ח] מקריב קרבנו קרי ליה, הלכך הוו להו בכלל "המקריב לא יחשב". ורבי אליעזר פוסל. התם מפרש בהדיא: שסתם מחשבת גוי לעבודה זרה. ואע"ג [ט] דלאו איהו שחיט לה — פסול. שאין כשר להצניע. במסכת שבת, כגון דם נדה או איסור [י] (או) הנאה. ואין מצניעין כמוהו. שכשר הוא להצניעו אם היה [יא] שיעורו, אבל שיעורו של זה מועט הוא, ואין אדם חושבו להצניעו. ובא אחר והוציאו. בשבת לרה"ר — חייב, דחשיב מלאכה מפני מחשבתו של זה שהוכשר לו והצניעו. ותרווייהו. רבי אליעזר ור"ש בן אלעזר. השתא בחוץ. בעבודה זרה ושבת, דלא כתיבא בהו מחשבה בהדיא, אמרינן: זה מחשב וזה עושה — [יב] הוי מחשבה. בפנים. בקרבנות, דמחשבה בהו כתיבא, מיבעיא? בפנים הוא דאמר. משום דעיקר [יג] מחשבות בקרבנות כתיבא. אבל בחוץ. כגון עבודה זרה ושבת — לא. בעבודה זרה מיבעיא. דעבודה זרה דומיא דעבודת פנים חייב בה רחמנא, כדאמרי' ב"ארבע מיתות" (סנהדרין ס:): "זובח לאלהים יחרם בלתי לה'" — [יד] עבודות הראויות למקום חייב בהו בעבודה זרה, בין שדרכה בכך בין שאין דרכה בכך. הלכך, לענין מחשבה נמי איכא למיגמרה מבפנים. מלאכת מחשבת אסרה תורה. שנסמכה [טו] שבת לפרשת המשכן ב"ויקהל". ומלאכת מחשבת — שהעושה אותה מתכוין למלאכה גמורה, אלא ששגג בשבת, או סבור שמלאכה זו מותרת. *וזה — שיעור זה חשוב בעיניו, אינו מתכוין למלאכה.

הדרן עלך בית שמאי

קדשי קדשים. כולן בכלל: חטאות ואשמות ועולה ושלמי ציבור. ומיהו, משום דחלוקין במתן דמים או [טז] בהקטרתן הדר תני להו כל חד וחד באפי נפשיה לפרש הלכותיהן. שחיטתן בצפון. ובגמ' מפרש מ"ט לא תנא "וקבול דמן", ומ"ש דתנן חטאות הפנימיות ברישא. פר ושעיר של יום הכפורים כו'. בגמ' יליף טעמא מנא לן דשחיטתן וקיבול דמן [יז] בכלי שרת בצפון. בכלי שרת. דכתיב [יח] בעולה בסיני: "וישם באגנות" (שמות כד), וממנה למדו כל הזבחים בהיקש ליטעון כלי. הזיה על בין הבדים. עומד בין שני בדי ארון ומזה א' למעלה וז' למטה כנגד [יט] עוביה של כפרת, ולא היו נוגעים בה. ועל הפרכת. כדכתיב: "וכן יעשה לאהל מועד" (ויקרא טז). ועל מזבח הזהב. כדכתיב: "ויצא אל המזבח" וגו' ב"אחרי מות". מתנה אחת מהן מעכבת. כדאמרי' בפ' "בית שמאי" (לעיל דף לו:). שירי הדם היה שופך על יסוד כו'. יליף בגמ'. ואם לא נתן. שירים הללו ליסוד — לא עיכב הכפרה. ובגמ' יליף לה בברייתא: יכול יעכבנו כו'. פרים הנשרפים. פר העלם ופר כהן משיח, שאין נאכלין לכהנים אלא נשרפין חוץ לירושלים, כדכתיב בהו: "אל שפך הדשן ישרף" (ויקרא ד). וילפינן בסדר יומא (דף סח.) שהוא חוץ לירושלים. ושעירים הנשרפים. שעירי עבודה זרה שהוקשו לפר העלם לכל דבריהם, בפרק "בית שמאי" (שם). הזיה על הפרוכת. כתיב בהו. אבל בין הבדים לא כתיב בהו כדכתיב בפר יום הכפורים: "והזה באצבעו על פני הכפרת" וגו' (ויקרא טז). מתנה

מסורת הש"ס: חולין יג. לא: מנחות קי. — [חולין לח:] — ל"ג — שבת טו. לא. חולין לח: — נ"ל דתניא — [ברכות יג. חגיגה י: ב"ק כו. ס. סנהדרין סב. כריתות יט:] — ס"א וזה שאין שיעור זה חשוב — שבת לא.

תוספות

מנין למתעסק בקדשים שהוא פסול. פ"ק דחולין (דף יג.) פירש בקונטרס: כגון מתעסק בסכינו להגביהו כ] [או] לזורקו. וקשה: דכה"ג אפילו בחולין פסול לרבנן דפליגי עליה דרבי נתן, ובעו כוונה. ואפי' מתכוין לחתיכה, כגון זרק סכין לנועצה בכותל, דחשיב מתכוין לחתיכה כדמוכח פ"ב דחולין (דף לא:) — אפ"ה פסלי רבנן עד שיתכוין לחתיכת כא] סימנין, אף על גב דאינו מתכוין לשחיטה להתיר בשר ודאי מכשרי, כדקאמר התם: ורבנן, נהי דלא בעו כוונה לזביחה לחתיכה מיהא בעינן, פירוש: לחתיכת סימנין, אבל חתיכה אחרת — לא, דזרק סכין לנועצה בכותל מתכוין לחתיכה הוא ופסלי רבנן! ונראה: האי מתעסק דקדשים — היינו מתכוין לחתיכת סימנין ולא לשם זביחה, דבחולין כשר ובקדשים פסול. ועוד יש מתעסק אחר, כגון משום חולין, כב] דהיינו כסבור שהן חולין. וכולהו מ"ושחט את בן הבקר" נפקי.

הדרן עלך בית שמאי

איזהו מקומן. קדשי קדשים שחיטתן בצפון. ה"ר אפרים היה מדקדק מכאן דלא בעינן כג] סכין בשחיטה, מדלא קתני "שחיטתן בכלי שרת בצפון", כדקתני גבי קבלה "וקיבול דמן בכלי שרת בצפון". ומתוך כך אתיא שפיר הא דאמר בפ"ק דחולין (דף ג.): כגון שבדק קרומית של קנה ושחט בה, כד] דלא בעי כלי שרת. כה] וכן משמע קצת בפסחים פ' "ואלו דברים" (דף סו.) שהיה כל אחד מביא סכינו מתוך ביתו. כו] ואי אפשר לומר כן, דבסוף "התודה" (מנחות פב:) ובסוף "דם חטאת" (לקמן צז:) דריש מדכתיב: "ויקח את המאכלת" דעולה טעונה כלי, [א] וילפינן כז] מיניה כולהו. ובסוטה פרק "היה מביא" (דף יד:) משמע דסכין כח] מקדש ליה לדם. ועוד: בריש "התודה" (מנחות עח:) איכא למ"ד סכין אלימא מכלי שרת, דאף על גב דלית לה תוך מקדשא. והיא קרומית של קנה — איכא למימר שתקנה ועשאה כלי, וכר' יוסי בר' יהודה דאמר בפרק "היה מביא" (סוטה יד:) דעושין כלי שרת דעץ. והיא ד"אלו דברים" (פסחי' סו.) [ב] — אימר: כל אחד הקדיש סכינו בערב שבת. והאי דלא תנן הכא כט] "שחיטתן בכלי שרת בצפון" כדתנן בקבלה — לא דמי, דבקבלה נמי לא הזכיר הכלי אלא משום דבעי שיהא גם הכלי בצפון, ל] לאפוקי אם הבהמה בצפון והכלי בדרום והדם מקבלו בתוכו. תדע, דבכל הנהו דבעו צפון קתני לא] "שחיטה כו' וקיבול דמן בכלי שרת בצפון", וגבי קדשים קלים ששחיטתן בכל מקום בעזרה לא קתני "וקיבול דמן בכלי שרת", אע"ג דבעי קבלה בכלי שרת. וכן לעיל פרק שני (דף כו.) דתניא: קדשים קלים שחיטתן בפנים וקבול דמן בכלי שרת בפנים — אתא לאשמועינן שצריך שיהא הכלי בפנים, לאפוקי אם רוב הכלי בחוץ [ג] ומיעוטה בפנים, אע"פ שאין הדם בפנים נפסל ביוצא, דמקבל במיעוט שבפנים. אי נמי, משום דאיכא אשם מצורע שמתקבל ביד איצטריך למיתני

עין משפט נר מצוה

סב א מיי' פ"א מהל' פסה"מ הלכה ג:
סג ב מיי' פי"ד מהל' פסה"מ הלכה א:
סד ג מיי' פ"ב מהל' שחיטה הלכה כב סמג עשין סג טוש"ע י"ד סימן ד סעיף ג:
א ד מיי' פ"ה מהלכות מעה"ק הלכה ב:
ב ה מיי' שם הל' א:
ג ו מיי' שם הלכה יב ופ"ד מהלכות ערב יוה"כ הלכה ב:
ד ז מיי' פ"ה מהלכות מעה"ק הלכה יג:

שיטה מקובצת

א] לדעתכם זבחו אות י' נמחק: ב] דתניא כלל: ג] זה ותרווייהו: ד] לית ליה: ה] כעין פנים: ו] מתנה אחת מהן מעכבת. הקשה הר"ר אליעזר מטריויש פתח בהזאות וסיים במתנות וי"ל דלרבותא נקט לא מבעיא הזאות דמעכבות בכל מקום שהן אפילו במזבח החיצון כגון בפרה ובנגעים כדאמר לעיל אפילו מתנות שאין מעכבות על מזבח החיצון דאם נתנם במתנה אחת יצא מ"מ מעכבות על מזבח הפנימי וכן משמע בגמ' דצריך קרא גם לארבע מתנות: ז] ראיה זו כבר ידענו כו' דנפקא לן מינה ולא עיכוב: ח] אלמא בעלים קרי ליה מקריב הלכך הוו להו: ט] דלאו איהו שחיט ליה פסול: י] תיבת או ל"ש ונמחק: יא] היה בו שיעור אבל: יב] עושה הויא מחשבה: יג] דעיקר מחשבה בקרבנות: יד] לה' לבדו: טו] שנסמכה פרשת שבת לפרשת מלאכת המשכן בויקהל ומאי מלאכת מחשבת: טז] או בהקטרת אימוריהן הדר: יז] דמן בצפון ותיבות בכלי שרת נמחק: יח] דכתיב בעולת סיני וישם: יט] כנגד עוביו של כפורת ולא היו נוגעים בו הס"ד: כ] בסכינו להגביהו ולזורקו וקשה כו' דר' נתן בפ"ק דחולין ובעו כוונה: כא] סימנין אבל מתכוון לחתיכות סימנין אע"ג. ס"א אפילו לא נתכוון לשחיטה כיון דנתכוון לחתיכת סימנין מכשרי רבנן כדמוכח בפ"ב דחולין דקאמר ורבנן נמי נהי כו': כב] משום חולין דהכא דפסלוהו דהיינו קסבר שהן חולין דפסול משום מתעסק

וכולהו: כג] בשחיטה סכין כלי שרת מדלא: כד] בה ואע"ג דמיירי שתקנה ועשה כלי דודאי כלי בעינן כדמוכח בבמה דוכתי מ"מ לא משתמע שתהא כלי שרת שהרי אין עושין כלי שרת של עץ. מהר"פ: כה] (שרת שהרי אין עושין כלי שרת עץ) ואפ"ה שוחטין בקרומית: כו] ביתו מי שפסחו טלה תוחב לו בצוארו ומי שפסחו גדי תוחב לו בין קרניו: כז] וילפינן כולהו מעולה ובסוטה: כח] מקדשא ליה לדם כו' למ"ד דסכין מקדשא אלימא מכלי שרת דאע"ג דלית ליה תוך מקדשא והיא דקרומית של קנה כו' כלי שרת וכרבי יוסי: כט] הכא דשחיטתן בכלי שרת בצפון משום דפשיטא ליה דכל העבודה בעינן כלי שרת וכ"ת למה תנן וקבול דמן בכלי שרת לא דמי [דלא תני] אלא משום דבעי שיהא הכלי שרת כולה בצפון לאפוקי דאי הוי רובא בדרום ומיעוטו בצפון אע"פ שהוא מקבל באותו מיעוט שבצפון מ"מ [כשהוא מקבל] הדם בכלי בטל אגב רוב הכלי שבדרום דאגד ליה אגד ולא הוי קבלה בצפון אבל בשעת שחיטה אינו צריך להיות הסכין כולו בצפון דהא אפילו אם הסכין רובו בדרום רק ששוחט במיעוט הסכין שבצפון כשרה וגם א) הבהמה בטלה אגב הסכין והרי יש שחיטה בצפון מיהו אמת דלא בעינן כלי שרת וראיה מתוספתא דמנחות כו' ואינו רוצה לומר [דאינה טעונה] כלי ממש שהרי בעולה [טעון כלי] מויקח [את] המאכלת אלא דאינה טעונה כלי שרת קאמר [וקשה] למורי דמאי [שנא] שחיטה משאר עבודות וכ"ת משום דכשרה בזר הרי בלילה כשרה בזר וטעונה כלי שרת ותירץ דבלילה דאינה כי אם בקדשים אע"ג דכשרה בזר הויא כשאר קדשים לענין כלי שרת אבל שחיטה הואיל ושייכא בחולין כמו בקדשים ולכך אע"פ שהצריך כלי לא בעינן כלי שרת וא"ת כיון דגלי קרא בשחיטה דבעי כלי מויקח את המאכלת א"כ מנין לנו לומר (שיהא) [שלא יהא] אותו כלי כלי שרת מידי דהוי [אקבלה] דבעינן כלי שרת משום דגלי קרא וישם באגנות בעולת סיני וי"ל דודאי מוישם באגנות נפקי לן כלי לאפוקי שלא יקבל ביד אבל שיהיה כלי שרת דהיינו שהוקדש בכלי לאו מהתם נפקא אלא מדכתיב ועשית מזרקותיו גבי כלי המזבח שנעשו מתרומת המשכן אבל שחיטה מי כתיב ועשית סכיניו הלכך לא בעיא כלי שרת בשחיטה ומיהו הביסא של מנחות צריכה להיות כלי שרת מדכתיב גבי מזרקות שניהם מלאים סולת למנחה אלמא היו נותנים המנחה במזרקות שהיו כלי שרת כדפי' כיון שהם כתובים גבי כלי המזבח כך נראה למורי הר"פ: ל] לאפוקי כו' בתוכו וא"ת כיון שאין הכלי בצפון תיפוק ליה משום דבעינן קבלה בצפון וכיון שהכלי בדרום א"כ הוי הקבלה עצמה בדרום וי"ל דאתי למעוטי היכא דרוב הכלי בדרום ומיעוטו בצפון וקיבל במיעוטו שבצפון אפ"ה פסול כיון שרוב הכלי בדרום ובגמרא איכא תרי קראי חד למקבל וחד לכלי שרת כלומר דקבלה עצמה טעונה צפון והשתא אי הוי תני וקיבול דמן בצפון ה"א כיון שמקבל במיעוט כלי שבצפון דסגי בכך לכך תני כלי שרת בצפון לומר לך דבעינן רוב הכלי בצפון שהדם מתקבל בתוכו ולכן שדינן ליה בתר רוב הכלי אבל גבי סכין לא שייך למימר האי טעמא ותדע דכל החדוש דקתני וקיבול דמן בכלי שרת בצפון משום הכי הוא דהא גבי קדשים קלים [לא תני וקבול דמן בבכלי שרת] וכן משמע התם דקאמר סכין מקדשא ליה לצואר בהמה אלמא משמע דכלי שרת הוא ויש לדחות דלעולם הסכין אינו כלי שרת והא דקאמר התם סכין מקדשא ליה לשחיטה אינו רוצה לומר שהוא כלי שרת אלא משום שהוא ראוי לשחוט וכן משמע בפרק התודה דלא בעינן כלי שרת לשחיטה דקאמר גבי סכין ועדיפא מכלי שרת דאף על גב דלית ליה תוך מקדשא ואי הוי כלי שרת הול"ל ועדיפא משאר כלי שרת אבל ר"ל עדיפא מכלי שרת ממש דהואיל והצריך הכתוב כלי לשחיטה ואף על גב דלית ליה תוך. לשון תוספות אחרות מתלמיד מהר"פ ז"ל: לא] תיבות שחיטה כו' נמחק:

א) מלה לנ"ל וגם הסכין בטל אגב הבהמה

הגהות הב"ח

(א) גמ' בפנים הוא דאמר בחוץ לא אמר ר"ש:

הגהות צ"ק [א] נ"א וילפינן כולהו מעולה: [ב] נ"א יש לומר דכל אחד כו': [ג] ומיעוטה בפנים ומקבל הדם במיעוט שבפנים אף על פי שאין הדם בפניה נפסל ביוצא א"נ כו' וכן הוא בתוספות חולין דף ג ע"א וע"ש:

ה א מיי' פ"ז מהלכות מעה"ק הלכה ב ופ"ד מהלכות עיה"כ הל' ב:
ו ב ג ד מיי' פ"ד מהל' מחוסרי כפרה הל' ב:

למיתני בכולהו קדשים: וקיבול דמן בכלי שרת י] בצפון. ומיהו, יש לדקדק מהא בתוספתא דמנחות: חומר בקמילה מבשחיטה, שהקמילה טעונה כלי והשחיטה אינה טעונה כלי יא] אלא אפי' קרומית של קנה. ועל כרחיך לא קאמר דלא תבעי כלי כלל, דהא אמרינן: מה עולה טעונה כלי כו', אלא דלא בעי כלי שרת קאמר. ומיהו, יש לפרש: דלא חיישינן לכלי יפה קאמר, יב] דלא פסלה קרומית של קנה משום "הקריבהו נא לפחתך", כדפריך התלמוד בסוטה פרק "היה מביא" (דף יד:) גבי כפיפה מצרית. דדורון הוא שדרך להביא בכלי נאה, אבל בשחיטה לא חיישינן. אי נמי, כפיפה מצרית מכוערת יותר מקרומית של קנה.

אלו ואלו נשרפין אבית הדשן. פירש בקונטרס: דפר יום הכיפורים אתי מהיקשא דפר העלם, כדאמר בפרק "בית שמאי" (לעיל לט.): "לפר" – זה פר יום הכיפורים. ואם תאמר: והא אין דבר הלמד בהיקש חוזר ומלמד בהיקש, ופר העלם בגופיה לא כתיב ביה "אל בית הדשן", ומפר כהן המשיח אתי, כדכתיב בפר העלם (ויקרא ד): "כאשר שרף את הפר הראשון" – והיינו היקש, כמו "ושחט החטאת במקום העולה" דקרי ליה היקש לקמן (דף מח.). ולפירש"י דפרק "בית שמאי" (לעיל מ.) דילפינן פר יום

מתנה אחת מהן מעכבת. שירי הדם היה שופך על יסוד מערבי של מזבח החיצון, ואם לא נתן — לא עיכב. א] אאלו ואלו נשרפין אבית הדשן.§ גמ' וניתני נמי: וקיבול דמן בכלי שרת בצפון! כיון דאיכא אשם מצורע דקיבול דמו ביד הוא — שייריה. ולא? והא קתני ב] לה לקמן: אשם נזיר ואשם מצורע — שחיטתן בצפון, וקבול דמן בכלי שרת בצפון! ג] מעיקרא סבר: קיבול דמו ביד הוא, שייריה. וכיון ד] דלא סגי ליה אלא בכלי — הדר תנייה. *דתניא: °"ולקח", (ויקרא יד) יכול בכלי? ת"ל: "ונתן", מה נתינה בעצמו של כהן — באף לקיחה בעצמו של כהן. יכול אף למזבח כן? ת"ל: °"כי כחטאת האשם (שם) הוא", מה חטאת טעונה כלי — גאף אשם טעון כלי. נמצאת אתה אומר: *דאשם מצורע שני כהנים מקבלין את דמו, אחד ביד ואחד בכלי, זה שקיבלו בכלי — בא לו ה] אצל מזבח, וזה שקיבלו ביד — בא לו אצל מצורע.§

פר

מתנה אחת מהן מעכבת. כדאמרן בפ' "בית שמאי" (לעיל לט.) מ"ועשה ו] כאשר עשה". אלו ואלו. של יום הכפורים ושאר הנשרפין. נשרפין אבית הדשן. למקום שמוליאין שם את הדשן של מזבח החיצון, דכתיב ביה: "והוציא את הדשן אל מחוץ למחנה" (ויקרא ו). ובפרים הנשרפים כתיב: (תורה אור) "אל שפך הדשן" (שם ד) ושל יום הכפורים ז] הקישו לפר העלם, כדאמרינן בפרק "ב"ש" (לעיל לט.): "לפר" – זה פר יום הכפורים. גמ' וניתני נמי ברישא. גבי סתם ח] של קדשי קדשים "וקבול דמן", כי היכי דתנא שחיטתן. אשם מצורע קיבול דמו ביד. כדיליף לקמן, שמקבל דמו לתוך כפו. שייריה. משום דלא פסיקא ליה למיתנייה בהדי כללי דשאר קדשים, שכל קבול דמן בכלי. וכיון דלא סגי ליה נמי. בלא קבלת כלי, כדיליף לקמן: שני כהנים מקבלין את דמו, אחד ביד ואחד בכלי – הדר תנייה בהדיא, ולא כללו. ולקח. באשם מצורע כתיב: "ולקח הכהן מדם האשם ונתן על תנוך" וגו' (ויקרא יד). מה נתינה בעצמו של כהן – באצבעו, דכתיב "אצבע" גבי שמן, ויליף דם מיניה. יכול אף למזבח. דם אשם מצורע הנזרק למזבח, דמרבינן ליה לקמן בדין מתן דמים ואימורין למזבח, ואע"ג דלאו בגופיה כתיבא. כי כחטאת האשם הוא ט]. באשם מצורע כתיב, כדין חטאת דין אשם זה בעבודת כהן: מה חטאת טעונה תלי תחלת דמה, דילפינן לקיחה לקיחה בתורת כהנים, כתיב בחטאת: "ולקח הכהן מדם החטאת" (ויקרא ד), וכתיב בעולת סיני: "ויקח משה חצי הדם וישם באגנות" (שמות כד) – אף אשם זה טעון כלי, אף על פי שאמרנו בו קבלה ביד.

בעולה

הכיפורים ל"את בדם וטבילה" מפר כהן משיח – אם כן יג] *ניחא דמצינו למילף נמי שריפת בית הדשן. אבל לפר"ת דהתם קשיא! ויש לומר: דאיכא תרי היקישי בפר העלם: "ועשה כאשר עשה לפר" דדרשינן מיניה פרק "בית שמאי" (גם זה שם) – זה פר כהן משיח, בין לעכב בהזאות *כמשיח בין לאגמורי יותרת ושתי הכליות בפר העלם ממשיח, הוא הדין דניגמר לענין שריפה פר העלם ממשיח. וכי הדר וכתב בפר העלם יד] "וכאשר שרף" (הילכך) – הוה ליה כמאן דכתיב בגופיה. ועוד יש לומר: הא דנשרפין חוץ לג' מחנות יליף לקמן בסוף "טבול יום" (דף קה:) מדכתיב תלת "אל מחוץ טו] למחנה" – *שלישית אי כתב בכולהו, ואין זה אלא כגילוי מילתא בעלמא ד"מחוץ למחנה" דכתב בכל חד וחד – טז] במחנה שלישית קאמר. הילכך אתי שפיר פר יום הכיפורים מפר העלם, ואייתר לו התם יז] "מחוץ למחנה" דכתיב בפר יום הכיפורים, לרבנן – לומר לך: כיון שילא מחוץ למחנה אחת השורפו מטמא בגדים, ולרבי שמעון לג"ש, ללמד יח] מפרה – מה כאן שלשה מחנות, מה להלן שלשה מחנות אף להלן למזרחה של ירושלים אף כאן למזרחה של ירושלים. ומיהו, בית הדשן ודאי קשה, דנהי דשלשה מחנות הוי כמאן דכתיב בגופיה, דאפשר חוץ לג' מחנות שלא במקום דשן, ואם כן הא יט] לא כתיב בגופיה בית הדשן דבעי מקום דשן הוי דבר הלמד בהיקש ואינו חוזר ומלמד בהיקש! ושמא גם זה חשוב גילוי מילתא בעלמא היא, דכל הנשרפין חוץ לשלש מחנות נשרפין במקום הדשן. *(אחר) השתא אתי שעיר יוה"כ, דלא איתקש לפר העלם. אי נמי, כולהו ולמינן בית הדשן בג"ש ד"מחוץ למחנה" מכהן משיח. כ] ואין לפרש דאתי מריבויא ד"חטאת" "חטאת" דכתיב בפר ושעיר של יום הכפורים, דדרשינן לקמן בסוף "התערובת" (דף פג.): "ואת פר החטאת ואת שעיר החטאת יוציא אל מחוץ למחנה ושרפו" מה ת"ל "חטאת" "חטאת"? שיכול כא] דאין לי למטמא בגדים ונשרפין בבית הדשן אלא אלו בלבד, מנין לרבות פר כהן משיח ופר העלם דבר של ציבור ושעירי עבודה זרה – ת"ל: "חטאת" "חטאת", דברי רבי יהודה. דעל כרחין נשרפין אבית הדשן כדי נסבה, דהא עיקר "על שפך הדשן" בפר כהן משיח כתיב, אלא משום מטמא בגדים נקט דלא כתיב בהו. וכן כב] מוכיח דר' מאיר כג] פליג עליה וקאמר: אינו לריך, הרי הוא אומר "לכפר", שאין תלמוד לומר לכפר – לימד על כל המתכפרים בפנים ששורפן מטמא בגדים. ושמא כי היכי דיליף מריבויא ד"חטאת" "חטאת" טומאת בגדים בכולהו מפר ושעיר של יום הכפורים – הכי נמי הוה יליף מינייהו מההוא ריבויא גופיה בית הדשן, *מפר ושעיר של יום הכפורים. **מה** נתינה בעצמו של כהן. פי' בקונטרס: מדכתיב אצבע גבי שמן, ויליף דם כד] מינייהו. ותימה: א"כ הוי היקשא מבנין אב, ולקמן (דף נז.) מיבעיא לן אי דבר הלמד בבנין אב חוזר ומלמד בהיקש! *ונראה לי: לקיחה מנתינה נמי הוי בנין אב, *וילפינן מנתינה דידיה ולא מנתינה דשאר קרבנות, ולקמן אמרינן דילפינן שפיר בנין אב מבנין אב. ברו"ך. **אף** לקיחה ולקח כה] מדם האשם בעצמו של כהן. תימה: דגבי חטאת נמי כתיב (ויקרא ד) "ולקח ונתן", ולא אמר: מה נתינה בעצמו של כהן אף לקיחה בעצמו של כהן! ושמא הכא דריש משום דמייתר, דכתיב במצורע (שם יד) עשיר ועני. ואע"ג דבתורת כהנים דריש מקמאי – אבתרא סמיך. ונראה לי דבחטאת כתיב: "ולקח מדם החטאת באצבעו ונתן" – אם כן לאו בידו מקבל, דבאצבע לא אפשר לקבל. אלא על כרחין בכלי קאמר, ו"באצבעו" היינו דעביד כו] אוזן לשפת מזרק, כדאמר לעיל פרק שני (דף כד.). אבל באשם לא כתיב באצבע. ומשום דלא נימא: "ולקח באצבעו" היינו וטבל דוקא, ולא איירי בקבלה – להכי איצטריך לגזירה שוה דגמרינן מ"ויקח חצי הדם וישם באגנות" בת"כ. ברו"ך. **מה** חטאת טעונה כלי כו'. פירש בקונטרס: דילפינן לקיחה לקיחה, בתורת כהנים כתיב בחטאת "ולקח כז] הכהן מדם החטאת" וכתיב בעולת סיני "ויקח משה חצי הדם וישם באגנות". ותימה: הוה ליה דבר הלמד בגזירה שוה כח] חוזר ומלמד בהיקשא ד"כחטאת האשם", ובעיא היא לקמן (דף נ.) ולא איפשיטא למאן דאמר בתר מלמד כט] אזלינן! ומיהו, בתוס פירש בקונטרס דילפינן לקיחה לקיחה, דלקמן בסוף "דם חטאת" (דף לז:) משמע דאתיא בהיקשא ד"זאת התורה" מזבחי שלמי ציבור. דקאמר: מה עולה טעונה כלי – אף כל טעון כלי. מאי כלי? אילימא מזרק – בזבחי שלמי ציבור נמי כתיב "ויקח משה חצי הדם וישם באגנות", פירוש: וכיון דהדר איתקש כולהו לשלמים דכתיב בהאי קרא, וילפינן מיניה התם: מה שלמים מפגלין ומתפגלין – כלי נמי תילף משלמים, דהתם נמי שלמים הוו בסיני. ומיהו, מכל מקום קשה עדיין: דהוה ליה דבר הלמד בהיקש, ואינו חוזר ומלמד בהיקש! יש לומר: דבההוא היקשא ד"וזאת התורה" כתב נמי אשם ואיתקוש *כמו של שלמים, וכל אשמות בכלל אפילו אשם מצורע, אלא דהוה אמינא דמעטיה קרא מקבלת כלי, ל] *ונדרשיה ביד דבעצמו של כהן – הלכך אתא "כחטאת האשם" לגלויי דלא בא הכתוב להוציאו מקבלת כלי לגמרי. לא] וקשה: גזירה שוה דלקיחה מסיני למה לי? לילף כולהו משלמים! יש לומר: דחטאת ילפינן משלמים לקבלת כלי מהיקשא, וגזירה שוה דלקיחה לקיחה איצטריך למיהוי כמאן דכתיב בגופיה דחטאת, והדר ילפינן אשם מחטאת בהיקשא ד"כחטאת האשם". לב] ולא גמרינן מעיקרא אשם משלמים בהיקשא ד"זאת התורה" כדילפינן לענין פיגול – דאם כן גזרה שוה דלקיחה לקיחה למה *[לי]?

איידי

יומא סח.

תוספתא דנגעים פ"ה

גליון הש"ס

תום' ד"ה מה חטאת וכו' לאצטריך למהוי כמאן דכתיב בגופיה. וכעין זה לאמרינן לעיל מח ע"א:

ניחא נ"ק

נ"א כמשיח בפר העלם בין כו' נ"ק

נ"ק מ"ז

נ"א ושלישית לא כתב בכולהו ואין זה אלא גילוי כו' נ"ק

אחד והשתא נ"ק

כפר נ"ק

[עיין ביומא דף סא ע"ב דמתרלו בע"א]

*דילפינן נ"ק

נמי לשלמים נ"ק

מדרשא דונתן דבעצמו נ"ק

ועי' נ"ק ורש"ק [ועי' תוס' יומא סא: ד"ה זה חטאת]

שיטה מקובצת

א] אלו ואלו כו'. פ"ה בפר כהן משיח כתיב בהדיא בית הדשן ופר העלם איתקש לפר כהן משיח ושעירי עבודת כוכבים הוקשו לפר העלם וכן פר יוה"כ אתי מהיקשא דפר העלם וקשה דבפר העלם גופיה לא כתיב כו' א) וי"ל דבפר העלם איכא תרי היקישא דכתיב ועשה כאשר עשה ושרף כאשר שרף הלכך הוי כאילו כתיב בגופיה ומיהו קשה שעיר יוה"כ מהיכא אתא אי משום דאיתקש לפר יוה"כ הא פר יוה"כ גופיה בהיקשא אתא לכך נראה דאין זה אלא גלוי מלתא בעלמא דכל הנשרפין יהיו נשרפין בבית הדשן שהרי שריפה חוץ לג' מחנות כתיב בגופייהו רק צריכין ללמוד שנשרפין אבית הדשן וכל בית הדשן הוי חוץ לשלש מחנות כדילפינן בפ' טבול יום וגלוי מלתא ילפינן מדבר הלמד בהיקש. לשון מהר"פ: ב] תיבת לה נמחק: ג] מעיקרא סבר כו' וא"ת וכי התנא לא היה יודע מסקנא דברייתא וי"ל דהה"פ סברתו היתה מעיקרא דלא תני בכלל שאר קדשים משום דאשם מצורע מקצת קבלתו ביד ושאר קדשים כל קבול דמן בכלי והלכך שיריה: ד] וכיון דחזא דלא: ה] לו וזרקו על המזבח תיבת אצל נמחק: ו] מועשה לפר: ז] הכפורים הוקשו לפר: ח] סתם כל קדשי קדשים: ט] הוא לכהן באשם: י] תיבת בצפון נמחק ומיהו יש לדקדק מהא דאמרינן בתוספתא: יא] כלי אלמא אפילו: יב] קאמר ולא פסלה: יג] כן ניחא דמצינו: יד] העלם כאשר שרף: טו] למחנה חד בפר כהן משיח וחד בפר העלם וחד בדישון דלא איצטרכי כולהו דהא לאקושי ליתן מתנה שלישית איכתיבו כולהו ואין זה: טז] וחד למחנה שלישית: יז] התם נמי מחוץ: יח] ללמד על הפרה מה כאן חוץ לשלשה מחנות ומה להלן: יט] הדשן מיהא לא כתיב בגופיה דאי אפשר חוץ לג' מחנות כו' דבעי במקום דשן הוי כו' נשרפין במקום אחד. תוס'. השתא. ותי' הדשן נמחק ומתיבת השתא עד תיבת ואין לפרש מוקף בח"ל: כ] משיח ע"כ. ואין: כא] שיכול אין לי: כב] וכן ס"א וכי מוכיח: כג] מאיר דפליג: כד] דם מיניה: כה] ולקח הכהן מדם: כו] דעביד ליה אזן לשפת מזרק כדאמרינן לעיל בפרק: כז] ולקח אהרן מדם ותיבת הכהן נמחק: כח] שוה וחוזר ומלמד: כט] אזלינן ועוד קשה למה לי לאקושי חטאת לאשם תיפוק ליה כדאמר לקמן דזאת התורה כו' ושלמים הוו בסיני כדאמר לקמן מה עולה טעונה כלי אף כל כו' ופריך מאי כלי אילימא מזרק בזבחי שלמי צבור כתיב ויקח משה וגו' פי' והוקשו לשלמים וא"כ ה"נ אשם תיפוק ליה מהיקשא דאשם וי"ל דקושיא שניה מתרץ לראשונה דודאי מההיא דלקמן לא הייתי יודע אשם מצורע הואיל ויצא מכלל שאר אשמות לידון בעצמו של כהן להכי אהני היקשא דחטאת כאשם להחזירו לכלל שאר אשמות להטעינו כלי דלא הוי השתא חוזר ומלמד בהיקשא דאין זה רק גלוי מלתא בעלמא לומר גם זה לא יצא מהיקשא לגמרי משלמים לומר דלא צריך כלי רק להזאות מצורע אבל לעולם מתנות מזבח צריך קבלה בכלי כמו בשאר אשמות ומיהו קשה למה לי ג"ש דקיחה קיחה לחטאת תיפוק ליה מהיקשא דשלמים ואמר מורי דהו"א כיון דחטאת יצא מן הכלל דמתן דמו באצבע ושאר כל הקרבנות בכלי ה"ה לענין קבלה דלא הוי כשאר קרבנות קמ"ל ג"ש דקיחה קיחה אבל אכתי קשה למה לי להקיש אשם מצורע לחטאת תיפוק ליה כמו כן מקיחה קיחה דסיני דבאשם גופיה כתיב קיחה ותירץ דהו"א דאתא קרא וליפקא מג"ש דמקשינן לקיחה לנתינה שיהא בעצמו של כהן ה"ה לענין מזבח קמ"ל ס"א וי"ל דכיון דאיכא היקשא דלקיחה איתקש דבעינן בעצמו של כהן אבל השתא מדהדריה (מבחטאת כאשם) [מכחטאת האשם] לכלל שאר אשמות א"כ נוקי היקשא דלקיחה לנתינה לענין הזאות מצורע דוקא ע"כ כתוב בס"א וא"ת גבי חטאת נמי נימא דאיתקש לקיחה לנתינה דכתיב ולקח הכהן מדם החטאת באצבעו ונתן על קרנות המזבח והנתינה דחטאת היא באצבע וי"ל דהתם גבי חטאת אצבע הפסיק הענין שלא להקיש לקיחה לנתינה. העתקתי לשון מהר"פ ז"ל: ל] כלי מדרשה דבעצמו: לא] לגמרי תוספות וקשה: לב] האשם ומכל מקום קשה אמאי לא גמרינן מעיקרא כו' למה ע"כ הס"ד:

א) עיין בתוספות ד"ה אלו.

דאתיא

ז א מיי' פ"ע מהלכות שגגות הלכה יא:

"פָּר וְשָׂעִיר שֶׁל יוֹם הַכִּפּוּרִים" כו'.§ מִכְּדֵי צָפוֹן בְּעוֹלָה כְּתִיב, נִיתְנֵי עוֹלָה בְּרֵישָׁא! חַטָּאת, אַיְּידֵי א] *דְּאָתֵי מִדְּרָשָׁא חֲבִיבָא לֵיהּ. וְנִיתְנֵי חַטָּאוֹת הַחִיצוֹנוֹת! ב] אַיְּידֵי דְּנִכְנָס דָּמָן לִפְנַי וְלִפְנִים חֲבִיבָא לֵיהּ. וְ"צָפוֹנָה" בְּעוֹלָה הֵיכָא כְּתִיבָא? °"וְשָׁחַט אוֹתוֹ עַל יֶרֶךְ הַמִּזְבֵּחַ צָפוֹנָה". אַשְׁכַּחַן בֶּן צֹאן, בֶּן בָּקָר מְנָא לָן? אָמַר קְרָא: "וְאִם מִן הַצֹּאן" – *וָי"ו מוֹסִיף עַל עִנְיָן רִאשׁוֹן, וְיִלְמַד עֶלְיוֹן מִתַּחְתּוֹן. הָנִיחָא לְמ"ד מְלַמְּדִין, ג] אֶלָּא לְמ"ד אֵין מְלַמְּדִין מַאי אִיכָּא לְמֵימַר? *דְּתַנְיָא: °"וְאִם נֶפֶשׁ" וגו' – לְחַיֵּיב עַל סְפֵק מְעִילוֹת אָשָׁם תָּלוּי, דִּבְרֵי רַבִּי עֲקִיבָא, וַחֲכָמִים אפּוֹטְרִין; מַאי לָאו בְּהָא קָא מִיפַּלְגִי, ד] מָר סָבַר: לְמֵידִין, וּמָר סָבַר: אֵין לְמֵידִין? אָמַר רַב פַּפָּא: דְּכוּלֵּי עָלְמָא לְמֵידִין, וְהַיְינוּ טַעְמָא דְּרַבָּנַן: נֶאֱמַר כָּאן "מִצְוֹת" וְנֶאֱמַר *בְּחַטַּאת חֵלֶב "מִצְוֹת", מַה לְּהַלָּן דָּבָר שֶׁחַיָּיבִין עַל זְדוֹנוֹ כָּרֵת וְעַל שִׁגְגָתוֹ חַטָּאת – אַף כָּאן שֶׁחַיָּיבִין עַל זְדוֹנוֹ כָּרֵת וְעַל שִׁגְגָתוֹ חַטָּאת. וְרַבִּי עֲקִיבָא: מַה לְּהַלָּן ה] בִּקְבוּעָה – אַף כָּאן בִּקְבוּעָה, לְאַפּוּקֵי חַטַּאת דְּטוּמְאַת מִקְדָּשׁ וְקָדָשָׁיו דְּעוֹלֶה וְיוֹרֵד הוּא. וְרַבָּנַן: *אֵין גְּזֵירָה שָׁוָה לְמֶחֱצָה. ו] וְר"ע נַמִּי, אֵין גְּזֵירָה שָׁוָה לְמֶחֱצָה! אִין הָכִי נַמִּי. וְהָכָא בְּהָא קָמִיפַּלְגִי, ר"ע סָבַר: "וְאִם נֶפֶשׁ" כְּתִיב, *וָי"ו מוֹסִיף עַל עִנְיָן רִאשׁוֹן. וְרַבָּנַן נַמִּי, הָכְתִיב: "וְאִם נֶפֶשׁ"! לֵימָא בְּהָא קָמִיפַּלְגִי, *דְּמָר סָבַר: *)הֶיקֵּשׁ עָדִיף, וּמָר סָבַר: גְּזֵירָה שָׁוָה עֲדִיף? לָא, דְּכ"ע דְּהֶיקֵּשׁ עֲדִיף, ז] וְאָמְרִי לָךְ רַבָּנַן: תַּחְתּוֹן הוּא דְּגָמַר מֵעֶלְיוֹן – לְאָשָׁם בְּכֶסֶף שְׁקָלִים, שֶׁלֹּא תֹּאמַר: לֹא יְהֵא סְפֵיקוֹ חָמוּר מִוַּדָּאוֹ, מַה וַּדָּאוֹ חַטָּאת בַּת דַּנְקָא – אַף סְפֵיקוֹ אָשָׁם בַּר דַּנְקָא. וְרַבִּי עֲקִיבָא, ח] הָא סְבָרָא מְנָא לֵיהּ? נָפְקָא לֵיהּ °מִ"זֹּאת תּוֹרַת הָאָשָׁם" – תּוֹרָה אַחַת לְכָל הָאֲשָׁמוֹת. תֵּינַח מַאן דְּאִית לֵיהּ "תּוֹרַת", ט] מַאן דְּלֵית לֵיהּ "תּוֹרַת" מֵהֵיכָא גָּמַר? גָּמַר °"בְּעֶרְכְּךָ" "בְּעֶרְכְּךָ". תֵּינַח הֵיכָא דִּכְתִיב "בְּעֶרְכְּךָ", אֲשַׁם שִׁפְחָה חֲרוּפָה דְּלָא כְּתִיב בֵּיהּ "בְּעֶרְכְּךָ", מַאי אִיכָּא לְמֵימַר? גָּמַר "בְּאֵיל" "בְּאֵיל".§ י] חַטָּאת מְנָא לָן דְּבָעְיָא צָפוֹן – דִּכְתִיב: °"וְשָׁחַט אֶת הַחַטָּאת בִּמְקוֹם הָעוֹלָה". אַשְׁכַּחַן שְׁחִיטָה, יא] קַבָּלָה מְנָא לָן? דִּכְתִיב: °"וְלָקַח הַכֹּהֵן מִדַּם הַחַטָּאת". מְקַבֵּל עַצְמוֹ מְנָא לָן? אָמַר קְרָא "וְלָקַח" – לוֹ יב] יִקַּח. אַשְׁכַּחַן לְמִצְוָה, לְעַכֵּב מִנַּיִן? קְרָא אַחֲרִינָא כְּתִיב: °"וְשָׁחַט אוֹתוֹ בִּמְקוֹם אֲשֶׁר יִשְׁחַט אֶת הָעוֹלָה"; וְתַנְיָא: יג] *הֵיכָן עוֹלָה נִשְׁחֶטֶת – בַּצָּפוֹן, אַף זֶה בַּצָּפוֹן. וְכִי

*) [עי' פירושו בתוספות ברכות נ. ד"ה אלא]

רש"י

בְּעוֹלָה כְּתִיב. גַּבֵּי עוֹלַת צֹאן בְּ"וַיִּקְרָא": "וְשָׁחַט אוֹתוֹ עַל יֶרֶךְ הַמִּזְבֵּחַ צָפוֹנָה". מִדְּרָשָׁא. מֵהֶיקֵּשָׁא, דִּכְתִיב: "בִּמְקוֹם אֲשֶׁר תִּשָּׁחֵט הָעוֹלָה" (ויקרא ד). עֶלְיוֹן. פָּרָשַׁת בֶּן בָּקָר לְמַעְלָה מִפָּרָשַׁת בֶּן צֹאן. הָנִיחָא לְמַאן דְּאָמַר לְמֵדִין. עֶלְיוֹן מִתַּחְתּוֹן עַל יְדֵי וָי"ו הַמּוֹסִיף. וְאִם נֶפֶשׁ. גַּבֵּי אָשָׁם תָּלוּי כְּתִיב בְּוַיִּקְרָא: "וְאִם נֶפֶשׁ כִּי תֶחֱטָא" וגו', וּלְמַעְלָה הֵימֶנָּה פָּרָשַׁת מְעִילָה וַדָּאִית, שֶׁיָּדַע לְאַחַר זְמַן שֶׁנֶּהֱנָה מִן הַהֶקְדֵּשׁ בְּשׁוֹגֵג, יד] וְחַיָּיבִין עָלֶיהָ אָשָׁם וַדַּאי. עַל סְפֵק מְעִילוֹת. הֶקְדֵּשׁ וְחוּלִּין לְפָנָיו, וְנֶהֱנָה מֵאֶחָד מֵהֶם כִּסָבוּר שֶׁנֵּיהֶם חוּלִּין, וְעַכְשָׁיו אֵינוֹ יוֹדֵעַ מֵאֵיזֶה מֵהֶן נֶהֱנָה – מֵבִיא אָשָׁם תָּלוּי לְהָגֵן טו] מִן הַיִּסּוּרִין, עַד שֶׁיִּוָּדַע לוֹ שֶׁוַּדַּאי מָעַל, וּמֵבִיא אָשָׁם וַדַּאי, וְגַם הוּא אַיִל בְּכֶסֶף שְׁקָלִים. לְמֵדִין. עֶלְיוֹן מִתַּחְתּוֹן, פָּרָשַׁת הֶקְדֵּשׁ מִפָּרָשַׁת אָשָׁם תָּלוּי שֶׁתַּחְתֶּיהָ, לְמֵימְרָא דְּהַנֶּהֱנֶה מִן הַהֶקְדֵּשׁ נַמִּי מַיְיתֵי אָשָׁם תָּלוּי עַל סְפֵיקוֹ. נֶאֱמַר מִצְוֹת. בְּאָשָׁם תָּלוּי: "וְעָשְׂתָה אַחַת מִכָּל מִצְוֹת" (ויקרא ה) וְכֵן בְּחַטָּאת. מַה חַטָּאת. בָּאָה עַל שִׁגְגַת זְדוֹן כָּרֵת, כִּדְיָלְפִינַן בְּהוֹרָיוֹת (דף ח.), אַף אָשָׁם תָּלוּי עַל סְפֵק דָּבָר שֶׁזְּדוֹנוֹ כָּרֵת וְשִׁגְגָתוֹ חַטָּאת. וְרַבִּי עֲקִיבָא. גָּמַר לָהּ לְהַךְ גְּזֵירָה שָׁוָה הָכִי: מַה חַטָּאת טז] קָרְבָּן קָבוּעַ לְעָנִי כְּעָשִׁיר – אַף אָשָׁם תָּלוּי אֵינוֹ בָּא אֶלָּא עַל סְפֵק חַטָּאת קָבוּעַ. לְאַפּוּקֵי. סְפֵק נִכְנַס טָמֵא לַמִּקְדָּשׁ סָפֵק לֹא נִכְנַס, הוֹאִיל וּוַדַּאי בְּעוֹלֶה וְיוֹרֵד – אֵין מֵבִיא עַל סְפֵיקוֹ אָשָׁם תָּלוּי. אֵין גז"ש לְמֶחֱצָה. וְכִי הֵיכִי יז] דְּגָמְרִינַן לָהּ לְגַבֵּי הָא מִילְּתָא – גְּמוֹר מִינֵּיהּ נַמִּי דְּאֵינוֹ בָּא אֶלָּא עַל סְפֵק כָּרֵת. וְאָמְרִי לָךְ רַבָּנַן. הֶיקֵּשׁ לְהָכִי אֲתָא: יח] תַּחְתּוֹן הוּא דְּגָמַר מֵעֶלְיוֹן, לִקְנוֹת אָשָׁם בִּשְׁתֵּי סְלָעִים. דְּגַבֵּי אֲשַׁם מְעִילוֹת כְּתִיב: "בְּעֶרְכְּךָ כֶּסֶף שְׁקָלִים", וְגָמַר אָשָׁם תָּלוּי מִינֵּיהּ, שֶׁלֹּא תֹּאמַר: לֹא יְהֵא סְפֵיקוֹ שֶׁל כָּרֵת חָמוּר מִוַּדָּאוֹ. דַּנְקָא. יט] שְׁתוּת כְּלוֹמַר, מָעָה כֶּסֶף שֶׁהוּא שְׁתוּת שֶׁל דִּינָר. וְלָאו דַּוְוקָא נָקַט, אֶלָּא כ] דָּמִים קַלִּים בְּעָלְמָא, שֶׁלֹּא נִיתַּן לָהּ קִצְבָּה. תֵּינַח מַאן דְּאִית לֵיהּ תּוֹרַת. בִּשְׁמַעְתָּא קַמַּיְיתָא דִּמְנָחוֹת (דף ג:). בְּעֶרְכְּךָ בְּעֶרְכְּךָ. בְּאָשָׁם תָּלוּי וּבַאֲשַׁם גְּזֵילוֹת כְּתִיב: "בְּעֶרְכְּךָ לְאָשָׁם", וְגָמְרִינַן מֵ"עֶרְכְּךָ" דַּאֲשַׁם מְעִילוֹת דִּכְתִיב בֵּיהּ: "בְּעֶרְכְּךָ כֶּסֶף שְׁקָלִים". גָּמַר בְּאֵיל בְּאֵיל. *כְּתִיב בֵּיהּ: כא] "בְּאֵיל הָאָשָׁם", וּבְחַד מֵהָנָךְ נַמִּי כְּתִיב: "בְּאֵיל הָאָשָׁם". וַאֲשַׁם נָזִיר וַאֲשַׁם מְצוֹרָע כב] נַמִּי לָא מְרַבֵּינַן, מִשּׁוּם דִּכְתִיב: "כֶּבֶשׂ בֶּן שְׁנָתוֹ", וּמִדְּאַיִל שֶׁהוּא בֶּן שְׁתֵּי שָׁנִים בָּא בִּשְׁתֵּי סְלָעִים – כֶּבֶשׂ בֶּן שָׁנָה בָּא בְּסֶלַע. כּוּלָּהּ כג] שְׁמַעְתִּין בִּכְרֵיתוֹת (דף כב:). אֶת הַחַטָּאת. יְתֵירָא הוּא, דְּהָא בְּחַטָּאת קָאֵי, וַהֲוָה לֵיהּ לְמִכְתַּב "וְשָׁחַט אוֹתָהּ", לָמָּה לִי "אֶת הַחַטָּאת" – בִּנְיַן אָב כד] לְכָל שֶׁשְּׁמוֹ חַטָּאת שֶׁטָּעוּן צָפוֹן, דְּלָא תֵּימָא דַּוְוקָא שְׂעִירַת יָחִיד דִּכְתִיב גַּבֵּיהּ. וְלָקַח הַכֹּהֵן. בָּתַר "וְשָׁחַט" כְּתִיב בְּחַטַּאת יָחִיד, וּמַשְׁמַע: כה] בִּמְקוֹם הָעוֹלָה נַמִּי יִלָּקַח. וְהַךְ לְקִיחָה – קַבָּלָה, דְּגָמַר בְּגז"ש בְּת"כ: נֶאֱמַר כָּאן לְקִיחָה וְנֶאֱמַר לְהַלָּן לְקִיחָה "וַיִּקַּח מֹשֶׁה חֲצִי הַדָּם וַיָּשֶׂם בָּאַגָּנוֹת" (שמות כד). מְקַבֵּל עַצְמוֹ. שֶׁצָּרִיךְ לַעֲמוֹד בַּצָּפוֹן, וְלֹא יַעֲמוֹד בַּדָּרוֹם וְיוֹשִׁיט יָדוֹ כו] בַּצָּפוֹן סָמוּךְ לוֹ אֵצֶל אֶמְצַע עֲזָרָה שֶׁהַדָּרוֹם וְהַצָּפוֹן נֶחְלָקוּ שָׁם וִיקַבֵּל, מְנָלַן? דְּהָא אָמַר לְקַמָּן: אִם עָמַד בַּדָּרוֹם וְקִיבֵּל בַּצָּפוֹן – פָּסוּל. וְלָקַח לוֹ כז] יִקַּח. סָרְסֵיהוּ לְמִקְרָא, וְדָרְשֵׁהוּ: אֶת עַצְמוֹ יִקַּח לִמְקוֹם הַדָּם. קְרָא אַחֲרִינָא כְּתִיב. דְּדָרֵישׁ לֵיהּ תַּנָּא לְעִיכּוּבָא, כִּדְתַנְיָא. "וְשָׁחַט אוֹתוֹ" וגו' – בִּשְׂעִיר נָשִׂיא כְּתִיב. אַף זֶה בַּצָּפוֹן. הַאי קְרָא מַגְמַר עֲלֵיהּ.

תוספות

אידי כח] [דאתי מדרשא] חביבא ליה. ואם תאמר: אם כן ליתני עולה לבסוף, כדפריך בשמעתא קמייתא דיבמות (דף ג.) גבי אחות אשה! ויש לומר: איידי כט] דאתיא עולה בציבור – תניא בהדי חטאות דבאות בציבור, והדר תניא אשם דאינו אלא ביחיד.

אשכחן בן צאן בן בקר מנלן. תימה: דלעיל פרק "כל הפסולין" (דף לג:) דרשינן: "בן הבקר לפני ה'" – ואין השוחט לפני ה'. ולא אמרינן: בן צאן מנין. ולכמה דרשות לא מצרכינן תרי קראי לבן בקר ולבן ל] צאן! ושמא אהך דרשא לא] הוי"ו מוסף סמיך. אי נמי: משום דבבן צאן כתיב "אותו" למעוטי – איצטריך הכא לרבויי. מיהו, בההיא ד"בן הבקר לפני ה'" לב] וסמיכה והפשט – ניחא דלא קאמר: בן צאן מנין, דפשיטא דילפינן תחתון מעליון. אבל עליון מתחתון ס"ד דלא יליף. **מה** להלן דבר שחייבין על זדונו כרת. ואם תאמר: היכי יליף מגזירה שוה "מצות" "מצות"! הא חטאת חלב גופה בהיקישא ילפא, לג] כדאמר: *הוקשה כל התורה לעבודה זרה! וי"ל: דכי האי גוונא לא חשיב למד בהיקש אינו חוזר ומלמד *בהיקש, כיון דאי לאו היקשא הוה מוקמינא ליה בכל דבר, ולא אתא היקשא אלא לד] למימר דלא איירי אלא בדבר שיש בו כרת. **דכולי** עלמא היקשא עדיפא. וא"ת: והאמרינן פ' "השולח" (גיטין דף מא:) דכ"ע גזירה שוה עדיפא! לה] וי"ל: הא דקאמר דכ"ע היקש עדיף – היינו לענין א) דטוב לנו לעשות הגז"ש למחצה ממה שנבטל ההיקש לגמרי. אבל התם, דמקיש "או חופשה" דהיינו שטר ל"הפדה לא נפדתה" דהיינו כסף לומר משחרר חצי עבדו בשטר מועיל כמו בכסף, וקאמר גזירה שוה ד"לה" "לה" מאשה עדיפא, מה אשה חציה לא מועיל. והתם לא נתבטל ההיקש, דשמא צריך לו] למילי אוחרי. ועוד י"ל: דשטר בשפחה כנענית *לא קמ"ל אלא בגזירה שוה ד"לה" "לה" מאשה, לכך קאמר דגזירה שוה עדיפא, דטוב לעשות גזירה שוה דתהוי שטר בשפחה כמו גט דאשה שלא להועיל חציה, מלעשותו כמו כסף שסמוך לו "והפדה", דהא מגט אשה נפקא שטר שחרור. ועיקר, ברו"ך.

וחטאת בת דנקא. פי' בקונטרס: לאו דווקא, אלא דמים קלים, שלא ניתן קצבה. והדין עמו, דבהדיא איתא בפ' בתרא דכריתות (דף כז.), גבי: מפני מה לא נתנה תורה שיעור במחוסרי כפרה. ופריך: אלא מעתה חטאת חלב תהא לה קצבה. וא"ת: הא בפ' "מחוסרי כפרה" (כריתות דף י:) משמע דהוי בסלע, גבי האומר "הרי עלי בסלע למזבח" – יביא כבש, שאין לך דבר שקרב בסלע אלא כבש. והאי סלע היינו בלא נסכים, דקאמר דחס רחמנא עליה למיהוי לז] [חד] משיתסר בעשירות! וי"ל: דהתם למלוה מן המובחר ב).

תינח למאן דאית ליה זאת תורת. פלוגתא בשמעתא קמייתא במנחות (דף ג:). והכי נמי הוה מצי למיבעי לרבנן: מנא להו אשם בכסף שקלים בכל אשמות, כיון דלית להו "זאת תורת"?

גמר בערכך בערכך. וא"ת: רבנן, לח] אי אית להו גזירה שוה ד"בערכך בערכך", א"כ "[ואם] נפש" למה ליך? ואי לית להו, א"כ אשם לט] גזילות בכסף שקלים מנא להו? ואומר ר"ת: דאע"ג דאית להו, מ] איצטריך "ואם נפש" שלא יהא ספיקו חמור מודאו. דכי האי גוונא אמר פ' "דם שחיטה" (כריתות כב:): ורבנן אע"ג דכתיב "זאת תורת" איצטריך "ואם נפש" כו', דאי מ"תורה אחת" – הני מילי לשאר אשמות, אבל אשם תלוי לא יהא חמור ספיקו מודאו. וא"ת: לרבנן, מגזירה שוה ד"בערכך" נמי נילף אשם תלוי בספק מעילות! וי"ל: ד"בערכך" לא משמע מא] להקיש, אלא לענין כסף שקלים. ומהאי טעמא נמי איצטריך לר"ע "ואם נפש" לספק מב] מעילות.

אשם שפחה חרופה מג] באיל איל. ובתורת כהנים יליף אשם שפחה לכסף שקלים מגזירה שוה "אשם אשם", *יכול אף אשם נזיר ומצורע כו' – ת"ל "הוא". והיינו טעמא דממעט אשם נזיר ומצורע טפי משאר אשמות, משום דבאין כבש שהוא בן שנה, כדפירש רש"י.

א) [וע"ע תוס' ברכות נ. ד"ה אלא ותוס' יבמות נט. ד"ה דומיא] ב) [ועי' ביתר ביאור תוס' מנחות קז: ד"ה כבש ותוס' כריתות י: ד"ה מכלל]

הג"ה

שיטה מקובצת

א] דאתיא מדרשא: ב] החיצונות ברישא איידי דהני נכנס דמן: ג] מלמדין עליון מתחתון אלא למ"ד אין למדין מאי: ד] מיפלגי דמר סבר: ה] להלן קבועה אף כאן קבועה: ו] למחצה לימא בהא קא מיפלגי דמר סבר יש ג"ש למחצה ומר סבר אין ג"ש למחצה דכ"ע אין ג"ש למחצה והיינו טעמא דר"ע דכתיב ואם נפש ורבנן הכתיב ואם נפש כו' והשאר נמחק: ז] עדיף. נ"א לעולם אימא לך (דכ"ע) [דכו"ע] דהיקש נמי עדיף ואמרי לך כו' כל כתוב בספרי כתיבת יד: ח] עקיבא האי סברא מנא ליה. תימה מאי קושיא.

תורה אור

*וְכִי מִכָּאן אַתָּה לָמֵד? וַהֲלֹא אכְּבָר נֶאֱמַר °"בִּמְקוֹם אֲשֶׁר תִּשָּׁחֵט הָעוֹלָה תִּשָּׁחֵט הַחַטָּאת"! הָא לְמָה יָצָא – לִקְבּוֹעַ לוֹ מָקוֹם, שֶׁאִם לֹא שְׁחָטָהּ בַּצָּפוֹן – פָּסוּל. אַתָּה אוֹמֵר לְכָךְ יָצָא, אוֹ אֵינוֹ אֶלָּא שֶׁזֶּה טָעוּן צָפוֹן וְאֵין אַחֵר טָעוּן צָפוֹן? תַּלְמוּד לוֹמַר: "וְשָׁחַט אֶת הַחַטָּאת בִּמְקוֹם הָעוֹלָה", זֶה בָּנָה אָב לְכָל חַטָּאוֹת שֶׁיְּהוּ טְעוּנוֹת צָפוֹן. אַשְׁכַּחַן שְׂעִיר נָשִׂיא בֵּין לְמִצְוָה בֵּין לְעַכֵּב. שְׁאָר חַטָּאוֹת נַמִי אַשְׁכַּחַן לְמִצְוָה, לְעַכֵּב מְנָא לָן? דִּכְתִיב בִּכְשָׂבָה וּכְתִיב בִּשְׂעִירָה. א] אֶלָּא "אוֹתוֹ" לָמָּה לִי? מִיבְּעֵי לֵיהּ לִכְדְתַנְיָא: *אוֹתוֹ בַּצָּפוֹן, וְאֵין שְׂעִיר נַחְשׁוֹן בַּצָּפוֹן. ב] וְתַנְיָא: *°"וְסָמַךְ יָדוֹ עַל רֹאשׁ הַשָּׂעִיר" – לְרַבּוֹת שְׂעִיר נַחְשׁוֹן לִסְמִיכָה, דִּבְרֵי ר' יְהוּדָה. ר' שִׁמְעוֹן אוֹמֵר: ג] לְרַבּוֹת שְׂעִירֵי עֲבוֹדָה זָרָה לִסְמִיכָה. ס"ד אָמִינָא: הוֹאִיל וְאִיתְרַבּוּ לִסְמִיכָה – אִיתְרַבּוּ נַמִי לְצָפוֹן, קָא מַשְׁמַע לָן. מַתְקִיף לָהּ רָבִינָא: הָנִיחָא לְר' יְהוּדָה, ד] לְר"ש מַאי אִיכָּא לְמֵימַר? א"ל מָר זוּטְרָא בְּרֵיהּ דְּרַב ה] טָבֵי לְרָבִינָא: וּלְר' יְהוּדָה מִי נִיחָא? לְמַאי דְּאִיתְרַבֵּי – אִיתְרַבֵּי, וּמַאי דְּלָא אִיתְרַבֵּי – לָא אִיתְרַבֵּי! וְכִי תֵּימָא, וְאִי לָא מַעֲטֵיהּ קְרָא, הֲוָה אָמִינָא: תֵּיתֵי בְּבִנְיַן אָב – אִם כֵּן, סְמִיכָה גּוּפַהּ תֵּיתֵי מִבִּנְיַן אָב! אֶלָּא ו] מִדּוֹרוֹת לָא גָּמְרִי' – ה"נ מִדּוֹרוֹת לָא גָּמְרִינַן! וְאֶלָּא: אוֹתוֹ בַּצָּפוֹן, וְאֵין שׁוֹחֵט בַּצָּפוֹן. שׁוֹחֵט מִדְּרַבִּי אַחְיָא נָפְקָא. דְּתַנְיָא, *ר' אַחְיָא אוֹמֵר: °"וְשָׁחַט אוֹתוֹ עַל יֶרֶךְ הַמִּזְבֵּחַ צָפֹנָה" מַה תַּלְמוּד לוֹמַר? לְפִי שֶׁמָּצִינוּ ז] עוֹמֵד בַּצָּפוֹן וּמְקַבֵּל בַּצָּפוֹן, וְאִם עָמַד בַּדָּרוֹם וְקִיבֵּל בַּצָּפוֹן בפָּסוּל, יָכוֹל אַף זֶה כֵּן? ת"ל: "אוֹתוֹ" – אוֹתוֹ בַּצָּפוֹן וְאֵין הַשּׁוֹחֵט גבַּצָּפוֹן! אֶלָּא: אוֹתוֹ בַּצָּפוֹן וְאֵין בֶּן עוֹף בַּצָּפוֹן. ח] דְּתַנְיָא: יָכוֹל יְהֵא בֶּן עוֹף טָעוּן צָפוֹן? וְדִין הוּא: וּמָה בֶּן צֹאן שֶׁלֹּא קָבַע לוֹ הַכֹּהֵן – קָבַע לוֹ צָפוֹן, בֶּן עוֹף שֶׁקָּבַע לוֹ כֹּהֵן – אֵינוֹ דִּין שֶׁיִּקְבַּע לוֹ צָפוֹן? ת"ל: "אוֹתוֹ". מַה לְבֶן צֹאן שֶׁכֵּן קָבַע לוֹ כְּלִי! אֶלָּא: אוֹתוֹ בַּצָּפוֹן ט] וְאֵין פֶּסַח בַּצָּפוֹן. דְּתַנְיָא, ר' אֱלִיעֶזֶר בֶּן יַעֲקֹב אוֹמֵר: יָכוֹל יְהֵא פֶּסַח טָעוּן צָפוֹן? וְדִין הוּא: וּמָה עוֹלָה, שֶׁכֵּן לֹא קָבַע לוֹ זְמַן לִשְׁחִיטָתוֹ – קָבַע לוֹ צָפוֹן, פֶּסַח שֶׁקָּבַע לוֹ זְמַן לִשְׁחִיטָתוֹ – אֵינוֹ דִּין שֶׁיִּקְבַּע לוֹ צָפוֹן? ת"ל: "אוֹתוֹ". *מַה לְעוֹלָה שֶׁכֵּן כָּלִיל! מֵחַטָּאת. *מַה לְחַטָּאת שֶׁכֵּן מְכַפֶּרֶת עַל חַיָּיבֵי כְרֵיתוֹת! מֵאָשָׁם. מַה לְאָשָׁם שֶׁכֵּן קָדְשֵׁי קָדָשִׁים! י] מִכּוּלָּן נַמִי, שֶׁכֵּן קָדְשֵׁי קָדָשִׁים! לְעוֹלָם כִּדַאֲמָרַן מֵעִיקָּרָא: אוֹתוֹ בַּצָּפוֹן וְאֵין שׁוֹחֵט בַּצָּפוֹן. וּדְקַשְׁיָא לָךְ: מִדְּרַבִּי אַחְיָא נָפְקָא לָן – לָאו לְמַעוּטֵי שׁוֹחֵט בַּצָּפוֹן, אֶלָּא: אֵין שׁוֹחֵט בַּצָּפוֹן, אֲבָל מְקַבֵּל בַּצָּפוֹן. מְקַבֵּל יא] מִ"לָקַח" "וְלָקַח" נָפְקָא! "לָקַח" וְ"לָקַח" לָא מַשְׁמַע לֵיהּ. אַשְׁכַּחַן שְׁחִיטָה בְּעוֹלָה יב] לְמִצְוָה, קַבָּלָה נַמִי לְמִצְוָה אַשְׁכַּחַן, שְׁחִיטָה וְקַבָּלָה לְעַכֵּב מְנָלַן? אָמַר רַב אַדָּא בַּר אַהֲבָה, וְאִיתֵּימָא רַבָּה בַּר שֵׁילָא: ק"ו, וּמַה חַטָּאת הַבָּאָה מִכֹּחַ עוֹלָה – מְעַכֶּבֶת, עוֹלָה שֶׁבָּאָה חַטָּאת מִכֹּחָהּ – אֵינוֹ דִּין שֶׁמְּעַכֶּבֶת? מַה לְחַטָּאת שֶׁכֵּן מְכַפֶּרֶת עַל חַיָּיבֵי כָרֵיתוֹת! אֲמַר רָבִינָא: הָא קַשְׁיָא לֵיהּ לְרַב אַדָּא בַּר אַהֲבָה: כְּלוּם מָצִינוּ *טָפֵל חָמוּר מִן הָעִיקָּר? אֲמַר לֵיהּ מָר זוּטְרָא בְּרֵיהּ דְּרַב מָרִי לְרָבִינָא: וְלָא? וַהֲרֵי

רש"י

וְכִי מִכָּאן. יג] צָרִיךְ לְלַמֵּד לָזֶה בִּפְנֵי עַצְמוֹ? וַהֲלֹא כָּל הַחַטָּאוֹת בִּכְלַל "תּוֹרַת הַחַטָּאת" – "בִּמְקוֹם אֲשֶׁר תִּשָּׁחֵט הָעוֹלָה" וגו'! יד] לִקְבּוֹעַ. לִשְׁנוֹת עָלָיו, לְעַכֵּב קִיבּוּעוֹ בְּכָךְ. אוֹ אֵינוֹ. בָּא לְעַכֵּב, אֶלָּא לִכְתּוֹב בּוֹ "אוֹתוֹ" דְּהָוֵי מִיעוּטָא, וּלְלַמֵּד: זֶה בַּצָּפוֹן וְאֵין שָׂעִיר אַחֵר בַּצָּפוֹן, כְּגוֹן שְׂעִירֵי יוה"כ, וּשְׂעִירֵי עֲבוֹדָה זָרָה, וְשֶׁל מוּסְפֵי הַמּוֹעֲדוֹת. וּמָה אֲנִי מְקַיֵּים "תִּשָּׁחֵט הַחַטָּאת" – בִּשְׁאָר בְּהֵמוֹת חוּץ מִשְּׂעִירִים, דְּ"אוֹתוֹ" כְּתִיב לְמַעוּטִינְהוּ. תַּלְמוּד לוֹמַר. בִּשְׂעִירַת יָחִיד (ויקרא ד): "וְשָׁחַט אֶת הַחַטָּאת", דַּהֲוָה לֵיהּ לְמִכְתַּב "וְשָׁחַט אוֹתָהּ" – בִּנְיַן אָב הוּא לְכָל טו] חַטָּאוֹת. וְעִיכּוּבָא מִיהָא לָא נָפְקָא לָן מִינֵּיהּ, דְּאִיכָּא לְמֵימַר לְמִצְוָה אִיצְטְרִיךְ, וּלְהָבִיא שְׂעִירֵי חַטָּאוֹת דְּלָא לְמַעוּטִינְהוּ מֵ"אוֹתוֹ" דִּשְׂעִיר נָשִׂיא. וּלְקַמָּן פָּרֵיךְ: וְאֶלָּא "אוֹתוֹ" לָמָּה לִי? שְׁאָר חַטָּאוֹת נַמִי לְמִצְוָה. אַשְׁכַּחַן מִ"תִּשָּׁחֵט הַחַטָּאת". דִּכְתִיב בִּכְשָׂבָה וּכְתִיב בִּשְׂעִירָה. טז] בְּכוּלָּם כְּתִיב: "בִּמְקוֹם אֲשֶׁר יִשָּׁחֵט הָעוֹלָה", וְסַגִּי לֵיהּ בִּשְׂעִירָה וְתֵילַף מִינֵּיהּ כִּשְׂבָּה לְמִצְוָה, וְכִי הֲדַר כְּתָבֵיהּ בִּכְשָׂבָה – תְּנֵהוּ לְעִנְיַן לִפְנִימִיּוֹת וְלִשְׂעִירֵי הָרְגָלִים לְעִיכּוּבָא. וְאֵין שְׂעִיר נַחְשׁוֹן. שְׂעִירֵי חֲנוּכַּת הַנְּשִׂיאִים, שֶׁלֹּא בָּאוּ עַל חֵטְא. *לִכְדְתַנְיָא. דְּאִיתְרַבֵּי לִסְמִיכָה, וְס"ד לְרַבּוּיֵי נַמִי לִשְׁחִיטָה בַּצָּפוֹן, לְהָכִי כְּתִיב "אוֹתוֹ" לְמַעוּטֵי. עַל רֹאשׁ הַשָּׂעִיר. בִּשְׂעִיר נָשִׂיא כְּתִיב, וַהֲוָה לֵיהּ לְמִכְתַּב "עַל רֹאשׁוֹ". לְרַבּוֹת שְׂעִירֵי עֲבוֹדָה זָרָה לִסְמִיכָה. מִשּׁוּם דְּמַעֲטִינְהוּ ר' יְהוּדָה יז] לִסְמִיכָה בְּמַסֶּ' מְנָחוֹת (דף צב.) *מֵהַאי דְּשָׂעִיר הַמִּשְׁתַּלֵּחַ, דִּכְתִיב: "וְסָמַךְ אַהֲרֹן אֶת שְׁתֵּי יָדָיו עַל רֹאשׁ הַשָּׂעִיר הַחַי" (ויקרא טז) – הַחַי טָעוּן סְמִיכָה, וְאֵין שְׂעִירֵי עֲבוֹדָה זָרָה טְעוּנִין סְמִיכָה. וְר"ש דָּרֵשׁ: הַחַי טָעוּן סְמִיכָה בְּאַהֲרֹן, וְאֵין שְׂעִיר עֲבוֹדָה זָרָה טָעוּן סְמִיכָה בְּאַהֲרֹן אֶלָּא בְּזִקְנֵי הָעֵדָה, וּמְרַבֵּי לֵיהּ מֵהָכָא. הָנִיחָא לְרַבִּי יְהוּדָה. דִּמְרַבֵּי לֵיהּ לִסְמִיכָה, אִיצְטְרִיךְ לְמַעוּטֵי יח] צָפוֹן. לְמַאי דְּלָא אִיתְרַבֵּי לָא אִיתְרַבֵּי. דְּהָא רִבּוּיָא גַּבֵּי סְמִיכָה כְּתִיב, וְצָפוֹן מֵהֵיכָא תֵּיתֵי? הָכִי גָּרְסִינַן לְהָךְ סוּגְיָא בִּמְנָחוֹת (דף נה:): וְכִי תֵּימָא אִי לָא מַעֲטֵיהּ קְרָא הֲוָה אָמִינָא תֵּיתֵי בְּבִנְיַן אָב א"כ סְמִיכָה גּוּפָהּ לִשְׁתּוֹק קְרָא מִינֵּיהּ וְתֵיתֵי מִבִּנְיַן אָב. בְּבִנְיַן אָב. מִ"וְשָׁחַט אֶת הַחַטָּאת". סְמִיכָה גּוּפָהּ נַמִי תֵּיתֵי מִבִּנְיַן אָב. דִּכְתִיב: "וְסָמַךְ יט] עַל רֹאשׁ הַחַטָּאת", וּמָצֵי לְמִכְתַּב "עַל רֹאשׁוֹ", (א) אֶלָּא בִּנְיַן אָב הוּא לְכָל שֶׁשְּׁמוֹ חַטָּאת שֶׁיִּטְעוֹן סְמִיכָה. אֶלָּא כ] כו'. מַסְקָנָא דְּקוּשְׁיָא הִיא: סְמִיכָה מַאי טַעְמָא אִיצְטְרִיךְ לְרַבּוּיֵי – מִשּׁוּם דְּאִי לָא רִבּוּיָא לָא הֲוָה גָּמְרִינַן קָדְשֵׁי שָׁעָה בְּבִנְיַן אָב מִקָּדְשֵׁי דוֹרוֹת. הָכִי נַמִי כא] מִשְּׁחִיטַת צָפוֹן לָמָּה לִי "אוֹתוֹ" לְמַעוּטֵי? כָּל כַּמָּה דְּלָא לֵימָא קְרָא – לָא גָּמְרִי בְּבִנְיַן אָב! וְלֹא שׁוֹחֵט בַּצָּפוֹן. אֵין צָרִיךְ שֶׁיַּעֲמוֹד בַּצָּפוֹן, שֶׁאִם רָצָה – עוֹמֵד בַּדָּרוֹם אֵצֶל צָפוֹן, וְיוֹשִׁיט יָדוֹ בַּצָּפוֹן וְיִשְׁחוֹט. לְפִי שֶׁמָּצִינוּ שֶׁהַמְקַבֵּל כו'. כב] מִ"לָקַח" "וְלָקַח" כִּדְלְעֵיל. ה"ג: אֶלָּא אוֹתוֹ בַּצָּפוֹן וְאֵין בֶּן עוֹף בַּצָּפוֹן דְּתַנְיָא יָכוֹל יְהֵא בֶּן עוֹף טָעוּן צָפוֹן וְדִין הוּא כו' ת"ל אוֹתוֹ מַה לְבֶן צֹאן כו'. וְאֵין בֶּן עוֹף. מְלִיקַת תּוֹרִין וּבְנֵי יוֹנָה. שֶׁלֹּא קָבַע לוֹ כֹּהֵן. דִּשְׁחִיטָה בְּזָר כְּשֵׁרָה. בֶּן עוֹף כג] קָבַע לוֹ כֹּהֵן. [דִּכְתִיב] "וְהִקְרִיבוֹ הַכֹּהֵן אֶל הַמִּזְבֵּחַ וּמָלַק אֶת רֹאשׁוֹ" וגו' (ויקרא א). שֶׁכֵּן קָבַע לוֹ כְּלִי. סַכִּין לִשְׁחִיטָה, מִ"וַיִּקַּח אֶת הַמַּאֲכֶלֶת" (לקמן דף נז:) וְהָתָם עוֹלָה הֲוַאי, וְכֵן מִזְרָק לְקַבֵּל. תֹּאמַר בְּבֶן עוֹף שֶׁנִּמְלָק בְּצִפּוֹרֶן. וְלֹא פֶּסַח בַּצָּפוֹן. דְּלָא כד] תֵּתְיֵיהּ בְּקַל וָחוֹמֶר: הוֹאִיל וְקָבַע זְמַן לִשְׁחִיטָתוֹ בֵּין הָעַרְבַּיִם – יִקְבַּע לוֹ מָקוֹם נַמִי לַצָּפוֹן. "מִדְּרַבִּי אֱלִיעֶזֶר בֶּן יַעֲקֹב נָפְקָא" לָא גָּרַס, אֶלָּא הָכִי גָּרְסִינַן: וְלֹא פֶּסַח בַּצָּפוֹן דְּתַנְיָא רַבִּי אֱלִיעֶזֶר בֶּן יַעֲקֹב אוֹמֵר כו'. וְכֵן מְצָאתִיהָ בִּסְפָרִים הָרִאשׁוֹנִים. אֵינוֹ דִּין שֶׁיִּקְבַּע לוֹ צָפוֹן תַּלְמוּד לוֹמַר אוֹתוֹ גָּרְסִינַן. מֵחַטָּאת. אִי לָאו דְּמַעֲטֵיהּ הֲוָה מַיְיתִינַן לֵיהּ מֵחַטָּאת, שֶׁאֵינָהּ כָּלִיל וּטְעוּנָה צָפוֹן. מִכּוּלְּהוּ נַמִי כה] שֶׁכֵּן קָדְשֵׁי קָדָשִׁים. כְּלוֹמַר, וְאִי בָּעֵי לְאַתּוּיֵי נַמִי מִכּוּלְּהוּ בְּ"מַה הַצַּד" אִיכָּא לְמִיפְרְכֵיהּ לְהָא פִּירְכָא "שֶׁכֵּן קָדְשֵׁי קָדָשִׁים". לָאו לְמַעוּטֵי שׁוֹחֵט בַּצָּפוֹן. "אוֹתוֹ" דִּגְבֵי שָׂעִיר – לָאו לְמַעוּטֵי שׁוֹחֵט בַּצָּפוֹן קָאָמְרִי, דְּוַדַּאי מֵ"אוֹתוֹ" דְּרַבִּי אַחְיָא נָפְקָא. כו] אֶלָּא לְרַבּוּיָא מִדּוּקְיָא דְּמִיעוּטָא דְּשׁוֹחֵט בַּצָּפוֹן דִּמְקַבֵּל בַּצָּפוֹן, דְּהָכִי דָּרְשִׁינַן: "אוֹתוֹ" בַּצָּפוֹן וְאֵין שׁוֹחֵט בַּצָּפוֹן, אֲבָל מְקַבֵּל בַּצָּפוֹן. קַבָּלָה נַמִי אַשְׁכַּחַן. כִּדַאֲמָרַן: אֲבָל מְקַבֵּל בַּצָּפוֹן. כז] הָא קַשְׁיָא לֵיהּ. כְּלוֹמַר, מֵהַאי כח] טַעַם דַּיֵּיק קַל וָחוֹמֶר דִּידֵיהּ. טָפֵל חָמוּר מִן הָעִיקָּר. לָמֵד חָמוּר מִן הַמְלַמֵּד, כְּגוֹן חַטָּאת שֶׁבָּאָה מִכֹּחַ עוֹלָה, דְּעִיקַּר צָפוֹן בְּעוֹלָה כְּתִיב. וַהֲרֵי

תוספות

הגה"ה אותו בצפון ולא שוחט בצפון. תימה: ל"ל קרא? הא אפילו "לפני ה'" לא בעי, כדדרשינן לעיל בריש "כל הפסולין" (דף לב:): "בן הבקר לפני ה'" – ולא שוחט לפני ה'! ויש לומר: דהכא סובר כר"ש התימני, דדריש התם כט] האי *כתוב בענין אחר.

מה לבן צאן שכן קבע לו כלי. ותימה: דלא פריך הכי בפ"ק *דקדושין (דף לו:): ל] ומה בן צאן שלא קבע לו כהן לשחיטתו קבע לו כהן להזאתו, בן עוף שקבע לו כהן במליקתו – אינו דין שיקבע לו כהן בהזאתו! ויש לומר: דהתם *דכל דינו בכהן – לא שייך למיפרך מכלי. לא] ול"נ: כיון דהדין הוי מהזאה – לא שייך למיפרך מכלי דשחיטה. וא"ת: וליעביד הכא קל וחומר ממקום: ומה בן צאן שלא קבע לו מזבח בשחיטתו – קבע לו מקום צפון, לב] בן עוף שקבע לו מזבח במליקתו כדדרשינן (לקמן דף סה.): מה הקטרה בראשו של מזבח אף מליקה – אינו דין שיקבע לו צפון? וזה אין לומר, לג] דסד"א דבן עוף כיון דחטאת קרייה רחמנא ליבעי צפון לד] ד"זאת תורת החטאת", דשמא ד"זאת תורת" לא הוי אלא לנשחטות*.

אלא אין שוחט בצפון אבל מקבל בצפון. תימה: הא נמי מדרבי אחיא נפקא, מדאיצטריך למעוטי שוחט – מכלל דמקבל בצפון, דאי לא דמקבל בצפון – למה לי קרא למעוטי שוחט, כדקאמר רבי אחיא: לפי שמצינו שמקבל בצפון, יכול אף זה כן! ושמא רבי אחיא דריש "ולקח" – לו יקח, אבל אנן לא דרשינן ליה.

קבלה נמי למצוה אשכחן. פי' בקונט', כדאמר: אבל מקבל בצפון. וקשה: דמ"אותו" דכתיב גבי עולה דרשינן ולא שוחט בצפון, ומ"אותו" דכתיב גבי חטאת דרשינן: אבל מקבל בצפון, וא"כ מקבל למצוה בעולה מנא לן? וגבי אשם צריכי תרי קראי למצוה, לקבלה ומקבל. ועוד: לה] עיכובא במקבל בחטאת מנא לן? דלא מצינו שנה אלא על השחיטה ועל הקבלה, אבל לא על המקבל! וי"ל: *מכיון דאשכחן למצוה מקבל כקבלה – ה"ה לעכב. וכי האי גוונא אמרינן בפ"ק (לעיל ד.): נאמרה זביחה בחטאת ונאמרה זביחה בשלמים, מה התם לא חלקת כו'. והרי

אֵ] וַהֲרֵי מַעֲשֵׂר, דְּהוּא נִפְדֶּה, וְאִילּוּ לָקוּחַ בְּכֶסֶף מַעֲשֵׂר אֵינוֹ נִפְדֶּה. דִּתְנַן: *אהַלָּקוּחַ בְּכֶסֶף מַעֲשֵׂר שֶׁנִּטְמָא — יִפָּדֶה, ר' יְהוּדָה אוֹמֵר: יִקָּבֵר; בֵ] (נִטְמָא — אִין, לֹא נִטְמָא — לָא!) הָתָם לָא אַלִּימָא קְדוּשָּׁתֵיהּ לְמִיתְפַּס פִּדְיוֹנֵיהּ. וַהֲרֵי תְּמוּרָה, דְּאִילּוּ *קָדָשִׁים לָא חָיְילִי עַל בַּעַל מוּם קָבוּעַ, וְאִילּוּ באִיהִי חָיְילָא! תְּמוּרָה מִכֹּחַ קָדָשִׁים קָא אָתְיָא, וְקָדָשִׁים מִכֹּחַ חוּלִּין קָאָתֵי. הֲרֵי פֶּסַח, דְּהוּא אֵינוֹ גטָעוּן סְמִיכָה וּנְסָכִים וּתְנוּפַת חָזֶה וָשׁוֹק, וְאִילּוּ מוֹתָר דִּידֵיהּ טָעוּן סְמִיכָה וּנְסָכִים וּתְנוּפַת חָזֶה וָשׁוֹק! גֵ] פֶּסַח בִּשְׁאָר יְמוֹת הַשָּׁנָה שְׁלָמִים הוּא. וְאִיבָּעֵית אֵימָא: אָמַר קְרָא "הָעוֹלָה" — דֵ] בִּמְקוֹמָהּ תְּהֵא. אָשָׁם דמִנַּלַן דְּבָעֵי צָפוֹן? דִּכְתִיב: °"בִּמְקוֹם אֲשֶׁר יִשְׁחֲטוּ אֶת הָעוֹלָה יִשְׁחֲטוּ אֶת הָאָשָׁם". אַשְׁכַּחַן שְׁחִיטָה, קַבָּלָה מְנָא לַן? הֵ] "וְאֶת דָּמוֹ יִזְרוֹק" — קִבּוּל דָּמוֹ נַמִי בַּצָּפוֹן. מְקַבֵּל עַצְמוֹ מְנָא לַן? "דָּמוֹ" — "וְאֶת דָּמוֹ". אַשְׁכַּחַן לְמִצְוָה, לְעַכֵּב וֵ] מְנָא לַן? קְרָא אַחֲרִינָא כְּתִיב: °"וְשָׁחַט אֶת הַכֶּבֶשׂ". זֵ] וְהַאי לְהָכִי הוּא דַּאֲתָא? הַאי מִיבָּעֵי לֵיהּ לִכְדְתַנְיָא: *דָּבָר שֶׁהָיָה בִּכְלָל וְיָצָא לִידּוֹן בַּדָּבָר הֶחָדָשׁ — אִי אַתָּה חֵ] רַשַּׁאי לְהַחֲזִירוֹ לִכְלָלוֹ עַד שֶׁיַּחֲזִירֶנּוּ הַכָּתוּב לִכְלָלוֹ בְּפֵירוּשׁ, כֵּיצַד? °"וְשָׁחַט אֶת הַכֶּבֶשׂ בִּמְקוֹם אֲשֶׁר יִשְׁחַט אֶת הַחַטָּאת וְאֶת הָעוֹלָה בִּמְקוֹם הַקֹּדֶשׁ כִּי כַּחַטָּאת טֵ] הָאָשָׁם הוּא" וגו', יֵ] שֶׁאֵין ת"ל "כַּחַטָּאת הָאָשָׁם", מַה ת"ל "כַּחַטָּאת הָאָשָׁם"? לְפִי שֶׁיָּצָא אֲשַׁם מְצוֹרָע לִידּוֹן בַּדָּבָר הֶחָדָשׁ, בְּבוֹהֶן יָד וּבוֹהֶן רֶגֶל וְאֹזֶן יְמָנִית, יָכוֹל לֹא יְהֵא טָעוּן מַתַּן דָּמִים וְאֵימוּרִין לְגַבֵּי מִזְבֵּחַ? תַּלְמוּד לוֹמַר: "כַּחַטָּאת הָאָשָׁם הוּא", מַה חַטָּאת טְעוּנָה מַתַּן דָּמִים וְאֵימוּרִין לְגַבֵּי מִזְבֵּחַ — יאֵ] אַף אֲשַׁם מְצוֹרָע טָעוּן מַתַּן דָּמִים וְאֵימוּרִין לְגַבֵּי מִזְבֵּחַ. אִם כֵּן, נִכְתּוֹב בְּהַאי וְלָא נִכְתּוֹב בְּהַאי. הָנִיחָא אִי סְבִירָא לַן: יָצָא לִידּוֹן בַּדָּבָר הֶחָדָשׁ — אִיהוּ הוּא דְּלָא גָּמַר מִכְּלָלוֹ, אֲבָל

(מסורת הש"ס: ויקרא ו | שם יד | שם)

רש"י

וַהֲרֵי מַעֲשֵׂר שֵׁנִי דְּהוּא נִפְדֶּה. אֲפִי' בִּירוּשָׁלַיִם אִם נִטְמָא, כִּדְיָלְפִינַן (ב"מ דף נג:) מִ"לֹּא תוּכַל שְׂאֵתוֹ", וְאֵין "שְׂאֵת" אֶלָּא אֲכִילָה, שֶׁנֶּאֱמַר: "וַיִּשָּׂא מַשְׂאוֹת". אֵינוֹ נִפְדֶּה. אַלִּיבָּא דְּר' יְהוּדָה. אַלְמָא: אִיכָּא טָפֵל חָמוּר מֵעִיקָּר. הָתָם מִשּׁוּם דְּלָא אַלִּים. וְלָא חוּמְרָא הוּא. קָדָשִׁים לָא חָיְילִי יבֵ] (עֲלֵיהּ). תְּחִילַּת הֶקְדֵּשׁ אֵינוֹ חָל עַל בַּעַל מוּם קָבוּעַ לִיקַדֵּשׁ קְדוּשַּׁת הַגּוּף, אֶלָּא קְדוּשַּׁת דָּמִים בְּעָלְמָא, וְיוֹצְאִין לְחוּלִּין גְּמוּרִין בְּפִדְיוֹן, וַאֲפִילּוּ לִיגָּזֵז וְלֵיעָבֵד, כִּדְתַנְיָא יגֵ] פֶּרֶק "הוֹצִיאוּ לוֹ" בְּסֵדֶר יוֹמָא (דף נ:): חוֹמֶר בִּתְמוּרָה, שֶׁהַתְּמוּרָה חָלָה עַל בַּעַל מוּם קָבוּעַ, וְאֵין יוֹצֵא לְחוּלִּין לִיגָּזֵז וְלֵיעָבֵד, מַה שֶּׁאֵין כֵּן בְּזֶבַח. דְּגַבֵּי תְּמוּרָה כְּתִיב "טוֹב בְּרָע" — ידֵ] הִשְׁוָה בַּעַל מוּם לְתָם לְעִנְיַן תְּמוּרָה, עַל כּוּלָּם נֶאֱמַר "וְהָיָה הוּא וּתְמוּרָתוֹ יִהְיֶה קֹּדֶשׁ". אֲבָל זֶבַח רִאשׁוֹן, אִם קָדַם הֶקְדֵּשׁוֹ אֶת מוּמוֹ — קָדוֹשׁ קְדוּשַּׁת הַגּוּף, וְאֵינוֹ יוֹצֵא לְחוּלִּין לִיגָּזֵז *וְלֵיעָבֵד, טוֵ] כִּדְתַנְיָא בִּבְכוֹרוֹת (דף יד.): כָּל הַקֳּדָשִׁים שֶׁקָּדַם מוּמָן לְהֶקְדֵּשָׁן — טזֵ] נִפְדֶּה. וְיָלֵיף לָהּ מִקְרָאֵי. קָדָשִׁים מִכֹּחַ חוּלִּין קָאָתוּ. לֹא חָלָה עֲלֵיהֶם קְדוּשָּׁה קוֹדֶמֶת. אֲבָל תְּמוּרָה בָּאָה מִכֹּחַ קְדוּשָּׁה קוֹדֶמֶת, הִלְכָּךְ לָאו טָפֵל חָמוּר מִן הָעִיקָּר הוּא, דְּהָא חוּמְרָא דְּעִיקָּר הוּא. שְׁלָמִים הוּא. וְלָא מוֹתַר פֶּסַח מִיקְּרֵי לְמִיחְשְׁבֵיהּ טָפֵל. וְאִיבָּעֵית אֵימָא. עִיכּוּבָא דְּעוֹלָה מֵהָכָא. דִּכְתִיב בִּמְקוֹם יזֵ] כו' הָעוֹלָה. חָזַר וְשָׁנָה. לִימֵּד: מָקוֹם שֶׁקְּבָעַתּוֹ לְעוֹלָה — לְעוֹלָם הוּא מְקוֹמָהּ. יִשְׁחֲטוּ אֶת הָאָשָׁם וְאֶת דָּמוֹ. בִּמְקוֹם שְׁחִיטָתוֹ תְּהֵא קַבָּלַת דָּמוֹ. דָּמוֹ וְאֶת דָּמוֹ. מִדְּמָלֵי לְמִיכְתַּב "יִשְׁחֲטוּ אֶת הָאָשָׁם וְדָמוֹ יִזְרוֹק", וּכְתִיב "וְאֶת דָּמוֹ" — "אֶת" לְרַבּוֹת אֶת הַמְקַבֵּל. וְשָׁחַט אֶת הַכֶּבֶשׂ וגו'. בַּאֲשַׁם מְצוֹרָע כְּתִיב, שָׁנָה הַכָּתוּב עָלָיו לְעַכֵּב. לִכְדְתַנְיָא כו'. דְּצָרִיךְ לְהַחֲזִירוֹ לִכְלָלוֹ. הִלְכָּךְ, לְעִנְיַן שְׁחִיטַת צָפוֹן נַמִי בָּעֵי לְהַחֲזִירוֹ, דְּאִי לָא הֲדַר כְּתָבֵיהּ בְּגַוֵּיהּ, כִּי הֵיכִי דְּאַהַדְרֵיהּ לְמַתַּן דָּמוֹ — הֲוָה אָמֵינָא לָא לִיבָּעֵי צָפוֹן. אִי אַתָּה יָכוֹל לְהַחֲזִירוֹ לִכְלָלוֹ. שֶׁיְּהֵא עוֹד כִּשְׁאָר הַכְּלָל. שֶׁיָּצָא אֲשַׁם מְצוֹרָע. מִכְּלַל "זֹאת תּוֹרַת הָאָשָׁם", דַּהֲוָה כְּתַב בְּכוּלְּהוּ "וְאֶת דָּמוֹ יִזְרוֹק עַל *הַמִּזְבֵּחַ". יחֵ] אַף כָּאן לִשְׁחִיטַת צָפוֹן נַמִי, לְהַחֲזִירוֹ הוּא דְּשָׁנָה עָלֵיהּ. לִכְתּוֹב. שְׁחִיטַת צָפוֹן בַּאֲשַׁם מְצוֹרָע, וְלָא נִכְתּוֹב גַּבֵּי "זֹאת תּוֹרַת הָאָשָׁם", וְנִגְמַר כּוּלָּן מִינֵּיהּ. יטֵ] וּמִדִּכְתָבֵיהּ הָכָא וְהָכָא — לְעִיכּוּבָא הוּא. אֲבָל

(מסורת הש"ס: פסחים לח. ב"מ נג. מעשר שני פ"ג מ"י סנהדרין קיב. | תמורה יז: | יבמות ז. | גי' הב"ח ולעבד אבל קדם מומן להקדישן לאין קדושת הגוף עליהם אלא קדושת דמים כדתנן כו' כל"ל וכ"ה בס"י | גי' הב"ח המזבח הס"ד ואח"כ מ"ה א"כ לכתובינהו לשחיטת צפון כו' הס"ד וכל"ל)

תוספות

והרי מעשר דהוא נפדה. אפילו בירושלים אם נטמא, כדילפינן מ"לא תוכל שאתו" ואין "שאת" אלא אכילה, ואילו לקוח בכסף מעשר שני אינו נפדה אליבא דר' יהודה, כן] אלמא: איכא טפל חמור מעיקר, כך פי' בקונטרס. ובספרי פרשת "עשר תעשר" מפרש טעמא דרבי יהודה: משום דכתיב ["הכסף"] – כסף ראשון ולא כסף שני. והא דאמר בריש "הזהב" (ב"מ דף מה.) גבי סלעין דינרין, ד"כסף" "כסף" ריבה – יש לחלק בזה שנגמר כאן פדיונו לגמרי *וקנה כאן] פדיונו מעשר, ואם היה טהור – לא היה נפדה, ותנן במסכת מעשר שני פ' שלישי (מ"י) אמרו לו לר' יהודה: מה אם מעשר שני עצמו שנטמא הרי הוא נפדה, הלקוח בכסף מעשר שנטמא אינו דין שיפדה? אמר להם: לא, אם אמרתם במעשר שני עצמו – שכן נפדה טהור ברחוק מקום, תאמרו בלקוח בכסף מעשר שאינו נפדה טהור ברחוק מקום. ואית ספרים דגרסי הכא: נטמא – אין, לא נטמא – לא. ומייתי ראייה מרבנן דטפל חמור מעיקר, פירוש: נטמא נפדה לרבנן, לא נטמא – אינו נפדה אפי' חוץ לירושלים, אע"פ שמעשר עצמו נפדה, והיינו חוץ לירושלים, דבירושלים אין מעשר טהור נפדה. ובתוספתא דמעשר שני משמע כפי' הקונטרס, דעל מילתא דר' יהודה כבן] פרכינן האי לישנא שעושה טפל חמור מן העיקר. והכי איתא התם: הלקוח בכסף מעשר כו', אמרו לו לרבי יהודה: תחמיר בטפילה יותר מן העיקר? כגן] ולגירסת הספרים "לא נטמא לא", ומוכיח דרבנן נמי סברי טפל חמור מן העיקר גבי מעשר טהור חוץ לירושלים, כדן] קשה: *)דאי פרכי רבנן לר' יהודה – תיקשי להו לדידהו, כיון דקורא טפל חמור מן העיקר האי דלקוח טהור אינו נפדה ומעשר כהן] עצמו נפדה! אבל לגירסת הקונטרס ניחא, דאיכא למימר דהאי לא מיקרי טפל חמור מן העיקר, דמעשר עצמו טהור נפדה ברחוק מקום כדי *לפדות בדמים בירושלים בקר וצאן יין ושכר, כדכתיב: "ונתת הכסף בכל אשר תאוה נפשך", אבל אם לקח פירות בו חוץ לירושלים כדי לאוכלם בירושלים – לא יפדה, כמו שלא היה פודה מה שהיה לוקח בירושלים. ולגירסת הספרים כון] "לא נטמא לא" קשה לפירוש הקונטרס דפרק "הזהב" (ב"מ דף נה:) גבי מחללין אותו כסף על נחשת נחשת על הפירות ויחזור ויפדה את הפירות, כזן] וחכמים אומרים יעלו פירות ויאכלו בירושלים. ופי' בקונטרס: וחכמים אומרים לא הזקיקוהו לחזור לחללם, כמו ת"ק, אלא אם רצה – יעלה פירות עצמו, דהקלו בו. משמע מתוך פירושו דר"מ מחמיר, דלא שרי נחשת על הפירות אא"כ יחזור ויפדה את הפירות ויעלה הכסף לירושלים. והכא משמע שזו היא קולא כשחוזר ופודה את הפירות, ומשמע דאפילו איסורא איכא למאי דגרסי' "לא נטמא לא", דאינו נפדה טהור ברחוק מקום, ומשנה שלימה היא במסכת כחן] מעשרות (פ"ג מ"י). ושם הארכתי בפרק "הזהב" (ב"מ דף נה: ד"ה ויחזור). **פסח** בשאר ימות השנה שלמים הוא. וא"ת: הרי אחד עשר, כטן] שטפל חמור מן העיקר, כדאמרינן בפ' "שתי מדות" (מנחות נא:): "האחד" – זה אחד עשר, שלא מלינו לו בכל התורה טפל חמור מן העיקר! וי"ל, כדמשני הכא: מותר הפסח שלמים הוי – ה"נ אחד עשר שלמים הוי, דכל דיני שלמים עליו, כדמשמע בבכורות (דף סא.) לן] *מדמצריך קרא. דמותר הפסח נמי בעי קרא, כדדרשינן פרק קמא (לעיל ט.): "אם כשב" – להביא פסח שעברה שנתו ושלמים הבאין מחמת פסח לכל מלות שלמים, שיטענו סמיכה ונסכים ותנופת חזה ושוק. והא דקרי ליה לאן] טפל – לאו דווקא. **לעכב** מנא לן דכתיב ושחט את הכבש. למקבל לא ידעינן עיכובא*. **לפי** שיצא אשם מצורע לידון בדבר החדש כו'. מה שחטאת לבן] מצורע טעונה נסכים ושאר חטאות אין טעונין – לא חשיב דבר חדש. וכן אוב וידעוני שיש כרת מה שאין כן בשאר מכשפים, מדלא תני בל"ו כריתות, ואפ"ה גמרינן סקילה מאוב וידעוני בשאר מכשפים פרק קמא דיבמות (דף ד.) ופרק "ארבע מיתות" (סנהדרין דף סז:). ואי מקרי כרת דכתיב באוב וידעוני דבר חדש, היכי גמר מינייהו סקילה למ"ד לגן] כללו לא גמר מיניה? וזה הקשה ה"ר יעקב מאורלינ"ש. אלא, *לא קרוי דבר חדש אלא כשסותר כללו, כי הכא, דשאר אשמות כל הדם למזבח, ואשם מצורע – לדן] הדם ממנו לבהונות. וכגון אשת אח בפרק קמא דיבמות (דף ז.), שנאסרו כל העריות וזו הותרה, וזהו דבר החדש שסותר כללו. אבל מה שחטאת להן] מצורע טעונה נסכים – אינו סותר מכללו, אלא תוספת הוא על הקרבן. וא"ת: למאן דאמר כללו גמר מיניה – יהיו כל אשמות טעונין מתן בהונות, ולילפו נמי כולהו עריות מאשת אח! וי"ל: דלא גמר מיניה אלא מידי דלא חידש בו, כגון שחיטת לפון. אבל החידוש – לא גמר מיניה, כדפירש בקונטרס, דא"כ לא היה עוד כאן דבר חדש. ועוד: דאם כן היה יוצא לידון בדבר החדש כיוצא בו ללמד על הכלל כולו. **נכתוב** בהאי ולא נכתוב בהאי לון]. תימה: ושאר אשמות היכי ילפי מאשם מצורע? מה לאשם מצורע שכן בא להתיר!

אי

*) נ"א דאפרכי רבנן לר"י כו' כל"ל נ"ק

(מסורת הש"ס: נ"ק | כ"א וקנה פירות במעשר שני ואם היה כו' כל"ל נ"ק ועי' בב"י כתוס' נג ע"ב | גי' הב"ח והא דמצריך קרא מותר הפסח נמי כו' | עי' רש"ק וש"ק)

עין משפט נר מצוה

יא א מיי' פ"ו מהלכות מעשר שני הלכ' ח ב:

יב ב מיי' פ"ג מהלכות תמורה הלכה ה:

יג ג מיי' פ"ג מהלכות מעשה קרבנות הלכ' ו:

יד ד מיי' שם פ"ה הלכה ג:

שיטה מקובצת

אֵ] עי' בהשמטות בסוף המסכת: בֵ] תיבות נטמא אין לא נטמא לא נמחק: גֵ] ושוק מותר פסח: דֵ] העולה העולה במקומה: הֵ] מנא לן ת"ל ואת דמו. וי"ו מוסיף על ענין ראשון במקום שחיטתו תהא קבלת דמו וע"כ משום קבלה אתיא דלא אתיא בשביל זריקה דזריקה אינה בצפון. לשון הר"פ ומשמע שהוא לשון רש"י שלו: וֵ] לעכב מנלן. וא"ת מאי בעי כיון דאקיש אשם לעולה א"כ אף לעכב אקשינן דאין היקש למחצה ועיכובא דעולה ידעינן מהעולה במקומה תהא וכן קשה למה לי דשנה הכתוב בחטאת לעכב (בחטאת) תיפוק ליה מדאיתקש לעולה ובעולה כתיב עיכובא מהעולה במקומה תהא וי"ל דודאי אי הוי ההיקש כתיבא בלשון [זה] החטאת כעולה וכן גבי אשם הוי כתיב האשם כעולה אז הוי משמע דאיתקש חטאת לעולה לגמרי גם לעכב וכן אשם לעולה גם לעכב אבל השתא דכתיב במקום אשר ישחטו העולה ישחטו את האשם אינו מקיש לגמרי האשם לעולה אלא למאי דכתיב בפסוק בהדיא דהיינו ישחטו דמשמע למצוה ולא לעכב וכן גבי חטאת דכתיב במקום העולה תשחט את החטאת ומשמע תשחט למצוה דוקא קאמר וסברא הוא דלא עדיף הך דהקישו לשחיטה דעולה מאילו הוה כתיב צפון באשם פעם אחת בהדיא דהוה למצוה ולא לעכב. כך נראה למורי מהר"פ ז"ל: זֵ] הכבש במקום אשר ישחט את החטאת ואת העולה חֵ] יכול להחזירו לכללו: טֵ] כחטאת. גליון כלומר כדין חטאת הוא אשם זה ובאשם מצורע כתיב ע"כ: יֵ] שאין ת"ל כחטאת האשם. גליון דאם לשחיטה בצפון הרי כבר נאמר ושחט את הכבש במקום אשר ישחט את העולה ואם למתן דמים ואכילתו הרי כל אשמות בכלל וזאת תורת האשם וכתיב בכולהו ואת דמם תזרוק על המזבח ומה ת"ל כחטאת כו'. ע"כ: יאֵ] אף אשם מצורע כו' אלמא דצריך קרא להחזירו לכללו משום מתן דמים ואימורים כמו כן איצטריך ושחט את הכבש שכתוב באשם מצורע להחזירו לכלל שאר אשמות לצפון וא"כ הק"ל עיכובא מנ"ל ומשני א"כ נכתוב בהא פי' צפון באשם מצורע ולא לכתוב בשאר אשמות צפון ולא נכתוב זאת תורת האשם ונגמור כולו מיניה ומדכתביה הכא והכא ש"מ לעיכובא הוא דכתביה כפ"ה ותימה דהיכא גמר שאר אשמות מאשם מצורע גופיה מהיקשא הוא דאתיא והויא ג"ש מן ההיקש ואיכא מ"ד דבר הבא בהיקש אינו חוזר ומלמד בג"ש ועוד נמי איכא למיפרך מה לאשם מצורע שכן בא להתיר א"נ שכן עמו דמים אחרים וי"ל דלמ"ד דגמרי כללו מיניה סבירא ליה דהוי דבר שבכלל ויצא מן הכלל (ס"א ללמד לא על עצמו יצא אלא כו' וגבי האי מדה לא פרכינן מידי כמו בשאר למודים שבתורה) לדברים שאינה חידוש והוו אחת מן המדות השוות שבתורה וכיון דהוי מדה שוה שבתורה ליכא למיפרך עליה מידי: טעון גליון פי' ואי לאו דאהדריה קרא הוי אמינא למאי דנפק נפק דהיינו בבהן יד ורגל ולמאי דלא נפק לא נפק ואין טעון מתן דמים ואימורים ע"כ: יבֵ] חיילי וכו' תחלת ותיבת עליה נמחק: יגֵ] כדתניא בפרק הוציאו לו כו' שהתמורה חלה על בעל מום: ידֵ] ברע וגו' השוה: טוֵ] וליעבד ואם קדם מומו להקדישו אינו קדוש קדושת הגוף ויוצא לחולין ליגזז וליעבד כדתנן: טזֵ] להקדישן נפדים ויליף: יזֵ] תיבת כו' ל"ש ונמחק: יחֵ] המזבח הס"ד ומה"ד א"כ דשחיטת צפון: יטֵ] מיניה בדין לא ללמד על עצמו יצא אלא ללמד על הכלל כולו יצא: כֵ] יהודה עיין בפ"ג דמע"ש באות' משנה בהר"ש: כאֵ] פירות ממעות מעשר ותיבת פדיונו נמחק: כבֵ] פרכי רבנן האי לישנא: כגֵ] העיקר א"ל מצינו שהתמורה חמורה מן העיקר ולגירסת הספרים (תוס') [דגרסי] לא: כדֵ] לירושלם ע"כ קשה דאדפרכי רבנן: כהֵ] ומעשר טהור: כוֵ] תיבות לא ניטמא לא נמחק: כזֵ] הפירות דברי ר"מ וחכמים אומרים: כחֵ] במס' מעשר שני אות ו' ת' נמחק: כטֵ] עשר. שקראו עשירי דטעון נסכים והעשירי שקראו אינו טעון נסכים והרי מצינו שטפל: לֵ] בבכורות מיהו צריך קרא דמותר הפסח: לאֵ] ליה התם: לבֵ] שחטאת ואשם מצורע טעונין נסכים ושאר חטאות ואשמות אין טעונין כו' וידעוני שיש בהם כרת משא"כ כו' מדלא תנן בכלל ל"ו כריתות: לגֵ] למ"ד כללו לא גמר מיניה זה פי' ה"ר יעקב: לדֵ] מצורע נותן ממנו לבהונות: להֵ] שחטאת ואשם מצורע טעונים נסכים אינו סותר כללו אלא: לוֵ] בהאי פי' ולא לכתוב צפון בשאר אשמות ונילף מאשם מצורע דהא סבירא ליה השתא דכללו נמי גמר מיניה כדקאמר בסמוך אלא להכי כתביה בשאר אשמות לעכב הבא והבא:

גליון הש"ס

תוס' ד"ה לפי וכו' לא קרוי דבר חדש. עי' לקמן נז ע"א רש"י ד"ה ה"ג וכשנאמרו:

אֲבָל כְּלָלוֹ גָּמַר מִינֵּיהּ א] (לְצָפוֹן) — שַׁפִּיר, אֶלָּא אִי סְבִירָא לָן דְּלָא הוּא גָּמַר מִכְּלָלוֹ וְלָא כְּלָלוֹ גָּמַר מִינֵּיהּ, הַאי לְגוּפֵיהּ אִיצְטְרִיךְ! ב] כֵּיוָן דְּאַהַדְרֵיהּ אַהַדְרֵיהּ. אֲמַר לֵיהּ מָר זוּטְרָא בְּרֵיהּ דְּרַב מָרִי לְרָבִינָא: אֵימָא, ג] כִּי אַהַדְרֵיהּ קְרָא לְגַבֵּי מַתַּן דָּמִים וְאֵימוּרִין דְּבָעֵי כְּהוּנָּה, אֲבָל שְׁחִיטָה דְּלָא בָּעֲיָא כְּהוּנָּה — לָא ד] מִיבָּעֵי צָפוֹן! א"כ, נֵימָא קְרָא: "כִּי כַּחַטָּאת הוּא", מַאי "כַּחַטָּאת הָאָשָׁם" — כִּשְׁאָר אֲשָׁמוֹת יִהְיֶה. לָמָּה לִי לְאַקְשׁוּיֵי לְחַטָּאת, לָמָּה לִי לְאַקְשׁוּיֵי לְעוֹלָה? אֲמַר רָבִינָא: אִיצְטְרִיךְ, אִי אַקְשֵׁיהּ לְחַטָּאת וְלָא אַקְשֵׁיהּ לְעוֹלָה, הֲוָה אָמִינָא: ה] חַטָּאת מֵהֵיכָן לָמְדָה — מֵעוֹלָה, דָּבָר הַלָּמֵד בְּהֶיקֵּשׁ חוֹזֵר וּמְלַמֵּד בְּהֶיקֵּשׁ. א"ל מָר זוּטְרָא בְּרֵיהּ דְּרַב מָרִי לְרָבִינָא: וְנִיקַשְׁיֵהּ לְעוֹלָה וְלָא נִיקַשְׁיֵהּ ו] לְחַטָּאת! הֲוָה אָמִינָא: *דָּבָר הַלָּמֵד בְּהֶיקֵּשׁ חוֹזֵר וּמְלַמֵּד בְּהֶיקֵּשׁ; וְכִי ז] תֵּימָא נִיקְשֵׁי אַקּוּשֵׁי לְחַטָּאת — נִיחָא לֵיהּ דְּמַקִּישׁ לֵיהּ לְעִיקָּר וְלָא נַקִּישׁ לֵיהּ לַטָּפֵל. לְהָכִי אַקְשֵׁיהּ לְחַטָּאת וְאַקְשֵׁיהּ לְעוֹלָה — לְמֵימַר: דָּבָר הַלָּמֵד בְּהֶיקֵּשׁ ח] שֶׁאֵינוֹ חוֹזֵר וּמְלַמֵּד בְּהֶיקֵּשׁ. רָבָא אָמַר: מֵהָכָא, דִּכְתִיב: °"כַּאֲשֶׁר יוּרַם מִשּׁוֹר זֶבַח הַשְּׁלָמִים", לְמַאי [ויקרא ד] הִלְכְתָא? אִי לְיוֹתֶרֶת הַכָּבֵד וּשְׁתֵּי הַכְּלָיוֹת — בְּגוּפֵיהּ כְּתִיב. ט] (אָמַר רַב פַּפָּא) מִשּׁוּם דְּבָעֵי אַגְמוּרֵי יוֹתֶרֶת הַכָּבֵד וּשְׁתֵּי הַכְּלָיוֹת י] מִפַּר הֶעְלֵם דָּבָר שֶׁל צִבּוּר לִשְׂעִירֵי עֲבוֹדָה זָרָה; יא] בְּגוּפֵיהּ לָא כְּתִיב, וּמִפַּר כֹּהֵן מָשִׁיחַ הוּא דְּגָמַר — לְהָכִי אִיצְטְרִיךְ "כַּאֲשֶׁר יוּרַם" דְּנֶיהֱוֵי כְּמַאן דִּכְתַב בְּגוּפֵיהּ, °וְלָא נֶיהֱוֵי דָּבָר הַלָּמֵד בְּהֶיקֵּשׁ חוֹזֵר וּמְלַמֵּד בְּהֶיקֵּשׁ. אֲמַר לֵיהּ רַב פַּפָּא לְרָבָא: וְלִיכְתְּבֵיהּ בְּגוּפֵיהּ וְלָא נַקִּישׁ! אִי כָּתַב בְּגוּפֵיהּ וְלָא אַקִּישׁ — הֲוָה אָמִינָא: *דָּבָר הַלָּמֵד בְּהֶיקֵּשׁ חוֹזֵר וּמְלַמֵּד בְּהֶיקֵּשׁ; וְכִי תֵּימָא נַקְשֵׁי אַקּוּשֵׁי — נִיחָא לֵיהּ דִּכְתַבֵיהּ בְּגוּפֵיהּ מִדְּאַקִּישׁ לֵיהּ אַקּוּשֵׁי. לְהָכִי כַּתְבֵיהּ וְאַקְשֵׁיהּ, לְמֵימְרָא: דָּבָר הַלָּמֵד בְּהֶיקֵּשׁ אֵין חוֹזֵר וּמְלַמֵּד בְּהֶיקֵּשׁ. (היק"ש וגזיר"ה שו"ה ק"ל וחומ"ר, יב] סִימָן): דָּבָר הַלָּמֵד בְּהֶיקֵּשׁ אֵין חוֹזֵר וּמְלַמֵּד *מֵהֶיקֵּשׁ, אִי מִדְּרָבָא, אִי מִדְּרָבִינָא. דָּבָר הַלָּמֵד בְּהֶיקֵּשׁ מַהוּ שֶׁיְּלַמֵּד בִּגְזֵירָה שָׁוָה? תָּא שְׁמַע: *רַבִּי נָתָן בֶּן אַבְטוֹלְמוֹס אוֹמֵר: אמִנַּיִן לִפְרִיחָה בִּבְגָדִים שֶׁהִיא טְהוֹרָה? נֶאֱמַר קָרַחַת וְגַבַּחַת בִּבְגָדִים, וְנֶאֱמַר קָרַחַת וְגַבַּחַת בְּאָדָם, מַה לְהַלָּן פָּרַח בְּכוּלּוֹ טָהוֹר — אַף כָּאן פָּרַח בְּכוּלּוֹ טָהוֹר. וְהָתָם מְנָא לָן? דִּכְתִיב: °"מֵרֹאשׁוֹ וְעַד רַגְלָיו", וְאִיתְקַשׁ רֹאשׁוֹ לְרֶגֶל, מַה לְהַלָּן יג] כּוּלּוֹ הָפַךְ לָבָן [שם יג] פָּרַח בְּכוּלּוֹ — טָהוֹר, אַף כָּאן כּוּלּוֹ הָפַךְ לָבָן פָּרַח בְּכוּלּוֹ — טָהוֹר. *אָמַר ר' יוֹחָנָן: בְּכָל הַתּוֹרָה כּוּלָּהּ יד] לְמֵידִין לָמֵד מִלָּמֵד, חוּץ מִן הַקֳּדָשִׁים שֶׁאֵין דָּנִין לָמֵד מִלָּמֵד. טו] דְּאִם כֵּן, לֹא יֹאמַר צְפוֹנָה בְּאָשָׁם וְתֵיתֵי בְּג"ש טז] דְּקָדְשֵׁי קָדָשִׁים מֵחַטָּאוֹת; °לָאו לְמֵימְרָא, דְּדָבָר הַלָּמֵד בְּהֶיקֵּשׁ אֵין חוֹזֵר וּמְלַמֵּד בִּגְזֵירָה שָׁוָה? וְדִלְמָא מִשּׁוּם דְּאִיכָּא לְמִיפְרַךְ: מַה לְחַטָּאת שֶׁכֵּן מְכַפֶּרֶת עַל חַיָּיבֵי כְרֵיתוֹת! יז] קָדְשֵׁי קָדָשִׁים יְתֵירֵי כְּתִיבֵי.§ *דָּבָר הַלָּמֵד מֵהֶיקֵּשׁ חוֹזֵר וּמְלַמֵּד בְּקַל וָחוֹמֶר, מִדְּתַנְיָא

רש"י

אֲבָל כְּלָלוֹ גָּמַר מִינֵּיהּ. מִידֵּי דְּלָא חִידֵּשׁ בּוֹ. כְּגוֹן שְׁחִיטַת צָפוֹן, אִי הֲוָה כְּתִיבָא בֵּיהּ וְלָא הֲוָה כְּתִיבָא בִּשְׁאָר אֲשָׁמוֹת — גָּמְרִי לֵיהּ שְׁאָר אֲשָׁמוֹת מִינֵּיהּ, יח] דְּלָאו חִידּוּשׁ הוּא, אֶלָּא יָצָא מִן הַכְּלָל הוּא, וְלִמֵּד עַל דָּבָר שֶׁלֹּא נֶאֱמַר בַּכְּלָל. (א) וְהֵיכִי יט] יָצָא לִידּוֹן בְּדָבָר הֶחָדָשׁ — כְּגוֹן מַתַּן דָּמִים שֶׁבָּזֶה לַמִּזְבֵּחַ, וּבָזֶה שִׁינָּה וְאוֹמֵר לִבְהוֹנוֹת. כֵּיוָן דְּאַהַדְרֵיהּ כ] כו'. וּכְתִיב: "כִּי כַּחַטָּאת הָאָשָׁם הוּא" כְּדִין חַטָּאת כָּךְ דִּין אָשָׁם כא]. אַהַדְרֵיהּ. לִכְלָלוֹ, בֵּין לְמַתַּן דָּמִים בֵּין לִשְׁחִיטַת צָפוֹן, וְלֹא הָיָה צָרִיךְ לִכְתּוֹב בּוֹ שְׁחִיטַת צָפוֹן אֶלָּא לְעִיכּוּבָא. דְּבָעֵי כְּהוּנָּה. שֶׁאֵינָהּ כְּשֵׁירָה בְּזָר. אֲבָל כב] לְמֵידָה דִּשְׁחִיטָה, דְּלָאו עֲבוֹדַת כֹּהֵן הִיא — לָא אַהַדְרֵיהּ, דְּהָא בַּחֲזָרָתוֹ כְּתִיב "כַּחַטָּאת הָאָשָׁם הוּא לַכֹּהֵן" — לְעִנְיַן עֲבוֹדוֹת שֶׁבַּכֹּהֵן. א"כ נֵימָא קְרָא כִּי כַּחַטָּאת הוּא. לַכֹּהֵן. כִּשְׁאָר אֲשָׁמוֹת יִהְיֶה. הִלְכָּךְ לְעִנְיַן צָפוֹן נַמִי אַהַדְרֵיהּ, וְכִי כְּתִיב כג] בֵּיהּ שְׁחִיטָה בַּצָּפוֹן, דִּקְרָא לְעִיכּוּבָא אֲתָא, וּשְׁאָר אֲשָׁמוֹת נַמִי מִינֵּיהּ יָלְפִינַן לְעִיכּוּבָא. לָמָּה לִי לְאַקְשׁוּיֵי בִּשְׁחִיטָתוֹ לְחַטָּאת וּלְעוֹלָה. דִּכְתִיב: "בִּמְקוֹם אֲשֶׁר יִשְׁחֲטוּ אֶת הַחַטָּאת וְאֶת הָעוֹלָה". מֵהֵיכָן כד] לָמְדוּ. לִשְׁחִיטַת צָפוֹן. אִי אַקְשֵׁיהּ לְעוֹלָה וְלָא אַקְשֵׁיהּ לְחַטָּאת הֲוָה אָמִינָא. בְּעָלְמָא דָּבָר הַלָּמֵד בְּהֶיקֵּשׁ חוֹזֵר וּמְלַמֵּד בְּהֶיקֵּשׁ. וְכִי תֵימָא. אִם אִיתָא דְּחוֹזֵר וּמְלַמֵּד בְּהֶיקֵּשׁ — נַקְשֵׁיהּ לְחַטָּאת וְלָא לְעוֹלָה! מְשַׁנֵּינַן לָךְ: נִיחָא לֵיהּ לְאַקְשׁוּיֵי לְעִיקַּר כו'. לְמֵימְרָא. מִדְּאִיצְטְרִיךְ לְמֶיהְדַּר כה] וְאַקּוּשֵׁי לְעוֹלָה, ש"מ, דָּבָר הַלָּמֵד בְּהֶיקֵּשׁ אֵין חוֹזֵר וּמְלַמֵּד בְּהֶיקֵּשׁ, וּמֵהָכָא נָפְקָא לָן בְּכָל דּוּכְתָּא. כַּאֲשֶׁר יוּרַם. בְּאֵימוּרֵי פַר כֹּהֵן מָשִׁיחַ כְּתִיב. מִשּׁוּם דְּבָעֵי אַגְמוּרֵי יוֹתֶרֶת הַכָּבֵד וּשְׁתֵּי כְלָיוֹת כו'. שֶׁהָיָה צָרִיךְ לִלְמֹד מִפַּר הֶעְלֵם תּוֹרַת כו] אֵימוּרֵיהֶן לִשְׂעִירֵי עֲבוֹדָה זָרָה, דְּאִיתְקוּשׁ אַהֲדָדֵי לְעִנְיַן הַקְטָרַת אֵימוּרִין כִּדְאָמְרִינַן בְּפֶרֶק "ב"ש" (לעיל מא.): "אִשֶּׁה לַה' וְחַטָּאתָם עַל שִׁגְגָתָם". וּפַר הֶעְלֵם דָּבָר בְּגוּפֵיהּ לָא כְּתִיב יוֹתֶרֶת וּכְלָיוֹת, וּמִפַּר כֹּהֵן מָשִׁיחַ גָּמַר בְּהֶיקֵּשׁ, כִּדְאָמְרַן בְּפֶרֶק "בֵּית שַׁמַּאי" (שם לט:): "וְעָשָׂה לַפָּר כַּאֲשֶׁר עָשָׂה לְפַר" — זֶה פַּר כֹּהֵן מָשִׁיחַ, אַקְשִׁינְהוּ לַהֲדָדֵי. לְהָכִי אִיצְטְרִיךְ כַּאֲשֶׁר יוּרַם. בְּפַר כֹּהֵן מָשִׁיחַ. וְאִם אֵינוֹ עִנְיָן לוֹ — תְּנֵהוּ לְעִנְיַן פַּר הֶעְלֵם, דְּנֶיהֱוֵי כְּמַאן דִּכְתִיבֵי בְּפַר הֶעְלֵם גּוּפֵיהּ, דְּלָא לֶיהֱוֵי דָּבָר הַלָּמֵד בְּהֶיקֵּשׁ חוֹזֵר וּמְלַמֵּד בְּהֶיקֵּשׁ. וְאִי קַשְׁיָא: הָא נָפְקָא לָן הַךְ דְּרָשָׁא מִ"וְעָשָׂה לַפָּר" — זֶה פַּר הֶעְלֵם דָּבָר, כִּדְאָמְרַן בְּפֶרֶק "ב"ש" (ב) (לעיל מא.)! ה"מ לְתַנָּא דְּבֵי ר' יִשְׁמָעֵאל, דְּאָמַר: "לַפָּר" — זֶה פַּר הֶעְלֵם. אֲבָל לְתַנָּא דְּבֵי רַב דְּאָמַר: "וְעָשָׂה לַפָּר" זֶה פַּר יוֹם הַכִּיפּוּרִים, אִיצְטְרִיךְ "כַּאֲשֶׁר יוּרַם" לְהַךְ דְּרָשָׁה. וְנִכְתְּבֵיהּ בְּגוּפֵיהּ. דְּפַר הֶעְלֵם בְּהֶדְיָא, וְלָא לִיקַשְׁיֵהּ לְפַר כֹּהֵן מָשִׁיחַ, הוֹאִיל וְסוֹף סוֹף כז] טָרַח וְכָתַב "כַּאֲשֶׁר יוּרַם" יְתֵירָא לְהָכִי! הֲוָה אָמִינָא דָּבָר הַלָּמֵד בְּהֶיקֵּשׁ חוֹזֵר וּמְלַמֵּד בְּהֶיקֵּשׁ. בְּעָלְמָא, דְּלָא הֲוָה יָלְפִינַן מֵהָכָא מִידֵּי. דָּבָר הַלָּמֵד בְּהֶיקֵּשׁ כו'. מִשּׁוּם דְּבָעֵי לְמִיבְּעֵי בָּעֲיָא עֲלָהּ, הֲדַר נָקֵיט לָהּ. אִי מִדְּרָבָא. מִ"כַּאֲשֶׁר יוּרַם". אִי מִדְּרָבִינָא. מֵאָשָׁם מְצוֹרָע, דְּאִיצְטְרִיךְ לְאַקּוּשֵׁי לְחַטָּאת וּלְעוֹלָה. לִפְרִיחָה. אִם פָּרְחָה הַצָּרַעַת בְּכָל הַבֶּגֶד. מַה לְהַלָּן פָּרַח כח] בְּכוּלָּהּ טָהוֹר. כִּדְכְתִיב: "אִם פָּרוֹחַ תִּפְרַח" וגו' (ויקרא יג). וְהָתָם. גַּבֵּי קָרַחַת וְגַבַּחַת דְּאָדָם, מְנָלַן דִּטְהוֹרָה פְּרִיחָה? דְּאִילּוּ פְּרִיחָה כִּי כְּתִיבָא — בְּנֶגַע עוֹר בָּשָׂר כְּתִיב. וְאִילּוּ קָרַחַת וְגַבַּחַת כְּתִיבֵי גַּבֵּי נְתָקִין דִּמְקוֹם שֵׂעַר דְּרֹאשׁ וְזָקָן, שֶׁאֵין סִימָּנֵיהֶן שָׁוִין לְנִגְעֵי עוֹר בָּשָׂר, שֶׁזֶּה בְּשֵׂעָר לָבָן וָזֶה בְּשֵׂעָר צָהוֹב. וְאִיתְקַשׁ רֹאשׁוֹ. נִתְקֵי הָרֹאשׁ. אַף כָּאן כו'. אַלְמָא נְתָקִין בְּהֶיקֵּשָׁא יָלְפִינַן לְהוּ, וְחוֹזְרִין וּמְלַמְּדִין כט] עַל הַבְּגָדִים בְּג"ש! א"ר יוֹחָנָן. מֵהָכָא לָא תֵּיתֵי רְאָיָה, דְּלָאו קֳדָשִׁים הוּא, דְּאַף הֶיקֵּשׁ מְלַמֵּד בְּהֶיקֵּשׁ ל] חוּץ מִקֳּדָשִׁים. וְתֵדַע לָךְ שֶׁהַמִּדָּה הַזֹּאת שֶׁהֲבֵאתָה אֵינָהּ לְמֵידָה בְּקָדָשִׁים. דְּא"כ הוּא. דְּדָבָר הַלָּמֵד בְּהֶיקֵּשׁ חוֹזֵר וְלָמֵד בְּג"ש. לֹא יֹאמַר צָפוֹן בְּאָשָׁם וְתֵיתֵי בְּג"ש. דְּנֶאֱמַר לא] "קָדְשֵׁי קָדָשִׁים" בְּחַטָּאת וְנֶאֱמַר קָדְשֵׁי קָדָשִׁים בְּאָשָׁם. קָדְשֵׁי קָדָשִׁים יְתֵירֵי כְּתִיבֵי. בְּהוּ, וַהֲוָה לֵיהּ גְּזֵירָה שָׁוָה מוּפְנָה מִשְּׁנֵי לְדָדִין, וְאֵין מְשִׁיבִין עָלֶיהָ. גַּבֵּי חַטָּאת כְּתִיב: "תִּשָּׁחֵט הַחַטָּאת קֹדֶשׁ קָדָשִׁים הִוא", וּבְאָשָׁם כְּתִיב: "זֹאת תּוֹרַת הָאָשָׁם קֹדֶשׁ קָדָשִׁים הוּא", וּבִתַרְוַויְהוּ כְּתִיב בְּ"וַיִּקַּח קֹרַח": "לְכָל חַטָּאתָם וּלְכָל אֲשָׁמָם אֲשֶׁר יָשִׁיבוּ לִי קֹדֶשׁ קָדָשִׁים לְךָ" לב]. מִדְּתַנְיָא

תוספות

אי אקשיה לעולה ולא אקשיה לחטאת. תימה: לן לא לכתוב "את החטאת", ואי דבר הלמד בהיקש חוזר ומלמד בהיקש — אמאי אקשיה לעולה כלל? תיפוק ליה לד] *מ"חטאת האשם", דמה חטאת לצפון מעכב — אף אשם כן! וי"ל: דאי לא כתב לצפון לא הוה אמינא לה] הא הדרה קרא לשחיטת לצפון למידי דלא בעיא כהונה. ו"האשם" לא דרשינן ליה כלל, דהא לא כתב "כאשם" דהוה משמע כשאר אשם דעלמא לצפון יהא זה, אבל "האשם" משמע: האשם זה יהא כחטאת למתן דמים לו] למזבח. וכן *יש להקשות: אי דבר הלמד בהיקש חוזר ומלמד בהיקש — לא נכתוב לצפון כלל, ותיתי לז] [באשמות] מ"כחטאת וכאשם" כי היכי דילפינן מיניה סמיכה בפרק קמא (לעיל יא.). *ועוד ניליף שאר אשמות מאשם מצורע ואשם מצורע מהיקישא דכחטאת! וי"ל: דלא הוה אמינא דאהדריה קרא לשחיטת צפון, ולא הוה דרשינן לח] "כאשם" — כשאר אשם (כיון דלא כתב כאשם), כיון דלא כתב צפון בהדיא בשאר אשמות.

כאשר יורם למאי הלכתא. תימה: הא איצטריך לכדדרשינן בסוף "כל הבשר" (חולין דף קיז.): זה בא ללמד ונמצא למד, מה פר כהן משיח יש בו מעילה — אף שור זבח השלמים יש בו מעילה! וי"ל: דמאי לאקשויי לזבח השלמים ולא ליכתוב "כאשר יורם", לט] ד"כאשר יורם" משמע דאתא לרבויי הרמה, אחרת. אי נמי, ההיא ד"כל הבשר" (שם) כתנא דבי רבי ישמעאל, דנפקא ליה דרשא דהכא מ"ועשה לפר" — זה פר העלם, מ] כדאמר פרק "בית שמאי" (לעיל דף מא.). אבל לתנא דבי רב דאמר "ועשה לפר" זה פר יום הכיפורים, איצטריך "כאשר יורם" (*להך דרשא).

ונכתביה בגופיה. תימה, כדאמר פרק "ב"ש" (גם זה שם:): משל למלך בשר ודם מא] שסרחה עליו מדינה ומיעט בסרחונס מפני מב] חיבתן! וי"ל: דבשביל חיבתן לא היה לו לגלגל אלו דרשות למילף מהיקשא. ומ"מ ילפינן מיניה מג] חיבתן, מדלא אשמעינן בדוכתא אחרינא דבר הלמד מהיקש אינו חוזר ומלמד בהיקש.

קדשי קדשים יתירי כתיבי. תימה: כיון דילפינן גזרה שוה מהדדי, למה לן היקשות דלעיל מד] בחטאת ואשם? לא

עין משפט נר מצוה

טו א מיי' פי"ב מהלכות טומאת צרעת הלכה ח:

ג"ל מכחטאת נ"ק

גי' הג"ק אין להקשות כו' ותיתי מכחטאת כאשם

נ"א

גי' נ"ק וניליף שאר כו' די"ל דלא

מסורת הש"ס

[לקמן נח. לעיל מה. יומא נז. מנחות כח. שח. פכ:]

יומא נז.

[נ"ל בהיקש]

סנהדרין פז: [נדה יט. ושם איתא ר' יונתן וכ"ה בילקוט]

שבועות י. תמורה כח:

[לעיל מח.]

הגהות הב"ח

(א) רש"י ד"ה אבל כללו וכו' ולהכי יצא: (ב) ד"ה להכי איצטריך וכו' בפ' ב"ש תנינא לתנא דבי ר' ישמעאל:

גליון הש"ס

גמ' ולא ניהוי דבר הלמד בהיקש. ע"ל דף נ ע"ב תוד"ה ולאב"ח: שם לאו למימרא דדבר הלמד כו'. עי' לעיל דף מח ע"א תוד"ה מה להלן:

שיטה מקובצת

א] תיבת לצפון נמחק: ב] איצטריך והאי לגופיה איצטריך כיון: ג] עי' בהשמטות בסוף המסכת: ד] לא תיבעי. ה] ס"א לא אהדריה א"כ כו': ו] עי' בהשמטות בסוף המסכת: ז] עי' בהשמטות בסוף המסכת: ח] [illegible] לעיקר תיבת ליה ל"ש ונמחק: ט] בהיקש אינו חוזר ומלמד בהיקש רבא אמר דבר הלמד בהיקש אינו חוזר ומלמד בהיקש מהכא: י] כתיב אלא משום ותיבות אמר רב פפא נמחק: י] הכליות כו'. ואע"ג דלעיל נפקא לן יותרת ושתי הכליות לשעירי ע"ז מלפר י"ל היינו לתנא דבי ר' ישמעאל אבל הכא אירי אליבא דרבי. מהר"ם: יא] זרה ופר העלם דבר של צבור בגופיה לא כתיב: יב] וחומר ובנין אב סימן: יג] מה להלן פרח בכולו טהור אף כאן פרח בכולו טהור: יד] כולה דנין למד מלמד: טו] דאם כן כו' א) ממילתיה דר' יוחנן בא להוכיח שמדה שהביא למעלה אינה נוהגת בקדשי'. ת"א: טז] בקודש קדשים מחטאת לאו. ס"י למאי הלכתא כתביה רחמנא לאו: יז] קדש קדשים יתירא כתיבי. תימה כיון דאיכא ג"ש וילפינן מהדדי למה לן היקשות דלעיל דכחטאת האשם דכתיב גבי מצורע להחזירו לכללו תיפוק ליה מקדש הקדשים דהא כתיב קדש קדשים גבי אשם מצורע ונילף ליה בג"ש דקדש קדשים מחטאת להחזירו לכללו להטעינו מתן דמים ואימורים וי"ל דכיון שיצא אשם מצורע מן הכלל לידון בדבר החדש אי אתה יכול להחזירו לכללו בפירוש מכח הך ג"ש דקדש קדשים לא הוי חזרה בפירוש אפי' את"ל דג"ש חשיבא כמו היקש מ"מ האי ג"ש דקדש קדשים איצטריך למילי אחרינא [ולא להחזירו לכללו] לקמן לגבי פגימת המזבח דקאמר אשכחן שירי מנחה קדשי קדשים מנין ת"ל קדש קדשים ולכך לא הוי חזרה בפירוש מכח [הך] ג"ש אבל היקש דכחטאת האשם כולו להחזירו הוא דאתא ולכך חשיבא חזרה בפירוש. ומיהו קשה לעיל בפ"ק למה לי היקשא דכחטאת האשם גבי סתם אשם תיפוק ליה מג"ש דקדש קדשים לומר דטעון סמיכה לרבנן דר' אליעזר ולר"א לשלא לשמו ואמר מורי דשמא ג"ש לא ניתנה לדרוש רק גבי שחיטה משום דקדש קדשים דכתיב בין בסתם אשם בין באשם מצורע גבי שחיטה הוא דכתיב אבל מכחטאת האשם דכתיב גבי סתם אשם דרשינן שפיר מיניה סמיכה דלגמרי מקיש הכתוב אשם לחטאת בהך היקשא כדכתיב כחטאת האשם תורה אחת לכם ועוד יש לומר דגבי סמיכה כתיב קרבנו דהוי מיעוט והוה מוקמינן ג"ש לדברים אחרים אבל השתא דאייתור היקשא לסמיכה מוקמינן (ג"ש) קרבנו לדרשא אחריתי וכן לר' אליעזר צריך היקש לשלא לשמו לאפוקי מהך היקשא דשלמים דזאת התורה: יח] מיניה דלאו חידוש: יט] והיכא דמי יצא: כ] דאהדריה וכתב כי כחטאת: כא] אשם זה הס"ד: כב] אבל לגבי שחיטה דלאו: כג] כתיב שחיטה בצפון רישא דקרא ותיבת ביה נמחק: כד] מהיכן למדה: כה] ולאקושי לעולה: כו] תורת אימורין לשעירי כו' דאתקוש להדדי לענין הקטרת אימורין כו' שגגתם הרי לך כשגגתם חטאתם ופר העלם: כז] סוף חזר וטרח: כח] פרח בכולו טהור: כט] ומלמדין בג"ש על הבגדים הס"ד: ל] בהיקש בבכל התורה חוץ: לא] קדש קדשים בחטאת ונאמר קדש קדשים באשם הס"ד ומה"ד קדש קדשים יתירי: לב] לך הוא הס"ד: לג] תימה אי דבר הלמד כו' והשאר נמחק: לד] ליה מכחטאת האשם: לה] האי דהדריה קרא למידי דלא בעיא כהונה והאשם כשאר אשם הוה דרשינן ליה כלל תום': לו] דמים ואימורין למזבח וכן יש להקשות ע"כ וא"ת אכתי אי דבר: לז] ותיתי מכחטאת האשם: לח] דרשינן האשם כשאר אשם יהא כיון: לט] יורם אלא כאשר יוזבח השלמים באמורי' פרק: מא] ידע שזעם על אוהבו ומיעט בסרחונו: מב] מפני חיבתו: מג] מיניה חיבתו וליכא למימר דכוליה להכי הוא דאתא לאשמועינן דדבר הבא בהיקש כו': מד] כחטאת האשם הס"ד:

א) גרלה דל"ל ממילתיה דר"י הוא ובא להוכיח וכו'.

מדתנא דבי ר' ישמעאל. דבר הלמד בהיקש מהו שילמד בבנין אב? אמר רבי ירמיה: לא לכתוב צפונה באשם ותיתי מבנין אב א] מחטאת, למאי הלכתא כתביה – לאו למימרא, דדבר הלמד בהיקש אין חוזר ומלמד בבנין אב? וליטעמיך, תיתי מבנין אב מעולה! ב] מאי טעמא לא אתי – משום דאיכא למיפרך: מה לעולה שכן כליל – חטאת נמי איכא למיפרך: מה לחטאת שכן מכפרת על חייבי כריתות. חדא מחדא לא אתיא, תיתי ג] חדא מתרתי! מהי תיתי? לא נכתוב רחמנא ד] עולה ותיתי מחטאת ואשם – מה להנך שכן מכפרין; לא נכתוב רחמנא בחטאת ותיתי מהנך – מה להנך שכן זכרים; לא נכתוב באשם ותיתי מהנך – מה להנך שכן ישנן בציבור כביחיד. דבר הלמד בגז"ש מהו *שילמד בהיקש? אמר רב פפא: ה] °"וזאת תורת זבח השלמים [וגו'] אם על תודה" – אלמדנו לתודה שבא מן המעשר, *מדאשכחן בשלמים דאתו ממעשר; שלמים גופייהו מנא לן – דכתיב: °"שם" °"שם". א"ל מר זוטרא בריה דרב מרי לרבינא: *מעשר דגן חולין בעלמא הוא! א"ל: (א) אמר אמרה *למד קדש ומלמד קדש? דבר הלמד בג"ש *מהו שילמד בג"ש? אמר רמי בר חמא: תניא °"סלת מרבכת" – למדנו גלרבוכה שבאה סולת. חלות ו] מניין? ת"ל: ד"חלות" "חלות". הרקיקין מניין? ת"ל: "מצות" "מצות". אמר ליה רבינא: ממאי ד"מצות מצות" מחלות גמר? דלמא ממאפה תנור גמר! אלא אמר רבא, *תניא: °"וקרבו ופרשו והוציא" – מלמד שמוציאו שלם. יכול ישרפנו שלם? נאמר כאן: ז] °"ראשו וכרעיו", ונאמר להלן: °"ראשו וכרעיו", מה להלן ע"י ניתוח – אף כאן על ידי ניתוח. אי מה להלן בהפשט – אף כאן ח] נמי בהפשט! תלמוד לומר: "וקרבו ופרשו". מאי תלמודא? א"ר פפא: כשם שפרשו בקרבו – כך בשרו בעורו. ותניא, *רבי אומר: נאמר כאן עור ובשר [ופרש] ונאמר

ויקרא ו | דברים כז | דברים יד | ויקרא ז | שם ד | שם | שם א

רש"י

מדתני דבי רבי ישמעאל. בפרק "כ"ס" (לעיל דף מט.): ומה במקום שלא הושוו קרבן לקרבן. ט] ואוקימנא התם דקסבר ר' ישמעאל דבר הלמד בהיקש חוזר ומלמד בקל וחומר. בבנין אב. "מה מלינו". י] וכולן שאילות הללו בקדשים נשאלו, וארבעה שאילות בכל מדה ומדה. כגון: דבר הלמד בהיקש, מהו שילמד בהיקש ובקל וחומר ובבנין אב. ודבר הלמד בגזרה שוה, מהו שילמד בהיקש ובג"ש וק"ו ובבנין אב. ודבר הלמד יא] בבנין אב, מהו שילמד בכולן. וליטעמיך. אי משום הא כתביה – לייתי מעולה, דכתיב בה בהדיא. שכן מכפרת כו'. ואין לך לפרש יב] שאילתייהו מכאן. מחדא לא אתיא כו'. יג] מילתא בפני נפשה היא, ולאו למיפשט בעיין. עולה לגבי חטאת ואשם לא חשיבה כפרת עשה דידיה כפרה. למדנו לתודה. מכאן בהיקש משלמים שבאה מן המעשר, אם פירש בשעת נדרו ע"מ להביאה ממעות מע"ש. שם שם. בשלמים כתיב (דברים כז): "וזבחת שלמים ואכלת שם", ובמעשר כתיב (שם יד): "ואכלת לפני ה' אלהיך במקום אשר יבחר לשכן שמו שם מעשר דגנך תירושך ויצהרך ובכורות". חולין הוא. ואנן בקדשים קמיבעיא לן. אמר אמרה. כלומר למד קדש ומלמד קדש? בתמיה. וכי שניהן צריכין שיהו טו] בקדשים? הואיל ולמד קדש, כגון שלמים – שפיר מיפשט בעיין, דבתר למד אזלינן. ומר זוטרא סבר בתר מלמד טז] אזלינן. והיינו דאמרינן בעלמא (לעיל דף מט:): הניחא למ"ד בתר למד אזלינן. למדנו יז] רבוכה. חלות מרובכות במים תחילה שבתודה, שבאה סולת ולא קמח. חלות שבתודה מניין. שבשלשה מינין מצה יש בה: חלות, רקיקין, רבוכה. חלות שבה מניין שהן סולת? ת"ל חלות חלות. נאמר בחלות "חלות" ונאמר ברבוכה "חלות". מצות מצות. נאמר ברקיקין "מצות" ונאמר בחלות "מצות", וילפינן רקיקין מחלות, וחלות יח] למדו מרבוכה, ושניהם בגז"ש. וממאי. דרקיקין דתודה "מצות" מחלות דתודה גמרי? דלמא ממצות דכתיב גבי רקיקין יט] מנחת מאפה גמר. והתם סלת בהדיא כתיב, "סלת חלות מצות בלולות בשמן ורקיקי מצות משוחים בשמן" (ויקרא ב). כ] מלמד שמוציא את כל הפר שלם. דאי במנותח – היאך כא] הכל יוציא בהוצאה אחת, הנתחים וקרבו ופרשו? נאמר כאן כב] ראשו וכרעיו. "על ראשו ועל כרעיו" (שם ד). ונאמר להלן ראשו וכרעיו. בעולת *גבי נאן כתיב: "וערך הכהן את הראש", וכתיב: "וקרבו וכרעיו ירחץ" כג] (שם א). מה להלן ע"י ניתוח. היה מקטירו, דניתוח כתיב ביה. אף שריפה של זה ע"י ניתוח. ובפר כהן משיח קאי. כשם שפרשו בקרבו כו'. דאיתקש שריפת עורו ובשרו לשריפת קרבו ופרשו. מה פרשו בקרבו. דדבר מגונה הוא להוציאו ולשורפו בעין.

תוספות

לא נכתוב רחמנא בעולה ותיתי מחטאת ואשם כד]. פי': ולכתוב בהדיא לפון בחטאת ואשם. ואם תאמר: ולכתוב בזבחי שלמי לבור ונילף עולה מינייהו! וי"ל: דאיכא למיפרך, דמה לזבחי שלמי ליבור – שכן זמנו קבוע. ועוד דחטאת לא אתי כה] מיניה – שכן זכרים. ואשם – שכן אינו בליבור. וא"ת: למה לי לאקושי לקמן (דף נה.) זבחי שלמי ליבור לעולה? תיפוק לי בבנין אב! וכי תימא: לאשמועי' שהם קדשי קדשים כעולה – הוי מצי למילף מדאיתקש לחטאת! כו] וי"ל: דאיכא למיפרך שכן תדיר, *כדמפרש בפרק "תמיד נשחט" (פסחים דף סה.). אי נמי: מה לשם שלמים – שכן אינן טעונין לפון. וא"ת: בפ"ק דשבועות (דף ט. ושם) דיליף שעיר דר"ח משעיר חילון, דאינו מכפר אלא על טומאת מקדש וקדשיו, דקאמר: הואיל וזה בא לזמן קבוע. ובשעיר הנעשה בחוץ קאמר, כדפירש התם בקונטרס, דאי מפנימי כז] הוה ליה למיפרך: שכן נכנס דמה לפני ולפנים! ועוד: דאדרבה, נילף משעיר המשתלח דמכפר בשאר עבירות. אבל השתא, אי מחילון גמר – ניחא, דדמו אהדדי טפי משעיר המשתלח. והשתא, אי מחילון גמר – א"כ תפשוט דדבר הלמד בהיקש חוזר ומלמד בבנין אב, דחילון גופיה לא ידענא אלא מהיקשא דפנימי! וי"ל: דהא אמרינן התם דגילוי מילתא בעלמא הוא. וא"ת: והיכי גמר בפ"ב דבילה (דף כ.) סמיכה בשלמי חובה בבנין אב כח] (משלמי נדבה) [מעולת חובה]? והא עולת חובה מ"כמשפט" ילפא, דהיינו היקש! וי"ל: דקושיא בעלמא הוא, דפריך התם: ממאי דבית הלל כו' דלמא מעולת חובה גמרי. כלומר, אם תימלי לומר דדבר הלמד בהיקש חוזר ומלמד בבנין אב. ועו"ק: כט] ב"הקומץ רבה" (מנחות דף כא:) נאמר הבא מנחה והבא מלח, ונאמר הבא מנחה והבא עלים, מה עלים משל ליבור – אף מלח משל ליבור. ועלים גופייהו לא ידעינן אלא מדאיתקש למזבח, דכתיב (ויקרא א): "על העלים אשר על האש אשר על המזבח" מה מזבח משל ליבור וכו'?

אם על תודה כו'. הקשה ה"ר יעקב מאורליינ"ש: בפרק "דם חטאת" (לקמן דף לח.) ובפ' "התודה" (מנחות דף פג.) דאמר: מה חטאת אינה באה אלא מן החולין – למה לי? הא שלמים ותודה שני כתובין הבאין כאחד, ואין מלמדין! עוד קשה: היכי יליף התם מחטאת, כיון דאיכא שלמים ותודה דבאין מן המעשר, דלא ילפינן בהיקשא ד"זאת התורה" אלא דבר שיכול לנהוג בכל הנזכרים בפסוק. דמהאי טעמא מיבעי לן קרא בפ"ב דבילה (דף כ.) ל] עולת חובה טעונה סמיכה, ולא ילפינן *מהיקשא ד"זאת התורה" – משום דסמיכה לא בעי בכולהו, דבכור ומעשר לא בעו סמיכה, כדתנן פרק "שתי מדות" (מנחות דף צב.)! וי"ל: דכל חובה מקשינן לחטאת, מה חטאת דבר שבחובה ואינו בא אלא מן החולין, לא] כדמוכח בפרק "התודה" (שם דף פג.). ול"ע: מנחת נדבה דאינה באה אלא מן החולין מנ"ל? וא"ת: בפ"ק דחגיגה (דף ח.) דדריש: "מסת" – מלמד שאדם מביא חגיגתו מן החולין, למה לי? הלא חובה היא, ותיפוק לי מהיקשא! וי"ל: משום דקאמר התם דחגיגה באה נמי מן המעשר, איצטריך "מסת" למימר דאינה באה הכל מן המעשר, אלא מן החולין ומן המעשר מתרוייהו. אי נמי: משום דכתיב "כאשר יברכך" בסיפיה דקרא, סלקא דעתך דאתיא לב] ממעשר, להכי איצטריך "מסת". אמר אמרה. לג] ורבינו שמואל מפרש: אימר אמרת, שמא אתה רוצה לומר ששניהם בעינן קדש? ורבינו תם גריס: אמי אמרה. ואמי שם חכם. לד] וביבמות פרק "הערל" (דף פ.) היינו דשמעתא ליה לאמי כל שממעי אמו לקוי. ובכתובות (דף מד:) לה] אמר רבא: תני אמי בתולת ישראל ולא בתולת גריס. וא"ת: דלמר זוטרא לא איפשיטא בעיא, ובסוף "אלו מנחות" (מנחות עו.) אמרינן: לחמי תודה ונזירות באות עשר עשר. לחמי תודה – בהדיא כתיב בהן. פירוש: דכתיב "ממנו אחד מכל קרבן תרומה לה'", ואמר בפרק "התודה" (שם דף עז:): נאמר כאן "תרומה", ונאמר להלן בתרומת מעשר "תרומה", מה להלן אחד מעשרה – אף כאן אחד מעשרה. ונזירות – מהיקש, דאמר מר: "על זבח תודת שלמיו" – לרבות שלמי נזיר. פי': לכל דין לחמי תודה, לעשרה קבין ירושלמית וחלי לוג שמן, ושיהיו באות י'. אלמא, דין דתודה אתיא בג"ש חוזרת ומלמדת בהיקש! לו] *ותו: בההיא שמעתא לעיל ילפינן דכל המנחות באות עשר בבנין אב מלחמי תודה, דאתיא בג"ש מתרומת מעשר, ואם כן תפשוט דבר הלמד בג"ש חוזר ומלמד בבנין אב! ובההיא שמעתא גופה פריך התם: אי ס"ל דדבר הלמד בג"ש חוזר ומלמד בבנין אב – נילף מחביתין! וי"ל: דתרומת מעשר דהתם חולין הוא, כדקאמר הכא: מעשר דגן חולין הוא. ומיהו, הך קשיא לז] לרבינא, דס"ל הכא בתר למד אזלינן, ובסמוך אמרינן תיקו! ודוחק לומר דלרבינא איפשטא ליה כמו כן בעיא דלקמן דמנחות. מה להלן ע"י ניתוח שלא בהפשט. ואם תאמר: היכי יליף מההיא דדבר הלמד בג"ש חוזר ומלמד בג"ש, דילפינן פר יום הכפורים בנתוח שלא בהפשט מפר כהן משיח, וניתוח דפר כהן משיח גמרינן מעולה? הלא כה"ג אפילו למד בהיקש חוזר ומלמד בהיקש, לח] כיון דהוי הימנו ודבר אחר. לט] דשלא בהפשט בפר כהן משיח – מדאיתקש עור ובשר לפרש יליף, כדפירש בקונטרס, *ודבר הלמד בהיקש אינו חוזר ומלמד בגזירה שוה! ושמא אין זה היקש אלא גילוי מילתא בעלמא. וי"ל: דשלא בהפשט

עין משפט נר מצוה

טז א מיי' פי"ז מהל' מעשה"ק הל' יז:
יז ב מיי' פ"ז מהל' מעשר שני הל' יב:
יח ג ד ה מיי' פ"ב מהל' מעשה הקרבנות הלכה ב:

גי' רש"ק כלפרים פ' אלו דברים וע"ש דף מו ע"א

מסורת הש"ס

מנחות פב.
[לעיל מה. לקמן ס: מעות יט. תמורה כח.]
[יומא סח.]
[שם סז.]
עי' רש"י יומא סח. ד"ה ונאמר להלן וכו'

הגהות הב"ח

(א) גמ' אמר ליה אמר אמרה. נ"ב כי עי' תוס' דף מח ע"א.

גליון הש"ס

גמ' מהו שילמד בהיקש. עי' לעיל דף יא ע"א תוס' ד"ה למד קדש. שם למד קדש. עי' לעיל דף מח ע"א תוס' ד"ה ... רש"י ד"ה ... תוס' ד"ה ...

שיטה מקובצת

א] מחטאת למאי הלכתא כתביה רחמנא כו'. תימה דהיכא בעי למילף לענין בנין אב הא איצטריך לאשמועינן דדבר הלמד בהיקש אינו חוזר ומלמד בג"ש כדקאמר לעיל ולעולם חוזר ומלמד בבנין אב וי"ל דמ"מ שפיר מוכח דאי סובר חוזר ומלמד בבנין אב א"כ לשתוק מצפונה דאשם דאין לו לכתבו שלא לצורך ובמקום אחר ישמעינו דאין היקש חוזר ומלמד. והקשה הר"ם דהיכא מוכח זה דלמא ניחא ליה למיכתביה בגופה מדמקשינן ליה אקשי דהא קאמר לעיל כי האי סברא דבשלמא לעיל גבי לא לכתוב צפון באשם ותיתי בקדשי קדשים מחטאת דאיכא למיפרך הכי דהוא ג"ש חשיבא כתיב בגופה כמו היקש דכתיב במקום אשר (תשחטו) [ישחטו את] העולה (תשחטו) [ישחטו את] האשם אבל הכא גבי בנין אב קשיא דודאי היקש חשיב כתיב בגופה יותר מבנין אב ותירץ דדוקא היינו קודם שידעו שהקדשים חלוקים מן החולין לענין למד מלמד אז דהיינו לעיל בסברא קלה כדי להשוותו לחולין אבל מאחר שלמדנו שההיקש מהיקש נשתנה מחולין אז יש לקיים המדות ולא לדחות בסברא קלה. מהר"ם: ב] מעולה אלא מעולה מאי: ג] תיבת חדא נמחק: ד] רחמנא בעולה ותיתי: ה] א"ר פפא תניא וזאת תורת זבח השלמים וגו' אם על תודה יקריבנו למדנו לתודה שהיא באה מן המעשר כו' ממעשר ושלמים גופייהו מנא ליה: ו] חלות שבתודה מנין ת"ל חלות כו' ס"א לג"ש מה חלות האמורות ברבוכה סולת אף חלות האמורות בבולן סולת ורקיקין לא נאמר בהן סולת מנין שיהו סולת ת"ל מצות מצות מה מצות האמורות בבולן סולת אף מצות האמורות בהן סולת: ז] ראש וכרעים ונאמר להלן ראש וכרעים: ח] תיבת נמי נמחק: ט] לקרבן כו' ואוקימנא התם דקסבר תנא דבי רבי ישמעאל: י] מצינו וכל שאילות הללו: יא] הלמד בק"ו מהו שילמד בהיקש ובג"ש בק"ו ובבנין אב ודבר הלמד בבנין אב מהו כו': יב] שאלתינו: יג] כו' אי דבר הלמד בהיקש [illegible]

חוזר ומלמד בבנין אב ותיתי חדא בבנין אב מתרתי דחדא כתיבא וחדא ילפא בהיקשא הס"ד ואח"כ מה"ד שכן מכפרת. עולה לגבי: יד] אמר אמרה. אמר האומר למד: טו] שיהו קדשים: טז] מלמד נמי אזלינן: יז] למדנו לרבוכה. שבתודה חלות מבושלות במים תחלה שבאה ותיבת שבתודה נמחק: יח] וחלות למדנו: יט] רקיקין דמנחת מאפה: כ] בשמן הס"ד ומה"ד והוציא משמע ההוצאה אחת הס"ד ומה"ד מלמד: כא] היאך יוציא הכל בהוצאה: כב] כאן ראש וכרעים: כג] ירחץ וגו': [illegible]

וְנֶאֱמַר לְהַלָּן עוֹר וּבָשָׂר וּפֶרֶשׁ, א] מַה לְּהַלָּן ע"י נִיתּוּחַ שֶׁלֹּא בְּהֶפְשֵׁט — אַף כָּאן ע"י נִיתּוּחַ שֶׁלֹּא בְּהֶפְשֵׁט. דָּבָר הַלָּמֵד בִּגְזֵירָה שָׁוָה מַהוּ שֶׁיְּלַמֵּד בְּק"ו? ק"ו: וּמַה הֶיקֵּשׁ שֶׁאֵינוֹ מְלַמֵּד ב] בְּהֶיקֵּשׁ, אִי מִדְּרָבָא אִי מִדְּרָבִינָא — מְלַמֵּד בְּקַל וָחוֹמֶר, מִדְּתָנָא דְּבֵי רַבִּי יִשְׁמָעֵאל; גז"ש הַמְלַמֶּדֶת בְּהֶיקֵּשׁ, מִדְּרַב פַּפָּא — אֵינוֹ דִּין שֶׁתְּלַמֵּד בְּק"ו? הָנִיחָא לְמַאן דְּאִית לֵיהּ דְּרַב פַּפָּא, אֶלָּא לְמַאן דְּלֵית לֵיהּ דְּרַב פַּפָּא מַאי אִיכָּא לְמֵימַר? אֶלָּא קַל וָחוֹמֶר: וּמַה הֶיקֵּשׁ שֶׁאֵין מְלַמֵּד בְּהֶיקֵּשׁ, אִי מִדְּרָבָא אִי מִדְּרָבִינָא — מְלַמֵּד בְּק"ו, מִדְּתָנָא דְּבֵי רַבִּי יִשְׁמָעֵאל; ג] גְּזֵירָה שָׁוָה הַמְלַמֶּדֶת בִּגז"ש חֲבֵירְתָהּ, *מִדְּרָמִי בַּר חָמָא — אֵינוֹ דִּין שֶׁתְּלַמֵּד בְּק"ו? *דָּבָר הַלָּמֵד בִּגז"ש מַהוּ שֶׁיְּלַמֵּד בְּבִנְיַן אָב? תֵּיקוּ. דָּבָר הַלָּמֵד בְּקַל וָחוֹמֶר מַהוּ שֶׁיְּלַמֵּד בְּהֶיקֵּשׁ? ק"ו: וּמַה גְּזֵירָה שָׁוָה שֶׁאֵינָהּ לְמֵדָה ד] בְּהֶיקֵּשָׁא, מִדְּר' יוֹחָנָן — מְלַמֵּד בְּהֶיקֵּשׁ, מִדְּרַב פַּפָּא; קַל וָחוֹמֶר הַלָּמֵד מֵהֶיקֵּשׁ, מִדְּתָנָא דְּבֵי ר' יִשְׁמָעֵאל — אֵינוֹ דִּין שֶׁיְּלַמֵּד בְּהֶיקֵּשׁ? הָנִיחָא לְמַאן דְּאִית לֵיהּ דְּרַב פַּפָּא, אֶלָּא לְמַאן דְּלֵית לֵיהּ דְּרַב פַּפָּא מַאי אִיכָּא לְמֵימַר? תֵּיקוּ. דָּבָר הַלָּמֵד בְּקַל וָחוֹמֶר מַהוּ שֶׁיְּלַמֵּד בִּגְזֵירָה שָׁוָה? קַל וָחוֹמֶר: וּמַה גְּזֵירָה שָׁוָה שֶׁאֵינָהּ לְמֵידָה בְּהֶיקֵּשָׁא, מִדְּרַבִּי יוֹחָנָן — מְלַמֵּד בִּגְזֵירָה שָׁוָה, ה] מִדְּרָמִי בַּר חָמָא; קַל וָחוֹמֶר הַלָּמֵד בְּהֶיקֵּשׁ, מִדְּתָנָא דְּבֵי רַבִּי יִשְׁמָעֵאל — אֵינוֹ דִּין ו] שֶׁתְּלַמֵּד בִּגז"ש? *דָּבָר הַלָּמֵד בְּקַל וָחוֹמֶר מַהוּ שֶׁיְּלַמֵּד בְּקַל וָחוֹמֶר? ק"ו: וּמַה גְּזֵירָה שָׁוָה שֶׁאֵינָהּ לְמֵידָה בְּהֶיקֵּשׁ, מִדְּר' יוֹחָנָן — ז] מְלַמֵּד בְּק"ו, כְּדַאֲמַרַן; ק"ו הַלָּמֵד מֵהֶיקֵּשׁ, מִדְּתָנָא דְּבֵי רַבִּי יִשְׁמָעֵאל — אֵינוֹ דִּין שֶׁיְּלַמֵּד בְּקַל וָחוֹמֶר? וְזֶהוּ ק"ו בֶּן ק"ו. ח] בֶּן בְּנוֹ שֶׁל ק"ו הוּא! אֶלָּא ק"ו: וּמַה הֶיקֵּשׁ שֶׁאֵינוֹ לָמֵד בְּהֶיקֵּשׁ, אִי מִדְּרָבָא אִי מִדְּרָבִינָא — מְלַמֵּד בְּק"ו, מִדְּתָנָא דְּבֵי רַבִּי יִשְׁמָעֵאל; ק"ו הַלָּמֵד מֵהֶיקֵּשׁ, מִדְּתָנֵי דְּבֵי רַבִּי יִשְׁמָעֵאל — אֵינוֹ דִּין שֶׁיְּלַמֵּד בְּק"ו? וְזֶהוּ ק"ו בֶּן קַל וָחוֹמֶר. דָּבָר הַלָּמֵד בְּקַל וָחוֹמֶר מַהוּ שֶׁיְּלַמֵּד בְּבִנְיַן אָב? אָמַר רַבִּי יִרְמְיָה, תָּא שְׁמַע: *מָלַק וְנִמְצֵאת טְרֵיפָה, ר"מ אוֹמֵר: אֵינָהּ מְטַמְּאָה בְּבֵית הַבְּלִיעָה, רַבִּי יְהוּדָה אוֹמֵר: *מְטַמְּאָה בְּבֵית הַבְּלִיעָה. אָמַר ר' מֵאִיר: קַל וָחוֹמֶר, וּמַה נִּבְלַת בְּהֵמָה שֶׁמְּטַמְּאָה בְּמַגָּע וּבְמַשָּׂא — שְׁחִיטָתָהּ מְטַהֶרֶת טְרֵיפָתָהּ מִטּוּמְאָתָהּ, נִבְלַת עוֹף שֶׁאֵין מְטַמֵּא בְּמַגָּע וּבְמַשָּׂא — אֵינוֹ דִּין שֶׁתְּהֵא שְׁחִיטָתָהּ מְטַהֶרֶת טְרֵיפָתָהּ מִטּוּמְאָתָהּ? מַה מָּצִינוּ בִּשְׁחִיטָה שֶׁמַּכְשַׁרְתָּהּ בַּאֲכִילָה — מְטַהֶרֶת

וְנֶאֱמַר לְהַלָּן. בְּפַר כֹּהֵן מָשִׁיחַ (ויקרא ד), וְנֶאֱמַר כָּאן בְּפַר וְשָׂעִיר שֶׁל יוֹם הַכִּיפּוּרִים (שם טז): "וְאֵת פַּר הַחַטָּאת וְאֵת שְׂעִיר הַחַטָּאת וגו' וְאֶת עוֹרוֹתָם וְאֶת בְּשָׂרָם וְאֶת פִּרְשָׁם". מה לְהַלָּן. בְּפַר כֹּהֵן מָשִׁיחַ. ע"י נִיתּוּחַ. דִּיָּלְפִינַן מִג"ש מֵעוֹלָה. ק"ו. כְּלוֹמַר, מִק"ו נִלְמַד לְפָרֵשׁ לְךָ שְׁאֵילָה זוֹ.
ה"ג: וּמַה הֶיקֵּשׁ שֶׁאֵינוֹ מְלַמֵּד בְּהֶיקֵּשׁ כו'. וְל"ג "לָמֵד". ג"ש הַמְלַמֶּדֶת בְּהֶיקֵּשׁ גָּרְסִי', וְלָא גָּרְסִי' "לְמֵדָה". מִדְּרַב פַּפָּא. "וְזֹאת תּוֹרַת זֶבַח הַשְּׁלָמִים" כו', דְּפָשַׁט רַב פַּפָּא ט] מִינֵּיהּ לִגְזֵירָה שָׁוָה חוֹזֶרֶת וּמְלַמֶּדֶת בְּהֶיקֵּשׁ. הָנִיחָא לְמַאן דְּאִית לֵי' דְּרַב פַּפָּא. דְּאָמַר: בָּתַר לָמֵד אָזְלִינַן. אֶלָּא לְמַאן דְּאָמַר. בָּתַר מְלַמֵּד אָזְלִינַן – לָא אַשְׁכַּחַן גז"ש חוֹזֶרֶת וּמְלַמֶּדֶת בְּהֶיקֵּשׁ, דְּהָתָם מַעֲשֵׂר י] חוּלִּין הוּא הַמְלַמְּדָהּ. בִּגז"ש חֲבֵירְתָהּ. מַה שֶּׁאֵין הֶיקֵּשׁ עוֹשֶׂה כֵּן בְּהֶיקֵּשׁ חֲבֵירוֹ. מִדְּרָמִי בַּר חָמָא. "סֹלֶת מוּרְבֶּכֶת חַלּוֹת". שֶׁאֵינָהּ לְמֵידָה מִן הַהֶיקֵּשׁ גָּרְסִי'. מִדְּר' יוֹחָנָן. לֹא יֹאמַר לְפוֹנָה בְּאָשָׁם, מִשָּׁם לָמַדְנוּ שֶׁאֵין דָּבָר הַלָּמֵד בְּהֶיקֵּשׁ מְלַמֵּד בִּגז"ש. שֶׁאֵינָהּ לְמֵידָה בְּהֶיקֵּשׁ. כְּלוֹמַר, מִן הַהֶיקֵּשׁ. יא] מְלַמֵּד בְּק"ו. כִּדְאָמַר לְעֵיל, מִק"ו: וּמַה הֶיקֵּשׁ שֶׁאֵינוֹ לָמֵד מִן הַהֶיקֵּשׁ מְלַמֵּד בְּק"ו, גז"ש הַמְלַמֶּדֶת מִגז"ש חֲבֵירְתָהּ, מִדְּרָמִי בַּר חָמָא וכו'. וְזֶהוּ ק"ו בֶּן קַל וָחוֹמֶר. ק"ו זֶה שֶׁאָנוּ מְבִיאִין כָּאן לְדוֹרְשׁוֹ בַּתּוֹרָה לְלַמֵּד ק"ו – מִק"ו אָנוּ לְמֵידִין אוֹתוֹ, מִדָּבָר שֶׁאַף הוּא לֹא לְמַדְנוּהוּ אֶלָּא בְּק"ו. דְּהָא מַיְיתֵי לָהּ מִגז"ש הַמְלַמֶּדֶת בְּק"ו, וְהִיא גּוּפָהּ לָא יָדְעִינַן לָהּ אֶלָּא ע"י ק"ו, דִּבְק"ו יָלְפִינַן לְעֵיל. וּפָרְכִינַן: בֶּן בְּנוֹ שֶׁל ק"ו הוּא. שֶׁאֲפִי' הָיִינוּ לְמֵידִין אוֹתוֹ מִדָּבָר שֶׁלֹּא לְמַדְנוּהוּ ע"י ק"ו – יב] הוּא הָיָה עַצְמוֹ בֶּן ק"ו, שֶׁהֲרֵי בְּק"ו אָנוּ לְמֵדִין אוֹתוֹ, כְּדַאֲמַרַן לְעֵיל יג] בְּק"ו: וּמַה גז"ש כו', עַכְשָׁיו שֶׁאַף גז"ש שֶׁאָנוּ לְמֵידִין אוֹתוֹ מִמֶּנּוּ לְדוֹרְשָׁהּ בַּתּוֹרָה, אַף הִיא לֹא לְמֵדָה שֶׁתְּלַמֵּד בְּק"ו אֶלָּא מִק"ו, נִמְצָא שֶׁאַתָּה מֵבִיא מִדַּת קַל וָחוֹמֶר בַּתּוֹרָה מִכֹּחַ שְׁנֵי קַלִּין וַחֲמוּרִין, וְהו"ל בְּנוֹ שֶׁל ק"ו וּבֶן בְּנוֹ שֶׁל ק"ו. [illegible] כּוּלֵּי הַאי לֵית לָן לְמֵילַף וּמֵיזַל! אֶלָּא. לָא תַּרְבֵּיהּ מִגְּזֵירָה שָׁוָה הַמְלַמֶּדֶת בְּק"ו, דְּהִיא גּוּפָהּ מִק"ו אָתְיָא לָן. אֶלָּא יָלֵיף לֵיהּ מֵהֶיקֵּשׁ הַמְלַמֵּד בְּק"ו, דְּנָפְקָא לָן מִמַּתְנִיתָא דְּתָנֵי דְּבֵי רַבִּי יִשְׁמָעֵאל דִּגְמָרָא גָּמַר לָהּ דְּדָבָר יד] הַמְלַמֵּד בְּהֶיקֵּשׁ חוֹזֵר וּמְלַמֵּד בְּקַל וָחוֹמֶר. וְהַשְׁתָּא לָא הָוֵי אֶלָּא קַל וָחוֹמֶר בֶּן קַל וָחוֹמֶר, כִּי אִיךְ דִּלְעֵיל, דִּגְזֵירָה שָׁוָה מְלַמֶּדֶת בְּקַל וָחוֹמֶר מִקַּל וָחוֹמֶר. מְטַמְּאָה בְּבֵית הַבְּלִיעָה. כְּדִין נִבְלַת עוֹף טָהוֹר, דְּאֵין מְלִיקַת טְרֵיפָה בְּקָדָשִׁים מְטַהֶרֶת מִידֵי נְבֵלָה. וְהוּא הַדִּין נַמִּי לְשׁוֹחֵט עוֹף חוּלִּין טְרֵיפָה – מְטַמְּאָה לְרַבִּי יְהוּדָה. שָׁלֹשׁ מַחֲלוֹקֶת בַּדָּבָר: לר"מ אַחַת שְׁחִיטַת טו] עוֹף שֶׁל חוּלִּין וְאַחַת מְלִיקָה בְּקָדָשִׁים מְטַהֲרוֹת טְרֵיפָתָן מִידֵי נְבֵלָה, וּלְר' יְהוּדָה זוֹ וָזוֹ אֵינָהּ מְטַהֶרֶת, וּלְר' יוֹסֵי שְׁחִיטָה מְטַהֶרֶת וְלֹא מְלִיקָה. וְכֵן טז] מְפָרֵשׁ בְּמַסֶּכֶת טְהָרוֹת בְּפֶרֶק "שְׁלֹשׁ עֶשְׂרֵה דְּבָרִים". שְׁחִיטָתָהּ מְטַהֶרֶת טְרֵיפָתָהּ מִטּוּמְאָתָהּ. כִּדְאָמְרִינַן בְּ"הָעוֹר וְהָרוֹטֶב" (חולין דף קכח:): "וְכִי יָמוּת מִן הַבְּהֵמָה" וגו' – מִקְצַת בְּהֵמָה מְטַמְּאָה וּמִקְצַת בְּהֵמָה אֵינָהּ מְטַמְּאָה, וְאֵיזוֹ זוֹ – טְרֵיפָה שֶׁשְּׁחָטָהּ. נִבְלַת עוֹף יז] אֵינוֹ מְטַמֵּא בְּמַגָּע וּבְמַשָּׂא. מִבַּחוּץ, דִּכְתִיב (ויקרא כב): "לְטָמְאָה בָהּ" – אֵין לְךָ אֶלָּא הָאָמוּר בָּהּ: אֲכִילָה, וְלֹא מַגָּע וּמַשָּׂא. אֵינוֹ דִּין שֶׁתְּהֵא שְׁחִיטָתָהּ מְטַהֶרֶת טְרֵיפָתָהּ מִטּוּמְאָתָהּ. וְהַשְׁתָּא דְּקי"ל שְׁחִיטָה דִּמְטַהֶרֶת בְּחוּלִּין מִק"ו, הָדְרָא וּמִיגַּמְרָא לַמְּלִיקָה דְּקָדָשִׁים בְּבִנְיַן אָב. מַה מָּצִינוּ בִּשְׁחִיטָה שֶׁמַּכְשֶׁרֶת. יח] לֶאֱכוֹל בְּחוּלִּין, וּמְטַהֶרֶת טְרֵיפָתָהּ מִטּוּמְאָתָהּ, אַף מְלִיקָה כו'. הָכִי

בהפשט נקט אגב אורחיה, ולא צריך למילף, יט] דמגופיה דפר יום הכפורים שמעינן, דכתיב (ויקרא טז): "ושרפו באש את עורותם ואת בשרם ואת פרשם", דאיתקש עורם ובשרם לפרשם.
אלא למאן דל"ל דרב פפא מאי איכא למימר. ורב אדא בר אהבה דיליף לעיל לפון דמעכב בעולה מק"ו מחטאת, והדר יליף אשם מדאיתקש לעולה – כ] היינו למצוה, דלמצוה בעולה כתיב.* ומיהא מדאיתקש תרי זימני אעולה הוא דילפינן עיכובא באשם. וא"ת: דבפ' "אמר להם הממונה" (יומא דף לב.) משמע דקידוש ידים ורגלים הבא בק"ו חוזר ומלמד בהיקש, דקאמר ר"ש בן אלעזר: ק"ו, ומה במקום שאין טעון טבילה טעון קידוש, מקום שטעון טבילה – אינו דין שטעון קידוש? כו' והדר קאמר: מקיש פשיטה ללבישה, מה לבישה טעון קידוש – אף פשיטה טעון קידוש! וי"ל: דהאי לא איקרי קדשים, אלא גוף הקרבן דוקא.
בן בנו של ק"ו הוא. כא] וכולי האי לית לן למילף ולמיזל. וקשה: כיון דק"ו כב] הוא, אמאי לא נילף שפיר כל כמה דמצינן למילף, כי היכי דילפינן בג"ש אפילו הן מאה? ויש לפרש: כג] בן בנו של ק"ו הוא, משום דמעיקרא הוא דמבעיא ליה אי דבר הלמד בק"ו *חוזר ומלמד בג"ש, היאך בא להוכיח מדהוו בק"ו בג"ש שמלמדת בק"ו ע"י ק"ו, א"כ אתה רוצה לדון ק"ו ע"י ק"ו מדבר הבא בקל וחומר – הלא זאת היא שאילתך שאתה מסופק בה!
רבי יהודה אומר מטמאה בגדים בבית הבליעה. פי' בקונטרס: דבמס' טהרות (פ"א) משמע דלר"מ אחת שחיטה בעוף של חולין ואחת מליקה בקדשים מטהרות טרפותן מידי נבלה, ולרבי יהודה זו וזו אינה מטהרת. וא"ת: דבפרק "אלו טריפות" (חולין דף נו.) אמרינן: רבי יהודה בדיק בידא, ור' נחמיה בדיק במחטא, וא"ל מאן דבדיק במחטא למאן דבדיק בידא: עד מתי אתה מאכיל נבילות לישראל! נבילות ס"ד? הא שחוטות נינהו. מאי קשיא? לרבי יהודה ודאי נבילות הוין, כדמשמע הכא דשחיטת עוף אינה מטהרת! וי"ל: דלא הו"ל למיפרך אליבא דרבי יהודה, כיון דרבנן פליגי עליה.
מה נבלת בהמה שמטמאה במגע ובמשא כו'. תימה: מה לנבלת בהמה שאינה מטמאה כד] בבית הבליעה! וי"ל: דעיקר טעמא דר"מ מהיקשא ד"זאת תורת הבהמה והעוף" כדלקמן פ' "חטאת העוף" (דף סט:), כדפי' בקונט'.
מה מצינו בשחיטה של עוף שמכשרתה באכילה וכו'. ודאי: ולא היא, תרוייהו משחיטת חולין גמרי, פי': מליקת קדשים ב"מה מצינו" משחיטת עוף שאינה כי אם בחולין, ושחיטת עוף של חולין – בק"ו משחיטת בהמת חולין. ותימה: היאך גמר מליקת עוף משחיטת עוף? מה לשחיטה שכן מכשרת בחולין! ועוד קשה: דמנא ליה דמליקת עוף משחיטת עוף גמר? כה] דלמא משחיטה דבהמה גמר! ונראה לי: דאם כן הוה גמר בק"ו, כדגמר שחיטת עוף. והיינו טעמא דלא

יט א מיי' פ"ז מהל' פסולי המוקדשין הלכה ג:

גי' נ"ק ומהא דלאיתקש תרי זימנין לעולה הוא כו'
גי' נ"ק אי מדרמי בר חמא אי מדרבא אינו דין
חוזר ומלמד בק"ו היאך בא להוכיח מדהוו בק"ו כו' נ"ק

[מנחות עו.]
עי' רש"ק
לקמן דף סט.

גליון הש"ס
גמ' מאי איכא למימר תיקו. עיין לקמן דף נה ע"א תוס' ד"ה אלא [illegible] תוס' ד"ה אלא בר אהבה. עי' לקמן דף נה ע"א תוס' ד"ה מה עולה.

שיטה מקובצת
א] מה להלן כו' שלא בהפשט אלמא דדבר הלמד בג"ש חוזר ומלמד בג"ש [דבר כו']. וא"ת דהיכי יליף מהכא לדבר הלמד בג"ש כו' דלמא דשאני הכא משום דניתן לדרוש לענין שלא בהפשט דאינו בא מג"ש בפר כהן משיח אתי ניתוח בהדי אגב גררא דהוי הימנו ודבר אחר ומלמדים הימנו ועוד קשה דשלא בהפשט גופיה היכא יליף בג"ש בפר יוה"כ מפר כהן משיח [הא] בפר כהן משיח גופיה לא כתיב הפשט בהדיא אלא ילפינן ליה בהיקש עור ובשר לקרבו ופרשו והיאך חוזר ומלמד בג"ש וי"ל דקושיא חדא מתרצה לחברתה דמדחזינן דילפינן מיניה שלא בהפשט אע"ג דהתם מהיקשא הוא דאתא א"כ ש"מ דדבר הלמד בג"ש חוזר ומלמד בג"ש והוי ניתוח כמו דכתיב בגופיה לגבי הכי ונילף בג"ש לפר ושעיר יוה"כ מפר כהן משיח וכיון דילפינן מיניה ניתוח מהשתא נילף נמי שלא בהפשט מהתם דהוי הימנו ודבר אחר. ס"א וי"ל קושיא חדא מתרצה לחברתה ואדרבה לגבי שלא בהפשט הימנו ודבר אחר הוא דלא מצי למילף שלא בהפשט אלא עם ניתוח דילפינן ניתוח בג"ש מעולה הלכך כי הדר יליף

ניתוח בפר יוה"כ בג"ש דדבר הלמד בג"ש חוזר ומלמד בג"ש יליף עמו הפשט והוי הימנו ודבר אחר ולא הוי היקש חוזר ומלמד בג"ש ועי"ל דשלא בהפשט לא ילפינן מפר כהן משיח אלא בגופייהו כתיב את עורותם. כו' ואיתקש בשרם לפירשם ואע"ג (דכתיב) [דלא כתיב] קרבם מ"מ נימא מה פירשם אינו שורפם בפני עצמה בלא קרבם אף בשרם שורפם בעורם והא דקאמר שלא בהפשט אגב ניתוח נקט לה. לשון תוס' מהר"פ: ב] מלמד מן ההיקש אי כן ג"ש המלמדת בג"ש חבירתה כו'. פ"ה מה שאין ההיקש עושה כו' וא"ת הא לא משום יפוי כח דמלמד הוא דג"ש מלמדת בג"ש אלא משום כח נלמד דלמד בקל ומש"ה לא תהא מלמד בקל ותדע דכמו דאין ההיקש מלמד בהיקש כמו כן ג"ש אינה מלמדת בהיקש אע"ג דג"ש מלמדת בג"ש אלמא לא משום כח המלמד הוא וי"ל דק"ו דעביד הוי אף מג"ש וה"ק ומה היקש שאינו מלמד לא בהיקש חבירו ולא בג"ש מלמד בק"ו ג"ש מלמדת בג"ש אע"פ שאינה מלמדת בהיקש אינו דין שתלמוד בק"ו כיון שהיא עושה מה שאין היקש עושה שמלמדת בג"ש ואע"ג דאינה מלמדת בהיקש כמו כן היקש אינו מלמד בהיקש: ד] שאינה למדה מן ההיקש [כו' ק"ו] הלמד מן היקש: ה] בגז"ש חבירתה מדרמי: ו] דין שילמד: ז] מלמדת בק"ו מדתרביצא. ה"ג מלמדת בק"ו מדתרביצא היינו הא דאמרי' לעיל דבר הלמד בג"ש מהו שילמד בק"ו מה היקש שאינה למד מן ההיקש מלמד בק"ו [illegible] ג"ש המלמדת בג"ש חבירתה מדרמי בר חמא (כולה) [כו'] ולפי שלא הוזכר בה שם חכם אלא מפי כל החבורה נזרקה קרי לה לישנא דתרביצא בית המדרש שמרביצין בו תורה. תיבת כדאמרן נמחק: ח] בן בנו של ק"ו הוא. נ"ל דה"פ כלומר אתה רוצה להוכיח דבר זה בק"ו מג"ש שמלמדת בק"ו והיא גופה שמלמדת בק"ו לא ידעת רק מכח ק"ו דלעיל. וא"כ אין לפשוט משם שהרי מזה אתה מסופק בתחלת דינך ועל זה אנו דנין אם דבר הלמד בק"ו אם חוזר ומלמד בק"ו וכיון שאתה עושה ק"ו מאותה מדה מג"ש שמלמדת בק"ו שזה הדבר עצמו אתה למד לעיל בק"ו א"כ כל עיקר דינך בדבר הלמד בק"ו שחוזר ומלמד בק"ו ואם אינו מלמד בק"ו א"כ אין להוציא בפה אותו ק"ו שבא מג"ש המלמדת בהיקש. לשון מהר"פ: ט] מינה דג"ש: י] מעשר דמחולין הוא: יא] מדבור המתחיל מלמד בק"ו כו' עד סה"ד נמחק: יב] ק"ו הואי הוא: יג] לעיל ק"ו וגם ג"ש כו' ממנו לדרוש מדה זו בתורה: יד] דדבר הלמד בהיקש: טו] אחת שחיטת העוף: טז] מפורש במס': יז] עוף טהור אינו: יח] שמכשרת לאכילה בחולין ומטהרת מליקה כו' לקמן בפ' חטאת העוף מייתי לה ופריך בגמ' ור"מ לית ליה דין: יט] למילף בפר יוה"כ מפר כהן משיח דמגופיה: כ] לעולה מצינו למימר דס"ל כרב פפא א"נ לא דמי דלמצוה. ותיבות היינו למצוה נמחק: כא] הוא. [illegible] כב] [illegible]

[illegible]

*) [נ"ל דמג"ל למליקת עוף משחיטת עוף גמר ושחיטת עוף משחיטת בהמה דלמא מליקת עוף משחיטת בהמה גמר [illegible] (ועי' תוס' בסמוך [illegible])

מְטַהֶרֶת טְרֵיפָתָהּ מִטּוּמְאָתָהּ, אַף מְלִיקָה שֶׁמַּכְשַׁרְתָּהּ בַּאֲכִילָה – תְּטַהֵר טְרֵיפָתָהּ מִטּוּמְאָתָהּ. ר' יוֹסֵי אוֹמֵר: דַּיָּהּ כְּנִבְלַת בְּהֵמָה טְהוֹרָה, שֶׁשְּׁחִיטָתָהּ מְטַהַרְתָּהּ וְלֹא מְלִיקָתָהּ. א] וְלָא הִיא, הָתָם תֶּיהֱוֵי הִיא, מִשְּׁחִיטָה דְּחוּלִּין ב] קָאָתְיָין. דָּבָר הַלָּמֵד בְּבִנְיַן אָב מַהוּ שֶׁיְּלַמֵּד בְּהֶיקֵּשׁ וּבִג"ש וּבְק"ו וּבְבִנְיַן אָב? פְּשׁוֹט מֵהָא חֲדָא: *מִפְּנֵי מָה אָמְרוּ: לָן בְּדָם כָּשֵׁר – שֶׁהֲרֵי לָן בְּאֵימוּרִין כָּשֵׁר, ג] לָן בְּאֵימוּרִין כָּשֵׁר – שֶׁהֲרֵי לָן בְּבָשָׂר כָּשֵׁר, *יוֹצֵא – הוֹאִיל וְיוֹצֵא כָּשֵׁר בְּבָמָה, טָמֵא – הוֹאִיל וְהוּתַּר בַּעֲבוֹדַת צִיבּוּר, חוּץ לִזְמַנּוֹ – הוֹאִיל וּמְרַצֶּה לְפִיגּוּלוֹ, חוּץ לִמְקוֹמוֹ – הוֹאִיל וְהוּקַּשׁ לְחוּץ לִזְמַנּוֹ, שֶׁקִּיבְּלוּ פְּסוּלִין וְזָרְקוּ ד] דָּמָן – בְּהָנָךְ פְּסוּלִין דַּחֲזוּ לַעֲבוֹדַת צִיבּוּר. *וְכִי דָּנִין דָּבָר שֶׁלֹּא בְּהֶכְשֵׁירוֹ מִדָּבָר שֶׁבְּהֶכְשֵׁירוֹ? תָּנָא, ה] *מִ"זֹּאת תּוֹרַת הָעוֹלָה" רִיבָּה, סָמֵיךְ לֵיהּ. "שְׁיָרֵי הַדָּם" כו'. מַאי טַעְמָא? ו] אָמַר קְרָא: °"אֶל יְסוֹד מִזְבַּח הָעוֹלָה אֲשֶׁר פֶּתַח אֹהֶל מוֹעֵד" – ז] *הַהוּא דְּפָגַע בְּרֵישָׁא. ת"ר: ח] "אֶל יְסוֹד מִזְבַּח הָעוֹלָה" – וְלֹא יְסוֹד מִזְבַּח הַפְּנִימִי, "אֶל יְסוֹד מִזְבַּח הָעוֹלָה" – אֵין לוֹ יְסוֹד לַפְּנִימִי עַצְמוֹ, "אֶל יְסוֹד מִזְבַּח הָעוֹלָה" – תֵּן יְסוֹד לַמִּזְבֵּחַ שֶׁל עוֹלָה. אוֹ אֵינוֹ אֶלָּא: ט] מִזְבְּחָהּ שֶׁל עוֹלָה יְהֵא לִיסוֹד? אָמַר ר' יִשְׁמָעֵאל: קַל וָחוֹמֶר, מַה שִּׁירַיִים שֶׁאֵין מְכַפְּרִין – טְעוּנִין יְסוֹד, תְּחִלַּת עוֹלָה שֶׁמְּכַפֶּרֶת – אֵינוֹ דִּין שֶׁטְּעוּנָה יְסוֹד? אָמַר רַבִּי עֲקִיבָא: מַה שִּׁירַיִים שֶׁאֵין מְכַפְּרִין, וְאֵין בָּאִין לְכַפָּרָה – י] טְעוּנָה יְסוֹד, תְּחִלַּת עוֹלָה שֶׁמְּכַפֶּרֶת וּבָאָה לְכַפָּרָה – אֵינוֹ דִּין שֶׁטְּעוּנָה יְסוֹד? יא] א"כ, מַה ת"ל "אֶל יְסוֹד מִזְבַּח הָעוֹלָה" – תֵּן יְסוֹד לְמִזְבְּחָהּ שֶׁל עוֹלָה. אָמַר מָר: "אֶל יְסוֹד מִזְבֵּחַ" (א) – יב] וְלֹא יְסוֹד מִזְבַּח הַפְּנִימִי. הָא מִיבָּעֵי לֵיהּ לְגוּפֵיהּ! °מֵ"אֲשֶׁר פֶּתַח אֹהֶל מוֹעֵד" נָפְקָא. "אֶל יְסוֹד מִזְבַּח הָעוֹלָה" – תֵּן

תורה אור: ויקרא ד | שם

רש"י

הָכִי גָּרְסִי': וְלָא הִיא הָתָם תֶּיהֱוֵי יג] מִשְּׁחִיטָה דְּחוּלִּין קָאָתְיָא. וְהָכִי פֵּירוּשׁוֹ: הָתָם עִיקַּר טַעְמָא דְּר"מ לָא יָלֵיף בְּבִנְיַן אָב אֶלָּא מֵהֶיקֵּשׁ דְּ"זֹאת תּוֹרַת הַבְּהֵמָה וְהָעוֹף" כִּדְלְקַמָּן בְּפֶרֶק "חַטַּאת הָעוֹף" (דף סט:) יד] אָמְרִינַן: ר"מ קְרָא אַשְׁכַּח וְדָרַשׁ. וְאִי נַמִי תֶּיהֱוֵי, דְּגָמַר לָהּ בְּבִנְיַן אָב כִּדְקָתָנֵי בְּמַתְנִי' – לָא מִיפְשְׁטָא בָּעֲיָין, דְּהָא ר"מ מְלִיקָה בְּקָדָשִׁים מִשְּׁחִיטָה דְּחוּלִּין גָּמַר, טו] הֲוָה לֵיהּ מְלַמֵּד דְּחוּלִּין, וּלְמַאן דְּלֵית לֵיהּ דְּרַב פַּפָּא, אַף עַל גַּב דְּלָמֵד קֹדֶשׁ לָאו רְאָיָיה הִיא. פְּשׁוֹט מֵהָא. מַתְנִי' חֲדָא מֵהָנָךְ בָּעֲיָא. מִפְּנֵי מָה אָמְרוּ. לְקַמָּן הִיא בְּפֶ' "הַמִּזְבֵּחַ [מְקַדֵּשׁ]" (דף פד:) לְרַבִּי יְהוּדָה דְּדָרֵישׁ "זֹאת הִיא הָעוֹלָה" – הֲרֵי אֵלּוּ מִיעוּטִין: פְּרָט לְנִשְׁחֲטָה בַּלַּיְלָה, וְשֶׁנִּשְׁפַּךְ דָּמָהּ, וְשֶׁיָּצָא דָּמָהּ חוּץ לַקְּלָעִים. וּפָרֵיךְ: מָה רָאָה לְהוֹצִיא אֶת אֵלּוּ וּלְהַכְשִׁיר אֶת הַשְּׁאָר? מִפְּנֵי מָה אָמְרוּ לָן בַּדָּם כָּשֵׁר. שֶׁאִם עָלָה לֹא יֵרֵד – שֶׁהֲרֵי טז] כָּשֵׁר בְּאֵימוּרִין, אִם לָנוּ אֵימוּרִין וְעָלוּ לַמִּזְבֵּחַ לֹא יֵרְדוּ. וְלָן בְּאֵימוּרִין יז] לָמָּה כָּשֵׁר שֶׁהֲרֵי לָן בְּבָשָׂר כָּשֵׁר. גְּמוּר מִן הַתּוֹרָה שֶׁזְּמַן אֲכִילַת שְׁלָמִים שְׁנֵי יָמִים. אַלְמָא אֵימוּרִין גָּמְרִי *בְּבִנְיַן אָב יח] עַל הַדָּם. טָמֵא. אֵיבְרֵי עוֹלָה טְמֵאִין, מִפְּנֵי מָה אִם עָלוּ לֹא יֵרְדוּ? הוֹאִיל וּמְרַצֶּה לְפִיגּוּלוֹ. הוֹאִיל וַחֲשׁוּבָה הַרְצָאַת דָּמוֹ לְחַיֵּיב עָלָיו מִשּׁוּם פִּיגּוּל כְּמוֹ שֶׁקָּרְבוּ מַתִּירָיו בְּהֶכְשֵׁר – לְפִיכָךְ אֵימוּרֵי פִּיגּוּל שֶׁעָלוּ לֹא יֵרְדוּ. שֶׁקִּבְּלוּ פְּסוּלִין. יט] אִם זָרְקוּ אֶת דָּמוֹ, מִפְּנֵי מָה אִם עָלוּ הַדָּם אוֹ הָאֵימוּרִין לֹא יֵרְדוּ? בְּהָנָךְ פְּסוּלִין. מַכְשִׁירִים דַּחֲזוּ לַעֲבוֹדַת צִבּוּר, כְּגוֹן כֹּהֵן טָמֵא. וְכִי דָּנִין דָּבָר כו'. דְּקָא יָלְפַתְּ כ] בְּאֵימוּרִין שֶׁלֹּא בְּהֶכְשֵׁירָם, מִנָּלַן *בְּבָשָׂר דְּהֶכְשֵׁירוֹ בְּכָךְ וְזוֹ הִיא מִצְוָתוֹ. וְתוּ: הֵיכִי יָלֵיף יוֹצֵא בַּמִּקְדָּשׁ מִיּוֹצֵא בְּבָמָה – שֶׁכּוּלּוֹ יוֹצֵא הוּא, שֶׁאֵין שָׁם קְלָעִים, אֶלָּא ע"פ הַשָּׂדֶה. זֹאת תּוֹרַת הָעוֹלָה. תּוֹרָה אַחַת לְכָל הָעוֹלִין, כא] אִם עָלוּ לֹא יֵרְדוּ, כִּדְכְתִיב: "עַל מוֹקְדָה כָּל הַלַּיְלָה". וְכָל רְאָיוֹת הַלָּלוּ, מִשּׁוּם דִּמְמַעֵט מִ"זֹּאת הִיא הָעוֹלָה" תְּלָתָא פְּסוּלֵי, מַיְיתֵי מֵהָנָךְ מַאי שְׁנָא הָנֵי מֵהָנֵי. *וְהָעִיקָּר מִקְּרָא, וְאַסְמַכְתָּא בְּעָלְמָא הוּא. מַאי טַעְמָא. אֶל יְסוֹד מַעֲרָב כב] הוּא? דִּכְתִיב בְּפַר כֹּהֵן מָשִׁיחַ (ויקרא ד): "אֶל יְסוֹד מִזְבַּח הָעוֹלָה אֲשֶׁר פֶּתַח אֹהֶל מוֹעֵד" – יְסוֹד שֶׁכְּנֶגֶד הַפֶּתַח, וְזוֹ הִיא מַעֲרָבוֹ שֶׁל מִזְבֵּחַ שֶׁהוּא כְּנֶגֶד פֶּתַח הַהֵיכָל. וּלְקַמָּן בְּבָרַיְיתָא (דף נב.) נָפְקָא לָן פַּר יוֹם הַכִּפּוּרִים מֵרִיבּוּיָא דְּ"הַפָּר" שֶׁטָּעוּן מַתַּן דָּם לַיְּסוֹד. כג] *בְּפַר כֹּהֵן מָשִׁיחַ וּבְשָׂעִיר כְּתִיב (ויקרא טז): "וְעָשָׂה אֶת דָּמוֹ כַּאֲשֶׁר עָשָׂה לְדַם הַפָּר". אֶל יְסוֹד מִזְבַּח הָעוֹלָה. חָמֵשׁ פָּרָשִׁיּוֹת הֵן בְּחַטָּאת: שֶׁל פַּר כד] כֹּהֵן מָשִׁיחַ וְשֶׁל *הֶעְלֵם – שֶׁהֵן פְּנִימִיּוֹת, וְשֶׁל שְׂעִיר נָשִׂיא, וְשֶׁל כִּבְשַׂת יָחִיד, וְשֶׁל שְׂעִירַת יָחִיד – שֶׁהֵן חִיצוֹנִיּוֹת. בִּשְׁתַּיִם הַפְּנִימִיּוֹת וּבִשְׂעִיר נָשִׂיא כְּתִיב בִּשְׁפִיכַת שְׁיָרֵיהֶן: "אֶל יְסוֹד מִזְבַּח הָעוֹלָה", בִּשְׁתַּיִם הַחִיצוֹנוֹת כְּתִיב: "אֶל יְסוֹד כה] מִזְבֵּחַ" סְתָמָא, וְקָדָרֵישׁ תַּנָּא תְּלָתָא "אֶל *)מִזְבַּח הָעוֹלָה" לָמָּה פֵּירֵשׁ הַכָּתוּב. וְה"ג לָהּ בְּת"כ: "אֶל יְסוֹד מִזְבַּח הָעוֹלָה" שֶׁל פַּר כֹּהֵן מָשִׁיחַ – וְלֹא יְסוֹד מִזְבַּח הַפְּנִימִי. "אֶל יְסוֹד מִזְבַּח הָעוֹלָה" שֶׁל פַּר הָעֵדָה, שֶׁאֵין ת"ל – **)אֵין לוֹ יְסוֹד לַפְּנִימִי עַצְמוֹ. כְּשֶׁהוּא אוֹמֵר: "אֶל יְסוֹד מִזְבַּח הָעוֹלָה" בִּשְׂעִיר נָשִׂיא, שֶׁאֵין תַּלְמוּד לוֹמַר, כו] שֶׁאִם אֶת שְׁיָרָיו לֹא קִיבֵּל מִזְבַּח הַפְּנִימִי שְׁיָרֵי מִזְבַּח הַחִיצוֹן יְקַבֵּל? דָּבָר אַחֵר: וְכִי יֵשׁ לוֹ יְסוֹד לַפְּנִימִי עַצְמוֹ? אִם כֵּן, מַה תַּלְמוּד לוֹמַר "אֶל יְסוֹד מִזְבַּח הָעוֹלָה" – תֵּן יְסוֹד לְמִזְבְּחָהּ שֶׁל עוֹלָה. וְהָכָא נַמִי כז] בָּעֵינַן תְּלָתָא לְמִיגְרַס, וְהָכִי גָּרְסִי', וּפֵירוּשׁוֹ: "אֶל יְסוֹד מִזְבַּח הָעוֹלָה" הָאָמוּר בְּפַר כֹּהֵן מָשִׁיחַ – וְלֹא יְסוֹד מִזְבַּח הַפְּנִימִי, שֶׁלֹּא תֹּאמַר: בִּמְקוֹם מַתַּן כח] הַקְּרָנוֹת שָׁם יִהְיוּ שְׁפִיכַת שְׁיָרָיו. אֶל יְסוֹד מִזְבַּח הָעוֹלָה. הָאָמוּר בְּפַר כט] הָעֵדָה, דְּלָא צָרִיךְ תּוּ דְּהָא אִיתְקוּשׁ לַהֲדָדֵי, אֶלָּא לְלַמּוֹד בָּא שֶׁאֲפִילּוּ יְסוֹד אֵין לוֹ לַפְּנִימִי. וְהָכִי מִידְרִישׁ: הוֹאִיל וּמְיוּתָּר לִדְרָשָׁא – יְסוֹד יִהְיֶה לְמִזְבַּח הָעוֹלָה וְלֹא לַפְּנִימִי. אֶל יְסוֹד מִזְבַּח הָעוֹלָה. הָאָמוּר בִּשְׂעִיר נָשִׂיא, שֶׁאֵין ת"ל, כִּדְמִתְפָּרֵשׁ בְּת"כ בְּהֶדְיָא מִתְּרֵי טַעֲמֵי: [חֲדָא – דְּהָא] שְׁיָרֵי דָּמִים שֶׁל ל] עַצְמָן שֶׁל פְּנִימִי כְּגוֹן בְּפַר מָשִׁיחַ וְעֵדָה, לֹא קִיבֵּל הַפְּנִימִי כִּדְאָמְרַן, שְׁיָרָיו שֶׁל חִיצוֹן יְקַבֵּל? בִּתְמִיָּה. וְעוֹד: לָמַדְנוּ שֶׁאֵין לוֹ יְסוֹד. וּלְקַמָּן (דף נב.) נַמִי הָכִי פָּרְשִׁינַן לָהּ בִּשְׁמַעְתִּין. אִם כֵּן מַה תַּלְמוּד לוֹמַר "אֶל יְסוֹד מִזְבַּח הָעוֹלָה" – תֵּן יְסוֹד לְמִזְבְּחָהּ שֶׁל עוֹלָה, תֵּן תּוֹרַת לא] שְׁפִיכַת שִׁירַיִם יְסוֹד לְהִלְכוֹת מִזְבְּחָהּ שֶׁל עוֹלָה, שֶׁיְּהֵא הַמִּזְבֵּחַ טָעוּן בְּעוֹלָה וּבְכָל דָּמִים הַנִּיתָּנִין עָלָיו שְׁפִיכַת שִׁירַיִם אֶל הַיְּסוֹד, אִם נִשְׁאַר בִּכְלִי כְּלוּם כְּשֶׁזּוֹרֵק מִמֶּנּוּ שְׁתֵּי זְרִיקוֹת לִשְׁתֵּי קְרָנוֹת – יִשְׁפְּכֶנּוּ לַיְּסוֹד. וּמִשּׁוּם דִּבְעוֹלָה לָא כְּתִיב שְׁפִיכַת שִׁירַיִם אִיצְטְרִיךְ לְמֵילַף מֵהָכָא. אוֹ אֵינוֹ אֶלָּא לְמִזְבְּחָהּ שֶׁל עוֹלָה יְהֵא יְסוֹד. אוֹ אֵינוֹ בָּא לְלַמֵּד כְּלוּם עַל שְׁפִיכַת שִׁירַיִם שֶׁל עוֹלָה וְשֶׁל שְׁאָר דָּמִים, אֶלָּא בָּא לְלַמֵּד עַל לב] הִלְכוֹת הַמִּזְבֵּחַ בְּמַתַּן דָּמָהּ שֶׁל עוֹלָה, שֶׁיִּתֵּן שְׁתֵּי מַתְּנוֹתֶיהָ כְּנֶגֶד הַיְּסוֹד, וּלְמַעוּטֵי קֶרֶן מִזְרָחִית דְּרוֹמִית שֶׁאֵין לוֹ יְסוֹד, כִּדְאָמְרִינַן בְּהַאי פִּירְקִין לג] (דף נג.). אָמַר רַבִּי יִשְׁמָעֵאל מִקַּל וָחוֹמֶר. נָפְקָא לָן הָא, וְלָא בָּעֵי קְרָא. מַה שִּׁירַיִם שֶׁל חַטָּאת שֶׁאֵין מְכַפְּרִין טְעוּנִין יְסוֹד כו'. וְרַבִּי עֲקִיבָא גָּמַר לָהּ לְהָא קַל וָחוֹמֶר הָכִי: וּמָה שִׁירַיִם כו', וּלְקַמֵּיהּ מְפָרֵשׁ מַאי בֵּינַיְיהוּ לד] כו'. הַאי מִיבָּעֵיָא לֵיהּ לְגוּפֵיהּ. שֶׁיִּשְׁפְּכֵם לִיסוֹד מִזְבַּח הַחִיצוֹן. וּמִיהוּ, כָּל שֶׁכֵּן אִם רָצָה יִתְּנֵם עַל הַפְּנִימִי, דְּמֵהֵיכָא יָלֵיף מִיעוּטָא? וְאִי קַשְׁיָא: הָא יָלְפִינַן מִבָּרַיְיתָא דְּאֵין לוֹ יְסוֹד לְגַמְרֵי! הַהוּא מִיַּיתּוּרָא דִקְרָא, וְאִי דָּרְשַׁתְּ קַמָּא לְגוּפֵיהּ וְתִנְיָינָא לְמִיעוּטָא – תּוּ לָא מְיַיתַּר שֵׁנִי לְהָכִי אֶלָּא מִקְרָא שְׁלִישִׁי, וְתוּ לֵית לָךְ דְּרָשָׁא שְׁלִישִׁי. מֵאֲשֶׁר פֶּתַח אֹהֶל מוֹעֵד נָפְקָא. דְּהַיְינוּ חִיצוֹן. וַהֲוָה מָצֵי לְמִיכְתַּב "אֶל יְסוֹד הַמִּזְבֵּחַ אֲשֶׁר פֶּתַח אֹהֶל מוֹעֵד", "מִזְבַּח הָעוֹלָה" לָמָּה לִי – לְמִיעוּטָא. הָכִי

*) אל יסוד מזבח נ"ק **) אלא ללמד שאין יסוד. כ"ה בתו"כ

תוספות

לָא גָמַר – דְּאִיכָּא תְּרֵי שִׁינּוּיֵי: מְלִיקָה מִשְּׁחִיטָה, וְעוֹף מִבְּהֵמָה. בְּרוּ"ךְ. וְעוֹד קָשֶׁה: הֵיכִי דָּיֵיק לְדָבָר הַלָּמֵד בְּק"ו חוֹזֵר וּמְלַמֵּד בְּבִנְיַן אָב? אֵימָא דִּשְׁחִיטַת עוֹף אָתְיָא בְּבִנְיַן אָב מִשְּׁחִיטַת בְּהֵמָה, וְדָבָר הַלָּמֵד בְּבִנְיַן אָב חוֹזֵר וּמְלַמֵּד בְּבִנְיַן אָב, לה] כִּדְמַסְקָא בִּשְׁמַעְתָּא! וְנִרְאֶה דְּלִישָּׁנָא דְּמַתְנִי' קָדַיֵּיק, דִּפְשִׁיטָא דְּעִיקַּר טַעְמוֹ שֶׁל ר"מ מֵהֶיקֵּשָׁא דְּ"זֹאת לו] הַתּוֹרָה" כִּדְלְקַמָּן, וּפְשִׁיטָא לֵיהּ דְּ"בַמֶּה מְלִינוּ" מֵעוֹף יָלֵיף, דְּאִי מִבְּהֵמָה – לָמָּה לִי לְאֵיתוּיֵי בְּק"ו.

פשוט מהא חדא לז]. תימה: דתרתי תפשוט, דכיון דמלמד בבנין אב חבירו – אם כן מלמד בק"ו: לח] ומה היקש שאינו מלמד בהיקש, *אי מדרבינא – מלמד בק"ו מדתנא דבי רבי ישמעאל, בנין אב המלמד בבנין אב חבירו – אינו דין שילמד בק"ו? וכה"ג עביד ק"ו לעיל לט].

מפני מה אמרו לן בדם כשר. תימה: היכי דייק מהכא דבנין אב חוזר ומלמד בבנין אב? דילמא לן הדם לאחר שקיעת החמה יליף מלן דאימורין, דלא פסילי בשקיעת החמה אלא בעמוד השחר, והדר יליף לן דאימורין הנפסלים בעמוד השחר דאם עלו לא ירדו מלן בשר! ויש לומר: דפשיטא ליה דאע"ג דיליף באימורים שלא מ] הכשירו מהכשירו דבשר – דם המתיר עדיף, ולא ילפינן דם שלא בהכשירו מהכשירו. תדע, מדלא ילפינן מעיקרא לן דם מלן בשר*.

אשר פתח אהל מועד. יסוד שכנגד הפתח, וזהו מערבו של מזבח, מא] *שיהו כנגד פתח ההיכל. כך פי' בקונטרס. ולא גרים מה שכתוב בספרים "ההוא דפגע ברישא", משום דמשמע מטעם שאין מעבירין על המצות ולא מן הפסוק "פתח אהל מועד", והלא גבי חטאת אית דאמרי שירי הדם על יסוד מערבי לקמן (דף נג.), ואמר טעמא: ילמוד סתום מן המפורש, מחטאת פנימי – משמע דמפורש בהדיא. ועוד: דאית דאמרי על יסוד דרומי, וקאמר: ילמוד ירידתו מן הכבש מב] בסמוך לו ליציאתו מן ההיכל בסמוך לו – מהיכן פשוט לו זה יותר מזה? והלא בתרווייהו שייך טעמא דאין מעבירין על המצות! ועוד: אמרינן לקמן (דף נח:) מג] *על קדשי קדשים: שירים בהדיא כתיב בהו "אשר פתח אהל מועד". ומיהו הא גופא קשיא: דלמה לי קרא ד"פתח אהל מועד"? תיפוק לי דאין מעבירין על המצות, כדאשכחן טעם זה בפ"ק דיומא (דף טו:) דפריך: מאי שנא דיהיב מזרחה לפונה ברישא, *וגבי דישון מזבח פנימי והמנורה אמר: דישון מזבח קודם משום דאין מעבירין, *וכן עבורי דרעא אטוטפתא אסור! ויש לומר: דלא שייך אין מעבירין על המצות אלא כשיש שתי מצות לפניו, כגון דישון מזבח פנימית ומנורה, או כגון מצות קרנות שאינו יודע מהיכן יתחיל, אבל לקבוע מקום אשפיכת שירים – לא קבעינן מהאי טעמא, אי לאו דגלי קרא בהדיא*).

*) וע"ע תוס' במנחות סד: ד"ה אב"א ותוס' במגילה ו: ד"ה מסתבר

*) [נ"ל בבנין אב חוזר ומלמד בבנין אב. תימה כו']

עין משפט נר מצוה

כ א מיי' פ"ה מהלכות מעשה הקרבנות הל"ו:

מסורת הש"ס

לקמן פד: | מנחות ו: מח: לקמן סח: סט. פד: | [לקמן סט. פד:] | גי' נ"ק בבנין אב והדר מגמר בבנין אב על הדם | נ"ל מבשר | גי' נ"ק וקרא עיקר וטעמיה אסמכתא כו' | כפר נ"ק | נ"ל העדה | יומא לג: סס: | נ"ל אי מדרבנא אי מדרבינא | אזאת צ"ק | [וע"ע תוס' לקמן פד: ד"ה ומוליא] | שהוא נ"ק

הגהות הב"ח

(א) גמ' אמר מר אל יסוד מזבח העולה ולא:

שיטה מקובצת

דאפי' לר"פ בעי מידת למד וחד מלמד קודש שהרי כששאלנו לעיל דבר הלמד בג"ש מהו שיחזור וילמד בהיקש ופשיט ליה משלמים שבא ממעשר בג"ש וחזר שלמים ומלמד על תודה הרי כאן דאפילו לרב פפא בעי למד וחד מלמד קודש דתודה למד ושלמים מלמד קדשים הם ואילו הכא לא הוי אלא למד קודש (דזו) [זו] היא מליקה ושאר כל המלמדים חולין דהא יליף מליקה משחיטת עוף דחולין ושחיטת עוף דחולין משחיטת בהמת קדשים ותדע דא"כ דלא אליבא דרב פפא מיפשט בעיין הוי ליה למימר כדלעיל הניחא לרב פפא אלא למאן דלית ליה כו': טו] שהרי לן כשר: יז] באימורין מפני מה כשר: יח] בבנין אב מבשר והדר מגמרי בבנין אב על: יט] פסולין או זרקו את דמו: כ] ילפת לן באימורים שהוא שלא בהכשירו מלן בבשר שהכשירו בכך וכו' ותו דילפת יוצא במקדש מיוצא דבמה שכולו יוצא הוא: כא] העולים שאם עלו לא ירדו כו' ראיות הללו לר' יהודה משום דממעט כו' מייתי ראיה להנך דלא תימא מאי שנא הני מהני ועיקר אסמכתא אקרא שמביא הס"ד והשאר נמחק: כב] מערב דכתיב תיבת הוא ומחק: כג] ליסוד כפר כהן: כד] פר כהן משיח ושל פר העלם: כה] יסוד המזבח סתמא: כו] לומר אם את כו' אות ש' נמחק: כז] נמי תלתא בעי' למיגרס והכי גרסי' ופירושא אל יסוד:

שיטה מקובצת

א] לא היא כו'. פ"ה וה"ג כו' וקשה דא"כ הל"ל כדלעיל הניחא לרב פפא אלא למאן דלית ליה לדרב פפא כו' לכך נראה לרשב"ם דשאני הכא דאפי' למ"ד בתר מלמד אזלינן מודה הכא דלא אזלינן אלא בתר למד כיון דליכא אלא חד למד דקודש ולמד ומלמד דחולין אבל לעיל במלתיה דרב פפא איכא למד תודה ואיכא מלמד שלמים דהיינו קדשים. תוס': ג] כשר מפני מה אמרו לן: ד] וזרקו את דמן: ה] תנא אותו תורת כו': אלמא דדבר הלמד בבנין אב חוזר ומלמד בבנין אב דשמעינן דיליף דלן בדם כל הלילה כשר משום דבשר ואימורים כשר כל הלילה והתם ילפינן דילפינן דם מאימורים ואימורים מבשר דלמא לן בדם מלן בשר יליף וי"ל דכולי האי לא הוי יליף לן דם שלא בהכשירו מלן דבשר דהכשר בשלמים לשני ימים ולילה אחת ואע"ג דילפינן אימורים מבשר משום דאימורים בשר נינהו שלא בהכשר מיוצא דבמה דהכשר גמור וי"ל דשאני התם דדם מדם יליף אבל דם מבשר הכשר גמור ודאי לא יליף וא"ת תרתי מצי למיפשט דכיון דבנין אב יליף בבנין אב א"כ נימא מלמד בהיקש כו' וי"ל דמגלן דהמלמד גורם שתאמר כמו כן יועיל ללמד על ק"ו דלמא הנלמד על נלמד וליכא למימר דמן הכל עושה הק"ו ונאמר בהיקש שאינו מלמד לא על היקש ולא על שט לעיל אי היקש מלמד בבנין אב. הר"פ: ו] דכתיב אל. (עיין נהשמטה נסוף המס'): ז] מועד ח תיבות ההוא דפגע ברישא נמחק: ח] תנו [רבנן] הראב"ד גרים גירסא אחרת בת"כ ופי' כו' יהא יסוד: י] לכפרה טעונים יסוד: יא] יסוד הא מה אני מקיים אל ותיבות א"כ מה ת"ל עולה ולא: יג] תיהוי היא משחיטת דחולין כו' לא בבנין אב יליף לה אלא מהיקש כו': יד] דאמרי' דגמר לה: טו] הוה ליה מלמד חולין ולמאן דל"ל דר"פ דאע"ג דלמד קדש לאו ראיה היא. זה כת"י וכתוב תוס' (לפני) [על] זה ואני אומר דאפי' לרב פפא ראיה היא ושפיר מיפשטן בעיין

כח] מתן דם הקרנות שם כו' שיריו וא"כ יש לנו לומר שיהא שפיכת שירים של פנימיות לכך אתא לומר שיהא על יסוד מזבח העולה: כט] בפר העלם דלא צריך תו דהא איתקוש לפר כהן משיח אלא ללמד בא שאפי': ל] דמים של פנימי עצמו כגון דפר משיח ועדה כו' ועוד הרי למדנו שאין לו יסוד כו' הכי מפרשי' לה: לא] תורת יסוד דהיינו שפיכת שירים למזבח של עולה: לב] על תחלת הלכות: לג] פירקין. גליון דליכא למימר לכל הדמים של מזבח העולה להטעינן תחלתן יסוד דהא איכא חטאת דתחלתן לקרנות: לד] תיבת כו' נמחק: לה] בבנין אב כדמשמע בשמעתא ונראה דמלישנא דמתניתין קדייק: לו] דזאת תורת הבהמה והעוף כדלקמן: לז] חדא. פי' בתרייתא דדבר הלמד בבנין אב*)כו': לח] בק"ו מק"ו ומה היקש כו' מדרבינא אי מדרבא: לט] לעיל בגז"ש המלמדת בג"ש חבירתה וי"ל דלמאי דפי' לעיל ניחא דהתם יליף מג"ש בתחלת הדין אבל הכא אינו יכול לעשות ק"ו בתחלת הדין מבנין אב עצמו ותאמר דהיקש אינו מלמד על בנין אב דהא מבעיא לן לעיל ולא אפשיט. לשון הר"פ: מ] שלא בהכשירו מהכשירו כו' ולא ילפינן דם מאימורין כיון דאיכא תרתי שלא בהכשירו מהכשירו ודם מבשר תדע מדלא: מא] מזבח שהוא כנגד: מב] הכבש מציאתו מן ההיכל מה יציאתו מן ההיכל בסמוך לו אף ירידתו מן הכבש בסמוך לו מהיכן כו': מג] לקמן בריש קדשי קדשים שירים:

תן ד] לה יסוד למזבח של עולה. פירש בקונטרס: כל דמים הניתנין על מזבח החיצון טעון שפיכת שירים ליסוד. ומשום דבעולה לא כתיבא שפיכת שירים ליסוד איצטריך למילף הכא. או אינו מדבר כלל בשירים, אלא למזבחה של עולה יהא ה] ליסוד, לתחילת דמים שיהו מתנות של כל הזבחים כנגד היסוד. אמר רבי ישמעאל ו] כו'. וקרא לא איצטריך לתחילת מתנות כנגד היסוד, דמקל וחומר דשירים של חטאת אתו. אלא על כרחיך להצריך שירים ליסוד לכל הזבחים אתי קרא, כך פירש בקונטרס. וקשה: דלעיל בפרק "ב"ש" (דף לז.) נפקא לן מקראי אחריני, מ"דם זבחיך ישפך", ולרבי מ"בדם". וטפי הוה ליה לאיתויי הך דרשא ז] *דלעיל על רבי עקיבא ורבי ישמעאל דפליגי, שהרי אית להו הך דרשא, וקרא דלעיל *)מייתי לרבי ישמעאל

תֵּן יְסוֹד לַמִּזְבֵּחַ שֶׁל עוֹלָה". דְּאִי סָלְקָא דַעְתָּךְ כְּדִכְתִיב, הָנֵי לָמָּה לִי א] קְרָא — לְשִׁירַיִם, שִׁירַיִם? הָא בָּרַאי עָבֵיד לְהוּ! וְכִי תֵּימָא, ב] דְּאַפֵּיךְ מֵיפַךְ, דְּבָרַאי

הָכִי גָּרְסִינַן: אֶל יְסוֹד מִזְבַּח הָעוֹלָה תֵּן יְסוֹד לְמִזְבְּחָהּ שֶׁל עוֹלָה ג] וְאִי סָלְקָא דַעְתָּךְ כִּדְכְתִיב הָנֵי לָמָּה לִי *[קְרָא לְשִׁירַיִים] שִׁירַיִם הָא בָּרָאֵי עָבֵיד לְהוּ וְכִי תֵּימָא דְאַפֵּיךְ מֵיפַךְ דְּגוּאֵי לְבָרָאֵי וּדְבָרָאֵי לְגוּאֵי הָא אֵין לוֹ יְסוֹד לַפְּנִימִי עַצְמוֹ אוֹ

ורבי עקיבא דהכא! ועוד קשה: דלקמן בסוף פירקין (דף נו:) ילפינן יסוד בתחילת מתנות בכור מעשר ופסח בגזירה שוה דזריקה זריקה מעולה, ולמה לי? תיפוק לי בקל וחומר דרבי ישמעאל ורבי עקיבא דהכא: ומה שירים שאין מכפרין כו', כי היכי דילפינן מהאי קל וחומר עולה ושלמים! וכי תימא: משום דשייכי בכפרה יותר מבכור שהוא בא חובה – נילף בקל וחומר כי האי גוונא: ומה שירים שאין מעכבין טעונין יסוד, תחילת *עולה שמעכבת אינו דין שטעונה יסוד? ועוד: שירים טעונין יסוד מהאי קרא, או מקרא דלעיל – תחילתן לא כל שכן? ועוד: דקאמר אתיא זריקה מעולה, אמאי נקט עולה טפי משלמים או שאר קרבנות? הלא כולהו מקל וחומר דהכא אתו, והוה ליה למימר: אתיא זריקה זריקה משאר קרבנות! ועוד, דקאמר התם: ועולה גופא מנא לן דכתיב "אל יסוד המזבח העולה" – הא תחילת מתנות מקל וחומר, ח] וקרא אתי לשירים ליסוד. ובקונטרס דחק לקמן, ופירש דכדי נסבה. ועוד קשה: היכי עביד קל וחומר משירים? נימא: חטאת תוכיח, ט] שמכפרת ואינה טעונה יסוד, אף אני אביא כל תחילת דמים מחטאת! י] ויש לומר: לפי שהיא על ארבע קרנות, וליכא למימר יסוד בכולהו. ועוד אמרינן לקמן בפירקין (דף נג.): נאמר "סביב" בחטאת ונאמר "סביב" בעולה. ופריך: אי מה חטאת ארבע מתנות על ארבע קרנות – אף עולה טעונה כו', יא] (והא) אמרת עולה טעונה יסוד. מהיכן פשוט לו בעולה טפי מבחטאת? הא בחטאת נמי איכא ק"ו דעולה! ועוד: עולת העוף שהיתה נעשית על קרן מזרחית דרומית, כדלקמן (שם) אמאי לא תהא טעונה יסוד מקל וחומר: ומה שירים דחטאת העוף שאין מכפרין טעונין יסוד, תחילת עולה שמכפרת אינו דין שטעונה יסוד? ומפרש רבינו חיים: דמקרא דהכא ליכא למילף שפיכת שירים יב] לדמים החיצונים אלא לעולה דווקא, כדמפרש בקרא. וקרא ד"ודם זבחיך ישפך" (דברים יב) לא אתא אלא לנאכלין, דכתיב בסיפיה "והבשר תאכל" וכן "והנשאר בדם" כתיב בחטאת העוף הנאכלת. *וקרא ד"אל יסוד מזבח" אתא לאשמועינן בעולה שיש לו תורת יסוד. יג] (או אינו כו') כלומר, תחילת מתנותיה של עולה יהא כנגד היסוד. ומסיק: מי כתיב "אל יסוד העולה", דמשמע תחילת דמים? "יסוד מזבח העולה" כתיב, דמשמע שירים! והדר אמר: דדילמא כתיב "מזבח" דלא תימא אזקיפה דיסוד, אלא אגגו. ועל זה קאמר רבי ישמעאל דמקל וחומר אתי, דכיון דכתיב ביה יסוד בפירוש – מקל וחומר ידענא דהוי אגגו, ואם כן על כרחין לשירים של עולה דליהוי איסוד קאתי. יד] ומהשתא אתיא תחילת עולה בקל וחומר משירים דידיה. אבל משירים של חטאת לא עבדינן קל וחומר *בתחילת דמים בקרבן אחר, כי אם על שירים של אותו קרבן עצמו גמרינן תחילת מתנותיו. ושאר קרבנות דלא כתיב בהו יסוד – אתו בג"ש "זריקה זריקה" מעולה, כמו בכור ומעשר. והא דבעי לקמן (דף נז.) אבכור כנגד היסוד מנא לן – משום דעליה קאי. אי נמי: לאחר שפירש כל הקרבנות קבעי: כנגד היסוד מנא לן, טו] וקאתיא זריקה זריקה מעולה אכולהו. אבל מקל וחומר (דחטאת) לא אתי, כיון דלא כתיב ביה יסוד בפירוש, דהאי קל וחומר לא אתי אלא לגלויי דיסוד דקאמר – אגגו קאמר, ולא שייך למימר חטאת תוכיח אהאי קל וחומר. ומיהו קשה: לתנא דברים "בית שמאי" (לעיל דף לז.) דדריש טז] שפיכה במעשר ופסח מ"ודם זבחיך ישפך", מנא ליה יסוד? הא לא כתיב בהו זריקה! *ואכתי קשה לי: כי היכי דילפינן תחילת עולה מקל וחומר דשירים דידיה – הכי נמי נילף שאר קרבנות לתחילת דמים משירים דידהו, דאתי מ"ודם זבחיך", ולמה לי לקמן למילף בכור ומעשר בגזירה שוה מעולה? ותו, דלקמן דקאמר: ועולה גופה מנא לן – דכתיב "אל יסוד מזבח העולה", קשה כמו לפירוש רש"י. וגם אינו מתורץ "אמרת עולה טעונה יסוד", מהיכא פשוט לו יותר מחטאת? ויש ליישב פירוש זה: דתחילת עולה כנגד יסוד לא גמר כלל מקל וחומר, אפילו משירים יז] דידיה. אלא מקרא ד"אל יסוד מזבח העולה" ידעינן תחילת דמים ליסוד, ו"מזבח" דמיותר – לגג לא איצטריך, דמקל וחומר אתי, אם כן דרשינן מיניה לשירים ליסוד. אבל קל וחומר לא אתי כלל אלא לגגו, היכא דכתיב יסוד. השתא אתי הכל שפיר. אך קשה קצת: דדרשינן מן הפסוק תרתי מילי: תחילת דמים, ומיתורא ד"מזבח" דרשינן שירים. יח] ואימא לשירים לחודא אתי! ויש לומר: דקודם יש לי להעמיד פשטא דקרא לתחילת מתנות, והייתור לשירים. יט] ברוך. ויש עוד לפרש בע"א: תן יסוד למזבח של עולה – שכל תחילת מתן דמים שעל מזבח העולה יהיו כנגד היסוד, בר מחטאת דכתיב כ] בהדיא קרנות, דגזירת הכתוב הוא. או אינו אלא מזבח של עולה יהא ליסוד. כלומר, דווקא דעולה ולא דשאר קרבנות! ופריך: מי כתיב כא] "ליסוד העולה", דמשמע עולה דווקא? "מזבח העולה" כתיב, דמשמע כל דמים של מזבח העולה! הדר קאמר: דילמא כתיב "מזבח העולה" משום גג יסוד! ועלה קאמר רבי ישמעאל: גג אתי בקל וחומר. והאי קל וחומר לא אתי אלא לגלויי דיסוד דקאמר קרא – אגגו קאמר, ולא שייך למימר חטאת תוכיח. ומסיק: תן יסוד למזבח של עולה. והא דלריך לקמן גזירה שוה דזריקה זריקה – משום דתחילת מתן דמים ליסוד מדרשא כב] "למזבחה של עולה" לא ידעינן אלא דומיא דעולה שהן דורון ומכפר – לאפוקי בכור ומעשר ופסח. אי נמי: דומיא דעולה – דשתי מתנות שהן ארבע. ואפילו ילפינן שירים דידהו ליסוד מ"ודם זבחיך ישפך", או מדרבי – מכל מקום תחילת דמים לא ידעינן בקל וחומר. כג] משירים לא אתו – דאיכא למימר חטאת תוכיח, ולקמן דקאמר: אמרת עולה טעונה יסוד – משום דעיקר קרא בעולה כתיב. ואם תאמר: אכתי כד] לא דרשינן מתן דמים ליסוד מזבח למעשר ופסח מ"ודם זבחיך ישפך", הא לא כתיב בהו זריקה, ומנא לן כה] יסוד? וכי תימא מבנין אב דבכור – אם כן תיפשוט דדבר הלמד בגזירה שוה חוזר ומלמד בבנין אב! ויש לומר: כיון דגלי לן קרא גזירה שוה כו] במתנת בכור – אם כן תן יסוד למזבחה של עולה בכל דמים איירי, אפילו באותן שבמתנה אחת כז] *איתנהו, כמעשר ופסח. ומיהו, עולת העוף לא אתיא, דלא מיירי קרא אלא בנזבחים. ואם תאמר: דלקמן (דף נג.) מפרש דקרן דרומית מזרחית לא היה לה יסוד, לפי שלא כח] היה בחלקו של טורף, והרצועה יוצאה מחלקו של יהודה ונכנסת לחלקו של בנימין. למאן דאמר ירושלים לא נתחלקה כט] (*היכי גמרינן מההיא) ברייתא דרצועה כדמוכח בפ"ק דיומא (דף יב.), דאם כן לכוליה מזבח היה לו יסוד מזבח, ואם כן כל הני קראי למה לי? ל] הא אין מזבח בלא יסוד, כדאמר לקמן פרק "קדשי קדשים" (דף סב.) דכבש ויסוד וריבוע מעכבין! ושמא אפי' למאן דאמר לא נתחלקה הכי לא] גמרינן דלא היה לו יסוד. וצריך לדקדק לקמן*) דבעי למימר רבי יהודה אף בדמים שיכול לזרוק על הרלפה, מאי עביד להו להני קראי דמוכחי דעולה טעונה יסוד וגג יסוד? לב] ויש לומר: דקודם דקדיש דוד הרלפה, או אם נעקרה הרלפה סמוך למזבח, או לא קדיש עד ארעית תהומא. *הכי גרסינן: מאשר פתח אהל מועד נפקא. ואף על גב דדרשינן ליה ליסוד מערבי – תרתי שמע מינה לג].

דבראי

*) נ"א לייתי אר' ישמעאל כו'

*) [קף ס.]

[גי' צ"ק לעיל על ר' ישמעאל דפליגי שהרי איתא ליה הך דרשא וקרא דלעיל לייתי על ר"ע דהכא]. ונ"א על הך דרשא דלעיל ר"ע

גי' צ"ק קרא לשירים הא בראי כו' וכ"ת דכי אפיך

נ"א טולין

צ"ל ופריך או אינו אלא מזבחה של עולה תהא ליסוד וקרא דאל יסוד מזבח כו' [תורת יסוד כלומר]

תחלת דמים דקרבן אחר כי אם משירים של כו' צ"ק

צ"ק מ"ז

ועוד קשה צ"ק

צ"ל והיינו מעשר ופסח

נ"א ופליג אההיא ברייתא [כו' א"כ] וגי' צ"ק לא גמרינן כההיא ברייתא כו' א"כ לכוליה כו' יסוד וא"כ

[שייך לע"א]

שיטה מקובצת

א] למה לי לשירים הא. תיבות קרא שירים נמחק: ב] וכי תימא. ס"י אי לא כתיב בעולה אלא אל יסוד המזבח סתמא הו"א דנפיך מיפך: ג] עולה דאי ס"ד כדכתיב הני למה לי לשירים הא בראי עביד להו וכ"ת דנפיך מיפך: ד] תן יסוד תיבת לה נמחק: ה] יהא יסוד אות ל' נמחק: ו] ישמעאל קרא לא איצטריך: ז] דרשא לעיל על כו' שהרי הכא אית להו הך דרשא ואקראי. נ"א וקראי דלעיל מייתרי לדרבי ישמעאל כו': ח] מק"ו אתי וקרא: ט] שמכפרת. ס"א שמעכבת: י] מחטאת תום' ויש לומר כו' בכולהו ע"כ ועוד אמרי': יא] תיבת והא נמחק: יב] שירים לכל דמים החיצונים: יג] תורת יסוד וה"ק תן יסוד למזבח של עולה כלומר לזריקת עולה שעל המזבח כדכתיב וזרקו על המזבח תן לו יסוד שישפוך שירים ליסוד או אינו אלא למזבחה של עולה תהא יסוד כלומר כו' ס"א ופריך או אינו כו' כלומר: יד] קאתי והשתא אתיא כו' משירים דידה. תום' אבל משירים כו' בתחלת דמים לקרבן אחר כי אם משירים של אותו קרבן כו' מתנותיו ע"כ ושאר: טו] מנא לן וקאמר אתיא זריקה: טז] דדריש מתן דמים ואימורין במעשר ופסח מודם כו' מק"ו דשירים דידה ה"נ: יז] משירים דידה אלא מקרא דאל יסוד העולה תיבת מזבח נמחק: יח] ואימא לשירים לחודה אתי נ"א שירים אל יסוד אתי: יט] תיבת ברוך נמחק: כ] דכתיב ביה בהדיא ד' קרנות: כא] כתיב אל יסוד העולה: כב] מדרשא דלמזבחה של עולה כו' שהוא דורון ומכפר תיבת שהן נמחק: כג] בק"ו דתחלת דמים משירים לא אתו: כד] אכתי תנא דדריש מתן. תיבות לא דרשינן נמחק: כה] ומנא לן כנגד יסוד: כו] גז"ש במתנות בכור: כז] ואתי מעשר. תיבת ואיתנהו נמחק: כח] שלא היתה בחלקו של טורף דרצועה יוצאה: כט] לא נתחלקה פליג אההיא ברייתא דרצועה יוצאה כדמוכח כו': ל] למה לי לאשמועינן דעולה טעונה יסוד הא: לא] הכי גמירי: לב] יסוד. תום' וי"ל דקודם כו' למזבח אי לא קדוש עד ארעית תהומא. ע"כ: לג] ש"מ דמ"מ אין מקרא יוצא מידי פשוטו דמשמע דהוי מזבח החיצון וליכא למימר דכולה להכי הוא דאתא ומנלן יסוד מערבי די"ל דא"כ לכתוב אשר לפני אהל מועד או אשר בחצר מאי ת"ל פתח ש"מ ליסוד מערבי כדאמרי' לקמן. הר"פ:

כא א מיי' פ"ה מהל' מעה"ק הל"י:
כב ב מיי' שם פ"ט הלכה ד:
כג ג מיי' שם פ"ה הלכה ז:
כד ד מיי' פ"ד מהל' עשה"ק הל"כ:

דְּבָרַאי לְגַוַּאי וּדְגַוַּאי לְבָרַאי — הָא אֵין לוֹ יְסוֹד לִפְנִימִי עַצְמוֹ. "אוֹ אֵינוֹ אֶלָּא מִזְבֵּחַ שֶׁל עוֹלָה יְהֵא א] לִיסוֹד". מִי כְּתִיב "אֶל יְסוֹד הָעוֹלָה"? ב] "אֶל יְסוֹד מִזְבַּח הָעוֹלָה" כְּתִיב! אִי הֲוָה כְּתִיב "אֶל יְסוֹד הָעוֹלָה" — הֲוָה אָמִינָא ג] בִּזְקִיפָה אֶל יְסוֹד, הָשְׁתָּא דִּכְתִיב "אֶל יְסוֹד מִזְבַּח הָעוֹלָה" — [א]אַגַּגּוֹ דִּיסוֹד. ד] א"ר יִשְׁמָעֵאל: גַּג יְסוֹד לָמָּה לִי קְרָא? ק"ו הוּא: וּמַה ה] שְׁיָרֵי חַטָּאת שֶׁאֵינָהּ מְכַפֶּרֶת — טְעוּנָה גַּג יְסוֹד, תְּחִלַּת עוֹלָה שֶׁמְּכַפֶּרֶת — אֵינוֹ דִּין שֶׁטְּעוּנָה גַּג יְסוֹד? אָמַר רַבִּי עֲקִיבָא: וּמַה ו] שְׁיָרֵי חַטָּאת שֶׁאֵין מְכַפְּרִין וְאֵין בָּאִין לְכַפֵּר — טְעוּנָה גַּג יְסוֹד, תְּחִלַּת עוֹלָה שֶׁמְּכַפֶּרֶת וּבָאָה לְכַפֵּר — אֵינוֹ דִּין שֶׁטְּעוּנָה גַּג יְסוֹד? אִם כֵּן, מַה ת"ל "אֶל יְסוֹד מִזְבַּח הָעוֹלָה" — תֵּן יְסוֹד לְמִזְבֵּחַ שֶׁל עוֹלָה. מַאי בֵּינַיְיהוּ? אָמַר רַב אַדָּא בַּר אַהֲבָה: שִׁירַיִם מְעַכְּבִים אִיכָּא בֵּינַיְיהוּ, מָר סָבַר: מְעַכְּבִי, וּמָר סָבַר: לָא מְעַכְּבִי. *רַב פָּפָּא אָמַר: [מגילה כו.] דְּכוּלֵּי עָלְמָא [ב]שִׁירַיִם אֵין מְעַכְּבִים, וְהָכָא בְּמִיצּוּי חַטָּאת ז] הָעוֹף מְעַכֵּב קָא מִיפַּלְגִי, מָר סָבַר: [ג]מְעַכֵּב, וּמָר סָבַר: לֹא מְעַכֵּב. תַּנְיָא כְּוָותֵיהּ דְּרַב פָּפָּא: °"וְאֵת כָּל ח] (*הַדָּם) ["הַפָּר"] יִשְׁפֹּךְ", [ויקרא ד] מַה ת"ל "הַפָּר" — לִימֵּד [ד]עַל פַּר יוֹם הַכִּיפּוּרִים שֶׁטָּעוּן מַתַּן דָּמִים לַיְסוֹד, דִּבְרֵי *רַבִּי. אָמַר רַבִּי יִשְׁמָעֵאל: קַל וָחוֹמֶר, ט] וּמָה אִם מִי שֶׁאֵין נִכְנָס דָּמוֹ י] לִפְנִים חוֹבָה — טָעוּן יְסוֹד, מִי שֶׁנִּכְנָס דָּמוֹ לִפְנִים חוֹבָה — אֵינוֹ דִּין שֶׁטָּעוּן יְסוֹד? אָמַר רַבִּי עֲקִיבָא: וּמַה מִי שֶׁאֵין דָּמוֹ נִכְנָס לִפְנַי וְלִפְנִים יא] בֵּין לְחוֹבָה בֵּין לְמִצְוָה — טָעוּן יְסוֹד, מִי שֶׁנִּכְנָס דָּמוֹ חוֹבָה לִפְנַי וְלִפְנִים אֵינוֹ דִּין שֶׁטָּעוּן יְסוֹד? יָכוֹל יב] יְעַכְּבֶנּוּ — ת"ל: °"וְכִלָּה מְכַפֵּר אֶת הַקֹּדֶשׁ" [שם טז] — שֶׁלְּמוּ כָּל הַכַּפָּרוֹת כּוּלָּן, דִּבְרֵי רַבִּי יִשְׁמָעֵאל. קַל וָחוֹמֶר לְפַר כֹּהֵן מָשִׁיחַ (מִשְּׂעִיר נָשִׂיא) מֵעַתָּה: וּמַה מִי שֶׁאֵין נִכְנָס דָּמוֹ לִפְנִים לֹא חוֹבָה וְלֹא מִצְוָה — טָעוּן יְסוֹד, מִי שֶׁנִּכְנָס דָּמוֹ לִפְנִים בֵּין לְחוֹבָה בֵּין לְמִצְוָה — אֵינוֹ דִּין שֶׁטָּעוּן יְסוֹד? יָכוֹל יְעַכְּבֶנּוּ — תַּלְמוּד לוֹמַר: "וְאֵת כָּל (*הַדָּם) [הפר] יִשְׁפֹּךְ" [נ"ל דם] — נִתְּקוֹ הַכָּתוּב יג] לַעֲשֵׂה, וַעֲשָׂאוֹ שְׁיָרֵי מִצְוָה, לוֹמַר לָךְ: שִׁירַיִם אֵין מְעַכְּבִין. וְסָבַר רַבִּי יִשְׁמָעֵאל מִיצּוּי חַטַּאת הָעוֹף מְעַכֵּב? וְהָתַנְיָא דְּבֵי רַבִּי יִשְׁמָעֵאל: °"וְהַנִּשְׁאָר בַּדָּם יִמָּצֵה" [שם ה] — טו] וְהַנִּשְׁאָר יִמָּצֵה, וְשֶׁאֵינוֹ

[מגילה כו.] [נ"ל ר"ע וכ"ה בילקוט] [בס"י ליתא]

תורה אור

רש"י

אוֹ אֵינוֹ טז] כו' (א). וְאִי ס"ד לְגוּפֵיהּ אֲתָא, הָנֵי לָמָּה לִי? מַה בָּא לְלַמְּדֵנוּ, לְשִׁירַיִם יז] אֲשֶׁר יִשָּׁפֵךְ שְׁיָרָיו לְמִזְבֵּחַ הַחִיצוֹן? פְּשִׁיטָא דְּעָלָיו יִשָּׁפְכִם, דְּהָא תְּחִלַּת מַתְּנוֹתָיו בַּחוּץ נַעֲשׂוּ! וְכִי תֵּימָא: אִי (לָא) כְּתִיב "אֶל יְסוֹד מִזְבַּח" יח] סְתָמָא הֲוָה אָמֵינָא נִשְׁפַּךְ מִיפַּךְ: שְׁיָרֵי הַדָּם הַפְּנִימִיִּים הִצְרִיךְ הַכָּתוּב לִשְׁפּוֹךְ בַּחוּץ, וּמֵהֶם אַתָּה לוֹמֵד שֶׁשְּׁיָרֵי הַחִיצוֹן יִתְּנוּ לַפְּנִימִי — הָא אֵין לוֹ יְסוֹד לַפְּנִימִי עַצְמוֹ, הִילְכָּךְ עַל כָּרְחָךְ תֵּן יְסוֹד לְמִזְבֵּחַ שֶׁל עוֹלָה קָאָמַר יט]. מִי כְּתִיב אֶל יְסוֹד הָעוֹלָה אֶל יְסוֹד מִזְבַּח הָעוֹלָה כְּתִיב. בִּשְׁלָמָא אִי דָּרְשַׁתְּ לֵיהּ לִיתֵּן תּוֹרַת שְׁפִיכַת שִׁירַיִים לְכָל דָּמִים הַחִיצוֹנִים — שַׁפִּיר כְּתִיב "מִזְבַּח הָעוֹלָה" לִיתֵּן תּוֹרַת יְסוֹד לְמִזְבַּח הָעוֹלָה, לְכָל דָּמִים הַנִּזְרָקִים עָלָיו. אֶלָּא אִי לִתְחִילַּת כ] דָּמִים קָא דָּרְשַׁתְּ לֵיהּ — תּוּ לֵיכָּא לְמֵימַר לִיתֵּן תּוֹרָה כְּנֶגֶד הַיְסוֹד לְמִזְבַּח הָעוֹלָה לְכָל דָּמָיו, דְּהָא כא] חַטָּאת טְעוּנָה מַתָּן עַל אַרְבַּע קְרָנוֹת וְקֶרֶן דְּרוֹמִית מִזְרָחִית בִּכְלָל, וְעַל כָּרְחָךְ אַעוֹלָה לְחוּדֵיהּ תִּדְרְשֵׁיהּ — הֲוָה לֵיהּ לְמִיכְתַּב "אֶל יְסוֹד הָעוֹלָה", שֶׁתְּהֵא הָעוֹלָה כְּנֶגֶד הַיְסוֹד, "מִזְבַּח הָעוֹלָה" מַאי הִיא? כב] בִּזְקִיפָה דִּיסוֹד. שֶׁיִּזְרוֹק תְּחִילַּת מַתְּנוֹת הָעוֹלָה בַּעֲלִיַּית אַמָּה שֶׁמִּן הָאָרֶץ עַד הַכְּנִיסָה, שֶׁהִיא כָּנוּס אַמָּה, דְּכוּלָּהּ הַהוּא אַמָּה בֵּין בְּגוֹבְהָהּ בֵּין בִּכְנִיסָה יְסוֹד מִיקְרְיָא. הָשְׁתָּא דִּכְתִיב: "אֶל יְסוֹד הַמִּזְבֵּחַ" — יְסוֹד שֶׁהוּא דּוֹמֶה לְמִזְבֵּחַ, דְּהַיְינוּ גַּג שֶׁל יְסוֹד. כג] שִׁירַיִים מְעַכְּבִין אִיכָּא בֵּינַיְיהוּ. ר' יִשְׁמָעֵאל סָבַר: כַּפָּרָה הוּא דְּלָא מְכַפְּרֵי, אֲבָל עִכּוּבֵי מְעַכְּבִי. רַבִּי עֲקִיבָא דְּמוֹסִיף "וְאֵין בָּאִין לְכַפָּרָה" — אַשְׁמְעִינַן דְּאֵין מַתַּן דָּמִים שֶׁל כד] מַתָּנוֹת תָּלוּי בָּהֶן, דְּלָא מְעַכְּבֵי לְהוּ שִׁירַיִים לַהֲזָאוֹת. דְּכוּלֵּי עָלְמָא שִׁירַיִים כה] לָא מְעַכְּבֵי. בַּחַטָּאוֹת, וַאֲפִי' פְּנִימִיּוֹת. וְהָנָךְ שִׁירַיִים דְּאִיפְּלוּג בְּהוּ ר' יִשְׁמָעֵאל וְר' עֲקִיבָא — בְּמִיצּוּי חַטַּאת הָעוֹף, כו] שֶׁהוּא שְׁיָרֵי הַזָּאָתוֹ, דִּכְתִיב: "וְהִזָּה מִדַּם הַחַטָּאת עַל קִיר הַמִּזְבֵּחַ וְהַנִּשְׁאָר בַּדָּם" וגו' (ויקרא ה). תַּנְיָא כְּוָותֵיהּ דְּרַב פָּפָּא כז]. דְּאִית לֵיהּ לְר' יִשְׁמָעֵאל נַמִי לָא מְעַכְּבֵי שִׁירַיִם. וְאֵת כָּל דַּם הַפָּר. בְּכֹהֵן מָשִׁיחַ כְּתִיב. "וְאֵת כָּל הַדָּם יִשְׁפּוֹךְ" הָיָה יָכוֹל לִכְתּוֹב, מַה ת"ל "הַפָּר" כו'. א"ר יִשְׁמָעֵאל כו'. לֹא לַחֲלוֹק הוּא בָּא, אֶלָּא לְלַמֵּד שֶׁאֵין שִׁירַיִים מְעַכְּבִין בּוֹ. וְהָכִי קָאָמַר: פַּר יוה"כ מִק"ו הוּא בָּא וּכְתָבוֹ הַכָּתוּב. יָכוֹל לְעַכֵּב כְּתָבוֹ לְךָ? ת"ל: "וְכִלָּה מְכַפֵּר" כו', מַסְקָנָא דְּמִילְּתָא דְּרַבִּי יִשְׁמָעֵאל כח] אָתְיָא. מִי שֶׁאֵין נִכְנָס דָּמוֹ לִפְנִים חוֹבָה. כְּגוֹן פַּר כֹּהֵן מָשִׁיחַ, כט] שֶׁכְּנִיסַת דָּמוֹ לִפְנִים אֵינָהּ חוֹבָה קְבוּעָה, שֶׁלֹּא הָיָה מִצְוָה לַחֲטוֹא וּלְהָבִיא חַטָּאת. טָעוּן יְסוֹד. שְׁפִיכַת שִׁירַיִים. מִי שֶׁנִּכְנָס דָּמוֹ לִפְנִים חוֹבָה. פַּר יוֹם הַכִּפּוּרִים, שֶׁהוּא חוֹבָה קְבוּעָה בְּכָל שָׁנָה. וְרַבִּי עֲקִיבָא בָּא לְהוֹסִיף עַל דְּבָרָיו: עַד שֶׁאַתָּה לוֹמְדוֹ מֵהֵיכָל שֶׁדַּם פַּר נִכְנָס לוֹ מִצְוָה — לֵךְ וְלָמְדוֹ מִלִּפְנַי וְלִפְנִים, שֶׁאֵינוֹ נִכְנָס לוֹ לֹא לְחוֹבָה וְלֹא לְמִצְוָה, וְזֶה נִכְנָס לוֹ אֲפִילּוּ לְחוֹבָה — אֵינוֹ דִּין ל] שֶׁיִּטְעוֹן? יָכוֹל יְעַכְּבֶנּוּ. דְּנֶיהֱוֵי כְּמִי שֶׁשָּׁנָה עָלָיו הַכָּתוּב לְעַכֵּב, שֶׁהֲרֵי לֹא הוּצְרַךְ לִכְתּוֹב וּכְתָבוֹ. תַּלְמוּד לוֹמַר. בְּ"אַחֲרֵי מוֹת": "וְכִלָּה מְכַפֵּר" — שֶׁלְּמוּ כָּל הַכַּפָּרוֹת כּוּלָּן בָּעֲבוֹדוֹת הַלָּלוּ הָאֲמוּרוֹת בָּעִנְיָן, וּשְׁפִיכַת שִׁירַיִים לֹא נֶאֶמְרוּ שָׁם. קַל וָחוֹמֶר לְפַר כֹּהֵן מָשִׁיחַ מֵעַתָּה. מֵאַחַר שֶׁבָּאנוּ לִכְלָל קַל וָחוֹמֶר, לא] יֵשׁ לָנוּ לִדְרוֹשׁ קַל וָחוֹמֶר כַּיּוֹצֵא בּוֹ, וְלוֹמַר שֶׁשִּׁירַיִים מְעַכְּבִין בְּפַר כֹּהֵן מָשִׁיחַ מֵרִיבּוּי הַכָּתוּב, שֶׁהֲרֵי בְּקַל וָחוֹמֶר הָיָה לָמֵד לִשְׁפִיכַת שִׁירַיִים מִשְּׂעִיר נָשִׂיא, יָכוֹל יְעַכְּבוּ מֵעַתָּה — תַּלְמוּד לוֹמַר: לב] "וְכִלָּה". וּמַה מִי שֶׁאֵין נִכְנָס דָּמוֹ לִפְנִים. כְּגוֹן שְׂעִיר נָשִׂיא וְחַטַּאת יָחִיד, שֶׁאֵין נִכְנָסִים לַהֵיכָל לֹא חוֹבָה וְלֹא מִצְוָה — טְעוּנִין יְסוֹד, פַּר מָשִׁיחַ שֶׁנִּכְנָס דָּמוֹ לִפְנִים מִצְוָה — אֵינוֹ דִּין שֶׁטָּעוּן יְסוֹד? נִרְאֶה בְּעֵינַי דְּלָא גָּרְסִינַן בְּהַאי מַסְקָנָא "בֵּין לְחוֹבָה בֵּין לְמִצְוָה", אֶלָּא לְמִצְוָה גְּרֵידְתָּא. וְאִי גָּרְסִינַן לָהּ — לֹא תִּיקְשֵׁה מַדְּתָנָא בְּרֵישָׁא עַל דַּם פַּר מָשִׁיחַ שֶׁאֵינוֹ נִכְנָס לִפְנִים חוֹבָה, וְכָאן הוּא שׁוֹנֶה בֵּין חוֹבָה בֵּין מִצְוָה; לְגַבֵּי פַּר יוֹם הַכִּפּוּרִים לָא הָוֵי כְּנִיסַת פַּר לג] מָשִׁיחַ חוֹבָה — שֶׁאֵינוֹ חוֹבָה כְּמוֹתוֹ, אֲבָל לְגַבֵּי שְׂעִיר נָשִׂיא דְּלָא עָיֵיל לֵיהּ כְּלָל — קָרֵי לָהּ לִכְנִיסַת פַּר מָשִׁיחַ "חוֹבָה". וּבְמַסֶּכֶת סוֹטָה (דף מד:) אָמְרִינַן כְּהַאי גַּוְונָא: מִצְוָה לְגַבֵּי רְשׁוּת — חוֹבָה קָרֵי לֵיהּ. יָכוֹל יְעַכְּבֶנּוּ. מֵעַתָּה, דְּנֶיהֱוֵי כְּמִי שֶׁשָּׁנָה עָלָיו לְעַכֵּב? ת"ל וְאֵת כָּל דַּם הַפָּר וגו' נִתְּקוֹ הַכָּתוּב. מִסֵּדֶר שְׁאָר הָעֲבוֹדוֹת, וַעֲשָׂאוֹ שְׁיָרֵי מִצְוָה. שֶׁשִּׁנָּה בְּהִילּוּךְ לְשׁוֹנוֹ, לד] שֶׁכָּל הָעֲבוֹדוֹת כְּתִיב "וְלָקַח" "וְהִזָּה" "וְנָתַן עַל קַרְנוֹת", וְכָאן לֹא כְּתִיב לה] "וְשָׁפַךְ דָּמוֹ אֶל יְסוֹד", אֶלָּא שִׁנָּה בְּמַשְׁמָעָהּ — לְנַתְּקוֹ מִכְּלַל שְׁאָר הָעֲבוֹדוֹת, לוֹמַר שֶׁאֵינָהּ חוֹבָה לו] כְּמוֹ אוֹתָם לְעַכֵּב.

תוספות

דבראי לגואי. וא"ת: הא אמר ר' עקיבא לקמן (דף פא:) דכל דמים שהכנים לפנים פסולין! וי"ל: דשירים אין מכפרין לרבי עקיבא, ולא קרינן בהו "לכפר בקודש". **גג** יסוד למה לי קרא ק"ו לז]. הקשה ה"ר חיים: לקמן פרק "התערובת" (דף פא.) אמרינן גבי דם חטאת שנתערב בדם עולה דפליגי רבי אליעזר ורבנן, אמר אביי: לא שנו אלא תחילת חטאת ועולה, אבל סוף חטאת ותחילת עולה — דברי הכל מקום עולה מקום שירים, פירוש: דאם נתערבו שירי חטאת בתחילת עולה — לכולי עלמא יתנם למטה מן החוט, דמקום תחילת מתן עולה כשר לשירי חטאת, ויזרקם לקיר המזבח ומאליהם שותתין ליסוד, ואין כאן שנוי מקום. א"ל רב יוסף, הכי אמר רב יהודה: שיריים צריכין אילטבא. פירוש: שישפכם על גג היסוד ממש העשוי כאילטבא, ולא יזרקם לקיר הזקוף כמשפט עולה. דמשמע דעולה אינה טעונה גג יסוד! וי"ל: דהאי דבעינן הכא בתחילת עולה גג יסוד — לא אתא אלא למעוטי אמה לח] אדמה התחתונה של מזבח שמן הארץ עד הכניסה, אבל קיר הזקוף של מעלה לט] עד היסוד — פשיטא דעדיף מ] (בעולה) מגג יסוד ממש, דחודה עדיף, משום דבעינן שתי מתנות שהן ארבע. **לימד** על פר יוה"כ שטעון מתן דמים ליסוד. לעיל פרק "בית שמאי" (דף מ:) גבי "ועשה לפר כאשר עשה" דריש סמיכה ושירי הדם בפר יוה"כ. ותימא: להאי *תנא, סמיכה מנא ליה? ושם פירשנו.

ומה מי שאין נכנס דמו לפנים חובה. תימה: מה לפר כהן משיח שכן מכפר על עבירת מצוה ידועה, כדפריך לעיל פ' "בית שמאי" (דף מ:) מא] וי"ל: דסמיך אהאי דאתי בקל וחומר משעירי רגלים ושעירי ראשי חדשים, דדבר הלמד בהיקש חוזר ומלמד בק"ו. **יכול** יעכבנו מב]. דלית לן למימר "טרח וכתב לה קרא" כל כמה דאיכא למידרש.

ל"ק מ"ז

נ"ל דם

גי' הל"ק תנא דהכא סמיכה כו'

הגהות הב"ח

(א) רש"י ד"ה או אינו וכו' וה"פ ואי ס"ד כצ"ל והד"א עם דיבור הקודם:

שיטה מקובצת

א] יהא יסוד מי כתיב: ב] עי' בהשמטות בסוף המסכת: ג] אמינא אזקיפה דיסוד השתא דכתיב אל יסוד המזבח משמע יסוד שהוא דומה למזבח דהיינו גג של יסוד. ואזקיפה דמזבח דממעט הכא היינו שלא יזרוק תחילת מתנות העולה בעליית אמה שמן הארץ עד הכניסה כו' עד יסוד מקרייא אבל הזקיפה שהיא מן הגג עד חוט הסיקרא לא ממעט דאדרבה דהא מוכח לקמן [בפ' התערובת] דשם מקום מתנות העולה ולא על גג יסוד ממש. תו"א: ד] אמר ר' ישמעאל (על) גג היסוד כו'. לעיל פ"ה דעיקר היסוד בתחילת [מתן] דם העולה ילפינן מקו"ח דחטאת וגג יסוד [ג"כ] נפקא לן מהאי קו"ח וכאן לא פי' כלום וקשה לפ"ה כיון דעיקר יסוד מחטאת יליף איכא למיפרך חטאת תוכיח ששיריה ליסוד ואין תחילת דמה ליסוד רק על הקרנות ונראה להר"ר חיים כו' ומיהו אכתי למסקנא כו' ותירץ כו' מ"מ קשה לפי הר"ר חיים דמשמע דתחילת דמו העולה נפקא לן מקו"ח ולקמן מייתי אל יסוד מזבח העולה לתחילת דמו לכך נראה לריב"א דבין תחילת דם ובין שירים נפקא דטעונים יסוד מפשטיה דקרא כדמוכח לקמן וקו"ח לא איצטריך כי אם לגג יסוד ותלמודא לא דייק כו' תוס' אחרות: ה] ומה שירים שאינן מכפרים טעונים גג: ו] ומה שירים שאין מכפרין ואין באין לכפרה טעונין גג יסוד כו' ובאה לכפרה אינו דין שטעונה גג יסוד ומה ת"ל אל יסוד: ז] חטאת העוף לקמן דף ס"ה ע"ב: ח] ואת כל דם הפר כו'. פ"ה דהפר מיותר דה"מ למיכתב כו' וא"ת תיפוק ליה מדאתקיש לפר העלם ובפר העלם כתיב יסוד וי"ל דלא איתקש אלא לעבודות המעכבות כפרה כדאמר בפ' ב"ש וא"ת מ"מ תיפוק לי מוכן יעשה דיליף מיניה שירים התם וי"ל דדריש ליה לקרנות וא"ת א"כ דוכן יעשה אתא לקרנות סמיכה בפר יוה"כ מנלן דלא איתקש לפר העלם אלא לעבודות המעכבות הכפרה וי"ל דמדכתיב וסמך ידו על ראש הפר בפר כהן משיח דהוי ליה למיכתב וסמך ידו על ראשו מה ת"ל לפר לרבות פר יוה"כ לסמיכה וא"ת יותרת וב' הכליות בפר יוה"כ מנ"ל [וי"ל] מכל חלב פר החטאת לרבות פר יוה"כ אבל בהיקש לא ידעינן אלא העבודות האמורו' בענין: ט] ומה מי שאין נכנס כו' תימה אמאי לא מייתי קו"ח דפרק ב"ש ומה במקום שלא השוה כו' וי"ל דמהאי קו"ח לא מצי למילף הכא דבר חדש דלא משמע מהתם אלא דבר המפורש בהם ומהאי דהכא חשיב טפי למילף דבר חדש וא"ת מ"מ האי קו"ח אמאי לא מייתי התם וי"ל דמהאי קו"ח לא משמע כי אם חומרא ולעיל בעי למילף נמי קולא להכשיר אִמִין שבאצבע: י] דמו חובה לפנים טעון יסוד מי שנכנס דמו חובה לפנים אינו דין שטעון יסוד: יא] ולפנים לא לחובה ולא למצוה טעון יסוד מי שנכנס דמו לפני ולפנים בין לחובה ובין למצוה אינו דין: יב] יעכבנו עיין רש"י לעיל (דף יג ע"א) ובתוס' (דף לט ע"ב): יג] כל דם הפר ישפך נתקו הכתוב פי' דלא כתיב ושפך דהוה משמע עיכובא אלא כתיב ישפוך לומר דלא מעכבי אע"פ שהוא א) [פנימי לחובה] היינו בפכ"מ [ובפר יוה"כ אפ"ה לא] וכן בפר העלם לא מעכבי כדאמרי' לעיל בפ' ב"ש מקרא דונסלח וא"ת ולמה לי ונסלח תיפוק ליה משום דכתיב בפר העלם ישפך כמו בפר כהן משיח וי"ל דלפ"ה ניחא דהא דקאמר הכא ישפך נתקו היינו משום דשינה הכתוב דבכל שאר עבודות כתיב ונתן והזה משמע דבא לומר דלא מעכבי אבל גבי פר העלם לא שייך האי טעמא דכמו כן כתיב יתן וא"כ לא שנה הכתוב בשפיכת שירים וא"ת ולמה לי ישפך בפכ"מ תיפוק ליה מונסלח

שיטה מקובצת

דדרשינן לעיל בפר העלם דשירים אין מעכבין והרי איתקש פר כהן משיח לפר העלם וי"ל כיון דאיכא הכא קו"ח וגם פסוק הו"א דשינה הכתוב לעכב קמ"ל ישפך נתקו [הכתוב וכו'] וא"ת א"כ קשה איפכא למה לי ונסלח לעיל בפר העלם דשירים אין מעכבין תיפוק ליה מהכא כיון דאיתקשו וי"ל דלא הוקשו אלא להקל ולא להחמיר כלומר לריבוי עבודות ולא למעט וא"ת והא איתקש לעיל להכשיר אִמִין שבאצבע היינו להקל וי"ל דהיינו דוקא לתיקון עבודו' המפורשות בו כבר ולא לדבר חדש כמו שירים: יד] תיבת לעשה נמחק: טו] ימצה הנשאר ימצה: טז] כו' ס"א כמו אמר מר הוא זה ופרושי קא מפרש אמאי קאמרינן תן יסוד למזבח של עולה משום דאי כו' דאי ס"ד דהכתוב לגופיה אתא [שכל] שיריה [יתן] ליסוד ובשעיר נשיא משתעי קרא הני למה לי: מה בא זה ללמדנו אי: יז] לשירים שישפך שיריו למזבח: יח] מזבח העולה אלא אל יסוד מזבח: יט] קאמר וכדי לגלות לשירי הדם של כל הזבחים שישפך שיהי' הדם ליסוד: כ] לתחילת מתן דמים: כא] דהא איכא חטאת שטעונה מתן על ארבע כו' מזרחית בכלל שלא היה לו יסוד ועל כרחך: כב] מה"ד אזקיפה דיסוד: כג] יסוד הס"ד ומה"ד שאינן מכפרין טעונין גג יסוד דכתיב בהו אל יסוד המזבח דמשמע גג הס"ד: כד] של הזאות תלוי בהן כו': כה] שירים. בחטאת לא מעכבי ואפי' דפנימיות ותיבת בחטאות נמחק: כו] העוף קאמר שהוא: כז] פפא דאמר דלר' ישמעאל ותיבות דאית ליה נמי נמחק: כח] ישמעאל להא אתיא: כט] פר כהן משיח נכנס לו למצוה: ל] דין שטעון יסוד הס"ד: לא] וחומר זה יש: לב] ת"ל כו': לג] פר כהן משיח: לד] לשונו שבכל העבודות: לה] ישפך את דמו אל: לו] חובה כמותם לעכב הס"ד: לז] ק"ו הוא הקשה: לח] תיבת אדמה נמחק: לט] תיבת עד נמחק: מ] דעדיף לעולה אות ב' נמחק: מא] שמאי וי"ל דאין זה פירכא דצד חומרא אלא פירכא דהשואות. מהר"פ: מב] יעכבנו פ"ה דהאי ק"ו למצוה ועיכובא מפשטיה דקרא דאל יסוד מזבח העולה שהרי ליכא למימר טרח וכתב לה קרא כיון דאיכא לאוקמי בעיכובא מפשטיה דקרא. מהר"פ:

א) נראה דצ"ל אע"פ שנכנס דמו לפנים חובה דהא מיירי בפר כהן משיח ובפר יוה"כ.

כה א מיי' פ"ב מהל' פסה"מ הל"ח:
כו ב ג מיי' שם הל"ח:
כז ד מיי' שם הל"ג:
כח ה מיי' פ"ה מהל' מעה"ק הל"ז:

וְשֶׁאֵינוֹ נִשְׁאָר — לֹא יִמָּצֵה! תְּרֵי תַּנָּאֵי וְאַלִּיבָּא דְּר' יִשְׁמָעֵאל. אָמַר רָמִי בַּר חָמָא: הַאי תַּנָּא סָבַר שִׁירַיִם מְעַכְּבִי. דְּתַנְיָא: °"הַכֹּהֵן הַמְחַטֵּא אוֹתָהּ", אוֹתָהּ שֶׁנִּיתַּן דָּמָהּ לְמַעְלָה, וְלֹא אוֹתָהּ שֶׁנִּיתַּן דָּמָהּ לְמַטָּה. אָמַרְתָּ: וְכִי מֵאַיִן בָּאתָה? מִכְּלָל שֶׁנֶּאֱמַר: °"וְדַם זְבָחֶיךָ יִשָּׁפֵךְ עַל מִזְבַּח" וגו' אלָמַדְנוּ לַנִּיתָּנִין בְּמַתַּן אַרְבַּע, שֶׁאִם נְתָנָן בְּמַתָּנָה אַחַת — כִּיפֵּר, יָכוֹל אַף הַנִּיתָּנִין לְמַעְלָה שֶׁנְּתָנָן לְמַטָּה כִּיפֵּר? וְדִין הוּא: נֶאֶמְרוּ דָּמִים א] לְמַעְלָה וְנֶאֶמְרוּ דָּמִים לְמַטָּן, ב] מַה דָּמִים הָאֲמוּרִים לְמַטָּן בשֶׁנְּתָנָן לְמַעְלָן — לֹא כִּיפֵּר, אַף דָּמִים הָאֲמוּרִים לְמַעְלָן גאִם ג] נָתַן לְמַטָּה — לֹא כִּיפֵּר! לֹא, אִם אָמַרְתָּ ד] בַּתַּחְתּוֹנִים שֶׁנִּיתָּנִין בִּנְתִינָה לְמַעְלָה — שֶׁאֵין סוֹפָן לְמַעְלָן, לֹא כִּיפֵּר, תֹּאמַר בָּעֶלְיוֹנִים שֶׁנְּתָנָן לְמַטָּה, *שֶׁיֵּשׁ מֵהֶן קָרֵב לְמַטָּה? דָּמִים (שִׁירַיִים) הַפְּנִימִיִּים יוֹכִיחוּ, *שֶׁיֵּשׁ מֵהֶן קָרֵב בַּחוּץ, וְאִם נְתָנָן בַּתְּחִלָּה בַּחוּץ — לֹא כִּיפֵּר! לֹא, אִם אָמַרְתָּ בְּדָמִים הַפְּנִימִיִּים — שֶׁאֵין מִזְבֵּחַ הַפְּנִימִי מְמָרְקָן, תֹּאמַר בָּעֶלְיוֹנִים — שֶׁהֲרֵי קְרָנוֹת מְמָרְקוֹת אוֹתָן, ה] אִם נְתָנָן לְמַטָּה כְּשֵׁרִים! ת"ל: "אוֹתָהּ" — אוֹתָהּ שֶׁנִּיתַּן ו] דָּמִים לְמַעְלָה, וְלֹא שֶׁנִּיתַּן דָּמָהּ לְמַטָּה. מַאי "שֶׁאֵין מִזְבֵּחַ הַפְּנִימִי מְמָרְקָן"? לָאו ז] אֵלּוּ שִׁירַיִם? א"ל רָבָא: אִי הָכִי, תֵּיתֵי בְּק"ו: מַה שִׁירַיִם הַפְּנִימִיִּים שֶׁסּוֹפָן חוֹבָה בַּחוּץ, עֲשָׂאָן בַּתְּחִלָּה בַּחוּץ — לֹא כִּיפֵּר, הַנִּיתָּנִין לְמַעְלָה שֶׁאֵין סוֹפָן חוֹבָה לְמַטָּה, וַעֲשָׂאָן בַּתְּחִלָּה לְמַטָּה — אֵינוֹ דִּין שֶׁלֹּא כִּיפֵּר? אֶלָּא, אֵין מִזְבֵּחַ הַפְּנִימִי מְמָרְקָן בִּלְבָד, אֶלָּא פָּרוֹכֶת. ח] *תָּנוּ רַבָּנַן: °"וְכִלָּה מִכַּפֵּר", אִם כִּיפֵּר — כִּלָּה, וְאִם לֹא כִּיפֵּר — לֹא כִּלָּה, *דִּבְרֵי ר' עֲקִיבָא. אָמַר לוֹ רַבִּי יְהוּדָה: מִפְּנֵי מָה לֹא נֶאֱמַר: אִם כִּלָּה — כִּיפֵּר, אִם לֹא כִּלָּה — לֹא כִּיפֵּר, *שֶׁאִם חִיסֵּר אַחַת מִכָּל הַמַּתָּנוֹת דלֹא עָשָׂה וְלֹא כְלוּם? *מַאי בֵּינַיְיהוּ? רַבִּי יוֹחָנָן וְרַבִּי יְהוֹשֻׁעַ בֶּן לֵוִי, חַד אָמַר: מַשְׁמָעוּת דּוֹרְשִׁין אִיכָּא בֵּינַיְיהוּ. וְחַד אָמַר: *שִׁירַיִים ט] מְעַכְּבִין אִיכָּא בֵּינַיְיהוּ. תִּסְתַּיֵּים דְּר' יְהוֹשֻׁעַ בֶּן לֵוִי הוּא דְּאָמַר שִׁירַיִים דִּמְעַכְּבִי, דְּא"ר יְהוֹשֻׁעַ בֶּן לֵוִי: לְדִבְרֵי הָאוֹמֵר שִׁירַיִים מְעַכְּבִין, מֵבִיא פַּר אֶחָד וּמַתְחִיל בַּתְּחִלָּה בִּפְנִים. אַטּוּ ר' יוֹחָנָן לֵית לֵיהּ הָא סְבָרָא? וְהָאָמַר ר' יוֹחָנָן: *תָּנָא ר' נְחֶמְיָה כְּדִבְרֵי הָאוֹמֵר שִׁירַיִם מְעַכְּבִין! אֶלָּא כְּדִבְרֵי הָאוֹמֵר וְלָאו י] לְהָנֵי תַּנָּאֵי, הָכָא נַמִי כְּדִבְרֵי הָאוֹמֵר וְלָאו לְהָנֵי תַּנָּאֵי.§ **מתני'** חַטָּאוֹת הַצִּבּוּר וְהַיָּחִיד; אֵלּוּ הֵן חַטָּאוֹת הַצִּבּוּר: שְׂעִירֵי רָאשֵׁי חֳדָשִׁים וְשֶׁל מוֹעֲדוֹת; שְׁחִיטָתָן בַּצָּפוֹן, וְקִיבּוּל דָּמָן בִּכְלֵי שָׁרֵת בַּצָּפוֹן, הוְדָמָן טָעוּן אַרְבַּע מַתָּנוֹת עַל אַרְבַּע קְרָנוֹת. כֵּיצַד?

עָלָה

תורה אור: ויקרא ו | דברים יב | ויקרא טז

נ"א שכן סופן למטה | נ"א שסופן להיות בחוץ | יומא ס: ולעיל מ. | סנהדרין ד: | [מנחות טז:]

אותה שנתן דמה למעלה ולא אותה שנתן דמה למטה. וא"ת: א"כ היכי פריך לעיל בריש "בית שמאי" (דף לח.): אימא וכפר אע"פ שלא נתן למעלה אלא למטה! לו] וי"ל: דהוה דריש "אותה" לדרשא אחריתי, כדדריש לעיל בפ"ק (דף י:): "אותה" לז] למעלה ולא אחרת למעלה. א"נ, הוה מפרש: אותה יאכלנה – אבל למטה לא יאכלנה, ולעולם כיפר. ולא שייכא כאן לח] דההיא דשמואל (לעיל ד' כו:) דכיון שהגיע דם למזבח נתכפר. **מה** דמים האמורים למטה אם נתנן למעלה לא כיפר. פירש בקונט' דבחטאת העוף כתיב "היא", שאם שינה בה פסלה. ותימה: הא לט] בבהמה נמי כתיב "היא", ונימא כמו כן שאם שינה בה פסלה! **תאמר** בניתנין למעלה שסופן למטה. תימה מ] מעולת העוף שסופן למטה, ותנן לקמן בפ' "חטאת העוף" (דף סו.) עשאה למטה כמעשה כולן – מא] פסולה! ומיהו, היא גופה לא ידעינן מנא לן.

כוליה

וְשֶׁאֵינוֹ נִשְׁאָר. כְּלוֹמַר, אִם יָצָא כָּל הַדָּם בַּהַזָּאָה – אֵין צָרִיךְ מִילּוּי. הַאי תַּנָּא סָבַר שִׁירַיִים מְעַכְּבִין גָּרְסִינַן. הַמְחַטֵּא אוֹתָהּ יא]. הַזּוֹרֵק אֶת דָּמָהּ. וּבִכְלָלָהּ דְּ"זֹאת תּוֹרַת הַחַטָּאת" כְּתִיב. "אוֹתָהּ" מִיעוּטָא הִיא, אִם *מְחַטְּאָה אֶת דָּמָהּ כְּהִלְכָתוֹ שֶׁכָּתַבְתִּי לְךָ יב] *בְּדָהּ קְרָנוֹת, דְּהַיְינוּ לְמַעְלָה – הוּא דְּהַוַּאי חִיטּוּי וְנֶאֱכֶלֶת, אִי לָא – לָא. וְכִי מֵאַיִן בָּאתָ. לְהַכְשִׁיר, שֶׁנִּזְקַקְתָּ לְהָבִיא מִקְרָא לִפְסוֹל. יִשָּׁפֵךְ. יג] שְׁפִיכָה אַחַת, וְנֶאֱמַר "וְהַבָּשָׂר תֹּאכֵל". נֶאֶמְרוּ דָּמִים לְמַטָּה. מִחוּט הַסִּיקְרָא, בְּחַטַּאת הָעוֹף: "וְהִזָּה מִדַּם הַחַטָּאת" (ויקרא ה), וְדָרְשִׁינַן לֵיהּ לְקַמָּן (דף סד:): זֶה קִיר הַתַּחְתּוֹן. וְנֶאֱמַר דָּמִים לְמַעְלָה. בְּחַטַּאת בְּהֵמָה. מַה דָּמִים הָאֲמוּרִים לְמַטָּה שֶׁנְּתָנָן לְמַעְלָה לֹא כִּיפֵּר. דְּהָא כְּתִיב בְּהַזָּאָתוֹ "חַטָּאת הִיא", שֶׁאִם שִׁינָּה בָּהּ פָּסוּל. דְּהָכִי אָמְרִינַן לְקַמָּן (דף סו.): עֲשָׂאָהּ לְמַעְלָה כְּמַעֲשֵׂה כוּלָּן – פָּסוּל. שֶׁכֵּן סוֹפָן לְמַטָּה. שִׁירַיִם נִיתָּנִין לַיְּסוֹד. שֶׁסּוֹפָן לַחוּץ. שְׁפִיכַת שְׁיָרֵיהֶם. וְאִם עֲשָׂאָן בַּתְּחִילָּה בַּחוּץ לֹא כִּפֵּר. דְּעִיכּוּבָא כְּתִיב בְּהוּ *כִּדְרָבִינָא מִ"וְעָשָׂה כַּאֲשֶׁר עָשָׂה". שֶׁאֵין מִזְבֵּחַ הַפְּנִימִי מְמָרְקָן. שֶׁאֵין שָׁם גְּמַר מַתַּן דָּמִים, שֶׁעוֹדָן צְרִיכִין עֲבוֹדָה יד] אַחַת, הִילְכָּךְ חֲמִירִי. וּלְקַמָּן מְפָרֵשׁ וְאָזֵיל מַאי הִיא. תֹּאמַר בַּנִּיתָּנִין לְמַעְלָה טו] בַּקְּרָנוֹת שֶׁמְּמָרְקוֹת אוֹתוֹ. שֶׁהוּא גְּמַר מַתַּן דְּמֵיהֶם לְעַכֵּב, דְּהָא לְכוּלֵּי עָלְמָא שִׁירַיִים הַחִיצוֹנִים לָא מְעַכְּבִי, הִילְכָּךְ לָא חֲמִירִי, טז] וְיִכָּשְׁרוּ לְמַטָּן – לְהָכִי אִיצְטְרִיךְ "אוֹתָהּ". מַאי שֶׁכֵּן אֵין מִזְבֵּחַ הַפְּנִימִי מְמָרֵק אוֹתוֹ יז] [לָאו]. דִּשְׁפִיכַת שִׁירַיִים מְעַכְּבִי בְּהוּ? אֲמַר לֵיהּ רָבָא. לְרָמִי בַּר חָמָא. אִי הָכִי. דְּשִׁירַיִים יח] מִבַּחוּץ מְעַכְּבִי בְּהוּ – כָּל שֶׁכֵּן דְּאָתְיָא מִקַּל וָחוֹמֶר, וְלָא בָּעֵי קְרָא. וּמַה דָּמִים הַפְּנִימִיִּים שֶׁסּוֹף שְׁיָרֵיהֶם חוֹבָה לַחוּץ לְעַכֵּב, עֲשָׂאָן בַּתְּחִילָּה בַּחוּץ כו'. הָכִי גָּרְסִינַן: אֶלָּא אֵין מִזְבֵּחַ הַפְּנִימִי מְמָרְקָן בִּלְבַד אֶלָּא פָּרֹכֶת. דְּדָמָן טָעוּן תְּחִילַּת הַזָּיָיה עַל הַפָּרוֹכֶת. יט] הוֹאִיל וּטְעוּנִין שְׁתֵּי עֲבוֹדוֹת בִּפְנִים – חֲמִירֵי לְעַכֵּב מִלַּעֲשׂוֹתָן בַּחוּץ, תֹּאמַר בַּנִּיתָּנִין לְמַעְלָן, שֶׁכֵּן קְרָנוֹת מְמָרְקוֹת אֶת עֲבוֹדוֹתֵיהֶן הָעֶלְיוֹנוֹת, וְאֵין טְעוּנִין שְׁתֵּי עֲבוֹדוֹת. כ] אֲבָל בְּשִׁירַיִים לָא קָאָמַר דְּלִיעַכְּבוּ. ה"ג: ת"ר וְכִלָּה מְכַפֵּר וגו'. וּלְקַמֵּיהּ מְפָרֵשׁ מַאי קָאָמְרִי וּמַאי בֵּינַיְיהוּ. מִפְּנֵי מָה לֹא נֶאֱמַר. מִפְּנֵי מָה לֹא נִדְרְשֶׁנּוּ כְּסֵדֶר מִכְתָּבוֹ. מַשְׁמָעוּת דּוֹרְשִׁין כו'. כא] תַּרְוַויְיהוּ לְלַמֵּד עַל הַמַּתָּנוֹת שֶׁמְּעַכְּבוֹת קָאָמְרִי, אֶלָּא מָר מַשְׁמַע לֵיהּ הָכִי, וּמָר מַשְׁמַע לֵיהּ הָכִי. רַבִּי עֲקִיבָא מַשְׁמַע לֵיהּ כב] מִדְּסֵיפָא לְרֵישָׁא מִדְרִישׁ, בְּכַפָּרָה דְּהַיְינוּ בְּמַתָּנוֹת תְּלוּיָה הַשְׁלָמָה וְשִׁירַיִם לָא מְעַכְּבִי. וְר' יְהוּדָה נַמִי שִׁירַיִם לָא מְעַכְּבִי אִית לֵיהּ, וְה"ק: מ"ט תִּדְרְשֵׁיהּ הָכִי, דְּהַשְׁתָּא לָא שָׁמְעִינַן כג] מִינֵּיהּ שֶׁכָּל מַתְּנוֹתָיו מְעַכְּבוֹת, דְּאִיכָּא לְמֵימַר בְּכַפָּרַת מַתָּנָה אַחַת קָאָמַר, דּוּמְיָא דְּחַטָּאוֹת הַחִיצוֹנוֹת. אֶלָּא דְּרוֹשׁ הָכִי: אִם כִּלָּה הַכֹּל כְּמָה כד] שֶׁכָּתַב – הוּא דְּכִיפֵּר, וְאִם לֹא כִּלָּה כָּל מַה שֶּׁבָּעִנְיָן – לֹא כִּיפֵּר. וְלָמַדְנוּ שֶׁאִם חִיסֵּר אַחַת מִן הַמַּתָּנוֹת – לֹא עָשָׂה כְּלוּם. וְשִׁירַיִים לָא מְעַכְּבִי, שֶׁאֵינָן אֲמוּרִין בְּעִנְיָן זֶה, דְּגַבֵּי פַּר כֹּהֵן מָשִׁיחַ הוּא דְּאִתְרַבֵּי פַּר יוֹם הַכִּיפּוּרִים לִשְׁיָרִים. (א) וּלְרַבִּי יְהוּדָה אִיצְטְרִיךְ לְמֵילַף עִיכּוּב מַתָּנוֹת מֵהָכָא, מִשּׁוּם כה] דְּקָאָמַר: כִּי כְּתִיבָא "חוּקָּה" – בִּדְבָרִים הַנַּעֲשִׂין בְּבִגְדֵי לָבָן לִפְנַי וְלִפְנִים הוּא דִּכְתִיב. שִׁירַיִים מְעַכְּבִי אִיכָּא בֵּינַיְיהוּ. וּלְרַבִּי עֲקִיבָא לָא מְעַכְּבִי. וְה"ק: אִם כִּיפֵּר מַה שֶּׁאָמוּר בָּעִנְיָן – כִּלָּה, דִּכְתִיב "חוּקָּה" לְעִיכּוּבָא. אֲבָל שִׁירַיִים שֶׁאֵינָהּ אָמוּר בָּעִנְיָן – לָא מְעַכְּבִי. וְאָתָא רַבִּי יְהוּדָה לְמֵימַר: כו] כִּלָּה כָּל צָרְכֵי עֲבוֹדוֹתָיו, וְאַף הַמְלַמְּדִין לוֹ מִמָּקוֹם אַחֵר – כִּיפֵּר, וְאִם לֹא כִּלָּה – לֹא כִּיפֵּר, שֶׁאִם חִיסֵּר אַחַת מִכָּל הַמַּתָּנוֹת כו', וַאֲפִילּוּ כז] בְּמַתַּן יְסוֹד מַשְׁמַע. לְדִבְרֵי הָאוֹמֵר שִׁירַיִים מְעַכְּבִי כו'. אִם גָּמַר כח] מַתְּנוֹת כּוּלָּן וְנִשְׁפַּךְ הַדָּם – מֵבִיא פַּר אַחֵר וּמַתְחִיל (ב) בַּהֵיכָל, כְּדֵי שֶׁיְּהוּ לוֹ שִׁירַיִים. דְּאע"ג דְּקָאָמְרִי': גָּמַר מַתָּנוֹת כט] מִבִּפְנִים וְנִשְׁפַּךְ הַדָּם – מֵבִיא פַּר אַחֵר וְיַתְחִיל בַּפָּרֹכֶת, גָּמַר מַתָּנוֹת שֶׁעַל הַפָּרֹכֶת וְנִשְׁפַּךְ הַדָּם – יָבִיא פַּר אַחֵר וְיַתְחִיל בַּמִּזְבֵּחַ, וְאֵין צָרִיךְ לְהַתְחִיל עֲבוֹדָה שֶׁהִשְׁלִים, שֶׁכּוּלָּן כַּפָּרָה ל] בִּפְנֵי עַצְמָן. לְדִבְרֵי הָאוֹמֵר שִׁירַיִים מְעַכְּבִין *וְלָא אָמְרִי': אִם גָּמַר מַתְּנוֹת מִזְבֵּחַ הַפְּנִימִי וְנִשְׁפַּךְ הַדָּם יָבִיא אַחֵר וְיִשְׁפּוֹךְ עַל יְסוֹד הַחִיצוֹן, דְּאִם כֵּן לָאו הַיְינוּ שִׁירַיִם. אֶלָּא בַּמִּזְבֵּחַ יַתְחִיל, שֶׁיַּעֲשׂוּ שִׁירַיִים וְיִשְׁפְּכֵם בַּחוּץ. אַלְמָא לְרַבִּי יְהוֹשֻׁעַ בֶּן לֵוִי אִיכָּא לְמַאן דְּאָמַר שִׁירַיִים מְעַכְּבִין. אַטּוּ ר' יוֹחָנָן מִי לֵית לֵיהּ הַךְ סְבָרָא. דְּאִיכָּא לְמַאן דְּאָמַר שִׁירַיִים מְעַכְּבִין. וְהָא אָמַר רַבִּי יוֹחָנָן. לא] בְּפֶרֶק "הַשּׁוֹחֵט" (לקמן דף קיא.). תָּנָא רַבִּי נְחֶמְיָה כְּדִבְרֵי הָאוֹמֵר כו'. דְּקָתָנֵי, רַבִּי נְחֶמְיָה אוֹמֵר: שְׁיָרֵי הַדָּם לב] שֶׁהִקְרִיבוֹ בַּחוּץ – חַיָּיב. וְאָמַר רַבִּי יוֹחָנָן עֲלָהּ: תָּנָא רַבִּי נְחֶמְיָה לְמִילְּתֵיהּ כְּדִבְרֵי הָאוֹמֵר שִׁירַיִים מְעַכְּבִין. אַלְמָא לְרַבִּי יוֹחָנָן נַמִי אִיכָּא דְּאִית לֵיהּ הָכִי! אֶלָּא מַאי לג] מְשַׁנֵּי עֲלָהּ דְּרַבִּי יוֹחָנָן, כִּי מוֹקְמָן לָהּ כְּר' יְהוֹשֻׁעַ בֶּן לֵוִי – מִבָּעֵית לְשַׁנּוּיֵי אַדְּרַבִּי יוֹחָנָן "לְדִבְרֵי הָאוֹמֵר" דְּקָאָמַר – אַתַּנָּאֵי אֲחֵרִים קָאֵי, וְלָא אַהָנֵי תַּנָּאֵי דִּלְעֵיל קָאֵי, לד] אַרַבִּי יְהוּדָה וְרַבִּי עֲקִיבָא. הָכָא נַמִי, אִיכָּא לְמֵימַר דְּרַבִּי יוֹחָנָן הוּא דְּאָמַר שִׁירַיִים מְעַכְּבִים אִיכָּא בֵּינַיְיהוּ, וְהָא דְּקָאָמַר רַבִּי יְהוֹשֻׁעַ בֶּן לֵוִי "לְדִבְרֵי הָאוֹמֵר" – לָאו אַהָנֵי תַּנָּאֵי קָאֵי. **מתני'** אֵלּוּ הֵן חַטָּאוֹת צִיבּוּר. שֶׁשָּׁנוּ צְרִיכִים לְהַזְכִּירָם, שֶׁהֲרֵי הַפְּנִימִיּוֹת, פַּר הָעֵדָה וּשְׂעִירֵי עֲבוֹדָה זָרָה – כְּבָר נִשְׁנוּ. שְׂעִירֵי רָאשֵׁי חֳדָשִׁים וְשֶׁל מוֹעֲדוֹת. שֶׁהֵן עַל מִזְבֵּחַ הַחִיצוֹן. שְׁחִיטָתָן בַּצָּפוֹן. שֶׁהֲרֵי לָמַדְנוּ בִּבְנְיָן אָב לְכָל לה] חַטָּאוֹת. אַרְבַּע מַתָּנוֹת כו'. כִּדְיָלְפִינַן מִ"קְרָנוֹת" "קַרְנוֹת" בְּפֶרֶק "בֵּית שַׁמַּאי" (לעיל דף לז:).

עָלָה

נ"ל חטאת נ"ק | נ"ל כד' | נ"ל וכדדרבינן נ"ק | [בילקוט איתא דברי ר' יהודה אמר לו ר' נחמיה מפני מה וכו'] | [יומא ס:] | [לעיל מב: לקמן קיא. מנחות טז: יומא ס:] | נ"ל לא

שיטה מקובצת

א] דמים למטה ונאמרו דמים למעלה: ב] מה דמים האמורים למטה. פ"ה בחטאת העוף כתיב היא ותימה כו' ועוד קשה מאי קאמר שכמו שמתנה אחת כיפר כך הייתי אומר בניתנין למעלה שנתנן למטה כיפר וכי מה ענין זה לזה לכך נראה לריב"א דה"פ וכי מאין באתה מודם זבחיך ישפך דמשמע במתנה אחת בשפיכה אחת וה"ה דמשתעי קרא בכל הזבחים אפי' בחטאת וכתיב ביה ישפך דהיינו משמע למטה דשפיכה על היסוד דלשון שפיכה משמע ששופך על גבי דבר אחד היינו על גבי יסוד והיינו למטה ומחמת האי קרא הייתי אומר שנתנו למטה כיפר ולא משום שנדמה זה לנתינה במתנה אחת על כן איצטריך אותה למעלה ולא למטה וחוזר ואומר דין הוא כלומר שיהא פסול בלא פסוק מטעם דנאמרו דמים כו' נתנו למעלה לא כיפר לא מפני מיעוט הוא אלא מסברא כיון ששינה את מקומו אף דמים האמורים כו' ומורי אמר דלא קשה מידי לפירש"י מהיא דשעיר נשיא דאותה היא כתיב קודם מתן דמים ולא שייך לומר שאם שינה קודם מתן דמים פסול דלא משתעי בענין דם אבל היא דחטאת העוף כתיב גבי מתן דם. מהר"פ: ג] אם נתנן: ד] לא אם אמרת בניתנין למטה שכן אין סופן למעלה תאמר בניתנין למעלה שכן סופן למטה דמים הפנימים יוכיחו שסופן לחוץ ואם נתנן כו' והשאר נמחק: ה] אותן הואיל וקרנות ממרקין אותן אם: ו] שניתן דמיה למעלה: ז] לאו אלא שירים א"ל רבא כו' בק"ו ומה שירים הפנימים: ח] פרוכת. ס"א כדתנו רבנן: ט] שירים מעכבי איכא בינייהו: י] ולאו אהני תנאי כו' האומר ולאו אהני תנאי: יא] אותה בחטאת בהמה כתיב כך גירסת מהר"פ: יב] לך בארבע קרנות: יג] ישפך בשפיכה אחת: יד] עבודה אחרת: טו] שכן קרנות ממרקות אותו: טז] חמירי ויוכשרו למטן: יז] ממרק אותן לאו אלא שירים. כלומר דשירים ממרקין אותן אלמא דשפיכת שירים: יח] שבחוץ מעכבי בהו בדמים הפנימים כל שכן: יט] והואיל וטעונין: כ] עבודות למעלה: כא] ותרויהו. גירסת רש"י דמהר"פ ותרויהו אית להו דשירים לא מעכבי וסברי שכל המתנות מעכבות אלא מר משמע [ליה] מתנות שהשלמה תלויה בהם אם כיפר כילה אע"פ שלא [עשה] שירים דשירים [לא] מעכבי ור' יהודה נמי [לא מעכבי] לשירים ור"ע למילף עיכובא הכא לא איצטריך [דהא] כתיב חוקה לעיכובא [ור"י] לטעמיה דאמר כי כתיב חוקה כו': כב] מסיפא לרישא מידריש וה"ק בכפרה דהיינו: כג] שמעינן מיניה שכל כו' למימר דכפרה מתנה אחת: כד] כמה שאמר בענין הוא דכיפר: כה] משום דסבר כי כתיבא: כו] למימר אם כילה: כז] ואפילו מתן יסוד במשמע: כח] גמר המתנות כולן: כט] מתנות שבפנים: ל] כפרה כפרה בפני עצמו לדברי כו' מעכבין לא אמרינן אם גמר כו' על יסוד מזבח החיצון דא"כ לאו כו' במזבח שבהיכל יתחיל כדי שיעשו השאר שירים וישפכם: לא] יוחנן לקמן בפ' השוחט: לב] שהקריבן בחוץ: לג] מאי תשני עלה דר"י כו' כריב"ל מבעיא לן לשנויי אדר"י: לד] קאי דהיינו ר"י ור"ע: לה] לכל החטאות הס"ד: לו] למטה והא ממעט מאותה: לז] אותה דמה למעלה: לח] כאן ההיא דשמואל דכיון שהגיע דם לאויר מזבח נתכפר הבעלים הס"ד: לט] בחטאת בהמה בשעיר נשיא נמי כתיב: מ] תימה ולילף מעולת העוף שסופה למטה: מא] פסולה וי"ל דחטאת העוף נמי לא ידעינן רק מקרא דהכא דאותה דגבי חטאת בהמה וכיון דגלי גלי. מהר"פ:

הגהות הב"ח

(א) רש"י ד"ה משמעות דורשין וכו' פר יוה"כ לשיריים הס"ד ואח"כ מ"ה שיריים מעכבי וכו' מכל המתנות כו' ולר' יהודה איצטריך למילף וכו' לפני ולפנים הוא דכתיב ואפי' במתן יסוד משמע: (ב) ד"ה לדברי האומר וכו' ומתחיל במזבח כדי שיהו לו שיריים:

יסוד

אעָלָה בַּכֶּבֶשׁ, וּפָנָה לַסּוֹבֵב, וּבָא לוֹ לְקֶרֶן דְּרוֹמִית מִזְרָחִית, מִזְרָחִית צְפוֹנִית, צְפוֹנִית מַעֲרָבִית, מַעֲרָבִית דְּרוֹמִית. בשְׁיָרֵי הַדָּם הָיָה שׁוֹפֵךְ עַל א] יְסוֹד דְּרוֹמִית. וְנֶאֱכָלִין גלִפְנִים מִן הַקְּלָעִים, לְזִכְרֵי כְהוּנָּה, בְּכָל מַאֲכָל, לְיוֹם וָלַיְלָה עַד חֲצוֹת.§ **גמ'** הֵיכִי עָבֵיד? רַבִּי יוֹחָנָן וְרַבִּי אֶלְעָזָר, חַד אָמַר: נוֹתֵן אַמָּה אֵילָךְ וְאַמָּה אֵילָךְ, וְחַד אָמַר: מְחַטֵּא וְיוֹרֵד כְּנֶגֶד חוּדּוֹ שֶׁל קֶרֶן. אַלִּיבָּא דְּרַבִּי אֶלְעָזָר בְּר"ש, דְּאָמַר: הִיא עַצְמָהּ אֵינָהּ נַעֲשֵׂית אֶלָּא בְּגוּפָהּ שֶׁל קֶרֶן — דְּכוּלֵּי עָלְמָא לָא פְּלִיגִי. כִּי פְּלִיגִי — אַלִּיבָּא דְּרַבִּי, מָר סָבַר: אַמָּה אֵילָךְ וְאַמָּה אֵילָךְ כְּנֶגֶד ב] קֶרֶן הוּא, וּמָר סָבַר: כְּנֶגֶד חוּדָּהּ — אִין, טְפֵי — לָא. מֵיתִיבֵי: חַטַּאת הַצִּיבּוּר וְהַיָּחִיד ג] כֵּיצַד מַתַּן דָּמָן? הָיָה עוֹלֶה לַכֶּבֶשׁ, וּפָנָה לַסּוֹבֵב וּבָא לוֹ לְקֶרֶן דְּרוֹמִית מִזְרָחִית, דוְטוֹבֵל בְּאֶצְבָּעוֹ הַיְמָנִית הַמְיוּמֶּנֶת שֶׁבְּיָמִין, מִן הַדָּם שֶׁבְּמִזְרָק, ד] וְחוֹמֵר בְּגוּדָלוֹ מִלְמַעְלָה וּבְאֶצְבָּעוֹ קְטַנָּה מִלְּמַטָּה, וּמְחַטֵּא וְיוֹרֵד כְּנֶגֶד חוּדָּהּ שֶׁל קֶרֶן עַד ה] שֶׁמְּכַלֶּה כָּל הַדָּם שֶׁבָּאֶצְבַּע וְכֵן כָּל קֶרֶן וָקֶרֶן! הָכִי קָאָמַר: המִצְוָה בְּחוּדָּהּ, אִי עָבַד אַמָּה אֵילָךְ וְאַמָּה אֵילָךְ לֵית לָן בָּהּ.§ מַאי רַבִּי, וּמַאי רַבִּי אֶלְעָזָר בְּר' שִׁמְעוֹן? *דְּתַנְיָא: דָּמִים הָעֶלְיוֹנִים נִיתָּנִין מֵחוּט הַסִּיקְרָא וּלְמַעְלָה, דָּמִים הַתַּחְתּוֹנִים נִיתָּנִין מֵחוּט הַסִּיקְרָא וּלְמַטָּן, דִּבְרֵי רַבִּי. רַבִּי אֶלְעָזָר בְּרַבִּי שִׁמְעוֹן אוֹמֵר: בַּמֶּה דְּבָרִים אֲמוּרִין — בְּעוֹלַת הָעוֹף, אֲבָל בְּחַטַּאת בְּהֵמָה — הִיא עַצְמָהּ אֵין נַעֲשֵׂית אֶלָּא עַל גּוּפָהּ שֶׁל קֶרֶן. אָמַר רַבִּי אַבָּהוּ: מַאי טַעְמָא דְּרַבִּי — דִּכְתִיב: °"וְהַהַרְאֵל אַרְבַּע ו] אַמּוֹת וּמֵהַהַרְאֵל וּלְמַעְלָה" וגו'; אַרְבַּע אַמּוֹת הוּא דְּהָוְיָא? אָמַר רַב אַדָּא בַּר אַהֲבָה: ז] וּמְקוֹם קְרָנוֹת אַרְבַּע. מְקוֹם קְרָנוֹת ד' הָוְיָא?! אֶלָּא אֵימָא: רְשׁוּת קְרָנוֹת ד'.§ *תְּנַן הָתָם: יחוּט שֶׁל סִיקְרָא חוֹגְרוֹ בְּאֶמְצַע, לְהַבְדִּיל בֵּין דָּמִים הָעֶלְיוֹנִים לַדָּמִים הַתַּחְתּוֹנִים. מְנָא הָנֵי מִילֵּי? אָמַר רַב ח] אַחָא בַּר רַב קְטִינָא, שֶׁנֶּאֱמַר: °"וְהָיְתָה הָרֶשֶׁת עַד חֲצִי הַמִּזְבֵּחַ" — הַתּוֹרָה נָתְנָה מְחִיצָה לְהַבְדִּיל בֵּין דָּמִים הָעֶלְיוֹנִים לַדָּמִים הַתַּחְתּוֹנִים.§ "שְׁיָרֵי הַדָּם" כו'.§ *ת"ר: "אֶל יְסוֹד מִזְבֵּחַ" — זֶה יְסוֹד דְּרוֹמִי. אַתָּה אוֹמֵר: זֶה יְסוֹד דְּרוֹמִי, אוֹ אֵינוֹ אֶלָּא יְסוֹד ט] מַעֲרָבִי? וְיִלְמַד סָתוּם מִן הַמְפוֹרָשׁ! אָמַרְתָּ: יִלְמַד יְרִידָתוֹ מִן הַכֶּבֶשׁ י] *לִיצִיאָתוֹ מִן הַהֵיכָל, מָה יְצִיאָתוֹ מִן הַהֵיכָל — בְּסָמוּךְ לוֹ, °אַף יְרִידָתוֹ מִן הַכֶּבֶשׁ — בְּסָמוּךְ לוֹ.§ *תַּנְיָא, רַבִּי יִשְׁמָעֵאל אוֹמֵר: זֶה וָזֶה יְסוֹד מַעֲרָבִי. ר' שִׁמְעוֹן בֶּן יוֹחַאי אוֹמֵר: זֶה וָזֶה יְסוֹד דְּרוֹמִי; בִּשְׁלָמָא לְמַאן דְּאָמַר יא] יְסוֹד מַעֲרָבִי — קָסָבַר: יִלְמַד סָתוּם מִן הַמְפוֹרָשׁ. אֶלָּא לְמַאן דְּאָמַר יב] יְסוֹד דְּרוֹמִי, מ"ט? א"ר אַסִּי, קָסָבַר הַאי תַּנָּא: יג] *כּוּלֵּיהּ מִזְבֵּחַ בַּצָּפוֹן קָאֵי. יד] ל"א: כּוּלֵּיהּ פֶּתַח בַּדָּרוֹם קָאֵי. תָּנָא

(יחזקאל מג) (שמות כז)

רש"י

עָלָה בַּכֶּבֶשׁ וּפָנָה לַסּוֹבֵב. מִפְּנֵי שֶׁדָּמָהּ נִיתָּן לְמַעְלָה עַל הַקְּרָנוֹת וּבְאֶצְבַּע צָרִיךְ לַעֲמוֹד עַל גַּבֵּי סוֹבֵב. אֲבָל בְּכָל שְׁאָר הַדָּמִים, שֶׁהֵן הַתַּחְתּוֹנִים, מִן הַחוּט טו] וּלְמַטָּה וּבְקֶרֶן זָוִית הַמִּזְבֵּחַ – עוֹמֵד עַל הָרִצְפָּה, וְזוֹרֵק מִן הַכְּלִי לַמִּזְבֵּחַ, וְכָל מָקוֹם שֶׁיַּגִּיעַ לַמִּזְבֵּחַ כָּשֵׁר. וּבָא לוֹ לְקֶרֶן דְּרוֹמִית מִזְרָחִית. שֶׁבָּהּ הוּא פּוֹגֵעַ רִאשׁוֹן, כִּדְקַיְימָא לָן לְקַמָּן (דף סג:): כָּל פִּינּוֹת שֶׁאַתָּה פּוֹנֶה יְהוּ דֶּרֶךְ יָמִין, וְהַכֶּבֶשׁ בַּדָּרוֹם, וּכְשֶׁעוֹלֶה בּוֹ וּפָנָיו לַמִּזְבֵּחַ – הָוֵי יְמִינוֹ טז] לַמִּזְרָח, וּבָא לִימִינוֹ לַמִּזְרָח. וּבָא לְאוֹתוֹ קֶרֶן וְהוֹלֵךְ וּמַקִּיף בַּסּוֹבֵב דֶּרֶךְ יָמִין וּפָנָיו לַמִּזְבֵּחַ: מִן הַדָּרוֹם לַמִּזְרָח, וּמִמִּזְרָח לַצָּפוֹן, וּמִצָּפוֹן לַמַּעֲרָב, דְּהַיְינוּ דֶּרֶךְ יָמִין. עַל יְסוֹד יז] דְּרוֹמִית. בַּגְּמָרָא יָלֵיף לָהּ. לִפְנִים מִן הַקְּלָעִים. לְפִי שֶׁבַּמִּשְׁכָּן הָיוּ קְלָעִים הֶיקֵּף לַחֲצַר אֹהֶל מוֹעֵד, וּבִמְקוֹם הַקְּלָעִים הָיְתָה חוֹמַת הָעֲזָרָה * יח] בְּבֵית שְׁלֹמֹה אוֹ בֵּית עוֹלָמִים. וּבְחַטָּאת כְּתִיבָא יט] "בַּחֲצַר אֹהֶל מוֹעֵד בְּמָקוֹם קָדוֹשׁ תֵּאָכֵל" כ] (ויקרא ו). לְזִכְרֵי כְהוּנָּה. דִּכְתִיב: "הַכֹּהֵן הַמְחַטֵּא אוֹתָהּ" כא] (שם) – לְאַפּוֹקֵי נָשִׁים שֶׁאֵינָן רְאוּיוֹת לְחִיטּוּי. וּבְ"וַיִּקַּח כב] קֹרַח" גַּבֵּי חַטָּאת וְאָשָׁם וּמִנְחָה כְּתִיב: "כָּל זָכָר יֹאכַל אוֹתוֹ". בְּכָל מַאֲכָל. מִשּׁוּם דְּקָתָנֵי בְּפֶסַח: וְאֵינוֹ נֶאֱכָל אֶלָּא צָלִי לְקַמָּן (דף נו:), כג] תָּנֵי בְּכוּלְּהוּ "וּבְכָל מַאֲכָל". לְיוֹם וָלַיְלָה. כִּדְיָלְפִינַן בְּפֶ' שְׁלִישִׁי (לעיל דף לו.): "וּבְשַׂר זֶבַח תּוֹדַת שְׁלָמָיו" – כד] לָמַדְנוּ שֶׁנֶּאֱכֶלֶת לְיוֹם אֶחָד, חַטָּאת וְאָשָׁם מִנַּיִן – תַּלְמוּד לוֹמַר "זֶבַח". וּבְקָדָשִׁים לַיְלָה הוֹלֵךְ אַחַר הַיּוֹם, דִּכְתִיב: "לֹא יַנִּיחַ מִמֶּנּוּ עַד בֹּקֶר" (ויקרא ז). עַד חֲצוֹת. סְיָיג עָשׂוּ חֲכָמִים לַתּוֹרָה לְהַרְחִיק אָדָם מֵעֲבֵירַת כָּרֵת, כִּדְתְנַן בִּבְרָכוֹת בְּפֶרֶק קַמָּא (דף ב.): כָּל הַנֶּאֱכָלִין לְיוֹם אֶחָד מִצְוָתָן כו'. **גמ'** הֵיכִי עָבֵיד. מַתְּנַת אֶצְבַּע בְּקֶרֶן. אַמָּה אֵילָךְ כה]. כְּשֶׁהוּא עוֹמֵד אֵצֶל זָוִית הַמִּזְבֵּחַ נוֹתֵן בְּתוֹךְ אַמָּה שֶׁל מִקְצוֹעַ לְאֵיזֶה רוּחַ שֶׁיִּרְצֶה, אוֹ לַדָּרוֹם אוֹ לַמִּזְרָח, בְּקֶרֶן דְּרוֹמִית מִזְרָחִית. וְכֵן בְּכָל קֶרֶן. מְחַטֵּא וְיוֹרֵד. לְשׁוֹן הַכָּתוּב: "הַכֹּהֵן הַמְחַטֵּא אוֹתָהּ" (ויקרא ו). אַלִּיבָּא דְּרַבִּי אֶלְעָזָר כו]. לְקַמָּן מַיְיתֵי פְּלוּגְתַּיְיהוּ. הִיא עַצְמָהּ. כְּלוֹמַר, כָּל עַצְמָהּ וְעִיקַּר מִצְוָתָהּ אֵינוֹ אֶלָּא שָׁם. דְּכ"ע לָא פְּלִיגִי. דְּלָא בָּעֵינַן כז] חוּדָּהּ. דְּקֶרֶן כְּתִיב, וְאַמָּה עַל אַמָּה בְּרוּם אַמָּה הַנָּתוּן בְּרֹאשׁ הַמִּזְבֵּחַ בְּכָל זָוִית וְזָוִית, בְּכָל מָקוֹם שֶׁבָּהּ קָרוּי קֶרֶן. כִּי פְּלִיגִי אַלִּיבָּא דְּרַבִּי. דְּמַכְשַׁר לָהּ מֵחוּט הַסִּיקְרָא וּלְמַעְלָה, וְאַע"ג כח] דְּלָאו בְּקֶרֶן. מָר סָבַר. כִּי הֵיכִי דְּקֶרֶן הָוְיָא אַמָּה עַל אַמָּה אַף כָּל שֶׁתַּחְתָּיו כְּנֶגְדּוֹ הָוֵי קֶרֶן. וּמָר סָבַר. *כֵּיוָן דִּקְרָא לָאו אַקְּרָנוֹת מַמָּשׁ קָפִיד, בִּשְׁאָר הַמִּזְבֵּחַ לֹא שַׁיָּיךְ לְשׁוֹן קֶרֶן. אֶלָּא בְּחוּדָּהּ שֶׁל זָוִית. הַמְיוּמֶּנֶת שֶׁבְּיָמִין. אֶצְבַּע הָרְגִילָה כט] לִמְלָאכָה, וְלֹא שְׁאָר אֶצְבָּעוֹת מוּכָנוֹת לְהוֹשִׁיט וְלִטְבּוֹל, הַיְינוּ שֶׁאֵצֶל גּוּדָל. מְיוּמֶּנֶת = אמנט"ר בְּלַעַ"ז. וְחוֹמֵר ל] בְּגוּדָלוֹ וּבְאֶצְבַּע קְטַנָּה. מוֹשֵׁךְ אֶת הַדָּם שֶׁבָּאֶצְבַּע כְּלַפֵּי לְמַטָּה, שֶׁיִּפּוֹל כּוּלּוֹ לַמִּזְבֵּחַ. חוֹמֵר. לְשׁוֹן "נֶחֶמְרוּ בְּנֵי מֵעֶיהָ" (חולין דף נד.) **דנורי"ר בְּלַעַ"ז. וּמְחַטֵּא. זְרִיקַת חַטָּאת קָרוּי חִיטּוּי, כְּמוֹ "הַכֹּהֵן הַמְחַטֵּא אוֹתָהּ". כְּנֶגֶד חוּדָּהּ לא]. רַבִּי הִיא, דְּמַכְשַׁר לְמַטָּה מִן הַקֶּרֶן, לְהָכִי תָּנָא לָהּ בְּחוּדָּהּ. בר"א. דְּדָמִים הָעֶלְיוֹנִים כְּשֵׁרִין לְמַעְלָה מִן הַחוּט מִיָּד. בְּעוֹלַת הָעוֹף. שֶׁנַּעֲשֵׂית לְמַעְלָה, כִּדְאָמְרִינַן בְּפֶרֶק "קָדְשֵׁי קָדָשִׁים" (לקמן דף סד:). אֲבָל חַטַּאת בְּהֵמָה. דִּכְתִיב בָּהּ קֶרֶן בְּהֶדְיָא, אֵינָהּ נַעֲשֵׂית כו'. וְהַהַרְאֵל. מִזְבֵּחַ. אַרְבַּע אַמּוֹת הוּא דְּהָוֵאי. בִּתְמִיָּה, וְכִי אֵין גּוֹבְהוֹ אוֹ רָחְבּוֹ אֶלָּא אַרְבַּע אַמּוֹת? מְקוֹם קְרָנוֹת אַרְבַּע. כְּלוֹמַר, הַקְּרָנוֹת תּוֹפְסִין אַרְבַּע אַמּוֹת בַּמִּזְבֵּחַ, דְּכָל קֶרֶן אַמָּה עַל אַמָּה. וּמְקוֹם קְרָנוֹת אַרְבַּע הָוְיָא. בִּתְמִיָּה, וַהֲרֵי אֵין הַקְּרָנוֹת אוֹכְלִין בַּמִּזְבֵּחַ אֶלָּא שְׁתֵּי אַמּוֹת מִן הַמִּזְרָח לַמַּעֲרָב, וּשְׁתַּיִם מִן הַדָּרוֹם לַצָּפוֹן – הַיְינוּ שְׁתַּיִם עַל שְׁתַּיִם! אֶלָּא. עַל כָּרְחָךְ ה"ק קְרָא: רְשׁוּת קְרָנוֹת אַרְבַּע. כְּלוֹמַר, שָׁם *רְשׁוּת הַקְּרָנוֹת תּוֹפֶסֶת לְמַטָּה מֵהֶן אַרְבַּע אַמּוֹת, דְּהַיְינוּ עַד הַחוּט, דְּכוּלֵּיהּ לג] הָוֵי קֶרֶן. הָרֶשֶׁת. כְּעֵין לִיוּר מְלוּוֶּרֶת בִּקְלִיעָה, וְשֶׁל נְחֹשֶׁת לג] הָוְיָא בְּתַחְתָּיו שֶׁל מִזְבֵּחַ, עֲשׂוּי כְּנָפָה, וְגָבְהָהּ עַד חֶצְיוֹ שֶׁל מִזְבֵּחַ. הַתּוֹרָה נָתְנָה מְחִיצָה. מִדְּקָפִיד אַחֲצִי מִזְבֵּחַ. אֶל יְסוֹד הַמִּזְבֵּחַ. הָאָמוּר בְּחַטָּאת הַחִיצוֹנָה. אוֹ אֵינוֹ אֶלָּא יְסוֹד מַעֲרָבִי. כִּדְאַשְׁכְּחַן בַּפְּנִימִיּוֹת לְעֵיל: "אֲשֶׁר פֶּתַח אֹהֶל מוֹעֵד", וְיִלְמַד סָתוּם מִן הַמְפוֹרָשׁ. יִלְמַד יְרִידָתוֹ מִן הַכֶּבֶשׁ. בַּחִיצוֹנוֹת וּשְׁיָרֵי הַדָּם בְּיָדוֹ, מִיצִיאָתוֹ מִן הַהֵיכָל לד] [וּשְׁיָרַיִים הַפְּנִימִיִּים בְּיָדוֹ: מַה יְּצִיאָתוֹ מִן הַהֵיכָל] – בִּיסוֹד מַעֲרָבִי שֶׁהוּא סָמוּךְ לוֹ. אַף יְרִידָתוֹ מִן הַכֶּבֶשׁ. נִשְׁפָּכִין לִיסוֹד דְּרוֹמִי, שֶׁהוּא סָמוּךְ לוֹ. זֶה וָזֶה. חִיצוֹנִים וְהַפְּנִימִים. סָתוּם. הַחִיצוֹנִים. מְפוֹרָשׁ. פְּנִימִים, שֶׁכָּתוּב בָּהֶן יְסוֹד מַעֲרָבִי, דִּכְתִיב: "אֲשֶׁר פֶּתַח אֹהֶל מוֹעֵד". לה] מ"ט. הָא כְּתִיב בַּפְּנִימִיִּים: "אֶל יְסוֹד אֲשֶׁר פֶּתַח אֹהֶל מוֹעֵד"! קָסָבַר כּוּלֵּיהּ מִזְבֵּחַ בִּצְפוֹן פֶּתַח הַהֵיכָל קָאֵי. לו] וְאֵין הַמִּזְבֵּחַ לִפְנֵי הַפֶּתַח כְּלוּם אֶלָּא אַמָּה שֶׁל יְסוֹד דְּרוֹמִי. אִי נַמִי בִּצְפוֹן הָעֲזָרָה קָאֵי, וְהָווּ חָמֵשׁ אַמּוֹתָיו כְּנֶגֶד הַפֶּתַח *וְאַמָּה אַחַת מֵהֶן יְסוֹד דְּרוֹמִי, אִשְׁתַּכַּח דְּכִי נָפֵיק מִן הַפֶּתַח רוֹאֶה יְסוֹד דְּרוֹמִי לְפָנָיו מְכוּוָּן בְּאֶמְצַע הַפֶּתַח. וְאִית דְּגָרַס: כּוּלֵּיהּ פֶּתַח בַּדָּרוֹם מִזְבֵּחַ קָאֵי וְהָא הִיא, כָּל פֶּתַח הַהֵיכָל לִדְרוֹמוֹ שֶׁל מִזְבֵּחַ הוּא.

(לעיל י:) (בכורות יז: מנחות לז:) (יומא נט.) (תוספתא דיומא פ"ג ע"ש) (לקמן נח. סג:)

בית עולמים ובחטאת כו' נ"ק · לעיל י: · נ"ל מיציאתו · נ"א כיון דקרא אקרנות כו' · ורשות נ"ק · ואחת מהן נ"ק

תוספות

כוליה מזבח בצפון קאי. פירש בקונטרס: בצפון פתח ההיכל קאי, ואין מן המזבח לפני פתח ההיכל כלום אלא אמה של יסוד דרומית. א"נ: בצפון העזרה קאי, *והוו חמש כנגד הפתח אחת מהן יסוד דרומי, אישתכח דכי נפיק מן לז] הפתח יסוד דרומי לפניו מכוון באמצע הפתח. וכלשון זה אחרון נראה, דלקמן פרק "קדשי קדשים" (דף נח.) מוכח דלמאן דאמר כוליה מזבח בצפון קאי – לח] *האי חמש אמות כנגד הפתח, דהא תנן (תמיד דף כט.): מערכה שניה של קטרת היה משוך מן הקרן כלפי צפון ארבע אמות – מוקי לה כרבי יוסי, דבעי לפני הפתח, וקסבר כוליה מזבח בצפון קאי.

וסימניך

עין משפט נר מצוה

כט א ב מיי' פ"ה מהל' מעה"ק הל"י:

ל ג מיי' שם פ"ז הלכה א:

לא ד ה מיי' שם פ"ה הל"ז:

לב ו מיי' פ"ב מהל' בית הבחירה הל"ט:

נ"ל והוו חמש אמותיו כנגד הפתח ואחת מהן כו' נ"ק

נ"ק הוי חמש כו' דהא דתנן כו' נ"ק

גליון הש"ס

גמ' אף ירידתו. ע"ל דף פא ע"א תוד"ה אבל:

שיטה מקובצת

א] יסוד דרומי: ב] קרן נמי קרן הוא כו' מיתיבי. חטאות הצבור: ג] כיצד סדר מתן כו' לכבש ופונה לסובב: ד] וחומר. ס"א וסומך ס"א וחומר בגודלו מכאן ובאצבעו מכאן והרמב"ם ז"ל גרים כן בפ"ה מהלכות מעשה הקרבנות אלא שהוא כתב שם וסומך באצבעו הגדולה מכאן ובגודל מכאן וצ"ע: ה] שיכלה כל כו' מצוה מחודה: ו] אמות ומהריאל ולמעלה הקרנות ארבע: ז] מקום קרנות ארבע ומקום קרנות: ח] רב חנא בר תיבת אחא נמחק: ט] מערבי וילמוד סתום: י] הכבש מיציאתו מן: יא] דאמר זה וזה יסוד: יב] דאמר זה וזה יסוד [דרומי] מ"ט אמר רב אשי: יג] כולה מזבח בצפון קאי פ"ה ואית דגרסי כו' וקשה לפי זה דלקמן בפ' קדשי קדשים מוכח דלמאן דאמר כוליה מזבח בצפון קאי הוי חמש אמות דרומית כנגד הפתח כו' לכך נראה כלשון אחר שבקונטרס דכוליה מזבח בצפון קאי וצפון העזרה מתחיל באמצע הפתח שהוא רחב עשר אמות נמצא ה' אמות דרומית של מזבח כנגד הפתח ואחת מהן יסוד דרומית וא"כ כשיוצא מן הפתח רואה יסוד דרומי לפניו מכוון כנגד אמצע הפתח ורגילות של אדם לצאת באמצע הפתח ודוחק הוא וכי לעולם הוא יוצא באמצע הפתח ועוד קשה מנלן דאותה אמה היא יסוד לפי שהיא כנגד הפתח אימא דגם ד' אמות מערבית שכנגד הפתח הוו יסוד דאי משום שכל יסוד מערבי לא היה כנגד הפתח מה בכך הלא כי נמי מזבח ממוצע היה מנלן דיסוד מערבי כולו מיקרי כנגד הפתח והלא אורכו ל"ב אמות ורוחב חלל הפתח עשר אמות נמצא דעשר אמות הוו כנגד הפתח ועוד נשאר י"א אמות מכאן וי"א אמות מכאן שלא כנגד הפתח ומ"מ מיקרי כולו יסוד כנגד הפתח משום דמקצתו ככולו ואמר מורי דלמ"ד בצפון קאי איכא לאוקמי פתח אהל מועד ברוח דרומי שכל יסוד שלו כנגד הפתח דאמה דרומית של כל רוח דרומית הוי כנגד הפתח ועוד דלא הוי יסוד לרוח דרומית רק אמה ראשונה של צד מערב כדאמר לקמן והילכך לא מיקרי רוח מערבי כנגד הפתח כיון שאין יסוד שלו כנגד הפתח אבל למ"ד דמזבח ממוצע באמצע הפתח שפיר מיקרי רוח מערבית שכנגד הפתח לפי שלא היה לו שום רוח אחר כנגד הפתח רק רוח מערבי שבאמצעיתו הוא עשר אמות כנגד הפתח כל רוחב הפתח: ס"א ודוחק הוא כו' וא"כ מנלן דיסוד דרומי מיקרי פתח אהל מועד לכן נראה דיסוד דרומי מיקרי יותר פתח אהל מועד מיסוד מערבי לפי שכולו כנגד הפתח אבל יסוד מערבי אינו כנגד הפתח כי אם ה' אמות וכ"ת א"כ כי נמי מזבח ממוצע מנלן דיסוד מערבי כולו מיקרי יסוד שכנגד הפתח והרי אורך היסוד של מערבי אורכו ל"ב אמות וחלל פתח ההיכל הוי עשר אמות נמצא יסוד המזבח מערבי עודף לכל צד על חלל הפתח י"א אמות אלא ודאי אמרינן מקצתו ככולו כי נמי כולו בצפון קאי מקצת יסוד מערבי ככולו וי"ל דודאי כי קאי באמצע העזרה הוי מקצתו ככולו לפי שלא היה רוח אחר של מזבח אפי' מקצתו כנגד הפתח אבל כי קאי בצפון א"כ רוח דרומי מיקרי פתח אהל מועד לפי שהוא כולו כנגד הפתח ולא מערבי שאינו כנגד הפתח כי אם מקצתו כך נראה למורי. מהר"פ: יד] תיבות ל"א בדרום קאי נמחק: טו] ולמטה עומד על הרצפה אצל זוית המזבח: טז] למזרח ופונה לימינו למזרח ובא לו לאותו קרן: יז] דרומי: יח] בבית עולמים תיבות שלמה או בית נמחק: יט] א) תיבות בחצר אהל מועד אין כאן מקומו ונמחק: כ] תאכל בחצר אהל מועד: כא] אותה וגו' לאפוקי: כב] קרח כתיב גבי כו' ומנחה כל זכר: כג] תנא ואות י' נמחק: כד] למדנו לתודה שנאכלת: כה] אילך ואמה אילך כשהוא: כו] דר' אלעזר כו' לקמן: כז] חודה משום דקרן: כח] ואע"ג דלאו בקרן: כט] למלאכה בלא שאר אצבעות כלומר מוכנת להושיט ולטבל והיינו: ל] בגודלו למעלה ובאצבע הקטנה מושך כו' כלפי מטה: לא] חודה של קרן רבי כו' להכי לא תנא בחודה: לב] הויא דקרן: לג] הויא בתחתיתו: לד] ההיכל ושירים הפנימים בידו מה יציאתו מן ההיכל ביסוד: לה] מ"ט דהא כתיב בפנימים אל יסוד מזבח העולה אשר: לו] ואין מן המזבח כו' אמותיו של מזבח כנגד הפתח ואחת מהן יסוד דרומי וצפון העזרה מתחיל באמצע הפתח ההיכל שהיה רחב הפתח י' אמות ואשתכח דכי נפיק מן הפתח ס"א ורגילות לצאת באמצע הפתח ומש"ה קרי פתח אהל מועד אמה של יסוד דרומי טפי מד' אמות הנשארות ואית: לז] הפתח רואה יסוד: לח] קאי היו חמש:

א) נראה דט"ס נפל בכאן וצ"ל ובחטאת כתיבא במקום קדוש תאכל בחצר אהל מועד הס"ד ואח"כ מתחיל אות כ' אותה וגו'.

לג א מיי' פ"ה מהל' מעה"ק הל"ו:
לד ב מיי' פ"ו שם הל"ח:
לה ג מיי' פ"ה שם הלכה ו:
לו ד מיי' פ"ב מהל' בית הבחירה הל"י:

תורה אור

תָּנָא דְּבֵי ר' יִשְׁמָעֵאל *כְּרַבִּי שִׁמְעוֹן בֶּן יוֹחַי א] אוֹמְרִים: זֶה וָזֶה יְסוֹד מַעֲרָבִי, וְסִימָנֵיךְ: *מִשַּׁכּוּ גַּבְרֵי לְגַבְרָא.§ **מתני'** הָעוֹלָה קָדְשֵׁי קָדָשִׁים, שְׁחִיטָתָהּ בַּצָּפוֹן, וְקִיבּוּל דָּמָהּ בִּכְלִי שָׁרֵת בַּצָּפוֹן, אוְדָמָהּ טָעוּן שְׁתֵּי מַתָּנוֹת שֶׁהֵן אַרְבַּע, בוּטְעוּנָה הֶפְשֵׁט וְנִיתּוּחַ וְכָלִיל לָאִשִּׁים.§ **גמ'** עוֹלָה מ"ט ב] תָּנֵי לֵיהּ קָדְשֵׁי קָדָשִׁים? מִשּׁוּם דְּלָא כְּתִיב בָּהּ (לַה') "קָדְשֵׁי קָדָשִׁים הִיא".§ "וְדָמָהּ טָעוּן שְׁתֵּי מַתָּנוֹת". הֵיכִי ג] עָבֵיד? אָמַר רַב: נוֹתֵן וְחוֹזֵר וְנוֹתֵן. וּשְׁמוּאֵל אָמַר: מַתָּנָה ד] אַחַת גכְּמִין גַּמָּא נוֹתֵן. ה] כְּתַנָּאֵי: יָכוֹל יִזְרְקֶנּוּ זְרִיקָה אַחַת? ת"ל: "סָבִיב". אִי סָבִיב, יָכוֹל יַקִּיפֶנּוּ כְּחוּט? ת"ל: "וְזָרְקוּ"; הָא ו] כֵּיצַד – כְּמִין גַּמָּא, (*וְדָמָהּ טָעוּן) שְׁתֵּי מַתָּנוֹת שֶׁהֵן אַרְבַּע. *ר' יִשְׁמָעֵאל אוֹמֵר: נֶאֱמַר כָּאן "סָבִיב" וְנֶאֱמַר לְהַלָּן °"סָבִיב", מָה לְהַלָּן – פִּיסּוּק וְאַרְבַּע מַתָּנוֹת, אַף כָּאן – פִּיסּוּק וְאַרְבַּע מַתָּנוֹת. אִי מָה לְהַלָּן אַרְבַּע מַתָּנוֹת עַל אַרְבַּע קְרָנוֹת, אַף כָּאן אַרְבַּע מַתָּנוֹת עַל אַרְבַּע קְרָנוֹת? אָמַרְתָּ: עוֹלָה טְעוּנָה יְסוֹד, דוְקֶרֶן מִזְרָחִית דְּרוֹמִית לֹא הָיָה לָהּ יְסוֹד. מ"ט? אָמַר ר' אֶלְעָזָר: *לְפִי שֶׁלֹּא הָיְתָה בְּחֶלְקוֹ שֶׁל טוֹרֵף. דְּאָמַר רַב שְׁמוּאֵל בַּר רַב יִצְחָק: מִזְבֵּחַ אוֹכֵל בְּחֶלְקוֹ שֶׁל יְהוּדָה אַמָּה. *אָמַר רַבִּי לֵוִי בַּר חָמָא *אָמַר רַבִּי חָמָא בְּרַבִּי חֲנִינָא: רְצוּעָה הָיְתָה יוֹצְאָה מֵחֶלְקוֹ שֶׁל יְהוּדָה וְנִכְנֶסֶת בְּחֶלְקוֹ שֶׁל ז] בִּנְיָמִין, וְהָיָה בִּנְיָמִין הַצַּדִּיק מִצְטַעֵר עָלֶיהָ בְּכָל יוֹם לְנוֹטְלָהּ, שֶׁנֶּאֱמַר: חוֹפֵף

ויקרא ח

[רש"י]

תָּנָא דְּבֵי רַבִּי יִשְׁמָעֵאל. ח] הָיוּ שׁוֹנִין כְּרַבִּי שִׁמְעוֹן בֶּן יוֹחַי: זֶה וָזֶה יְסוֹד מַעֲרָבִי. תַּלְמִידֵי רַבִּי יִשְׁמָעֵאל הָיוּ שׁוֹנִין מִשְׁנָה שֶׁנִּשְׁנֵית בְּבֵית מִדְרָשׁוֹ שֶׁל רַבִּי שִׁמְעוֹן דְּזֶה וָזֶה יְסוֹד ט] מַעֲרָבִי, כְּרַבִּי יִשְׁמָעֵאל. וְסִימָנֵיךְ. שֶׁלֹּא תַּחֲלִיף הַגִּירְסָא, לוֹמַר: זֶה וָזֶה דְּרוֹמִי. מִשַּׁכּוּ גַּבְרֵי לְגַבְרָא. תַּלְמִידֵי ר' יִשְׁמָעֵאל שֶׁהֵן מְרוּבִּין מָשְׁכוּ אֶת ר"ש לוֹמַר כְּדִבְרֵי רַבָּן. **מתני'** הָעוֹלָה קָדְשֵׁי קָדָשִׁים. הִיא, לִיפָּסֵל בְּיוֹצֵא וּבִטְבוּל יוֹם וּבִמְחוּסַּר כִּפּוּרִים, וּמוֹעֲלִין בָּהּ י]. שְׁתֵּי מַתָּנוֹת. בְּקֶרֶן מִזְרָחִית צְפוֹנִית וּבְקֶרֶן מַעֲרָבִית דְּרוֹמִית שֶׁכְּנֶגְדָּהּ בַּאֲלַכְסוֹן. וְהָכִי תְּנַן בְּמַסֶּכֶת תָּמִיד (דף ל:): בָּא לוֹ לְקֶרֶן מִזְרָחִית צְפוֹנִית נוֹתֵן מִזְרָחִית צְפוֹנִית, מַעֲרָבִית דְּרוֹמִית נוֹתֵן מַעֲרָבִית דְּרוֹמִית. וְטַעְמָא – מִשּׁוּם דְּקֶרֶן מִזְרָחִית דְּרוֹמִית לֹא הָיָה לָהּ יְסוֹד, כִּדְאָמְרִינַן בְּשַׁמַּעְתִּין, וְעוֹלָה טְעוּנָה יא] תּוֹרַת מַתַּן דָּמָהּ כְּנֶגֶד הַיְּסוֹד, וְכִדְרַבִּינַן לְעֵיל (דף נג.) מִק"ו מִשְּׁיָרֵי חַטָּאת, הִילְכָּךְ בָּעֵי יב] [הָנָךְ] תַּרְתֵּי דַּאֲמָרַן. שְׁתֵּי מַתָּנוֹת שֶׁהֵן ד'. בָּעֵינַן, כְּדֵי שֶׁיְּהֵא מַתַּן הַדָּם בְּד' רוּחוֹת הַמִּזְבֵּחַ. וְהָא לָא מַשְׁכַּחַתְּ לָהּ אֶלָּא בִּשְׁתֵּי קְרָנוֹת הָעוֹמְדוֹת יג] [זוֹ] בַּאֲלַכְסוֹנָהּ שֶׁל זוֹ, דְּאִי בִּשְׁתַּיִם שֶׁבְּרוּחַ אַחַת – לָא הָוֵי דָּם אֶלָּא בְּג' רוּחוֹת שֶׁל מִזְבֵּחַ, וְלָא קָרֵינַן בֵּיהּ "סָבִיב". שֶׁהֵן אַרְבַּע. בַּגְּמָ' מְפָרֵשׁ הֵיכִי עָבֵיד. **גמ'** מַאי טַעְמָא תָּנֵי בָּהּ קָדְשֵׁי קָדָשִׁים, הָאִי דְּלָא תָּנֵי גַּבֵּי חַטָּאוֹת וַאֲשָׁמוֹת, דַּהֲווּ נָמֵי קָדְשֵׁי קָדָשִׁים. וּמְשַׁנֵּי: מִשּׁוּם דְּלָא כְּתִיב בָּהּ. אִיצְטְרִיךְ לְאַשְׁמוּעִינַן דְּאַף עַל פִּי כֵן קָדְשֵׁי קָדָשִׁים הִיא, דְּהָא כּוּלָּהּ לַגָּבוֹהַּ וְאֵין לְךָ קָדְשֵׁי קָדָשִׁים כָּזֶה. וּבְקָדָשִׁים קַלִּים גּוּפַיְיהוּ, מַאי דְּאָזֵיל מִינַּיְיהוּ לַגָּבוֹהַּ קָדְשֵׁי קָדָשִׁים הוּא, כִּדְתְנַן לְקַמָּן יד] בְּפֶ' "הַתָּדִיר" (דף פט.): מַעֲשֵׂר קוֹדֵם לְעוֹפוֹת מִפְּנֵי שֶׁהוּא מִין זֶבַח, וְיֵשׁ בּוֹ קָדְשֵׁי קָדָשִׁים – דָּמוֹ וְאֵימוּרָיו. הֵיכִי עָבֵיד. דְּנַעֲשִׂים הַשְּׁתַּיִם טו] שֶׁהֵן אַרְבַּע. נוֹתֵן וְחוֹזֵר וְנוֹתֵן. זוֹרֵק מִן הַכְּלִי וְלַמִּזְבֵּחַ בְּרוּחַ זוֹ שֶׁל קֶרֶן וְכֵן בְּרוּחַ הַשְּׁנִיָּה שֶׁל קֶרֶן, וְכֵן לַקֶּרֶן שֶׁכְּנֶגְדָּהּ בַּאֲלַכְסוֹן. וְנִמְצָא מִן הַדָּם לְד' רוּחוֹת שֶׁל מִזְבֵּחַ, מַתָּנָה לְכָל רוּחַ. כְּמִין גַּמָּא. זוֹרֵק טז] נֶגֶד הַפִּינָּה מִן הַכְּלִי וְהַדָּם מִתְפַּשֵּׁט לִשְׁתֵּי רוּחוֹת הַפִּינָּה, וַהֲרֵי הוּא כְּמִין גַּאם – אוֹת יְוָנִית עֲשׂוּיָה כְּכַף יז] פְּשׁוּטָה (א). וְזָרְקוּ אֶת הַדָּם עַל הַמִּזְבֵּחַ סָבִיב. בְּעוֹלָה כְּתִיב, וְכֵן כְּתִיב בִּשְׁלָמִים וְאָשָׁם. ת"ל וְזָרְקוּ. וְאֵין זְרִיקָה אֶלָּא מֵרָחוֹק. וּבְחוּט אִי אֶפְשָׁר לְהַקִּיף, אֶלָּא בְּאֶצְבַּע וּבִנְגִיעָה. וְדָמָהּ טָעוּן כו'. כְּמִין גַּמָּא, וּבִשְׁתֵּי קְרָנוֹת שֶׁבַּאֲלַכְסוֹן, דְּאִיכָּא סָבִיב לְאַרְבַּע רוּחוֹת הַמִּזְבֵּחַ, וּבִזְרִיקָה. וְנֶאֱמַר לְהַלָּן סָבִיב. יח] בְּחַטָּאוֹת הַמִּלּוּאִין דִּ"כַלֵּי אֶת אַהֲרֹן". מָה לְהַלָּן פִּיסּוּק ד' מַתָּנוֹת. ד' נִפְסָקוֹת זוֹ מִזּוֹ, דְּהָא עַל אַרְבַּע קְרָנוֹת נוֹתֵן. אַף כָּאן. אע"פ *שֶׁבִּשְׁתֵּי קְרָנוֹת – יט] פִּיסּוּק בָּעֵינַן. וְהַיְינוּ כְּדְרַב, נוֹתֵן וְחוֹזֵר וְנוֹתֵן. עוֹלָה טְעוּנָה יְסוֹד. תְּחִילַּת כ] מַתְּנוֹתֶיהָ צְרִיכָה נֶגֶד הַיְּסוֹד, שֶׁיְּהֵא יְסוֹד הַמִּזְבֵּחַ תַּחַת מְקוֹם מַתָּנָה. וּמִקַּל וָחוֹמֶר מַיְיתֵינָהּ לְעֵיל בְּפִירְקִין (דף נג.). לֹא הָיָה לָהּ יְסוֹד. לְקַמֵּיהּ מְפָרֵשׁ הֵיכִי דָּמֵי. הִילְכָּךְ בְּקֶרֶן מִזְרָחִית צְפוֹנִית הָיָה מַתְחִיל. כא] מַאי טַעַם. לֹא הָיָה לָהּ יְסוֹד. טוֹרֵף. בִּנְיָמִין, דִּכְתִיב בֵּיהּ: "זְאֵב יִטְרָף" (בראשית מט), כב] שֶׁנִּתְנַבֵּא יַעֲקֹב עָלָיו: "בַּבֹּקֶר יֹאכַל עַד" (שם) – "בְּאַחְסַנְתֵּיהּ תִּיתְבְּנֵי מַדְבְּחָא". וְאוֹתָהּ הַקֶּרֶן לֹא הָיְתָה בְּחֶלְקוֹ, כִּדְמְפָרֵשׁ וְאָזֵיל. דְּאָמַר רַב שְׁמוּאֵל בַּר רַב יִצְחָק מִזְבֵּחַ הָיָה כג] אוֹכֵל בְּחֶלְקוֹ שֶׁל יְהוּדָה אַמָּה. אַמָּה בְּמִזְרָחוֹ אַמָּה בִּדְרוֹמוֹ, עַל כָּל הָאוֹרֶךְ בְּעוֹבִי אַמָּה. אֶלָּא שֶׁלֹּא הָיְתָה אַמָּה כד] שֶׁבַּמִּזְרָח עַל פְּנֵי כָּל הַמִּזְרָח, שֶׁכְּשֶׁמַּגִּיעַ לְקֶרֶן מִזְרָחִית צְפוֹנִית הָיְתָה כָּלָה בְּסָמוּךְ כה] לְקֶרֶן אַמָּה. וְכֵן אֲכִילַת הָאַמָּה הַדְּרוֹמִית לֹא הָיְתָה מְהַלֶּכֶת עַל פְּנֵי כָּל הַדָּרוֹם, שֶׁכְּשֶׁמַּגַּעַת לְקֶרֶן דְּרוֹמִית מַעֲרָבִית כָּלָה כו] בְּסָמוּךְ לַקֶּרֶן אַמָּה. כִּדְתְנַן לְקַמָּן (דף נד.): הַיְּסוֹד מְהַלֵּךְ עַל פְּנֵי כָּל הַצָּפוֹן וְעַל פְּנֵי כָּל הַמַּעֲרָב, אוֹכֵל בַּמִּזְרָח אַמָּה אַחַת וּבַדָּרוֹם אַמָּה אַחַת, נִמְצָא יְסוֹד לְג' קְרָנוֹת כָּזֶה. רְצוּעָה הָיְתָה יוֹצְאָה מֵחֶלְקוֹ שֶׁל יְהוּדָה. לִדְרוֹמוֹ שֶׁל מִזְבֵּחַ. שֶׁחֶלְקוֹ שֶׁל יְהוּדָה כז] הָיְתָה בַּמִּזְרָח, כִּדְתַנְיָא (יומא דף יב.): מֶה הָיָה בְּחֶלְקוֹ שֶׁל יְהוּדָה – הַר הַבַּיִת (בִּכְנִיסָתוֹ), וְהַלְּשָׁכוֹת שֶׁבּוֹ, וְהָעֲזָרוֹת. עֶזְרַת נָשִׁים כּוּלָּהּ, כח] (וְעֶזְרַת) וּשְׁנַיִם וְעֶשְׂרִים אַמָּה שֶׁל מְקוֹם דְּרִיסַת רַגְלֵי הַכֹּהֲנִים, וּמְקוֹם דְּרִיסַת רַגְלֵי יִשְׂרָאֵל, מִיקְרוּ עֲזָרוֹת. נִמְצָא חֶלְקוֹ שֶׁל יְהוּדָה בְּמִזְרַח הַמִּזְבֵּחַ וּבְלַדּוֹ [לַדָּרוֹם]. וְהַמִּזְבֵּחַ אוֹכֵל בְּחֶלְקוֹ אַמָּה בַּמִּזְרָח – כט] מִלְּבַד אַמָּה שֶׁל קֶרֶן מִזְרָחִית צְפוֹנִית ל] הָיְתָה כּוּלָּהּ חֶלְקוֹ שֶׁל יְהוּדָה, שֶׁהָיְתָה אוֹתָהּ אַמָּה בְּרָחוֹק מִן הַקֶּרֶן אַמָּה. וְהָרְצוּעָה הָיְתָה יוֹצְאָה בַּדָּרוֹם לַמִּזְבֵּחַ וְנִכְנֶסֶת בְּחֶלְקוֹ שֶׁל בִּנְיָמִין, שֶׁמִּמְּקוֹם הַדְּרִיסָה לא] וּלְמַעְלָה הָיָה חֶלְקוֹ שֶׁל בִּנְיָמִין, אֶלָּא שֶׁרְצוּעָה זוֹ הָיְתָה לִיהוּדָה בָּאָה בְּתוֹךְ חֶלְקוֹ שֶׁל בִּנְיָמִין בִּדְרוֹמוֹ שֶׁל מִזְבֵּחַ, וּמִזְבֵּחַ אוֹכֵל בָּהּ אַמָּה. וְהִיא לב] אַמָּה שֶׁהִיא כְּנִיסַת הַיְּסוֹד רָאוּי לִהְיוֹת בָּהּ, כִּדְאָמַר מָר (מדות פרק ג מ"א): עָלָה אַמָּה וְכָנַס אַמָּה – זֶהוּ יְסוֹד. כָּל אוֹרֶךְ כּוֹתֶל מִזְרָחִי בְּעוֹבִי אַמָּה הָיָה אוֹכֵל חֶלְקוֹ שֶׁל יְהוּדָה, וְכֵן כּוֹתֶל דְּרוֹמִי, לְבַד אַמָּה סָמוּךְ לְקֶרֶן דְּרוֹמִית מַעֲרָבִית לג].

[תוספות]

וסימניך משכינהו גברי לגברא. פירש בקונטרס: תלמידי רבי ישמעאל שהם מרובים משכו את רבי שמעון לומר כדברי רבם. ותימה: דלקמן פרק בתרא (דף קיט:) אמרינן: וסימניך משכינהו *גברא לגברי. דר' שמעון דאמר זו וזו ירושלים – משכינהו (ב) לרבי ישמעאל. והשתא מה סימניך הוא זה, כיון דפעמים אמרינן איפכא? ונראה כדגרסינן בספרים ישנים: וזה וזה יסוד דרומי, וסימניך משכינהו גברי לגברא. רבי שמעון בן יוחי קרי "גברי", לפי שנזכר שמו ושם אביו, ור' ישמעאל שהוא יחידי קרי "גברא". וגרסינן נמי פרק בתרא (שם): וסימניך משכינהו גברי לגברא, וכן בערוך בערך משך.

העולה קדשי קדשים כו'. תימה: לד] דלא תני שפיכות שיריים בעולה. והלא כל הדמים טעונין יסוד, לה] *כדדרשינן "העולה" למזבחה של עולה לפירוש הקונטרס. ובריש "בית שמאי" (לעיל דף לז.) אמרינן: מנין לכל הדמים שטעונין מתן דמים ליסוד. ועוד: דבמסכת תמיד (דף ל:) תנן: שירי הדם היה שופך על יסוד דרומי! לו] ותירץ ה"ר משה מפונטויז"א: משום דעולה בזריקת כלי, וזימנין דלית בה שירים. לז] *בחטאת דבאצבע – אי אפשר בלא שיריים. ולא נהירא, דכולה חטוחה מוכחת דמלוק במתן שיריים, לח] וה"ר יעקב מאורליינ"ש פירש: דכיון לט] דשמעי' תנא דפנימיים ביסוד מערבי, מ] וגם התחיל בחיצונים למיתני יסוד דרומי – הוא הדין בכולהו. ואע"ג דקתני בכל פנימיים – היינו משום דהתחיל בפנימיים, וצריך למיתני בחיצונים, ואין רוצה להפסיק.

קדשי קדשים. פי' בקונטרס: ליפסל ביוצא ובטבול יום מא] ומועלין בה. ולא היה לו לפרש לענין טבול יום ומחוסר כפורים – שזה הדין נוהג בכל קדשים אפילו קלים. אבל יוצא ומעילה ניחא, דקדשים קלים לא (מבטלי) מיפסלי ביוצא, ואין בהן מעילה מב]: **משום** דלא כתיב בה קדשי קדשים. תימה: מג] ומהאי טעמא הוה ליה למימר גבי זבחי שלמי צבור, דהא לא כתב בהו קדשי קדשים. וילפינן להו לקמן (דף נה.) מדאיתקש לעולה, מה עולה קדשי קדשים! **נאמר** כאן סביב כו'. הא דאיצטריך לעיל לאקושי חטאת לעולה לענין צפון, משום דמהך גזירה שוה ד"סביב" ליכא למילף, דלא שייכא אלא לענין מתנות. דהא חטאת שנכנס דמה לפנים פסולה ודמה טעון כיבוס, מה שאין כן בעולה.

מה להלן פיסוק מתנות כו'. תימה: כי היכי דדרשינן בפרק קמא (לעיל ד' י:): אותה דמה למעלה, ולא אחרת דמה למעלה – הכא נמי נימא: אותה בפיסוק מתנות, ולא אחרת בפיסוק מתנות! מד] ואי

[נ"ל ברבי]
[לקמן קיט: יומא נט.]
רש"ק מ"ז
[בת"כ ליתא]
[לעיל י: לקמן לז:]
יומא יב. מגילה כו. לקמן קיח: [אדר"נ פל"ה וע"ש בפי' בנין יהושע הטעם על לפיכך ובילקוט הברכה דף ש"א ע"ד]
[נ"ל שהוא בשתי]

גברי לגברא נ"ק
נ"א כדדרשינן לעיל תן יסוד למזבח של עולה
נ"ל אבל בחטאת דבאצבע כו' נ"ק
[ע' תוס' יומא יב. ד"ה ירושלים ותוס' מגילה כו. ד"ה ורצועה]
[ביומא יב. איתא דתניא והיא ברייתא ועי' תוס' לעיל נח:]

שיטה מקובצת

א] תיבת אומרים נמחק: ב] תני ביה קדשי קדשים משום דלא כתיב בה קדשי ותי' לה' נמחק תימה א"כ למה לא תני כמו כן אצל זבחי שלמי צבור ולקמן ילפינן להו מהיקשא דעולה וי"ל כיון דתני בעולה לא צריך למיתני בזבחי שלמי צבור דהא מהיקשא דעולה ילפינן אבל גבי עולה דלא כתיב בה רק דידעינן מסברא כדפ"ה לפי שכולה כליל הילכך צריך למיתני בה קדשי קדשים: ג] עביד רב אמר נותן: ד] אחת נותן כמין א): ה] כתנאי. וזרקו את הדם וגו' יכול ב) תיבת נותן נמחק: ו] כיצד דמה טעון שתי: ז] בנימין ג) ס"א ובה היה מזבח בנוי: ח] ישמעאל ברבי ר' שמעון: ט] וזה יסוד ד) דרומי: י] בה גליון פי' בין לפני זריקה בין לאחר זריקה ובקדשי' קלים ליכא מעילה אלא באימורים לפני זריקה. ע"כ: יא] טעונה תחילת מתן בעי הנך תרתי: יב] העומדות זו באלכסונה: יד] בפרק כל התדיר: טו] השתים ארבע ותיבת שהן נמחק: טז] זורק כנגד הפינה: יז] פשוטה שלנו: יח] סביב בחטאת אות ו' נמחק: יט] קרנות הוא נותן פיסוק כו' כדרב דאמר נותן וחוזר ונותן: כ] תחילת מתנותיה צריך כנגד היסוד שיהא יסוד למזבח תחת מקום המתנה בקל וחומר אייתינא לה לעיל: כא] מאי טעמא אות מ' נמחק: כב] שנתנבא עליו יעקב בבקר כו' באחסנתא יתבני: כג] אוכל כלומר תופס בחלקו כו' במזרחו ואמה בדרומו: כד] אמה למזרח על: כה] בסמוך אמה לקרן: כו] כלה סמוך לקרן: כז] יהודה היה במזרח: כח] כולה ועזרת ישראל שנים ועשרים אמה של עזרה מקום דריסת רגלי ישראל ומקום דריסת רגלי כהנים מיקרו: כט] במזרח אלא שלצד קרן תיבות מלבד אמה של נמחק: ל] היה כלה חלקו של יהודה אותה אות ו' ותיבת שהיתה נמחק: לא] הדריסה ולמערב היה תיבת ולמעלה נמחק: לב] אמה שהיה כניסת: לג] מערבית ולבד אמה סמוך לקרן מזרחית צפונית: לד] תימה אמאי לא תני: לה] כדדרשינן לעיל תן יסוד למזבחה תיבת העולה נמחק: לו] דרומי ס"א ותירץ הר"ר מאורליינ"ש דלא רצה לשנות בכל קרבן וכ"ת למה פירש אותן בחטאת י"ל דהוצרך לפרש פנימיות וחיצוניות אבל לאחר דגלי באחד מהן גלי בכל מקום: לז] שירים אבל בחטאת: לח] שירים ואפי' בעולה צריך ליזהר בזריקה שישאר מן הדם ותירץ הר"ר מאורליינ"ש דלא חשש התנא לאשמועינן שירים בכולו דאטו כי רוכלא ליזל ולחשוב ותני ליה פנימיות וחיצוניות לאפוקי ממ"ד זו וזו יסוד דרומי או זו וזו יסוד מערבי והא דתני בכל הפנימים זה לפי שרוצה לשנותו בחיצוניות ליסוד דרומי ובתר דתנייה ליסוד דרומי בחיצוניות ולא רצה להפסיק ובתר דתנא ושייר ובתמיד תנא מה ששייר הכא וכן שייר מקום זריקה שלא פירש כאן ובתמיד מפרש דהיינו קרן מזרחית צפונית ומערבית דרומית. לשון מהר"פ: לט] דאשמועינן תנא כו' מערבי וחיצוניות לא חש תו למיתני (דכל) [דאטו] כרוכלא ליחשוב לכל החיצונים כיון דאשמועינן לאפוקי ממ"ד כולהו ביסוד מערבי או כולהו ביסוד דרומי: מ] מתיבת וגם עד תיבת ואף בס"א אינו: מא] יום ובמחוסר כפורים ומועלין: מב] מעילה וקדשי קדשים מועלין בהן בין לפני זריקת דמים ובין אחר זריקת דמים ואפי' מחיים ושייך איסור יוצא אף בירושלים: מג] תימא דמהאי טעמא: מד] מתנות ונראה דאתיא גז"ש ומפקא ליה ממיעוט ומוקמינן ליה למיעוט דאין אחרת למעלה:

הגהות הב"ח

(א) רש"י ד"ה כמין גמא וכו' פשוטה הס"ד ואח"כ מ"ה סביב וזרקו: (ב) תוס' ד"ה וסימניך וכו' משכינהו לתלמידי ר' ישמעאל:

א) נראה דצ"ל כמין גמא כתנאי ותיבות נותן נמחק. ב) נראה דכך תיבת נותן נמחק שייך לאות ד'. ג) וכן הגי' ביומא דף יב ע"א. ד) הכבר נ"ע דגי' רש"י בזולא דזה וזה יסוד מערבי ועי' בתוס' ד"ה וסימנך ואולי לט"ס יש בכאן.

ומזמצה

תורה אור

(דברים לג) "חופף עליו כל היום", *לפיכך זכה בנימין הצדיק ונעשה אושפיזכן להקב"ה, שנאמר: (שם) "ובין כתפיו שכן". מיתיבי: *עולת העוף אכיצד היתה נעשית? היה מולק את ראשה ממול עורפה ומבדיל, וממצה א] דמה על קיר המזבח; ואי אמרת לא היה לה יסוד – באוירא בעלמא הוא דקא עביד? אמר רב נחמן בר יצחק: אימר כך התנו, אוירא דבנימין, קרקע דיהודה. מאי לא הוה לה יסוד? רב אמר: בבנין, לוי אמר: בדמים. רב מתרגם: "באחסנתיה יתבני מדבחא", ב] לוי מתרגם: "באחסנתיה יתבני מקדשא", מקום מקודש לדמים. תא שמע: *בהיסוד היה מהלך על פני כל הצפון ועל פני כל המערב, אוכל בדרום אמה אחת ובמזרח אמה אחת! מאי אוכל? נמי בדמים. תא שמע: *גהמזבח היה שלשים ושתים על שלשים ושתים! הכא במאי עסקינן – מן הצד. ת"ש: *נמצא פורח (א) אמה על יסוד ואמה על סובב! אימא: כנגד אמה יסוד ג] ועל אמה סובב.§ תא שמע, דתני לוי: כיצד בונין את המזבח? דמביאין מלבן שהוא שלשים ושתים על שלשים ושתים וגובהו אמה, ומביא ד] חלוקי אבנים מפולמות, בין גדולות בין קטנות, ומביא סיד וקוניא וזפת וממחה ושופך, *וזה הוא ה] מקום יסוד. וחוזר ומביא מלבן שהוא שלשים ו] אמה על שלשים אמה וגובהו חמש אמות, ומביא חלוקי אבנים כו'. *)וחוזר ומביא (ב) מלבן שהוא כ"ח על כ"ח אמות וגובהו ג' אמות, ומביא חלוקי כו', והוא מקום המערכה. וחוזר ומביא מלבן שהוא אמה על אמה, ומביא חלוקי אבנים מפולמות בין גדולות בין קטנות, ומביא זפת וקוניא, וממחה ושופך, וזהו קרן, וכן לכל קרן וקרן! ז] וכי תימא

דגייז

*) וזהו סובב וחוזר כו' ל"ק

רש"י

חופף. כמו: נזיר חופף ומפספס (שבת דף נ:), *דפרוטי"ר *דגרנטו"ר בלע"ז, כאדם המחשב ודואג. ומבדיל. בשתי סימנין, ולא כחטאת שהיא בסימן אחד. ולקמן יליף לה בפרק "קדשי קדשים" (דף סה.). וממצה מדמה ח]. *(ומקיף = מחבר, כמו: אין מקיפין שתי חביות (ביצה דף לב:)). דוחק בית מליקתו לקיר, והוא מתמצה ע"י ט] דוחקו בקיר. ולקמן אמרינן שעל קרן מזרחית דרומית י] היא נעשית. ואי אין לה יסוד, נמצא כשהוא מולקה – באויר היא נמלקת, והדם נופל לארץ לאיבוד. וא"ת: יא] נופל על הסובב, שהרי למעלה היא נעשית! הא קתני התם: עשאה למטה מרגליו אפי' אמה אחת כשרה, דלא קפיד אלא אלמעלה מן החוט. באוירא בעלמא קעביד. בתמיה. אימר כך וכו'. ואיכא למימר: למעלה מג', דלאו קרקע הוא, עשוי כמין בליטה קטנה כנגד אותה הקרן, לקבל בה דם עולת העוף שלא יפול לארץ. וקיר מזבח מיקרי, אבל יסוד לא מיקרי להכשיר הקרן למתן דמים הצריכין ליתן כנגד היסוד, שאין יסוד אלא המיוסד בארץ. רב אמר בבנין. בקרן דרומית מערבית בנו היסוד אמה באורך הדרום, וחדלו להם כל הדרום וכל המזרח עד אמה סמוך לקרן לפונית מזרחית, כדאמרן (לקמן): אוכל במזרח אמה ובדרום אמה. לוי יב] אומר בדמים. יסוד היה על פני כל המזרח, אבל לא נותנין דמים בחלקו של יהודה. יתבני מדבחא. בניינא גופיה משמע. יג] אוכל. = תופס. במזרח אמה אחת. ובמקצוע לפונית מזרחית משוך לצד מזרח אמה ולא יותר, כמו שפירשתי למעלה. קשיא ללוי, דהא יד] בניינא משמע. על שלשים ושתים. קשיא לרב, דמשמע ריבוע היה. מן הצד. לאו טו] בארבעת רבעין קחשיב, אלא מצד צפון היה ל"ב. אבל מזרח ודרום לא היה אלא ל"א על ל"א, דקרן דרומית מזרחית חסרה לה אמה לדרום ואמה למזרח. נמצא פורח על אמה יסוד ועל אמה סובב. טז] ולקמן הוא בפרק "קדשי קדשים" (דף סב:), דרמינן מתניתין אהדדי, דתנן חדא: כבש היה לדרומו של מזבח אורך ל"ב, והמזבח ל"ב אורך – הרי אורך המזבח והכבש ס"ד. וכי מני להו אהדדי תנן: הכבש והמזבח ס"ב. יז] והא שיתין וארבע הוי תפסין בקרקע העזרה, והתם לגבי תפיסת הקרקע קא מני להו! ומשנינן: נמצא שראש הכבש פורח ועולה על שתי אמות של כניסת היסוד יח] וסובב, ונמצא שתי אמות העליונות נבלעות בל"ב של מזבח. מדקתני: "פורח על אמה של יסוד" מכלל יט] דאיכא כניסת כ] היסוד לדרום, קשיא לרב דאמר ד"אוכל במזרח אמה אחת ובדרום אמה אחת" דקתני, ותו לא – בבנין קאמר. והכבש בדרום הוא, ויש תחתיו כניסת יסוד כא] המזבח! אימא כנגד אמה יסוד. כנגד מקום שהכניסה ראויה להיות, ולא שהיתה שם. ומיהו, שתי אמות נבלעות לתוך ל"ב של מזבח, שהיה נכנס לתוך כב] הפנימי שכנגד בליטה שהיסוד התחיל בה, לאכול בה בדרום אמה אחת. מלבן. כג] הוא דפוס מרובע עשוי מארבע קרשים, וכל אחת כד] ארוכה ל"ב, כעין *אנשטר"א שעושין לכירים. ורוחב הקרש אמה, והוא גובהו של מלבן, כה] וממלאהו אבנים וסיד וזפת וקוניא עד שמשווהו לגובה המלבן. מפולמות. = לחות. קוניא. = כו] ניתוך אבר, כעין שעושין לצפוי כלי חרס שקורין *פולמי"ר. וממחה. = *איספרידיי"ר בלע"ז. ושופך כז] בתוך המלבן על אבנים, ונדבקים יחד על ידי אלו. וזה היסוד הראשון ששנינו בו: עלה אמה. וחוזר ומביא כו'. ומושיבו על זה, וממלאהו. נמלאת כניסת אמה – זה (ג) יסוד, כולט אמה כח] זה סובב. וחוזר ומביא כו'. וזהו סובב על זה היה כהן מהלך, כדמפרש ואזיל. שהמלבן השלישי שהושיבו על זה קצר ממנו שתי אמות על שתי אמות, נמצא האמצעי כולט מתחת העליון אמה בכל צד. מקום המערכה. כלומר, ראש המזבח. וחוזר ומביא מלבן של אמה כו'. ומושיבו בזוית המזבח מלמעלה. קתני מיהא: מלבן התחתון של ל"ב על ל"ב, אלמא יסוד כולט בו מד' רוחותיו!

דגייז

תוספות

ואי אמרת לא היה לו יסוד באוירא בעלמא קעביד. בתמיה, דלקמן (דף סד:) אמרי' שעל קרן מזרחית דרומית היא נעשית. ואי אין לה יסוד, נמלא כשהוא מולקה – באויר היא נמלקת, והדם נופל לארץ לאיבוד. ואם תאמר: נופל הוא על הסובב, שהרי למעלה היא נעשית! הא קתני התם: עשאה למטה מרגליו ואפילו אמה אחת כשרה, דלא קפיד אלא למעלה מן החוט. כך פירש בקונטרס. ונראה שלא היה כתוב בהך ברייתא "שירי הדם היה שופך ליסוד", מדלא מדקדק בקונטרס אלא מהא שהדם הולך לאיבוד. וקשה: דאם כן הוה ליה לאקשויי ממתני' ד"קדשי קדשי" (שם סד:), דתנן: בא לו לקרן דרומית מזרחית היה מולק ראשה כו'! וברוב ספרים גורסין כאן: שירי הדם היה שופך ליסוד. ומפרש ה"ר חיים: דודאי גרסי' ליה, ומכח זה פריך, דעל כרחין לאותו קרן שמולק שם היה שופך שירי הדם כט] קרי לה יסוד, מדלא קתני שהיה הולך לקרן דרומית מערבית שהיה בו יסוד לשפוך שירים. ועוד: דלקמן פ' "קדשי קדשים" (גם זה שם.) מפרש שעושה אותה באותו קרן לפי שהוא קרוב לבית הדשן, ויכול לזרוק משם מוראה ונוצה. ואם היה זקוק לילך לקרן אחר לשפוך שירים – מה היה מרויח, כיון שהיה צריך לחזור? ואין לומר דלאחר זריקת מוראה ונוצה היה הולך לשפוך שירים, דאם היה מאחר כל כך – היה דם כלה. אלא על כרחין במקומו היה שופך ליסוד, ולכך פריך: ואי אמרת לא היה לה יסוד באוירא בעלמא קעביד! ומשני: אימר כן התנו, אוירא דבנימין, ועשו כמין בליטה, ועל אותה בליטה היה שופך שירים. ומיהו, קשה: דאי חשיב יסוד – לענין שאר דמים נמי יחשב יסוד! וי"ל: דלא חשיב יסוד אלא לענין דמים הניתנין למעלה מחוט הסיקרא, אבל לענין דמים הניתנין למטה, אי מכשרת ליה להוא קרן – זימנין דאתי למיתב תחת אותה בליטה ונמצא נותן תחת היסוד. אבל דמים העליונים – לעולם הם למעלה מן הבליטה. ומיהו, קשה: דאם כן היכי ממעט הכא עולה דלא ל] הוה ארבע קרנות *בחטאת משום דטעונה יסוד *לענין דמים העליונים? ונראה לרבינו תם: דלא גרסינן "שירי הדם היה שופך ליסוד", ד"שופך" משמע מן הכלי, מדלא תני "מתמצה ליסוד" כדקתני גבי חטאת העוף. לא] ועוד: דבמתני' דלקמן פרק "קדשי קדשים" (דף סד:) קתני בחטאת העוף שירי הדם, ובעולת העוף לא תני – משמע דלית ליה שירים. והא דמרבינן לעיל שירים בכל הקרבנות – היינו לב] לבד מעולת העוף. וכיון דנעשית מלותו – מה לנו במה שהדם נופל אחר כך לארץ והולך לאיבוד? דכל דמים נמי לאחר שנשפכו ליסוד הולכין לאיבוד אחרי כן! ועוד, כשמתרץ: כך התנו אוירא, ופירש בקונטרס: שהיה עושה כמין בליטה במזבח לקבל דמים – היה לו להתלמוד לפרש זה! ונראה לר"ת: דפריך ממליקה עצמה, דבעי בראשו של מזבח דומיא דהקטרה כדלקמן, ואי עביד ליה באויר דיהודה – אם כן לג] אינה עולה לקדשי מזבח! ומשני: דאוירא דבנימין, וקדיש האויר בקדושת מזבח. ואף על גב דהקטרה באויר אי אפשר – לא חייש אלא בהא דליהוי קדושת מזבח. ומיהו, למאן דאמר (לקמן דף סה.): אין עושין מערכה על גבי סובב – נראה דמליקה נמי לא מהניא התם, אף על גב דקדוש בקדושת מזבח. והכא איירי למאן דאמר עושין מערכה על גבי סובב.

רב אמר בבנין. אף על גב דלמטה לא הוי רבוע, למעלה במקום המערכה הוי רבוע. וקשה קצת *)לישנא דמתני' לרב, דתנן במסכת יומא (דף יב.): דרצועה יוצאה מחלקו של יהודה ונכנסת לחלקו של בנימין ובה מזבח בנוי, משמע שהיה בה מבנין.

מפולמות. לד] כגון דגים מפולמין, פרק "אין לדין" (ביצה כד:).

*) נ"ל לישנא דמתניתא לרב דתניא

דגייז

מסורת הש"ס

שייך במתני' לקמן דף סד:

[סוטה לז.]

לקמן סד.

מדות פ"ג מ"א

שם [מנחות לז:]

לקמן סב:

נ"ק מ"ז

נ"א זהו יסוד וחוזר ומביא מלבן שהוא ל' אמות ושני טפחים על ל' אמות ושני טפחים וגובהו ה' כו' וזהו סובב וחוזר ומביא מלבן של כ"ח אמות וד' טפחים על כ"ח אמות וד' טפחים וגובהו ג' כו'

עין משפט נר מצוה

לז א מיי' פ"ו מהלכות מעשה"ק הלכה כ:

לח ב מיי' פ"ב מהל' בית הבחירה הל' ו:

לט ג מיי' שם הל' ה:

מ ד מיי' שם הלכה יז:

שיטה מקובצת

א] וממצה מדמה על קיר המזבח נטל את הראש ומקיף בית מליקתו למזבח ואי: ב] מדבחא מקום דמים לוי: ג] יסוד וכנגד אמה [סובב]: ד] ומביא חלקי אבנים: ה] תיבת מקום נמחק: ו] שלשים ושני טפחים על שלשים ושני טפחים וגבהו חמש אמות ומביא חלקי אבנים מפולמות וכו' וממחה ושופך וחוזר ומביא מלבן של עשרים ושמונה אמות וד' טפחים על שמונה ועשרים וד' טפחים וגבהו שלש ומביא חלקי כו' וממחה ושופך וזהו מקום מערכה וחוזר ומביא מלבן כו' ומביא חלקי אבנים: ז] תיבות וכי תימא ל"ש ונמחק: ח] מדמה א) כו' ומקיף: ט] ע"י שדוחקו בקיר: י] היתה נעשית אות א' נמחק: יא] וא"ת הוא נופל: יב] לוי אמר: יג] משמע הס"ד ומה"ד מקום המקודש לדמים פירוש היסוד היה בכל המזבח אך הדמים אין ניתנין רק בחלקו של בנימין הס"ד ומה"ד אוכל. תופס במזרח אמה אחת דבמקצוע צפונית: יד] דהא בבניינא משמע: טו] בארבעה רבעיו קחשיב אלא כו' היה ל"ב ומצד מערב ל"ב אבל מזרח: טז] לקמן הוא: יז] ס"ב ופריך והא שתין וארבע הוי תפס בקרקע: יח] היסוד והסובב ונמצא ב' אמות העליונות של כבש נבלעות בל"ב: יט] מכלל ס"א מכלל דאיכא כניסת יסוד בדרום שהרי הכבש בדרום היה וקשיא לרב דאמר בבנין כלומר שברוח דרומית וברוח מזרח לא היה שם יסוד בנוי והכא משמע שהיה שם בנוי: כ] כניסת יסוד: כא] יסוד במזבח הס"ד: כב] שהיה נכנס לתוך הפגימה שכנגד בליטה שהיסוד התחיל לאכול בה בדרום: כג] תיבת הוא נמחק: כד] ארכה ל"ב: כה] מלבן וממלאו: כו] קוניא. אבר ניתוך כעין כו' שקורין פולמיה הס"ד: כז] ושופך לתוך המלבן על האבנים ונדבקין יחד על ידי אלו וזה הוא היסוד: כח] אמה זו סביב: כט] תיבות קרי לה נמחק: ל] דלא הויא מארבע קרנות כחטאת משום דטעונה יסוד הא חשבא ליה יסוד לענין דמים: לא] העוף ועולת

הגהות הב"ח

(א) גמ' נמצא פורח על אמה יסוד ועל אמה סובב: (ב) שם ומביא מלבן כ"ב ועיין בסוכה דף מה ע"א: (ג) רש"י ד"ה וחוזר ומביא כו' ומושיבו וכו' יסוד הס"ד ותיבות כולט אמה זה סובב נמחק:

העוף אין דמו בכלי ועוד דלא היה בו שירים כיון דבעי מיצוי: לב] היינו ס"א דוקא בבהמה דכתיב בקרא: לג] כן חול הוא לענין קדושת מזבח ותיבות אינה עולה לקדשי נמחק: לד] מפולמות. לחות כמו דגים מפולמים:

א) נראה דל"ל מדמה כו' נטל את הראש ומקיף בית מליקתו מקיף מחבר וכו'.

דגייז ליה — "אבנים שלמות" כתיב! אדמחית מידי מתותיה ושקיל ליה. דאי לא תימא הכי, הא א] דאמר רב כהנא: באבנים של קרנות חלולות היו, דכתיב: °"ומלאו כמזרק כזויות מזבח" (זכריה ט), הכא נמי — "אבנים שלמות" אמר רחמנא! אלא: דמחית מידי מתותיה ושקיל ליה, ה"נ, דמחית מידי מתותיה ושקיל ליה. דרש רבא, מאי דכתיב: °"וילך *דוד ושמואל וישבו בנויות ברמה" (ש"א יט), וכי מה ענין נויות אצל רמה? אלא, שהיו יושבין ברמה, ועוסקין בנויו של עולם; אמרי: כתיב °"וקמת ועלית אל המקום" (דברים יז) — *מלמד שבית המקדש גבוה מכל ארץ ישראל, וארץ ישראל גבוהה מכל ארצות. לא הוו ידעי ב] דוכתיה היכא, אייתו ספר יהושע, בכולהו ג] כתיב: °"וירד" "ועלה הגבול" (יהושע יח) "ותאר הגבול", בשבט בנימין "ועלה" כתיב, "וירד" לא כתיב. אמרי: ש"מ הכא הוא מקומו. סבור למבנייה בעין עיטם דמדלי, אמרי: ד] ניתתי ביה *קליל, כדכתיב: °"ובין כתפיו שכן" (דברים לג). ה] ואיבעית אימא: גמירי דסנהדרין בחלקו דיהודה, ושכינה בחלקו דבנימין, ואי מדלינן ליה — מתפליג טובא, מוטב דניתתי ביה פורתא, כדכתיב: "ובין כתפיו שכן". ועל דבר זה נתקנא דואג האדומי בדוד, כדכתיב: °"כי קנאת ביתך אכלתני" (תהלים סט), וכתיב: °"זכור ה' לדוד את כל ענותו (שם קלב) אשר נשבע לה' וגו' אם אבא ו] באהל ביתי אם אתן שנת לעיני לעפעפי תנומה עד אמצא מקום לה' וגו' הנה שמענוה באפרתה מצאנוה בשדה יער", "באפרתה" — *זה יהושע דקאתי מאפרים, "מצאנוה בשדה יער" — זה בנימין, דכתיב: °"בנימין זאב יטרף" (בראשית מט). §

מתני' זבחי שלמי צבור גואשמות; אלו הן אשמות: אשם גזילות, אשם מעילות, אשם שפחה חרופה, אשם נזיר, אשם מצורע, אשם תלוי; שחיטתן בצפון, וקיבול דמן בכלי שרת בצפון, דודמן טעון שתי מתנות שהן ארבע, הונאכלין לפנים מן הקלעים, ולזכרי כהונה, זלכל מאכל, חליום ולילה טעד חצות. §

גמ'

רש"י

דגייז ליה. אחר שנעשה סתר הבנין מעל חלקו של יהודה. ופרכינן: והא אבנים שלמות כתיב. שיהא חלק ולא פגימות, ואי אפשר לסתירה להיות חלקה. דמחית מידי מתותיה. כלומר, במקומו על (כנגד) חלקו של יהודה הניח עץ ז] ארוך ועוביו כעובי המלבן וחלק, [והניח] נ"ק בתוך המלבן, ולא יכול להדביק עם חלוקי האבנים ע"י שפיכת המיחוי של סיד וקוניא. ולכשייבש קלט נטלו, ונשאר מקומו חלק. קרנות של מזבח חלולות היו. נקבים נקבים עמוקים ח] בארבעתן, שיפול דם החטאת ויבלע לתוכו. כמזרק כזויות מזבח. אלמא בית קיבול יש ט] כמזרקים. דמחית מידי מתותיה. מקלות וקסמין י] [דקים] נתן בין חלוקי האבנים, וכשייבש הוציאם ונשארו מקומות בנקבים יא] חלוקים, ולא הוצרך לפגוס בפגימות לנקבים. יב] *שהן יושבים ברמה. בעירו של שמואל. נויו של עולם. למצוא מקום לבית הבחירה מן התורה. ועלית. יג] "בכל שעריך" קרי עלייה ומשם לבית המקדש, מלמד שבית המקדש היה גבוה מכל ארץ ישראל. וארץ ישראל גבוהה מכל הארצות. לא מיבעיא לן הכא, ולאו מהכא נפקא לן אלא מקרא אחרינא, דכתיב (ירמיה טז כג): "לא יאמר עוד חי וגו' כי אם חי ה' אשר העלה ואשר הביא את בני ישראל מארץ צפון ומכל יד] המקומות אשר הדחתים שם" וגו'. דוכתיה. מקומו היכן? מקום הגבוה בא"י בגבול מי הוא. אייתו ספר יהושע. לבדוק בגבולי השבטים, ולא טו] פירשו שם באחד מכל השבטים פיאות גבוליהם לארבע רוחותיהם, חוץ משבט יהודה ובנימין, שנתפרשו שם כל הגבולים מסובבין טז] ברוחותיה ומקצועותיה. גבול יהודה לדרומה של ארץ ישראל, וארץ אדום גבולו לדרום על פני כולו. ואורך גבול יהודה מן המזרח למערב על פני אורך כל גבולה של א"י, ים המלח למזרח וים הגדול למערב, והן מן גבולי ארץ ישראל בפרשת "אלה מסעי". וגבול צפוני של יז] ארץ יהודה לא היה מכוון לארכו, אלא התחיל למזרח מן הירדן ועולה למערב, ומרחיב יח] מאמצעו ופונה באלכסון לצפון, ועולה *מדביר ומרחיב לצד צפון אל יט] הכתף היבוסי היא ירושלים. ומשהתחיל מן המזרח *מוגה והולך עד ירושלים. כתיב ועלה הגבול ולא כתיב וירד. ועוד כתיב כ] בעלייה אחת מירושלים (א) עד ראש ההר על פני גיא בן הינום. ומשם עד הים שהוא לרוח מערב כתיב: "ותאר הגבול וירד הגבול". *ולא כתיב ועלה. ונחלת בנימין בצפונה של נחלת יהודה, וגבול נגב לבנימין הוא גבול צפונה ליהודה, אלא שאין אורך נחלת בנימין מן המזרח ועד הים, אלא עד ירושלים, ועד ההר אשר על כא] גיא בן הינום ועד קרית *יערים. *)כתיב ועלה ותאר ולא כתיב וירד. "ותאר" אינה לא עליה ולא ירידה. למדנו שראש ההר אשר על כב] גיא בן הינום הוא גבוה מן הכל ולמעלה מירושלים, דמירושלים ולשם כתיב "ועלה". סבור למיבנייה בעין עיטם. נראה בעיני שהוא מעין מי נפתוח האמור שם אחר עליית ההר אשר על פני גיא בן הינום, אשר לא נכתב ירידה בינתיים. ניתתי ביה קליל. נעשה אותו נמוך מעט, ונבנהו בירושלים שהיא למטה, כדכתיב "כתפיו" ולא כתיב כג] ראשו. *ואיבא דאמרי. האי דלא כד] בנאה בעין עיטם – משום דרחיק שם נחלת בנימין מנחלת יהודה יותר משיעור הר הבית, ואפשר לסמוך לשכת הגזית לעזרה. ואנן בעינן סנהדרין בעזרה, דכתיב: "וקמת ועלית" וגו', וצריכה להיות בחלקו של יהודה, כדמפרש ואזיל: גמירי סנהדרין בחלקו של יהודה, כדכתיב (בראשית מט): "ומחוקק מבין רגליו". אשר עינה את עצמו לעסוק ולדעת, ונשבע ונדר: "אם אבא באהל" וגו'. **מתני'** זבחי שלמי צבור. כבשי עצרת. אשם גזילות. האמור בשבועת הפקדון (ויקרא ה). אשם מעילות. הנהנה מן ההקדש. אשם שפחה חרופה. הבא על שפחה כנענית המיועדת לעבד עברי. אשם נזיר. שנטמא במת, דכתיב ביה: "והזיר לה' את ימי נזרו" וגו' (במדבר ו). אשם תלוי. ספק שגג בכרת ספק לא חטא. והוא כתוב בויקרא גבי אשם מעילות. "אשם ודאי" ל"ג, שכל אלו שהוזכרו אשמות ודאין הן, חוץ מאשם תלוי. שתי מתנות שהן ארבע. דבאשם נמי כה] בעינן זריקת סביב, דכתיב: "במקום אשר ישחטו" וגו' (ויקרא ז). ונאכלין לפנים מן הקלעים. דכתיב באשם ב"ויקח קרח": "לכל אשמם וגו' בקדש הקדשים תאכלנו" וגו'. וזבחי שלמי צבור בגמרא מפרש מנא ליה.

*) [וע"ע תוס' סוכה מט. ד"ה שכל ותוס' מס' ע"ז כג: ד"ה בקשו ותוס' גיטין סח. ד"ה איכא ותוס' חולין יח. ד"ה וכמה]

תוספות

דגייז ליה. תימה: מעיקרא ליעבד מלבן בענין זה.

אבנים שלמות כו'. תימה, דהוה ליה לאקשויי: "לא תניף עליהם ברזל" אמר רחמנא! ויש לומר: שהתלמוד קיצר כאן, ורוצה לומר כמו שמדקדק התלמוד במסכת ע"ז פרק "רבי ישמעאל" (דף נב:) גבי אבני מזבח ששקצום אנשי יון: ליתברינהו – "אבנים שלמות" אמר רחמנא, לינסרינהו – "לא תניף עליהם ברזל" כתיב. ואם תאמר: וליעביד על ידי שמיר! דבבית שני הוה שמיר, כדמוכח בסוטה פרק "עגלה ערופה" (דף מח.). דקתני: משמתו נביאים הראשונים – בטל אורים ותומים, כו] [והיינו בית ראשון]. משחרב בית המקדש – בטל השמיר, והיינו בית שני, דאי בית ראשון – ליערבינהו וליתנינהו, דמשמתו נביאים הראשונים היינו חורבן הבית, כדתניא בגמרא: משחרב בית המקדש בטלו אורים ותומים, והיינו בית ראשון, דחמשה דברים חסר בית שני מבית ראשון, כדאיתא ביומא (דף כא:). ובטל השמיר היינו לאחר בית שני. וכן הא דקאמר רבן שמעון בן גמליאל התם: משחרב בית המקדש ניטל טעם כז] פירות, ומסתמא בבית שני שחרב בימיו איירי. תדע, דאשכחן בבית שני שהיו פירותיהם מתברכים בימי שמעון בן שטח, שנעשו חיטין ככליות של שור הגדול (תענית דף כג.). ועוד יש להביא ראיה דהוה שמיר בבית שני מעובדא דדמא בן נתינה *שמו דפרק קמא דקדושין (דף לא.), ובפרק שני דמסכת ע"ז (דף כג:) שבקשו ממנו חכמי ישראל אבנים לאפוד, ואבני אפוד בעו שמיר, כח] כדמוכח פרק "עגלה ערופה" (סוטה דף מח:) מדכתיב "במלואותם". ואפי' רבי יהודה דפליג עליה ואמר: שמיר שבו בנה שלמה את בית המקדש – מודה דאבני אפוד נמי בעו שמיר, כדמוכח פרק "מי שאחזו" (גיטין דף סח.) גבי בנין בית המקדש שעשה שלמה, דקאמר: היכי נעביד – איכא שמיר דאייתי משה לאבני אפוד. והיא על כרחין רבי יהודה היא, דלר' נחמיה לא הוה בעי שמיר למקדש. ועובדא כט] דבן נתינה בבית שני, דקאמר: הדר לשנה אחרת נולדה לו פרה אדומה בעדרו, ושבע פרות היו, הראשונה עשה משה, שניה עשה עזרא, כדתנן במסכת פרה (פ"ג מ"ה). וכמו כן קשה בפרק "רבי ישמעאל" במסכת ע"ז (דף נב:), אמאי גנזו בית חשמונאי אבני מזבח ששקצום אנשי יון, כיון דאפשר על ידי שמיר! ויש לומר: דשמיר אין עושה אותן שלמות שלא תחגור בה הצפורן. ופרק קמא דחולין (דף יח.) אמרינן: וכמה כדי פגימת המזבח – כדי שתחגור בה צפורן. ומיהו קשה: ל] בית המקדש כתיב "אבן שלמה מסע נבנה", וקאמר רבי יהודה דהוה שמיר לבית המקדש!*).

ומלאו כמזרק בזוית מזבח. הוה מלי לאתויי מתני' דמסכת מדות (פ"ג מ"ג): ובקרן מערבית דרומית היו שני נקבים כמין שני חוטמין דקין, לא] (א) שהדמים היו נתונים על יסוד דרומית יורדין בהן ומתערבין באמה ויוצאין לנחל קדרון. אלא ניחא ליה לאיתויי דרב כהנא משום לב] קרא. ובקונטרס פירש שהנקבים היו בד' קרנות, שיפול דם חטאת לתוכן ויבלע. ותימה לפירושו, שלא היו המתנות למעלה, אלא כנגד חודה מבחוץ.

(א) נ"ל שהדמים שהיו נתונים על יסוד מערבי ועל יסוד דרומי יורדין כו' נ"ק

זבחי

עין משפט נר מצוה

מא א מיי' פ"ב מהל' בית הבחירה הל' טז:
מב ב מיי' שם הל' ח:
מג ג מיי' פ"א מהל' מעה"ק הל' ג:
מד ד מיי' שם הל' ו:
מה ה ו מיי' פ"ט מהל' מעה"ק הלכה א ופ"י שם הל' ג:
מו ז מיי' שם פ"י הל' י:
מז ח מיי' שם הל' ז:
מח ט מיי' שם הל' ח:

מסורת הש"ס

נ"ק
נ"ל הוא
סנהדרין פז. [קדושין סט.]
שהיו נ"ק
[תרגום יונתן של יוקח נא מעט מים קליל מיא]
נ"ל שמביא בפ"ק כו'
[גיר' הערוך ערך הנה זה ספר יהושע ע"ש פי' נכון]
מדבריה נ"ק
ומוגה והולך עד ירושלים כתב ועלה והד"א נ"ק
ולא כתב ועלה כו' והד"א נ"ק
יערים כתב ועלה והד"א נ"ק
*)עיין חלופי גרסאות
ואיכבעית אימא הכי נ"ק

הגהות הב"ח

(א) רש"י ד"ה כתיב ועלה וכו' ועוד כתיב עליה אחת מירושלים אל ראש ההר אשר על פני:

שיטה מקובצת

א] דאמר רב כהנא קרנות של מזבח חלולות היו (תיבת אבנים נמחק) וי"מ קרנות המזבח חלולות היו כדתנן במס' מדות בקרן מערבית דרומית היו שני נקבים כמין שני חוטמין דקין שהדמים הניתנים על יסוד מערבי ועל יסוד דרומי יורדין בהם ומתערבים באמה ויוצאין לנחל קדרון: ב] מקומו היכא ותיבת דוכתיה נמחק: ג] בכולהו כתיבי שבטים וירד הגבול ותאר הגבול ובשבט בנימין כתיב ועלה פי' מעין עיטם ואילך לדרום הוא גבול שאר שבטים וכל הצפון עד עין עיטם גבול בנימין ובאותן גבולים שמעין עיטם ואילך לדרום כתיב וירד ובגבול בנימין שבצפון עד עין עיטם כתיב ועלה נמצא שעין עיטם גבוה מכולם לשון רש"י בנספחות מהר"פ: ד] ניתתי. גליון כמו תיתי ניהלי האמור לעיל (דף יט ע"א): ה] שכן ואיבא דאמרי: ו] באהל ביתי אם אתן שנת לעיני וא"ת והיאך היה נודר כך הלא אמרו בנדרים הנודר שלא לישן שלשה ימים מכין אותו ויישן לאלתר ויש לפרש דקאי אאהל ביתי וה"ק אם אתן שנת לעיני באהל ביתי אבל לא היה נודר שלא לישן כלל: ז] עץ גדול וארוך ועוביו: ח] עמוקים היו בארבעתן שיפול דם החטאת ויבלע: ט] יש להם כמזרקים: י] קסמין חלקים: יא] בנקבים חלולים ולא הוצרך לפגום בהם פגימות לנקבם הס"ד: יב] מה"ד שהיו יושבין: יג] ועלית מכל שעריך קרי עלייה משם לבית המקדש: יד] ומכל הארצות אשר הדיחם שמה וגו' הס"ד ומה"ד מקומו היכא מקום הגבוה מכל א"י בגבול מי הוא: טו] פירש שם: טז] מסובבין ברוחותיהם ומקצועותיהם גבול: יז] תיבת ארץ מוקף בחצאי לבנה: יח] ומרחיב ס"א מתחיל מקרוב לאמצע לפנות לצד צפון ומרחיב ועולה אל כתף היבוסי היא ירושלים: יט] אל כתף היבוסי היא ירושלים כו' המזרח מתחיל ועולה עד: כ] ועוד כתוב בו עלייה אחת מירושלים לההר אשר על פני גיא בן הינום ועד קרית יערים: כא] על פני גיא כו' יערים והיינו דקאמר הכא דבכולהו כתיב וירד הגבול ותאר הגבול ובשבט בנימין ועלה כתיב וירד לא כתיב והיינו שכל תחומי יהודה הנזכרים בצפון שהם מגבלות נחלת בנימין ולהלן לצפון ולצד מערב וסמוכים לצד דרומי של שאר שבטים כתיב בהו וירד הגבול ותאר הגבול ולא כתיב ועלה וכל מה שבגבול צפוני של יהודה סמוך לנחלת בנימין מן המזרח עד קרית יערים כתיב ועלה וכו' והד"א: כב] על פני גיא בן הינום הוא הגבוה מן הכל והוא למעלה מירושלים: כג] כתיב בראשו: כד] דלא בנה בעין: כה] זריקה סביב בצוו באשם אחרון במקום אשר: כו] תיבות והיינו בית ראשון נמחק: כז] טעם. ס"א באה ונתנה לעובדי עבודה ומסתמא בבית שני שחרב בימיו איירי הרע דקאמר נמי בגמרא: כח] כדמוכח פרק: כט] ועובדא דדמא בן נתינה בבית שני הוה דקאמר התם לשנה אחרת: ל] כדאמר ר' נחמיה פרק ותיבת כדמוכח נמחק: לא] משום דמייתי קרא ובקונטרס פירש כו' חטאת ויבלע לתוכו ותימה: לב] קשה דבבית המקדש: לג] שהדמים הניתנים על יסוד דרומית הם יורדין בהן:

גמ' מְנָא לָן דְּבָעֵי צָפוֹן? דְּתָנֵי א] רַבָּה בַּר רַב חָנָן קַמֵּיהּ דְּרָבָא: °"וַעֲשִׂיתֶם שְׂעִיר עִזִּים אֶחָד לְחַטָּאת", ב] מַה חַטָּאת בַּצָּפוֹן – אַף אשַׁלְמֵי צִבּוּר בַּצָּפוֹן. אֲמַר לֵיהּ רָבָא: •וְכִי חַטָּאת מֵהֵיכָן לְמֵדָה – מֵעוֹלָה, ג] *דָּבָר הַלָּמֵד בְּהֶיקֵּשׁ חוֹזֵר וּמְלַמֵּד בְּהֶיקֵּשׁ? אֶלָּא, ד] *מִדְּתָנֵי רַב מָרִי בְּרֵיהּ דְּרַב כָּהֲנָא: °"עַל עוֹלוֹתֵיכֶם וְעַל זִבְחֵי שַׁלְמֵיכֶם", מָה עוֹלָה קָדְשֵׁי קָדָשִׁים – אַף זִבְחֵי שַׁלְמֵי צִבּוּר קָדְשֵׁי קָדָשִׁים, מָה עוֹלָה בַּצָּפוֹן – אַף זִבְחֵי שַׁלְמֵי צִבּוּר בַּצָּפוֹן. ה] אֶלָּא הֶיקֵּשָׁא קַמָּא לְמַאי אָתָא? כִּי חַטָּאת, מַה חַטָּאת אֵינָהּ נֶאֱכֶלֶת אֶלָּא לְזִכְרֵי כְהוּנָּה – באַף זִבְחֵי שַׁלְמֵי צִבּוּר ו] לְזִכְרֵי כְהוּנָּה. אֲמַר לֵיהּ אַבַּיֵי: אִי ז] הָכִי, גַּבֵּי אֵיל נָזִיר, דִּכְתִיב: °"וְהִקְרִיב אֶת קָרְבָּנוֹ לַה' כֶּבֶשׂ בֶּן שְׁנָתוֹ תָמִים אֶחָד לְעוֹלָה וְכַבְשָׂה אַחַת בַּת שְׁנָתָהּ ח] [תְּמִימָה] לְחַטָּאת וְאַיִל אֶחָד [תָּמִים] לִשְׁלָמִים", הָכִי נַמִי נֵימָא ט] דְּהִקִּישׁ הַכָּתוּב לְחַטָּאת: מַה חַטָּאת אֵינָהּ נֶאֱכֶלֶת אֶלָּא לְזִכְרֵי כְהוּנָּה – אַף אֵיל נָזִיר נַמִי אֵינוֹ נֶאֱכָל אֶלָּא לְזִכְרֵי כְהוּנָּה? הָכִי הָשְׁתָּא?! הָתָם, כֵּיוָן דִּכְתִיב: °"וְלָקַח הַכֹּהֵן אֶת הַזְּרוֹעַ בְּשֵׁלָה מִן הָאַיִל" – גמִכְּלָל דְּכוּלֵּיהּ בְּעָלִים אָכְלִי לֵיהּ. דזְרוֹעַ בְּשֵׁלָה מִיהָא לָא י] לִיתְאֲכִיל אֶלָּא לְזִכְרֵי כְהוּנָּה! קַשְׁיָא. וְאִיבָּעֵית אֵימָא: יא] קָדְשֵׁי אִקְרִי, קָדְשֵׁי קָדָשִׁים לָא יב] אִיקְרוּ. וְאֶלָּא לְמַאי הִלְכְתָא אִיתַּקַּשׁ? אָמַר *רָבָא: *השֶׁאִם גִּלַּח עַל אֶחָד יג] מִשְּׁלָשְׁתָּן – יָצָא.§

מתני' הַתּוֹדָה וְאֵיל נָזִיר קָדָשִׁים קַלִּים; שְׁחִיטָתָן ובְּכָל מָקוֹם בָּעֲזָרָה, זוְדָמָן טָעוּן שְׁתֵּי מַתָּנוֹת שֶׁהֵן אַרְבַּע, חוְנֶאֱכָלִין בְּכָל הָעִיר, לְכָל אָדָם, בְּכָל מַאֲכָל, לְיוֹם וְלַיְלָה עַד חֲצוֹת. הַמּוּרָם מֵהֶם כַּיּוֹצֵא בָהֶן, אֶלָּא טשֶׁהַמּוּרָם נֶאֱכָל לַכֹּהֲנִים, לִנְשֵׁיהֶם וְלִבְנֵיהֶם וּלְעַבְדֵיהֶם.§

גמ' ת"ר: יד] °"אֶת חֲזֵה הַתְּנוּפָה וְאֵת שׁוֹק הַתְּרוּמָה תֹּאכְלוּ בְּמָקוֹם טָהוֹר", אָמַר רַבִּי נְחֶמְיָה: וְכִי רִאשׁוֹנִים בְּטוּמְאָה אֲכָלוּם? אֶלָּא, טָהוֹר מִכְּלָל שֶׁהוּא טָמֵא, טָהוֹר – מִטּוּמְאַת מְצוֹרָע, וְטָמֵא – מִטּוּמְאַת זָב, וְאֵיזֶה זֶה – יזֶה מַחֲנֵה יִשְׂרָאֵל. וְאֵימָא: טָהוֹר – מִטּוּמְאַת זָב, וְטָמֵא – מִטּוּמְאַת מֵת, וְאֵיזֶה זֶה – זֶה מַחֲנֵה לְוִיָּה! אָמַר אַבַּיֵי: אָמַר קְרָא °"וַאֲכַלְתֶּם אוֹתָהּ בְּמָקוֹם קָדוֹשׁ" – אוֹתָהּ בְּמָקוֹם קָדוֹשׁ, וְלֹא אַחֶרֶת בְּמָקוֹם קָדוֹשׁ, אַפְּקָהּ טו] לְמַחֲנֵה לְוִיָּה; הֲדַר כְּתִיב: "בְּמָקוֹם טָהוֹר" – אַפְּקָהּ לְמַחֲנֵה יִשְׂרָאֵל. רָבָא אָמַר: אוֹתָהּ בְּמָקוֹם קָדוֹשׁ וְלֹא אַחֶרֶת בְּמָקוֹם קָדוֹשׁ – אַפְּקָהּ לְגַמְרֵי; הֲדַר כְּתַב טז] רַחֲמָנָא: "תֹּאכְלוּ בְּמָקוֹם טָהוֹר" – עַיְּילָא לְמַחֲנֵה יִשְׂרָאֵל. וְאֵימָא: עַיְּילָא לְמַחֲנֵה לְוִיָּה! לַחֲדָא מְעַיְּילִינַן, לְתַרְתֵּי לָא מְעַיְּילִינַן. אִי הָכִי, אַפּוּקֵי נַמִי, *לַחֲדָא מַפְּקִינַן, מִתַּרְתֵּי לָא מַפְּקִינַן! וְעוֹד, °"לֹא תוּכַל לֶאֱכוֹל בִּשְׁעָרֶיךָ" כְּתִיב! אֶלָּא, מְחַוַּורְתָּא כְּדַאֲבַיֵי.§

מתני' *שְׁלָמִים קָדָשִׁים קַלִּים; שְׁחִיטָתָן בְּכָל מָקוֹם בָּעֲזָרָה, וְדָמָן טָעוּן שְׁתֵּי מַתָּנוֹת שֶׁהֵן אַרְבַּע, וְנֶאֱכָלִין בְּכָל הָעִיר, לְכָל אָדָם, בְּכָל מַאֲכָל, לִשְׁנֵי יָמִים וְלַיְלָה אֶחָד. הַמּוּרָם מֵהֶם כַּיּוֹצֵא בָהֶם, אֶלָּא שֶׁהַמּוּרָם נֶאֱכָל לַכֹּהֲנִים, לִנְשֵׁיהֶם וְלִבְנֵיהֶם וּלְעַבְדֵיהֶם.§

גמ' ת"ר: °"וּשְׁחָטוֹ פֶּתַח אֹהֶל מוֹעֵד", °"וְשָׁחַט אוֹתוֹ לִפְנֵי אֹהֶל מוֹעֵד" – לְהַכְשִׁיר אֶת כָּל הָרוּחוֹת •בְּקָדָשִׁים קַלִּים. יז] ק"ו לַצָּפוֹן: וּמַה קָּדְשֵׁי קָדָשִׁים שֶׁלֹּא הוּכְשְׁרוּ בְּכָל הָרוּחוֹת – הוּכְשְׁרוּ בַּצָּפוֹן, קָדָשִׁים קַלִּים שֶׁהוּכְשְׁרוּ בְּכָל הָרוּחוֹת – אֵינוֹ דִּין שֶׁהוּכְשְׁרוּ בַּצָּפוֹן? רַבִּי אֱלִיעֶזֶר אוֹמֵר: לֹא יח] נֶאֱמַר הַכָּתוּב אֶלָּא לְהַכְשִׁיר צָפוֹן. שֶׁיָּכוֹל, וַהֲלֹא דִּין הוּא: וּמַה קָּדָשִׁים קַלִּים שֶׁהוּכְשְׁרוּ בְּכָל הָרוּחוֹת – לֹא הוּכְשַׁר מְקוֹמָן אֵצֶל קָדְשֵׁי קָדָשִׁים, קָדְשֵׁי קָדָשִׁים שֶׁלֹּא הוּכְשְׁרוּ אֶלָּא בַּצָּפוֹן – אֵינוֹ דִּין שֶׁלֹּא הוּכְשַׁר מְקוֹמָן אֵצֶל קָדָשִׁים קַלִּים? ת"ל: יט] "אֹהֶל מוֹעֵד".

בְּמַאי

רש"י

גמ' וַעֲשִׂיתֶם שְׂעִיר עִזִּים וגו'. גַּבֵּי שְׁתֵּי הַלֶּחֶם וְכִבְשֵׂי עֲצֶרֶת כ] כְּתִיב, וְסֵיפֵיהּ דִּקְרָא "וּשְׁנֵי כְבָשִׂים" וגו'. וְעַל זִבְחֵי שַׁלְמֵיכֶם וגו'. עַל כָּרְחָךְ בְּשַׁלְמֵי צִבּוּר כְּתִיב, שֶׁאֵין קָרְבַּן יָחִיד טָעוּן כְּלֵי שִׁיר, שֶׁאֵין אוֹמְרִים שִׁיר עַל קָרְבַּן יָחִיד, כִּדְאָמַר בַּעֲרָכִין (דף י:). קָדְשֵׁי קָדָשִׁים. כא] נִפְסָלִים בִּטְבוּל יוֹם וּבְיוֹצֵא (וּבְלִינָה). הֶיקֵּשָׁא קַמָּא. דְּאִיתַּקַּשׁ לְחַטָּאת. ה"ג מַה חַטָּאת כב] כו'. כֵּיוָן דִּכְתִיב וְלָקַח הַכֹּהֵן אֶת הַזְּרוֹעַ. סֵיפֵיהּ דִּקְרָא: "קֹדֶשׁ הוּא לַכֹּהֵן" – ש"מ הַשְּׁאָר לַבְּעָלִים כג]. *קֹדֶשׁ אִיקְּרִי. זְרוֹעַ בְּשֵׁלָה. וּמִדְּלָא כְּתִיב "קָדְשֵׁי קָדָשִׁים" ש"מ לָא אִיתְקוּשׁ לְחַטָּאת לְהָכִי דְּתֶיהֱוֵי (א) עֲלֵי' *חוּמְרָא דְּקֹדֶשׁ קָדָשִׁים, דִּבְהֶדְיָא מְעַטֵּיהּ כד] מִדִּכְתִיב "קֹדֶשׁ" וְלָא כְּתִיב קָדָשִׁים. וְגַבֵּי שַׁלְמֵי צִבּוּר, אַע"ג דִּכְתִיב בְּהוּ כה] נַמִי "קֹדֶשׁ יִהְיוּ לַה' לַכֹּהֵן" (ויקרא כג) וְלָא כְּתִיב "קָדְשֵׁי קָדָשִׁים", כֵּיוָן דִּכְתִיב "לַה'" – לָאו לְמַעוּטֵיהּ כו] הוּא מֵהֶיקֵּשָׁא, דְּאִיכָּא לְמֵימַר כְּמַאן דִּכְתִיב קָדְשֵׁי קָדָשִׁים דָּמֵי. אֶלָּא לְמַאי הִלְכְתָא אִיתַּקַּשׁ. אֵיל נָזִיר לְחַטָּאת. שֶׁאִם גִּילַּח עַל אַחַת מִשְּׁלָשְׁתָּן יָצָא. וְחַטָּאת הוּא דְּיָלְפָא מִשְּׁלָמִים: מָה אֵיל נָזִיר אִם הֱבִיאוֹ יְחִידִי בְּלֹא חַטָּאת וְעוֹלָה יָצָא, דִּכְתִיב (במדבר ו): "וְאַחַר יִשְׁתֶּה הַנָּזִיר יָיִן", וְאָמַר מַר בְּסִיפְרֵי: כז] אַחַר מַעֲשֶׂה יְחִידִי, וְהַיְינוּ שְׁלָמִים. שֶׁעִיקַּר תִּגְלַחְתּוֹ שֶׁל נָזִיר תְּלוּיָה בִּשְׁלָמָיו, שֶׁהֲרֵי כח] הוּזְקְקוּ לוֹ לְשַׁלֵּחַ שְׂעָרוֹ תַּחַת הַדּוּד, כִּדִכְתִיב (שם): "עַל הָאֵשׁ אֲשֶׁר תַּחַת זֶבַח הַשְּׁלָמִים", וְתַנְיָא בְּסִיפְרֵי: כט] "וְגִלַּח הַנָּזִיר פֶּתַח אֹהֶל מוֹעֵד" – בִּשְׁלָמִים הַכָּתוּב מְדַבֵּר, כְּלוֹמַר, גִּילּוּחוֹ שֶׁל נָזִיר ע"י דָּבָר שֶׁנֶּאֱמַר בּוֹ "וְשָׁחַט פֶּתַח אֹהֶל מוֹעֵד", וְהַיְינוּ שְׁלָמִים בְּוַיִּקְרָא. אוֹ אֵינוֹ אֶלָּא כְּמַשְׁמָעוֹ, שֶׁיְּגַלֵּחַ פֶּתַח אֹהֶל מוֹעֵד מַמָּשׁ! אִם אָמַרְתָּ כֵּן דֶּרֶךְ בִּזָּיוֹן כו'. **מתני'** קָדָשִׁים קַלִּים. אֵין ל] (לְךָ) מוֹעֲלִין בָּהֶן. בְּכָל מָקוֹם. אֵין טְעוּנִין צָפוֹן. וְנֶאֱכָלִין בְּכָל הָעִיר. בַּגְּמָ' מְפָרֵשׁ. לְכָל אָדָם. לְזָרִים. לְיוֹם וְלַיְלָה. בְּתוֹדָה כְּתִיב: "בְּיוֹם קָרְבָּנוֹ יֵאָכֵל לֹא יַנִּיחַ מִמֶּנּוּ עַד בֹּקֶר", וְתַנְיָא: "תּוֹדַת שְׁלָמָיו" – לְרַבּוֹת שַׁלְמֵי נָזִיר. הַמּוּרָם מֵהֶן. מִן הַתּוֹדָה – *חָזֶה וְשׁוֹק כִּשְׁאָר שְׁלָמִים, דְּהָא אִיתַּקַּשׁ לִשְׁלָמִים כְּדַאֲמָרַן: "זֶבַח הַשְּׁלָמִים אִם עַל תּוֹדָה" (ויקרא ז), וְאַרְבַּע חַלּוֹת מִד' מִינִין שֶׁבָּהּ, כִּדִכְתִיב: "אֶחָד מִכָּל קָרְבָּן וגו' לַכֹּהֵן הַזּוֹרֵק" וגו' (שם). וּמוּרָם מֵאֵיל נָזִיר – זְרוֹעַ בְּשֵׁלָה, וְחָזֶה וְשׁוֹק נַמִי בֵּיהּ כְּתִיבִי, וְחַלַּת מַצָּה אַחַת וּרְקִיק מַצָּה אֶחָד. כַּיּוֹצֵא בָּהֶן – וְנֶאֱכָלִין בְּכָל הָעִיר לְיוֹם וְלַיְלָה. אֶלָּא. שֶׁאֵינוֹ לַבְּעָלִים אֶלָּא לַכֹּהֲנִים. וְלִנְשֵׁיהֶם. כִּדִכְתִיב (ויקרא י): "וְאֵת חֲזֵה הַתְּנוּפָה וגו' אַתָּה וּבָנֶיךָ וּבְנוֹתֶיךָ". **גמ'** תֹּאכְלוּ בְּמָקוֹם טָהוֹר. בְּפָרָשַׁת "וַיְהִי בַּיּוֹם הַשְּׁמִינִי" כְּתִיב. וְכִי הָרִאשׁוֹנִים בְּטוּמְאָה אֲכָלוּם. קָרְבָּנוֹת הָרִאשׁוֹנִים שֶׁנֶּאֶמְרוּ תְּחִילָּה בָּעִנְיָן, כְּגוֹן שְׂעִירִים וּמִנְחָה. טָהוֹר מִכְּלָל שֶׁהוּא טָמֵא. מִדְּלָא כְּתִיב "קֹדֶשׁ" ש"מ טָהוֹר בְּמִקְצָת קָאָמַר וְלָא מִן הַכֹּל. הָא כֵּיצַד? בַּמַּחֲנֶה הַטָּהוֹר מִטּוּמְאַת מְצוֹרָע – שֶׁאֵין מְצוֹרָע נִכְנָס לוֹ, וְטָמֵא מִטּוּמְאַת זָב – שֶׁהַזָּבִין נִכְנָסִין שָׁם. וְאֵיזֶה זֶה – זֶה מַחֲנֵה יִשְׂרָאֵל בַּמִּדְבָּר, כָּל דֶּגֶל בְּתוֹךְ אֲסִיפַת דִּגְלוֹ, וּבֵית עוֹלָמִים – תּוֹךְ יְרוּשָׁלַיִם. דְּאָמְרִינַן בִּפְסָחִים (דף סז.): מְצוֹרָע מִשְׁתַּלֵּחַ חוּץ לְג' מַחֲנוֹת. זָב נִכְנָס לְמַחֲנֵה יִשְׂרָאֵל אֲבָל לֹא לְמַחֲנֵה לְוִיָּה, וְהוּא בַּמִּדְבָּר חֲנִיַּית הַלְוִיִּם סָבִיב לְמִשְׁכַּן הָעֵדוּת, בְּבֵית עוֹלָמִים הַר הַבַּיִת. וּטְמֵא מֵת מוּתָּר לִיכָּנֵס בְּמַחֲנֵה לְוִיָּה, שֶׁנֶּאֱמַר: "וַיִּקַּח מֹשֶׁה אֶת עַצְמוֹת יוֹסֵף עִמּוֹ" (שמות יג), עִמּוֹ בִּמְחִיצָּתוֹ. אוֹתָהּ. בְּמִנְחָה כְּתִיב בְּהַהוּא עִנְיָנָא. וְאֵין אַחֶרֶת. וְאֵין לַחְמֵי תוֹדָה בְּמָקוֹם קָדוֹשׁ. אַפְּקָהּ. מִמַּחֲנֵה שְׁכִינָה שֶׁקְּרֵבָה בְּתוֹכָהּ, לְמַחֲנֵה לְוִיָּה. הֲדַר כְּתִיב "בְּמָקוֹם טָהוֹר" לְהָקֵל וְלוֹמַר טָהֳרָה כָּל דְּהוּ, לא] דְּלָא אִיצְטְרִיךְ, פְּשִׁיטָא דִּבְטוּמְאָה מַמָּשׁ לָא אָכְלֵי לָהּ. אַפְּקָהּ לְגַמְרֵי. וַאֲפִי' חוּץ לַחוֹמָה (ב) כְּמַשְׁמָע, (בִּשְׁעָרֶיךָ) חוּץ לִירוּשָׁלַיִם. וְעוֹד לֹא תוּכַל לֶאֱכוֹל בִּשְׁעָרֶיךָ כְּתִיב. וְהֵיכִי אָמְרִינַן לב] אַפְּקֵיהּ לְגַמְרֵי? **מתני'** בְּכָל מָקוֹם. אַף בַּדָּרוֹם. וּבַגְּמָרָא יָלֵיף לָהּ. בְּכָל הָעִיר. כְּדַאֲמָרַן לְעֵיל בְּחָזֶה וְשׁוֹק דְּשַׁלְמֵי יוֹם שְׁמִינִי. לִשְׁנֵי יָמִים וְלַיְלָה אֶחָד. דְּהָכִי כְּתִיב בְּהוּ. וּבַגְּמָרָא מַיְיתֵי לָהּ. **גמ'** וּשְׁחָטוֹ כו'. לג] כָּל שָׁלֹשׁ פָּרָשִׁיּוֹת בִּשְׁלָמִים: חֲדָא בְּבֶן בָּקָר, וַחֲדָא לד] בְּבֶן כֶּשֶׂב, וַחֲדָא בְּעֵז. בְּקַמַּיְיתָא כְּתִיב: "וּשְׁחָטוֹ פֶּתַח אֹהֶל מוֹעֵד", וּבְתַרְתֵּי כְּתִיב "לִפְנֵי אֹהֶל מוֹעֵד". לְהַכְשִׁיר לה] כָּל הָרוּחוֹת שֶׁבָּעֲזָרָה. ד"לִפְנֵי" מַשְׁמַע כָּל שֶׁלִּפְנֵי הַהֵיכָל וְשֶׁבַּצְּדָדִין. לְקַמֵּיהּ יָלֵיף לו] וּמְפָרֵשׁ לָהּ. קַל וָחוֹמֶר לַצָּפוֹן. לְיֶרֶךְ מִזְבֵּחַ צְפוֹנִי הַקָּבוּעַ לְעוֹלָה וּלְקָדְשֵׁי קָדָשִׁים. וּמִשּׁוּם פְּלוּגְתָּא דִּפְלִיג רַבִּי אֱלִיעֶזֶר עֲלָהּ וְאָמַר: צָפוֹן אִיצְטְרִיךְ קְרָא בְּהֶדְיָא לְרַבּוּיֵי לִשְׁחִיטַת קָדָשִׁים קַלִּים, אִיצְטְרִיךְ לְת"ק לְמֵימַר הַאי קַל וָחוֹמֶר לַצָּפוֹן. לז] לֹא בָא אֶחָד מִן הַכְּתוּבִין הַלָּלוּ אֶלָּא לְהַכְשִׁיר צָפוֹן. לח] לְקַמֵּיהּ מְפָרֵשׁ מַאי פְּלוּגְתַּיְיהוּ. שֶׁיָּכוֹל וַהֲלֹא דִּין הוּא. שֶׁלֹּא יְהֵא צָפוֹן בִּכְלַל "לִפְנֵי אֹהֶל מוֹעֵד" לְהַכְשִׁירוֹ לִשְׁחִיטַת שְׁלָמִים. שְׁלֹשָׁה הָרוּחוֹת הַכְּשֵׁירוֹת לָהֶם לֹא הוּכְשְׁרוּ לִשְׁחִיטַת קָדְשֵׁי קָדָשִׁים לט]. לֹא הוּכְשַׁר מְקוֹמָן.

בְּמַאי

תוספות

זבחי שלמי צבור מנא לן. לעיל (דף נ. ד"ה לא) פירשנו אמאי לא אתי בבנין אב. **מה** חטאת בצפון כו'. ולענין מתנות ליכא מ] לאקשויי לחטאת, כדדרשינן לעיל פרק קמא (דף י:): אותה דמה למעלה ואין אחרת דמה למעלה. **מה** עולה בצפון. וא"ת: עיכובא מנא לן? דבעולה לא ידעינן עיכובא אלא מק"ו דחטאת, כדקאמר רב אדא בר אהבה לעיל (דף מח:) שלא יהא טפל חמור מן העיקר, ודבר הלמד בקל וחומר אינו חוזר ומלמד בהיקש (לעיל נ:). אם לא נאמר •דס"ל כרב פפא מא]. **אלא** היקשא קמא למאי אתא. לא מצי למימר לענין ארבע מתנות על ארבע קרנות כדפרי'. מב] וכי תימא: לענין פיסוק מתנות, דנותן וחוזר ונותן, כדקאמר רבי ישמעאל בעולה לעיל מג] (דף נג:)! כיון דאיתקש נמי לעולה – אין לנו לשנות מעולה. **מה** חטאת אינה נאכלת אלא לזכרי כהונה. תימה: דלקמן פ' "דם חטאת" (דף צז:) ופ' "התודה" (מנחות דף פג:) נפקא לן מקרא *אחרינא. וא"ת: כיון דאיתקש לחטאת, אם כן יפסלו שלא לשמה כחטאת! ולרבנן דדרשי בפ"ק (לעיל דף י:) "אותה" מד] ניחא, אבל לר' אליעזר קשה! וצריך לדקדק בפ' "התכלת" (מנחות דף מח:) דגמר שלמי חובה משלמי נדבה ולא מקשינן לחטאת. **שאם** גלח על אחת משלשתן יצא. תימה דצריך קרא בנזיר מה] *המשלח שערו תחת הדוד של חטאת, תיפוק לי מהך היקשא.

שלמים

עין משפט נר מצוה

מט א מיי' פ"ה מהל' מעה"ק הל' ג:
נ ב מיי' שם פ"י הל' ג:
נא ג ד מיי' פ"ט שם הל' יא:
נב ה מיי' פ"ח מהל' נזיר הלכה ב:
נג ו מיי' פ"ה מהל' מעה"ק הלכה ב:
נד ז מיי' שם הל' ו:
נה ח מיי' פ"י שם הלכה ה:
נו ט מיי' שם הל' ד:
נז י מיי' שם הלכה ה:

[ועי' תוס' לקמן נז: ד"ה מה מנחה]

מסורת הש"ס

קדשי איקרי נ"ק
[לעיל מט: וש"נ]
[ערכין יא: ע"ש בתוס']
כל תומרא נ"ק
נ"א רבינא
[נזיר כח: מה. וש"נ]
נ"א חזה ושוק שניתן לכהנים כשאר שלמים דהא איתקש תודה לשלמים כדאמרן זאת תורת זבח השלמים כו'
*מנחות ג.

שיטה מקובצת

א] דתני רבא בר רב חנן: ב] לחטאת הקישו הכתוב לחטאת מה חטאת בצפון אף זבחי שלמי: ג] מעולה וכי דבר: ד] אלא אמר רבא מדרתני: ה] בצפון ואלא היקשא קמא למה לי אמר רבא מה חטאת כו' והשאר נמחק: ו] צבור אינם נאכלין אלא לזכרי כהונה: ז] עי' בהשמטות בסוף המסכת: ח] שנתה תמימה לחטאת ואיל אחד תמים: ט] נימא דהיקשו הכתוב: י] לא ניתכול אות ל' ואות א' ל"ש: יא] קדשי איקרי. פ"ה גבי שלמי צבור כיון דכתיב לה' כמאן דכתיב קדש קדשים דמי וקשה א"כ למה לי היקשא דשלמי צבור לעולה לומר דהוי קדשי קדשים תיפוק ליה משום דכתיב לה' ותירץ מורי דלא מהני לה' אלא לומר דלא אתא קודש ומפיק להו מהיקשא ולעשותו קדשי קדשים על ידי היקשא. תו' מהר"פ: יב] לא איקרי ואלא כו' אמר רבינא תיבת רבא ל"ש: יג] משלשתן. (מנחות דף ס ע"א) ועיקר (המשנה) [במשנה] (נזיר דף מה ע"א): יד] ת"ר ואת חזה: טו] אפקה ממחנה שכינה למחנה: טז] כתב במקום טהור ותיבות רחמנא תאכלו נמחק: יז] קלים וק"ו: יח] לא בא הכתוב תיבת נאמר נמחק: יט] לומר ושחטו פתח אהל מועד לפני אהל מועד: כ] כתוב וסיפא דקרא ושני כבשים וגו' לזבח שלמים הס"ד: כא] ליפסל בטבול יום: כב] חטאת [אינה] נאכלת כו': כג] לבעלים ואקשינן זרוע בשלה לא יאכל אלא לזכרי כהונה ואנן תנן המורם מהן כיוצא בהן אלא כו' קשיא הס"ד ומה"ד קדש איקרו זרוע בשלה קדש בלחוד איקרו ומדלא כתיב קדש קדשים ש"מ דלא איתקש לחטאת: כד] מעטיה קרא: כה] תיבת נמי נמחק: כו] למעוטי מהיקשא הוא: כז] בספרי (נזיר דף מו ע"א): כח] שהרי הזקיקו לו להניפם ולשלח שערו: כט] בסיפרי (נזיר דף מה ע"א):

הגהות הב"ח

(א) רש"י ד"ה קדש וכו' דתיהוי לה תומרא: (ב) ד"ה אפקה לגמרי וכו' כמשמע בס"ד ואח"כ מ"ה ועוד לא תוכל לאכול בשעריך כתיב ובשעריך חוץ לירושלים והיכי אמרי':

גליון הש"ס

גמ' וכי חטאת מהיכן למדה. ע"ל דף נ ע"ב תד"ה ולאו: שם בקדשים קלים ק"ו לצפון. ע"ל דף נח ע"א תוד"ה כולה: תום' ד"ה מה עולה וכו' דס"ל כרב פפא. לעיל דף נ ע"ב ועי' תוס' שם ד"ה תלת:

ל] תיבת לך נמחק: לא] דהו דאי להחמיר לא איצטריך: לב] אמרי' אפקה: לג] תיבת כל נמחק: לד] וחדא בכשב ותיבת בבן נמחק: לה] להכשיר את כל: לו] יליף לה ומפרש הס"ד: לז] לצפון הס"ד ומה"ד לא בא הכתוב אלא להכשיר צפון. לא בא כו': לח] צפון ולקמיה: לט] קדשים ת"ל אהל מועד כו' ות"ק לית ליה קו"ח דר' אליעזר דמה לקדשי קדשים שהם חמורים ולכך לא הוכשרו בהן שאר הרוחות: מ] לאקושי: מא] פאה דאמר חוזר ומלמד בהיקש וללישנא דהעולה במקומה תהא ניחא דעיכוב בגופיה כתיב והואיל ואיתקש בהיקש גמור איתקש אף לעיכובא ושאני לעיל דלא כתיב אלא ושחט אותה תהא אלא למצוה. מהר"פ: מב] תיבות וכי תימא נמחק: מג] לעיל דכיון דאיתקש: מד] אותה דחטאת למעט כל שאר קדשים מפסול שלא לשמו ניחא ולר"א דלא דריש אותה אה"נ דסבר דשלמי צבור פסולין שלא לשמן וה"נ איכא תנא בפ' התכלת דפסיל שלמי צבור שלא לשמן והשתא מוקמינן ליה כר"א. מהר"פ: מה] בנזיר דמשלח:

בְּמַאי קָא מִיפַּלְגִי? תַּנָּא קַמָּא סָבַר: תְּלָתָא קְרָאֵי כְּתִיבִי, חַד – לְגוּפֵיהּ, דְּנִיבְעֵי פֶּתַח אֹהֶל מוֹעֵד, וְחַד – לְהַכְשִׁיר צְדָדִין, א] וְחַד – לִפְסוֹל צִידֵּי צְדָדִין; וְצָפוֹן לָא אִיצְטְרִיךְ קְרָא. וְר׳ אֱלִיעֶזֶר סָבַר: חַד – לְגוּפֵיהּ, דְּנִיבְעֵי פֶּתַח אֹהֶל מוֹעֵד, וְחַד – לְהַכְשִׁיר צָפוֹן, וְחַד – לְהַכְשִׁיר צְדָדִין; וְצִידֵּי צְדָדִין לָא אִיצְטְרִיךְ קְרָא. מַאי שְׁנָא הָכָא ב] דִּכְתִיב: "פֶּתַח אֹהֶל מוֹעֵד", וּמַאי שְׁנָא הָתָם דִּכְתִיב: "לִפְנֵי אֹהֶל מוֹעֵד"? קמ"ל כִּדְרַב יְהוּדָה אָמַר שְׁמוּאֵל. *דְּאָמַר רַב יְהוּדָה אָמַר שְׁמוּאֵל: אשְׁלָמִים שֶׁשְּׁחָטָן קוֹדֶם שֶׁיִּפָּתְחוּ דַּלְתוֹת הַהֵיכָל – פְּסוּלִין, שֶׁנֶּאֱמַר: °"וּשְׁחָטוֹ פֶּתַח אֹהֶל מוֹעֵד" – בִּזְמַן שֶׁהוּא פָּתוּחַ, וְלֹא בִּזְמַן שֶׁהוּא נָעוּל. ג] אִיתְּמַר נַמִי, אָמַר מָר עוּקְבָא בַּר חָמָא אָמַר רַבִּי יוֹסֵי בְּרַבִּי חֲנִינָא: שְׁלָמִים שֶׁשְּׁחָטָן קוֹדֶם שֶׁיִּפָּתְחוּ דַּלְתוֹת הַהֵיכָל – פְּסוּלִין, שֶׁנֶּאֱמַר: "וּשְׁחָטוֹ פֶּתַח אֹהֶל מוֹעֵד" – בִּזְמַן ד] שֶׁפֶּתַח הַהֵיכָל פָּתוּחַ, וְלֹא בִּזְמַן שֶׁהוּא נָעוּל. בְּמַעֲרָבָא מַתְנֵי הָכִי, אָמַר רַב ה] יַעֲקֹב בַּר אַחָא אָמַר רַב אַשִׁי: שְׁלָמִים שֶׁשְּׁחָטָן קוֹדֶם שֶׁיִּפָּתְחוּ דַּלְתוֹת הַהֵיכָל – פְּסוּלִים. ו] *וּבַמִּשְׁכָּן – קוֹדֶם שֶׁיַּעֲמִידוּ לְוִיִּם אֶת הַמִּשְׁכָּן, וּלְאַחַר שֶׁיְּפָרְקוּ לְוִיִּם אֶת הַמִּשְׁכָּן – פְּסוּלִים. פְּשִׁיטָא: במוּגָף – כְּנָעוּל דָּמֵי, וִילוֹן מַאי? א"ר זֵירָא: ז] גהוּא עַצְמוֹ אֵין נַעֲשֶׂה אֶלָּא כְּפֶתַח ח] פָּתוּחַ. גּוֹבְהָהּ מַאי? ת"ש, דְּתַנְיָא, *ר׳ יוֹסֵי בְּר׳ יְהוּדָה אוֹמֵר: שְׁנֵי פִשְׁפָּשִׁין הָיוּ בְּבֵית הַחֲלִיפוֹת ט] וְגוֹבְהָן שְׁמוֹנֶה, כְּדֵי לְהַכְשִׁיר אֶת הָעֲזָרָה כּוּלָּהּ לַאֲכִילַת קָדְשֵׁי קָדָשִׁים, וְלִשְׁחִיטַת קָדָשִׁים קַלִּים; מַאי לָאו דְּאִיכָּא קַמַּיְיהוּ[א] שְׁמוֹנָה? לָא, י] דְּגָבְהוּ נִינְהוּ שְׁמוֹנָה. מֵיתִיבִי: * דכָּל הַשְּׁעָרִים שֶׁהָיוּ שָׁם, גּוֹבְהָן עֶשְׂרִים אַמָּה וְרׇחְבָּן עֶשֶׂר אַמָּה! פִּשְׁפָּשִׁין שָׁאנֵי. וְהָאִיכָּא צְדָדִין! יא] דְּמְעַיֵּיל לְהוּ בְּקֶרֶן זָוִית. אֲחוֹרֵי בֵּית הַכַּפּוֹרֶת מַאי? תָּא שְׁמַע, דְּאָמַר רָמִי בַּר רַב יְהוּדָה אָמַר רַב: לוּל קָטָן הָיָה אֲחוֹרֵי בֵּית הַכַּפּוֹרֶת יב] גָּבוֹהַּ שְׁמוֹנֶה אַמּוֹת, כְּדֵי לְהַכְשִׁיר אֶת הָעֲזָרָה לַאֲכִילַת קָדְשֵׁי קָדָשִׁים וְלִשְׁחִיטַת קָדָשִׁים קַלִּים. יג] וְהַיְינוּ דִּכְתִי׳: °"שְׁנַיִם לַפַּרְבָּר". *מַאי "לַפַּרְבָּר"? אָמַר רַבָּה בַּר רַב שֵׁילָא: כְּמַאן דְּאָמַר: "כְּלַפֵּי יד] בַּר". א"ר יְהוּדָה אָמַר שְׁמוּאֵל: אֵין חַיָּיבִין מִשּׁוּם טוּמְאָה אֶלָּא עַל

אוֹרֶךְ

תורה אור: ויקרא ג – דה"א כו

רש"י

בְּמַאי קָמִיפַּלְגִי. מַאי קָמְרַבֵּי ת"ק בְּחַד מֵהָנָךְ קְרָאֵי דְּמַיְיתֵי לָפוֹן מִק"ו, דַּאֲתָא רַבִּי אֱלִיעֶזֶר לְמֵימַר: לָא תְּרַבְּיֵיהּ מִינֵּיהּ, דִּקְרָא לַצָּפוֹן אִיצְטְרִיךְ? דְּנִיבָּעֵי פֶּתַח אֹהֶל מוֹעֵד. כִּדְאָמְרִי׳ לְקַמָּן, שֶׁאִם אֵין שָׁם פֶּתַח, טו] [כְּגוֹן] קוֹדֶם שֶׁיִּפָּתְחוּ הַדְּלָתוֹת, וְקוֹדֶם שֶׁיַּעֲמִידוּ הַלְוִיִּם אֶת הַמִּשְׁכָּן, וּלְאַחַר שֶׁפֵּירְקוּהוּ – לֹא הָיָה שׁוֹחֵט. וְחַד לְהַכְשִׁיר צְדָדִין. כָּל רוֹחַב הָעֲזָרָה. דְּלָא תֵּימָא כְּנֶגֶד הַפֶּתַח דַּוְקָא, לְהָכִי הֲדַר כְּתַב "לִפְנֵי", וְלָא כְּתִיב פֶּתַח. וְכָל הָאֲוִיר בִּכְלַל "לִפְנֵי", דְּלָא כְּתִיב כְּנֶגֶד. וְחַד לִפְסוֹל צִידֵּי צְדָדִין. כְּגוֹן לְשָׁכוֹת, וַאֲפִילּוּ תּוֹכָן קֹדֶשׁ פְּסוּלוֹת לִשְׁחִיטָה, כִּדְלְקַמָּן. דְּלָא תֵּימָא: מִדְּ"פֶתַח" לָאו דַּוְקָא – "לִפְנֵי" נַמִי לָאו דַּוְקָא, אֶלָּא שֶׁיְּהֵא אֹהֶל טז] נָטוּי. לְהָכִי הֲדַר כְּתִיב "לִפְנֵי", לְמֵימְרָא דְּדַוְקָא הוּא, וְלֹא לְשָׁכוֹת. יז] צָפוֹן לָא אִיצְטְרִיךְ קְרָא. דְּמִק"ו קָאָתֵי. וְחַד לְהַכְשִׁיר צָפוֹן. דְּק"ו מְעוּטֵי מְמַעִיט לֵיהּ לְאִידָךְ גִּיסָא. וְק"ו דְּרַבָּנַן לָא דָּרֵישׁ, דְּאִיכָּא לְמֵימַר: *לְהַאי קָבַע לָפוֹן וּלְהַאי שְׁאָר רוּחוֹת, דְּמַאי קְדוּשָּׁתֵיהּ דְּלָפוֹן מִדָּרוֹם? אֶלָּא דִּקְבִיעַת מָקוֹם בְּעָלְמָא הוּא. וְצִידֵּי צְדָדִין. לִפְסוֹל לָא אִיצְטְרִיךְ קְרָא (א) אַחֲרִינָא יח]. [ב] לִפְנֵי. כְּתִיב בִּקְרָא קַמָּא. בִּזְמַן שֶׁהוּא פָּתוּחַ. לְשׁוֹן "פֶּתַח" אֵינוֹ אֶלָּא הֶחָלָל, וְהַפּוֹתֵחַ וְהַנּוֹעֵל קָרוּי "דֶּלֶת". מוּגָּף. סָגוּר וְלֹא נָעוּל, כְּמוֹ הַגָּפַת דְּלָתוֹת (ערכין דף יא:). וִילוֹן. פָּרוּשׂ כְּנֶגֶד הַפֶּתַח, מִי הָוֵי כְּנָעוּל אוֹ לָא? הוּא עַצְמוֹ. וִילוֹן עַצְמוֹ אֵינוֹ חָשׁוּב אֶלָּא כְּפֶתַח פָּתוּחַ, דְּלִצְנִיעוּתָא בְּעָלְמָא עָבֵיד. גּוֹבְהָהּ. כְּגוֹן תֵּל אוֹ עֵץ מוּטָּל כְּנֶגֶד הַפֶּתַח מַפְסִיק בֵּין פֶּתַח לִשְׁחִיטָה [וְהַפֶּתַח פָּתוּחַ, מַאי?]. שְׁנֵי פִשְׁפָּשִׁין הָיוּ בְּבֵית הַחֲלִיפוֹת. (עוֹדֵף) שֶׁהָאוּלָם עוֹדֵף עַל רוֹחַב הַהֵיכָל לַצָּפוֹן וְלַדָּרוֹם ט"ו אַמָּה לְכָל צַד, וְאׇרְכּוֹ יט] לַמִּזְרָח מִן הַמַּעֲרָב אֵינוֹ אֶלָּא י"א אַמּוֹת. *וּבְכוֹתֶל הַמַּעֲרָבִי שֶׁל אוֹתוֹ עוֹדֵף הָיוּ חַלּוֹנוֹת לִגְנוֹז סַכִּינִין מִבַּחוּץ, וְלָכֵן קָרוּי הֶחָלָל כְּנֶגְדּוֹ עַד כּוֹתֶל מַעֲרָבִי שֶׁל הָעֲזָרָה "בֵּית הַחֲלִיפוֹת". וּבְאוֹתָן שְׁנֵי כְּתָלִים הָיוּ שְׁנֵי פְּתָחִים קְטַנִּים. וְהָכִי נַמִי תַּנְיָא לָהּ בַּתּוֹסֶפְתָּא בְּהֶדְיָא: ר׳ יוֹסֵי בְּר׳ יְהוּדָה אוֹמֵר: שְׁנֵי פִשְׁפָּשִׁין הָיוּ בְּבֵית הַחֲלִיפוֹת וּפְתוּחִין לַמַּעֲרָב. וְקָסָבַר אוּלָם נַמִי קָרוּי "אֹהֶל מוֹעֵד". לְהַכְשִׁיר אֶת כָּל הָעֲזָרָה. אֶת כָּל שְׁאָר הָעֲזָרָה שֶׁאֵינוֹ בִּכְלַל "לִפְנֵי אֹהֶל מוֹעֵד" עַל יְדֵי פֶּתַח רִאשׁוֹן, וְהָווּ לִידֵי לְדָדִין, כְּגוֹן מִכְּנֶגֶד (זָוִיּוֹת) כּוֹתֶל הָאוּלָם וְלַמַּעֲרָב בַּצָּפוֹן וּבַדָּרוֹם כ] לְבֵית הַחֲלִיפוֹת, וּבֵית הַחֲלִיפוֹת עַצְמוֹ. וְאֵלּוּ שְׁנֵי פִשְׁפָּשִׁין מַכְשִׁירִין כָּל בֵּית הַחֲלִיפוֹת לְאׇרְכּוֹ וּלְרׇחְבּוֹ, דְּקָרֵינַן מֵהַשְׁתָּא "לִפְנֵי". וּלְקַמָּן פָּרֵיךְ: הָא אִיכָּא לְדָדִין! לַאֲכִילַת קָדְשֵׁי קָדָשִׁים. קס"ד הַשְׁתָּא דְּלַאֲכִילָה נַמִי בָּעֵיָא כא] פְּנִים. וּלְקַמָּן אָמְרִינַן: סְמֵי מִכָּאן אֲכִילָה. ה"ג: מַאי לָאו דְּאִיכָּא קַמַּיְיהוּ גּוֹבְהָהּ שְׁמוֹנֶה. שֶׁהָיָה כְּנֶגְדָּן תֵּל גָּבוֹהַּ שְׁמוֹנָה, וש"מ גּוֹבְהָהּ לָא פָּסֵיל. לָא דְּגָבְהִי אִינְהוּ שְׁמוֹנֶה. גּוֹבְהָן שֶׁל פְּתָחִים ח׳ אַמּוֹת. פִּשְׁפָּשִׁין שָׁאנֵי. שֶׁהֵן פְּתָחִים קְטַנִּים וְאֵין מְשַׁמְּשִׁין כְּנִיסָה וִיצִיאָה, אֶלָּא לְאַכְשׁוּרֵי כב] בִּשְׁמָא בְּעָלְמָא. וְהָא אִיכָּא צְדָדִין. הַיְינוּ אֲוִיר שֶׁבֵּין כּוֹתֶל אוּלָם לְכוֹתֶל הָעֲזָרָה לַדָּרוֹם וְלַצָּפוֹן, דְּהָווּ לְהוּ אֲחוֹרֵי אוֹתָם פְּתָחִים וְלָא הָווּ "לִפְנֵי"! כג] דְּפֶתַח לְהוּ בְּקֶרֶן זָוִית. שֶׁל אוּלָם, מִקְצָת הַפֶּתַח פּוֹנֶה לַצָּפוֹן וּמִקְצָתוֹ לַמַּעֲרָב. וְכֵן בַּדָּרוֹם. אֲחוֹרֵי בֵּית הַכַּפֹּרֶת. אַחַת עֶשְׂרֵה אַמָּה הָיָה אֲוִיר כד] [ג] עַד חוֹמַת הָעֲזָרָה לַמַּעֲרָב, כָּזֶה* מַאי. בְּמַאי מִתְכַּשַׁר לִשְׁחִיטָה, דְּקָאָמַר כָּל הָעֲזָרָה כְּשֵׁרָה? לוּל. כְּמִין חַלּוֹן פָּתוּחַ מִן הַתָּא שֶׁאֲחוֹרֵי בֵּית הַכַּפֹּרֶת לָאֲוִיר הָעֲזָרָה. וְהַיְינוּ דִּכְתִיב שְׁנַיִם לַפַּרְבָּר. כה] (בְּסֵפֶר עֶזְרָא) (ד"ה א כו) מִשְׁתָּעֵי בְּמִסְפַּר כו] הַשּׁוֹמְרִים שֶׁהֶעֱמִידוּ בַּמִּקְדָּשׁ לְכָל הַפְּתָחִין. וְקָאָמַר: שְׁנֵי שׁוֹמְרִים הֶעֱמִידוּ לַבָּר, וְהַיְינוּ לְאוֹתוֹ לוּל. כְּמַאן דְּאָמַר כְּלַפֵּי לְבַר גָּרְסִינַן. כְּלַפֵּי חוּץ אֲחוֹרֵי כָּל כּוֹתְלֵי הַהֵיכָל כז] וְקׇדְשֵׁי קָדָשִׁים. אֵין חַיָּיבִין מִשּׁוּם טוּמְאָה. הַנִּכְנָס טָמֵא לְהַר הַבַּיִת אֵינוֹ חַיָּיב אֶלָּא אִם כֵּן נִכְנַס לְתוֹךְ הֶיקֵּף חֲלַל הָעֲזָרָה. וְהוּא הָיָה

תוספות

שְׁלָמִים ששחטן קודם פתיחת ההיכל. מפורש בפ״ק דעירובין (דף ב.) ובפ׳ "התכלת" (מנחות דף מט:). הוא עצמו אין נעשה אלא כפתח פתוח.[ד] שהוילון כח] משמשת עשוי לצניעות בעלמא, שלא יסתכלו בהיכל בשעת שחיטה. דאי משום לאחר שחיטה – הרי יכולין כט] לסגור הדלתות.

גּוֹבְהָהּ מאי. תימה: אי גובהה חשיב הפסק, א״כ כנגד המזבח יפסל, שמפסיק! ל] ואין לומר משום דרואה פתח מלמעלה למזבח, דהא סלקא דעתך השתא דגובהה שמנה מפסיק. דליכא למימר משום דגובהה שמנה היה סותם כל הפתח, דהא סבור שהיה הפתח גובה עשרים אמה כדפריך בסמוך.[ה] וצ״ע: דביומא פ״ק (דף טז:) לא] גבי כהן השורף פרה שהיה כותל מזרחי נמוך שיוכל לראות פתח אהל מועד, וקאמר התם דדרך פלגא אמתא עילאה היה יכול לראות. ושמא היינו דוקא לב] הזאה שהיתה מעומד, אבל שחיטה[ו] היתה מיושב, ואכתי תיקשי מכנגד המזבח אמאי כשר לשחוט, כדאמר כל העזרה כולה כשרה לשחיטה.

שְׁנֵי פשפשין היו בבית החליפות. במסכת מדות (דף לה:) לג] דאולם עודף עליו חמש עשרה אמה מן הצפון וחמש עשרה אמה מן הדרום, והוא היה נקרא בית החליפות, והיו לו שני פשפשין להכשיר את כל העזרה. דאותו אויר עד כותל מערבי קרוי עזרה, ולא כמו שפי׳ בקונטרס לד] שהכל קרוי בית החליפות עד כותל מערבי. לה] ובפרק "הניזקין" (גיטין נד:) גבי כהן גדול ביוה״כ דקאמר דחזיניה בפשפש, ופי׳ בקונטרס: דשני פשפשין היו לו] *באותם החליפות. ותימה גדול[ז] פירושו, דדרך פשפשין לא היה יכול לראות לז] כלל! ופי׳ רבינו ריב״א: דחזיני׳ דרך פשפש – שיעשו פשפשין לראות אם פיגל ואם לאו. וגם זה קשה, דלעיל פרק "כל הפסולין" (דף לג.) פריך: וניעביד פשפש – לח] "הכל בכתב מיד ה׳ עלי השכיל"! ומפרש ה״ר יעקב מאורלינ״ש: דההוא פשפש היינו דרך הלול שאחורי בית הכפרת, שירצה משם לט] דרך בית קדש הקדשים, ובהיכל יכול לראות דרך פתח הגדול לאולם.

שְׁנַיִם [ח] לפר. גבי שומרין מייתי להאי קרא בפ״ק דתמיד (דף כז.). תימה לי: אחורי הכפרת היאך יכול לשחוט? הא אינו יכול לראות שם פתח אהל מועד דרך מ] חלון דלפר בר, דהא איכא שני פרכות בין היכל ובין קדשי הקדשים, ובפרכת לא היה שום פתח אלא אחת פרופה מן הדרום ואחת מן הצפון! ויש לומר: דהלול קרי פתח, ורואה בו קדשי קדשים דלא גרע מאהל מועד. כמו אחורי בית החליפות, שהיו פשפשין וקרויין פתח וע״י כן כשר לשחוט עד כותל מערבי לפי שרואה בהן האולם שקרוי אהל מועד, למאן דאמ׳ א) קדושת היכל ואולם חדא מילתא. ב) ולא נ״ל, דבשלמא שני פשפשין דבית החליפות הוו שני פתחים קטנים ומשמשין כניסה ויציאה, ומיקרו פתח, אבל מא] לפר בר חלון קטן ולא פתח מקרי. ובסוף "התערובות" (לקמן פב:) קרי ליה דרך משופש ולא מיקרי ביאה דרך שם. ואי הוה נקב בפתחו של היכל – לא היה יכול לשחוט אם היה הפתח נעול על סמך אותו נקב קטן. ברו״ך.

א) [לעיל יח.] ב) נ״א הגהה ולא נ״ל כו׳

עין משפט נר מצוה

נח א ב ג מיי׳ פ״ה מהל׳ מעה״ק הל׳ ה׳:
נט ד מיי׳ פ״ה מהל׳ בית הבחירה הל׳ ה:

שיטה מקובצת

א] וחד לפסול צידי צדדין. פ״ה דס״ד דמדפתח אהל מועד לאו דוקא כו׳ עד לפני אהל מועד א) לומר דצידי צדדין דהיינו בית החליפות פסולים אם לא היו להם פשפשין דאם לאו קרא דהכא הייתי אומר דהוא כשר אפילו בלא פשפשין לכך צריך קרא לפסול צידי צדדין ולכך קאמר בסמוך דצריך פשפשין להכשיר צידי צדדין דהיינו בית החליפות דאין [לומר] דצידי צדדין דהכא דפסלינן להו לאו היינו בית החליפות אלא לשכות א״כ למה לי קרא להכי תיפוק ליה משום דאמרינן בשמעתין דלשכות לא קדישי אבל [נראה (דצידי) דצדדין] היינו כל מה שאינו כנגד הפתח דהיינו כל רוחב שלפני אהל מועד למזרח והא דפריך לקמן והא איכא צדדין גבי בית החליפות אין הפירוש כי הכא דהכא מכשירין בצדדין בלא פתח דקרן זויות משום [דמיקרי] לפני אהל מועד אלא הוי פי׳ דלקמן כמו צידי צדדין דפסיל הכא אם לא יהיה בו פשפש ולכך מצריך לקמן לפתוח בקרן זוית והא דקרי ליה צדדין היינו משום דפי׳ תחילה אחורי הבליטה של עדיפת אולם על ההיכל דהיו שם פשפשין להכשיר העזרה ולהכי בעי על צידי בליטה והא איכא צדדין אויר שבין כותל האולם לכותל העזרה לדרום ולצפון שהעזרה עודפת על האולם לדרום ולצפון דהוי להו אחורי אותם פתחים ולא הוי לפני [אהל מועד] ומשני דפתח בקרן זוית של אולם מקצת הפתח פונה לצפון ומקצתו למערב דהיינו בית החליפות למערב וכן לדרום מקצת פונה למערב ומקצת לדרום צידי צדדין קרוי לכל מה שכנגד כותל ג) פתח בית המקדש מב׳ רוחותיו וצדדין נקרא כל מה שאינו כנגד חלל הפתח דהיינו כל רוחב החצר כו׳. תוס׳ אחרות: ב] דכתיב ושחטו פתח אהל מועד ומאי שנא בכולהו דכתב בהו לפני אהל מועד מילתא אגב אורחא קא משמע לן: ג] נעול. וא״ת תיפוק ליה דנשחטו קודם התמיד של שחר ואמרינן מנין ג) שלא יהא דבר קודם תמיד של שחר ת״ל העולה עולה ראשונה וי״ל דהיינו למצוה אבל פסול ליכא: ד] בזמן שפתוח ולא בזמן: ה] רב אחא בר יעקב אמר: ו] פסולים שנאמר ושחטו פתח אהל מועד בזמן שפתוח ולא בזמן שהוא נעול תנ״ה שלמים ששחטן קודם שיפתחו דלתות היכל פסולים

שיטה מקובצת

דודאי גובהו של מזבח אינו מפסיק כיון דלצורך קרבנות הוא. לשון מהר״פ: ט] וגובה שמונה להכשיר את כל העזרה: י] לא דגביהי אינהו שמונה: יא] צדדין אמר רב אדא בר אהבה דפתח ליה בקרן זויות תיבת דמעייל נמחק: יב] הכפורת להכשיר את כל העזרה והשאר נמחק: יג] קלים ושנים היו והיינו: יד] כלפי לבר: טו] פתח כגון קודם: טז] אהל מועד נטוי: יז] מה״ד וצפון לא: יח] אחרינא דלפני כתיב בקרא קמא דמשמע צדדין ולא צידי צדדין והד״א: יט] וארכו מן המזרח למערב אינו אלא: כ] ובדרום לצד בית החליפות עצמן ואלו שני כו׳ דקרינן ביה מהשתא לפני: כא] בעי׳ לפני ולקמן: כב] לאכשורי בשלמים בעלמא: כג] לפני שום פתח והיכי קתני להכשיר כל העזרה הס״ד ומה״ד דפתח ליה:

כו] במספר השוערים שהעמידו כו׳ הס״ד: כח] תיבת משמשת ... העזרה א״כ גם מזרחו של מזבח ... אמרינן דאולם: לד] בקונטרס ... לה] מערבי של העזרה ובפרק: ... פשפש ומשני הכל: לט] תיבת ... אות ל׳ נמחק:

הגהות הב״ח

(א) רש״י ד״ה וצידי צדדין וכו׳ אחרינא דלפני כתיב בקרא קמא משמע לצדדין ולא לצידי צדדין:

א) אולי נ״ל עד למימרא דוקא הוא ולא לשכות ...

הגהות צ״ק

[א] גובה שמונה: [ב] הד״א וכצ״ל קרא אחרינא לפני כתיב בקרא קמא דמשמע לצדדין ולא לצידי צדדין וכו״ד: [ג] מחומת העזרה: [ד] נ״ל שהוילון אינו משמש רק עשוי לצניעות כו׳: [ה] והא דאמרי׳ ביומא פ״ק: [ו] שחיטה מיושב אכתי: [ז] לפירושו: [ח] לפר בר:

מסורת הש״ס

עירובין ב. יומא סב: | דהא דקבע להאי לצפון ולהאי שאר רוחות משום קדושתיה דלצפון מדרום ולאו דקביעות מקום בעלמא הוא נ״ך | [ע׳ תוס׳ מנחות נה. ד״ה מר אמר] | [לקמן נו.] | נ״ק מ״ו | (מנחות לה:) יומא טז. מדות פ״ב מ״ג ע״ש | דה״א כו

היתה אורך קפ"ז על רוחב קל"ה, כדתנן במסכת *מדות (דף לה.). למעוטי הנכנס ללשכות הבנויות חולה לו ופתוחות לתוכו, שלא נתקדשו בקדושת עזרה בשירי מנחה ובשר של פגעים ובאורים ותומים, שמקדשים בהן את העזרה, ובהליכה סביב, כדאמרינן בשבועות (דף יד.). ה"ג: תני תנא קמיה דרב נחמן כל העזרה היתה אורך קפ"ז על רוחב קל"ה אמר ליה הכי אמר לי אבא כו'. ואוכלין שם קדשי קדשים. *דהכי הוא [ט] דהוה קדושה בקדושת חצר אהל מועד לאכילת קדשי קדשים, וטפי מהכי לא קדיש עזרה. והוא חלל כל העזרה, ובתוכו היכל ואולם ובית קדשי הקדשים, והפתח לאחורי בית הכפורת, וי"א אמה אויר מאחוריו. ושוחטין שם קדשים קלים *גרסינן. [י] וחייבין עליו משום טומאה. החלונות. עובי חלל החלונות שבחומות העזרה סביב מבפנים, ועובי החומה בראשה למעלה. תנינא. דקדישי, והיכי מצי למעוטינהו? ה"ג: אלא למעוטי לשכות אי דבנויות בחול ופתוחות לקדש [יא]. שהכהנים נכנסין לשם ואוכלין שם קדשי קדשים ושירי מנחה תלמוד לומר בחצר אהל מועד כו'. ול"ג: "ושוחטין שם קדשים קלים" הכא. וגם אחר לשון הכתוב בספרים שבוש הוא. וכן הגהתי מספרו של רבינו. הא אנן תנן תוכן קדש. וליחייב עלייהו משום טומאה! מדרבנן. מצות חכמים היא שלא יכנסו להן בטומאה, אבל כרת וקרבן ליכא. והתניא מנין ללשכות כו'. ומדמרבינן להו לענין אכילה – ש"מ קדושתם הן מן התורה. דאי מדרבנן, וקרא אסמכתא הוא – היאך הקילו חכמים [יב] לעקור דבר ולהכשיר מקום חול לאכילת קדשי קדשים? חצרות הרבה. במקום קדוש בחצר אהל מועד. לאכילה שאני. דרבי בה קרא חצרות הרבה. ואין שוחטין שם קדשים קלים. דהא בעינן "לפני אהל מועד", למעוטי לדי לדדין. לאו אמרת. דקתני בה אין שוחטין, אלמא לאו קדישי, תני נמי: אין חייבין משום טומאה. מי לא עסקינן [יג] דאיכא שחיטה כנגד הפתח. כשהיה פתחו מכוון כנגד פתחי בית החליפות. קדשי שעה שאני. גזירת הכתוב היתה במילואים. אבל קדשי דורות איתרבו, כדאמר: התורה ריבתה חצרות הרבה. ביום שאתה זובח אתה מקריב ביום שאי אתה זובח אי אתה מקריב. הכי גרסינן לה בכולה סוגיא, [יד] כך מצאתי מוגה. והכי פירושא: "ביום הקריבו את זבחו" – שתהא הקרבה וזביחה ביום אחד, ולא מהניא ליה הלנה בראש המזבח לאכשורי [טו] לזריקה למחר. לגופיה

תורה אור

אורך מאה ושמונים ושבע על רוחב מאה ושלשים וחמש. תני תנא קמיה דרב נחמן: [א]כל העזרה היתה קפ"ז על רוחב קל"ה. אמר ליה: הכי אמר [א] לי אבא: כגון זה, כהנים נכנסין לשם ואוכלין שם קדשי קדשים, ושוחטין שם קדשים קלים, וחייבין משום טומאה. למעוטי מאי? אילימא למעוטי חלונות דלתות ועובי החומה – תנינא: *[ב]החלונות ועובי החומה כלפנים! ואלא למעוטי לשכות; [ב] ואי בנויות בחול ופתוחות לקדש – *והתנן: [ג]תוכן קודש! מדרבנן. ודאורייתא לא? והתניא: [ג] [ד]לשכות בנויות בחול ופתוחות לקדש, מנין שהכהנים נכנסין לשם ואוכלין שם קדשי קדשים ושירי מנחה – תלמוד לומר: °"בחצר אהל מועד יאכלוה", ויקרא ו התורה ריבתה חצירות הרבה [ד] אצל אכילה אחת! אמר רבא: [ה]לאכילה שאני. אבל לענין טומאה לא? והתניא: *לשכות הבנויות לחול ופתוחות לקודש – כהנים נכנסין לשם ואוכלין שם קדשי קדשים, ואין שוחטין שם קדשים קלים, וחייבין משום טומאה! לאו אמרת: [ו]אין שוחטין? תני נמי: אין חייבין. בשלמא אין שוחטין – בעינא כנגד הפתח, וליכא. אלא אין חייבין אמאי? ולטעמיך, אין שוחטין, מי לא עסקינן [ה] דאיכא שחיטה כנגד הפתח? דאי ליכא – למאי איצטריך? אלא אף על גב *דקא שחיט כנגד הפתח תני אין שוחטין, משום דלא [ו] קדיש; תני נמי: אין חייבין. ולאכילה לא בעינן כנגד הפתח? והתניא, *רבי יוסי ברבי יהודה אומר: שני פשפשין היו בבית החליפות גובהן שמונה, [ז] כדי להכשיר את העזרה לאכילת קדשי קדשים ולשחיטת קדשים קלים! אמר רבינא: סמי מכאן אכילה. והכתיב: °"בשלו את הבשר פתח אהל מועד ושם תאכלו אותו"! שם ח קדשי שעה שאני.§ אמר רב יצחק בר אבודימי: [ח] מנין [ז]לדם *שנפסל בשקיעת החמה – שנאמר: °"ביום הקריבו את זבחו יאכל", שם ז ביום שאתה זובח אתה מקריב, ביום שאי אתה זובח – אי אתה מקריב. האי מיבעי ליה לגופיה

קדשי שעה שאני. [טז] דתלאו הכתוב באהל מועד, דכתיב (ויקרא ח): "ומפתח אהל מועד לא תצאו שבעת ימים".

מנין לדם שנפסל בשקיעת החמה. פירש בקונטרס דלא מהניא ליה הלנה בראש המזבח לאכשורי למחר לזריקה. ותימה: הניחא למאן דאמר *אין לינה מועלת בראשו של מזבח, אלא למאן דאמר מועלת, למה לי קרא בלילה אין יכול לזרוק, ד"ביום צוותו" כתיב (שם ז), ולמחר מיפסיל בעמוד השחר כאימורים! וכי תימא דאיצריך קרא משום אימורין, דקיימא לן (לקמן דף פד.) אם עלו לא ירדו, וקמ"ל בדם דירדו. ואליבא דמאן? אי לר"ג – האמר לקמן פרק "המזבח מקדש" (דף פג.) דלא ירד אף בדם, ואי לרבי יהושע – הא אמר דאין המזבח מקדש פסולין שלא ירדו אלא בהקטרה, ואם כן קרא דהכא למה לי? ויש לומר: דאיצטריך קרא לפסול דם בלינה, משום דהוה אמינא דלא מיפסיל, כי היכי דאין חייבין עליו משום פיגול ונותר. ומיהו, אין טעם זה נכון: והרי עלים ולבונה לר' שמעון (לעיל דף מו:) דאין חייבין עליהם משום נותר, ומיפסלי בלינה היכא דקדשו בכלי! ועוד, דהוה ליה למימר: מנין לדם שנפסל בלינה! ויש לפרש: שקיעת החמה – היינו תחילת שקיעה, קודם צאת הכוכבים, [יז] כדאמר דמשקיעת החמה ועד צאת הכוכבים ד' מילין בפרק "מי שהיה טמא" (פסחים צד.), וחשוב יום לענין [יח] שמצותן ביום, ומפסוק מיותר ממעט ליה הכא מ"ביום הקריבו". [יט] ובכל דוכתא חשוב יום עד צאת הכוכבים, כדאמר: אף על פי שאין ראיה לדבר זכר לדבר "ואנחנו עושים במלאכה וחציים מחזיקים ברמחים מעלות השחר ועד צאת הכוכבים", ואומר "והיה לנו הלילה משמר והיום מלאכה" בפ"ב דמגילה (דף כ:). והשתא לא הוי כמו שקיעת החמה דמסכת תענית (דף יב.): [כ] כל תענית שלא שקעה עליו חמה אינו תענית, וקבלה בידינו בצאת הכוכבים. וב"מי שהיה טמא" (פסחים דף צג:) נמי הכי משמע דנפסל הדם בשקיעת החמה שקודם צאת הכוכבים ארבע מילין, דחשיב דרך רחוקה מן המודיעים משום דלא מטי לירושלים עד תחילת שקיעת החמה, דקעבר [כא] עליה זמן שחיטת הפסח. (ואין) לדחות: ההיא ד"מי שהיה טמא" – רבנן עבוד הרחקה כדי שלא יבא לידי הלנת דם וכדי לזרוס בפסח, והעמידו דבריהם במקום כרת. והאי דלא חשיב ליה בפסחים בהדי איך בפ' "האשה" (דף צג.) – ה"נ לא חשיב חתיכת יבלתו והבאתו מחוץ לתחום, דלא חשיב אלא דברים של חידוש. והא דאמר בשמעתא [כב] דנאכלין ליום אחד מחשבים בדמו משתשקע החמה – היינו תחילת שקיעה [כג] ומדאורייתא, ולא צאת הכוכבים, דומיא [כד] דאימורין ובשר דחשיב לקמן בהדי דם. ו"משתשקע החמה" דלקמן לא הוי כמו משתשקע החמה [כה] בעלמא. דרגיל רבינו תם לפרש ד"שקיעה" דווקא משמע תחילת שקיעה, אבל "משתשקע" משמע סוף שקיעה. משום דקשה ליה דבסוף פרק "במה מדליקין" (שבת דף לד:) [כו] משמע משקיעת חמה עד לילה תלתא ריבעי מיל, ובפרק "מי שהיה טמא" (פסחים דף צד.) משמע דמשתשקע החמה עד צאת הכוכבים ארבע מילין וחשיב ליה במדידת היום, [כז] *דמפרש רבינו תם ד"משקיעה" משמע תחילת שקיעה, שהחמה מתחלת ליכנס בעובי הרקיע. *ואתי שפיר דאיידי דבסמוך קתני גבי [כח] בשר קדשים קלים: ובבשרם משתשקע החמה של יום שני, דהיינו על כרחך צאת הכוכבים – תני נמי האי לישנא גבי דם, אף על גב שחלוקין זה מזה.

[ועיין תוס' שבת לה. ד"ה תרי תילתי מיל ותוס' פסחים צד. ד"ה ר' יהודה ותוס' מנחות כ: ד"ה נפסל].

אור

עין משפט נר מצוה

ס א מיי' פ"ה מהלכות בית הבחירה הלכה ד:

[לקמן פז.]

סא ב מיי' פ"ו מהל' בית הבחירה הלכה ט ופ"י מהלכות מעה"ק הלכה ה:

סב ג ד ה ו מיי' פ"ו מהל' בית הבחירה הלכה ח:

סג ז מיי' פ"א מהל' פסה"מ הלכה לג ופ"ד מהלכות מעה"ק הלכה א:

פסחים פו. מעשר שני פ"ג מ"ח יומא כה.

שיטה מקובצת

א] אמר אבא כגון זו כהנים אוכלין שם קדשי קדשים כו' וחייבין עליהן משום טומאה כו' למעוטי חלונות ועובי החומה: ב] לשכות אי דבנויות: ג] והתניא מנין ללשכות בנויות כו' לקדש שהכהנים נכנסין: ד] חצרות הרבה לאכילה אמר רבא לאכילה שאני וטומאה לא והא אנן תנן תוכן קדש מדרבנן ודאורייתא לא והתניא מנין ללשכות הבנויות בחול ופתוחות לקדש שהכהנים נכנסים לשם: ה] עסקינן דקא שחיט כנגד הפתח דאי שלא כנגד הפתח למאי אצטריך: ו] דלא קדשי תני: ז] גובהן שמונה להכשיר את כל העזרה כולה לאכילת: ח] מנין לדם שנפסל בשקיעת החמה. וא"ת ותיפוק ליה משום דאינו ראוי לכפרה רק באותו יום דהא בלילה אינו ראוי לזריקה משום דכתיב ביום צוותו ואם למחר הרי הוא נפסל בלינה בעמוד השחר בלא טעמא דשקיעת החמה ופ"ה דבעי היכא שהעלתוהו מיד אחר שקיעת החמה קודם עמוד השחר בראשו של מזבח דלינה אינה מועלת בו וקשה הניחא למ"ד אין לינה (פוסלת) [מועלת] בראשו של מזבח אלא למ"ד מועלת מאי איכא למימר ופר"ת דמיירי הכא בתחלת שקיעה ואע"ג דמתחלת שקיעה ועד צאת הכוכבים ד' מילין הוא ואכתי יממא אפ"ה נפסל מתחלת שקיעת החמה מקרא דביום הקריבו דאם [אינו] ענין ללילה דמביום צוותו נפקא תנהו ענין לתחלת שקיעת החמה.

מסורת הש"ס

[לעיל נה:]

[מנחות כ:]

פסחים פה:

תוספתא למעשר שני פ"א ע"ש

מהר"פ: ט] הוא דהויא קדוש אות ה' ה' נמחק: י] גרסי' הס"ד ומה"ד למעוטי מאי דאין חייבין עליו: יא] לקדש והא אנן תנן תוכן קדש מדרבנן ומדאורייתא לא והתניא מנין ללשכות הבנוית בחול ופתוחות לקדש שהכהנים: יב] חכמים על דבר תורה להכשיר מקום חול: יג] עסקינן דקא שחיט כנגד: יד] סוגיא וכך מצאתי מוגה והכי פירושא: טו] לאכשורי זריקה למחר: טז] שאני. תימה כיון דתרווייהו נאכלים בעזרה כדמייתי לעיל תלמודא מתאכלו במקום טהור תרווייהו נמי לשוו לפתח אהל מועד ועוד דבשום מקום לא אמרינן קדשי שעה שאני להחמיר אלא להקל וי"ל דה"ק שאני קדשי שעה דהיינו מילואים דגזירת הכתוב בכל מקום באהל מועד שנאמר ומפתח אהל מועד לא תצאו שבעת ימים אבל קדשי דורות איתרבו כדאמרן התורה ריבתה חצרות הרבה. מהר"פ: יז] הכוכבים כדאמרינן: יח] לענין ביום צוותו ומפסוק כו' תיבת שמצוותן נמחק: יט] הקריבו דאם אינו ענין ללילה דמביום צוותו נפקא תנהו לענין לתחילת שקיעת החמה: כ] דאמרינן כל: כא] תיבת עליה נמחק: כב] דאמר בשמעתא משום דנאכלין: כג] תיבת ומדאורייתא נמחק: כד] דומיא דבשר דחשיב לקמן: כה] החמה דבעלמא: כו] מדליקין פליגי אי משקיעת החמה עד לילה (תרי) [תלתא] ריבעי אי לא ובפרק מי שהיה טמא: כז] היום ומפרש ר"ת: כח] תיבת בשר נמחק:

האידנא

אור לשלישי גרס, כמו "אור לי"ד". ד"לאור שלישי" משמע לילה שאחר שלישי, כמו "לאור עיבורו" דבשמעתא קמייתא דפסחים (דף ג:).

ת"ל עד יום. פי' בקונטרס: "ביום זבחכם יאכל וממחרת, והנותר עד יום השלישי" – בעוד שהוא יום תאכלנו. וקשה: ד"הנותר" הפסיק הענין! וה"ר חיים מפרש: "עד יום השלישי" – ולא יום השלישי בכלל. א"כ אינו נאכל בליל שלישי.

ונאכלין בכל העיר. פירש בקונטרס: כדכתיב בפרשת "ראה אנכי": "והבאתם שמה עולותיכם וזבחיכם ואת מעשרותיכם", ותניא בספרי, רבי עקיבא אומר: בשתי מעשרות הכתוב מדבר, אחד מעשר בהמה ואחד מעשר דגן, וכתיב בההוא קרא "ובכורות בקרכם וצאנכם". ומדלא קבע בהו מחילה – שמע מינה דנאכלין בכל העיר. ותימה גדול לפי': דהא כתיבי נמי התם כג] חטאות ואשמות דבעו קלעים. והכי תניא בספרי: "מעשרותיכם", ר"ע אומר: בשתי מעשרות הכתוב מדבר, אחד מעשר דגן ואחד מעשר בהמה, "ותרומת ידכם" – אלו הביכורים, כענין שנאמר: "ולקח הכהן הטנא מידך", "ובכורות" – זה הבכור, "בקרכם וצאנכם" – אלו חטאות ואשמות, "ואכלתם שם לפני ה' אלהיכם" – כד] אלו המחילה. *ויש לתמוה: אמאי לא בעי בכור ומעשר מחילה כיון דכתיב בהו "לפני ה'", כמו שחיטה דדרשינן (לעיל דף לב.) "לפני ה'" בעזרה? ועוד *אמרינן בתמורה בסוף "אלו קדשים" (דף כא:): אם ללמוד על הבכור שנאכל לפנים כה] (מן הקלעים) מן החומה – אינו צריך, שהרי כבר נאמר "לפני ה' אלהיך תאכלנו", וא"כ, ליבעי לפנים מן הקלעים כשחיטה! ונראה דנפקא לן מדכתיב "לא תוכל לאכול בשעריך מעשר דגנך וגו' ובכורות בקרכם וצאנכם", דמשמע: בשעריך הוא דלא תוכל לאכול, הא בירושלים – אכול ומעשר בהמה גמר העברה העברה מבכור. ומיהו קשה: דבההוא קרא נמי הא כתיבי חטאות ואשמות, כדדרשינן בפ' בתרא דמכות (דף יז.): "בקרך וצאנך" – אלו חטאות ואשמות! ונראה לפרש דנפקא לן מדמקשינן בגמ' לחזה ושוק של שלמים כו] הנאכלין לשני ימים, והוא הדין לענין שנאכלין בכל העיר. ותודה ואיל נזיר ושלמים נפקא לן קרא דחזה ושוק של מילואין.

לשני ימים. פי' בקונט': בבכור יליף לה בגמ', מעשר לא ידענא מהיכא. ושוב כז] הגיה, דיליף העברה העברה מבכור. ותימה: א"כ תפשוט מהכא לדבר הלמד בהיקש חוזר ומלמד בגז"ש, כח] ולעיל אמרינן דאינו חוזר ומלמד בגז"ש מדרבי יוחנן! כט] ונראה דמעשר יליף משלמים בבנין אב: מה שלמים קדשים קלים – אף מעשר קדשים קלים. דבכור נמי הוה אתי משלמים אי לאו משום דמתנה לכהן, וא"כ מעשר דלא הוי מתנה לכהן משלמים אתי.

הפסח אינו נאכל כו'. תימה: ליתני נמי דאינו נאכל אלא על מצות ומרורים! ותירץ ה"ר חיים: דלא חשיב אלא דבר שכנגדו ל] בקדשים, והוא חלוק מהם, דשאר קדשים נאכלין ביום ובלילה לא] עד היום ולכל אדם בכל מאכל, ופסח אינו נאכל אלא בלילה עד חצות ולמנויו וצלי. אי נמי: לא תנא מצות ומרורים, דאין מעכבין. א"נ: לאו מצוה דגופיה לב]. למה

לגופיה! אם כן, נימא קרא: "ביום זבחו יאכל", "הקריבו" למה לי? ש"מ: ביום שאתה זובח אתה מקריב, ביום שאי אתה זובח – אי אתה מקריב. ודילמא ה"ק רחמנא: אי קריב דם האידנא – א] ניתאכיל בשר האידנא ולמחר, אי קריב דם למחר – ב] ניתאכיל בשר למחר וליומא אוחרא! אם כן, נימא קרא: "ביום הקריבו יאכל", "זבחו" למה לי? שמע מינה: ביום שאתה זובח אתה מקריבו, ביום שאי אתה זובח – אי אתה מקריבו.§ איתמר: המחשב לאור שלישי, חזקיה אמר: כשר, רבי יוחנן אמר: פסול. חזקיה אמר כשר – דהא לא אינתיק לשריפה, רבי יוחנן אמר: פסול – דהא אידחי ליה מאכילה. האוכל לאור שלישי, חזקיה אמר: פטור – ג] דלא אינתיק לשריפה, רבי יוחנן אמר: חייב – דהא אידחי לי' מאכילה. תניא כוותיה דרבי יוחנן: ד] אקדשים הנאכלין ליום אחד – ●מחשבין בדמן משתשקע החמה, ובבשרן ובאימוריהן – משיעלה עמוד השחר. ה] קדשים הנאכלין לשני ימים ולילה אחת – מחשבין בדמן משתשקע החמה, ובאימוריהן משיעלה עמוד השחר, ו] ובבשרן משתשקע החמה של שני ימים.§ ת"ר: יכול *יהו נאכלין לאור שלישי? ודין הוא: זבחים נאכלין ליום אחד וזבחים נאכלין לשני ימים, ז] מה זבחים הנאכלין ליום אחד – לילה אחריהן, אף זבחים הנאכלין לשני ימים – ח] לילה אחריהן! תלמוד לומר: °"והנותר עד יום" – בבעוד יום הוא נאכל, ואינו נאכל לאור שלישי. יכול ישרף מיד? ודין הוא: זבחים נאכלין ליום אחד, וזבחים נאכלין לשני ימים, מה זבחים הנאכלין ליום אחד – תיכף לאכילה שריפה, אף זבחים הנאכלין לשני ימים – תיכף לאכילה שריפה! ת"ל: °"ביום השלישי באש ישרף", גביום אתה שורפו, ואי אתה שורפו בלילה.§ **מתני'** הבכור והמעשר והפסח קדשים קלים; שחיטתן בכל מקום בעזרה, דודמן טעון מתנה אחת, ובלבד שיתן כנגד היסוד. שינה באכילתן: ההבכור נאכל לכהנים, והמעשר לכל אדם, ט] ונאכלין בכל העיר, בכל מאכל, לשני ימים ולילה אחד. זהפסח אינו נאכל אלא בלילה, חואינו נאכל אלא עד חצות, טואינו נאכל אלא למנויו, יואינו נאכל אלא צלי.§ **גמ'** מאן תנא? אמר רב חסדא: ר' יוסי הגלילי היא, דתניא, *ר' יוסי הגלילי אומר: י] "חלבו" לא נאמר, אלא: "חלבם", "דמו" לא נאמר, אלא: "דמם", לימד על בכור ומעשר ופסח שטעונין מתן דמים ואימורין לגבי מזבח. כנגד היסוד מנא לן? א"ר *אליעזר: אתיא זריקה זריקה מעולה, ועולה

לגופיה. ללמד יא] זמן אכילת שלמים ביום זביחתו וממחרת. ה"ג: א"כ נימא קרא ביום זבחו יאכל הקריבו למה לי ש"מ ביום שאתה זובח אתה מקריב כו'. דלמא הכי קאמר רחמנא כו'. ה"ג: אם כן נימא קרא יב] וביום הקריבו יאכל וזבחו למה לי ש"מ ביום שאתה זובח אתה מקריב כך הגהתי מספרו של רבי. ודלמא הכי קאמר רחמנא כו'. דלא תלה רחמנא זמן אכילה בזביחה אלא בזריקה, לאוכלו ביום זריקתו וממחרת. המחשב לאור שלישי. יג] בשחיטת שלמים, על מנת לאכול מן הבשר לאור שלישי, ליל שני לזביחה יד]. כשר. דלא הוי חוץ לזמנו. דלא אינתיק ליה. מזמנו לגמרי, ולהיות זמן שריפתו עכשיו עד לצפרא, כדתני' לקמן בשמעתין. האוכל לאור שלישי. מבשר קרבן כשר. פטור. מקרבן שגגת נותר. לא אינתיק לשריפה. הלכך לאו נותר הוא. מחשבין בדמן משתשקע החמה טו]. אם שחט על מנת לזרוק דמן משתשקע החמה – פיגול. ובאכילת בשר ובהקטרת אימוריהם, אם חישב בשחיטה על מנת לאכול מבשרן או להקטיר מאימוריהן משיעלה עמוד השחר – פיגול, דהיינו חוץ לזמן דידהו. ה"ג: והנאכלין לשני ימים ולילה אחד מחשבין בדמן משתשקע החמה ובאימורין משיעלה עמוד השחר ובבשרן משתשקע החמה של שני ימים. והיינו לאור שלישי, כר' יוחנן. לענין דם ואימורין קדשי קדשים וקדשים קלים שוין, דדם ואימורין לעולם קדשי קדשים הם. לילה אחריהם. דכתיב בתודה (ויקרא ז): "לא יניח ממנו עד בקר" – טז] [הא] כל הלילה נאכל, אף כאן בשלמים תהא לילה אחר יום המחרת. עד יום. גבי אכילה כתיב ב"קדושים תהיו": "ביום זבחכם יאכל וממחרת והנותר עד יום" – בעוד שהוא יום תאכלנו. יכול ישרף מיד. לאור שלישי, הואיל ועבר זמן אכילתו. מה להלן. בנאכלין ליום אחד, תיכף לאכילה שריפה, דכתיב גבי מילואים: "ואם יותר מבשר המילואים" וגו'. יז] ב"לו את אהרן" כתיב, ובהאי קרא לא כתיב אכילה אלא שריפה, ולהכי לא כתיב "עד יום" אלא "ביום". **מתני'** והמעשר. מעשר בהמה. מתנה אחת. דלא כתיב בהו "סביב", אלא "ואת דמם תזרוק" כתיב בבכור, והנך נמי יח] מהכא ילפינן כדאמרינן בגמ'. כנגד היסוד. במקום שיש יסוד תחתיו, למעוטי מזרח ודרום. שינה באכילתן. אע"פ ששוה הכתוב את מתן דמם, שינה באכילתן זה מזה. הבכור נאכל לכהנים. כדכתיב: "ובשרם יהיה לך" (במדבר יח). והמעשר לכל אדם. שלא מצינו יט] לו בתורה שינתן לכהן. ונאכלין בכל העיר בכל מאכל גרס. ולא גרסי' "לכל אדם", דהא קתני בכור כ] לכהנים. בכל העיר. כדכתיב: "והבאתם שמה עולותיכם וזבחיכם ואת מעשרותיכם" (דברים יב), ותניא בספרי: ר' עקיבא אומר בשתי מעשרות הכתוב מדבר, אחד מעשר בהמה ואחד מעשר דגן, וכתיב (א) בההוא קרא: "ובכורות בקרכם וצאנכם". ומדלא קבע כא] בהו מחיצה – שמע מינה בכל העיר נאכלין. לשני ימים ולילה אחד. בבכור יליף לה בגמ', מעשר לא ידענא מהיכא. אלא בלילה. כדכתיב: "בלילה הזה" (שמות יב). ואינו נאכל אלא עד חצות. בגמ' יליף לה. למנוייו. שנמנו בדמי לקיחתו, כדכתיב: "לפי אכלו תכוסו" (שם). **גמ'** מאן תנא. למה מעשר ופסח בזריקה? כב] מדמשוי מתן דמים בכור ומעשר ופסח, דקתני: שינה באכילתן – מכלל דמתן דמים לא שינה. ובבכור כתיב: "ואת דמם תזרוק" (במדבר יח). דמו לא נאמר. "אך בכור שור" וגו'. אבל לר' ישמעאל פסח בשפיכה, דנפקא ליה מתן דמים לפסח מ"ודם זבחיך ישפך" (דברים יב).

תורה אור: ויקרא יט; שם

עין משפט נר מצוה: סד [illegible] סה [illegible] סו [illegible] סז [illegible] סח [illegible] סט [illegible] ע [illegible] עא [illegible] עב [illegible] עג [illegible]

שיטה מקובצת: א] האידנא אכול בשר: ב] למחר אכול בשר: ג] פטור רבי יוחנן אמר חייב חזקיה אמר פטור דלא: ד] זבחים הנאכלין. [illegible]

מסורת הש"ס: פסחים ג. [illegible]; לעיל לז. פסחים סד:; [נ"ל אלעזר]

הגהות הב"ח: (א) רש"י ד"ה בכל העיר וכו' וכתיב נ"ב בההוא קרא:

גליון הש"ס: גמ' מחשבין בדמן משתשקע החמה. עיין לעיל דף כט ע"א תוס' ד"ה למקום:

[illegible]

ועולה גופה מנלן – א] דכתיב: "אל יסוד מזבח העולה", ב] למד על עולת חובה שטעונה יסוד. אי מה להלן ג] שתי מתנות שהן ארבע – אף כאן שתי מתנות שהן ארבע! אמר אביי: ד] למה לי למכתב "סביב" בעולה, "סביב" בחטאת? *הוו שני כתובין הבאין כאחד, *וכל שני כתובין הבאין כאחד אין מלמדין. הניחא למ"ד אין מלמדין, אלא למ"ד מלמדין מאי איכא למימר? הוי ה] אשם שלשה, ושלשה ודאי אין מלמדין.§ ו] "הבכור נאכל לכהנים".§ ת"ר: מנין לבכור שנאכל לשני ימים ולילה – ז] שנאמר: "ובשרם יהיה לך כחזה התנופה וכשוק הימין", הקישו הכתוב לחזה ושוק של שלמים: מה שלמים נאכלין לשני ימים ולילה אחד – אף בכור נאכל לשני ימים ולילה אחד. וזו שאלה נשאלה לפני חכמים בכרם ביבנה: בכור לכמה נאכל? נענה ר"ט ואמר: לשני ימים ולילה אחד. היה שם תלמיד אחד שבא לבית המדרש ח] לפני חכמים תחלה, ור' יוסי הגלילי שמו. אמר לו: רבי, מנין לך? אמר לו: בני, שלמים קדשים קלים ובכור קדשים קלים, מה שלמים נאכלין לשני ימים ולילה אחד – אף בכור נאכל לשני ימים ולילה אחד. אמר לו: רבי, בכור – מתנה לכהן, וחטאת ואשם מתנה לכהן, מה חטאת ואשם ליום ולילה – אף בכור ליום ולילה! אמר לו: ט] נדון דבר מ(תוך) דבר ונלמד דבר מ(תוך) דבר: מה שלמים אין באין על חטא – אף בכור אינו בא על חטא, מה שלמים נאכלים לשני ימים ולילה אחד – אף בכור נאכל לשני ימים ולילה אחד. אמר לו: רבי, נדון דבר מדבר י] ילמד דבר מדבר: חטאת ואשם מתנה לכהן, יא] ובכור מתנה לכהן, מה חטאת ואשם אין באין בנדר ונדבה – אף בכור אינו בנדר ונדבה, מה חטאת ואשם נאכלין ליום יב] אחד – אף בכור נאכל ליום אחד! קפץ ר"ע ונסתלק ר"ט. אמר לו: הרי הוא אומר: "ובשרם יהיה לך" – יג] הקישן הכתוב לחזה ושוק של שלמים, מה שלמים נאכלין לשני ימים ולילה אחד – אף בכור נאכל לשני ימים ולילה אחד. אמר לו: יד] היקשתו לחזה ושוק של שלמים, ואני מקישו לחזה ושוק של תודה: מה תודה נאכלת ליום ולילה – אף בכור נאכל ליום ולילה! אמר לו: הרי הוא אומר: "ובשרם יהיה לך", שאין ת"ל טו] "לך יהיה", ומה ת"ל "לך יהיה" – *הוסיף הכתוב הויה אחרת בבכור. וכשנאמרו דברים לפני ר' ישמעאל, אמר להן: *צאו ואמרו לו טז] לר"ע: טעיתה, תודה מהיכן למדה – משלמים, [וכי] דבר הלמד בהיקש *חוזר ומלמד יז] בהיקש? הא אין עליך לידון בלשון אחרון אלא בלשון ראשון. ור' ישמעאל, האי "לך יהיה" מאי עביד לי'? *לימד על בכור בעל מום שהוא מתנה לכהן, *שלא מצינו בכל התורה. יח] ור"ע? יליף ליה מ"בשרם" – חד תם, וחד בעל מום. ור' ישמעאל? מבשרם דהנך בכורות קאמר. במאי קמיפלגי? מ"ס: *הימנו ודבר אחר – הוי היקש, ומ"ס: לא הוי היקש. בשלמא למ"ד לא הוי היקש – היינו דכתיב: "וכן יעשה לאהל מועד", *כשם שמזה לפני ולפנים אחת למעלה ושבע למטה מדם הפר – כך א מזה בהיכל, וכשם שלפני ולפנים אחת למעלה ושבע למטה מדם השעיר – כך ב מזה בהיכל. אלא למ"ד הוי היקש מאי איכא למימר? יט] *מקומות הוא דגמרי מהדדי. ואיבעית

רש"י

ועולה גופה מנלן. כדי נסבה, דהא מק"ו ילפינן לעיל בפירקין (דף נג.), והאי קרא לדרשא אחרינא כ] אוקימנא. וקיצור דברים הוא דנקט לה מקרא, דאי לאו ק"ו, הוה ילפינן לה כא] מינה. אי מה כו' אף כאן. *דבכור זריקה זריקה מעולה ילפינן, מה להלן ד' מתנות שתים שהן ארבע. סביב בחטאת. במילואים, ובעולה. מ"סביב" שמעינן ביה ד' מתנות, כב] שסובב בדמה *רוחות המזבח. אין מלמדין. ואע"ג דהכא לאו בבנין אב אנו באין ללמוד, אשמעינן אביי דשני כתובין הבאין כאחד אין מלמדין אפי' בג"ש אותו דבר שנכתב בשניהן. ובשרם יהיה לך. בבכור כתיב. לחזה ושוק של שלמים. ולקמיה פריך: כג] לשל תודה אקשינן. בכרם. ת"ח יושבין שורות ככרם, כך מפורש בברכות ירושלמי. שבא לבית המדרש תחלה. היא היתה תחילת ביאתו לפניהם ביבנה. וחטאת ואשם מתנה לכהן. אבל שלמים לבעלים. נדון דבר מדבר. כלומר, שכמותו ודומה לו. אין באין על חטא. כחטאת ואשם. אינו בא בנדר ובנדבה. לאפוקי שלמים דבאין בנדר ובנדבה. ונסתלק. נשתתק. הקישו הכתוב. ואין משיבין על ההיקש. הוסיף לך הכתוב כו'. כלומר, מודה אני לדבריך שלחזה ושוק של תודה כד] צריכין אנו להקישו, דתפסת מועט תפסת. מיהו, מדהדר הכתוב בסיפיה דקרא "לך יהיה", דלא איצטריך, דהא כתיב ברישיה "יהיה לך" – הוסיף לו הכתוב הויה אחרת, כמו זו הבאה לו בהיקש. ה"ג: וכשנאמרו דברים לפני ר' ישמעאל אמר להם צאו ואמרו לו כה] לר"ע טעית תודה מהיכן למדה משלמים כו] ודבר הלמד בהיקש חוזר ומלמד בהיקש אין עליך כו'. טעיתה במה שחזרת בך מהיקש שלמים ואתה מקישו לתודה, דלא למדו הכתוב אלא משלמים. דאי מתודה – חזה ושוק לא כתיב בה, אלא מדאיתקש תודה לשלמים נפקא לן בה חזה ושוק בת"כ. דתניא: לפי שיצאה תודה לידון בדבר החדש, שטעונה לחם, יכול אין לך בה אלא חידושה – כז] ת"ל: "תורת זבח השלמים אם על תודה" מה שלמים טעונים סמיכה ונסכים ותנופת חזה ושוק – אף תודה כו'. ודבר הלמד בהיקש כח] יחזור וילמד על הבכור בהיקש. ליאכל ליום ולילה? אין עליך לדונו בלשון אחרון. להקישה לחזה ושוק של תודה. אלא בלשון ראשון. לשל שלמים. שלא מצינו. ללמדו בכל התורה כולה אלא מכאן. דהנך בכורות. בכור שור בכור כשב בכור עז, כט] וכל לשון רבים דקרא – עלייהו קאי לר' ישמעאל. וה"נ אמרינן גבי "ואת דמם ואת חלבם" לר' ישמעאל בפרק "ב"ש" (לעיל לז.). במאי קמיפלגי. רבי ישמעאל ור"ע? דע"כ אין היקש חוזר מלמד בהיקש, ור"ע מ"ט גמיר לה? הימנו ודבר אחר. אכילת חזה ושוק של תודה ליום ולילה – הימנו ודבר אחר *העמידוה. קלת המלמד כתב בה – דכתיב בתודה יום ולילה, וקלת היא למדה ממקום אחר, ל] מאי היא – חזה ושוק דלא כתיב בה. רבי ישמעאל סבר היקש הוא. נמלא מה שחזה ושוק לא] נאכלין ליום ולילה מן ההיקש למד. ור"ע סבר: הואיל ויום ולילה בתודה כתיב, אע"ג דחזה ושוק למדה לב] בהיקש – לא הויא זמן אכילת חזה ושוק של תודה דבר הלמד בהיקש. כשם שמזה לפני ולפנים כו'. ולפני ולפנים גופיה אחת למעלה ושבע למטה בפר ושעיר – בהימנו ודבר אחר גמר לג] דבפנים למעלה בפר לא כתיב ביה מניינא, דכתיב (ויקרא טז): "והזה באצבעו על פני הכפרת וקדמה ולפני הכפרת יזה שבע פעמים", לד] ושבע למטה הוא דכתיבא ביה. ובשעיר חטאת למעלה הוא דכתיבא "והזה אותו על הכפרת ולפני הכפרת", "אותו" – חדא משמע, לה] ולפני הכפרת לא כתיב שבע. וגמירי בהיקשא מהדדי, דכתיב: "ועשה את דמו כאשר עשה לדם הפר". אלמא עבודת פר ושעיר בפנים לו] בהימנו ודבר אחר ילפינן, דמקצת עבודה כל אחד כתובה בו, ומקצתה למד מחבירו. והדר מיגמר היכל מפנים בהיקשא ד"כן יעשה לאהל מועד". אלמא הימנו ודבר אחר לא כהיקשא חשיב לה. אלא למ"ד הוי היקש. היכי הדר היכל וגמר מיניה בהיקשא? מקומות הוא דגמירי מהדדי. ואין זה לז] חוזר ומלמד בהיקש. דבהיקש קמא בהמות איתקוש, ובהיקשא בתרא מקומות איתקוש. אבל גבי תודה ובכור – *חזה ושוק של תודה לח] הוקשה לבכור, והיא עצמה למידה משלמים בהיקש. ה"ג

תוספות

למה לי למכתב סביב בעולה סביב בחטאת הוו שני כתובים. לט] "סביב" בעולה איצטריך, לכדאמר לעיל: יכול יזרקנו זריקה אחת – ת"ל "סביב". אלא "סביב" דחטאת קאמר ל"ל, דארבע קרנות כתיב ביה. מ] ומיהו, לרבי ישמעאל קשה: דאיצטריך לגזירה שוה, דיליף מיניה פיסוק ד' מתנות בעולה, כדאמר לעיל. ועוד: למ"ד לעיל (דף נג.) בחטאת נותן אמה אילך ואמה אילך, איצטריך בחטאת "סביב" לגופיה, שלא תאמר דסגי בשתי מתנות *ברוחב אחת בשתי קרנות! ושמא "סביב" דעולה הוא *דמייתי, דטובא "סביב" כתיב בעולה בפרשת ויקרא. מא] ועוד: דעולה אתיא זריקה זריקה משלמים. ואני מקישו לחזה ושוק של תודה. משום דלחומרא מקשינן. וכי דבר הלמד בהיקש חוזר ומלמד בהיקש. תימה: ונקשיה לחזה ושוק של איל נזיר דכתיב בהדיא, ונאכל ליום ולילה, כדמרבינן לעיל מב] *בפ"ק (דף ד) ובפרק "כל הפסולין" (דף לו.). מג] וכ"ת דהאי דמרבינן מ"בשר זבח תודת שלמיו" חשיב היקשא – מד] א"כ היכי יליף לה לעיל מחטאת ואשם דילפינן *מההוא קרא? ולעיל (דף נ.) איבעיא לן אי דבר הלמד בהיקש חוזר ומלמד בבנין אב ולא איפשיטא! ויש לומר: דמסתברא לאקושי לתודה שנוהגת בכל בהמה מה] *בבכור, ולא לאיל נזיר דאינו נוהג אלא באיל. א"נ, בשוק הימין כתב *ותודה ילפי' משלמים דכתיב בהו "ימין", אבל איל נזיר לא כתיב ביה ימין. ואיבעית

שיטה מקובצת

א] דכתיב אל יסוד כו' פ"ה דכדי נסבא כו' היינו לשיטתו דלעיל אבל לפי' ריב"א אתי שפיר ואע"ג דאוקימנא לעיל בשירים בעולה לפי' רבינו חיים מ"מ [אמרינן נמי] בתחלת עולה דהוא פשטיה דקרא לפי' ריב"א ולפירוש רבינו חיים וא"ת אכתי תחלת דמים דכל הקרבנות כנגד היסוד מגלן לפי' רבינו חיים דלא [אתא] קרא דאל יסוד העולה רק בעולה וי"ל דילפינן להו נמי בג"ש דזריקה מעולה כמו בכור ומעשר ה"ה נמי לכל הקרבנות אלא משום דהוי קבעי על הבכור אי נמי א) לאחר שפי' כל הקרבנות קבעי הכא כנגד היסוד מגלן ואכולהו קרבנות קאי וא"ת ולמאן דדריש בכור ומעשר מדם זבחיך ישפך לומר דהם בשפיכה שהם כנגד היסוד מגליה כיון דלא שייך ג"ש דזריקה ואין סברא לומר דפליג בהא דהא לא אשכחן שום תנא דפליג אלא בשפיכה אבל כנגד היסוד לא אשכחן שום תנא דפליג ועוד דמתני' דקתני כנגד היסוד מסברא אתי ככולי עלמא ותירץ ריב"א דיסוד גופיה נפקא מישפך דלשון שפיכה משמע ששופך על גבי דבר אחר והיינו על גבי היסוד דהיינו דבר חלק אבל מאן דיליף להו מאת דמם תזרוק לא הוי ידעינן כנגד היסוד אלא מג"ש דזריקה. תו' מהר"פ: ב] על תיבות למד על עולת שטעונה יסוד נרשם מלמעלה קו להורות שאין זה מדברי התלמוד (ותיבת חובה נמחק): ג] להלן ארבע מתנות אף כאן ארבע מתנות (ועל תיבות שהן ארבע נרשם קו): ד] למה לי למכתב סביב בעולה כו'. תימה והלא אינם שוין דעולה היינו ב' מתנות כו' ועוד דהיא למטה וחטאת למעלה אלא אחטאת קאמר כו'. לשון מהר"פ: ה] אשם שלשה. תימה דלא מצינו למילף אשם מעולה דאיכא למיפרך מה לעולה שכן כליל וי"ל דבאשם נמי כתיב זריקה וילפינן בג"ש מעולה שטעונה יסוד לתחלת דמו וה"ה דהמ"ל הוי שלמים ג' כתובים הבאים [כאחד] דנאמר בהם זריקה וסביב: ו] ונאכלים בכל העיר וכו'. ת"ר מנין: ז] ולילה אחת שנאמר: ח] תיבות לפני חכמים נמחק: ט] א"ל בני נדון דבר מדבר ונלמד דבר מדבר שלמים קדשים קלים ואין באין על חטא ובכור קדשים קלים ואינו בא על חטא: י] ונלמד דבר: יא] מתנה לכהן ואינן באים בנדר ונדבה ובכור מתנה לכהן ואין בא בנדר ונדבה מתיבות מה חטאת כו' עד תיבת ונדבה נמחק: יב] ליום ולילה אחד אף בכור נאכל ליום ולילה אחד: יג] לך וגו' הקישן: יד] לו אתה היקשתו: טו] ת"ל יהיה לך ומה ת"ל יהיה לך הוסיף: טז] לו לעקיבא: יז] בהיקש. וא"ת ולילף בכור בהיקשא דחזה ושוק דאיל נזיר דכתיב בגופיה זמן אכילתו כדדרשינן מזבח תודת שלמיו לרבות שלמי נזיר לעיל וליכא למימר דגם זה חשיב היקש דאיתקש לתודה ואע"ג דאיכא יתורא דא"כ חטאת ואשם נמי לא נפקא אלא מהאי קרא וכיון דחשיב היקש היכא ילפינן בכור לעיל מבנין אב דחטאת ואשם והלא דבר הלמד בהיקש אינו חוזר ומלמד בבנין אב ולעיל לא איפשט לן וי"ל דמחזה ושוק דאיל נזיר לא מצי יליף משום דהתם יש זרוע בשלה שגם הוא מתנה לכהן ובהאי קרא דבכור לא כתיב כי אם חזה ושוק דמשמע דמקיש בכור לחזה ושוק גרידא דליכא בהדיה דבר אחר שהוא מתנה לכהן. לשון מהר"פ: יח] התורה כולה ור"ע יליף ליה מובשרם כו' ורבי ישמעאל ובשרם דהנך: יט] מקומות הוא כו' דבהיקש קמא איתקש פר ושעיר ובהיקש בתרא מקשינן היכל לבין הבדים הלכך היקשא בתרא לא הוי מעין היקשא קמא: כ] אחרינא אוקמינא: כא] לה תלמודא מהכא ב) כלומר אי דבכור והד והד"א: כב] מתנות שיסבב בדמה ארבע רוחות: כג] פריך דלמא לחזה ושוק של תודה: כד] תודה הוקש תיבות צריכין אנו להקישו נמחק: כה] לו לעקיבא טעית: כו] משלמים דבר הלמד אות ו' נמחק: כז] חידושה בלבד ת"ל וזאת תורת זבח השלמים וגו': כח] בהיקש היאך חוזר ומלמד על בכור: כט] עז דכתיבי בקרא וכל לשון רבים דקרא לר' ישמעאל עלייהו קאי והכי נמי: ל] אחר דלא כתיב בה חזה ושוק הס"ד: לא] ושוק של תודה נאכלין ליום כו' למד הלכך אינה חוזרת ומלמדת בהיקש הס"ד: לב] למדה בה בהיקש: לג] גמר דלמעלה ותיבת דבפנים נמחק: לד] פעמים שבע למטה כו' ובשעיר אחת למעלה בלחוד כתיבא והזה אותו: לה] משמע ושבע למטה לא כתיב וגמירי תיבות ולפני הכפורת נמחק: לו] בפנים בהיקש בהימנו ודבר אחר ילפינן דמקצת עבודות כל אחד ואחד כתובות בו ומקצתו הוא למד מחבירו והדר מיגמר פנים אהיכל בהיקשא דכן כו' לא היקשא חשיב ליה הס"ד: לז] זה קרוי חוזר: לח] תודה עצמה הוקשה: לט] דאסביב דעולה לא קאי דאיצטריך לאתויי לכדאמר: מ] ביה ואם אינו ענין לגופיה תנהו ענין לעולה והוי ב' כתובים בעולה ואין מלמדין ומיהו לר"י קשה דאצטריך סביב לגזירה: מא] עיין בהשמטות בסוף המסכת: מב] לעיל בפרק כל הפסולין ותיבות בפ"ק נמחק: מג] ואין לומר דהאי תיבות וכ"ת ל"ש: מד] היקשא דא"כ: מה] כבכור ולא לאיל נזיר שאינו נוהג:

עין משפט נר מצוה

עד א ב מיי' פ"ה מהלכות מעה"ק הל' יב ופ"ג מהלכות עיה"כ הלכה ה:

הגהות בגליון

נ"ל ברוח נ"ק | גי' הג"ק דמייתר | [קדושין כד. וש"נ] | מה שנרשם כאן בפ"ק דמרבי' שלמי נזיר ליתא ועי' לעיל דף ד ע"א וצ"ל כדמרבינן לעיל בפ' כל הפסולין נ"ק | נ"ל נמי מהאי קרא | נ"ל כבכור | נ"ל כבכור ותודה נ"ק

מסורת הש"ס

נ"ל כיון דבכור נ"ק | [פסחים סה. ע"ש] | גי' הג"ק ד' רוחות המזבח | [עי' תוס' פסחים סז: ד"ה אתיא] | [בכורות כז:] | [שם כח.] | [יומא עה: ע"ש] | [לעיל מט: וש"נ] | [בכורות כז: לעיל לז:] | *[שבת פג: וש"נ] | [מנחות עח. יומא נז.] | [יומא נז.] | [שם] | נ"ל הוא קלת התלמוד כו' פי' קלת הלימוד נ"ק | נ"ק חזה ושוק של בכור הוקשה לתודה והיא כו' כצ"ל

ואיבעית

א) אולי צ"ל לאחר שפירש דבכור ומעשר ופסח טעונין מתן דמים ואימורין ככל הקרבנות קבעי הכא וכו'. ב) נראה דצ"ל מהכא הס"ד ומה"ד אי מה כו' אף כאן כלומר אי דבכור כו'.

עה א מיי' פ"ח מהל' תמידין ומוספין הלכה ד:

ואיבעית אימא חוץ מפנים בחדא זימנא גמיר. פירש בקונטרס: דכולה מילתא דהיכל בעי למילף מפנים, ואיידי דניתן היקש לדרוש בדברים המפורשים בפנים, כגון למטה בפר ולמעלה בשעיר – נדרש ולמד בבת אחת אף הלמד בפנים בהיקש עמו. וגבי היקש דלעיל נמי, אם היינו צריכין ללמוד לבכור תנופת חזה ושוק וזמן אכילה, והוקש בכור לתודה עצמה ללמוד שיהן ממנה, מתוך שתודה מלמדת עליו זמן אכילה דכתיב בה – מלמדת עליו נמי חזה ושוק שלמדתו בהיקש משלמים. אבל עכשיו, שלא הוקש לתודה אלא לחזה ושוק לא] וללמוד ממנו זמן אכילה לבדו, אם אתה אומר לחזה ושוק של תודה הקישו הכתוב – לב] בו עצמו לא למדו בתודה אלא בהיקש. ע"כ לשון הקונט'. וקשה לפירושו מהא דאמר לעיל (דף מט:) דיותרת ושתי הכליות דעבודה זרה הוי דבר הלמד בהיקש, ואינו חוזר ומלמד בהיקש, *אע"ג לג] דכתיבא ההיא היקשא לדברים דכתיבי בפר העלם גופיה, כגון הזאות וכמה דברים, ולא אמרי' בחד זימנא גמיר. ועוד: אמרי' לעיל (דף נה.) דלא ילפינן זבחי שלמי ציבור לצפון מחטאת, משום דהוי דבר הבא בהיקש ואינו חוזר ומלמד בהיקש – *אף על גב דצריכא ההיא, לד] וילפינן בהיקשא לה] [*דנאכל לזכרי כהונה]! ותי' ר"י: דמאחת למעלה דכתיב בשעיר יליף מבחוץ, בין בפר בין בשעיר, לו] דהכי משמע: "וכן יעשה" בחוץ, בין בפר בין בשעיר. וכן *בשבע דלמטה דכתיבי בפר בפנים – ילפינן (בין) בחוץ, בין לז] בפר [בין] בשעיר, כלומר בכל הבהמות. ורבינו חננאל פירש בפרק "הוציאו לו" (יומא נז.) בחדא זימנא גמיר – דכי גמרינן שיהיו כל עשיותיו שוות בין בפנים בין בחוץ, שכל הזאות שיעשו מהם בכל מקום שיהיו שוות. ואית ספרים דגרסי: חוץ ופנים בחד זימנא גמר*. **היינו** דכתיב ממושבותיכם תביאו. גבי שתי הלחם כתיב, וילפינן מינה חלות חמץ לח] *לתודה, דמה כאן בשתי הלחם עשרון לחלה – אף כאן חמץ שבתודה עשרון לחלה. ומנין חלות שבתודה ילפינן דהוו עשר בג"ש דתרומה תרומה מתרומת מעשר. אלמא איכא י' עשרונות לי' חלות של חמץ. והדר ילפינן לט] מיניה מחמץ דכנגד חמץ הבא מצה – והוו להו י' עשרונות לג' מינים של מצה, דהיינו מ] ג' עשרון ושליש *לכל מין חלה וחלה של מצה. ואע"ג דמנין של חלות לאו בגופיה דחמץ כתיב – חשיב ליה מא] *בחמץ, כדפירש בקונטרס, משום דדבר הלמד בג"ש חוזר ומלמד בהיקש. א"נ: משום דתרומת מעשר חולין הוא. א"נ, משום דפריך בפ' "התודה" (מנחות עז:): ואימא ב' עשרונות ותו לא, כשתי הלחם! וקאמר: ת"ל "תהיינה". וגרסי' התם: מאי תלמודא? אמר ר' יצחק בר אבדימי: "תהיינה" כתיב, *עשרה עשרונות דבר הכתוב. ומריבוי ב' יודין דריש, דחד יו"ד מב] יתיר משמע עשרה, ומסתברא דהאי יו"ד ד"תהיינה" אלחמי תודה קאי, דאי אשתי הלחם – "שתים שני עשרונים" כתיב. והיינו הימנו ודבר אחר, די' עשרונות בדידיה כתיב, ד"תהיינה" מג] משמע י' חלות, ועשרון מ"תביאו" קא יליף. ובלשון אחרון פירש בקונטו' במנחות (גז"ש). ואית ספרים דגרסי התם: אמר רב יצחק בר אבדימי תהיינה כתיב, ותו לא. ול"ג: עשר עשרונות דבר הכתוב. ודריש משום ד"תהיינה" מיעוטא הוא, דמשמע: הני דוקא שני עשרונים, ולא אחר שני עשרונות. וכ"נ, דיו"ד לא מד] *מייתינן למידרש, דכמו שיאמר מ"תעשה" לשון יחיד "תעשינה" לשון רבים, כך יאמר מ"תהיה" "תהיינה", יו"ד אחת של עיקר ויו"ד אחת של שימוש. ואם תאמר: ומג"ש דתרומת מעשר היכי יליף לי' חלות? דלמא עביד חדא חלה מה] אחת גדולה ויטול הימנה פרוסה לתרומה! וי"ל: דהא אמרינן (פסחים דף לז:) "אחד" – שלא יטול פרוסה. ועוד: דרשינן התם שיהו כל הקרבנות שוין, אלמא דבעי להנך חלות דליהוו *כחלות של תרומה. **להרחיק** מן העבירה. לנאכלין לשני ימים ולילה אחד לא עשו חכמים הרחקה עד חצות, דניכר הוא מתי יהיה שקיעת החמה. אבל בלילה אינו ניכר מו]. **ואיבעית אימא** כי התם כו'. בקונטרס לא גרס "ואיבעית אימא". ויש לפרש, דדייק מדלא קתני "עד חצות" לבסוף, ותני ליה באמצע, ש"מ דהוי דאורייתא כמו לילה ומנויו וצלי. ויש לדקדק דהלכה כר' אלעזר בן עזריה, דסתם לן תנא כוותיה במתני' וב"ערבי פסחים" (פסחים קכ:) ובפ"ק דברכות (דף ט.). וצריך ליזהר אמצה, משום דקאמר רבא בסוף "ערבי פסחים": אכל מצה אחר חצות לרבי אלעזר בן עזריה לא יצא ידי חובתו [ועיין תוספות פסחים קכ: ד"ה אמר רבא ותוספות מגילה כא. ד"ה לאיתויי]. **הדרן עלך איזהו מקומן**

ה"ג: ואיבעית אימא חוץ מפנים בחד זימנא גמיר. והכי איתא בסדר יומא בפרק "הוציאו לו" (דף נז.). כלומר: נהי נמי דהיקש מקומות כהיקש בהמות הואיל והיקש יבן לורך פנים הוא, אפ"ה לא דמי להנהו דלעיל, דאילו היכל כולה מילתא קא בעי למילף מפנים, ואיידי דניתן היקש לידרש בדברים המפורשים בפנים, יגן כמו למטה בפר ולמעלה בשעיר – נדרש ידן ולמד בבת אחת ובא אף מה שלמד בפנים בהיקש עמו. וגבי היקש *דלעיל נמי, אם טון כתוב *בתודה והוקש בכור לתודה (ג) ללמוד לו חזה ושוק, ולמדתה בהיקש – אי הוי טזן הוקש בכור לתודה עצמה והיה למד ממנה תנופת חזה ושוק ואכילת יום ולילה, יזן דמתוך שיכולה ללמוד עליו זמן לאכילה שהוא כתוב בה מלמדת נמי עליו תנופת חזה ושוק. יחן אבל השתא לתודה עצמה לא הקישה הכתוב, אלא לחזה ושוק שבתודה, ובתודה עצמה לא למדתה אלא בהיקש. היינו דכתיב ממושבתיכם וגו'. גבי שתי הלחם דעצרת יטן כתיב, והוצרכנו במסכת מנחות (דף עז:) ללמוד מהם כמה עשרונות יש בלחמי תודה. ובגופה נכתב י' חלות בכל מין אבל לא נתפרש מכמה היא החלה, ומייתי לה לחלות חמץ שבתודה כן משתי הלחם שאף הן חמץ, והכתוב הקיש כל הבאות של חמץ כאן שיהיו שוות. ומקרא יתירא ד"תביאו" ילפי' לה, דלא איצטריך, דכתיב: "והקרבתם מנחה חדשה ממושבתיכם כבן תביאו לחם תנופה" ולא איצטריך "תביאו", מה ת"ל "תביאו" – כל חמץ שאתה מביא ממקום אחר יהא כזה, עשרון לחלה, כדכתיב: "שתים שני עשרונים". אי מה כגן להלן. אלו שני *עשרונים, אף אלו כל י' חלות שבה שני עשרונים. ת"ל תהיינה. התם מפרש מאי כדן למודה בפ' "התודה". למדנו עשרה. עשרונות לחמץ, דהא י' חלות למודות בה בג"ש מתרומת מעשר: מה תרומת מעשר אחד מעשר – אף תרומת תודה "והקריב ממנו אחד מכל קרבן מכל מין תרומה לה'" אחד מעשר, הרי י' חלות. ובהיקש כהן "תביאו" למדנו שהחלה בעשרון – הרי למדנו י' עשרונות לחמץ. כון הימנו ודבר אחר, י' חלות למדנו בהן כבר, ובהיקש הן למידות עשרון לחלה. עשרה. בעשרון לשלשת מינין שבמצה, מנין? ת"ל על חלת לחם חמץ. מנה הכתוב מינין שבמצה, וכתב אחריהן "על חלת לחם חמץ" – הרי היקש. אלמא, חמץ שלמדנו בו עשרה עשרונות בהימנו ודבר אחר, חוזר ומלמד על המצה בהיקש עשרה עשרונות! **תביאו רבויא הוא.** לרבות חמץ שבתודה שכל שתים כזן שבו יהו שתים עשרונים, והוי כמאן דכתיב כחן בגופיה בלחמי תודה, ולאו משתי הלחם גמרי. כטן והיכי דמי דליהוי הימנו ודבר אחר – כגון אי איתקוש חמץ דתודה לשתי הלחם בקרא אחרינא דלא מפרש לן בה עשרון לחלה, וילפינן תודה משתי הלחם בהיקש לעשרון לחלה, ובדידיה כתיבי עשר חלות. **מאן תנא.** דאינו נאכל אלא עד חצות. **עד שעת חפזון.** שהם נחפזים ללכת, והיינו לאור הבוקר, כדכתיב (שמות יב): "ואתם לא תצאו איש מפתח ביתו עד בקר". **יכול יהא נאכל כשאר כל הקדשים.** ביום זביחתו קודם שתחשך יתחיל לאוכלו אם ירצה? ת"ל כו'. **להרחיק את האדם.** כדתנן בכולהו עד חצות. **א"כ מאי אלא.** ליתני: ונאכל עד חצות, כדתנא בכולהו! **כי התם.** דומיא דלילה ומנויו וצלי תנייה, דהוו דאורייתא. "איבעית אימא" לא גרסינן. וה"ג: א"כ מאי אלא כי התם מה התם דאורייתא כו'.

הדרן עלך איזהו מקומן

תורה אור

א] וְאִיבָּעֵית אֵימָא: חוּץ מִפְּנִים בְּחַד זִימְנָא גָּמֵיר. בִּשְׁלָמָא לְמ"ד (א) ב] *הָוֵי הֶיקֵּשׁ — הַיְינוּ דִּכְתִיב: °"מִמּוֹשְׁבוֹתֵיכֶם תָּבִיאוּ לֶחֶם תְּנוּפָה", *שֶׁאֵין ת"ל "תָּבִיאוּ", מַה ת"ל "תָּבִיאוּ"? כׇּל שֶׁאַתָּה מֵבִיא מִמָּקוֹם ג] (לְמָקוֹם) אַחֵר הֲרֵי הוּא כָּזֶה, מַה לְּהַלָּן עִשָּׂרוֹן לְחַלָּה — אַף כָּאן עִשָּׂרוֹן לְחַלָּה. אִי מַה לְּהַלָּן שְׁנֵי עֶשְׂרוֹנִים, אַף כָּאן שְׁנֵי עֶשְׂרוֹנִים! ת"ל: "תִּהְיֶינָה". ד] וְלָמַדְנוּ א עֲשָׂרָה לְחָמֵץ, עֲשָׂרָה לְמַצָּה מִנַּיִן? ת"ל: °"עַל חַלֹּת לֶחֶם חָמֵץ" — ה] נֶגֶד חָמֵץ הָבֵא מַצָּה; אֶלָּא לְמַאן דְּאָמַר ו] (ב) (*לָא) הָוֵי הֶיקֵּשׁ, מַאי אִיכָּא לְמֵימַר? "תָּבִיאוּ" ז] יְתֵירָא הִיא. § "הַפֶּסַח אֵינוֹ נֶאֱכָל". מַאן תַּנָּא? *אָמַר רַב יוֹסֵף: רַבִּי אֶלְעָזָר בֶּן עֲזַרְיָה הִיא. דְּתַנְיָא, רַבִּי אֶלְעָזָר ח] [בֶּן עֲזַרְיָה] אוֹמֵר, נֶאֱמַר כָּאן: °"בַּלַּיְלָה [הַזֶּה]" וְנֶאֱמַר לְהַלָּן: °"וְעָבַרְתִּי בְאֶרֶץ מִצְרַיִם בַּלַּיְלָה הַזֶּה", מַה לְּהַלָּן עַד חֲצוֹת — אַף כָּאן עַד חֲצוֹת. א"ל ר"ע: וַהֲלֹא כְּבָר נֶאֱמַר: "וַאֲכַלְתֶּם אוֹתוֹ בְּחִפָּזוֹן" — עַד שְׁעַת חִפָּזוֹן! א"כ, מַה ת"ל "בַּלַּיְלָה הַזֶּה"? שֶׁיָּכוֹל יְהֵא כְּכׇל הַקֳּדָשִׁים הַנֶּאֱכָלִים בַּיּוֹם? ת"ל: "בַּלַּיְלָה", בַּלַּיְלָה ט] יְהֵא נֶאֱכָל וְאֵינוֹ נֶאֱכָל בַּיּוֹם. א"ל אַבַּיֵי: וּמִמַּאי דְּרַבִּי אֶלְעָזָר ב"ע, וּדְאוֹרַיְיתָא? דִּלְמָא דְּרַבָּנַן, י] וּלְהַרְחִיק מִן הָעֲבֵירָה! א"כ, מַאי "אֶלָּא יא] עַד חֲצוֹת"? [אֶלָּא] כִּי הָתָם, מַה הָתָם דְּאוֹרַיְיתָא — אַף כָּאן נַמִי דְּאוֹרַיְיתָ'.§

הדרן עלך איזהו מקומן

הגהות הב"ח

(א) גמ' בשלמא למ"ד לא הוי היקש: (ב) שם אלא למ"ד הוי היקש: (ג) רש"י ד"ה ה"ג ואיבעית אימא וכו' אם כתוב בתודה והוקש בכור לתודה עצמה והיה למד ממנה וכו' ללמוד לו חזה ושוק ולמד תה בהיקש אי הוי הוקש בכור לתודה נמחק:

גליון הש"ס

תוס' ד"ה היינו וכו' משום דדבר הלמד בג"ש חוזר ומלמד בהיקש. עיין לעיל דף נ ע"א תוס' ד"ה אמר. ול"ע:

שיטה מקובצת

א] ואיבעית אימא חוץ מפנים כו'. פרש"י דכיון שצריך ללמוד מבין הבדים דבר שנכתב בגופו בהיקשא ילפינן נמי דבר שלא נכתב בגופו דאתי מהיקשא דהכל גמרינן בחדא זימנא אבל לעיל לא צריך ללמוד א) מתודה אלא ליום ולילה וזה לא נכתב בתודה אלא מהיקשא אתי ודוקא אם היינו צריכים ללמוד בבכור (דתנופת וחזה) [תנופת חזה] ושוק וזמן אכילה והוקש בכור לתודה עצמה [היינו יכולים] ללמוד שתיהן ממנה שהתודה שמלמדת עליו זמן אכילתה הכתוב בה מלמדת עליו נמי חזה ושוק שלמדתו מהיקש משלמים ולא נהירא דכיון דאפילו למ"ד הימנו ודבר אחר הוי היקש לא חשיב היקש בכה"ג כדפי' א"כ אמאי איצטריך לעיל לפר לפר העלם לאגמורי ליותרת הכבד ושתי הכליות לשעירי עבודת כוכבים והא איצטריך היקשא להזאות דכתיב בגופיה דפר העלם ודברים אחרים ולא אמרינן בחדא זימנא גמר לכך נראה דה"פ חוץ מפנים כו' דילפינן אהל מועד מבין הבדים בין לפר [בין] לשעירים כמה שכתוב בהדיא בתרוייהו בפנים דהיינו אחת למעלה בשעיר ושבע למטה בפר ועל זה קאמר וכן יעשה לפר ושעיר הנעשים באהל מועד כמו שמצינו מפורש (בהיכל) [בפנים] בשניהם דהיינו שבע למטה ואחת למעלה ולא ילפינן פר מפר ושעיר משעיר אלא ילפינן פר חיצון משעיר ופר דפנים וכן ילפינן שעיר דחיצון מפר ושעיר דפנים מכל אחד ילפינן מה שכתוב בו בפירוש. תוספות מהר"פ: ב] דאמר לא הוי: ג] ממקום אחר יהא כזה ותיבות למקום הרי הוא נמחק: ד] תהיינה למדנו אות ו' נמחק: ה] חמץ כנגד חמץ: ו] דאמר הוי תיבת לא נמחק: ז] תביאו ריבויא תיבות יתירא היא נמחק: ח] אלעזר בן עזריה אומר כו' בלילה הזה: ט] בלילה הוא נאכל תיבת יהא נמחק: י] להרחיק את האדם מן: יא] על תיבות עד חצות נרשם עליו קו: יב] והיקש בהמות תיבת צורך: יג] בפנים כגון למטה תיבת כמו נמחק: יד] נדרש ונלמד בבת: טו] אם היינו צריכים ללמוד בבכור תנופת חזה ושוק וזמן אכילה מתיבת כתוב עד תיבת הוי הוקש בכור נמחק: טז] והוקש בכור: יז] ולילה מתוך שיכולים ללמוד עליו זמן אכילה שהוא: יח] ושוק שלמדתו בהיקש משלמים אבל השתא שלא הוקש לתודה אלא לחזה ושוק של תודה הימנו וללמוד הימנו זמן אכילה לבדו אם אתה אומר לחזה ושוק של תודה הקישן הכתוב הלא הן עצמן לא למדו בתודה אלא בהיקש הס"ד: יט] דעצרת דהא חמץ כתיב והוצרכנו: כ] שבתודה בהיקש משתי: כא] חמץ יחד שיהו שוות אות י' ל"ש: כב] ממושבותיכם לחם תיבת תביאו נמחק: כג] מה אלו על תיבת להלן נרשם עליו מלמעלה קו: כד] מאי תלמודא: כה] ובהיקש דתביאו: כו] לחמץ בהימנו ודבר אחר המנין של חלות למדין שלא בהיקש והוי כהימנו דקי"ל דבר הלמד בג"ש חוזר ומלמד בהיקש ומדות החלות הוי דבר אחר שלמדנום בהיקש משתי הלחם (גירסת רש"י של הר"פ ז"ל) [כך] וזה אנו קורין הימנו ודבר אחר שחלות מצה למדין מחמץ שהן עשרה והוי כמאן דכתיב בגופיה דמיא וזה קרוי הימנו ודבר אחר קרוי והן עשרון דדבר זה למדנו בחמץ מג"ש והוי כמאן דכתיב בגופיה דמיא (מסברא) [מתביאו] דכתיב גבי שתי הלחם [ע"כ]: כז] שתים שבה: כח] בגופייהו דלחמי תודה: כט] גמרי דהא בההוא קרא דכתיב ריבויא לתודה והיכי: ל] מפרש ביה תיבת בה נמחק: לא] ושוק לבדו תיבות וללמוד ממנו זמן אכילה נמחק: לב] הכתוב הוא עצמו: לג] אע"ג דצריכא ההיא תיבת דכתיבא נמחק: לד] ההיא ילפותא למילף שהן קדשי קדשים ונאכלים לזכרי כהונה דכתיב בגופיה ור"י פי' דמאחת למעלה דכתיב בשעיר בפנים ילפינן: לה] בהיקשא דוכן יעשה בין בפנים בין בחוץ בין בפר נמחק: לו] בשעיר וכן משבע דלמטה ומתיבת דהכי עד תיבת (דכתיב) [וכן] נמחק (ס"א דהכי משמע ליה וכן יעשה באהל מועד בשתי בהמות כמו שעשה אחת למעלה בשעיר וכן כאשר עשה בפר בפנים למטה יעשה לשני הבהמות באהל מועד ור"ח כו'): לז] בין בחוץ בין בפנים בין בפר: לח] חמץ שבתודה דמה: לט] ילפינן מצה מחמץ דכנגד: מ] דהיינו שליש עשרון לכל חלה וחלה: מא] ליה הימנו כדפי' תיבת בחמץ נמחק: מב] תיבת יתיר ל"ש: מג] דתהיינה דמשמע י' חלות אתביאו קאי ובלשון: מד] לא מייתרא למידרש: מה] תיבת אחת נמחק: מו] עיין בהשמטות בסוף המסכת:

א) נראה דצ"ל לא צריך ללמוד מחזה ושוק של תודה אלא ליום ולילה וחזה ושוק לא נכתב וכו'.

וליבא

קָדְשֵׁי קָדָשִׁים שֶׁשְּׁחָטָן בְּרֹאשׁ הַמִּזְבֵּחַ, רַבִּי יוֹסֵי אוֹמֵר: כְּאִילּוּ נִשְׁחֲטוּ בַּצָּפוֹן. ר' יוֹסֵי בְּר' יְהוּדָה אוֹמֵר: מֵחֲצִי הַמִּזְבֵּחַ וְלַדָּרוֹם – כַּדָּרוֹם, מֵחֲצִי הַמִּזְבֵּחַ וְלַצָּפוֹן – כַּצָּפוֹן. **גמ'** אָמַר רַב אַסִּי א"ר יוֹחָנָן, *אוֹמֵר הָיָה ר' יוֹסֵי: כּוּלֵּיהּ מִזְבֵּחַ בְּצָפוֹן קָאֵי. וּמַאי "כְּאִילּוּ"? מַהוּ דְּתֵימָא: בָּעֵינַן "עַל יֶרֶךְ" [א] וְלֵיכָּא, קמ"ל. אֲמַר לֵיהּ רַבִּי זֵירָא לְרַב אַסִּי: [ב] אֶלָּא מֵעַתָּה, לְר' יוֹסֵי בְּרַבִּי יְהוּדָה הָכִי נַמִי [ג] דְּחֶצְיוֹ בַּצָּפוֹן וְחֶצְיוֹ בַּדָּרוֹם? וְכִי תֵּימָא הָכִי נַמִי – [ד] וְהָא אַתְּ הוּא דַּאֲמַרְתְּ מִשְּׁמֵיהּ דְּרַבִּי יוֹחָנָן: מוֹדֵי רַבִּי יוֹסֵי בר"י שֶׁאִם שְׁחָטָן [ה] כְּנֶגְדָּן בַּקַּרְקַע פְּסוּלָה! אֲמַר לֵיהּ: הָכִי קָאָמַר רַבִּי יוֹחָנָן: שְׁנֵיהֶם מִקְרָא אֶחָד דָּרְשׁוּ: "וְזָבַחְתָּ עָלָיו אֶת עוֹלֹתֶיךָ וְאֶת שְׁלָמֶיךָ". ר' יוֹסֵי סָבַר: כּוּלּוֹ לְעוֹלָה וְכוּלּוֹ לִשְׁלָמִים, [ו] וְרַבִּי יוֹסֵי בְּר' יְהוּדָה סָבַר: [ז] חֶצְיוֹ לְעוֹלָה וְחֶצְיוֹ לִשְׁלָמִים; דְּאִי ס"ד כּוּלּוֹ לְעוֹלָה כָּשֵׁר, הַשְׁתָּא כּוּלּוֹ לְעוֹלָה כָּשֵׁר – כּוּלּוֹ לִשְׁלָמִים מִבַּעְיָא? וְאִידָךְ: אִיצְטְרִיךְ, ס"ד אָמֵינָא: עוֹלָה הוּא דְּדָחִיק [ח] לֵיהּ מָקוֹם, אֲבָל שְׁלָמִים דְּלָא דָּחִיק לֵיהּ מָקוֹם – אֵימָא לָא, קמ"ל. גּוּפָא, אָמַר רַב אַסִּי אָמַר רַבִּי יוֹחָנָן: מוֹדֵי רַבִּי יוֹסֵי בְּרַבִּי יְהוּדָה שֶׁאִם שְׁחָטָן [ט] כְּנֶגְדָּן בַּקַּרְקַע פְּסוּלוֹת. אֲמַר לֵיהּ רַב אַחָא מִדִּיפְתִּי לְרָבִינָא: מַאי "כְּנֶגְדָּן בַּקַּרְקַע"? [י] אִילֵימָא אַמָּה יְסוֹד וְאַמָּה סוֹבֵב – הַאי גּוּפֵיהּ [יא] מִזְבֵּחַ הוּא! וְעוֹד, מַאי "כְּנֶגְדָּן בַּקַּרְקַע"? וְכ"ת, דַּעֲבִיד מְחִילּוֹת בַּקַּרְקַע וְשָׁחֵיט בְּהוּ – וְכִי הַאי גַּוְונָא מִי הָוֵי מִזְבֵּחַ? וְהָתַנְיָא: "מִזְבַּח אֲדָמָה תַּעֲשֶׂה לִּי" – *שֶׁיְּהֵא מְחוּבָּר [יב] מֵאֲדָמָה, שֶׁלֹּא יִבְנֶנּוּ לֹא עַל גַּבֵּי מְחִילּוֹת וְלֹא עַל גַּבֵּי כִיפִּין! לָא צְרִיכָא, [יג] דְּבַצְרֵיהּ בְּצוּרֵי. אָמַר רַבִּי זֵירָא: אֶפְשָׁר אִיתָא לְהָא דְּרַבִּי יוֹחָנָן וְלָא תְּנֵינָא לַהּ בְּמַתְנִי'? נָפֵק, דַּק וְאַשְׁכַּח, *דִּתְנַן: בֵּירְרוּ מִשָּׁם עֲצֵי תְאֵינָה יָפִים לְסַדֵּר מַעֲרָכָה שְׁנִיָּה שֶׁל קְטֹרֶת, כְּנֶגֶד קֶרֶן מַעֲרָבִית דְּרוֹמִית, מָשׁוּךְ מִן הַקֶּרֶן כְּלַפֵּי צָפוֹן אַרְבַּע אַמּוֹת, בְּאוֹמֶד חָמֵשׁ סְאִין גֶּחָלִים, וּבְשַׁבָּת בְּאוֹמֶד שְׁמוֹנָה סְאִין גֶּחָלִים; שֶׁשָּׁם הָיוּ נוֹתְנִין שְׁנֵי בָזִיכֵי לְבוֹנָה שֶׁל לֶחֶם הַפָּנִים. וּמַאי סִימָנָא? רַבִּי יוֹסֵי הִיא, דְּתַנְיָא: רַבִּי

רש"י

קדשי קדשים. כאילו נשחטו בצפון. בגמ' יליף טעמא. **גמ'** אמר רבי יוחנן אומר היה כו'. גמרא גמיר לה רבי יוחנן. מאי כאילו. הא ודאי בצפון נשחטו! אלא מעתה כו'. קס"ד דרבי זירא דממתני' גמיר לה רבי יוחנן להא [יד] ד"אומר היה רבי יוסי". מודה רבי יוסי ברבי יהודה. אע"ג שמכשיר [טו] במזבח מחציו לצפון – מודה הוא שאם שחטו כנגד אותו מקום מתחתיהם בקרקע [טז] פסולות. ולקמיה מפרש היאך יכול לשחוט תחת המזבח. א"ל. רב אסי, הכי קאמר ר' יוחנן כו'. כלומר: "אומר היה רבי יוסי" דקאמר ר' יוחנן לעיל – לאו ממתני' גמר, אלא הכי גמר לה מרבותיו. ומתניתין לאו במקום מזבח פליגי, דנימא רבי יוסי [יז] כוליה בצפון, ור' יוסי בר' יהודה נימא חציו לצפון, אלא [יח] מדרשא דקרא. ה"ג: כולו לעולה וכולו לשלמים. כולו ראוי לשחיטת עולה, דקדושת צפון עליו מגזירת הכתוב. וכולו ראוי לשלמים, שהשלמים כשירין אף בצפון, מק"ו דפירקין דלעיל (דף נה.). דדחיק לה מקום. שמקומן קטן ודחוק, שאין כשר לה אלא צפון, ופעמים שעולות מרובות וצר להם המקום, [יט] והכשיר להן הכתוב ראש המזבח. מאי כנגדן בקרקע. הא ליכא לפרושי: כנגדן ברצפה למזרח המזבח ולמערבו – [כ] דאם כן לא הוה קשיא מילתא לרב אסי לעיל, דמהכא ליכא למילף דלית ליה לרבי יוסי ברבי יהודה חצי המזבח עומד בצפון, [כא] דאפילו הוא צפון נמי פסיל ליה לרבי יוסי [ברבי יהודה], ואפילו סמוך לכותל העזרה צפוני פוסל אם משוך מכנגד זוית המזבח צפונה למזרח או למערב, דדרשינן "על ירך", כדאמר בפ"ב (לעיל כו.): איזהו צפון – מקיר מזבח צפוני עד כותל עזרה צפונית כנגד המזבח כולו, אבל משוך מכנגד המזבח – לא. הלכך, על כרחך האי "כנגדו" דקיימינן מינה דמקום המזבח לאו צפון הוא – [כב] תחתיו קאמר, ומאי היא? אי נימא. אם שחטן על כניסת הסובב והיסוד – האי לאו כנגדן הוא, אלא מזבח ממש, ומכשר בה רבי יוסי בר' יהודה, כדקתני: מחצי המזבח לצפון [כג]. כיפין. = אולמים, ארקמלו"ט. בדבצריה בצורי. אם [כד] נמלך לקצר את המזבח, ונשאר מקום של צפון פנוי, ושחט שם – פסולות. ואע"ג דירך הוא – פסיל ליה. אלמא סבירא ליה בדרום עזרה הוא, דאי לא – אמאי פסיל ליה? **אפשר איתא להא דר' יוחנן.** דקאמר: אומר היה רבי יוסי כוליה מזבח בצפון קאי, ולא תנינן לה שום רמז במשנה בששה סדרים? דק ואשכח. במשנת תמיד. בירורו משם. מדיר העצים. עצי תאנה יפין. בשל תאנה היו רגילין. וטעם אגדה הוא, שבו היתה תקנה לאדם הראשון, [כה] "ויעשו להם חגורות". מערכה שניה של קטרת. אצל מערכה גדולה היו מסדרין מערכה קטנה, ליטול ממנה גחלים להכניס על מזבח הפנימי שלשה קבין לכל בקר וערב, להקטיר עליהם [כו] קטרת. ובמסכת יומא בפרק "טרף בקלפי" (דף מה:) בסופיה ילפינן מקרא דעל מזבח החיצון צריך להיות מערכה לכך. כנגד [כז] מערבית דרומית. של מזבח, ומשוך לצד צפון להרחיקו מן הקרן ד' אמות. וטעם מפרש לקמיה מאי שנא הקרן זה, ומ"ט מושכו הימנה ולצפון ד' אמות. משוך מן הקרן כלפי צפון ארבע אמות גרס. וכן מצינו בסדר המשנה [כח] במשנת תמיד. באומד חמש סאין גחלים. לפי אומד ה' סאין גחלים היו נותנין שם עצים. כך [כט] שיעורו לחתות בתוכו בראש המזבח [ב] שהוא חלק מחתה של סאה, לר' יוסי דאמר בסדר יומא (דף מג:): בכל יום חותה בשל סאה ומערה בתוך ג' קבין. בשבת היו מסדרין שם לפי אומד ח' סאין. לפי שצריך להקטיר הבזיכין על מזבח החיצון. שעל מזבח הפנימי אין הקטר אלא [ל] של קטרת שחרית וערבית, כדכתיב: "לא תעלו עליו קטרת זרה" וגו' (שמות ל). **ומאי סימנא.** מהו [ג] הסימן [לא] שהוקבע להם למערכה שניה ולהקטרת הבזיכין – קרן מערבית דרומית, ומשוך ארבע אמות מן הקרן ולצפון?

א) נ"א מן ונראה לי עד סה"ד שייך לסוף דף סג ע"ב   ב) נ"א אכתי הוה אמינא לצד דרום כו' הקישא לחטאת ליסוד מוכח דהוי מערב כיון דכתיב כו' וע' בתוס' מנחות סח ע"ב

תוספות

קדשי קדשים ששחטן בראש המזבח. מדאורייתא שוחט לכתחלה, כדדרשינן [לב] מ"וזבחת עליו". ושמא הא דנקט דיעבד – מדרבנן, שלא תרבין גללים. **כולן** לשלמים. ואע"ג דקסבר ליה כולו מזבח בצפון קאי – [לג] אפילו הכי *איצטריך לן לעיל קרא להכשיר צפון לשלמים. דמהכא לא נפקא, דעל [לד] המזבח גזירת הכתוב הוא, כי היכי דמכשר רבי יוסי ברבי יהודה מחציו ולצפון לעולה, אע"ג דכנגדן בקרקע פסולות, דדרום הוא. אלא דעל המזבח גזירת הכתוב. **משוך** מן הקרן כלפי צפון ארבע אמות. בכולה שמעתא משמע דגחלים דיום הכפורים צריך ליקח כנגד הפתח. וצריך לומר דהיינו לכתחילה, אבל דיעבד כשר אפילו דהאי גיסא ודהאי גיסא, כדאמר בפרק "טרף בקלפי" (יומא מה: מו. ע"ש ד"ה אבל): ואיצטריך מ"על המזבח" ואיצטריך "מלפני ה'". [לה] וא"ת: מהיכא תיתי עיכובא, דאיצטריך קרא לאכשורי בדיעבד? אין זה בדברים הנעשים בבגדי[ד] לבן לא בפנים ולא בחוץ, ובין לרבי יהודה ובין לרבי נחמיה *ליכא עיכובא! וי"ל: דאיצטריך משום דלצורך פנים כפנים דמי, [לו] כקטורת שחפנה קודם שחיטת הפר שלא עשה ולא כלום, [ה]ד"חוקה" כתיב בה (ויקרא טז), דלצורך פנים כפנים דמי. וא"ת: הכא משמע דלא מקרי "לפני ה'" אלא במערב, וכן גבי נר מערבי בפ' "שתי הלחם" (מנחות דף לח:). ואילו בסוף "כל המנחות [באות מצה"] (שם סא.) אמרינן: "לפני ה'" – במזרח, גבי תנופת לוג שמן של מצורע ואשמו. וכן גבי שחיטה כתיב "לפני ה'", ושריא בכל מקום בעזרה! וי"ל: דשחיטה ותנופת לוג אשם כתיב "לפני ה'" למעוטי בחוץ, דתנופת אשם מחיים. אבל גבי גחלים כתיב (ויקרא טז) "מעל המזבח", ונרות היו בהיכל, אם כן "לפני ה'" למה לי? [לז] לאו משום דבעינן במערב? ומיהו, קשה: דבההוא שמעתא ד"כל המנחות באות מצה" (גם זה שם) פריך עלה: והאמרת במערב "לפני ה'", פי': גבי הגשת מנחה, בפירקין וברים "הקומץ רבה" (מנחות דף יט:)! ומשני: הני מילי – מנחות דאיקרי חטאת, וחטאת טעונה יסוד, וקרן דרומית מזרחית לא היה לה יסוד, אבל הכא "לפני ה'" קרינא ביה, משמע דאי לא בעיא יסוד – הוה מכשרנא קרן דרומית מזרחית להגשה, ואע"ג דכתיב "לפני[ו] ה'"! א) ונראה לי ברו"ך: דאי לא כתיב "לפני ה'" בהגשת מנחה, אע"ג דכתיב בה "אל פני המזבח" דהיינו דרום, וגם איתקש לחטאת העוף ליסוד – ב) אכתי [לח] אמצע לצד דרום באמה של יסוד רחוק מקרן מערבי. אבל קשה: [לט] בלא היקשא לחטאת [מ] בעינן ליסוד מערב, כיון דכתיב "לפני ה'" לגלות מערב, כמו גבי גחלי יום הכיפורים, וגם כתיב "פני המזבח" דמשמע דרום. וכן איתא לקמן בפירקין (דף סג:)! ברו"ך.

רבי

עין משפט נר מצוה

א א מיי' פ"ג מהלכות פסה"מ הלכה ח:
ב ב מיי' פ"ה מהלכות בית הבחירה הל' יג ופ"ב שם הלכה טז:
ג ג מיי' פ"ב מהלכות תמידין ומוספין הלכה ח:

מסורת הש"ס

לעיל נג. [לקמן סג.]
שמות כ
[לקמן סח.]
תמיד כט.
[יומא ס.]

גליון הש"ס

תוס' ד"ה כולו לשלמים כו' איצטריך לן לעיל. ע' לעיל דף נה ע"א.

שיטה מקובצת

א] וליכא. ואם תאמר ואימא אה"נ דבפרק (קבלה) [ב' דף כו.] מוכח דבעינן על ירך לעכב וי"ל דהתם היינו לענין אויר דתלה ושחט לגבי הכי הוי דוקא על ירך אבל כאן לאו באויר שחיט ועי"ל דה"ק קמ"ל דעל ירך מיקרי: ב] אלא מעתה לר"י בר יהודה ה"נ. (פי' משמע) דחציו בצפון [כו'] והא את כו'. וא"ת ותקשי דא"כ הל"ל כאילו בצפון לר"י [בר"י] כמו לת"ק משום מהו דתימא בעינן על ירך וליכא קמ"ל וי"ל דאה"נ אלא סמיך אהא דקאמר ת"ק כבר כאלו ולפיכך לא חש ר"י [בר"י] למימר כאלו ועוד נראה למהר"ם דדוקא לת"ק דמכשיר בכוליה מזבח אפילו לצד דרום אפילו לצד הכבש שנקרא פני המזבח שייך למתני כאלו משום דאין זה על ירך על אותו צד שבדרום ומ"מ מכשרינן משום דצפון הוא ולפיכך שייך למימר כאלו אבל לר"י בר"י דאמר מחציו ולצפון כצפון הא ודאי דבאותו חצי נקרא ירך כדמוכח לקמן דלצד הכבש הוי פני המזבח ולאידך צד מיקרי ירך: ג] נמי חציו ואות ד' נמחק: ד] והא את הוא דאמרת כו'. וא"ת דלמא משום הכי פסיל כנגד צפון משום דאזיל לטעמיה דאמר בפ' קבלה איזה צפון מקיר המזבח צפוני ועד כותל העזרה צפוני וכנגד כל המזבח כולו אלמא דאפילו סמוך לכותל העזרה צפוני פסול אם משוך מכנגד זוית המזבח למזרח או למערב ולכך פסול מכנגד המזבח ברצפה במזרחו או במערבו דהיינו כנגד חצי המזבח דמצד צפון וי"ל דהא דקאמר כנגדן בקרקע פסולה אינו רוצה לומר על הרצפה אלא כנגדן מתחתיהן כדמפרש בסמוך: ה] שחטן כנגדו בקרקע פסולים א"ל הכי אמר ר' יוחנן שניהם מקרא אחד דרשו. וא"ת כיון שאמת הוא דבצפון קאי א"כ למה לי וזבחת עליו לומר כולו לעולה וי"ל דמשום דמ"מ ס"ד למיפסליה משום דאין זה על ירך: ו] ורבי יוסי בר יהודה חלקיהו חציו כו'. פי' אע"ג דבדרום קאי כוליה מ"מ גזירת הכתוב היא אבל תימה למה לי קרא לחציו לשלמים דאפילו יהיה דרום מה בכך הרי דרום כשר לשלמים וי"ל דכיון דרבייה לעולה הו"א לעולה דוקא ולא לשלמים ולכך הוצרך להכשיר לשלמים: ז] סבר חלקיהו חציו: ח] לה מקום אבל כו' דלא דחיקי להו מקום: ט] שחטן כנגדו בקרקע פסולים א"ל: י] אילימא אמה יסוד ואמה כו'. פ"ה דליכא לאוקומי כנגדן בקרקע כו' אלא ע"כ כנגדן מתחתיו ובמאי אי באמה יסוד כו' האי גופיה דמזבח הוא ותימה דמשמע דאי לאו גופיה דמזבח ניחא ומי ניחא אכתי היכי מוכח דקסבר דלאו בצפון קאי מדפסיל באמה יסוד ואמה סובב הא כי נמי בצפון קאי מ"מ ראוי לפסול באמה יסוד משום דאין זה על ירך המזבח כיון דלא חשיב כגוף המזבח דדוקא לעיל בראש המזבח בחציו לצפון הוי ממש על ירך המזבח וי"ל דלמאי דפי' לעיל ניחא דר"י בר"י סמוך אכאלו דקאמר ת"ק וא"כ מעל ירך לא ממעיט כי אם אויר כדפי' לעיל אבל גבי המזבח וכן מחילות חשיב שפיר על ירך כיון שאינו באויר: יא] דמזבח הוא ועוד מאי בקרקע ותיבת כנגדן נרשם עליו קו: יב] מחובר באדמה שלא: יג] דבצרי בצורי: יד] להא דאמר אומר היה: טו] שמכשיר בראש המזבח מחציו: טז] פסולים ולקמיה: יז] אלא בדרשא דקרא: יח] לפיכך הכשיר להן: יט] ובמערבו וטעמא משום דלא מכשיר צפון אלא מכותל המזבח צפונה עד כותל העזרה צפוני כנגד המזבח לבד כדאיתא לעיל פ' שני: כ] תיבת מילתא נמחק: כא] דאפילו היה כולו בצפון פסיל ליה רבי יוסי ברבי יהודה דאפילו סמיך לכותל העזרה הצפוני פוסל אם משוך קמעא מכנגד זוית המזבח למזרח של מזבח. או כו' ועל תיבת צפונה נרשם קו למעלה: כב] הוא בקרקע תחתיו: כג] לצפון כצפון הס"ד: כד] נמלכו לקצר את המזבח כדאמר לקמן ונשאר מחציו של צפון פנוי כו' פסיל ליה כוליה בדרום אלמא: כה] הראשון שנאמר ויעשו: כו] עליהם הקטרת ובמסכת כו' צריך לעשות המערכה לכך: כז] כנגד קרן מערבית דרומית של מזבח החיצון משוך לצד צפון כו' מאי שנא האי קרן ותיבת זה ל"ש: כח] המשנה במס' תמיד ותיבת במשנת נמחק: כט] כך שיערו: ל] אלא לקטורת ותי' של נמחק: לא] הסימן הזה שהוקבע: לב] כדדרשינן בגמרא מוזבחת: לג] קאי וכשרה לשלמים אפילו: לד] דעל ראש המזבח: לה] וא"ת מהיכא כו' דאיצטריך התם קרא לאכשורי אין זה מדברים הנעשים: לו] דמי. ס"א דהוא בשביל הקטרת: לז] לי אי לאו: לח] אכתי אמצא אות ע' ל"ש: לט] בלא. גליון פי' למה לי היקשא דחטאת לומר דמנחה טעונה יסוד תיפוק לי יסוד מלפני ה' דהוי בקרן מערבית דרומית ששם היה יסוד: מ] לחטאת ליסוד מערב ידענא כיון:

הגהות צ"ק [א] כולו: [ב] נ"ל שהיה לוקח: [ג] סימנא שהוקבע כו': [ד] לבן בפנים וליכא עיכובא לר' יהודה כנ"ל כו': [ה] אע"ג דלא כתיב בה חוקה דלצורך פנים כו': [ו] ה' א"כ לפני ה' למה לי ונראה:

רַבִּי יוֹסֵי אוֹמֵר: זֶה סִימָן, א] כָּל הַנִּיטָּל בִּפְנִים לִינָּתֵן בַּחוּץ — אֵינוֹ נוֹתֵן אֶלָּא בְּסָמוּךְ שֶׁאֵין לִפְנִים, *וְכָל הַנִּיטָּל בַּחוּץ לִינָּתֵן לִפְנִים — אֵינוֹ נִיטָּל אֶלָּא בְּסָמוּךְ שֶׁאֵין לִפְנִים; "כָּל הַנִּיטָּל בִּפְנִים לִינָּתֵן בַּחוּץ" מַאי נִיהוּ? אִילֵימָא שִׁירַיִם — בְּהֶדְיָא כְּתִיב בְּהוּ: °"אֶל יְסוֹד מִזְבַּח הָעוֹלָה אֲשֶׁר פֶּתַח (ויקרא ד) אֹהֶל מוֹעֵד"! וְתוּ: "כָּל הַנִּיטָּל בַּחוּץ לִינָּתֵן בִּפְנִים" מַאי נִיהוּ? אִילֵימָא גֶּחָלִים שֶׁל יוֹם הַכִּיפּוּרִים — בְּהֶדְיָא כְּתִיב בְּהוּ: °"וְלָקַח מְלֹא הַמַּחְתָּה גַּחֲלֵי (שם טז) אֵשׁ" ב] וגו'! אֶלָּא: כָּל הַנִּיטָּל בִּפְנִים לִינָּתֵן בַּחוּץ — שְׁנֵי בְזִיכֵי לְבוֹנָה שֶׁל לֶחֶם הַפָּנִים, דְּגָמְרִי מִשִּׁירַיִם. הַנִּיטָּל בַּחוּץ לִינָּתֵן בִּפְנִים — גֶּחָלִים דְּכָל יוֹמָא וְיוֹמָא, דְּגַמְרָן מִגֶּחָלִים שֶׁל יוֹם הַכִּפּוּרִים; וּמַאי קָסָבַר? אִי קָסָבַר כּוּלֵּיהּ מִזְבֵּחַ בַּדָּרוֹם קָאֵי — עֶשְׂרִים וְשֶׁבַע בָּעֵי לְמֵיתֵי, וְאִי נַמִּי קָסָבַר *קְדוּשַּׁת הֵיכָל וְאוּלָם חֲדָא הִיא — עֶשְׂרִים וְתַרְתֵּי בָּעֵי ג] מֵיתֵי! וְאִי קָסָבַר חֶצְיוֹ בַּצָּפוֹן וְחֶצְיוֹ בַּדָּרוֹם — חַד סְרֵי בָּעֵי לְמֵיתֵי, ד] וְאֶלָּא קָסָבַר: קְדוּשַּׁת הֵיכָל וְאוּלָם חֲדָא ה] מִילְּתָא הִיא — שִׁית בָּעֵי לְמֵיתֵי! אֶלָּא לָאו מִשּׁוּם דְּקָסָבַר כּוּלֵּיהּ מִזְבֵּחַ בַּצָּפוֹן קָאֵי, וְהָנֵי אַרְבַּע אַמּוֹת — אַמָּה יְסוֹד, וְאַמָּה סוֹבֵב, וְאַמָּה מְקוֹם קְרָנוֹת, וְאַמָּה מְקוֹם רַגְלֵי הַכֹּהֲנִים, דְּכִי ו] מְסַגּוּ לְקַמֵּיהּ טְפֵי — תּוּ לֵיכָּא פֶּתַח. אָמַר רַב אַדָּא בַּר אַהֲבָה: הָא מַנִּי — רַבִּי יְהוּדָה הִיא. *דְּתַנְיָא, ר"י אוֹמֵר: מִזְבֵּחַ מְמוּצָּע וְעוֹמֵד בְּאֶמְצַע הָעֲזָרָה, ז] וּשְׁלֹשִׁים וּשְׁתַּיִם אַמּוֹת הָיוּ לוֹ, עֶשֶׂר אַמּוֹת כְּנֶגֶד פִּתְחוֹ שֶׁל הֵיכָל, ח] אַחַת עֶשְׂרֵה אַמָּה מִיכָּן וְאַחַת עֶשְׂרֵה אַמָּה מִיכָּן, נִמְצָא מִזְבֵּחַ מְכוּוָּן כְּנֶגֶד הֵיכָל. ט] סוֹף סוֹף לְרַבִּי יְהוּדָה חַד סְרֵי בָּעֵי לְמֵיתֵי! וְאִי קָסָבַר: י] קְדוּשַּׁת הֵיכָל וְאוּלָם חֲדָא יא] מִילְּתָא הִיא — שִׁית בָּעֵי לְמֵיתֵי! מִי סָבְרַתְּ הָנֵי אַרְבַּע אַמּוֹת בַּהֲדֵי אַמָּה יְסוֹד וְאַמָּה סוֹבֵב? אַרְבַּע אַמּוֹת בַּר מֵאַמָּה יְסוֹד וְאַמָּה סוֹבֵב. וְנוֹקְמָהּ כְּרַבִּי יוֹסֵי, וּבִמְמוּצָּע! מִשּׁוּם דְּרַבִּי יְהוּדָה שָׁמַעְנָא לֵיהּ מְמוּצָּע בְּהֶדְיָא. וְרַב שֵׁרֵבְיָא אָמַר: הָא מַנִּי — רַבִּי יוֹסֵי הַגְּלִילִי הִיא, דְּתַנְיָא, רַבִּי יוֹסֵי הַגְּלִילִי אוֹמֵר, מִתּוֹךְ שֶׁנֶּאֱמַר: °"וְנָתַתָּ אֶת הַכִּיּוֹר בֵּין אֹהֶל מוֹעֵד" (א) וְגוֹמֵר, יב] °"וְאֵת (שמות שם) מִזְבַּח

רַבִּי יוֹסֵי הִיא דְּתַנְיָא רַבִּי יוֹסֵי אוֹמֵר זֶה סִימָן. בְּיָדְךָ: כָּל הַנִּיטָּל מִבִּפְנִים לִינָּתֵן בַּחוּץ. וּלְקַמֵּיהּ מְפָרֵשׁ מַאי נִיהוּ. אֵינוֹ נוֹתֵן אֶלָּא בְּסָמוּךְ שֶׁאֵין לִפְנִים. אֵינוֹ נִיתָּן בַּחוּץ עַל הַמִּזְבֵּחַ הַחִיצוֹן אֶלָּא בְּסָמוּךְ לְצַד פְּנִים, שֶׁאֵין בַּמִּזְבֵּחַ הַחִיצוֹן מָקוֹם הַסָּמוּךְ לִפְנִים יוֹתֵר מִמֶּנּוּ. וְכָל הַנִּיטָּל מֵעַל (תורה אור) מִזְבֵּחַ הַחִיצוֹן לִיתֵּן בִּפְנִים אֵינוֹ נִיטָּל אֶלָּא מִמָּקוֹם שֶׁהוּא סָמוּךְ לִפְנִים. שֶׁאֵין מָקוֹם בְּכָל מִזְבֵּחַ הַחִיצוֹן סָמוּךְ מִמֶּנּוּ. כָּל הַנִּיטָּל בִּפְנִים לִינָּתֵן בַּחוּץ מַאי נִיהוּ אִי נֵימָא שְׁיָרֵי הַדָּם. דְּחַטָּאוֹת הַפְּנִימִיּוֹת – ל"ל לְרַבִּי יוֹסֵי לְשַׁוְּיֵיהּ בְּהוּ כְּלָלָא? הָא בְּהֶדְיָא כְּתִיב בְּהוּ. דְּנִיתָּנִין בַּיְסוֹד שֶׁכְּנֶגֶד הַפֶּתַח, דִּכְתִיב: "יִשְׁפֹּךְ אֶל יְסוֹד מִזְבַּח הָעוֹלָה אֲשֶׁר פֶּתַח". וְתוּ כָּל הַנִּיטָּל בַּחוּץ לִינָּתֵן בִּפְנִים מַאי נִיהוּ אִי נֵימָא גֶּחָלִים שֶׁל יוֹם הַכִּיפּוּרִים. שֶׁמַּכְנִיסִין בְּמַחְתָּה לִפְנַי וְלִפְנִים לְהַקְטִיר בָּהֶן מְלֹא חָפְנָיו קְטֹרֶת סַמִּים דַּקָּה, דְּאַף הֵם נִיטָּלִין מִמִּזְבֵּחַ הַחִיצוֹן, כִּדְכְתִיב: "מֵעַל הַמִּזְבֵּחַ מִלִּפְנֵי ה'" – מִצַּד הַמַּעֲרָב, וְדָרְשִׁינַן בְּיוֹמָא (דף מה:): אֵיזֶהוּ מִזְבֵּחַ שֶׁמִּקְצָתוֹ לִפְנֵי ה' וְאֵין כּוּלּוֹ לִפְנֵי ה' — זֶהוּ מִזְבֵּחַ הַחִיצוֹן. וְיָהֵיב לוֹ בָּהּ רַבִּי יוֹסֵי כְּלָלָא וְסִימָנָא, דְּאֵין נִיטָּל אֶלָּא מִמָּקוֹם שֶׁאֵין סָמוּךְ הֵימֶנּוּ יג] וְלִפְנִים. בְּהֶדְיָא כְּתִיב בְּהוּ. "מִלִּפְנֵי ה'", דְּהַיְינוּ לְצַד פְּנִים. אֶלָּא כָּל הַנִּיטָּל בִּפְנִים לִינָּתֵן בַּחוּץ שְׁנֵי בְזִיכֵי לְבוֹנָה. הַנִּיטָּלִין בַּשַּׁבָּת מִן הַשֻּׁלְחָן לִיתֵּן עַל מִזְבֵּחַ הַחִיצוֹן. וְאַשְׁמְעִינַן ר' יוֹסֵי שֶׁנִּיתָּנִין כְּנֶגֶד הַפֶּתַח, דְּגָמְרִי מִשִּׁירַיִם הַפְּנִימִיִּים. וְהַנִּיטָּל בַּחוּץ לִינָּתֵן בִּפְנִים גֶּחָלִים דְּכָל יד] יוֹם. הַנִּיטָּלִין מִמַּעֲרָכָה שְׁנִיָּה שֶׁל קְטוֹרֶת לִינָּתֵן עַל מִזְבֵּחַ הַפְּנִימִי. וְאַשְׁמְעִינַן רַבִּי יוֹסֵי דְּנִיטָּלִין מִכְּנֶגֶד הַפֶּתַח, דְּגָמְרִי מִגֶּחָלִים שֶׁל יוה"כ שֶׁקָּבַע לָהֶן טו] כְּנֶגֶד הַפֶּתַח לִנְטִילָתָן. וְהַיְינוּ סִימָנָא דְּתָנָא תַּנָּא בְּמַסֶּכֶת תָּמִיד לְמַעֲרָכָה שְׁנִיָּה טז] שֶׁהִיא לִנְטִילַת גֶּחָלִים וּלְהַקְטָרַת בָּזִיכִין – שֶׁתְּהֵא בְּקֶרֶן דְּרוֹמִית מַעֲרָבִית, וּמְשׁוּכָה לַצָּפוֹן אַרְבַּע אַמּוֹת, שֶׁתְּהֵא מְכוּוֶּנֶת כְּנֶגֶד הַפֶּתַח, וּמִינָּהּ פַּשְׁטִינַן יז] דְּלר' יוֹסֵי כּוּלֵּיהּ מִזְבֵּחַ בַּצָּפוֹן קָאֵי. וּמַאי קָסָבַר. יח] שֶׁקָּבַע לִמְשִׁיכַת הַמַּעֲרָכָה מִן הַקֶּרֶן ד' אַמּוֹת. אִי קָסָבַר כּוּלֵּיהּ מִזְבֵּחַ בַּדָּרוֹם עֲזָרָה קָאֵי. וּמְשִׁיכַת ד' יט] הָאַמּוֹת לְקָרְבָהּ כְּנֶגֶד הַפֶּתַח הוּא בָּא. כ"ז אַמּוֹת בָּעֵי לְמֵיתֵי. כ] וְלִמְשׁוֹךְ מִקֶּרֶן מַעֲרָבִית דְּרוֹמִית וְלַצָּפוֹן, וְחוּץ לְאוֹתָן כ"ז אַמּוֹת סִידּוּר הַמַּעֲרָכָה. שֶׁהֲרֵי הַפֶּתַח בְּאֶמְצַע הָעֲזָרָה הָיָה, וַעֲשָׂרָה אַמּוֹת רׇחְבּוֹ, כא] וְחָמֵשׁ בַּצָּפוֹן וְה' בַּדָּרוֹם. וְכֵיוָן שֶׁהַמִּזְבֵּחַ בַּדָּרוֹם – נִמְצָא שֶׁאֵין מִמֶּנּוּ לִפְנֵי הַפֶּתַח אֶלָּא ה' אַמּוֹת (ב) צְפוֹנִיּוֹת שֶׁלּוֹ, שֶׁכֻּלָּהּ כְּנֶגֶד אֶמְצַע הַפֶּתַח. נִשְׁאֲרוּ לוֹ מל"ב [אַמּוֹת] שֶׁלּוֹ כ"ז, וְאֶת כּוּלָּן אַתָּה צָרִיךְ לִמְשׁוֹךְ הַמַּעֲרָכָה מִכְּנֶגֶד כב] קֶרֶן יְסוֹד הַמִּזְבֵּחַ הַדְּרוֹמִי וְלַצָּפוֹן, קוֹדֶם שֶׁהִגִּיעַ לַפֶּתַח. וא"נ קָסָבַר קְדוּשַּׁת הֵיכָל וְאוּלָם חֲדָא הִיא. כג] וּמִשֶּׁתַּגִּיעַ כְּנֶגֶד פֶּתַח הָאוּלָם קָרֵינַן "לִפְנֵי ה'". וּפֶתַח הָאוּלָם עוֹדֵף לְכָל רוּחַ עַל פֶּתַח הַהֵיכָל ה' אַמּוֹת לְכָל צַד, שֶׁהָיָה רׇחְבּוֹ כ' אַמּוֹת, כִּדְתְנַן בְּמַסֶּכֶת מִדּוֹת – (דף לו.) כ"ב בָּעֵי מַיְיתֵי. וְאִי נַמִּי קָסָבַר חֶצְיוֹ שֶׁל מִזְבֵּחַ בַּצָּפוֹן וְחֶצְיוֹ בַּדָּרוֹם. וְגָא לְמוֹשְׁכָהּ עַד כְּנֶגֶד כד] הַהֵיכָל. חַד סְרֵי בָּעֵי מַיְיתֵי. שֶׁהֲרֵי ט"ז אַמּוֹתָיו בַּדָּרוֹם, נִמְצְאוּ מֵהֶן י"א [אַמּוֹת] כה] מְזָוִית דְּרוֹמִית שֶׁל פֶּתַח וְלַדָּרוֹם. וְאִי נַמִּי קְדוּשַּׁת הֵיכָל וְאוּלָם חֲדָא הִיא שִׁית מִיהָא בָּעֵי לְמֵיתֵי. אֶלָּא עַל כָּרְחָךְ לָא מַשְׁכַּחַתְּ לָהּ שֶׁתְּהֵא מְשִׁיכַת ד' אַמּוֹת הַלָּלוּ לְקָרֵב כְּנֶגֶד הַפֶּתַח, אֶלָּא נָתַן לָךְ מִדָּה כו] בְּשִׁיעוּר שֶׁלֹּא תִּמְשְׁכֶנָּה יוֹתֵר מִכָּאן, שֶׁכׇּל מַה שֶּׁאַתָּה יָכוֹל לְקׇרְבָהּ אֵצֶל קֶרֶן דְּרוֹמִית הֲוֵי מְקַרְבָהּ, וּבְכָךְ אַתָּה מְכַוְּונָהּ כְּנֶגֶד הַפֶּתַח. וְד' אַמּוֹת הַלָּלוּ ע"כ הוּא מוֹשְׁכָהּ לַצָּפוֹן, לְפִי שֶׁאֵין לוֹ מָקוֹם לְסַדֵּר עֲלֵיהֶן. כז] וְקָסָבַר כּוּלֵּיהּ בַּצָּפוֹן קָאֵי, וְאֵין מִמֶּנּוּ לִפְנֵי הַפֶּתַח אֶלָּא חֲמִשָּׁה (ג) דְּרוֹמִיּוֹת, וּמֵהֶן אַמָּה יְסוֹד, וְאַמָּה סוֹבֵב, וְאַמָּה מְקוֹם הַקֶּרֶן, וְאַמָּה הִילּוּךְ לַכֹּהֲנִים הַמְסַדְּרִין אֶת הַמַּעֲרָכָה וּמַקִּיפִין בֵּין קֶרֶן לַמַּעֲרָכָה וְאֵין לוֹ מָקוֹם לְסַדֵּר. וְלִימֶּדְךָ שֶׁיְּסַדֵּר חוּצָה לָהֶן מִיָּד, כְּדֵי שֶׁתְּהֵא אַמָּה מִן הַמַּעֲרָכָה כְּנֶגֶד הַפֶּתַח, דְּכִי מַסְגֵּי לַצָּפוֹן טְפֵי – תּוּ לֵיכָּא פֶּתַח. אָמַר רַב אַדָּא בַּר אַהֲבָה. לְעוֹלָם לָא תֵּידוּק מִינָּהּ לְרַבִּי יוֹסֵי כח] בַּצָּפוֹן קָאֵי, אֶלָּא (אֵימָא) רַבִּי יְהוּדָה הִיא דְּאָמַר חֶצְיוֹ בַּצָּפוֹן וְחֶצְיוֹ בַּדָּרוֹם: עֶשֶׂר אַמּוֹת אֶמְצָעִיּוֹת שֶׁלּוֹ הָיוּ כְּנֶגֶד פִּתְחוֹ שֶׁל הֵיכָל, וי"א אַמּוֹת כט] מְזָוִית הֵיכָל וְלַצָּפוֹן, וּכְנֶגְדָּן לַדָּרוֹם. נִמְצָא מְכוּוָּן כְּנֶגֶד רוֹחַב חֲלָלוֹ שֶׁל הֵיכָל *וְעוֹבִי כְּתָלָיו, שֶׁהַהֵיכָל חֲלָלוֹ כ' אַמָּה וְעוֹבִי ל] שֶׁל כּוֹתֶל ו' אַמּוֹת. וְהָכִי תְּנַן לָהּ בְּמַסֶּכֶת מִדּוֹת (דף לז.). כִּדְאַקְשִׁינַן לְעֵיל. לא] סוֹף סוֹף. וּמִלְמַעְלָה בְּרֹאשׁ הַמִּזְבֵּחַ קַמַּקְשֵׁי לב] לְהוּ. וְנִמְצָא לִפְנֵי הַפֶּתַח, שֶׁהֲרֵי נִמְשָׁךְ ו' אַמּוֹת. וְלֹא הוּזְכְּרוּ ד' אַמּוֹת אֵלּוּ אֶלָּא לְקׇרְבָן לַפֶּתַח, דִּבְלָאו מֵהָכִי לָאו כְּנֶגֶד הַפֶּתַח הוּא. וְנוֹקְמָהּ כְּר' יוֹסֵי לג] *בְּאֶמְצַע. לָמָּה לָךְ לְמִשְׁקְלָהּ מֵרַבִּי יוֹסֵי, דִּשְׁמַעְתְּ לֵיהּ דְּאָמַר: אֵין נִיתָּנִין אֶלָּא בְּסָמוּךְ שֶׁאֵין לִפְנִים? מִכְּדֵי לד] *לְהִיסְּתֵר דּוּקְיָא דְּרַבִּי זֵירָא קָא אָתֵית, דְּבָעֵי לְמֵידַק לה] מִינֵּיהּ לְרַבִּי יוֹסֵי דְּכוּלֵּיהּ מִזְבֵּחַ בַּצָּפוֹן קָאֵי – אֵימָא הָכִי: לְעוֹלָם קָסָבַר חֶצְיוֹ בַּדָּרוֹם וְחֶצְיוֹ בַּצָּפוֹן, וּמִי סָבְרַתְּ בַּהֲדֵי אַמָּה יְסוֹד כו'! וּמְשַׁנֵּי: לְרַבִּי יְהוּדָה שָׁמְעִינַן לֵהּ מְמוּצָּע בְּהֶדְיָא. וְאִי מִשּׁוּם דְּאַיְירֵי רַבִּי יוֹסֵי בְּנִיטָּלִין בִּפְנִים וְנִיתָּנִין בַּחוּץ, וְנִיטָּלִין בַּחוּץ וְנִיתָּנִין בִּפְנִים – הָא כּוּלֵּי עָלְמָא אִית לְהוּ. וְרַב שֵׁרֵבְיָא אָמַר. ד' אַמּוֹת דְּקָתָנֵי – בַּהֲדֵי אַמָּה יְסוֹד וְאַמָּה סוֹבֵב קָאָמַר, וְדוּק מִינָּהּ כִּדְקָאָמְרַתְּ לו] דְּמִזְבֵּחַ בַּצָּפוֹן קָאֵי. וּמִיהוּ, לְרַבִּי יוֹחָנָן לָא תְּסַיְּיעֵיהּ מִינָּהּ, דְּנֵימָא רַבִּי יוֹסֵי בֶּן חֲלַפְתָּא הִיא מִשּׁוּם דְּשָׁמְעִינַן לֵיהּ דְּאַיְירֵי בְּנִיטָּלִין וְנִיתָּנִין, דְּהַהוּא לְכוּלֵּי עָלְמָא אִית לְהוּ. וְהָא דְּתָמִיד – כְּרַבִּי יוֹסֵי הַגְּלִילִי מוֹקְמִינַן, לז] דִּשְׁמָעִינַן לֵיהּ דְּאָמַר מִזְבֵּחַ בַּצָּפוֹן קָאֵי. אֲבָל לְרַבִּי יוֹסֵי סְתָמָא, דְּהוּא רַבִּי יוֹסֵי בֶּן חֲלַפְתָּא, דְּלָא שְׁמַעְתְּ לֵיהּ דְּאָמַר – לָא תּוֹקְמָהּ, דְּדִלְמָא כְּרַבִּי יְהוּדָה ס"ל. בַּכִּיּוֹר. מִתּוֹךְ שֶׁנֶּאֱמַר: "בֵּין אֹהֶל מוֹעֵד וּבֵין הַמִּזְבֵּחַ", וְכָתוּב אֶחָד אוֹמֵר: לח] מִזְבַּח

רבי יוסי היא. וא"ת: מי מצית מוקמת לה לסדר תמיד כר"י הא תנן בסוף מסכת תמיד (דף לג.): עירן לתוך של זהב ונתפזר ממנה קב גחלים. ולרבי יוסי היה מתפזר יותר, כדתנן פרק "טרף בקלפי" (יומא דף מג:), רבי יוסי אומר: בכל יום היה חותה בשל סאה ומערה לשל שלשת קבין! וי"ל: נהי דהא לא כרבי יוסי – הך כרבי יוסי אתיא שפיר. ולא דמי להא דדייקינן בפ"ק דיומא (דף טז:): ואי ס"ד מדות רבי יהודה היא כו'. קדושת היכל ואולם חדא היא. והתלמוד מסופק בכל מקום, לעיל ספ"ק (דף יז.) וביומא פ' "טרף בקלפי" (דף מד:) ובריש עירובין (דף ב.). הא מני ר' יוסי הגלילי היא. הוה מצי למימר רבי אלעזר היא, דאמר לקמן בפירקין (דף סג:) דקסבר כוליה מזבח בצפון קאי. וא"ת: דמשמע הכא דמאן דלית ליה כוליה מזבח בצפון קאי – הוי כיור בין אהל מועד ובין המזבח. ובתוספתא פרק קמא דכלים: נכנסים בין האולם ולמזבח שלא רחוץ ידים ורגלים, וחכמים אומרים: אין נכנסין! ושמא סבר לה כרבי מאיר דאמר נכנסין.

פנוי

א] סימן בידך כל הניטל כו' אינו ניתן אלא: ב] מעל המזבח מלפני ה' ותיבת וגו' נמחק: ג] בעי למיתי ואי: ד] למיתי וא"נ קסבר תיבת ואלא נמחק: ה] תיבת מילתא נמחק: ו] דכי מסגי לקמיה: ז] העזרה עשר ועל תיבות ושלשים ושתים אמות היו לו נרשם קו: ח] היכל ואחת: ט] היכל וכתליו סוף: י] קסבר נמי קדושת: יא] תיבת מילתא נמחק: יב] וגו' וכתי' א) את אות ו' נמחק: יג] הימנו לפנים הס"ד: יד] דכל יומא ויומא הניטלין: טו] להן מקום כנגד: טז] למערכה שניה להקטרת בזיכין והשאר נמחק: יז] פשטינן לר' יוסי דכוליה מזבח: יח] קסבר שהצריך משיכת המערכה מן הקרן ד' אמות לצפון הס"ד: יט] ד' האמות נרשם נקודה על ה' מלמעלה: כ] למיתי ולהמשיך מקרן: כא] רוחבו חמש בצפון וחמש בדרום וכיון שכל המזבח בדרום נמצא שאין ממנו כנגד הפתח אלא ה' אמות צפוניות שלו שהרי כלה הוא כנגד כו': כב] מכנגד זוית יסוד ותיבת קרן נמחק: כג] היא ומשהגיע כנגד פתח האולם כו' עודף על רוחב פתח ההיכל ה' אמות לכל צד שהרי רחבו כ' אמות אות ת' ותיבת לכל נמחק: כד] כנגד פתח ההיכל: כה] ממזוזת דרומית: כו] מידה לשיעור: כז] עליהן. דקסבר כוליה מזבח בצפון קאי ואין ממנו כנגד הפתח אלא חמשה אמות דרומית ומהן אמה כו' מקום הקרנות ואמה למקום הילוך רגלי כהנים המסדרין את כו' בין הקרן למערכה ואין לו שום מקום כנגד הפתח אלא אמה אחת ולימדך שעל אותה אמה יתחיל המערכה שהיא משוכה מן הקרן ארבע אמות ולא יתרחק מן הקרן יותר דכי מסגי כו' ומתיבת שיסדר כו' עד תיבת הפתח נמחק: כח] יוסי דמזבח בצפון קאי אלא ר"י ותיבת אימא נמחק: כט] אמות ממזוזת: ל] של כל כותל: לא] סוף כו' כדאקשי: לב] להו אבל מן היסוד שש אמות הוא נמשך ותיבו' ונמצא לפני הפתח שהרי נמחק: לג] יוסי בממוצע. כלומר למה לך (למתוקמא) [לאוקמי] דלא כר' יוסי דשמענא ליה דאמר כל הניטל בפנים כו' כיון דלא באתה [רק] לדחות סייעתא דר"י מהכא דליכא למידק לר' יוסי דכוליה מזבח בצפון קאי א"כ כי אוקמת כר"י ובממוצע תוכל לומר דקסבר חציו בצפון וחציו בדרום ומשני משום דר' יהודה כו' ואע"ג דר' יוסי איירי בניטלים כו' נימא דלכ"ע אית להו האי סברא דרבי יוסי דר' יוסי אמרה אליבא דכ"ע: ורב שרביא אמר כו' כלומר הא ודאי דדייקינן מיניה דכוליה מזבח בצפון קאי ור' יוסי דאיירי בניטלים בפנים אינו שונה אותה ברייתא ולא הוי סייעתא לר' יוחנן אלא לר' יוסי הגלילי היא דסבר דכל הניטלים דכ"ע אית להו. נוסחאת רש"י של מהר"פ: לד] מכדי לאפוקי מדוקיא דר' זירא: לה] מינה לר': לו] כדקאמרת דכוליה מזבח: לז] מוקמינן ליה דשמעינן: לח] אומר את:

כל נ"ק

הגהות הב"ח

(א) גמ' את הכיור בין אהל מועד וגו' וכתוב אחד אומר ואת מזבח העולה: (ב) רש"י ד"ה כ"ז אמות וכו' נמצא שאין ממנו לפני הפתח אלא ה' אמות דרומיות שלו נ"ב ועל תיבת ממנו נ"ב ר"ל ממזבח ועל תיבת שלו נ"ב ר"ל של מזבח: (ג) ד"ה וא"נ וכו' חמשה דרומיות נ"ב ר"ל של מזבח:

[לעיל יז. וש"נ]

יומא טז.

נ"ק

גליון הש"ס

תוס' ד"ה הא וכו' ושמא ס"ל כר"מ כו'. ק"ל הא ר' יוסי ס"ל בשמעתין דכוליה מזבח בצפון ואפ"ה ס"ל במתני' ספ"א דכלים דאין נכנסין שלא רחוץ בין אולם ולמזבח וצ"ע:

נ"ק מ"ז

נ"א ועובי של כל כותל נ"ק

ובממוצע נ"ק

לסתור נ"ק

א) ר"ל קרא דונתת את מזבח העולה לפני פתח משכן אהל מועד (שמות מ' פסוק ו') וכרש"י העתיק קרא דפסוק כ"ע שם.

"מִזְבַּח הָעוֹלָה שָׂם פֶּתַח טז] אוֹהֶל מוֹעֵד" וְאֵין כִּיּוֹר מַפְסִיק בֵּינְתַיִים – לָמַדְתָּ מִשְּׁנֵי הַמִּקְרָאוֹת הַלָּלוּ שֶׁצָּרִיךְ לִיתְּנוֹ כָּל מַה שֶּׁיָּכוֹל לְקָרְבוֹ בָּאֲוִיר שֶׁבֵּין מִזְבֵּחַ לְאֹהֶל מוֹעֵד, וּבִלְבַד שֶׁלֹּא יְהֵא מַפְסִיק בֵּין מִזְבֵּחַ וְלַפֶּתַח. הֵיכָן הָיָה נָתוּן מָשׁוּךְ קִימְעָא. מִזָּוִית הַמִּזְבֵּחַ וְלַדָּרוֹם. נִמְצָא שֶׁאֵינוֹ כְּנֶגֶד הַמִּזְבֵּחַ כְּלָל, אֶלָּא כְּבֵין אֹהֶל מוֹעֵד וְלַמִּזְבֵּחַ. תורה אור

מִזְבַּח הָעוֹלָה" וגו' – מִזְבֵּחַ בְּפֶתַח אֹהֶל מוֹעֵד, וְלֹא כִּיּוֹר בְּפֶתַח אֹהֶל מוֹעֵד; הֵיכָן הָיָה נוֹתְנוֹ – *אבֵּין הָאוּלָם וְלַמִּזְבֵּחַ, מָשׁוּךְ קִימְעָא כְּלַפֵּי הַדָּרוֹם. מַאי קָסָבַר? אִי קָסָבַר א] כּוּלֵּיהּ מִזְבֵּחַ בַּדָּרוֹם קָאֵי – נוֹקְמֵיהּ מִכּוֹתֶל הֵיכָל וְלַדָּרוֹם (א) בֵּין אוּלָם לַמִּזְבֵּחַ. וְאִי נַמִי קָסָבַר: *קְדוּשַּׁת הֵיכָל וְאוּלָם חֲדָא הִיא – נוֹקְמֵיהּ מִכּוֹתֶל אוּלָם וְלַדָּרוֹם ב] בְּבֵין אוּלָם לַמִּזְבֵּחַ. אִי נַמִי קָסָבַר: חֶצְיוֹ בַּצָּפוֹן וְחֶצְיוֹ בַּדָּרוֹם – נוֹקְמֵיהּ מִכּוֹתֶל הֵיכָל וְלַדָּרוֹם בֵּין אוּלָם ג] וְלַמִּזְבֵּחַ. וְאִי נַמִי קָסָבַר: קְדוּשַּׁת הָאוּלָם וְהֵיכָל חֲדָא הִיא – נוֹקְמֵיהּ מִכּוֹתֶל אוּלָם וְלַדָּרוֹם ד] בֵּין אוּלָם וְלַמִּזְבֵּחַ! אֶלָּא לָאו מִשּׁוּם דְּקָסָבַר: כּוּלֵּיהּ מִזְבֵּחַ בַּצָּפוֹן. ה] *כִּי נַמִי מוֹקְמַתְּ לָהּ מִכּוֹתֶל הֵיכָל וְלַצָּפוֹן, ה"ל בֵּין אוּלָם וְלַמִּזְבֵּחַ; וְנוֹקְמָהּ מִכּוֹתֶל אוּלָם וְלַצָּפוֹן ו] בְּבֵין אוּלָם וְלַמִּזְבֵּחַ! אָמַר קְרָא: "צָפוֹנָה" – שֶׁיְּהֵא ז] צָפוֹן פָּנוּי מִכֵּלִים. מַאן תַּנָּא דְּפָלֵיג עֲלֵיהּ דְּר' יוֹסֵי הַגְּלִילִי? ר"א בֶּן יַעֲקֹב הִיא. דְּתַנְיָא, ח] *ר"א בֶּן יַעֲקֹב אוֹמֵר: "צָפוֹנָה" – שֶׁיְּהֵא צָפוֹן פָּנוּי מִכְּלוּם, וַאֲפִילּוּ מִן הַמִּזְבֵּחַ. אָמַר רַב: במִזְבֵּחַ שֶׁנִּפְגַּם – כָּל הַקֳּדָשִׁים שֶׁנִּשְׁחֲטוּ שָׁם פְּסוּלִין, *מִקְרָא ט] הוּא בְּיָדֵינוּ וּשְׁכַחְנוּהוּ. כִּי סְלֵיק ◦רַב כָּהֲנָא, אַשְׁכְּחֵיהּ לְר"שׁ בְּרַבִּי דְּקָאָמַר מִשּׁוּם ר' יִשְׁמָעֵאל בְּר' יוֹסֵי: מִנַּיִן לְמִזְבֵּחַ שֶׁנִּפְגַּם שֶׁכָּל הַקֳּדָשִׁים שֶׁנִּשְׁחֲטוּ שָׁם פְּסוּלִין – שֶׁנֶּאֱמַר: ◦"וְזָבַחְתָּ עָלָיו אֶת עוֹלֹתֶיךָ וְאֶת שְׁלָמֶיךָ"; וְכִי עָלָיו אַתָּה זוֹבֵחַ? אֶלָּא, י] כְּשֶׁהוּא שָׁלֵם וְלֹא כְּשֶׁהוּא חָסֵר. אֲמַר: הַיְינוּ קְרָא דְּאִישְׁתְּמִיט לֵיהּ לְרַב. וְרַבִּי יוֹחָנָן אָמַר: אֶחָד זֶה וְאֶחָד זֶה פְּסוּלִין. בְּמַאי פְּלִיגִי? *רַב סָבַר: גבַּעֲלֵי חַיִּים אֵינָן נִדְחִים, וְר' יוֹחָנָן סָבַר: *בַּעֲלֵי חַיִּים נִדְחִין. מֵיתִיבֵי: כָּל הַקֳּדָשִׁים שֶׁהָיוּ עַד שֶׁלֹּא נִבְנָה הַמִּזְבֵּחַ, וְאַחַ"כ נִבְנָה הַמִּזְבֵּחַ – פְּסוּלִין; דנִבְנָה? דְּחוּיִין מֵעִיקָּרָא נִינְהוּ! אֶלָּא: עַד שֶׁלֹּא נֶהֱרַס יא] הַמִּזְבֵּחַ; נֶהֱרַס? הָא אִיזְקוּן לְהוּ! אֶלָּא, *עַד שֶׁלֹּא נִפְגַּם הַמִּזְבֵּחַ, יב] וְאַחַר כָּךְ נִפְגַּם הַמִּזְבֵּחַ – פְּסוּלִין! וְלָא תְּרוּצֵי קָא מְתָרְצַתְּ? יג] אֵימָא: שֶׁנִּשְׁחֲטוּ. וְהָאָמַר רַב גִּידֵּל אָמַר רַב: המִזְבֵּחַ שֶׁנֶּעֱקַר – מַקְטִירִין קְטֹרֶת בִּמְקוֹמוֹ. כִּדְאָמַר רָבָא: יד] *מוֹדֶה הָיָה ר' יְהוּדָה בְּדָמִים. הָכָא נַמִי, מוֹדֶה רַב בְּדָמִים. מַאי ר' יְהוּדָה? דְּתַנְיָא: ◦"בַּיּוֹם הַהוּא קִדַּשׁ הַמֶּלֶךְ טו] תּוֹךְ הֶחָצֵר וגו' כִּי מִזְבַּח (*שֶׁעָשָׂה מֹשֶׁה) קָטֹן מֵהָכִיל" – דְּבָרִים כִּכְתָבָן, דִּבְרֵי רַבִּי יְהוּדָה. א"ל רַבִּי יוֹסֵי: וַהֲלֹא

ה"ג יז] בת"כ וּבְמַס' מִדּוֹת. וּמִדְּאַצְטְרִיךְ לֵיהּ רַבִּי יוֹסֵי הַגְּלִילִי לְמָשְׁכוֹ מִכְּנֶגֶד הַמִּזְבֵּחַ וְלַדָּרוֹם, (ב) וְהוּא אֵינוֹ צָרִיךְ לְהַרְחִיקוֹ אֶלָּא מִבֵּין הַמִּזְבֵּחַ וְלַפֶּתַח – פָּשׁוּט מִינֵּיהּ דְּכוּלֵּיהּ מִזְבֵּחַ בַּצָּפוֹן קָאֵי וּלְפִיכָךְ עַל כָּרְחוֹ הוּא מוֹשְׁכוֹ מִכְּנֶגֶד הַמִּזְבֵּחַ כּוּלּוֹ, שֶׁאִם נְתָנוֹ כְּלָל כְּנֶגֶד הַמִּזְבֵּחַ – א"א שֶׁלֹּא יַפְסִיק בֵּינוֹ וְלַפֶּתַח, כִּדְמְפָרֵשׁ וְאָזֵיל. דְּמַאי קָסָבַר. שֶׁלֹּא קִיֵּים אֶת הַמִּקְרָא שֶׁכָּתַב: "בֵּין אֹהֶל מוֹעֵד וּבֵין הַמִּזְבֵּחַ" וְהוּא מוֹשְׁכוֹ קִימְעָא? אִי כּוּלֵּיהּ בַּדָּרוֹם. הַרְבֵּה מִן הַמִּזְבֵּחַ יֵשׁ בַּדָּרוֹם כְּנֶגֶד יח] הֵיכָל שֶׁלֹּא כְּנֶגֶד הַפֶּתַח, וְהָיָה לוֹ לְתִתּוֹ שָׁם. לוֹקְמֵיהּ מִכּוֹתֶל הֵיכָל וְלַדָּרוֹם. כְּלוֹמַר, מִשֶּׁמַּתְחִיל כּוֹתֶל פֶּתַח הַהֵיכָל לִיסְּתֵם לַדָּרוֹם, דְּהַיְינוּ בֵּין פֶּתַח הָאוּלָם וְלַמִּזְבֵּחַ, וּכְנֶגֶד הַהֵיכָל, שֶׁפֶּתַח הָאוּלָם עוֹדֵף עַל שֶׁל הֵיכָל ה' אַמּוֹת כ] לַדָּרוֹם. וְא"נ סָבַר קְדוּשַּׁת אוּלָם וְהֵיכָל חֲדָא הִיא. וּפֶתַח אוּלָם כְּפֶתַח הֵיכָל, וְהוּלְרַךְ לְמוֹשְׁכוֹ אַף מִכְּנֶגֶד פִּתְחוֹ שֶׁל אוּלָם. נוֹקְמֵיהּ מִסְּתִימַת כּוֹתֶל אוּלָם וְלַדָּרוֹם. דְּה"ל אַכַּתִּי כְּבֵין הָאוּלָם וְלַמִּזְבֵּחַ. דְּכֵיוָן דְּכוֹתֶל אוּלָם כְּכוֹתֶל הֵיכָל – קָרֵי בֵּיהּ בֵּין אֹהֶל מוֹעֵד וְלַמִּזְבֵּחַ, וּמִיקַּיְימִי קְרָאֵי שַׁפִּיר. וְאִי נַמִי קָסָבַר חֶצְיוֹ בַּצָּפוֹן כו'. יֵשׁ לוֹ ט"ז אַמָּה בַּדָּרוֹם, צֵא מֵהֶן ה' אַמּוֹת שֶׁל פֶּתַח – עֲדַיִין יֵשׁ לוֹ מָקוֹם י"א אַמָּה לְתִתּוֹ שָׁם, מִכּוֹתֶל מְזוּזַת הֵיכָל כא] דָּרוֹם. וְא"נ קָסָבַר קְדוּשַּׁת אוּלָם וְהֵיכָל חֲדָא הִיא. וְהוּלְרַךְ לְמוֹשְׁכוֹ אַף מִכְּנֶגֶד פֶּתַח אוּלָם, נוֹקְמֵיהּ מִמְּקוֹם סְתִימַת פֶּתַח אוּלָם וְלַדָּרוֹם, כב] כְּבֵין הָאוּלָם וְלַמִּזְבֵּחַ, דַּעֲדַיִין יֵשׁ שָׁם מָקוֹם ו' אַמּוֹת. אֶלָּא לָאו מִשּׁוּם דְּקָסָבַר כּוּלֵּיהּ מִזְבֵּחַ בַּצָּפוֹן. קָאֵי, וּדְרוֹמוֹ שֶׁל מִזְבֵּחַ *כּוּלּוֹ לִפְנֵי הַפֶּתַח. וְאִם הָיָה נוֹתְנוֹ כְּנֶגֶד הַמִּזְבֵּחַ כְּלָל – נִמְצָא מַפְסִיק בֵּין מִזְבֵּחַ כג] לַפֶּתַח. וְנוֹקְמֵיהּ בֵּין הַמִּזְבֵּחַ וְלַהֵיכָל בַּצָּפוֹן. *בִּסְתִימַת כּוֹתֶל הַהֵיכָל, כד] בִּמְזוּזַת צְפוֹנִית וְלַצָּפוֹן. קָסָבַר קְדוּשַּׁת הֵיכָל כו'. וְאֵינוֹ רַשַּׁאי לְהַפְסִיק בֵּין פֶּתַח אוּלָם וְלַמִּזְבֵּחַ. וְכִי מוֹקְמַתְּ לֵיהּ מִכּוֹתֶל הֵיכָל וְלַצָּפוֹן – ה"ל מַפְסִיק בֵּין אוּלָם וְלַמִּזְבֵּחַ. שֶׁיְּהֵא פָּנוּי מִכֵּלִים. גָּרַס הָכָא. וְכִיּוֹר כְּלִי הוּא. (ג) צְפוֹנָה. מִדַּהֲוָה לֵיהּ לְמִיכְתַּב "עַל יֶרֶךְ הַמִּזְבֵּחַ צָפוֹן", וּכְתִיב "צָפוֹנָה" – לִדְרָשָׁא אֲתָא. מַאן תַּנָּא דְּפָלֵיג כו'. וְאוֹמֵר כּוּלֵּיהּ בַּדָּרוֹם קָאֵי. בְּדר"א גָּרְסִינַן "פָּנוּי מִכְּלוּם". *שֶׁנִּשְׁחֲטוּ שָׁם. בָּעֲזָרָה. כְּשֶׁהוּא שָׁלֵם. וְהַאי "עָלָיו" – בְּגִינוֹ וּבִשְׁבִילוֹ קָאָמַר. אֶחָד זֶה וְאֶחָד זֶה. בֵּין שֶׁנִּשְׁחֲטוּ בִּשְׁעַת כה] פְּגִימָתָן, בֵּין שֶׁנִּשְׁחֲטוּ אַחַר תִּיקּוּנוֹ – פְּסוּלִין כָּל הַקֳּדָשִׁים שֶׁהָיוּ קְדוֹשִׁין בְּאוֹתָהּ שָׁעָה, לְפִי שֶׁנִּרְאוּ וְנִדְחוּ. וְקָסָבַר: בַּעֲלֵי חַיִּים נִדְחִין כִּשְׁחוּטִין. עַד שֶׁלֹּא נִבְנָה. מַשְׁמַע, קוֹדֶם כו] שֶׁלֹּא בְּנָאוּהוּ בְּנֵי הַגּוֹלָה. דְּחוּיִין מֵעִיקָּרָא הֵן. שֶׁכְּשֶׁהוּקְדְּשׁוּ לֹא נִרְאוּ. שְׁמַע מִינֵּיהּ דִּחוּי מֵעִיקָּרוֹ הָוֵי דִּחוּי, וְתִקְשֶׁה לְמַאן דְּאָמַר לָא הָוֵי דִּחוּי! נֶהֱרַס. מַשְׁמַע בִּימֵי כז] נְבוּכַדְנֶצַּר הָיוּ. כח] אִיזְקִין לְהוּ. עַד שֶׁלֹּא נִבְנָה בַּיִת שֵׁנִי. וּפְשִׁיטָא דִּפְסוּלִין, דְּגַבֵּי מוּמִין קָתָנֵי כט] לְהוּ בִּבְכוֹרוֹת (דף מא.): הַזָּקֵן וְהַחוֹלֶה וְהַמְזוֹהָם! בְּמִזְבֵּחַ פְּנִימִי קָמַיְירֵי. וְקָא סָלְקָא דַּעְתָּךְ דְּהוּא הַדִּין לְחִיצוֹן. קַשְׁיָא דְּרַב אַדְּרַב, דְּאָמַר לְעֵיל: כָּל הַקֳּדָשִׁים שֶׁנִּשְׁחֲטוּ שָׁם – פְּסוּלִין. מוֹדֶה רַבִּי יְהוּדָה בְּדָמִים. דְּבָעֵינַן מִזְבֵּחַ. דְּבָרִים כִּכְתָבָן. שֶׁקִּדֵּשׁ אֶת הָרִצְפָּה כּוּלָּהּ לְשֵׁם מִזְבֵּחַ לְהַקְטִיר עָלֶיהָ, לְפִי שֶׁהָיָה הַמִּזְבֵּחַ קָטָן מֵהָכִיל עוֹלוֹת וּשְׁלָמִים שֶׁהִקְרִיבוּ לַחֲנוּכַּת הַמִּזְבֵּחַ. וְאָמְרִינַן לְקַמָּן: ל] לְרַבִּי יְהוּדָה הָכִי מַשְׁמַע קְרָא: כִּי מִזְבַּח אֲבָנִים אֲשֶׁר תַּחַת מִזְבַּח הַנְּחוֹשֶׁת קָטָן הָיָה. אָמַר לוֹ רַבִּי יוֹסֵי וַהֲלֹא כְּבָר נֶאֱמַר. בַּמִּזְבֵּחַ לא] שֶׁעָשָׂה מֹשֶׁה בַּמִּדְבָּר, שֶׁהָיָה בְּנוֹב וְגִבְעוֹן. אֶלֶף

פנוי מכלים. אע"פ שמזבח שעשה משה לב] (אינו פנוי) *[כלי] היה, כדאמר: דנין כלי מכלי ואין דנין כלי מבנין – משאר כלים קאמר, ד"לפונה" *אמזבח קאי. ואע"פ שהיה בצפון נסכין וקלונסות ושולחנות, מסתמא הא דאמרה תורה פנוי מכלום – משום שחיטה הוא, והני צורך שחיטה נינהו. **שיהא** צפון פנוי מכלים. אפילו מן המזבח. צריך לדקדק במתני' דמדות (דף לג) שלא תקשה, דרבי אליעזר בן יעקב ס"ל הכא כוליה מזבח בדרום קאי, ובפ"ק דיומא (דף טז.) מוקמינן מתני' דמדות כר"א בן יעקב. **וכי** עליו אתה זובח. אע"ג דלעיל דרשינן "עליו" ממש, הכא דייק משום ד"וזבחת עליו" לג] משמע שמצוה לזבוח עליו. וכן לקמן (דף ס.) גבי "ואכלוה מצות אצל המזבח" לד] משמע שמצוה, אלא כשהוא שלם ולא כשהוא חסר. **עד** שלא נבנה המזבח. דחויין מעיקרא הן. לה] אלא עד שלא נפגם ונפגם. ומשני: לא תרוצי מתרצת לה. ותימה: דא"כ משמע דפירכא קמייתא דחויין מעיקרא הוו, ואפילו לר' יוחנן. ואמאי? והא ר' יוחנן סבר גבי בהמה של ב' שותפין (קדושין דף ז.) דחוי מעיקרא הוי דחוי. ועוד תקשי ליה ממתני' ד"מי שהיה טמא" (פסחים דף לז:): המפריש נקבה לפסחו, דקאמר: דחוי מעיקרו הוי דחוי! ויש לומר: דהתם אין בידו לתקן מיקרי דחוי, כדפרישית פ"ק (לעיל דף יב:*), אבל הכא בידו לתקן *המזבח, לו] ולכך משמע ליה הכא דכ"ע לא הוי דחוי מידי לז] דהוה אמחוסר זמן בגופו ובבעלים, כגון יולדת זב ומצורע שהפרישו קרבנם קודם זמנם – ה"נ מפריש קרבנו להקריב לכשיבנה בהמ"ק, לח] והוי כמחוסר זמן, ולא חשיב נדחה. וכן מוכח לקמן פ"ב (דף קיד.) דחובות שהקדישן בגלגל – לגבי שילה היו מחוסר זמן וקרבי בשילה, דלא אמרינן דחויין הן. וקשה לי: דבפ"ק (לעיל דף יב.) פריך לבן בתירא פסח היכי משכחת לה? אי *אפרשי' בצפרא – דחוי מעיקרא הוא, שאינו ראוי לשלמים לבן בתירא, הואיל לט] ומקצתו הוא ראוי לפסח בחצות. מה בכך? כיון דבידו להשהותו עד חצות, למה לא יהא כשר כמו *מקדיש אותו לאחר שחיטת בנו, שראוי למחר. ומקדיש בגלגל חובות שכשרין בשילה. ברו"ך. וא"ת: אכתי, כיון דהוי כמחוסר זמן כי ליכא מזבח, דפריך דחויין מעיקרא הן, אמאי אמר ר' יוחנן בפ' "השוחט והמעלה" (לקמן דף קז:) דהמעלה בזמן הזה בחוץ – חייב, דקדושה ראשונה קידשה לעתיד לבא? הא אינו ראוי לפתח אהל! ותנן נמי פרק בתרא (לקמן דף קיב:): אותו ואת בנו ומחוסר זמן בחוץ – אינו אפילו בלא תעשה לרבנן. ואם כן, לרבי יוחנן אמאי מחייב משום שחוטי חוץ? ותו: הא עדיפא מינה אמרינן ביומא פרק "שני שעירי" (דף סג.) דשלמים ששחטן *)קודם פתיחת דלתות ההיכל

*) בחוץ קודם נ"ק

מסורת הש"ס

[מדות פ"ג מ"ו]

[לעיל יד. וש"נ]

[יומא לז.]

[ע"ז נב:]

[לעיל יב. פסחים לח. יומא סד. קדושין ז: כריתות כז. כח. תמורה כו: לקמן עג:]

כלה נ"ק

[ע' תוס' מנחות נט: ד"ה כל שבידו]

מסתימת נ"ק

[לקמן ס.]

נ"ל הנחושת אשר לפני ה'

עי' רש"ק שכתב סד"ה שנשחטו כו' עד מלת קאמר הס"ד ובעל פנים מאירות הגיה עליו והוכיח כן מתוך סוגית גירסת הש"ס הכא

הגהות הב"ח

(א) גמ' מכותל היכל ולדרום דהיינו בין: (ב) רש"י ד"ה ה"ג וכו' ולדרום והא אינו צריך: (ג) ד"ה צפונה נ"ל קודם ד"ה שיהא פנוי:

נ"א ונוקמיה בין היכל ולצפון קסבר קדושת היכל ואולם חדא כי נמי כו'

גליון הש"ס

גמ' רב כהנא אשכחיה. עיין גיטין דף פד ע"ב תוס' ד"ה רי"א:

עין משפט נר מצוה

גי' רש"ק. וגר' נ"ק אינו פנוי היה ונקרא כלי כלדאמרינן ולא מזבח קאמר נ"ק

ד א מיי' פ"א מהלכות בית הבחירה הל' ו:

ה ב מיי' פ"ג מהלכות פסה"מ הלכה כב:

ו ג מיי' שם הלכה כג ופט"ו מהל' מעה"ק הלכה ז:

ז ד מיי' פ"ג מהלכות פסה"מ הלכה כב:

ח ה מיי' פ"ב מהלכות תמידין ומוספין הל' ב:

[ד"ה וש"מ]

נ"א המזבח ויהא נראה כשהמזבח יהא בנוי ולכך משמע כו' וכן הוא בס"י ועי' נ"ק

[לקמן עג: יומא סד. פסחי' עג: נח. קדושין ז:]

דאפרשיה לאלונתא לחוי כו' נ"ק

שיטה מקובצת

א] כוליה מזבח בדרום קאי. ה"ה דהוי מצי למבעי אי בדרום קאי מאי משוך קימעא הא צריך למשוך כל הדרום ולכל הפחות ה' אמות כנגד הפתח דהא בעינן ולא כיור בפתח אהל מועד: ב] ולדרום כבין אולם: ג] למזבח ואי נמי קסבר קדושת היכל ואולם: ד] ולדרום כבין: ה] בצפון קאי ונוקמיה מכותל היכל ולצפון קסבר קדושת היכל ואולם חדא הוא וכי נמי. ס"א כי נמי מוקמת לה מכותל היכל ולדרום הוי ליה בין האולם ולמזבח ונוקמיה מכותל היכל ולצפון בין אהל מועד ולמזבח ואי נמי קסבר קדושת היכל ואולם חדא היא נוקמיה מכותל אולם ולצפון כבין אולם ולמזבח אמר קרא כו' אבל גירסת רש"י אינו כן: ו] ולצפון כבין אולם: ז] צפונה שיהא פנוי מכלום. וא"ת א"כ למה לי להזכיר הברייתא ואת מזבח העולה שם פתח אוהל מועד לומר דאין כיור פתח אהל מועד תיפוק א) ליה משום דאם יעמוד [הכיור] בין המזבח לפתח אהל מועד לצפון הואיל דבעינן צפון דכוליה מזבח בצפון קאי ובעינן צפון פנוי מכלום וליכא וי"ל דאי לאו דמפסיק הוה מעמידו שפיר בין ההיכל ובין המזבח תוך חלל פתח האולם דלא מקרי צפון כדקאמר לעיל דאפילו בית החליפות לא מקרי צפון ולכן מייתי מקרא דאת מזבח העולה כו' דמשמע דבעינן שלא יהא כיור מפסיק בין מזבח לפתח אהל מועד. מהר"ם: ח] ר"א בן יעקב אומר צפונה כו'. תימה דבמס' מדות תנן הכיור היה בין האולם ולמזבח משוך כלפי דרום ואמרינן ביומא מאן תנא מדות ראב"י והכא אית ליה לראב"י דמזבח לאו בצפון קאי וא"כ היכא אתיא ההיא דמדות כותיה דהא לכאורה סבר ההיא דמדות דמזבח בצפון קאי כדדייקינן בהך דר"י הגלילי וי"ל דההיא דמדות איכא למימר דר"ל משוך מן הדרום ה' אמות ממזבח בכותל ההיכל לדרום וקסבר כוליה מזבח בדרום קאי אבל הכא דקתני משוך קימעא ליכא לפרושי הכי במשוך מכנגד הפתח דוקא קאמר ולעולם הוי בין המזבח לכותל ההיכל דא"כ אמאי נקט קימעא אפילו טובא נמי יכול למשכו מכנגד הפתח דאכתי נשאר הרבה מן המזבח לקיומי ונתת את הכיור בין אהל מועד ובין המזבח אלא ודאי משוך קימעא דקאמר משוך ב) מכנגד הפתח קאמר ולכך דוקא קימעא לפי שצריך לקרבו כל מה שנוכל נגד אויר שבין המזבח להיכל ולאולם כדי לקיים בין אהל [מועד] ומזבח ואת"ל שאין להרחיקו מן הכותל כל כך מ"מ לא סגי בקימעא דכיון דאפתח קאי צריך שיהא משוך מתחילת המזבח ה' אמות כשיעור הפתח: ט] מקרא היה בידינו: י] אלא עליו כשהוא: יא] המזבח ואח"כ נהרס המזבח פסולים נהרס (נ"א היכא אסקא להו אלא עד שלא נהרס המזבח ונבנה): יב] המזבח ונפגם ואחר כך נתקן תיבת נפגם נמחק: יג] מתרצת תני נמי שנשחטו ותיבת אימא נמחק: יד] רבא מודי רבי יהודה בדמים הכי נמי מודי רב: טו] המלך את תוך החצר וגו' כי מזבח הנחשת אשר לפני ה' קטן מהכיל: טז] שם פתח משכן אהל: יז] ה"ג לה בת"כ ובמס' מדות ומדאצטריך ליה ריה"ג למושכו מכנגד המזבח: יח] כנגד כותל היכל: יט] וכנגד כותל ההיכל: כ] אמות לכל צד הס"ד: כא] ולדרום הס"ד: כב] ולדרום בין: כג] מזבח ולפתח הס"ד: כד] ההיכל אמזוזת צפונית: כה] בשעת פגימתו: כו] קודם שבנוהו בני תיבת שלא נמחק: כז] נבוכדנצר תיבה אחת: כח] הא אזקין להו עד שנבנה בית שני: כט] תיבת להו נמחק: ל] לקמן דלר"י: לא] במזבח הנחשת שעשה משה במדבר שהיה בבמה (נ"א בנוב וגבעון): לב] משה כלי היה (תיבות אינו פנוי נמחק) כדאמרי' לקמן דנין כלי כו' מבנין הכא פנוים משאר כלים: לג] משמע. ס"א דוקא עליו: לד] המזבח וכי אצל המזבח אוכלים כלומר דוקא ולא במקום אחר [אלא כו'] ותיבות משמע שמצוה נמחק: לה] מתיבת אלא עד תיבת וא"ת אכתי מוקף בחצאי לבנה: לו] ולכך יהא נראה כשהמזבח יהא בנוי ומתוקן ולכך משמע: לז] מידי (דלא) דהוי אמחוסר זמן בין בגופו בין בבעלים דכי מצו חזו הדרי כשרין כגון: לח] בית המקדש הוי כמחוסר: לט] הואיל והוא ראוי ותיבת ומקצתו נמחק:

א) נראה דל"ל משום דאם יעמוד הכיור בין המזבח כנגד פתח אוהל מועד ע"כ צריך להעמידו בצפון העזרה דהא כוליה מזבח וכו' ב) נראה דל"ל משוך מכנגד המזבח קאמר.

והלא? כבר נאמר: °"אלף עולות יעלה שלמה על המזבח ההוא", א] ואילו בבית עולמים הוא אומר: °"ויזבח שלמה את זבח השלמים אשר זבח לה' בקר עשרים ושנים אלף", וכשאתה מגיע לחשבון עולות ולמנין אמות – זה גדול מזה! אלא מהו "קטן מהכיל" – כאדם האומר לחבירו: "פלוני ננס הוא", ופסול לעבודה. ור' יהודה, שפיר קאמר ר' יוסי! ר' יהודה לטעמיה, דאמר: מזבח שעשה משה גדול היה. דתניא: °"חמש אמות אורך וחמש אמות רוחב" – דברים ככתבן, דברי ר' יוסי. ר' יהודה אומר: נאמר כאן °"רבוע" ונאמר להלן °"רבוע", מה להלן – מאמצעיתו היה מודד, אף כאן – מאמצעיתו היה מודד. והתם מנלן? דכתיב: *°"והאריאל שתים עשרה ב] אמה" – לכל רוח, *או אינו אלא י"ב על י"ב? כשהוא אומר: "אל ארבעת רבעיו" – מלמד שמאמצע הוא מודד. ג] ור' יוסי: כי גמר גזירה שוה – בגובהה הוא דגמיר. דתניא: °"ושלש אמות קומתו" – דברים ככתבן, דברי רבי יהודה. רבי יוסי אומר, נאמר כאן: °"רבוע" ונאמר להלן: "רבוע", מה להלן גובהו פי שנים כארכו – אף כאן פי שנים כארכו. אמר ליה רבי יהודה: *(והלא כבר נאמר: ד] "ואת החצר מאה אמה וקומה חמש אמות" וגו',) אפשר כהן עומד ע"ג המזבח ועבודה בידו, וכל העם רואין אותו מבחוץ? אמר לו ר' יוסי: והלא כבר נאמר: °"ואת קלעי החצר ואת מסך ה] שער החצר אשר על המשכן ועל המזבח", ו] *אמה משכן י' אמות – אף מזבח י' אמות. ואומר: °"קלעים חמש עשרה אמה

אלף עולות יעלה שלמה וגו' וכשאתה מגיע לחשבון עולות ז] ולמנין אמות. שהיה מזבח אבנים של שלמה עודף עליו, זה של שלמה גדול משל משה לפי אורך העולות. שהרי מזבח של משה כתיב ביה: "ה' אמות אורך וה' אמות רוחב" צא מהם מקום הקרנות אמה לכל צד ומקום הילוך רגלי הכהנים אמה לפנים מן הקרנות סביב ח] המערכה – נמצא מקום המערכה אמה על אמה. הכי אמרינן לקמן בפירקין (דף סב.): יסוד וסובב לא היו ממעטין בארכו ורחבו, לפי ט] שמקיפין ובולטין סביביו מעשה רשת נחושת, והוא היה סובבו. ובמזבח שעשה שלמה היה מקום המערכה *כ' על כ' לרבי יוסי, כדתנן במסכת מדות י] (דף לה:). חלקהו לכ' רצועות כל אחת ואחת ברוחב אמה ואורך עשרים – הרי ד' מאות יא] אורך ברוחב אמה. ואין לך אמה על אמה שאינה מחזקת לבער אלף יב] ליום, שהיתה אש של שמים ממהרת לאכול – הרי ד' מאות אלף. אלא מהו אומר קטן מהכיל. לאו במזבח אבנים קאמר, ומשום יג] ההוא יומא. אלא למזבח הנחשת קאמר, ובא לפוסלו לעולם, יד] שסילקו. ומה שתלה הכתוב קטנו בעולות של אותו היום – לישנא מעליא נקט. כאדם שאומר לחבירו. כאדם שנפסל. ננס פלוני. לישנא מעליא, ולא אמר "נפסל פלוני". טו] ונפסל לעבודה. לאו טז] מסקנא ד"אדם אומר", אלא רבי יוסי קאמר לה: ואותו פלוני פסול לעבודה, והוא קורא לו ננס. שפיר קא"ר יוסי. ול"ל לקדושי רצפה? מזבח של משה גדול היה. וכשאתה מגיע לחשבון עולות ומנין אמות שבשניהם – נמצא של שלמה קטן לפי הערך. ונאמר להלן רבוע. בשל יחזקאל, שנתנבא על בית שני או על העתיד: "רבוע אל ארבעת רבעיו". מה להלן. מדה האמורה בו מאמצעיתו הוא מודד, כדמפרש ואזיל. אף כאן מודד ה' על ה' מאמצעיתו. לכל רוח, נמצא י' על י'. צא מהן אמה מכאן ואמה מכאן לקרנות, וכן למקום הילוך – הרי ו' על ו' מקום המערכה. ושל שלמה כ' על כ' מקום המערכה. עשה ממנו ג' רצועות של ו' יז] רוחב – נשארו שתי אמות באורך עשרים. חלוק ג' הרצועות יח] לרחבו [לחתיכות רבועות של שש שש], תמצא בכל אחת ג' חתיכות רבועות של שש שש – הרי תשע. ועוד נשארו בכל אחת ב' אמות באורך ששה, יט] קרבם זו אצל זו – הרי ו' על ו', הרי עשר חתיכות רבועות. ועוד צרף הרצועה הארוכה עשרים ורחבה ב' – ותמצא ו' על ו', הרי י"א. כ] וב' אמות על ב' אמות. נמצא של משה אחד מי"א כשל שלמה, ומגיע לחשבון י"א אלפים עולות ותו לא, כא] ובחנוכתו כתיב: "בקר כ"ב אלף וצאן כב] *כ"ב אלף". והאריאל. מקום מערכה של מזבח. שתים עשרה. "אל ארבעת רבעיו" – מלמד שמאמצעיתו מודד. ורבי יוסי. דאמר: דברים ככתבן. כי גמיר ג"ש. ד"רבוע" "רבוע" – בגובהה הוא דגמר. ולאו מ"רבוע" דיחזקאל, אלא מ"רבוע" דכתיב במזבח הפנימי, כג] דתניא: "וג' אמות קומתו" כו' (שמות כז) – כד] ובמזבח הנחשת כתיב. ונאמר להלן רבוע. במזבח הזהב: "אמה ארכו ואמה רחבו רבוע ואמתים קומתו" (שם ל). אף כאן גובהו פי שנים בארכו. הרי י' אמות. *ובסיפא מפרש ר' יוסי מאי "וג' קומתו". והלא כבר נאמר וקומה ה' אמות. דאין גובה היקף הקלעים של חצר אלא ה' אמות. אפשר כן. שיהא כהן בראש המזבח ועבודה בידו כו'. מה משכן. צריך כה] קלעים לחצר סביביו מוקף גובה י' אמות, דהא הכי הוה גובהה דכתיב (שם כו): "י' אמות אורך הקרש". אף מזבח. צריך כו] היקף לכדי י' אמות. ואומר קלעים ט"ו אמה

היכל – פטור, דאינו ראוי לפתח אהל מועד, *דמחוסרי מעשה, וכ"ש זה! ועוד: אמרינן בפ"ק דמס' ע"ז (דף יג:) דאם הקדיש והחרים והעריך בזמן הזה – בהמה תעקר, דהיינו נועל דלת בפניה והיא מתה מאליה כדאיתא התם. ופריך: ונישחטינהו מישחט. ופי' בקונטרס: משום שחוטי חוץ לא מחייב, דמיירי בקדשי בדק הבית דאין חייבין משום שחוטי חוץ, כדמוכח לקמן (דף קיג:) ובפרק "שני שעירי" (יומא דף סג:). וקשה: דאי בקדשי בדק הבית – כז] מאי פריך: ונישוייה גיסטרא, כח] ומשני: מפני שנראה כמטיל מום בקדשים? כט] וליכא למימר דיש איסור מטיל מום אף בבהמה תמימה לקדשי בדק הבית, כדאמר: המתפיס תמימים לבדק הבית אינן יוצאין מידי מזבח לעולם. דהיינו מדרבנן משום קנס, כדמוכח פרק "המנחות והנסכים" (מנחות קא.) דקאמר: משום דלא שכיחי תמימים תקנו שיהיו למזבח. לכך נראה דמיירי בקדשי מזבח, ולא מחייבי משום שחוטי חוץ – משום דאינו ראוי לפתח אהל מועד, או משום דהוי דחוי, או משום דמחוסר זמן. ודוחק לומר דההיא דמס' ע"ז כמ"ד הותרו הבמות, דהא סתם מתניתין לקמן (דף קיב:) דירושלים אין אחריה היתר. ובפ"ק דמגילה (דף י.) פריך מינה *לר' יוחנן דאמר שמעתי שמקריבין בבית חוניו. ונראה לתרץ: דר' יוחנן דמחייב לקמן מעלה בחוץ – מיירי בהעלאת קטרת, דלא מחוסר מעשה, כדאמר בשמעתין: מזבח שנעקר – מקטירין קטרת במקומו. א"נ, בהעלאת מנחה שקמלה בכלי שרת בפנים ל] אע"פ שאין בית. דאזבחים דוקא בעי מזבח, כדכתיב "וזבחת עליו". וניחא השתא הא דנקט ר' יוחנן "מעלה בזמן הזה", ולא נקט שוחט בזמן הזה. ואין לתרץ דר' יוחנן כרבי יהודה *דשרי להקטיר ברצפת העזרה, דלא מיסתבר דלישרי רבי יהודה בשעה שהמזבח פגום אלא בשעה שהמזבח כשר. ועוד יש לתרץ: דלקמן ר' יוחנן מיירי כשבנה המזבח במקומו והעלה בחוץ. כיון דקדשי לעתיד לבא. לא] *וההיא דפ"ק דע"ז (דף יג:) יש להקשות: בקדשי בדק הבית אמאי נועל דלת בפניה לרבא? ונשחטיה או נשוייה גיסטרא! אלא פי' רבינו הקדוש: דמדרבנן אסור להטיל בהם מום גזירה אטו קדשי מזבח, כדאמר ב"ראשית הגז" (חולין דף קלה.) דקדשי בדק הבית אסורין בגיזה ועבודה, גזירה אטו קדשי מזבח. וא"כ יש ליישב פי' רש"י דפריך בקדשי בדק הבית: ונשחטיה משחט ונשוייה גסטרא, ומשני: נראה כמטיל מום, דאסור גזירה אטו קדשי מזבח. וא"ת: מאי טעמא פטרינן שלמים ששחטן לב] קודם פתיחת דלתות ההיכל לג] בחוץ *(לעיל דף נה:)? והלא בפנים כי האי גוונא אם עלו לא ירדו, לפי מה שפי' הקונטרס לקמן לד] קודם שיעמידו לוים את המשכן ולאחר שפרקו לוים את המשכן – דשלמים דוקא בעי פתיחת דלתות ההיכל ולא שאר קדשים. וכיון דשאר קדשים כשרין – א"כ שלמים נמי, אם עלו לא ירדו, וחייב בחוץ כמו הלן והיוצא ושנשחט חוץ לזמנו וחוץ למקומו דחייב עליהן בחוץ הואיל ומתקבל בפנים! וי"ל: דהתם מיירי בהעלאה, דכיון שהשחיטה נעשית בפנים כהלכתה – מיחייב בהעלאה, כיון דמתקבל בפנים. אבל הכא, דאין השחיטה כהלכתה – לא. ואפילו אם תימצי לומר דפסח והחטאת ששחטן שלא לשמן בחוץ חייב – הבהמה ראויה לפנים לכתחילה, אבל אלו קדשים אינן ראויין לפנים לכתחילה. *הא אזקינן להו. וגבי מומין תנן בבכורות (דף מא.) הזקן. והא דאמר *)(אלה הדברים רבה): חיים כלכם היום ק"ל ואומר מפרים שהתנדבו הנשיאים לשאת הארון במדבר, שחיו עד שלמה שהקריבן לגבוה – הוראת שעה היתה. והלא כבר נאמר אלף עולות יעלה שלמה. וא"ת: מנא ליה דאמזבח הנחשת לה] קאמר? הא ג' מזבחות הוו, כדאמר לקמן (דף סא:) של נוב ושל גבעון, וגדול היה! וי"ל: דסמיך אקרא (דה"ב ג א) דכתיב בהדיא על מזבח הנחשת שעשה בצלאל. *מה משכן עשר אמות. תימה: כיון דאיכא היקשא, גזירה שוה דרבות למה לי? לו] ואומר קלעים ט"ו אמה אל הכתף. פי' בקונטרס: וקס"ד בגובה קאמר, וה"ה לכל החצר. וקשה לר"ת: היכי מצי למימר דאגובה קאי? והא מוכח קרא בהדיא דברחבה מיירי, דקחשיב מעיקרא החצר לפאת לז] ים חמשים אמה, ואחר כך מפרש חמש עשרה אמה קלעים לכתף שאצל השער, ולכתף השנית חמש עשרה קלעים, ואחר כך לשער החצר מסך עשרים

*) [נ"ל במדבר רבה סדר נשא פ' יב]

שיטה מקובצת

א] ההוא ובבית עולמים תיבת ואילו ל"ש: ב] י"ב ארך בי"ב רחב רבוע אל ארבעת רבעיו ותניא והאריאל שתים עשרה לכל ותיבת אמה נמחק: ג] מודד י"ב אמה לכל רוח: ד] נאמר ארך החצר מאה באמה וגו' וקומה ה' אמות אפשר: ה] מסך פתח השער: ו] המזבח סביב מה: ז] עולות של חנוכת המזבח: ח] סביב מן המערכה: ט] לפי שבולטין חוצה לו ומקיפין ובולטין סביביו: י] מדות והוא שנאמר בדברי הימים ויעש שלמה מזבח נחשת כ' אמה ארכו וכ' אמה רחבו ושל אבנים היה ולפי שהיה לעולה תחת מזבח הנחשת של משה קרא לו מזבח הנחשת ועשרים על עשרים דקרא אמקום [המערכה] קאי כמו והריאל שתים עשרה ארך בשתים עשרה רחב דאמקום מערכה קאמר במזבח בית שני חלק עשרים על עשרים לארכו לכ' רצועות ותיבת חלקהו נמחק: יא] מאות אמות ארך: יב] אלף עולות ליום: יג] ומשום קרבנות דההוא יומא אלא למזבח הנחשת דמשה קאמר: יד] שסילקו. ס"א וקראו שם ננס ופסול כאדם שאומר לחבירו על כהן ננס הוא ופסול לעבודה וסילקו וגנזו ועשה חילופו מזבח אבנים והוא שנאמר קדש את תוך החצר להציב בו בנין אבנים למזבח כי שם עשה את העולה כי מזבח של משה ננס ופסול לפי שלא היה ראוי לרוב עולות של אותו היום וזה שנאמר בדברי הימים כי מזבח הנחשת של משה שעשה שלמה תחתיו מזבח אחר קטן מהכיל (שפיר): טו] מה"ד ופסול לעבודה: טז] לעבודה לאו ס"א אינו ר"ל דאדם אומר לחבירו פלוני ננס ופסול לעבודה אלא ופסול לעבודה ר"י קאמר לה: יז] ו' ו' רוחב: יח] הרצועות. (ס"א לרחבן תמצא בכל אחת שלש חתיכות רבועות של שש שש) לרחב' לחתיכות רבועות של שש תמצא שלש בכל אחת הרי תיבות ג' חתיכות רבועות של שש שש נמחק: יט] ששה יצרף שלש חתיכות הקטנים ותמצא חתיכה רבוע ו' כו' ותיבות קרבם זו אצל זו הרי נמחק: כ] י"א רצועות שש על שש וב': כא] לא כיון דשל משה אלף ותו לא ובחנוכתו: כב] וצאן מאה ועשרים אלף: כג] הפנימי דמשה: כד] במזבח הנחשת: כה] צריך קלעי החצר שסביביו גבוה י' ותיבת מוקף נמחק: כו] צריך להיות מוקף קלעים גובה עשר ותיבות היקף לכדי נמחק: כז] הבית כי פריך תיבת מאי ל"ש: כח] מאי משני מפני אות ו' נמחק: כט] מתיבת וליכא כו' עד תיבות לכך נראה מוקף בחצאי לבנה: ל] בפנים דמקריבין אע"פ: לא] לבא ובההיא מתיבת ובההיא עד ותיבת וא"ת מ"ט מוקף ח"ל: לב] ששחטן בחוץ קודם: לג] תיבת בחוץ נמחק: לד] לקמן גבי קודם: לה] הנחשת קריב ליה שלא היה מקום המערכה אלא אמה דלמא מזבח דנוב וגבעון קאמר דהיה גדול יותר כדאמרינן לקמן ג' מזבחות הוו שם בנוב ובגבעון וי"ל כו'. מהר"פ: לו] לי תיפוק ליה מהיקשא דהכא וי"ל דאי לאו ג"ש לא הוה דרשינן הך היקשא לסתור משמעות הפסוק שכתוב בהדיא ג' אמות קומתו א"נ הך היקשא לאו אגובה דמזבח קאי אלא אגובה דקלעים כדפ"ה ובא לתרץ קושיתו של רבי יהודה שהקשה מן הפסוק דכתיב גבי קלעים וקאמר ה' אמות לפיכך בא לתרץ ולומר דמה משכן עשר אמות אף קלעים שהוא סביב המזבח עשר אמות ולפיכך לא היה נראה הכהן מבחוץ. מהר"פ: לז] לפאת קדמה מזרחה רחב חמשים אמה:

וכ"ש זה דמחוסר מעשה גדול ועוד כו' נ"ק

[מנחות נז:]

[אחד עשר תיבות הללו ליתא בילקוט]

ס"ל דשרי נ"ק

עיין נ"ק שמהפך סגי' כאן

[בכף נה ליתא אבל הוא סיומא דמימרא דרב יהודה אמר שמואל ביומא דף סג.]

נ"א ארך החצר מאה באמה וקומה חמש אמות אפשר כו' נ"ק

[שבת לב.]

ועיין רש"ק ונ"ק

אַמָּה אֶל הַכָּתֵף. אֵצֶל הַשַּׁעַר. *וְקס"ד בְּגוֹבְהָהּ קָאָמַר, וְה"ה לְכָל הֶחָצֵר. מִשְּׂפַת מִזְבֵּחַ וּלְמַעְלָה. לְמַעְלָה מִן הַמִּזְבֵּחַ הָיָה גּוֹבְהָן ה' אַמּוֹת. מִשְּׂפַת סוֹבֵב וּלְמַעְלָה. עַד מְקוֹם הַקְּרָנוֹת. וּלְמַטָּה הֵימֶנּוּ ו' אַמּוֹת, וְגוֹבַהּ הַקֶּרֶן אַמָּה. וְר' יְהוּדָה. ו] אוֹמֵר דְּבָרִים כִּכְתָבָן, כִּי גָּמֵיר ג"ש ז] דְּ"רָבוּעַ" "רָבוּעַ" – בְּרָחְבָּהּ, דְּגָמֵיר לְמֵימַר דְּמֶאֶמְצָעִיתוֹ מוֹדֵד, וּמִמִּזְבֵּחַ דִּיחֶזְקֵאל ח] וּכְדִלְעֵיל. וּלְרַבִּי יְהוּדָה. נְהִי נַמִּי דִּדְבָרִים כִּכְתָבָן – הָא קָא מִיתְחֲזֵי כֹּהֵן, דְּהָא גּוֹבְהוֹ שָׁלֹשׁ וּקְלָעִים אֵינָן אֶלָּא חָמֵשׁ, וְהוּא עַצְמוֹ ג' אַמּוֹת – נִמְצָא רֹאשׁוֹ לְמַעְלָה מִן הַקְּלָעִים! בִּשְׁלָמָא לְרַבִּי יְהוּדָה הַיְינוּ דִּכְתִיב קִידֵּשׁ. הַמֶּלֶךְ ט] אֶת [תּוֹךְ הֶחָצֵר] וגו', שֶׁהוּצְרְכָה כָּל הָרִצְפָּה לְקַדְּשָׁהּ לְשֵׁם מִזְבֵּחַ. וּקְדוּשָּׁתָהּ בְּשִׁירֵי מִנְחָה וּבְשִׁיר, כִּדְאָמְרִי' בִּשְׁבוּעוֹת (דף יד.). מַאי קִידֵּשׁ. אֶת תּוֹךְ הֶחָצֵר. וּמְשַׁנֵּי: קִדְּשׁוֹ לְשֵׁם עֲזָרָה, לְהַעֲמִיד בּוֹ מִזְבַּח אֲבָנִים. בִּשְׁלָמָא לְר' יוֹסֵי. דְּאָמַר: שֶׁל שְׁלֹמֹה גָּדוֹל וְשֶׁל מֹשֶׁה קָטָן. הַיְינוּ דִּכְתִיב קָטָן. אַמִּזְבַּח הַנְּחֹשֶׁת. וְהָכִי קָאָמַר: הֶעֱמִיד מִזְבַּח אֲבָנִים, כִּי מִזְבַּח הַנְּחֹשֶׁת קָטָן י]. אֶלָּא לְרַבִּי יְהוּדָה. דְּאָמַר: כּוּלָּהּ רִצְפָּה קִידֵּשׁ, יא] דְּמִזְבַּח שְׁלֹמֹה לֹא יָכוֹל לְהָכִיל הָעוֹלָה. מַאי קָטָן. דִּכְתִיב אַמִּזְבַּח הַנְּחֹשֶׁת? הָא דִּשְׁלֹמֹה גּוּפֵיהּ קָטָן הֲוָה! הָכִי קָאָמַר כו'. וּמִשּׁוּם דְּקָאֵי בִּמְקוֹם מִזְבַּח הַנְּחֹשֶׁת וְחִילּוּפוֹ הוּא, קָרֵי לֵיהּ "מִזְבַּח הַנְּחֹשֶׁת". וּבְדִבְרֵי הַיָּמִים (ב ד) קָרֵי לֵיהּ הָכִי בְּהֶדְיָא "וַיַּעַשׂ (הַמֶּלֶךְ) מִזְבַּח נְחֹשֶׁת כ' אַמָּה אָרְכּוֹ וְכ' אַמָּה רָחְבּוֹ", וְאַמְּקוֹם הַמַּעֲרָכָה קָאֵי. בְּמַאי קָמִיפַּלְגִי. ר' יוֹסֵי דְּגָמֵיר "רָבוּעַ" "רָבוּעַ" מִמִּזְבַּח הַזָּהָב, וְרַבִּי יְהוּדָה דְּגָמֵיר לָהּ מִשֶּׁל יְחֶזְקֵאל. כְּלִי מִכְּלִי. מִזְבַּח הַנְּחֹשֶׁת יב] וְהַזָּהָב כֵּלִים הֵם. מוֹדֶה ר' יְהוּדָה בְּדָמִים. דְּאַע"ג דְּאָמַר רַבִּי יְהוּדָה כָּל הָעֲזָרָה מְקוּדֶּשֶׁת – הָנֵי מִילֵּי לְהַקְטִיר חֲלָבִים, אֲבָל לִזְרִיקַת דָּמִים – לָא. מִדַּם הַתַּעֲרוֹבֶת. שֶׁל פְּסָחִים מֵעַל הָרִצְפָּה. בְּגִינוֹ = בִּשְׁבִילוֹ. וְכִי אֵצֶל הַמִּזְבֵּחַ אֲכָלוּהָ. וַהֲלֹא כָּל הָעֲזָרָה כְּשֵׁרָה לְכָךְ, דִּכְתִיב בְּמִנְחָה: יג] "מַצּוֹת תֵּאָכֵל בְּמָקוֹם קָדוֹשׁ" (ויקרא ו). קֹדֶשׁ קָדָשִׁים. בג"ש דְּ"קֹדֶשׁ קָדָשִׁים" יָלְפִי מֵהֲדָדֵי. מִשּׁוּם ג'

תורה אור

(שמות כז) אַמָּה אֶל הַכָּתֵף". וּמַה ת"ל: א] °"ה' אַמּוֹת" – מִשְּׂפַת (שם) מִזְבֵּחַ וּלְמַעְלָה, וּמַה ת"ל: °"וְשָׁלֹשׁ אַמּוֹת קוֹמָתוֹ" – מִשְּׂפַת סוֹבֵב וּלְמַעְלָה. וְר' יְהוּדָה, כִּי גָּמֵיר גְּזֵירָה שָׁוָה – בְּרָחְבָּהּ הוּא דְּגָמֵיר. ב] וּלְרַבִּי יְהוּדָה, הָא קָא מִיתְחֲזֵי כֹּהֵן! נְהִי דְּכֹהֵן מִיתְחֲזֵי, עֲבוֹדָה דְּבִידוֹ לָא מִיתְחֲזֵי. בִּשְׁלָמָא לְרַבִּי יְהוּדָה – הַיְינוּ (מ"א ח) דִּכְתִיב: °"קִידֵּשׁ", אֶלָּא לְרַבִּי יוֹסֵי מַאי "קִידֵּשׁ"? לְהַעֲמִיד בָּהּ מִזְבֵּחַ. בִּשְׁלָמָא לְרַבִּי יוֹסֵי – הַיְינוּ דִּכְתִיב "קָטֹן", אֶלָּא לְרַבִּי יְהוּדָה מַאי "קָטֹן"? הָכִי (מפתח נ"ק) קָאָמַר: מִזְבַּח אֲבָנִים שֶׁעָשָׂה שְׁלֹמֹה תַּחַת מִזְבַּח הַנְּחֹשֶׁת – קָטָן הֲוָה. בְּמַאי פְּלִיגִי? מָר סָבַר: דָּנִין חוּץ מֵחוּץ, וְאֵין דָּנִין חוּץ מִפְּנִים. וּמָר סָבַר: דָּנִין כְּלִי מִכְּלִי, וְאֵין דָּנִין כְּלִי מִבִּנְיָן. אָמַר רָבָא: מוֹדֶה רַבִּי יְהוּדָה בְּדָמִים. דְּתַנְיָא, *רַבִּי יְהוּדָה אוֹמֵר: כּוֹס אֶחָד הָיָה מְמַלֵּא מִדַּם הַתַּעֲרוֹבוֹת וְשׁוֹפְכוֹ עַל גַּבֵּי מִזְבֵּחַ, שֶׁאִם יִשָּׁפֵךְ דָּמוֹ שֶׁל אַחַת מֵהֶן – נִמְצָא זֶה מַכְשִׁירוֹ; וְאִי סָלְקָא דַּעְתָּךְ סָבַר רַבִּי יְהוּדָה כּוּלָּהּ עֲזָרָה מִיקַּדְשָׁא, הָא אִיתְעֲבִידָא לֵיהּ מִצְוָותֵיהּ. וְדִלְמָא מִשּׁוּם דְּקָסָבַר: שְׁפִיכָה מִכֹּחַ הָאָדָם בָּעֵינַן! אִם כֵּן, נִשְׁקְלֵיהּ וְנִשְׁפְּכֵיהּ אַדּוּכְתֵּיהּ. וְדִלְמָא מִשּׁוּם דְּבָעֵינַן מִצְוָה מִן הַמּוּבְחָר. ג] אָמַר רַבִּי אֶלְעָזָר: אמִזְבֵּחַ שֶׁנִּפְגַּם – אֵין אוֹכְלִין •בְּגִינוֹ שְׁיָרֵי (ויקרא ו) מִנְחָה, שֶׁנֶּאֱמַר: °"וְאִכְלוּהָ מַצּוֹת אֵצֶל הַמִּזְבֵּחַ", וְכִי אֵצֶל הַמִּזְבֵּחַ אֲכָלוּהָ? אֶלָּא, בִּזְמַן שֶׁהוּא שָׁלֵם וְלֹא בִּזְמַן שֶׁהוּא חָסֵר. אַשְׁכְּחַן שְׁיָרֵי מִנְחָה, בקָדְשֵׁי קָדָשִׁים מְנָלַן? ד] ת"ל: "קֹדֶשׁ קָדָשִׁים". גקָדָשִׁים קַלִּים ה] מְנַיִן? אָמַר אַבַּיֵי: אָתְיָא מִדְּרָשָׁא דְּר' יוֹסֵי. דְּתַנְיָא, *ר' יוֹסֵי אוֹמֵר: ג' דְּבָרִים מִשּׁוּם ג'

עשרים אמה! יד] ובשמעתא קמייתא דעירובין (דף ג:) קשה טפי, דפריך: בין לרבנן בין לר' יהודה לילפו מפתח שער החצר. ופי' שם בקונטרס שני לשונות. ופי' בלשון שני, דפריך טו] שיחשב פתח ברחב עשרים, ומשני: "פתח שער החצר" איקרי, פתח סתמא לא איקרי. ואיבעית אימא: כי כתיב "חמש עשרה" – (א) בגובהה כתיב. והכתיב "וקומה ה' אמות"! ההוא משפת מזבח ולמעלה. ופי' שם בקונטרס דהיינו כר' יוסי דשמעתין. וזו היא תימה, דלא מצינן למימר חמש עשרה אמה בגובה כתיב, אלא ברחבה, כדפרישית. ועוד קשה: דאי מרחבה פריך התם, הוה ליה למימר הכי: אלא הא דתנן הרחב מעשר אמות ימעט – נילף מפתח שער החצר, כיון דעד השתא איירי בגובהה! ועוד: לר' יהודה אמאי הוצרך להקשות מפתח החצר? *פתח אולם דקאי ביה הוה ליה לאקשויי! ועוד: מאי קושיא מפתח טז] החצר? התנן: יש לו צורת הפתח – א"צ למעט. וחצר צורת הפתח הוה ליה, שהיו העמודים משני צדדים וכלונסות על גביהן שהקלעים תלויין בהן![א] ומיהו, בסמוך יז] (ב) (קשה) כי פריך: ור' יהודה מפתחו של אולם גמר? והתנן וכו' – לא משני: שאני פתחו של אולם דה"ל צורת הפתח. יח] [ובע"כ צ"ל] דכיון דאליבא דרב קיימא – לא משני הכי, דאיהו תני במתני' "צריך למעט", כדאמר התם. *ומהאי טעמא יט] פריך [שפיר] השתא. ועוד: (ג) דשער חצר לא ה"ל צורת הפתח, שהכלונסות היו על הווין שקבועין בעמודין מבחוץ, ואמרינן התם בפ"ק (דף יא.): צורת הפתח שעשאה מן הצד – לא עשה כלום. ומפרש כ] רבינו: דמגובהה פריך התם, דלא יחשב פתח ביתר מה' אמות. כא] ומסתברא היא לן טפי למילף מפתח החצר ממאי דנילף מפתח ההיכל. דפתח כב] המשכן על כרחין שלא כדין איקרי "פתח כג] אהל מועד", וחידוש הוא, דלא הוו ליה גיפופי, שהיה פרוץ לפניו במלואו. הלכך, פתח ההיכל שהיה במקומו – דלמא שלא כדין נמי איקרי פתח. ובתר הכי גרס: איבעית אימא קלעים ט"ו אמה, כד] וכי כתיב "וקומה ברוחב ה' אמות" – משפת קלעים ולמעלה. והביא שינויא כרבי יוסי דהכא, ול"ג "ט"ו אמה בגובהה הוא דכתיב", וגם לא גרס "אל הכתף", דלא קאי אחמש עשרה דכתיב בקרא, דההוא לא מיתוקמא אלא ברחבה. אלא פירוש הוא, כלומר: הקלעים היו גבוהין חמש עשרה שלא יראו עבודה שבידו, כרבי יוסי דאמר מזבח י' אמות. והאי דכתיב בקלעים: "וקומה ה' אמות" – ודאי משפת מזבח ולמעלה. והאי קרא דמייתי: "וקומה ברוחב ה' אמות" (היינו) להוכיח גובה פתח כ' אמה – כה] היינו ההוא דכתיב גבי מסך בסוף "ויקהל", ומפרש דמשפת קלעים ולמעלה קאמר, שהקלעים היו גבוהין סביב החצר לצפון ודרום ומערב וכן לצד המזרח. כו] [שכמו] שהקלעים היו ט"ו רוחב מימין הפתח וכן משמאל הפתח – כמו כן היו גבוהין ט"ו אמה. ועל מסך הפתח כתיב: "רוחב כ' אמה וקומה ה' אמות ברוחב לעומת קלעי החצר", פירוש: שהמסך כל רוחב כ' היה גבוה ה' אמות מאחר קלעי החצר, אשתכח המסך גבוה כ', וזו היא כז] אמת גובהו של פתח. והביא שינויא בתרא ליתיה אלא לרבנן, דהא לרבי יהודה לא מתוקם כלל. ואע"ג דקאי התם לשנויי לרבנן ולרבי יהודה, שינויא קמא יתיישב לרבי יהודה, דשנינן: "פתח" סתמא לא איקרי. דהכי נמי לא מיתוקם ההוא שינויא כרבי יוסי דהכא, אלא כרבי יהודה דפליג עליה. והכא בשמעתין גרסי': מה משכן י' אמות אף מזבח י' אמות, קלעים ט"ו. ולא גרסינן כח] נמי "אל הכתף", דלאו קרא מייתי. ובברייתא דמלאכת המשכן לא גרסינן כלל "קלעים ט"ו" במילתא דר' יוסי. ופירושא בעלמא הוא, כלומר: הקלעים היו גבוהין ט"ו אמה שלא יראה כהן ועבודה בידו. ומה ת"ל "ה' אמות משפת מזבח" כו'. ור"ת מפרש בספר הישר דלשמואל עצמו פריך: נילף מפתח שער החצר, כט] מנא ליה ד"ושחטו פתח אהל מועד" אפתח היכל קאי? ואי אפשר לומר כן כלל, כדמוכחי כמה קראי בפרשת "אלה פקודי" ובשאר מקומות. וקצת קשה לפירוש ל] ר"ת: דפריך מגובה חמש, דמאי משני: "פתח שער" איקרי, פתח סתמא לא איקרי? כיון דנקרא שער – כ"ש דאיקרי פתח, דפתח קטן משער. עוד נילף מפתח עזרה שנקרא "פתח" (יחזקאל מא) והיה גובהו עשרים*. **הכי** קאמר מזבח אבנים שעשה שלמה תחת מזבח הנחשת. תימה: דבפ' "במה בהמה" (שבת דף נה.) אמרינן: "ויעמוד אצל מזבח הנחשת", מזבח הנחשת מי הוה? אמר להן הקב"ה: התחילו ממקום שאומרים שירה לפני בכלי נחשת. ואמאי לא אמר כי הכא? וי"ל: דהתם מה לו להזכיר מזבח הנחשת כלל. **מודה** רבי יהודה בדמים. תימה: מאי קס"ד מעיקרא? והא קרן לא] ורבוע יסוד* מעכבין!* **קדשים** קלים מנין. תימה: דלא יליף מהיקשא מ"זאת התורה". **אתיא** מדרשא דרבי יוסי. תימה: ל"ל ג"ש ד"קדש קדשים"? לב] ועוד,*) לג] [קדשים קלים] גופה נילף ממעשר! וכי תימא: מה למעשר שכן טעון וידוי וכסף וצורה – בכור יוכיח, ועוד: דבהאי קרא דמייתי דמקיש מעשר לבכור, נמי כתיב חטאת ואשם. דתניא בספרי פרשת "ראה אנכי": "בקרכם וצאנכם" – אלו חטאות ואשמות. וכן בקרא ד"לא תוכל לאכול בשעריך" דריש פרק בתרא דמכות (דף יז.): "בקרך וצאנך" – לד] אלו חטאות ואשמות.

מאי

*) נ"א ועוד והיא גופה וקאי אשירי מנחה וגי' הצ"ק וכ"כ בעל פנים מאירות דה"ג [תימה] דקדשי קדשים גופיה נילף ממעשר וכו' והשאר נמחק]

עין משפט נר מצוה: י א ב ג מיי' פ"ג מהל' פסה"מ הל' כב כג:

מסורת הש"ס: וקסבר נ"ק | נ"ק | פסחים סה. [לעיל לה: ע"ש מנחות נט: ע"ש תוספתא פסחים פ"ד] | [תוס' סנהדרין פ"ג מכות יט. תמורה כח.] | [וע"ע תוספות עירובין ב: ד"ה בין ור"ה ולאו"א] | נ"ל יסוד כתיב שמעכבין רש"ק | *ועי' תוס' לעיל נה: סד"ה תן לה:

הגהות הב"ח

(א) תוס' ד"ה ואומר וכו' חמש עשרה אמה בגובהה וכו': (ב) בא"ד ומיהו בסמוך נמי קשה כי פריך וכו' והתנן וכו' לא משני וכו' צורת הפתח אלא נ"ל דכיון: (ג) בא"ד ועוד י"ל דשער החצר:

גליון הש"ס

גמ' אין אוכלין בגינו שירי מנחה. ולאחר שחרב ונבנה עי' תוס' בכ"מ דף נג ע"ב ד"ה לא פליג:

שיטה מקובצת

א] [וקומה] חמש אמות (מקומתו) משפת: ב] דגמיר לה ולר"י: ג] המובחר. ה"ה דהמ"ל משום דבעינן יסוד: ד] מנלן אתיא קדש קדש. תיבות ת"ל נמחק: ה] קלים מנלן אמר תיבת מנין נמחק: ו] יהודה. דאמר דברים: ז] ג"ש דרבוע רבוע ברחבה הוא דגמר: ח] דיחזקאל גמיר לה וכדלעיל: ט] תיבות את תוך החצר ל"ש: י] קטן נגם היה הס"ד: יא] קידש דאף מזבח של שלמה: יב] הנחשת ומזבח הזהב כלים הם: יג] במנחה בחצר אהל מועד יאכלוה הס"ד ומה"ד קדש קדש. בג"ש דקדש קדש ילפי מהדדי הס"ד ותיבות מצות תאכל משום נמחק: יד] אמה ועוד דהו"ל לר"י למימר ההוא ברחבה הוא דכתיב. ר"פ: טו] דפריך ארחבה שיחשב: טז] מפתח שער החצר: יז] בסמוך קשה כי פריך כו' והתנן כו' ואמאי לא משני: יח] הפתח וי"ל דכיון: יט] טעמא נמי פריך: כ] ומפרש רבינו (תם) [אא"ה נ"ל שצ"ל רבינו חננאל א) ועי' לקמן בסוף הדבור עכ"ה] דאגובהה אות מ נמחק: כא] אמות דמסתברא: כב] דפתח אהל מועד על כרחין: כג] פתח וחידוש כו' תיבות אהל מועד נמחק: כד] אמה גובהה וכי: כה] אמה והיינו ההוא: כו] המזרח מימין. תיבות [שכמו] שהקלעים היו ט"ו רוחב נמחק: כז] היא מדת גובהו תיבת אמת נמחק: כח] ולא גרסינן ואומר ול"ג נמי: כט] החצר ומנא ליה: ל] לפירוש רבינו דפריך. תיבת ר"ת נרשם עליו קו (ועיין למעלה באות כ') ועי' בספר הישר סי' רפו: לא] קרן וכבש ורבוע יסוד שמעכבין הס"ד: לב] קדשים. ס"א הא כתיב בהאי קרא דמייתי והבאתם שמה וגו' ועוד: לג] קדשי קדשים גופיה תיבת קלים נמחק: לד] וצאנך. ולמאי דפי' ריב"א לעיל (דף נו ע"א) דאכילה לא קיימי אחטאות ואשמות דכתיב אתם ובתיכם ניחא. מהר"פ:

א) וכ"ה באמת כפי' הר"ח למסכת עירובין (דף ב ע"ב) שנדפס לפנינו בש"ס הזה שם:

הגהות צ"ק

[א] ומיהו הא לא קשיא דכיון דאליבא דרב קיימא דאיהו תני במתני' צריך למעט בסמוך ומהאי טעמא כי פריך בסמוך ור"י מפתחו של אולם גמר והתנן כו' ולא משני שאני פתחו של אולם דה"ל צורת הפתח כדאמר התם ומהאי טעמא (דאין) [דיש] לו צורת הפתח כיון דאליבא דרב קיימא לא משני הכי ועוד דשער כו' כצ"ל:]

יא א מיי' פ"ז מהלכות בית הבחירה הל' טו ופסק להלכון שם ע"ש:

ג' זְקֵנִים, א] וְזֶה אֶחָד מֵהֶן. *רַבִּי יִשְׁמָעֵאל אוֹמֵר: אֵיכוֹל יַעֲלֶה אָדָם מַעֲשֵׂר שֵׁנִי לִירוּשָׁלַיִם וְיֹאכְלֶנּוּ בַּזְּמַן הַזֶּה? וְדִין הוּא: בְּכוֹר טָעוּן הֲבָאַת מָקוֹם וּמַעֲשֵׂר טָעוּן הֲבָאַת מָקוֹם, מַה בְּכוֹר אֵינוֹ אֶלָּא בִּפְנֵי הַבַּיִת — אַף מַעֲשֵׂר אֵינוֹ אֶלָּא בִּפְנֵי הַבַּיִת. מַה לִּבְכוֹר שֶׁכֵּן טָעוּן מַתַּן דָּמִים וְאֵימוּרִים לְגַבֵּי מִזְבֵּחַ! בִּיכּוּרִים יוֹכִיחוּ. מַה לְבִיכּוּרִים שֶׁכֵּן טְעוּנִין הֲנָחָה! ת"ל: *°"וַהֲבֵאתֶם שָׁמָּה עוֹלוֹתֵיכֶם" וגו', מַקִּישׁ מַעֲשֵׂר לִבְכוֹר, מַה בְּכוֹר אֵינוֹ אֶלָּא בִּפְנֵי הַבַּיִת — אַף מַעֲשֵׂר אֵינוֹ אֶלָּא בִּפְנֵי הַבַּיִת. וְנִיהֲדַר דִּינָא, וְנֵיתֵי בְּ"מָה הַצַּד"! מִשּׁוּם דְּאִיכָּא לְמִיפְרַךְ: מָה לְהַצַּד הַשָּׁוֶה שֶׁבָּהֶן — שֶׁכֵּן יֵשׁ בָּהֶן צַד מִזְבֵּחַ. ב] מַאי קָסָבַר? אִי קָסָבַר *קְדוּשָּׁה רִאשׁוֹנָה קִידְּשָׁה לִשְׁעָתָהּ וְקִידְּשָׁה לֶעָתִיד לָבֹא — אֲפִילּוּ בְּכוֹר נַמִי, ג] וְאִי קָסָבַר: לֹא קִידְּשָׁה לֶעָתִיד לָבֹא — ד] אֲפִילּוּ בְּכוֹר נַמִי תִּיבָּעֵי! אָמַר רָבִינָא: לְעוֹלָם קָסָבַר לֹא קִידְּשָׁה. וְהָכָא בְּמַאי עָסְקִינַן — בִּבְכוֹר שֶׁנִּזְרַק דָּמוֹ קוֹדֶם חוּרְבַּן הַבַּיִת, וְחָרַב הַבַּיִת, וַעֲדַיִין בְּשָׂרוֹ קַיָּים; וְאִיתַּקַּשׁ בְּשָׂרוֹ לְדָמוֹ, מַה דָּמוֹ בְּמִזְבֵּחַ אַף בְּשָׂרוֹ בְּמִזְבֵּחַ; וְאָתֵי מַעֲשֵׂר וְיָלֵיף מִבְּכוֹר. *וְכִי דָּבָר הַלָּמֵד בְּהֶיקֵּשׁ חוֹזֵר וּמְלַמֵּד בְּהֶיקֵּשׁ? מַעֲשֵׂר דָּגָן חוּלִּין הוּא. הָנִיחָא לְמ"ד *בָּתַר לָמֵד אָזְלִינַן, אֶלָּא לְמ"ד בָּתַר מְלַמֵּד אָזְלִינַן, מַאי אִיכָּא לְמֵימַר? דָּם וּבָשָׂר חֲדָא מִילְּתָא הִיא. כִּי סְלֵיק רָבִין אַמְרַהּ לִשְׁמַעְתָּא קַמֵּיהּ דְּרַבִּי יִרְמְיָה. אֲמַר: *בַּבְלָאֵי טַפְשָׁאֵי, אַמְּטוֹל דְּיָתְבִי בְּאַרְעָא חֲשׁוֹכָא אָמְרִי שְׁמַעְתָּא דְּמַחְשְׁכָא! לָא שְׁמִיעַ לְהוּ הָא *דְּתַנְיָא: בִּשְׁעַת סִילּוּק מַסָּעוֹת קָדָשִׁים נִפְסָלִין, וְזָבִים וּמְצוֹרָעִים מִשְׁתַּלְּחִים חוּץ לַמְּחִיצָה; וְתַנְיָא אִידָךְ: בִּשְׁנֵי מְקוֹמוֹת קָדָשִׁים נֶאֱכָלִים; ה] מַאי לָאו — ו] הָא בְּקׇדְשֵׁי קָדָשִׁים, הָא — בְּקָדָשִׁים קַלִּים? אָמַר רָבִינָא: ז] אִידִי וְאִידִי בְּקָדָשִׁים קַלִּים, וְלָא קַשְׁיָא:

הא

רש"י

ג' זְקֵנִים. דָּבָר אֶחָד מִפִּי כָּל זָקֵן וְזָקֵן. ר' יִשְׁמָעֵאל אוֹמֵר כו'. זוֹ הִיא אַחַת מֵהֶן. יָכוֹל יַעֲלֶה אָדָם מַעֲשֵׂר שֵׁנִי. דְּקָסָבַר: קְדוּשַּׁת הָאָרֶץ לֹא בָּטְלָה, וּצְרִיכָה הַפְרָשַׁת מַעַשְׂרוֹת מִן הַתּוֹרָה. ח] וְקָאָמַר: יָכוֹל יֹאכְלֶנּוּ עַכְשָׁיו בִּירוּשָׁלַיִם בְּלֹא פִּדְיוֹן? ת"ל וכו'. וּלְקַמֵּיהּ פָּרֵיךְ: מַאי שְׁנָא בְּכוֹר דִּפְשִׁיטָא לֵיהּ, וּמַאי שְׁנָא מַעֲשֵׂר דְּמִיבָּעְיָא לֵיהּ? שֶׁכֵּן טָעוּן מַתַּן דָּמִים. הִלְכָּךְ צָרִיךְ בַּיִת וּמִזְבֵּחַ. בִּכּוּרִים יוֹכִיחוּ. שֶׁאֵין טְעוּנִין מַתַּן דָּמִים, וּצְרִיכִין בַּיִת, כִּדְכְתִיב: ט] "לִפְנֵי מִזְבַּח" (דברים כו). שֶׁכֵּן טָעוּן הֲנָחָה. הִלְכָּךְ בָּעוּ בַּיִת, דְּהוּזְקְקוּ לַמִּזְבֵּחַ לְכָךְ. ת"ל כו'. וּלְקַמֵּיהּ פָּרֵיךְ: וְלִיהֲדַר דִּינָא, וְלֵיתֵי בְּמָה הַצַּד! צַד מִזְבֵּחַ. זֶה לְמַתַּן דָּמִים וְאֵלּוּ לַהֲנָחָה. מַאי קָסָבַר. הַאי תַּנָּא דְּפָשֵׁיט לֵיהּ בְּכוֹר י] מִמַּעֲשֵׂר. אִי קָסָבַר קְדוּשָּׁה רִאשׁוֹנָה שֶׁל בַּיִת קִידְּשָׁה לִשְׁעָתָהּ וְקִדְּשָׁה לֶעָתִיד לָבֹא. כִּי הֵיכִי דְּס"ל בִּקְדוּשַּׁת הָאָרֶץ. וְקָמִיבָּעֵי לֵיהּ: מִי קָרֵינָא בֵּיהּ "לִפְנֵי אֱלֹהֶיךָ" אוֹ לָא, וְקָפָּשֵׁיט מַעֲשֵׂר מִבְּכוֹר. אֲפִילּוּ בְּכוֹר נַמִי. אֲפִילּוּ בְּכוֹר יַקְרִיב וְיֹאכַל, דְּהָא מַאן דְּאִית לֵיהּ קִדְּשָׁה לֶעָתִיד לָבֹא — אִית לֵיהּ שֶׁמַּקְרִיבִין אע"פ שֶׁאֵין בַּיִת, כִּדְאָמְרִינַן בִּמְגִילָּה יא] (דף י.). ה"ג: וְאִי קָסָבַר לֹא קִדְּשָׁה אֲפִי' בְּכוֹר נַמִי תִּיבָּעֵי. וְאִי קָסָבַר קְדוּשַּׁת בַּיִת בָּטְלָה יב] לָהּ, וּמִיבָּעֵי *לָהּ בְּמַעֲשֵׂר הוֹאִיל וְאֵינוֹ צָרִיךְ לְבַיִת, מִי מִיתְאֲכִיל בִּירוּשָׁלַיִם וְ"לִפְנֵי ה'" קָרֵינָא בֵּיהּ אוֹ לָא. וַאֲפִילּוּ בְּכוֹר בה"ג נַמִי תִּיבָּעֵי לֵיהּ. כְּגוֹן יג] *שֶׁקָּרְבוּ דָּמָיו וְאֵימוּרָיו, וְחָרַב הַבַּיִת וּבְשָׂרוֹ קַיָּים, מַהוּ שֶׁיֹּאכְלוּהוּ? אָמַר רָבִינָא לְעוֹלָם קָסָבַר לֹא קִדְּשָׁה. וְהָכָא דְּקָפָּשֵׁיט לֵיהּ מַעֲשֵׂר מִבְּכוֹר — בִּבְכוֹר שֶׁאֵינוֹ צָרִיךְ לְבַיִת, דּוּמְיָא דְּמַעֲשֵׂר יד] קָפָּשֵׁיט לֵיהּ דִּפְשִׁיטָא לֵיהּ גַּבֵּיהּ דְּלָא *מִיתְכִיל. דְּאִיתַּקַּשׁ בְּשָׂרוֹ לְדָמוֹ. טו] "וְאֶת דָּמָם תִּזְרֹק וְאֶת חֶלְבָּם תַּקְטִיר וּבְשָׂרָם יִהְיֶה לָּךְ" (במדבר יח), וְיָלֵיף מִינֵּיהּ: בְּשָׁעָה שֶׁאַתָּה רָאוּי לִזְרוֹק אֶת הַדָּם אַתָּה אוֹכֵל אֶת הַבָּשָׂר, וְלֹא אַחַר שֶׁנֶּהֱרַס הַמִּזְבֵּחַ. וְכִי. בָּשָׂר הַלָּמֵד בְּהֶיקֵּשׁ מִן הַדָּם, חוֹזֵר וּמְלַמֵּד בְּהֶיקֵּשׁ עַל הַמַּעֲשֵׂר? טז]. לִשְׁמַעְתָּא. הָא דְּאַבַּיֵי, דְּאָמַר: קָדָשִׁים קַלִּים נִפְסָלִין בִּפְגִימַת הַמִּזְבֵּחַ, וּמַיְיתֵי לָהּ מִדְּרָשָׁא דְּרַבִּי יוֹסֵי. בִּשְׁעַת סִילּוּק הַמַּסָּעוֹת. כְּשֶׁמּוֹרִידִין אֶת הַמִּשְׁכָּן וּמְסַלְּקִין אֶת הַמִּזְבְּחוֹת, בְּעֵת הַמַּסָּעוֹת בַּמִּדְבָּר. קָדָשִׁים נִפְסָלִים. בְּשַׂר קׇדְשֵׁי קָדָשִׁים. °וְקָא סָלְקָא יז] דַּעְתָּךְ: מִפְּנֵי סִילּוּק הַמִּזְבֵּחַ הוּא, מִדְּקָתָנֵי: וְזָבִין וּמְצוֹרָעִין מִשְׁתַּלְּחִין, שֶׁאֵין מְצוֹרָע נִכְנָס לְדִגְלֵי הַשְּׁבָטִים, וְלֹא זָב לְמַחֲנֵה לְוִיִּם נוֹשְׂאֵי הָאָרוֹן, כִּדְאָמְרִינַן לְקַמָּן (דף סא:): אע"פ שֶׁנָּסַע אֹהֶל מוֹעֵד הוּא, אַלְמָא נִפְסָלִין דְּקָאָמַר — לָאו מִשּׁוּם דְּמִיפַּסְלֵי בְּיוֹצֵא הוּא, דְּהָא אֹהֶל מוֹעֵד חָשֵׁיב לֵיהּ. יח] וְתַנְיָא אִידָךְ גָּרֵיס. בִּשְׁנֵי מְקוֹמוֹת יט] נֶאֱכָלִין. אַחַד בִּמְקוֹמָן בַּמַּחֲנוֹת הָאֲמוּרוֹת בָּהֶן — כְּשֶׁהַמִּשְׁכָּן בִּמְקוֹמוֹ, וְאַחַד בְּכׇל מָקוֹם שֶׁיְּהֵא שָׁם דֶּרֶךְ הֲלִיכָתָן — מִשֶּׁנָּסְעוּ. וְקַשְׁיָין אַהֲדָדֵי. מַאי לָאו. קַמַּיְיתָא בְּקׇדְשֵׁי קָדָשִׁים, וְהָא בְּקָדָשִׁים קַלִּים? הָכִי גָּרְסִינַן: מַאי לָאו הָא בְּקׇדְשֵׁי קָדָשִׁים הָא בְּקָדָשִׁים קַלִּים. אִידִי וְאִידִי קָדָשִׁים קַלִּים וְלָא קַשְׁיָא. קַמַּיְיתָא

רַבִּי

תוספות

מאי קסבר האי תנא. דפשיטא ליה בכור טפי ממעשר? אי קסבר קדשה לעתיד לבא בקדושת הארץ, וקמבעיא ליה אי קרינא ביה "לפני ה'" אי לא — אפי' בכור נמי יקרב ויאכל, דמאן דאית ליה קדשה קסבר דמקריבין אע"פ שאין בית, כדאיתא פ"ק דמגילה (דף י.). ואי קסבר לא קדשה, דבטלה קדושת כ] *הארץ, ומבעיא ליה במעשר משום דאינו צריך לבית כא] ומיתאכיל בירושלים אי קרינא ביה "לפני ה'" אי לא — אפי' בכור נמי תיבעי היכא דהוי כעין מעשר, כגון בכי ה"ג שאינו צריך לבית, שקרבו דמיו ואימוריו וחרב הבית ובשרו קיים, מהו שיאכלוהו! ומסיק דקסבר לא קידשה, והא דפשיטא ליה בבכור — משום דאיתקש בשרו לדמו, ולא אכיל בשר אלא בשעה הראויה לזריקת דם, ולא משנהרס. זו היא גירסת הקונטרס ופירושו. ואם תאמר: אי קסבר לא קדשה, היכי משכחת מעשר שני דאורייתא, כיון דבטלה קדושת הארץ? כב] וי"ל: דאי קסבר לא קידשה — מוקמינן ליה למעשר שגדל בפני הבית, כמו שפירש בקונטרס כג] [גבי] בכור שקרבו דמו ואימוריו וחרב הבית ובשרו קיים. א"נ, אפי' קסבר לא קדשה — הני מילי קדושת הבית, אבל קדושת הארץ לא בטלה, ונתחייבו בתרומות ומעשרות, כדאשכחנא (לקמן דף קיב:) כשחרב שילה, שבטלה קדושת הבית ולא בטלה קדושת הארץ. וא"ת: כיון דלא קידשה והותרו הבמות — כד] יהא נאכל בכל ערי ישראל, ולספרים דגרסי' לקמן בפ' בתרא (דף קיב:): באו לנוב וגבעון — הותרו הבמות, מעשר נאכל בכל ערי ישראל! וי"ל: דלפי אותה גירסא לא מתוקם הכא אלא במעשר שגדל לפני הבית, והוזקק להבאת מקום, כה] ואינו נאכל בכל ערי ישראל. וקשה לפירוש הקונטרס: מאי דוחקיה דרבינא לומר לא קדשה, ופליג אכוליה התלמוד דקים לן ירושלים אין אחריה היתר, כדתנן בפרק בתרא (גם זה שם)? לימא דלעולם קסבר קדשה, כו] ובכור שנזרק דמו ונפגם המזבח — דאין בשרו נאכל בפגימת המזבח! ומיהו, מצי למימר דלישנא דברייתא קשיתיה, דקתני: מה בכור אינו אלא בפני הבית, דמשמע בית ממש צריך, ואי קדשה — למה לי בית? הלא מקריבין אע"פ שאין בית, ואין צריך רק מזבח, משום דאיתקש בשרו לדמו. אבל ה"ה דלעולם מצי סבר קדשה, דכיון דנזרק דמו ואח"כ חרב — אין אוכלין בשרו, משום דאיתקש לדמו. *מיהו, האי בפני הבית — היינו בפני מזבח, ולאו בית ממש קאמר. אבל קשה: מאי קאמר "אפילו בכור נמי תיבעי"? ולא *)תבעי מעשר? אדרבה, כיון דלא קדשה, פשיטא כז] לא קרינא ביה "לפני ה'", דמחילה לאכול דאורייתא! ועוד: דבכור פשיטא דמפסיל ביוצא כשחרב הבית ונפלו מחילות, כיון דלא קדשה, ומה צריך כלל כח] היקישא דבשר ודם? וכי תימא: כשחרב הבית ונהרס המזבח, אבל חומות ירושלים כט] קיימת, ולא בטלה קדושתה לענין קדשים קלים ומעשר שני — זהו תימה לומר, דהא ירושלים לא נתקדשה אלא בשביל הבית, ואיך יתכן שקדושת הבית תבטל וקדושת ירושלים קיימא? לכך נראה כמו גירסת הספרים: אי קסבר קדשה — אפילו בכור נמי, ואי קסבר לא קדשה — אפילו מעשר נמי. אמר רבינא: לעולם קסבר קדשה וכו'. והכי פריך: אפילו בכור נמי משכחת לה בלא חומות ירושלים ובלא חומות עזרה, כמו שפירש בקונטרס דמקריבים אע"פ שאין בית, כלומר, יבנה המזבח ויזרוק הדם ויאכל הבשר. אבל בלא מזבח — פשיטא ליה דאינו יכול להקריב, כדאמרי' לעיל (דף נט.): מודה רב בדמים, אע"פ שהבית קיים, וכל שכן בזמן הזה. ואי קסבר לא קדשה קדושה הבית לבנות המזבח, וכל שכן קדושת ירושלים, אבל קדושת הארץ קיימת להתחייב בתרומה ומעשר כמו בנוב וגבעון — אפילו מעשר יהא ל] פסול, פשיטא דאין לו היתר בירושלים! ולא גרסינן לקמן פ' בתרא (דף קיב:): מעשר שני נאכל בכל ערי ישראל. ואי גרסינן ליה, צריך לומר דהכי פריך: אפילו מעשר**) שני יהא פשיטא דאין חייב להעלותו, ואמאי קאמרת "יכול יעלה אדם",

דמשמע

*) נ"ל מיבעיא נ"ק **) מעשר יהא כו'

הָא רַבִּי יִשְׁמָעֵאל, הָא רַבָּנַן. וְאִיבָּעֵית אֵימָא: הָא וְהָא בְּקָדְשֵׁי קָדָשִׁים, וּמַאי "בִּשְׁנֵי מְקוֹמוֹת" – קוֹדֶם שֶׁיַּעֲמִידוּ לְוִיִּם אֶת הַמִּשְׁכָּן, וּלְאַחַר

ר' יִשְׁמָעֵאל. דְּיָלֵיף בָּשָׂר מִדָּם, א] בַּתְרַיְיתָא – רַבָּנַן. וְאִיבָּעֵית אֵימָא. בַּתְרַיְיתָא נַמִי בְּקָדְשֵׁי קָדָשִׁים. וּשְׁנֵי מְקוֹמוֹת. לָאו לְאַחַר שֶׁנָּסְעוּ, דְּנִסְתַּלֵּק הַמִּזְבֵּחַ קָאָמַר. אֶלָּא חַד מִינַּיְיהוּ כִּדְאִיתָא בְּעוֹד ב] הַמִּשְׁכָּן נָטוּי כְּמִשְׁפָּטוֹ, וְחַד לְאַחַר שֶׁפֵּירְקוּ קְרָשִׁים וְקַלְעֵי הֶחָצֵר, וַעֲדַיִין הַמִּזְבֵּחַ בִּמְקוֹמוֹ. וְקוֹדֶם שֶׁיַּעֲמִידוּ לְוִיִּם אֶת ג] מִשְׁכָּן דְּנָקַט הָכָא – לָאו דַּוְקָא נָקַט, חֲדָא – דְּלָא *מַשְׁכַּחַתְּ לָהּ, שֶׁהֲרֵי קוֹדֶם שֶׁיִּסְּעוּ בְּנֵי קְהָת נוֹשְׂאֵי הַמִּזְבְּחוֹת הָיוּ חוֹנִין בְּנֵי גֵרְשׁוֹן וּמְרָרִי נוֹשְׂאֵי הַמִּשְׁכָּן וּמְקִימִין אוֹתוֹ, וּבִנְסִיעָתָם הָיוּ מוֹרִידִין אֶת הַמִּשְׁכָּן תְּחִילָּה. *וְנוֹשְׂאִין בְּנֵי גֵרְשׁוֹן וּמְרָרִי אַחַר *דֶּגֶל ד] אֶחָד וּבְנֵי קְהָת אַחֲרֵי שְׁנֵי דְגָלִים, כְּדֵי שֶׁיְּהוּ קוֹדְמִין בְּנֵי גֵרְשׁוֹן בַּחֲנִיָּיתָן, וּמַעֲמִידִין אֶת הַמִּשְׁכָּן לִפְנֵי בּוֹא בְּנֵי קְהָת. כְּדִכְתִיב אַחַר מַסַּע דֶּגֶל בְּנֵי יְהוּדָה: "וְהוּרַד הַמִּשְׁכָּן" וגו' (במדבר י), וְאַחַר שְׁנֵי דְגָלִים כְּתִיב (שם): "וְנָסְעוּ הַקְּהָתִים נוֹשְׂאֵי הַמִּקְדָּשׁ" – דְּהַיְינוּ אָרוֹן וּמִזְבְּחוֹת וּכְלֵי הַשָּׁרֵת, וְהֵקִימוּ בְּנֵי גֵרְשׁוֹן אֶת הַמִּשְׁכָּן עַד בּוֹאָם שֶׁל בְּנֵי קְהָת. ה] וְעוֹד, אִי בְּשֶׁשִּׁינּוּ אֶת הַסֵּדֶר מוֹקְמַתְּ לָהּ – הֵיכִי שָׁחֲטֵי קָרְבָּנוֹת קוֹדֶם שֶׁיַּעֲמִידוּ מִשְׁכָּן? הָא אָמַר בְּ"אֵיזֶהוּ מְקוֹמָן" (לעיל דף נה:) ו] בִּשְׁלָמִים שֶׁשְּׁחָטָן קוֹדֶם שֶׁיַּעֲמִידוּ לְוִיִּם כו' – פְּסוּלִין! וְאִי ז] גָּרְסַתְּ לָהּ – מוֹקֵי לָהּ בְּשֶׁשִּׁינּוּ אֶת הַסֵּדֶר, וְהַהוּא דְ"אֵיזֶהוּ מְקוֹמָן" – שְׁלָמִים דַּוְקָא קָאָמַר, מִשּׁוּם דִּכְתִיב בְּהוּ (ויקרא ג): "וּשְׁחָטוֹ פֶּתַח אֹהֶל מוֹעֵד", וְלָא יָלֵיף שְׁאָר קָדָשִׁים מִינַּיְיהוּ.

מַהוּ

דמשמע דמספקא ליה אי חייב להעלותו לירושלים או לא? כיון דלא קידשה – יהא נאכל בכל ערי ישראל, כדתנן לקמן (שם), ואמאי לריך לאקושי לבכור דמה בכור אינו מעלהו אף מעשר אינו מעלהו! אמר רבינא: לעולם קסבר קדשה. ולא איירי כלל בחובת העלאה, אלא אם יכול לאוכלו בזמן הזה או לא. וילפינן אכילת מעשר מאכילת בכור, דמה אכילת בכור בעיא מזבח משום דאיתקש בשרו לדמו – אף אכילת מעשר בעיא מזבח, ואין שום מעשר נאכל בזמן הזה. ואית ספרים דגרסי: אי לא קדשה – אפילו מעשר נמי לא. וה"פ: אפילו מעשר נמי לא יהא נאכל. כלומר, דמדקבעית במעשר בזמן הזה – *א"כ במעשר שהוזקק להבאת מקום ח] קבעי', אבל לאחר חורבן – ההוא שמא לא נתחייב כלל במעשר, כיון דלא קדשה. ואפילו נתחייב במעשר כמו בנוב וגבעון – מ"מ פשיטא דנאכל בכל ערי ישראל לפי הגירסא דלקמן, כדפרישית. אלא כי קבעי באותו שגדל בפני הבית וחרב הבית – ט] והוא פשיטא דאינו נאכל! אמר רבינא: לעולם קסבר קדשה, ובבכור שנזרק דמו קודם חורבן הבית עסקינן, וחרב הבית ועדיין בשרו קיים, ואיתקש בשרו לדמו. וא"ת: והא כתיב (במדבר יח): "ואת דמם תזרוק ואת חלבם תקטיר", אלמא איתקש י] בההוא קרא להקטרת חלב, ואמרי' לעיל:* דמזבח שנעקר – מקטירין קטורת במקומו, וה"ה אימורין!

וי"ל: דקולא וחומרא – לחומרא מקשינן, ומקשינן בשרו יא] לדמו. והשתא מהך דרשא יליף לכל הקדשים, דאם נפגם המזבח – אין נאכלין. וא"ת: לפי גירסא זו דגרס "קדשה" – קשיא דר' ישמעאל אדר' ישמעאל, דלקמן פ' בתרא (דף קיט.) תניא, רבי ישמעאל אומר: זה וזה, מנוחה ונחלה, שילה ופי' בקונטרס: דבקדושת ירושלים גופה ס"ל דלא קדשה, ויש אחריה *היתר, מדלא קרי ליה נחלה, כדאיתא בפ"ק דמגילה (דף י.): שמעתי שמקריבין בבית חוניו בזמן הזה, ואוקמינן כרבי ישמעאל מיהו בזה לא דק בפירושו, דההיא דמגילה (גו"ש) רבי ישמעאל ברבי יוסי, והיא דלקמן רבי ישמעאל בן אלישע בר פלוגתיה דר"ע. אבל מ"מ על כרחין *קסבר לא קדשה, דכיון דמוקי קרא דנחלה בשילה – א"כ מנא ליה דירושלים אין אחריה היתר? וי"ל: דשמא נפקא ליה מקרא אחרינא. והרב רבי חיים מפרש: דרבי ישמעאל סבר קדשה, והאי דקאמר: זה וזה שילה – אתא לאשמועינן דשילה אין אחריה היתר, דלא כמ"ד יש אחריה היתר, והיינו משום דדריש: "מנוחה" – זו שילה, "נחלה" – זו ירושלים, ומדלחקו קדריש ליתן היתר בין זו לזו. ופליג אמתני' דקתני שילה יש אחריה היתר, דתנן (לקמן דף קיב:): באו לנוב וגבעון כו'. ואין נראה כלל, שהרי יב] מוכיחים דבנוב וגבעון הותרו הבמות גבי שמואל "והוא יברך את הזבח" (שמואל א ט), וגם קרי ליה בפסוק "במה". אבל אחר ירושלים לכולי עלמא לא הותרו הבמות, ואפי' מאן דאית ליה לא קדשה – מ"ס דאין אחריה היתר. וכן משמע פ"ק דמגילה (גו"ש), א"ר יצחק: שמעתי שמקריבין בבית חוניו בזמן הזה. וקאמר דהדר ביה מהא דתניא: ירושלים אין אחריה היתר. ואמאי הדר ביה? הא קאמר התם כתנאי אי קדשה לעתיד לבא אי לא קדשה, ומעיקרא מאי סבר ולבסוף מאי סבר? אלא ודאי מעיקרא סבר דלמ"ד לא קדשה – הותרו הבמות, והדר ביה ממתניתין דמגילה וממתניתין דלקמן בפ' בתרא (דף קיב:), דירושלים אין אחריה היתר, דמשמע – לכולי עלמא, אפילו למ"ד לא קדשה. ותנאי דמייתי התם בקדשה ולא קדשה – לא קאי אדרבי יצחק, אלא ריהטא דהתלמוד הוא, משום יג] *דאיירי קדושה ראשונה קדשה לשעתה וקדשה לעתיד לבא דנקיט כתנאי, ומייתי פלוגתא דבתי ערי חומה דדמי לקדושת הארץ דמשוי להו *אהדדי. ובפ"ב דערכין (דף לב:) גבי מקיש ביאתם בימי עזרא לביאתם בימי יהושע, וכמה תנאי היא יכול להביא דאיכא דאית ליה קדשה ואיכא דאית ליה לא קדשה. ור"מ בפ"ק דחולין (דף ו:) קסבר לא קדשה גבי בית שאן, ורבי ישמעאל דהכא, ורבי יוסי דסדר עולם בפרק "הערל" (יבמות דף פב:). יד] וא"ת: ומנא ליה לקמן דרבי יוחנן סבר קדשה משום דמחייב מעלה בזמן הזה? לעולם אימא לך דסבר לא קדשה, אפ"ה אין אחריה היתר, כדפי'! וי"ל: דאי לא קדשה – לא מחייב, טו] דאינו ראוי לפתח אהל מועד, דנדחו לגמרי. אבל אי קדשה – לא נדחו, דיכול לבנות מזבח במקומו ויקריב עליו. או מיירי ר' יוחנן בקטרת, דלא בעי מזבח כדפי' לעיל. ואין להקשות לפי' הקונטרס דגרס הכא "לא קדשה", ובסוף "הערל" (גו"ש) שמעינן לרבי יוסי דקדשה בברייתא דסדר עולם! טז] ויש חילוק, כדפי' לעיל, דאפילו בטלה קדושת הבית – קדושת הארץ לא בטלה, כדאשכחן בנוב וגבעון. א"נ: תני ולא סבר ליה, כדבעי למימר פרק "יוצא דופן" (נדה דף מו:). א"נ: הא דידיה הא דרביה, דהכא משמיה דרבי ישמעאל. וא"ת: למאי דגרס "קדשה", הא ר"ל ס"ל אליבא דרבי יוסי (יבמות דף פב.) תרומה בזמן הזה דרבנן! וי"ל: כדפרישית לעיל, דאפשר אפילו לא בטלה קדושת הבית – קדושת הארץ בטלה. ותדע, דרבי יהושע שמעי' ליה יז] עיגול בעיגולין עולה בפ"ק דבילה (דף ד.), ובסוף "הערל" (יבמות דף פב.) מוכח לר"ל יח] למ"ד עולה – קסבר תרומה בזמן הזה דרבנן. ושמעינן ליה לרבי יהושע בכמה דוכתי דאמר: שמעתי שמקריבים אע"פ שאין בית. יט] ●ותימה הוא לומר שקדושת הבית קיימת להקריב קרבן בלא במה, ולא יתחייב בתרומה. אבל לעיל דאמר איפכא – אתי שפיר, כמו בנוב וגבעון. והכא י"ל דרבי יוסי משום רבי ישמעאל קאמר ולא ס"ל. ומר' יהושע י"ל *דסבר דאינו מקדש אלא ו' דברים בלבד – לכן יעלו העיגולין. ור"א דמספקא ליה בפרק "ידיעות הטומאה" (שבועות דף טז.) ובפ"ק דמגילה (דף י.) אי סבר קדשה או לא קדשה, ושמעי' ליה בפ"ק דחגיגה (דף ג:) גבי עמון ומואב מעשרין מעשר עני בשביעית, דקסבר לא קדשה. ומיהו, אין ראיה, משום ד"הרבה כרכים" לאו מדברי ר"א, כ] כדפרישית פ"ק דיבמות (דף טז. ד"ה עמון), וליתיה כא] במסכת ידים (פ"ד מ"ג). *קדשים נפסלין. פי' בקונטרס: קס"ד מפני סילוק המזבח הוא, מדקתני: זבין ומצורעין משתלחין, שאין מצורע נכנס לדגלי השבטים, ולא זב למחנה הלוים נושאי ארון. כדאמר לקמן: אע"פ שנסע – אהל מועד הוא. אלמא נפסלין דקאמר – לאו משום דמפסלי ביוצא הוא, דהא אהל מועד חשיב ליה. וא"ת, כב] דלמאי דמוקי לה השתא בקדשי קדשים, אפילו בלא סילוק מזבח אלא סילוק קלעי החצר לחוד נפסלין קדשי קדשים ביוצא, דבהדיא מוכח בפ' "שתי הלחם" (מנחות דף צה.) דבשעת כג] מסעות אין קרוי מחנה שכינה קיים, ולחם הפנים ושאר קדשי קדשים מיפסלי ביוצא, דנסע אהל מועד הוא – לאו דוקא לענין מחנה שכינה. אבל לגבי קדשים קלים – ודאי לא מיפסלי ביוצא משום מסע המחנות, דלענין מחנה ישראל ומחנה לויה, אע"פ שנסע – אהל מועד הוא, דמחניהם קיימים בדגלי השבטים, כדמוכח לקמן פ' בתרא (דף קטז:). ולכך זבין ומצורעין משתלחין, וקדשים קלים אין נפסלין ביוצא. ואתקפתא הוי מדקתני נאכלין בשני מקומות, דמיירי בקדשים קלים, ואע"פ שאין מזבח במקומו. **הא** ר' ישמעאל והא רבנן. היינו תנאי דפליגי עליה דר' ישמעאל בתמורה פרק "ואלו קדשים" (דף כא.) ודרשי' ליה לקרא בע"א. **קודם** שיעמידו המשכן. פרש"י: לאו דוקא קודם, אלא לאחר שהעמידו הכל, המשכן והמזבח. דאין לפרש ממש קודם שהעמידו המשכן, כיון שכבר העמידו המזבח במקומו אוכלין קדשי קדשים. הלא תחילה נוסעין בני גרשון ומעמידין המשכן, ואח"כ בני קהת מעמידין המזבח, ואם שינו הסדר והעמידו המזבח תחילה – היאך שחטו קדשים קודם העמדת המשכן? הא אמרן (יומא דף סג:): שלמים ששחטן קודם פתיחת ההיכל פסולין! וי"ל: שלמים דוקא כתיב בהו "ושחטו פתח אהל מועד". כל זה פי' רש"י. וק"ל (ברו"ך): הא תנן גבי תמיד (תמיד דף ל:): לא היה שוחט עד ששמע שער הגדול שנפתח, אלמא ילפינן שאר קרבנות שאין שוחטין משלמים! ואין נראה לומר דהיינו מדרבנן, דהא בהיקשא ד"זאת התורה" נילף לפסולא משלמים. וגם אין לומר בשלמים גופייהו אינו פוסל רק מדרבנן, דלא שנה הכתוב לעכב, דהא אמרי' פ' "שני שעירי" (יומא דף סג:) דשלמים ששחטן בחוץ קודם פתיחת דלתות ההיכל – פטור. אלמא: מן התורה אינו ראוי לפתח אהל מועד, דפסול דרבנן חייב בחוץ. ואפילו בפסול דאורייתא חייב בחוץ היכא דאם עלו לא ירדו, כדמוכח פרק "השוחט והמעלה" (לקמן קט.). וזהו הוכחה דשאר קדשים נמי פסולין בפנים קודם פתיחת דלתות ההיכל. דאי כשירין – א"כ בשלמים אם עלו לא ירדו, דקרוי פסולו בקודש היכא דאית ליה הכשירא בעלמא – א"כ הוא דבשלמים ●אם עלו לא ירדו – אמאי פטור בחוץ? אלא ודאי בשאר קדשים נמי פסולין. אם לא תאמר כיון דלא נפתחו קודם השחיטה דלתות ההיכל – חשיב שוחט שלמים שלא במקומן וירדו, אע"ג דשאר קדשים אין נפסלין מן התורה. ודמי לקדשי קדשים ששחטן בדרום, בפ"ק דמעילה (דף ג.), דכמאן דמנקיון דמו, וירדו [לרבי יהודה], אע"ג דקדשים קלים שחיטתן כד] בדרום כשירין, אבל לר"ש לא ירדו כדאיתא התם. א"כ ההיא ד"שני שעירי" דפטר בחוץ – כרבי יהודה. ●וגם אין לומר דקודם שפירקו המשכן כלל שחטו וזרקו את הדם ואחרי כן פירקוהו, ושינו הסדר בשעת חנייה והעמידו המזבח וקלעי החצר תחילה, וקאמר בשמעתא דקודם שיעמידו קרשי המשכן יאכלו קדשי קדשים – הלא מיד שפירקוהו נפסלו ביוצא הקדשי קדשים, ולא אמרינן נסע אהל מועד הוא לגבי מחנה שכינה. אלא ודאי קודם שהעמידו – לאו דוקא, אלא העמידו הכל. וחידושא הוי אלאחר שיפרקו, כדקאמר: קמ"ל אע"פ דנסע – אהל מועד הוא ואע"פ שנפרק המשכן, כיון שקלעי החצר והמזבח במקומן. ברו"ך.

ולאחר

גי' הצ"ק משכחת לה שיהא המזבח מונח קודם העמדת המשכן שהרי כו' כצ"ל

צ"ל ונוסעין דגל ראשון כו' אחרי דגל שני כדי צ"ק

במעשר בזמן הזה אם הוזקק להבאת מקום מאי קבעית אי דגדל לאחר החורבן ההוא כו' צ"ק

[דף נט.]

היתר כדאמרינן בפ"ק צ"ק

גי' הצ"ק קסבר לא קדשה מדלא קרי ליה נחלה ועוד דכיון דמוקי כו'

דאיירי דנקט קדושה ראשונה קדשה לשעתה ולא קדשה לעתיד לבא נקיט כתנאי כו' כצ"ל

*אהדדי בפ"ב צ"ק

[ועי' בתוס' יבמות פח. ד"ה שאני שונה כו' דהו סברא זו ע"ש]

שייך לעיל דף ס ע"ב

שיטה מקובצת

א] מדם וא"כ בשעת סילוק המחנות כיון שאי אפשר לזרוק את הדם אין הבשר נאכל בתרייתא רבנן דלא ילפי בשר מדם הס"ד: ב] בעוד שהמשכן נטוי: ג] המשכן דנקט הכא לאו דוקא נקט אלא איידי דנקט לאחר שיפרקו נקט [נמי קודם שיעמידו] דלא משכחת לה שיהא המזבח מונח קודם העמדת המשכן שהרי קודם: ד] דגל ראשון ובני קהת אחרי דגל שני כדי: ה] קהת ואי בששינו ותיבת ועוד נמחק: ו] מקומן שלמים ששחטן כו' פסולין ואי כששחטו כבר משעת נסיעה והביאו עמם הבשר א"כ מיפסלא להו ביוצא: ז] ואי גרסת. ס"א ואם תמצ' לומר קודם שיעמידו הלוים את המשכן דוקא קאמר מוקמינן כו': ח] קבעית דההוא דגדל לאחר ותיבת אבל נמחק: ט] הבית וההיא פשיטא: י] איתקש נמי: יא] לדמו וא"ת הואיל ומוקי ליה בבכור שנזרק דמו א"כ היכא קאמר בברייתא בכורים יוכיחו והא בכורים דהוי כה"ג דמעשר שנזרעו קודם החורבן ולא מחוסר רק אכילה דהיינו כשהניחו לפני המזבח קודם חורבן הבית אז ודאי נאכלים שפיר לאחר חורבן הבית וכמו שאין אתה למד מעשר מבכור רק בדמי ליה דלא מיחסר רק אכילה כמו כן אין לעשות יוכיח מבכורים רק בדדמי ליה דלא מיחסר רק אכילה וי"ל דדוקא גבי היקשא דבכור ומעשר איכא למימר דלא איתקש אלא לבכור דכוותיה אבל שייך שפיר לומר ביכורים יוכיחו אף מאותם שלא הניחם קודם חורבן הבית כיון שבבנין הבית היה למד. כך נראה למהר"ם תו' מהר"פ: יב] שהרי קראי מוכיחים: יג] דאיירי בקדושה ראשונה כו' לבא הוא דנקט כתנאי כו' דבתי ערי חומה ולאו משום דדמיא ליה דיש חילוק בין קדושת בית לבתי עירי חומה אבל ודאי קדושת בתי ערי חומה דמיא לקדושת אות ד' נמחק: יד] הערל קסבר קדשה ולקמן נמי בפרק השוחט והמעלה גבי פלוגתא דר"י ור"ל דהמעלה בזמן הזה מייתי פלוגתא דר"א ור"י דמקריבין אע"פ שאין בית ולא מייתי דר"מ דבית שאן ור' ישמעאל דהכא ור' יוסי דסדר עולם וא"ת ומנא ליה לקמן בפרק השוחט והמעלה דר': טו] מחייב כרת דאינו: טז] עולם דיש חילוק: יז] ליה דעיגול בעיגולין: יח] דמ"ד עולה: יט] מתיבת ותימה עד תיבת ור"א דמספקא ליה מוקף בח"ל: כ] ר"א הוא כדפי': כא] וליתיה במילתיה במס': כב] וא"א לומר כן דלמאי: כג] דבשעת סילוק מסעות אין מחנה שכינה: כד] שחיטתן כשרין בדרום אבל:

מהו

גליון הש"ס

תוס' ד"ה (בעמוד הקודם) מאי וכו' ותימה הוא לומר שקדושת הבית קיימת. עי' לקמן דף סב ע"א תוס' ד"ה ואחד: **תוס'** ד"ה קודם וכו' אם עלו לא ירדו אמאי פטור בחוץ. עי' לעיל דף נט ע"א תוס' ד"ה עד: **בא"ד** וגם אין לומר דקודם שפירקו וכו' נפסלו ביוצא הק"ק קי"ל הא גם בקדשים קלים כה"ג פסול מאכילה כיון דבעת סילוק מסעות הוי פגם מזבח ואידחי מאכילה ואינו חוזר ונראה כמ"ש תוס' בדיבור הסמוך בד"ה ולאחר ובד"ה אע"פ:

יב א מיי' פ"ב מהלכות בית הבחירה הל' ה:
יג ב מיי' שם פ"א הלכה יג ופ"ב שם הלכה טז:

תורה אור

וּלְאַחַר שֶׁיָּפְרְקוּ הַלְוִיִּם אֶת הַמִּשְׁכָּן; א] *מַהוּ דְּתֵימָא אִיפְסִיל לְהוּ בְּיוֹצֵא, קָא מַשְׁמַע לָן. *וְאֵימָא הָכִי נַמִי! אָמַר קְרָא: °"וְנָסַע אֹהֶל מוֹעֵד", *אַף עַל פִּי שֶׁנָּסַע – אֹהֶל מוֹעֵד הוּא. אָמַר רַב ב] הוּנָא אָמַר רַב: מִזְבֵּחַ שֶׁל שִׁילֹה שֶׁל אֲבָנִים הָיָה. ג] *דְּתַנְיָא: ר"א בֶּן יַעֲקֹב אוֹמֵר, מַה תַּלְמוּד לוֹמַר: °"אֲבָנִים" °"אֲבָנִים" °"אֲבָנִים" שָׁלֹשׁ פְּעָמִים? אֶחָד שֶׁל שִׁילֹה, וְאֶחָד שֶׁל נוֹב וְגִבְעוֹן, וּבֵית עוֹלָמִים. מְתִיב רַב ד] אַחָא בַּר אַמִי: *אֵשׁ שֶׁיָּרְדָה מִן הַשָּׁמַיִם בִּימֵי מֹשֶׁה – לֹא נִסְתַּלְּקָה מֵעַל מִזְבַּח הַנְּחֹשֶׁת אֶלָּא בִּימֵי שְׁלֹמֹה, וְאֵשׁ שֶׁיָּרְדָה בִּימֵי שְׁלֹמֹה – לֹא נִסְתַּלְּקָה עַד שֶׁבָּא מְנַשֶּׁה וְסִילְּקָהּ; וְאִם אִיתָא – מֵעִיקָּרָא הוּא דְּאִיסְתַּלַּק ה] לֵיהּ! הוּא דְּאָמַר כְּרַבִּי נָתָן. דְּתַנְיָא, רַבִּי נָתָן אוֹמֵר: מִזְבֵּחַ שֶׁל שִׁילֹה שֶׁל נְחוֹשֶׁת ו] הָיָה, חָלוּל וּמָלֵא אֲבָנִים. ר"נ בַּר יִצְחָק אָמַר: מַאי "לֹא נִסְתַּלְּקָה" – לֹא נִסְתַּלְּקָה ז] לְבַטָּלָה. מַאי הִיא? רַבָּנַן אָמְרִי: שְׁבִיבָא הֲוָה מְשַׁדְּרָא. רַב פַּפָּא אָמַר: אוּשְׁפִּיזָא הֲוָה נָקֵט, ח] וְזִימְנִין הָכָא וְזִימְנִין הָכָא. תְּנַן הָתָם: *וּכְשֶׁעָלוּ אבְּנֵי הַגּוֹלָה, הוֹסִיפוּ עָלָיו ד' אַמּוֹת מִן הַדָּרוֹם וְד' אַמּוֹת מִן הַמַּעֲרָב כְּמִין גַּמָּא. מַאי טַעְמָא? אָמַר רַב יוֹסֵף: מִשּׁוּם דְּלָא ט] סָפַק. אֲמַר לֵיהּ אַבַּיֵי: הַשְׁתָּא מִקְדָּשׁ רִאשׁוֹן, דִּכְתִיב בֵּיהּ: °"יְהוּדָה וְיִשְׂרָאֵל רַבִּים כַּחוֹל אֲשֶׁר עַל (שְׂפַת) הַיָּם" – י] סָפַק, מִקְדָּשׁ שֵׁנִי דִּכְתִיב בֵּיהּ: °"כָּל הַקָּהָל כְּאֶחָד אַרְבַּע רִבּוֹא" לָא יא] סָפַק?! א"ל: הָתָם – אֵשׁ שֶׁל שָׁמַיִם מְסַיַּיעְתָּן, הָכָא – אֵין אֵשׁ שֶׁל שָׁמַיִם מְסַיַּיעְתָּן. כִּי אֲתָא רָבִין אֲמַר ר"ש בֶּן פָּזִי יב] מִשּׁוּם בַּר קַפָּרָא: שִׁיתִין הוֹסִיפוּ. מֵעִיקָּרָא סְבוּר: "מִזְבַּח אֲדָמָה" – שֶׁהוּא אָטוּם בָּאֲדָמָה. וּלְבַסּוֹף סְבוּר: שְׁתִיָּה כַּאֲכִילָה. וּמַאי "מִזְבַּח אֲדָמָה" – *שֶׁהוּא מְחוּבָּר בָּאֲדָמָה; שֶׁלֹּא בִיבְנֻהוּ לֹא ע"ג כֵּיפִים, וְלֹא

(במדבר ב; שמות כ; דברים כז; מלכים א ד; עזרא ב)

רש"י

מַהוּ דְּתֵימָא כו'. כְּלוֹמַר, וְלֹא אֲכִילָה מִשֶּׁנֶּעֱקַר הַמִּזְבֵּחַ אֲתָא לְאַשְׁמוּעִינַן, אֶלָּא אֲכִילַת קָדְשֵׁי קָדָשִׁים בְּלֹא קְלָעִים אֲתָא לְאַשְׁמוּעִינַן. דְּלָא תֵּימָא כֵּיוָן שֶׁנִּסְתַּלְּקוּ קְלָעִים יֵשׁ כָּאן פְּסוּל יוֹצֵא. יג] אֲבָנִים ג"פ. "אִם מִזְבַּח אֲבָנִים" [וגו'], "מִזְבַּח אֲבָנִים לֹא תָנִיף" [וגו'], "אֲבָנִים שְׁלֵמוֹת תִּבְנֶה" וגו'. נוֹב וְגִבְעוֹן. חַד חָשֵׁיב לְהוּ, דִּשְׁנֵיהֶם בָּמָה וְאֵינָן קְדוֹשִׁים. לֹא נִסְתַּלְּקָה. שֶׁבִּשְׁעַת הַמַּסָּעוֹת כּוֹפִין עָלָיו פְּסַכְתֵּר, וּמַנִּיחִין אוֹתָהּ בִּמְקוֹמָהּ. אֶלָּא בִּימֵי שְׁלֹמֹה. שֶׁנִּסְתַּלְּקָה מִשָּׁם לְמִזְבַּח אֲבָנִים שֶׁעָשָׂה שְׁלֹמֹה. עַד שֶׁבָּא מְנַשֶּׁה וְסִילְּקָהּ גָּרַס. וְאִם אִיתָא מֵעִיקָּרָא הוּא דְּאִיסְתַּלַּק. מִשֶּׁהוּקַם הַמִּשְׁכָּן בְּשִׁילֹה וּבָנוּ מִזְבַּח אֲבָנִים הוּזְקְקָה לְהִסְתַּלֵּק מִמִּזְבֵּחַ שֶׁל נְחֹשֶׁת. הוּא דְּאָמַר. רַב הוּנָא דְּאָמַר כְּרַבִּי נָתָן. וְהָא דְּלָא אָמְרִי' הוּא דְּאָמַר כְּר"א בֶּן יַעֲקֹב – מִשּׁוּם דְּר' נָתָן הוּא דְּשָׁמְעִי' לֵיהּ בְּהֶדְיָא יד] מַעֲשֶׂה הָיָה כָּךְ, אֲבָל מִדְּר"א בֶּן יַעֲקֹב לָא שָׁמְעִינַן אֶלָּא דְּהוּכְשַׁר בְּשֶׁל אֲבָנִים. לֹא נִסְתַּלְּקָה לְבַטָּלָה. שֶׁתְּהֵא בְּטֵילָה מִמִּזְבַּח הַנְּחֹשֶׁת לְגַמְרֵי. שְׁבִיבָא הֲוָה מְשַׁדְּרָא. כְּשֶׁהָיוּ מַקְטִירִין עַל שֶׁל אֲבָנִים – הָיוּ זִיקִים וּלְהָבוֹת יוֹצְאוֹת מֵאֵשׁ שָׁמַיִם שֶׁעַל מִזְבַּח הַנְּחֹשֶׁת שֶׁל מֹשֶׁה, שֶׁאַף הוּא מוּנָּח שָׁם. תְּנַן הָתָם. בְּמַסֶּכֶת מִדּוֹת. ר' יוֹסֵי אוֹמֵר: בַּתְּחִילָּה בִּימֵי שְׁלֹמֹה לֹא הָיָה *אֶלָּא כ"ח. (א) כּוֹנֵס וְעוֹלֶה יְסוֹד וְסוֹבֵב וּמְקוֹם קְרָנוֹת וּמְקוֹם הִילּוּךְ, עַד שֶׁהָיָה מְקוֹם הַמַּעֲרָכָה כ' עַל כ'. וּכְשֶׁעָלוּ בְּנֵי הַגּוֹלָה הוֹסִיפוּ עָלָיו כו', נִמְצָא יְסוֹדוֹ ל"ב עַל ל"ב, וּמְקוֹם מַעֲרַכְתּוֹ כ"ד עַל כ"ד. גַּמָּא. גִּימֶל יְוָונִית, עֲשׂוּיָה כְּמִין כַּף פְּשׁוּטָה שֶׁלָּנוּ, טו] כִּדְפָרֵישִׁית, דָּרוֹם וּמַעֲרָב. הָכָא. בְּמִקְדָּשׁ שֵׁנִי, אֵין אֵשׁ שֶׁל שָׁמַיִם מְסַייַעְתָּן. כִּדְיָלְפִינַן בְּפ"ק דְּיוֹמָא (דף כא:): "וְאֶרְצֶה בּוֹ וְאֶכָּבֵד" מְחוּסָּר ה' – אֵלּוּ ה' דְּבָרִים שֶׁחָסֵר מִקְדָּשׁ שֵׁנִי, וְאֵשׁ אֶחָד מֵהֶן. וְאָמְרִינַן הָתָם: מֵיהֲוֵי הֲוָה, סִיּוּעֵי לָא מְסַייְעָא. טז] שִׁיתִּין הוֹסִיפוּ. קֶרֶן מַעֲרָבִית דְּרוֹמִית הוֹסִיפוּ לְמָשְׁכָהּ לַדָּרוֹם וְלַמַּעֲרָב, יז] שֶׁשָּׁם הָיוּ מְנַסְּכִין נְסָכִים, כִּדְאָמְרִינַן יח] (הָתָם) בְּמַתְנִי' דִּלְקַמָּן (דף סג.). וּבִימֵי שְׁלֹמֹה הָיָה כְּמִין בּוֹר כָּרוּי אֵצֶל הַמִּזְבֵּחַ בְּאוֹתָהּ זָוִית לֵירֵד הַנְּסָכִים בְּתוֹכוֹ, וְיוֹרְדִין מִן הַמִּזְבֵּחַ יט] וְלָרְצָפָה וְשׁוֹתְתִין שָׁם. *וְהֵם קָלְטוּ אוֹתוֹ הַבּוֹר לְתוֹךְ הַמִּזְבֵּחַ, וְעָשׂוּ נְקָבִים כְּנֶגְדָּן בְּרֹאשׁ הַמִּזְבֵּחַ, לֵירֵד הַנְּסָכִים שָׁם. אָטוּם בָּאֲדָמָה. שֶׁלֹּא יְהֵא חָלוּל. שְׁתִיָּה כַּאֲכִילָה. מָה אֲכִילָה מִתְעַכֶּלֶת בַּמִּזְבֵּחַ – אַף שְׁתִיָּה תִּבָּלַע בַּמִּזְבֵּחַ. אָמַר

תוספות

ולאחר שיפרקו הלוים את המשכן. אבל המזבח וקלעי החצר במקומן. אבל נסע מכל וכל – אין מחנה שכינה קיים לגבי קדשי קדשים, כדפרי'. ולחם הפנים נפסל ביוצא, כדאמר התם במסולק מסידור השלחן דכ"ע לא פליגי דנפסל ביוצא. ועוד: דאי כ] נפרק מכל וכל – תיפוק לי דמיפסל מטעם פגימת המזבח. וא"ת: ובמנחות (דף צה.) אמאי תלי טעמא ביוצא בלחם הפנים? תיפוק לי משום פגימת המזבח! כא] ואי חזרו והעמידו בו ביום ואז יאכלוהו – הא כיון שנדחה אינו חוזר ונראה לאכול! וכ"ת: חד מתרי טעמי נקט, א"כ היכי דייק התם: ש"מ יש סילוק מסעות בלילה, דאי ס"ד ביום מאי איריא משום יוצא? תיפוק לי דאיפסול ליה בלינה! וי"ל: דודאי סילוק מסעות פוסל, או משום יוצא או משום פגימת המזבח. והתם דייק: אם היה נפסל משום לינה קודם סילוק – נמצא דלא היה המסע פוסל. **אע"פ** שנסע אהל מועד הוא. וא"ת: בפ' "שתי הלחם" (מנחות דף צה.) כב] דמעיקרא פליגי בלחם הפנים במסולק אם נפסל במסעות, דמ"ד אינו נפסל דרש מדכתיב: "ונסע אהל מועד", אע"פ שנסע – אהל מועד הוא, אפילו למחנה שכינה, ואידך – ההוא לדגלים אתא. אמאי לא משני דאיצטריך לדרשא דהכא, או *למחנה ישראל דקיים, כדאמר פ' בתרא (לקמן קיז:)? ותירץ ה"ר חיים: דלפי סברתו קמהדר ליה, דס"ל דלא צריך קרא לדרשא דהכא ולדרשא דפ' בתרא, כיון דאית ליה דאפי' כי ליכא לא מזבח ולא קלעים – אפי' לחם הפנים שהוא קדשי קדשים לא מיפסיל, דקרינא ביה מחנה שכינה קיים, ולכך משני דלדגלים הוא דאתא. וא"ת: היכי תיסק אדעתא למימר התם דמסולק כשר ביוצא? מ"מ הא מסולק מיפסיל בפגימת מזבח! וכי תימא כשחזרו והעמידו המשכן בו ביום – ואיך יאכלוהו? הא כיון דנדחה – שוב אינו חוזר ונראה! וי"ל: דלא קיימא ההיא מסקנא. א"נ: אפי' בשעת שנשאו בכתף – מזבח הוא, *כיון דאמר: אע"פ שנסע אהל מועד הוא. **ארבע** אמות מן הדרום וד' אמות מן המערב. כך גירסת הקונטרס. וקשה לר"ת: כג] דא"כ היה המזבח *ד' אמות בחלקו של יהודה, דמסתמא בבית ראשון לא היה יסוד לקרן דרומית מזרחית לפי שלא היה בחלקו של טורף, כדאמר פ' "איזהו מקומן" (לעיל נג:), ואם בבית שני הוסיפו בדרום – א"כ בנו בחלקו של יהודה! וגרס ר"ת: מן הצפון מן המערב. והכי תנן במס' מדות (פ"ג מ"א). וקשה: דהא מסקי' הכא דמשום שיתין הוסיפו, שיהא הבור כד] קלוט מתוך המזבח. ושיתין בדרום היו, כדתנן בפירקין (לקמן סג.): בג' דברים היתה קרן מערבית דרומית משמשת למעלה: ניסוך המים והיין. *ועוד תנן במסכת מדות (פ"ג מ"ג): מקום היה שם, אמה על אמה וטבלא של שיש עליה, שבה יורדין לשיתין! ומלינו למידחק: ברוח מערבית היה לצד קרן דרומית. אבל קשה עוד: תניא במעילה פרק "ולד חטאת" (דף יא:) ומייתי לה בסוכה פרק "לולב" כה] (דף מח.): לול קטן היה בצד מערבו של כבש, אחד לשבעים שנה פרחי כהונה יורדין לשם ומביאין משם יין קרוש! לכך נראה כגירסת הספרים דגרסי דרום ומערב. ובבית ראשון היה להם יסוד לדרום, שהיה משוך בחלקו של טורף, חוץ מרוח מזרחית שלא נשתנה, שהיה בלא יסוד (עד) חלקו של יהודה כמו בבית שני. וקראי דממעטי בפרק "איזהו מקומן" (לעיל דף נג:) קרן שאין לה יסוד – משום בית שני נאמרו. אי נמי: אף בבית ראשון לא חשיב קרן דרומית קרן, כיון דלא הוה ליה יסוד משני לדדין כגון בצד מזרח. אי נמי: לפי שהיה עתיד להיות בלא יסוד בבית שני – לא היו נותנין דמים בו. כמו במזבח של משה, לפי שהיה עתיד להיות בלא יסוד בבית עולמים. ולא

מסורת הש"ס

[לקמן קטז:] | שם | [שם מנחות לה.] | [נ"ל תניא נמי הכי וכ"א בילקוט פרשת יתרו רמז ש"ו] | סדר עולם פרק טו | [לעיל נח.] | נ"א למחנה ישראל ולקדשים קלים כדאמרינן בפ"ב כו' נ"ק | נ"ל כמאן | אמה מערכה בחלקו כו' נ"ק

הגהות הב"ח

(א) רש"י ד"ה תנן התם וכו' לא היה אלא כ"ח וכונס אמה יסוד כצ"ל ותיבת ועולה נמחק:

נ"א אלא כ"ח על כ"ח וכונס ועולה כו' נ"ק מדות לה: [פ"ג מ"א]

נ"א והם הוסיפו הבנין עד שיהיה אותו הבור קלוט לתוך המזבח ופתחו הנקבים כנגדו כו'

נ"א ותנן במס' מדות למטה ברצפה באותו הקרן מקום היה כו' נ"ק

שיטה מקובצת

א] מהו דתימא כו'. פ"ה שפרקו המשכן הקרשים והיריעות והמזבח קיים זהו לפי שיטתו דלעיל דאינו נפסל אפילו כי הסיר הקלעים וקשה דהיכי קאמר אע"פ שנסע אהל מועד הוא ולא נפסל ביוצא [הא] אין לך יוצא גדול מזה כיון דמחוסר קלעים הוא אלא יש לפרש לאחר שפרקו הקרשים אבל הקלעים עומדים במקומן וא"ת מאי קמ"ל פשיטא דלא מיפסל משום יוצא הואיל והקלעים קיימין וי"ל כיון דאין הקלעים אלא מחמת המשכן שבתוכן א"כ משנסתלק קדושת המשכן בטלה קדושת קלעים ושייך משום יוצא קמ"ל אף על פי שנסע או"מ הוא הקלעים כיון שלא נסתלקו וההיא דשתי הלחם מיירי שנסתלקו הקלעים דמיפסלי משום יוצא. תוס' מהר"פ: ב] רב חסדא אמר רב ותיבת הונא נמחק: ג] היה. תניא ר"א אות ד' נמחק ס"א תניא נמי הכי כו': ד] רב אחדבוי בר אמי תיבת אחא נמחק: ה] דאסתלק לה: ו] היה חלול וכמו כן במדבר נמי היו ממלאין אותו בחנייתן והאש של שמים היה מונח על השפה וכשהיו נושאין אותו היו כופין עליו פסכתר כדי שלא ישרוף את הבגדים שהיו משימין על האש כשמביאין המזבח ממקום למקום. תו"א: ז] לבטלה היכי הוי רבנן ותיבות מאי היא נמחק: ח] הוה נקיט זמנין הכא: ט] דלא ספיק: י] הים ספיק מקדש: יא] לא ספיק א"ל: יב] תיבות משום בר קפרא נמחק: יג] תיבת אבנים נמחק: יד] בהדיא דאמר מעשה: טו] שלנו כדמפרש דרום: טז] מה"ד משום שיתין: יז] ולמערב כדאמרי' ששם: יח] תיבת התם נמחק: יט] המזבח לרצפה ושותתין שם ובני הגולה הוסיפו בבנין עד שהיה אותו הבור קולט לתוך המזבח ופתחו נקבים כנגדו: כ] דאי נסע ותיבת נפרק ל"ש: כא] מתיבת ואי עד תיבת וכ"ת חד מוקף בח"ל: כב] דפליגי בלחם תיבת דמעיקרא נמחק: כג] דא"כ. נ"א דע"כ אותן ד' אמות שהוסיפו בדרום היה בחלקו של טורף דאי בחלקו של יהודה לא הוכשר למזבח ולעיל אמרי' שלא היה לו יסוד בבית ראשון מן הדרום לפי שלא היה בחלקו של טורף לכך נראה דגרסי' מן הצפון כו' אלא לכך נראה כגירסת רש"י דרום ומערב והגיע עד חלקו של יהודה שבבית ראשון היה לו יסוד לרוח דרומית אבל במזרח לא היה לו יסוד לפי שהיה בחלקו של יהודה וכן מוכח לעיל הלשון דקאמר המזבח אוכל בחלקו של יהודה אמה ולא קאמר אמה מכאן ואמה מכאן משמע דוקא לצד אחד דהיינו לצד מזרח אבל בקרן דרומית היה בחלקו של טורף ומ"מ בקרן דרומית מזרחית לא היה בו יסוד לפי שלא היה ראוי אותו קרן למתן דמים משום דבעינן בדם שיהא מטפטף מכאן ומכאן על היסוד משני צדדין של הקרן והכא לא היה יסוד באותו קרן של צד מזרח לפי שהיה אוכל בחלקו של יהודה ולא היה יסוד בדרומי כי אם אמה אחת בקרן דרומית מערבית. תוס' מהר"פ: כד] הבור קולט בתוך המזבח: כה] לולב וערבה לול:

וְלֹא עַל גַּבֵּי מְחִילוֹת. אֲמַר רַב יוֹסֵף, לָאו הַיְינוּ
דְּתַנְיָא: °"וַיָּכִינוּ (אֶת) הַמִּזְבֵּחַ עַל מְכוֹנוֹתָיו" —
שֶׁהִגִּיעוּ לְסוֹף מִדּוֹתָיו? וְהָכְתִיב: °"הַכֹּל בִּכְתָב
מִיַּד ה' עָלַי הִשְׂכִּיל"! אֶלָּא אֲמַר רַב יוֹסֵף, קְרָא
א] אַשְׁכַּח וְדָרַשׁ: °"וַיֹּאמֶר דָּוִיד זֶה הוּא בֵּית ה'
הָאֱלֹהִים וְזֶה מִזְבֵּחַ ב] לְעוֹלָה לְיִשְׂרָאֵל", כִּי בַּיִת:
מַה בַּיִת שִׁשִּׁים אַמָּה — אַף מִזְבֵּחַ שִׁשִּׁים אַמָּה.
בִּשְׁלָמָא בַּיִת — מִינְכְּרָא צוּרָתוֹ, אֶלָּא מִזְבֵּחַ מְנָא
יָדְעִי? אָמַר רַבִּי אֶלְעָזָר: רָאוּ מִזְבֵּחַ בָּנוּי וּמִיכָאֵל
ג] הַשַּׂר הַגָּדוֹל עוֹמֵד וּמַקְרִיב עָלָיו. וְר' יִצְחָק
נַפָּחָא אָמַר: אֶפְרוֹ שֶׁל יִצְחָק רָאוּ שֶׁמּוּנָּח
בְּאוֹתוֹ מָקוֹם. ד] וְר' שְׁמוּאֵל בַּר נַחְמָנִי אָמַר: מִכָּל
הַבַּיִת כּוּלּוֹ הֵרִיחוּ רֵיחַ קְטֹרֶת, מִשָּׁם הֵרִיחוּ
רֵיחַ אֵבָרִים. אָמַר רַבָּה בַּר בַּר חָנָה א"ר יוֹחָנָן:
אשְׁלֹשָׁה נְבִיאִים עָלוּ עִמָּהֶם מִן הַגּוֹלָה, אֶחָד
שֶׁהֵעִיד לָהֶם עַל הַמִּזְבֵּחַ, וְאֶחָד שֶׁהֵעִיד לָהֶם
עַל מְקוֹם הַמִּזְבֵּחַ, וְאֶחָד שֶׁהֵעִיד לָהֶם
*שֶׁמַּקְרִיבִין אַף עַל פִּי שֶׁאֵין בַּיִת. בְּמַתְנִיתָא
תָּנָא, ר"א בֶּן יַעֲקֹב אוֹמֵר: שְׁלֹשָׁה נְבִיאִים עָלוּ
עִמָּהֶן מִן הַגּוֹלָה; אֶחָד שֶׁהֵעִיד לָהֶם עַל הַמִּזְבֵּחַ
וְעַל מְקוֹם הַמִּזְבֵּחַ, וְאֶחָד שֶׁהֵעִיד לָהֶם שֶׁמַּקְרִיבִין אַף עַל פִּי שֶׁאֵין בַּיִת,
וְאֶחָד שֶׁהֵעִיד לָהֶם עַל הַתּוֹרָה שֶׁתִּכָּתֵב אַשּׁוּרִית. ת"ר: *בקֶרֶן וְכֶבֶשׁ וִיסוֹד
וְרִיבּוּעַ — מְעַכְּבִין, מִדַּת אׇרְכּוֹ וּמִדַּת רׇחְבּוֹ וּמִדַּת קוֹמָתוֹ אֵין מְעַכְּבִין. מנה"מ?
אָמַר רַב הוּנָא, אָמַר קְרָא: °"הַמִּזְבֵּחַ", כׇּל מָקוֹם שֶׁנֶּאֱמַר "הַמִּזְבֵּחַ" — לְעַכֵּב. אֶלָּא מֵעַתָּה,
כִּיּוֹר לְרַבִּי, וְסוֹבֵב לְרַבִּי יוֹסֵי בְּרַבִּי יְהוּדָה, הָכִי נַמִּי דִּמְעַכֵּב? דִּכְתִ': °"וְנָתַתָּה אוֹתָהּ
תַּחַת כַּרְכֹּב הַמִּזְבֵּחַ מִלְּמָטָּה"; וְתַנְיָא: אֵיזֶהוּ כַּרְכּוֹב? רַבִּי אוֹמֵר: זֶה כִּיּוֹר, רַבִּי יוֹסֵי
בְּרַבִּי יְהוּדָה אוֹמֵר: זֶה הַסּוֹבֵב! אִין, *דְּתַנְיָא: אוֹתוֹ הַיּוֹם נִפְגְּמָה קֶרֶן מִזְבֵּחַ, וְהֵבִיאוּ
בּוּל שֶׁל מֶלַח וּסְתָמוּהוּ. ה] וְלֹא מִפְּנֵי שֶׁכָּשֵׁר לַעֲבוֹדָה, אֶלָּא שֶׁלֹּא יֵרָאֶה מִזְבֵּחַ
פָּגוּם. גשֶׁכׇּל מִזְבֵּחַ שֶׁאֵין לוֹ קֶרֶן וְכֶבֶשׁ וִיסוֹד וְרִיבּוּעַ — פָּסוּל. רַבִּי יוֹסֵי בְּרַבִּי
יְהוּדָה אוֹמֵר: אַף הַסּוֹבֵב. ת"ר: אֵיזֶהוּ כַּרְכּוֹב — בֵּין קֶרֶן לְקֶרֶן מְקוֹם הִילּוּךְ רַגְלֵי
הַכֹּהֲנִים אַמָּה. אַטּוּ הַכֹּהֲנִים בֵּין קֶרֶן לְקֶרֶן הֲווֹ אָזְלִי? אֶלָּא אֵימָא: דוּמְקוֹם הִילּוּךְ
רַגְלֵי הַכֹּהֲנִים אַמָּה. וְהָכְתִיב: °"תַּחַת כַּרְכֻּבּוֹ מִלְּמַטָּה עַד חֶצְיוֹ"! אָמַר רַב
נַחְמָן בַּר יִצְחָק: תְּרֵי הֲווּ, חַד לְנוֹי, וְחַד לַכֹּהֲנִים דְּלָא נִשְׁתָּרְקוּ. "מִדַּת אׇרְכּוֹ
וּמִדַּת רׇחְבּוֹ וּמִדַּת קוֹמָתוֹ אֵין מְעַכְּבִין". א"ר מָנִי: הוּבִלְבַד שֶׁלֹּא יִפְחֲתֶנּוּ
מִמִּזְבֵּחַ שֶׁעָשָׂה מֹשֶׁה. וְכַמָּה? אָמַר רַב יוֹסֵף: אַמָּה. ו] מְחַכּוּ עֲלֵיהּ: °"חָמֵשׁ אַמּוֹת
אֹרֶךְ וְחָמֵשׁ אַמּוֹת רוֹחַב רָבוּעַ יִהְיֶה הַמִּזְבֵּחַ"! אֲמַר לֵיהּ אַבָּיֵי: דִּלְמָא ימְקוֹם
מַעֲרָכָה קָאָמַר מָר? א"ל: *מָר דְּגַבְרָא רַבָּה הוּא יָדַע מַאי קָאָמֵינָא. קָרֵי עֲלַיְיהוּ:
בְּנֵי

עזרא ג | דה"א כח | שם כב | שמות כז | שם | שם לח | שם כז

רש"י

אָמַר רַב יוֹסֵף לָאו הַיְינוּ דְּתַנְיָא כו'. רַב יוֹסֵף חָלָה וְנֶעֱקַר לִמּוּדוֹ,
וּפְעָמִים שֶׁאָמַר דָּבָר, וְנִזְכַּר שֶׁשָּׁנָה הִיפֵּךְ, וְחָזַר בּוֹ (נדרים דף מא.).
וְהָכָא הָכִי אָמַר: הֵיכִי ז] אָמְרִינַן לְעֵיל מִשּׁוּם אֵשׁ שֶׁל שָׁמַיִם מְסַיַּיעְתָּן
לֹא הוּצְרְכוּ לְיוֹתֵר? לָאו הַיְינוּ דְּתַנְיָא. שֶׁאַנְשֵׁי כְּנֶסֶת הַגְּדוֹלָה הִגִּיעוּ
לְסוֹף מִדּוֹתָיו? לָהֶם נִגְלָה ח] מָקוֹם הַמְקוּדָּשׁ לַמִּזְבֵּחַ, מַה שֶּׁלֹּא נִגְלָה
לִשְׁלֹמֹה. וְהָכְתִיב הַכֹּל בִּכְתָב. שֶׁכׇּל מְקוֹמוֹת הַקְּדוֹשׁוֹת וּמִדּוֹתֵיהֶן נִכְתְּבוּ
לְדָוִד. אַלְמָא בְּמִקְדָּשׁ רִאשׁוֹן נַמִּי, הַאי דְּלֹא עֲשָׂאוּהוּ גָּדוֹל – לָאו מִשּׁוּם דְּלֹא
נִגְלָה לִשְׁלֹמֹה הַמָּקוֹם בְּמִדּוֹתָיו! אֶלָּא אֲמַר רַב יוֹסֵף קְרָא ט] אַשְׁכַּח וְדָרַשׁ.
שֶׁנֶּאֱמַר לְדָוִד שִׁשִּׁים אַמָּה בִּמְקוֹם הַמִּזְבֵּחַ, וּשְׁלֹמֹה לֹא הֵבִין לְדָרְשׁוֹ, וְהֵם
דְּרָשׁוּהוּ וְהוֹסִיפוּ עָלָיו לְפִי הַצּוֹרֶךְ לָהֶם. וְלִשִּׁשִּׁים אַמָּה לֹא הוּצְרְכוּ, י] דְּאָמְרִינַן
לְקַמָּן: מִדַּת אׇרְכּוֹ וְרׇחְבּוֹ וְקוֹמָתוֹ אֵין מְעַכְּבִין. מַה בַּיִת ס' אַמָּה. כִּדְכְתִיב
(מלכים א ו): "שִׁשִּׁים אַמָּה אׇרְכּוֹ", אַף מִזְבֵּחַ עַד שִׁשִּׁים אַמָּה יא] רָאוּי לוֹ,
וּמְקוּדָּשׁ הַמָּקוֹם אִם יִרְצוּ. בִּשְׁלָמָא בַּיִת. יָדְעוּ אַנְשֵׁי כְּנֶסֶת הַגְּדוֹלָה מַה
קָּדוֹשׁ לָעֲזָרָה מַה קָּדוֹשׁ לַהֵיכָל. שֶׁנִּיכָּרִים צוּרָתוֹ. יְסוֹדוֹת הַחוֹמוֹת.
מְנָא יָדְעִי. מְקוֹמוֹ הֵיכָא. שְׁלֹשָׁה נְבִיאִים. חַגַּי זְכַרְיָה וּמַלְאָכִי. אֶחָד
הֵעִיד לָהֶם עַל הַמִּזְבֵּחַ. יב] שֶׁיֵּשׁ לוֹ מָקוֹם לְהוֹסִיף עַד שִׁשִּׁים אַמָּה. עַל
מְקוֹם הַמִּזְבֵּחַ. הֵיכָן הָיָה. שֶׁמַּקְרִיבִין אע"פ שֶׁאֵין בַּיִת. דִּקְדוּשַּׁת הַבַּיִת קִדְּשָׁהּ
לְשַׁעְתָּהּ וְקִדְּשָׁהּ לֶעָתִיד לָבֹא. שֶׁתִּכָּתֵב אַשּׁוּרִית. שֶׁמִּתְּחִילָּה נִיתְּנָה לָהֶם
בִּכְתָב עִבְרִי, יג] כְּתַב לִיבּוֹנָאָה, כִּדְאָמַר בְּסַנְהֶדְרִין (דף כא:). וְרִיבּוּעַ. אִם
אֵין הַמִּזְבֵּחַ מְרוּבָּע. יד] שֶׁכׇּל מָקוֹם שֶׁנֶּאֱמַר הַמִּזְבֵּחַ לְעַכֵּב. דְּ"הַמִּזְבֵּחַ" מַשְׁמַע
כְּשֶׁהוּא כֵּן הוּא דְּמִיקְרֵי מִזְבֵּחַ, וְאִי לָא — לָא. וּבְקֶרֶן כְּתִיב (ויקרא ד): "קַרְנוֹת
הַמִּזְבֵּחַ". וּבִיסוֹד כְּתִיב (שם): "אֶל יְסוֹד הַמִּזְבֵּחַ". וּבַכֶּבֶשׁ כְּתִיב: "אֶל פְּנֵי
הַמִּזְבֵּחַ" (שם ו), וְהוּא הַכֶּבֶשׁ, שֶׁהוּא פָּנָיו שֶׁל מִזְבֵּחַ, שֶׁעוֹלִים לוֹ דֶּרֶךְ שָׁם,
כִּי הֵיכִי דְּחָשֵׁיב צַד מִזְרָחִית "פְּנֵי אֹהֶל מוֹעֵד" מֵחֲמַת שֶׁהַפֶּתַח שָׁם. וּבְרִיבּוּעַ
כְּתִיב (שמות כז) "רָבוּעַ יִהְיֶה הַמִּזְבֵּחַ". אֶלָּא מֵעַתָּה כִּיּוֹר לְרַבִּי כו'. דִּכְתִיב
בֵּיהּ "הַמִּזְבֵּחַ", הָכִי נַמִּי דִּמְעַכְּבִי לְרַבִּי, אִם לֹא עָשָׂה צִיּוּרִים שֶׁל פְּרָחִים
וְלִילִּים וּקְלָעִים סָבִיב לַמִּזְבֵּחַ? כְּמוֹ
"סִידוֹ וְכִיּוֹרוֹ"*. זֶה כִּיּוֹר. צִיּוּרִים סָבִיב לְמַעְלָה מֵאֶמְצָעוֹ. אוֹתוֹ הַיּוֹם. שֶׁנִּסֵּךְ כֹּהֵן לְדוֹקִי מֵי הֶחָג עַל רַגְלָיו, וּרְגָמוּהוּ כׇּל הָעָם, כִּדְאָמְרִינַן
בְּסוּכָּה (דף מח:). בּוּל שֶׁל מֶלַח. מְלֹא אֶגְרוֹף שֶׁל מֶלַח, שֶׁמַּעְתִּי. לֹא שֶׁכָּשֵׁר טו] לַעֲבוֹדַת. הַמִּזְבֵּחַ כׇּל זְמַן שֶׁהַקֶּרֶן פָּגוּם, כִּדְמְסַיֵּים וְאָזֵיל:
שֶׁכׇּל מִזְבֵּחַ שֶׁאֵין לוֹ כו'. אַף הַסּוֹבֵב וּמִדְּרַבִּי יוֹסֵי בְּרַבִּי יְהוּדָה נִשְׁמַע לְרַבִּי דְּכִיּוֹר מְעַכֵּב. אֵיזֶהוּ כַּרְכּוֹב. טז] וְקס"ד אַכַּרְכּוֹב דִּקְרָא
קָאֵי. כַּרְכּוֹב — לְשׁוֹן הֶיקֵּף חָרִיץ עֲגוּלָּה, כִּדְאָמְרִינַן בְּ"הַכֹּל שׁוֹחֲטִין" (חולין דף כה.): כׇּל שֶׁעָתִיד לְגָרֵר לְכַרְכֵּב. בֵּין קֶרֶן לְקֶרֶן. אַמָּה רוֹחַב שֶׁכְּנֶגֶד
בֵּין יז] קְרָנוֹת הָיְתָה עֲמוּקָּה וּבוֹלֶטֶת, גּוֹבַהּ מְעַט הָיָה סָבִיב לָהּ בִּשְׂפַת הַמִּזְבֵּחַ. מְקוֹם הִילּוּךְ רַגְלֵי הַכֹּהֲנִים אַמָּה. הָשְׁתָּא מַשְׁמַע: יח] וְהִיא
הָיְתָה אַמָּה שֶׁל מְקוֹם הִילּוּךְ. אַטּוּ כֹּהֲנִים בֵּין קֶרֶן לְקֶרֶן הֲווּ אָזְלִי. וַהֲלֹא כְּשֶׁיַּגִּיעוּ לְקֶרֶן הַקֶּרֶן מְעַכְּבָן יט] מֵהֶיקֵּף! אֶלָּא ה"ק בֵּין קֶרֶן לְקֶרֶן
וּמְקוֹם הִילּוּךְ רַגְלֵי הַכֹּהֲנִים. כ] כְּמִין חָרִיץ עָמוֹק מִמְּקוֹם הַמַּעֲרָכָה *מִשְּׂפַת הַמִּזְבֵּחַ סָבִיב, וּמַקִּיף אֶת מְקוֹם הַמַּעֲרָכָה. וְרׇחְבּוֹ שֶׁל חָרִיץ שְׁנֵי
אַמּוֹת, אַמָּה שֶׁל בֵּין הַקְּרָנוֹת וְאַמָּה שֶׁל מְקוֹם הִילּוּךְ. וְהָכְתִיב. גַּבֵּי מִכְבַּר מַעֲשֵׂה רֶשֶׁת נְחֹשֶׁת שֶׁנְּתָנוּהוּ תַּחַת כַּרְכּוּבּוֹ מִלְּמַטָּה עַד חֶצְיוֹ,
כא] הֶקִּיפוּהוּ לַמִּזְבֵּחַ מֵאֶמְצָעוֹ וּלְמַעְלָה לְבוּשׁ כְּמִין הֶיקֵּף שֶׁל כְּבָרָה, וְהוּא עָשׂוּי נְקָבִים נְקָבִים כִּכְבָרָה כב] וְרֶשֶׁת שֶׁל דַּגִּים, וּמַגִּיעַ לְמַעְלָה עַד
מִתַּחַת לַכַּרְכּוֹב. אַלְמָא כַּרְכּוֹב מִזְבֵּחַ סָבִיב הֲוָה, דְּאִי בְּרֹאשׁ הַמִּזְבֵּחַ — הֵיכִי קָרֵי לַמִּכְבָּר הַנָּתוּן סָבִיב הַקִּיר "תַּחַת כַּרְכֻּבּוֹ"? תְּרֵי הֲווּ.
שְׁנֵי סוֹבְבִין הָיוּ לוֹ לַמִּזְבֵּחַ שֶׁעָשָׂה מֹשֶׁה. חַד לְנוֹי וְחַד לַכֹּהֲנִים דְּלָא נִשְׁתָּרְקוּ. סָבִיב הַקִּיר, מִשֶּׁעָלָה שֵׁשׁ אַמּוֹת גּוֹבַהּ לְרַבִּי יוֹסֵי, דְּאָמַר
לְעֵיל (דף נט:): י' אַמּוֹת גּוֹבְהוֹ, הָיָה הֶיקֵּף כד] *הַבְּלִיטָה קְטַנָּה חוֹגַרְתּוֹ סָבִיב לְנוֹי, וְזֶהוּ סוֹבֵב וְכִיּוֹר דְּאִפְלִיגוּ בֵּיהּ רַבִּי וְר' יוֹסֵי בַּר'
יְהוּדָה לְעֵיל. וּמִתַּחַת לְאוֹתוֹ סוֹבֵב נָתְנוּ הַמִּכְבָּר, וְרׇחְבּוֹ מַגִּיעַ לְמַטָּה עַד חֲצִי הַמִּזְבֵּחַ, וְהוּא הָיָה סִימָן לְהַבְדִּיל בֵּין הַדָּמִים הָעֶלְיוֹנִים
לַדָּמִים הַתַּחְתּוֹנִים, *כִּדְאָמְרִינַן בְּ"אֵיזֶהוּ מְקוֹמָן" (לעיל דף נג.) מֵהַאי קְרָא הַתּוֹרָה נָתְנָה מְחִיצָּה כו'. וְחַד לַכֹּהֲנִים דְּלָא נִשְׁתָּרְקוּ.
וּלְמַעְלָה בְּרֹאשׁ הַמִּזְבֵּחַ הֶעֱמִיקוּ *סוֹבֵב כְּמִין חָרִיץ עָמוֹק דָּבָר מוּעָט, לִהְיוֹת לָהֶם שְׂפָתוֹ הֶיקֵּף מַעֲקֶה קָטָן סָבִיב, שֶׁלֹּא יַחֲלִיקוּ.
דִּלְמָא מְקוֹם מַעֲרָכָה קָאָמַר. דַּהֲוֵי אַמָּה כה] שֶׁבֵּין הַקְּרָנוֹת וּמְקוֹם הִילּוּךְ מְמַעֲטִין בּוֹ אַמָּתַיִם לְכׇל צַד, פָּשׁ לֵיהּ אַמָּה עַל אַמָּה.
בְּנֵי

[לקמן קז: מגילה י. שבועות טז: עדיות פ"ח משנה ו] | [לקמן קח: קכ.] | סוכה מח: [תוספתא שם פרק ג ע"ש] | [כתובות נ: עי' תוספות ערכין ה. ד"ה והא] | [ע"ז מז:]

תוספות

וְלֹא עַל גבי מחילות. בור של שיתין לא היה חשוב מחילה, כיון דהוא לורך מזבח. אף מזבח ששים אמה. והא דאמר (בסוף) [בריש] "כיסוי הדם" (חולין דף פג:): קמוסיף כו] אבניין – היינו כשהיה המזבח עד ששים. כז] א"נ, מגובה פריך התם. אי נמי, פריך קמוסיף – שלא יהא רבוע, שעל כל מליקת עוף אין יכולת לתת עפר בכל סביביו כדי לרבעו כמשפטו.

אחד שהעיד להם על המזבח. תימה: כח] קרא כתיב ביחזקאל (מג) *"והאריאל שתים עשרה אמות", אלמא מקום המערכה כ"ד על כ"ד, ומהאי קרא דרשינן במתני' דמדות כט] (פ"ג מ"א)! וי"ל: דאי לאו עדות היינו מפרשי' עם מקום קרנות, שלא לשנות ממזבח שלמה ל]. ואחד שמקריבין אע"פ שאין בית. דקדושת בית קידשה לשעתה ולעתיד. ולא דמי לקדושת הארץ, דקי"ל דבטלה, כדמוכח בפ"ק דחולין (ו:) גבי בית שאן. שיש חילוק ביניהם, כדפרישית לעיל (סא. ד"ה מאי).

מדת ארכו ומדת רחבו אין מעכבין. והא דכתיב: "הכל בכתב מיד ה' עלי השכיל" ומיירי אף גבי מזבח, כדאיתא פרק "כיסוי הדם" (חולין פג.) דמה בית ששים אף מזבח ששים – היינו שיהא קדוש עד ששים אם ירצו להרחיבו, ולא שיהא חובה לעשות כן.

בלמה

עין משפט נר מצוה

יד א מיי' פ"ב מהל' בית הבחירה הל' ד:

טו ב ג מיי' שם הל' יז:

טז ד מיי' שם הלכה ז:

יז ה ו מיי' שם הל' יז:

נ"ק (beside Tosafot line 3)

גי' הל"ק והאריאל שתים עשרה אמות ומהאי קרא דרשינן במתניתין דמדות שמן האמלעי הוא מודד י"ב אמה לכל רוח אלמא מקום המערכה כ"ד על כ"ד וא"כ עדותן ל"ל וי"ל כו' כל"ל

בליטה קטנה וחוגרתו כו' מלמטה עד חליו ל"ק

כדדרשינן ל"ק

סביב ל"ק

נ"א עד שפת המזבח וגיר' ל"ק לשפת המזבח

שיטה מקובצת

א] אשכחו ודרוש ויאמר: ב] (מזבח לעולה לישראל): ג] שר הגדול: ד] מקום ר' שמואל אות ו' נמחק: ה] וסתמוהו לא מפני אות ו' נמחק: ו] אמה אחיכו עליה: ז] היכי אמרי לעיל משום דאש של שמים: ח] נגלה המקים: ט] קרא אשכחו ודרוש: י] ואמרינן לקמן: יא] אמה יש לו מקום ראוי ומקודש אם ירצו הס"ד: יב] המזבח שמקומו מקודש עד ששים אמה הס"ד: יג] עברי שהוא כתב: יד] מה"ד כל מקום: טו] שכשר המזבח לעבודה כל: טז] כרכוב קס"ד אכרכוב דקרא קאי וכרכוב לשון: יז] בין הקרנות היתה עמוקה הרוצה ובליטת גובה: יח] משמע דהיא היתה אמה: יט] מעכבן מלהקיף המזבח הס"ד ומה"ד אלא: כ] הכהנים אמה היה יותר כמין חריץ ממקום המערכה עד שפת המזבח סביב: כא] חציו והקיפוהו למזבח: כב] ככברה כרשת של: כג] המזבח סביב היה כרכוב דאי: כד] היקף בליטה קטנה חוגרתו סביב ולנוי וזהו: כה] אמה על אמה שבין הקרנות למקום הילוך: כו] אבנין ומאי קפידא יש אם הוסיף והלא מוסיפין עד כ' אמה: כז] ששים וקא מוסיף עליו כל שעה בכסוי א"נ: כח] תימה הא קרא כתיב כו' עשרה אמה על י"ב אמה [אא"ה לשון הכתוב עשרה אורך בשתים עשרה רוחב עכ"ה]: כט] דמדות דהיה המזבח ל"ב על ל"ב ואם כן מה היו צריכים לעדות הנביא וי"ל: ל] שלמה שהיה מקום המערכה שלו כ' על כ':

גמרא

°"בְּנֵי קְטוּרָה". בְּנֵי אַחְתֵיהּ דְּרַבִּי טַרְפוֹן הֲווּ יָתְבִי קַמֵּיהּ דְּרַבִּי א] טַרְפוֹן, פְּתַח וַאֲמַר: °"וַיֹּסֶף אַבְרָהָם וַיִּקַּח אִשָּׁה וּשְׁמָהּ יוֹחֲנִי". אָמְרִי לֵיהּ: "קְטוּרָה" כְּתִיב! קָרֵי עֲלֵיהֶם: "בְּנֵי קְטוּרָה". אָמַר ב] אַבַּיֵי בַּר הוּנָא אָמַר רַב חָמָא בַּר גּוּרְיָא: ג] אגְּזִירִין שֶׁעָשָׂה מֹשֶׁה, אוֹרְכָּן אַמָּה וְרׇחְבָּן אַמָּה, וְעוֹבְיָין כְּמַחַק גּוֹדֶשׁ סְאָה. אָמַר רַבִּי יִרְמְיָה: בְּאַמָּה ד] גְּדוּמָה. אָמַר רַב יוֹסֵף, וְלָאו הַיְינוּ דְּתַנְיָא: °"עַל הָעֵצִים אֲשֶׁר עַל הָאֵשׁ אֲשֶׁר עַל הַמִּזְבֵּחַ" — שֶׁלֹּא יְהוּ עֵצִים יוֹצְאִין מִן הַמִּזְבֵּחַ כְּלוּם. תְּנַן הָתָם: *בכֶּבֶשׁ הָיָה לִדְרוֹמָהּ שֶׁל מִזְבֵּחַ, אוֹרֶךְ שְׁלֹשִׁים וּשְׁתַּיִם עַל רוֹחַב שֵׁשׁ עֶשְׂרֵה. מְנָא ה"מ? אָמַר רַב הוּנָא, אָמַר קְרָא: °"וְשָׁחַט אוֹתוֹ עַל יֶרֶךְ הַמִּזְבֵּחַ צָפֹנָה" — שֶׁיְּהֵא יָרֵךְ בַּצָּפוֹן וּפָנָיו בַּדָּרוֹם. אֵימָא: יָרֵךְ בַּצָּפוֹן וּפָנָיו בַּצָּפוֹן! אָמַר רָבָא: רְמִי גַּבְרָא אַאַפֵּיהּ. א"ל אַבַּיֵי: אַדְּרַבָּה, *תָּרֵיץ וְאוֹתֵיב גַּבְרָא! א"ל: °"רָבוּעַ" כְּתִיב. ה] וְהָא מִיבָּעֵי לֵיהּ דִּמְרַבַּע רִבּוּעֵי! מִי כְּתִיב "מְרוּבָּע"? וְלִיטַעֲמִיךְ, מִי כְּתִיב "רָבוּץ"? ו] א"ל: "רָבוּעַ" כְּתִיב, דְּמַשְׁמַע הָכִי וּמַשְׁמַע הָכִי. וְתַנָּא מַיְיתֵי לַהּ מֵהָכָא, דְּתַנְיָא, רַבִּי יְהוּדָה אוֹמֵר: ז] °"וּמַעֲלֹתֵיהוּ פְּנוֹת קָדִים" *גכׇּל פִּינּוֹת שֶׁאַתָּה פּוֹנֶה — לֹא יְהוּ אֶלָּא דֶּרֶךְ יָמִין, לַמִּזְרָח. וְאֵימָא: ח] שְׂמֹאל לַמִּזְרָח? לָא ס"ד, *דְּתָנֵי רָמֵי בַּר (*יְחִזְקִיָּה) יָם שֶׁעָשָׂה שְׁלֹמֹה, °"עוֹמֵד עַל שְׁנֵים עָשָׂר ט] (עַמּוּדִים) בָּקָר שְׁלֹשָׁה פֹנִים צָפוֹנָה וּשְׁלֹשָׁה פֹנִים יָמָּה וּשְׁלֹשָׁה פֹנִים נֶגְבָּה וּשְׁלֹשָׁה פֹנִים י] מִזְרָחָה", כׇּל פִּינּוֹת שֶׁאַתָּה פּוֹנֶה — לֹא יְהוּ אֶלָּא דֶּרֶךְ יָמִין, לַמִּזְרָח. הַהוּא מִיבָּעֵי לֵיהּ לְגוּפֵיהּ! א"כ, "פֹּנִים" "פֹּנִים" לָמָּה לִי? שָׁאַל רַבִּי שִׁמְעוֹן בֶּן יוֹסֵי בֶּן לָקוֹנְיָא אֶת ר' יוֹסֵי: אוֹמֵר הָיָה ר"ש בֶּן יוֹחַי, *דאֲוִיר יֵשׁ בֵּין כֶּבֶשׁ לַמִּזְבֵּחַ? אָמַר לוֹ: וְאַתָּה אִי אַתָּה אוֹמֵר כֵּן? וַהֲלֹא כְּבָר נֶאֱמַר: °"וְעָשִׂיתָ עֹלֹתֶיךָ הַבָּשָׂר וְהַדָּם", המָה דָּם בִּזְרִיקָה — אַף בָּשָׂר בִּזְרִיקָה! אָמַר לוֹ: שֶׁאֲנִי אוֹמֵר, עוֹמֵד בְּצַד מַעֲרָכָה וְזוֹרֵק. א"ל: כְּשֶׁהוּא זוֹרֵק, לְמַעֲרָכָה דְּלוּקָה הוּא זוֹרֵק אוֹ לְמַעֲרָכָה שֶׁאֵינָהּ דְּלוּקָה הוּא זוֹרֵק? הֱוֵי אוֹמֵר: לְמַעֲרָכָה דְּלוּקָה הוּא *זוֹרֵק; הָתָם מִשּׁוּם דְּלָא אֶפְשָׁר! יא] רַב פָּפָּא אָמַר: כִּי דָּם, מָה דָּם אֲוִיר קַרְקַע מַפְסִיקוֹ — אַף בָּשָׂר אֲוִיר קַרְקַע מַפְסִיקוֹ. וְאָמַר רַב יְהוּדָה: וּשְׁנֵי כְבָשִׁים קְטַנִּים יוֹצְאִין מִן הַכֶּבֶשׁ, יב] שֶׁבָּהֶן פּוֹנִים לַיְסוֹד וְלַסּוֹבֵב, וּמוּבְדָּלִין מִן הַמִּזְבֵּחַ מְלֹא נִימָא, מִשּׁוּם שֶׁנֶּאֱמַר: "סָבִיב". יג] וְרַבִּי אַבָּהוּ אָמַר: "רָבוּעַ". וְאִיצְטְרִיךְ לְמִכְתַּב "סָבִיב" וְאִיצְטְרִיךְ לְמִכְתַּב "רָבוּעַ", דְּאִי כָּתַב רַחֲמָנָא "סָבִיב" הֲוָה אָמֵינָא דְּעָגִיל מְעַגָּל — כָּתַב רַחֲמָנָא "רָבוּעַ", וְאִי כָּתַב רַחֲמָנָא "רָבוּעַ" הֲוָה אָמֵינָא דַּאֲרִיךְ וְקָטִין — כָּתַב רַחֲמָנָא "סָבִיב". תְּנַן הָתָם: *הַכֶּבֶשׁ וְהַמִּזְבֵּחַ שִׁשִּׁים וּשְׁתַּיִם. הָנֵי שִׁיתִּין יד] וְאַרְבְּעָה הָווּ! *ונִמְצָא פּוֹרֵחַ אַמָּה עַל טו] יְסוֹד וְאַמָּה עַל סוֹבֵב.

אָמַר

רש"י

בְּנֵי קְטוּרָה. בְּנֵי אַבְרָהָם הֵם, אֲבָל לֹא כְּזֶרַע יִצְחָק וְיַעֲקֹב. הָכִי גָּרְסִינַן: הֲווּ יָתְבִי קַמֵּיהּ דְּרַבִּי טַרְפוֹן. וְלָא הָווּ אָמְרִי מִידֵי. פְּתַח וַאֲמַר. כְּדֵי שֶׁיְּדַבְּרוּ. יוֹחֲנִי. מִילְּתָא בְּעָלְמָא הוּא דְּקָאָמַר, כְּדֵי לִפְתּוֹחַ פִּיהֶם. בְּנֵי קְטוּרָה. אֵינָם יוֹדְעִין לְדַבֵּר בַּהֲלָכָה. גְּזִירִין. שְׁנֵי גִּזְרֵי עֵצִים צָרִיךְ לְסַדֵּר בְּרֹאשׁ טז] הַמִּזְבֵּחַ הַמַּעֲרָכָה, לְתָמִיד שֶׁל שַׁחַר בְּכֹהֵן אֶחָד, יז] וּלְתָמִיד שֶׁל בֵּין הָעַרְבַּיִם בִּשְׁנֵי כֹהֲנִים, כִּדְקַיְימָא לָן בְּסֵדֶר יוֹמָא (דף כו:). אַמָּה אׇרְכּוֹ וְאַמָּה רׇחְבּוֹ. כְּמִידַּת מְקוֹם הַמַּעֲרָכָה. בְּאַמָּה גְּדוּמָה. קְצָרָה, שֶׁלֹּא יֵצְאוּ חוּץ לַמַּעֲרָכָה וִיעַכְּבוּ הַכֹּהֲנִים מִלְּהַקִּיף. לָאו הַיְינוּ דְּתַנְיָא כו'. וְאַמָּה גְּדוּמָה לָמָּה לִי? אֶלָּא אַמָּה מְלוּמְלֶמֶת. מְנָהֲנֵי מִילֵּי. שֶׁהַכֶּבֶשׁ בַּדָּרוֹם. יָרֵךְ. רַגְלַיִם. וּפָנָיו בַּדָּרוֹם, כְּאָדָם הַשּׁוֹכֵב אַרְכָּה וְרַגְלָיו לַצָּפוֹן – נִמְצָא רֹאשׁוֹ וּפָנָיו לַדָּרוֹם. אֵימָא יָרֵךְ בַּצָּפוֹן וּפָנָיו בַּצָּפוֹן. כְּאָדָם הַיּוֹשֵׁב זָקוּף. רְמִי גַּבְרָא אַאַפֵּיהּ. שִׁיעֵר בְּאָדָם הַשּׁוֹכֵב אַרְכָּה. אַדְּרַבָּה תָּרֵיץ וְאוֹתֵיב גַּבְרָא. זְקָפוּהוּ וְהוֹשִׁיבוּהוּ, וְנִמְצָא רֹאשׁוֹ וְרַגְלָיו לְרוּחַ אַחַת. רָבוּעַ כְּתִיב. דְּ"רָבוּעַ" בְּאָדָם רוֹבֵץ וּמוּשְׁכָּב שִׁיעֵר הַכָּתוּב. וְהַאי רָבוּעַ מִיבָּעֵי לֵיהּ דִּמְרַבַּע רִיבּוּעֵי. שֶׁיְּהֵא מְרוּבָּע וְלֹא עָגוֹל. יח] ה"ג: רָבוּעַ כְּתִיב דְּמַשְׁמַע הָכִי וּמַשְׁמַע הָכִי. הִלְכָּךְ תַּרְוַויְיהוּ יָלֵיף מִינָּהּ. וְתַנָּא. דִּבְרַיְיתָא מַיְיתֵי לַהּ. לְהָא יט] דְּאַיְיתֵי רַב הוּנָא מִ"יֶּרֶךְ הַמִּזְבֵּחַ" מַיְיתֵי תַּנָּא מֵהָכָא. כ] וּמַעֲלוֹתֵיהוּ פְּנוֹת קָדִים כׇּל פִּינּוֹת שֶׁאַתָּה פּוֹנֶה יְהוּ דֶּרֶךְ יָמִין לַמִּזְרָח. הַאי קְרָא בַּמִּזְבֵּחַ כְּתִיב בִּיחֶזְקֵאל, וְקָאָמַר כא] *שֶׁתָּמִיד כֶּבֶשׁ מַעֲלוֹתָיו בְּרוּחַ הָרְאוּיָה לִפְנוֹת הֵימֶנָּה לַמִּזְרָח, וּתְהֵא אוֹתוֹ הַפְּנִיָּיה לְיָמִין, וְאֵין לְךָ רוּחַ רְאוּיָה לְכָךְ אֶלָּא דָּרוֹם. וּפָרְכִינַן: וְאֵימָא דֶּרֶךְ שְׂמֹאל לַמִּזְרָח. נְהִי דִּ"פְנוֹת קָדִים" כְּתִיב בִּקְרָא, אֲבָל דֶּרֶךְ יָמִין לָא כְּתִיב בֵּיהּ. כב] הַעֲמִידֵהוּ בַּצָּפוֹן, וּכְשֶׁתַּגִּיעַ לְרֹאשׁ הַמִּזְבֵּחַ – פְּנֵה אֶל קֶרֶן מִזְרָחִית צְפוֹנִית, כג] וְדֶרֶךְ שְׂמֹאלוֹ! לָא ס"ד. שֶׁיְּהוּ פוֹנִים לִשְׂמֹאל, אֶלָּא כד] דֶּרֶךְ יָמִין. לֹא יְהוּ אֶלָּא דֶּרֶךְ יָמִין. כִּי מִינָּהּ דִּקְרָא, דְּקָחָשֵׁיב וְאָזֵיל דֶּרֶךְ יָמִין: מִצָּפוֹן לַמַּעֲרָב, וּמִמַּעֲרָב לַדָּרוֹם. וּכְשֶׁאַתָּה מַקִּיף שׁוּם דָּבָר וּפָנֶיךָ אֵלָיו וְאַתָּה סוֹבְבוֹ מִצָּפוֹן לַמַּעֲרָב – לִימִינְךָ אַתָּה הוֹלֵךְ. לַמִּזְרָח. מֵהַאי קְרָא לָא נָפְקָא לָן. כה] *וּמֵהָכָא נָפְקָא לָן דֶּרֶךְ יָמִין, וּמִקְּרָא דִּלְעֵיל דִּכְתִיב כו] "קָדִים" שָׁמְעִינַן לַמִּזְרָח, דְּלָא תֵּימָא דֶּרֶךְ יָמִין לַמַּעֲרָב, וִיהֵא כֶּבֶשׁ בַּצָּפוֹן. מִיבְּעֵיָא לֵיהּ לְגוּפֵיהּ. לְהוֹדִיעֲךָ מוֹשַׁב הַיָּם הֵיאָךְ, וּמִנַּיִן לְךָ לִלְמוֹד הֵימֶנּוּ לְפִינּוֹת הַמִּקְדָּשׁ בְּצׇרְכֵי עֲבוֹדָה? אֲוִיר יֵשׁ בֵּין כֶּבֶשׁ לַמִּזְבֵּחַ. שֶׁלֹּא הָיָה רֹאשׁ הַכֶּבֶשׁ נוֹגֵעַ בַּמִּזְבֵּחַ, אֶלָּא אֲוִיר מְעַט מַפְסִיק בֵּינֵיהֶם. ה"ג: אָמַר לוֹ וְאַתָּה אִי אַתָּה אוֹמֵר כֵּן. מָה דָּם. עוֹלָה כז] שֶׁעוֹמֵד בָּאָרֶץ וְזוֹרֵק מִן הַכְּלִי, כִּדְכְתִיב "וְזָרְקוּ", אַף בָּשָׂר בִּזְרִיקָה. אַלְמָא, אֲוִיר יֵשׁ וּמֵחֲמַת הָאֲוִיר כח] *הוּא צָרִיךְ זְרִיקָה, שֶׁעוֹמֵד בַּכֶּבֶשׁ וְזוֹרֵק אֶל עֵבֶר הָאֲוִיר לַמַּעֲרָכָה. אָמַר לוֹ שֶׁאֲנִי אוֹמֵר כט] זוֹרֵק עוֹמֵד בְּצַד הַמַּעֲרָכָה. בְּרֹאשׁ הַמִּזְבֵּחַ, וְזוֹרֵק. ל] וּלְהָכִי אֲתָא קְרָא. אָמַר לוֹ כְּשֶׁהוּא זוֹרֵק לְמַעֲרָכָה דְּלוּקָה הוּא זוֹרֵק כו'. כְּלוֹמַר, מִשּׁוּם הָא לָמָּה לִי קְרָא? פְּשִׁיטָא דְּעַל כׇּרְחוֹ הוּא זוֹרְקוֹ, שֶׁהֲרֵי אֵין יָכוֹל לְסַדֵּר סָבִיב עַל רָאשֵׁי הָעֵצִים שֶׁאֵין הַמַּעֲרָכָה דְּלוּקָה שָׁם, אֶלָּא הֵימֶנּוּ וָהָלְאָה מָקוֹם שֶׁהַמַּעֲרָכָה דּוֹלֶקֶת, וְהָתָם מִשּׁוּם דְּלָא אֶפְשָׁר הוּא. לא] *דְּע"כ כִּי אֲתָא קְרָא לְאַשְׁמוּעִינַן אֲתָא דְּיֵשׁ אֲוִיר בֵּין כֶּבֶשׁ לַמִּזְבֵּחַ. רַב פָּפָּא אָמַר. לָא מְגַלֵּית אָמְרַתְּ דְּהֶיקֵּשׁ לב] לְאַשְׁמוּעִינַן אֲתָא דְּעוֹמֵד בְּצַד הַמַּעֲרָכָה וְזוֹרֵק, דְּהַפְסָקָה אֲוִיר רִצְפָּה בָּעֵינַן, כִּי דָּם. מָה דָּם אֲוִיר קַרְקַע. הָרִצְפָּה מַפְסִיק בֵּינוֹ לַמִּזְבֵּחַ, אַף בָּשָׂר כו'. שְׁנֵי כְבָשִׁים קְטַנִּים יוֹצְאִין מִן הַכֶּבֶשׁ כו'. אוֹתוֹ שֶׁפּוֹנִין בּוֹ לַסּוֹבֵב לג] יָצָא בְּמִזְרָחוֹ שֶׁל כֶּבֶשׁ לְיָמִין, וְיוֹצֵא וּמַתְחִיל בְּשִׁיפּוּלוֹ שֶׁל כֶּבֶשׁ וְנִמְשָׁךְ וְעוֹלֶה בַּאֲלַכְסוֹן עַד שֶׁמַּגִּיעַ לַסּוֹבֵב. וְהַפּוֹנֶה לַיְסוֹד יוֹצֵא לְמַעֲרָבוֹ לד] לְהוֹלִיךְ בּוֹ שִׁירַיִם שֶׁל חַטָּאת, *שֶׁיּוֹרֵד מִן הַמִּזְבֵּחַ פּוֹנֶה לִשְׂמֹאלוֹ לִיסוֹד דְּרוֹמִי. וּמַתְחִיל לָצֵאת בְּשִׁיפּוּלוֹ שֶׁל כֶּבֶשׁ רָחוֹק מִן הַמִּזְבֵּחַ, כְּדֵי שֶׁיְּהֵא נוֹחַ לִשְׁפּוֹעַ וְלֵירֵד לַיְסוֹד. מִשּׁוּם שֶׁנֶּאֱמַר סָבִיב. שֶׁיְּהֵא הֶיקֵּף לַמִּזְבֵּחַ כׇּל דְּהוּ. וְאִי הָווּ מְחוּבָּרִין – שׁוּב אֵין לה] הֶיקֵּף, אֲפִילּוּ בְּחוּט אֵין אָדָם יָכוֹל לְסוֹבְבוֹ. רַבִּי אַבָּהוּ אָמַר רָבוּעַ. וְאִי מְחוּבָּרִין לָא הָוֵי בִּנְיָנוֹ מְרוּבָּע. וְאִיצְטְרִיךְ לְמִיכְתַּב סָבִיב וְאִיצְטְרִיךְ לְמִיכְתַּב רָבוּעַ. וְאַף עַל גַּב דְּאַפְקִינְהוּ לְתַרְוַויְיהוּ לְהָךְ דְּרָשָׁא שֶׁלֹּא יְהֵא בִּנְיָן אַחֵר מְחוּבָּר לוֹ. דְּעָגִיל מְעוּגָּל. וְלֹא יְהֵא לוֹ זָוִיּוֹת. דַּאֲרִיךְ וְקָטִין. אׇרְכּוֹ יוֹתֵר עַל רׇחְבּוֹ, וְזָוִיּוֹת יְהֵא לוֹ. כָּתַב רַחֲמָנָא סָבִיב. שֶׁיְּהוּ כׇּל סְבִיבָיו שָׁוִין. שִׁיתִּין וְאַרְבַּע הָווּ. דְּהָא תְּנַן לְעֵיל: אוֹרֶךְ הַכֶּבֶשׁ ל"ב אַמָּה. וְכֵן הַמִּזְבֵּחַ. וּמְשַׁנֵּי: נִמְצָא שֶׁרֹאשׁ הַכֶּבֶשׁ פּוֹרֵחַ וְעוֹלֶה עַל בְּנִיסַת הַיְסוֹד וְהַסּוֹבֵב. וּמַגִּיעַ לְרֹאשׁ הַמִּזְבֵּחַ, נִמְצְאוּ שְׁתֵּי אַמּוֹת הָעֶלְיוֹנוֹת שֶׁלּוֹ מוּבְלָעִים *בִּשְׁתֵּי אַמּוֹת לו].

ה"ג

תוספות

באמה גדומה. חסירה. ובערוך *פירש: גרומה ברי"ש, כמו "נותן לו את גירומיו" לז] (ב"ב פח:). ורב יוסף פריך ממתניתא שלא יהו לח] *עצים יוצאים. **אויר** קרקע מפסיקו. *קרקע לאו דוקא, לט] שהיה פורח אמה על יסוד ואמה על סובב. ובלאו קרא היה צריך אויר, משום שנאמר "סביב" כדבסמוך, אלא דסגי במשהו. אבל הכא בעינן אויר גדל וניכר שהוא לצורך אויר. **דאריך** וקטין. והא דכתיב: "חמש אמות אורך וחמש אמות רוחב" – למצוה, והאי קרא לעכב. ומיהו קשה, לעכב מ"המזבח" נפקא מ].

שיתין וד' הוו. *היינו כלוי, דאמר לעיל (דף נד.) בדמים. ונקיט כותיה משום תרגום דידן, דמתרגמינן: באחסנתיה יתבני מקדשא. אבל לרב דלא הוה ליה יסוד בבנין – הוה ליה מזבח מן הצפון ולדרום ל"א וכבש ל"ב – הרי ס"ג, ה"ל לשנויי שהיה פורח על הסובב אמה.

עין משפט נר מצוה

[ערך (רגם) [גרס] ה' ע"ש]

נ"ל עולים

יח א מיי' פ"ו מהלכות איסורי מזבח הל' ג:

יט ב מיי' פ"ב מהלכות בית הבחירה הל' יג:

כ ג מיי' פ"ו מהלכות מעה"ק הלכה יא:

כא ד מיי' פ"ב מהל' בית הבחירה הלכה יג:

עי' רש"ק ועי' בס' פנים מאירות שהגיה בנ"ע על תוס' דהא לעיל נב. פריך מיניה לרב ומשני אימא כנגד אמה יסוד וכנגד אמה סובב ע"ש

כב ה מיי' פ"ו מהלכות מעה"ק הלכה ד:

כג ו מיי' פ"ב מהלכות בית הבחירה הלכה יד:

כד ז מיי' שם הלכה יג:

יומא נח:

מסורת הש"ס

מדות פ"ג מ"ג

[תרגום של בשלום וכמישור בשלמא ובתרלותא עי' ערוך ערך תרכן]

סוטה טו: [סוכה מח] יומא עז: יז: נג. נו.

[נ"ל יחזקאל]

פסחים לד. עז. לקמן קד.

נ"ל שתעמוד נ"ק

זורקו והתם נ"ק

גליון הש"ס

תוס' ד"ה אויר וכו' קרקע לאו דוקא. עיין לקמן דף פז ע"ב תוספות ד"ה אויר:

מדות פ"ה מ"ח

לעיל נד.

דמהכא נ"ק

הוא זורק נ"ק

וע"כ נ"ק

נ"ל כשיורד נ"ק

בל"ג אמות של מזבח נ"ק

שיטה מקובצת

א] טרפון ולא הוו אמרי מידי פתח: ב] רבי אבין בר תיבת אביי נמחק: ג] גזירין שעשה משה אורכן אמה כו'. ואם תאמר והלא מקום המערכה לא היתה כי אם אמה על אמה וא"כ גיזרין מכסין כולה והיאך היו משימין הקיסמין וי"ל דהיו מניחין אותן על צידיהן והיו נותנין קיסמין בינתים להבעירם: ד] גדומה. פ"ה קצרה כמו גדמת ופריך [רב יוסף] דתניא ואם כן מצומצמת היו יכולים לעשות ואמאי עשו אותה קצרה. וקצת קשה דמשמע דפריך מפשטיה דקרא. לכך נראה כגירסת הערוך גרומה מלשון נותן לו את גירומיו דהיינו יתר על [המשקל] כלומר אמה גדולה והשתא פריך שפיר מהיא דשלא יהיו העצים יוצאים מן המזבח ואמה מצומצמת הוי ליה למעבד: ה] כתיב האי רבוע מיבעי תיבת והא ל"ש ונמחק: ו] רבוץ אלא רבוע תיבת א"ל ל"ש: ז] ומעלתהו פנות: ח] ואימא דרך שמאל למזרח כו' בר יחזקאל תיבת יחזקיה נמחק: ט] תיבת עמודים נמחק: י] ושלשה פונים קדמה כו' למזרח לא נפקא לן מהאי קרא אלא דרך ימין נפקא לן מהאי קרא וכ"ת דרך ימין למערב ויהא הכבש בצפון הא כתיב באידך קרא דלעיל פנות קדים תיבת מזרחה נמחק: יא] אפשר הוא רב: יב] שבהן פונים ליסוד פי' במערבה של כבש היה כבש קטן שבו פונין ליסוד וא"ת למה לי כבש קטן ירד למטה על הרצפה וישפוך שירים על היסוד וי"ל שמא יקרוש הדם אם יאחר כל כך: יג] סביב רבי ואות ו' נמחק: יד] עיין בהשמטות בסוף המסכת: טו] על היסוד ואמה על הסובב: טז] תיבת המזבח נמחק: יז] אחד ותמיד של: יח] (א"ל) ה"ג אלא רבוע: יט] להא מילתיה דאייתי רב הונא דכבש בדרום מירך המזבח מהכא הס"ד ותיבות מייתי תנא נמחק: כ] ומעלתהו: כא] וקאמר שתעמיד כבש שיהו מעלותיו ותיבת שתמיד נמחק: כב] ביה הלכך העמידהו: כג] צפונית דרך שמאל: כד] אלא לימין הס"ד: כה] לן אלא מהכא נפקא: כו] דכתיב פנות קדים שמעינן שיהיו הפניות של מזבח למזרח: כז] עולה בזריקה שעומד: כח] האויר הוזקק לזריקה שעומד כו' ותיבת הוא נמחק ותיבת צריך ל"ש: כט] אומר עומד תיבת זורק ל"ש: ל] וזורק וגזירת הכתוב הוא הס"ד: לא] הוא אלא ע"כ כי: לב] דהיקש אתא לאשמועינן דעומד וכו' וזורק דהפסקת אויר רצפה: לג] לסובב יוצא במזרחו של כבש בימין ומתחיל ויוצא בשפולו: לד] למערבו להוריד בו שירי דם חטאת כשיורד מן המזבח: לה] אין לו היקף: לו] אמות של מזבח הס"ד: לז] גירומיו כלומר גדולה ורב: לח] ממתניתא שלא יהו עצים: לט] דוקא (עיין בתוס' דף פז ע"ב) שהרי היה פורח על אמה יסוד ועל אמה סובב אלא ר"ל אויר בעלמא מפסיקו וא"ת ולמה לי היקש לכך הא כתיב סביב לומר שיהא ריבוע ויכולים להקיף בחוט וי"ל דר"ל אויר גדול וכו'. מהר"פ: מ] נפקא וי"ל דהו"א דוקא של משה צריך ארכו כרחבו אבל במקדש לא לכך צריך רבוע כזה:

אָמַר רָמִי בַּר חָמָא: א] (א) *כָּל כִּבְשֵׁי כְבָשִׁים שָׁלֹשׁ אַמּוֹת לְאַמָּה, ב] חוּץ מִכִּבְשׁוֹ שֶׁל מִזְבֵּחַ שֶׁהָיָה שָׁלֹשׁ אַמּוֹת וּמֶחֱצָה וְאֶצְבַּע וּשְׁלִישׁ אֶצְבַּע *בְּזַכְרוּתָא.§ **מתני'** ג] מְנָחוֹת הָיוּ נִקְמָצוֹת אבְּכָל מָקוֹם בָּעֲזָרָה, וְנֶאֱכָלוֹת לִפְנִים מִן הַקְּלָעִים, לְזִכְרֵי כְהוּנָּה, בְּכָל מַאֲכָל, לְיוֹם וְלַיְלָה עַד חֲצוֹת.§ **גמ'** *א"ר אֶלְעָזָר: מִנְחָה ד] שֶׁנִּקְמְצָה בבַּהֵיכָל — כְּשֵׁירָה, שֶׁכֵּן מָצִינוּ בְּסִילּוּק בָּזִיכִין. מְתִיב רַבִּי יִרְמְיָה: °"וְקָמַץ מִשָּׁם" — מִמָּקוֹם שֶׁרַגְלֵי הַזָּר עוֹמְדוֹת. בֶּן בְּתֵירָא אוֹמֵר: מִנַּיִן שֶׁאִם קָמַץ בִּשְׂמֹאל, ה] שֶׁיַּחֲזִיר וְיִקְמוֹץ בְּיָמִין — ת"ל: "מִשָּׁם", מִמָּקוֹם שֶׁקָּמַץ כְּבָר! אִיכָּא דְּאָמְרִי: הוּא מוֹתִיב לָהּ וְהוּא מְפָרֵק לָהּ, אִיכָּא דְּאָמְרִי: א"ל ר' ו] *עֲקִיבָא לְר' יִרְמְיָה בַּר תַּחֲלִיפָא: אַסְבְּרָא לָךְ, לָא נִצְרְכָא אֶלָּא לְהַכְשִׁיר כָּל הָעֲזָרָה כּוּלָּהּ; סָלְקָא דַּעְתָּךְ אָמִינָא: הוֹאִיל וְעוֹלָה קׇדְשֵׁי קָדָשִׁים וּמִנְחָה קׇדְשֵׁי קָדָשִׁים, מָה עוֹלָה טְעוּנָה צָפוֹן — אַף מִנְחָה טְעוּנָה צָפוֹן. *מַה לְּעוֹלָה, שֶׁכֵּן כָּלִיל! מֵחַטָּאת. מַה לְּחַטָּאת, שֶׁכֵּן מְכַפֶּרֶת עַל חַיָּיבֵי כְרֵיתוֹת! מֵאָשָׁם. מַה לְּאָשָׁם שֶׁכֵּן מִינֵי דָמִים! מִכּוּלְּהוּ. ז] מַה לְּכוּלְּהוּ שֶׁכֵּן מִינֵי דָמִים! אֶלָּא אִיצְטְרִיךְ, סד"א: הוֹאִיל וּכְתִיב °"וְהִגִּישָׁהּ אֶל הַמִּזְבֵּחַ", °"וְהֵרִים מִמֶּנּוּ בְּקוּמְצוֹ", מַה הַגָּשָׁה גבְּקֶרֶן מַעֲרָבִית דְּרוֹמִית — אַף קְמִיצָה בְּקֶרֶן מַעֲרָבִית דְּרוֹמִית, קָא מַשְׁמַע לָן. אָמַר רַבִּי יוֹחָנָן: *שְׁלָמִים שֶׁשְּׁחָטָן בַּהֵיכָל דכְּשֵׁרִים, שֶׁנֶּאֱמַר: °"וּשְׁחָטוֹ (אוֹתוֹ) פֶּתַח אֹהֶל מוֹעֵד", וְלֹא יְהֵא *טָפֵל חָמוּר מִן הָעִיקָּר. מֵיתִיבֵי, *רַבִּי ח] יוֹחָנָן בֶּן בְּתֵירָה אוֹמֵר: מִנַּיִן שֶׁאִם הִקִּיפוּ גוֹיִם אֶת כָּל הָעֲזָרָה, [ד] שֶׁהַכֹּהֲנִים נִכְנָסִין ט] לְשָׁם וְאוֹכְלִין שָׁם קׇדְשֵׁי קָדָשִׁים — ת"ל: °"בְּקֹדֶשׁ הַקֳּדָשִׁים תֹּאכְלֶנּוּ"; וְאַמַּאי? נֵימָא "בַּחֲצַר אֹהֶל מוֹעֵד יֹאכְלוּהָ", וְלֹא יְהֵא טָפֵל חָמוּר מִן הָעִיקָּר! הָכִי הַשְׁתָּא?! הָתָם, עֲבוֹדָה דְּאָדָם עוֹבֵד בִּמְקוֹם רַבּוֹ — אָמְרִינַן לֹא יְהֵא טָפֵל חָמוּר מִן הָעִיקָּר. אֲכִילָה, דְּאֵין אָדָם אוֹכֵל בִּמְקוֹם רַבּוֹ — י] לֹא יְהֵא טָפֵל חָמוּר מִן הָעִיקָּר לָא אָמְרִינַן.§ **מתני'** חַטַּאת הָעוֹף הָיְתָה נַעֲשֵׂית העַל קֶרֶן יא] דְּרוֹמִית מַעֲרָבִית. *וּבְכָל מָקוֹם הָיְתָה כְּשֵׁירָה, אֶלָּא זֶה הָיָה מְקוֹמָהּ. ושְׁלֹשָׁה דְּבָרִים הָיְתָה אוֹתָהּ קֶרֶן מְשַׁמֶּשֶׁת מִלְּמַטָּה, וּשְׁלֹשָׁה מִלְמַעְלָה, מִלְּמַטָּה: חַטַּאת הָעוֹף, וְהַגָּשׁוֹת, וּשְׁיָרֵי הַדָּם. וּמִלְמַעְלָן: נִיסּוּךְ הַיַּיִן, וְהַמַּיִם, וְעוֹלַת הָעוֹף כְּשֶׁהִיא רַבָּה בַּמִּזְרָח. *חכָּל הָעוֹלִין לַמִּזְבֵּחַ — עוֹלִין דֶּרֶךְ יָמִין וּמַקִּיפִין

רש"י

ה"ג: אָמַר רָמִי בַּר חָמָא כָּל כִּבְשֵׁי כְבָשִׁים שָׁלֹשׁ אַמּוֹת לְאַמָּה חוּץ מִכִּבְשׁוֹ שֶׁל מִזְבֵּחַ שֶׁהָיָה ג' אַמּוֹת וּמֶחֱצָה וְאֶצְבַּע וּשְׁלִישׁ אֶצְבַּע. כָּל כְּבָשִׁים גְּדוֹלִים וּקְטַנִּים שֶׁהָיוּ שָׁם הָיָה לָהֶן שִׁיפּוּעַ שָׁלֹשׁ אַמּוֹת לְאַמָּה גּוֹבַהּ, חוּץ מִכֶּבֶשׁ הַגָּדוֹל שֶׁל מִזְבֵּחַ, שֶׁעוֹלִין בּוֹ בְּמַשָּׂא אֵיבָרִים כְּבֵדִים וְהוּא חָלָק — צָרִיךְ שֶׁיְּהֵא מְשׁוּפָּע בְּיוֹתֵר וְנוֹחַ לַעֲלוֹת, לְכָךְ *הֶאֱרִיכוּהוּ ל"ב שִׁיפּוּעַ לְט' אַמּוֹת, יב] הֲרֵי לְכָל אַמָּה שָׁלֹשׁ אַמּוֹת וּמֶחֱצָה וְאֶצְבַּע וּשְׁלִישׁ אֶצְבַּע, כְּשֶׁתִּתֵּן לְכָל אַמָּה שָׁלֹשׁ וּמֶחֱצָה — הֲרֵי ל' וְאַחַת וּמֶחֱצָה, תֵּן עוֹד ט' אֶצְבָּעוֹת וְט' שְׁלִישֵׁי אֶצְבַּע — הֲרֵי י"ב אֶצְבָּעוֹת שֶׁהֵן ג' טְפָחִים, וְהֵן חֲצִי אַמָּה יג]. **מתני'** הָיוּ נִקְמָצוֹת בְּכָל מָקוֹם. וְאֵין יד] טְעוּנִין צָפוֹן. לִפְנִים מִן הַקְּלָעִים לְזִכְרֵי כְהוּנָּה. דִּכְתִיב: "לְכָל קׇרְבָּנָם וּלְכָל מִנְחָתָם וּלְכָל חַטָּאתָם" וגו', וְסָמִיךְ לֵיהּ: "בְּקֹדֶשׁ הַקֳּדָשִׁים תֹּאכְלֶנּוּ כָּל זָכָר יֹאכַל אוֹתוֹ" (במדבר יח). לְיוֹם וְלַיְלָה עַד חֲצוֹת. דְּיָלְפִינַן *מִמִּנְחַת לַחְמֵי תוֹדָה. **גמ'** שֶׁכֵּן מָצִינוּ בְּסִילּוּק בָּזִיכִין. שֶׁהֵן אַזְכָּרָה לְמִנְחַת לֶחֶם הַפָּנִים, כִּדְכְתִיב: "וְהָיְתָה לַלֶּחֶם לְאַזְכָּרָה" (ויקרא כד), וּמַתִּירִין אֶת הַלֶּחֶם. טו] וְסִילּוּקָן מֵעַל שֻׁלְחַן הַפָּנִים שֶׁבַּהֵיכָל — בִּמְקוֹם קְמִיצָה דִּמְנָחוֹת הַנִּקְמָצוֹת. מִמָּקוֹם שֶׁרַגְלֵי הַזָּר עוֹמְדוֹת. טז] לְעֵיל קָאֵי, וְהֵבִיאָהּ הַזָּר אֶל בְּנֵי אַהֲרֹן הַכֹּהֲנִים, "וְקָמַץ מִשָּׁם מְלֹא קוּמְצוֹ", מַשְׁמַע: מִמָּקוֹם שֶׁהַבְּעָלִים עוֹמְדִין שָׁם. וְקס"ד הַשְׁתָּא יז] לֶאֱסוֹר בֵּין הָאוּלָם קָאָתֵי, שֶׁאֵין זָר נִכְנָס לְשָׁם. שֶׁיַּחֲזִיר. הַקּוֹמֶץ לְתוֹךְ הַשִּׁירַיִם, וְלָא אָמְרִי' כְּבָר נִפְסְלָה. **לא נִצְרְכָא.** יח] הָא מִמְּקוֹם רַגְלֵי הַזָּר דְּקָאָמַר. **אֶלָּא** לְהַכְשִׁיר. דְּלָא לִיבָּעֵי עַל יֶרֶךְ הַמִּזְבֵּחַ צָפוֹנָה, אֶלָּא כָּל מְקוֹם דְּרִיסַת רַגְלֵי יִשְׂרָאֵל כָּשֵׁר לִקְמִיצָה, וְכָל שֶׁכֵּן עֶזְרַת כֹּהֲנִים וְהֵיכָל. שֶׁכֵּן כָּלִיל. וְהֵיכִי הֲוָה יָלְפִינַן מִינֵּיהּ? וּקְרָא לְמַעוּטֵי לָמָּה לֵיהּ? מֵחַטָּאת. אִי לָאו דְּמִיעֲטָהּ הֲוָה יָלְפִינַן לָהּ מֵחַטָּאת. וּפָרְכִינַן: מַה לְּחַטָּאת שֶׁכֵּן מְכַפֶּרֶת כו'. ה"ג: מַה לְּאָשָׁם שֶׁכֵּן מִינֵי דָמִים. מִכּוּלְּהוּ. יט] בָּעְיָא לְמִגְמְרֵיהּ בְּמִיהְדַּר דִּינָא, וְתֵיתֵי בְּ"מָה הַצַּד". מַה הַגָּשָׁה בְּקֶרֶן מַעֲרָבִית דְּרוֹמִית. קוֹדֶם קְמִיצָתָהּ כ] מַגִּיעָתָהּ בְּתוֹךְ כֶּלְיָהּ לְקֶרֶן מַעֲרָבִית דְּרוֹמִית שֶׁל מִזְבֵּחַ, כִּדְלְקַמָּן. שֶׁנֶּאֱמַר וּשְׁחָטוֹ פֶּתַח אֹהֶל מוֹעֵד וכו'. אַלְמָא, מִדְּתָלָה הֶכְשֵׁר עֲזָרָה לִשְׁלָמִים בְּפֶתַח אֹהֶל מוֹעֵד — שְׁמַע מִינַּהּ: אֹהֶל מוֹעֵד עִיקָּר, וַעֲזָרָה טָפֵל. וְלֹא יְהֵא טָפֵל חָמוּר מִן הָעִיקָּר. דְּכֵיוָן דְּטָפֵל חֲזֵי לְהוּ — כ"ש עִיקָּר. הִקִּיפוּ גוֹיִם. לְמִלְחָמָה, וְיוֹרִים חִיצִּים וְאַבְנֵי בְּלִיסְטְרָאוֹת לְתוֹךְ הָעֲזָרָה. בְּקֹדֶשׁ הַקֳּדָשִׁים. הֵיכָל בְּמַשְׁמַע. **וְאַמַּאי.** אִם אִיתָא דְּאָמְרִי' לֹא יְהֵא טָפֵל חָמוּר מִן הָעִיקָּר, לָמָּה לִי לְמִיכְתַּב הַאי קְרָא לְאַכְשׁוּרֵי הֵיכָל לַאֲכִילַת כא] קָדָשִׁים? הָא כְּתִיב בְּהוּ: "בַּחֲצַר אֹהֶל מוֹעֵד", *וְנֵימָא: לֹא יְהֵא טָפֵל חָמוּר מִן הָעִיקָּר! אֲכִילָה דְּאֵין אָדָם אוֹכֵל בִּמְקוֹם רַבּוֹ. דְּזִילוּתָא דְּרַבֵּיהּ הִיא לַעֲשׂוֹת כב] צׇרְכֵי עֶבֶד לְפָנָיו — לֹא יְהֵא טָפֵל חָמוּר לֵיכָּא לְמֵימַר, דְּלָאו חוּמְרָא הִיא אֶלָּא קוּלָּא, וְכֵן הַדִּין שֶׁיְּהֵא טָפֵל כג] *חָמוּר מִן הָעִיקָּר. **מתני'** חַטַּאת הָעוֹף הָיְתָה נַעֲשֵׂית כו'. בַּגְּמָ' יָלֵיף כד] מְנָא לֵיהּ. בְּכָל מָקוֹם הָיְתָה כְּשֵׁירָה כו'. בַּגְּמָ' פָּרֵיךְ מַאי קָאָמַר. מִלְּמַטָּה. לְמַטָּה מִן הַחוּט. **חַטָּאת.*** כה] יָלֵיף בַּגְּמָרָא שֶׁהִיא לְמַטָּה. הַגָּשׁוֹת. שֶׁל מְנָחוֹת קוֹדֶם קְמִיצָתָן, כִּדְכְתִיב: "וְהִגִּישָׁהּ". וּבַגְּמָ' יָלֵיף הָא קֶרֶן מְנָא לֵיהּ. וּשְׁיָרֵי הַדָּם. שֶׁל חַטָּאוֹת הַחִיצוֹנוֹת. וּבַגְּמָ' מְפָרֵשׁ לָהּ. נִיסּוּךְ הַמַּיִם וְהַיַּיִן. שֶׁשָּׁם הָיוּ כו] שִׁיתִּין, וְאִי אֶפְשָׁר לְנַסֵּךְ כִּי אִם שָׁם. וְעוֹלַת הָעוֹף כְּשֶׁהִיא רַבָּה בַּמִּזְרָח. דְּעִיקַּר מְקוֹמָהּ בְּקֶרֶן דְּרוֹמִית מִזְרָחִית, כִּדְמְפָרֵשׁ טַעְמָא בַּגְּמָרָא: מִפְּנֵי שֶׁקְּרוֹבָה לְבֵית הַדֶּשֶׁן לִזְרוֹק שָׁם מוּרְאָה וְנוֹצָה, כִּדְכְתִיב: "וְהִשְׁלִיךְ אוֹתָהּ וגו' אֶל מְקוֹם הַדָּשֶׁן" (ויקרא א). וּכְשֶׁהִיא רַבָּה שָׁם, שֶׁיֵּשׁ כֹּהֲנִים הַרְבֵּה בְּאוֹתוֹ הַקֶּרֶן עֲסוּקִין בְּעוֹלוֹת, וְאֵין לָזֶה מָקוֹם הַמּוּסָב לַעֲמוֹד, שֶׁהָעוֹלָה נַעֲשֵׂית לְמַעְלָה — בָּא לוֹ לְקֶרֶן מַעֲרָבִית דְּרוֹמִית, שֶׁאַף הִיא סְמוּכָה לְבֵית הַדֶּשֶׁן מִשְּׁאָר שְׁתֵּי הַקְּרָנוֹת, שֶׁבֵּית הַדֶּשֶׁן סָמוּךְ לַכֶּבֶשׁ הָיָה בְּמִזְרָחוֹ וְלִדְרוֹמוֹ שֶׁל מִזְבֵּחַ. וּמַקִּיפִין

תוספות

כל כבשי כבשים שלש אמות לאמה. כז] למ"ד (לעיל דף נח:) כוליה מזבח כח] בדרום קאי, יש תימה על מזבח הנחשת, למ"ד גובהו עשר כט] לא משכחת לכל היותר כי אם כ' אמות לט' אמות. דחצר שלפני המשכן חמשים אמה, כ"ה אמות חצי החצר וה' אמות מקום מזבח — פש ליה כ' אמה עד כותל דרומי. כי מטי כבש עד הכותל — לא משכחת לאמה אלא שתי אמות וטפח ואצבע ושליש אצבע. והוה ליה הילוך על ידי הדחק, כדמוכח בשבת (דף ק.) ובעירובין (דף נח:) במתלקט עשרה מתוך ארבע דהוי רשות היחיד. ולמ"ד דמזבח רחב עשר אמות — לא הוו אלא ט"ו אמה עד הכותל. ל] ורבי יוסי דאמר לעיל (דף נט:): מזבח גבוה עשר אמות ורחב חמש — לטעמיה, דאמר: כוליה מזבח בצפון קאי, והיה משוך כל כך לצד צפון עד דמשתיירי ל"ב אמה לכבש. ומיהו, א"כ לא היה כלל מן המזבח לפני פתח המשכן אי מזבח משוך יותר מכ"ה אמה. דמסתמא משכן הוה כמו בית עולמים, דגבי יום הכיפורים צריך "לפני ה'". ולרבי יהודה דאמר עשר רחבו — יש לומר דלדידיה שלש אמות קומתו ולא יותר, כדתניא לעיל (דף נט:).

חוץ מכבשו של מזבח שהיה שלש אמות ומחצה ואצבע ושליש אצבע *בזכרותא. זו היא גירסת הקונטרס, לא] ומכוון חשבון לט' אמות של מזבח. ורבותיו גורסים: ג' אמות ומחצה וחצי טפח ואצבע ושליש אצבע לב] בזכרותו. ופירש בקונטרס דלחשבון זה לא היה ראש הכבש שוה לראש המזבח אלא נמוך ממנו רביע אמה, דלחשבון גובה ט' יש לכבש יותר מל"ב אמה. ולא דק בקונטרס, דאין *גבוה אלא חומש אמה חסר משהו. והקשה בקונטרס: הרי אמרה תורה "לא תעלה במעלות על מזבחי"! ותירץ רבי נתן מדודיא: דבפרק "שתי הלחם" (מנחות לז:*) אמרינן דאמה של לג] [יסוד] גובה באמה בת חמשה. לד] ולפירוש הקונטרס, [קשה] דנמצא ראש הכבש גבוה מראשו של מזבח. ומיהו אין לחוש. אי נמי, לפירוש הקונטרס לה] אמות של כבש לפי אמות של מזבח לו].

שכן מצינו בסילוק בזיכין. ולא שייך למימר כאן טעם אחר: לז] ולא יהא טפל חמור מן העיקר, כדקאמר בשלמים דשלמים תלאן הכתוב בפתח אהל מועד. לח] ואם תאמר: ל"ל טעמא דבזיכין? אמאי ס"ד למיפסל, לפי מה שפירש בקונטרס לעיל ספ"ק (דף יד.): מודה ר"ש בחטאות הפנימיות לעבודה שאין יכול לבטלה, משום דלאו אורח ארעא לשחוט בהיכל. דמשמע דאי לאו הכי — היה יכול לשחוט בהיכל, אע"ג דחטאת בעי צפון. ואם כן קמילה תתכשר! וי"ל: דסלקא דעתך לפסול, לט] דדרשינן: מקום שרגלי הזר עומדות, להכשיר כל מקום שזר יכול לעמוד. דה"א לפסולי היכל קאתי, שאין זר יכול לעמוד שם. סלקא דעתך אמינא מ] אף מנחה טעונה צפון, לכך אתא קרא דממקום שרגלי הזר עומדות, להכשיר כל מקום שזר יכול לעמוד אפי' בדרום. אבל אין לפרש דדריש דרום מטעם דאין זר יכול לעמוד בצפון. חדא — דלעיל בפרק ב' (דף כ.) מוסיף מא] אף מקום דריסת רגלי ישראל דחשוב לפון. ועוד: אפי' למ"ד מרחק לפון — לא מסתבר שיהא זר אסור בצפון כנגד המזבח, אלא מב] מדרבנן, מעלה בעלמא. ויורדין

כה א ב מיי' פ"ב מהלכות מעה"ק הלכה יב:
כו ג מיי' שם הלכה ו ופי"ג שם הלכה יב:
כז ד מיי' פ"ה מהלכות מעה"ק הלכה ז:
[ד] מיי' פ"י מהלכות מעה"ק דין ג:
כח ה מיי' פ"ז מהל' מעה"ק הלכה ב:
כט ו מיי' שם הל' ט:
ל ז מיי' שם הלכה י:
לא ח מיי' שם הלכה יח:

מסורת הש"ס: עי' תוספי גרסאות | נ"א בזוטרתא [ועי' מ"ש תוס' מנחות מח: ד"ה ארכבעה] | [מנחות ח.] | [ועי' רש"י מנחות יח: ד"ה לאחר וכו'] | [לעיל מח.] | מנחות ח: | [לעיל מח: וש"נ] | [מנחות ח: ע"ש ושם איתא רבי יהודה בן בתירה ובספרים הישנים מצאתי מתיב רבי יוחנן] | [עי' לקמן סו. סז. מנחות כ:] | סוכה מח: | יאכלנה נ"ק | נ"א קל | העוף נ"ק | רש"ק גרס יעקב (וכ"ה מנחות ח:) | נ"א בזוכרותא | [ושם ד"ה לא חיק]

שיטה מקובצת

ז] ותיבת עקיבא נמחק: ז] מכולהו. ס"א מכולהו נמי שכן כו': ח] רבי יהודה תיבת יוחנן נמחק: ט] נכנסין להיכל ואוכלין שם קדשי קדשים ושירי מנחה ת"ל בקדש: י] רבו. ס"א טעמא דאהדריה קרא הא לא אהדריה קרא לא כו': יא] קרן מערבית דרומית: יב] אמות גובה הרי: יג] ע' בהשמטות בסוף המסכת: יד] ואין טעונות צפון: טו] הלחם בקומץ שמתיר את השירים וסילוקו מעל השולחן במקום ותיבות הפנים שבהיכל נמחק: טז] עומדות דעל מקום הזר קאי קרא דכתיב והביא: יז] השתא למעוטי היכל ואולם קאתי: יח] האי מקום שרגלי הזר עומדות דקאמר: יט] מכולהו ואי מכולהו בעי: כ] קמיצתה מגיעה ברגלי לקרן מערבית: כא] לאכילת קדשי קדשים: כב] לעשות עבדו צרכיו לפניו: כג] טפל קל מן העיקר: כד] תיבת מנא נמחק: כה] חטאת העוף יליף: כו] היו השיתין: כז] לאמה. משמע שכל כבש דינו להיות כך א"כ למ"ד: כח] מזבח לדרום העזרה קאי: כט] עשר ורחבו חמש לא משכחת כו' לט' אמות דגובה המזבח מלבד הקרנות שהיו אמה דחצר: ל] ושמא ר' יוסי אות ו' נמחק: לא] ומכוון החשבון לט': לב] בזכרותו פי' בשפוע בעובי הגודל והא דנקט בזכרותו כדי ליישב החשבון מצומצם ד' אצבעות לטפח משום דבסתם אצבעות הוי הטפח ששה אצבעות ופי': לג] של גובה יסוד באמה: לד] חמשה ס"א א"כ המזבח היה גבוה ט' אמות פחות טפח ואדרבה לגירסת רש"י קשה מהתם דנמצא כו': לה] הקונטרס יש ליישב דאמות של: לו] מזבח ושל מטה בת חמשה לשיעור יסוד ואינך בבת חמשה: לז] דלא יהא טפל חמור מן העיקר החצר מן האהל כדקאמר: לח] מועד אם כן עשה הפסוק הפתח טפל לאהל אבל הכא לא הזכיר אהל כלל אלא החצר וא"ת: לט] לפסול מהא דרשינן ממקום שרגלי הזר עומדות דה"א לפסול ההיכל קאתי כו' והשאר נמחק: מ] אמינא הואיל ועולה טעונה צפון אף: מא] מוסיף רבי לג' אף: מב] אלא מעלה מדרבנן בעלמא:

א] כל כבשי כבשים כו'. משמע דכל כבש דינו להיות כך ותימה דלמ"ד דכוליה מזבח בדרום העזרה קאי א"כ המזבח היה עומד באמצע חצר המשכן שהיתה חמשים על חמשים א"כ א) חצי העזרה לא היתה כי אם כ"ה אמה ולמ"ד שהמזבח גבוה עשר והמזבח היה רוחב ה' אמות וא"כ כי מטי הכבש עד כותל העזרה לא היה הכבש [אורך כי אם עשרים] אמה והמזבח היה גבוה ט' אמות מבלי מקום הקרנות ולחשבון ג' אמות לאמה היה לו לכבש להיות אורך כ"ז אמות וצריך להיות כל הכבש בדרום כדנפקא לן לעיל מירך המזבח צפונה ואפילו להדליק אינו ראוי הואיל ואינו מתלקט כו' וי"ל דר' יוסי [הוא] דאמר גבהו ט' אמה (פי' מבלי מקום הקרנות. עכ"ה) ור' יוסי לטעמיה דאמר כוליה מזבח בצפון קאי מיהו אכתי קשה דלא נשאר מן החצר לכבש רק כ"ה אמה וי"ל שהיה המזבח משוך לצד צפון כל כך שלא היה מן המזבח לפני אהל מועד רק ג' אמות ונשאר מן החצר כ"ז אמות לכבש דהיינו ג' אמות לאמה ודי בכך לפי שלא היה קבוע כל כך אבל ליכא למימר שלא היה כלל מן המזבח לפני המשכן דהא כתיב פתח אהל מועד: ב] עיין בהשמטות בסוף המסכת: ג] מתני' המנחות היו: ד] מנחה שקמצה: ה] שיחזיר. ס"א שהוא מחזיר ויחזור ויקמוץ: ו] ר' יעקב לג'

א) נ"ל כ' אמה חצי החצר וכו' עד כותל דרומי לא היה וכו'.

הגהות הב"ח (א) גמרא כל כבשי כבשים. נ"ב כאן יש לתמוה הפלא ופלא דלהרכה של הכבש היה ל"ב אמה וכמידות קחשיב רחבה של עזרה מקום הכבש ל"ב אמה וזה א"א לפי החשבון שאמרו חכמים כל אמתא בריבוע אמתא ותרי חומשי באלכסונא לפי זה החשבון יגיע ארכה של כבש לשלשים [והשאר חסר]:

גליון הש"ס גמ' כל כבשי כבשים. עיין תשובת מעיל צדקה סימן כח: **תוס'** ד"ה חוץ וכו' ותירץ ר' נתן וכו'. עיין בתשובת מהר"ם בר ברוך דפוס פראג סימן רל"ט ועיין בערוך ערך כבש. ועיין מנחות דף מח ע"ב תוספות ד"ה ד' בגודל:

לב א מיי' פ"ג מהל' מעה"ק הלכה יב: לג ב מיי' פ"ז שם הלכה ט:

וּמַקִּיפִין וְיוֹרְדִין דֶּרֶךְ שְׂמֹאל, חוּץ מִן הָעוֹלֶה לַג' א] אֵלּוּ, שֶׁהָיוּ עוֹלִין וְיוֹרְדִין עַל הֶעָקֵב.§

גמ' מְנָא ה"מ? ב] א"ר *יְהוֹשֻׁעַ, אָמַר קְרָא: °"לֹא יָשִׂים עָלֶיהָ שֶׁמֶן וְלֹא יִתֵּן עָלֶיהָ לְבוֹנָה כִּי חַטָּאת הִיא", חַטָּאת קְרוּיָה מִנְחָה, וּמִנְחָה קְרוּיָה חַטָּאת; מַה חַטָּאת טְעוּנָה צָפוֹן — אַף מִנְחָה טְעוּנָה צָפוֹן, וּמַה מִּנְחָה בְּקֶרֶן מַעֲרָבִית דְּרוֹמִית — ג] אַף חַטָּאת בְּקֶרֶן מַעֲרָבִית דְּרוֹמִית. וּמִנְחָה גּוּפָהּ מְנָלַן? ד] *דְּתַנְיָא: °"לִפְנֵי ה'", יָכוֹל בַּמַּעֲרָב? ת"ל: °"אֶל פְּנֵי הַמִּזְבֵּחַ"; אִי "אֶל פְּנֵי הַמִּזְבֵּחַ", יָכוֹל בַּדָּרוֹם? ת"ל: "לִפְנֵי ה'"; הָא כֵּיצַד? אמַגִּישָׁהּ בְּקֶרֶן מַעֲרָבִית דְּרוֹמִית כְּנֶגֶד חוּדָּהּ שֶׁל קֶרֶן, וְדַיּוֹ. ר"א אוֹמֵר: יָכוֹל יַגִּישֶׁנָּה לְמַעֲרָבָהּ שֶׁל קֶרֶן אוֹ לִדְרוֹמָהּ שֶׁל קֶרֶן? אָמַרְתָּ: *כָּל מָקוֹם שֶׁאַתָּה מוֹצֵא שְׁנֵי מִקְרָאוֹת, אֶחָד מְקַיֵּים עַצְמוֹ וּמְקַיֵּים חֲבֵירוֹ, וְאֶחָד מְקַיֵּים עַצְמוֹ וּמְבַטֵּל חֲבֵירוֹ — מַנִּיחִין זֶה שֶׁמְּקַיֵּים עַצְמוֹ וּמְבַטֵּל חֲבֵירוֹ, וְתוֹפְשִׂין ה] אֶת שֶׁמְּקַיֵּים עַצְמוֹ וּמְקַיֵּים חֲבֵירוֹ. ו] *כְּשֶׁאַתָּה אוֹמֵר (א) "אֶל פְּנֵי ה'" בַּמַּעֲרָב, ז] הֵיכָן קִיַּימְתָּ "אֶל פְּנֵי הַמִּזְבֵּחַ"? וּכְשֶׁאַתָּה אוֹמֵר "אֶל פְּנֵי הַמִּזְבֵּחַ" בַּדָּרוֹם — קִיַּימְתָּ "לִפְנֵי ה'". ח] בַּדָּרוֹם הֵיכָן קִיַּימְתָּ? אָמַר רַב אַשִׁי, קָסָבַר הַאי תַּנָּא: *כּוּלֵּיהּ מִזְבֵּחַ בַּצָּפוֹן קָאֵי.§ "בְּכָל מָקוֹם הָיְתָה כְּשֵׁרָה" [וכו'].§ מַאי קָאָמַר? אָמַר רַב אַשִׁי, ה"ק: בְּכָל מָקוֹם הָיְתָה כְּשֵׁרָה לִמְלִיקָתָהּ, אֶלָּא זֶה הָיָה מְקוֹמָהּ לְהַזָּאָתָהּ. תָּנֵינָא לְהָא דְּת"ר: ט] *מְלִיקָה בְּכָל מָקוֹם בַּמִּזְבֵּחַ — כְּשֵׁרָה, בהִיזָּה דָּמָהּ בְּכָל מָקוֹם — כְּשֵׁרָה, י] הִיזָּה וְלֹא מִיצָּה — כְּשֵׁרָה, וּבִלְבַד שֶׁיִּתֵּן מֵחוּט הַסִּיקְרָא וּלְמַטָּה מִדַּם הַנֶּפֶשׁ. מַאי קָאָמַר? ה"ק: מְלִיקָה בְּכָל מָקוֹם בַּמִּזְבֵּחַ — כְּשֵׁרָה, מִיצָּה דָּמָהּ בְּכ"מ בַּמִּזְבֵּחַ — כְּשֵׁרָה,

שֶׁאִם

רש"י

וּמַקִּיפִין דֶּרֶךְ שְׂמֹאל. מַקִּיפִים אֶת הַמִּזְבֵּחַ בִּשְׁבִיל צוֹרְכֵי עֲבוֹדָה, אוֹ לְמַתַּן דְּמֵי חַטָּאת אוֹ סִידּוּר הַמַּעֲרָכָה אוֹ הִיפּוּךְ אֵיבָרִים בְּצִינּוֹרָא. וְיוֹרְדִין הַמַּעֲרָבוֹ שֶׁל כֶּבֶשׁ, שֶׁהוּא שְׂמֹאל יא] לְעוֹלִים בַּמִּזְבֵּחַ בַּעֲלִיָּיתָן. לַג' דְּבָרִים אֵלּוּ. הַנַּעֲשִׂים בְּקֶרֶן מַעֲרָבִית דְּרוֹמִית: נְסָכִים, וְעוֹלַת הָעוֹף. יב] כְּשֶׁהוּא עוֹלֶה לַמִּזְבֵּחַ פּוֹנֶה לִשְׂמֹאל בְּאוֹתָהּ הַקֶּרֶן, וּכְשֶׁגָּמַר חוֹזֵר עַל הֶעָקֵב דֶּרֶךְ עֲלִיָּיתוֹ. וּבַגְּמָ' פָּרֵיךְ: הָא בָּעֵינַן דֶּרֶךְ יָמִין. וְלַג' דְּבָרִים הַנַּעֲשִׂים בָּהּ לְמַטָּן — אֵינוֹ עוֹלֶה וְאֵינוֹ מַקִּיף, אֶלָּא עוֹמֵד עַל הָרִצְפָּה יג] בַּקַּרְקַע. גמ' מְנָא הָנֵי מִילֵּי. דְּחַטַּאת הָעוֹף בְּקֶרֶן מַעֲרָבִית דְּרוֹמִית. לֹא יָשִׂים עָלֶיהָ וגו'. בְּמִנְחַת חוֹטֵא כְּתִיב, הַבָּאָה תַּחַת חַטַּאת הָעוֹף בְּדַלֵּי דַלּוּת, וְקַרְיֵיהּ רַחֲמָנָא חַטָּאת. יד] וְאַשְׁמְעִינַן נַמִי שֶׁהַחַטָּאת קְרוּיָה מִנְחָה, דְּהָכִי מַשְׁמַע נַמִי כִּי הַחַטָּאת נֶהֶפְכָה לִהְיוֹת מִנְחָה. מַה חַטָּאת טְעוּנָה צָפוֹן. יוֹדֵעַ אֲנִי שֶׁגִּירְסָא זוֹ טו] שִׁיבּוּשׁ, שֶׁהֲרֵי לֹא חַטַּאת הָעוֹף וְלֹא מִנְחָה טָעוּן צָפוֹן. וְא"ת: מִנְחַת חוֹטֵא חֲלוּקָה מִן הַשְּׁאָר, וּלְחַטַּאת בְּהֵמָה מַקִּישׁ לָהּ — הֲוָה לֵיהּ לְמִיתְנֵי בְּמַתְנִיתִין דְּקָתָנֵי לְעֵיל: הַמְּנָחוֹת נִקְמָצוֹת בְּכָל מָקוֹם בָּעֲזָרָה חוּץ מִמִּנְחַת חוֹטֵא. וְעוֹד: הֵיאַךְ אֶפְשָׁר? חַטַּאת הָעוֹף טז] שֶׁבָּאת תַּחַת חַטַּאת בְּהֵמָה אֵינָהּ טְעוּנָה צָפוֹן, שֶׁהֲרֵי נַעֲשֵׂית בְּקֶרֶן מַעֲרָבִית דְּרוֹמִית, יז] וּבְמִנְחָה הַבָּאָה תַּחַת הָעוֹף תִּטְעוֹן צָפוֹן? וְגִירְסָא אַחֲרִינָא גָּרְסִי' בָּהּ וְאֵינִי יוֹדֵעַ אֲמִיתָּהּ. וְנִרְאֶה בְּעֵינַי: מַה חַטָּאת פְּסוּלָה שֶׁלֹּא לִשְׁמָהּ — אַף מִנְחָה פְּסוּלָה שֶׁלֹּא לִשְׁמָהּ. וְה"נ יָלְפִינַן לָהּ בְּפ"ק דִּמְנָחוֹת (דף ד.). וּמַה מִּנְחָה. טְעוּנָה הַגָּשָׁה בְּקֶרֶן מַעֲרָבִית דְּרוֹמִית — אַף חַטַּאת הָעוֹף עֲבוֹדָתָהּ בְּקֶרֶן מַעֲרָבִית דְּרוֹמִית, וְהַזָּאַת דָּמָהּ הִיא עִיקַּר עֲבוֹדָתָהּ. לִפְנֵי ה'. "הַקְרֵב אוֹתָהּ בְּנֵי אַהֲרֹן לִפְנֵי ה'", הַיְינוּ שֶׁמַּגִּיעָהּ לַמִּזְבֵּחַ. אֶל פְּנֵי הַמִּזְבֵּחַ. דָּרוֹם, שֶׁשָּׁם הַכֶּבֶשׁ. וְדַיּוֹ. בְּמַסֶּכֶת סוֹטָה בְּפ"ב מְפָרֵשׁ מַאי יח] דַּיּוֹ, וְקָאָמַר שֶׁאֵינוֹ צָרִיךְ לְהַגִּיעַ גּוּפָהּ לַמִּזְבֵּחַ, אֶלָּא הַכְּלִי. רַבִּי אֱלִיעֶזֶר אוֹמֵר. מֵאַחַר שֶׁפֵּרֵט לְךָ הַכָּתוּב בְּהַגָּשָׁתָהּ שְׁתֵּי רוּחוֹת, יָכוֹל לְאֵיזֶה מֵהֶן שֶׁיִּרְצֶה? ה"ג: יָכוֹל יַגִּישֶׁנָּה לְמַעֲרָבָהּ יט] אוֹ לִדְרוֹמָהּ שֶׁל קֶרֶן. כּוּלֵּיהּ מִזְבֵּחַ בַּצָּפוֹן קָאֵי. נִמְצָא דְּרוֹמוֹ שֶׁל מִזְבֵּחַ כּוּלּוֹ לְנֶגֶד הַפֶּתַח, וְקָרֵינַן נַמִי בְּצַד דְּרוֹמוֹ "לִפְנֵי ה'". בְּכָל מָקוֹם הָיְתָה כְּשֵׁרָה לִמְלִיקָתָהּ. בֵּין לְמַעְלָה בֵּין לְמַטָּה. דְּכִי יָלְפִינַן לְמַטָּה בְּחַטַּאת הָעוֹף — כ] בְּהַזָּאָה הוּא דְּיָלְפִינַן לְקַמָּן בִּשְׁמַעְתִּין: "וְהִזָּה מִדַּם הַחַטָּאת עַל קִיר", וְאָמַר מָר: זֶה קִיר הַתַּחְתּוֹן. וְקֶרֶן מַעֲרָבִית דְּרוֹמִית נַמִי כא] בְּהַזָּאָה הוּא דְּיָלְפִינַן, דְּהָא מֵהַגָּשָׁה דְּמִנְחָה יָלֵיף, וְהַגָּשָׁתָהּ

תוספות

כב] ויורדין על העקב. לאו משום שלא ירבה בהילוך בחנם, דאם כן כשהיה בקרן דרומית מזרחית נמי. אלא היינו טעמא, דהכא חזרתו על העקב הויא לה דרך ימין.

מנחה קרויה חטאת וחטאת קרויה מנחה. תימה, דהוה לן למימר: מנחה קרויה חטאת, ואין חטאת קרויה מנחה. כדאמרינן פ"ק (לעיל ז:): תודה קרויה שלמים ואין שלמים קרויין תודה. ובמנחות פרק "התודה" (דף פ:): לחם איקרי תודה, תודה לא איקרי לחם! וי"ל: כג] דודאי לא מיקרי שם אחד לענין לשמה דפ"ק, ולענין ניתותרו המעות דפרק "התודה". אבל הכא דמהיקשא קדריש, דמנחה וחטאת איתקוש ודאי להדדי – איכא לאקושינהו שפיר כד].

מה חטאת טעונה צפון. פירש בקונטרס דגירסא זו משובשת היא, שהרי לא חטאת העוף טעונה צפון, כדאמר: ולא בן עוף בצפון, ולא מנחה טעונה צפון. וא"ת: מנחת כה] *חטאת חלוקה משאר מנחות, ולחטאת בהמה מקיש לה – הוה ליה למיתני במתניתין לעיל דקתני: כל המנחות נקמצות בכל מקום בעזרה חוץ ממנחת כו] חוטא. ועוד: *אפשר חטאת העוף הבאה בדלות תחת חטאת בהמה אינה טעונה צפון, שהרי נעשית בקרן מערבית דרומית, ומנחה הבאה תחת חטאת העוף תטען לצפון? כז] וגירסא אחרינא גרסינן בה ואיני יודע אמיתה. ונראה בעיני: מה חטאת פסולה שלא לשמה אף מנחה פסולה שלא לשמה. וה"נ ילפינן לה בפ"ק [דמנחות]. ע"כ לשון הקונטרס. וקשה לפירושו: כח] דודאי מעיקרא אמרי' בפ"ק דמנחות (דף ד.): בשלמא מנחת חוטא – חטאת קרייה רחמנא, אבל מנחת קנאות מנלן? אבל במסקנא אמרינן: אלא מנחת חוטא ומנחת קנאות דפסולות שלא לשמן מנלן? חטאת טעמא מאי דכתיב בה "היא" – ה"נ הא כתיב בה "היא"! כט] ועוד קשה לגירסת הספרים, דבפרק "איזהו מקומן" (לעיל מט:) מוכח דחטאת הטעונה לפון כעולה הוי היקש, אם כן היכי אתיא מנחה והדר ילפינן מחטאת? וכי דבר הלמד בהיקש חוזר ומלמד בהיקש? ועוד: כמו שהקשה בקונטרס, דאמירא לא הויא מנחה מחטאת העוף דאתיא במקומה, ואינה טעונה לפון. מיהו י"ל: הרי בתורת כהנים ילפינן דחטאת העוף פסולה שלא לשמה מן הפסוק, ולא ילפינן ממנחת חוטא דמפיק פסול מקרא אחרינא. ויש לדחות. מיהו, אמת דמנחה לא בעיא לפון ל] אלא הגשה בקרן מערבית דרומית כדבסמוך, לא] (ואי) והקמילה אינה טעונה לפון – אפי' מנחת חוטא נמי, כדמוכח בתוספתא דמנחות פ"ק: חומר בשחיטה שטעונה לפון מה שאין כן בקמילה. וכי תימא היינו במנחת נדבה, אבל במנחת חוטא טעונה לפון – מכל מקום אינו חומר לב] *בשחיטה לגמרי, שהרי בשחיטה נמי ליתא בלפון לג] בקלים. מיהו י"ל: דכללא בקדשי קדשים הוי דומיא דמנחה. וזהו דוחק. ועוד, דתני בסיפא: חומר בקמילה מבמליקה, שהקמילה דוחה שבת וטומאה – וליתני: שהקמילה טעונה לפון ולא מליקה. אף על גב דיש קמילה דלא בעיא לפון, כגון מנחת נדבה – כמו כן אינה דוחה שבת! מיהו נ"ל לדחות: דה"נ לא מיירי במנחת חוטא, דהא אינה דוחה שבת. אלא מיירי במנחת העומר ומנחת תמיד שהן בציבור, והן ודאי לא בעו לפון. אבל מנחת חוטא לד] בעי' לפון, דאיתקש לחטאת בהמה שבאה חליפתה בעשירות. ברו"ך. והרב רבי חיים גרים: מה חטאת העוף טעונה יסוד, דכתיב "והנשאר בדם ימצה אל יסוד המזבח" – אף מנחה טעונה הגשה כנגד היסוד. לה] והכי מוכח פרק "כל המנחות באות מצה" (מנחות דף סא.) [גבי] ואלו טעונות תנופה: לוג שמן של מצורע ואשמו. [דאמרינן התם] "לפני ה'" – במזרח. והאמרת "לפני ה'" במערב! פירוש: בהך לו] שמעתיה. ומשני: ה"מ מנחה דאיקרי חטאת, וחטאת טעונה יסוד, וקרן דרומית מזרחית לא היה לה יסוד, אבל הכא "לפני ה'" קרינא ביה. והשתא, כולה בדרום ליכא למימר – משום יסוד, וכולה במערב נמי לא – משום דכתיב (ויקרא ו): "אל פני המזבח" דהיינו דרום, מכל מקום איצטריך "לפני ה'" דלא תימא "אל פני המזבח" גזירת הכתוב הוא, אף על גב דלית ליה יסוד. ובריש פירקין *פירשתי מה שהקשה דגבי גמלים דיום הכיפורים קרי "לפני ה'" במערב דוקא. וא"ת: ושאר מנחות מנלן? וכי תימא: מדאיתקוש כל המנחות לחטאת ואשם בפרשת "צו", וילפינן משירי הדם שטעונין יסוד – אם כן מנחת חוטא לז] תיפוק לי מהתם! ועוד: מנלן דמקשינן לשירים? לקשינהו לתחילת דמים, לח] ולא בעי יסוד כחטאת! ויש לומר: דכתיב "לפני ה'" במנחת חוטא, ובכל המנחות נמי כתיב "לפני ה'", כי היכי דהאי "לפני ה'" כנגד היסוד – לט] [האי נמי כנגד היסוד]. ולא ג"ש ממש [היא], דדבר הלמד בהיקש מבעיא לן אי חוזר ומלמד בג"ש אי לא, אלא גלוי מילתא בעלמא הוא. מ] *ור"ת גרים: מה חטאת טעונה ימין – אף מנחה כן. והיינו דלא כר"ש, דאמר לעיל (דף כה.): בא לעובדה בכלי עובדה בשמאל. אי נמי, אפילו כרבי שמעון, וכגון שבא לעובדה ביד, דאמר עובדה בימין כחטאת. מא] הגה"ה

אף חטאת בקרן מערבית דרומית. תימה: דלא ילפינן מינה מליקה! ושמא לא ילפינן אלא מידי דאשכחן דבעי מזבח, כמנחה. וכן פירש בקונטרס בסמוך. בדרום קיימת א) כולה. ב) על כרחך רבי אליעזר אית ליה ההיא מב] ד"מה חטאת טעונה יסוד", דאי לאו הכי – מנא ליה דאמר מערבית? ותימה: אם כן "לפני ה'" למה לי? דרומית נפקא לן מ"אל פני המזבח", ומערבית – מדבעיא יסוד!

שאם

א) כ' נ"ק ב) עיין רש"ק

... המזבח וגם איכא יסוד וא"כ למה לי לפני ה' וי"ל דהו"א דמגישה באמה אחת שבדרום ... היה יסוד קמ"ל לפני ה' לומר שמגישה כנגד חודה של קרן אבל אכתי קשה בשאר ... אצל היסוד מלמטה אימא דמגישן מלמעלה אצל הקרן הואיל דמהיקשא דמנחה לחטאת ... מנחת חוטא וי"ל דבמנחת חוטא כתיב לפני ה' וכן במנחת נדבה וא"כ כי היכי דלפני ה' ... היינו למטה מן היסוד כמו כן לפני ה' דכתיב במנחת נדבה ר"ל מלמטה ומיהו ריב"א ... במנחת חוטא לפני ה'. (ס"א לכך פי' דכך צ"ל מדקאמר הכא דלפני ה' דנדבה חשבינן ... ת חוטא דאמנחת חוטא נמי קאי מייתורא דהמנחה כדפי' וע"כ הוי פי' דלפני ה' דמנחת ... יתקש לחטאת א"כ כי נמי קאי אנדבה כפשטיה לא ישתנה פירושו דאתרוייהו קאי) ... כתיב לפני ה' במנחת נדבה מרבינן מנחת חוטא מייתורא מאת המנחה להגשה לעיכוב ... סברא הוא דכמו דבמנחת חוטא ר"ל ליסוד כמו כן במנחת נדבה ר"ל ליסוד דהואיל דקאי ... נה פירושו: ה] ותופשין זה שמקיים תיבת את נמחק: ו] עיין בהשמטות בסוף המסכת: ... אל פני המזבח בדרום ותיבת היכן קיימת נמחק: ח] במערב היכן תיבת בדרום נמחק: ... י] תיבות היזה ולא מיצה כשרה נמחק: יא] שמאל העולים למזבח בעלייתן: יב] שכשעולה ... לשמאלו ותיבות כשהוא עולה ל"ש: יג] תיבת בקרקע נמחק: יד] חטאת מינה שמעינן

שאינו צריך להגיע המנחה גופה: יט] למערבה של קרן או: כ] העוף בהזאתה הוא: ... הוא דילפינן דהא כי גמר מהגשה דמנחה הזאה הוא דגמר ותיבת יליף נמחק: כב] ... העקב: כג] וי"ל דלאו דוקא נקט דודאי: כד] שפיר ודוחק הוא ונראה דבקונטרס דקדק ... מינה שהחטאת קרויה מנחה כי חטאת העוף נהפכת לבא תחתיה מנחת חוטא בדלי ד... קרויה מנחה כשהיא פוטר בדלי דלות ממנחת חוטא תחת חטאת העוף. מהר"פ: כה] מנ... כו] חוטא ועוד דמסתמא אקשינן מנחת חוטא שהיא בדלי דלות לחטאת העוף שלפניו ... לחטאת בהמה דעשיר דלפני פניו: כז] עיין בהשמטות בסוף המסכת: כח] לפירושו דא"כ ... חוטא פסולה שלא לשמה כי אם מהיקשא דחטאת וזה אינו דודאי: כט] היא אלמא דמ... ל] צפון אי בהגשה הלא היא בקרן תיבת אלא נמחק ול"ש: לא] כדבסמוך ואי הקמיצה: ל... לגמרי: לג] בצפון בקדשים קלים: לד] חוטא שמא בעי: לה] היסוד לאפוקי קרן דרומי... לו יסוד והכי מוכח כו' באות מצה דתנן ואלו טעונות תנופה כו' ואשמו ואמרינן בגמרא ... דשמעתין אות ה' נמחק: לז] חוטא נמי תיפוק: לח] דמים דלא בעיא: לט] היסוד האי ... ולא ג"ש ממש היא דדבר: מ] מתיבת ור"ת עד סוף הדבור מוקף ח"ל: מא] כחטא... מב] ההיא דרשא דמה חטאת כו' מנא ליה קרן דרומית מערבית ותיבת דאמרת נמ...

לד א מיי' פ"ב מהל' תמידין ומוספין הל"ב:
לה ב ג מיי' פ"ב מהל' מעשה הקרבנות הל"ב:

תורה אור

שֶׁאִם הִיזָּה וְלֹא מִיצָּה כְּשֵׁירָה, וּבִלְבַד שֶׁיִּתֵּן מֵחוּט הַסִּיקְרָא וּלְמַטָּה מִדַּם הַנֶּפֶשׁ.§ "שְׁלֹשָׁה דְּבָרִים" כו'.§ חַטַּאת הָעוֹף — הָא דַּאֲמַרַן, א] הַגָּשׁוֹת — דִּכְתִיב: °"וְהִגִּישָׁהּ אֶל (פְּנֵי) הַמִּזְבֵּחַ". ב] שְׁיָרֵי הַדָּם — דִּכְתִיב °"וְאֵת כָּל דַּם הַפָּר יִשְׁפּוֹךְ אֶל יְסוֹד הַמִּזְבֵּחַ".§ "מִלְמַעְלָה: נִיסּוּךְ הַמַּיִם וְהַיַּיִן, וְעוֹלַת הָעוֹף כְּשֶׁהִיא רַבָּה בַּמִּזְרָח".§ ג] מ"ט? רַבִּי יוֹחָנָן אָמַר: ד] מִפְּנֵי שֶׁקְּרוֹבָה מִבֵּית הַדֶּשֶׁן. אָמַר רַבִּי יוֹחָנָן: בֹּא וּרְאֵה כַּמָּה גָּדוֹל כֹּחָן שֶׁל כֹּהֲנִים, שֶׁאֵין לְךָ קַל בָּעוֹפוֹת יוֹתֵר מִמּוּרְאָה וְנוֹצָה, פְּעָמִים שֶׁהַכֹּהֵן זוֹרְקָן יוֹתֵר ה] מִבִּשְׁלֹשִׁים אַמָּה. *דִּתְנַן: אנָטַל מַחְתָּה שֶׁל כֶּסֶף וְעָלָה לְרֹאשׁ הַמִּזְבֵּחַ, וּפִינָּה אֶת הַגֶּחָלִים אֵילָךְ וָאֵילָךְ, וְחָתָה מִן הַמְאוּכָּלוֹת הַפְּנִימִיּוֹת וְיוֹרֵד. הִגִּיעַ לָרִצְפָּה, מַחֲזִיר פָּנָיו כְּלַפֵּי צָפוֹן וְהוֹלֵךְ לְמִזְרָחוֹ שֶׁל כֶּבֶשׁ ו] כְּעֶשֶׂר אַמּוֹת, צָבַר אֶת הַגֶּחָלִים עַל גַּבֵּי הָרִצְפָּה, רָחוֹק מִן הַכֶּבֶשׁ שְׁלֹשָׁה טְפָחִים, מָקוֹם שֶׁנּוֹתְנִין מוּרְאָה וְנוֹצָה וְדִישּׁוּן מִזְבֵּחַ הַפְּנִימִי וְהַמְּנוֹרָה. ז] הָנֵי טְפֵי מִתְּלָתִין וְחַד הָוְיָין! מָקוֹם ח] גַּבְרֵי לָא חָשֵׁיב.§ "כָּל הָעוֹלִים לַמִּזְבֵּחַ".§ מ"ט? אָמַר רַבִּי יוֹחָנָן: נְסָכִים — שֶׁמָּא יִתְעַשְּׁנוּ, וְעוֹלַת הָעוֹף — שֶׁמָּא תָּמוּת בֶּעָשָׁן. ט] וּרְמִינְהוּ: *בָּא לוֹ לְהַקִּיף אֶת הַמִּזְבֵּחַ, מֵאַיִן הוּא מַתְחִיל? במִקֶּרֶן דְּרוֹמִית מִזְרָחִית, מִזְרָחִית צְפוֹנִית, צְפוֹנִית מַעֲרָבִית, מַעֲרָבִית דְּרוֹמִית, י] וְנוֹתְנִין לוֹ יַיִן לְנַסֵּךְ! גאָמַר רַבִּי יוֹחָנָן: הַקָּפָה

(ויקרא ב) (שם ד) (תמיד לג:)

רש"י

וְהַגָּשָׁתָהּ לַמִּזְבֵּחַ הוּא דְּיָלֵיף יא] דּוּמְיָא דְּהַגָּשָׁה בְּמִנְחָה. וּמְלִיקָה נָמֵי בַּמִּזְבֵּחַ, יב] אֶלָּא הַזָּאָה וּמִילּוּי. *מַאי קָאָמַר. קָתָנֵי: הִזָּה דָּמָהּ בְּכָל מָקוֹם, וַאֲפִילּוּ לְמַעְלָה מִן הַחוּט, כְּשֵׁירָה. וַהֲדַר יג] תַּנְיָא: וּבִלְבַד שֶׁיִּתֵּן מֵחוּט הַסִּיקְרָא וּלְמַטָּה! וְהָא לֵיכָּא לְמֵימַר דְּהִזָּה יד] וְאַח"כ חָזַר וְהִזָּה לְמַטָּה קָא טו] מַכְשְׁרִי, דְּהָא "הִזָּה דָּמָהּ" קָתָנֵי — כָּל דָּמָהּ מַשְׁמַע, דְּלָא קָתָנֵי "הִזָּה מִדָּמָהּ". מִיצָּה דָּמָהּ. *שֶׁהַחַטָּאת טְעוּנָה מִילּוּי אַחַר הַזָּאָה, כִּדְכְתִיב: "וְהַנִּשְׁאָר בַּדָּם יִמָּצֵה" וגו' (ויקרא ה), שֶׁמַּקִּיף הַגּוּף לַמִּזְבֵּחַ וְדוֹחֵק בֵּית מְלִיקָתוֹ בַּקִּיר, וְהַדָּם מִתְמַצֶּה וְיוֹרֵד. בְּכָל מָקוֹם כְּשֵׁירָה. כִּדְמְפָרֵשׁ טַעְמָא, דְּמִילּוּי בְּחַטָּאת טז] לָאו עֲבוֹדָה הִיא לִיפָּסֵל בְּשִׁינּוּי, שֶׁאֲפִילּוּ עָקַר הַמִּילּוּי לְגַמְרֵי, שֶׁהִזָּה וְלֹא מִיצָּה — כְּשֵׁירָה, כְּדַאֲמַרַן בְּ"אֵיזֶהוּ מְקוֹמָן" (לעיל דף נב.): "וְהַנִּשְׁאָר יִמָּצֵה" — שֶׁאֵינוֹ נִשְׁאָר לֹא יִמָּצֵה. אַלְמָא אִיכָּא יז] דִּסְבִירָא דְּלָא מְעַכֵּב, וּמֵהַאי *קְרָא. וּבִלְבַד. יח] שֶׁיְּהֵא הַזָּאָה הַנַּעֲשֵׂית רִאשׁוֹן מֵחוּט הַסִּיקְרָא וּלְמַטָּה מִדַּם הַנֶּפֶשׁ. הָא דַּאֲמַרַן. דְּיָלְפִינַן לְעֵיל מִ"כִּי חַטָּאת הִיא" הָאָמוּר בְּמִנְחָה. אֶל פְּנֵי הַמִּזְבֵּחַ. וְדָרְשִׁינַן לְעֵיל דְּאַקֶּרֶן מַעֲרָבִית דְּרוֹמִית קָאֵי. אֶל יְסוֹד יט] הַמִּזְבֵּחַ. וְאָמְרִינַן בְּ"אֵיזֶהוּ מְקוֹמָן" (לעיל דף נג.): יִלְמַד יְרִידָתוֹ מִן הַכֶּבֶשׁ בַּחַטָּאוֹת הַחִיצוֹנוֹת מִיְּצִיאָתוֹ מִן הַהֵיכָל — כ] *בְּסָמוּךְ לוֹ, וְהַיְינוּ יְסוֹד דְּרוֹמִי. וּבְכָל הַדָּרוֹם אֵין לְךָ יְסוֹד אֶלָּא אַמָּה אַחַת בְּקֶרֶן מַעֲרָבִית דְּרוֹמִית, כִּדְאָמְרִינַן (שם דף נד.): אוֹכֵל בַּדָּרוֹם אַמָּה אַחַת. מִבֵּית הַדֶּשֶׁן. מָקוֹם שֶׁנּוֹתְנִין שָׁם בְּכָל בֹּקֶר תְּרוּמַת הַדֶּשֶׁן, שֶׁכָּתַב בָּהּ "וְשָׂמוֹ אֵצֶל הַמִּזְבֵּחַ", וְהוּא בְּמִזְרָחוֹ שֶׁל כֶּבֶשׁ. וּכְתִיב גַּבֵּי מוּרְאָה וְנוֹצָה (ויקרא א): "וְהִשְׁלִיךְ אוֹתָהּ אֵצֶל הַמִּזְבֵּחַ קֵדְמָה אֶל מְקוֹם הַדָּשֶׁן". וּלְקַמָּן מַיְיתֵי מִשְׁנָה מִמַּסֶּכֶת תָּמִיד דִּבְמִזְרָחוֹ שֶׁל כֶּבֶשׁ הֲוָה, וְהַיְינוּ כא] *לְקֶרֶן דְּרוֹמִית מִזְרָחִית. שֶׁאֵין לְךָ קַל בָּעוֹף. וְדָבָר שֶׁהוּא קַל מְאֹד אֵין נוֹחַ לְזוֹרְקוֹ לְמֵרָחוֹק. פְּעָמִים שֶׁכֹּהֵן זוֹרְקוֹ כו'. כְּשֶׁהִיא רַבָּה בַּמִּזְרָח, וְנַעֲשֵׂית בְּקֶרֶן מַעֲרָבִית דְּרוֹמִית צָרִיךְ לִזְרוֹק יוֹתֵר מִשְּׁלֹשִׁים אַמָּה. דִּתְנַן. בְּמַסֶּכֶת תָּמִיד: מִי שֶׁזָּכָה בִּתְרוּמַת הַדֶּשֶׁן כב] שֶׁל מַחְתָּה נָטַל מַחְתָּה שֶׁל כֶּסֶף וְעָלָה לְרֹאשׁ הַמִּזְבֵּחַ כו'. הִגִּיעַ לָרִצְפָּה. לְסוֹף הַכֶּבֶשׁ. מַחֲזִיר פָּנָיו לַצָּפוֹן. כג] כְּלַפֵּי הַמִּזְבֵּחַ, וְהוֹלֵךְ לְמִזְרָחוֹ שֶׁל כֶּבֶשׁ, וּמִתְקָרֵב לַמִּזְבֵּחַ עֶשֶׂר אַמּוֹת מִמָּקוֹם שֶׁכָּלָה הַכֶּבֶשׁ, דְּהַיְינוּ רָחוֹק כד] מֵעַל רֹאשׁ הַמִּזְבֵּחַ *כ"ב אַמָּה. צָבַר אֶת הַגֶּחָלִים כו'. אַלְמָא הָתָם הָוֵי בֵּית הַדֶּשֶׁן. וּכְשֶׁהוּא עוֹשֶׂה עוֹלַת הָעוֹף בְּקֶרֶן מַעֲרָבִית דְּרוֹמִית — צָרִיךְ לְזוֹרְקָהּ כה] כָּל אֲלַכְסוֹן שֶׁל כ"ב עַל כ"ב, שֶׁהֲרֵי[א] (א) מִדָּרוֹם לַצָּפוֹן אָמַרְנוּ דְּאִיכָּא כ"ב, וּמִמָּקוֹם שֶׁהוּא עוֹמֵד עַד מִזְרָחוֹ שֶׁל כֶּבֶשׁ אֵין פָּחוֹת *מִכ"ב. כו] וַאֲפִי' הוּא מִתְקָרֵב לַכֶּבֶשׁ כָּל אַמּוֹת רוֹחַב הַקֶּרֶן וְאֵין כָּאן אֶלָּא כ"א, תֵּן כְּנֶגְדָּהּ אַמָּה מְקוֹם מַעֲמָדוֹ כז] שֶׁהוּא מְרוּחָק מִן הַצָּפוֹן לַדָּרוֹם לְבֵית הַדֶּשֶׁן, שֶׁהוּא עוֹמֵד בְּרֹאשׁ הַמִּזְבֵּחַ וְלֹא בַּסּוֹבֵב. שֶׁכְּשֶׁהִיא נַעֲשֵׂית בַּמִּזְרָח עוֹמֵד בַּסּוֹבֵב לְפִי שֶׁיֵּשׁ לוֹ כֶּבֶשׁ קָטָן בַּמִּזְרָח לִפְנוֹת הֵימֶנּוּ לַסּוֹבֵב, אֲבָל לְצַד הַמַּעֲרָב אֵין לוֹ כח] [כֶּבֶשׁ] לִפְנוֹת לַסּוֹבֵב, וְצָרִיךְ לַעֲלוֹת עַל רֹאשׁ הַמִּזְבֵּחַ, כט] וְעוֹמֵד *בִּדְרוֹמָהּ שֶׁל קֶרֶן. וְהָכִי תְּנַן בְּמַסֶּ' סוּכָּה (דף מח.) גַּבֵּי נְסָכִים: עָלָה ל] וּפָנָה לִשְׂמֹאל, וְלֹא תְּנַן בָּהּ "וּפָנָה לַסּוֹבֵב". הֲרֵי מִשָּׁם וְלַכֶּבֶשׁ ה' אַמּוֹת, שֶׁהַכֶּבֶשׁ רָחָב ט"ז בְּאֶמְצַע הַמִּזְבֵּחַ — נִמְצָא רֹאשׁ הַמִּזְבֵּחַ עוֹדֵף עָלָיו לְכָל צַד ו' אַמּוֹת. הֲרֵי כ"ב אַמָּה עִם רוֹחַב הַקֶּרֶן. וְאַע"פ שֶׁזֶּה נִמְשַׁךְ לְצַד הַכֶּבֶשׁ לא] שֶׁל קֶרֶן — הֲרֵי נִתְרַחֵק כְּנֶגְדָּהּ אַמָּה *לַדָּרוֹם. נִמְצָא בֵּית הַדֶּשֶׁן עוֹמֵד כְּנֶגְדָּהּ בַּאֲלַכְסוֹן שֶׁל כ"ב עַל כ"ב, וְכָל אַמְּתָא בְּרִיבּוּעַ אַמְּתָא וּתְרֵי חוּמְשֵׁי בַּאֲלַכְסוֹנָא — נִמְצָא תּוֹסֶפֶת ח' אַמּוֹת וְד' חוּמָשִׁים, הֲרֵי שְׁלֹשִׁים אַמּוֹת וְד' טְפָחִים גְּדוֹלִים. וּבֵית הַדֶּשֶׁן הָיָה מָשׁוּךְ מִמִּזְרָחוֹ שֶׁל כֶּבֶשׁ שְׁלֹשָׁה טְפָחִים — הֲרֵי שְׁלֹשִׁים וְא' אַמָּה וָטֶפַח. וְהַיְינוּ דְּפָרֵיךְ: לב] טְפֵי (לֵיהּ) מִתְּלָתִין וַחֲדָא הָוְיָין. וּמְשַׁנֵּינַן: מְקוֹם גַּבְרָא לָא קָחָשֵׁיב. לג] [וְלָא הָוֵי] לְהוּ יוֹתֵר *מִשְּׁלֹשִׁים. מַאי טַעְמָא. הָעוֹלֶה לד] אֵין עוֹלֶה דֶּרֶךְ יָמִין וְיַקִּיף? וַהֲלֹא דֶּרֶךְ יָמִין מִצְוָה, כְּדַאֲמַרַן לְעֵיל. יִתְעַשְּׁנוּ. כְּשֶׁיַּקִּיף אֶת הַמַּעֲרָכָה בְּעָשָׁן הַמַּעֲרָכָה, וְקַיְ"ל בִּמְנָחוֹת (דף פו:): יַיִן מְעוּשָּׁן פָּסוּל. בָּא לוֹ לְהַקִּיף כו'. מִשְׁנָה הִיא בְּמַסֶּכֶת תָּמִיד גַּבֵּי כֹּהֵן גָּדוֹל, שֶׁאֵינוֹ כִּשְׁאָר כֹּהֲנִים לִזְכּוֹת בְּפַיִיס לַעֲבוֹדָה אַחַת, אֶלָּא עוֹבֵד לה] וְגוֹמֵר בְּכָל חֶפְצוֹ, כִּדְתְנַן בְּמַסֶּכֶת יוֹמָא (דף יז:): כֹּהֵן גָּדוֹל מַקְרִיב חֵלֶק בָּרֹאשׁ. אָמַר "עוֹלָה זוֹ אֲנִי מַקְרִיב". בִּזְמַן שֶׁהוּא לו] (מַקְרִיב) רוֹצֶה לְהַקְטִיר — מִי שֶׁזָּכוּ בְּהוֹלָכַת הָאֵיבָרִים מוֹשִׁיטִין לוֹ, וְהוּא עוֹמֵד בְּרֹאשׁ הַמִּזְבֵּחַ וְזוֹרְקָן לַמַּעֲרָכָה. וּלְאַחַר שֶׁגָּמַר בָּא לְהַקִּיף כו' עַד שֶׁמַּגִּיעַ לְקֶרֶן הַשִּׁיתִין, וְקַסָּלְקָא דַּעְתָּךְ וְהַיַּיִן בְּיָדוֹ, אַלְמָא: לָא חָיְישִׁינַן לְשֶׁמָּא נִתְעַשְּׁנוּ!

תוספות

שאם היזה ולא מיצה כשירה. הא דלא פריך מהכא במסכת מעילה פרק "חטאת העוף" (דף ח:) לרב אדא בר אהבה, *דאמר לז] דתני רב: מילה דמה, דמילוי חטאת העוף מעכב – דמצי למימר: הא מני – תנא דבי ר' ישמעאל היא, לח] דאמר אינו מעכב, לעיל פ' "איזהו מקומן" (דף נב:), כדאמר: תרי תנאי ואליבא דרבי ישמעאל. והא דפריך התם* לרב הונא דתני: "הזה" דמילוי אינו מעכב, ולא משני דאתא כההוא תנא דאמר אינו מעכב – ניחא ליה לשנויי טפי: לגלדין קתני. **הגשות** דכתיב והגישה. הוה ליה למימר: "כדאמרן", דמהאי קרא לחודיה לא נפיק.

שירי הדם דכתיב. נראה דהיינו שירים החיצונים, לט] דבעי קרן *מזרחית דרומית. מ]

מפני שקרובה מבית הדשן. תימה: ולמה הוא הולך עד הקרן, שהיה מרחיק מבית הדשן? *ואין לומר משום דכל דמים טעונין קרן, דהא אמר לעיל (דף ס.) גבי מודה רבי יהודה בדמים דניסקליה ונשפוך אדוכתיה, ואי כל דמים טעונין קרן – מאי קשיא ליה? **יותר** *מל"א אמות. פי' בקונטרס: כשהיתה מא] במזרח היה עומד בסובב, לפי שבמזרח היה כבש קטן שפנה על סובב. אבל במערב לא היה לו כבש לשמאל לפנות בו לסובב, וצריך לעלות לראש המזבח ולעמוד בדרומית של קרן. והכי תנן במסכת סוכה (דף מח.) גבי נסכים: עלה בכבש ופנה לשמאלו, ולא תנן בהו "ופנה לסובב". ונראה דאין משם ראי' שלא היה כבש לסובב מב] במערב, אם כן כשהיה נותן ארבע מתנות שבחטאת, ותנן פרק "איזהו מקומן" (לעיל דף נג.): "פנה לסובב" גבי חטאת, וכשהיה מגיע לקרן מערבית דרומית היה צריך לחזור על עקיבו! ולכך נראה דהיה מג] שם כבש. אבל קשה: דלא חשיב ליה לעיל (דף סב:) גבי שני כבשים קטנים יוצאים מן הכבש.

מן המאוכלות הפנימיות. אומר ר"ת: דגבי גחלים של יום הכפורים* לא גרסינן "מן המאוכלות מד] הפנימיות", דהכא חשבינן להו דשן, וביום הכפורים וכן בקטרת של כל השנה בעינן גחלים דוקא, כדאמר התם: א) "גחלי אש" יכול עוממות. **צבר** את הגחלים. משום דאמר "ושמו" – שלא יפזר. **דישון** מזבח הפנימי והמנורה. הקשה ריב"א: כיון דתרומת הדשן ודישון מזבח הפנימי והמנורה נבלעים במקומן, אמאי מועלין בזה יותר מזה? דבתרומת הדשן מועלין, כדאמר לעיל ס"פ "ב"ש" (דף מו.), ובדישון מזבח ומנורה תנן במעילה* דלא נהנים ולא מועלים! וי"ל: דשאני תרומת הדשן, דגלי קרא "ושמו". וכי תימא: כיון דנבלעין, היכי משכחת בהו מעילה? שמא לא היו נבלעין מיד. ור"ת אומר: דתרומת הדשן לא היה נבלע, מדלא חשיב להו ביומא (דף כא.) בהדי אינך דנבלעין, מה] ב) דישון מזבח הפנימי והמנורה. ואומר ה"ר יום טוב: דאין זו ראיה, דה"נ מו] בת"כ (סדר ויקרא פ' ט) דחשיב ג'[ב] בתי דשנים הן, אחד *בדרום דמוראה ונוצה ודישון מזבח הפנימי והמנורה, ולא חשיב תרומת הדשן, אף על פי שהיתה שם, מז] כדתנן בתמיד ג).

א) [פסחים עה:] ב) נ"ל גבי דישון נ"ק ג) [ועי' תוס' יבמות ק. ד"ה והשירים]

לו א מיי' פ"ז מהל' מעה"ק הל"ו:
לז ב מיי' שם הל"ז:
לח ג מיי' שם הל"ו:
לט ד מיי' שם הל"ח:
מ ה מיי' פ"ו מהל' מעה"ק הל"כ:
מא ו מיי' שם הל' כא:
מב ז מיי' שם הל' כב:
ל"ל כו' ל"ק
מג ח ט מיי' שם הל' כ:
מד י מיי' פי"ג מהל' פסה"מ הל"ה:
מה כ מיי' פט"ו שם הלכה א:
מו ל מיי' פט"ז שם הלכה א:

הקפה ברגל. ואין היין בידו. ולמגוה בעלמא, מפני שכל העולין לשאר דברים פונין לימין ומקיפין, וזה כח] להקטיר עולה, לפיכך מקיף ובא למקום שמנסכין שם ונותנין לו יין לנסך. אבל שאר כהנים, כו] שהזוכה בנסכים בפיים לא זכה לעבודה אחרת – עולה והיין בידו ופנה לשמאל וחוזר על העקב, כדנתני'. עולים דרך מזרח. כשהן עולין לכבש – במזרחו אצל שפתו עולין, שהרי דרך ימין יפנה, ולמה לו להאריך הילוכו כל רחבו של כבש? וכשהוא יורד – כז] יורד בשפת מערבו של כבש. ה"ג: חוץ מן העולה לג' דברים הללו שעולין דרך מערב ויורדין דרך מערב עולין דרך ימין ויורדין דרך ימין. שמאל הוא. מערבו של כבש כח] שמאל הוי כשהאיש פניו למזבח. מאי ימין. דקתני בסיפא – ימין דמזבח, שהמזבח פניו לדרום וימינו למערב. ומאי שמאל. דקתני ברישא – שמאל דגברא. אידי ואידי. דרישא ודסיפא.

תורה אור

א] הקפה ברגל. אמר רבא: דיקא נמי, דקתני: ב] נותנין לו יין לנסך, ולא קתני: אומר לו "נסך", ש"מ. ת"ר: כל העולין למזבח – עולין דרך ימין ויורדין דרך שמאל, עולין דרך מזרח ויורדין דרך מערב, חוץ מן ג] העולה לשלשה דברים הללו, שעולים דרך מערב ויורדין דרך מערב, עולין דרך ימין ויורדין דרך ימין. דרך ימין?! דרך שמאל הוא! אמר ד] רבינא: תני שמאל. רבא אמר: מאי ימין – ימין דמזבח, ומאי שמאל – שמאל דגברא. וניתני או אידי ואידי דמזבח, או אידי ואידי דגברא! קשיא.§ **מתני'** חטאת העוף ה] כיצד היה נעשית? (עלה לכבש ופנה לסובב, בא לו לקרן דרומית מזרחית) היה [א]מולק את ראשה ממול ערפה ו] ואינו מבדיל, ומזה מדמה על קיר המזבח. שירי הדם היה מתמצה על היסוד, ז] [ב]ואין למזבח אלא דמה, וכולה לכהנים.§ **גמ'** ת"ר: °"והזה מדם החטאת" – ח] מגוף החטאת. הא כיצד? ט] אוחז בראש ובגוף ומזה על קיר המזבח, ולא על קיר הכבש, ולא על קיר היכל, ולא על קיר אולם. ואיזה – [ג]זה קיר התחתון. י] או אינו אלא קיר העליון? ודין הוא: ומה בהמה שעולתה למטה – חטאתה למעלה, עוף שעולתו למעלה – אינו דין שחטאתו למעלה? ת"ל: °"והנשאר בדם ימצה אל יסוד המזבח" – קיר יא] שהשירין שלו מתמצים ליסוד, ואיזה זה – קיר התחתון. ונעביד מעילאי והדר נעביד מתתאי! אמר רבא: מי כתיב יב] "ימצה"? "ימצה" כתיב, דממילא משמע. אמר רב זוטרא בר טוביה אמר רב: כיצד מולקין חטאת העוף? אוחז יג] גפיו בשתי אצבעות, ושתי רגלים בשתי אצבעות, ומותח צוארה על יד] רוחב גודלו, ומולקה. במתניתא תנא ציפרא מלבר: [ד]אוחז גפיו בשתי אצבעות, ושני רגלים בשתי אצבעות, ומותח צוארו על רוחב שתי אצבעותיו, ומולק. וזו טו] *עבודה קשה שבמקדש. זו היא ותו לא? והאיכא: קמיצה וחפינה! אלא אימא: זו עבודה קשה מעבודות קשות שבמקדש.§ **מתני'** *[ה]עולת העוף כיצד טז] נעשית? עלה לכבש, ופנה לסובב, בא לו לקרן דרומית מזרחית. היה מולק את ראשה ממול ערפה ומבדיל, יז] ומיצה את דמה על קיר המזבח. [ו]נטל את הראש והקיף בית מליקתו למזבח, ?וספגו? במלח, וזרקו על גבי האשים. בא לו לגוף, והסיר את המוראה ואת הנוצה ואת בני המעיים היוצאין יח] עמם והשליכן לבית הדשן. [ז]שיסע ולא הבדיל, ואם הבדיל – כשר. יט] סופגו במלח, וזרקו על גבי האשים. לא הסיר המוראה ולא הנוצה כ] ואת בני מעיים היוצאין עמם, ולא ספגו במלח, כל ששינה בה מאחר שמיצה את דמה – כשירה. כא] *[ח]הבדיל בחטאת ולא הבדיל בעולה – פסול. [ט]מיצה כב] את דם הראש ולא מיצה דם הגוף – פסולה. דם הגוף ולא מיצה דם הראש – כשירה. [י]חטאת העוף שמלקה שלא לשמה, מיצה דמה שלא לשמה, כג] לשמה ושלא לשמה, או שלא לשמה ולשמה – פסול. [כ]עולת העוף – כשירה, ובלבד שלא עלתה לבעלים לשם חובה. *[ל]אחד חטאת העוף ואחד עולת העוף, שמלקן ושמיצה את דמן לאכול דבר שדרכו לאכול, ולהקטיר דבר שדרכו להקטיר, חוץ למקומו – פסול ואין בו כרת. חוץ לזמנו – פיגול וחייבין עליו כרת, ובלבד שיקריב המתיר כמצותו. כיצד *קרב המתיר כמצותו? מלק בשתיקה ומיצה הדם חוץ לזמנו, או שמלק חוץ לזמנו ומיצה הדם בשתיקה, או שמלק ומיצה הדם חוץ לזמנו – זהו שקרב המתיר כמצותו. כיצד לא קרב המתיר כמצותו? מלק חוץ למקומו כד] מיצה הדם חוץ לזמנו, או שמלק חוץ לזמנו ומיצה הדם חוץ למקומו, או שמלק ומיצה הדם חוץ למקומו;

חטאת

חטאת העוף כיצד היתה נעשית. משום דדם חטאת קודם לעולה, מפרש חטאת תחילה. **מגופה** של חטאת. מדכתיב "והזה מדם החטאת", ולא כתיב "ולקח", דמשמע בכלי.

אוחז בראש ובגוף ומזה*. תימה: דלא בעי הכא "מאי קאמר", כדקבעי פ"ק דחולין (דף כב.).

ואיזה זה קיר התחתון. דאי קיר העליון – פעמים שהוא מתמלה לסובב אם עושה למעלה מן הסובב, דקיר העליון הוי מן החוט עד הקרנות.

קמיצה וחפינה. בכולהו תנינא עבודה קשה.

והקריבו

מתני' ואינו מבדיל. הראש מן הגוף, אלא סימן אחד לבדו מולק, דכתיב בה: "ומלק את ראשו ממול ערפו ולא יבדיל" (ויקרא ה), וב"הכל שוחטין" (חולין דף כא:) ילפינן דבסימן אחד הוא. ומזה. אוחז בעוף עצמו ומזה. היה מתמצה. שמקיף כט] ומתקרב בית מליקתו למזבח, ודוחקו בקיר, והדם מתמצה ויורד ליסוד. שהרי למטה מן החוט היא נעשית, וכניסת הסובב למעלה הימנו. **גמ'** מגוף של חטאת. שלא יזה לא בכלי ולא באצבע. אלא אוחז בעוף עצמו ומזה. קיר התחתון. שלמטה מן החוט. בהמה שעולתה למטה. כדאמרן בפ"ק (לעיל דף י:), דכתיב בחטאת בהמה: "המחטא אותה" – אותה דמה למעלה, ואין אחרת דמה למעלה. חטאתה למעלה. דקרנות כתיבי בה. עוף שעולתו למעלה. כדיליף לקמן בפירקין (דף סה.). שהשירים שלו. כשמזה הדם שותת ומתמצה ליסוד. ואיזה זה קיר התחתון. ל] *פעמים שהוא מתמצה לסובב, כשהוא עושהו למעלה מן הסובב, דמן החוט עד הקרנות קיר העליון הוא. אבל קיר התחתון – כולו למטה מן הסובב, שהחוט למטה מן הסובב אמה. ונעביד מעילאי. ההזאה יעשה למעלה, והדין נותן כדאמרן, והדר נעביד מילוי מתתאי כדכתיב! מי כתיב לא] ימצה ימצה כתיב. אי הוה כתיב ימצה הוה משמע שמזהיר את הכהן שיחזור וימצה אחר ההזאה. השתא דכתיב ימצה משמע נמי לענין ההזאה, לב] דממילא יהיה דם מצוי אצל היסוד. אוחז שני גפיה בשתי אצבעות. גוף העוף על כפו מבפנים, ומכניס שני רגליה בין אצבע קטנה לג] זרת לקמיצה, ושני גפיה בין אמה לאצבע. ומותח צוארה. גרונה התחתון מותח על רוחב החיצון של גודל, שמכניס הצואר בין אצבע לגודל, נמצא הגרון לצד גודלו, ומותחו על גודלו והעורף מלמעלה, ומולק. ציפרא מלבר. כמו שאנו לד] *עושים על גב היד, אלא שהופך פניו של עוף לה] על גב ידו, שיהא העורף מלמעלה. מותח צוארו. הגרון על רוחב הפנימי של שתי אצבעותיו אצבע ואמה. גבי קמיצה נמי תניא זו היא עבודה קשה. שצריך למחוק בגודלו מלמעלה ובאצבעו קטנה למטה, שלא יהא הקומץ מבורץ. וכן בחפינת יום הכפורים נמי תניא. זו היא עבודה קשה. ותרוייהו בסדר יומא בפרק "הוציאו לו" (דף מז: ודף מט:). עבודה קשה מעבודות קשות. כלומר, אחת מעבודות קשות שבמקדש. **מתני'** עלה בכבש. לפי שנעשית למעלה, כדילפינן בגמרא. בא לו לקרן דרומית מזרחית. כדאמרן, שקרובה לבית הדשן. ומבדיל. בשני סימנין, כדיליף ב"הכל שוחטין" (חולין דף כא:). ערפה. גובה הראש. מול ערפה – למטה, לצד האגפיים, מול הרואה את העורף. והקיף את בית מליקתו למזבח. סומכו ודוחקו בקיר כדי שיתמצה הדם. ספגו במלח. מקנחו במלח הנמלח בראש המזבח, כדכתיב: "וכל קרבן מנחתך במלח תמלח". לו] ואומר ב"הקומץ רבה" (מנחות דף כא:) בג' מקומות המלח נתונה: בלשכת המלח, ועל גבי הכבש, ובראש המזבח. מוראה. זפק. נוצה. שנוטל העור שכנגד הזפק בנוצתה, עם הזפק.* שיסע. הגוף בין אגפיה. הבדיל בחטאת. במליקתה, לז] שמולק שני סימנין. או לא הבדיל בעולה – שמלקה בסימן אחד. פסול. דכל שינוי שהוא לפני עבודות הדם – פסולות. ובגמרא מפרש טעמא. מיצה דם כו'. מפרש טעמא בגמרא. לאכול דבר שדרכו לאכול. חטאת העוף. שדרכו להקטיר. עולת העוף. שלא לח] לשמן. אין מוציא עולה מידי פיגול, מפני שהיא כשירה בשלא לשמה.

גמ'

*מנחות יח. [יומא מז: מט:]

ס"א דאי קיר העליון פעמים כו'

[לעיל נב. מנחות לז:]

[עי' תוס' לקמן סה: ד"ה הבדיל]

[מעילה ט.]

[עי' תוס' לקמן סה: ד"ה כילד]

שוחטים ל"ק

הזפק הס"ד ואח"כ ד"ה חטאת העוף שמלקה שלא לשמה אבל עולת העוף שמלקה שלא לשמה אין מוציא עולתה מידי פיגול מפני שהיא כשרה בשלא לשמה הס"ד וכצ"ל ואח"כ ד"ה לאכול דבר שדרכו לאכול חטאת עוף הס"ד ואח"כ ד"ה שדרכו להקטיר עולת העוף הס"ד ל"ק

שיטה מקובצת

א] הקפה ברגל. פ"ה בלא יין וקשה לרש"י א"כ למה היה מקיף יפנה מיד לצד מערב לספלים לנסך ויחזור על העקב כמו שאר כהנים עושין שזוכין בניסוך על ידי פיים וי"ל דלא דמי דאחד משאר כהנים שהיה זוכה בנסכים בפיים לא היה מגיע בחלקו עבודה אחרת אבל כהן הגדול שהיה כמו כן מקטיר היה מקיף בשם שלא כדרכו [להעלות] אברים שצריך להקטיר ולא נהירא דהתם מוכח דהקף זה אחר כל ההקטרה לכך נראה לרבינו שמשון דלכך היה מקיף להראות שיש לו רשות יותר מלאחרים שהוא בן בית וכן איתא בפרק טרף בקלפי ששאר הכהנים היו עולים ויורדים בשפה של הכבש במזרח או במערב והכהן הגדול באמצע מהאי טעמא להראות שהיה יותר בן בית משאר הכהנים: ב] נתנו לו יין: ג] מן העולים לשלשה: ד] אמר רבא תני שמאל רבינא אמר: ה] כיצד היתה נעשית היה מולק כו' והשאר נמחק: ו] ואינו מבדיל דכיון דהכשר העוף בסימן אחד כל מה שימלוק מכאן ואילך קרוי הבדלה וא"ת א"כ לא היה לו למלוק רק רוב סימן אחד כיון דהכשרו דעוף ברוב סימן אחד וי"ל דאין זה אלא דיעבד אבל לכתחילה בעינן סימן שלם וא"ת כמו כן נמי מוכח בחולין דצריך לשחוט ב' סימנין לכתחילה וי"ל דטעמא לא הוי משום דאין זה אלא דיעבד אלא דמסברא יש לנו לומר כיון שהתחיל למלוק הסימן שימלקנו כולו: ז] היסוד אין למזבח אות ו' נמחק: ח] החטאת מגופו של חטאת: ט] עי' בהשמטות בסוף המסכת: י] התחתון אתה אומר קיר התחתון או: יא] שהשירים שלו מתמצין ליסוד. וא"ת ויעשה למעלה מן החוט באמה שלמטה מן הסובב ומשם ימצה ליסוד ולעולם בקיר העליון הוא וי"ל דא"כ הוי ג' מקומות במזבח דלמטה מן החוט הוי מקום דמים דעולת בהמה ולמעלה מן הסובב עולת העוף ולחטאת בהמה ולמטה מן הסובב באמה שבין הסובב לחוט הסיקרא לחטאת העוף וזה לא יתכן דהואיל חוט הסיקרא מפסיק בין דמים עליונים לתחתונים א"כ משמע דאין בו כי אם שני מקומות לדמים. מהר"פ: יב] כתיב ימצה ימצה כתיב ס"י מי כתיב ימצא ימצה כתיב ורש"י לא גרס כן: יג] אוחז שני גפיה בשתי: יד] רוחב גודלו. והעוף אחר ידו ומיעקם צואר העוף על גודלו ובאותו גודל עצמו מולק כי כל העבודות נעשות בימין ולכך היתה עבודה קשה ובמתנית' היתה העוף מלבר על גב היד וצואר העוף בין אצבע לגודל ומולק בגודל. תו"א: טו] ומולק וזו היא עבודה: טז] כיצד היתה נעשית: יז] ומצה: יח] היוצאין עמה והשליכן: יט] כשר ספגו במלח: כ] הנוצה ולא את בני המעיים היוצאים עמם ולא ספגן במלח: כא] הבדיל בחטאת ולא הבדיל בעולה פסול פ"ה בפ"ק דחולין האי דבעינן הבדלה בעולת העוף יליף מומלק והקטיר כדמשמע בגמרא אבל בחטאת העוף כתיב לא יבדיל וה"פ לא יבדיל יותר מכשיעור שחיטה והיינו סימן אחד בעוף וא"ת א"כ אם יבדיל [יותר] מרוב סימן אחד תיפסל דהוי יותר משיעור שחיטה וי"ל דמ"מ לכתחילה בעינן (רוב) סימן שלם וא"ת והא מוכח בחולין דלכתחילה בעינן שני סימנים בשחיטת העוף בפרק השוחט דמוקי דיעבד אוחאד בעוף משמע הא לכתחילה בעינן שנים אף בעוף לכך נראה דקרא דלא יבדיל קאי אדיעבד דשחיטה ולהכי סגי בחד ומ"מ בעינן סימן שלם ולא סגי ברוב דמסתמא לא הצריך הכתוב לומר דלא יבדיל להפסיק בתוך הסימן אלא לאחר שיסיים סימן שלם דמסברא לא איירי קרא בחצאין: כב] מיצה דם הראש ולא מיצה דם הגוף פסול דם: כג] או לשמה ושלא: כד] למקומו ומיצה הדם: כה] וזה אף הוא להקטיר: כו] כהנים הזוכים בנסכים בפיים ולא זכו לעבודה אחרת עולה בידו ופונה לשמאל וחוזר: כז] יורד הימנו יורד: כח] כבש הוי שמאל כשהאיש: כט] שמקיף ומקרב בית: ל] התחתון דאי קיר העליון פעמים: לא] כתיב ימצה ימצה כתיב: לב] הואה שיזה במקום דממילא יהיה הדם מתמצה על היסוד הס"ד: לג] תיבת זרת נמחק: לד] שאנו שוחטין שהעוף על ותיבת עושין נמחק: לה] לצד גב תיבת על נמחק: לו] תמלח וגו' ואמרינן בהקומץ: לז] במליקתה שמלק: לח] שלא לשמה אין:

ומיצה

גמ' והקריבו מה תלמוד לומר. בעולת העוף כתיב: "והקריבו הכהן אל המזבח", מה ת"ל? הא כתיב: "והקריב מן התורים" וגו' וליכתוב בתריה: "ומלק הכהן את ראשו על המזבח"! פרידין = גוזלות. לקבוע לו כהן. שלא ימלקנו זר. לא קבע לו כהן. דשחיטה בזר כשירה. קבע לה כלי. דנפקא לן מ"ויקח את המאכלת", לקמן באידך פירקין (דף צז:). ת"ל כהן ומלק אמר רבי עקיבא כו'. כולה ר' עקיבא קאמר לה. בעצמו של כהן. בציפורנו, ולא בסכין. בין יח] למעלה. מן החוט. מן הצואר. מן הגרון. ונאמר להלן. בחטאת [העוף]. והקטיר אותו. *"ושסע בכנפיו ולא יבדיל *והקטיר אותו", יט] אני יודע מה שנאמרה תחילה "ומלק את ראשו והקטיר" – בהקטרת הראש. דמו כולו. מדלא כתיב "ונמצה *מדמו". מאחר שהקטיר הוא ממצה. וא"ת: במילוי הגוף – לא מקיימא "דמו" כולו. ה"ג: ת"ל ומלק והקטיר ונמצה דמו וכי תעלה על דעתך משהקטיר ממצה אלא לומר לך מה הקטרה בראש המזבח אף המילוי בראש המזבח. ובא לקרן דרומית מזרחית גרסינן. למטה מרגליו. שהחוט למטה מן הסובב אמה. אלא בראש המזבח. דבעינן "והקטיר ונמצה דמו" – שיהא מילוי בקיר הסמוך למקום הקטרה. מאי בינייהו. כלומר: במאי קמיפלגי? הא ע"כ לת"ק גופיה אית ליה "והקטיר ונמצה דמו", דאי לאו ס"ל – קיר העליון מנא *ליה? עושה מערכה כו'. לת"ק הרוצה לעשות מערכה על גבי סובב ולהקטיר – כ] עושה, הילכך מילוי שתחת הסובב סמוך למקום הקטרה. כא] יכול יקדיר את העור בסכין, ויטלנו. לזפק לבדו בלא עור ובלא נוצה, כמו כב] שצולין עוף עושין? ונוטל את קורקבנה. "ונוצתה" לשון פרש ודבר מאוס הוא, כמו (איכה ד) "כי נצו גם נעו". בנוצתה שלה. כג] ולא יותר ממה שכנגד הזפק הא

תורה אור

חטאת העוף שמלקו שלא לשמה ומיצה א] הדם חוץ לזמנו, או שמלק חוץ לזמנו ומיצה דמו שלא לשמה, או שמלק ומיצה הדם שלא לשמה – זהו שלא קרב המתיר כמצותו. *לאכול כזית בחוץ כזית למחר, כזית למחר כזית בחוץ, כחצי זית בחוץ כחצי זית למחר, כחצי זית למחר כחצי זית בחוץ – פסול, ואין בו כרת. א"ר יהודה: זה הכלל, אם מחשבת הזמן קדמה למחשבת המקום – פיגול וחייבין עליו כרת, ואם מחשבת המקום קדמה למחשבת הזמן – פסול ואין בו כרת. ב] [*וחכ"א: זה וזה פסול ואין בו כרת]. *לאכול כחצי זית ולהקטיר כחצי זית – כשר, שאין אכילה והקטרה מצטרפין.§ **גמ'** *ת"ר: °"והקריבו", מה ת"ל? לפי שנאמר: °"והקריב מן התורים או מן בני היונה", יכול המתנדב עוף לא יפחות משני פרידין? ת"ל "והקריבו" – אפילו פרידה אחת יביא אל המזבח. מה ת"ל °"הכהן" – לקבוע לו כהן. שיכול, והלא דין הוא: ומה בן צאן שקבע לו צפון – לא קבע לו כהן, עוף שלא קבע לו צפון – אינו דין שלא יקבע לו כהן? ת"ל: ג] "אל הכהן", לקבוע לו כהן. יכול ימלקנו בסכין? ודין הוא: ומה אם שחיטה שלא קבע לה כהן – קבע לה כלי, מליקה שקבע לה כהן – אינו דין שיקבע לה כלי? ת"ל: ד] *°"כהן ומלק". אמר רבי עקיבא: וכי תעלה על דעתך שזר קרב לגבי מזבח? אלא מה ת"ל "כהן" – שתהא מליקה בעצמו של כהן. יכול ימלקנה בין מלמעלה בין מלמטה – ת"ל: "ומלק והקטיר", מה הקטרה בראש המזבח – אף מליקה בראש המזבח. "ומלק" – ה] ממול עורף. אתה אומר ממול עורף, או אינו אלא מן הצואר? ו] ודין הוא: נאמר כאן "ומלק" ונאמר להלן °"ומלק", מה להלן ממול עורף – אף כאן ממול עורף. אי מה להלן מולק ואינו מבדיל, אף כאן מולק ואינו מבדיל! ת"ל: "ומלק והקטיר", ז] מה הקטרה – הראש לעצמו והגוף לעצמו, אף מליקה – הראש לעצמו והגוף לעצמו. ומנין שהקטרת הראש בעצמו והגוף בעצמו? שנאמר: °"והקטיר אותו" – הרי הקטרת הגוף אמורה, הא מה אני מקיים °"והקטיר המזבחה" – בהקטרת הראש הכתוב מדבר. °"ונמצה דמו" – כולו, ח] "אל קיר המזבח" – ולא על קיר הכבש, ולא על קיר ההיכל. ט] ואיזה זה – זה קיר העליון. או אינו אלא קיר התחתון! ודין הוא: מה בהמה שחטאתה למעלה – עולתה למטה, עוף שחטאתו למטה – אינו דין י] שעולתו למטה? ת"ל: "ומלק והקטיר ונמצה דמו", וכי תעלה על דעתך יא] לאחר שהקטיר חוזר וממצה? אלא לומר לך: מה הקטרה בראש המזבח – אף מיצוי בראש המזבח. הא כיצד? היה עולה בכבש ופונה לסובב, ובא לו לקרן דרומית מזרחית, היה מולק את ראשה ממול ערפה ומבדיל, יב] וממצה מדמה על קיר המזבח. אם עשאה למטה מרגליו אפילו אמה – יג] כשירה. רבי נחמיה ורבי אליעזר בן יעקב אומרים: יד] כל עצמה אין נעשית אלא בראש המזבח. מאי בינייהו? אביי ורבא דאמרי תרוייהו: עושה מערכה ע"ג סובב איכא בינייהו.§ "בא לו לגוף" כו'.§ ת"ר: °"והסיר את מוראתו טו] בנוצתה" – זו זפק. יכול יקדיר בסכין ויטלנו? ת"ל: "בנוצתה" – טז] נוטל את הנוצה עמה. אבא יוסי בן חנן אומר: נוטלה ונוטל יז] קורקבנה עמה. דבי רבי ישמעאל תנא: "בנוצתה" – בנוצה שלה, קודרה בסכין כמין ארובה.§

שיסע

והקריבו מה תלמוד לומר. וא"ת: דבפ"ק דחולין (דף כא:) דריש כד] לדרשא אחרינא, הא איצטריך לכדדרשינן הכא! וי"ל: דהכא דריש מדסמכיה לתורים ובני יונה – ש"מ פרידה אחת. והתם דריש *מדסמכיה כה] ל"והקטיר". ואין לומר דדרשינן תרתי משום וי"ו ד"והקריבו", דהא בחולין הוא רבי ישמעאל דלא דריש וי"ו פ' "אלמנה" (יבמות דף סח:)*.

עוף שלא קבע לו צפון אינו דין שלא קבע לו כהן. וא"ת: קמילה תוכיח, דלא קבע לה צפון וקבע לה כהן! כו] ויש לומר: מה למנחה – שטעונה הגשה ותנופה *וקידוש קומץ כז] וכלי שרת. וא"ת: נילף מדאיתקש חטאת למנחה כדאמרינן לעיל! ונראה דמסתבר ליה דלא תהוי מליקה עבודה יותר משחיטה. **בן** עוף שקבע לו כהן אינו דין שיקבע לו כלי. וא"ת: קמילה תוכיח, שקבע לה כהן ולא קבע לה כלי! כח] וי"ל: מה למנחה – שכן אינה מיני דמים. וא"ת: מה לבן צאן – שכן מין זבח. אבל עוף לא חשיב ליה מין זבח בפ"ק (לעיל דף ח:)! וי"ל: דהיינו משום דקים לן שהוא ביד, אבל כט] אי הוה בכלי – הוה חשיב מין זבח. וא"ת: מה לבן צאן שכן טעון צפון! על כן נראה, דמעיקרא סמיך אהיקשא ד"זאת התורה", דילפינן מינה: מה עולה טעונה כלי. דעופות נמי כתיבי בההוא עניינא, מדפריך פ"ק דחולין (דף כב.): ביום – מ"ביום צוותו" נפקא. ובמגילה פרק "הקורא למפרע" (דף כ:) גבי כל היום כשר למליקה, דרשינן בגמרא מ"ביום צוותו".

תלמוד לומר הכהן ומלק ל] בעצמו של כהן. וא"ת: ונילף מדאיתקש לעיל חטאת העוף למנחה! וי"ל: חטאת איתקש, עולת העוף לא איתקש. ועוד: כיון דאיכא לאוקומי *היקש – לא מפקא מק"ו דהכא. ועוד: דאדרבה, נקיש בהיקשא ד"זאת התורה" לעולה דבעיא כלי.

וכי תעלה על דעתך שזר קרב למזבח. ואפילו מאן לא] דלית ליה הך סברא גבי הלכתא אליתא (יומא דף מה.) – משום דהא אפשר דקאי אארעא ועביד במפוחא.

אף מליקה בראש מזבח. *חטאת ועולה ילפי מהדדי גבי "מול עורף" ולענין בעצמו של כהן בג"ש, נאמר כאן "ומלק" ונאמר להלן "ומלק". אבל להצריך לחטאת מליקה בראש המזבח *כעולה – לא ילפינן, משום דעולה לא ילפא אלא מהיקשא דהקטרה, ודבר הלמד בהיקש אינו חוזר ומלמד בג"ש, מדרבי יוחנן, כדאמר פרק "איזהו מקומן" (לעיל דף מט:). וא"ת: בפ"ק דקדושין (דף לו.) דאמר דמליקה אינה כשירה בנשים, דאיתקש להקטרה, ובהקטרה כתיב "בני אהרן" ולא בנות אהרן. תינח מליקה דעולה, מליקה דחטאת מנלן? דבר הלמד בהיקש אינו חוזר ומלמד בג"ש! וי"ל: דגלוי מילתא בעלמא הוא, כהן ולא כהנת. וא"ת: ורבי *שמעון דנפקא ליה בפרק קמא דחולין (דף כא:) עולת העוף ממול עורף מהיקישא ד"כמשפט" חטאת העוף, ולית ליה ג"ש דהכא – א"כ מנא ליה בחטאת העוף דבעינן כהן שתהא בעצמו של כהן? וי"ל: דחטאת נמי ילפא מעולה, מהיקישא ד"כמשפט". **דמו** כולו. נראה דחטאת לא בעי דמו כולו, מדלא קתני בה הקיף בית *מליקה למזבח. **ואם** עשאה למטה מרגליו ואפילו אמה אחת כשירה. אף על גב דכתיב: "ומלק והקטיר ונמצה" – לא בעי מקום הקטרה ממש, כי היכי דלגבי דם חשיב לב] סמוך לקרן אמה אחת.

הבדיל

מז א ב ג מיי' פי"ג מהל' פסה"מ הלכה כ:
מח ד מיי' פט"ו מהל' מעה"ק הל"ט:
מט ה מיי' שם פ"ו הל' כג:
נ ו ז ח מיי' שם הל' כא:
נא ט מיי' שם הל' כ:
נב י ב מיי' שם הל"כ:

גי' הב"ח מדסמכיה לומלק והקטיר כו'
[ועי' בתוס' שם ד"ה כמאן כר"ע ובמנחות דף נח: ד"ה וי"ו כו' כתבו דאיכא למ"ד דלהגי דרשי לא דרשו וי"ו ולאחוז דרשה דרשו וי"ו ולפ"ז א"ל דר"י נמי הכי]
וקידוש בכלי שרת ב"ק
[נ"ע חכמים היינו ת"ק ועמ"ש לעיל כט: על הגליון]
נ"א היקש לדרשה אחרינא לא מפקא כו' ב"ק
וחטאת ב"ק
מעולה ב"ק
ל"ל ישמעאל
מליקתו ב"ק

לעיל כט:
מדכתיב ושסע ב"ק
נ"א והקטיר אותו הס"ד ואח"כ מה"ד ומה אני מקיים מה שנאמרה כו'
כס"י איתא הדם
[לעיל לה. וש"נ]
כריתות ט.
ליה ב"ק
הכהן ב"ק
חולין כב.
חולין כח:

גליון הש"ס

גמ' אם עשאה למטה מרגליו. ע"ל דף סד ע"ב תוספות ד"ה עולת.

שיטה מקובצת

א] ומיצה דמה חוץ לזמנה או שמלקה חוץ לזמנה ומיצה דמה שלא לשמה או שמלקה ומיצה דמה: ב] כרת וחכ"א זה וזה פסול ואין בו כרת לאכול: ג] תיבת אל נמחק: ד] ת"ל הכהן ומלק. כדמפרש ר"ע שתהא מליקה בעצמו של כהן דר"ע מילתא דת"ק אתא לפרושי אלא דת"ק אית ליה דמשמעות הכהן משמע תרתי שתהא מליקה בעצמו של כהן ולקבוע לו כהן ור"ע אית ליה דהכהן אתא לומר שתהא מליקה בעצמו של כהן אבל לקבוע לו כהן לא איצטריך דסברא הוא בלא פסוק דצריך כהן כדמפרש תלמודא אבל ודאי לא נשמע מהכהן תרתי: ה] ומלק שתהא מליקה ממול: ו] על תיבות ודין הוא נרשם עליו קו: ז] מה הקטרה הראש (בעצמו) [לעצמו] כו'. וא"ת אי מה הקטרה אינה מעכבת אף מליקה אם לא הבדיל בעולה אינה מעכבת וא"כ למה תנן אם לא הבדיל בעולה פסול ותירץ ריב"א דאה"נ נימא מליקה דומיא דהקטרה דאם לא הבדיל אלא בסימן אחד הוי כאילו לא מלק כלל וחיסר מצות מליקה ואז פסול ממילא אבל אם חיסר מצות הקטרה לא מיפסל בהכי אבל קשה דלעיל יליף נמי מה הקטרה בראש המזבח ועוד קשה דאמאי קאמר במתני' דאם שינה פסול נימא דומיא דהקטרה ואם לא הקטיר כשר וי"ל דהתם נמי הויא דומיא דהקטרה וה"פ מה הקטרה אם שינה בה ולא עשאה בראש המזבח חיסר מצות הקטרה והוי כאילו לא הקטיר כלל ואם לא הקטיר כלל פסול אף מליקה אם שינה בה חיסר מצות מליקה כאילו לא מלק כלל ואם לא מלק כלל פסול דאין כאן עבודה כלל: ח] כולו (ס"י אוחז בראש ובגוף וממצה בשניהם) על קיר תיבת אל נמחק: ט] ההיכל ולא על קיר האולם ואיזה: י] שתהא עולתו למטה: יא] וכי תעלה על דעתך מאחר שהקטיר כו' וא"ת אה"נ והמצאות דם הגוף קאמר דאכתי לא איירי קרא אלא בהקטרת הראש וי"ל דנמצה דמו משמע ליה כל דמו והא ליכא הואיל והקטיר הראש: יב] ומבדיל ס"י ודמה מתמצה על כו': יג] אמה אחת כשרה: יד] היא עצמה אינה נעשית אלא בראש: טו] תיבת בנוצתה נמחק: טז] בנוצתה נוטלה ונוטל: יז] ונוטל את: יח] בין מלמעלה: יט] אותו וגו' הס"ד ומה"ד ומה אני מקיים מה שנאמרה: כ] ולהקטיר בה עושה: כא] הקטרה היא הס"ד: כב] כמו שצולין העוף עושין: כג] שלה שלא יטול יותר ממה שכנגד: כד] דריש. ס"א לומר דחילק הכתוב בין חטאת העוף לעולת העוף א) היינו מוהקריב לזה ולא לאחר והכא דריש מדסמכיה והקריבו אל מן התורים: כה] מדסמכי' לומלק ותיבת לוהקטיר נמחק: כו] כהן דכתיב וקמץ הכהן וי"ל מה למנחה שכן טעונה הגשה: כז] בכלי שרת (אות ו' נמחק) לאחר קמיצה מה שאין כן בעוף ועוד אמר ריב"א דמליקה לשחיטה סברא לדמות שכן מיני דמים ולא לקמיצה דמנחה שאינה מיני דמים. תוס' אחרות: כח] כלי שהיה קימץ בידו אף אני אביא מליקה וי"ל דמה למנחה שטעונה הגשה. תוס' אחרות: כט] אבל ס"א כל כמה דלא ידעינן שהוא ביד שפיר מיחשב מין זבח כו': ל] ומלק שתהא מליקה בעצמו: לא] מאן דלית ליה. עי' לעיל בתוס' (דף יד ע"ב) ובתוס' יומא (דף כז ע"א): לב] חשיב קרן סמוך

א) אולי צ"ל וי"ל דהתם דריש מוהקריב כו'.

הָא כֵּיצַד? קוֹדֵר אֶת הָעוֹר סְבִיבוֹת הַזֶּפֶק כְּמִין אֲרוּבָּה, וְנוֹטֵל נוֹצָה וְעוֹר שֶׁכְּנֶגֶד הַזֶּפֶק עִם הַזֶּפֶק. אֲבָל בְּלֹא קְדֵירָה – לֹא שֶׁהָעוֹר נִמְשָׁךְ אַחֲרָיו, וְיוֹצֵא יוֹתֵר. וְכֵן הוּא אוֹמֵר. בְּשֶׁמְשׁוֹן, וְהָתָם מְפָרֵשׁ בְּהֶדְיָא דִּכְיָד הֲוָה. מַתְנִי'. דְּקָתָנֵי: הִבְדִּיל בִּמְלִיקַת חַטָּאת, שֶׁמְּלָקָהּ בִּשְׁנֵי סִימָנִין פָּסוּל – דְּלָא כְּרַבִּי אֶלְעָזָר.

"שִׁיסַּע וְלֹא הִבְדִּיל".§ ת"ר: "וְשִׁסַּע" – אֵין א] שִׁיסּוּעַ אֶלָּא בַּיָּד, וְכֵן הוּא אוֹמֵר: °"וַיְשַׁסְּעֵהוּ כְּשַׁסַּע הַגְּדִי".§ "לֹא הֵסִיר אֶת הַמּוּרְאָה" כו'.§ מַתְנִי' דְּלָא כְּרַבִּי אֶלְעָזָר בְּר"ש. דְּתַנְיָא, *א"ר אֶלְעָזָר בְּר"ש: שָׁמַעְתִּי ב] שֶׁמַּבְדִּילִין בְּחַטַּאת הָעוֹף. מַאי בֵּינַיְיהוּ? אָמַר רַב חִסְדָּא: ג] מִיצּוּי חַטַּאת הָעוֹף מְעַכֵּב אִיכָּא בֵּינַיְיהוּ. ת"ק סָבַר: מִיצּוּי חַטַּאת הָעוֹף מְעַכֵּב, וְכֵיוָן ד] דְּמִיצּוּי דָּם (א) – קָעָבֵיד מַעֲשֵׂה עוֹלָה בְּחַטַּאת הָעוֹף. וְר' אֶלְעָזָר בְּר"ש סָבַר: *מִיצּוּי חַטַּאת הָעוֹף לֹא מְעַכֵּב, ה] וּמְחַתֵּךְ בָּשָׂר בְּעָלְמָא הוּא. רָבָא אָמַר: שְׁהִיָּיה בְּסִימָן שֵׁנִי בְּעוֹלַת הָעוֹף ו] מְעַכֵּב אִיכָּא בֵּינַיְיהוּ; תַּנָּא קַמָּא סָבַר: שְׁהִיָּיה בְּסִימָן שֵׁנִי בְּעוֹלַת הָעוֹף – לֹא ז] מְעַכֵּב, וְאע"ג דְּשַׁהְיָיהּ – קָא עָבֵיד מַעֲשֵׂה עוֹלָה בְּחַטָּאת. וְרַבִּי אֶלְעָזָר בְּר"ש סָבַר: ח] מְעַכֵּב, וְכֵיוָן דְּשַׁהְיָיהּ – מְחַתֵּךְ בָּשָׂר בְּעָלְמָא הוּא. אַבַּיֵי אָמַר: רוֹב בָּשָׂר מְעַכֵּב אִיכָּא בֵּינַיְיהוּ. וּבִפְלוּגְתָּא דְּר' זֵירָא וְר' שְׁמוּאֵל בַּר רַב יִצְחָק, חַד אָמַר: שְׁהִיָּיה בְּסִימָן שֵׁנִי בְּעוֹלַת הָעוֹף ט] מְעַכֵּב אִיכָּא בֵּינַיְיהוּ, וְחַד אָמַר: רוֹב בָּשָׂר מְעַכֵּב אִיכָּא בֵּינַיְיהוּ. מִכְּלָל דְּבָעֵינַן (ג) י] דְּרוֹב בָּשָׂר בִּתְחִילָּה? אִין, יא] גוְהָתַנְיָא: *כֵּיצַד מוֹלְקִין חַטַּאת הָעוֹף? חוֹתֵךְ שִׁדְרָה וּמַפְרֶקֶת בְּלֹא רוֹב בָּשָׂר, עַד שֶׁמַּגִּיעַ לַוּוֹשֶׁט אוֹ לַקָּנֶה. יב] הִגִּיעַ לַוּוֹשֶׁט אוֹ לַקָּנֶה – חוֹתֵךְ סִימָן אֶחָד אוֹ רוּבּוֹ, וְרוֹב בָּשָׂר עִמּוֹ. וּבְעוֹלָה – שְׁנַיִם אוֹ רוֹב שְׁנַיִם. אֲמַרוּהָ קַמֵּיהּ דְּרַבִּי יִרְמְיָה, אֲמַר: יג] לָא שְׁמִיעַ לְהוּ הָא דְּא"ר שִׁמְעוֹן בֶּן אֶלְיָקִים מִשּׁוּם רַבִּי אֶלְעָזָר בֶּן פְּדָת מִשּׁוּם ר"א בֶּן שַׁמּוּעַ: אוֹמֵר הָיָה ר"א בְּר' שִׁמְעוֹן: שָׁמַעְתִּי בְּחַטַּאת הָעוֹף שֶׁמַּבְדִּילִין, יד] וּמַאי "לֹא יַבְדִּיל" – אֵין

תורה אור: שׁופטים יד

שֶׁמַּבְדִּילִין. שֶׁאִם הִבְדִּיל לֹא פָּסַל. מַאי בֵּינַיְיהוּ. כְּלוֹמַר, בְּמַאי קָמִיפַּלְגִי? טו] ת"ק סָבַר. מִילּוּי טז] בָּתַר הַזָּאָה בְּחַטַּאת הָעוֹף מְעַכֵּב. וְכֵיוָן דִּבְעַל כָּרְחוֹ מְמַצֶּה דָּם, אִי אָמְרַתְּ מַבְדִּיל – קָעָבֵיד כָּל מַעֲשֵׂה עוֹלָה בְּחַטָּאת: מְלִיקָה מוּבְדֶּלֶת, וּמִילּוּי, דְּעוֹלָה *מִילּוּי הוּא דְּעָבֵיד בָּהּ, וּלְקַמָּן (דף סו.) תְּנַן: דְּחַטַּאת הָעוֹף שֶׁעֲשָׂאָהּ כְּמַעֲשֵׂה עוֹלָה יז] לְשֵׁם חַטָּאת – פְּסוּלָה. וְר"א בְּר"ש סָבַר לֹא מְעַכֵּב. הִילְכָּךְ, אִם רָצָה לְהַבְדִּיל – יַבְדִּיל, וְלֹא יְמַצֶּה לְאַחַר הַבְדָּלָה, וְלָא עָבֵד לֵיהּ מַעֲשֵׂה עוֹלָה. וְאִי מִשּׁוּם דְּשִׁינָּה בְּהַבְדָּלָה, כֵּיוָן דְּלָאו מַעֲשֵׂה עוֹלָה – מָצֵי לְמֵימַר יח] בָּהּ חִיתּוּךְ בָּשָׂר בְּעָלְמָא הוּא. ה"ג: שְׁהִיָּיה בְּסִימָן שֵׁנִי בְּעוֹלַת הָעוֹף אִיכָּא בֵּינַיְיהוּ. בְּעוֹלַת הָעוֹף יט] הִצְרִיכוּ ב' סִימָנִים, וְשָׁהָה שִׁיעוּר שְׁהִיָּיה בֵּין סִימָן לְסִימָן אִיכָּא בֵּינַיְיהוּ, אִי פָּסֵיל בָּהּ כ] בִּשְׁהִיָּיה בֵּין סִימָן לְסִימָן כִּבְהֵמָה אוֹ לָא. ת"ק סָבַר שְׁהִיָּיה בְּסִימָן שֵׁנִי בְּעוֹלַת הָעוֹף לֹא פְּסָלָהּ. דְּלָא דָּמֵי לִשְׁחִיטַת בְּהֵמָה. דְּטַעְמָא דִּבְהֵמָה כא] בָּעֲיָא ב' סִימָנִים – מִשּׁוּם דְּלָא נָפְקָא חִיּוּתָא בְּסִימָן אֶחָד, הִילְכָּךְ יֵשׁ שְׁחִיטָה עַל שְׁנֵיהֶם, כב] אֲבָל עוֹף – בְּסִימָן אֶחָד פָּסְקָא חִיּוּתָא. כג] וְעוֹלַת הָעוֹף – מִצְוַת הַבְדָּלָה בְּעָלְמָא הוּא דְּאִיכָּא עֲלָהּ, אֲבָל שֵׁם מְלִיקָה אֵינוֹ חָל אֶלָּא עַל הָרִאשׁוֹן, וְלָא מְהַנְּיָא שְׁהִיָּיה לִפְסוֹל בַּשֵּׁנִי. וְחַטָּאת שֶׁהִבְדִּיל בָּהּ, אע"ג דִּבְלֹא שְׁהִיָּיה אִי אֶפְשָׁר בֵּין סִימָן לְסִימָן, כִּדְתָנֵי לְקַמָּן בְּשְׁמַעְתִּין, שֶׁבִּתְחִילָּה חוֹתֵךְ שִׁדְרָה וּמַפְרֶקֶת בְּלֹא רוֹב בָּשָׂר, הִגִּיעַ לַסִּימָן – חוֹתְכוֹ וְרוֹב בָּשָׂר עִמּוֹ. וַהֲוָה לֵיהּ חֲתִיכַת רוֹב בָּשָׂר, כד] אַף עַל גַּב דְּאִית בֵּיהּ שִׁיעוּר שְׁהִיָּיה, כֵּיוָן דִּבְעוֹלָה שְׁהִיָּיה בֵּין סִימָן לְסִימָן לָא פָּסְלָה, אִי כה] עֲבַדֵיהּ בְּחַטָּאת – עָבֵיד מַעֲשֵׂה עוֹלָה בְּחַטָּאת. וְר"א בְּר"ש סָבַר שְׁהִיָּיה בְּסִימָן שֵׁנִי בְּעוֹלַת הָעוֹף פָּסְלָה. הִלְכָּךְ, חַטָּאת שֶׁהִבְדִּיל בָּהּ, כֵּיוָן שֶׁא"א לָהּ בְּלֹא שְׁהִיָּיה בֵּין סִימָן לְסִימָן – אֵין כָּאן מַעֲשֵׂה עוֹלָה, דִּבְעוֹלָה שְׁהִיָּיה לֵיכָּא, וּמְחַתֵּךְ בָּשָׂר בְּעָלְמָא הוּא. רוֹב בָּשָׂר מְעַכֵּב אִיכָּא בֵּינַיְיהוּ. וּדְכוּלֵּי עָלְמָא שְׁהִיָּיה בְּעוֹלָה בְּסִימָן שֵׁנִי פָּסְלָה. וְהָכָא בְּהָא פְּלִיגֵי: לְת"ק חִיתּוּךְ רוֹב בָּשָׂר בְּחַטָּאת כו] לֹא מְעַכֵּב (א) אִי לָא מְחַתֵּיךְ לֵיהּ, וְאִי אָמְרַתְּ מַבְדִּיל – עָבֵיד לֵיהּ שְׁנֵי סִימָנִין בְּלֹא שְׁהִיָּיה, וְיֵשׁ כָּאן מַעֲשֵׂה עוֹלָה. כז] וְרַבִּי אֶלְעָזָר בְּרַבִּי שִׁמְעוֹן סָבַר: רוֹב בָּשָׂר בְּחַטָּאת מְעַכֵּב, כח] וַחֲתִיכָתוֹ אַחַר סִימָן רִאשׁוֹן הוּא, וְכֵיוָן דְּלָא סַגִּי בְּלֹא שְׁהִיָּיה בֵּינְתַיִים – אֵין כָּאן מַעֲשֵׂה עוֹלָה. מִכְּלָל דְּבָעֵינַן רוֹב כט] הַבָּשָׂר לְבַתְּחִילָּה. מִדְּקָמִיפַּלְגִי בְּעִיכּוּבָא – מִכְּלָל דְּכוּלְּהוּ מוֹדוּ לְכַתְּחִילָּה בָּעֵי לַחְתּוֹךְ רוֹב בָּשָׂר אַחַר הַסִּימָן. שִׁדְרָה = חוּט הַשִּׁדְרָה. מַפְרֶקֶת = עֶצֶם הַצַּוָּאר. בְּלֹא רוֹב בָּשָׂר. הַמַּקֶּפֶת סָבִיב. כִּדְאָמְרִינַן בְּ"הַכֹּל שׁוֹחֲטִין" (חולין דף כ:): נִשְׁבְּרָה מַפְרֶקֶת וְרוֹב בָּשָׂר עִמָּהּ – נְבֵלָה וּמְטַמְּאָה, וַאֲפִילּוּ מְפַרְכֶּסֶת. הִילְכָּךְ, אִי הֲוָה חוֹתֵךְ רוֹב בָּשָׂר קוֹדֶם הַסִּימָן – הָוְיָא ל] לֵיהּ מֵתָה, וְלָא מְהַנְּיָא בָּהּ מְלִיקָה. וְסִימָנִין הֲלָכָה לְמֹשֶׁה מִסִּינַי הֵן. שְׁנַיִם אוֹ רוֹב שְׁנַיִם. בְּ"הַכֹּל שׁוֹחֲטִין" (שם דף כא.) אָמְרִינַן: שְׁנַיִם – לְרַבָּנַן, רוֹב שְׁנַיִם – לְר"א בְּר"ש. וְהָתָם פְּלִיגִי בָּהּ בִּקְרָאֵי. אֲמָרוּהָ קַמֵּיהּ דְּר' יִרְמְיָה. לְהַךְ פְּלוּגְתָּא דְּהָנָךְ אֲמוֹרָאֵי, דִּפְלִיגִי בְּטַעֲמָא דְּר"א בְּרַבִּי שִׁמְעוֹן. אֵין

*הבדיל בחטאת ולא הבדיל בעולה פסול. בחטאת ניחא, כדדרשינן בת"כ: "חטאת היא", שאם מלקה שלא לשמה – פסולה. וס"ה דכל שהיא בה פסולה. אבל בעולה קשה, מנלן? ויעוד, דמהקטרה ילפא: מה הקטרה הראש בעצמו והגוף בעצמו – לא] אף כאן כו'. ומה הקטרה אינה מעכבת – אף הבדלה אינה מעכבת. וכן קשה ממליקת לב] *עוף שעשאה למטה, כיון דעשאה למטה – מהקטרה ילפא, דון מינה ומינה, וכי היכי דלא הקטיר למעלה כשר – לא מלק למעלה נמי כשר. *כיצד קרב המתיר. כל הנך משניות דהכא, ודפ"ק דמכילתא ודמנחות, צריכי לדקדק אמאי צריכי כולהו. קעביד מעשה עולה בחטאת. מה שזה למעלה וזה למטה לא חשיב ליה שינוי.

ורבי אלעזר בר"ש סבר מיצוי בחטאת לא מעכב. הילכך, אם רצה להבדיל – יבדיל ולא ימצה אחר הבדלה, ולא עביד מעשה עולה. לג] ואי משום דשינה *בהבדלה – [כיון דלא מילה] כמעשה עולה, א"כ כי מבדיל הוי חיתוך בשר בעלמא, כך פירש בקונטרס. וקשה: דבפ"ק דחולין (דף כא:) דדריש רבי אלעזר בר"ש: כמשפט חטאת העוף, מה להלן כשהוא לד] אוחז הראש בגוף ומזה, ויליף מיניה בעולת העוף שאין חותך אלא רוב שנים – היכי יליף? הא אי בעי מבדיל לגמרי בחטאת! והיינו יכולין לפרש: כשהוא לה] אוחז הראש בגוף ומזה – אם ירצה קאמר, *ומדקאמר: מה להלן בסימן אחד – היינו שאם ירצה לא יחתוך כ"א סימן אחד. אבל קשה מברייתא דהתם לעיל, לו] דקתני: שנים או רוב שנים, ומפרש התם: שנים – לרבנן, או רוב שנים – לר' אלעזר בר"ש. לוקמה כולה כרבי אלעזר בר"ש, דאי בעי – שנים, ואי בעי – רוב שנים! לז] ובפרק "העור והרוטב" (שם דף קכג.) נמי, גבי טלית שנקרעה רובה שוב אינה חיבור, וטהורה. ומוקי לה בטלית טבולת יום, דכיון דלא חס עלה ואטבלה – ליכא למימר דילמא חייס ולא קרע רובה, אבל כשאינה טבולת יום – גזרינן. ופריך: אלא מעתה לח] לרבי אלעזר בר"ש ליגזר *)דילמא לא אתי למיעבד *רובא! והשתא, לט] אי אין אסור לחתוך כל השנים – ל"ל למגזר שם כלל דילמא חייס? ונראה לפרש כל סוגיא זו בהבדלה שלאחר הזאה, אבל קודם הזאה – כולי עלמא לא פליגי דפסולה, דאמר קרא "לא יבדיל". ודוקא רבי שמעון בן אליקים דלקמן אית ליה הך סברא לרבי אלעזר בר"ש דיכול להבדיל כל השנים ואפילו קודם הזאה, ולית ליה איסור פסול בהבדלה כלל, *דהא מפרש "לא יבדיל" דקרא – אין צריך להבדיל. וסוגיא דחולין פרק קמא (דף כא:) והיא ד"העור והרוטב" (שם דף קכג.) – דלא כוותיה, אלא כרב חסדא ורבה ואביי. והכי פירושא דכולה שמעתא: מאי בינייהו, פי': מאי טעמייהו? אמר רב חסדא: מילוי חטאת העוף מעכב איכא בינייהו, דרבנן סברי מילוי חטאת העוף מעכב, וכשהזה עדיין לא נגמרה מצוותה, הילכך, כשהבדיל סימן שני לאחר הזאה – לא חשיב מחתך בשר בעלמא, ופסול משום שעשה מעשה עולה בחטאת, שיש כאן הבדלה בשנים קודם מילוי, כמו בעולה. ור"א בר"ש סבר דמילוי אינו מעכב, וכבר נגמרה כל מ] מצוותן, וכשמבדיל לאחר הזאה – אינו אלא מחתך בשר בעלמא. והשתא צ"ל מא] דרב חסדא [סבר] דשהייה בסימן שני בעולת העוף לא מעכב, דאי מעכב – אמאי פסול לרבנן כשהבדיל לאחר הזאה? אין כאן מעשה עולה, שהרי שהה, ואין הכשרה של עולה בכך, ואי אפשר לו לעשות הזאה בין מליקת סימן ראשון לסימן שני שלא ישהה. ורבה מפרש: שהייה בסימן שני בעולת העוף מעכב איכא בינייהו, דלרבנן לא מעכב ולרבי אלעזר בר"ש מעכב. ואביי מפרש דרוב בשר מעכב איכא בינייהו, ורבנן סברי רוב בשר לא מעכב, ולכך זימנין דלא חתיך רוב בשר עם סימן הראשון מב] (*מ"מ אסור להבדיל עם סימן הראשון אפילו לאחר הזאה) גזרינן אטו היכא דלא חתך רוב בשר. ור"א ברבי שמעון סבר רוב בשר מעכב, ולכך לא פסל, דאין כאן מעשה עולה, שכבר חתך רוב בשר עם סימן ראשון. וכשמבדיל לאחר ההזאה – מתה עומד ומבדיל, ופסול, מג] לאביי דפ"ק דחולין (דף כ:) דפריך: תקשי לך עולת העוף דבעיא שני סימנין, וכי מתה עומד ומולק? ולית ליה טעמא דכדי לקיים מצות הבדלה. והדר קאמר: אמרוה רבנן קמיה דרבי ירמיה, פי': הנך טעמי דרב חסדא ורבה ואביי. אמר להו: לא שמיעא להו הא דאמר ר"ש בן אליקים משום רבי אלעזר בן פדת, אומר היה ר"א ברבי שמעון: שמעתי שמבדילין בחטאת העוף, ומאי לא יבדיל – א"צ להבדיל. פי': ולא צריכין לכל הנך טעמי מד] דפריש רב חסדא ורבה ואביי, ואף קודם ההזאה מותר להבדיל. וא"ת: לדידהו דאסור להבדיל קודם הזאה ואפילו לרבי אלעזר בר"ש – א"כ מאי קאמר לעיל: מתניתין דלא כר"א בר"ש? הא לכאורה מתני' קודם הזאה, דומיא דרישא דקתני: חטאת העוף כיצד היתה נעשית? מלק ראשה ממול ערפה ואין מבדיל, ומזה מדמה על

*) נ"ל דילמא לא אתי למיעבד רובא והשתא א"א בשלמא אסור לחתוך כל השנים פריך שפיר דלא ליסגי ברוב מצומצם עד שיפסוק רוב הנראה לעינים פן יחוש לצמצם לפי שירא שלא יחתוך כל השנים אלא אי שרי לחתוך כל השנים למה לי למגזר כו'. מתוס' חולין דף כא ע"ב ד"ה ואינו מבדיל

כה] אבדיל בחטאת ע"י שהייה עביד ותיבת עבדי' נמחק: כו] בחטאת עם סימן ראשון לא מעכב וזימנין דלא מחתך ליה ותיבות אי לא נמחק: כז] עולה ס"א ואפילו מחתך ליה רוב בשר כיון דאי בעי לא עביד מעשה עולה שפיר קרינא ס"א ואפילו כשמחתך ליה לא הוי מעשה עולה מ"מ גזרינן הא אטו הא. ור"א: כח] תיבות וחתיכתו אחר סימן ראשון הוא נמחק: כט] רוב בשר לכתחילה כו' מודו דלכתחילה: ל] לה מתה: לא] בעצמו אם כן מה הקטרה אינה מעכבת: לב] ממליקת עולה שעשאה למטה דכיון דמהקטרה ילפי נימא דון מינה ומינה: לג] ואי משום דשינה בהבדלה כיון דלא מצית למימר כמעשה עולה א"כ: לד] כשהוא אחוז בגוף מזה ויליף: לה] אחוז הראש בגוף מזה אם ירצה קאמר והא דקאמר התם אי מה להלן: לו] לעיל מינה דקתני: לז] שנים כיון דמחטאת לא ילפינן רק דאינו חובה להבדיל וע"ק דבפ' העור והרוטב: לח] מעתה ס"א עולת העוף לראב"ש ליחוש דילמא חיים עליה ולא יעשה רוב שנים: לט] והשתא בשלמא אי (תיבת אין ל"ש) אסור לחתוך כל השנים פריך שפיר דלא ליסגי ברוב מצומצם עד שיפסוק רוב הנראה לעינים פן יחוש לצמצם לפי שירא שלא יחתוך כל השנים אלא אי שרי לחתוך כל השנים בעולה לגמרי א"כ מאי יש לחוש הלא יכול למלקו עד שיהא ברור לו שיש רוב שנים ואם יעלה בידו שימלוק כל השנים מ"מ כשר הוא ולמה לי למיגזר שם כלל דילמא חיים אלא ש"מ דבעולה קאמר דוקא רוב שנים ולא יבדיל לגמרי משום דילפינן מחטאת דאסור להבדיל: מ] כל מצוותה: מא] צ"ל לרב חסדא דשהייה: מב] הראשון דקודם הזאה וכשמבדיל אחר הזאה יש כאן מעשה עולה בחטאת ואפילו חתך רוב בשר עם סימן הראשון מ"מ אסור להבדיל אפילו לאחר ההזאה דגזרינן אטו היכא: מג] ופסול וכה"ג בעולה לאו הבדלה הוא דאביי לטעמיה דאית ליה הכי בפ"ק דחולין: מד] דפרישו דבפירושא דקרא פליגי דלמר שרי ולמר אסור ואפילו קודם הזאה פליגי וא"ת ולרב חסדא ורבא ואביי אמאי מוקי מתניתין דלא כראב"ש הא לכאורה כו' ומתיבות רב חסדא כו' עד תיבת הא לכאורה נמחק:

א) אולי צ"ל ס"א גרס כרש"י מיצוי חטאת העוף דבחטאת כו'

שיטה מקובצת

א] אין שיסוע: ב] ע"י בהשמטות בסוף המסכת: ג] מיצוי עיין דף נ"ב ע"ב: ד] וביון דקא מצי לדם כי מבדיל קא עביד: ה] לא מעכב הילכך מחתך בשר: ו] תיבת מעכב נמחק: ז] לא פסלא. תיבת מעכב נמחק: ח] סבר פסלא וביון. תיבת מעכב נמחק: ט] העוף פסלא תיבת מעכב נמחק: י] דבעינן רוב בשר: יא] אין דתניא: יב] לקנה חותך ס"י הגיע לוושט או לקנה חותך: יג] לא שמיע להו כו'.

הגהות הב"ח

(א) גמ' וכיון דמצוי דם מעכב קעביד מעשה: (ב) שם מכלל דבעינן רוב בשר: (ג) רש"י ד"ה רוב בשר וכו' לא מעכב אע"ג דלא מחתך:

גליון הש"ס

תוס' ד"ה הבדיל כו' לא מלק למעלה נמי כשר. עיין תוס' יומא דף ס ע"ב ד"ה אי מה מיצוים:

אין צריך להבדיל. א"ל רב אחא בריה דרבא לרב אשי: א] אלא מעתה, גבי בור דכתיב: °"ולא יכסנו", ה"נ דאין צריך לכסות? הכי השתא?! התם, כיון דכתיב: °"בעל הבור ישלם" – עלויה הוא דרמי לכסויי. אבל הכא, מכדי כתיב: "והקריבו", חלק הכתוב בין חטאת העוף לעולת העוף, ב] "לא יבדיל" למה לי? ש"מ: אין צריך להבדיל.§ "מיצה דם הגוף".§ ת"ר: "עולה" – אע"פ שמיצה דם הגוף ולא מיצה דם הראש. יכול ג] (א) מיצה דם הראש ולא מיצה דם הגוף? ת"ל: "הוא". מאי תלמודא? אמר רבינא: מסתברא, (ב) דרוב דמים בגוף שכיחי.§

תורה אור: שמות כא, שם

הדרן עלך קדשי קדשים

חטאת העוף שעשאה למטה, כמעשה חטאת לשם חטאת – כשירה. [א]כמעשה חטאת לשם עולה, כמעשה עולה לשם חטאת, כמעשה עולה לשם עולה – פסולה. [ב]עשאה למעלה כמעשה כולן – פסולה. עולת העוף שעשאה למעלה, כמעשה עולה לשם עולה – כשירה. [ג]כמעשה עולה לשם חטאת – כשירה, ובלבד שלא עלתה לבעליה. [ד]כמעשה חטאת לשם עולה, כמעשה חטאת לשם חטאת – פסולה. עשאה למטה כמעשה כולן – [ה]פסולה ד].§

גמ'

רש"י

אין צריך להבדיל. הילכך, אם הבדיל – לאו שינוי הוא. מכדי כתיב. בעולת העוף "והקריבו", ומינה נפקא לן לר"א ברבי שמעון הבדלה בעולת העוף ב"הכל שוחטין" (חולין דף כא.). ולא דרש "ומלק והקטיר" כדדרשי' לעיל מה הקטרה הראש בעצמו כו' דתיפוק ליה הבדלה מהכא, דהך סברא לית ליה שימלוק את ח] כולן, אלא דנקא רוב שנים, ויליף לה מקראי, ואפילו רבנן דפליגי עליה התם – עיקר הבדלה בעולה לא נפקא להו אלא מ"והקריבו", דמשמע: חלק את זה מן החטאת. הילכך, על כרחך "ולא יבדיל" האמור בחטאת למה ליה כלומר, מאי (ג) ו] קאמר לן? שמע מינה: א"צ להבדיל קאמר. הילכך נפקא לן העולה מ"והקריבו" דצריך להבדיל, ז] דהא חלק ביניהן, דאי אזהרה היא בחטאת שלא יבדיל – היכי נפקא לן בעולה מ"והקריבו" דצריך להבדיל? ח] אינו מוזהר שלא להבדיל הוא דנפקא לן מחילוקו, ולא ט] שטעון הבדלה. ד"א: האי למה לי. כמו י] "מאי היא", לשון קצר, מדאתא "והקריבו" לחלק – *למדנו הבדלה בעולה, שמע מינה: "ולא יבדיל" – אין צריך להבדיל קאמר, ואשמעי' "והקריבו" דחלק בעולה דצריך להבדיל. (דאי אזהרה היא בחטאת – יא] לא שמעי' מ"והקריבו" אלא דאינו מוזהר מלהבדיל בעולה, אבל מצות הבדלה לא נפקא לן).

ללמדנו נ"ק

הדרן עלך קדשי קדשים

חטאת העוף. במעשה חטאת. מליקה בסימן אחד, והזאה ומיצוי. במעשה עולה. בגמרא מפרש דשני במאי. עשאה למעלה במעשה כולן. כלומר, כמעשה אחד מכולן האמורין כאן, ואפילו כמעשה חטאת לשם חטאת. בגמרא מפרש דשני במאי. עשאה למטה במעשה כולן. כמעשה אחד מכל אלו, ואפילו כמעשה עולה לשם עולה יב].

גמ'

תוספות

קיר המזבח! ויש לומר: דמשמע ליה דמתני' פוסלת בכל ענין, אפי' לאחר הזאה, יג] מדקאמר רבי אלעזר בר"ש: שמעתי שמבדילין, והיינו דוקא לאחר הזאה, מכלל דרבנן פליגי עליה ואמרי אין מבדילין, אם כן מתני' דלא כוותיה. וא"ת: יד] ריש פ' "חטאת העוף": עשאה כמעשה עולה פסולה. וקאמר בגמרא: דשני במאי? אילימא דשני במליקה – נימא דלא כר"א בר"ש, דאי ר"א בר' שמעון – הא אמר שמעתי שמבדילין בחטאת העוף. מאי קשיא ליה? לרבי אלעזר בר"ש נמי משכחת לה, דהבדיל קודם הזאה! וי"ל: כיון דמוקמינן כמעשה עולה דשני במליקה, א"כ מדלא קתני כמעשה עולה קודם הזאה – ש"מ דאיירי בין קודם הזאה בין לאחר הזאה. ועוד: דלר' אלעזר בן פדת ור"ש בן אליקים ורבי ירמיה – טו] מכשר רבי אלעזר בר"ש אפילו קודם ההזאה, דמפרשים "לא יבדיל" דקרא – אין צריך להבדיל. ור"ת הגיה בגליון בספרו על מילתא דר"ש בן אליקים: ומאי לא יבדיל, דמשמע בין בשעת הזאה בין בשעת מילוי – אינו צריך להבדיל ואם הבדיל כשר, וכ"ש שמתמלה כל הדם. ושבקינן לקרא דאיהו דסיק ומוקי אנפשיה, דדוקא לא יבדיל בשעת הזאה, אבל בשעת מילוי, דלדם הוא צריך – אי בעי מבדיל אי בעי לא מבדיל, עכ"ל. משמע שרוצה לפרש דבשעת הזאה אסר קרא, ובשעת מילוי בעי למימר קרא דאין צריך. ותרווייהו משתמעי *מיניה, טז] (וש"מ) מדאפקיה קרא בלשון לאו קדריש דבשעת הזאה לא יבדיל. ולאסורא אף בשעת מילוי לא אתי קרא, דמ"והקריבו" הוה נפיק, יז] דדריש מיניה בחולין (דף כא.) שחילק הכתוב בין חטאת העוף לעולת העוף, לכך יש לפרש נמי דאתי קרא למימר דבשעת מילוי אם ירצה לא יבדיל. והא דאמר רבי ירמיה: לא שמיע להו, דמשמע שבא לחלוק על רב חסדא ורבא ואביי – היינו משום שבא ר' ירמיה להשמיענו דכשמבדיל לאחר הזאה אין כאן מעשה עולה בחטאת, שמצות חטאת נמי כך הוא, דקרא אין צריך להבדיל קאמר. וא"ת: לרב הונא דאמר משמיה דרב במעילה פרק "חטאת העוף" (דף ח:) דמילוי חטאת העוף אינו מעכב, ולהכי תני במתני' דהתם: הוזה דמה – אמאי פסלי רבנן כשהבדיל לאחר הזאה? הא אין כאן מעשה עולה בחטאת, דמחתך בשר בעלמא הוא כדפרישית, כיון דכבר נגמרו עבודת הדם, דמילוי אינו מעכב! ולפי מה שפירשתי ניחא, דדילמא רב הונא סבר כר"ש בן אליקים דמוקי פלוגתייהו קודם הזאה. אבל לפירוש ר"ת קשה: דאפילו לר"ש בן אליקים לא פליגי אלא לאחר הזאה! ויש לומר דרב הונא יעמיד מתני' דקתני הבדיל פסול – קודם הזאה, ואפילו כרבי אלעזר בר"ש. וסוגיא דשמעתא דקאמר: מתניתין דלא כרבי אלעזר בר"ש – אתיא כרב אדא בר אהבה, דאמר במעילה* משמיה דרב: מילוי חטאת העוף מעכב. יח] ורבנן פליגי עליה דר"א בר"ש אפילו לרב הונא, מדקאמר רבי אלעזר ברבי שמעון: שמעתי שמבדילין, משמע דפליגי רבנן עליה. ואע"ג דרב הונא סבר מילוי לא מעכב – מודה הוא יט] דפליגי רבנן עליה דרבי אלעזר ברבי שמעון, *סבר מילוי מעכב. וה"נ איכא חד תנא במעילה דסבר הכי. ומיהו *)מתני' לא אפשר למימר לרב הונא דסבר מעכב – דהא מהדר התלמוד לאוקומי כל סתמי דמתני' כוותיה, דאית ליה אינו מעכב. וא"ת: והא קתני מתני': חטאת העוף שמלקה לשמה ומילה דמה שלא לשמה – פסול. אלמא דמילוי מעכב! ויש לומר: דרב הונא לא הוה תני "מילה", אלא "היזה", כדתני במתניתין דמעילה: הוזה דמה. אבל סיפא דמתני' דמייתי התם במעילה: כ] אחד חטאת העוף ואחד עולת העוף כא] מלקן ומילה דמן כו' – לא מצי לשנויי *דהוא ושהיזה, דהא קתני בה נמי עולה, והזאה בעולה ליכא. לכך צריך לשנויי דלגלדין קתני.

אלא מעתה גבי בור דכתיב ולא יכסנו כו'. מכל לאוין שבתורה, כגון "לא תחסום" "לא תאכלו כל נבילה" "לא תלבש שעטנז" – לא קשיא ליה למאי כב] כתביה אם לא ללאו. אבל הא, דמסברא הוה אמינא דמבדיל לפי שצריך לדם, אמרינן דכי כתיב "לא יבדיל" – אין צריך להבדיל קאמר. וגבי בור נמי – מסברא הוה אמינא דחייב לכסותו, וכי כתיב "לא יכסנו" – אין צריך לכסותו קאמר.

מיניה דמדאפקיה קרא נ"ק

דף ח:

נ"ל וסברי מילוי כו' וכן הוא בתוס' חולין דף כא: ד"ה ואינו כו' וע"ש

לשנויי ושהיזה נ"ק

הדרן עלך קדשי קדשים

חטאת העוף. במעשה חטאת לשם חטאת כשירה. זו היא מצוותה, כג] ואגב אחריני נקטיה. למעלה במעשה כולן פסולה. כד] אף שעשה העבודה כתקנה. והיינו באכילה, אבל בעלים נתכפרו, לשמואל דאמר לעיל פרק ב' (דף כו:): כיון שהגיע דם למזבח – נתכפרו בעלים כה]. למטה במעשה כולן פסולה. בסוף פירקין לעיל (דף סה:) פירשתי דלא ידעינן מנא ליה עיכובא בעולה.

נימא

יו] נ"ל ומיהו רבנן דמתני' לא אפשר למימר לר"ה דסברי מעכב כו' נ"ק

עין משפט נר מצוה

א א מיי' פ"ז מהלכות פסולי המוקדשין הלכה ז:
ב ב מיי' שם הלכה ה:
ג ג ד מיי' שם הל' ח:
ד ה מיי' שם הלכה ו:

הגהות הב"ח

(א) גמ' יכול אע"פ שמיצה דם הראש: (ב) שם מסתברא רוב כצ"ל ואות ד' נמחק: (ג) רש"י ד"ה מכדי וכו' כלומר מאי קמ"ל:

שיטה מקובצת

א] אלא מעתה גבי בור כו'. וא"ת *)כו' וי"ל דהא דדריש לא יבדיל דאינו צריך להבדיל היינו משום דלדם הוא צריך לעשות ההזאה והמיצוי וא"כ סברא לומר דצריך הבדלה בחטאת יותר מבעולה דבעולה ליכא כי אם מיצוי בלבד ולכך קאמר לא יבדיל דאין צריך להבדיל אבל אם רצה מבדיל ולהכי פריך אלא מעתה כו' דאי כפשוטו לאשמועינן דצריך לכסותו פשיטא דכיון דחפרו צריך לכסותו ומשני הכי השתא כלומר גבי בור כיון דכתיב בעל הבור ישלם אלמא צריך לכסותו ומ"מ כתב ולא יכסנו לספור דברים בעלמא דאם לא כסהו חייב והא דדרשינן לא יבדיל לומר דאינו צריך להבדיל לאו משום דהוי ס"ד מבדיל מסברא כדס"ד אלא משום דמכדי כתיב והקריבו כו': ב] לא יבדיל למה לי. לפום רהיטא נראה דה"פ כיון דכתיב והקריבו לחלק בענין מליקה א"כ ממילא ידעינן דבחטאת לא יבדיל אלא בסימן אחד אבל לא יבדיל בשני סימנין כענין מליקה דעולה וא"כ על כרחך אתא לא יבדיל לומר דא"צ להבדיל וקשה דאילו לא הוי כתיב לא יבדיל היכא הוי ידעינן בעולה דעביד שני סימנין איפוך אנא ואימא דבחטאת עביד שני סימנין ובעולה סימן אחד ואי משום דדרשינן בעולה ומלק והקטיר מה הקטרה הראש בעצמו והגוף בעצמו זה אינו דהא לראב"ש קיימינן ובפ"ק דחולין משמע דלראב"ש לית ליה הך היקשא דקאמר התם דבעולה נמי כשהוא אחוז בראש בגוף כו' והיקשא דמליקה להקטרה מוקי ליה לומר מה הקטרה בראשו של מזבח כו' כדקאמר התם לת"ק דברייתא דכמשפט ורש"י דחק ופי' בענין אחר מכדי כתיב בעולה והקריבו ומינה דריש ראב"ש הבדלה בעולת העוף וא"כ הא דכתיב לא יבדיל בחטאת היינו דא"צ להבדיל קאמר א"כ והקריבו דכתיב לחלק בינהם לומר דבעולה צריך להבדיל יותר מבחטאת ועביד רוב שנים ומ"מ לא עביד שנים לגמרי והא כמשפט מקיש לענין זו דכשהוא אחוז הראש בגוף (אין) מזה כדקאמר התם דאי לא יבדיל להזהיר בחטאת מלהבדיל א"כ היכא נפקא בעולה מוהקריבו דצריך להבדיל דלמא לא נפקא לן מיניה אלא שאינו מוזהר מלהבדיל ולא שטעון הבדלה ופליאה גדולה איזו הוכחה היא זו מדקי"ל בעולה דחובה והיא גופיה מנ"ל שמתוך כן אתה דורש דלא יבדיל דאינו צריך להבדיל אימא דבעולה אינו חובה להבדיל ואתא והקריבו לומר דחלק מחטאת דבחטאת אסור להבדיל ובעולה אין אסור להבדיל. וע"ק לפי' לישנא דלמה לי לכך נראה למהר"ם דפי' קמא דפי' לא יבדיל כלומר בלאו הכי נמי ידעינן שפיר דאסור להבדיל מדכתיב והקריבו לומר דחלק מליקה דחטאת ממליקה דעולה ומליקה דעולה בהבדלה היא מהקישא דהקטרה והא דדריש ראב"ש התם דכשאחוז הראש בגוף מזה היינו לבתר דכתיב לא יבדיל וכיון דכתיב לא יבדיל וכמשפט א"כ יש לנו לעשות היקשא לענין דלא יבדיל והיקשא דמליקה להקטרה מוקמינן לה לראשו של מזבח והא דכתיב והקריבו לומר דבעולה לא סגי בסימן אחד אלא בעי רוב שנים אבל הכא מיירי אי לא כתיב לא יבדיל ואז ודאי יש לנו לדרוש היקשא דמלק והקטיר לגמרי אף לענין הראש בעצמו כו' וא"כ מוהקריבו שמעינן דבחטאת אסור להבדיל מדחלק הכתוב בין חטאת העוף לעולת העוף במליקה ואי משום כמשפט מוקמינן ליה לדרשא אחריתי. וקצת קשה למורי דנהי דלא יבדיל לא הוי איצטריך לאיסור הבדלה דחטאת כדפי' מ"מ איצטריך לכתוב לא יבדיל כדי לאקושי (חטאת לעולת העוף) [עולת העוף לחטאת] לאיסור הבדלה כדאמר ראב"ש בחולין מכמשפט דמכח הך היקשא לא דריש ראב"ש היקשא דמליקה להקטרה לענין הראש בעצמו והגוף בעצמו והדרא קושיא לדוכתיה מנ"ל דלא יבדיל דאינו צריך להבדיל קאמר ותירץ דטפי אית לן למימר א"צ להבדיל דהשתא איצטריך לגופיה דחטאת העוף לומר דלא יבדיל [אין] איסור להבדיל [ולא] לגלות בעולת העוף איסור הבדלה ולא לענין חטאת גופיה: ג] יכול אפי' מיצה: ד] פסולה. יכולן אין מטמאין אבית הבליעה ומועלין בהן חוץ מחטאת העוף שעשאה למטה כמעשה חטאת לשם חטאת: גמ' ומועלין בהן חוץ מחטאת כו'. דחטאת פסולה אין לה היתר לכהנים ועולה אפי' היא כשרה (לאו) בת מעילה היא אבל חטאת העוף שעשאה בהכשר אין מועלין בה דכל שיש לו היתר לכהנים אין מועלין כו' וא"ת ובחטאת העוף ששינה בה אמאי מועלין בה למ"ד במעילה היתר שחיטה שנינו והכא איכא היתר מליקה דהא בגמ' מוקמינן שינוי מקום דגבי חטאת בהזאה וי"ל דדוקא היתר שחיטה מוציאה מידי מעילה משום דלאחר שחיטה הובשר לקבל דם לאחר אבל בעוף דליכא קבלה לא מהני היתר מליקה לאפוקי מידי מעילה: ה] את כולו אלא: ו] מאי קמ"ל אלא ש"מ: ז] להבדיל דמחלק בינהן: ח] להבדיל. נוסחאת רש"י ממהר"פ נימא הכא דהקריב חלק לומר דבחטאת מוזהר שלא יבדיל אבל בעולה אינו מוזהר להבדיל אבל דצריך הבדלה לא תיפוק מיניה אלא על כרחך מדנפקא ליה מוהקריב חלק הבדלה בעולת העוף ש"מ ולא יבדיל כו': ט] שתטעון הבדלה. האי כו'. תיבות ה"א ל"ש ונמחק: י] מאי קאמר ולישנא קצר הוא תיבת היא נמחק: יא] בחטאת לומר שלא יבדיל לא: יב] עולה הס"ד ומה"ד וכולן. אע"פ שנפסלו מליקתן מטהרתן מידי נבלה ואין מטמאין בבית הבליעה. כדתן נבלת עוף טהור הס"ד ומה"ד ומועלין בהן. ואף בחטאת הואיל ונפסלו ואין בהן שעת היתר לכהנים לא יצא מידי מעילה שבהן הס"ד ומה"ד חוץ מחטאת העוף שעשאה למטה כמעשה חטאת לשם חטאת. הכשרה היא ויש בה שעת היתר לכהנים ושוב אין בה מעילה אפי' לזר הס"ד ומה"ד גמ': יג] הזאה. ס"א משום דראב"ש אמר שמעתי שמבדילין אמתני' קאמר ובא לחלוק עליה וא"ת: יד] וא"ת לקמן ריש פ' חטאת העוף דתנן עשאה למטה במעשה עולה כו': טו] ור' ירמיה פריך שפיר דהדידהו מכשר: טז] ושמא מדאפקיה: יז] נפיק כדדריש: יח] מעכב ואיכא רבנן דפליגי: יט] הוא דאיכא רבנן דפליגי עליה דר"א: כ] במעילה דקתני אחד: כא] העוף שמלקן ששינה דמן כו' לא מצי לשנויי דהוה תני ושהיזה תיבת דהוא ל"ש ונמחק: כב] למאי כתבינהו אם לא ללאו אבל האי דמסברא: כג] מצוותה והא הנקט שעשאה ברעבד אגב אחריני נקטיה: כד] תיבות אף שעשאה העבודה בתקנה נמחק: כה] בעלים. ועי"ל דלא קאמר שמואל אלא בזבחים אבל בעוף לא דקרא דמייתי לעיל גבי זבחים כתיב ואני נתתי לכם על המזבח לכפר הס"ד:

*) [גירסת דפוסים לקמיית התוס' כל"ה תנא. ונבי לאיון כו' לא קשיא ליה:]